Fabian Reimann

another freeman's journal, based on

H. G. Wells

The World Set Free

A History of Mankind

SPECTOR BOOKS

"And that first glimmering of speculation, that first story of achievement, that story-teller, bright-eyed and flushed under his matted hair, gesticulating to his gaping, incredulous listener, gripping his wrist to keep him attentive, was the most marvelous beginning this world had ever seen. It doomed the mammoths, and it began the setting of the snare that shall catch the sun ... "

H. G. WELLS @ WORLD'S END EDGE

It is noticeable in retrospect that Herbert George Wells' encounter with science fiction came before the break-up of the British empire. There at the expansionist peak, the end was already perfectly visible. With his first novel *The Time Machine, an Invention* (1895) the twenty-nine year old journalist with a social grievance looked far beyond the Boer War; with Charles Darwin he looked over the edge of the end of history itself, and returned to find fiction a very real thing, bearing a global message for a global audience. Ever since, like Mary Shelley and Edgar A. Poe, H. G. Wells has become a character of a genre he didn't know existed, yet in large part created. He might have been dismayed at the steampunk nostalgia enmeshing his memory today. Wells would come to stand for the Edwardian era; he took the most dismal view of that culture, seeing himself surrounded by the decaying remnants of a hypocritical Victorianism.

Does it really matter how the world ends? This committed socialist was open to whatever local apocalypse the immediate novel needed; but all his science fiction projects delineate inevitable trouble for humanity. *The Time Traveller's* Moorlocks and Eloi would haunt fantasy and sf ever after; but it was when the thought experiment of *The Time Machine* went deeper still, to our planet's eventual destruction, that it became a moon-landing moment for the world at large. Fantastic fiction delivered reality. It is often pointed out that the book got the end wrong, predicting—like mainstream science of the day—an eventual cooling out of the sun. But without that step away from the real, Wells might not have been able to make visible the infinity of science fiction lying beyond the end of a mere planet.

> The cold that smote to my marrow, and the pain I felt in breathing, overcame me. I shivered, and a deadly nausea seized me. Then like a red-hot bow in the sky appeared the edge of the sun. I got off the machine to recover myself. I felt giddy and incapable of facing the return journey. As I stood sick and confused I saw again the moving thing upon the shoal—there was no mistake now that it was a moving thing—against the red water of the sea. It was a round thing, the size of a football perhaps, or, it may be, bigger, and tentacles trailed down from it; it seemed black against the weltering blood-red water, and it was hopping fitfully about.

Out past the Apocalypse, that flopping, round object, avatar of the science fictional creative mind, had just begun to test its tentacles.

As the century turned, Wells continued to discover new local apocalypses, pairing speculative science with romance, publishing five of the finest works in the history of science fiction in short succession: *The Island of Doctor Moreau* (1896), *The Invisible Man, a Grotesque Romance* (1897), *War of the Worlds* (1898), and *The First Men in the Moon* (1901). The success of these works remains enormous and astonishing, each stamping particular traditions and story forms in the genre to be with its influence. Though the prolific Wells turned to the mainstream novel and non-fictional writings as the 20th century began, he never entirely gave up on the "scientific romance." *Food of the Gods, and How It Came to Earth* (1904) and *Days of the Comet* (1906) darkly complicated the formulas the earlier books established. By *The War in the Air, and Particularly How Mr. Bert Smallways Fared while it Lasted* (1908) Wells' increasing sciencefictional imagination of a real coming apocalypse had become eerily prophetic.

Written in the teeth of the Great War, as if to spite it—in his thirty-third novel, *The World Set Free: A Story of Mankind* (1914)—Wells for the first time attempted to imagine a way out, beyond an apocalypse.

The book before you now is unique in its author's bibliography. Bubbling with ideas and inventions on every page, it engages the past and the future globally, employing a pastiche of science writing, satire, short stories, future history and vision—but also contains a single central prediction, one that has proven bizarrely, even allegorically perfectly exactly correct.
He had already dealt with tanks and aeroplanes, and this novel builds on those early visions. Wells depicts a World War erupting in an imaginary 1956, ended only by the use of nuclear weapons. The destruction and trauma of the conflict initiates a "Great Change." Discovering the coming utopia is one of the pleasures of reading the book; I won't outline it here. Let us say those bombs imagined by Wells are in some sense quite different from real nuclear bombs as we have experienced them; they explode, as it were, into time. But this step into the imaginary opens John Martin-esque visions of bombed world capitals outmatching any spectacles of destruction Hollywood or history has yet devised.

In its prelude the book defines "fiction" as a "pointing a way to achievement." As is well documented online, the horror visions and realistic aftermath depicted by Wells inspired real world scientists to invent the bomb before the Nazis, and to keep its existence secret. Refugee Physicist Leó Szilárd read this book in London, and soon after discovered the nuclear chain reaction of the nuclear bomb.

“Knowing what it would mean—and I knew because I had read H. G. Wells—I did not want this patent to become public.” Szilárd contacted Einstein; they contacted the U. S. Government. Mostly forgotten today, this mere fiction, “romance” as Wells himself might have called it, is peculiarly responsible for the current livability of our planet.

Despite its dated, male-ist vision of history in general, at the time of this writing the novel is also strangely up to date with the current state of aggression in the armed patriarchal world. Our actual nuclear weapons live on, blowing out an eternal 1956, stiffening politics and ideology, crippling technological advance, poisoning sites long-term. They have left the Van Allen Belt circling the Earth, a permanent danger to any living being attempting to get to space or back ever since. The cultural burn continues as well. We have known since 1945 the end of all war and its eventual meaning; we have shown no inclination to assemble anything of the panache, imagination, and sheer global good will of that generation Wells imagines encountering such destruction.

Though perhaps we should look more closely at the fact the book re-appears now. With a “Slavic Fox” manipulating the world stage, everywhere “happy-rich people flying, heedless of the misfortunes of others,” with America newly impatient with “the monstrous and socially paralysing party systems that had sprung out of their absurd electoral arrangements," with a "War against Flies ... waged so successfully that this pestilential branch of life is nearly extinct," Wells' 1956 moment of crisis repeatedly chills with its familiarity, and points to our own need for "the Great Change."

Cold fusion technology promises unlimited free power; but it doesn't build the utopia that Wells imagines following the crisis. And so against our sense of this writer's having hit the edge of our own empire by breaking through his own exactly as the Great War he predicted gathered, rational readers will take the first steps towards survival Wells imagines beyond the collapse of capitalism extremely seriously.

> "Philosophy, discovery, art, every sort of skill, every sort of service, love; these are the means of salvation ... "

Mark von Schlegell, 2018

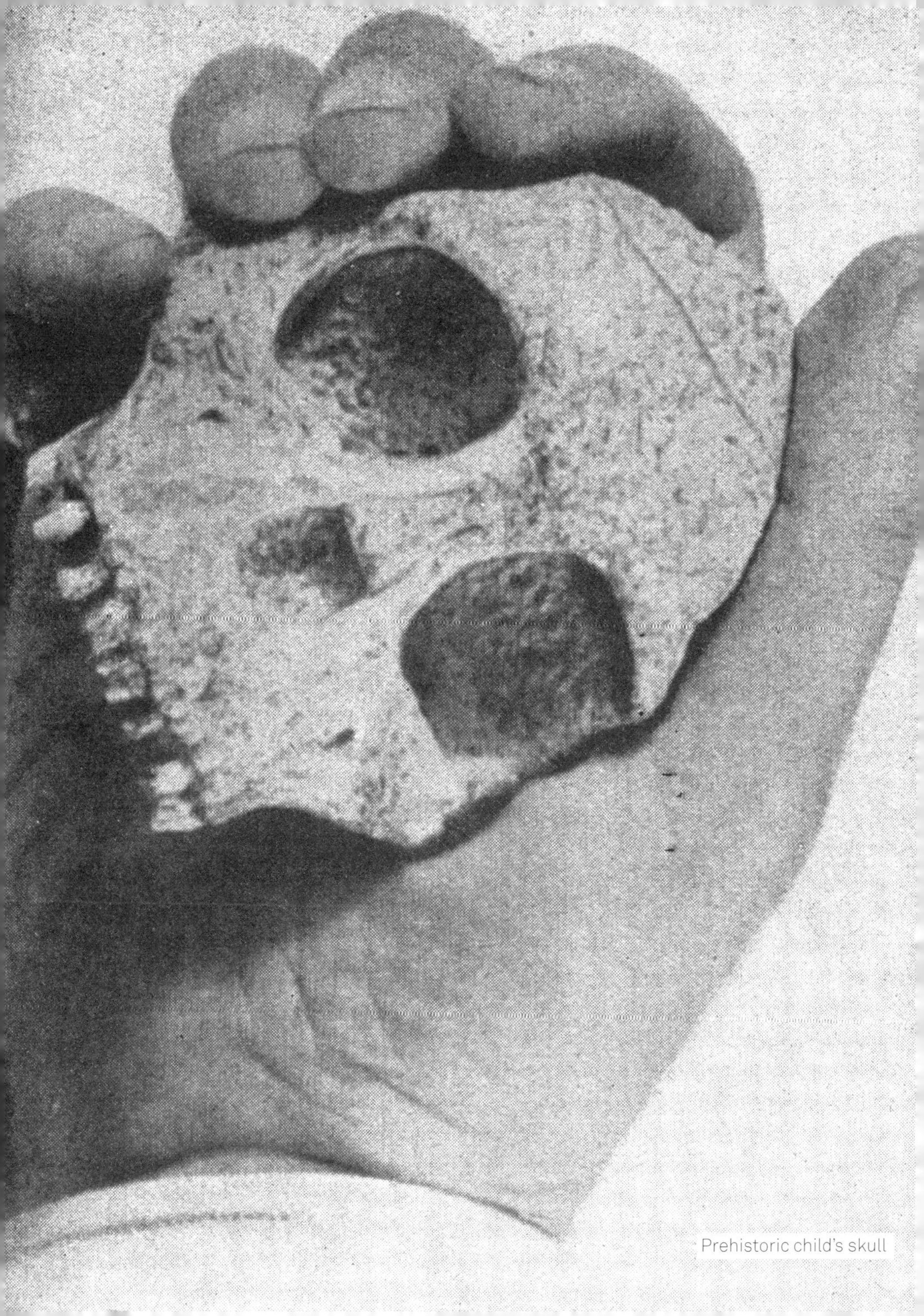
Prehistoric child's skull

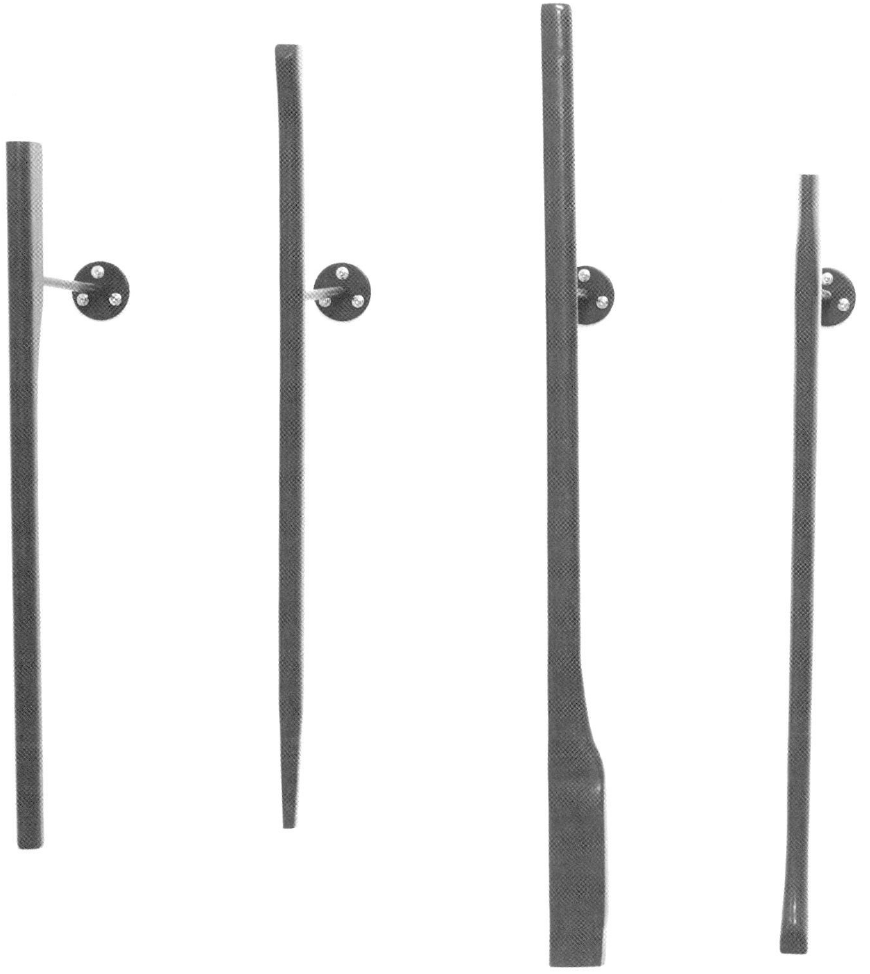

Hand Tool Interfaces, 2012

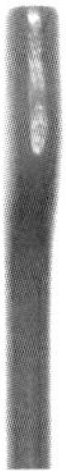
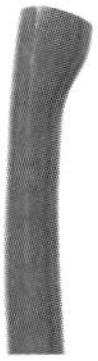
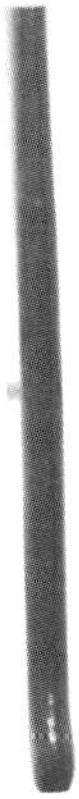
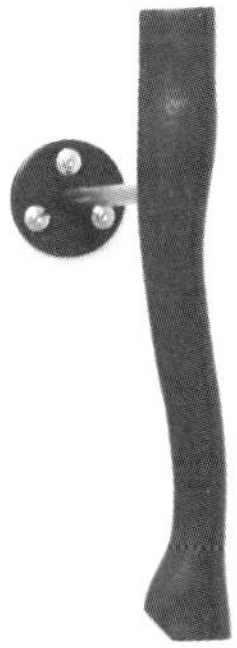

THE WORLD SET FREE

PRELUDE

THE SUN SNARERS

§ 1

THE history of mankind is the history of the attainment of external power. Man is the tool-using, fire-making animal. From the outset of his terrestrial career we find him supplementing the natural strength and bodily weapons of a beast by the heat of burning and the rough implement of stone. So he passed beyond the ape. From that he expands. Presently he added to himself the power of the horse and the ox, he borrowed the carrying strength of water and the driving force of the wind, he quickened his fire by blowing, and his simple tools, pointed first with copper and then with iron, increased and varied and became more elaborate and efficient. He sheltered his heat in houses and made his way easier by paths and roads. He complicated his social relationships

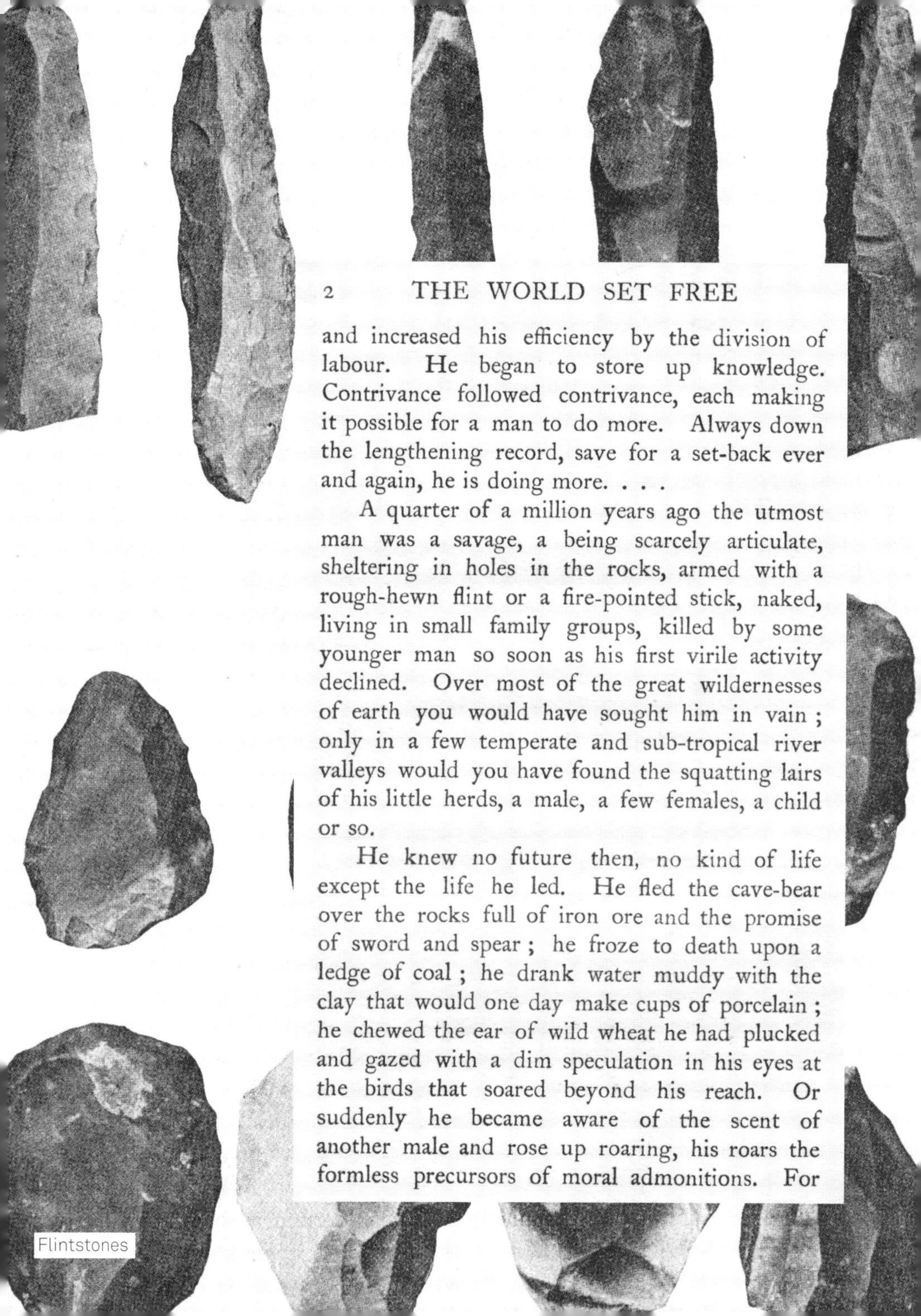

and increased his efficiency by the division of labour. He began to store up knowledge. Contrivance followed contrivance, each making it possible for a man to do more. Always down the lengthening record, save for a set-back ever and again, he is doing more. . . .

A quarter of a million years ago the utmost man was a savage, a being scarcely articulate, sheltering in holes in the rocks, armed with a rough-hewn flint or a fire-pointed stick, naked, living in small family groups, killed by some younger man so soon as his first virile activity declined. Over most of the great wildernesses of earth you would have sought him in vain ; only in a few temperate and sub-tropical river valleys would you have found the squatting lairs of his little herds, a male, a few females, a child or so.

He knew no future then, no kind of life except the life he led. He fled the cave-bear over the rocks full of iron ore and the promise of sword and spear ; he froze to death upon a ledge of coal ; he drank water muddy with the clay that would one day make cups of porcelain ; he chewed the ear of wild wheat he had plucked and gazed with a dim speculation in his eyes at the birds that soared beyond his reach. Or suddenly he became aware of the scent of another male and rose up roaring, his roars the formless precursors of moral admonitions. For

Flintstones

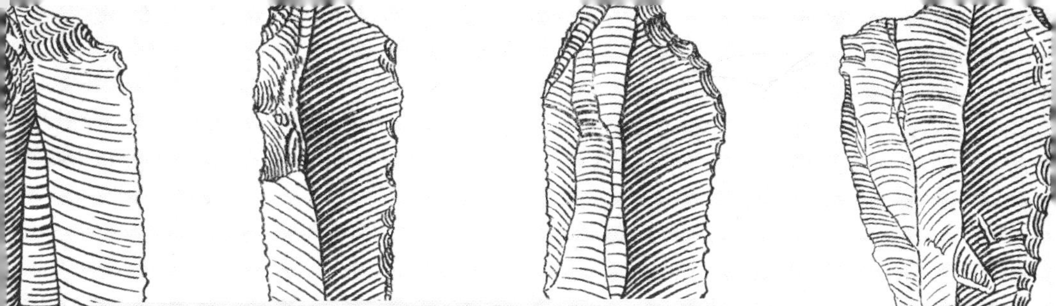

he was a great individualist, that original, he suffered none other than himself.

So through the long generations, this heavy precursor, this ancestor of all of us, fought and bred and perished, changing almost imperceptibly.

Yet he changed. That keen chisel of necessity which sharpened the tiger's claw age by age and fined down the clumsy Orchippus to the swift grace of the horse, was at work upon him—is at work upon him still. The clumsier and more stupidly fierce among him were killed soonest and oftenest ; the finer hand, the quicker eye, the bigger brain, the better balanced body prevailed ; age by age, the implements were a little better made, the man a little more delicately adjusted to his possibilities. He became more social ; his herd grew larger ; no longer did each man kill or drive out his growing sons ; a system of taboos made them tolerable to him, and they revered him alive and soon even after he was dead, and were his allies against the beasts and the rest of mankind. (But they were forbidden to touch the women of the tribe, they had to go out and capture women for themselves, and each son fled from his stepmother and hid from her lest the anger of the Old Man should be roused. All the world over, even to this day, these ancient inevitable taboos can be traced.) And now instead of caves came huts and hovels, and the fire was better tended and there were

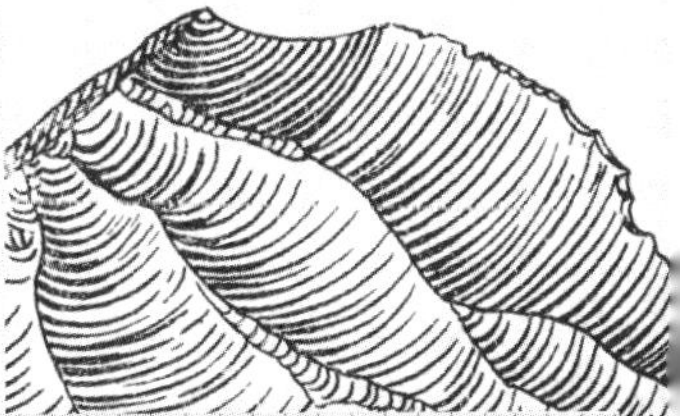

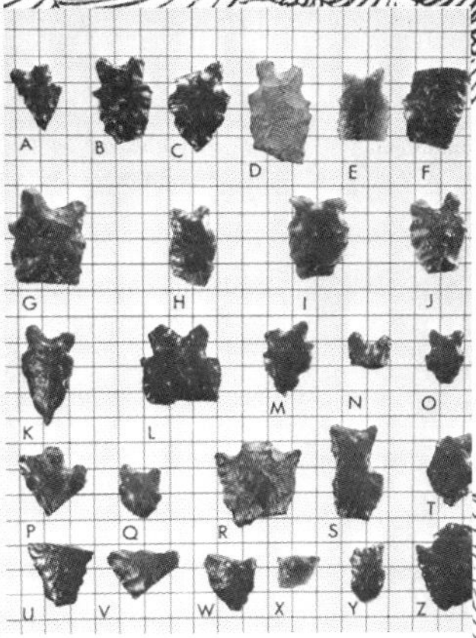

Inventory, test site stones

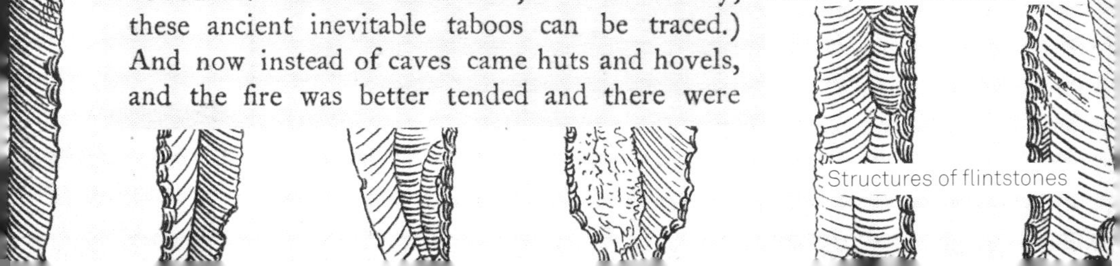
Structures of flintstones

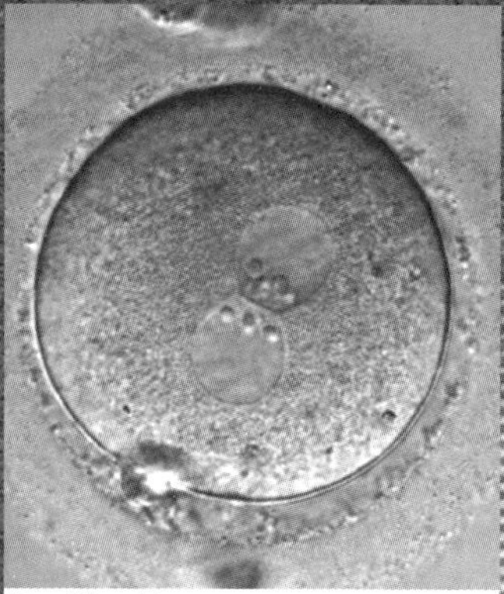

Fertilised human egg

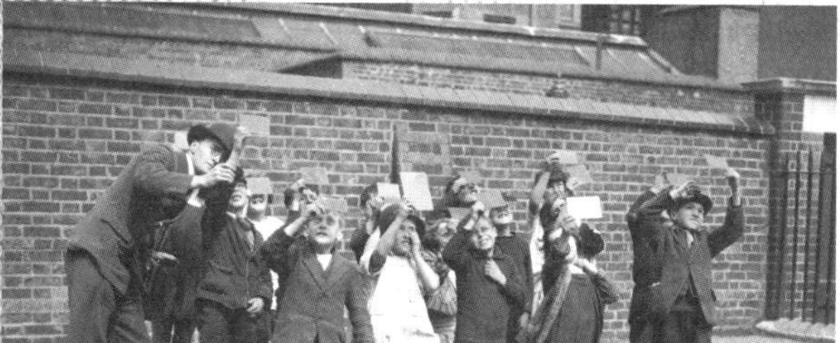

How to watch the sun, 1927

Sunspots

wrappings and garments; and so aided, the creature spread into colder climates, carrying food with him, storing food—until sometimes the neglected grass-seed sprouted again and gave a first hint of agriculture.

And already there were the beginnings of leisure and thought.

Man began to think. There were times when he was fed, when his lusts and his fears were all appeased, when the sun shone upon the squatting-place and dim stirrings of speculation lit his eyes. He scratched upon a bone and found resemblance and pursued it and began pictorial art, moulded the soft warm clay of the river brink between his fingers and found a pleasure in its patternings and repetitions, shaped it into the form of vessels and found that it would hold water. He watched the streaming river and wondered from what bountiful breast this incessant water came; he blinked at the sun and dreamt that perhaps he might snare it and spear it as it went down to its resting-place amidst the distant hills. Then he was roused to convey to his brother that once indeed he had done so—at least that someone had done so—he mixed that perhaps with another dream almost as daring, that one day a mammoth had been beset; and therewith began fiction—pointing a way to achievement—and the august prophetic procession of tales.

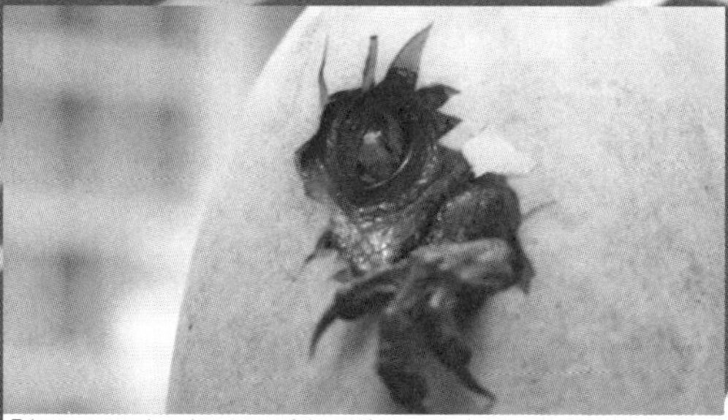
Dinosaur Junior cracking the egg (US 2015)

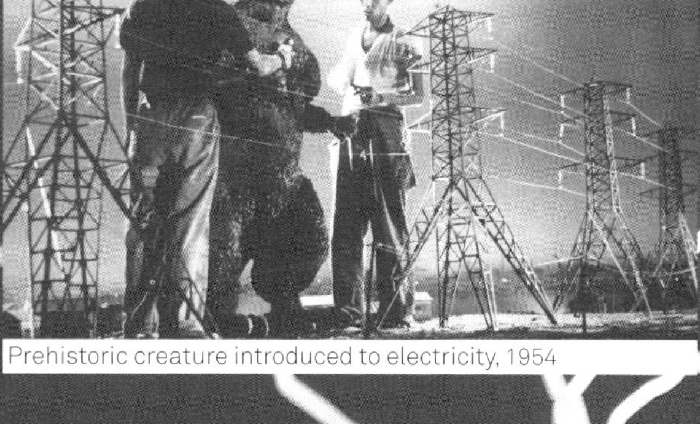
Prehistoric creature introduced to electricity, 1954

For scores and hundreds of centuries, for myriads of generations that life of our fathers went on. From the beginning to the ripening of that phase of human life, from the first clumsy eolith of rudely chipped flint to the first implements of polished stone, was two or three thousand centuries, ten or fifteen thousand generations. So slowly, by human standards, did humanity gather itself together out of the dim intimations of the beast. And that first glimmering of speculation, that first story of achievement, that story-teller bright-eyed and flushed under his matted hair gesticulating to his gaping incredulous listener, gripping his wrist to keep him attentive, was the most marvellous beginning this world has ever seen. It doomed the mammoths, and it began the setting of that snare that shall catch the sun.

§ 2

That dream was but a moment in a man's life, whose proper business it seemed was to get food and kill his fellows and beget after the manner of all that belongs to the fellowship of the beasts. About him, hidden from him by the thinnest of veils, were the untouched sources of Power, whose magnitude we scarcely do more than suspect even to-day, Power that could make his every conceivable dream come real. But the feet of the

Earth, approx. 180.000.000 years ago

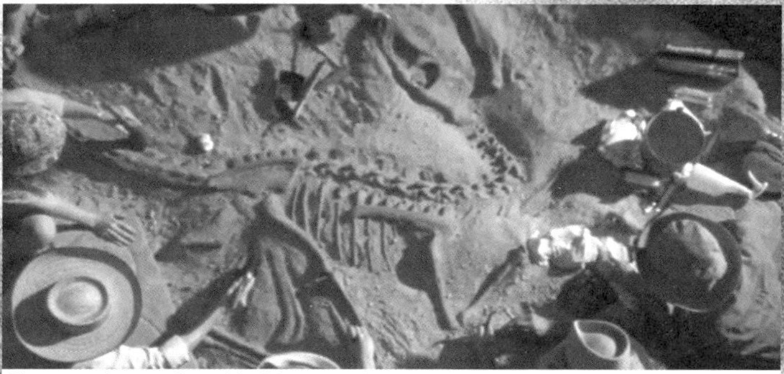
Dinosaur bones found in Montana (US 1993)

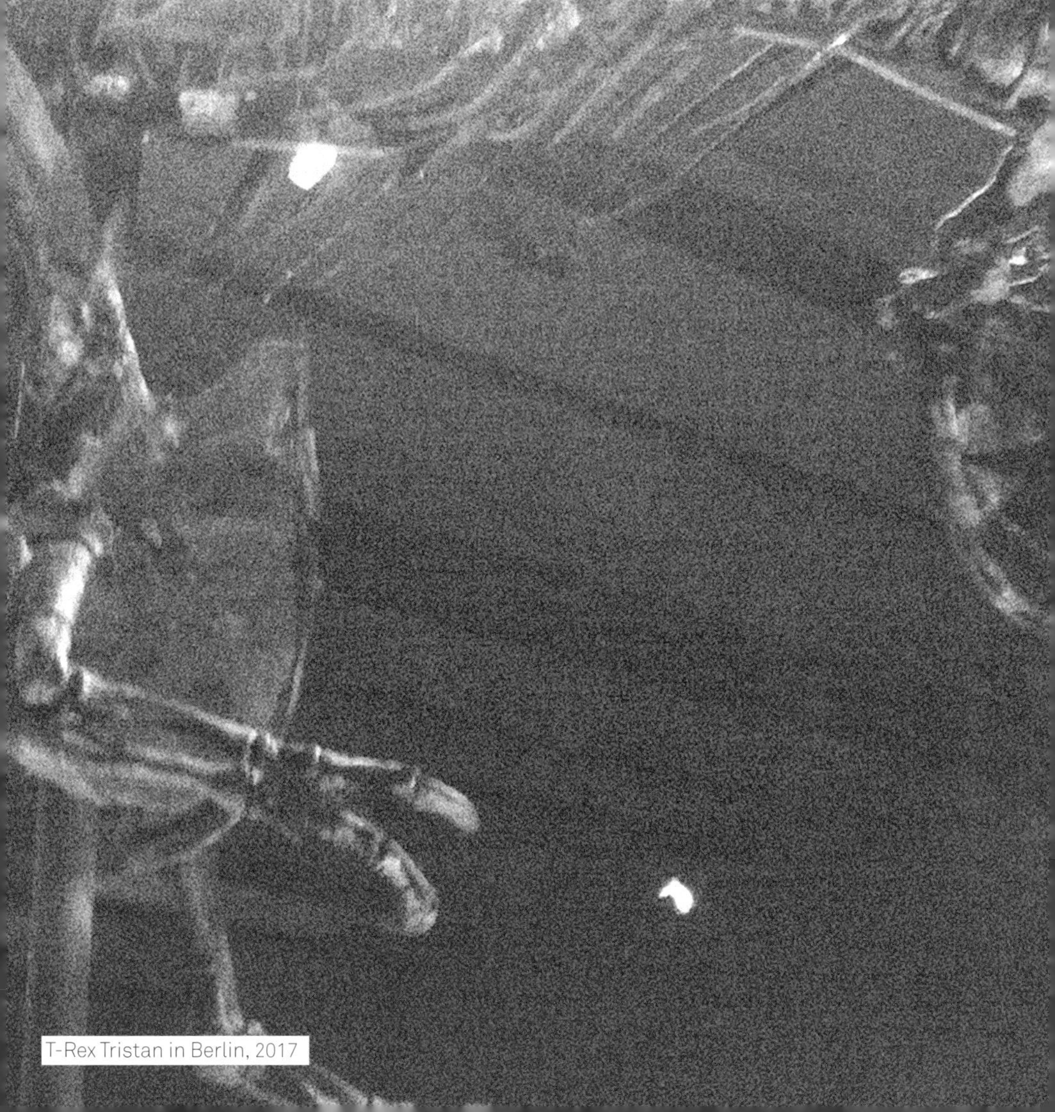
T-Rex Tristan in Berlin, 2017

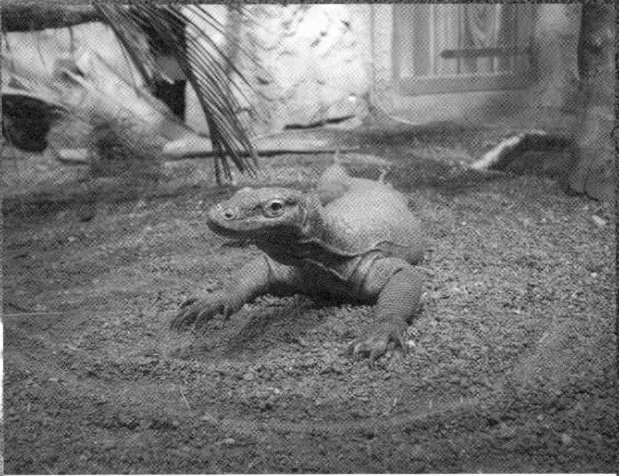

Relict of evolution, Leipzig Zoo, 2018

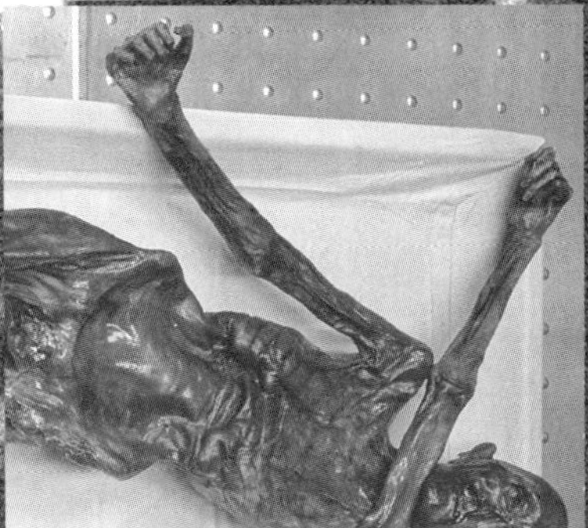

The Ötzi, found in the Alps, 1991

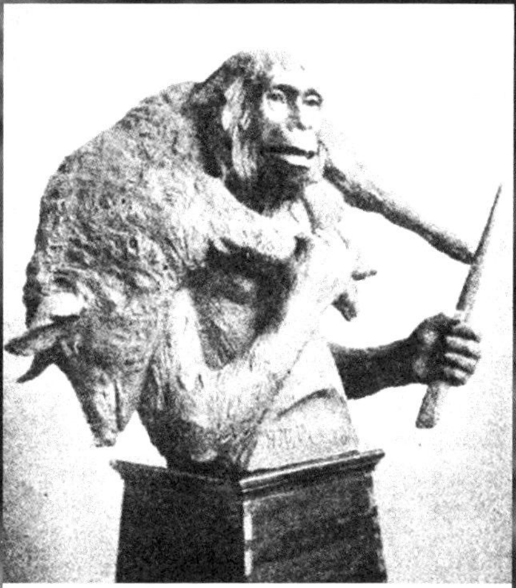

Homo heidelbergensis

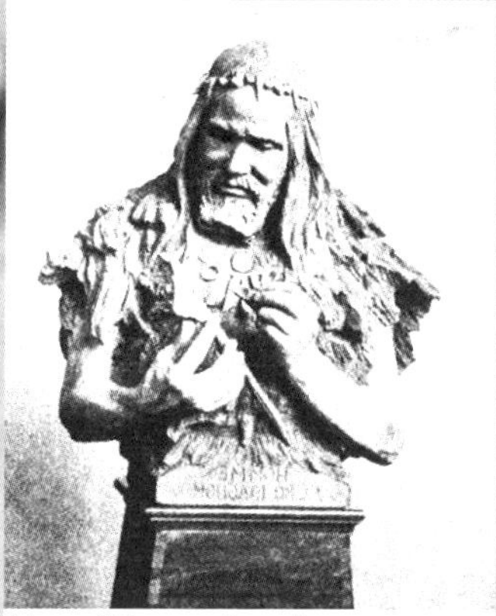

Man of the modern time

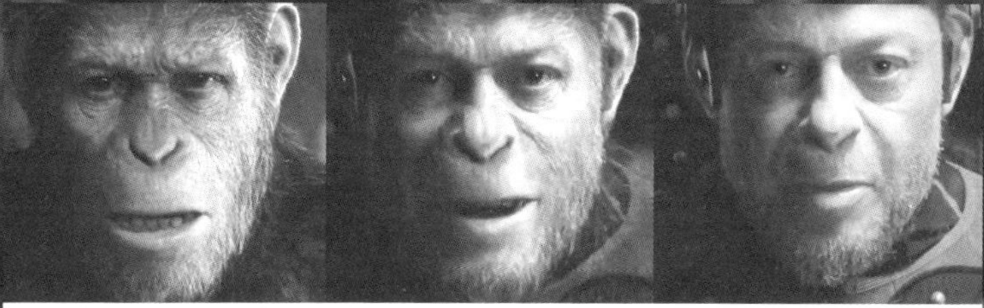

How the ape leader Caesar becomes the actor Andy Serkis, 2017

race were in the way of it, though he died blindly unknowing.

At last, in the generous levels of warm river valleys, where food is abundant and life very easy, the emerging human, overcoming his earlier jealousies, becoming, as necessity persecuted him less urgently, more social and tolerant and amenable, achieved a larger community. There began a division of labour, certain of the older men specialized in knowledge and direction, a strong man took the fatherly leadership in war, and priest and king began to develop their rôles in the opening drama of man's history. The priest's solicitude was seed-time and harvest and fertility, and the king ruled peace and war. In a hundred river valleys about the warm temperate zone of the earth there were already towns and temples, a score of thousand years ago. They flourished unrecorded, ignoring the past and unsuspicious of the future, for as yet writing had still to begin.

Very slowly did man increase his demand upon the illimitable wealth of Power that offered itself on every hand to him. He tamed certain animals, he developed his primordially haphazard agriculture into a ritual, he added first one metal to his resources and then another until he had copper and tin and iron and lead and gold and silver to supplement his stone, he hewed and carved wood, made pottery, paddled down his

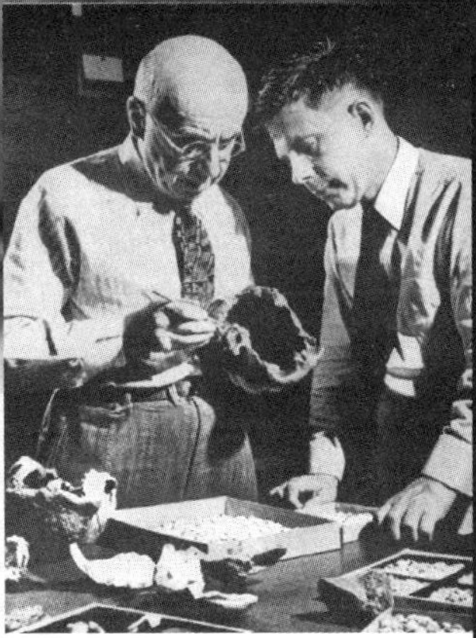

Solving puzzles

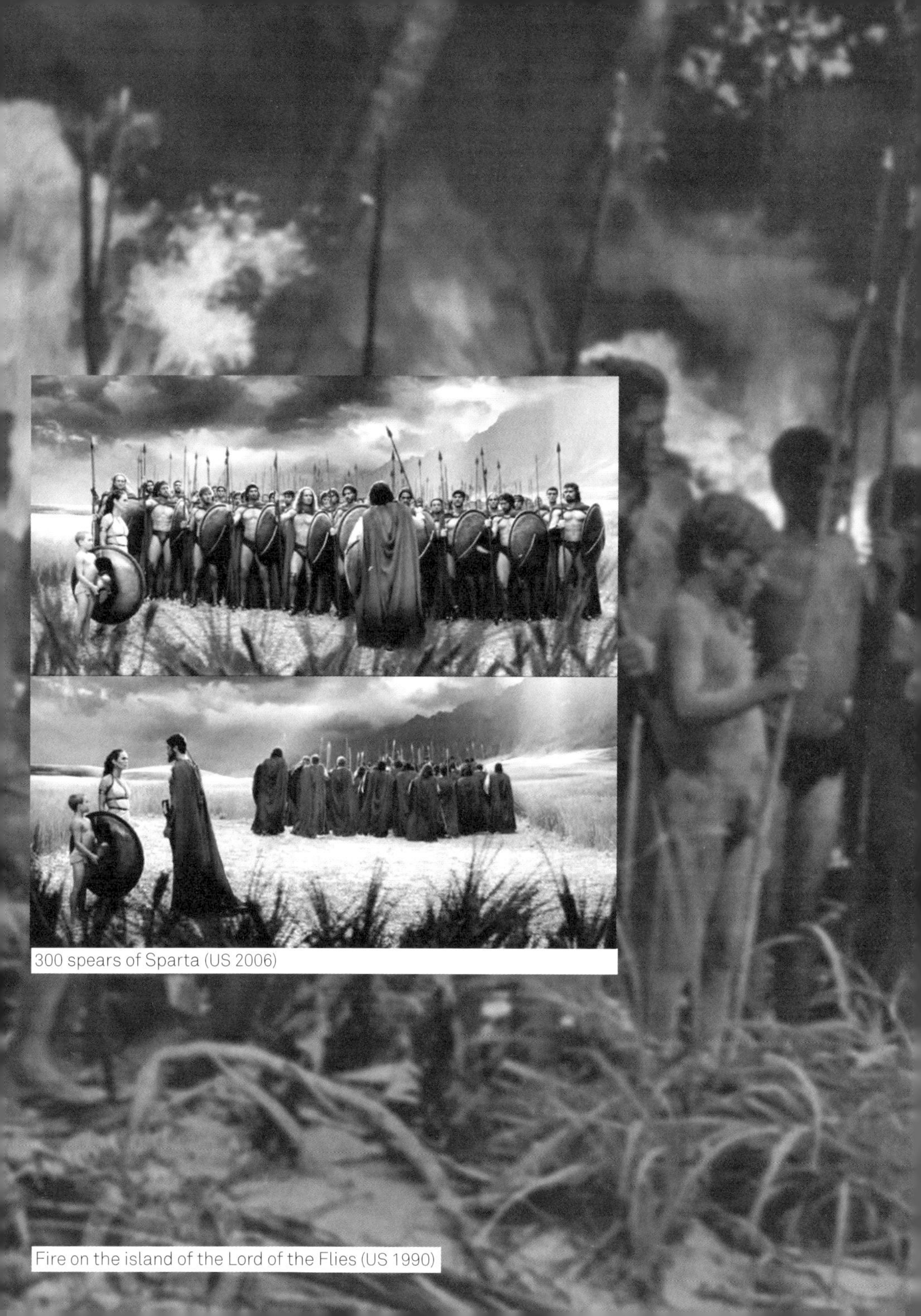

300 spears of Sparta (US 2006)

Fire on the island of the Lord of the Flies (US 1990)

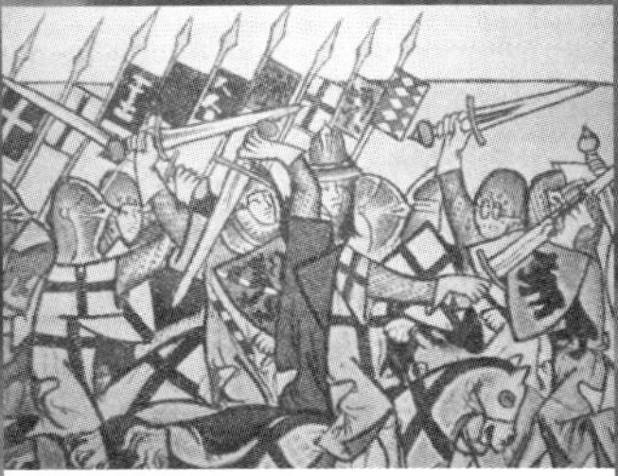
Knights of the 14th century

river until he came to the sea, discovered the wheel and made the first roads. But his chief activity for a hundred centuries and more, was the subjugation of himself and others to larger and larger societies. The history of man is not simply the conquest of external power ; it is first the conquest of those distrusts and fiercenesses, that self-concentration and intensity of animalism, that tie his hands from taking his inheritance. The ape in us still resents association. From the dawn of the age of polished stone to the achievement of the Peace of the World, man's dealings were chiefly with himself and his fellow man, trading, bargaining, law-making, propitiating, enslaving, conquering, exterminating, and every little increment in Power, he turned at once and always turns to the purposes of this confused elaborate struggle to socialize. To incorporate and comprehend his fellow men into a community of purpose became the last and greatest of his instincts. Already before the last polished phase of the stone age was over he had become a political animal. He made astonishingly far-reaching discoveries within himself, first of counting and then of writing and making records, and with that his town communities began to stretch out to dominion ; in the valleys of the Nile, the Euphrates and the great Chinese rivers, the first empires and the first written laws had their beginnings. Men specialized for fighting

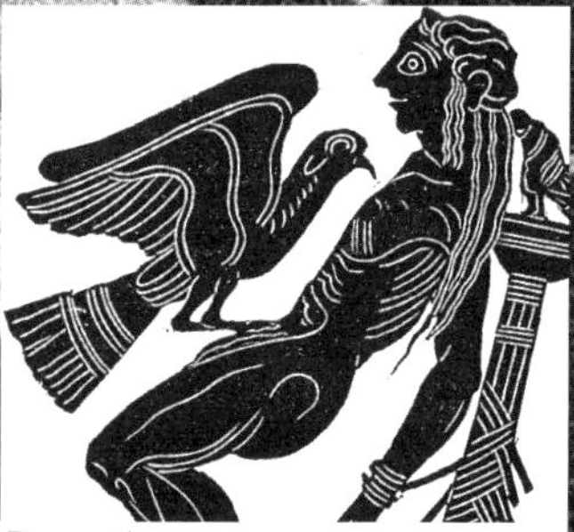
Prometheus

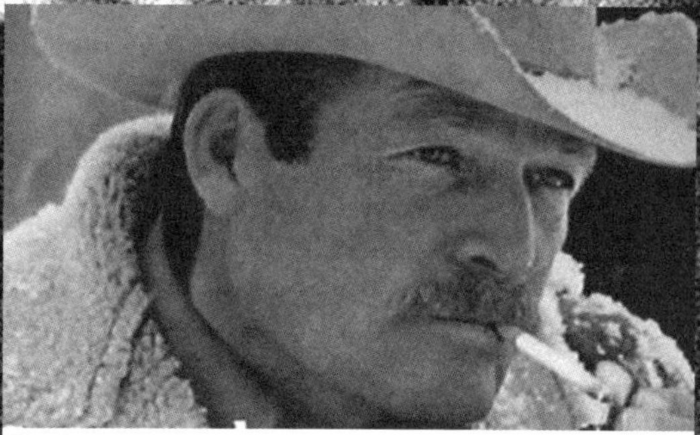
Smoker

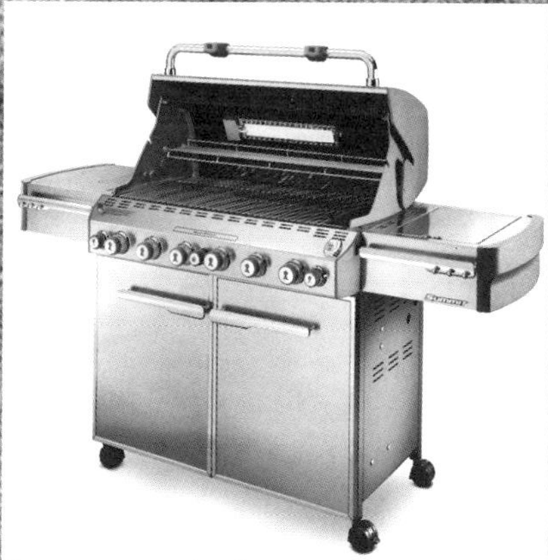
Contemporary barbeque

First time food is cooked by fire (FR 1978)

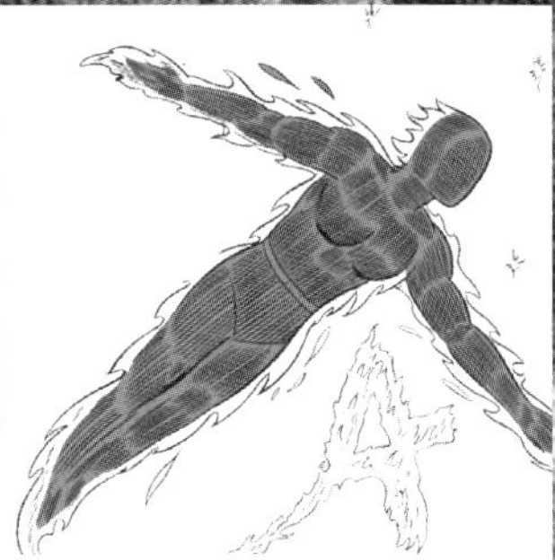

Human torch

and rule as soldiers and knights. Later as ships grew seaworthy, the Mediterranean which had been a barrier became a highway, and at last out of a tangle of pirate polities came the great struggle of Carthage and Rome. The history of Europe is the history of the victory and breaking up of the Roman Empire. Every ascendant monarch in Europe up to the last, aped Caesar and called himself Kaiser or Czar or Imperator or Kasir-i-Hind. Measured by the duration of human life it is a vast space of time between that first dynasty in Egypt and the coming of the aeroplane, but by the scale that looks back to the makers of the eoliths, it is all of it a story of yesterday.

Now during this period of two hundred centuries or more, this period of the warring states, while men's minds were chiefly preoccupied by politics and mutual aggression, their progress in the acquirement of external Power was slow—rapid in comparison with the progress of the old stone age, but slow in comparison with this new age of systematic discovery in which we live. They did not very greatly alter the weapons and tactics of warfare, the methods of agriculture, seamanship, their knowledge of the habitable globe, or the devices and utensils of domestic life between the days of the early Egyptians and the days when Christopher Columbus was a child. Of course there were inventions and

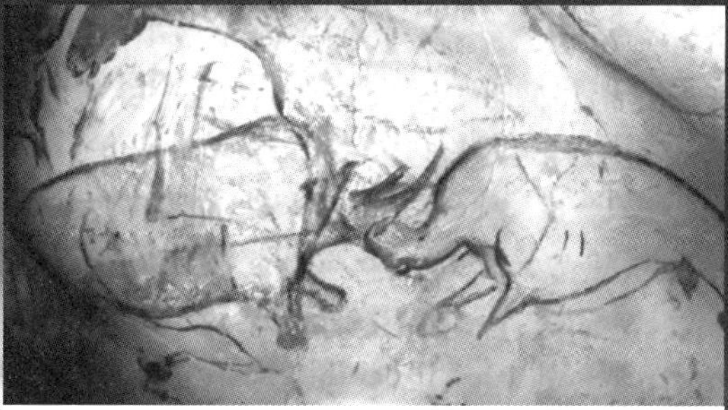

Bull fight drawn on a cave wall

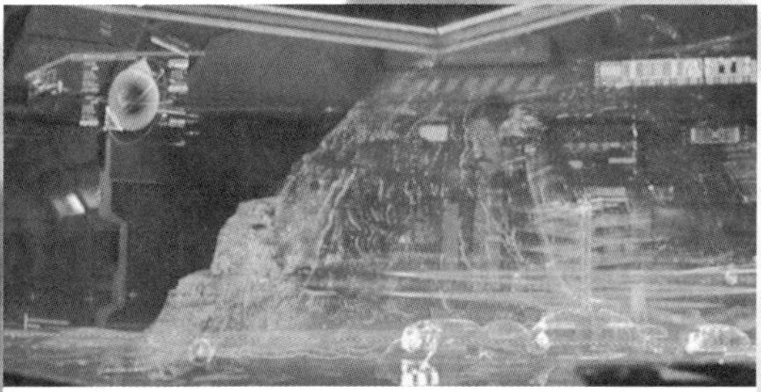

Scanning a cave on moon LV-223 (UK, US 2012)

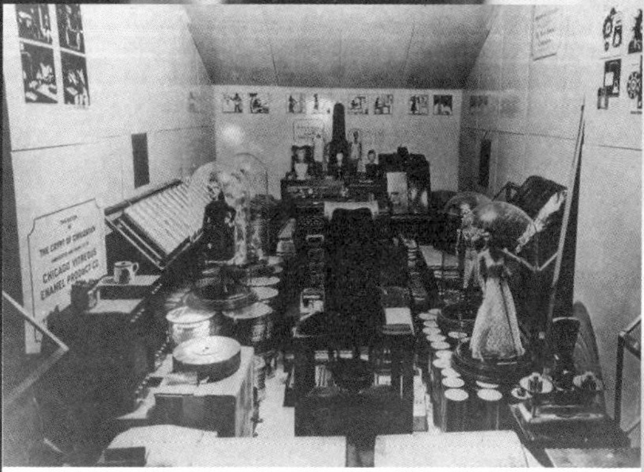

Crypt of Civilisation, to be opened in the year 8113

Cave of Chauvet (FR, DE, CA, UK, US 2010)

changes, but there were also retrogressions; things were found out and then forgotten again; it was on the whole a progress but it contained no steps; the peasant life was the same, there were already priests and lawyers and town craftsmen and territorial lords and rulers, doctors, wise women, soldiers and sailors in Egypt and China and Assyria and south-eastern Europe at the beginning of that period, and they were doing much the same things and living much the same life as they were in Europe in 1500 A.D. The English excavators of the year 1900 A.D. could delve into the remains of Babylon and Egypt and disinter legal documents, domestic accounts and family correspondence that they could read with the completest sympathy. There were great religious and moral changes throughout the period, empires and republics replaced one another, Italy tried a vast experiment in slavery, and indeed slavery was tried again and again and failed and failed and was still to be tested again and rejected again in the New World; Christianity and Mahometanism swept away a thousand more specialized cults, but essentially these were progressive adaptations of mankind to material conditions that must have seemed fixed for ever. The idea of revolutionary changes in the material conditions of life would have been entirely strange to human thought through all that time.

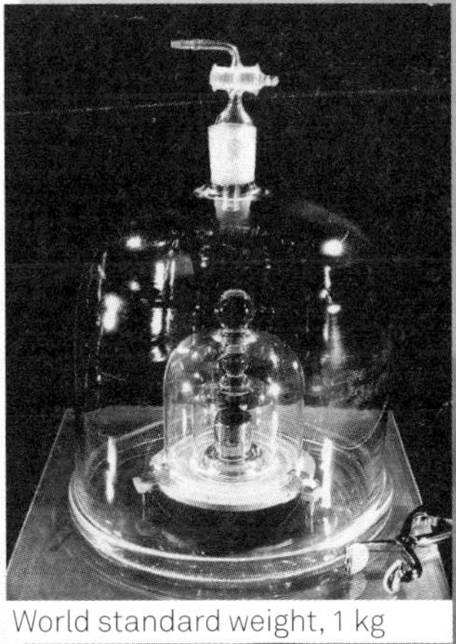

World standard weight, 1 kg

Yet the dreamer, the story-teller, was there still, waiting for his opportunity amidst the busy pre-occupations, the comings and goings, the wars and processions, the castle building and cathedral building, the arts and loves, the small diplomacies and incurable feuds, the crusades and trading journeys of the middle ages. He no longer speculated with the untrammelled freedom of the stone-age savage; authoritative explanations of everything barred his path; but he speculated with a better brain, sat idle and gazed at circling stars in the sky and mused upon the coin and crystal in his hand. Whenever there was a certain leisure for thought throughout these times, then men were to be found dissatisfied with the appearances of things, dissatisfied with the assurances of orthodox belief, uneasy with a sense of unread symbols in the world about them, questioning the finality of scholastic wisdom. Through all the ages of history there were men to whom this whisper had come of hidden things about them. They could no longer lead ordinary lives nor content themselves with the common things of this world once they had heard this voice. And mostly they believed not only that all this world was as it were a painted curtain before things unguessed at, but that these secrets were Power. Hitherto Power had come to men by chance, but now there were these seekers, seeking,

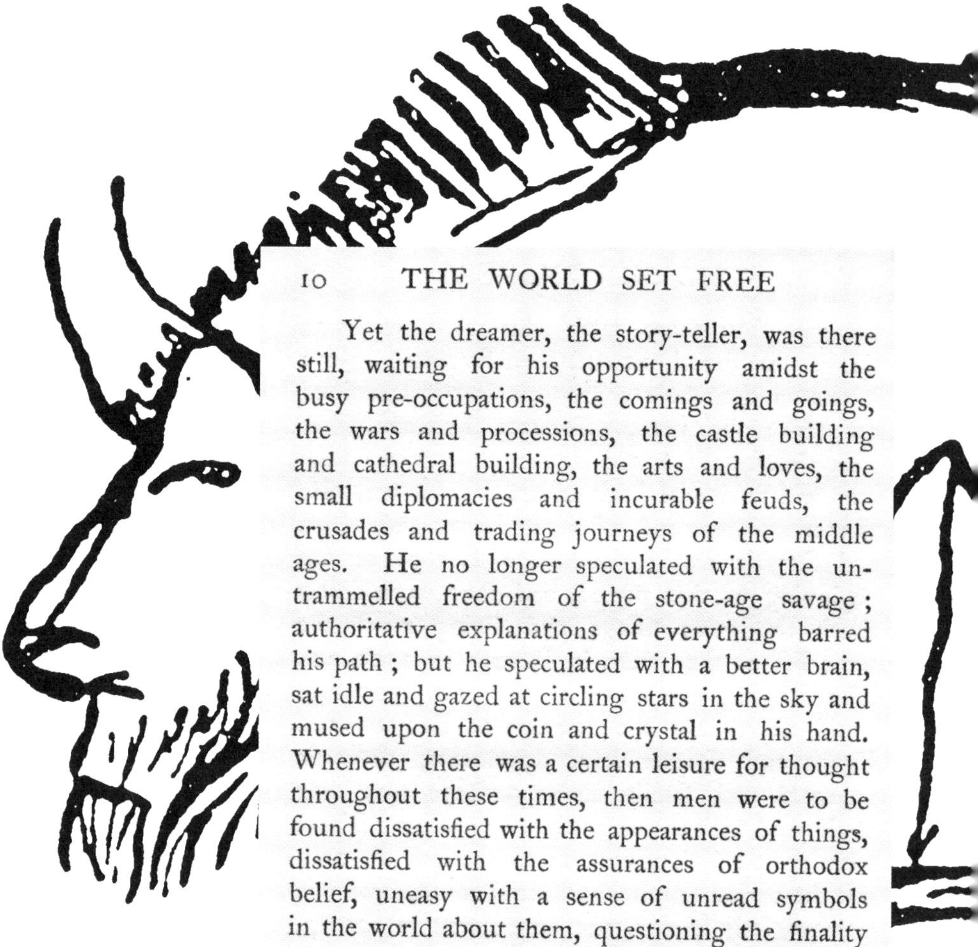

Cro-Magnon Bison

seeking among rare and curious and perplexing objects, sometimes finding some odd utilizable thing, sometimes deceiving themselves with fancied discovery, sometimes pretending to find. The world of every day laughed at these eccentric beings, or found them annoying and ill-treated them, or was seized with fear and made saints and sorcerers and warlocks of them, or with covetousness and entertained them hopefully; but for the greater part heeded them not at all. Yet they were of the blood of him who had first dreamt of attacking the mammoth; every one of them was of his blood and descent; and the thing they sought, all unwittingly, was the snare that will some day catch the sun.

§ 3

Such a man was that Leonardo da Vinci, who went about the court of Sforza in Milan in a state of dignified abstraction. His commonplace books are full of prophetic subtlety and ingenious anticipations of the methods of the early aviators. Dürer was his parallel and Roger Bacon—whom the Franciscans silenced—of his kindred. Such a man again in an earlier city was Hero of Alexandria, who knew of the power of steam nineteen hundred years

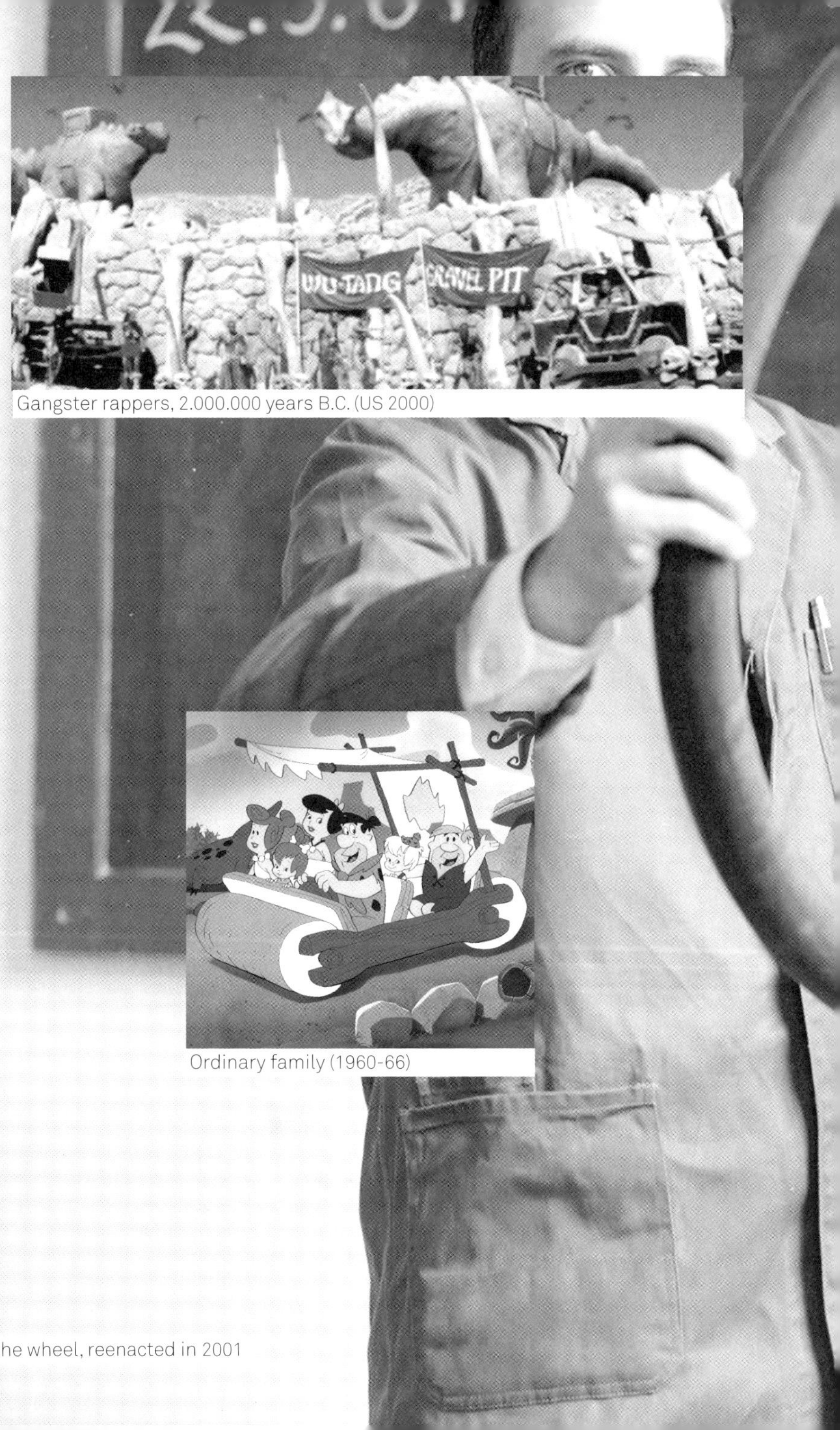

Gangster rappers, 2.000.000 years B.C. (US 2000)

Ordinary family (1960-66)

Invention of the wheel, reenacted in 2001

before it was first brought into use. And earlier still was Archimedes of Syracuse, and still earlier the legendary Daedalus of Cnossos. All up and down the record of history whenever there was a little leisure from war and brutality the seekers appeared. And half the alchemists were of their tribe.

When Roger Bacon blew up his first batch of gunpowder one might have supposed that men would have gone at once to the explosive engine. But they could see nothing of the sort. They were not yet beginning to think of seeing things; their metallurgy was all too poor to make such engines even had they thought of them. For a time they could not make instruments sound enough to stand this new force even for so rough a purpose as hurling a missile. Their first guns had barrels of coopered timber, and the world waited for more than five hundred years before the explosive engine came.

Even when the seekers found, it was at first a long journey before the world could use their findings for any but the roughest, most obvious purposes. If man in general was not still as absolutely blind to the unconquered energies about him as his paleolithic precursor, he was at best purblind.

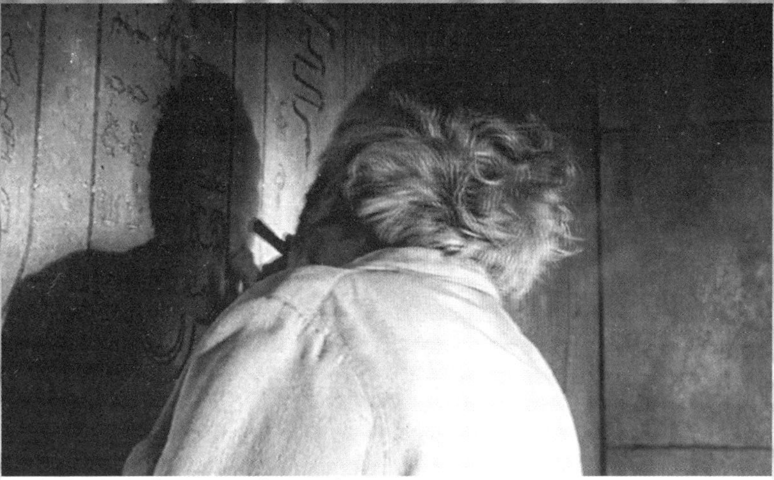

Archeologist in Egypt, 1914 (FR 1997)

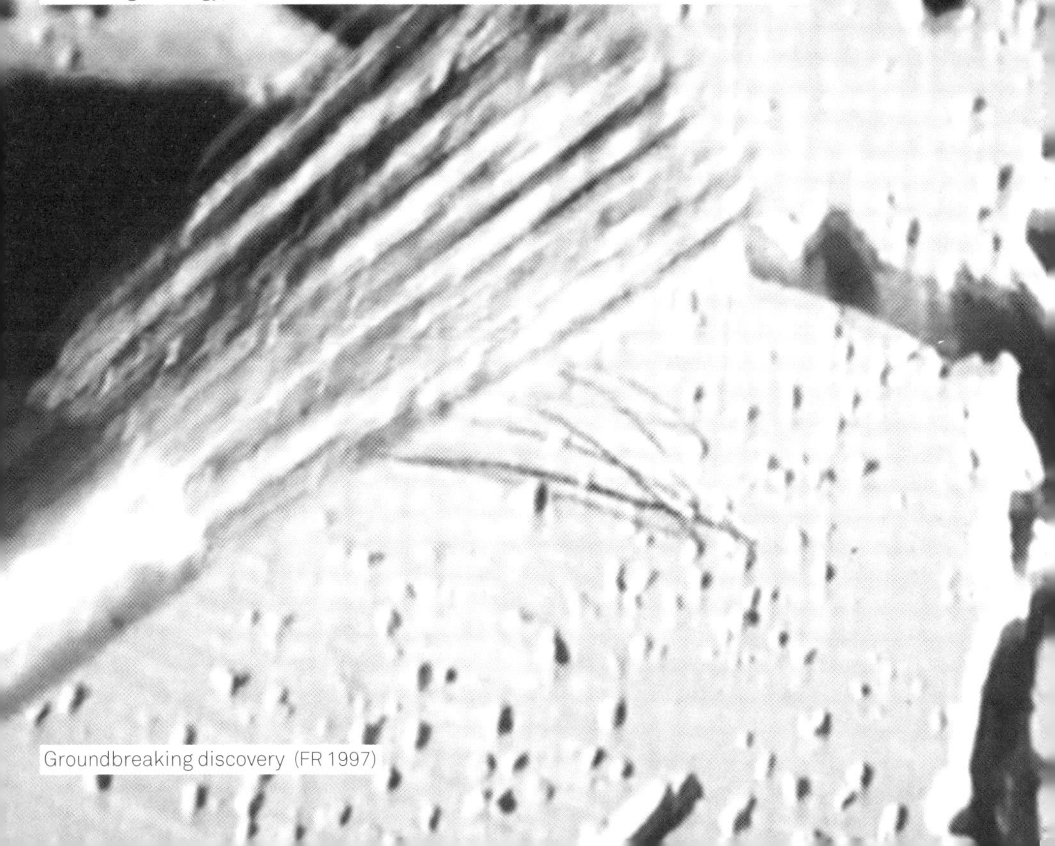

Groundbreaking discovery (FR 1997)

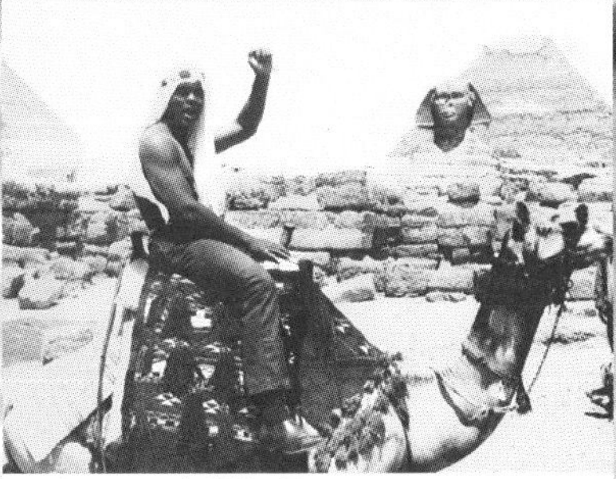

Muhammad Ali in Egypt, 1966

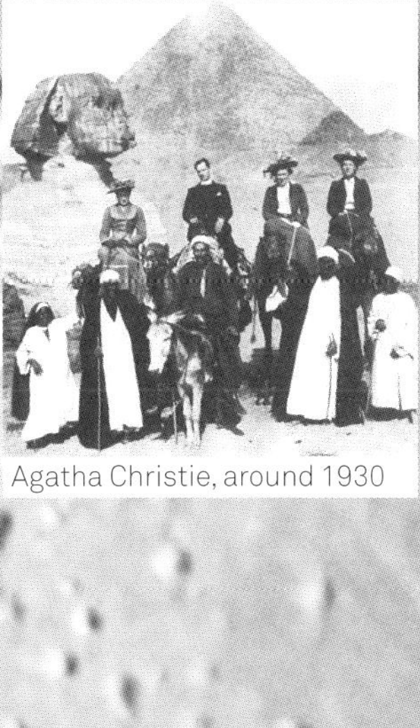

Agatha Christie, around 1930

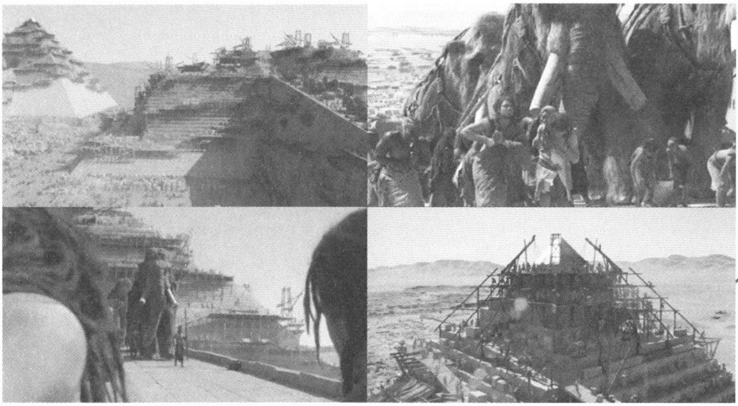

Building the Giza pyramids with mammuths (US, ZA 2008)

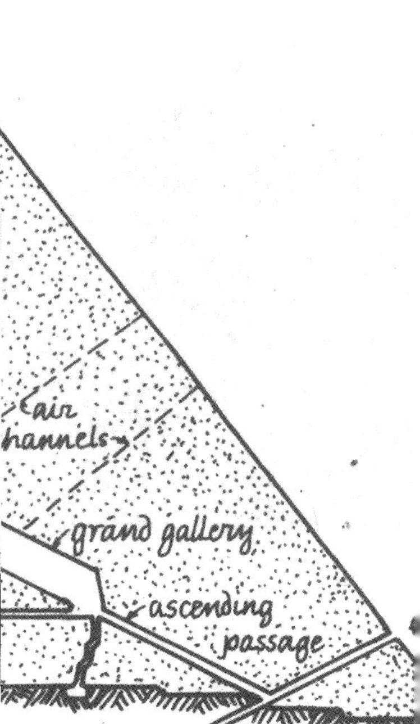

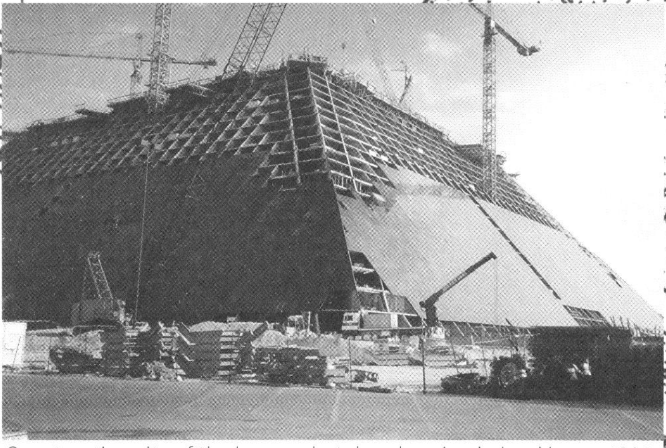

Construction site of the Luxor—hotel and casino in Las Vegas, 1992

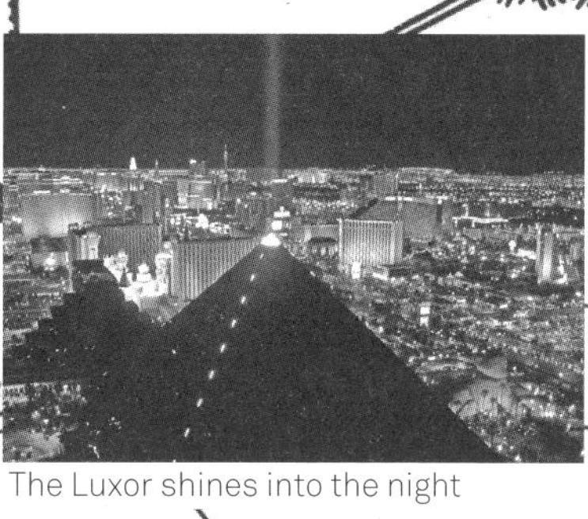

The Luxor shines into the night

Dimensions of the great pyramids

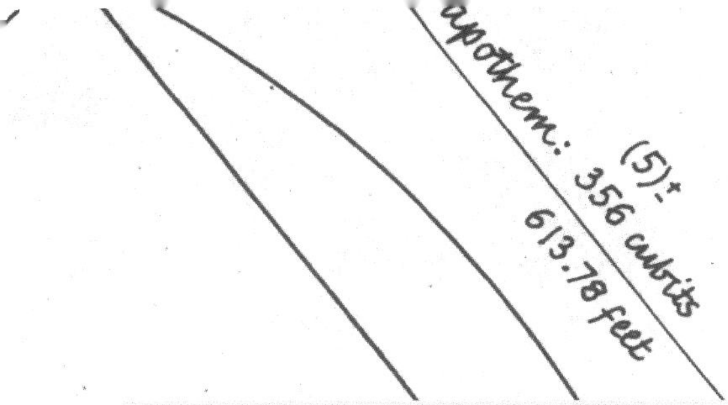

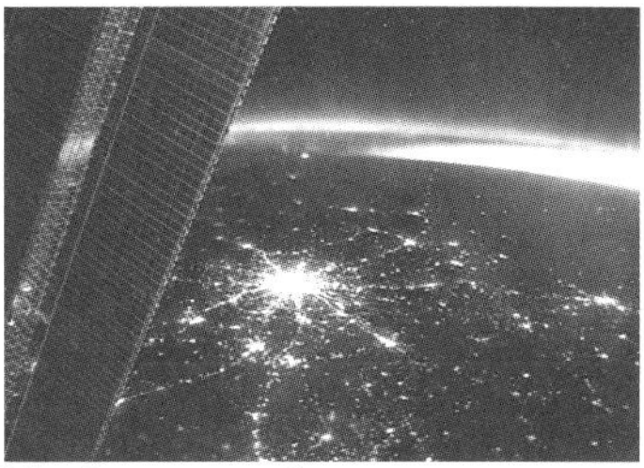
The Luxor seen from space

§ 4

The latent energy of coal and the power of steam waited long on the verge of discovery, before they began to influence human lives.

There were no doubt many such devices as Hero's toys devised and forgotten, time after time, in courts and palaces, but it needed that coal should be mined and burning with plenty of iron at hand before it dawned upon men that here was something more than a curiosity. And it is to be remarked that the first recorded suggestion for the use of steam was in war; there is an Elizabethan pamphlet in which it is proposed to fire shot out of corked iron bottles full of heated water. The mining of coal for fuel, the smelting of iron upon a larger scale than men had ever done before, the steam pumping engine, the steam-engine and the steam-boat, followed one another in an order that had a kind of logical necessity. It is the most interesting and instructive chapter in the history of the human intelligence, the history of steam from its beginning as a fact in human consciousness to the perfection of the great turbine engines that preceded the utilization of intra-molecular power. Nearly every human being must have seen steam, seen it incuriously for many thousands of years; the women in

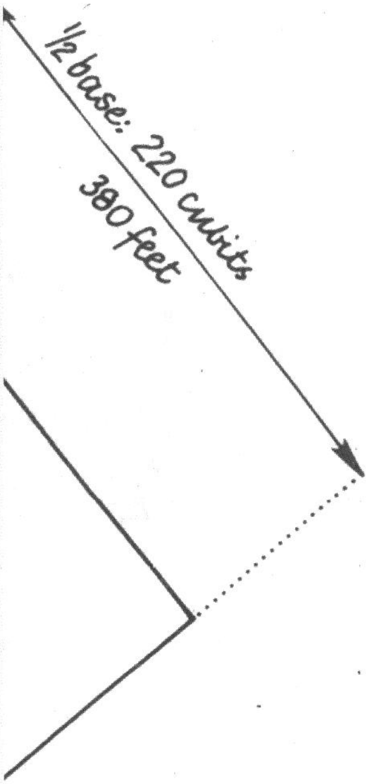

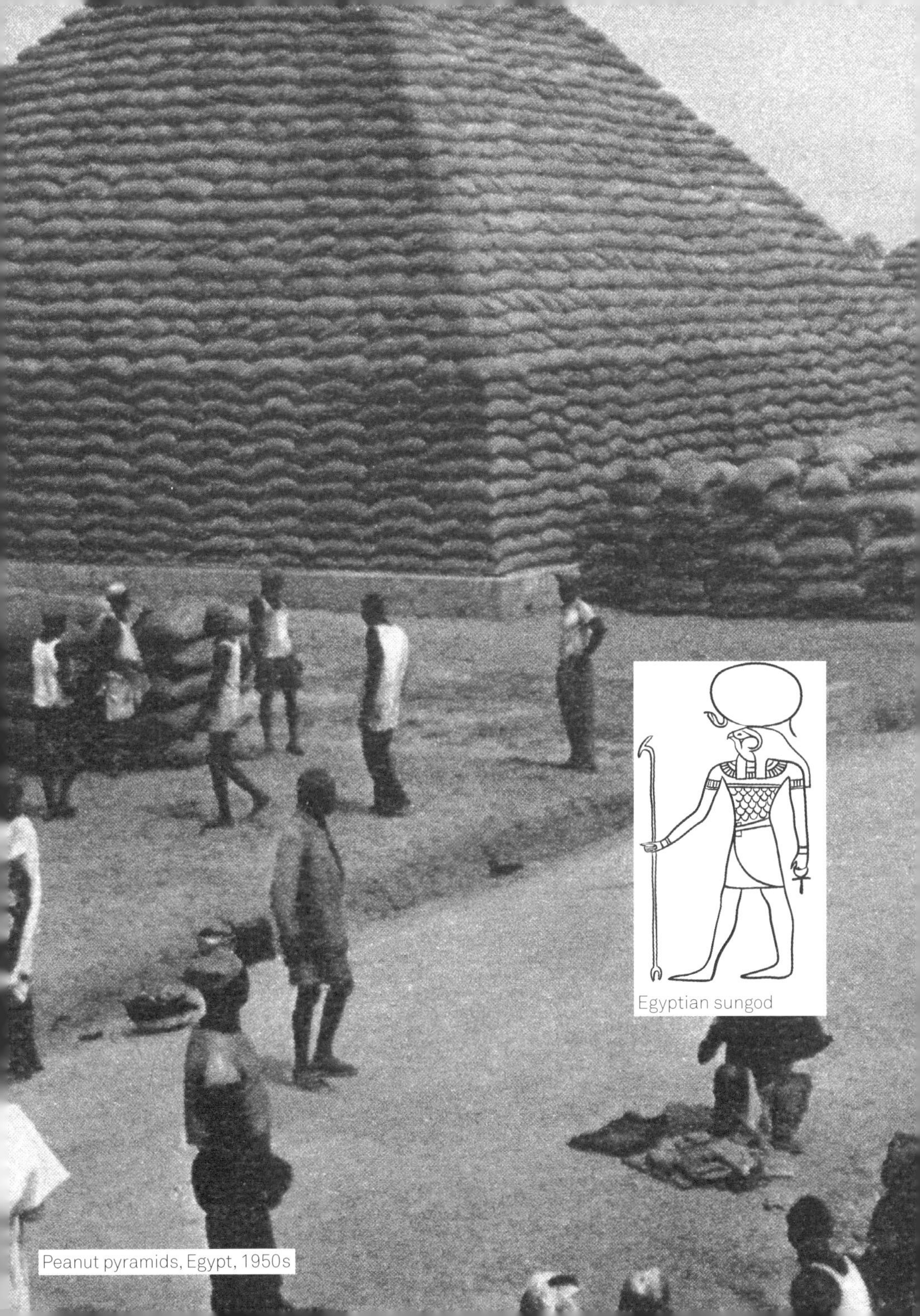

Peanut pyramids, Egypt, 1950s

Egyptian sungod

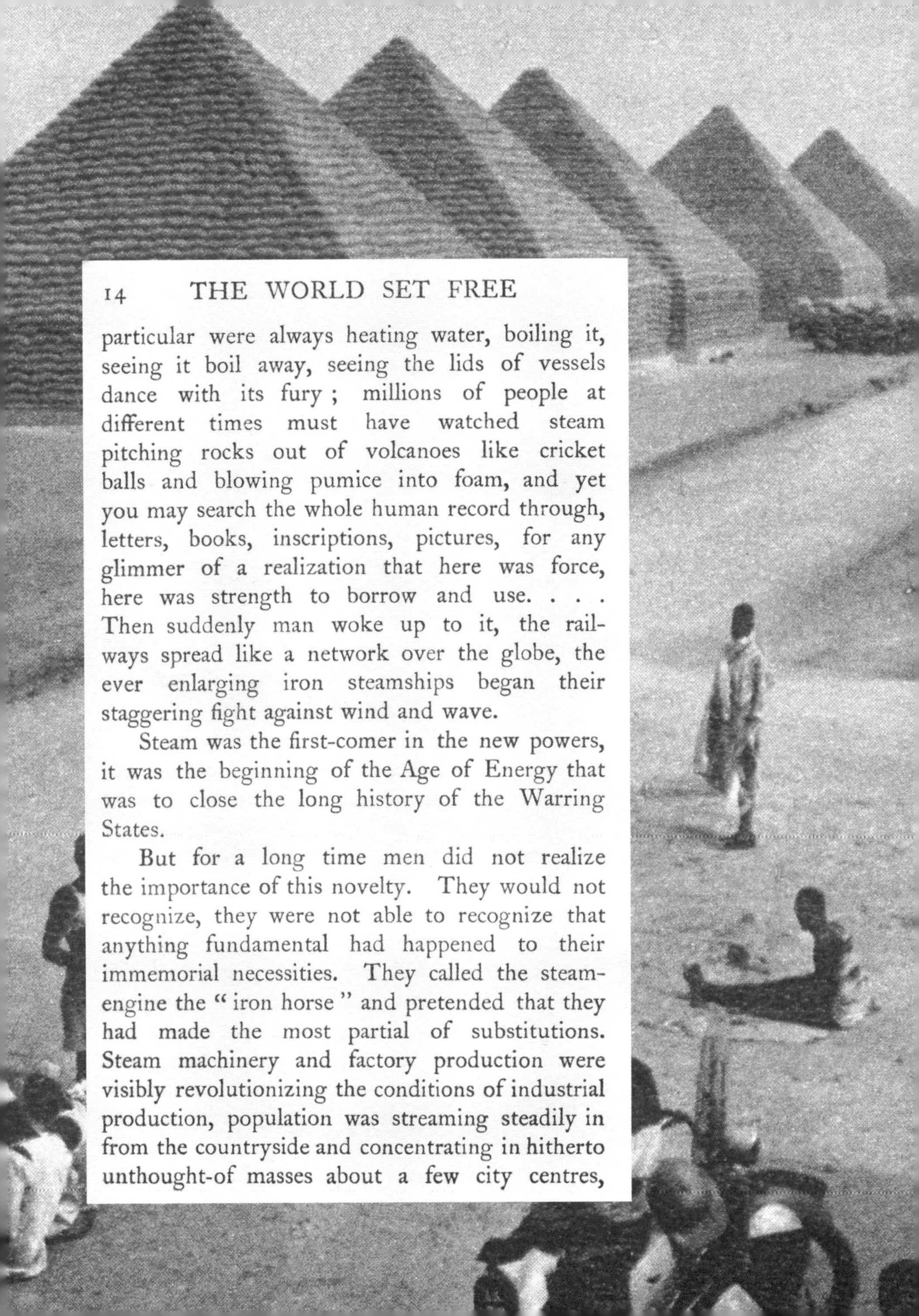

particular were always heating water, boiling it, seeing it boil away, seeing the lids of vessels dance with its fury ; millions of people at different times must have watched steam pitching rocks out of volcanoes like cricket balls and blowing pumice into foam, and yet you may search the whole human record through, letters, books, inscriptions, pictures, for any glimmer of a realization that here was force, here was strength to borrow and use. . . . Then suddenly man woke up to it, the railways spread like a network over the globe, the ever enlarging iron steamships began their staggering fight against wind and wave.

Steam was the first-comer in the new powers, it was the beginning of the Age of Energy that was to close the long history of the Warring States.

But for a long time men did not realize the importance of this novelty. They would not recognize, they were not able to recognize that anything fundamental had happened to their immemorial necessities. They called the steam-engine the "iron horse" and pretended that they had made the most partial of substitutions. Steam machinery and factory production were visibly revolutionizing the conditions of industrial production, population was streaming steadily in from the countryside and concentrating in hitherto unthought-of masses about a few city centres,

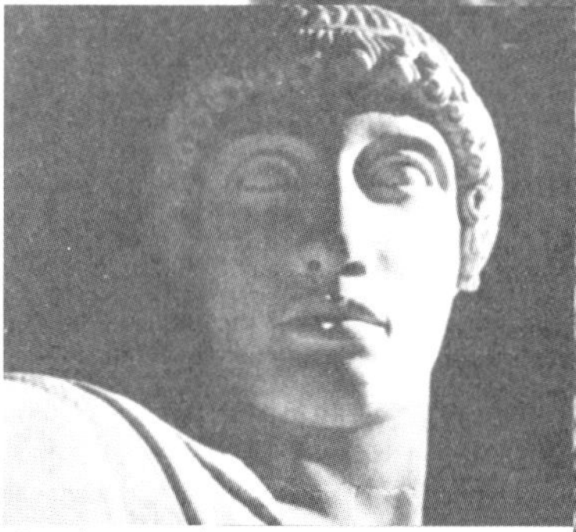

Greek sungod

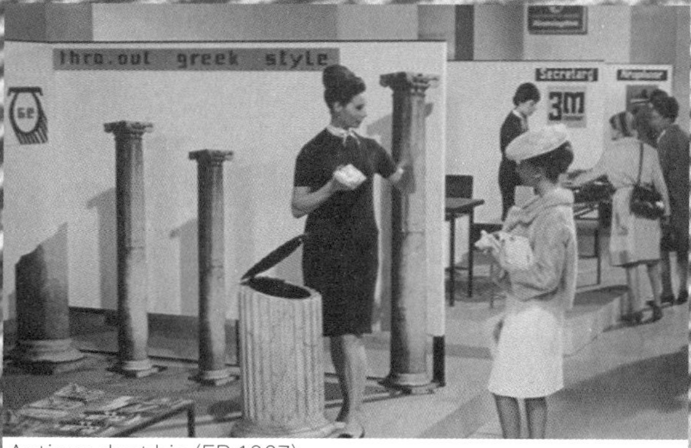

Antique dust bin (FR 1967)

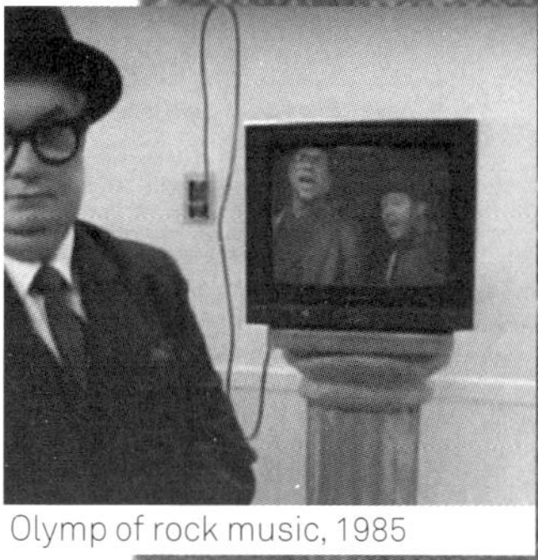

Olymp of rock music, 1985

Theatre

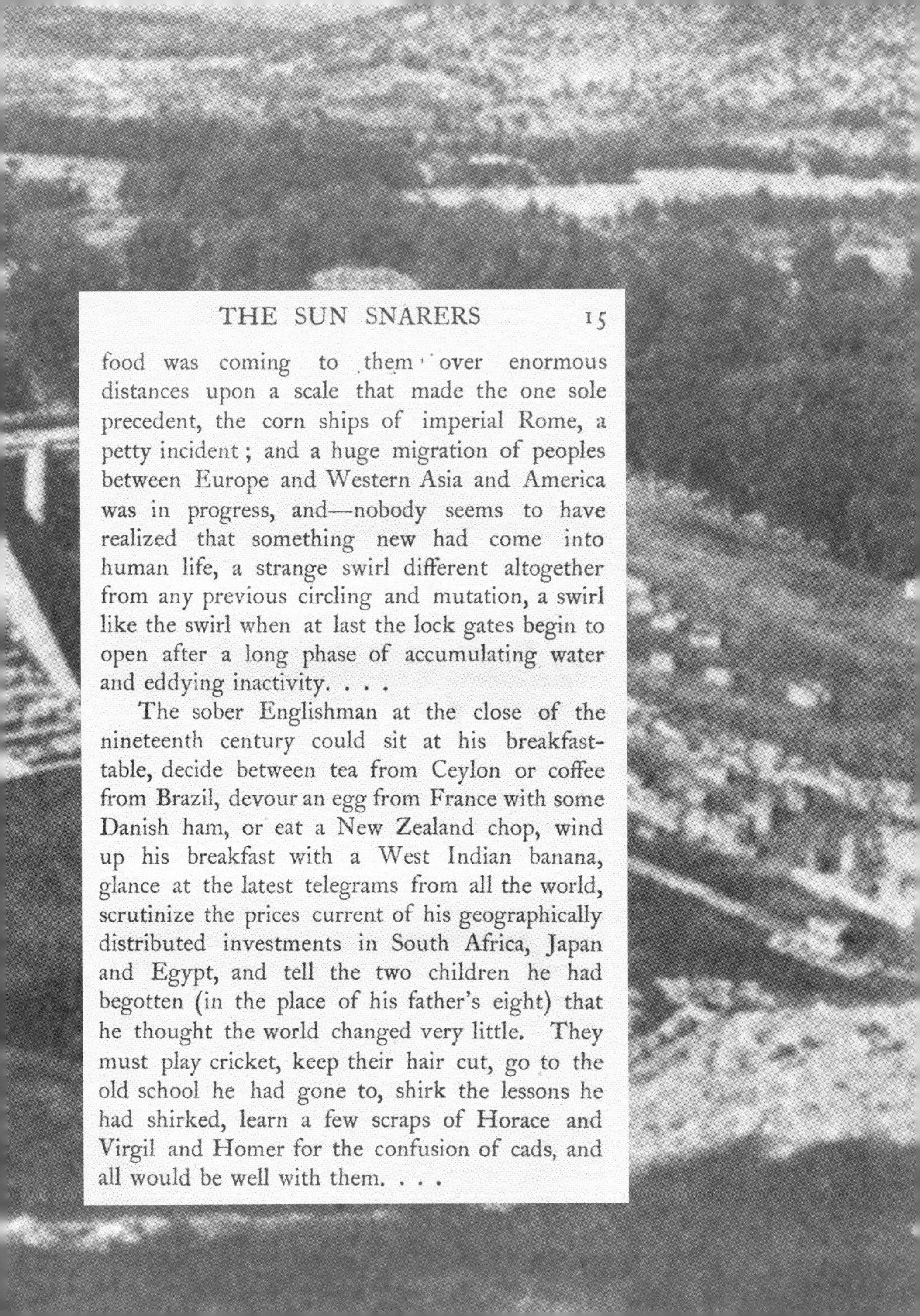

food was coming to them over enormous distances upon a scale that made the one sole precedent, the corn ships of imperial Rome, a petty incident; and a huge migration of peoples between Europe and Western Asia and America was in progress, and—nobody seems to have realized that something new had come into human life, a strange swirl different altogether from any previous circling and mutation, a swirl like the swirl when at last the lock gates begin to open after a long phase of accumulating water and eddying inactivity. . . .

The sober Englishman at the close of the nineteenth century could sit at his breakfast-table, decide between tea from Ceylon or coffee from Brazil, devour an egg from France with some Danish ham, or eat a New Zealand chop, wind up his breakfast with a West Indian banana, glance at the latest telegrams from all the world, scrutinize the prices current of his geographically distributed investments in South Africa, Japan and Egypt, and tell the two children he had begotten (in the place of his father's eight) that he thought the world changed very little. They must play cricket, keep their hair cut, go to the old school he had gone to, shirk the lessons he had shirked, learn a few scraps of Horace and Virgil and Homer for the confusion of cads, and all would be well with them. . . .

§ 5

Electricity, though it was perhaps the earlier of the two to be studied, invaded the common life of men a few decades after the exploitation of steam. To electricity also, in spite of its provocative nearness all about him, mankind had been utterly blind for incalculable ages.

Could anything be more emphatic than the appeal of electricity for attention ? It thundered at man's ears, it signalled to him in blinding flashes, occasionally it killed him, and he could not see it as a thing that concerned him enough to merit study. It came into the house with the cat on any dry day and crackled insinuatingly whenever he stroked her fur. It rotted his metals when he put them together. . . . There is no single record that anyone questioned why the cat's fur crackles or why hair is so unruly to brush on a frosty day, before the sixteenth century. For endless years man seems to have done his very successful best not to think about it at all ; until this new spirit of the Seeker turned itself to these things.

How often things must have been seen and dismissed as unimportant, before the speculative eye and the moment of vision came ! It was Gilbert, Queen Elizabeth's court physician, who first puzzled his brains with rubbed amber and

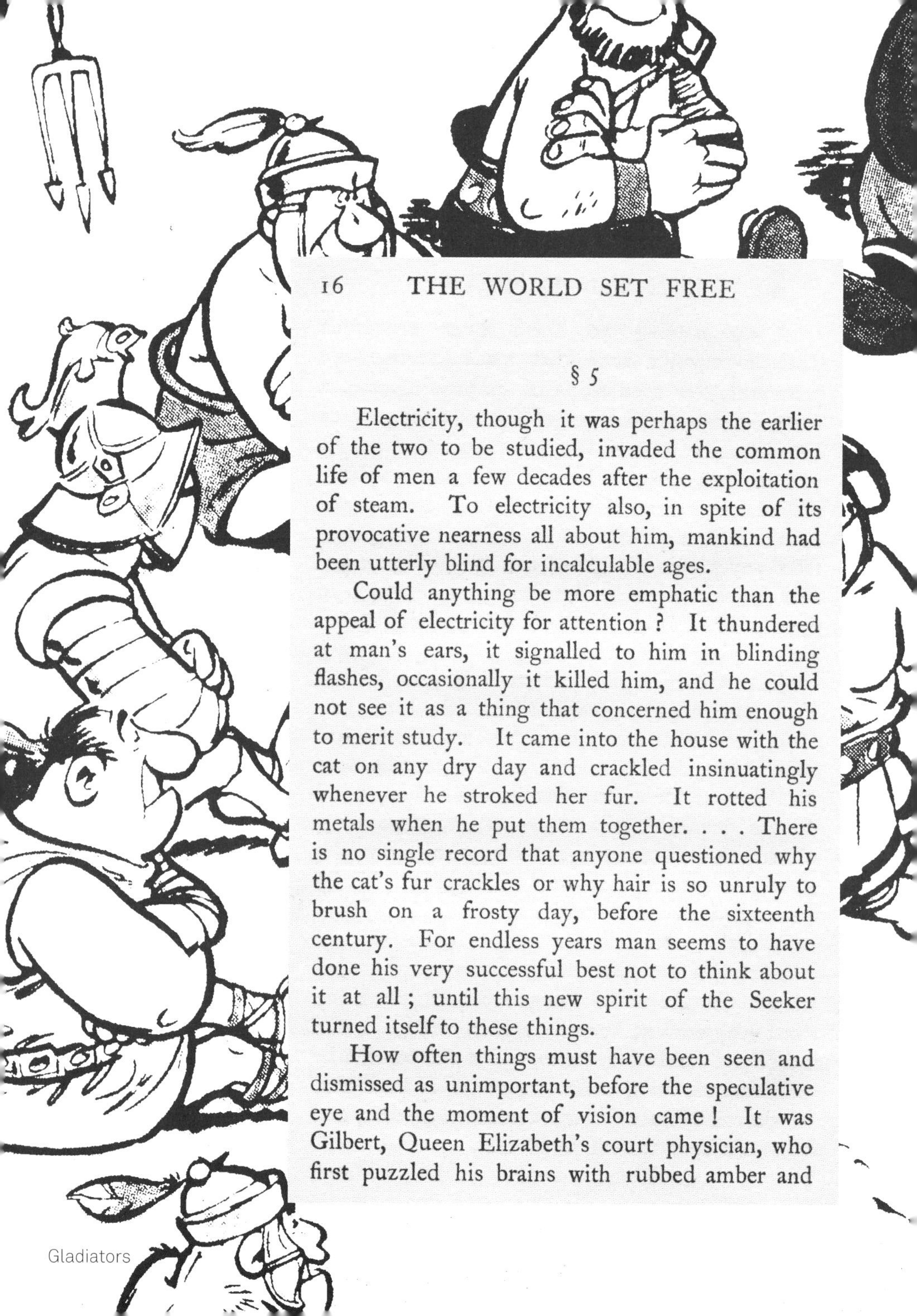

Gladiators

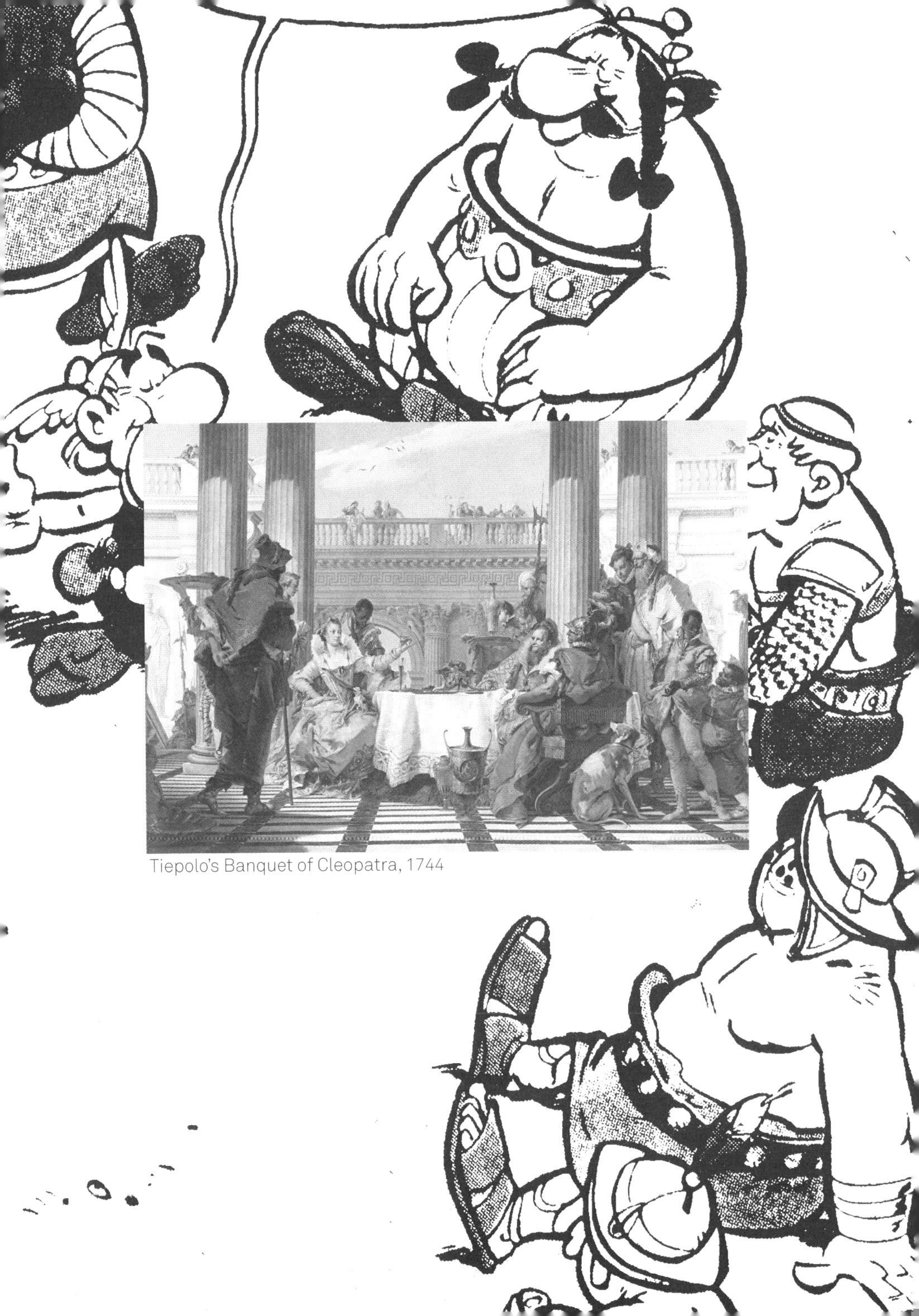

Tiepolo's Banquet of Cleopatra, 1744

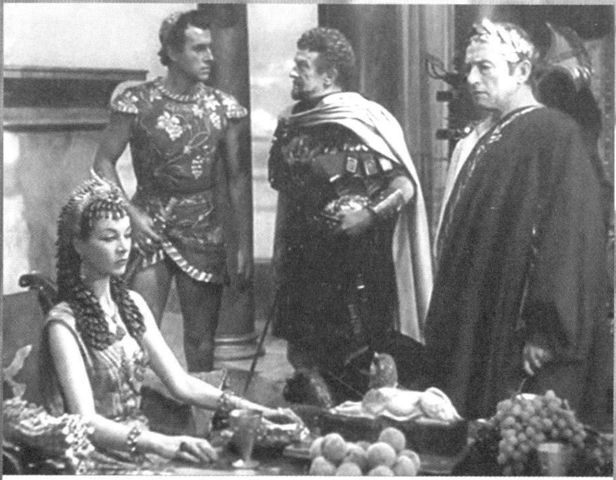

Another depiction of the Banquet of Cleopatra (UK 1945)

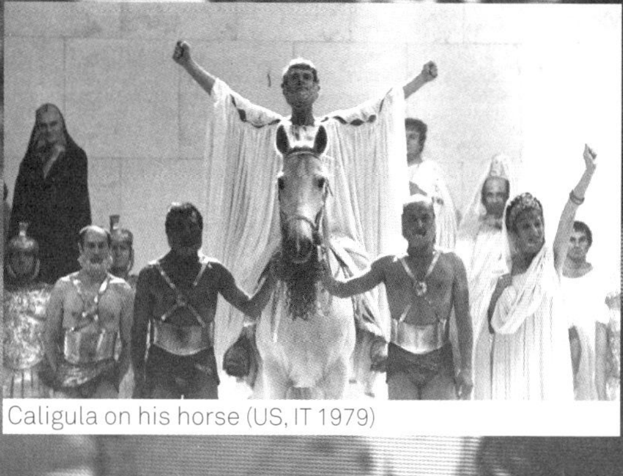

Caligula on his horse (US, IT 1979)

Colosseum, 2015

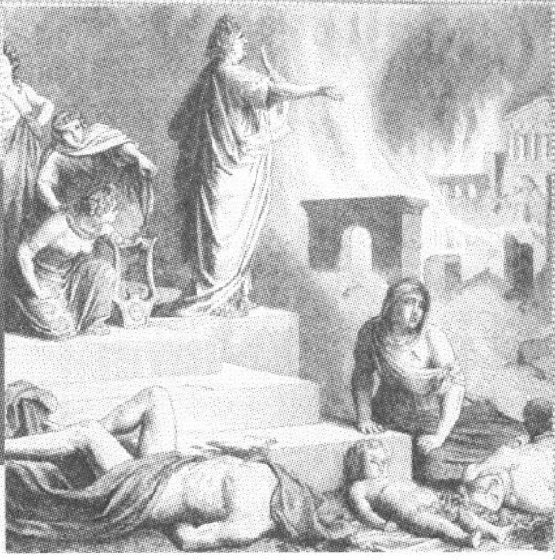

Nero watches Rome burning

bits of glass and silk and shellac and so began the quickening of the human mind to the existence of this universal presence. And even then the science of electricity remained a mere little group of curious facts for nearly two hundred years, connected perhaps with magnetism—a mere guess that—perhaps with the lightning. Frogs' legs must have hung by copper hooks from iron railings and twitched upon countless occasions before Galvani saw them. Except for the lightning conductor, it was 250 years after Gilbert before electricity stepped out of the cabinet of scientific curiosities into the life of the common man. . . . Then suddenly, in the half-century between 1880 and 1930, it ousted the steam-engine and took over traction, it ousted every other form of household heating, abolished distance with the perfected wireless telephone and the telephotograph. . . .

§ 6

And there was an extraordinary mental resistance to discovery and invention for at least a hundred years after the scientific revolution had begun. Each new thing made its way into practice against a scepticism that amounted at times to hostility. One writer upon these subjects gives a funny little domestic conversation that happened, he says, in the year 1898,

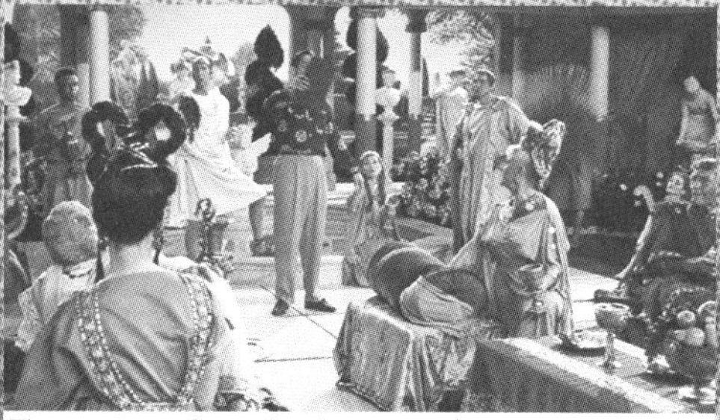

The setting of another banquet (UK, JP, US 2016)

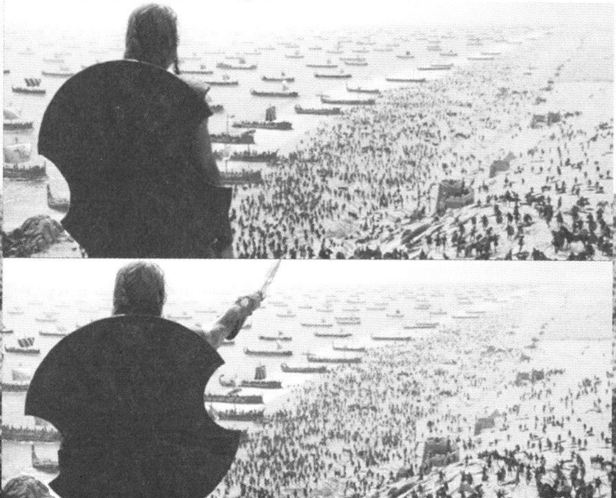

Setting of the attack against Troy (UK, MT, US 2004)

Ancient battleship

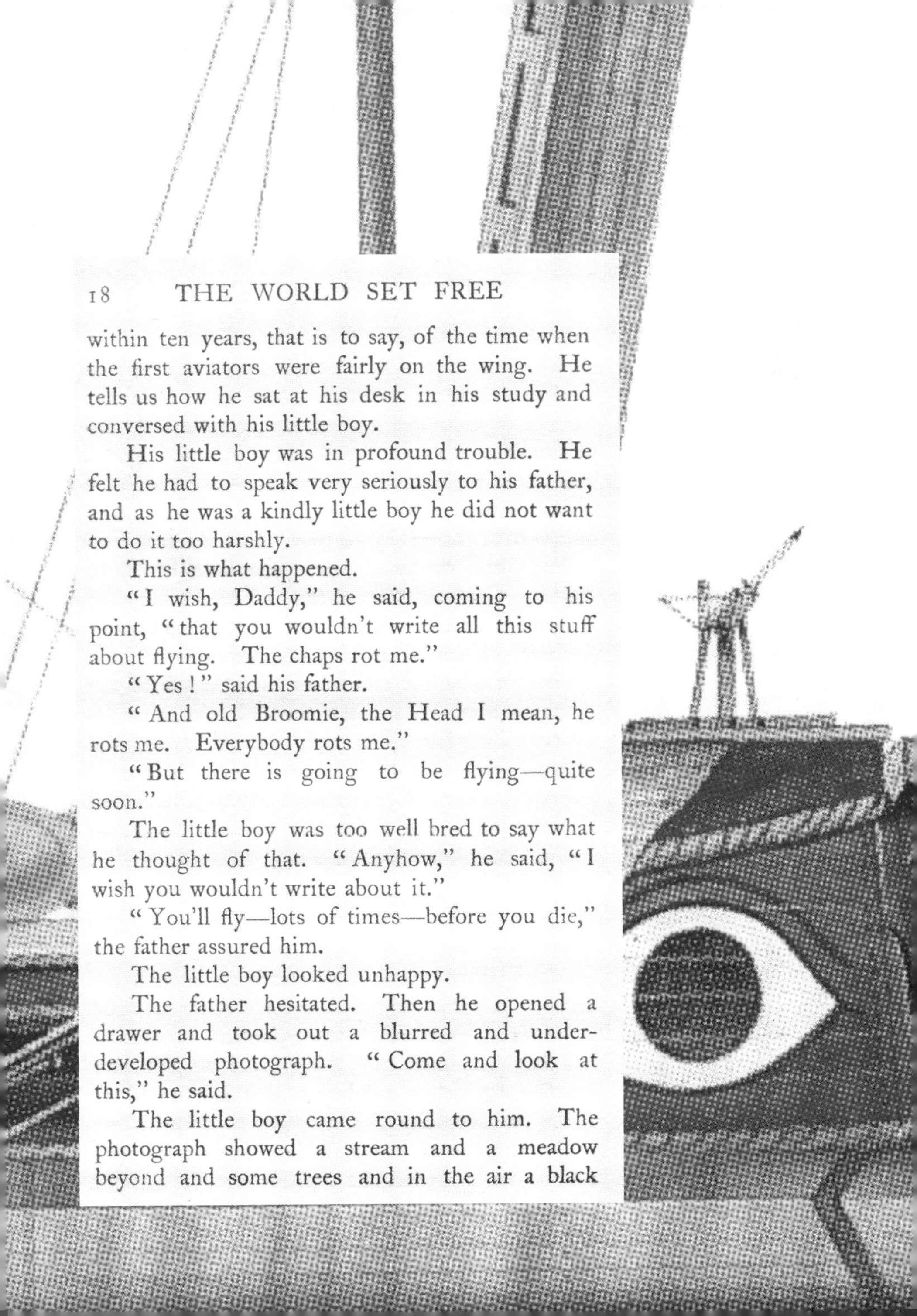

within ten years, that is to say, of the time when the first aviators were fairly on the wing. He tells us how he sat at his desk in his study and conversed with his little boy.

His little boy was in profound trouble. He felt he had to speak very seriously to his father, and as he was a kindly little boy he did not want to do it too harshly.

This is what happened.

"I wish, Daddy," he said, coming to his point, "that you wouldn't write all this stuff about flying. The chaps rot me."

"Yes!" said his father.

"And old Broomie, the Head I mean, he rots me. Everybody rots me."

"But there is going to be flying—quite soon."

The little boy was too well bred to say what he thought of that. "Anyhow," he said, "I wish you wouldn't write about it."

"You'll fly—lots of times—before you die," the father assured him.

The little boy looked unhappy.

The father hesitated. Then he opened a drawer and took out a blurred and under-developed photograph. "Come and look at this," he said.

The little boy came round to him. The photograph showed a stream and a meadow beyond and some trees and in the air a black

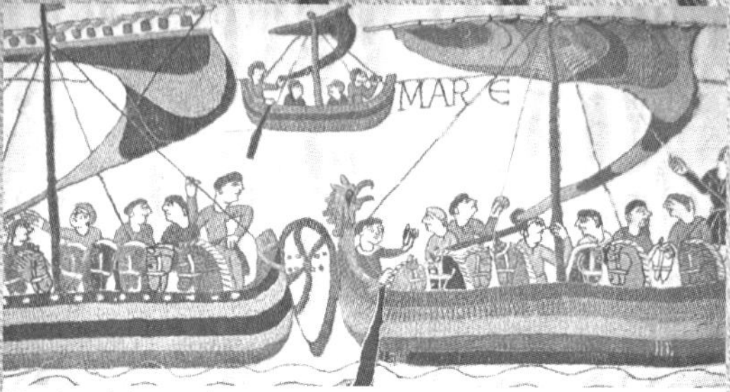

England, here they come...

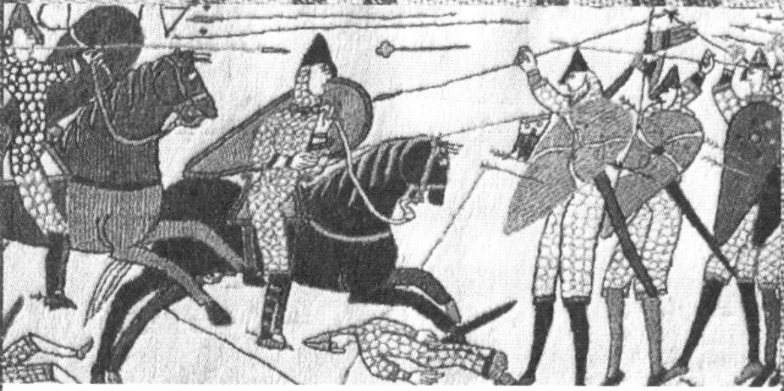

... and conquer.

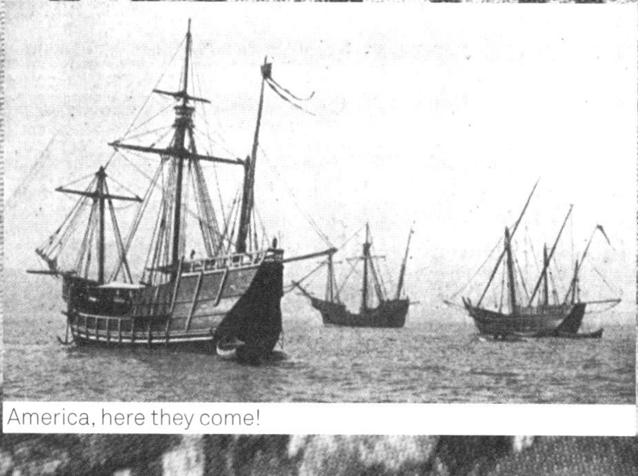

America, here they come!

Conclusion of peace, Breda, 1667 (detail)

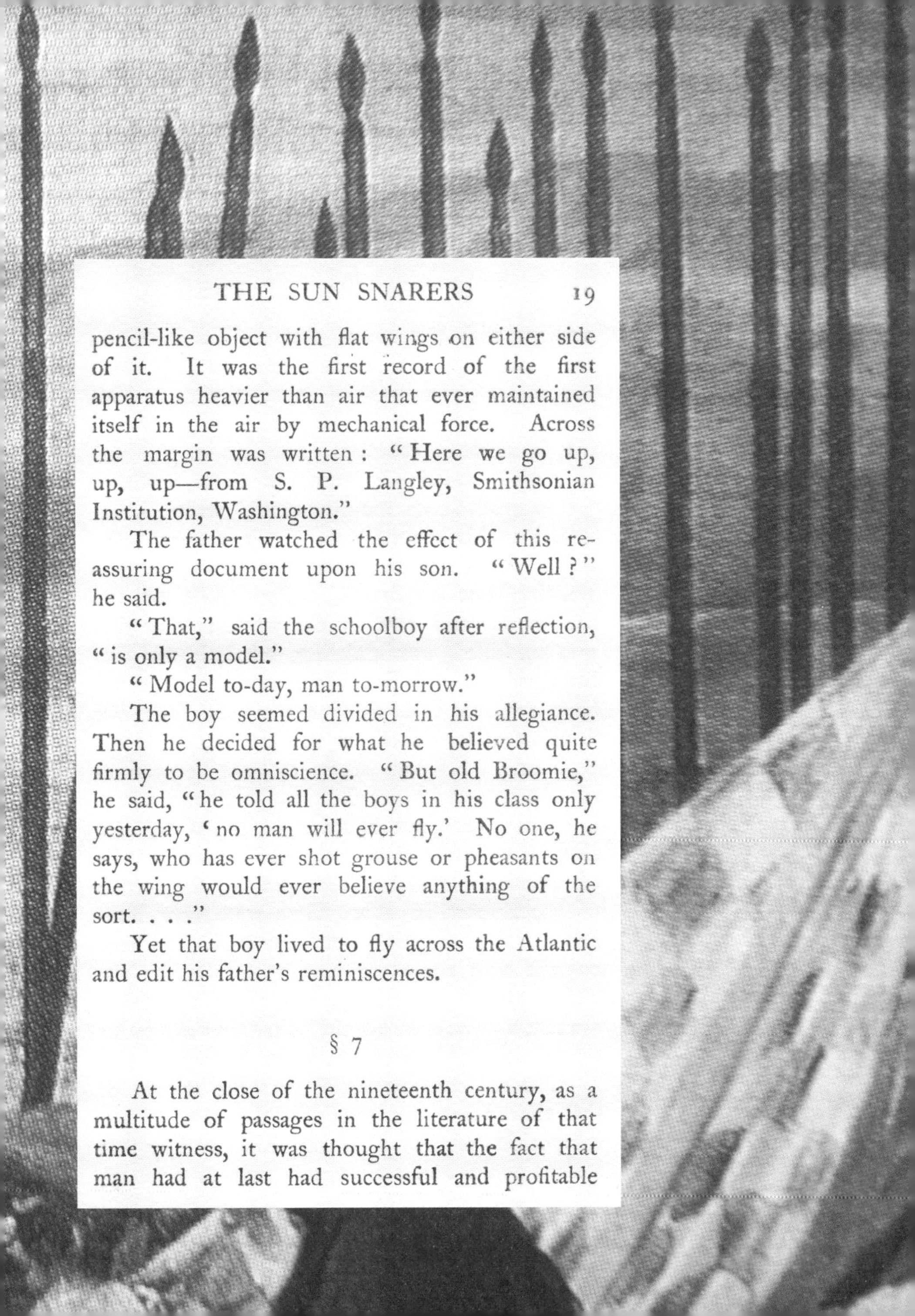

pencil-like object with flat wings on either side of it. It was the first record of the first apparatus heavier than air that ever maintained itself in the air by mechanical force. Across the margin was written: "Here we go up, up, up—from S. P. Langley, Smithsonian Institution, Washington."

The father watched the effect of this reassuring document upon his son. "Well?" he said.

"That," said the schoolboy after reflection, "is only a model."

"Model to-day, man to-morrow."

The boy seemed divided in his allegiance. Then he decided for what he believed quite firmly to be omniscience. "But old Broomie," he said, "he told all the boys in his class only yesterday, 'no man will ever fly.' No one, he says, who has ever shot grouse or pheasants on the wing would ever believe anything of the sort. . . ."

Yet that boy lived to fly across the Atlantic and edit his father's reminiscences.

§ 7

At the close of the nineteenth century, as a multitude of passages in the literature of that time witness, it was thought that the fact that man had at last had successful and profitable

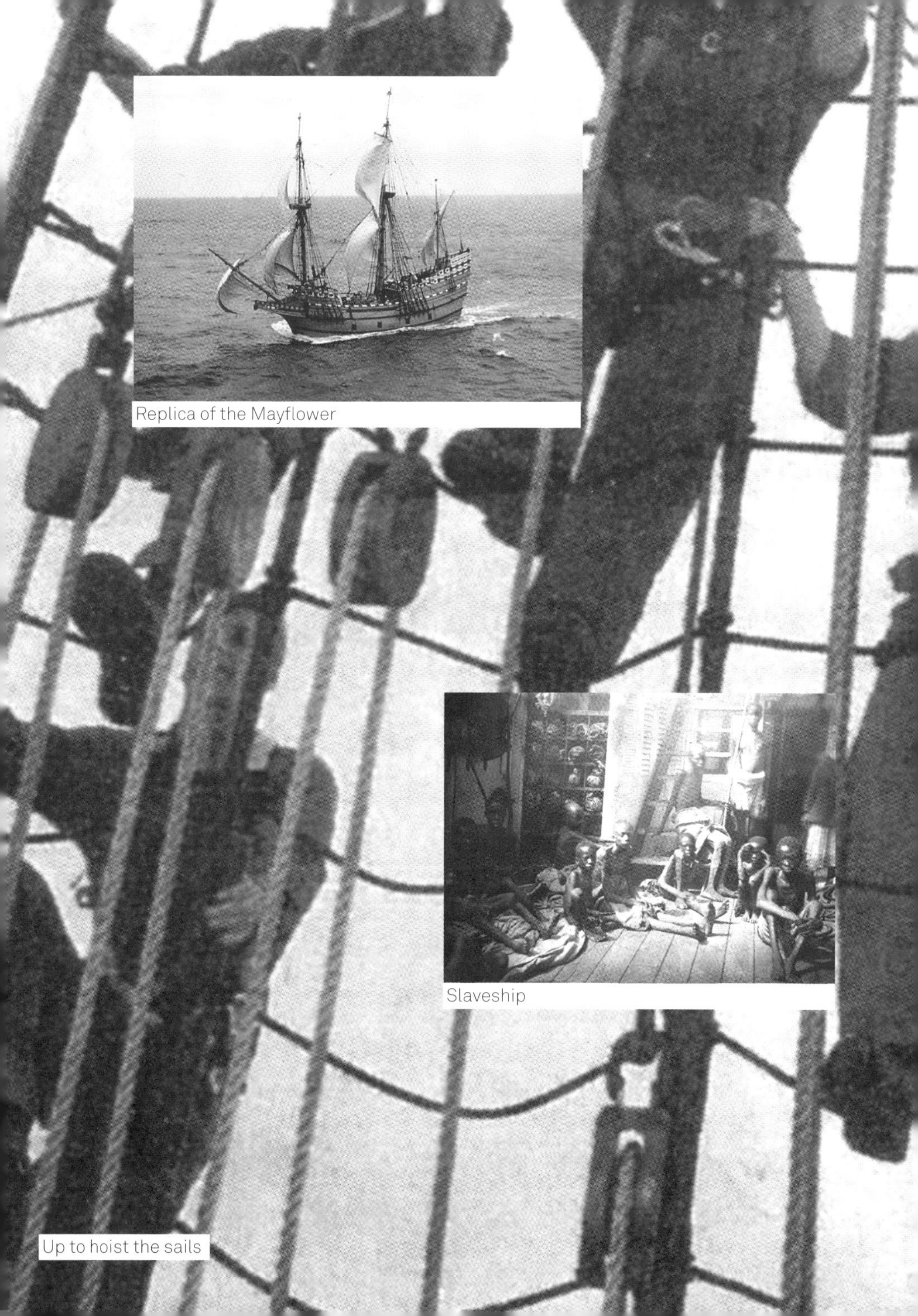
Replica of the Mayflower

Slaveship

Up to hoist the sails

dealings with the steam that scalded him and the electricity that flashed and banged about the sky at him, was an amazing and perhaps a culminating exercise of his intelligence and his intellectual courage. The air of "Nunc Dimittis" sounds in some of these writings. "The great things are discovered," wrote Gerald Brown in his summary of the nineteenth century. "For us there remains little but the working out of detail." The spirit of the seeker was still rare in the world; education was unskilled, unstimulating, scholarly and but little valued, and few people even then could have realized that Science was still but the flimsiest of trial sketches and discovery scarcely beginning. No one seems to have been afraid of science and its possibilities. Yet now where there had been but a score or so of seekers, there were many thousands, and for one needle of speculation that had been probing the curtain of appearances in 1800, there were now hundreds. And already Chemistry, which had been content with her atoms and molecules for the better part of a century, was preparing herself for that vast next stride that was to revolutionize the whole life of man from top to bottom.

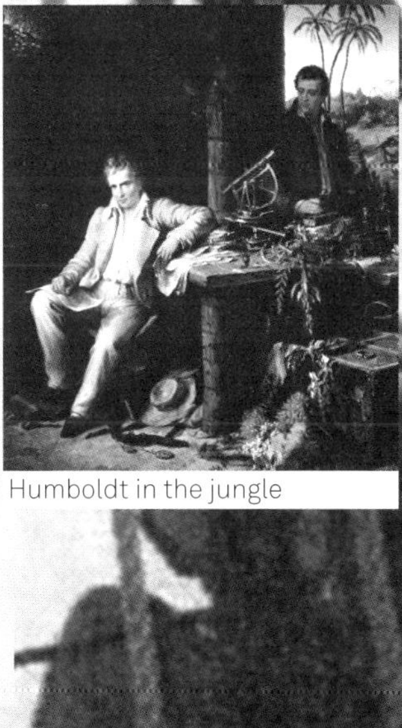
Humboldt in the jungle

One realizes how crude was the science of that time when one considers the case of the composition of air. This was determined by that strange genius and recluse, that man of mystery,

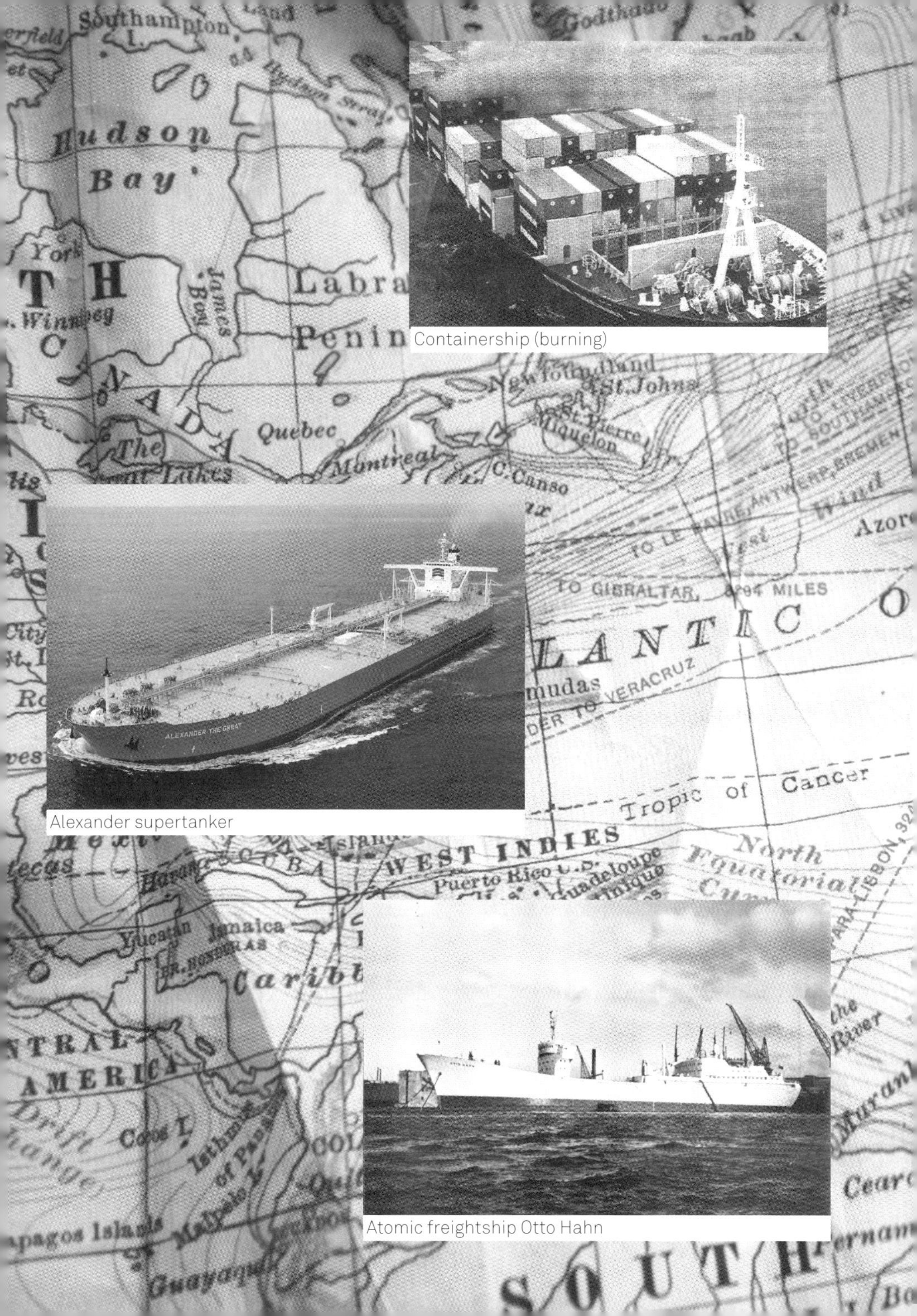

Containership (burning)

Alexander supertanker

Atomic freightship Otto Hahn

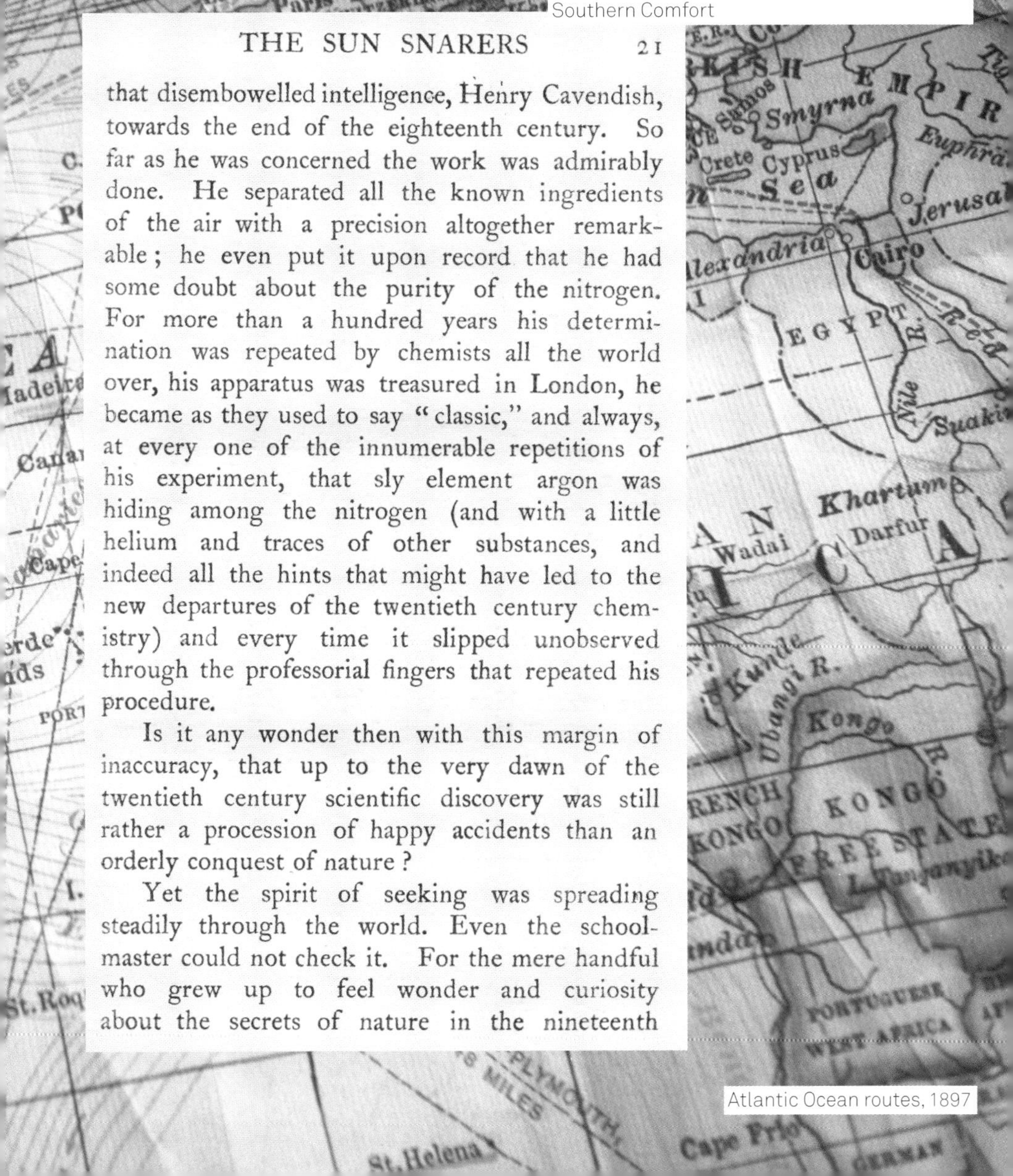

Atlantic Ocean routes, 1897

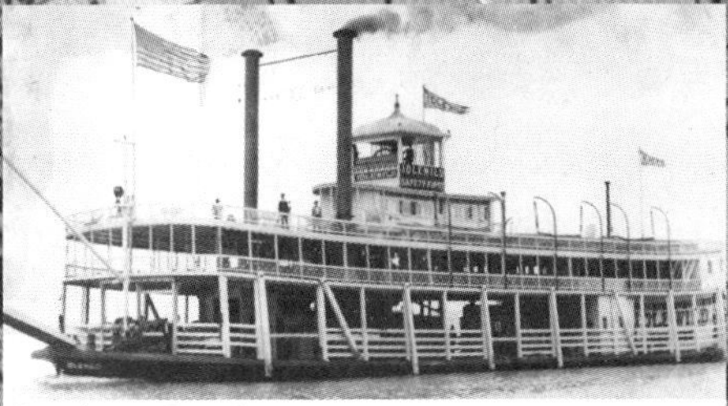

Southern Comfort

that disembowelled intelligence, Henry Cavendish, towards the end of the eighteenth century. So far as he was concerned the work was admirably done. He separated all the known ingredients of the air with a precision altogether remarkable; he even put it upon record that he had some doubt about the purity of the nitrogen. For more than a hundred years his determination was repeated by chemists all the world over, his apparatus was treasured in London, he became as they used to say "classic," and always, at every one of the innumerable repetitions of his experiment, that sly element argon was hiding among the nitrogen (and with a little helium and traces of other substances, and indeed all the hints that might have led to the new departures of the twentieth century chemistry) and every time it slipped unobserved through the professorial fingers that repeated his procedure.

Is it any wonder then with this margin of inaccuracy, that up to the very dawn of the twentieth century scientific discovery was still rather a procession of happy accidents than an orderly conquest of nature?

Yet the spirit of seeking was spreading steadily through the world. Even the schoolmaster could not check it. For the mere handful who grew up to feel wonder and curiosity about the secrets of nature in the nineteenth

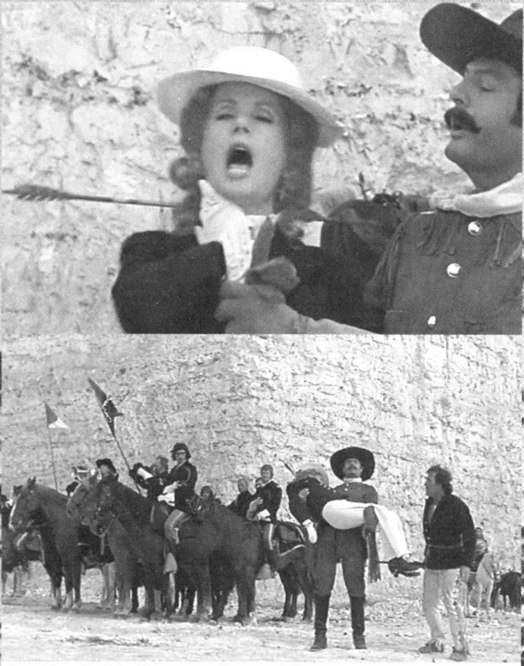
Another Little Big Horn (FR 1974)

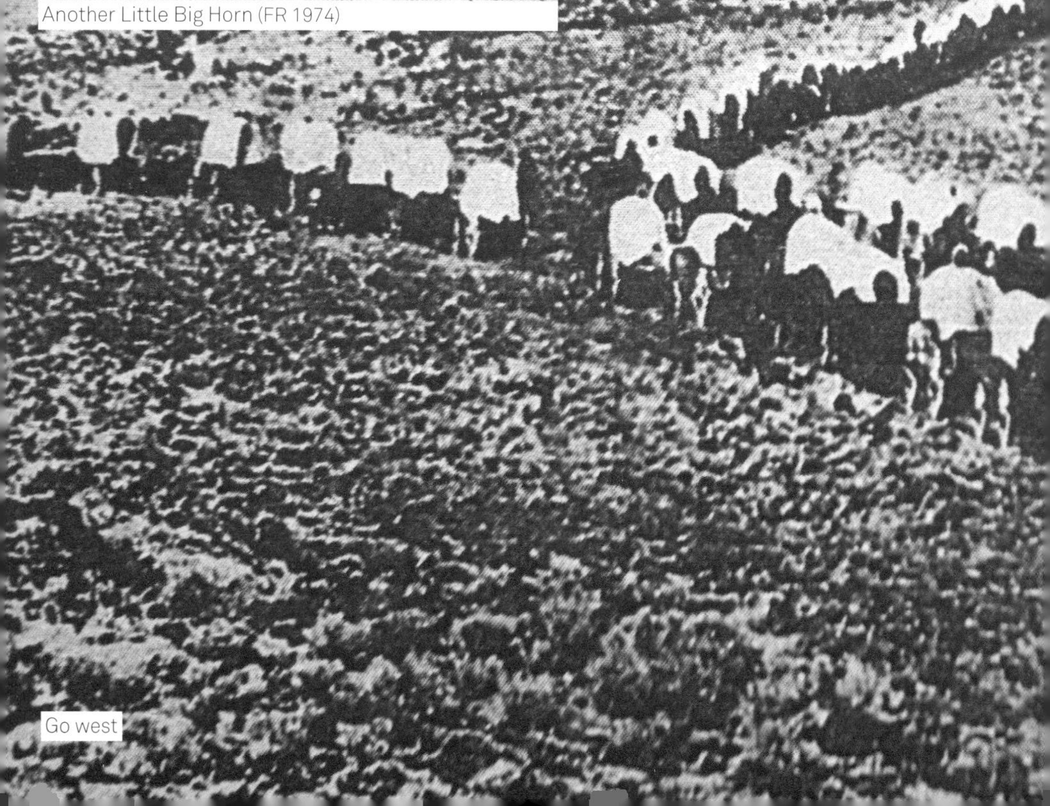
Go west

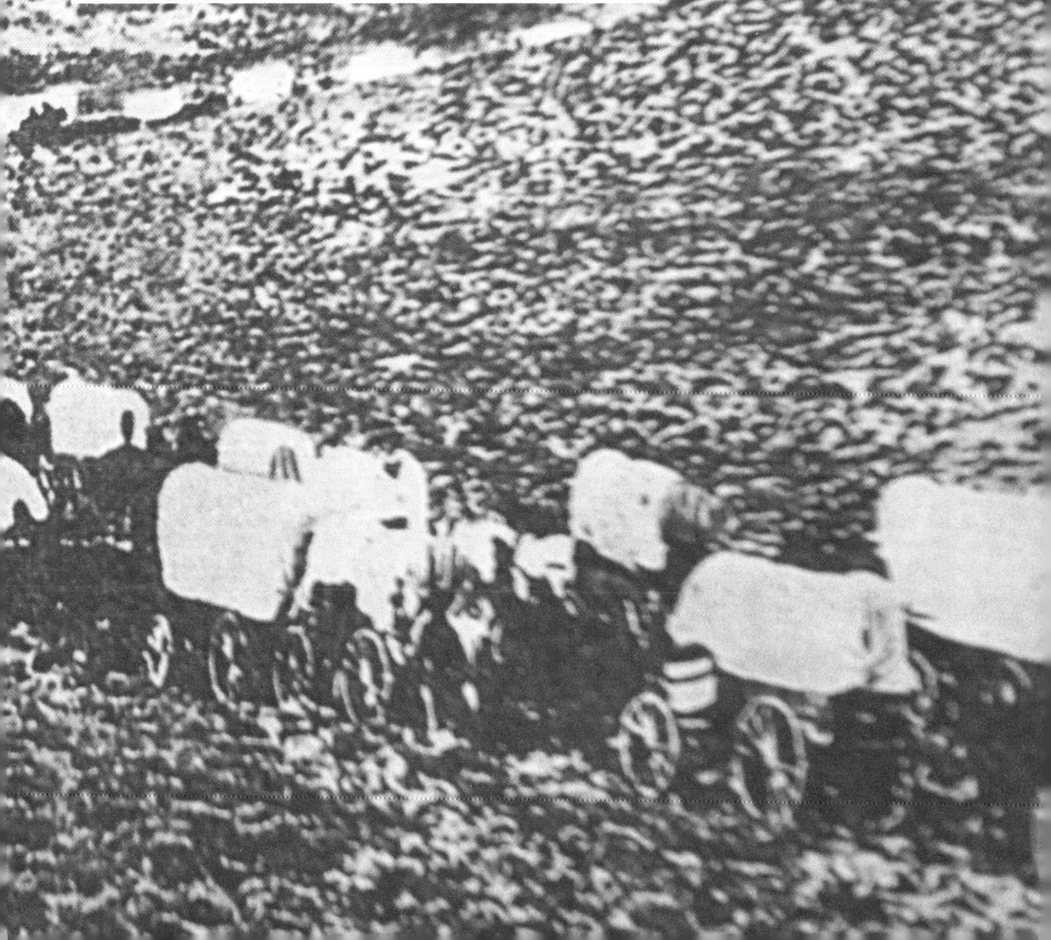

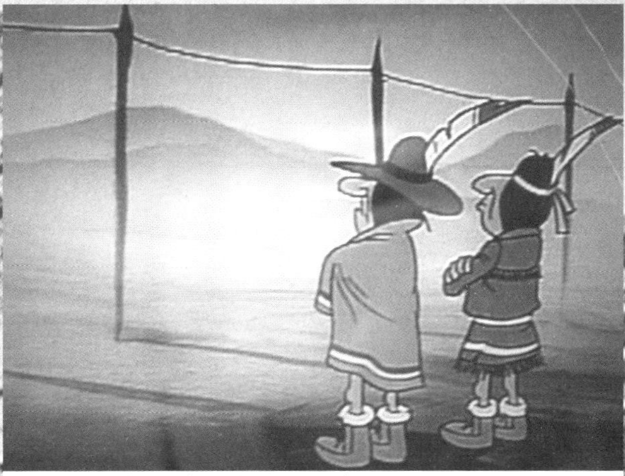

Wondering about the wire (FR 1983)

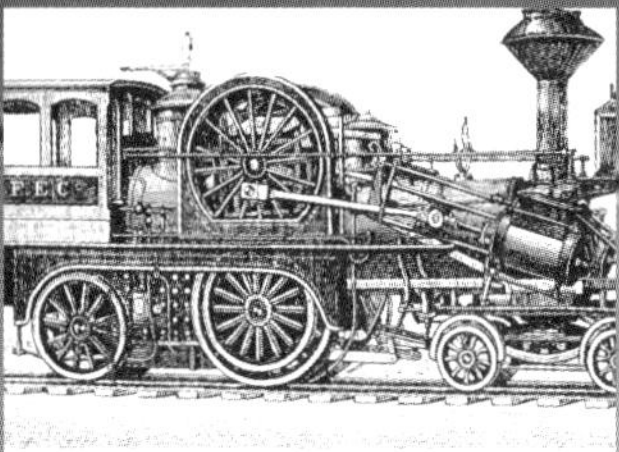
Steaming progress

century, there were now at the beginning of the twentieth myriads escaping from the limitations of intellectual routine and the habitual life, in Europe, in America, North and South, in Japan, in China and all about the world.

It was in 1910 that the parents of young Holsten, who was to be called by a whole generation of scientific men, "the greatest of European chemists," were staying in a villa near Santo Domenico between Fiesole and Florence. He was then only fifteen, but he was already distinguished as a mathematician and possessed by a savage appetite to understand. He had been particularly attracted by the mystery of phosphorescence and its apparent unrelatedness to every other source of light. He was to tell afterwards in his reminiscences how he watched the fireflies drifting and glowing among the dark trees in the garden of the villa under the warm blue night sky of Italy; how he caught and kept them in cages, dissected them, first studying the general anatomy of insects very elaborately, and how he began to experiment with the effect of various gases and varying temperature upon their light. Then the chance present of a little scientific toy invented by Sir William Crookes, a toy called the spinthariscope, on which radium particles impinge upon sulphide of zinc and make it luminous, induced him to associate the two sets

The wire sings (FR 1983)

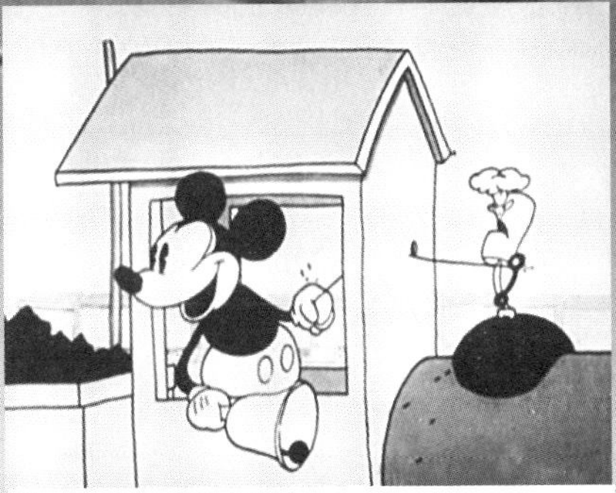
Choo-choo (US 1929)

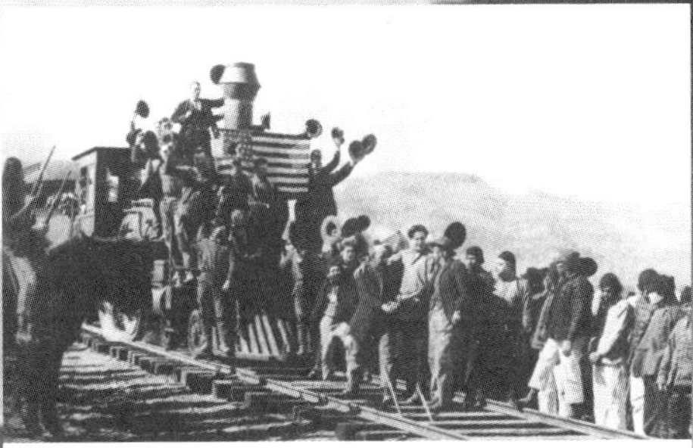
Birth of a Nation (US 1915)

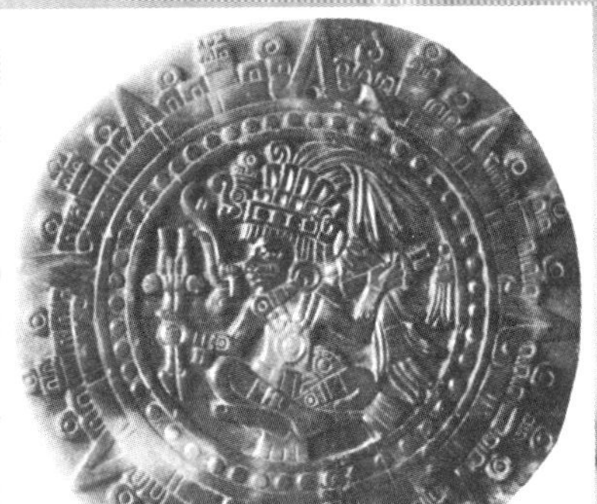
Alztec sungod

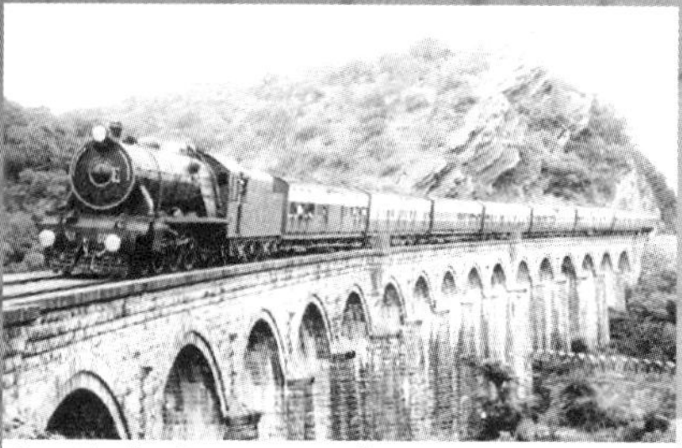
East India Company railway

of phenomena. It was a happy association for his enquiries. It was a rare and fortunate thing, too, that any one with the mathematical gift should have been taken by these curiosities.

§ 8

And while the boy Holsten was mooning over his fireflies at Fiesole, a certain professor of physics named Rufus was giving a course of afternoon lectures upon Radium and Radio-Activity in Edinburgh. They were lectures that had attracted a very considerable amount of attention. He gave them in a small lecture-theatre that had become more and more congested as his course proceeded. At his concluding discussion it was crowded right up to the ceiling at the back, and there people were standing, standing without any sense of fatigue, so fascinating did they find his suggestions. One youngster in particular, a chuckle-headed scrub-haired lad from the Highlands, sat hugging his knee with great sand-red hands and drinking in every word, eyes aglow, cheeks flushed and ears burning.

"And so," said the professor, "we see that this Radium, which seemed at first a fantastic exception, a mad inversion of all that was most established and fundamental in the constitution of matter, is really at one with the rest of the

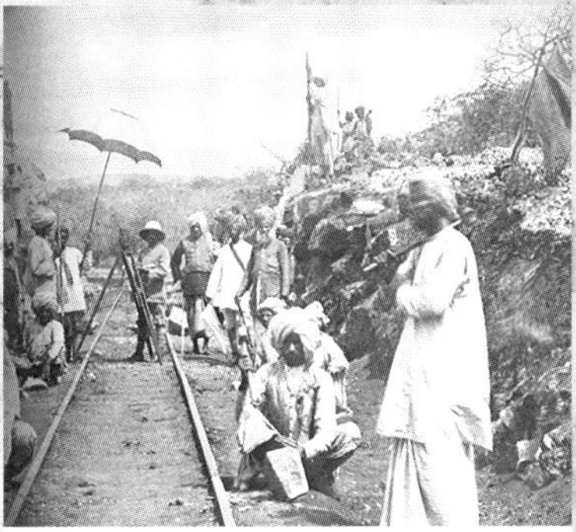
Indian railroad workers

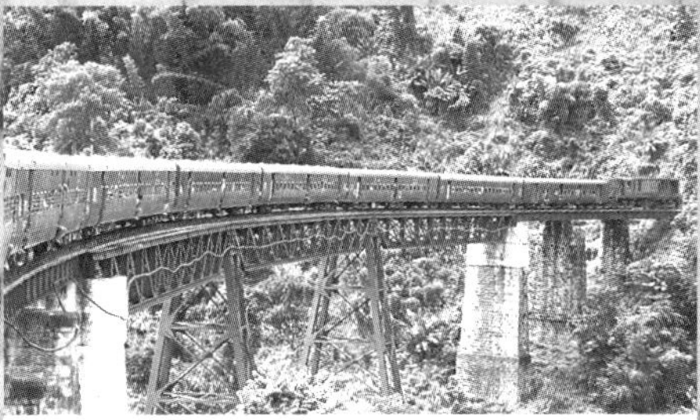
Cross country India

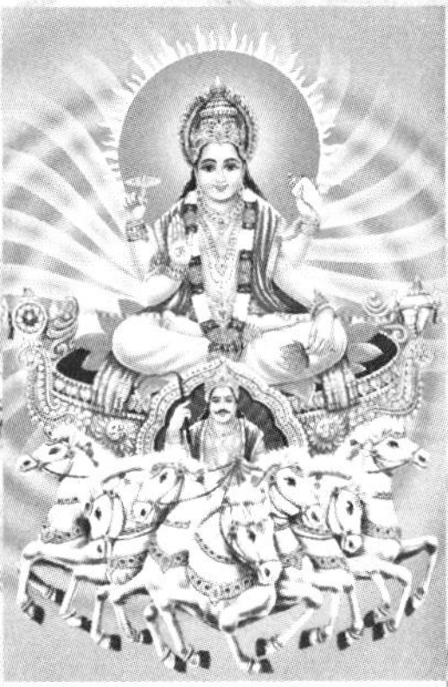
Indian sungod

Railway Rivals India (detail, 2015)

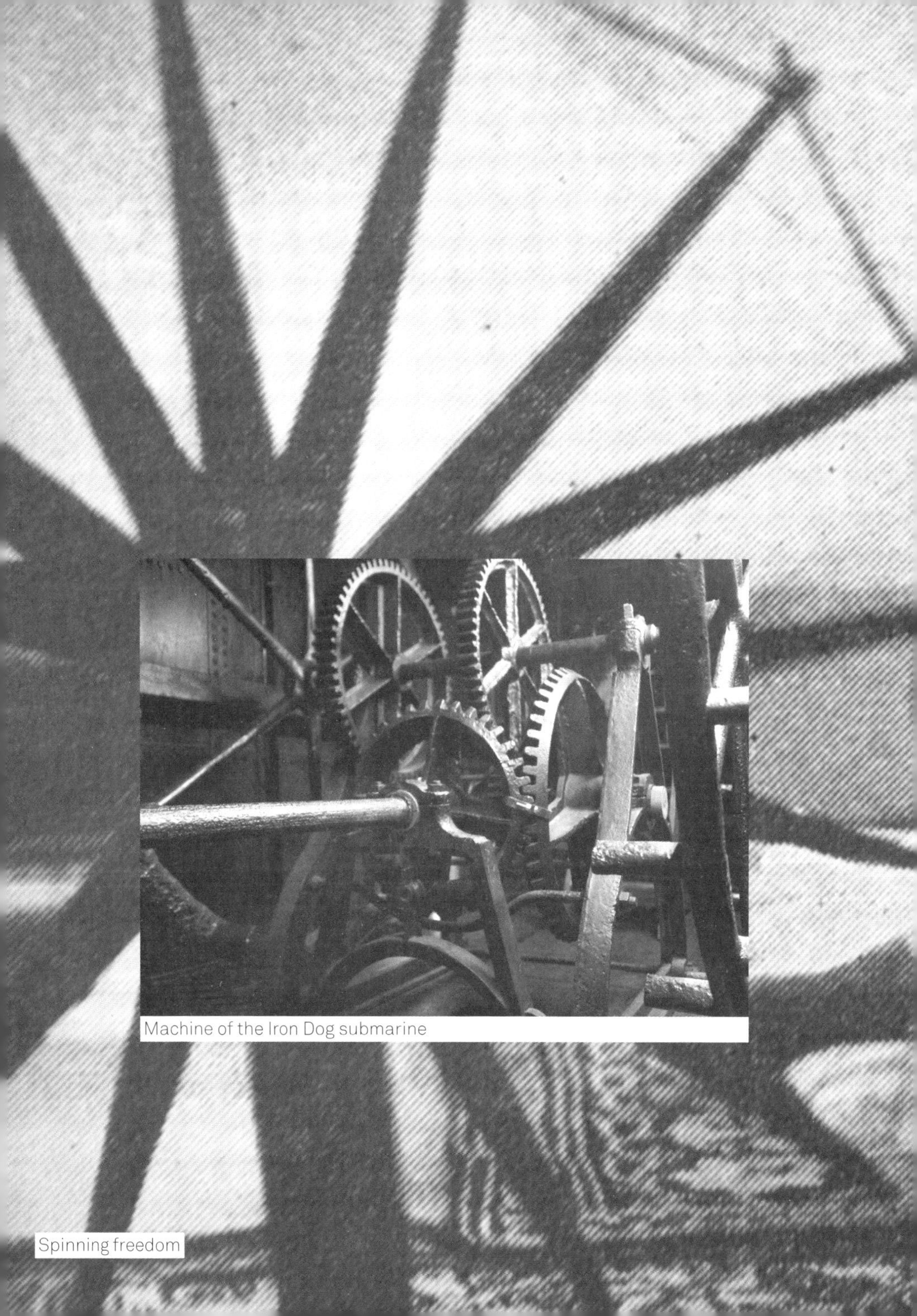

Machine of the Iron Dog submarine

Spinning freedom

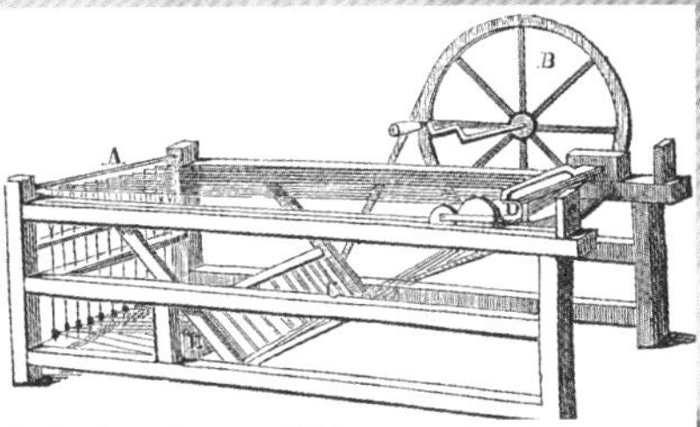

Spinning Jenny, 1884

elements. It does noticeably and forcibly what probably all the other elements are doing with an imperceptible slowness. It is like the single voice crying aloud that betrays the silent breathing multitude in the darkness. Radium is an element that is breaking up and flying to pieces. But perhaps all elements are doing that at less perceptible rates. Uranium certainly is ; thorium —the stuff of this incandescent gas mantle— certainly is ; actinium. I feel that we are but beginning the list. And we know now that the atom, that once we thought hard and impenetrable, and indivisible and final and—lifeless—lifeless, is really a reservoir of immense energy. That is the most wonderful thing about all this work. A little while ago we thought of the atoms as we thought of bricks, as solid building material, as substantial matter, as unit masses of lifeless stuff, and behold ! these bricks are boxes, treasure boxes, boxes full of the intensest force. This little bottle contains about a pint of uranium oxide ; that is to say about fourteen ounces of the element uranium. It is worth about a pound. And in this bottle, ladies and gentlemen, in the atoms in this bottle there slumbers at least as much energy as we could get by burning a hundred and sixty tons of coal. If at a word, in one instant I could suddenly release that energy here and now it would blow us and everything about us to

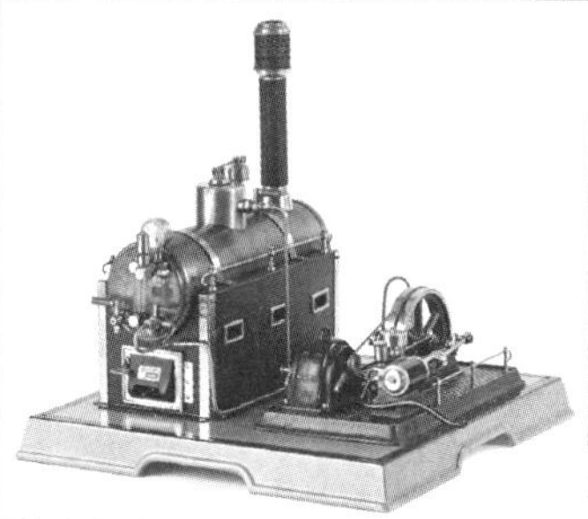

Model of a steam engine, 1939-52

fragments ; if I could turn it into the machinery that lights this city, it could keep Edinburgh brightly lit for a week. But at present no man knows, no man has an inkling of how this little lump of stuff can be made to hasten the release of its store. It does release it, as a burn trickles. Slowly the uranium changes into radium, the radium changes into a gas called the radium emanation, and that again to what we call radium A, and so the process goes on, giving out energy at every stage, until at last we reach the last stage of all, which is, so far as we can tell at present, lead. But we cannot hasten it."

"I take ye, man," whispered the chuckle-headed lad, with his red hands tightening like a vice upon his knee. "I take ye, man. Go on ! Oh, go on !"

The professor went on after a little pause. "Why is the change gradual ?" he asked. "Why does only a minute fraction of the radium disintegrate in any particular second ? Why does it dole itself out so slowly and so exactly ? Why does not all the uranium change to radium and all the radium change to the next lowest thing at once ? Why this decay by driblets ; why not a decay *en masse ?* . . . . Suppose presently we find it is possible to quicken that decay ?"

The chuckle-headed lad nodded rapidly.

Machine room of the Titanic

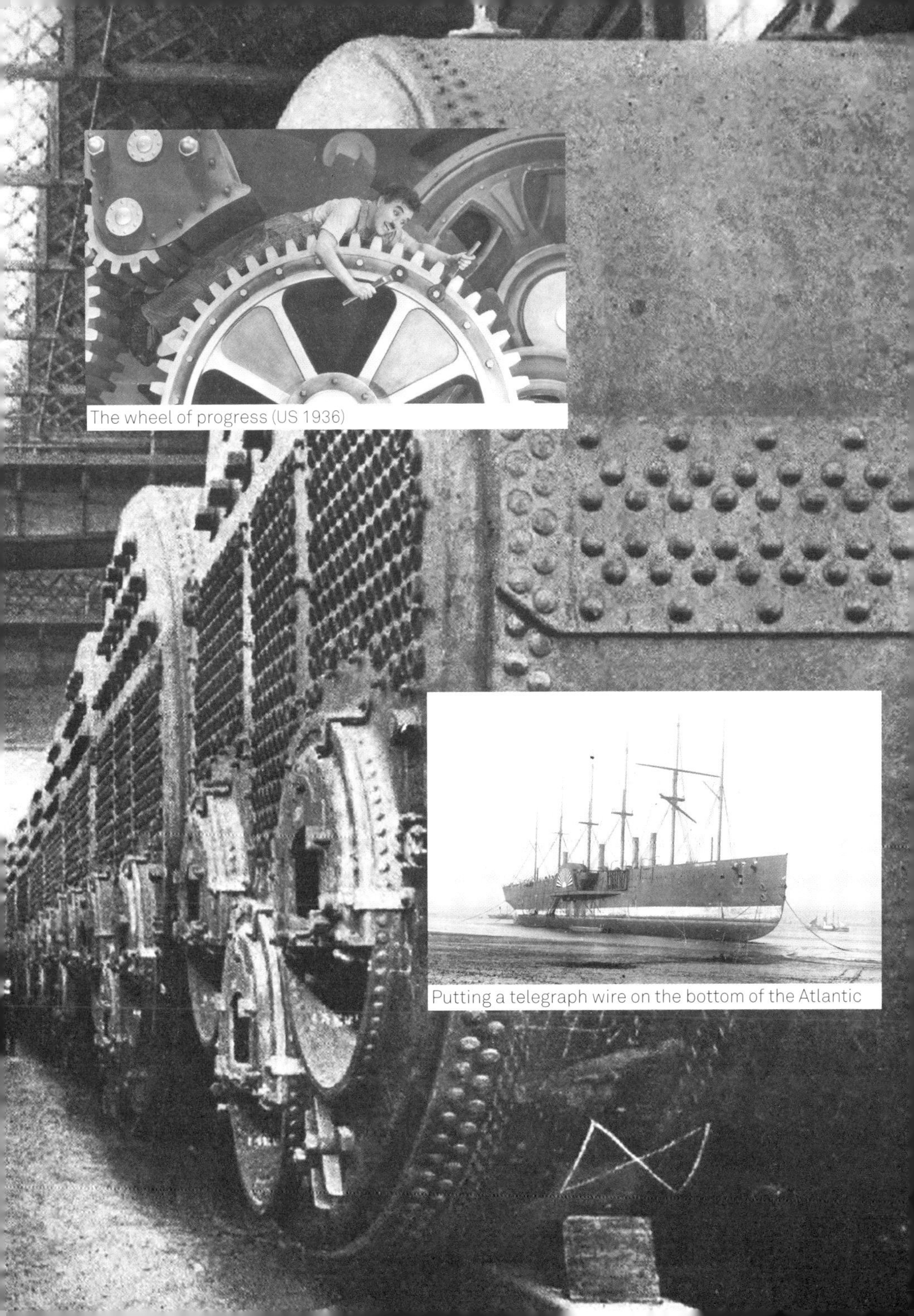

The wheel of progress (US 1936)

Putting a telegraph wire on the bottom of the Atlantic

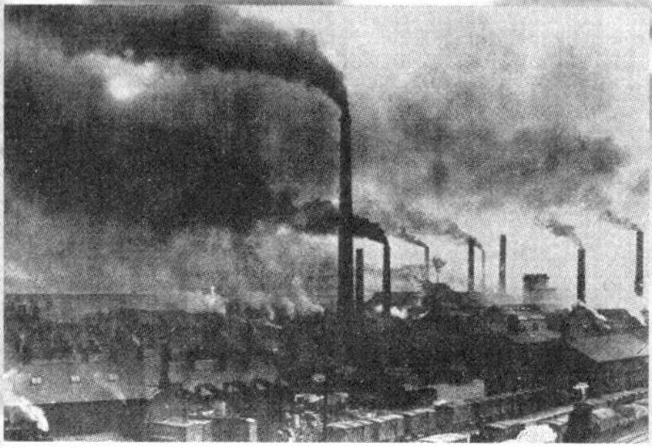
Smoke over London

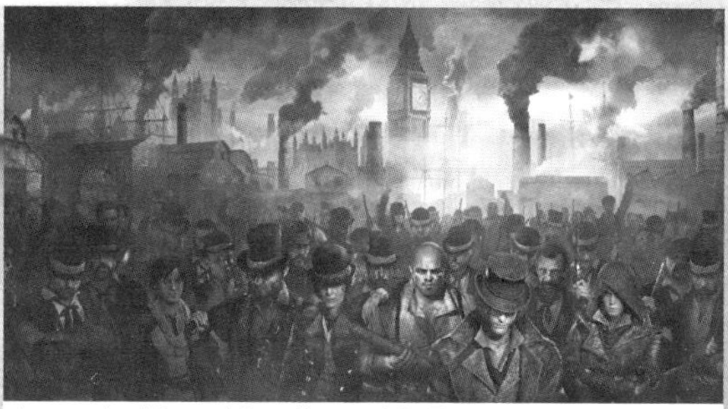
Assassins' Creed Syndicate, 2015

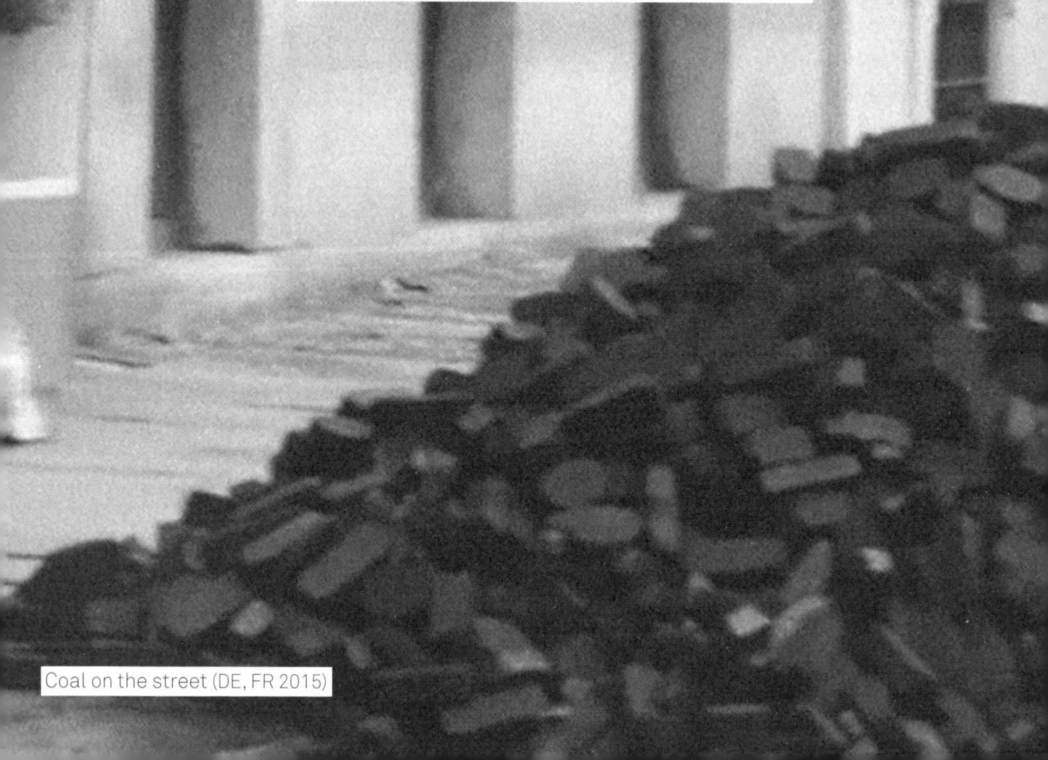
Coal on the street (DE, FR 2015)

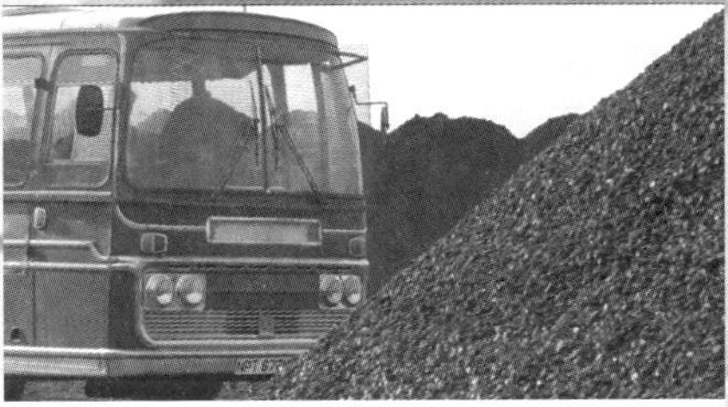

Coal miners' bus (UK 2000)

The wonderful inevitable idea was coming. He drew his knee up towards his chin and swayed in his seat with excitement. "Why not?" he echoed, "why not?"

The professor lifted his forefinger.

"Given that knowledge," he said, "mark what we should be able to do! We should not only be able to use this uranium and thorium; not only should we have a source of power so potent that a man might carry in his hand the energy to light a city for a year, fight a fleet of battleships or drive one of our giant liners across the Atlantic; but we should also have a clue that would enable us at last to quicken the process of disintegration in all the other elements, where decay is still so slow as to escape our finest measurements. Every scrap of solid matter in the world would become an available reservoir of concentrated force. Do you realize, ladies and gentlemen, what these things would mean for us?"

The scrub head nodded. "Oh! go on. Go on."

"It would mean a change in human conditions that I can only compare to the discovery of fire, that first discovery that lifted man above the brute. We stand to-day towards radio-activity exactly as our ancestor stood towards fire before he had learnt to make it. He knew it then only as a strange thing utterly beyond his

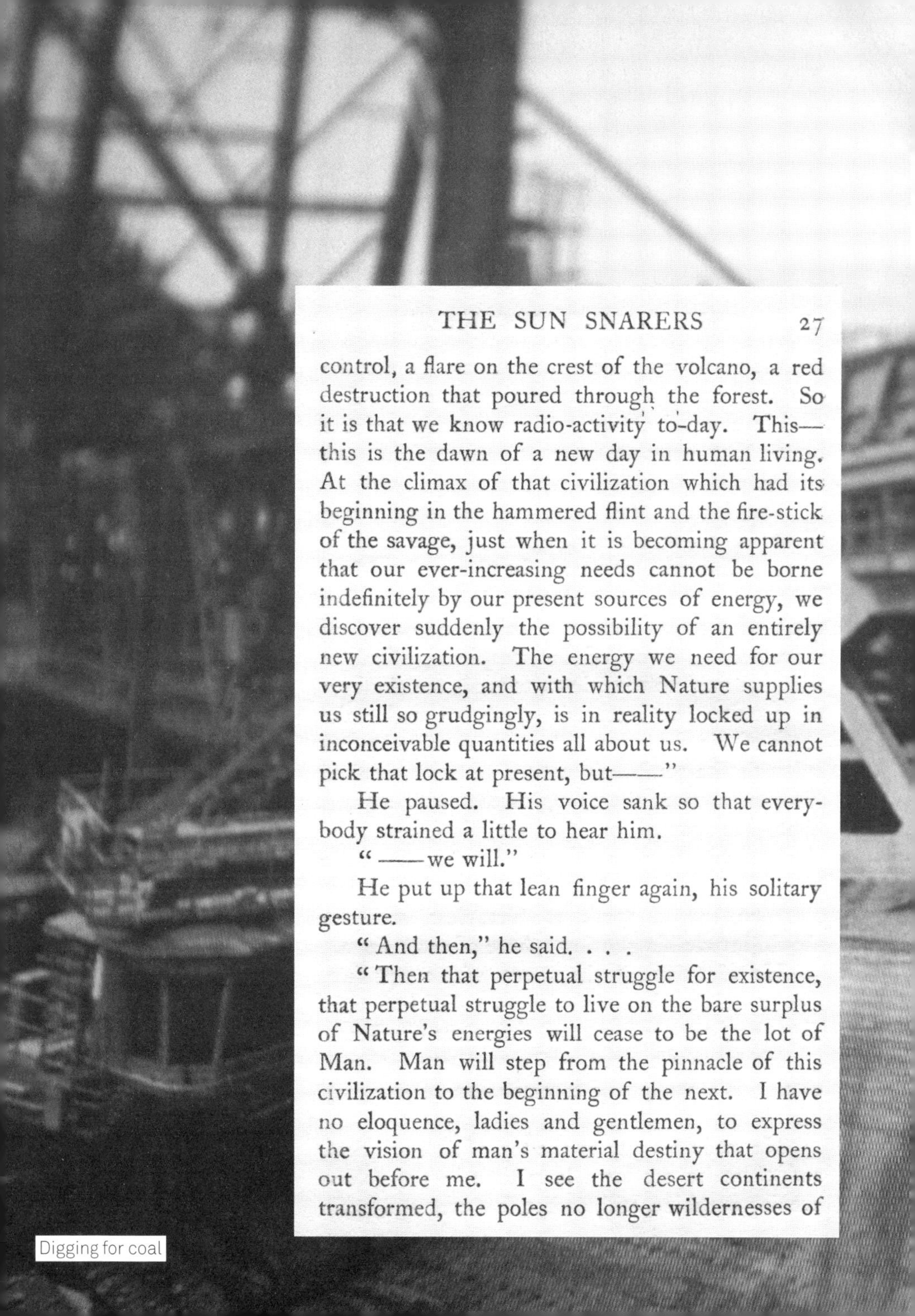

control, a flare on the crest of the volcano, a red destruction that poured through the forest. So it is that we know radio-activity to-day. This—this is the dawn of a new day in human living. At the climax of that civilization which had its beginning in the hammered flint and the fire-stick of the savage, just when it is becoming apparent that our ever-increasing needs cannot be borne indefinitely by our present sources of energy, we discover suddenly the possibility of an entirely new civilization. The energy we need for our very existence, and with which Nature supplies us still so grudgingly, is in reality locked up in inconceivable quantities all about us. We cannot pick that lock at present, but——"

He paused. His voice sank so that everybody strained a little to hear him.

"——we will."

He put up that lean finger again, his solitary gesture.

"And then," he said. . . .

"Then that perpetual struggle for existence, that perpetual struggle to live on the bare surplus of Nature's energies will cease to be the lot of Man. Man will step from the pinnacle of this civilization to the beginning of the next. I have no eloquence, ladies and gentlemen, to express the vision of man's material destiny that opens out before me. I see the desert continents transformed, the poles no longer wildernesses of

Digging for coal

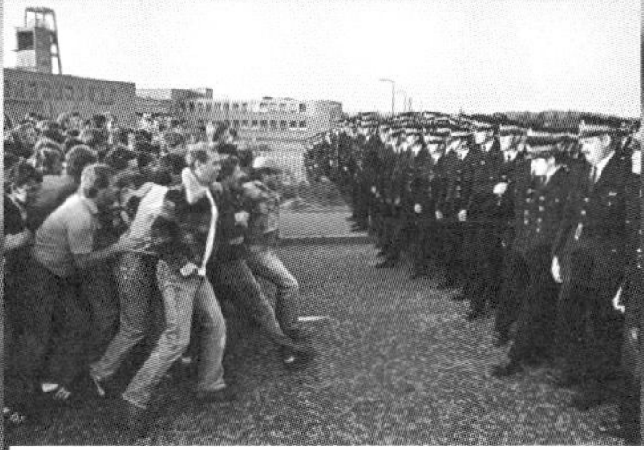

Durham coal miners' strike, 1985

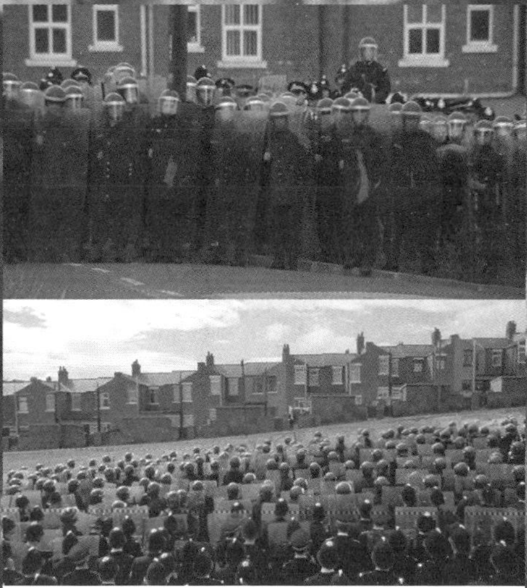

Coal miners' strike reenacted (UK 2000)

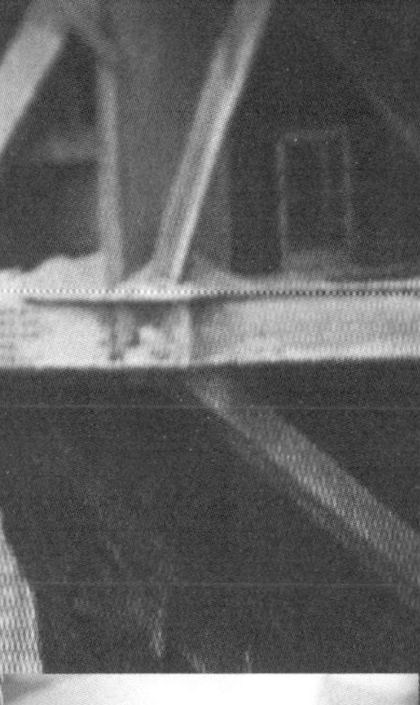

Standard coal

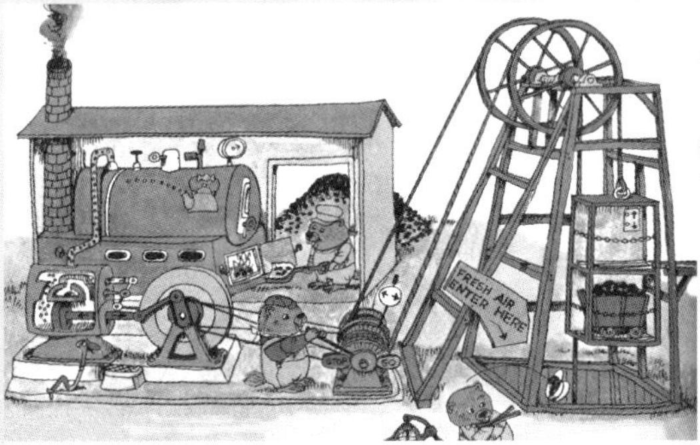

Steam power for coal mining

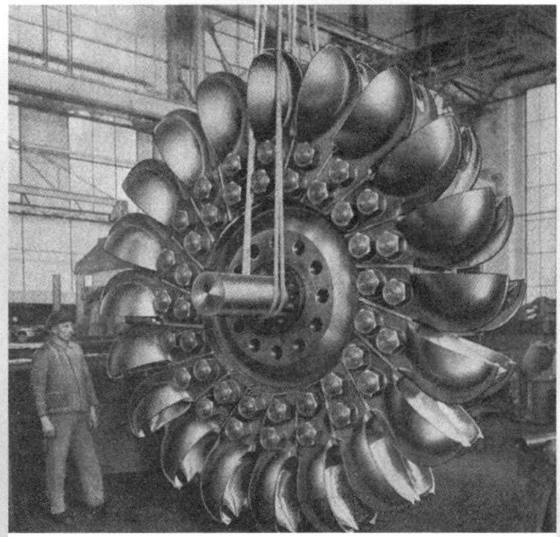
Turbine

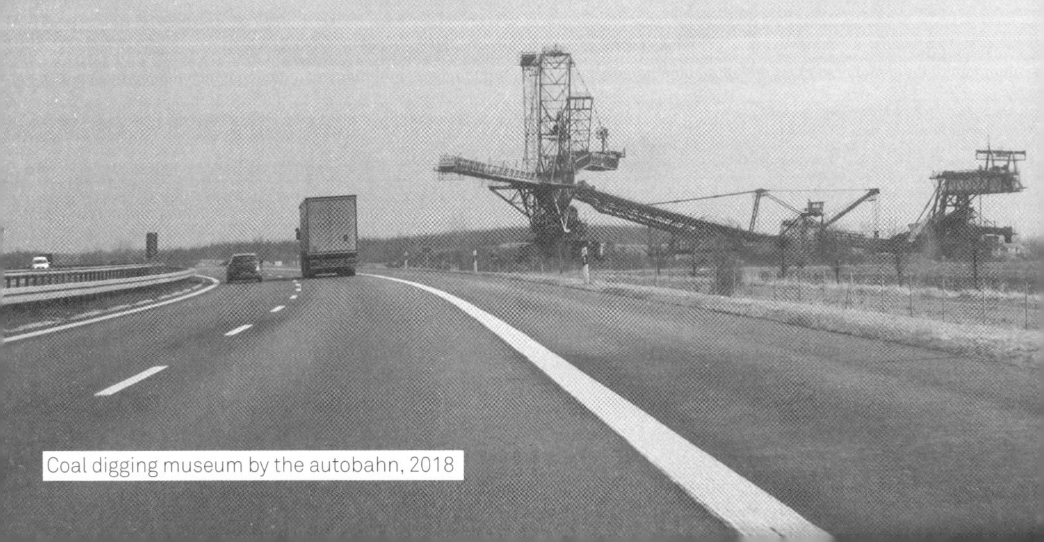
Coal digging museum by the autobahn, 2018

ice, the whole world once more Eden. I see the power of man reach out among the stars. . . ."

He stopped abruptly with a catching of the breath that many an actor or orator might have envied. . . .

The lecture was over, the audience hung silent for a few seconds, sighed, became audible, stirred, fluttered, prepared for dispersal. More light was turned on and what had been a dim mass of figures became a bright confusion of movement. Some of the people signalled to friends, some crowded down towards the platform to examine the lecturer's apparatus and make notes of his diagrams. But the chuckle-headed lad with the scrub hair wanted no such detailed frittering away of the thoughts that had inspired him. He wanted to be alone with them ; he elbowed his way out almost fiercely, he made himself as angular and bony as a cow, fearing lest someone should speak to him, lest someone should invade his glowing sphere of enthusiasm.

He went through the streets with a rapt face, like a saint who sees visions. He had arms disproportionately long, and ridiculous big feet.

He must get alone, get somewhere high out of all this crowding of commonness of everyday life.

He made his way to the top of Arthur's Seat, and there he sat for a long time in the golden evening sunshine, still, except that ever and again

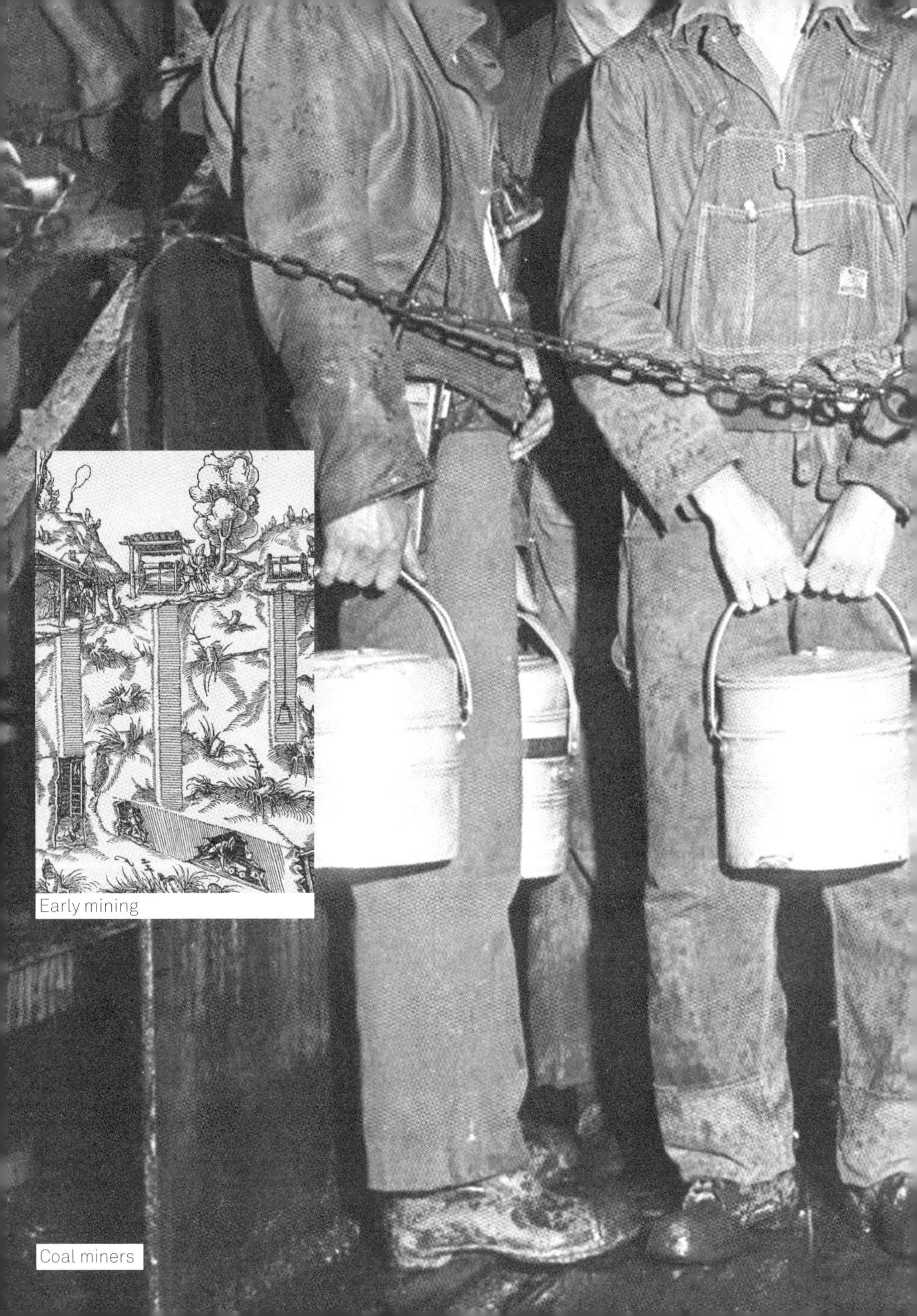

Early mining

Coal miners

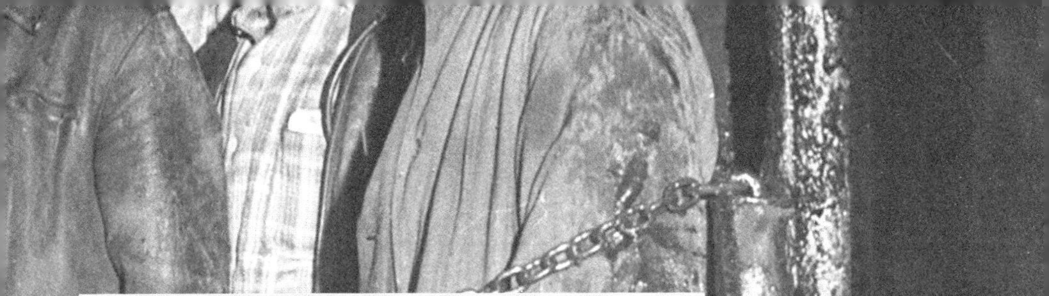

he whispered to himself some precious phrase that had stuck in his mind.

"If," he whispered, "if only we could pick that lock. . . ."

The sun was sinking over the distant hills. Already it was shorn of its beams, a globe of ruddy gold, hanging over the great banks of cloud that would presently engulf it.

"Eh!" said the youngster. "Eh!"

He seemed to wake up at last out of his entrancement, and the red sun was there before his eyes. He stared at it, at first without intelligence and then with a gathering recognition. Into his mind came a strange echo of that ancestral fancy, that fancy of a Stone Age savage, dead and scattered bones among the drift two hundred thousand years ago.

"Ye auld thing," he said,—and his eyes were shining, and he made a kind of grabbing gesture with his hand; "ye auld red thing. . . . We'll have ye *yet*."

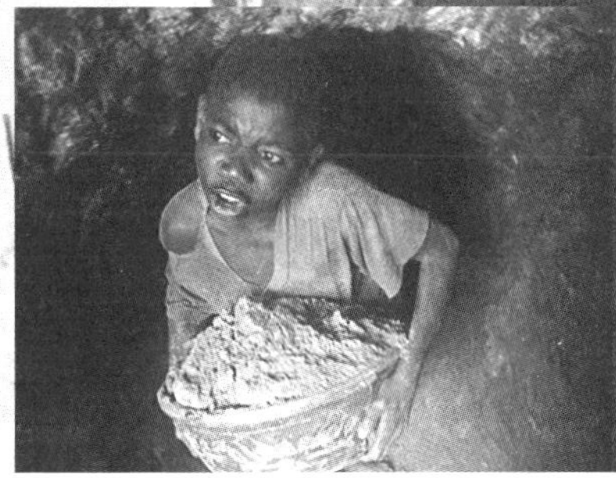

Contemporary working conditions

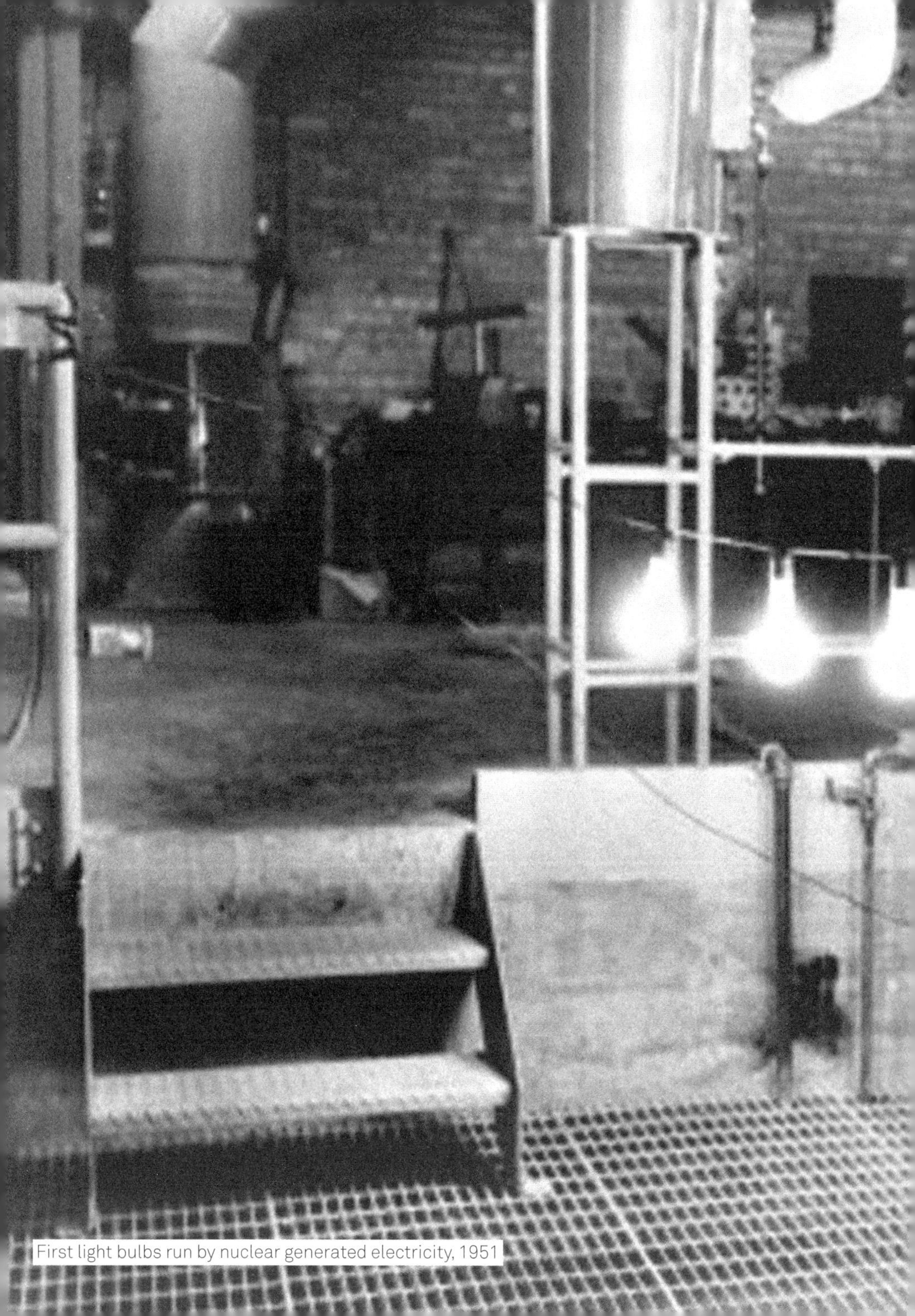

First light bulbs run by nuclear generated electricity, 1951

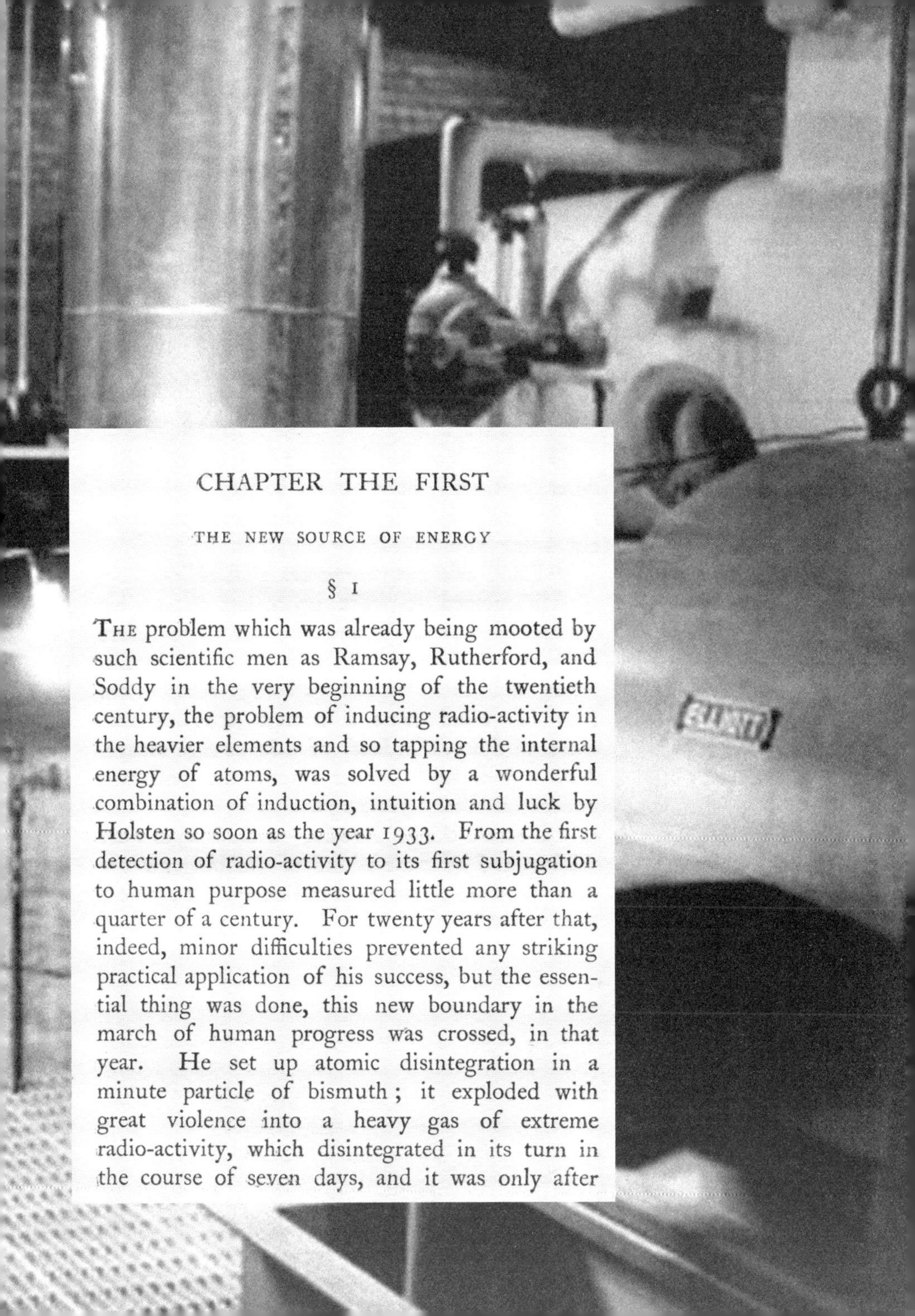

CHAPTER THE FIRST

THE NEW SOURCE OF ENERGY

§ 1

THE problem which was already being mooted by such scientific men as Ramsay, Rutherford, and Soddy in the very beginning of the twentieth century, the problem of inducing radio-activity in the heavier elements and so tapping the internal energy of atoms, was solved by a wonderful combination of induction, intuition and luck by Holsten so soon as the year 1933. From the first detection of radio-activity to its first subjugation to human purpose measured little more than a quarter of a century. For twenty years after that, indeed, minor difficulties prevented any striking practical application of his success, but the essential thing was done, this new boundary in the march of human progress was crossed, in that year. He set up atomic disintegration in a minute particle of bismuth; it exploded with great violence into a heavy gas of extreme radio-activity, which disintegrated in its turn in the course of seven days, and it was only after

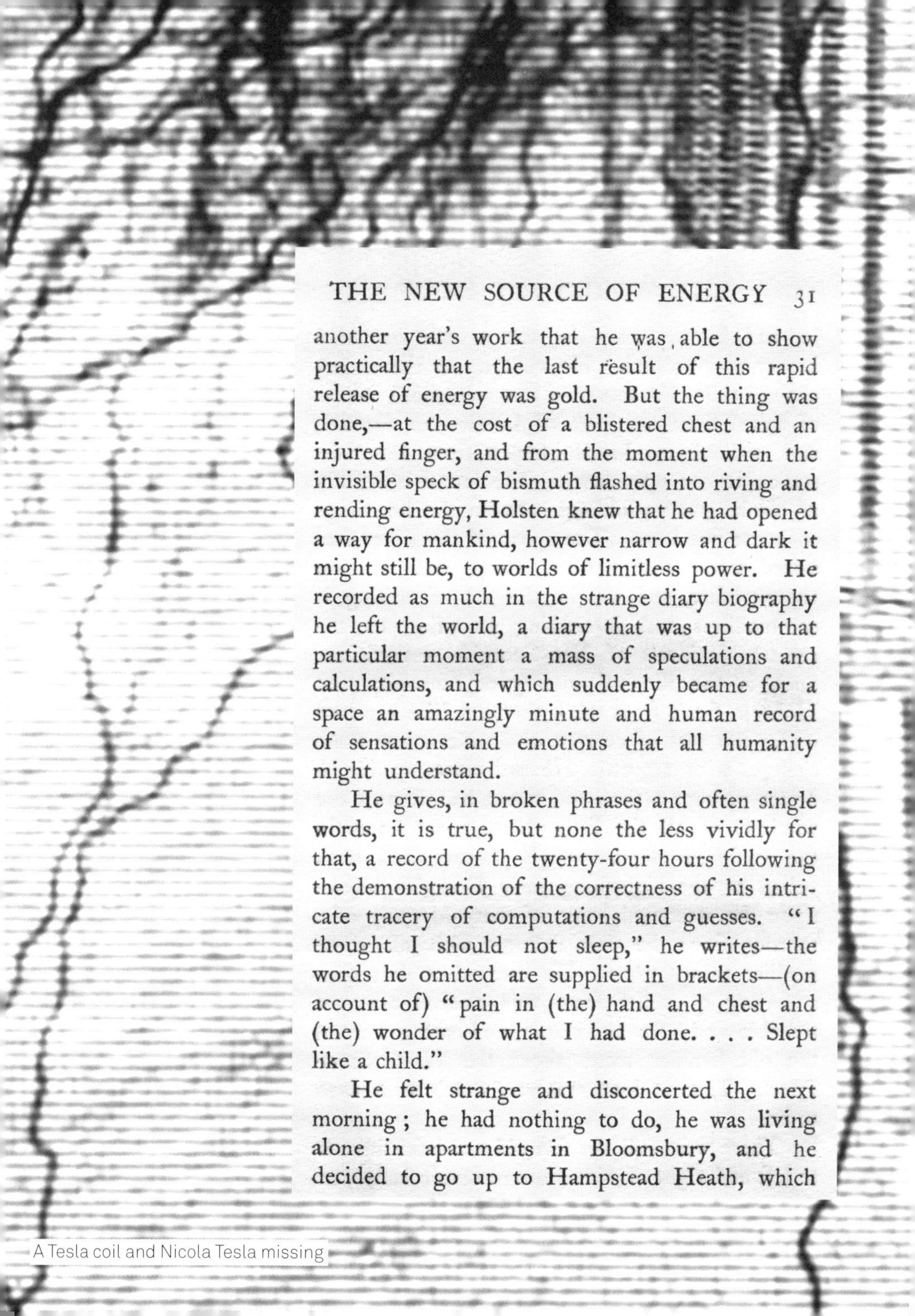

another year's work that he was able to show practically that the last result of this rapid release of energy was gold. But the thing was done,—at the cost of a blistered chest and an injured finger, and from the moment when the invisible speck of bismuth flashed into riving and rending energy, Holsten knew that he had opened a way for mankind, however narrow and dark it might still be, to worlds of limitless power. He recorded as much in the strange diary biography he left the world, a diary that was up to that particular moment a mass of speculations and calculations, and which suddenly became for a space an amazingly minute and human record of sensations and emotions that all humanity might understand.

He gives, in broken phrases and often single words, it is true, but none the less vividly for that, a record of the twenty-four hours following the demonstration of the correctness of his intricate tracery of computations and guesses. "I thought I should not sleep," he writes—the words he omitted are supplied in brackets—(on account of) "pain in (the) hand and chest and (the) wonder of what I had done. . . . Slept like a child."

He felt strange and disconcerted the next morning; he had nothing to do, he was living alone in apartments in Bloomsbury, and he decided to go up to Hampstead Heath, which

A Tesla coil and Nicola Tesla missing

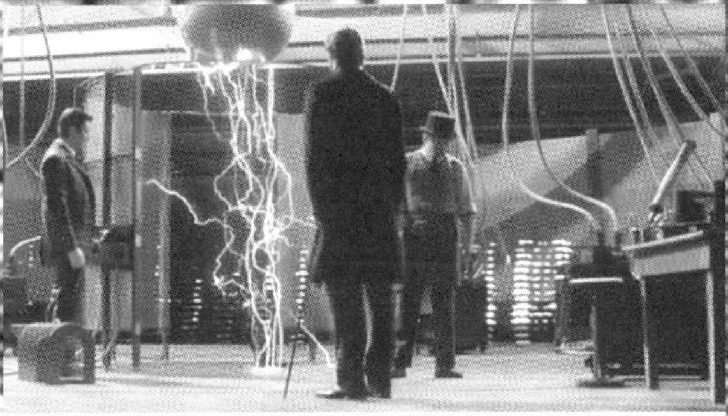

Technican and magican (US, UK 2006)

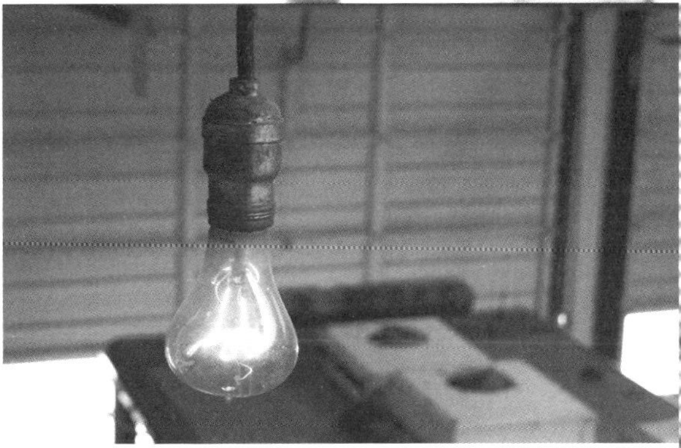

Working constantly since 1901, in 2010

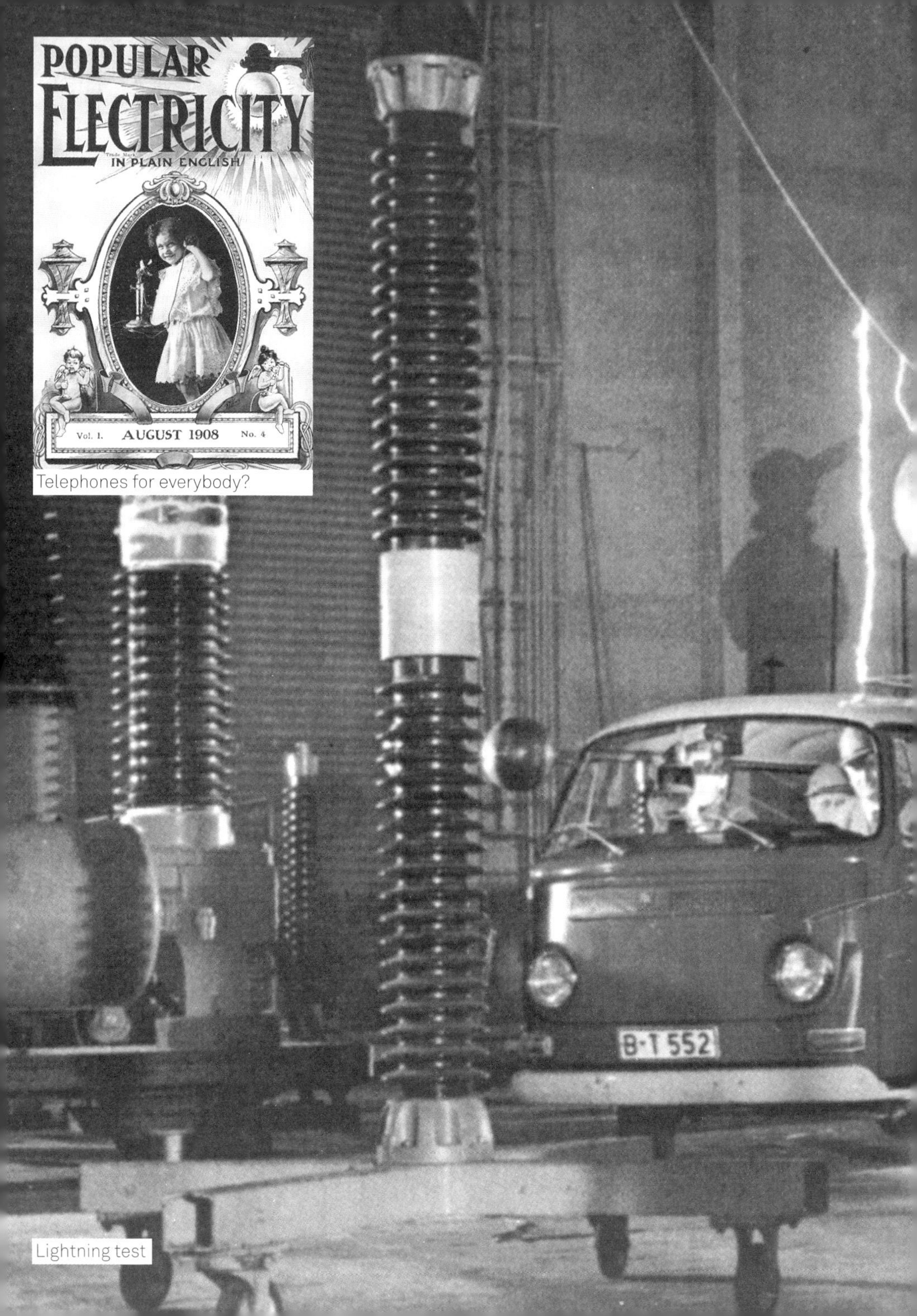

Telephones for everybody?

Lightning test

he had known when he was a little boy as a breezy play-ground. He went up by the underground tube that was then the recognised means of travel from one part of London to another, and walked up Heath Street from the tube station to the open heath. He found it a gully of planks and scaffoldings between the hoardings of house-wreckers. The spirit of the times had seized upon that narrow, steep, and winding thoroughfare, and was in the act of making it commodious and interesting according to the remarkable ideals of Neo-Georgian æstheticism. Such is the illogical quality of humanity that Holsten, fresh from work that was like a petard under the seat of current civilization, saw these changes with regret. He had come up Heath Street perhaps a thousand times, had known the windows of all the little shops, spent hours in the vanished cinematograph theatre, and marvelled at the high-flung early Georgian houses upon the westward bank of that old gully of a thoroughfare; he felt strange with all these familiar things gone. He escaped at last with a feeling of relief from this choked alley of trenches and holes and cranes, and emerged upon the old familiar scene about the White Stone Pond. That, at least, was very much as it used to be.

There were still the fine old red-brick houses to left and right of him; the reservoir had been

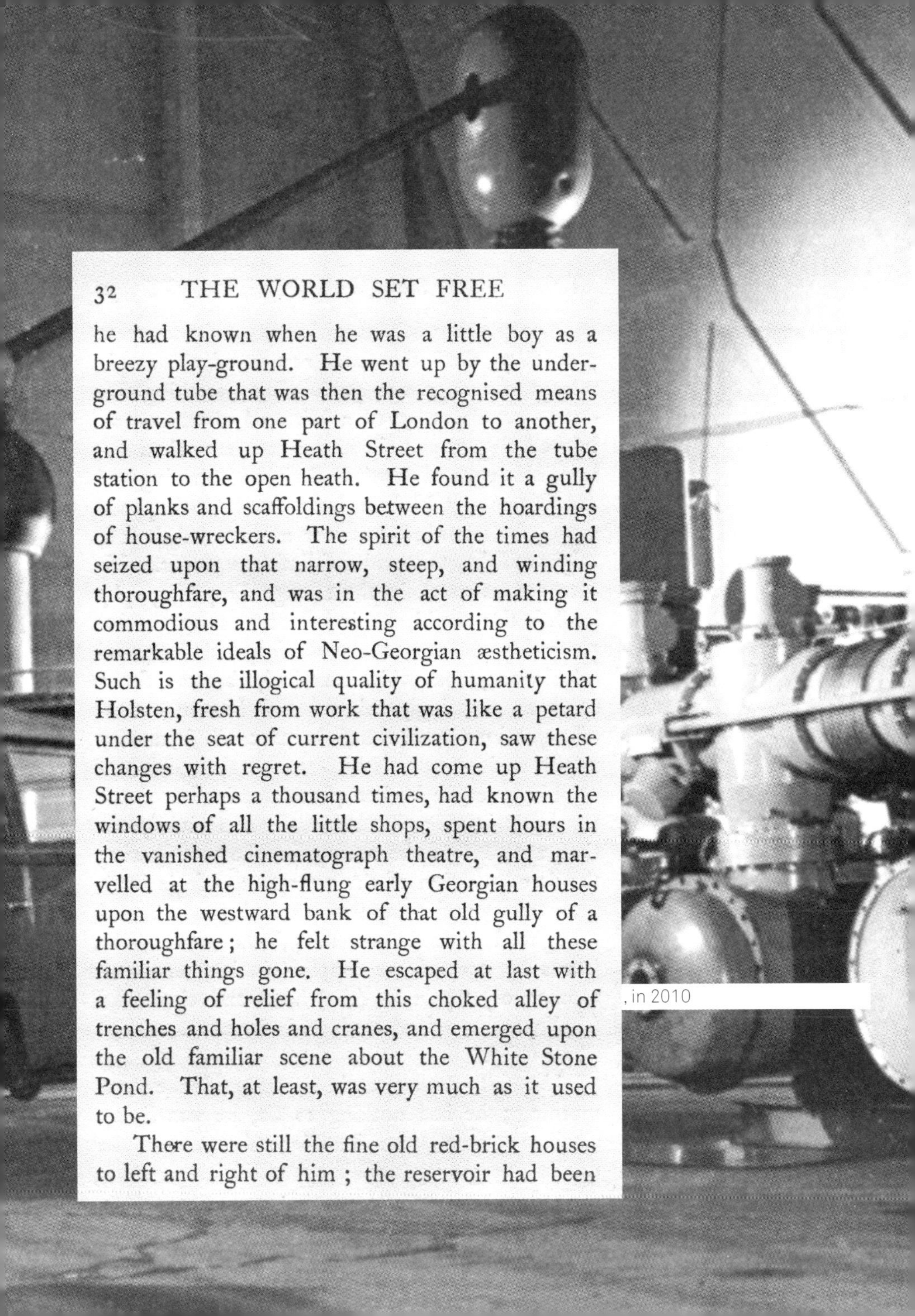

, in 2010

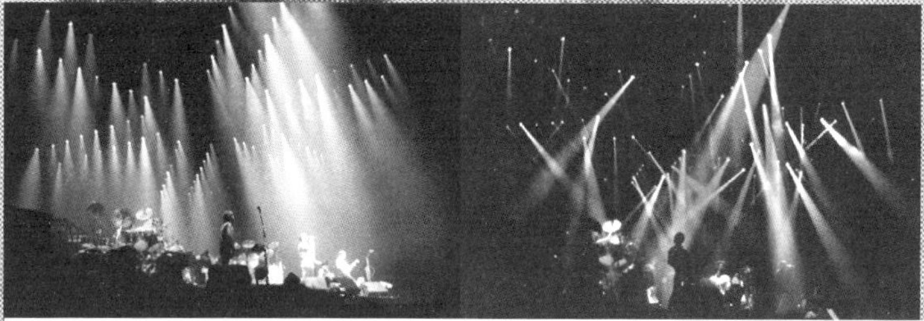

Genesis electric light show

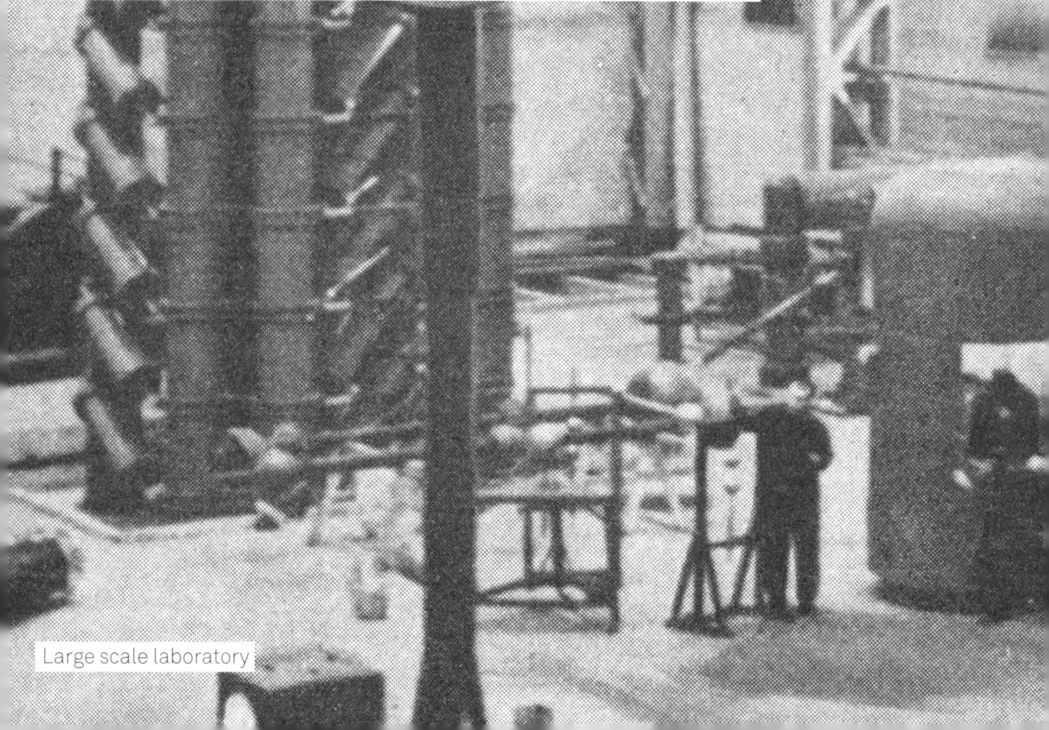

Large scale laboratory

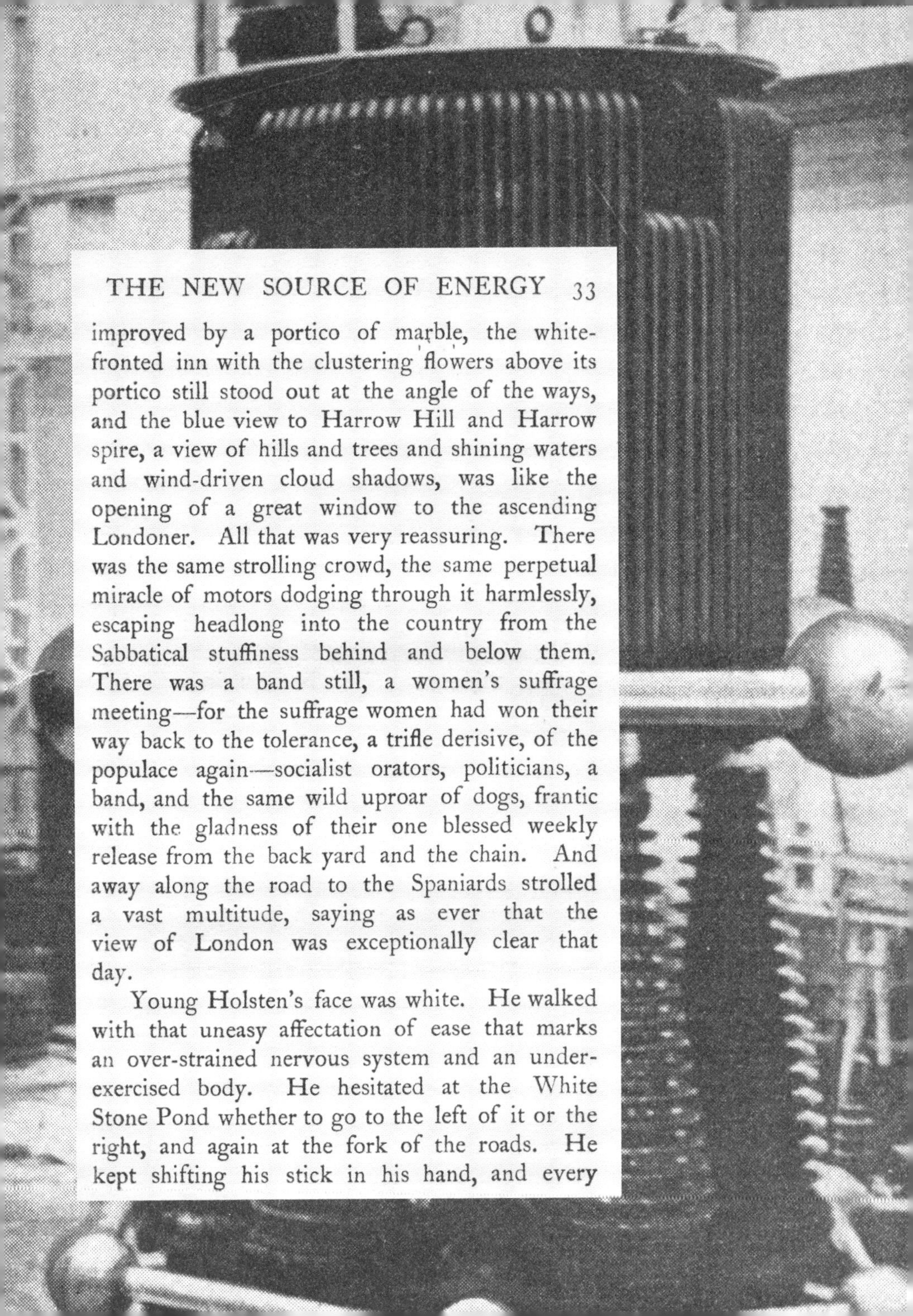

improved by a portico of marble, the white-fronted inn with the clustering flowers above its portico still stood out at the angle of the ways, and the blue view to Harrow Hill and Harrow spire, a view of hills and trees and shining waters and wind-driven cloud shadows, was like the opening of a great window to the ascending Londoner. All that was very reassuring. There was the same strolling crowd, the same perpetual miracle of motors dodging through it harmlessly, escaping headlong into the country from the Sabbatical stuffiness behind and below them. There was a band still, a women's suffrage meeting—for the suffrage women had won their way back to the tolerance, a trifle derisive, of the populace again—socialist orators, politicians, a band, and the same wild uproar of dogs, frantic with the gladness of their one blessed weekly release from the back yard and the chain. And away along the road to the Spaniards strolled a vast multitude, saying as ever that the view of London was exceptionally clear that day.

Young Holsten's face was white. He walked with that uneasy affectation of ease that marks an over-strained nervous system and an under-exercised body. He hesitated at the White Stone Pond whether to go to the left of it or the right, and again at the fork of the roads. He kept shifting his stick in his hand, and every

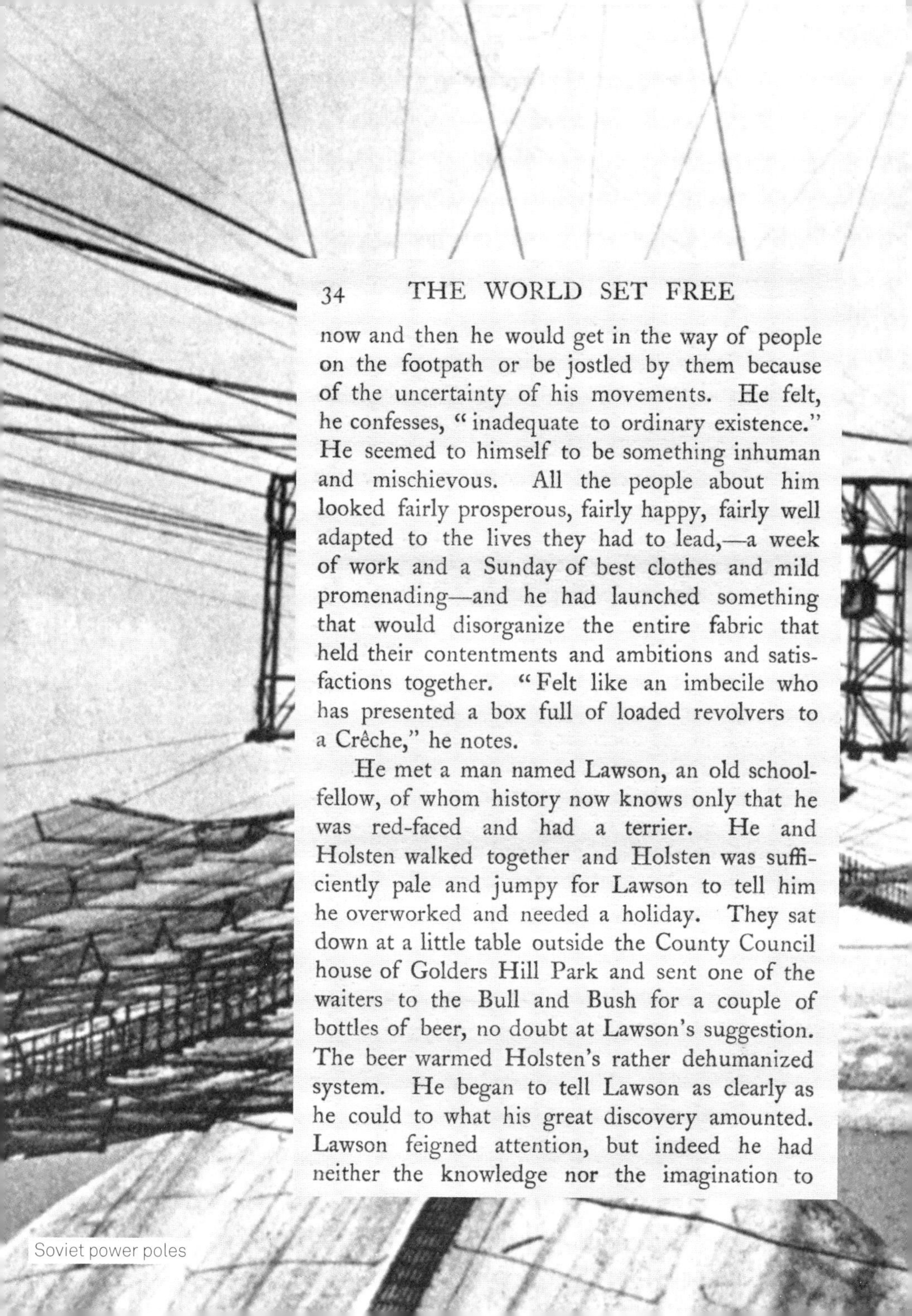

Soviet power poles

now and then he would get in the way of people on the footpath or be jostled by them because of the uncertainty of his movements. He felt, he confesses, "inadequate to ordinary existence." He seemed to himself to be something inhuman and mischievous. All the people about him looked fairly prosperous, fairly happy, fairly well adapted to the lives they had to lead,—a week of work and a Sunday of best clothes and mild promenading—and he had launched something that would disorganize the entire fabric that held their contentments and ambitions and satisfactions together. "Felt like an imbecile who has presented a box full of loaded revolvers to a Crêche," he notes.

He met a man named Lawson, an old schoolfellow, of whom history now knows only that he was red-faced and had a terrier. He and Holsten walked together and Holsten was sufficiently pale and jumpy for Lawson to tell him he overworked and needed a holiday. They sat down at a little table outside the County Council house of Golders Hill Park and sent one of the waiters to the Bull and Bush for a couple of bottles of beer, no doubt at Lawson's suggestion. The beer warmed Holsten's rather dehumanized system. He began to tell Lawson as clearly as he could to what his great discovery amounted. Lawson feigned attention, but indeed he had neither the knowledge nor the imagination to

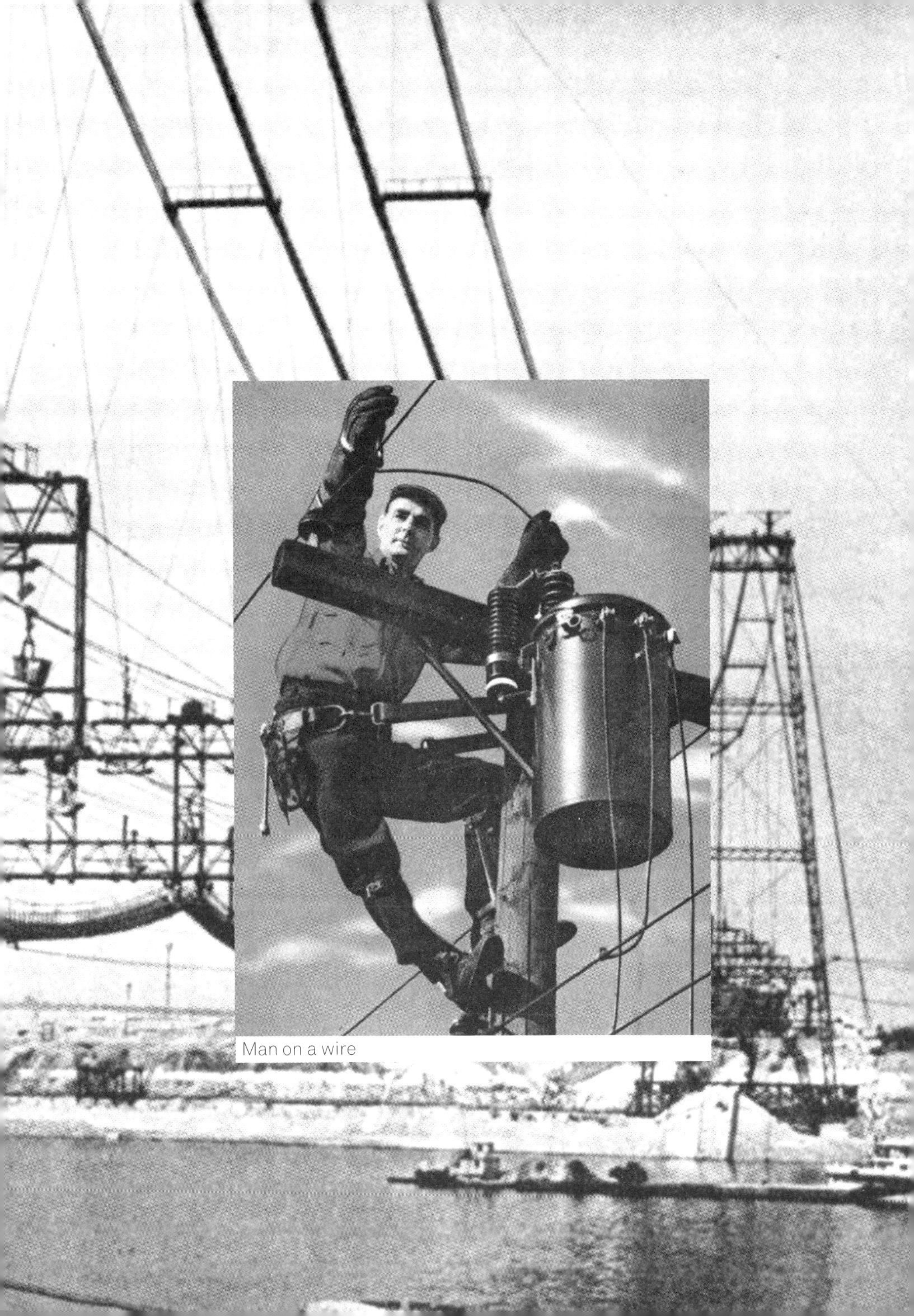

Man on a wire

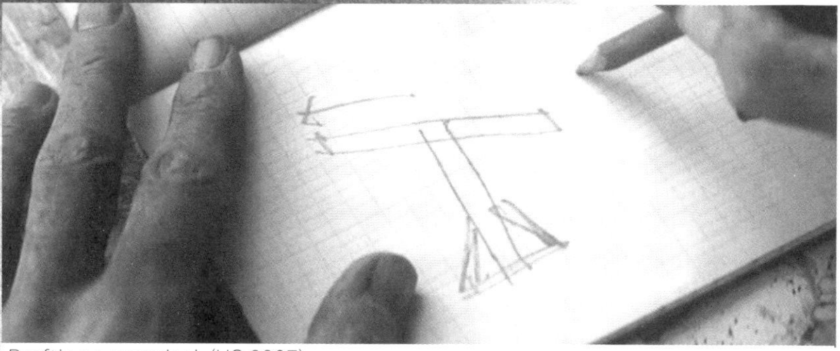
Drafting a pumpjack (US 2007)

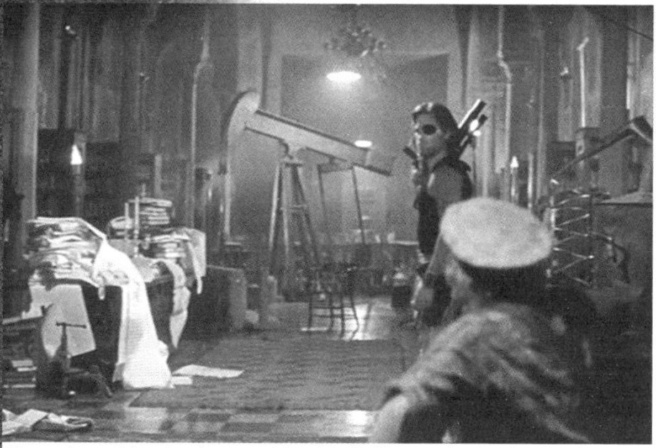
Pumping oil in the former New York library (UK, US 1981)

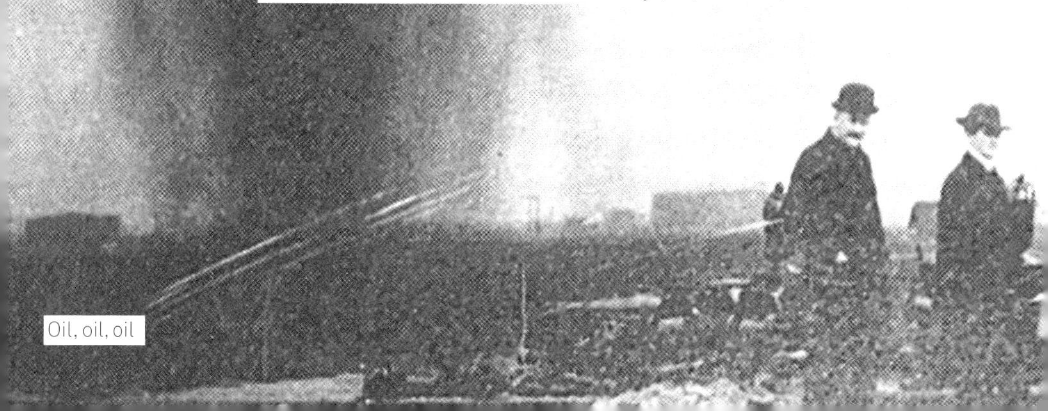
Oil, oil, oil

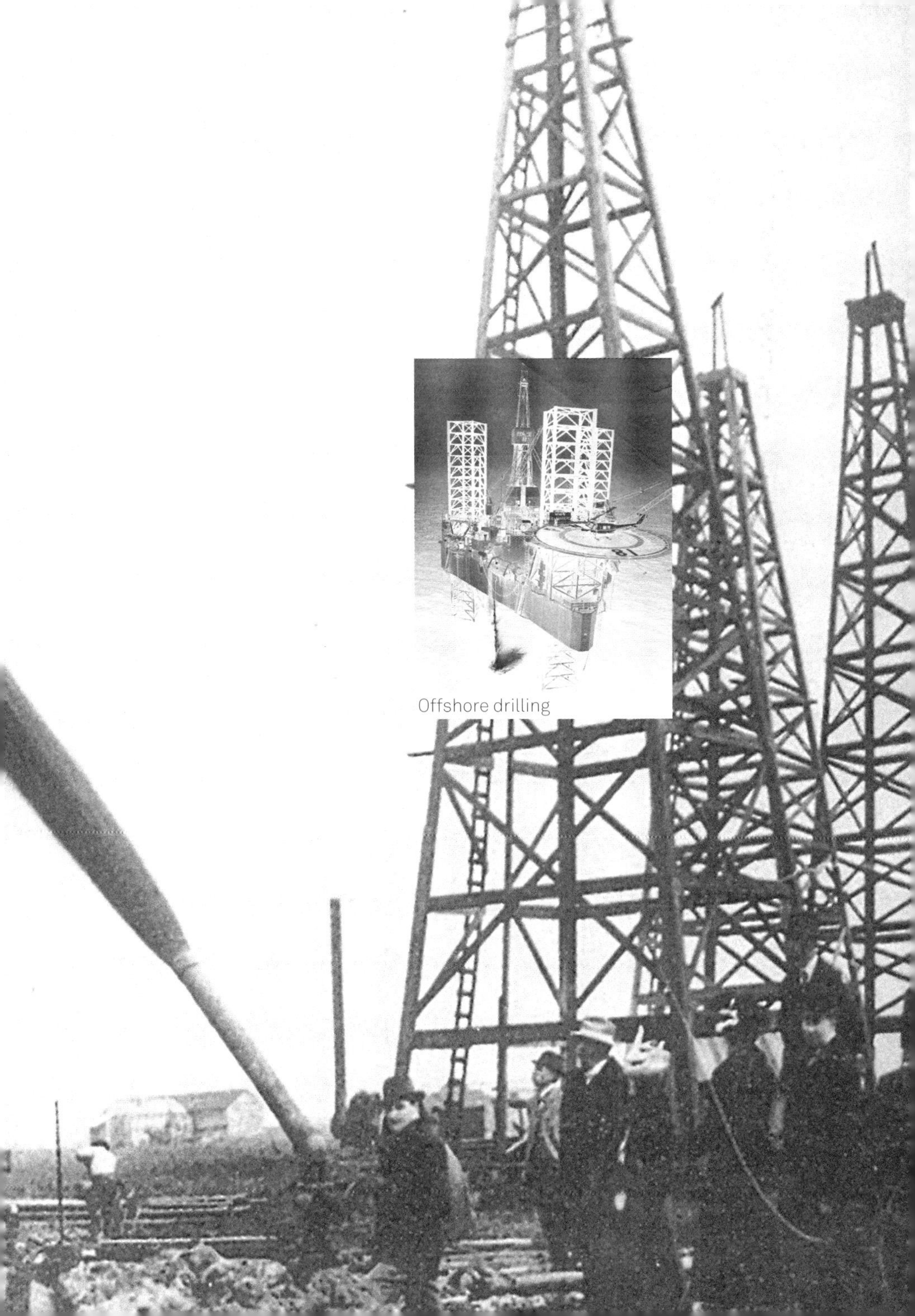

Offshore drilling

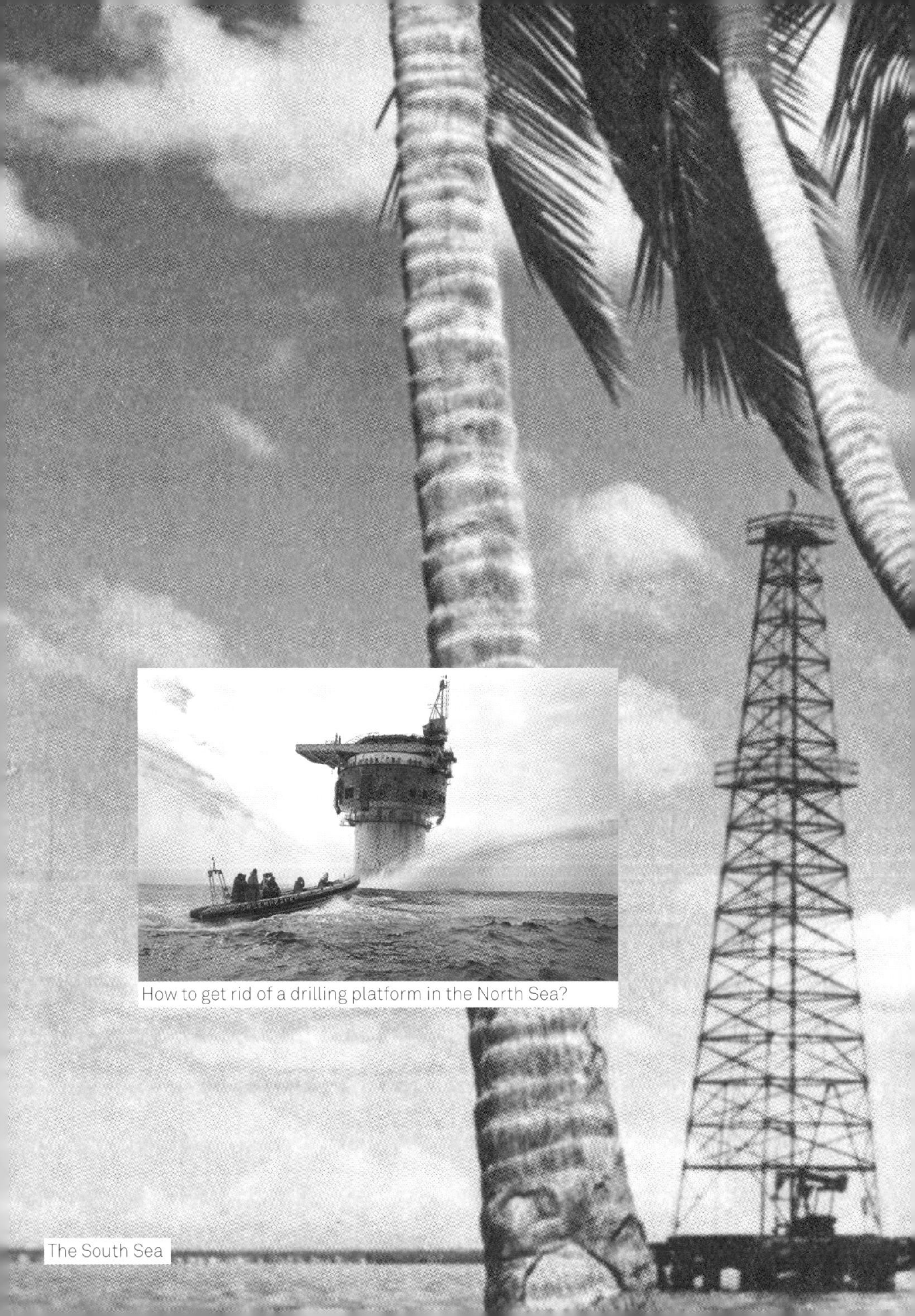

How to get rid of a drilling platform in the North Sea?

The South Sea

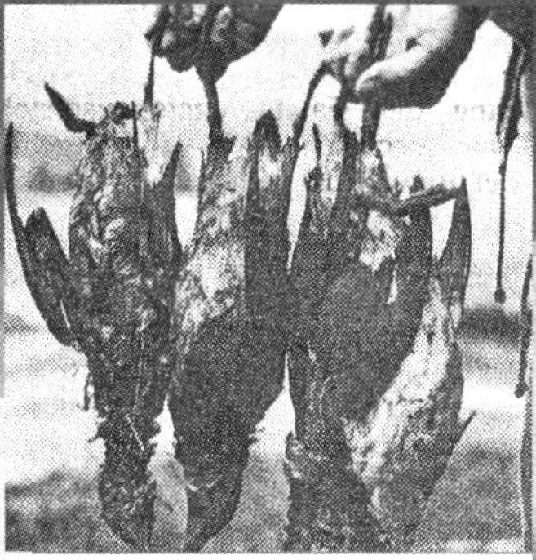

Oil pollution

understand. "In the end, before many years are out, this must eventually change war, transit, lighting, building and every sort of manufacture, even agriculture, every material human concern——"

Then Holsten stopped short. Lawson had leapt to his feet. "Damn that dog!" cried Lawson. "Look at it now. Hi! Here! *Phewoo—phewoo—phewoo!* Come *here*, Bobs! Come *here!*"

The young scientific man with his bandaged hand sat at the green table, too tired to convey the wonder of the thing he had sought so long, his friend whistled and bawled for his dog, and the Sunday people drifted about them through the spring sunshine. For a moment or so Holsten stared at Lawson in astonishment, for he had been too intent upon what he had been saying to realize how little Lawson had attended.

Then he remarked, "*Well!*" and smiled faintly and—finished the tankard of beer before him.

Lawson sat down again. "One must look after one's dog," he said with a note of apology. "What was it you were telling me?"

§ 2

In the evening Holsten went out again. He walked to Saint Paul's Cathedral and stood for

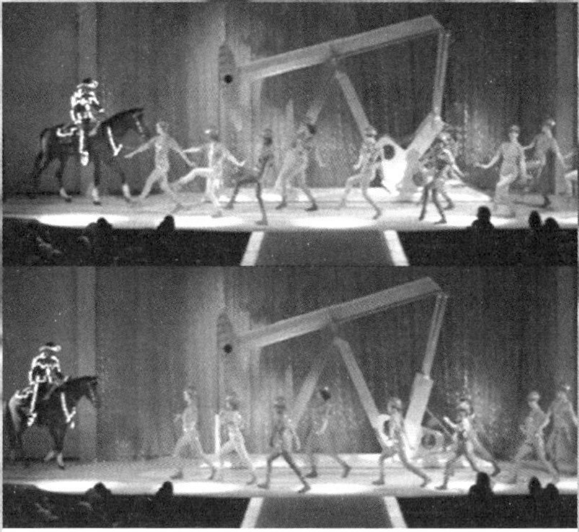

Pumping jack on a Las Vegas stage ...

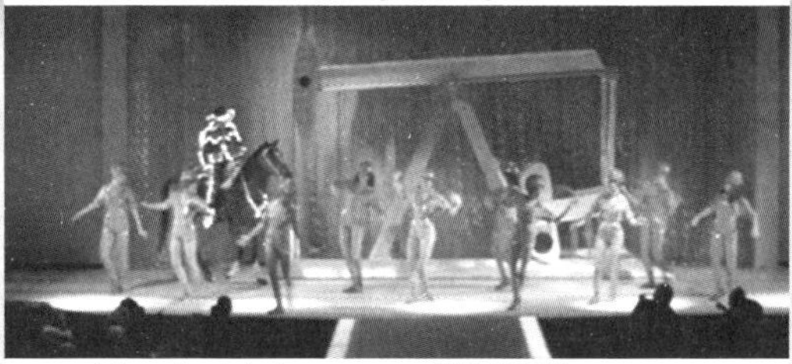

... and the electric horseman (US 1979)

The age of road cruising

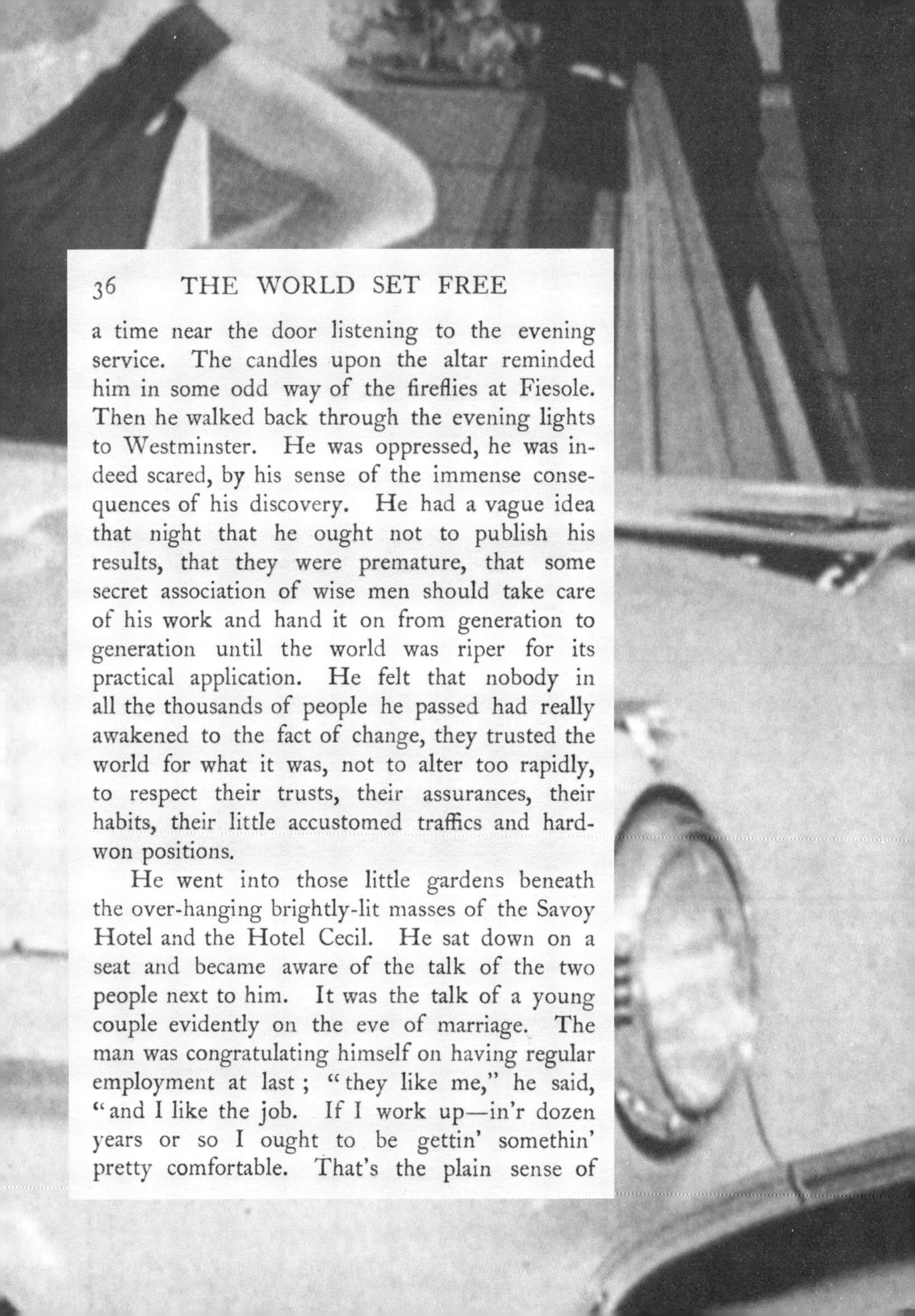

a time near the door listening to the evening service. The candles upon the altar reminded him in some odd way of the fireflies at Fiesole. Then he walked back through the evening lights to Westminster. He was oppressed, he was indeed scared, by his sense of the immense consequences of his discovery. He had a vague idea that night that he ought not to publish his results, that they were premature, that some secret association of wise men should take care of his work and hand it on from generation to generation until the world was riper for its practical application. He felt that nobody in all the thousands of people he passed had really awakened to the fact of change, they trusted the world for what it was, not to alter too rapidly, to respect their trusts, their assurances, their habits, their little accustomed traffics and hard-won positions.

He went into those little gardens beneath the over-hanging brightly-lit masses of the Savoy Hotel and the Hotel Cecil. He sat down on a seat and became aware of the talk of the two people next to him. It was the talk of a young couple evidently on the eve of marriage. The man was congratulating himself on having regular employment at last; "they like me," he said, "and I like the job. If I work up—in'r dozen years or so I ought to be gettin' somethin' pretty comfortable. That's the plain sense of

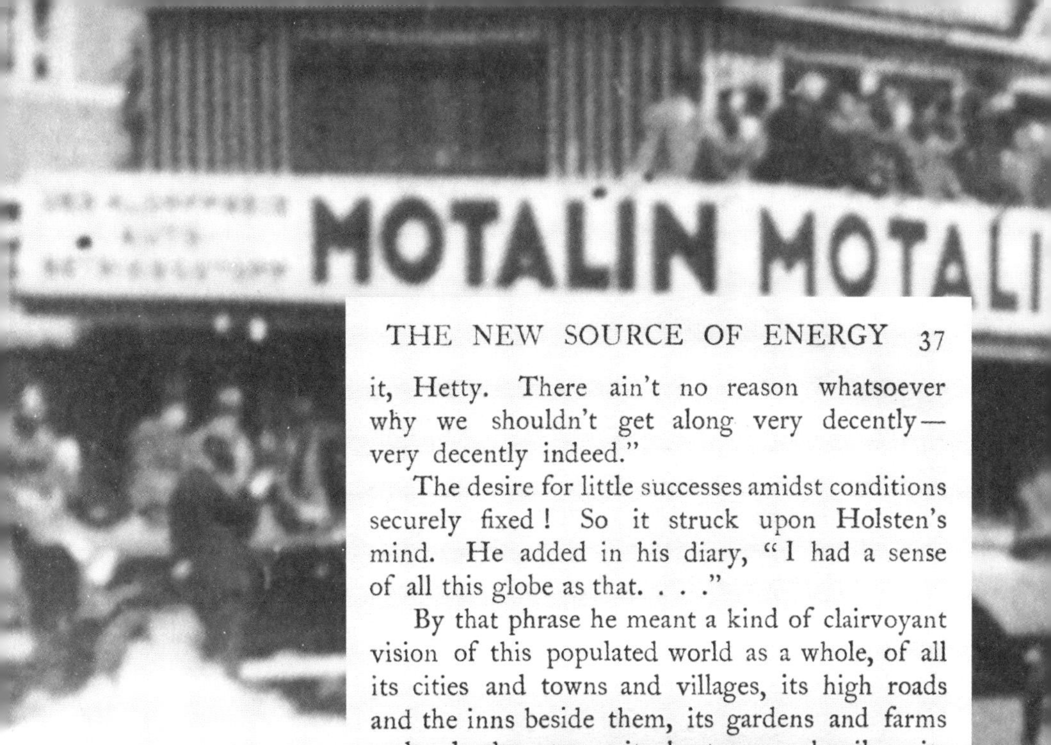

it, Hetty. There ain't no reason whatsoever why we shouldn't get along very decently—very decently indeed."

The desire for little successes amidst conditions securely fixed! So it struck upon Holsten's mind. He added in his diary, "I had a sense of all this globe as that. . . ."

By that phrase he meant a kind of clairvoyant vision of this populated world as a whole, of all its cities and towns and villages, its high roads and the inns beside them, its gardens and farms and upland pastures, its boatmen and sailors, its ships coming along the great circles of the ocean, its time-tables and appointments and payments and dues as it were one unified and progressive spectacle. Sometimes such visions came to him; his mind, accustomed to great generalizations and yet acutely sensitive to detail, saw things far more comprehensively than the minds of most of his contemporaries. Usually the teeming sphere moved on to its predestined ends and circled with a stately swiftness on its path about the sun. Usually it was all a living progress that altered under his regard. But now fatigue a little deadened him to that incessancy of life, it seemed now just an eternal circling. He lapsed to the commoner persuasion of the great fixities and recurrencies of the human routine. The remoter past of wandering savagery, the inevitable changes of to-morrow were veiled, and

Speeding record rocket car in 1928

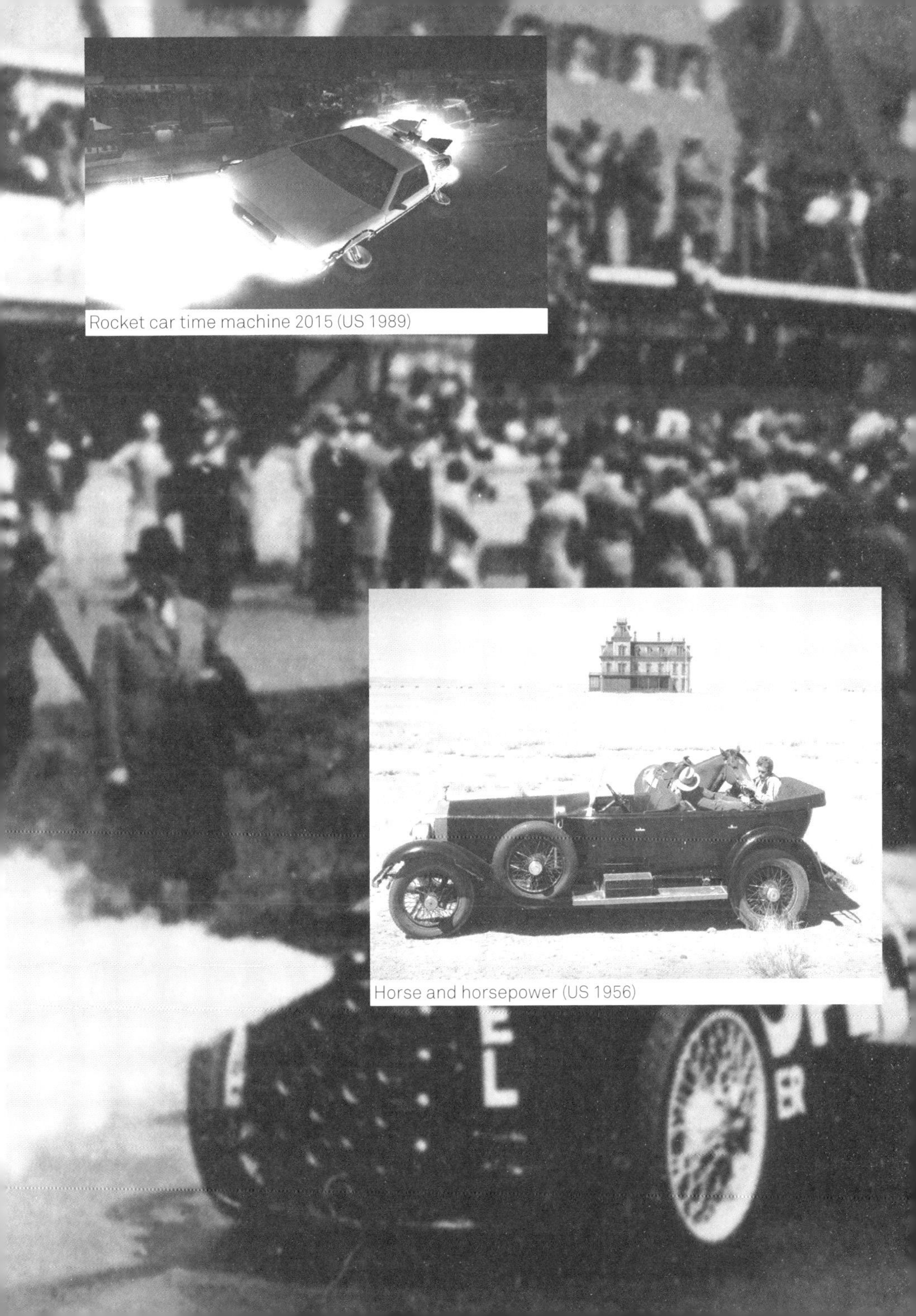

Rocket car time machine 2015 (US 1989)

Horse and horsepower (US 1956)

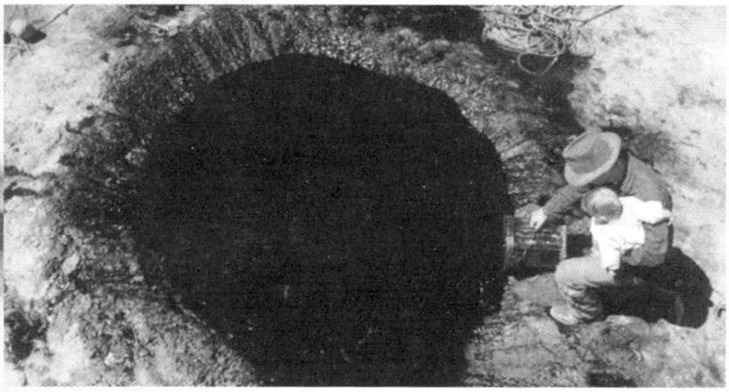
Oil pit (US 2007)

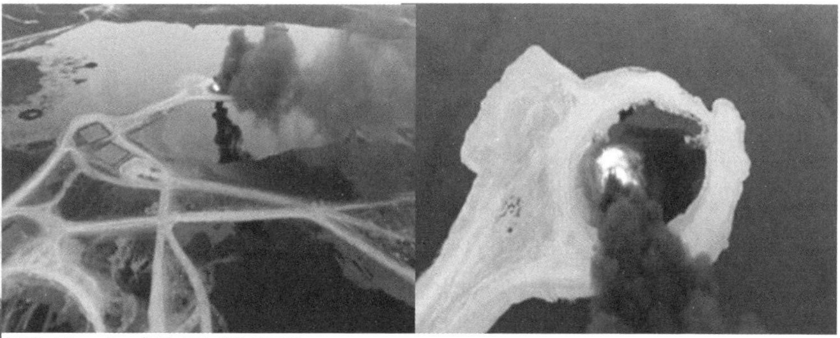
Oilfield on fire (FR, UK, DE 1992)

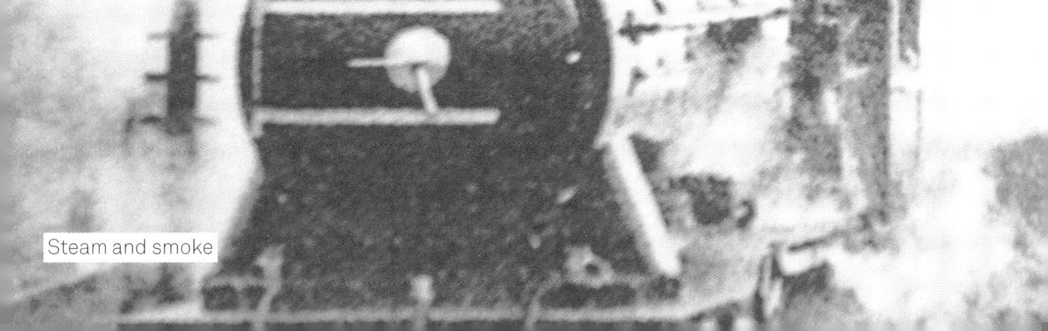
Steam and smoke

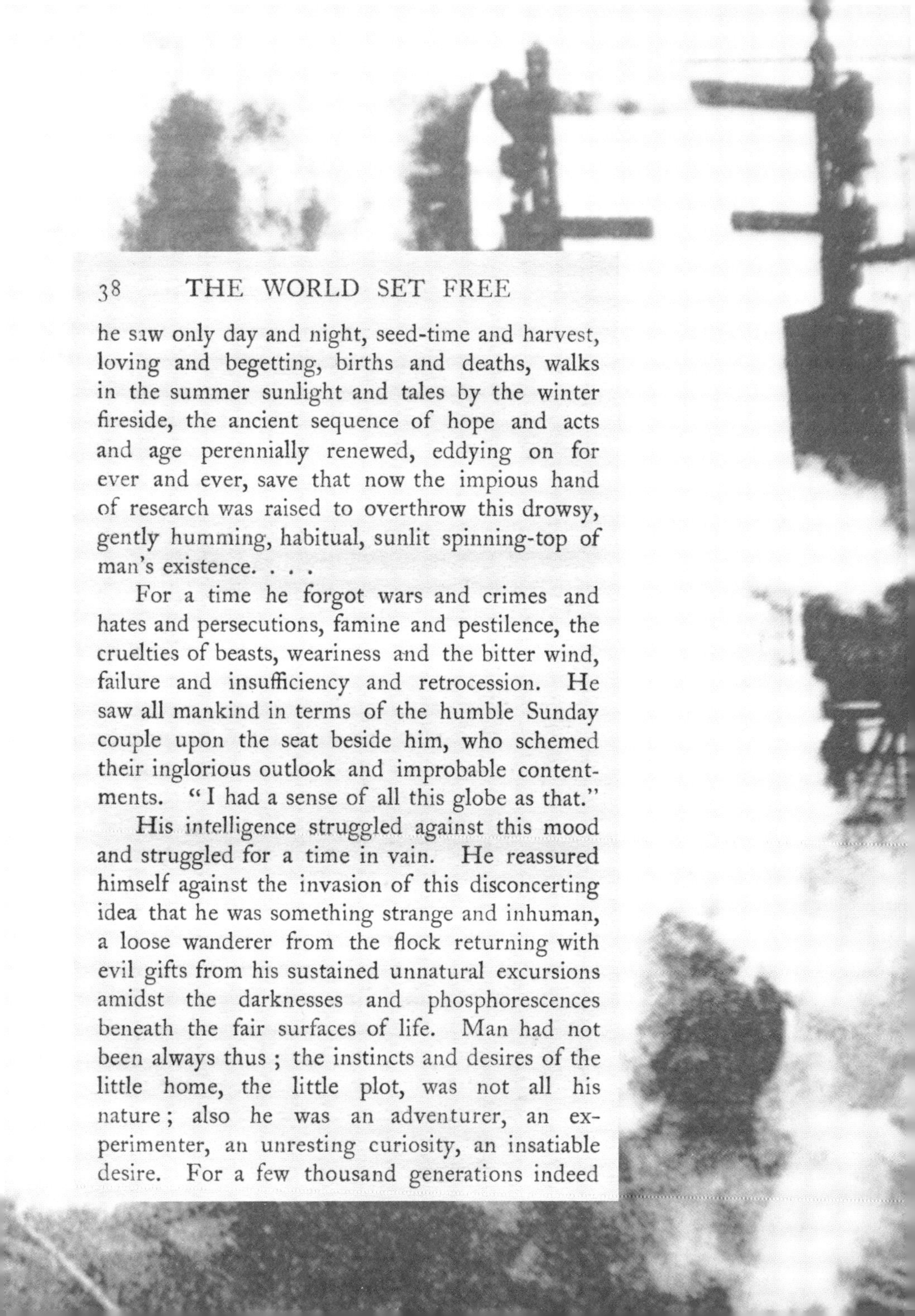

he saw only day and night, seed-time and harvest, loving and begetting, births and deaths, walks in the summer sunlight and tales by the winter fireside, the ancient sequence of hope and acts and age perennially renewed, eddying on for ever and ever, save that now the impious hand of research was raised to overthrow this drowsy, gently humming, habitual, sunlit spinning-top of man's existence. . . .

For a time he forgot wars and crimes and hates and persecutions, famine and pestilence, the cruelties of beasts, weariness and the bitter wind, failure and insufficiency and retrocession. He saw all mankind in terms of the humble Sunday couple upon the seat beside him, who schemed their inglorious outlook and improbable contentments. "I had a sense of all this globe as that."

His intelligence struggled against this mood and struggled for a time in vain. He reassured himself against the invasion of this disconcerting idea that he was something strange and inhuman, a loose wanderer from the flock returning with evil gifts from his sustained unnatural excursions amidst the darknesses and phosphorescences beneath the fair surfaces of life. Man had not been always thus; the instincts and desires of the little home, the little plot, was not all his nature; also he was an adventurer, an experimenter, an unresting curiosity, an insatiable desire. For a few thousand generations indeed

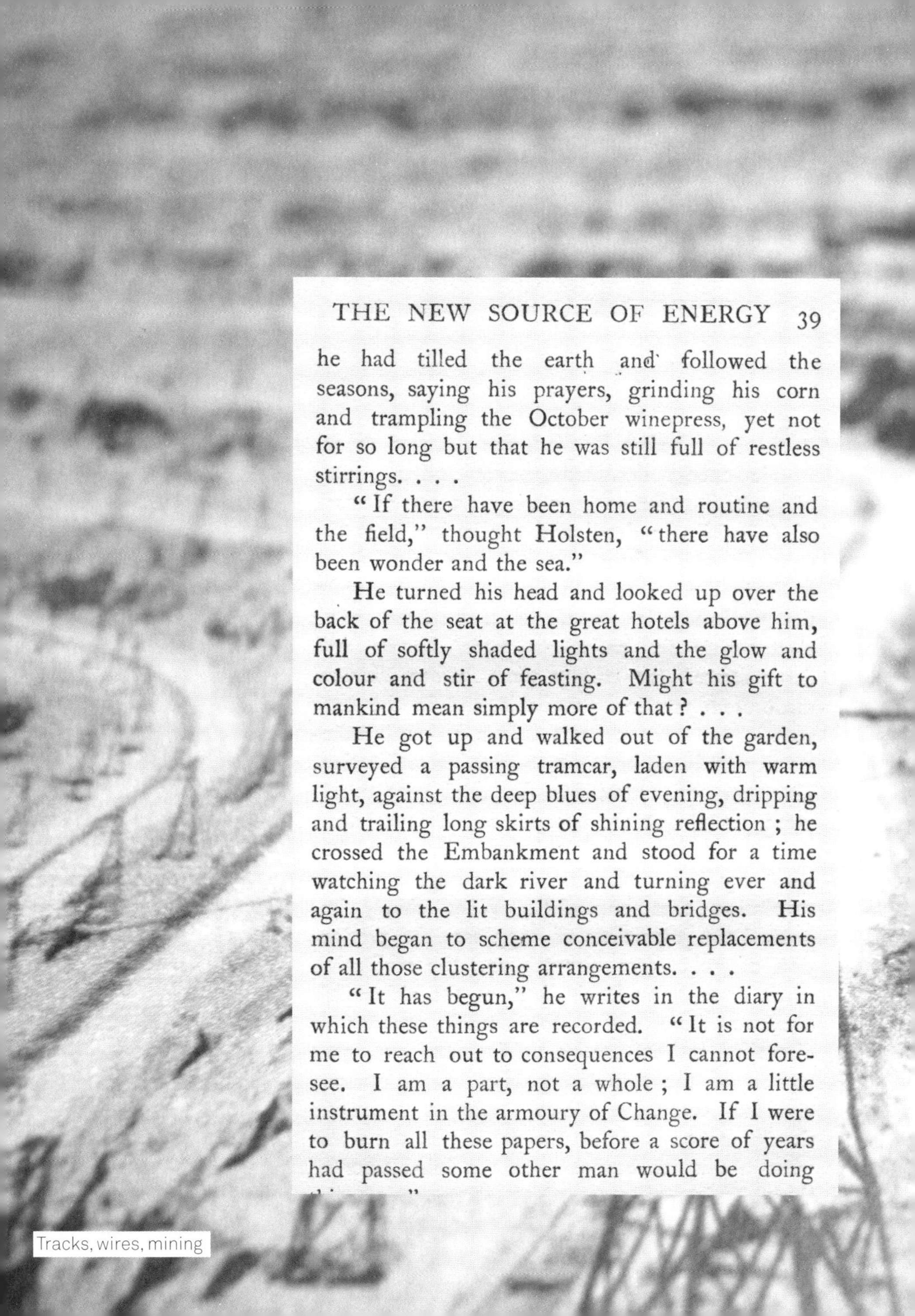

Tracks, wires, mining

he had tilled the earth and followed the seasons, saying his prayers, grinding his corn and trampling the October winepress, yet not for so long but that he was still full of restless stirrings. . . .

"If there have been home and routine and the field," thought Holsten, "there have also been wonder and the sea."

He turned his head and looked up over the back of the seat at the great hotels above him, full of softly shaded lights and the glow and colour and stir of feasting. Might his gift to mankind mean simply more of that? . . .

He got up and walked out of the garden, surveyed a passing tramcar, laden with warm light, against the deep blues of evening, dripping and trailing long skirts of shining reflection; he crossed the Embankment and stood for a time watching the dark river and turning ever and again to the lit buildings and bridges. His mind began to scheme conceivable replacements of all those clustering arrangements. . . .

"It has begun," he writes in the diary in which these things are recorded. "It is not for me to reach out to consequences I cannot foresee. I am a part, not a whole; I am a little instrument in the armoury of Change. If I were to burn all these papers, before a score of years had passed some other man would be doing

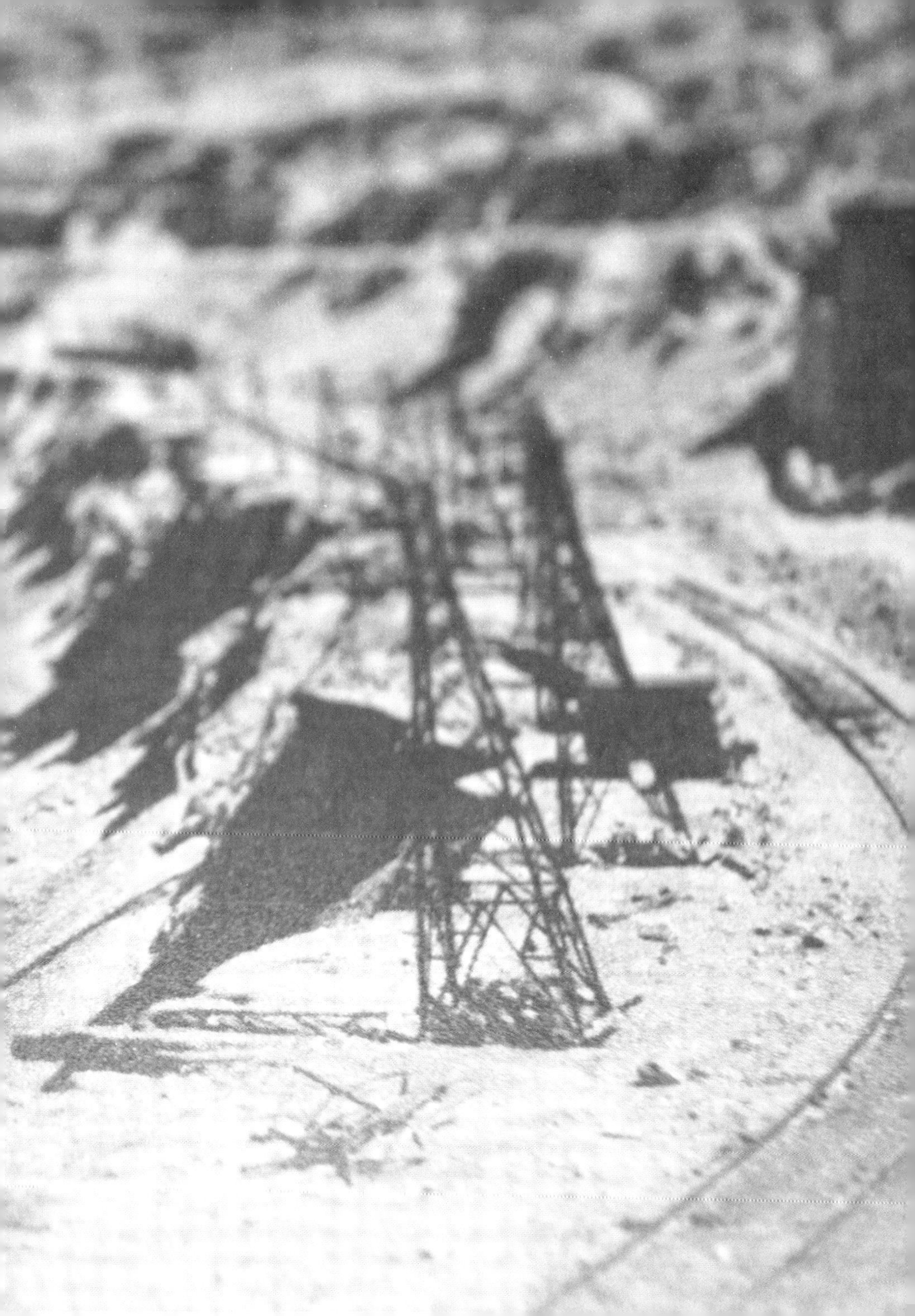

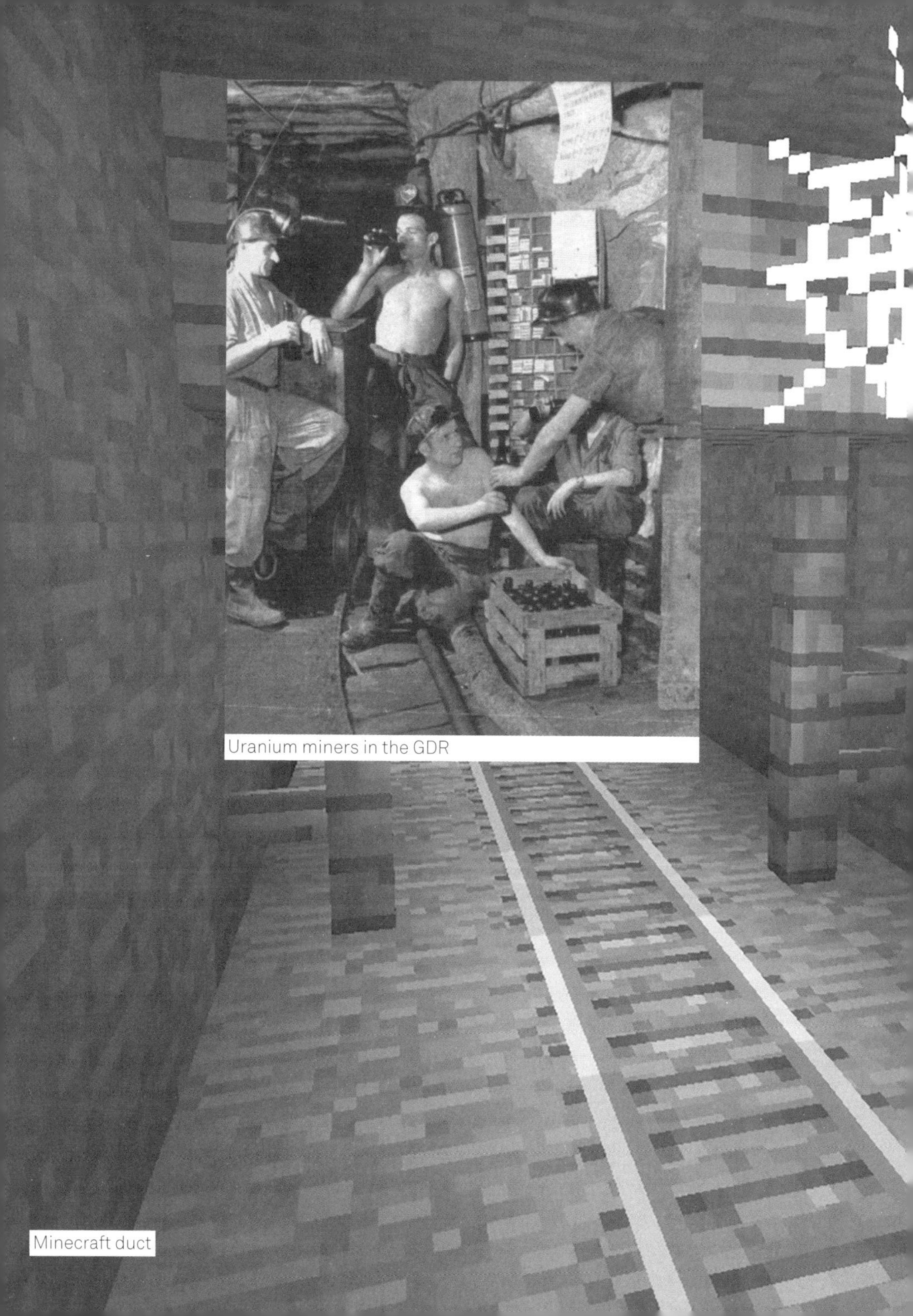
Uranium miners in the GDR

Minecraft duct

§ 3

Holsten, before he died, was destined to see atomic energy dominating every other source of power, but for some years yet a vast network of difficulties in detail and application kept the new discovery from any effective invasion of ordinary life. The path from the laboratory to the workshop is sometimes a tortuous one; electro-magnetic radiations were known and demonstrated for twenty years before Marconi made them practically available, and in the same way it was twenty years before induced radio-activity could be brought to practical utilization. The thing of course was discussed very much, more perhaps at the time of its discovery than during the interval of technical adaptation, but with very little realization of the huge economic revolution that impended. What chiefly impressed the journalists of 1933 was the production of gold from bismuth and the realization albeit upon unprofitable lines of the alchemist's dreams; there was a considerable amount of discussion and expectation in that more intelligent section of the educated publics of the various civilized countries which followed scientific development; but for the most part the world went about its business—as the inhabitants of those Swiss villages which live under the

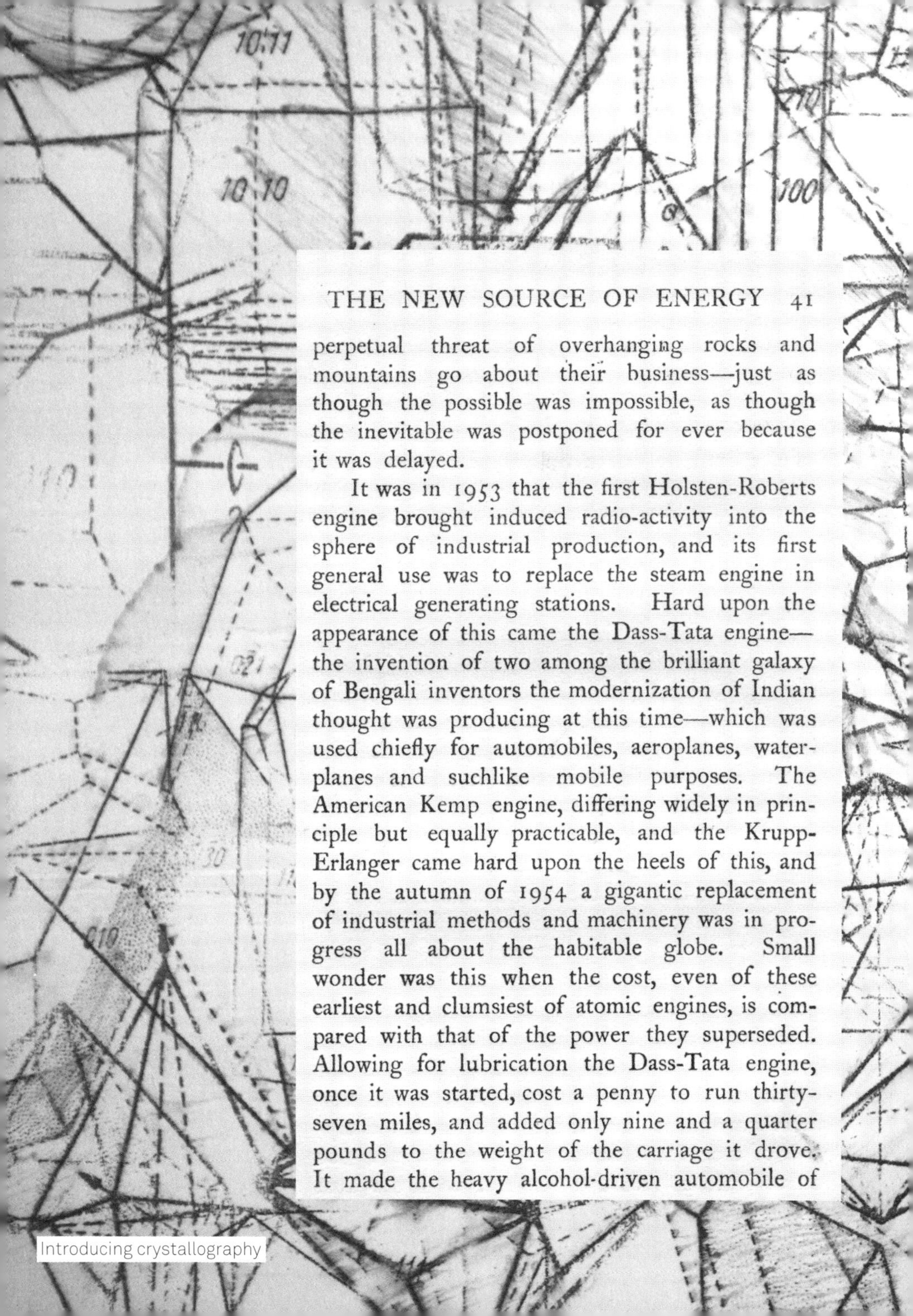

perpetual threat of overhanging rocks and mountains go about their business—just as though the possible was impossible, as though the inevitable was postponed for ever because it was delayed.

It was in 1953 that the first Holsten-Roberts engine brought induced radio-activity into the sphere of industrial production, and its first general use was to replace the steam engine in electrical generating stations. Hard upon the appearance of this came the Dass-Tata engine—the invention of two among the brilliant galaxy of Bengali inventors the modernization of Indian thought was producing at this time—which was used chiefly for automobiles, aeroplanes, waterplanes and suchlike mobile purposes. The American Kemp engine, differing widely in principle but equally practicable, and the Krupp-Erlanger came hard upon the heels of this, and by the autumn of 1954 a gigantic replacement of industrial methods and machinery was in progress all about the habitable globe. Small wonder was this when the cost, even of these earliest and clumsiest of atomic engines, is compared with that of the power they superseded. Allowing for lubrication the Dass-Tata engine, once it was started, cost a penny to run thirty-seven miles, and added only nine and a quarter pounds to the weight of the carriage it drove. It made the heavy alcohol-driven automobile of

Introducing crystallography

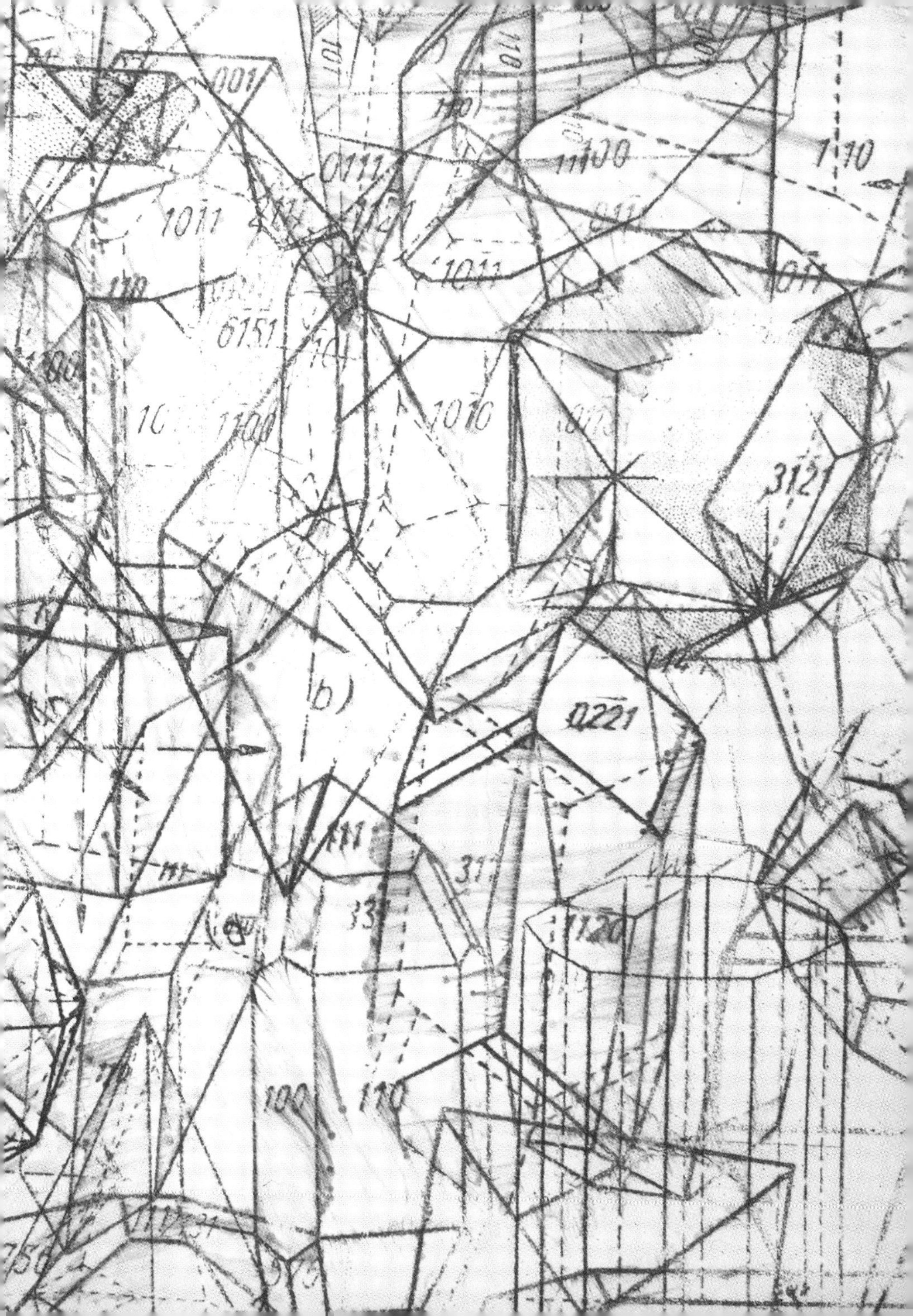
b)

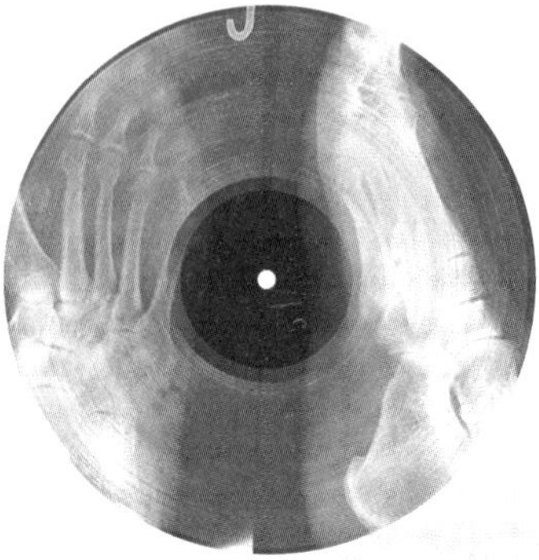

bootleg on x-ray film

First x-ray image

the time ridiculous in appearance as well as preposterously costly. For many years the price of coal and every form of liquid fuel had been clambering to levels that made even the revival of the draft horse seem a practicable possibility, and now with the abrupt relaxation of this stringency the change in appearance of the traffic upon the world's roads was instantaneous. In three years the frightful armoured monsters that had hooted and smoked and thundered about the world for four awful decades were swept away to the dealers in old metal, and the highways thronged with light and clean and shimmering shapes of silvered steel. At the same time a new impetus was given to aviation by the relatively enormous power for weight of the atomic engine, it was at last possible to add Redmayne's ingenious helicopter ascent and descent engine to the vertical propeller that had hitherto been the sole driving force of the aeroplane without overweighting the machine, and men found themselves possessed of an instrument of flight that could hover or ascend or descend vertically and gently as well as rush wildly through the air. The last dread of flying vanished. As the journalists of the time phrased it, this was the epoch of the Leap into the Air. The new atomic aeroplane became indeed a mania; everyone of means was frantic to possess a thing so controllable, so secure and so free from the dust

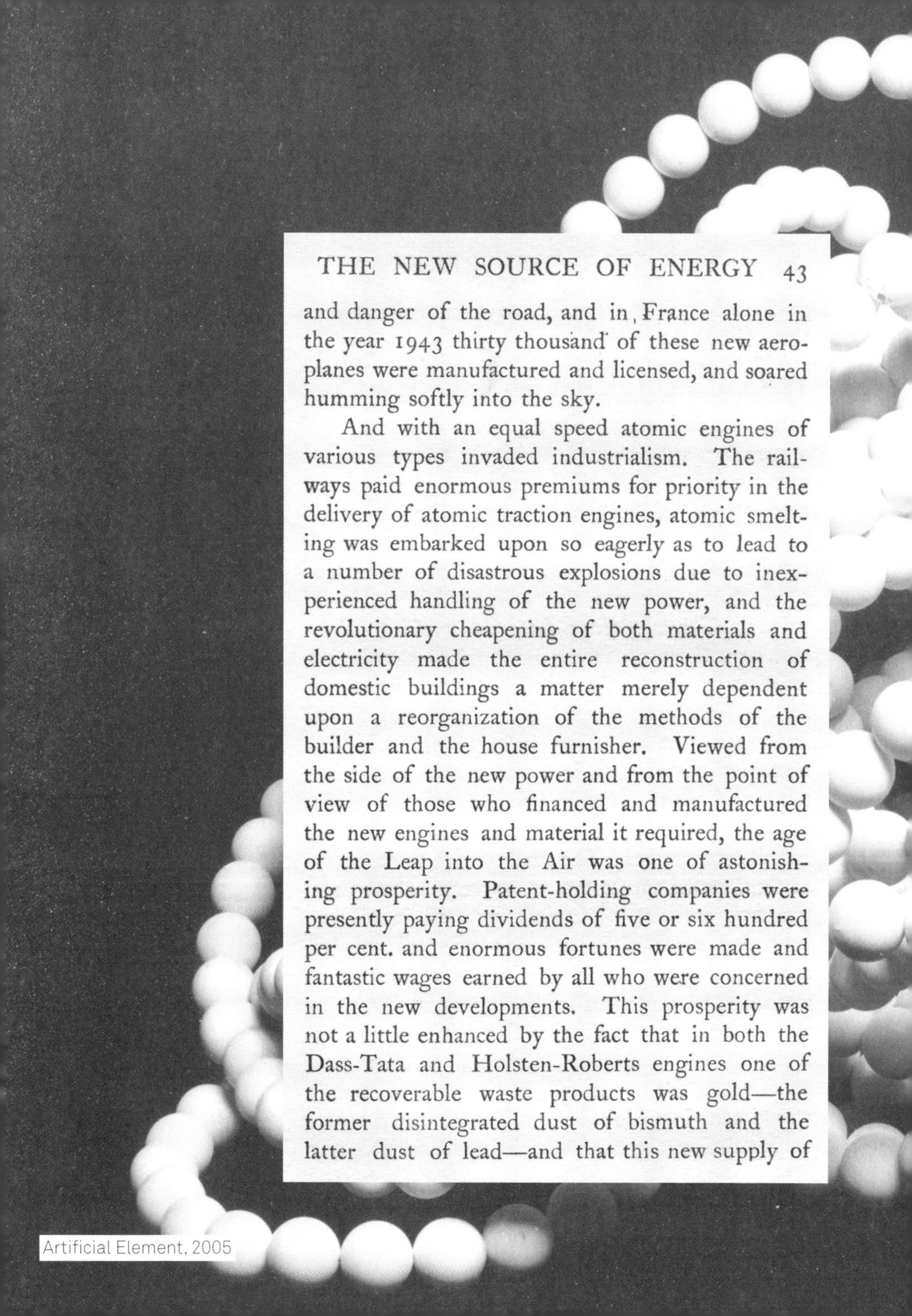

THE NEW SOURCE OF ENERGY 43

and danger of the road, and in France alone in the year 1943 thirty thousand of these new aeroplanes were manufactured and licensed, and soared humming softly into the sky.

And with an equal speed atomic engines of various types invaded industrialism. The railways paid enormous premiums for priority in the delivery of atomic traction engines, atomic smelting was embarked upon so eagerly as to lead to a number of disastrous explosions due to inexperienced handling of the new power, and the revolutionary cheapening of both materials and electricity made the entire reconstruction of domestic buildings a matter merely dependent upon a reorganization of the methods of the builder and the house furnisher. Viewed from the side of the new power and from the point of view of those who financed and manufactured the new engines and material it required, the age of the Leap into the Air was one of astonishing prosperity. Patent-holding companies were presently paying dividends of five or six hundred per cent. and enormous fortunes were made and fantastic wages earned by all who were concerned in the new developments. This prosperity was not a little enhanced by the fact that in both the Dass-Tata and Holsten-Roberts engines one of the recoverable waste products was gold—the former disintegrated dust of bismuth and the latter dust of lead—and that this new supply of

Artificial Element, 2005

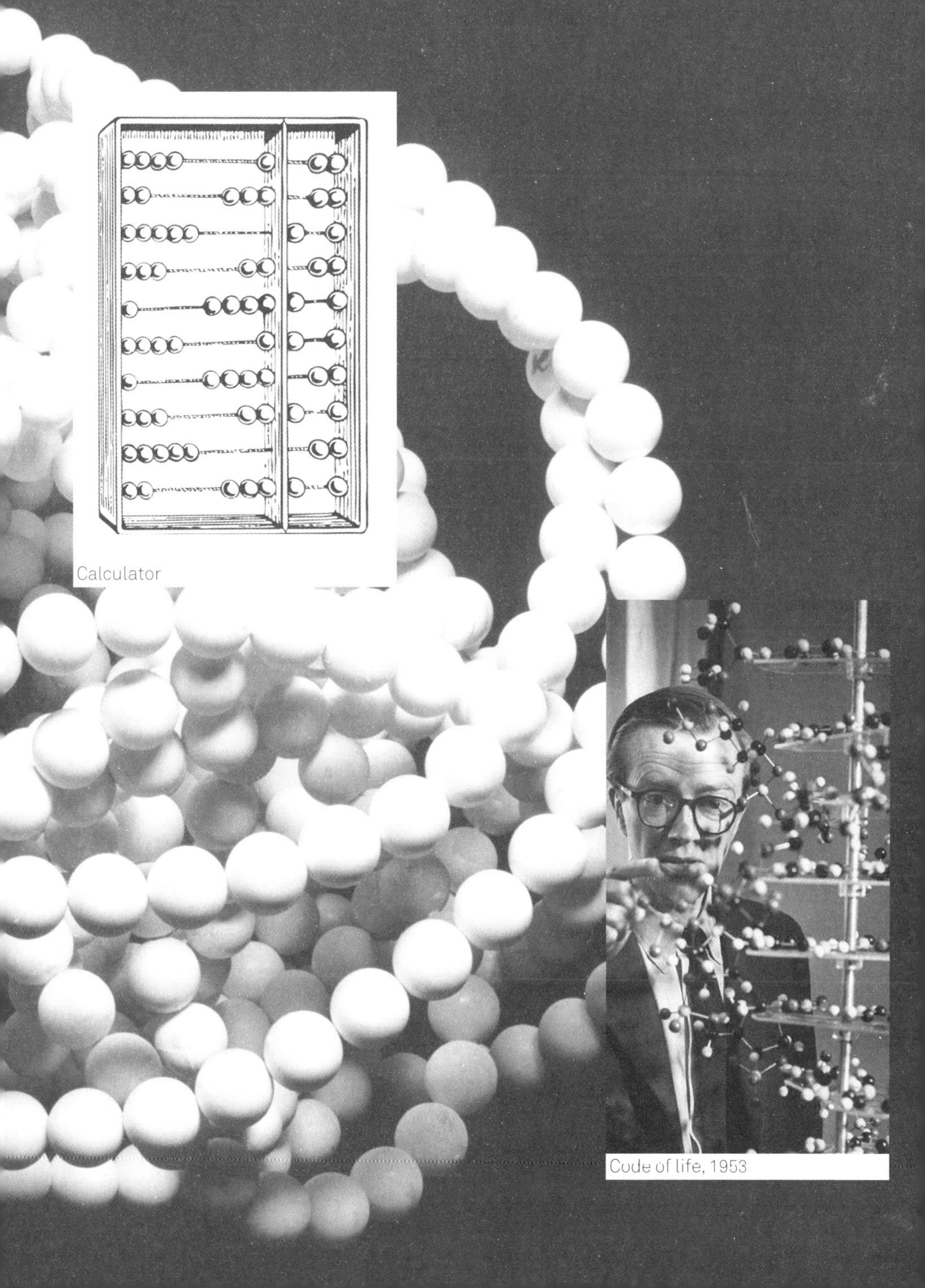

Calculator

Code of life, 1953

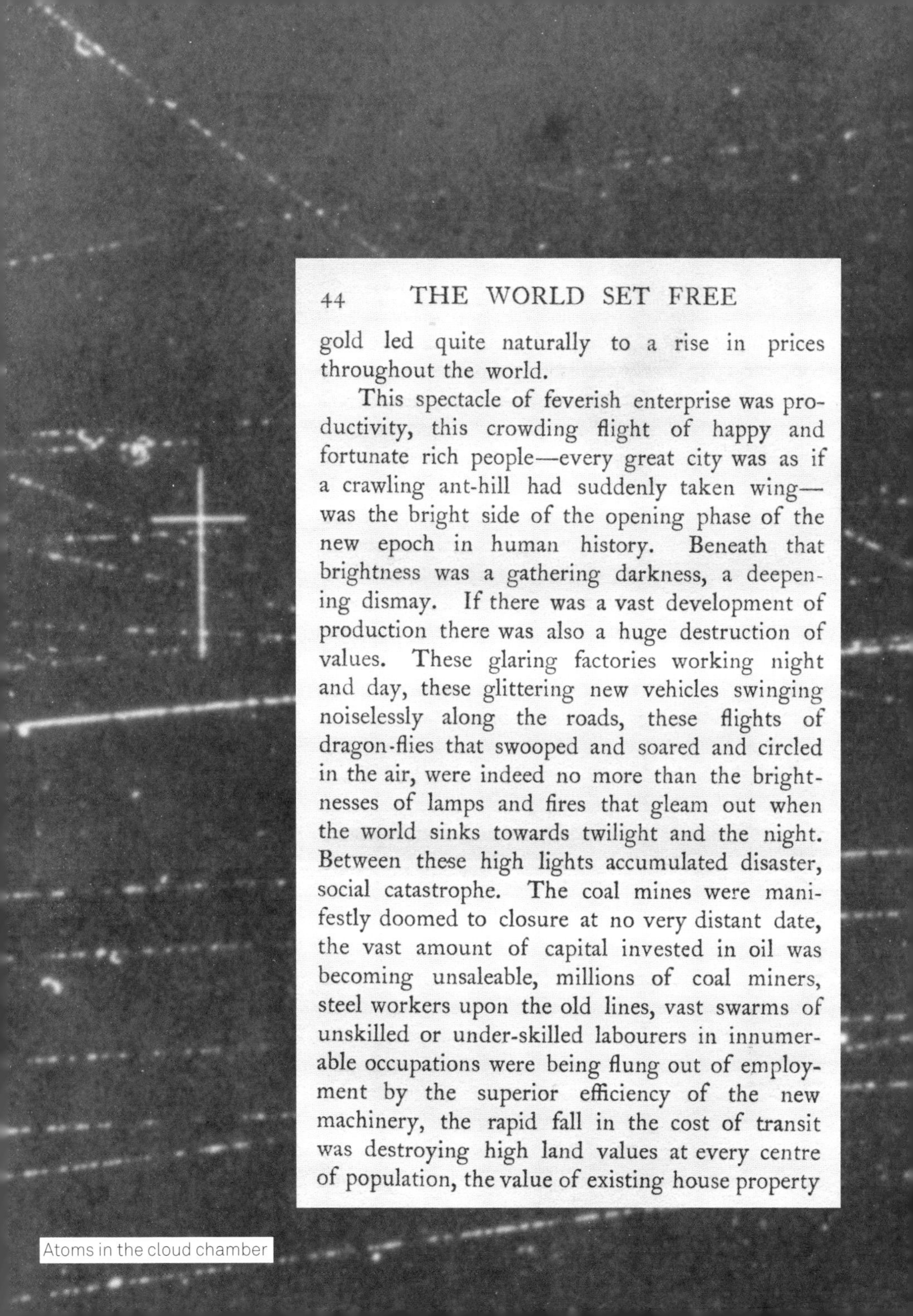

gold led quite naturally to a rise in prices throughout the world.

This spectacle of feverish enterprise was productivity, this crowding flight of happy and fortunate rich people—every great city was as if a crawling ant-hill had suddenly taken wing—was the bright side of the opening phase of the new epoch in human history. Beneath that brightness was a gathering darkness, a deepening dismay. If there was a vast development of production there was also a huge destruction of values. These glaring factories working night and day, these glittering new vehicles swinging noiselessly along the roads, these flights of dragon-flies that swooped and soared and circled in the air, were indeed no more than the brightnesses of lamps and fires that gleam out when the world sinks towards twilight and the night. Between these high lights accumulated disaster, social catastrophe. The coal mines were manifestly doomed to closure at no very distant date, the vast amount of capital invested in oil was becoming unsaleable, millions of coal miners, steel workers upon the old lines, vast swarms of unskilled or under-skilled labourers in innumerable occupations were being flung out of employment by the superior efficiency of the new machinery, the rapid fall in the cost of transit was destroying high land values at every centre of population, the value of existing house property

Atoms in the cloud chamber

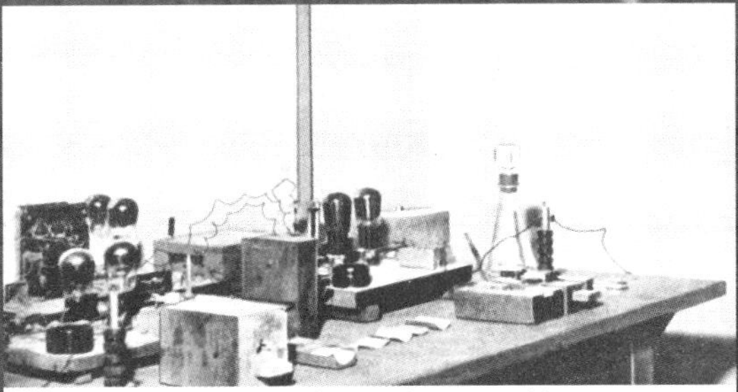
Where the first nuclear fission happened in 1936

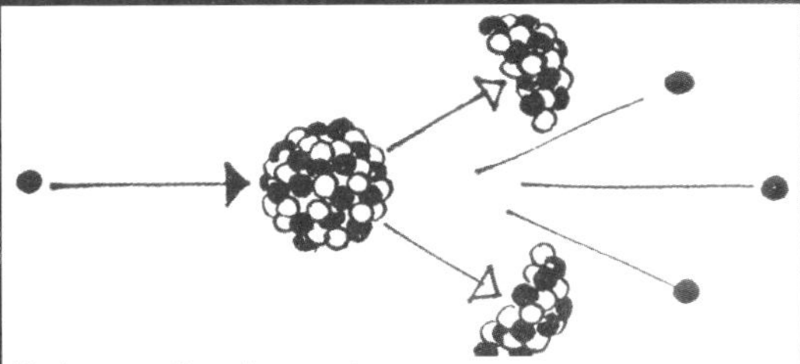
Understanding the crack

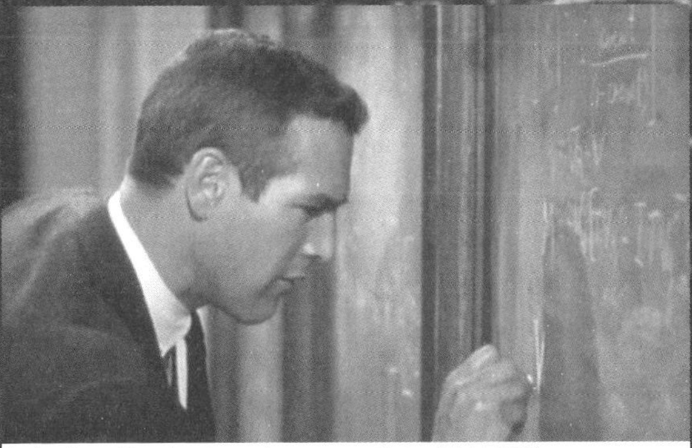
Leipziger Streit of nuclear scientists (UK 1966)

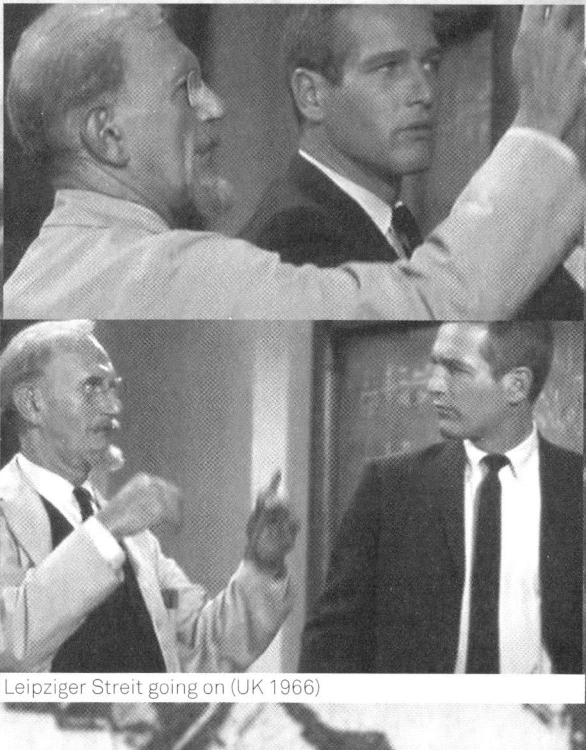

Leipziger Streit going on (UK 1966)

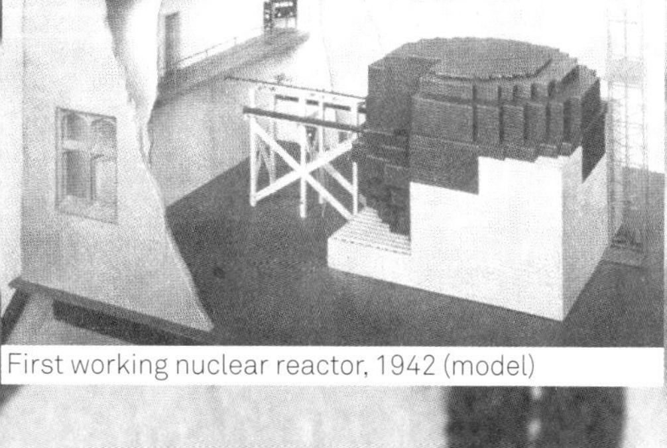

First working nuclear reactor, 1942 (model)

Experimental reactor Haigerloch, uranium cubes, 1945

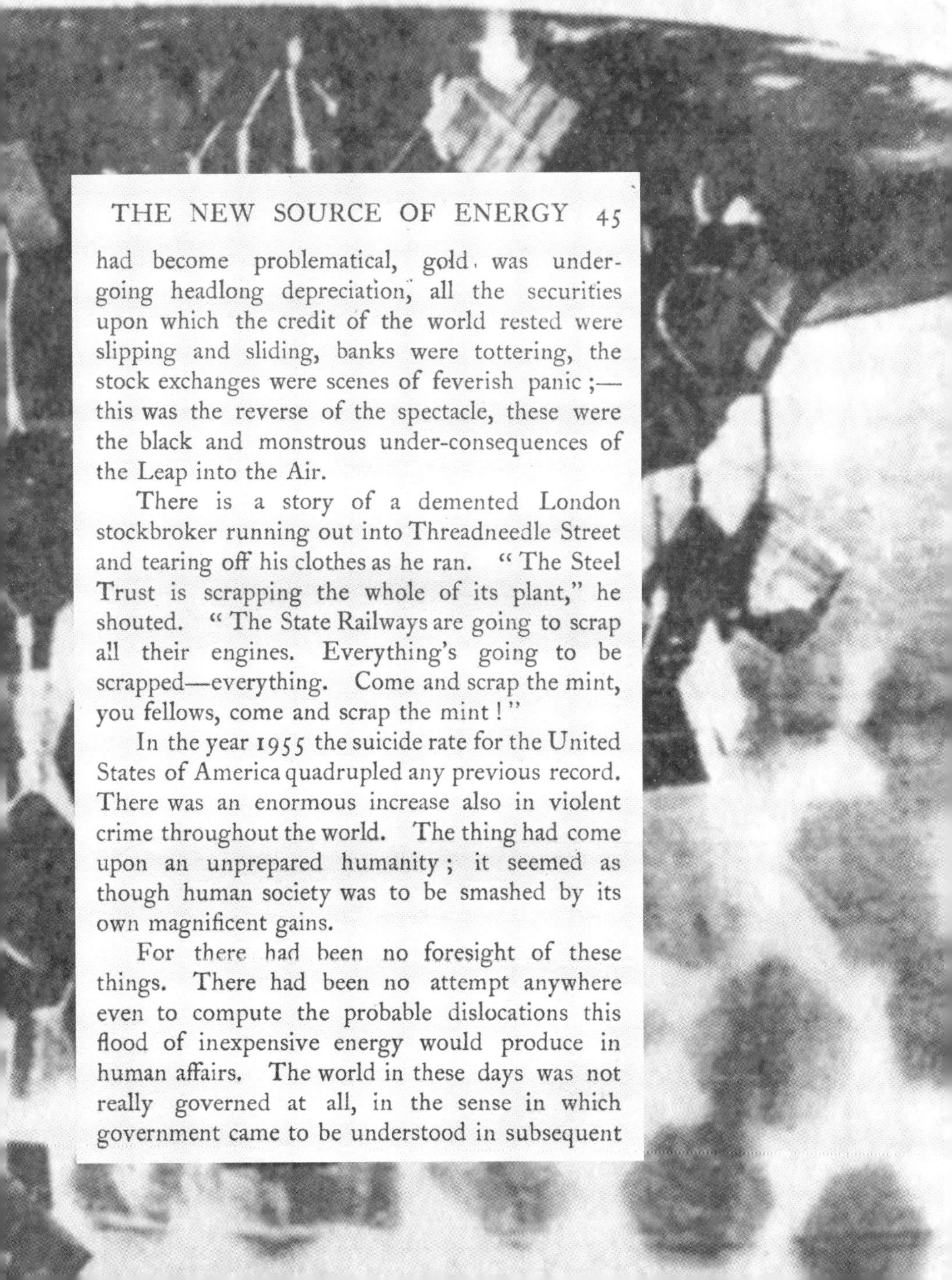

had become problematical, gold was undergoing headlong depreciation, all the securities upon which the credit of the world rested were slipping and sliding, banks were tottering, the stock exchanges were scenes of feverish panic ;— this was the reverse of the spectacle, these were the black and monstrous under-consequences of the Leap into the Air.

There is a story of a demented London stockbroker running out into Threadneedle Street and tearing off his clothes as he ran. "The Steel Trust is scrapping the whole of its plant," he shouted. "The State Railways are going to scrap all their engines. Everything's going to be scrapped—everything. Come and scrap the mint, you fellows, come and scrap the mint!"

In the year 1955 the suicide rate for the United States of America quadrupled any previous record. There was an enormous increase also in violent crime throughout the world. The thing had come upon an unprepared humanity; it seemed as though human society was to be smashed by its own magnificent gains.

For there had been no foresight of these things. There had been no attempt anywhere even to compute the probable dislocations this flood of inexpensive energy would produce in human affairs. The world in these days was not really governed at all, in the sense in which government came to be understood in subsequent

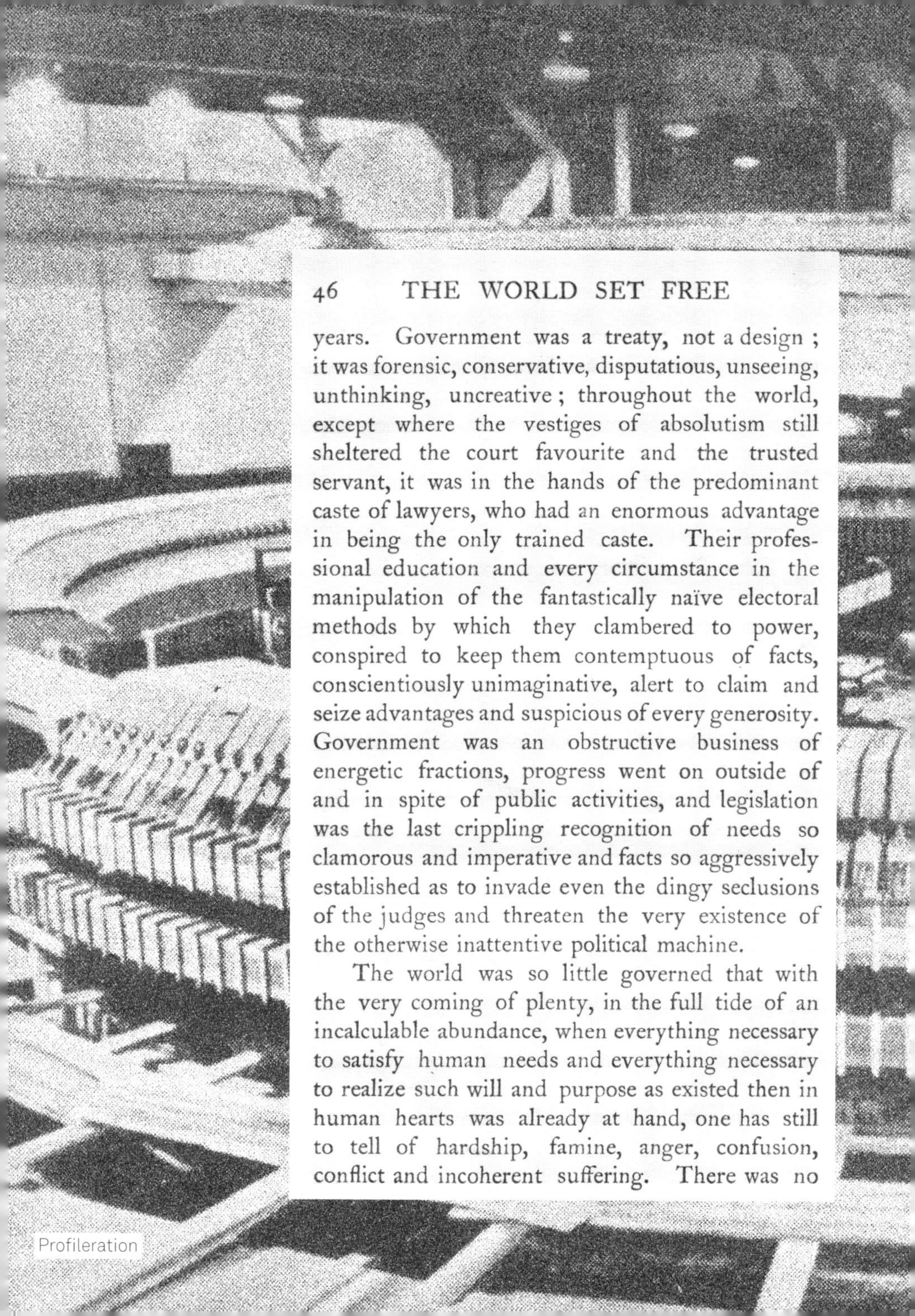

years. Government was a treaty, not a design; it was forensic, conservative, disputatious, unseeing, unthinking, uncreative; throughout the world, except where the vestiges of absolutism still sheltered the court favourite and the trusted servant, it was in the hands of the predominant caste of lawyers, who had an enormous advantage in being the only trained caste. Their professional education and every circumstance in the manipulation of the fantastically naïve electoral methods by which they clambered to power, conspired to keep them contemptuous of facts, conscientiously unimaginative, alert to claim and seize advantages and suspicious of every generosity. Government was an obstructive business of energetic fractions, progress went on outside of and in spite of public activities, and legislation was the last crippling recognition of needs so clamorous and imperative and facts so aggressively established as to invade even the dingy seclusions of the judges and threaten the very existence of the otherwise inattentive political machine.

The world was so little governed that with the very coming of plenty, in the full tide of an incalculable abundance, when everything necessary to satisfy human needs and everything necessary to realize such will and purpose as existed then in human hearts was already at hand, one has still to tell of hardship, famine, anger, confusion, conflict and incoherent suffering. There was no

Profileration

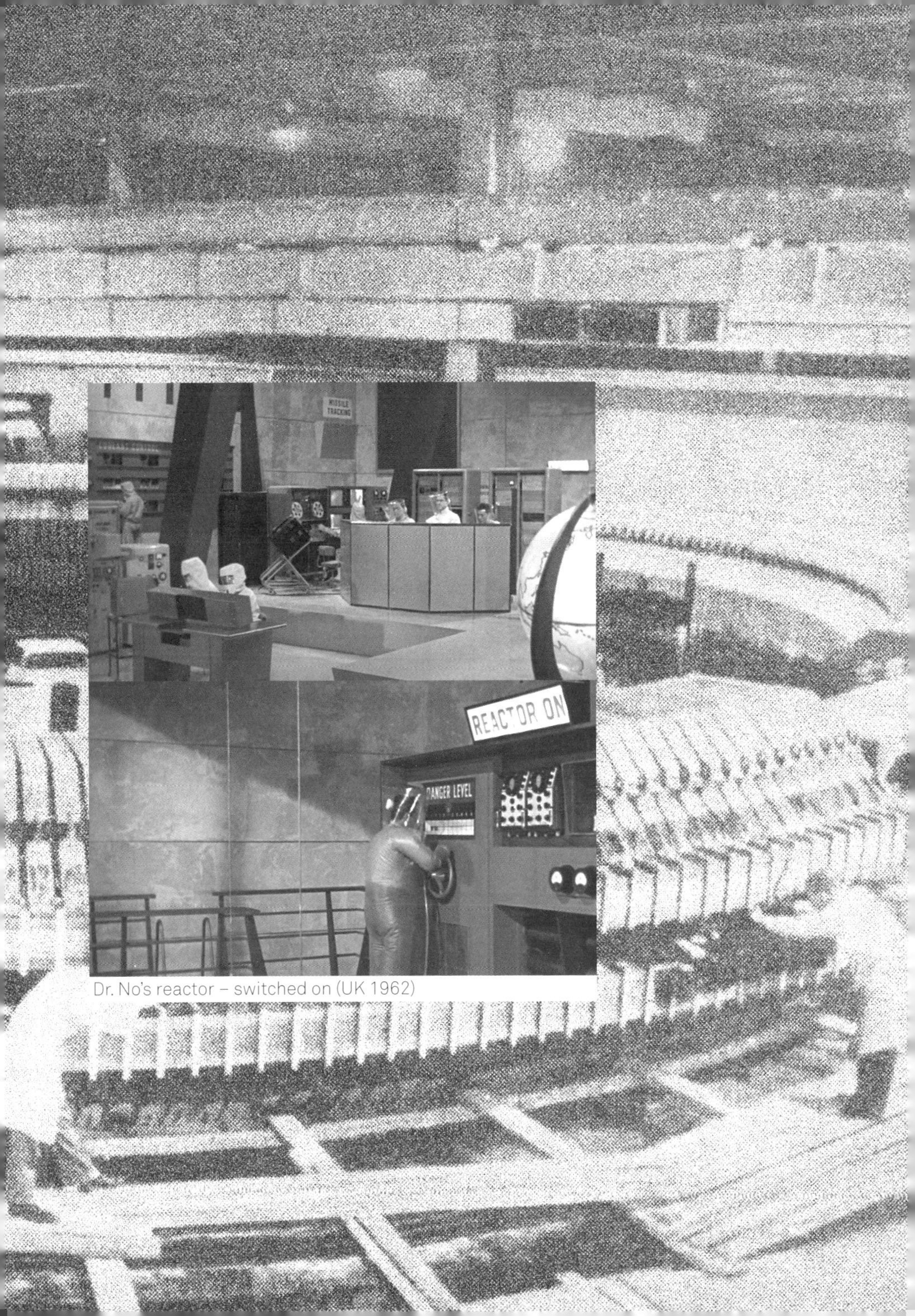

Dr. No's reactor – switched on (UK 1962)

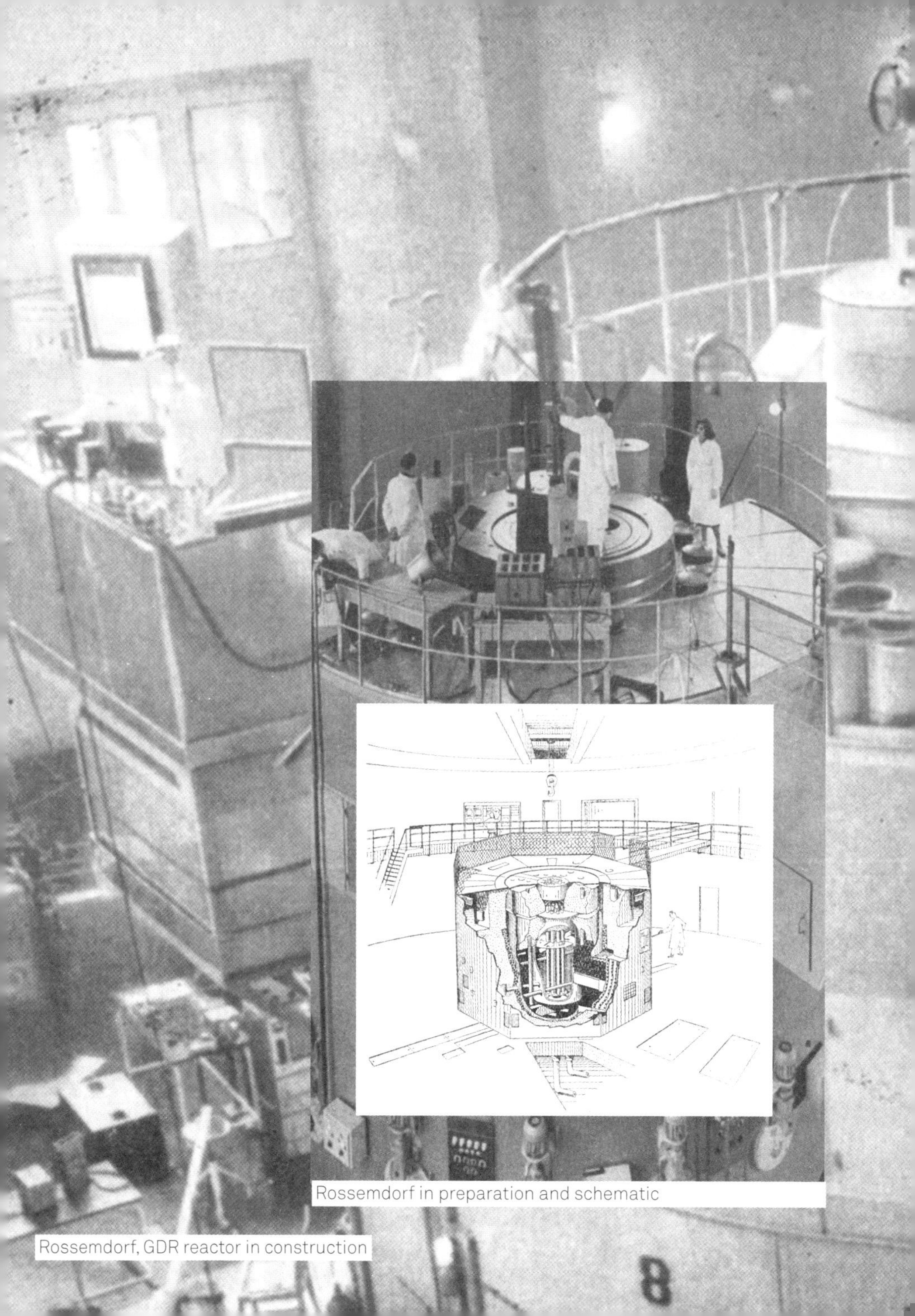

Rossemdorf in preparation and schematic

Rossemdorf, GDR reactor in construction

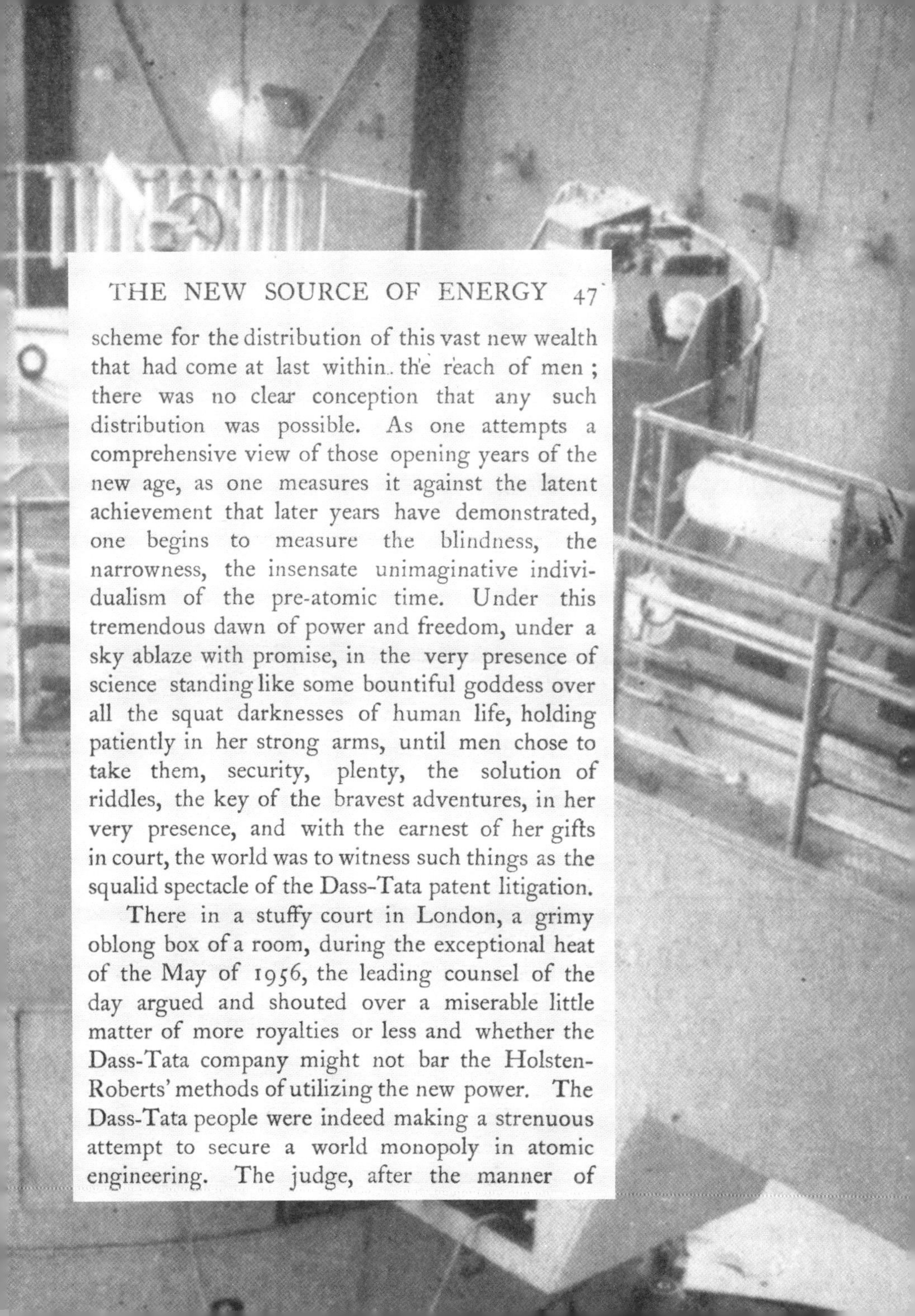

scheme for the distribution of this vast new wealth that had come at last within the reach of men; there was no clear conception that any such distribution was possible. As one attempts a comprehensive view of those opening years of the new age, as one measures it against the latent achievement that later years have demonstrated, one begins to measure the blindness, the narrowness, the insensate unimaginative individualism of the pre-atomic time. Under this tremendous dawn of power and freedom, under a sky ablaze with promise, in the very presence of science standing like some bountiful goddess over all the squat darknesses of human life, holding patiently in her strong arms, until men chose to take them, security, plenty, the solution of riddles, the key of the bravest adventures, in her very presence, and with the earnest of her gifts in court, the world was to witness such things as the squalid spectacle of the Dass-Tata patent litigation.

There in a stuffy court in London, a grimy oblong box of a room, during the exceptional heat of the May of 1956, the leading counsel of the day argued and shouted over a miserable little matter of more royalties or less and whether the Dass-Tata company might not bar the Holsten-Roberts' methods of utilizing the new power. The Dass-Tata people were indeed making a strenuous attempt to secure a world monopoly in atomic engineering. The judge, after the manner of

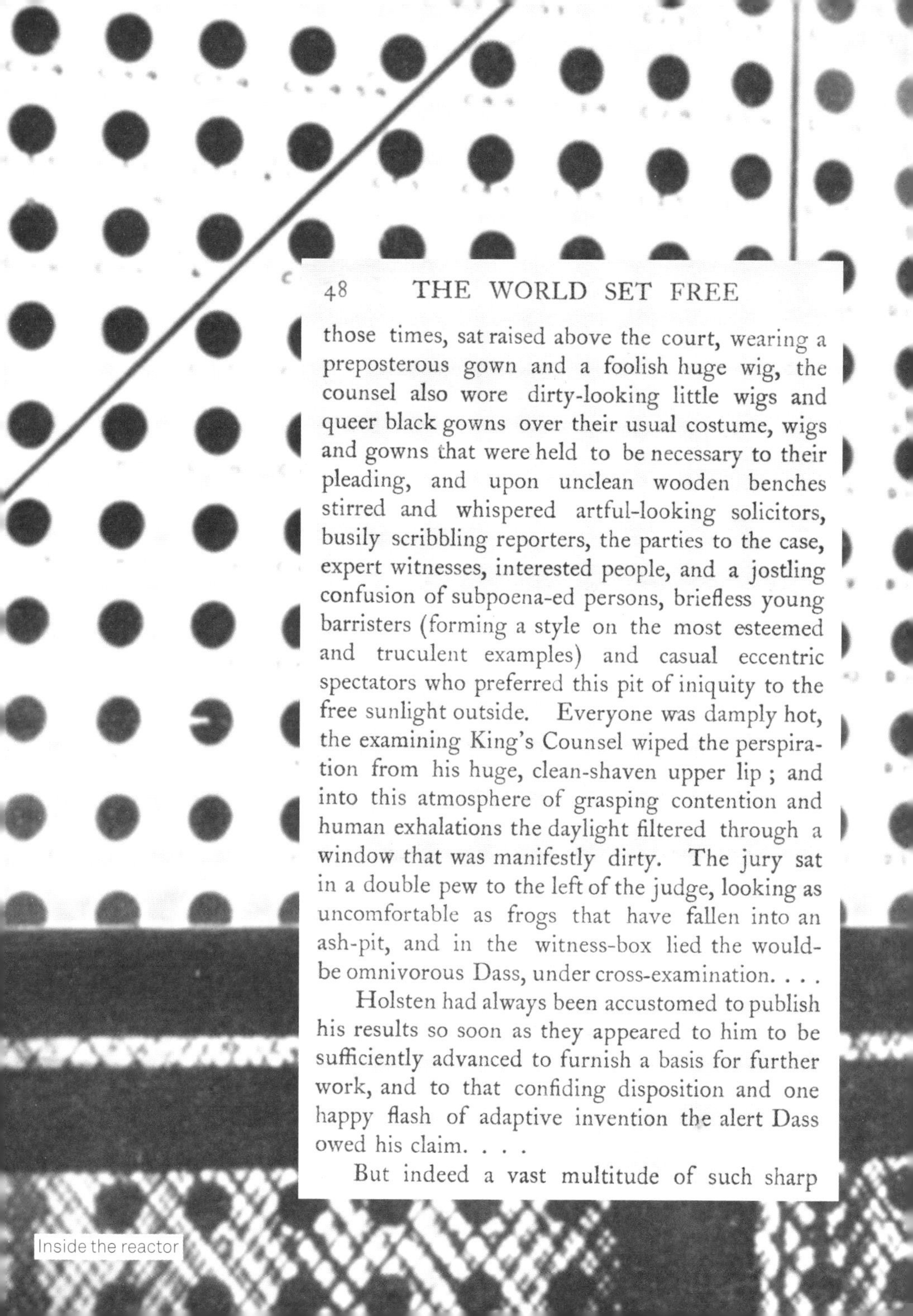

those times, sat raised above the court, wearing a preposterous gown and a foolish huge wig, the counsel also wore dirty-looking little wigs and queer black gowns over their usual costume, wigs and gowns that were held to be necessary to their pleading, and upon unclean wooden benches stirred and whispered artful-looking solicitors, busily scribbling reporters, the parties to the case, expert witnesses, interested people, and a jostling confusion of subpoena-ed persons, briefless young barristers (forming a style on the most esteemed and truculent examples) and casual eccentric spectators who preferred this pit of iniquity to the free sunlight outside. Everyone was damply hot, the examining King's Counsel wiped the perspiration from his huge, clean-shaven upper lip; and into this atmosphere of grasping contention and human exhalations the daylight filtered through a window that was manifestly dirty. The jury sat in a double pew to the left of the judge, looking as uncomfortable as frogs that have fallen into an ash-pit, and in the witness-box lied the would-be omnivorous Dass, under cross-examination. . . .

Holsten had always been accustomed to publish his results so soon as they appeared to him to be sufficiently advanced to furnish a basis for further work, and to that confiding disposition and one happy flash of adaptive invention the alert Dass owed his claim. . . .

But indeed a vast multitude of such sharp

Inside the reactor

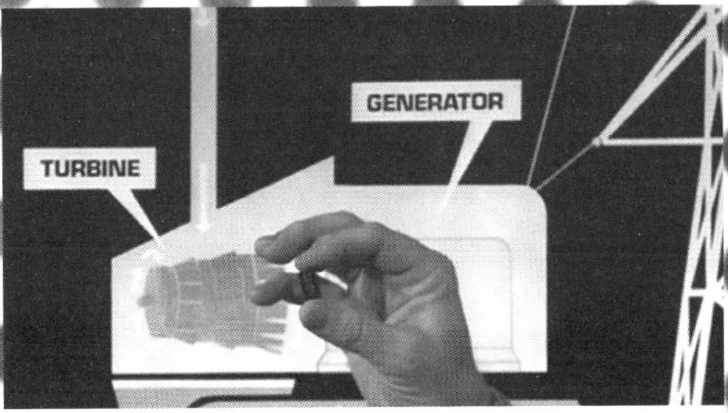

The powerful pill

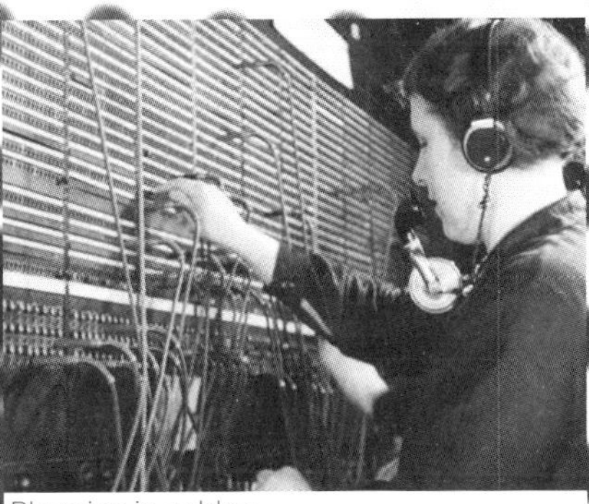
Plugging in cables

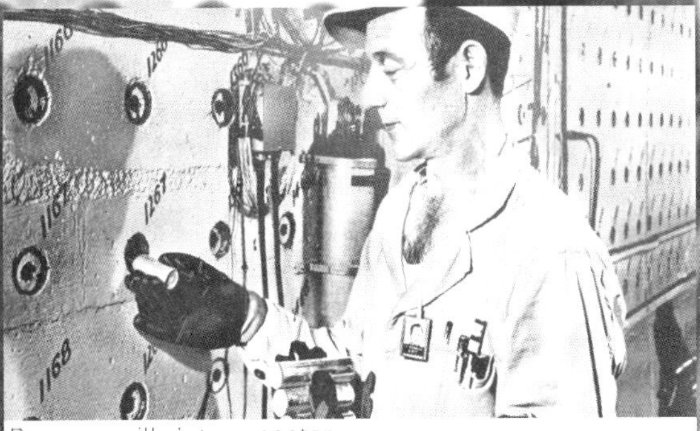
Dropping pills into a reactor

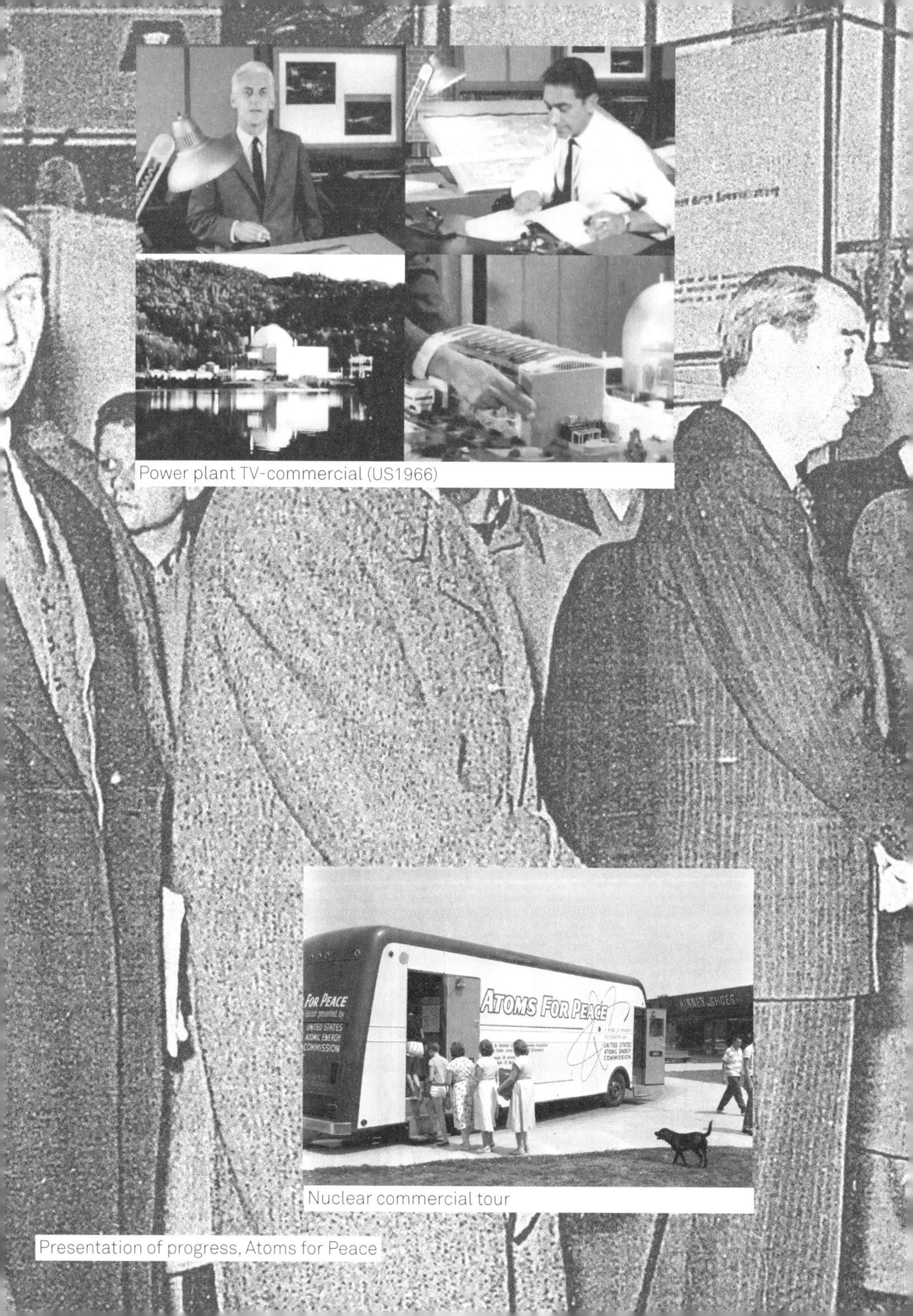

Power plant TV-commercial (US1966)

Nuclear commercial tour

Presentation of progress, Atoms for Peace

people were clutching, patenting, pre-empting, monopolising this or that feature of the new development, seeking to subdue this gigantic winged power to the purposes of their little lusts and avarice. That trial is just one of innumerable disputes of the same kind. For a time the face of the world festered with patent legislation. It chanced however to have one oddly dramatic feature in the fact that Holsten, after being kept waiting about the court for two days as a beggar might have waited at a rich man's door, after being bullied by ushers and watched by policemen, was called as a witness, rather severely handled by counsel, and told not to "quibble" by the judge when he was trying to be absolutely explicit.

The judge scratched his nose with a quill pen, and sneered at Holsten's astonishment round the corner of his monstrous wig. Holsten was a great man, was he? Well, in a law-court great men were put in their places.

"We want to know has the plaintiff added anything to this or hasn't he?" said the judge, "we don't want to have your views whether Sir Philip Dass's improvements were merely superficial adaptations or whether they were implicit in your paper. No doubt—after the manner of inventors—you think most things that were ever likely to be discovered are implicit in your papers. No doubt also you think too that most subsequent additions and modifications are merely superficial.

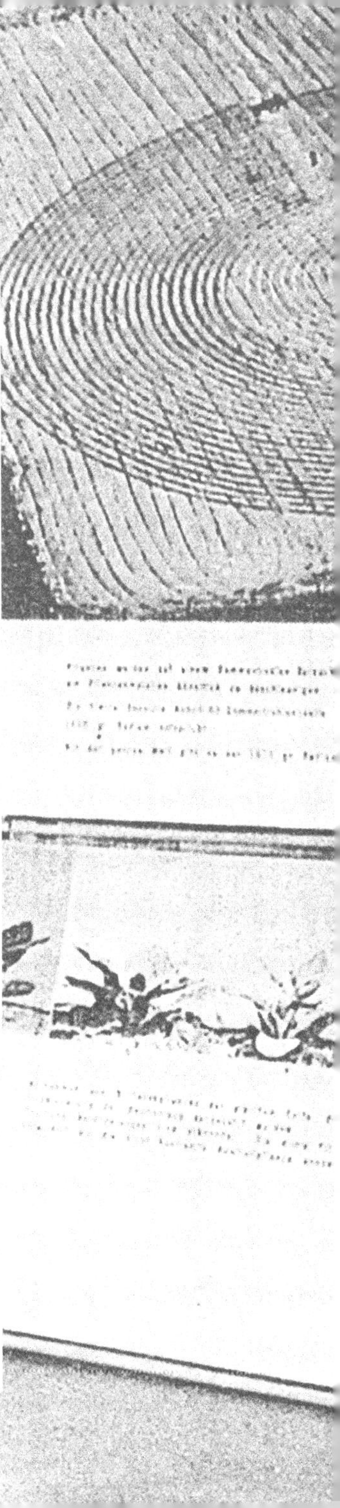

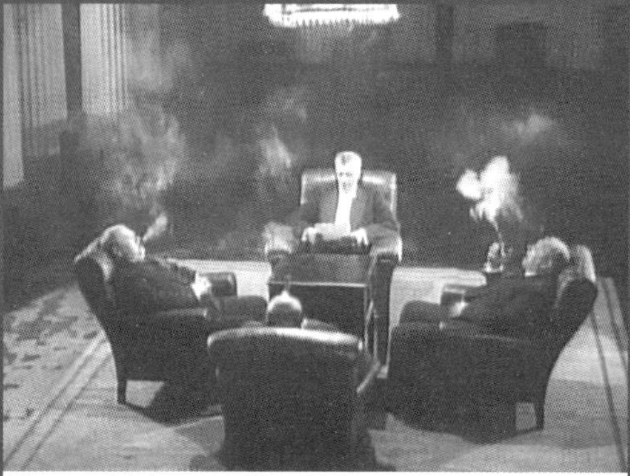

Eisenstein's bosses (SU 1925)

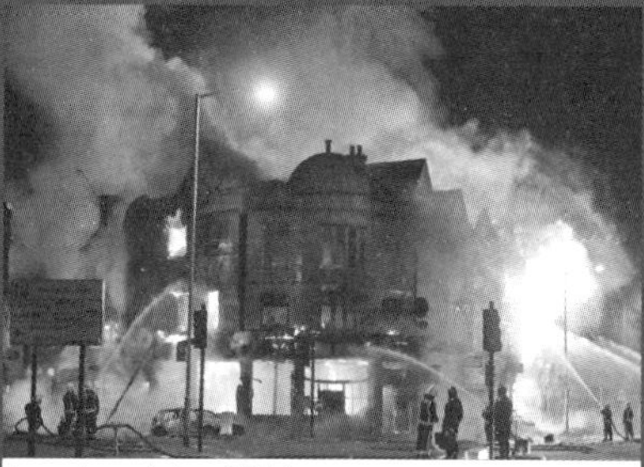

London riots, 2011

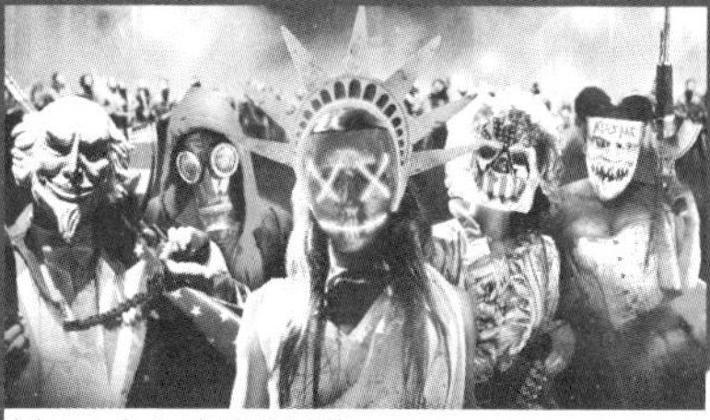

More riots (US 2016)

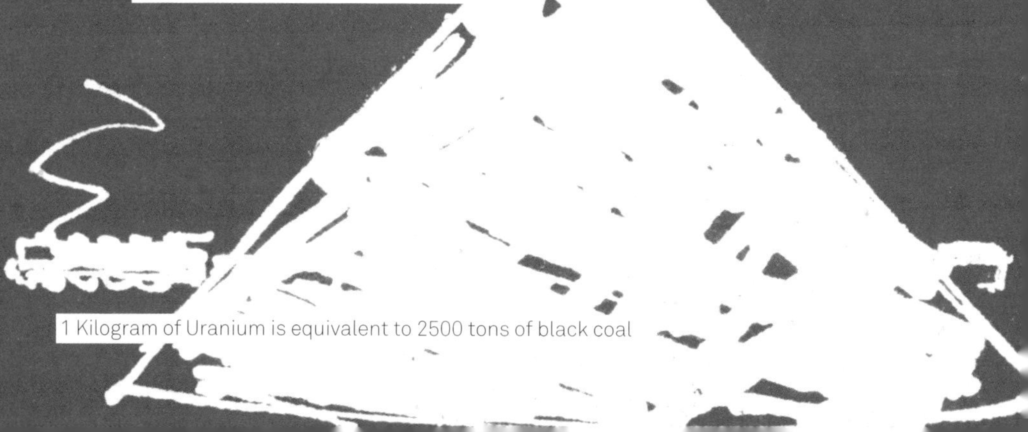

1 Kilogram of Uranium is equivalent to 2500 tons of black coal

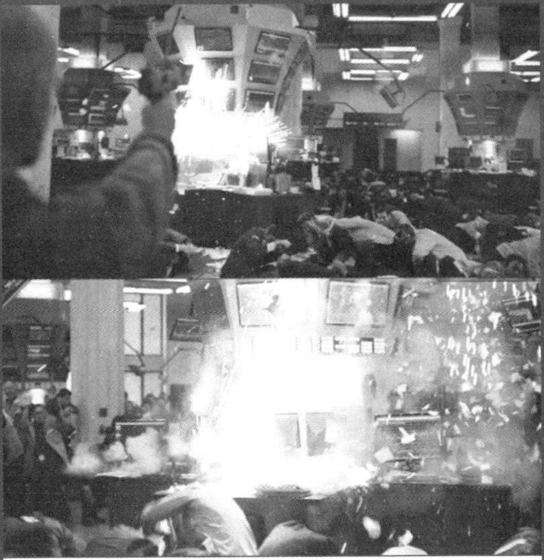

Wall Street piracy (UK, US 2012)

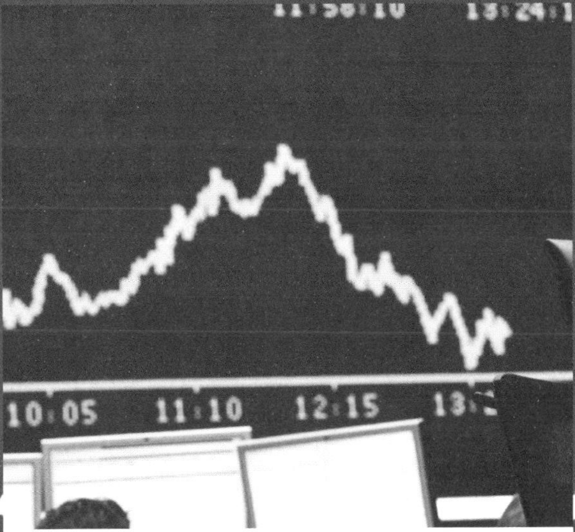

Wall Street crisis 2009

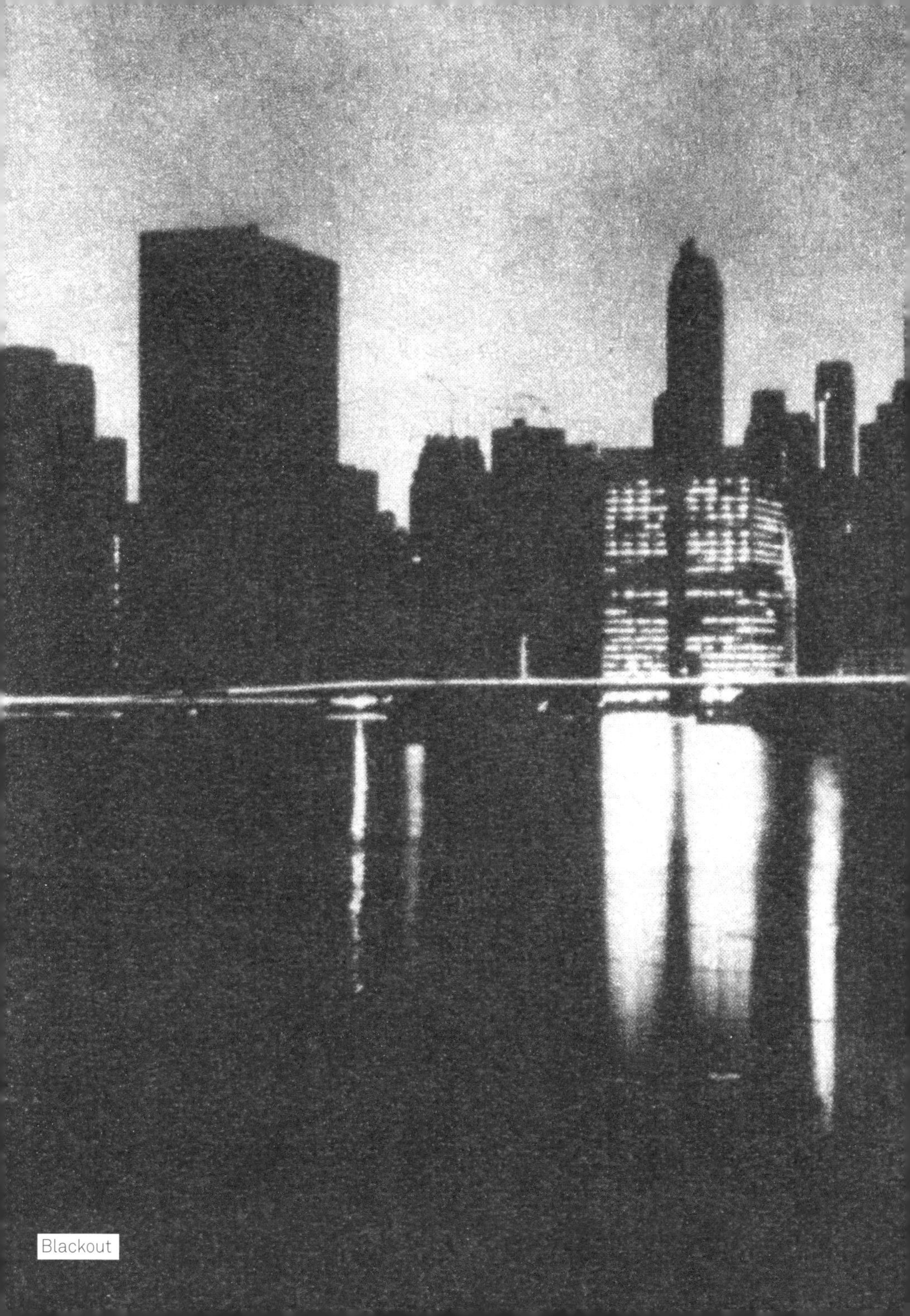

Blackout

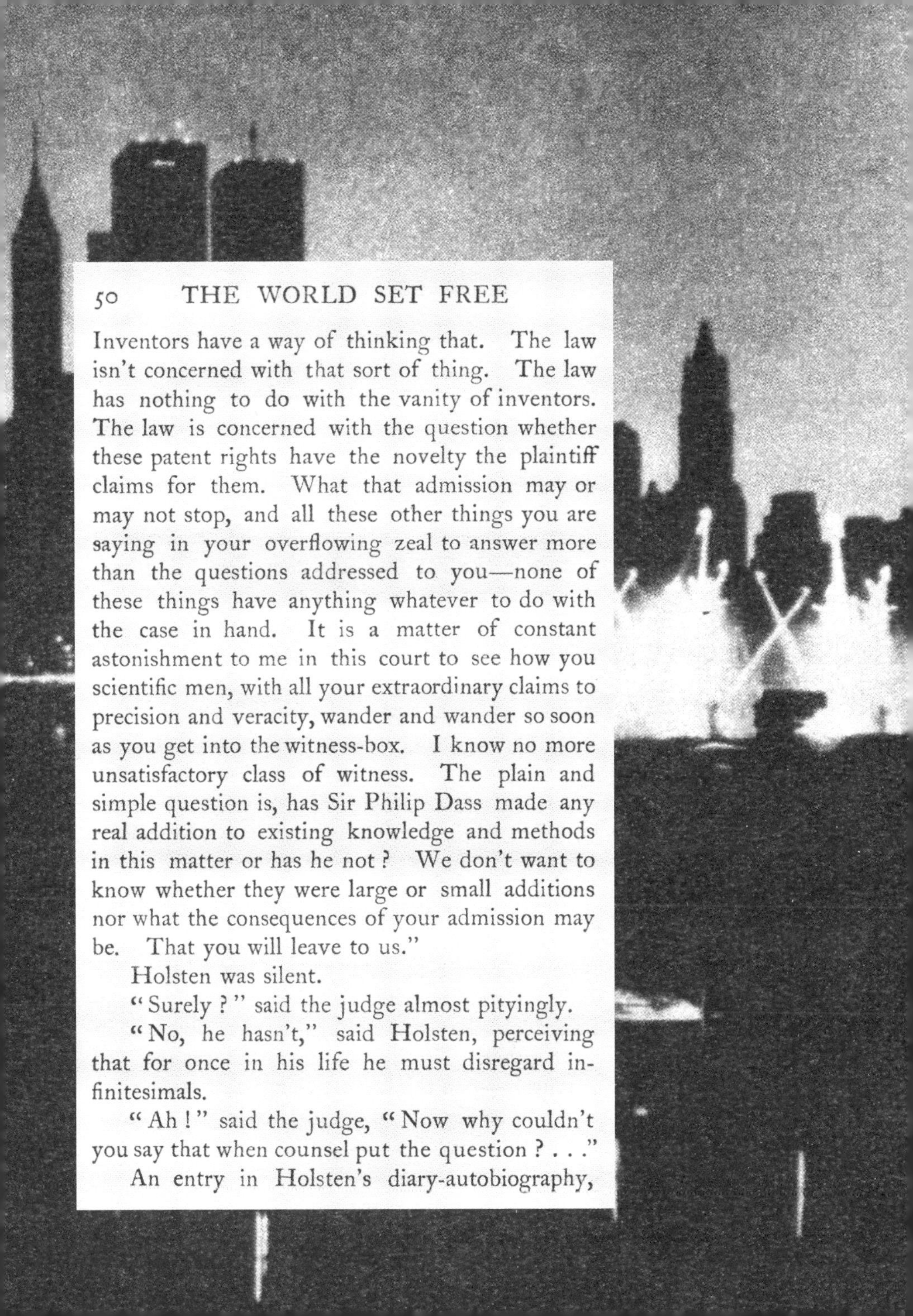

Inventors have a way of thinking that. The law isn't concerned with that sort of thing. The law has nothing to do with the vanity of inventors. The law is concerned with the question whether these patent rights have the novelty the plaintiff claims for them. What that admission may or may not stop, and all these other things you are saying in your overflowing zeal to answer more than the questions addressed to you—none of these things have anything whatever to do with the case in hand. It is a matter of constant astonishment to me in this court to see how you scientific men, with all your extraordinary claims to precision and veracity, wander and wander so soon as you get into the witness-box. I know no more unsatisfactory class of witness. The plain and simple question is, has Sir Philip Dass made any real addition to existing knowledge and methods in this matter or has he not? We don't want to know whether they were large or small additions nor what the consequences of your admission may be. That you will leave to us."

Holsten was silent.

"Surely?" said the judge almost pityingly.

"No, he hasn't," said Holsten, perceiving that for once in his life he must disregard infinitesimals.

"Ah!" said the judge, "Now why couldn't you say that when counsel put the question? . . ."

An entry in Holsten's diary-autobiography,

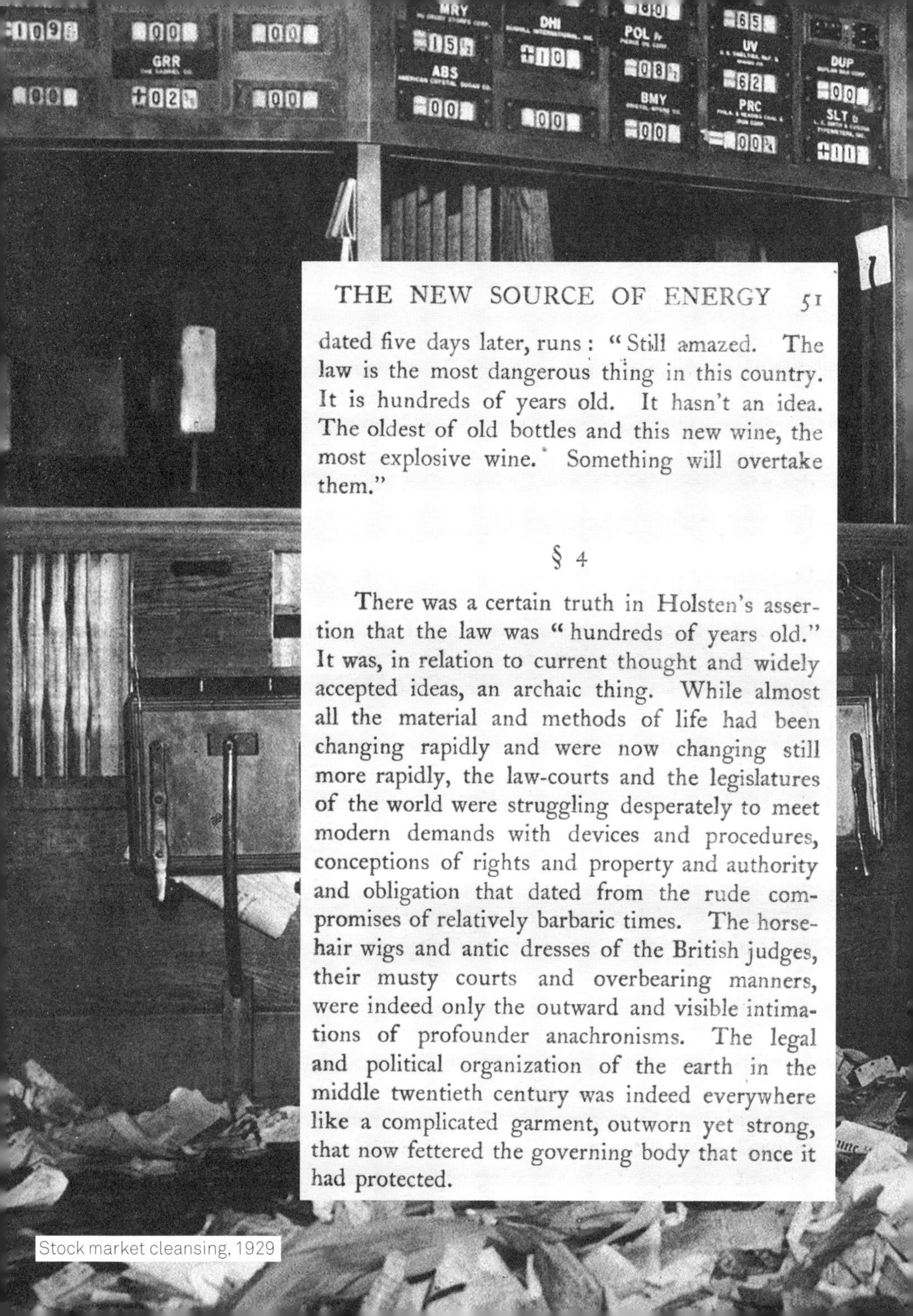

dated five days later, runs: "Still amazed. The law is the most dangerous thing in this country. It is hundreds of years old. It hasn't an idea. The oldest of old bottles and this new wine, the most explosive wine. Something will overtake them."

§ 4

There was a certain truth in Holsten's assertion that the law was "hundreds of years old." It was, in relation to current thought and widely accepted ideas, an archaic thing. While almost all the material and methods of life had been changing rapidly and were now changing still more rapidly, the law-courts and the legislatures of the world were struggling desperately to meet modern demands with devices and procedures, conceptions of rights and property and authority and obligation that dated from the rude compromises of relatively barbaric times. The horsehair wigs and antic dresses of the British judges, their musty courts and overbearing manners, were indeed only the outward and visible intimations of profounder anachronisms. The legal and political organization of the earth in the middle twentieth century was indeed everywhere like a complicated garment, outworn yet strong, that now fettered the governing body that once it had protected.

Stock market cleansing, 1929

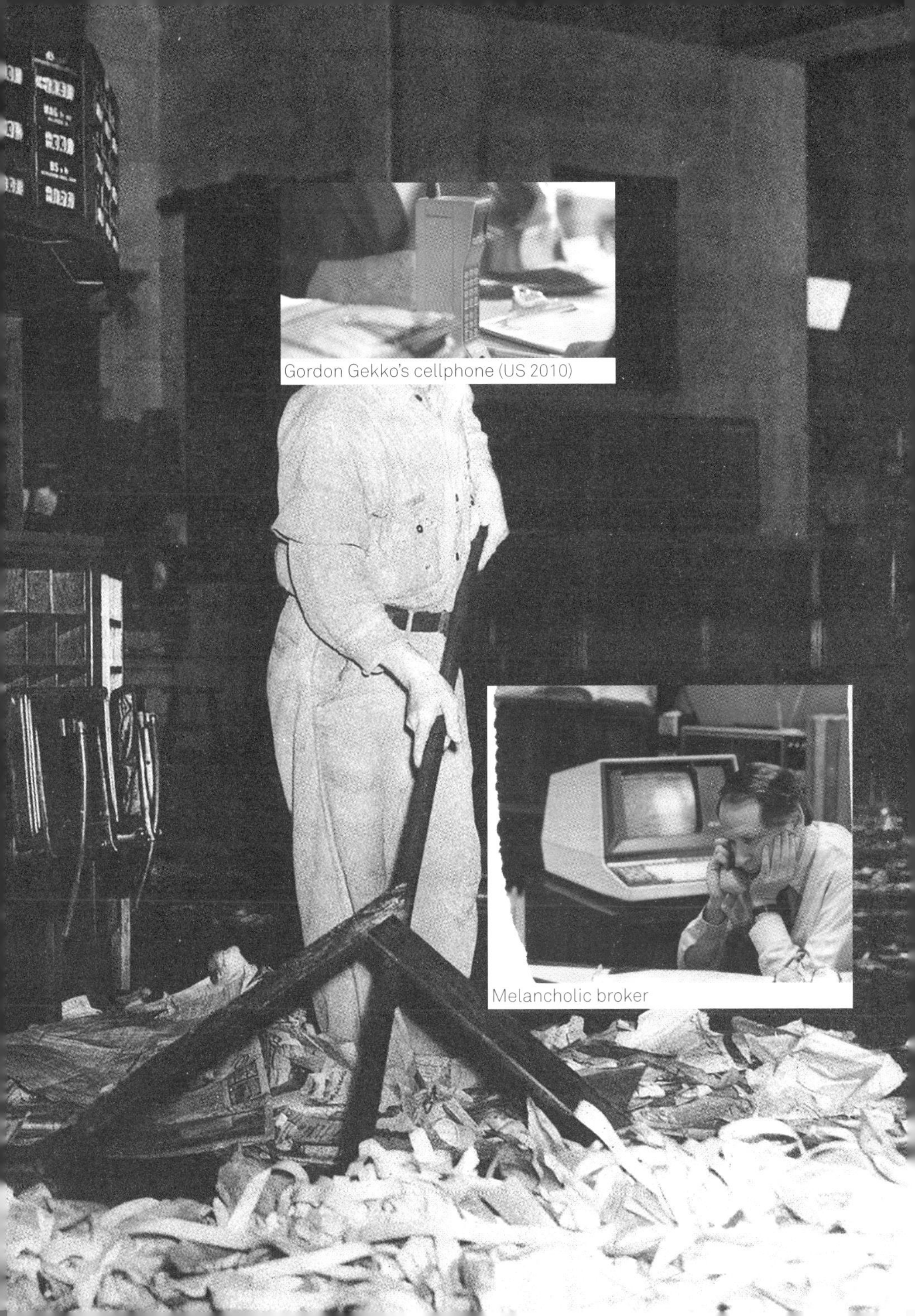

Gordon Gekko's cellphone (US 2010)

Melancholic broker

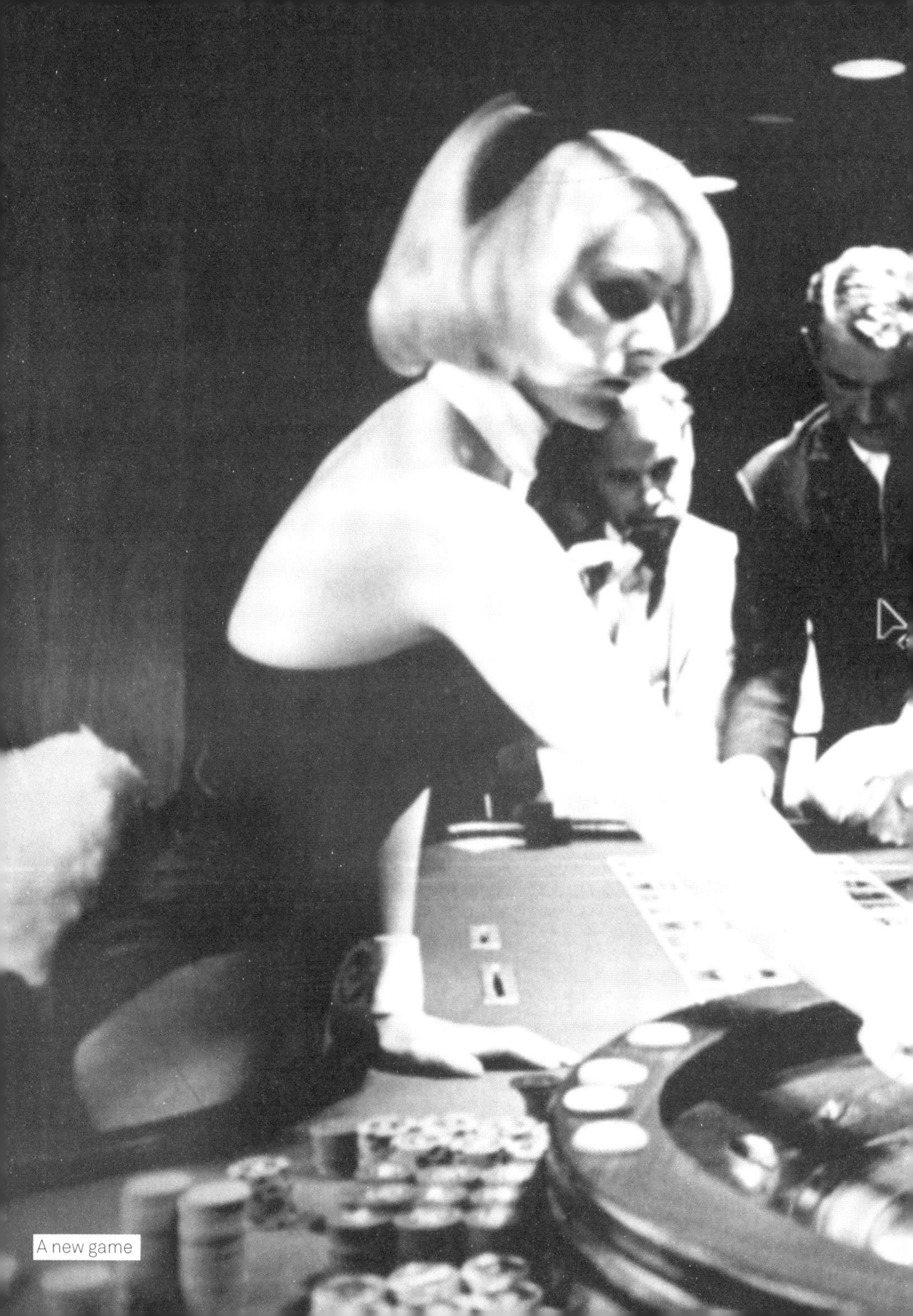

A new game

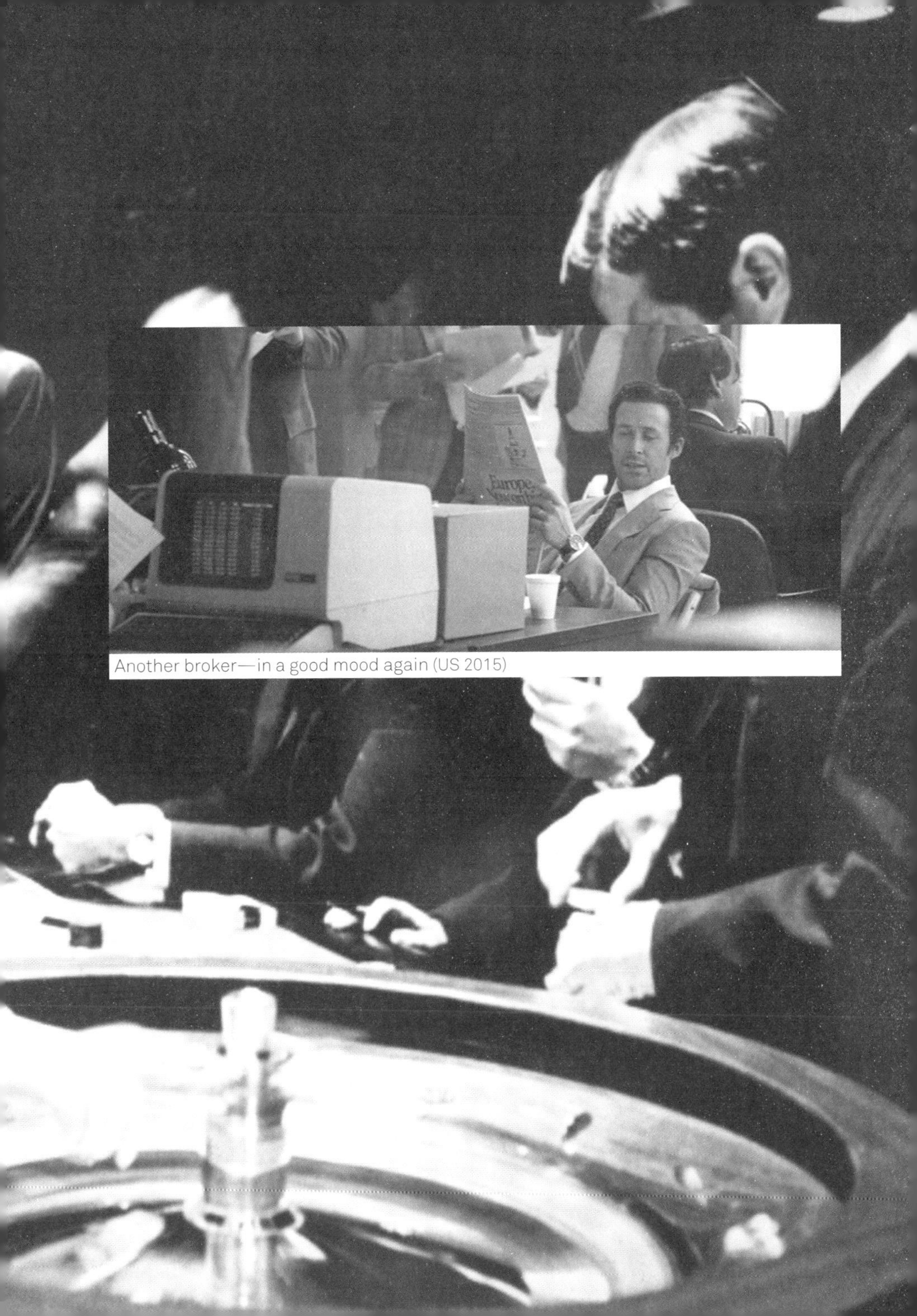

Another broker—in a good mood again (US 2015)

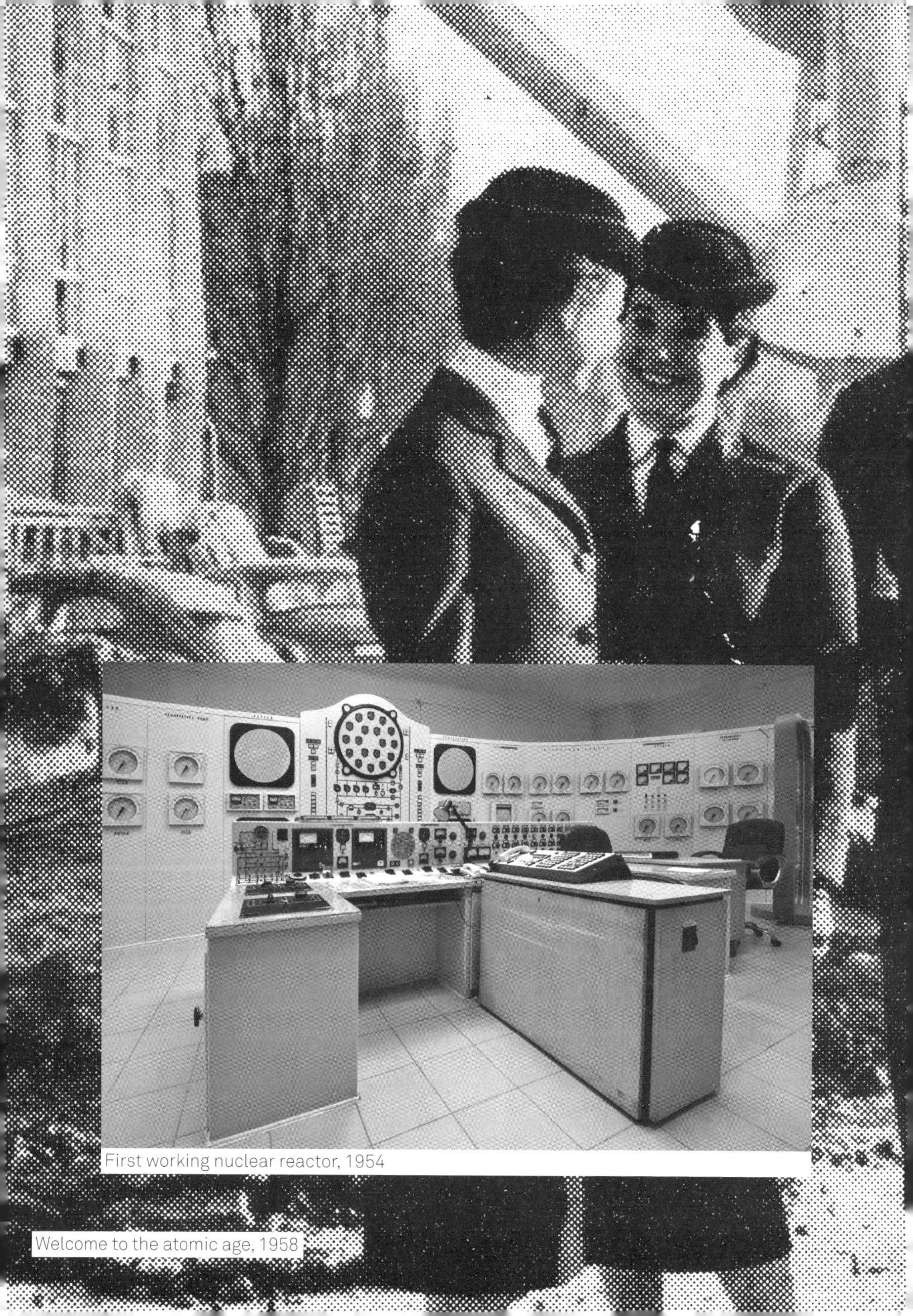

First working nuclear reactor, 1954

Welcome to the atomic age, 1958

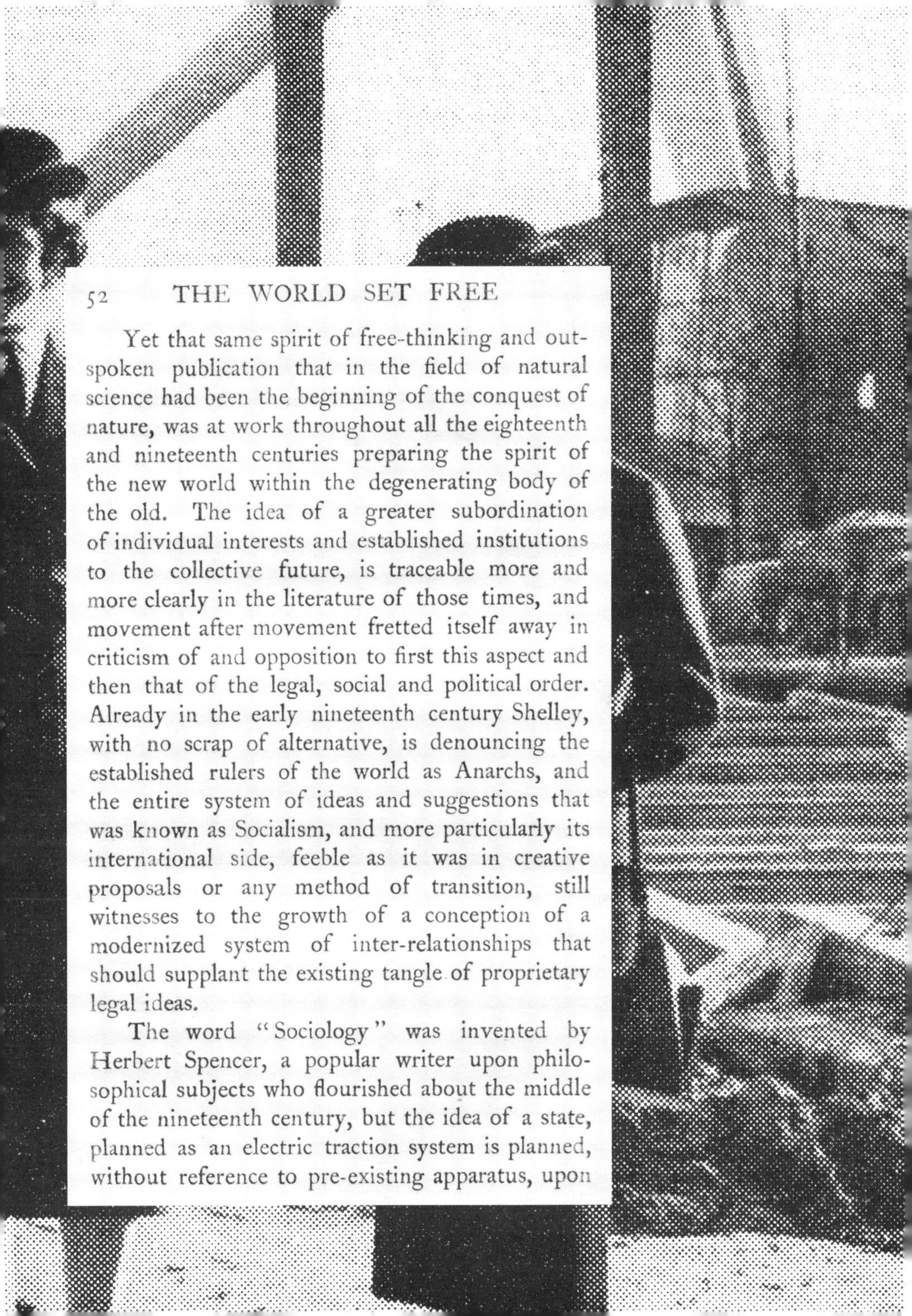

Yet that same spirit of free-thinking and outspoken publication that in the field of natural science had been the beginning of the conquest of nature, was at work throughout all the eighteenth and nineteenth centuries preparing the spirit of the new world within the degenerating body of the old. The idea of a greater subordination of individual interests and established institutions to the collective future, is traceable more and more clearly in the literature of those times, and movement after movement fretted itself away in criticism of and opposition to first this aspect and then that of the legal, social and political order. Already in the early nineteenth century Shelley, with no scrap of alternative, is denouncing the established rulers of the world as Anarchs, and the entire system of ideas and suggestions that was known as Socialism, and more particularly its international side, feeble as it was in creative proposals or any method of transition, still witnesses to the growth of a conception of a modernized system of inter-relationships that should supplant the existing tangle of proprietary legal ideas.

The word "Sociology" was invented by Herbert Spencer, a popular writer upon philosophical subjects who flourished about the middle of the nineteenth century, but the idea of a state, planned as an electric traction system is planned, without reference to pre-existing apparatus, upon

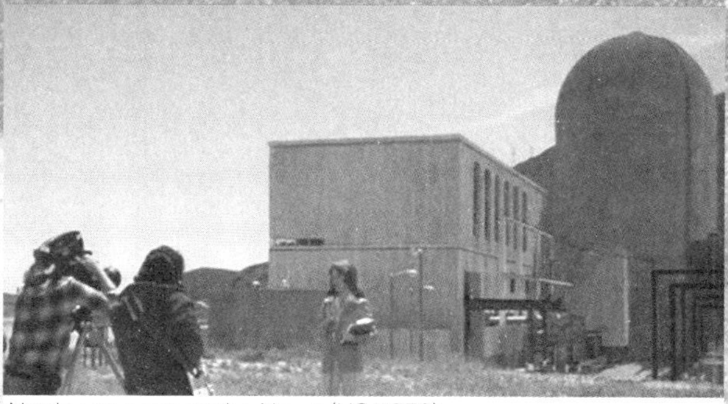

Nuclear power on the News (US 1979)

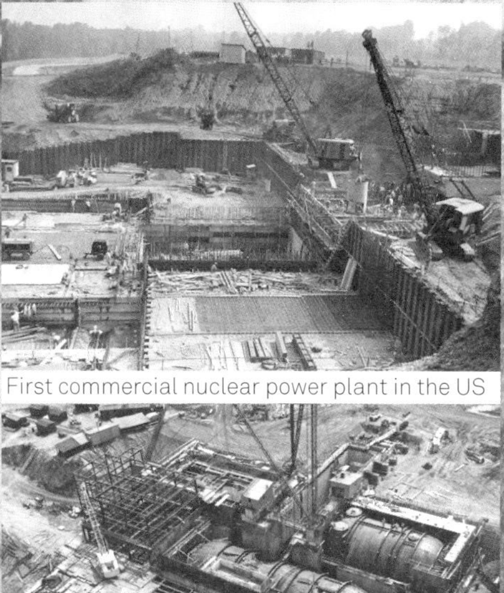

First commercial nuclear power plant in the US

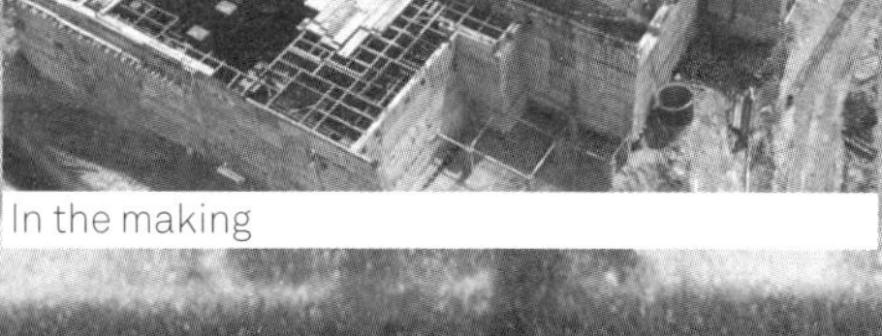

In the making

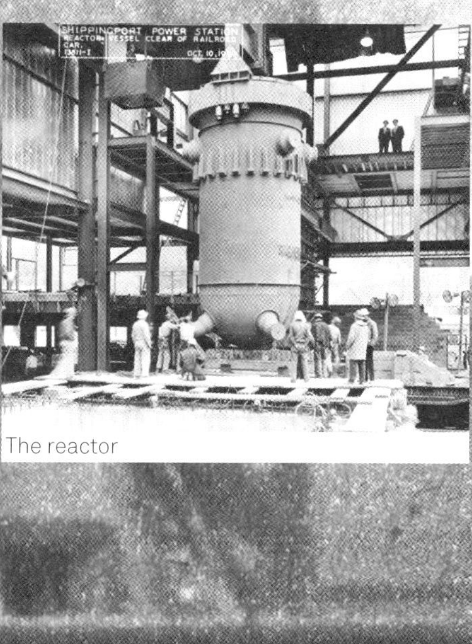

The reactor

Working the atomic age

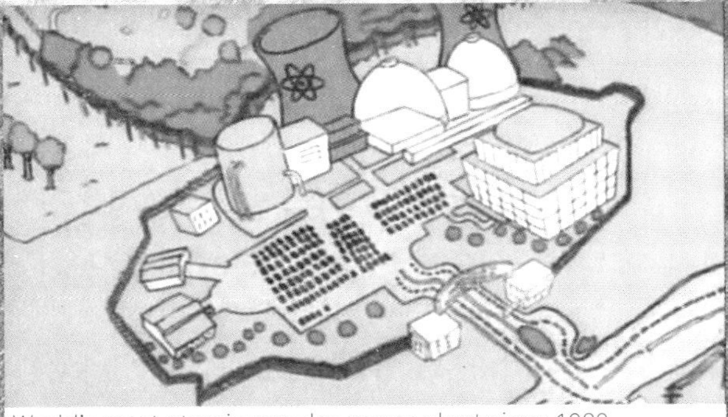

World's most atomic popular power plant since 1989

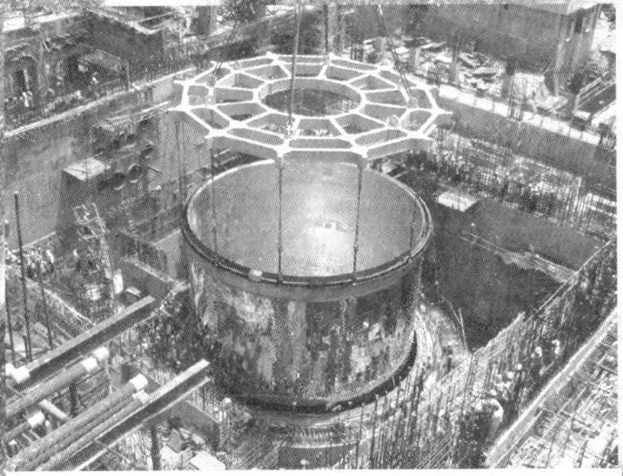

Pushing nuclear power in India, 2017

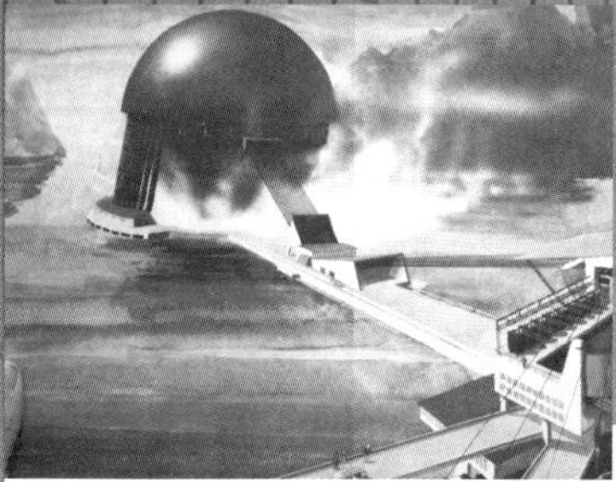

Shape of the future power plant, 1954

scientific lines, did not take a very strong hold upon the popular imagination of the world until the twentieth century. Then, the growing impatience of the American people with the monstrous and socially paralyzing party systems that had sprung out of their absurd electoral arrangements, led to the appearance of what came to be called the " Modern State " movement, and a galaxy of brilliant writers, in America, Europe and the East, stirred up the world to the thought of bolder rearrangements of social interaction, property, employment, education and government, than had ever been contemplated before. No doubt these Modern State ideas were very largely the reflection upon social and political thought of the vast revolution in material things that had been in progress for two hundred years, but for a long time they seemed to be having no more influence upon existing institutions than the writings of Rousseau and Voltaire seemed to have had at the time of the death of the latter. They were fermenting in men's minds, and it needed only just such social and political stresses as the coming of the atomic mechanisms brought about, to thrust them forward abruptly into crude and startling realization.

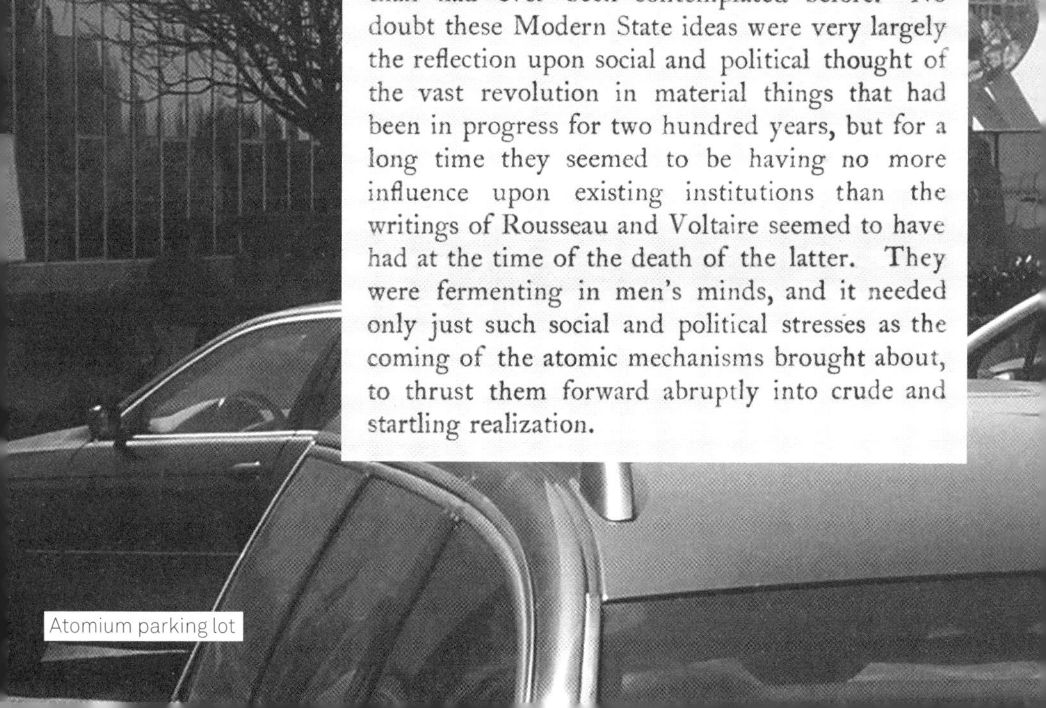

Atomium parking lot

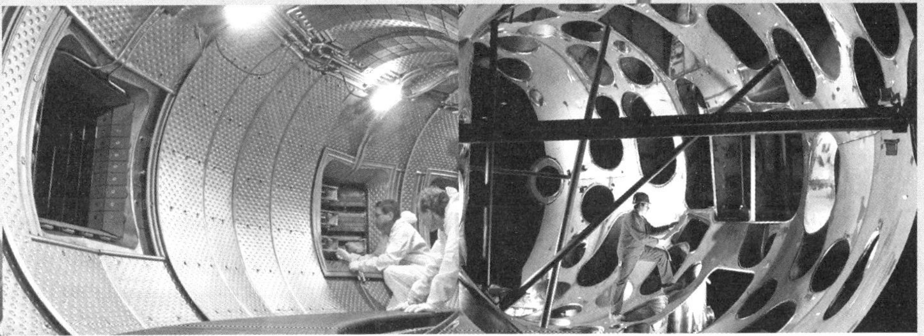

Next generation reactor, experiments in nuclear fusion since 2000

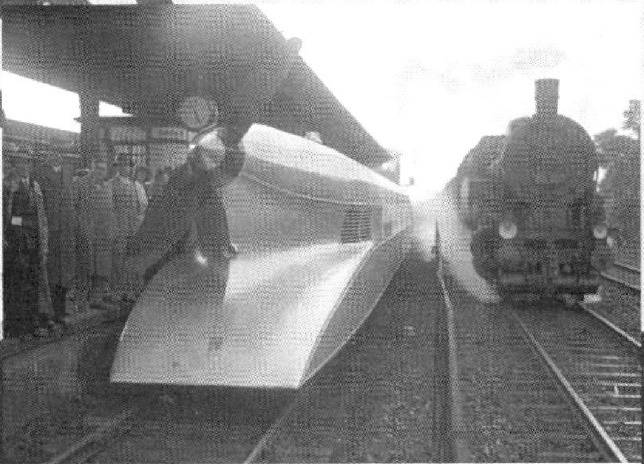

Experimental future train, the railway airship

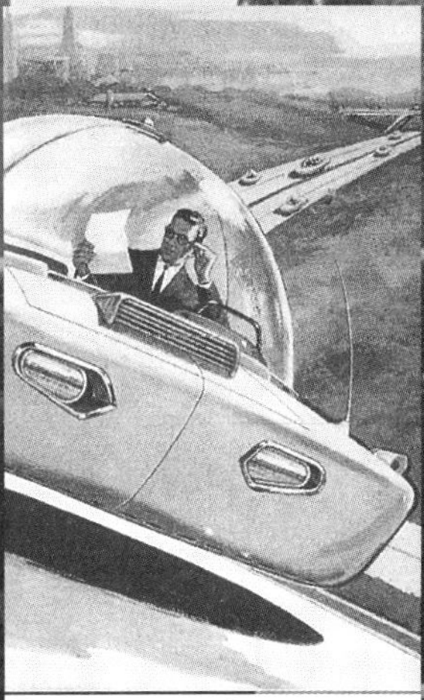

Future commuting

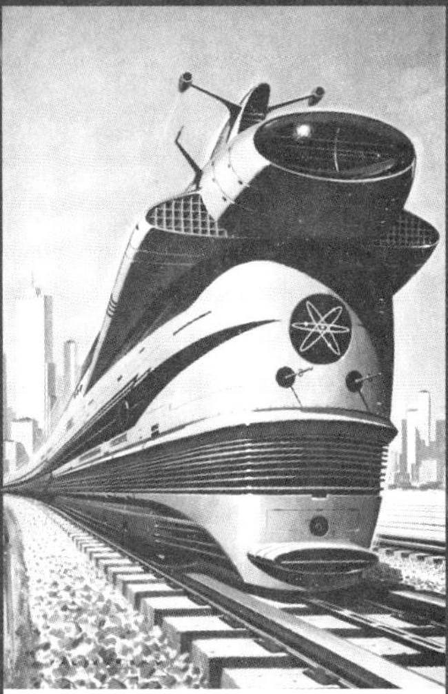

Atomic train, 1960

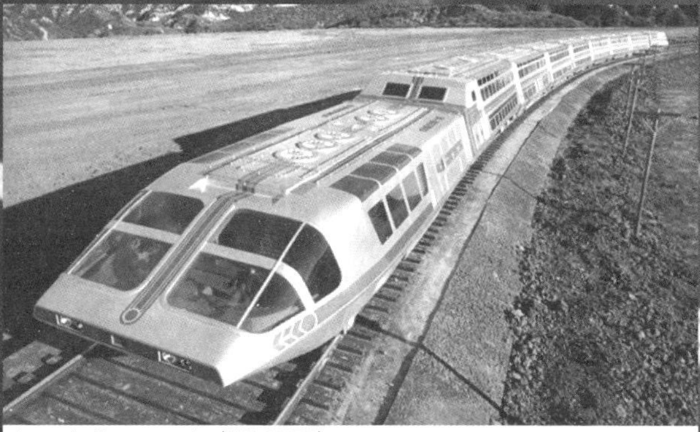

Atomic Supertrain (US 1979)

Dream of the atomic driving

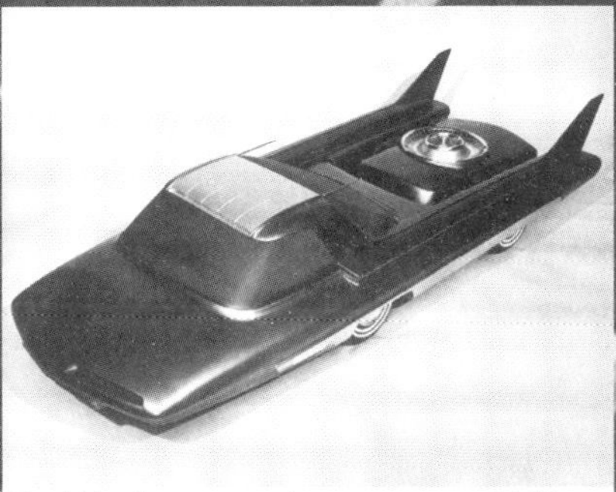

Ford Nucleon, atomic concept car 1958

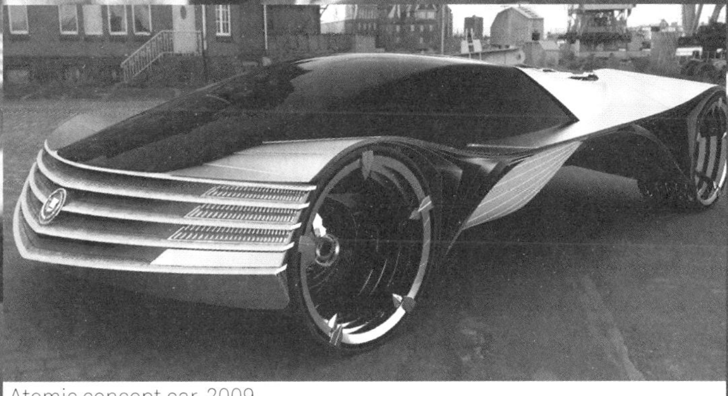

Atomic concept car, 2009

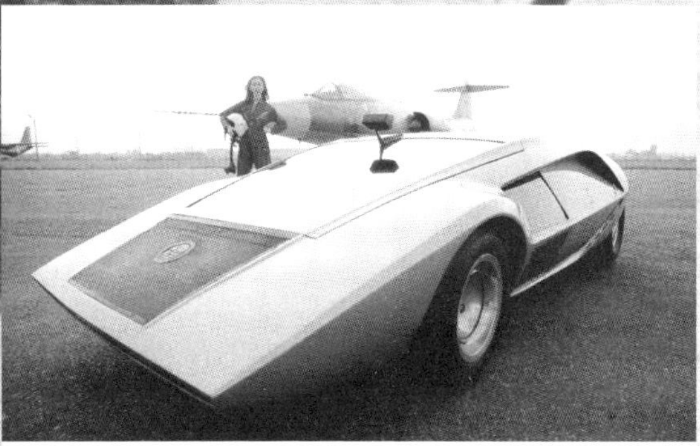

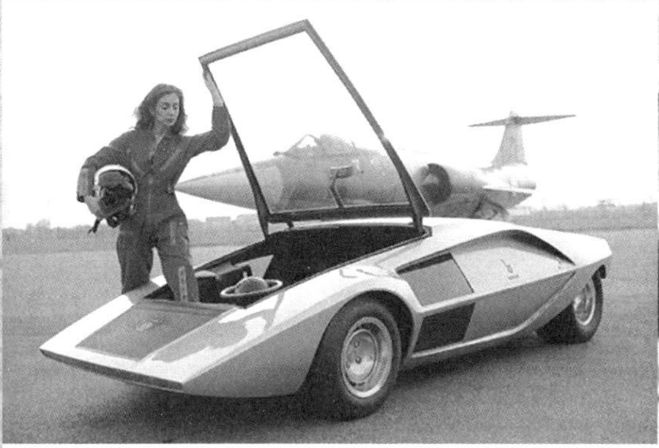

Street pilot, 1970

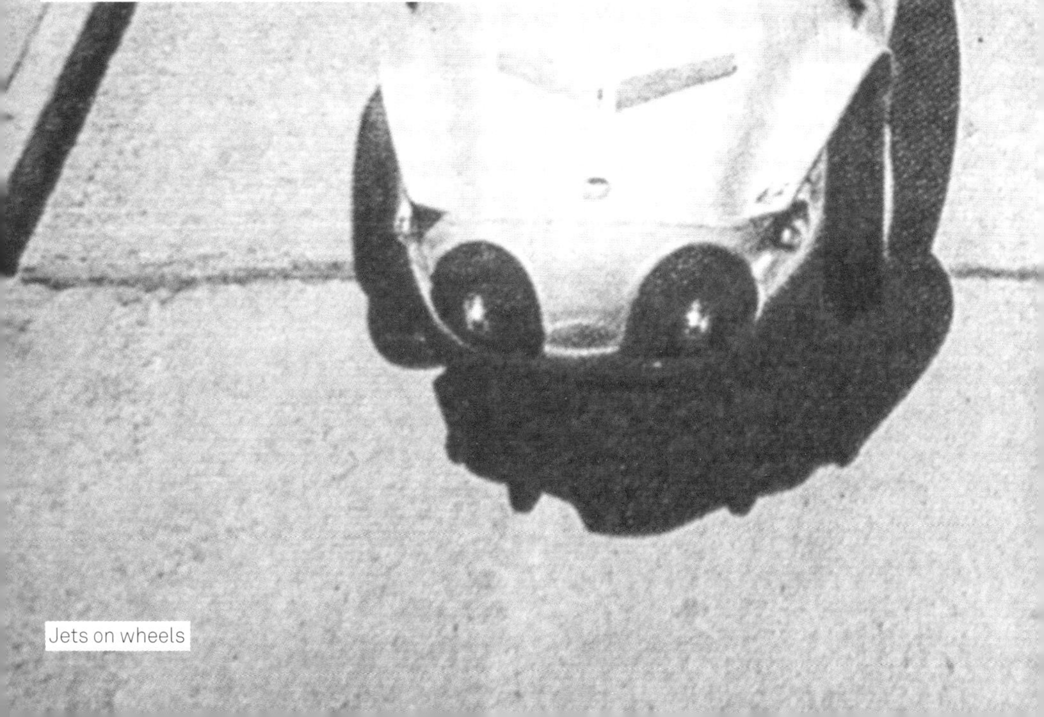

Jets on wheels

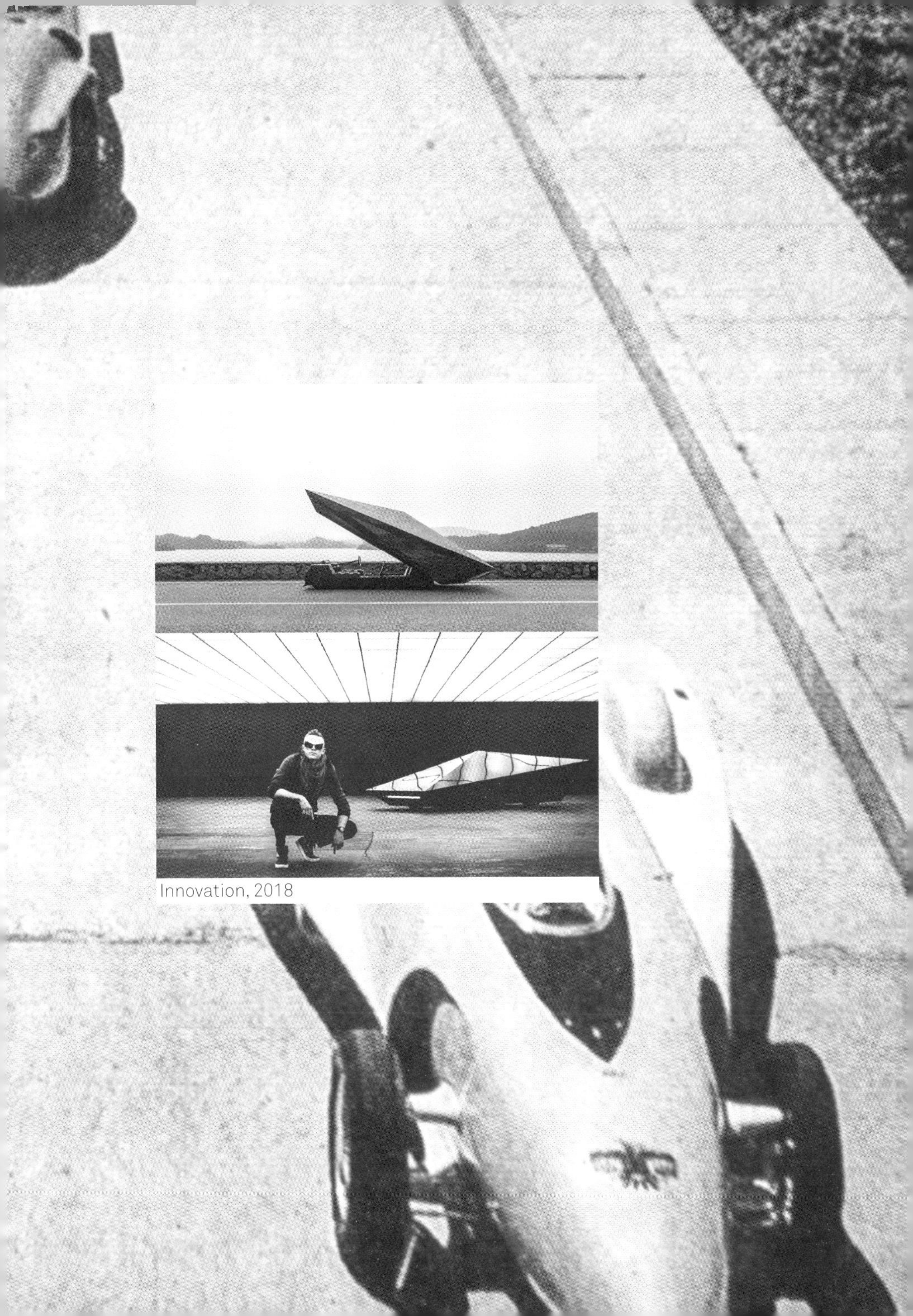

Innovation, 2018

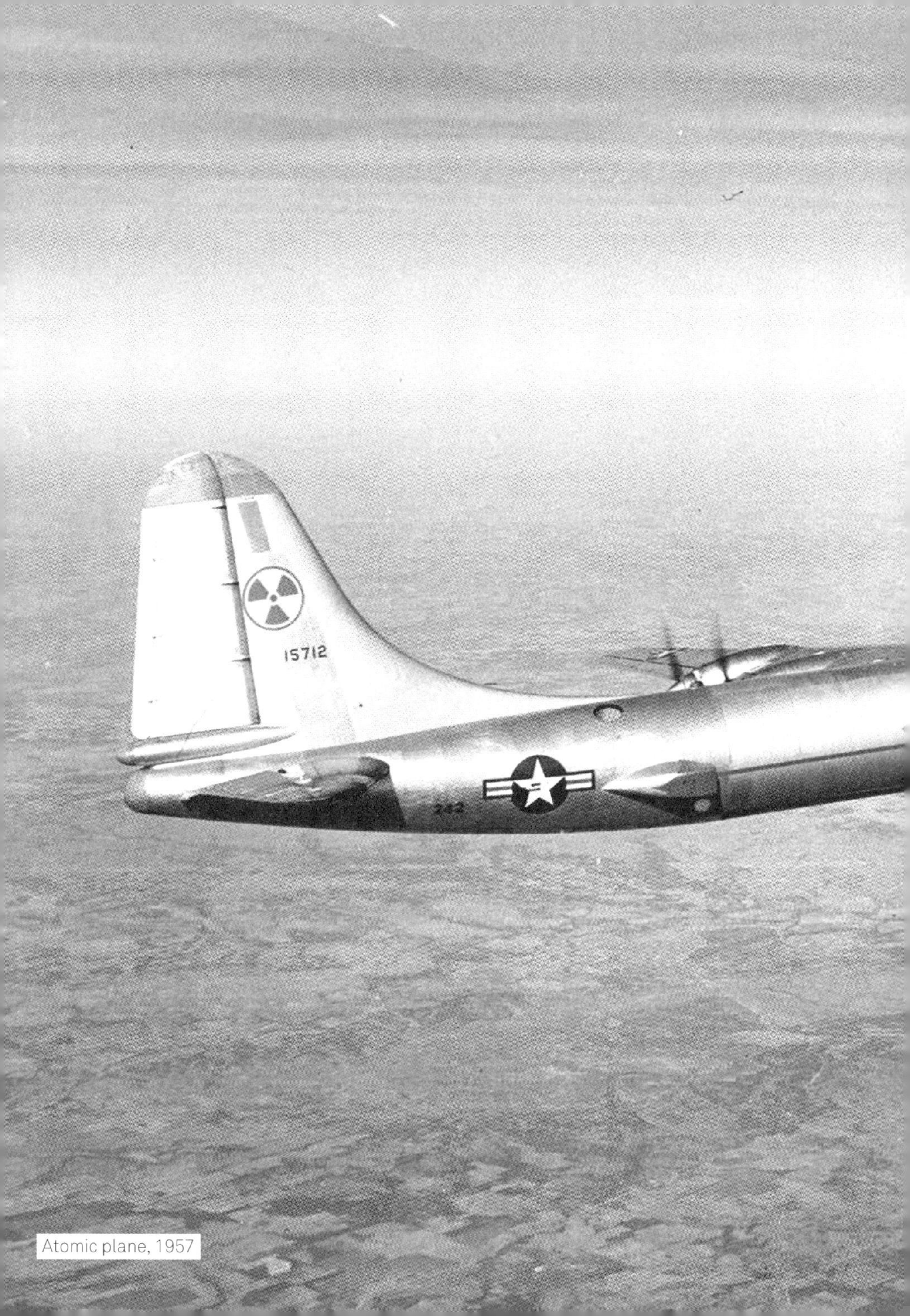

Atomic plane, 1957

§ 5

Frederick Barnet's Wander Jahre is one of those autobiographical novels that were popular throughout the third and fourth decades of the twentieth century. It was published in 1970 and one must understand Wander Jahre rather in a spiritual and intellectual than in a literal sense. It is indeed an allusive title carrying the world back to the *Wilhelm Meister* of Goethe, a century and a half earlier.

Its author, Frederick Barnet, gives a minute and curious history of his life and ideas between his nineteenth and his twenty-third birthdays. He was neither a very original nor a very brilliant man, but he had a trick of circumstantial writing; and though no authentic portrait was to survive for the information of posterity, he betrays by a score of casual phrases that he was short, sturdy, inclined to be plump, with a "rather blobby" face, and full, rather projecting blue eyes. He belonged until the financial *débâcle* of 1956 to the class of fairly prosperous people, he was a student in London, he aeroplaned to Italy and then had a pedestrian tour from Genoa to Rome, crossed in the air to Greece and Egypt and came back over the Balkans and Germany. His family fortunes, which were largely invested in bank shares, coal

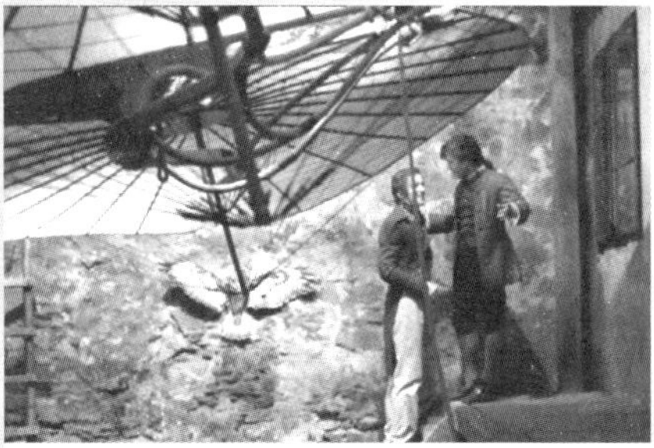

Flight pioneers, early 19th century (DE 1978)

mines and house property, were destroyed. Reduced to penury he sought to earn a living. He suffered great hardship, and was then caught up by the war and had a year of soldiering, first as an officer in the English infantry and then in the army of pacification. His book tells all these things so simply and at the same time so explicitly that it remains as it were an eye by which future generations may have at least one man's vision of the years of the Great Change.

And he was, he tells us, a "Modern State" man "by instinct" from the beginning. He breathed in these ideas in the class rooms and laboratories of the Carnegie Foundation school that rose, a long and delicately beautiful façade, along the South Bank of the Thames opposite the ancient dignity of Somerset House. Such thought was interwoven with the very fabric of that pioneer school in the educational renascence in England. After the customary exchange years in Heidelberg and Paris, he went into the classical school of London University. The older so-called "classical" education of the British pedagogues, probably the most paralysing, ineffective and foolish routine that ever wasted human life, had already been swept out of this great institution in favour of modern methods; and he learnt Greek and Latin as well as he had learnt German, Spanish and French, so that he wrote and spoke them freely and used them with

Aviation experiments

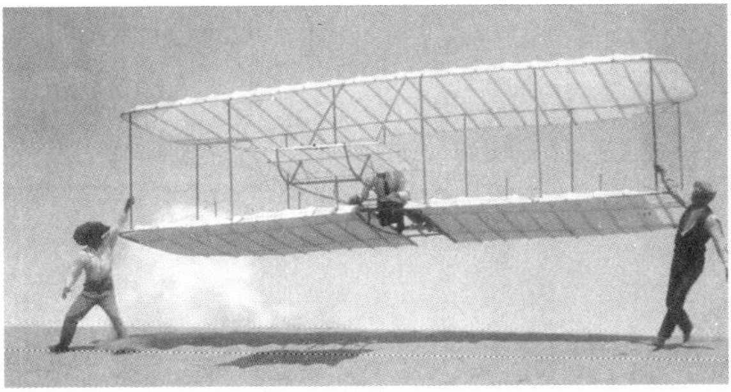

Wright brothers first flight, 1903

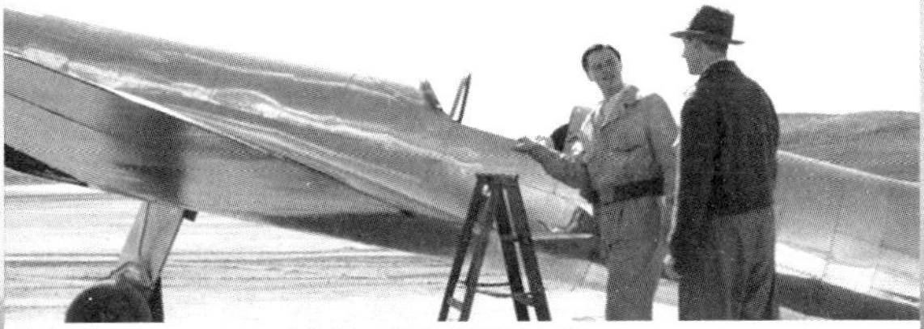

Aviation pioneers 1940s (US, DE 2004)

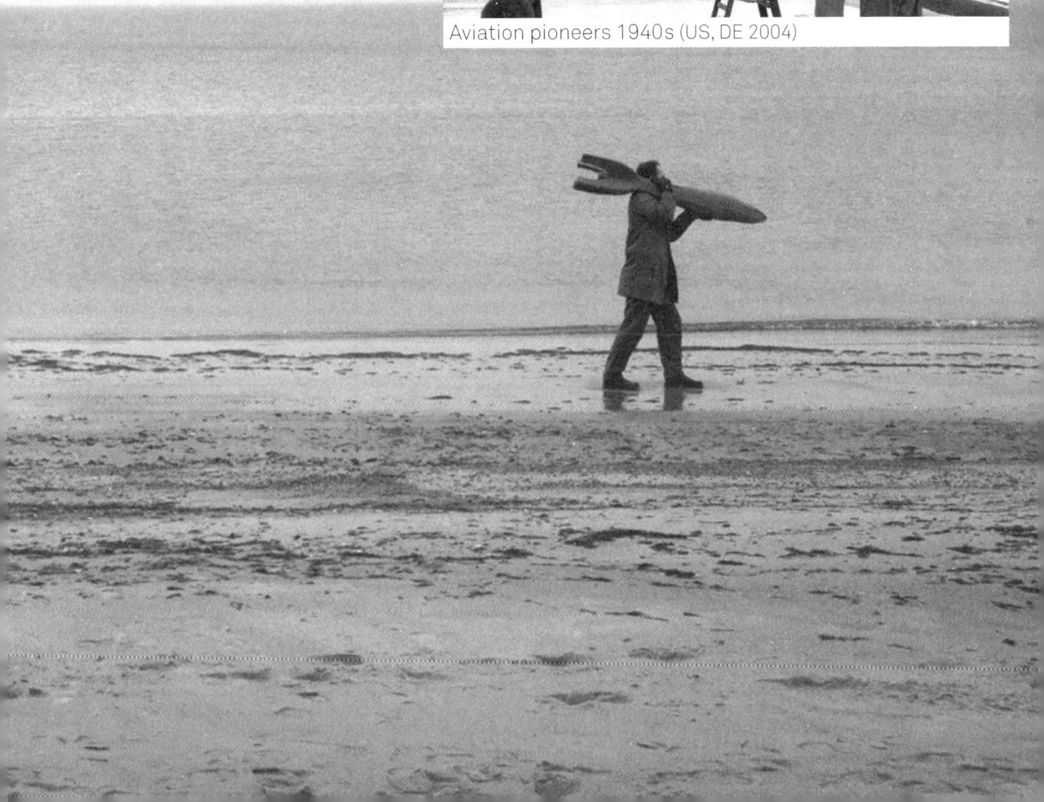

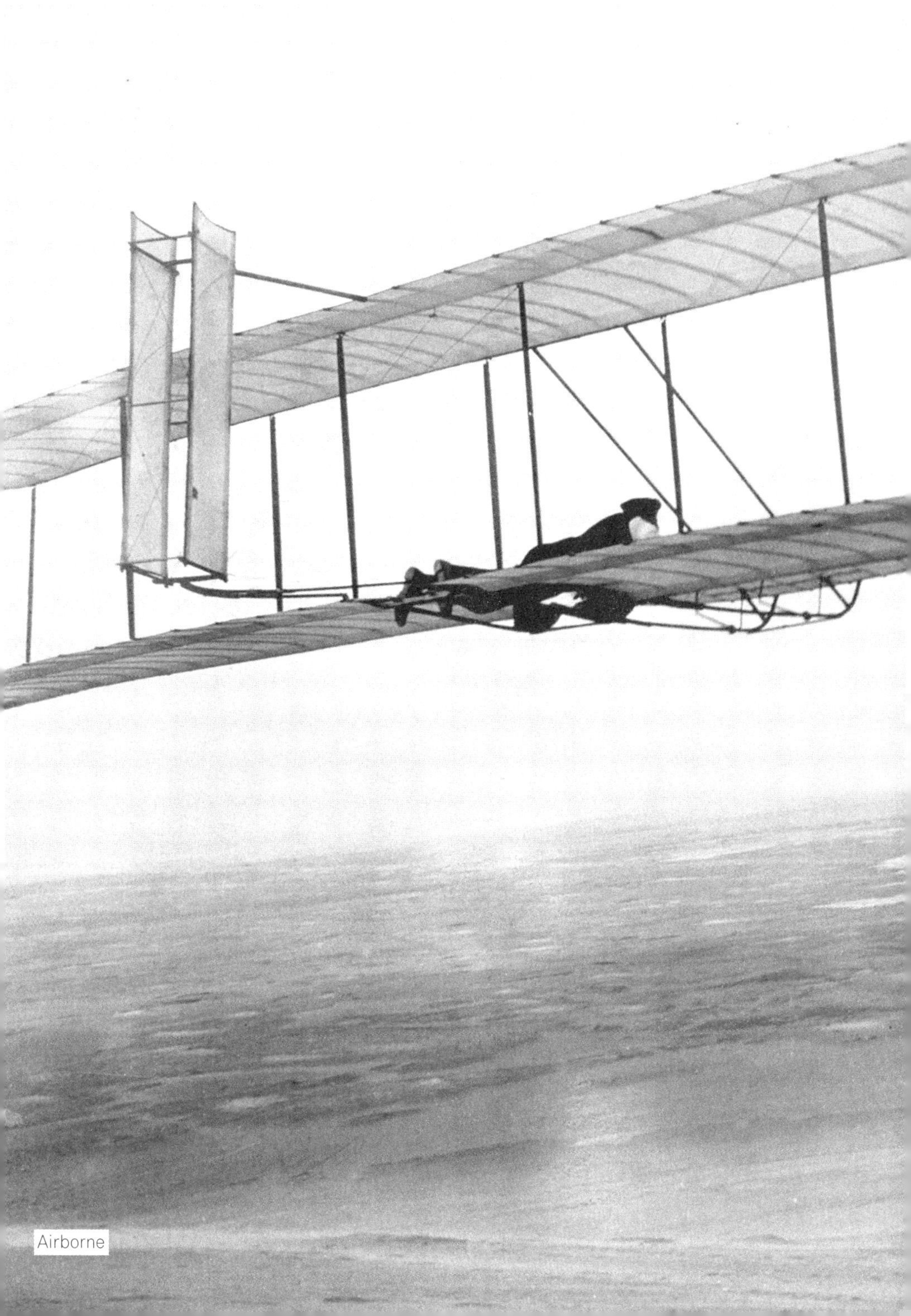
Airborne

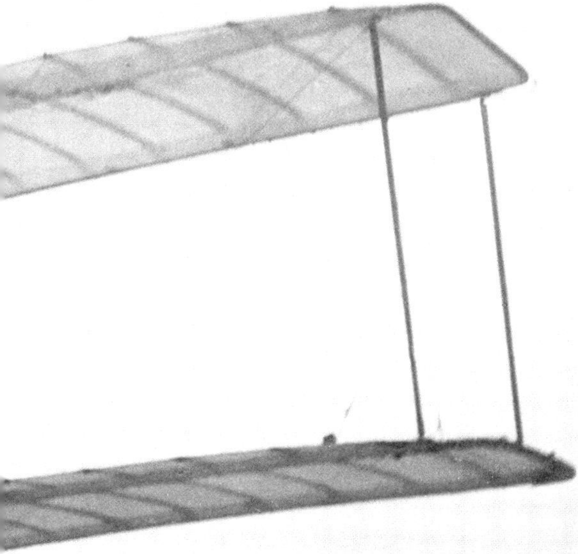

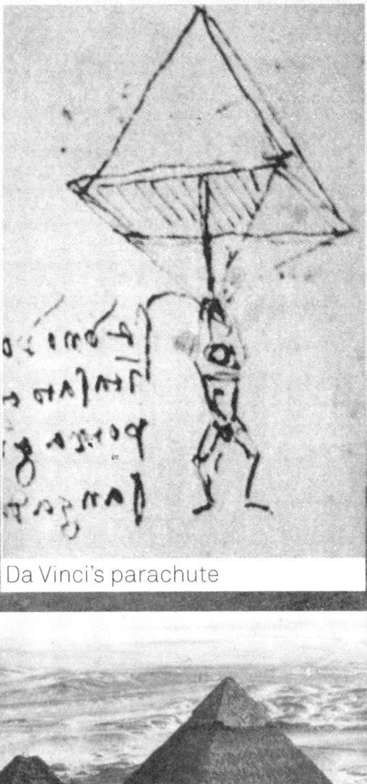

Da Vinci's parachute

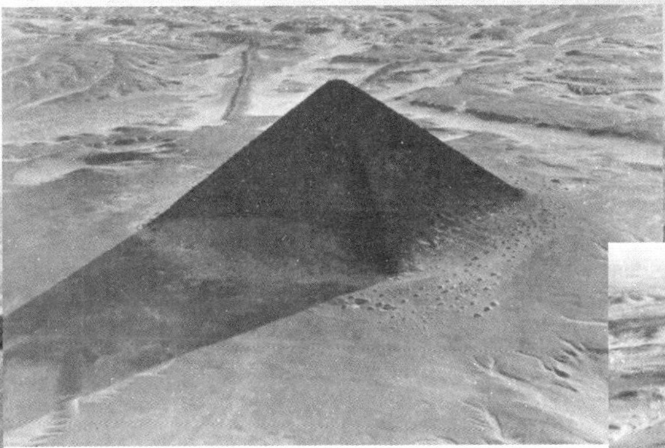

Airhip flight over Egypt, 1932

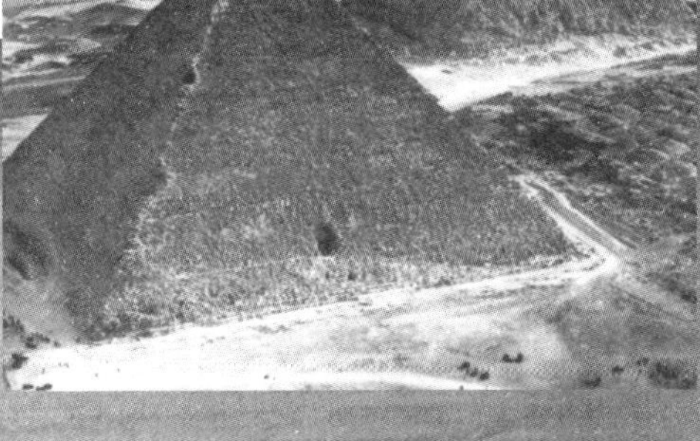

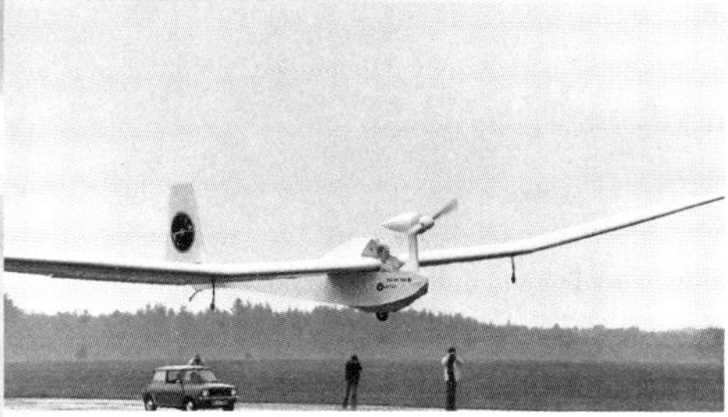
First solar plane's flight, 1979

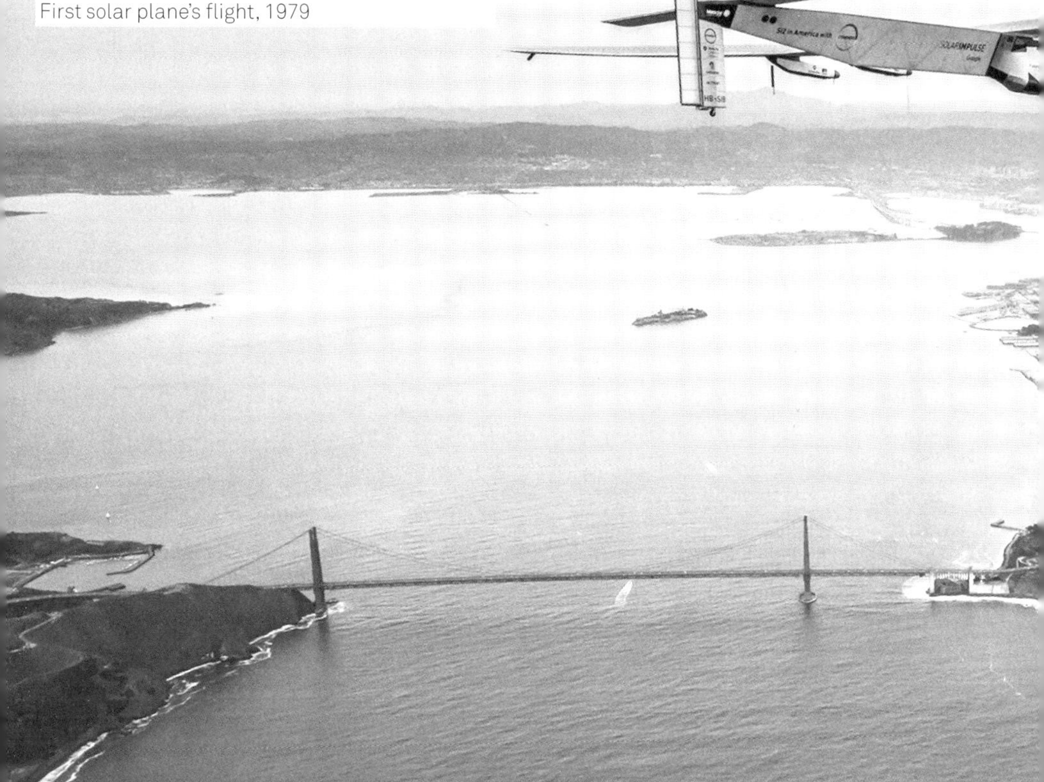
Around the world on solar power, 2015–16

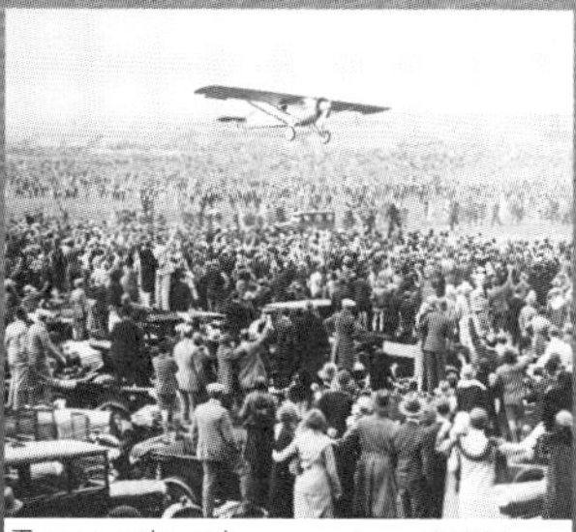
Transatlantic nonstop, 1927

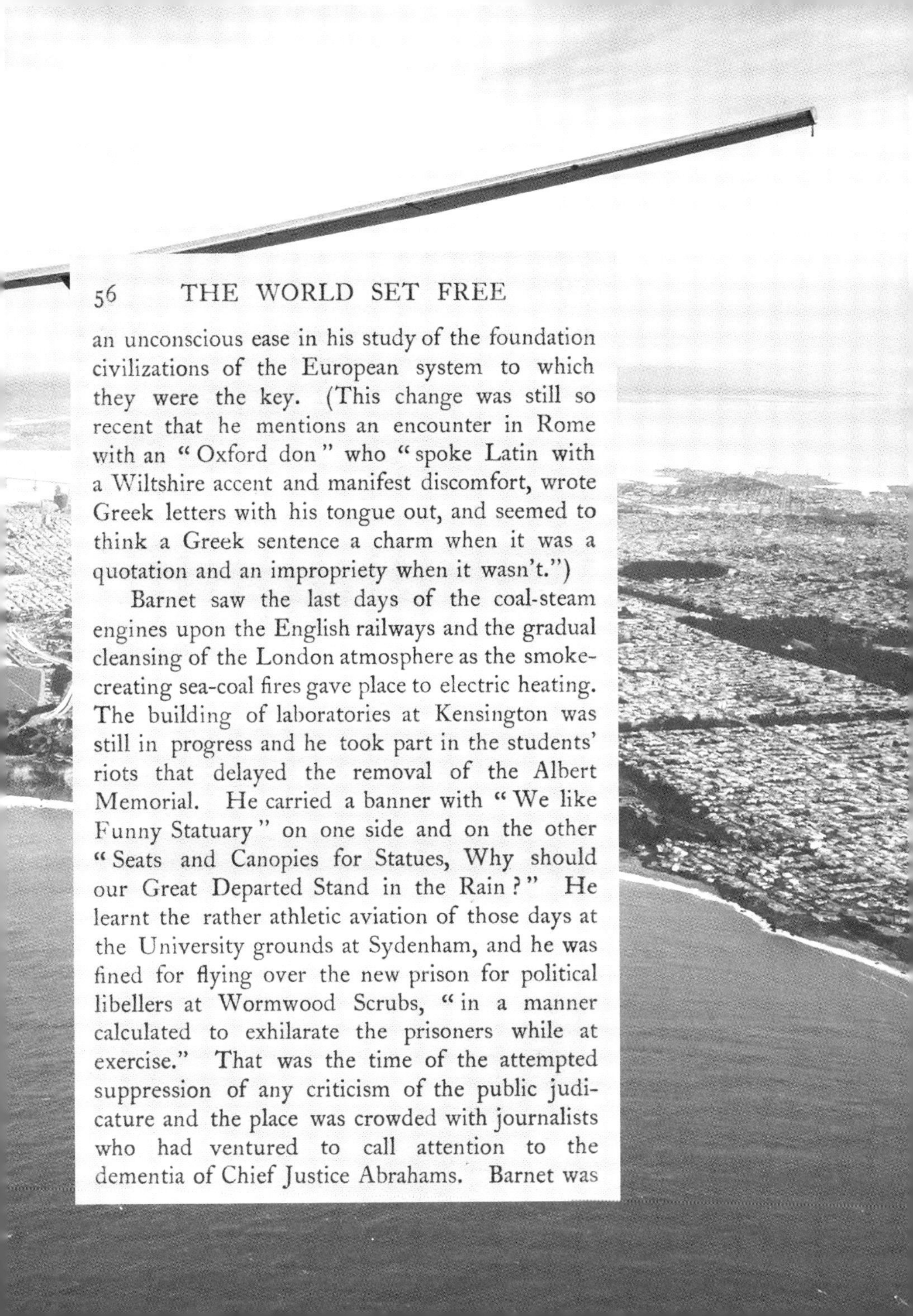

an unconscious ease in his study of the foundation civilizations of the European system to which they were the key. (This change was still so recent that he mentions an encounter in Rome with an "Oxford don" who "spoke Latin with a Wiltshire accent and manifest discomfort, wrote Greek letters with his tongue out, and seemed to think a Greek sentence a charm when it was a quotation and an impropriety when it wasn't.")

Barnet saw the last days of the coal-steam engines upon the English railways and the gradual cleansing of the London atmosphere as the smoke-creating sea-coal fires gave place to electric heating. The building of laboratories at Kensington was still in progress and he took part in the students' riots that delayed the removal of the Albert Memorial. He carried a banner with "We like Funny Statuary" on one side and on the other "Seats and Canopies for Statues, Why should our Great Departed Stand in the Rain?" He learnt the rather athletic aviation of those days at the University grounds at Sydenham, and he was fined for flying over the new prison for political libellers at Wormwood Scrubs, "in a manner calculated to exhilarate the prisoners while at exercise." That was the time of the attempted suppression of any criticism of the public judicature and the place was crowded with journalists who had ventured to call attention to the dementia of Chief Justice Abrahams. Barnet was

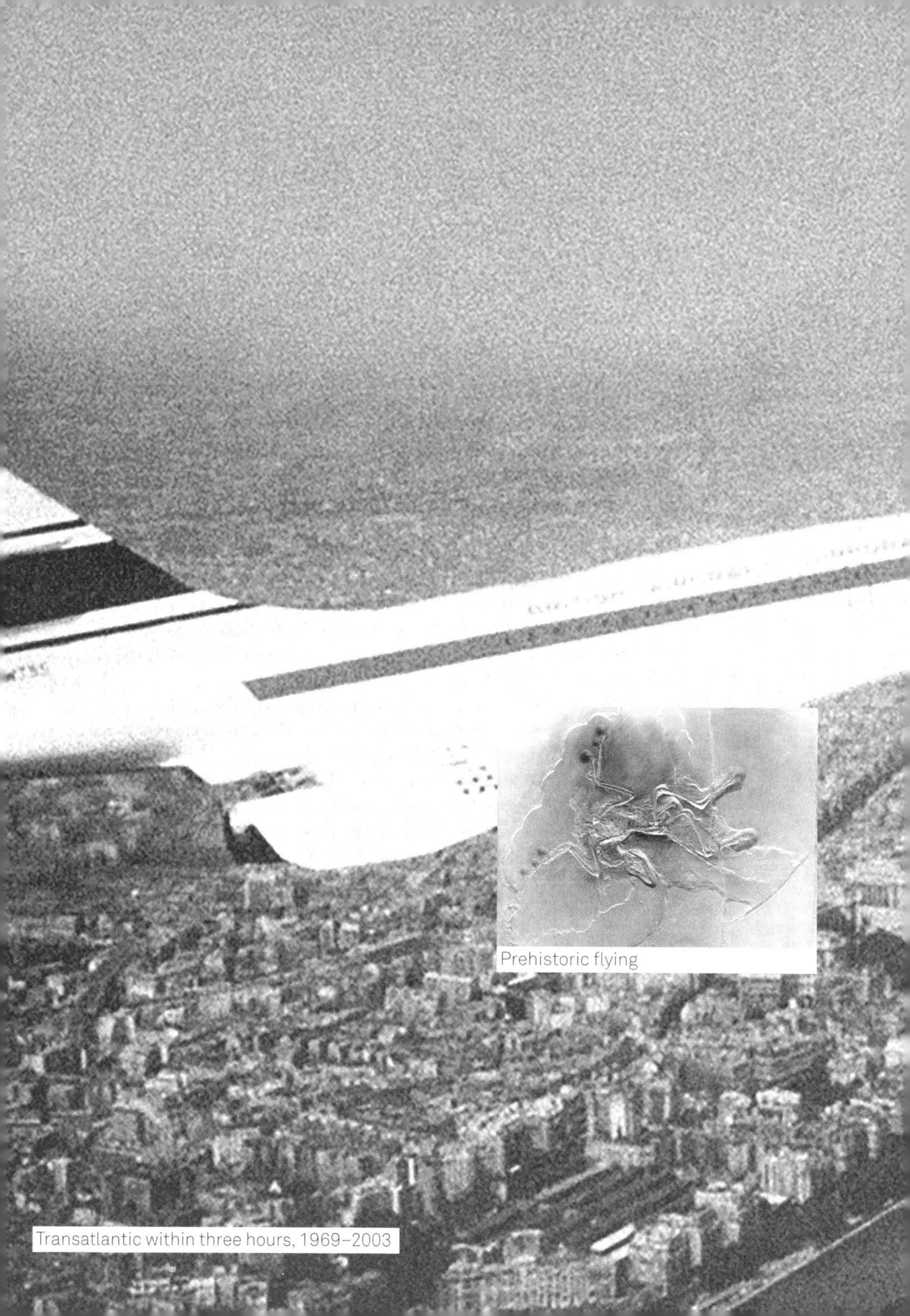

Prehistoric flying

Transatlantic within three hours, 1969–2003

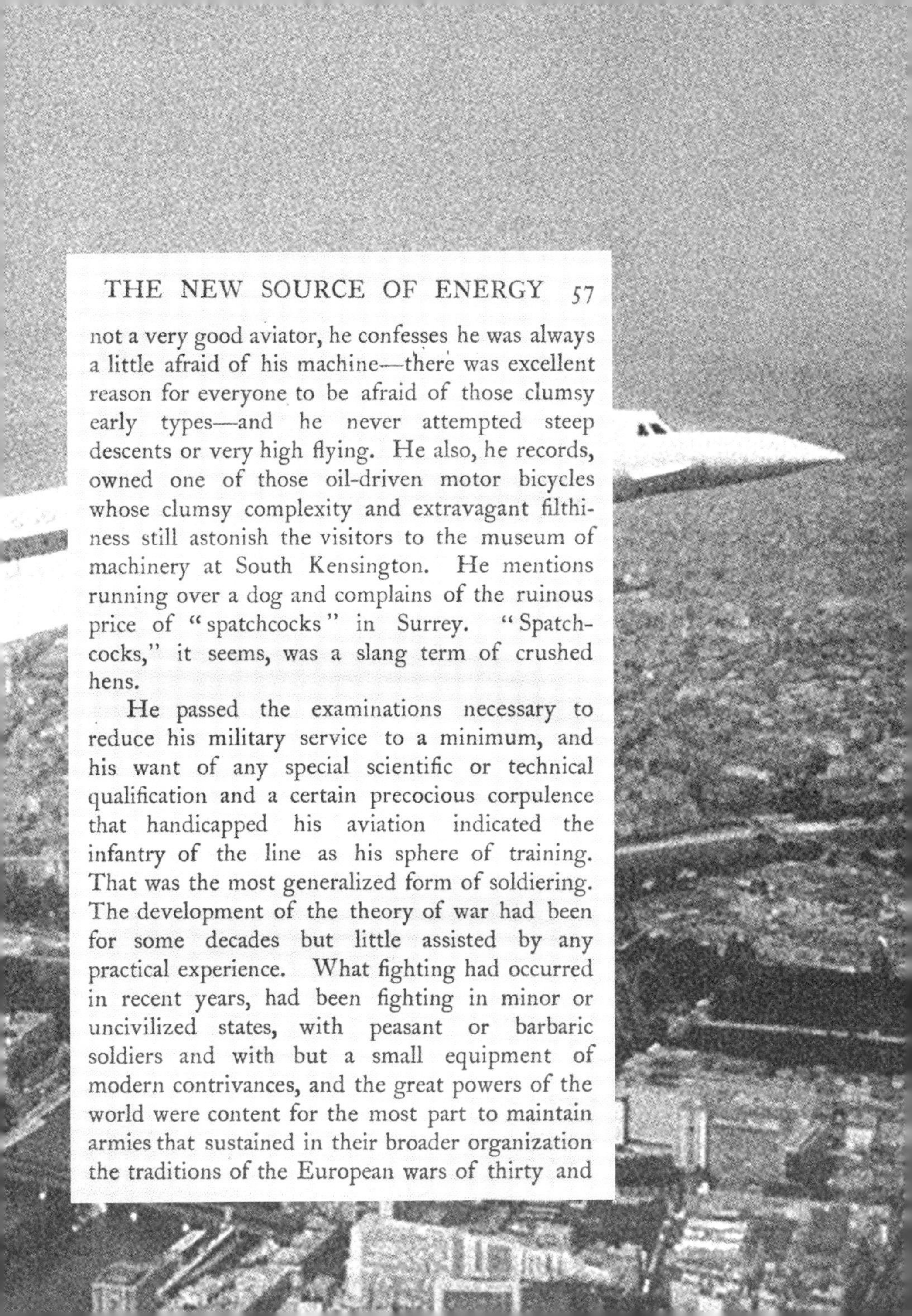

not a very good aviator, he confesses he was always a little afraid of his machine—there was excellent reason for everyone to be afraid of those clumsy early types—and he never attempted steep descents or very high flying. He also, he records, owned one of those oil-driven motor bicycles whose clumsy complexity and extravagant filthiness still astonish the visitors to the museum of machinery at South Kensington. He mentions running over a dog and complains of the ruinous price of "spatchcocks" in Surrey. "Spatchcocks," it seems, was a slang term of crushed hens.

He passed the examinations necessary to reduce his military service to a minimum, and his want of any special scientific or technical qualification and a certain precocious corpulence that handicapped his aviation indicated the infantry of the line as his sphere of training. That was the most generalized form of soldiering. The development of the theory of war had been for some decades but little assisted by any practical experience. What fighting had occurred in recent years, had been fighting in minor or uncivilized states, with peasant or barbaric soldiers and with but a small equipment of modern contrivances, and the great powers of the world were content for the most part to maintain armies that sustained in their broader organization the traditions of the European wars of thirty and

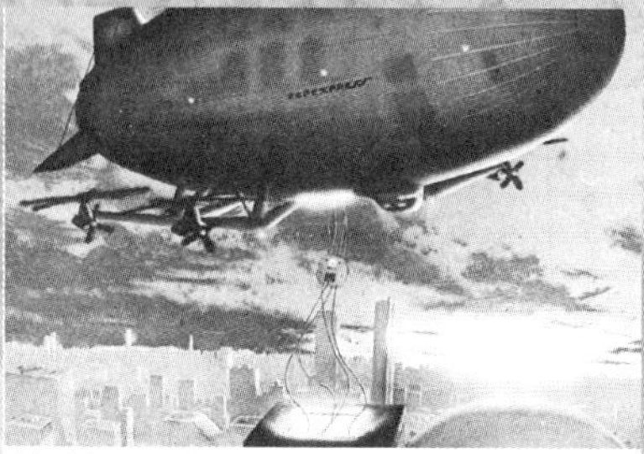

Airship carrier

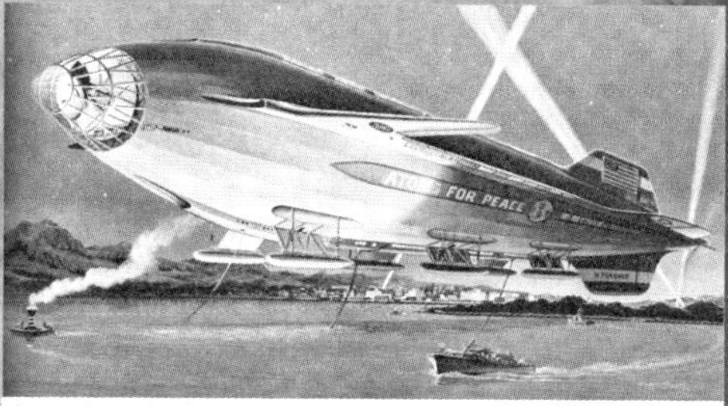

Atomica airship

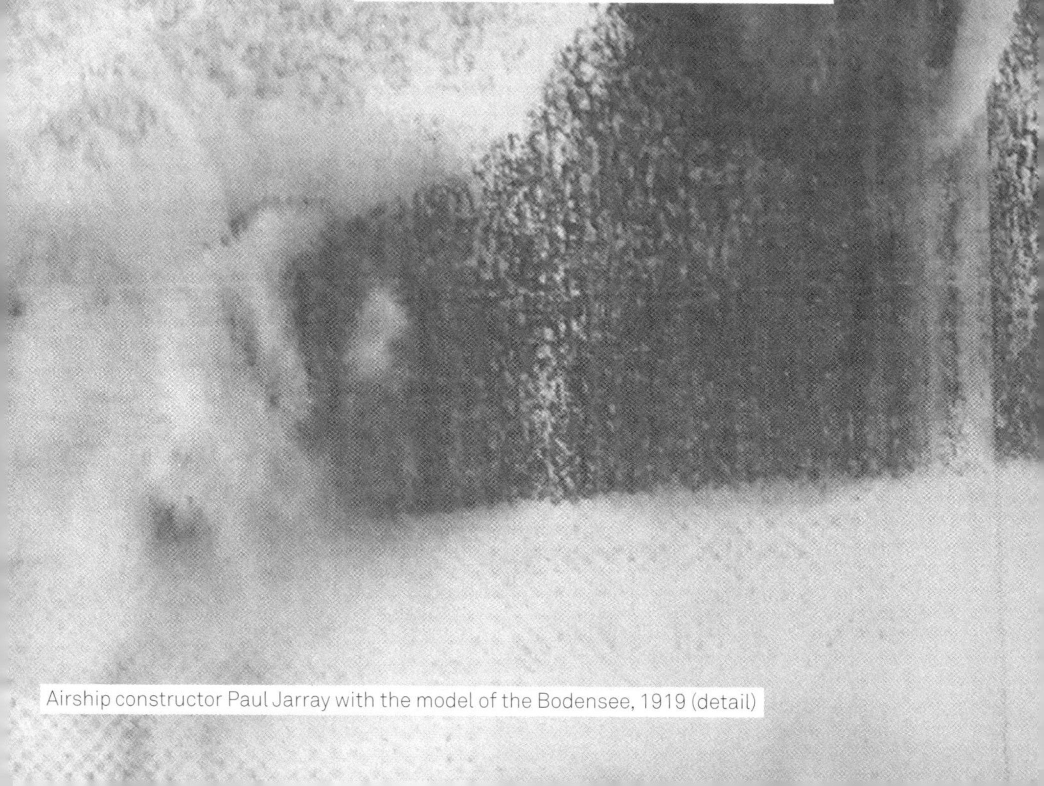

Airship constructor Paul Jarray with the model of the Bodensee, 1919 (detail)

forty years before. There was the infantry arm to which Barnet belonged and which was supposed to fight on foot with a rifle and be the main portion of the army. There were cavalry forces, (horse soldiers), having a ratio to the infantry that had been determined by the experiences of the Franco-German war in 1871. There was also artillery, and for some unexplained reason much of this was still drawn by horses; though there were also in all the European armies a small number of motor-guns with wheels so constructed that they could go over broken ground. In addition there were large developments of the engineering arm, concerned with motor transport, motor-bicycle scouting, aviation and the like.

No first-class intelligence had been sought to specialize in and work out the problem of warfare with the new appliances and under modern conditions, but a succession of able jurists, Lord Haldane, Chief Justice Briggs, and that very able King's Counsel Philbrick, had reconstructed the army frequently and thoroughly and placed it at last, with the adoption of national service, upon a footing that would have seemed very imposing to the public of 1900. At any moment the British Empire could now put a million and a quarter of arguable soldiers upon the board of Welt-Politik. The traditions of Japan and the Central European armies were more princely and less forensic; the Chinese still refused resolutely to become a

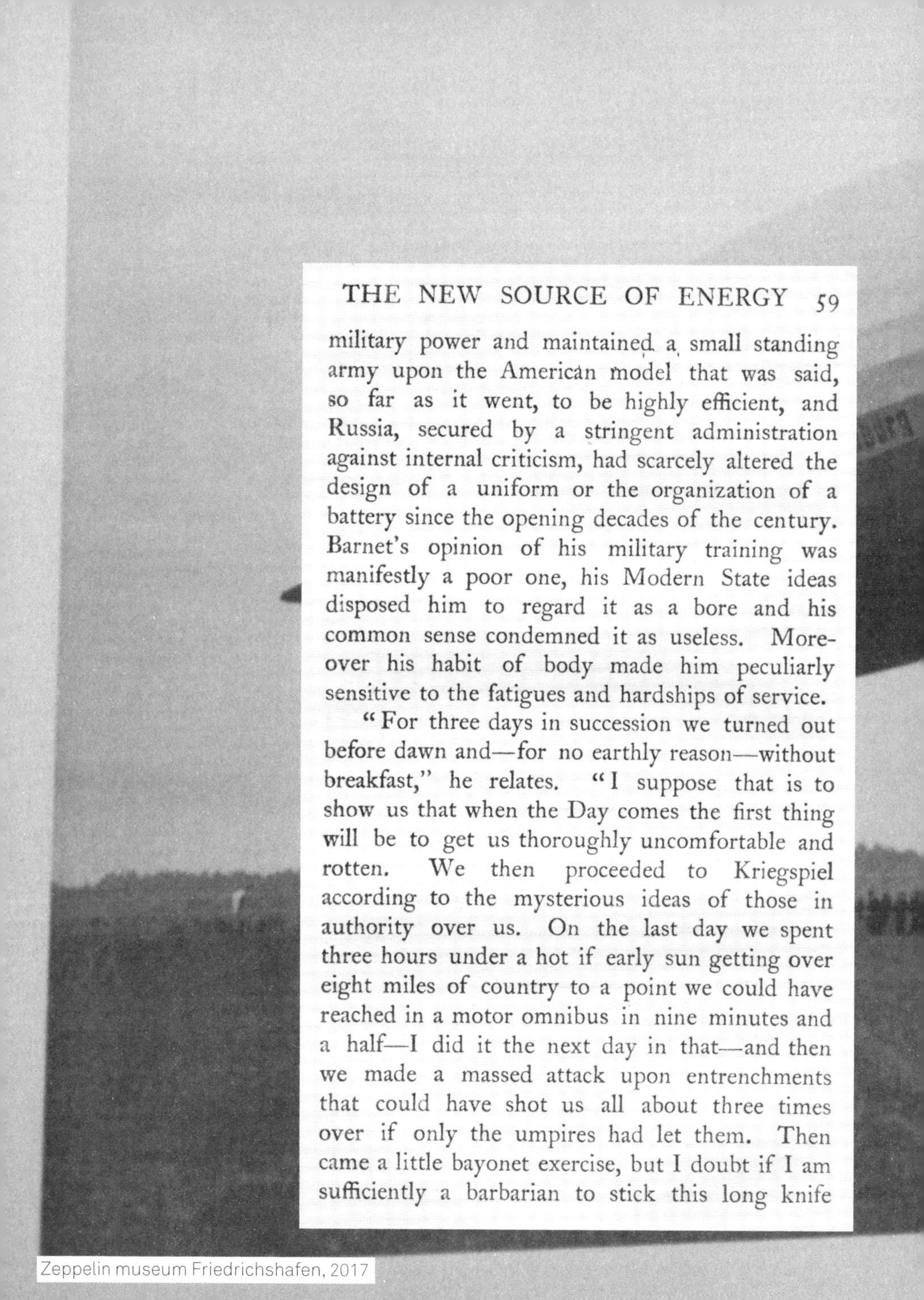

military power and maintained a small standing army upon the American model that was said, so far as it went, to be highly efficient, and Russia, secured by a stringent administration against internal criticism, had scarcely altered the design of a uniform or the organization of a battery since the opening decades of the century. Barnet's opinion of his military training was manifestly a poor one, his Modern State ideas disposed him to regard it as a bore and his common sense condemned it as useless. Moreover his habit of body made him peculiarly sensitive to the fatigues and hardships of service.

"For three days in succession we turned out before dawn and—for no earthly reason—without breakfast," he relates. "I suppose that is to show us that when the Day comes the first thing will be to get us thoroughly uncomfortable and rotten. We then proceeded to Kriegspiel according to the mysterious ideas of those in authority over us. On the last day we spent three hours under a hot if early sun getting over eight miles of country to a point we could have reached in a motor omnibus in nine minutes and a half—I did it the next day in that—and then we made a massed attack upon entrenchments that could have shot us all about three times over if only the umpires had let them. Then came a little bayonet exercise, but I doubt if I am sufficiently a barbarian to stick this long knife

Zeppelin museum Friedrichshafen, 2017

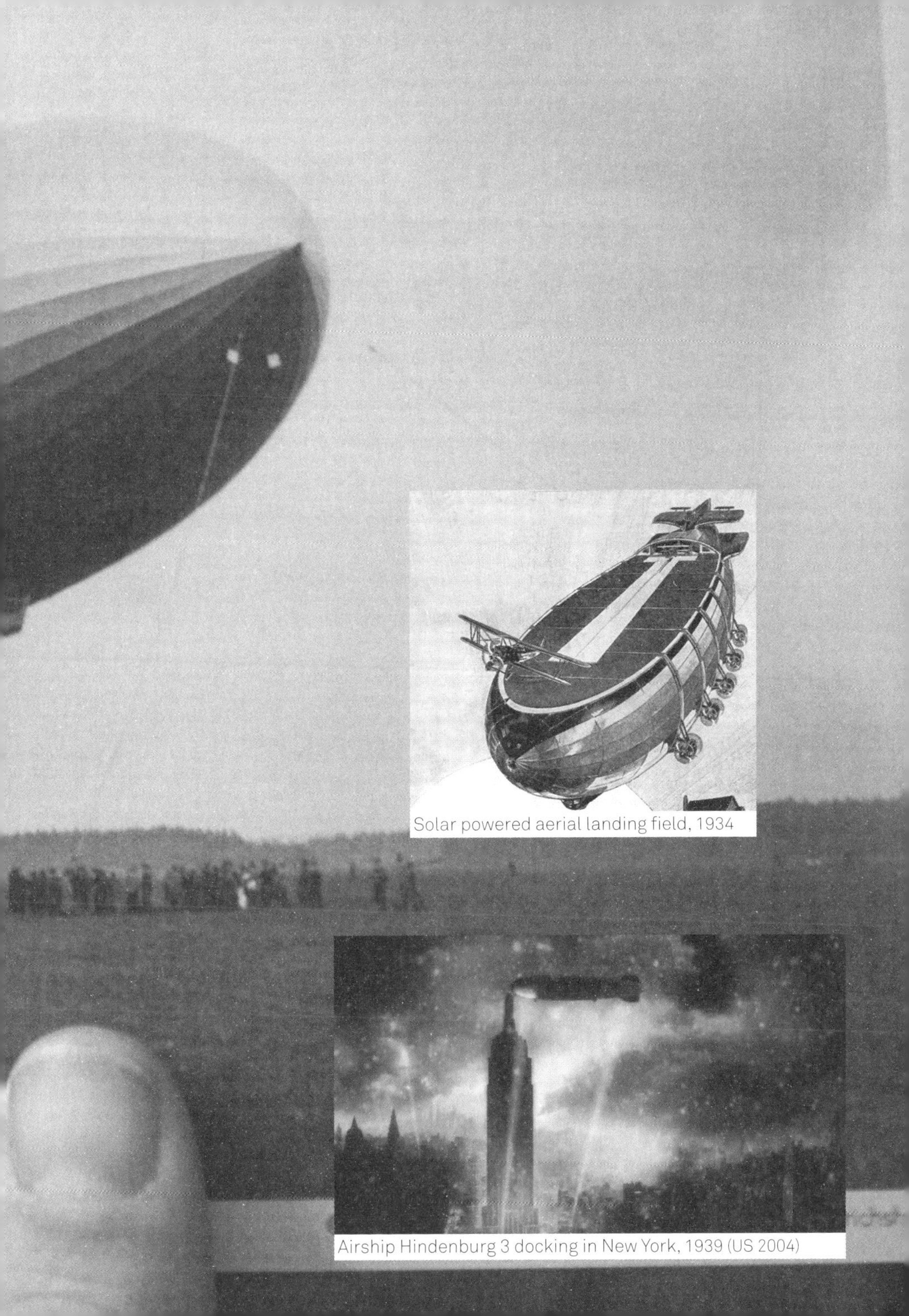

Solar powered aerial landing field, 1934

Airship Hindenburg 3 docking in New York, 1939 (US 2004)

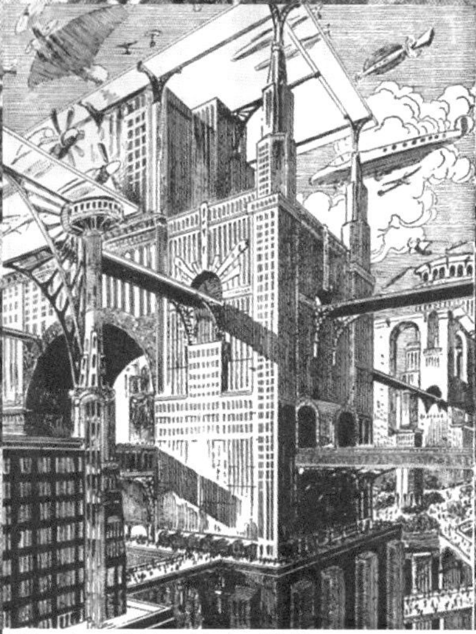

City airport New York, 1946

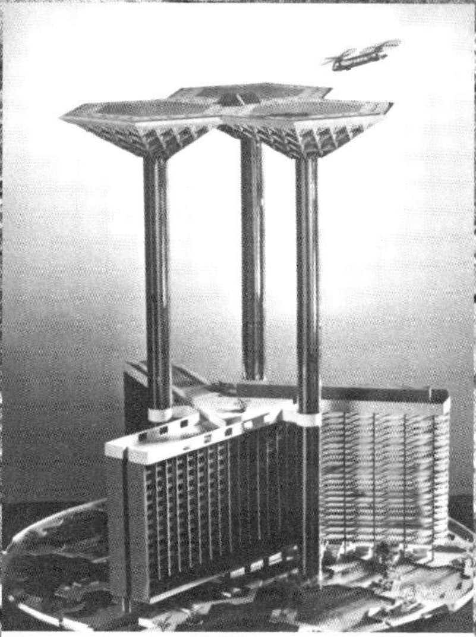

Skyport London, 1957

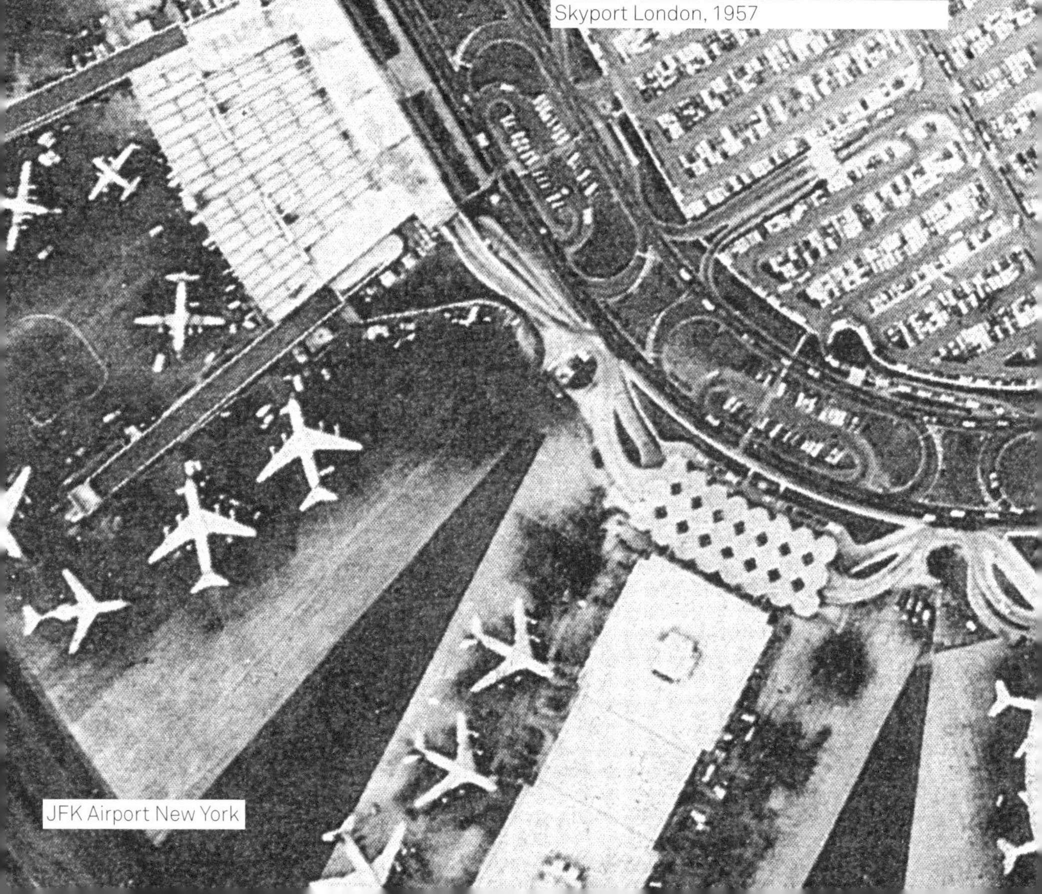

JFK Airport New York

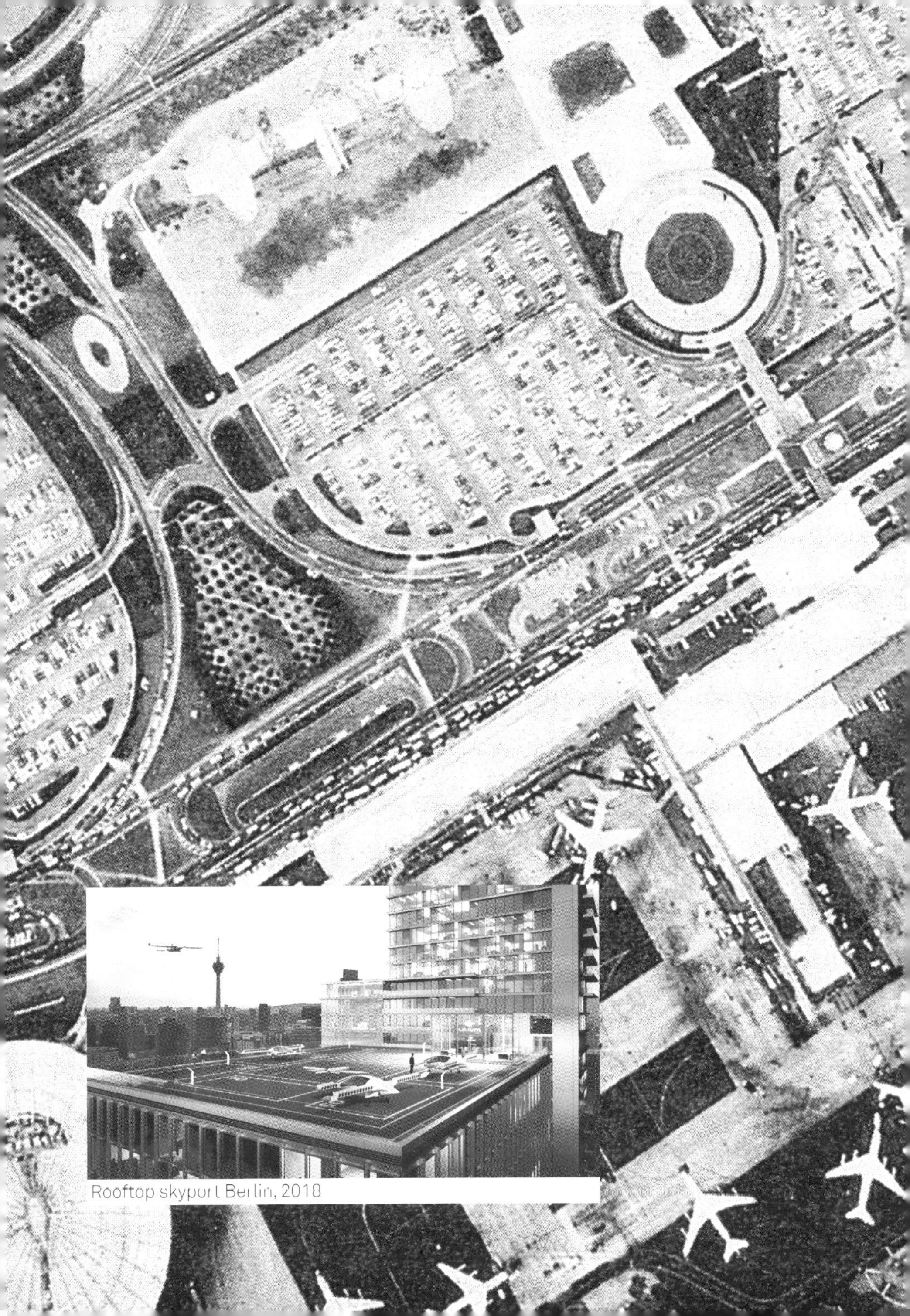

Rooftop skyport Berlin, 2018

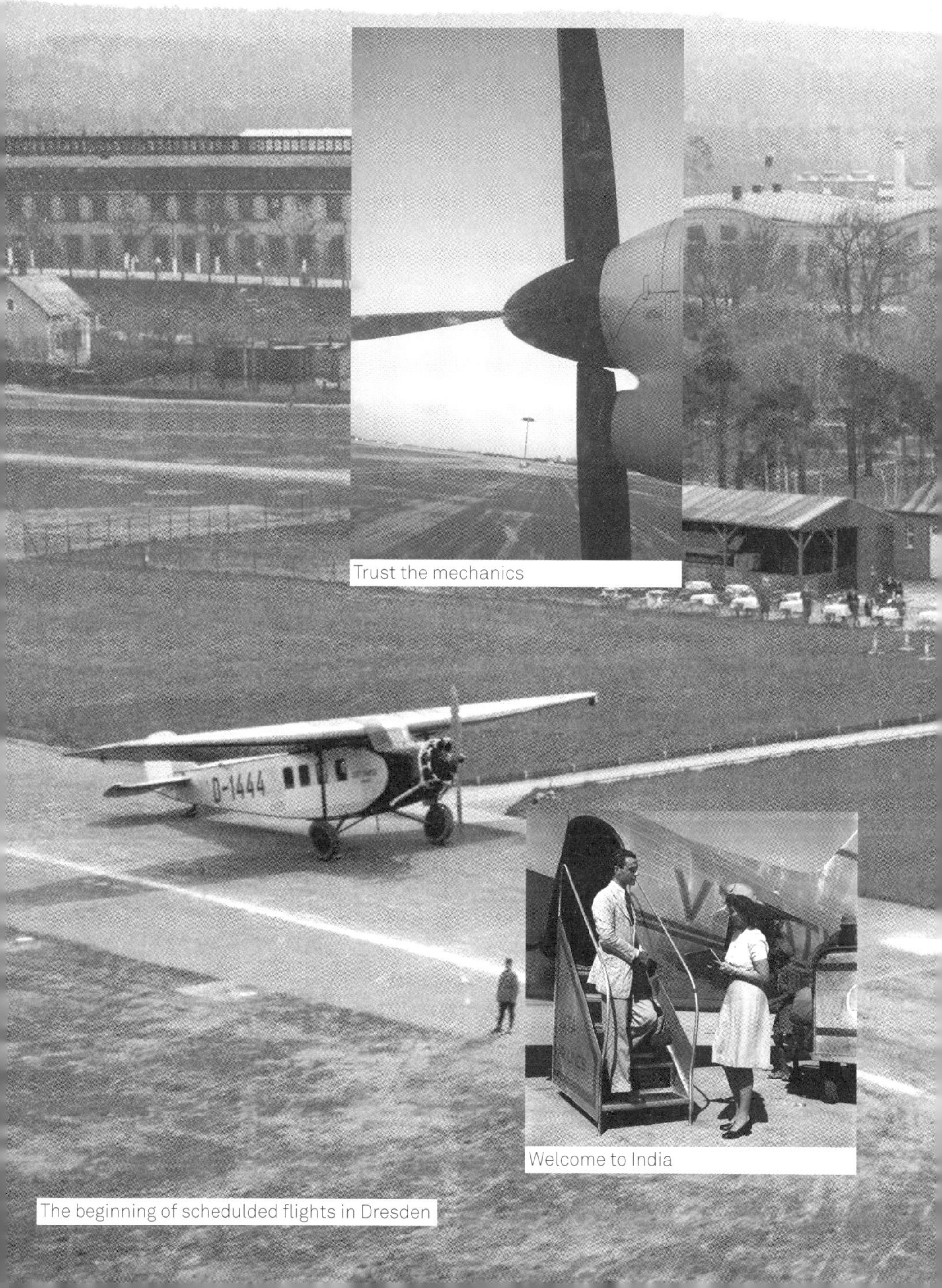

Trust the mechanics

Welcome to India

The beginning of schedulded flights in Dresden

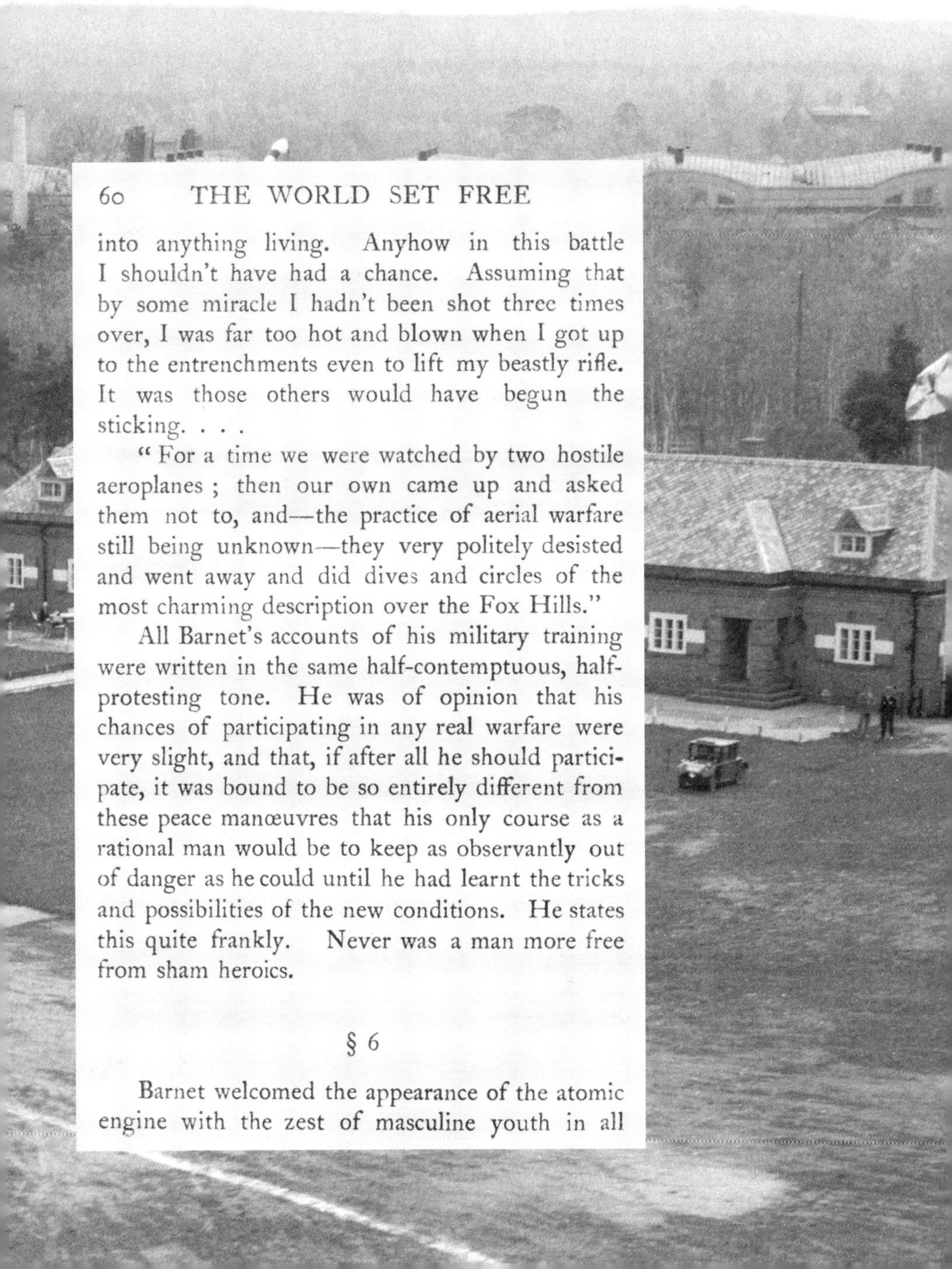

into anything living. Anyhow in this battle I shouldn't have had a chance. Assuming that by some miracle I hadn't been shot three times over, I was far too hot and blown when I got up to the entrenchments even to lift my beastly rifle. It was those others would have begun the sticking. . . .

"For a time we were watched by two hostile aeroplanes ; then our own came up and asked them not to, and—the practice of aerial warfare still being unknown—they very politely desisted and went away and did dives and circles of the most charming description over the Fox Hills."

All Barnet's accounts of his military training were written in the same half-contemptuous, half-protesting tone. He was of opinion that his chances of participating in any real warfare were very slight, and that, if after all he should participate, it was bound to be so entirely different from these peace manœuvres that his only course as a rational man would be to keep as observantly out of danger as he could until he had learnt the tricks and possibilities of the new conditions. He states this quite frankly. Never was a man more free from sham heroics.

§ 6

Barnet welcomed the appearance of the atomic engine with the zest of masculine youth in all fresh machinery, and it is evident that for some time he failed to connect the rush of wonderful new possibilities with the financial troubles of his family. "I knew my father was worried," he admits. That cast the smallest of shadows upon his delighted departure for Italy and Greece and Egypt with three congenial companions in one of the new atomic models. They flew over the Channel Isles and Touraine, he mentions, and circled about Mont Blanc—"These new helicopters, we found," he notes, "had abolished all the danger and strain of sudden drops to which the oldtime aeroplanes were liable,"—and then he went on by way of Pisa, Paestum, Ghirgenti and Athens to visit the pyramids by moonlight, flying thither from Cairo, and to follow the Nile up to Khartoum. Even by later standards it must have been a very gleeful holiday for a young man, and it made the tragedy of his next experiences all the darker. A week after his return his father, who was a widower, announced himself ruined, and committed suicide by means of an unscheduled opiate.

At one blow Barnet found himself flung out of the possessing, spending, enjoying class to which he belonged, penniless and with no calling by which he could earn a living. He tried teaching and some journalism, but in a little while he found himself on the underside of a world in which he had always reckoned to live in the

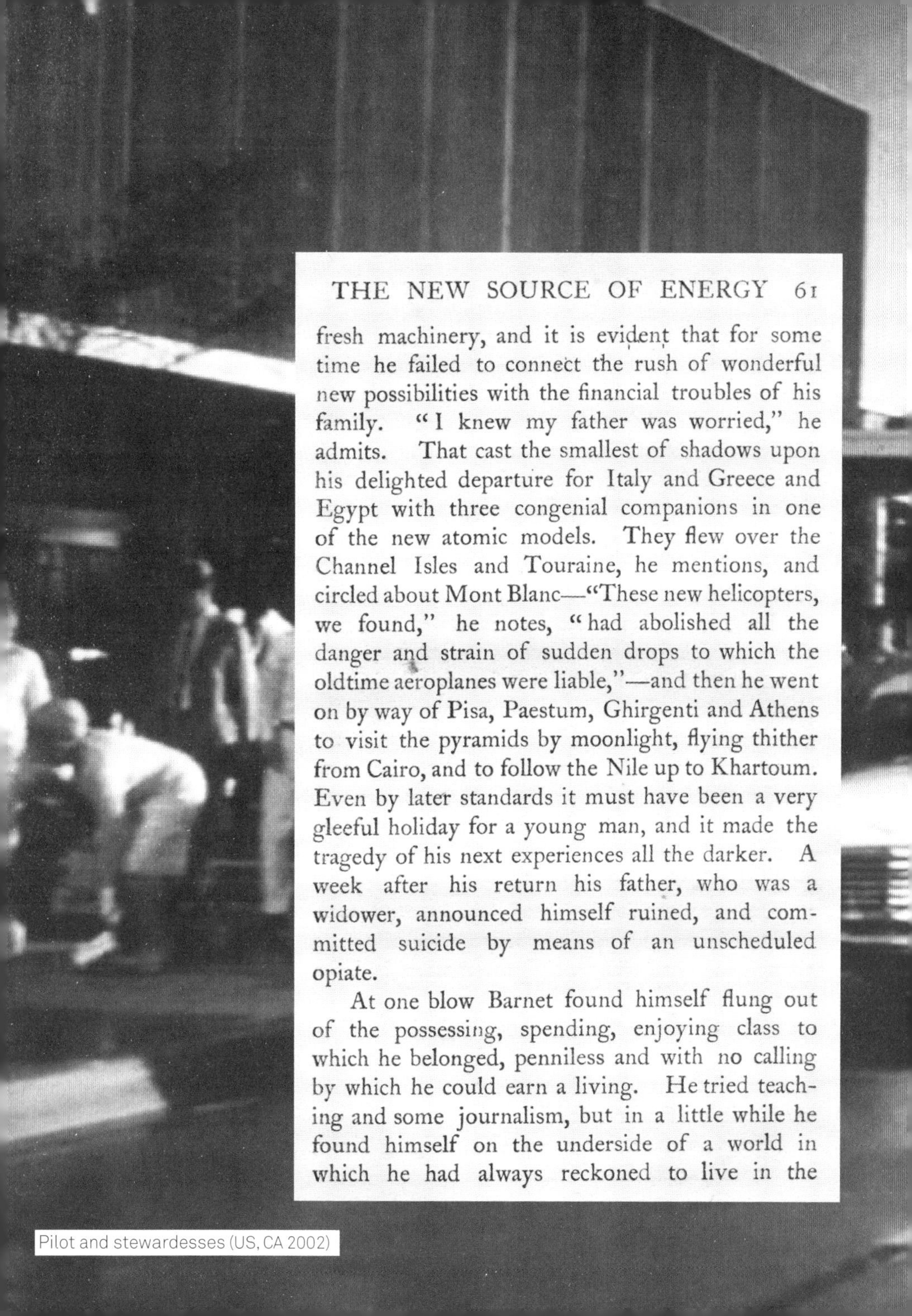

Pilot and stewardesses (US, CA 2002)

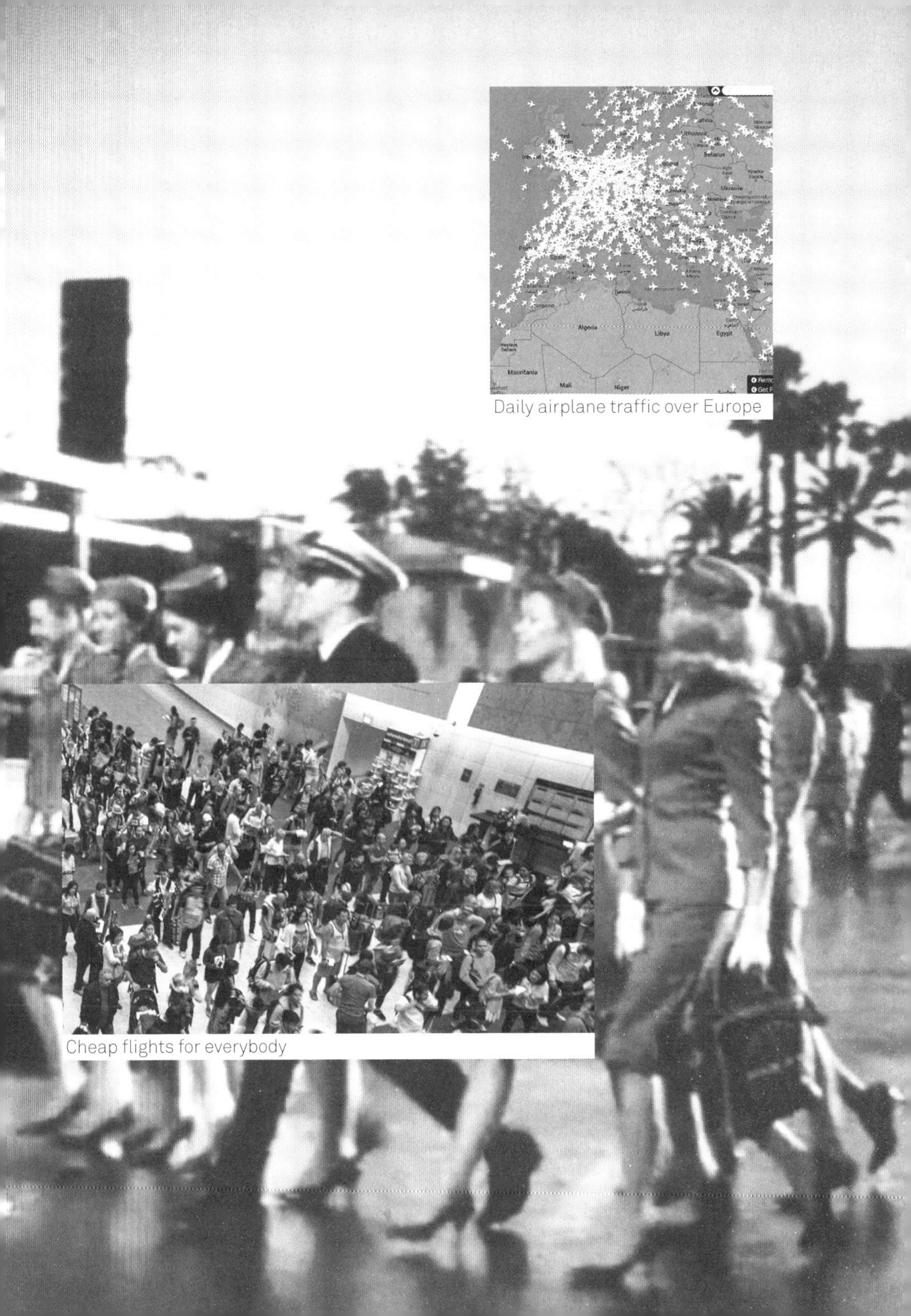

Daily airplane traffic over Europe

Cheap flights for everybody

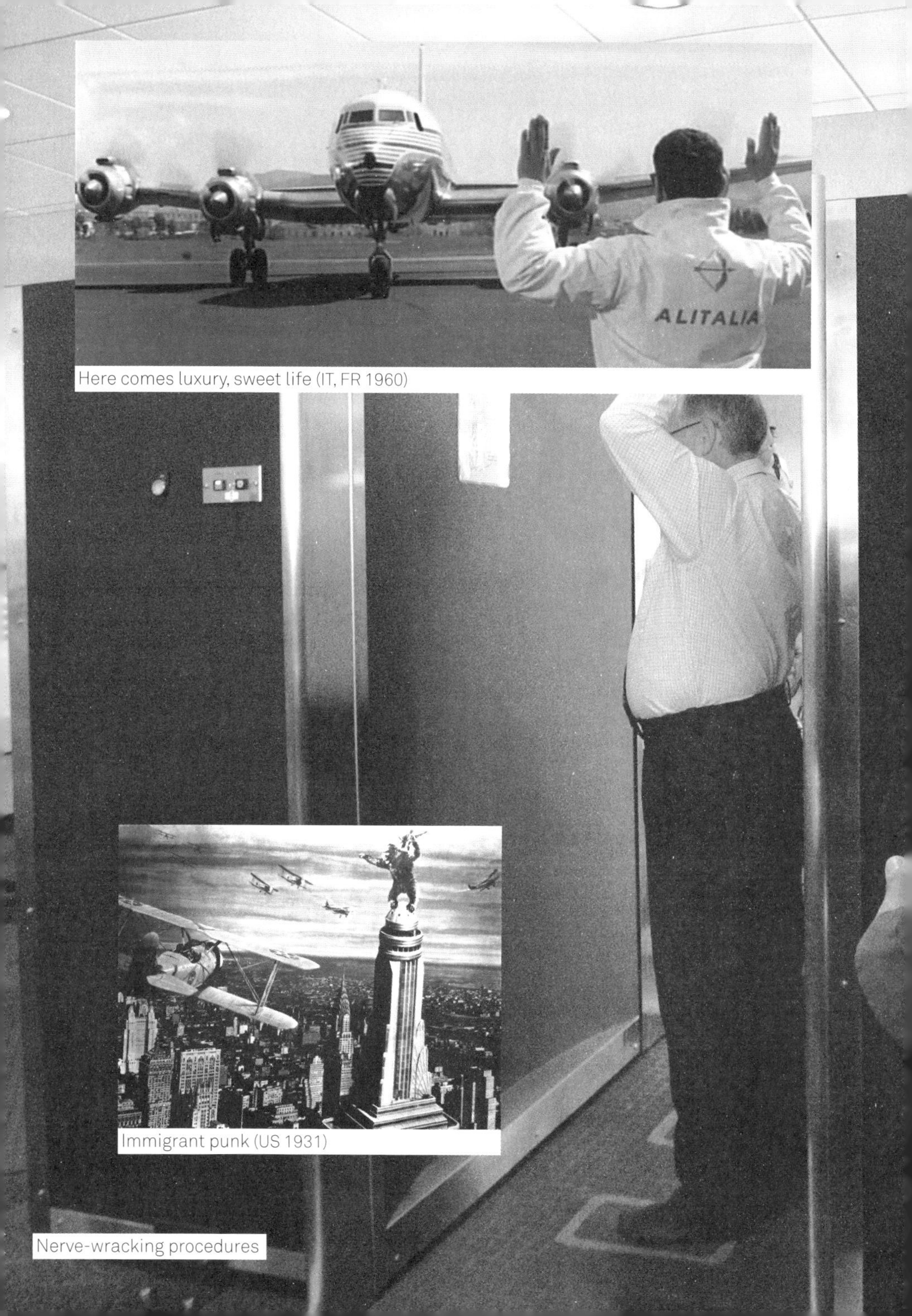

Here comes luxury, sweet life (IT, FR 1960)

Immigrant punk (US 1931)

Nerve-wracking procedures

sunshine. For innumerable men such an experience has meant mental and spiritual destruction, but Barnet, in spite of his bodily gravitation towards comfort, showed himself, when put to the test, of the more valiant modern quality. He was saturated with the creative stoicism of the heroic times that were already dawning, and he took his difficulties and discomforts stoutly as his appointed material, and turned them to expression.

Indeed, in his book he thanks fortune for them. "I might have lived and died," he says, "in that neat fool's paradise of secure lavishness above there. I might never have realized the gathering wrath and sorrow of the ousted and exasperated masses. In the days of my own prosperity things had seemed to me to be very well arranged." Now from his new point of view he was to find they were not arranged at all; that government was a compromise of aggressions and powers and lassitudes, and law a convention between interests, and that the poor and the weak though they had many negligent masters had few friends.

"I had thought things were looked after," he wrote. "It was with a kind of amazement that I tramped the roads and starved—and found that no one in particular cared."

He was turned out of his lodging in a backward part of London.

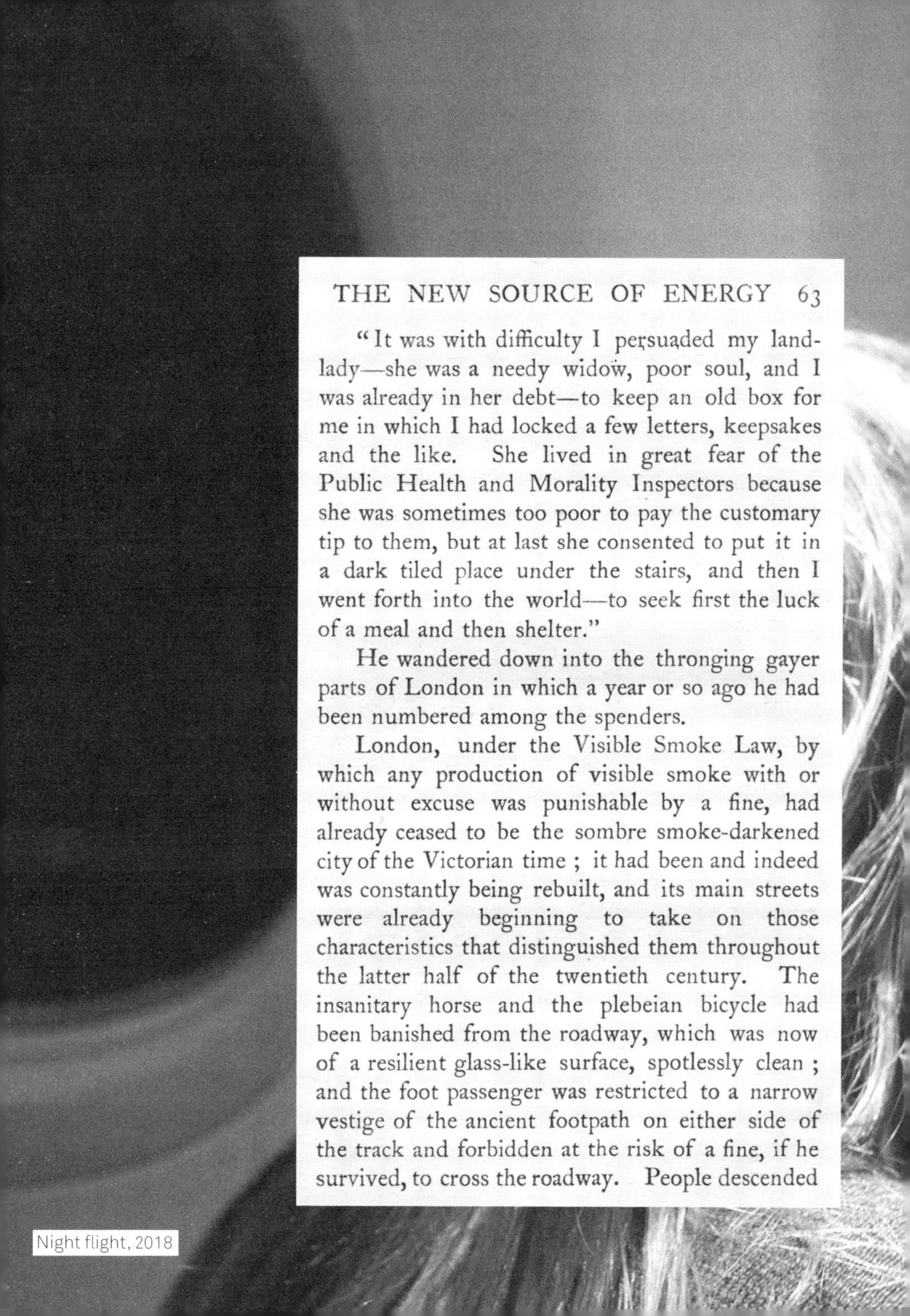

"It was with difficulty I persuaded my landlady—she was a needy widow, poor soul, and I was already in her debt—to keep an old box for me in which I had locked a few letters, keepsakes and the like. She lived in great fear of the Public Health and Morality Inspectors because she was sometimes too poor to pay the customary tip to them, but at last she consented to put it in a dark tiled place under the stairs, and then I went forth into the world—to seek first the luck of a meal and then shelter."

He wandered down into the thronging gayer parts of London in which a year or so ago he had been numbered among the spenders.

London, under the Visible Smoke Law, by which any production of visible smoke with or without excuse was punishable by a fine, had already ceased to be the sombre smoke-darkened city of the Victorian time; it had been and indeed was constantly being rebuilt, and its main streets were already beginning to take on those characteristics that distinguished them throughout the latter half of the twentieth century. The insanitary horse and the plebeian bicycle had been banished from the roadway, which was now of a resilient glass-like surface, spotlessly clean; and the foot passenger was restricted to a narrow vestige of the ancient footpath on either side of the track and forbidden at the risk of a fine, if he survived, to cross the roadway. People descended

Night flight, 2018

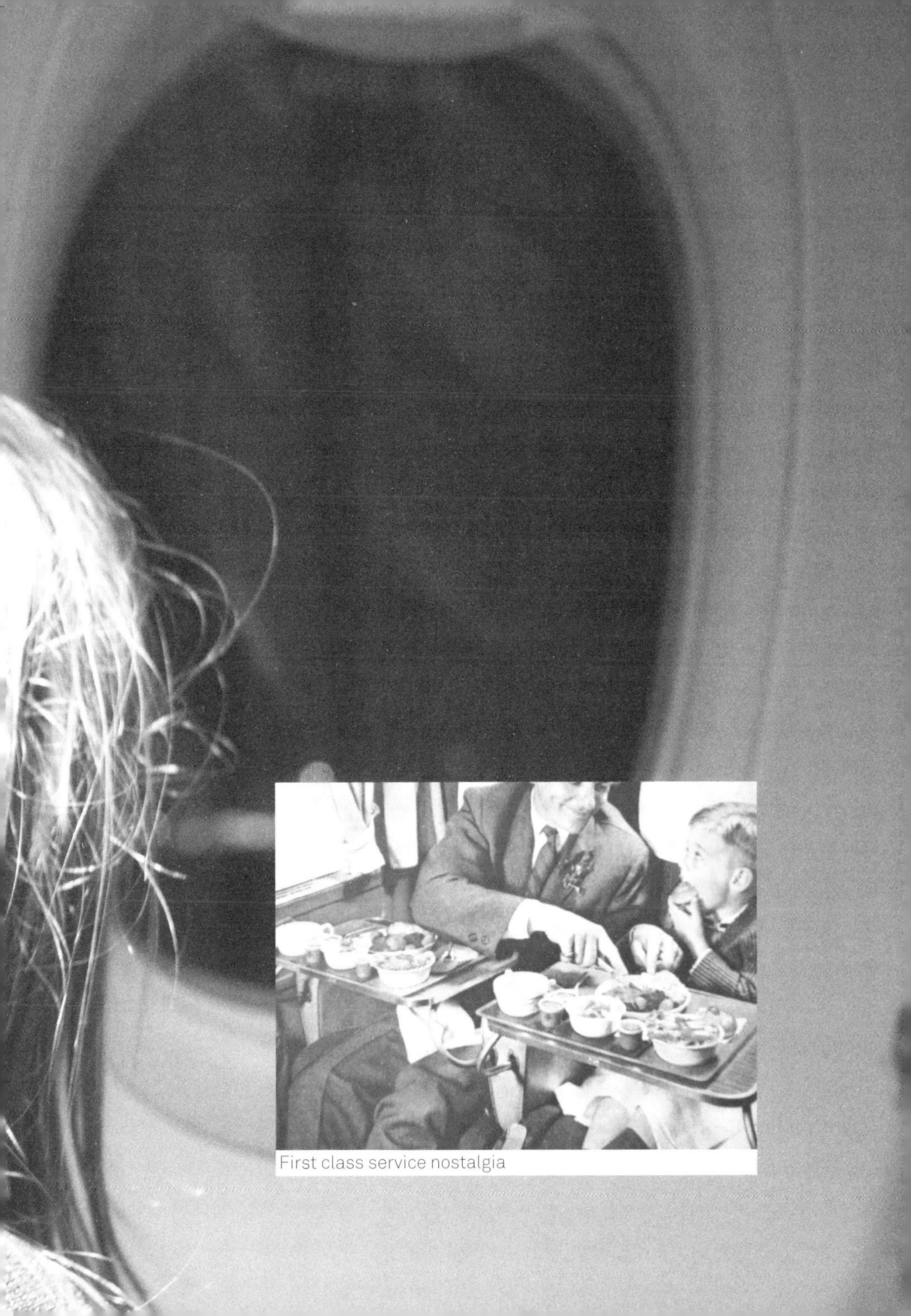

First class service nostalgia

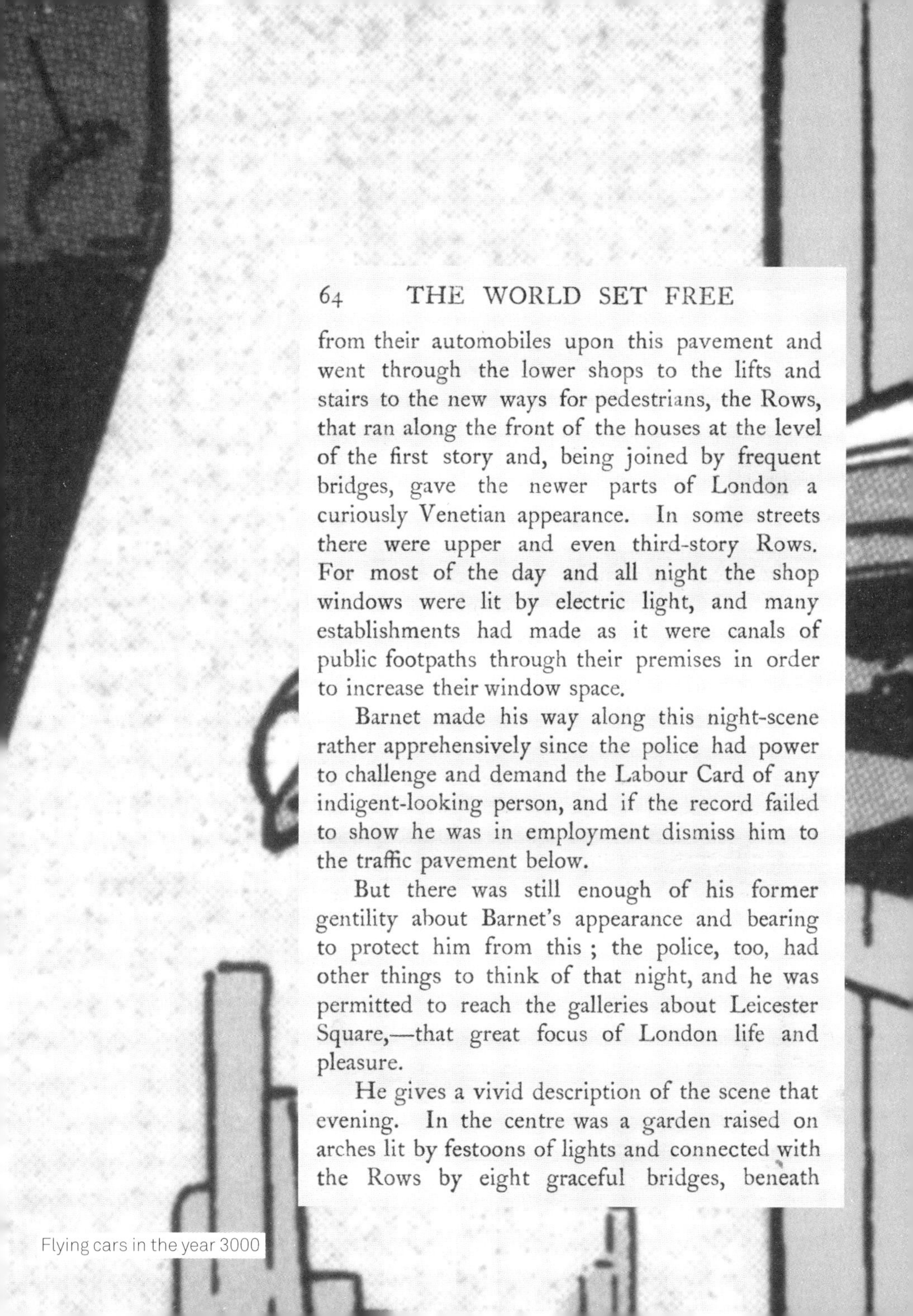

from their automobiles upon this pavement and went through the lower shops to the lifts and stairs to the new ways for pedestrians, the Rows, that ran along the front of the houses at the level of the first story and, being joined by frequent bridges, gave the newer parts of London a curiously Venetian appearance. In some streets there were upper and even third-story Rows. For most of the day and all night the shop windows were lit by electric light, and many establishments had made as it were canals of public footpaths through their premises in order to increase their window space.

Barnet made his way along this night-scene rather apprehensively since the police had power to challenge and demand the Labour Card of any indigent-looking person, and if the record failed to show he was in employment dismiss him to the traffic pavement below.

But there was still enough of his former gentility about Barnet's appearance and bearing to protect him from this ; the police, too, had other things to think of that night, and he was permitted to reach the galleries about Leicester Square,—that great focus of London life and pleasure.

He gives a vivid description of the scene that evening. In the centre was a garden raised on arches lit by festoons of lights and connected with the Rows by eight graceful bridges, beneath

Flying cars in the year 3000

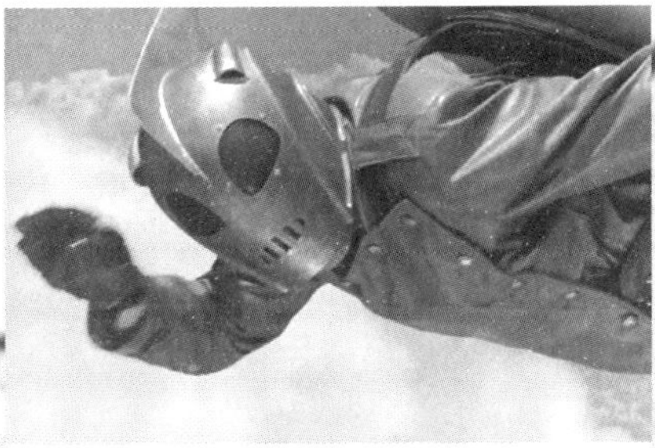

Say Hi! to the jetpack guy (US 1991)

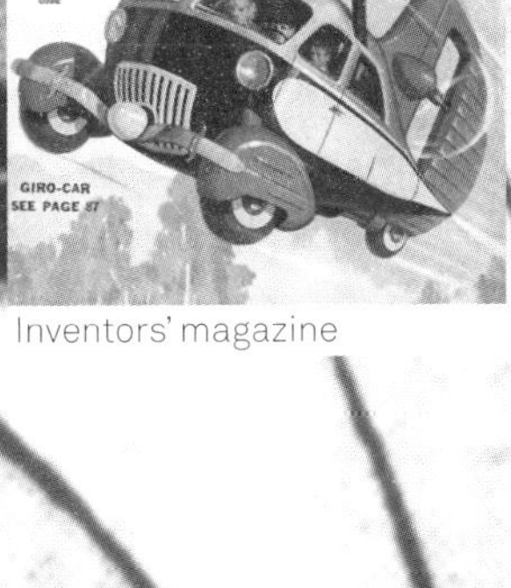

Inventors' magazine

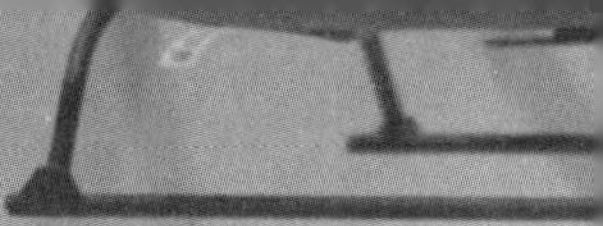

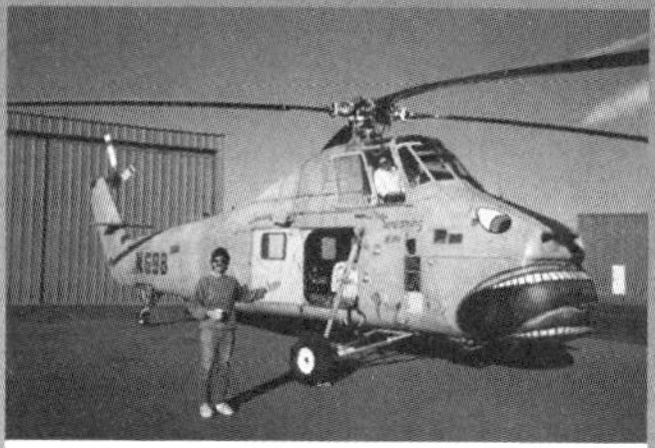
Screaming Mimi

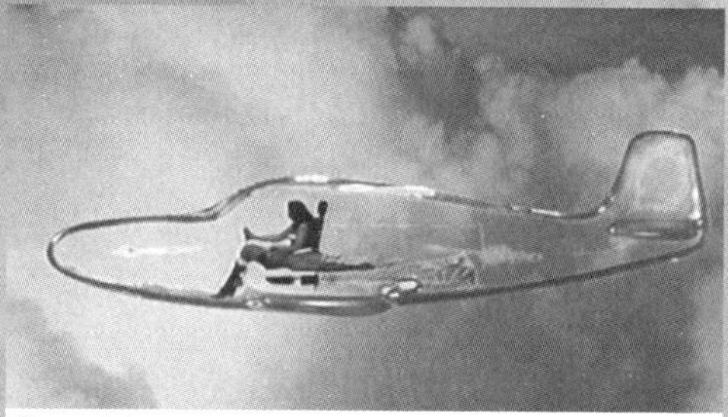
Glass jet

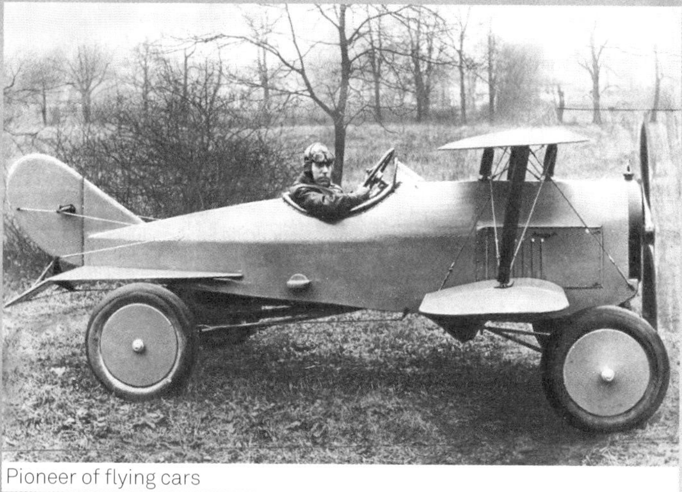
Pioneer of flying cars

Private aviation

which hummed the interlacing streams of motor traffic, pulsating as the current alternated between east and west and north and south. Above rose great frontages of intricate rather than beautiful reinforced porcelain, studded with lights, barred by bold illuminated advertisements, and glowing with reflections. There were the two historical music halls of this place, the Shakespear Memorial Theatre, in which the municipal players revolved perpetually through the cycle of Shakespear's plays, and four other great houses of refreshment and entertainment whose pinnacles streamed up into the blue obscurity of the night. The south side of the square was in dark contrast to the others; it was still being rebuilt, and a lattice of steel bars surmounted by the frozen gestures of monstrous cranes rose over the excavated sites of vanished Victorian buildings.

This framework attracted Barnet's attention for a time to the exclusion of other interests. It was absolutely still, it had a dead rigidity, a stricken inaction, no one was at work upon it and all its machinery was quiet; but the constructors' globes of vacuum light filled its every interstice with a quivering green moonshine and showed alert but motionless—soldier sentinels!

He asked a passing stroller, and was told that the men had struck that day against the use of an

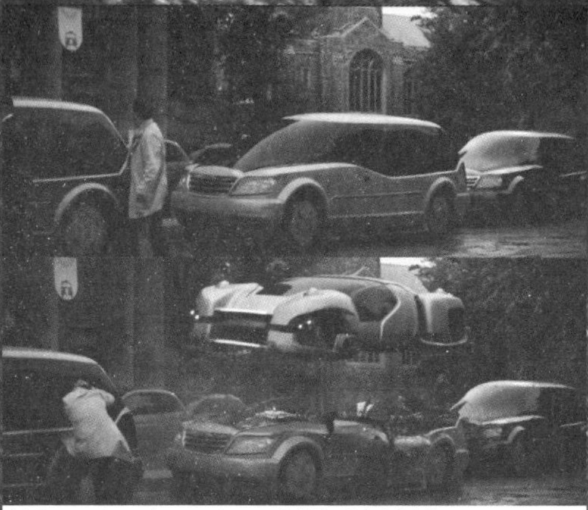
Airbound and steetbound (US, CA 2012)

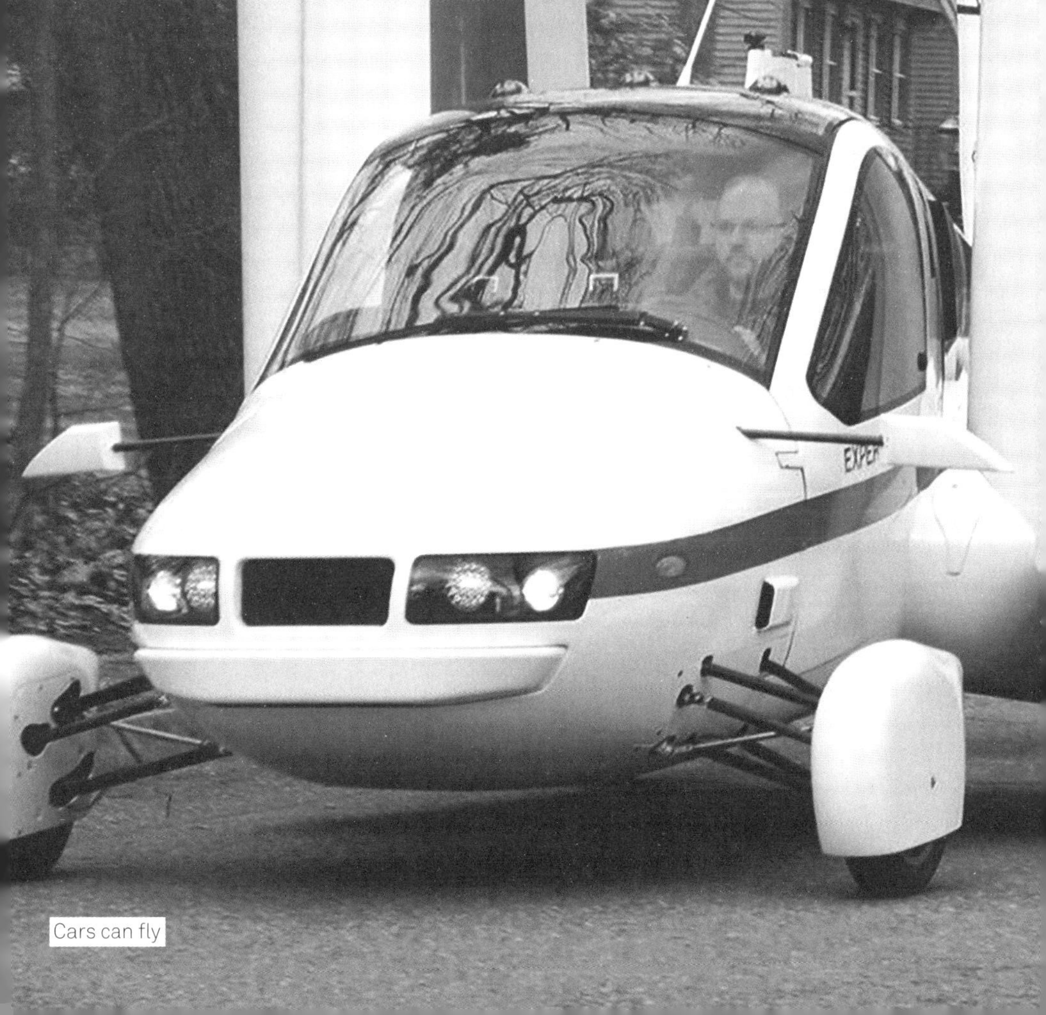
Cars can fly

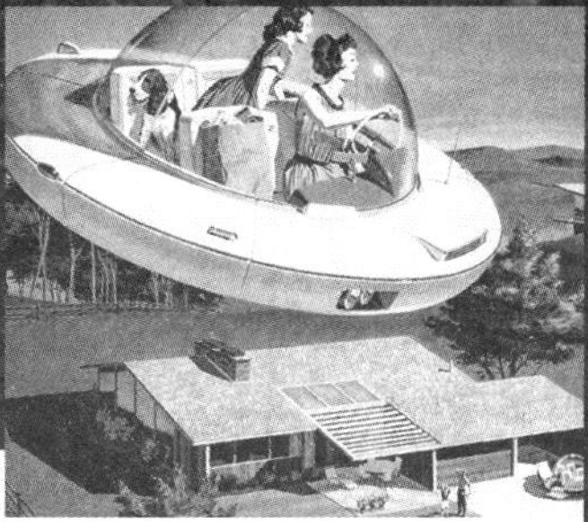
In suburbia

atomic riveter that would have doubled the individual efficiency and halved the number of steel workers.

"Shouldn't wonder if they didn't get chucking bombs," said Barnet's informant, hovered for a moment, and then went on his way to the Alhambra music hall.

Barnet became aware of an excitement in the newspaper kiosks at the corners of the square. Something very sensational had been flashed upon the transparencies. Forgetting for a moment his penniless condition he made his way over a bridge to buy a paper, for in those days the papers, which were printed upon thin sheets of metallic foil, were sold at determinate points by specially licensed purveyors. Half over he stopped short at a change in the traffic below; and was astonished to see that the police signals were restricting vehicles to the half roadway. When presently he got within sight of the transparencies that had replaced the placards of Victorian times, he read of the Great March of the Unemployed that was already in progress through the West End, and so without expenditure he was able to understand what was coming.

He watched, and his book describes this procession which the police had considered it unwise to prevent and which had been spontaneously organized in imitation of the Unemployed Processions of earlier times. He had

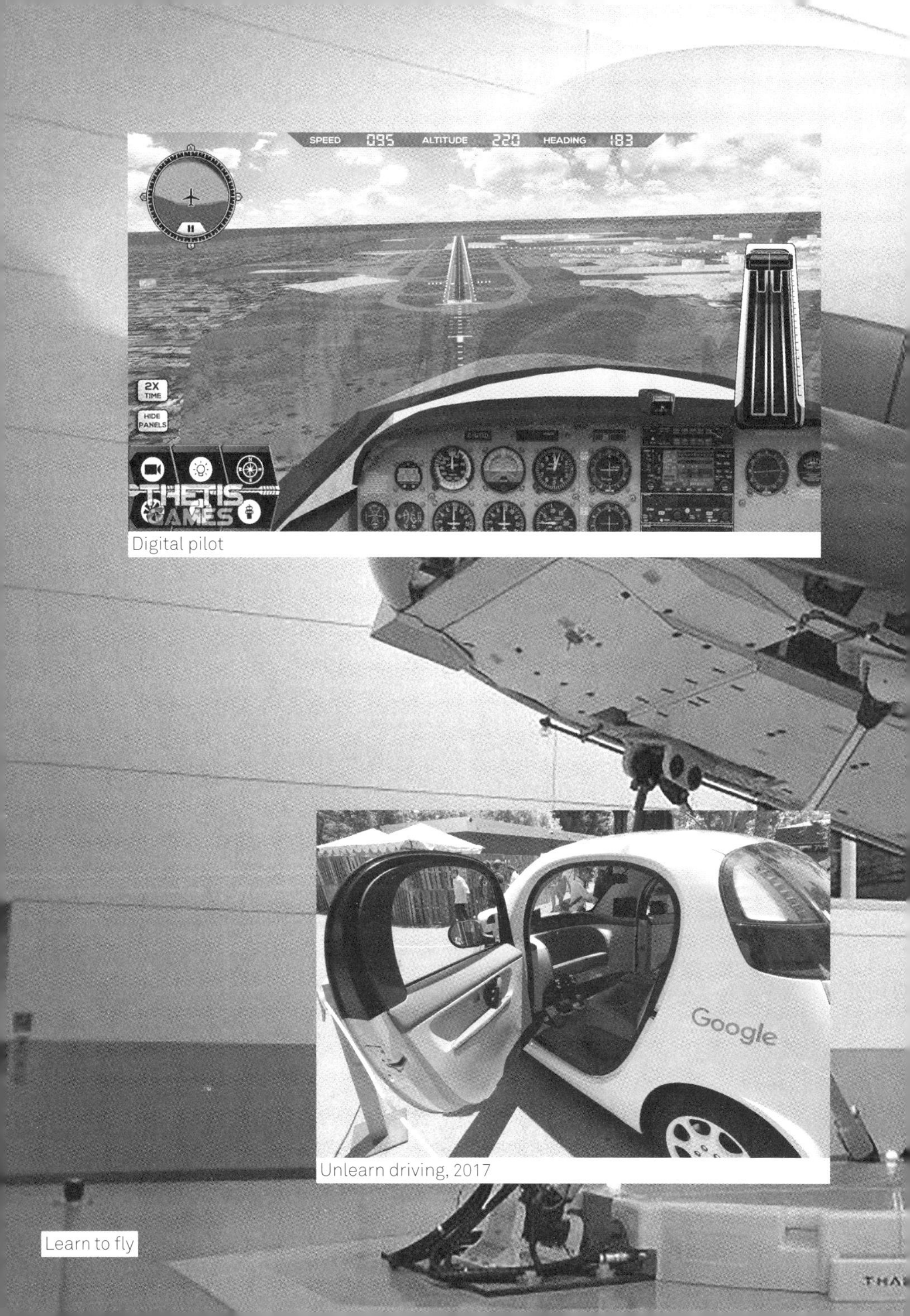

Digital pilot

Unlearn driving, 2017

Learn to fly

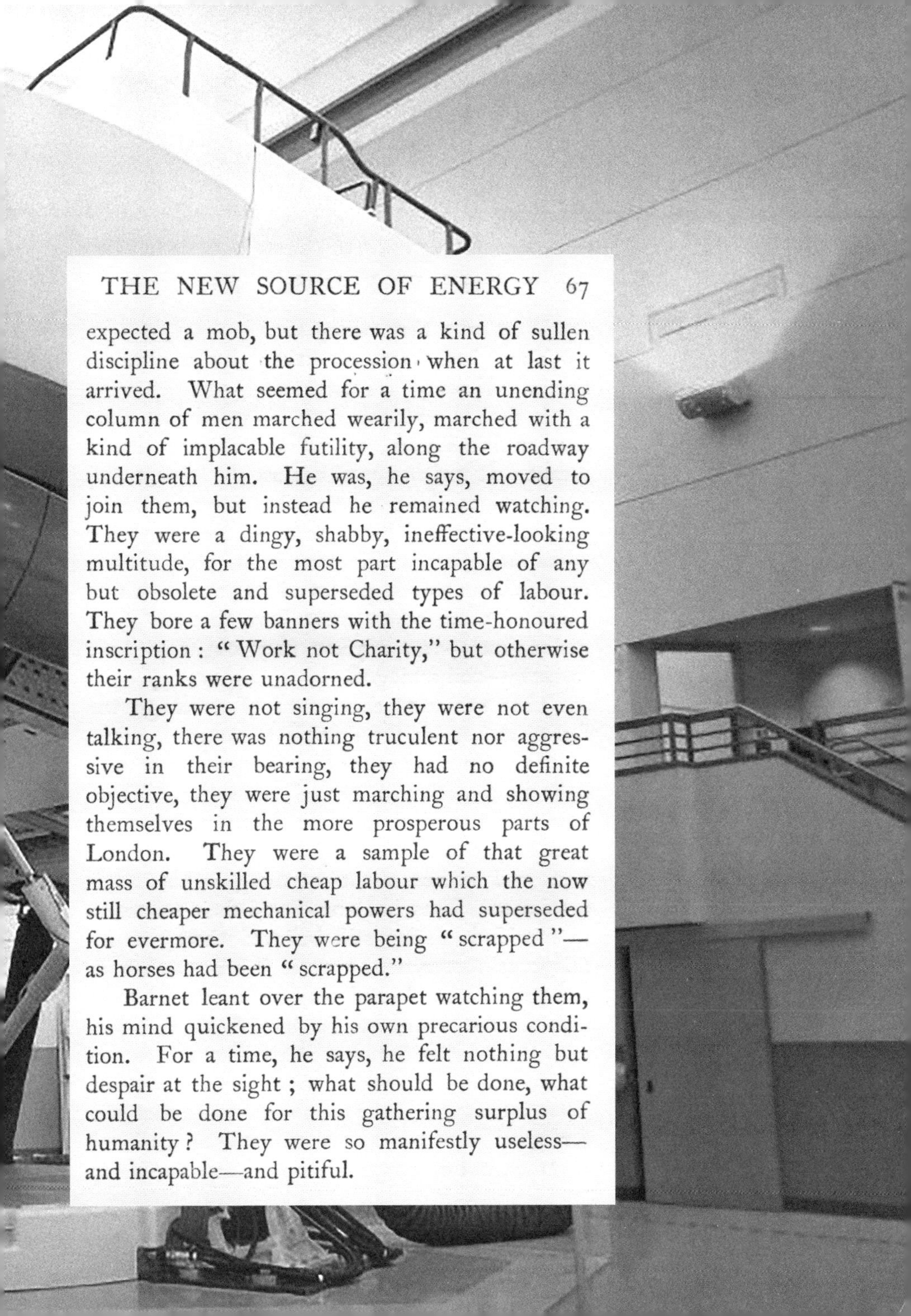

expected a mob, but there was a kind of sullen discipline about the procession when at last it arrived. What seemed for a time an unending column of men marched wearily, marched with a kind of implacable futility, along the roadway underneath him. He was, he says, moved to join them, but instead he remained watching. They were a dingy, shabby, ineffective-looking multitude, for the most part incapable of any but obsolete and superseded types of labour. They bore a few banners with the time-honoured inscription: "Work not Charity," but otherwise their ranks were unadorned.

They were not singing, they were not even talking, there was nothing truculent nor aggressive in their bearing, they had no definite objective, they were just marching and showing themselves in the more prosperous parts of London. They were a sample of that great mass of unskilled cheap labour which the now still cheaper mechanical powers had superseded for evermore. They were being "scrapped"—as horses had been "scrapped."

Barnet leant over the parapet watching them, his mind quickened by his own precarious condition. For a time, he says, he felt nothing but despair at the sight; what should be done, what could be done for this gathering surplus of humanity? They were so manifestly useless—and incapable—and pitiful.

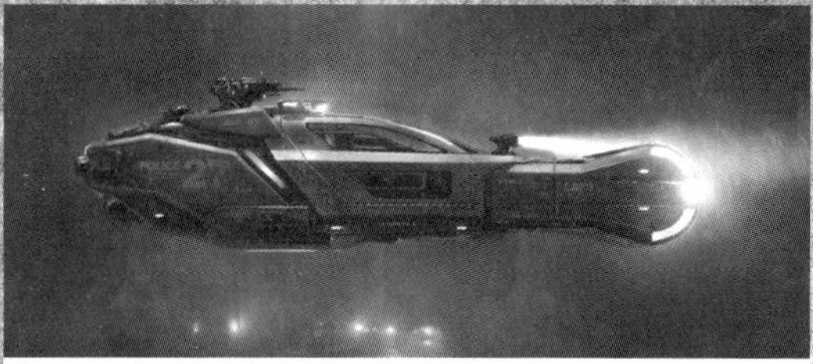
Peugeot in 2049 (US, UK, HU, CA 2017)

What were they asking for?

They had been overtaken by unexpected things. Nobody had foreseen——

It flashed suddenly into his mind just what the multitudinous shambling enigma below meant. It was an appeal against the unexpected, an appeal to those others who, more fortunate, seemed wiser and more powerful, for something —for *intelligence*. This mute mass, weary footed, rank following rank, protested its persuasion that some of these others must have foreseen these dislocations,—that anyhow they ought to have foreseen—and arranged.

That was what this crowd of wreckage was feeling and seeking so dumbly to assert.

"Things came to me like the turning on of a light in a darkened room," he says. "These men were praying to their fellow creatures as once they prayed to God! The last thing that men will realize about anything is that it is inanimate. They had transferred their animation to mankind. They still believed there was intelligence somewhere, even if it was careless or malignant. . . . It had only to be aroused to be conscience-stricken, to be moved to exertion. . . . And I saw too that as yet *there was no such intelligence*. The world waits for intelligence. That intelligence has still to be made, that will for good and order has still to be gathered together, out of scraps of impulse and wandering

Parade and airport in Moscow

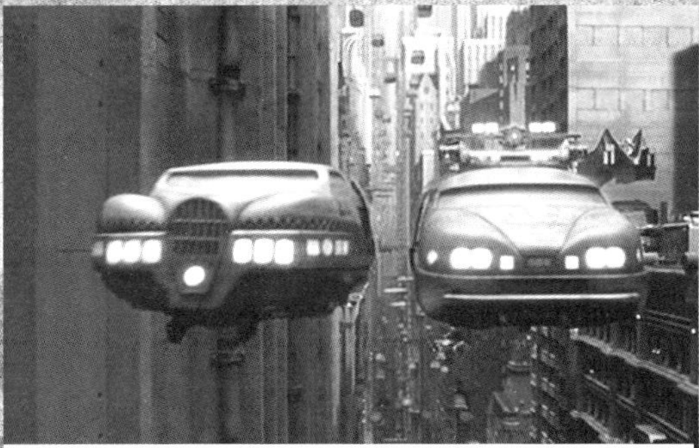

Speeding ticket (FR 1997)

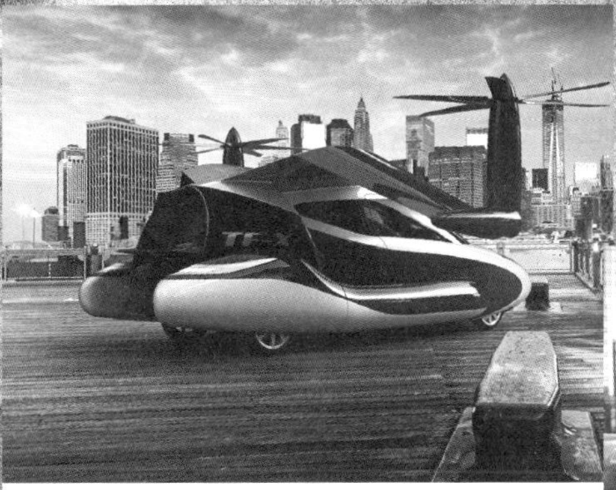

Drone taxi, 2017

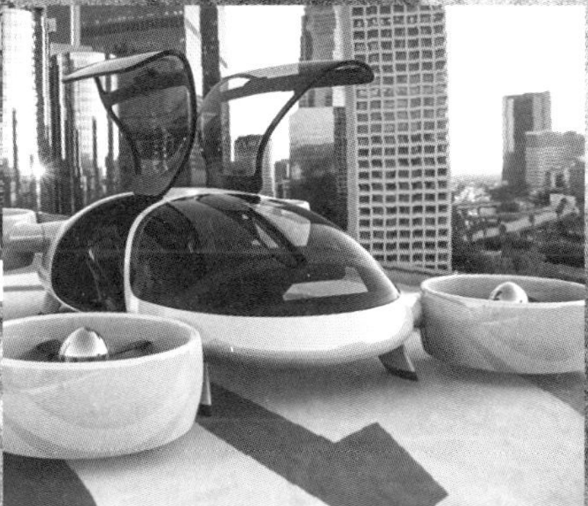

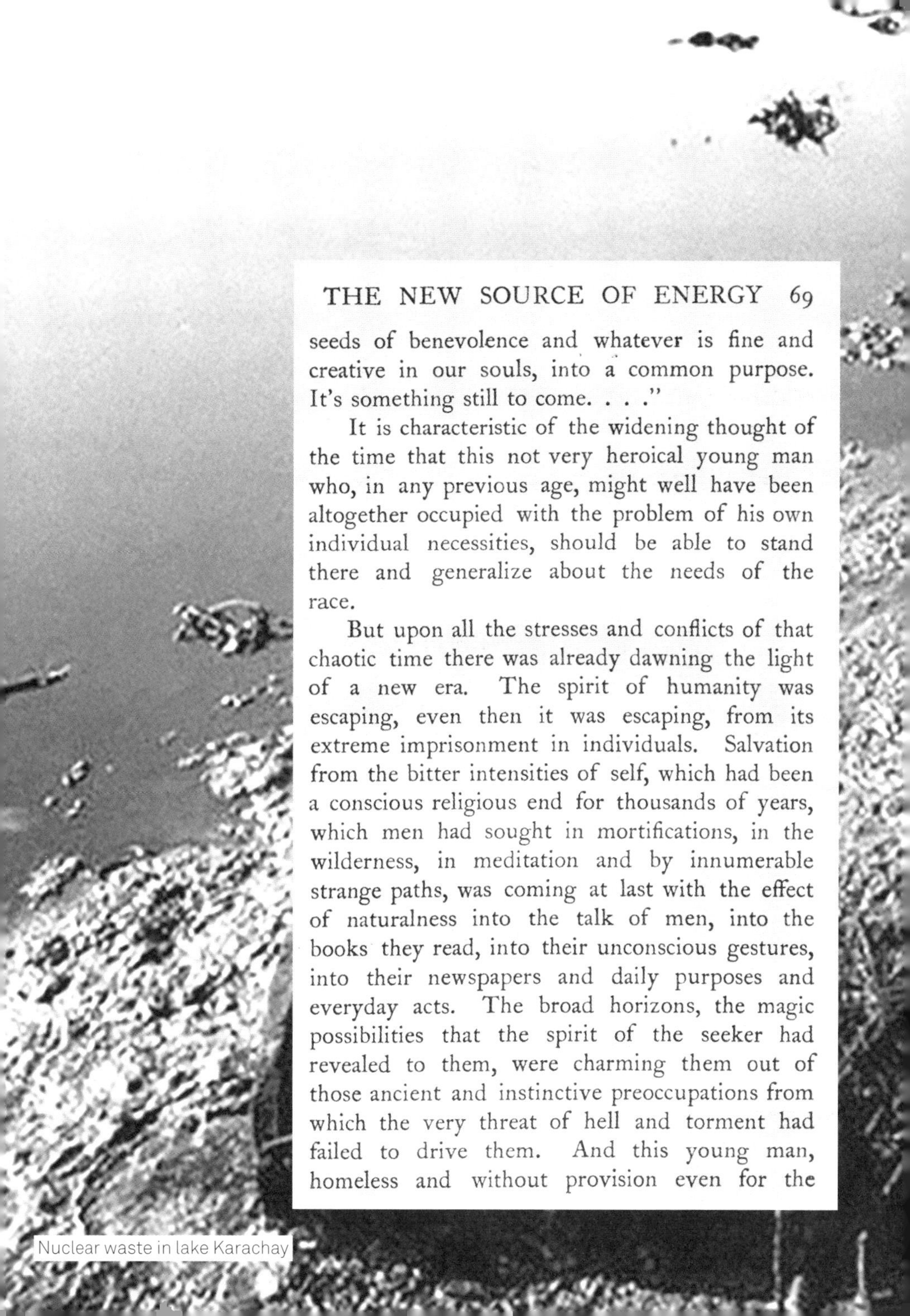

seeds of benevolence and whatever is fine and creative in our souls, into a common purpose. It's something still to come. . . ."

It is characteristic of the widening thought of the time that this not very heroical young man who, in any previous age, might well have been altogether occupied with the problem of his own individual necessities, should be able to stand there and generalize about the needs of the race.

But upon all the stresses and conflicts of that chaotic time there was already dawning the light of a new era. The spirit of humanity was escaping, even then it was escaping, from its extreme imprisonment in individuals. Salvation from the bitter intensities of self, which had been a conscious religious end for thousands of years, which men had sought in mortifications, in the wilderness, in meditation and by innumerable strange paths, was coming at last with the effect of naturalness into the talk of men, into the books they read, into their unconscious gestures, into their newspapers and daily purposes and everyday acts. The broad horizons, the magic possibilities that the spirit of the seeker had revealed to them, were charming them out of those ancient and instinctive preoccupations from which the very threat of hell and torment had failed to drive them. And this young man, homeless and without provision even for the

Nuclear waste in lake Karachay

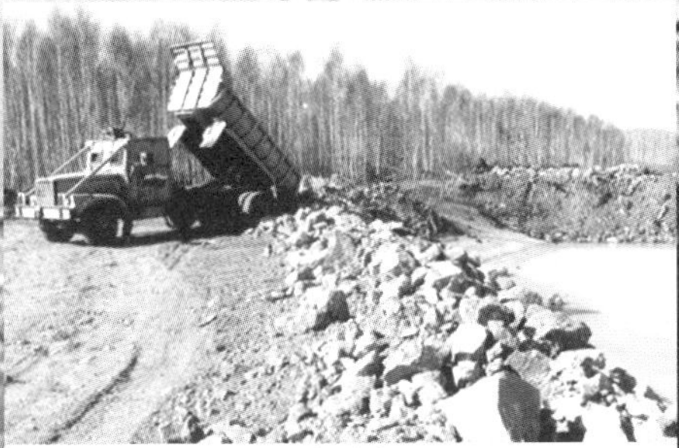

Dumping waste into the lake

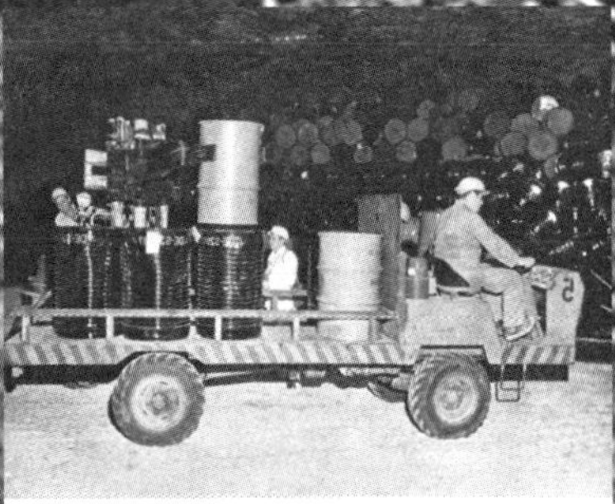

Storage of nuclear waste

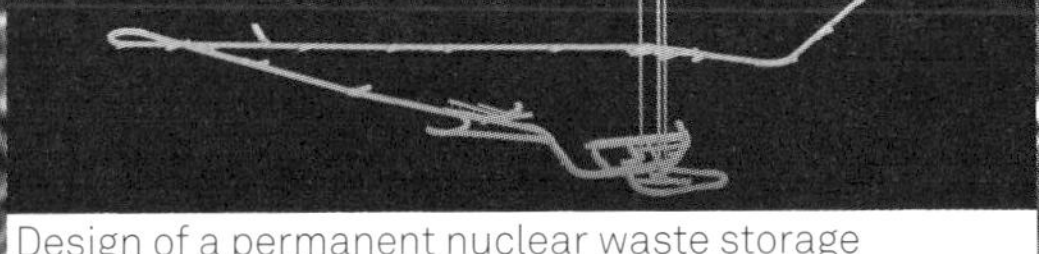

Design of a permanent nuclear waste storage

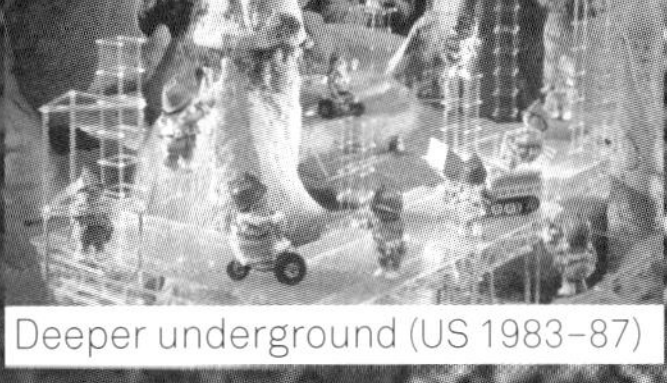

Deeper underground (US 1983–87)

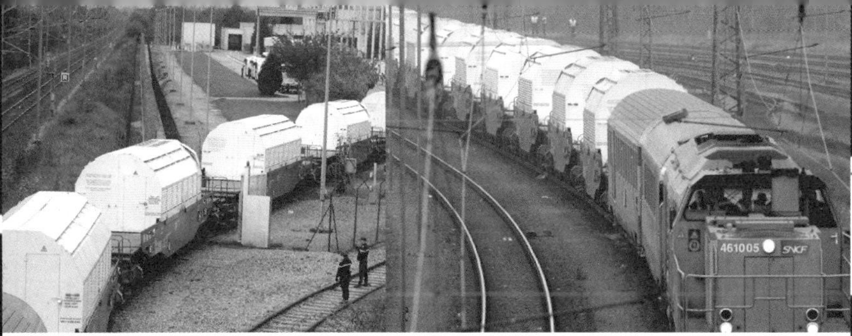

Trains carrying nuclear waste

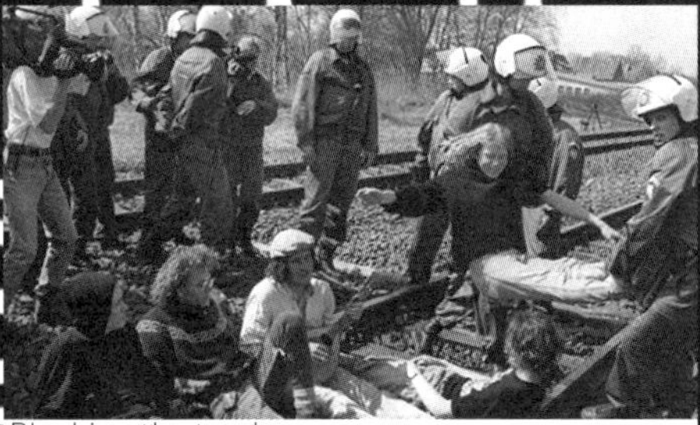
Blocking the tracks

Details of another atomic train

immediate hours, in the presence of social disorganization, distress and perplexity, in a blazing wilderness of thoughtless pleasure that blotted out the stars, could think as he tells us he thought.

"I saw life plain," he wrote. "I saw the gigantic task before us, and the very splendour of its intricate and immeasurable difficulty filled me with exaltation. I saw that we have still to discover government, that we have still to discover education, which is the necessary reciprocal of government, and that all this—in which my own little speck of a life was so manifestly overwhelmed—this and its yesterday in Greece and Rome and Egypt were nothing, the mere first dust swirls of the beginning, the movements and dim murmurings of a sleeper who will presently be awake. . . ."

§ 7

And then the story tells, with an engaging simplicity, of his descent from this ecstatic vision of reality.

"Presently I found myself again and I was beginning to feel cold and a little hungry."

He bethought himself of the John Burns Relief Offices which stood upon the Thames Embankment. He made his way through the galleries of the booksellers and the National Gallery, which had been open continuously day

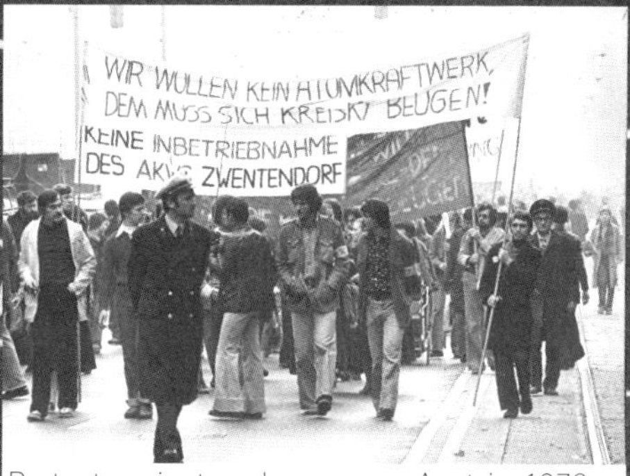

Protest against nuclear energy, Austria, 1978

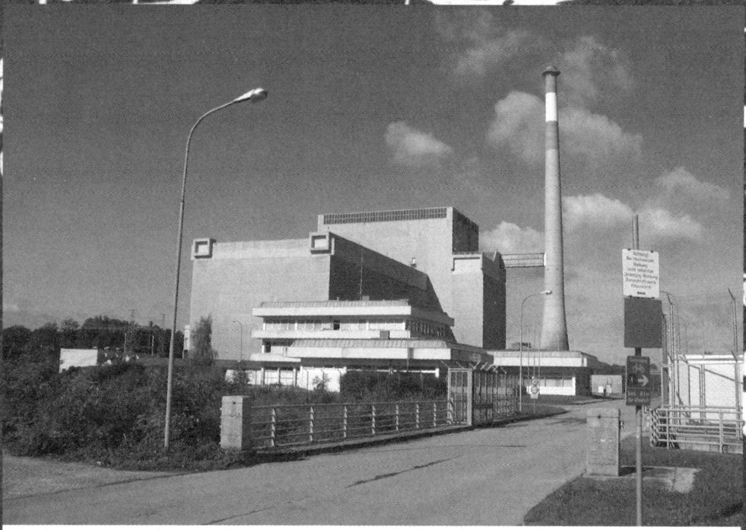

Nuclear power plant in Austria, never used after the populaton protested, 2008

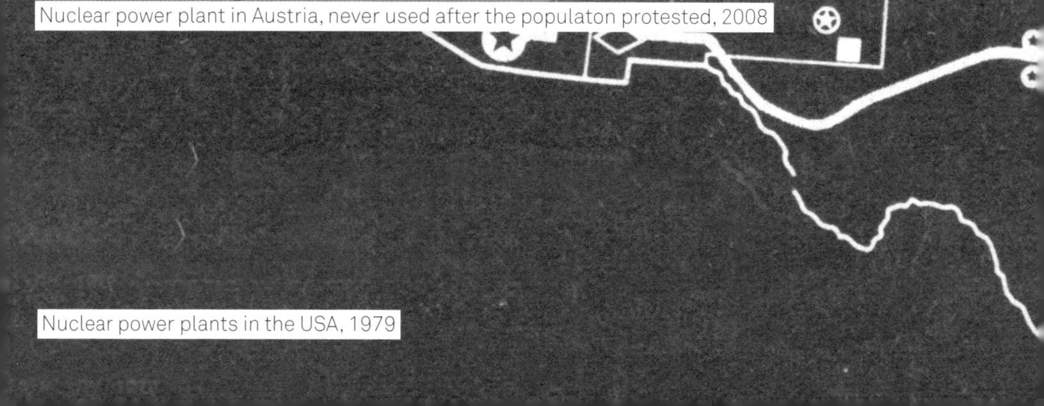

Nuclear power plants in the USA, 1979

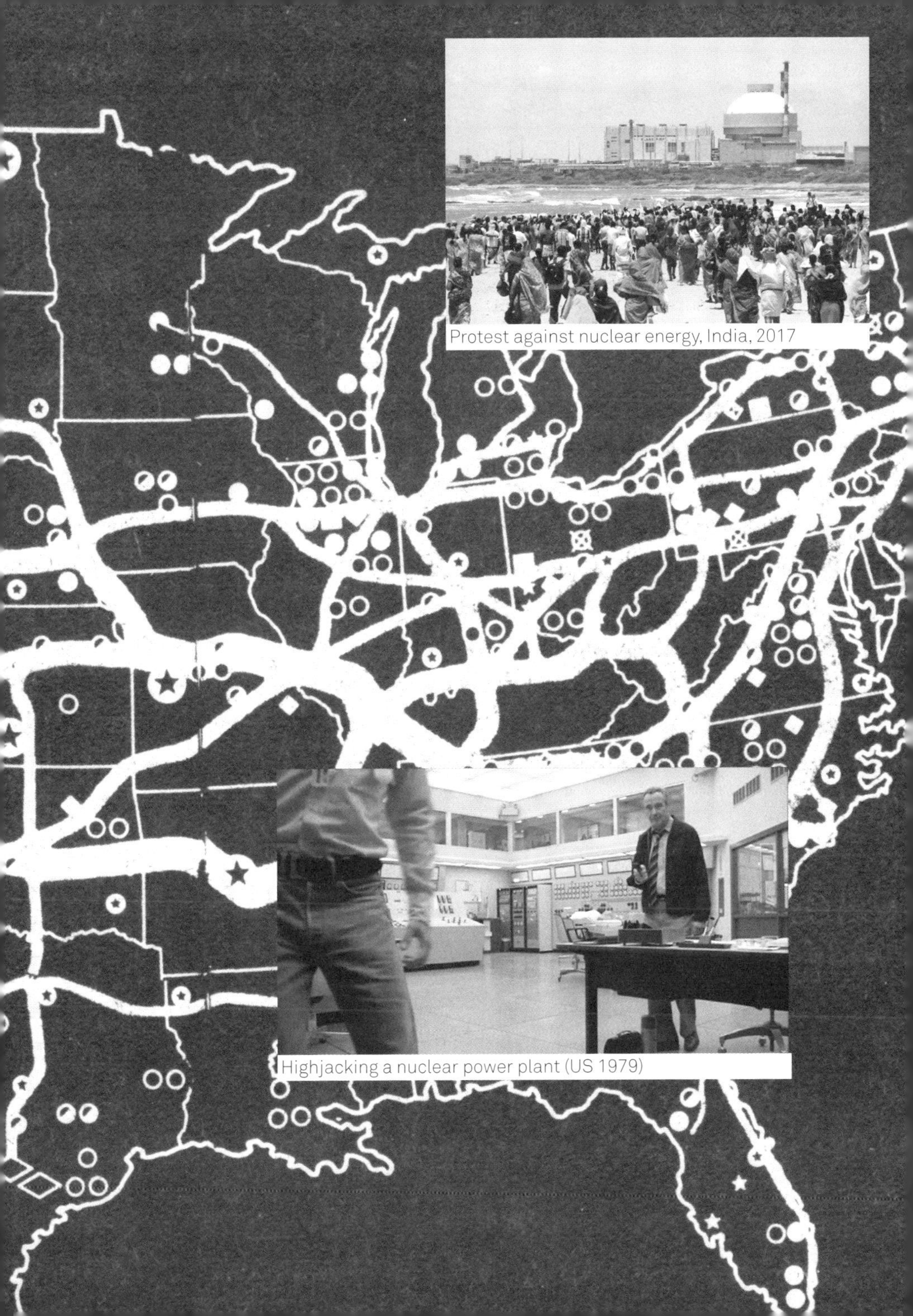

Protest against nuclear energy, India, 2017

Highjacking a nuclear power plant (US 1979)

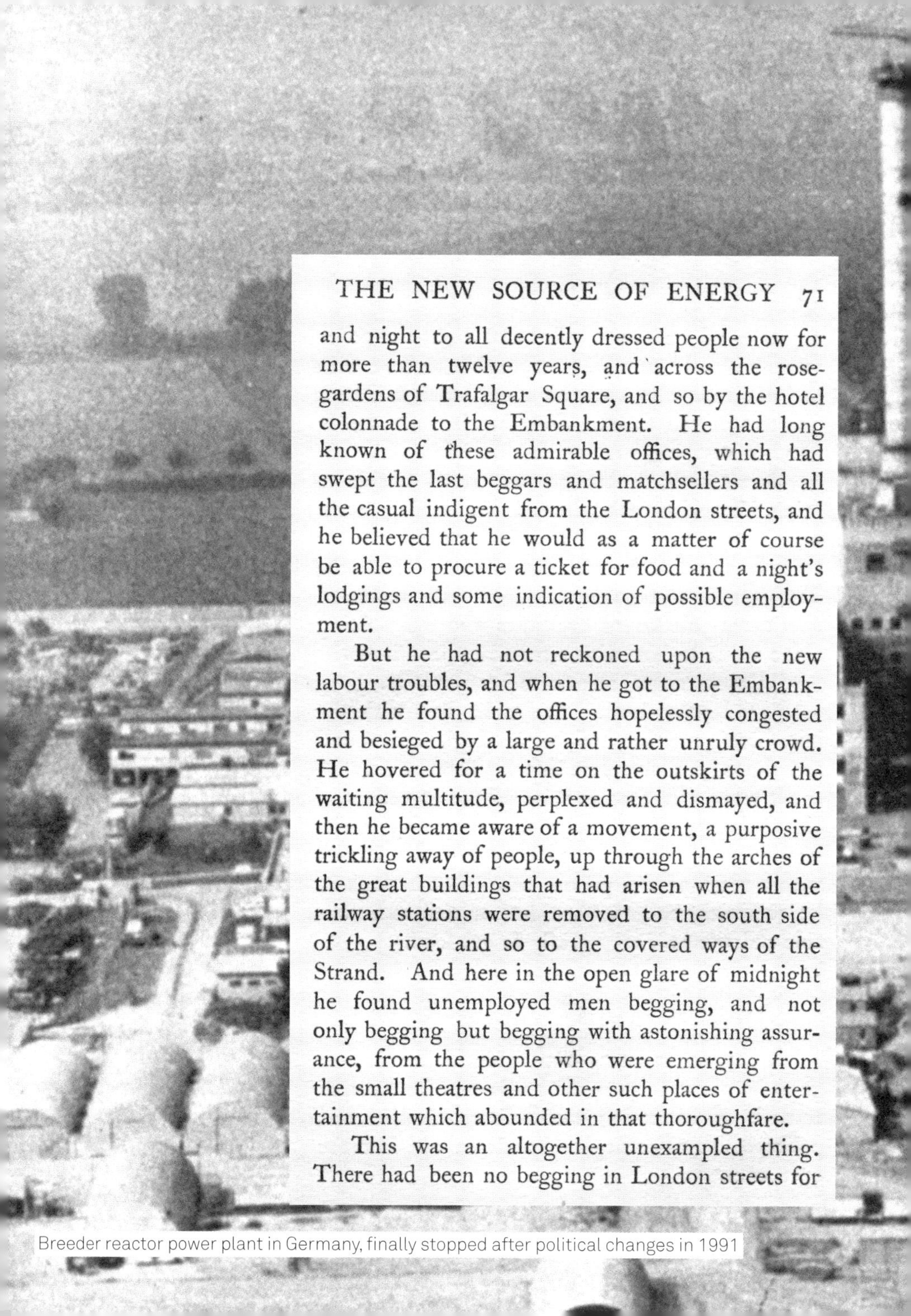

and night to all decently dressed people now for more than twelve years, and across the rose-gardens of Trafalgar Square, and so by the hotel colonnade to the Embankment. He had long known of these admirable offices, which had swept the last beggars and matchsellers and all the casual indigent from the London streets, and he believed that he would as a matter of course be able to procure a ticket for food and a night's lodgings and some indication of possible employment.

But he had not reckoned upon the new labour troubles, and when he got to the Embankment he found the offices hopelessly congested and besieged by a large and rather unruly crowd. He hovered for a time on the outskirts of the waiting multitude, perplexed and dismayed, and then he became aware of a movement, a purposive trickling away of people, up through the arches of the great buildings that had arisen when all the railway stations were removed to the south side of the river, and so to the covered ways of the Strand. And here in the open glare of midnight he found unemployed men begging, and not only begging but begging with astonishing assurance, from the people who were emerging from the small theatres and other such places of entertainment which abounded in that thoroughfare.

This was an altogether unexampled thing. There had been no begging in London streets for

Breeder reactor power plant in Germany, finally stopped after political changes in 1991

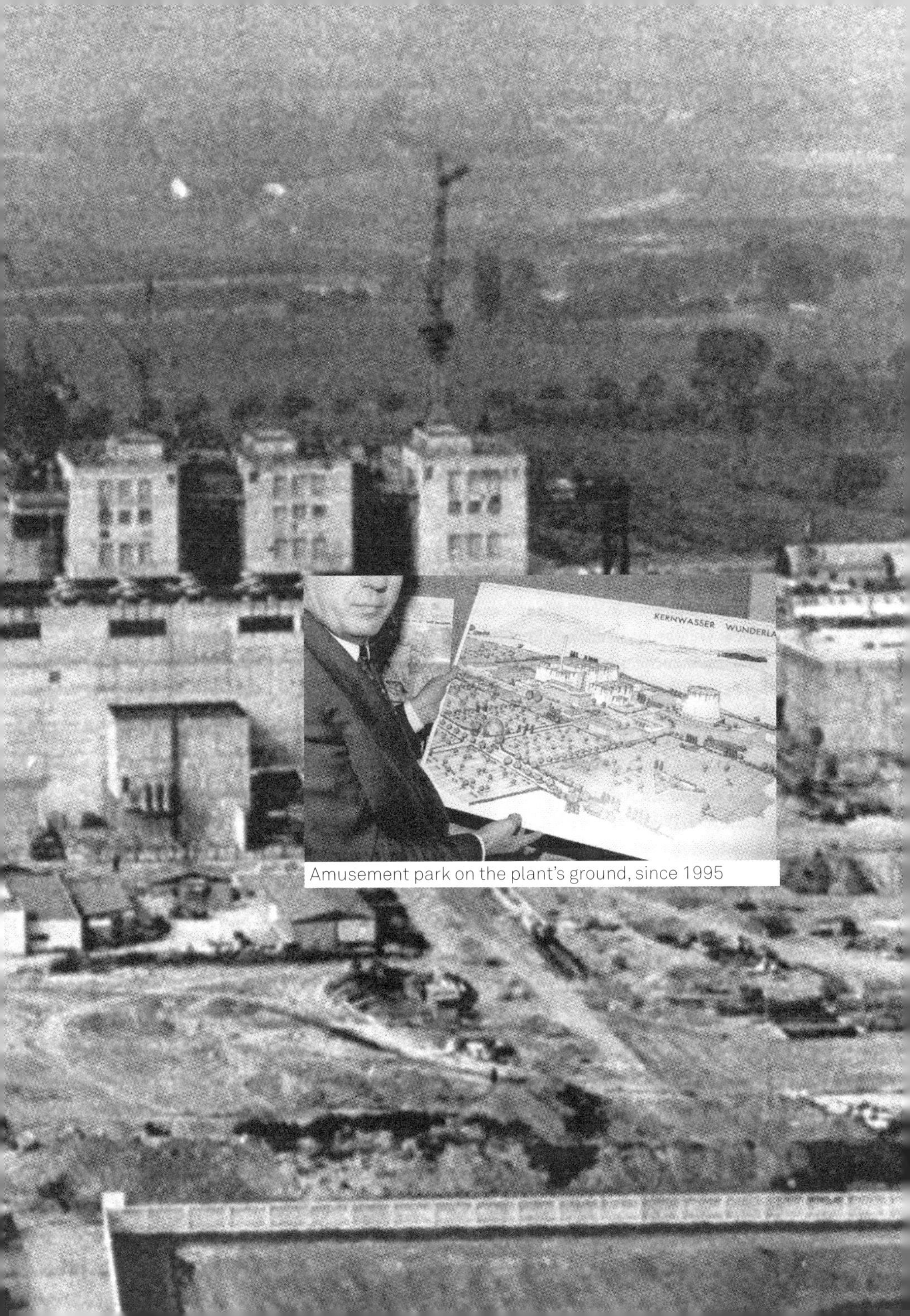

Amusement park on the plant's ground, since 1995

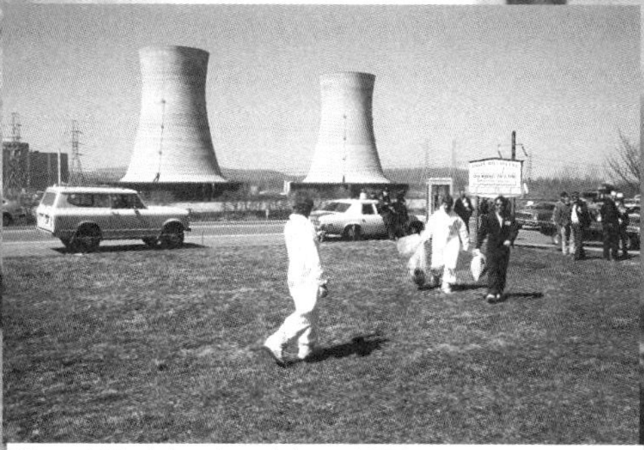

Three Mile Island accident, 1979

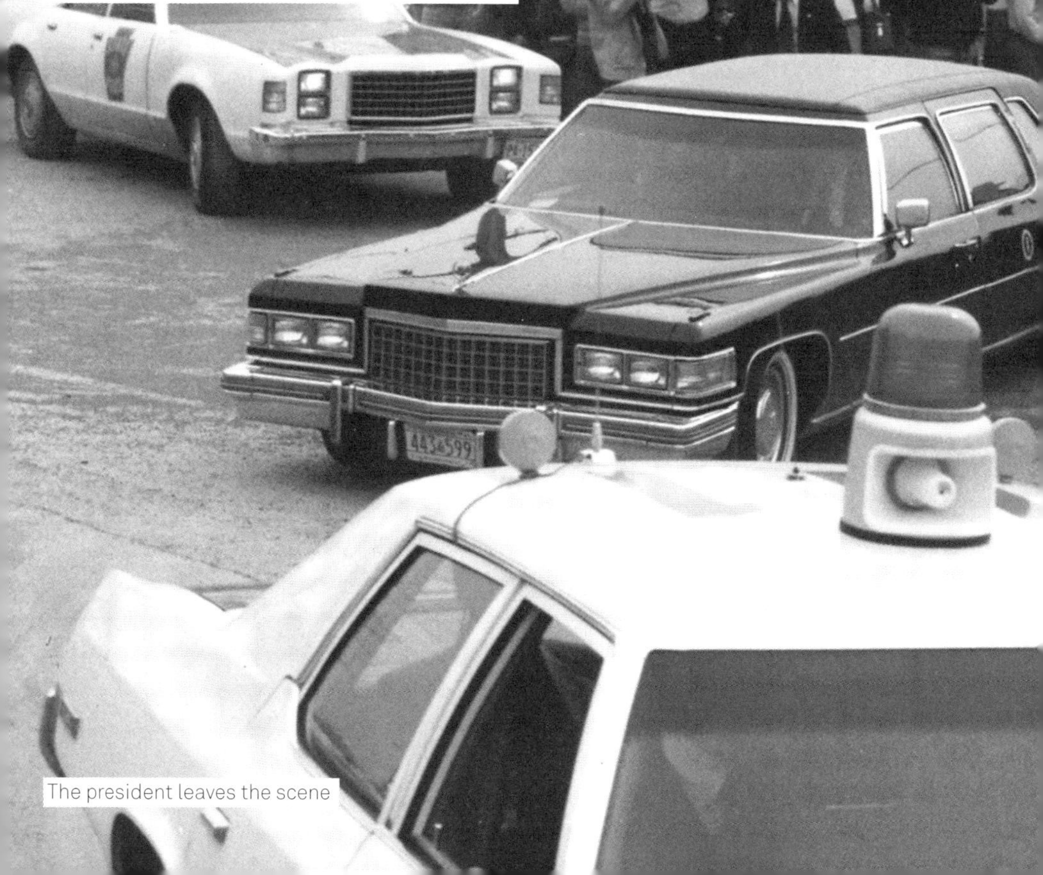

The president leaves the scene

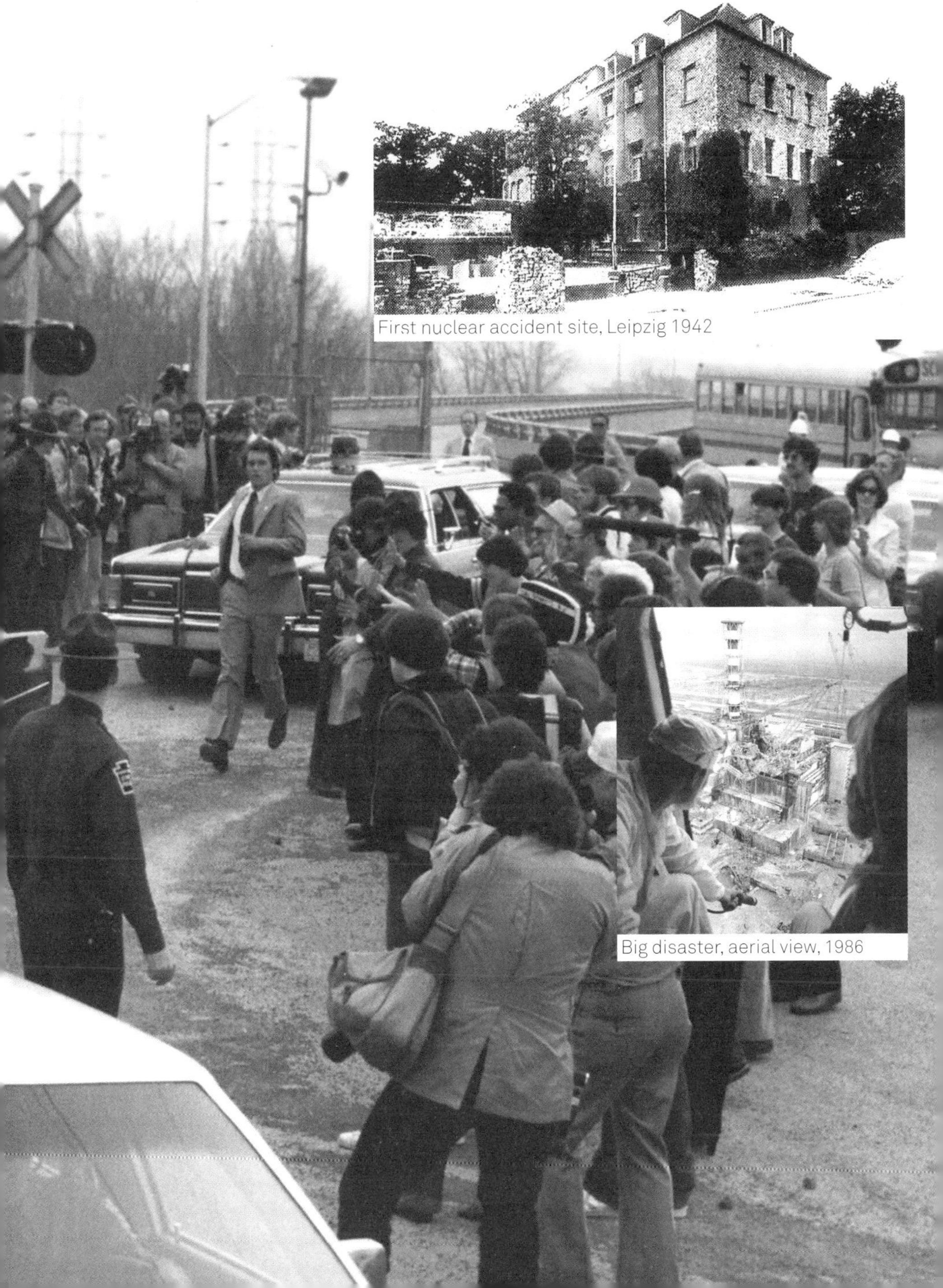

First nuclear accident site, Leipzig 1942

Big disaster, aerial view, 1986

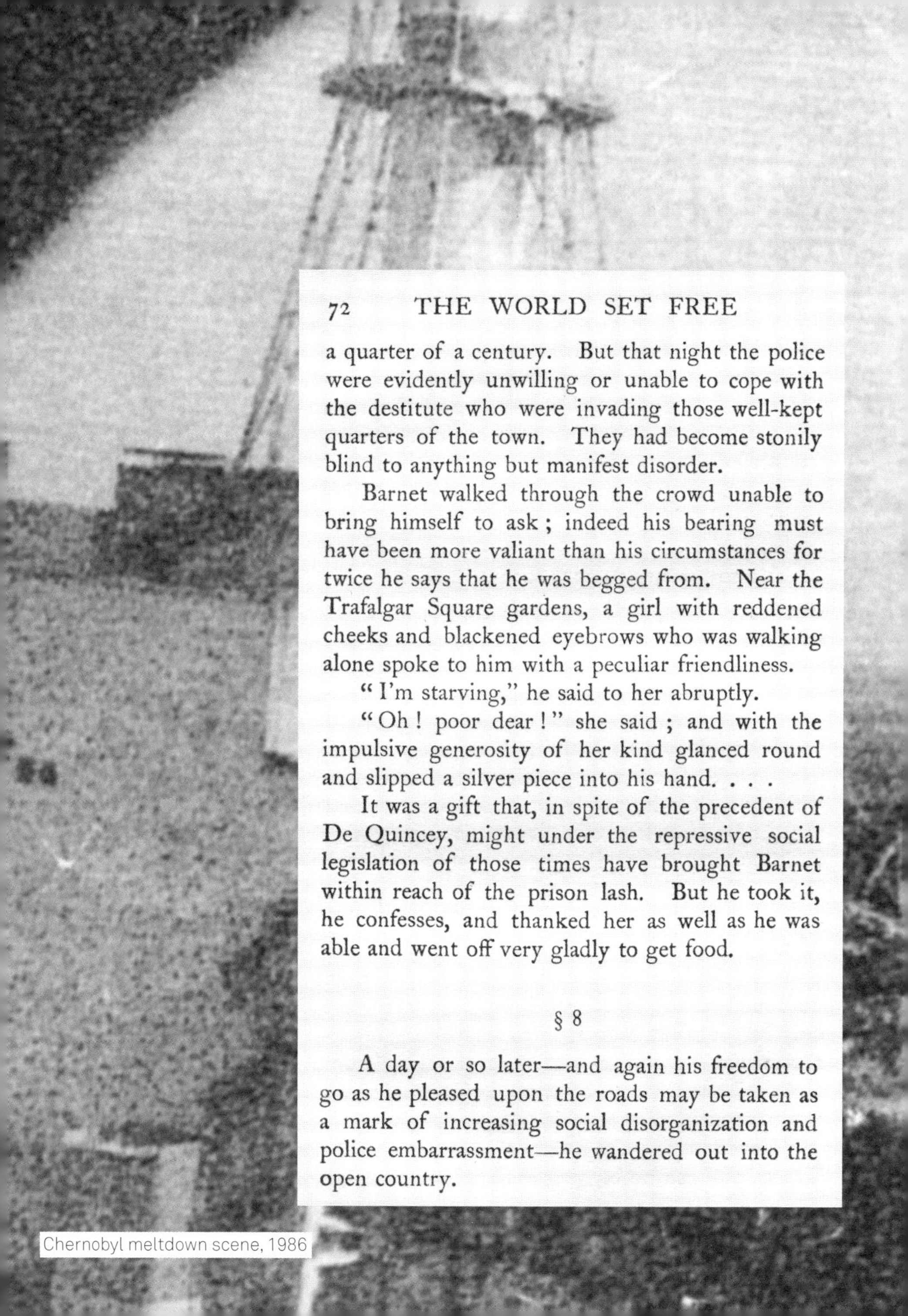

a quarter of a century. But that night the police were evidently unwilling or unable to cope with the destitute who were invading those well-kept quarters of the town. They had become stonily blind to anything but manifest disorder.

Barnet walked through the crowd unable to bring himself to ask ; indeed his bearing must have been more valiant than his circumstances for twice he says that he was begged from. Near the Trafalgar Square gardens, a girl with reddened cheeks and blackened eyebrows who was walking alone spoke to him with a peculiar friendliness.

"I'm starving," he said to her abruptly.

"Oh ! poor dear !" she said ; and with the impulsive generosity of her kind glanced round and slipped a silver piece into his hand. . . .

It was a gift that, in spite of the precedent of De Quincey, might under the repressive social legislation of those times have brought Barnet within reach of the prison lash. But he took it, he confesses, and thanked her as well as he was able and went off very gladly to get food.

§ 8

A day or so later—and again his freedom to go as he pleased upon the roads may be taken as a mark of increasing social disorganization and police embarrassment—he wandered out into the open country.

Chernobyl meltdown scene, 1986

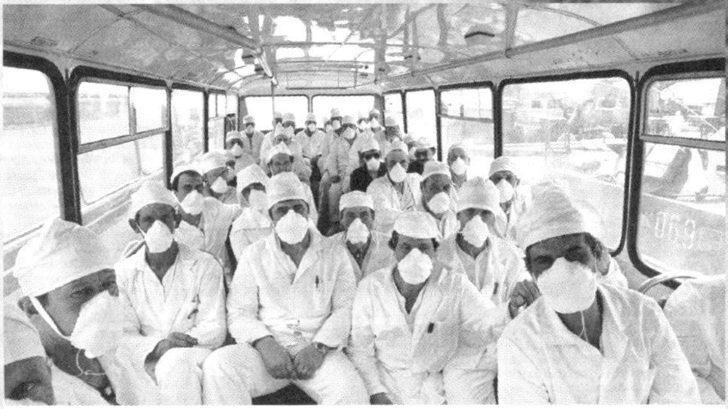

Chernobyl first helping crew

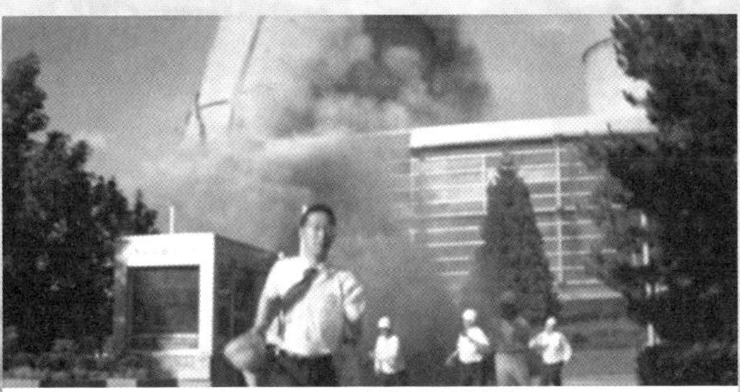

Nuclear catastrophe in Japan, (JP, US 2014)

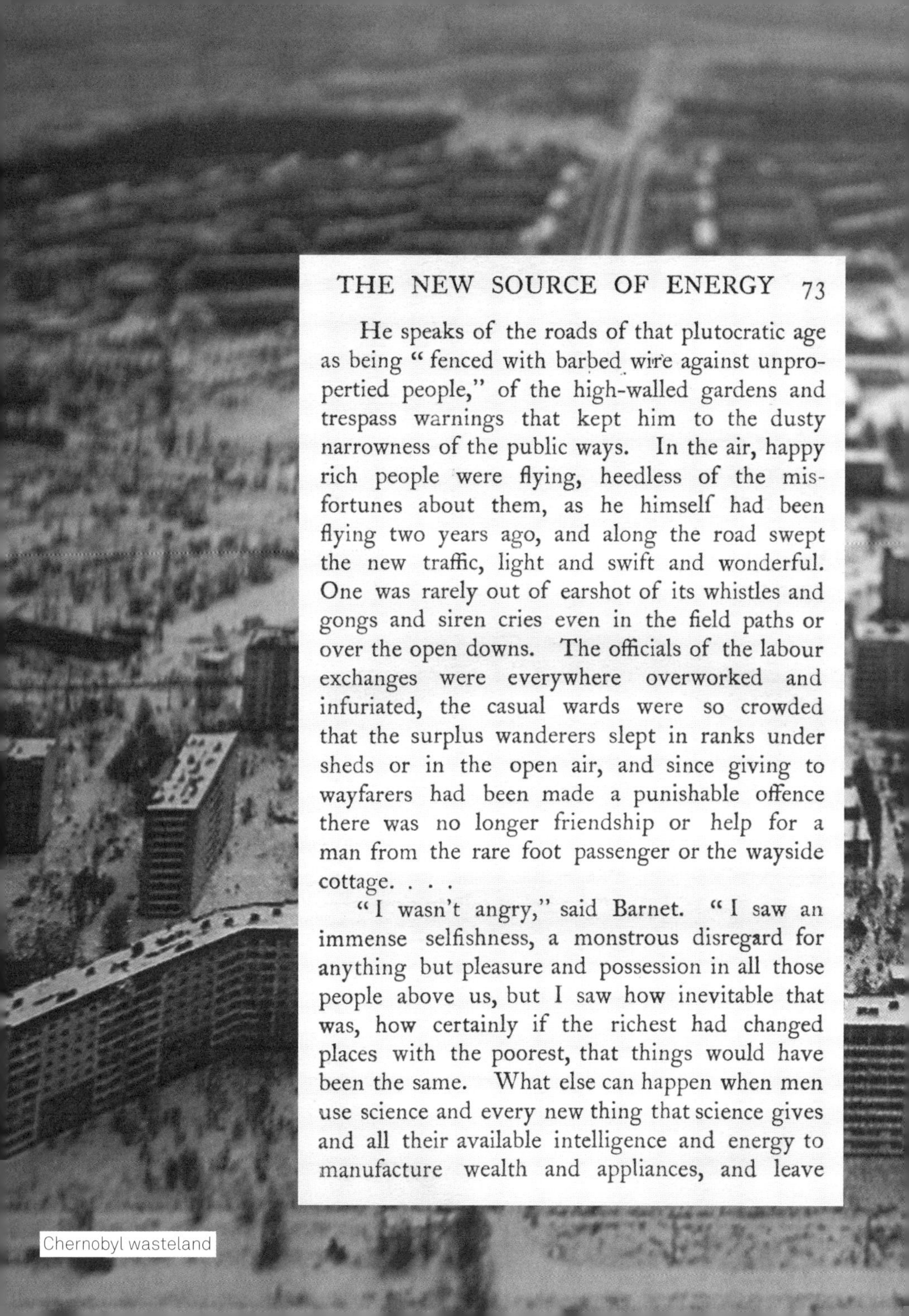

He speaks of the roads of that plutocratic age as being "fenced with barbed wire against unpropertied people," of the high-walled gardens and trespass warnings that kept him to the dusty narrowness of the public ways. In the air, happy rich people were flying, heedless of the misfortunes about them, as he himself had been flying two years ago, and along the road swept the new traffic, light and swift and wonderful. One was rarely out of earshot of its whistles and gongs and siren cries even in the field paths or over the open downs. The officials of the labour exchanges were everywhere overworked and infuriated, the casual wards were so crowded that the surplus wanderers slept in ranks under sheds or in the open air, and since giving to wayfarers had been made a punishable offence there was no longer friendship or help for a man from the rare foot passenger or the wayside cottage. . . .

"I wasn't angry," said Barnet. "I saw an immense selfishness, a monstrous disregard for anything but pleasure and possession in all those people above us, but I saw how inevitable that was, how certainly if the richest had changed places with the poorest, that things would have been the same. What else can happen when men use science and every new thing that science gives and all their available intelligence and energy to manufacture wealth and appliances, and leave

Chernobyl wasteland

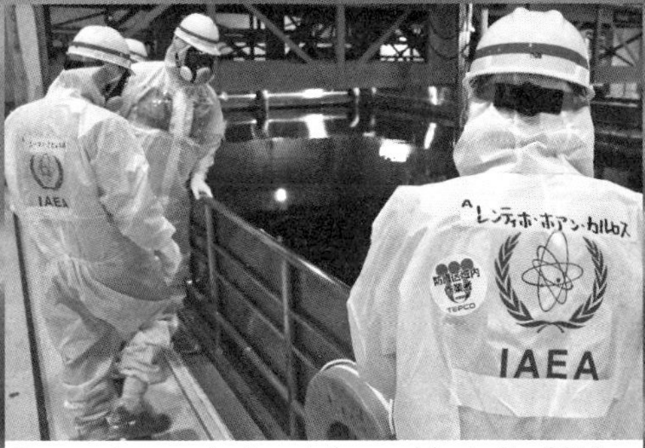

Research commission at the accident site, 2011

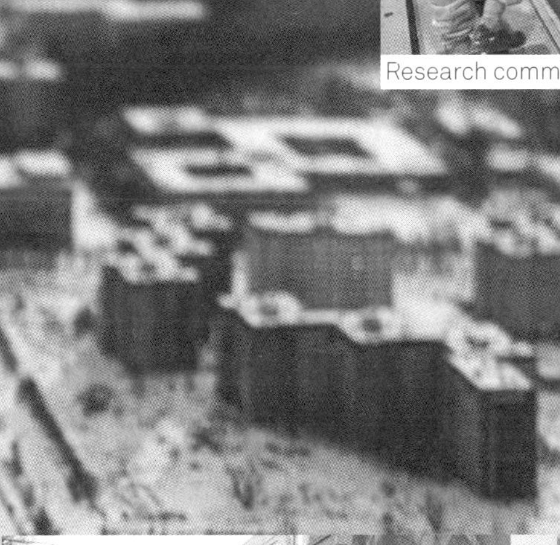
Chernobyl tourists (US 2012)

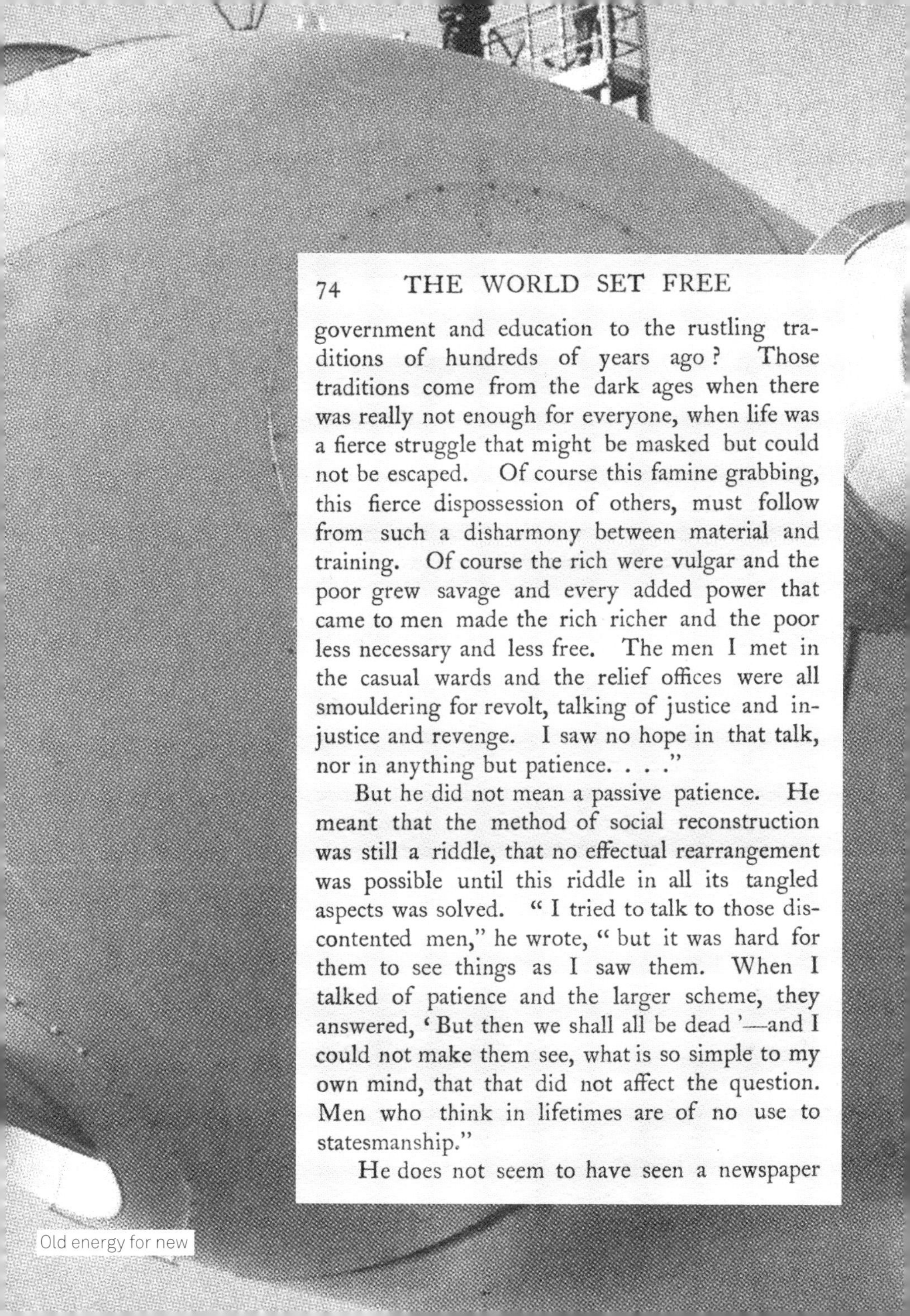

government and education to the rustling traditions of hundreds of years ago? Those traditions come from the dark ages when there was really not enough for everyone, when life was a fierce struggle that might be masked but could not be escaped. Of course this famine grabbing, this fierce dispossession of others, must follow from such a disharmony between material and training. Of course the rich were vulgar and the poor grew savage and every added power that came to men made the rich richer and the poor less necessary and less free. The men I met in the casual wards and the relief offices were all smouldering for revolt, talking of justice and injustice and revenge. I saw no hope in that talk, nor in anything but patience. . . ."

But he did not mean a passive patience. He meant that the method of social reconstruction was still a riddle, that no effectual rearrangement was possible until this riddle in all its tangled aspects was solved. "I tried to talk to those discontented men," he wrote, "but it was hard for them to see things as I saw them. When I talked of patience and the larger scheme, they answered, 'But then we shall all be dead'—and I could not make them see, what is so simple to my own mind, that that did not affect the question. Men who think in lifetimes are of no use to statesmanship."

He does not seem to have seen a newspaper

Old energy for new

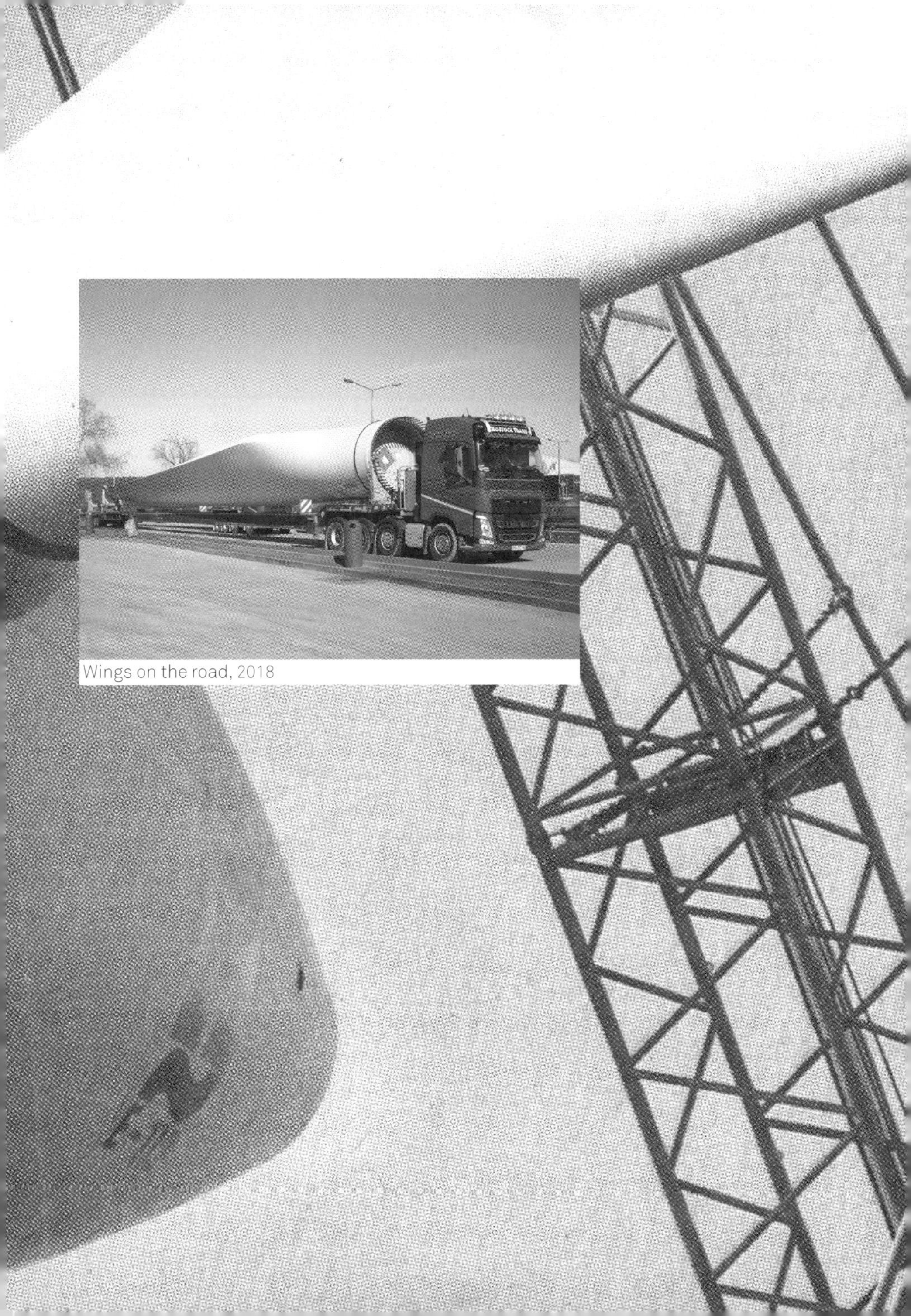

Wings on the road, 2018

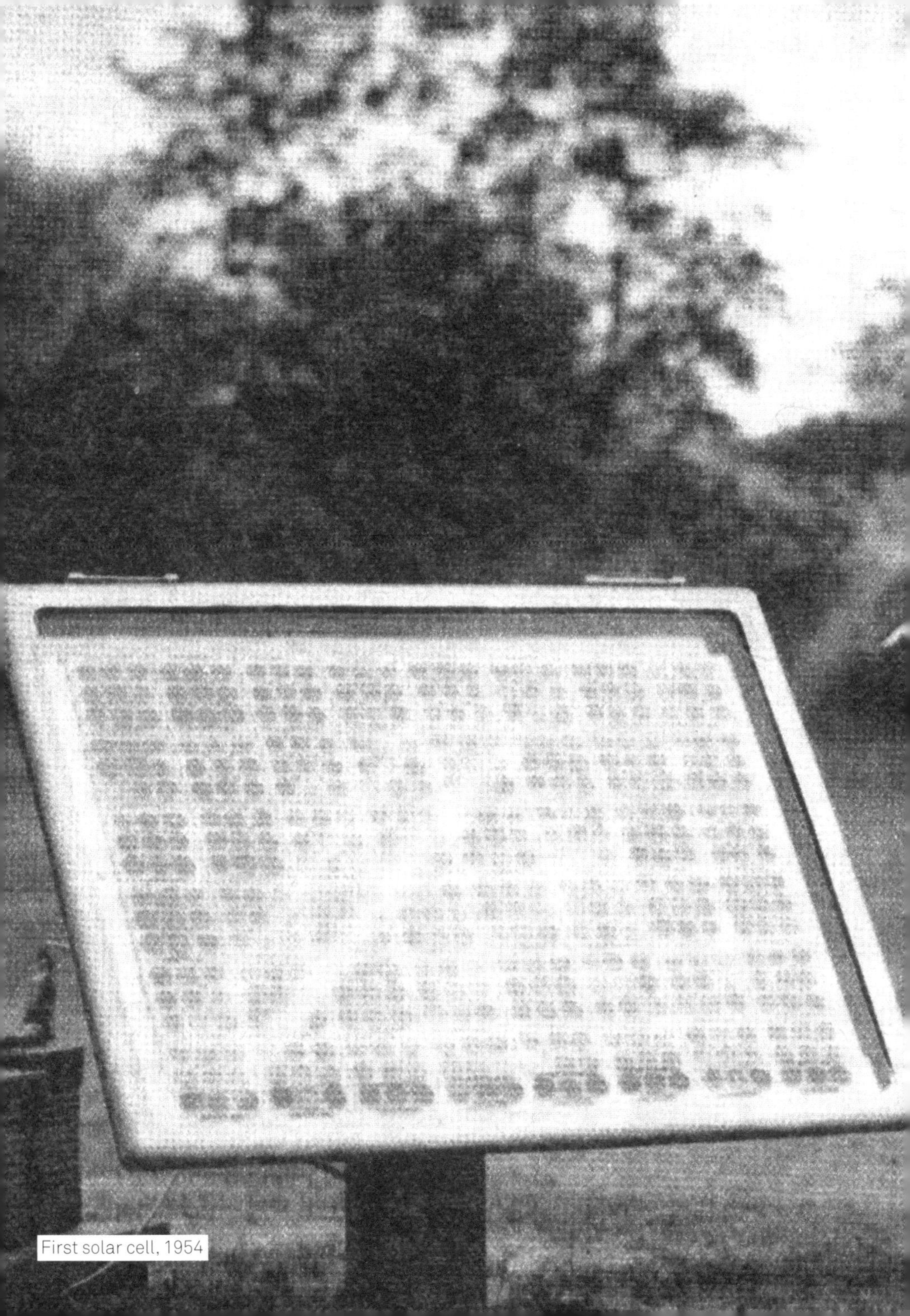

First solar cell, 1954

during those wanderings, and a chance sight of the transparency of a kiosk in the market-place at Bishop's Stortford announcing a "Grave International Situation" did not excite him very much. There had been so many grave international situations in recent years.

This time it was talk of the Central European powers suddenly attacking the Slav Confederacy, with France and England going to the help of the Slavs.

But the next night he found a tolerable meal awaiting the vagrants in the casual ward, and learnt from the workhouse master that all serviceable trained men were to be sent back on the morrow to their mobilisation centres. The country was on the eve of war. He was to go back through London to Surrey. His first feeling, he records, was one of extreme relief that his days of "hopeless battering at the underside of civilization" were at an end. Here was something definite to do, something definitely provided for. But his relief was greatly modified when he found that the mobilization arrangements had been made so hastily and carelessly that for nearly thirty-six hours at the improvised dépôt at Epsom he got nothing either to eat or to drink but a cup of cold water. The dépôt was absolutely unprovisioned, and no one was free to leave it.

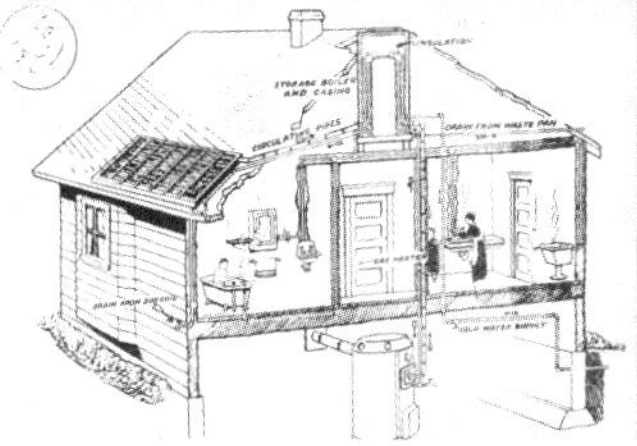
Solar house

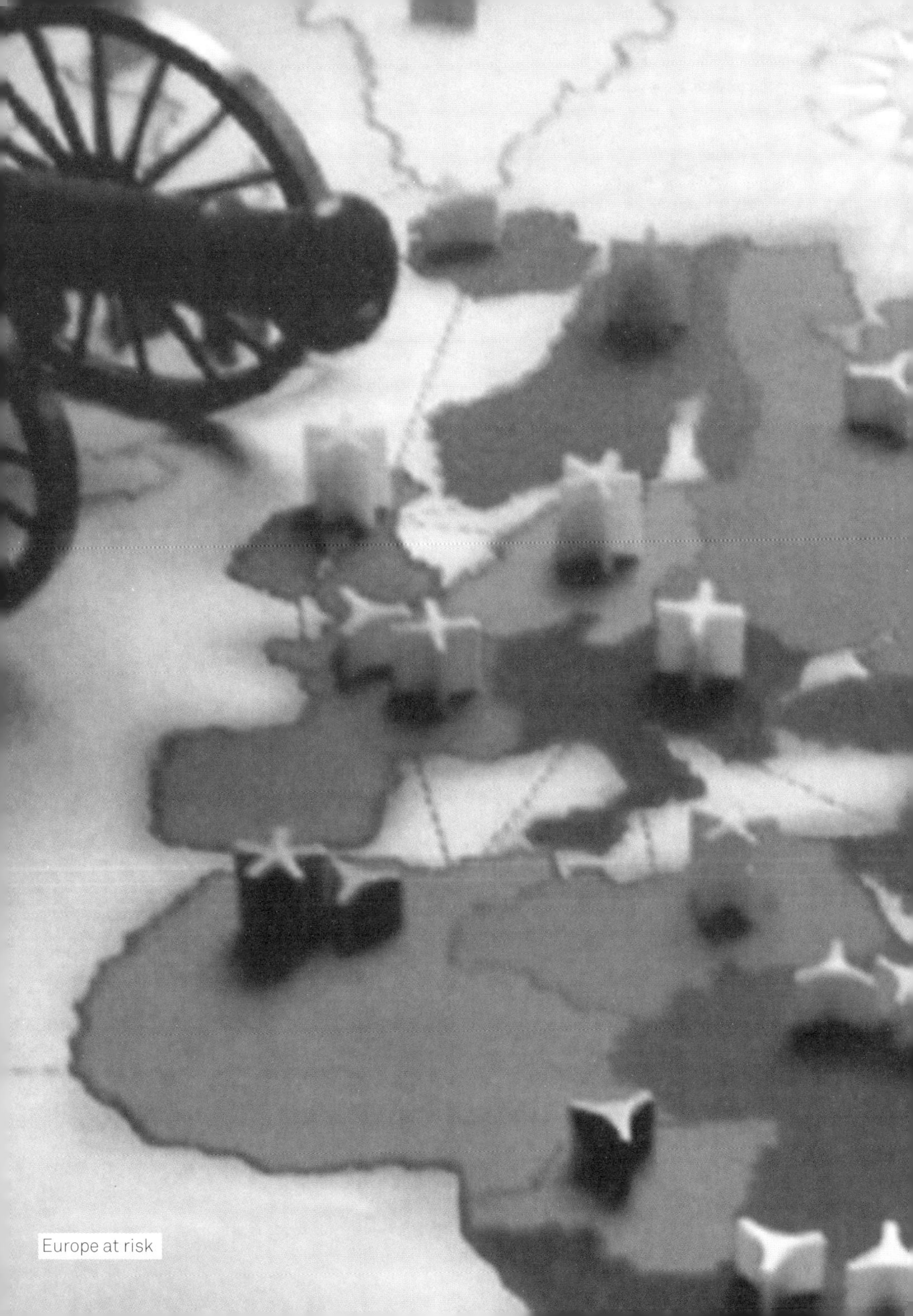

Europe at risk

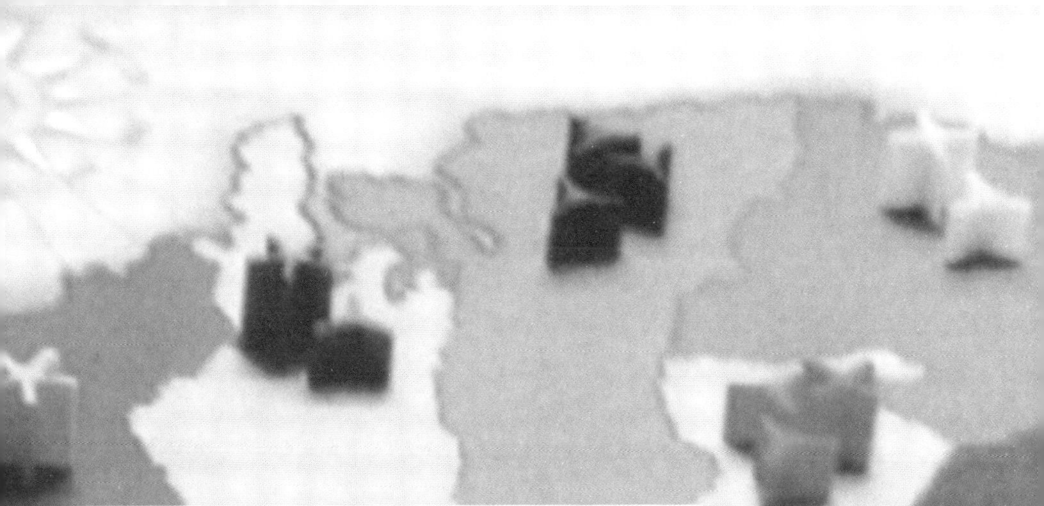

CHAPTER THE SECOND

THE LAST WAR

§ 1

VIEWED from the standpoint of a sane and ambitious social order, it is difficult to understand and it would be tedious to follow the motives that plunged mankind into the war that fills the histories of the middle decades of the twentieth century.

It must always be remembered that the political structure of the world at that time was everywhere extraordinarily behind the collective intelligence. That is the central fact of that history. For two hundred years there had been no great changes in political or legal methods and pretensions, the utmost change had been a certain shifting of boundaries and slight readjustment of procedure, while in nearly every other aspect of life there had been fundamental revolutions, gigantic releases and an enormous enlargement of scope and outlook. The absurdities of courts and the indignities of representative

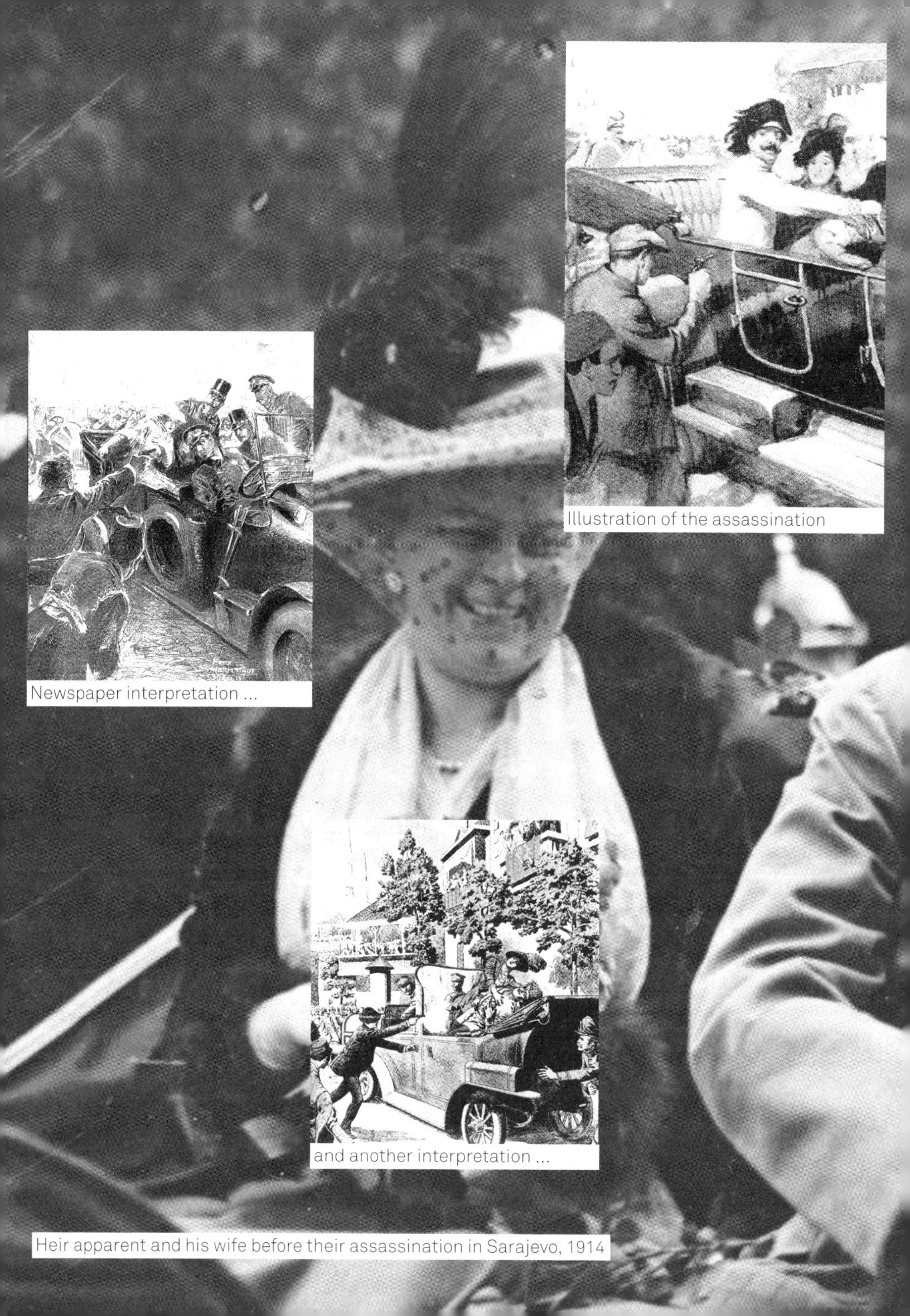

Illustration of the assassination

Newspaper interpretation ...

and another interpretation ...

Heir apparent and his wife before their assassination in Sarajevo, 1914

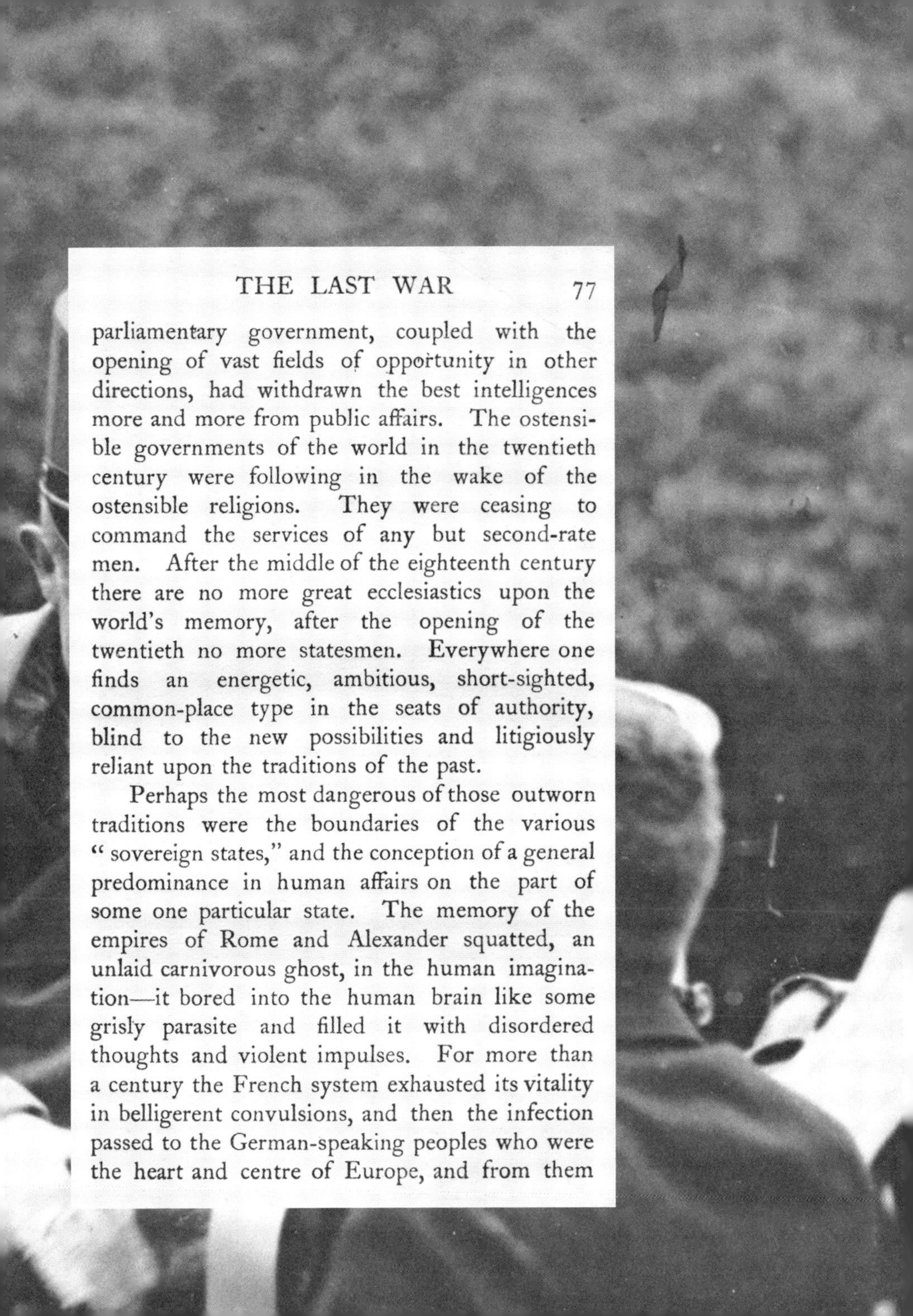

parliamentary government, coupled with the opening of vast fields of opportunity in other directions, had withdrawn the best intelligences more and more from public affairs. The ostensible governments of the world in the twentieth century were following in the wake of the ostensible religions. They were ceasing to command the services of any but second-rate men. After the middle of the eighteenth century there are no more great ecclesiastics upon the world's memory, after the opening of the twentieth no more statesmen. Everywhere one finds an energetic, ambitious, short-sighted, common-place type in the seats of authority, blind to the new possibilities and litigiously reliant upon the traditions of the past.

Perhaps the most dangerous of those outworn traditions were the boundaries of the various "sovereign states," and the conception of a general predominance in human affairs on the part of some one particular state. The memory of the empires of Rome and Alexander squatted, an unlaid carnivorous ghost, in the human imagination—it bored into the human brain like some grisly parasite and filled it with disordered thoughts and violent impulses. For more than a century the French system exhausted its vitality in belligerent convulsions, and then the infection passed to the German-speaking peoples who were the heart and centre of Europe, and from them onward to the Slavs. Later ages were to store and neglect the vast insane literature of this obsession, the intricate treaties, the secret agreements, the infinite knowingness of the political writer, the cunning refusals to accept plain facts, the strategic devices, the tactical manœuvres, the records of mobilizations and counter-mobilizations. It ceased to be credible almost as soon as it ceased to happen, but in the very dawn of the new age their state-craftsmen sat with their historical candles burning, and, in spite of strange new reflections and unfamiliar lights and shadows, still wrangling and planning to rearrange the maps of Europe and the world.

It was to become a matter for subtle inquiry how far the millions of men and women outside the world of these specialists sympathized and agreed with their portentous activities. One school of psychologists inclined to minimize this participation, but the balance of evidence goes to show that there were massive responses to these suggestions of the belligerent schemer. Primitive man had been a fiercely combative animal; innumerable generations had passed their lives in tribal warfare, and the weight of tradition, the example of history, the ideals of loyalty and devotion fell in easily enough with the incitements of the international mischief-maker. The political ideas of the common man were picked up haphazard, there was practically nothing in such

Marshall, decorated

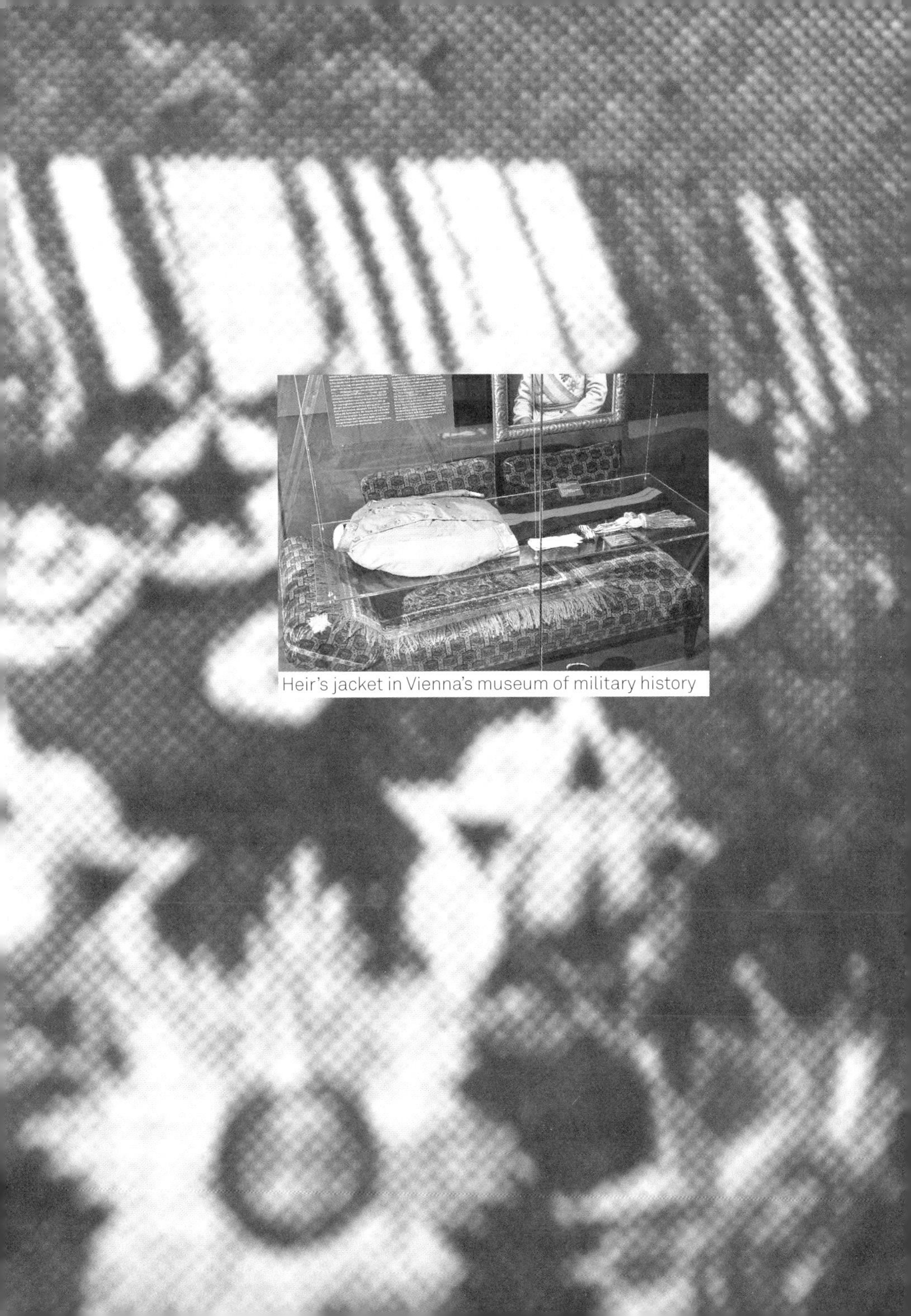

Heir's jacket in Vienna's museum of military history

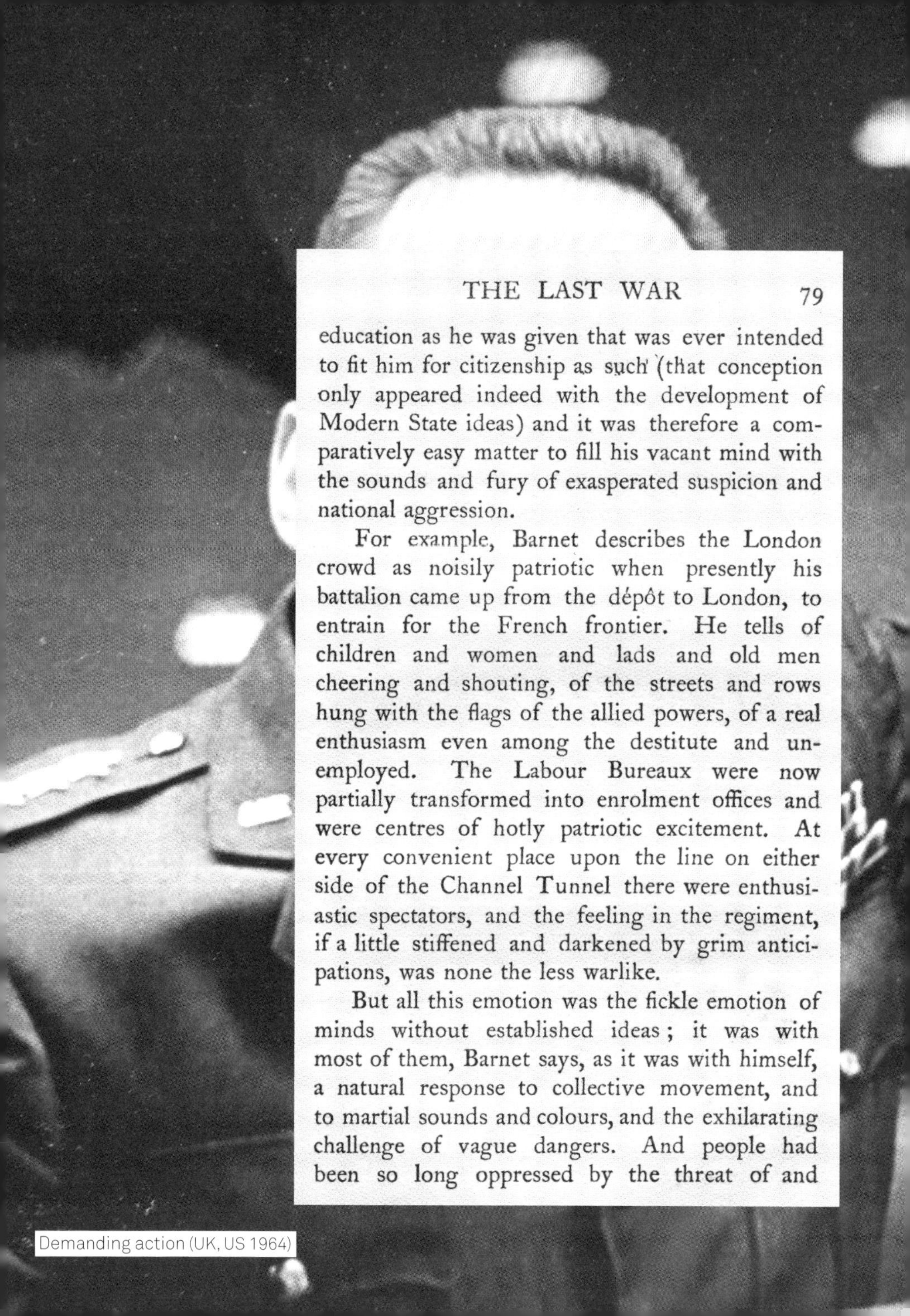

education as he was given that was ever intended to fit him for citizenship as such (that conception only appeared indeed with the development of Modern State ideas) and it was therefore a comparatively easy matter to fill his vacant mind with the sounds and fury of exasperated suspicion and national aggression.

For example, Barnet describes the London crowd as noisily patriotic when presently his battalion came up from the dépôt to London, to entrain for the French frontier. He tells of children and women and lads and old men cheering and shouting, of the streets and rows hung with the flags of the allied powers, of a real enthusiasm even among the destitute and unemployed. The Labour Bureaux were now partially transformed into enrolment offices and were centres of hotly patriotic excitement. At every convenient place upon the line on either side of the Channel Tunnel there were enthusiastic spectators, and the feeling in the regiment, if a little stiffened and darkened by grim anticipations, was none the less warlike.

But all this emotion was the fickle emotion of minds without established ideas ; it was with most of them, Barnet says, as it was with himself, a natural response to collective movement, and to martial sounds and colours, and the exhilarating challenge of vague dangers. And people had been so long oppressed by the threat of and

Demanding action (UK, US 1964)

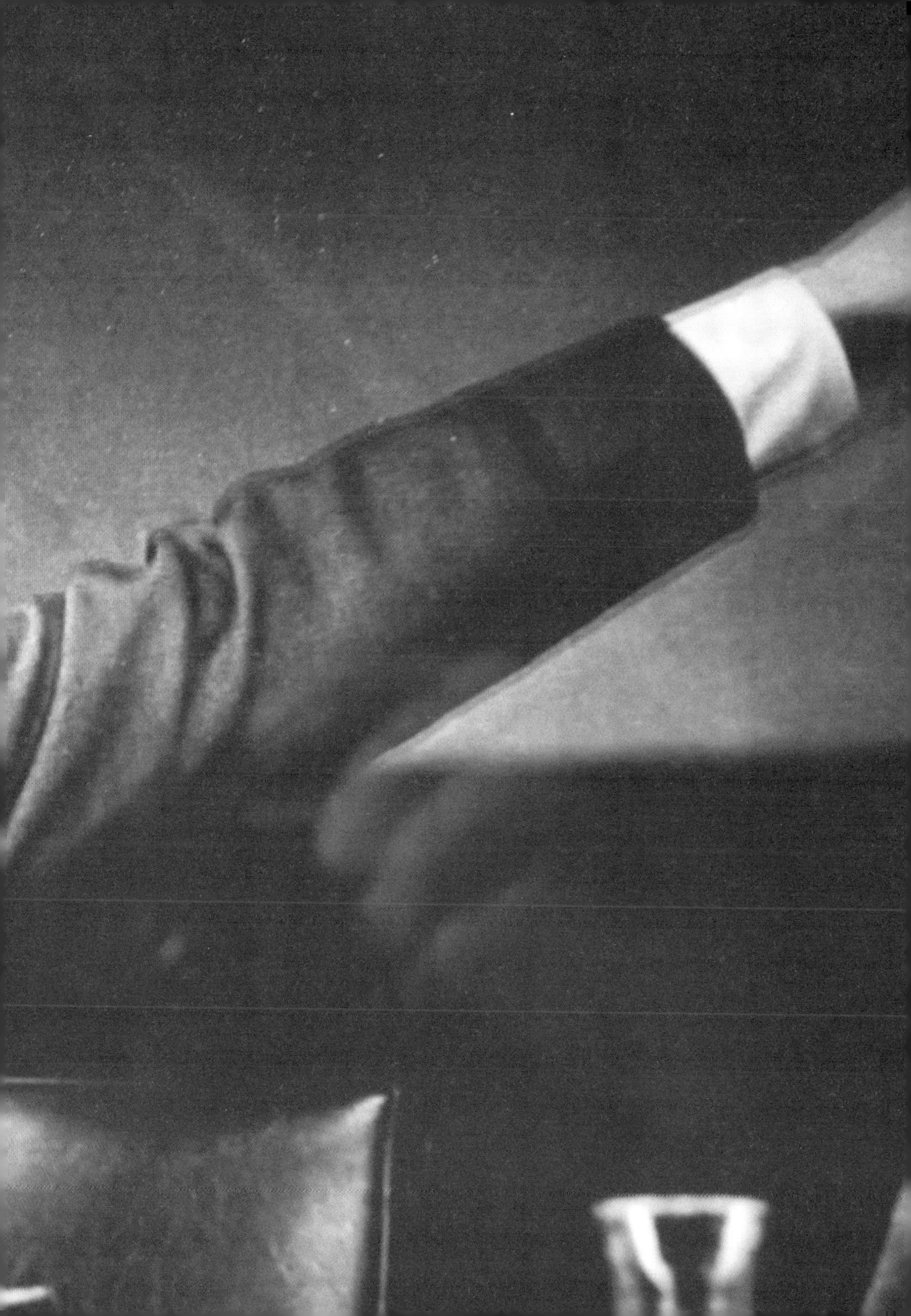

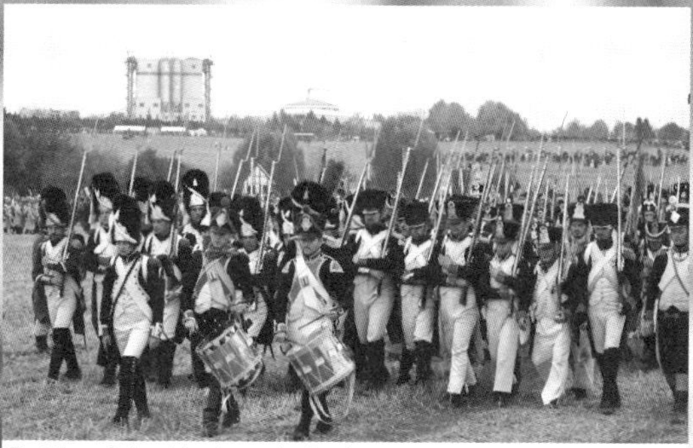

Battle of the Nations, Leipzig 2013

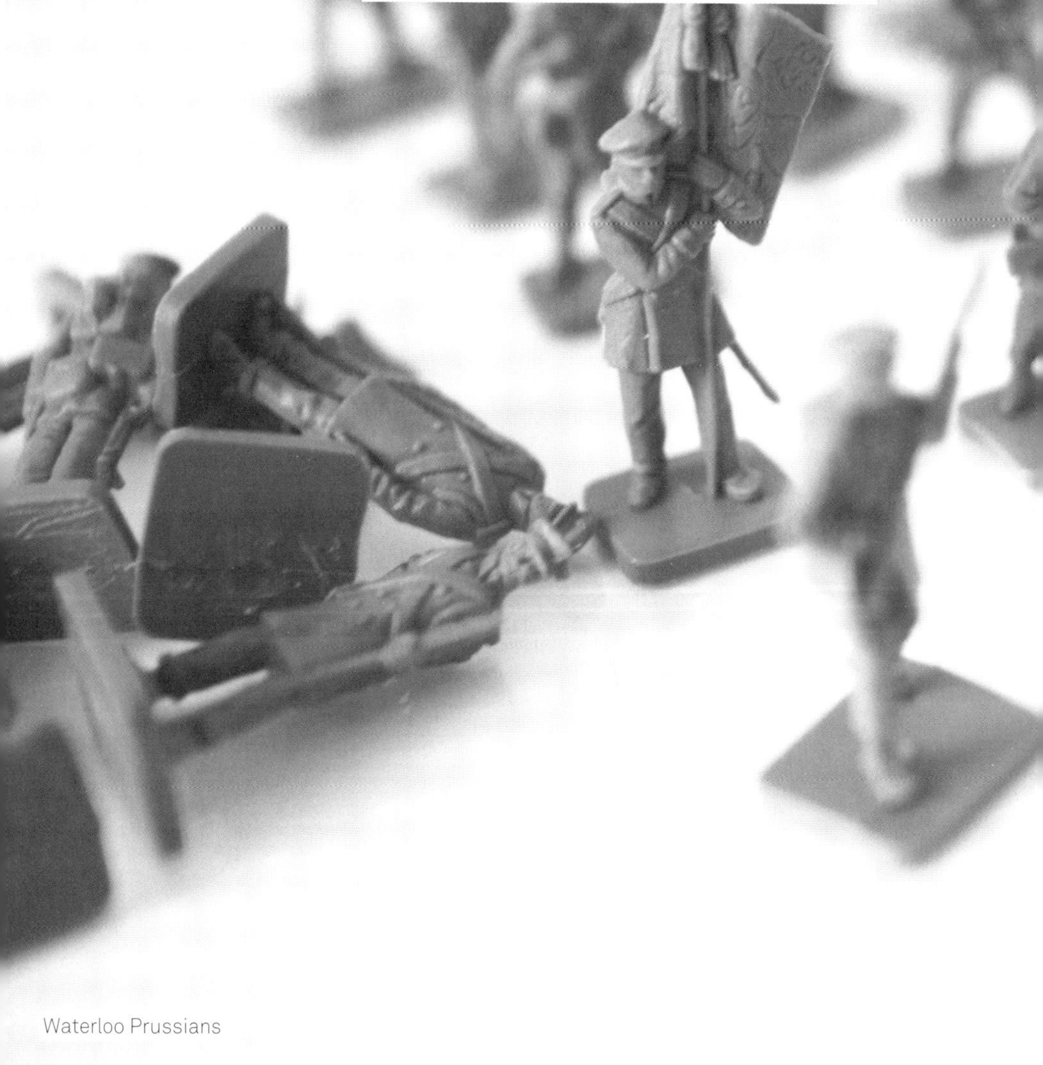

Waterloo Prussians

preparation for war that its arrival came with an effect of positive relief.

§ 2

The plan of campaign of the allies assigned the defence of the lower Meuse to the English, and the troop-trains were run direct from the various British dépôts to the points in the Ardennes where they were intended to entrench themselves.

Most of the documents bearing upon the campaign were destroyed during the war, from the first the scheme of the allies seems to have been confused, but it is highly probable that the formation of an aërial park in this region, from which attacks could be made upon the vast industrial plant of the lower Rhine, and a flanking raid through Holland upon the German naval establishments at the mouth of the Elbe, were integral parts of the original project. Nothing of this was known to such pawns in the game as Barnet and his company, whose business it was to do what they were told by the mysterious intelligences at the direction of things in Paris, to which city the Whitehall staff had also been transferred. From first to last these directing intelligences remained mysterious to the body of the army, veiled under the name of "Orders." There was no Napoleon, no Cæsar

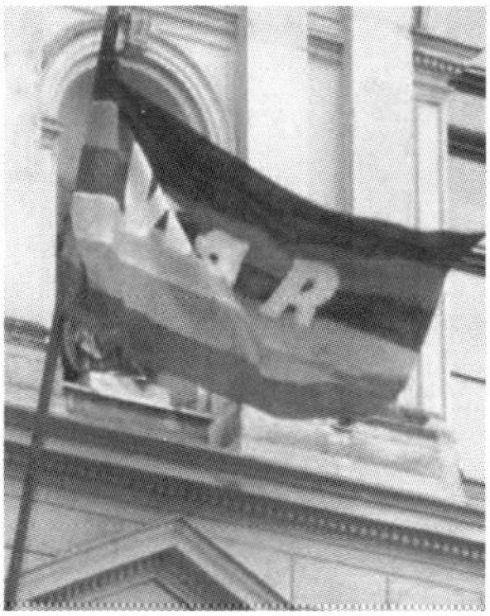

War flag, 2004

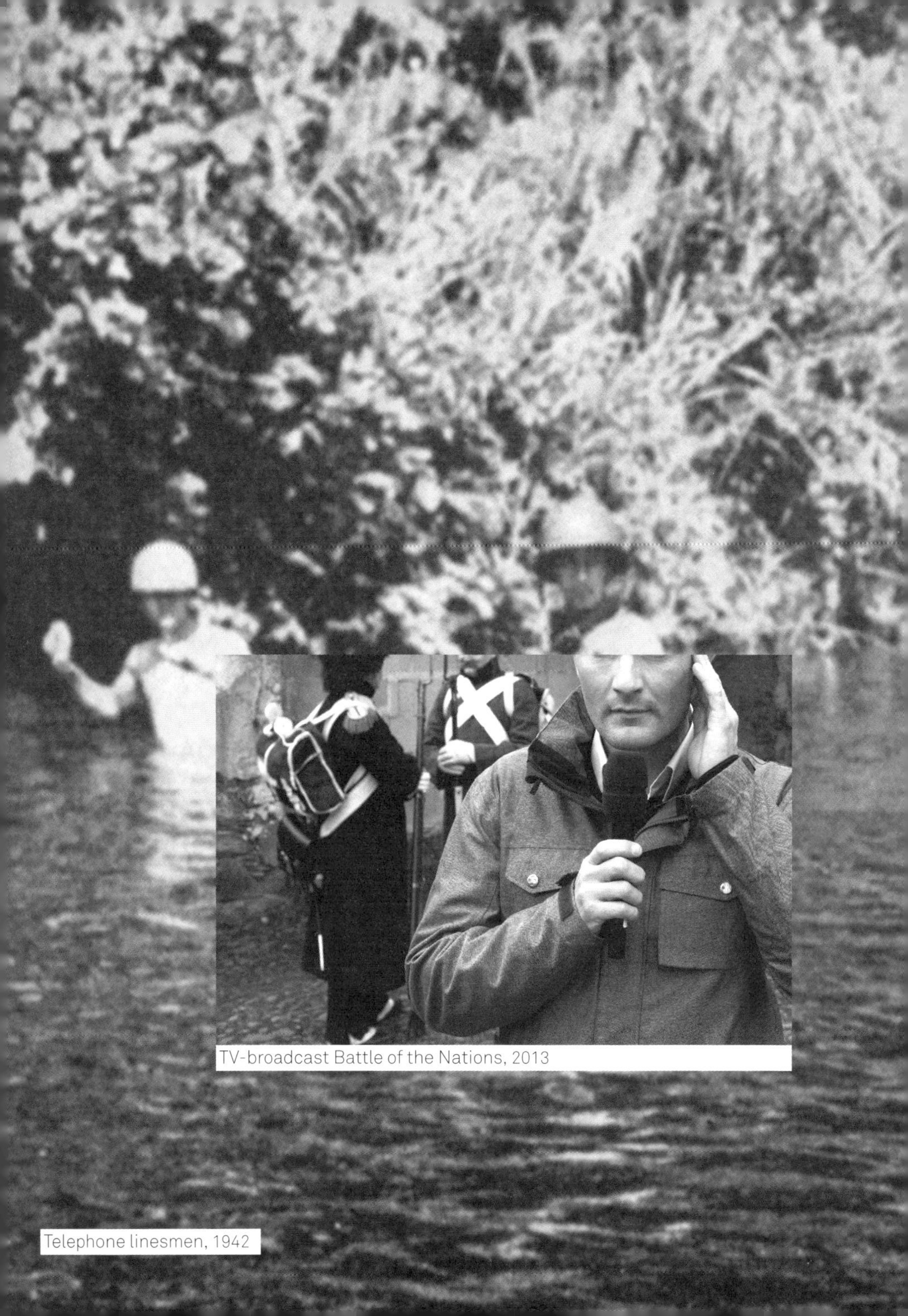

TV-broadcast Battle of the Nations, 2013

Telephone linesmen, 1942

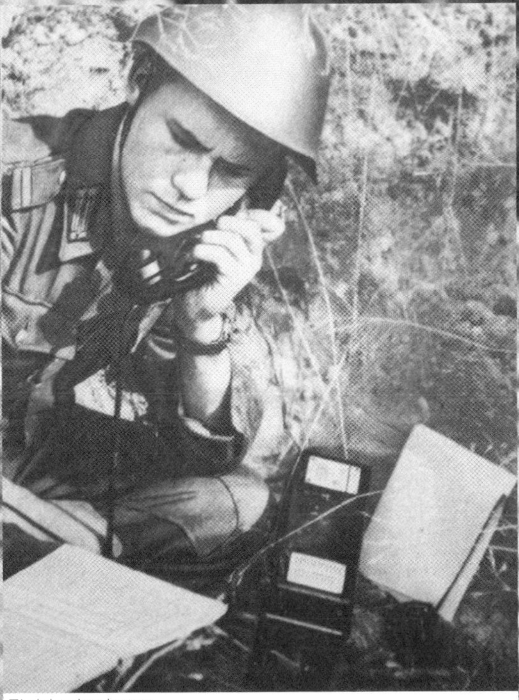

Field telephone

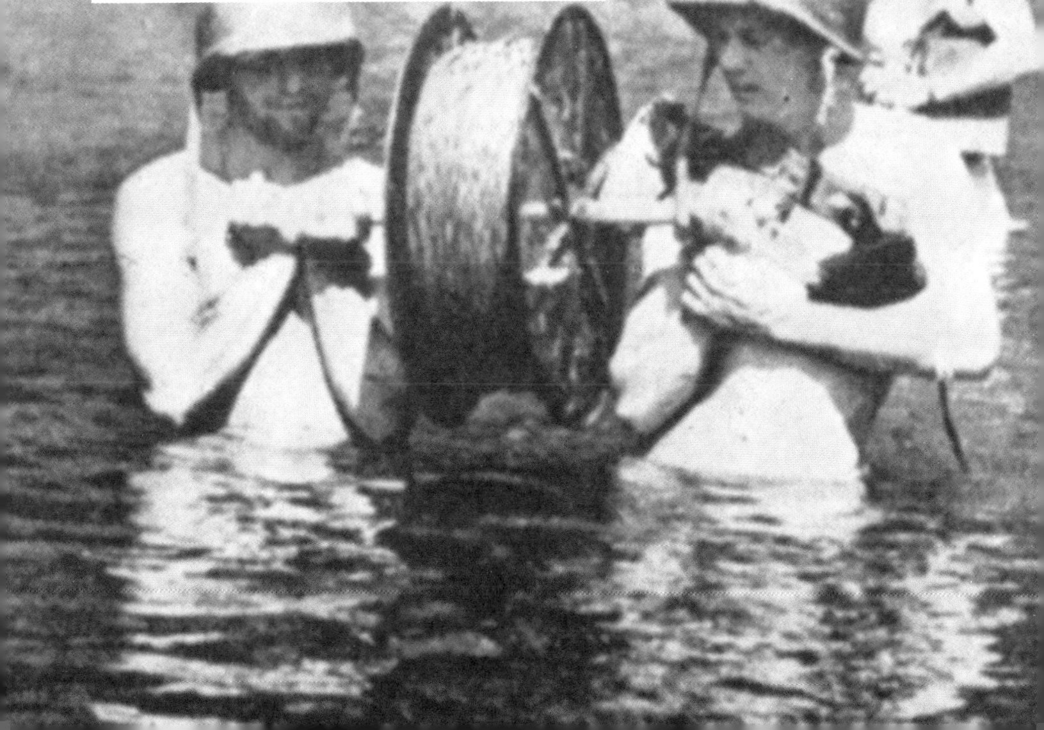

to embody enthusiasm. Barnet says, "We talked of Them. *They* are sending us up into Luxembourg. *They* are going to turn the Central European right."

Behind the veil of this vagueness the little group of more or less worthy men which constituted Headquarters was beginning to realize the enormity of the thing it was supposed to control. . . .

In the great hall of the War Control whose windows looked out across the Seine to the Trocadero and the palaces of the western quarter, a series of big-scale relief maps were laid out upon tables to display the whole seat of war, and the staff-officers of the control were continually busy shifting the little blocks which represented the contending troops, as the reports and intelligence came drifting in to the various telegraphic bureaux in the adjacent rooms. In other smaller apartments there were maps of a less detailed sort, upon which for example the reports of the British Admiralty and of the Slav commanders were recorded as they kept coming to hand. Upon these maps as upon chessboards Marshal Dubois, in consultation with General Viard and the Earl of Delhi, was to play the great game for world supremacy against the Central European powers. Very probably he had a definite idea of his game; very probably he had a coherent and admirable plan.

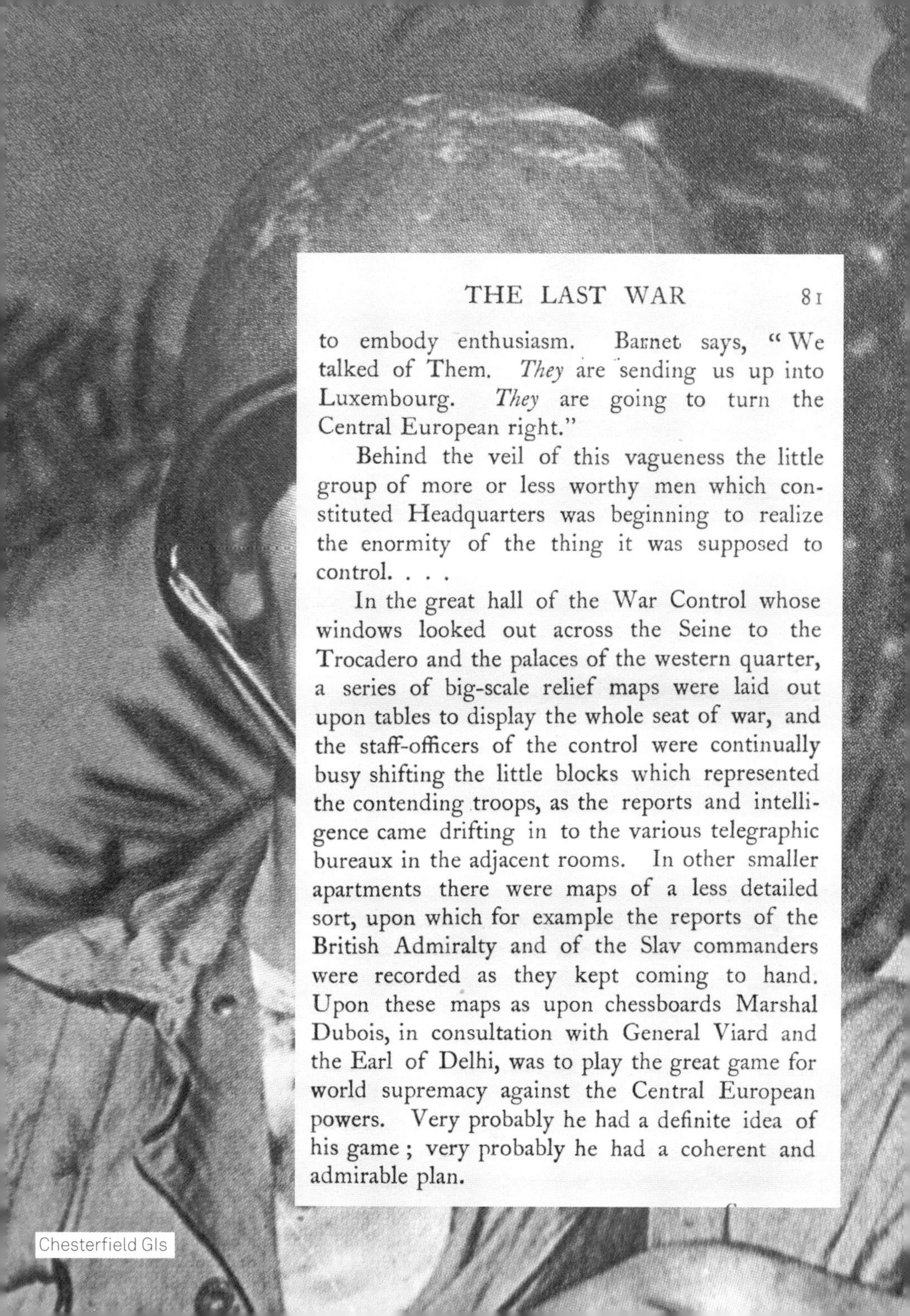

Chesterfield GIs

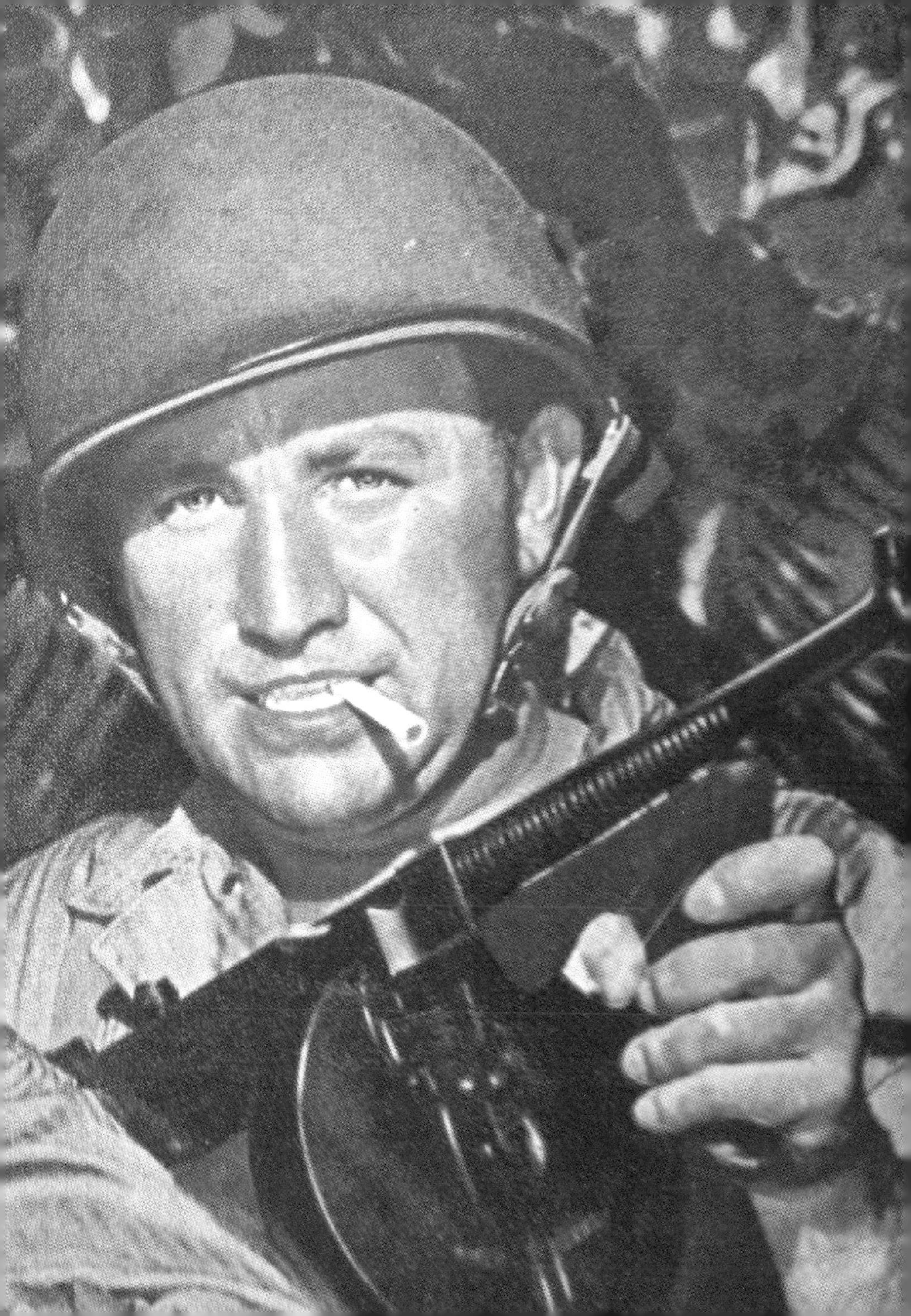

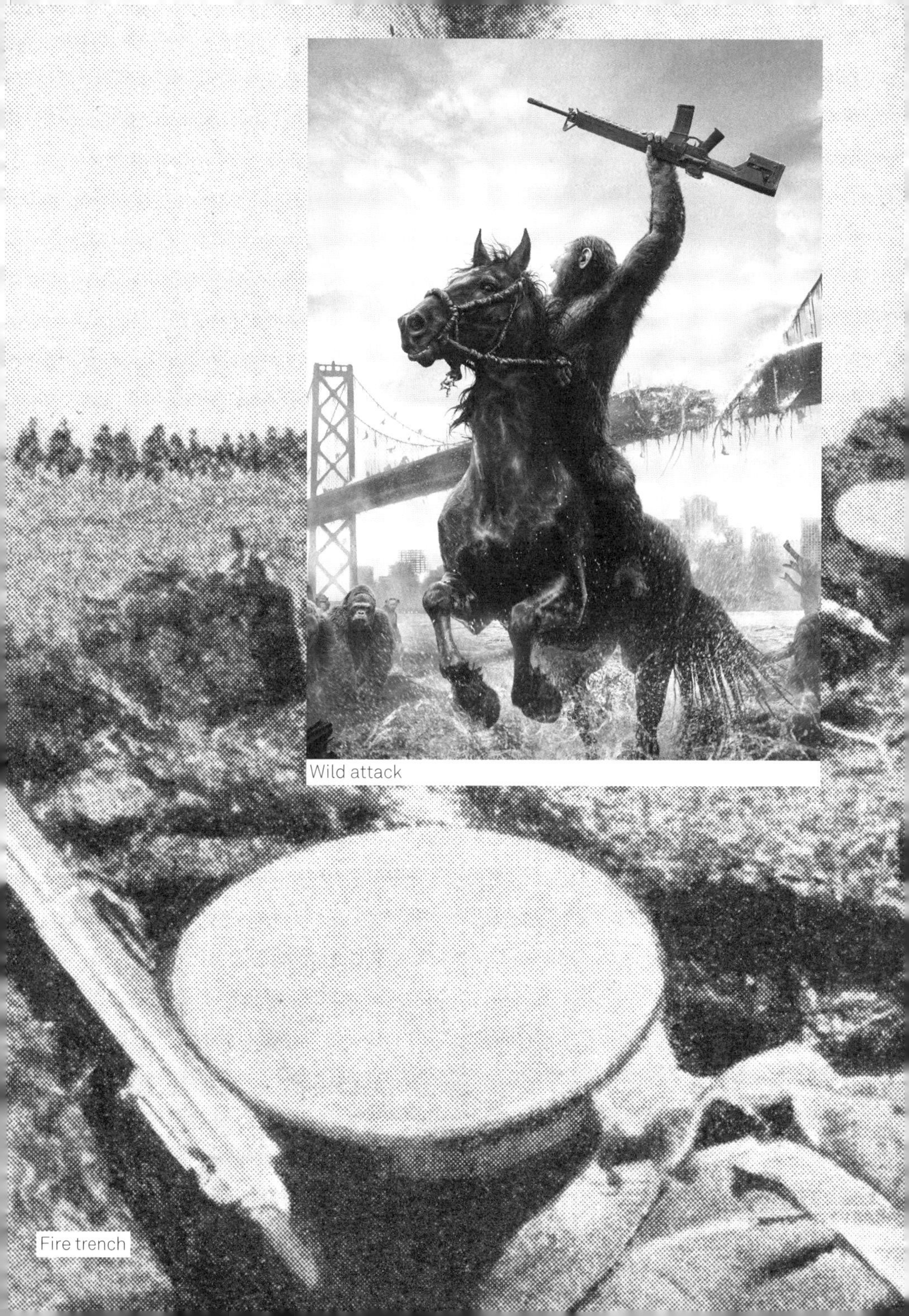

Wild attack

Fire trench

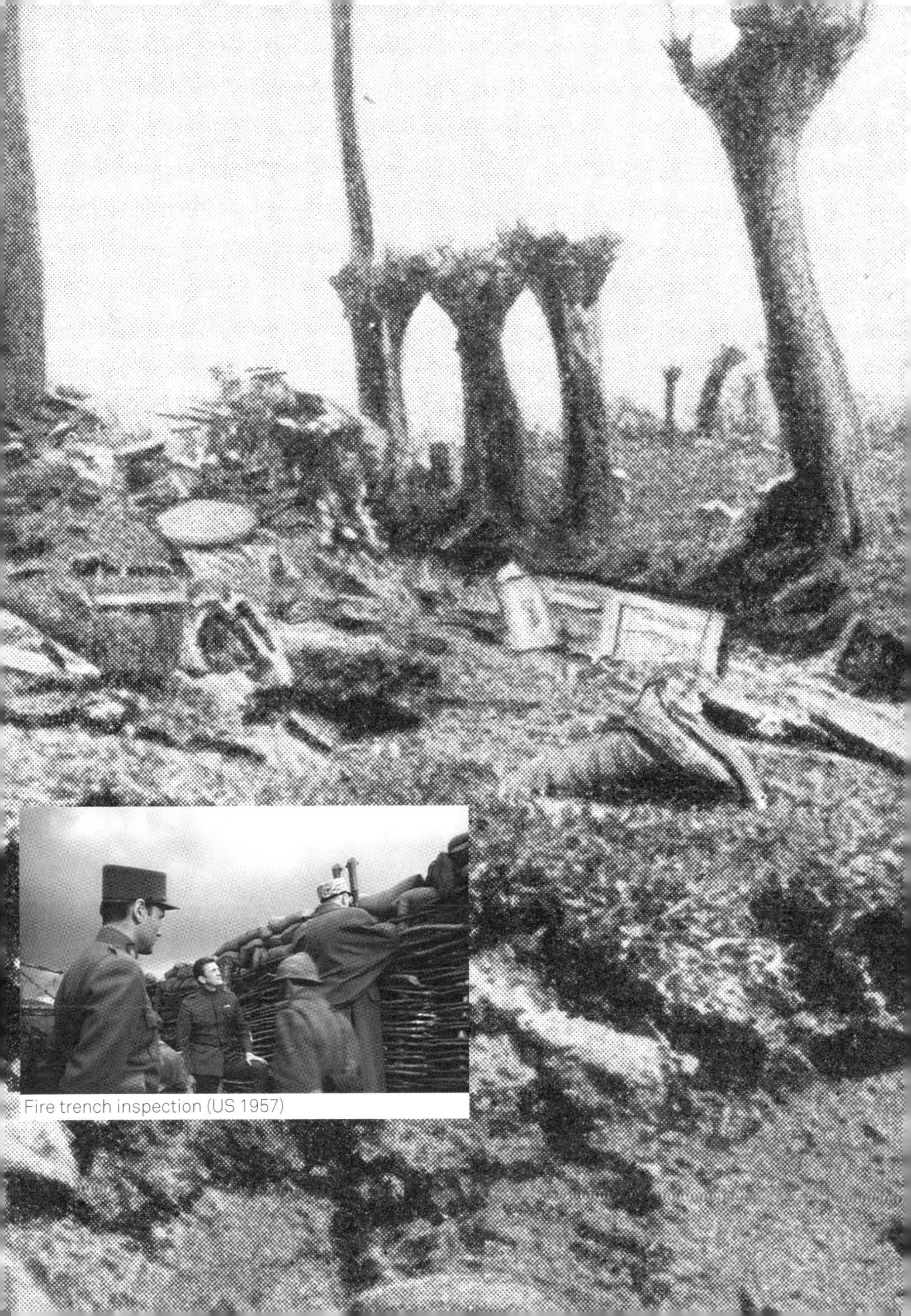
Fire trench inspection (US 1957)

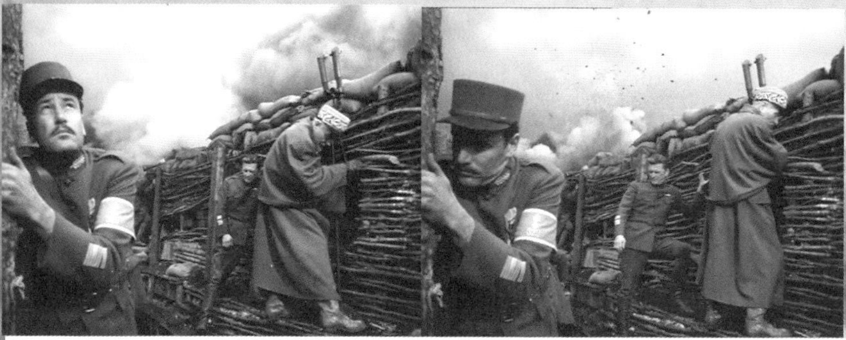

Fire trench under attack (US 1957)

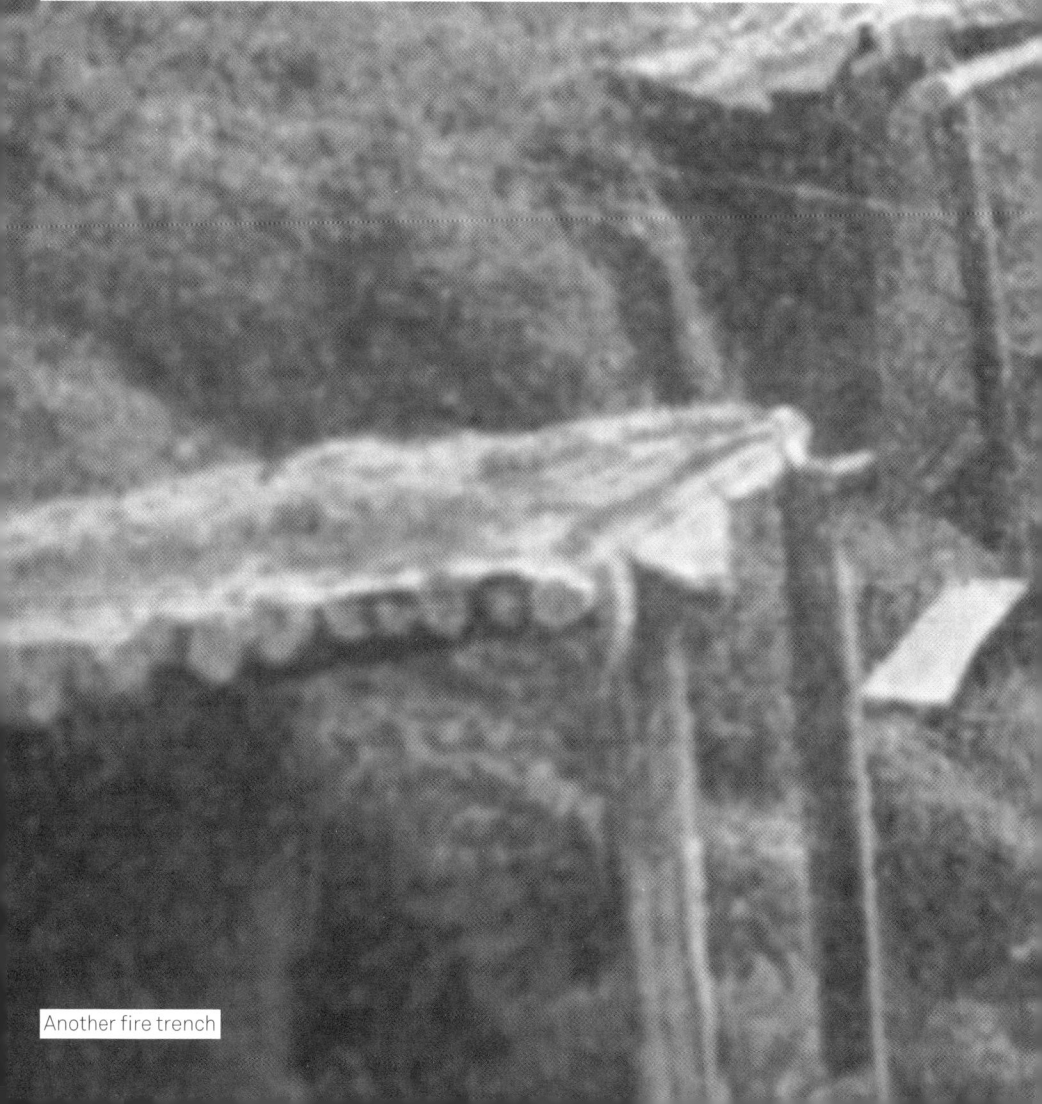

Another fire trench

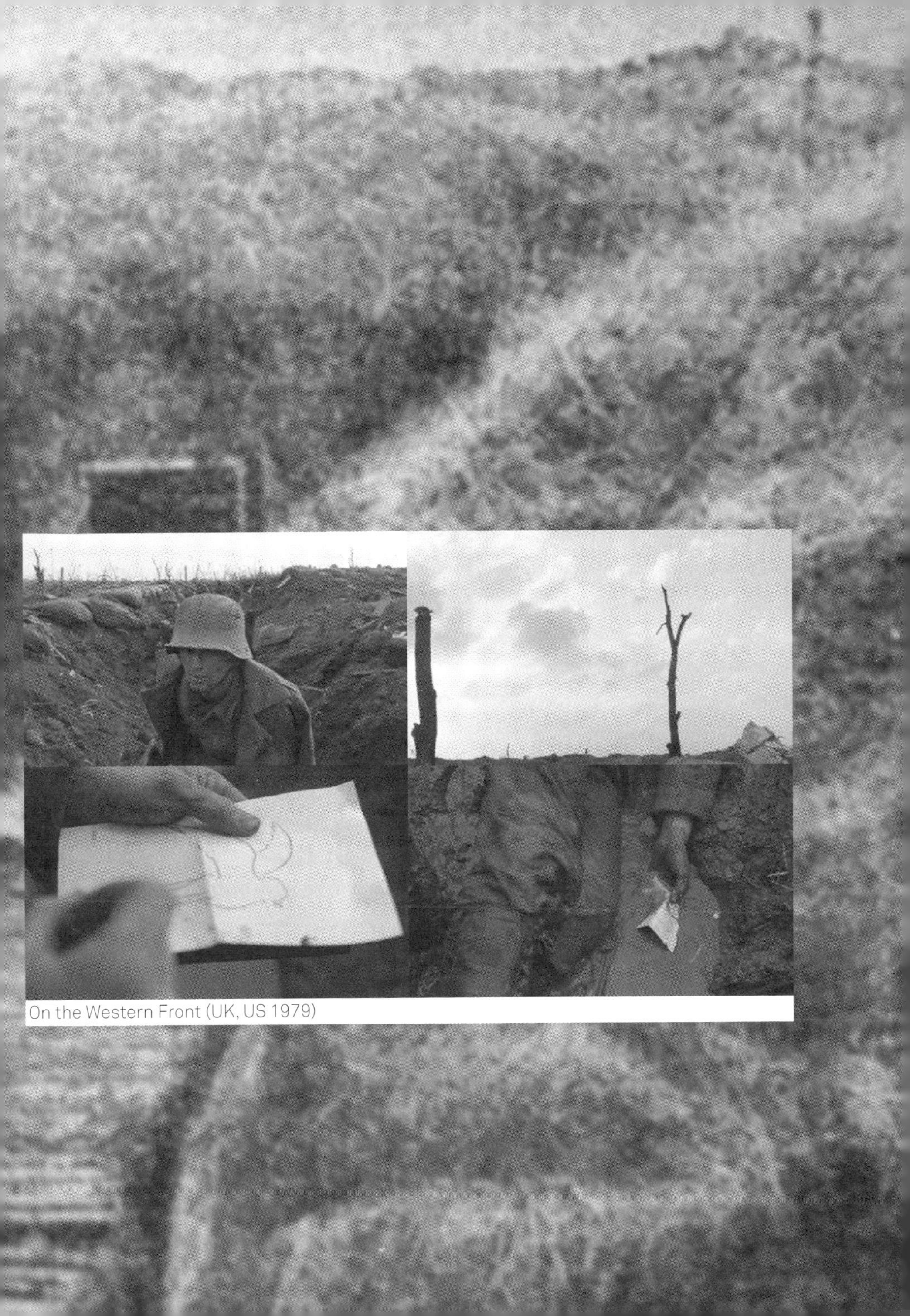

On the Western Front (UK, US 1979)

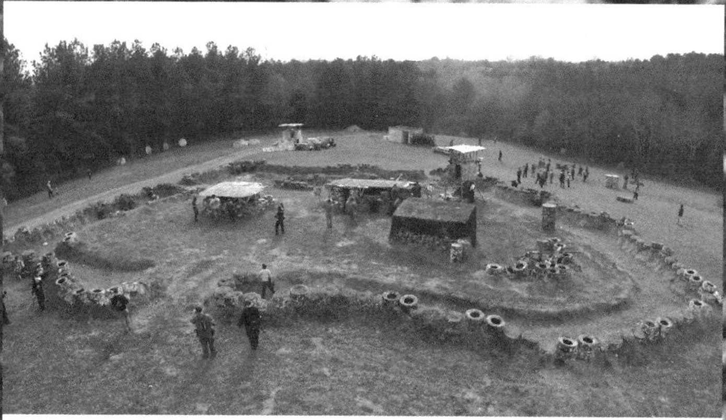

Fulda gap paintball scene

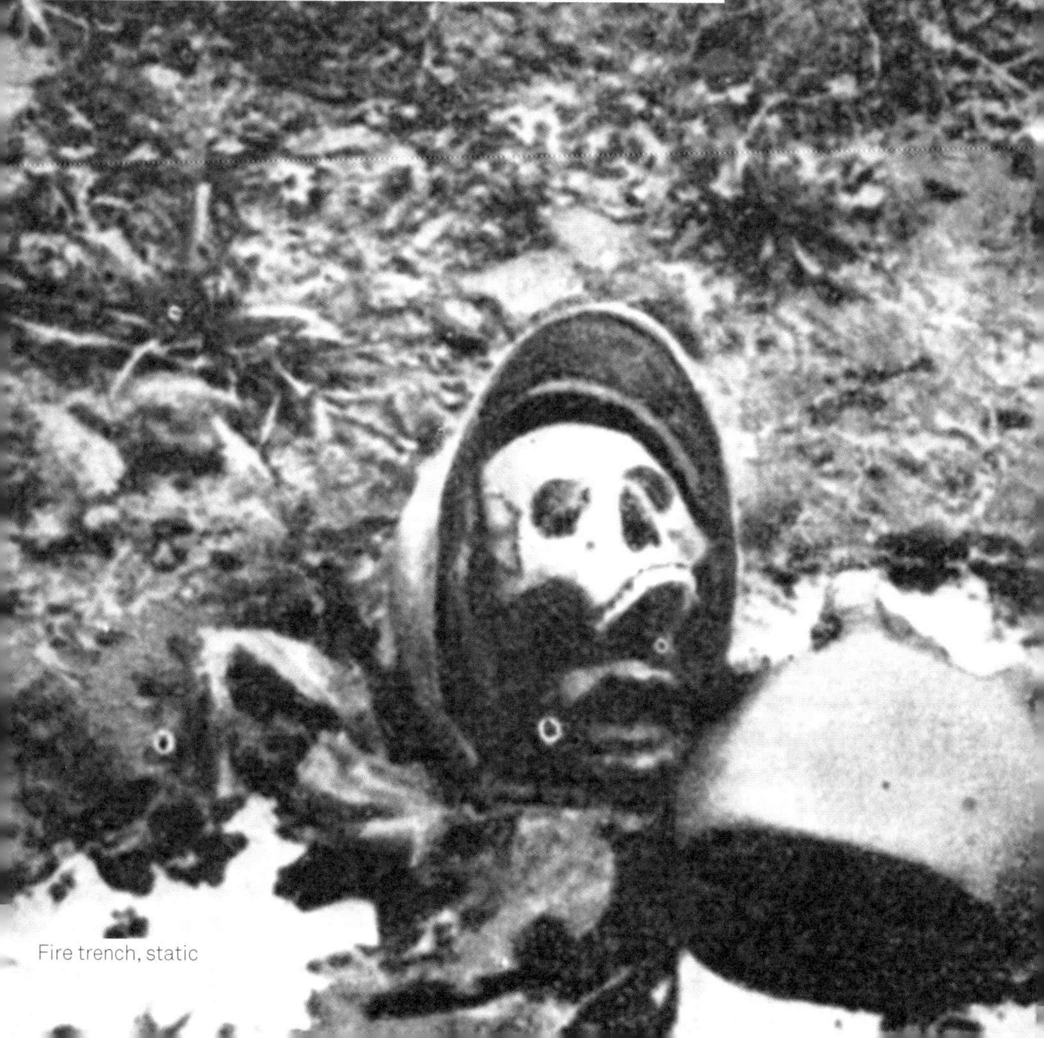

Fire trench, static

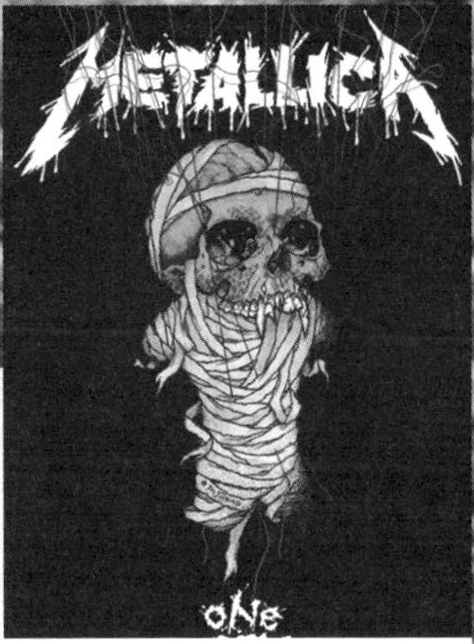

Johnny got his gun, 1988

But he had reckoned without a proper estimate either of the new strategy of aviation or of the possibilities of atomic energy that Holsten had opened for mankind. While he planned entrenchments and invasions and a frontier war, the Central European generalship was striking at the eyes and the brain. And while, with a certain diffident hesitation, he developed his gambit that night upon the lines laid down by Napoleon and Moltke, his own scientific corps in a state of mutinous activity was preparing a blow for Berlin. "These old fools!" was the key in which the scientific corps was thinking.

The War Control in Paris on the night of July the second was an impressive display of the paraphernalia of scientific military organization, as the first half of the twentieth century understood it. To one human being at least the consulting commanders had the likeness of world-wielding gods. . . .

She was a skilled typist, capable of nearly sixty words a minute, and she had been engaged in relay with other similar women to take down orders in duplicate and hand them over to the junior officers in attendance to be forwarded and filed. There had come a lull, and she had been sent out from the dictating room to take the air upon the terrace before the great hall and to eat such scanty refreshment as she had brought with her until her services were required again.

From her position upon the terrace this young woman had a view not only of the wide sweep of the river below her, and all the eastward side of Paris from the Arc de Triomphe to Saint Cloud, great blocks and masses of black or pale darkness with pink and golden flashes of illumination and endless interlacing bands of dotted lights under a still and starless sky, but also the whole spacious interior of the great hall with its slender pillars and gracious arching and clustering lamps was visible to her. There, over a wilderness of tables, lay the huge maps, done on so large a scale that one might fancy them small countries ; the messengers and attendants went and came perpetually, altering, moving the little pieces that signified hundreds and thousands of men, and the great commander and his two consultants stood amidst all these things and near where the fighting was nearest, scheming, directing. They had but to breathe a word and presently away there, in the world of reality, the punctual myriads moved. Men rose up and went forward and died. The fate of nations lay behind the eyes of these three men. Indeed they were like gods.

Most godlike of the three was Dubois. It was for him to decide ; the others at most might suggest. Her woman's soul went out to this grave, handsome, still, old man, in a passion of instinctive worship. . . .

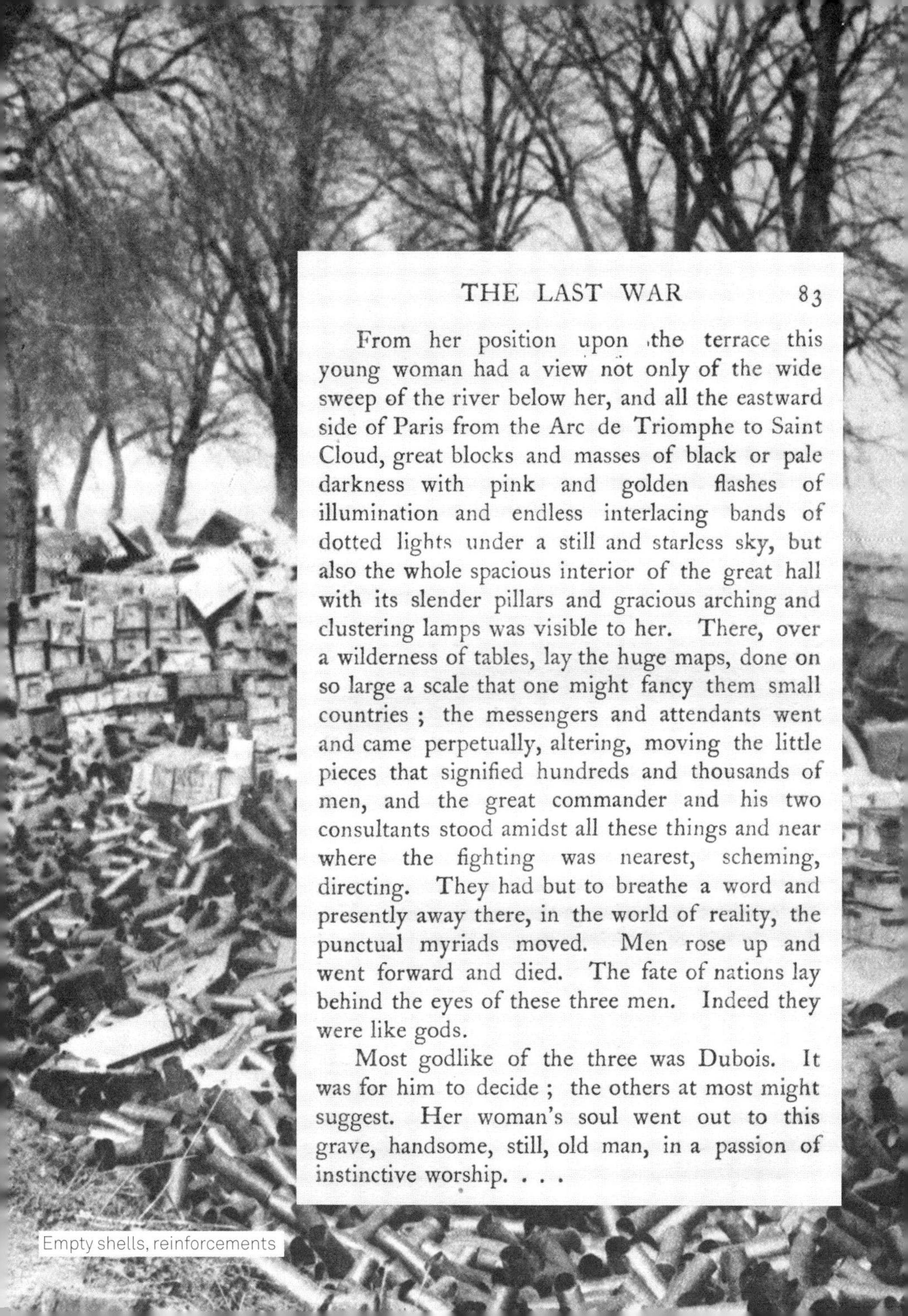

Empty shells, reinforcements

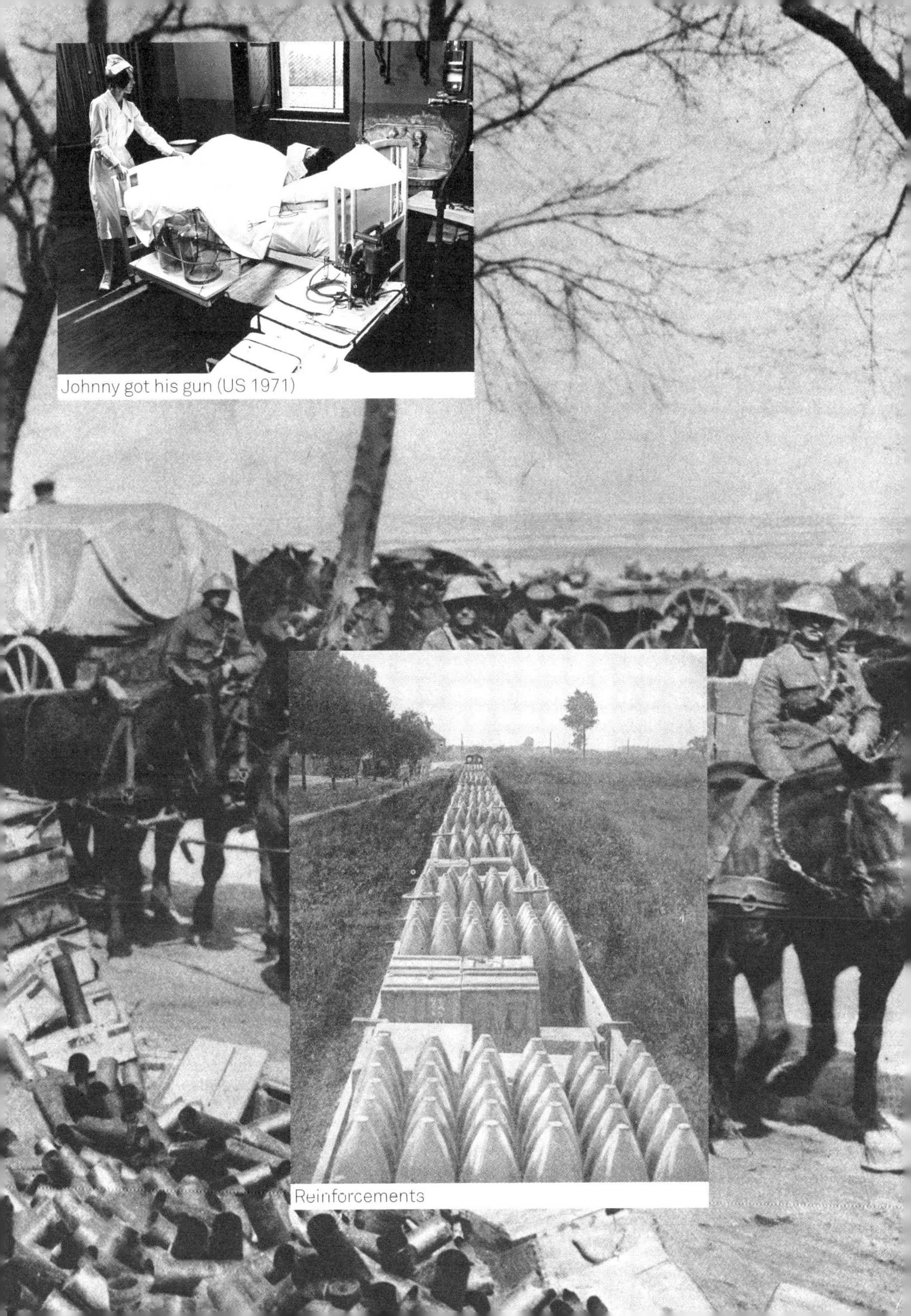

Johnny got his gun (US 1971)

Reinforcements

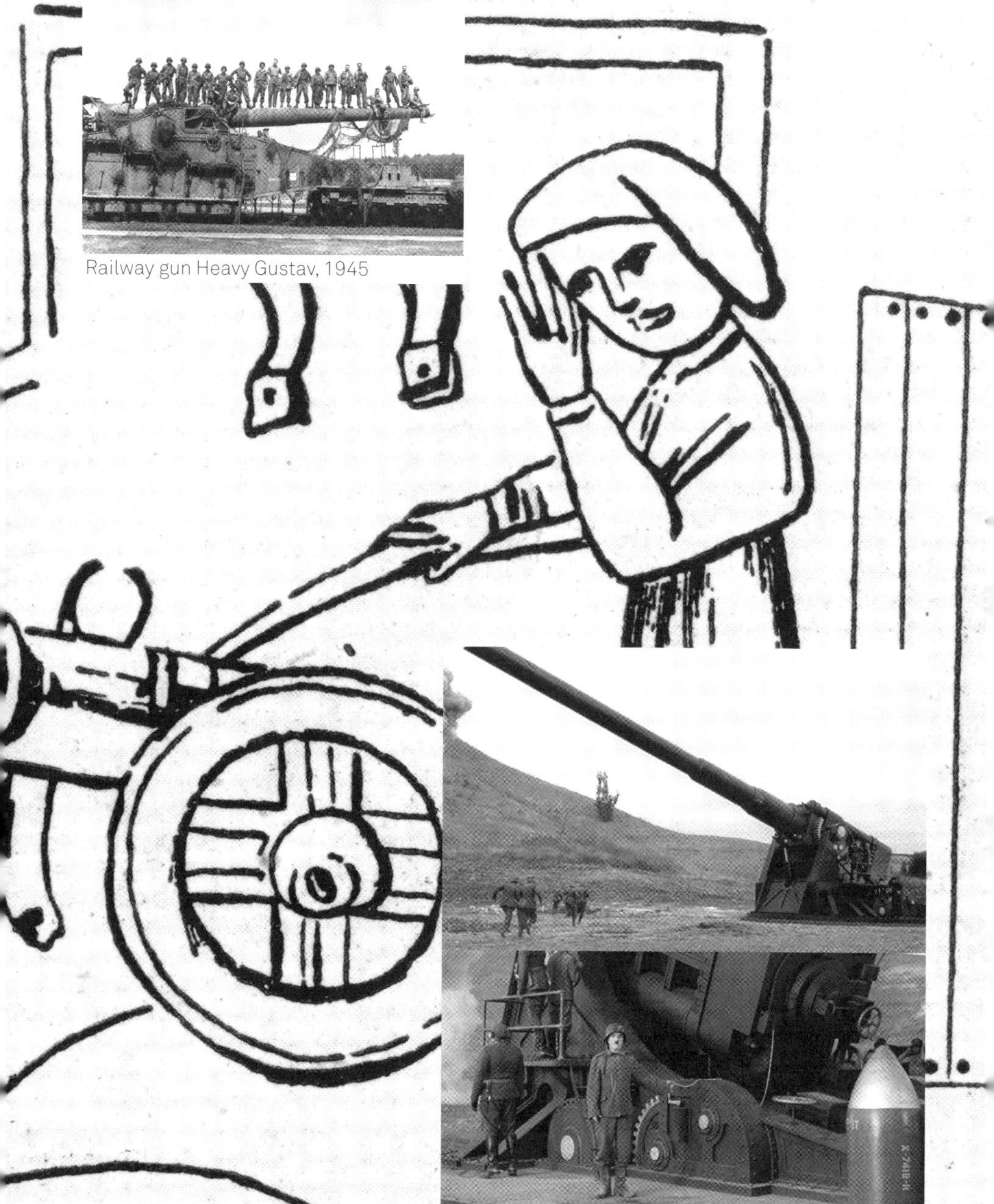

Railway gun Heavy Gustav, 1945

Very big gun (US 1940)

Medieval cannon

Once she had taken words of instruction from him direct. She had awaited them in an ecstasy of happiness—and fear. For her exaltation was made terrible by the dread that some error might dishonour her. . . .

She watched him now through the glass with all the unpenetrating minuteness of an impassioned woman's observation.

He said little, she remarked. He looked but little at the maps. The tall Englishman beside him was manifestly troubled by a swarm of ideas, conflicting ideas ; he craned his neck at every shifting of the little red, blue, black and yellow pieces on the board and wanted to draw the commander's attention to this and that. Dubois listened, nodded, emitted a word and became still again, brooding like the national eagle.

His eyes were so deeply sunken under his white eyebrows that she could not see his eyes ; his moustache overhung the mouth from which those words of decision came. Viard, too, said little ; he was a dark man with a drooping head and melancholy watchful eyes. He was more intent upon the French right, which was feeling its way now through Alsace to the Rhine. He was, she knew, an old colleague of Dubois ; he knew him better, she decided, he trusted him more than this unfamiliar Englishman. . . .

Not to talk, to remain impassive and as far

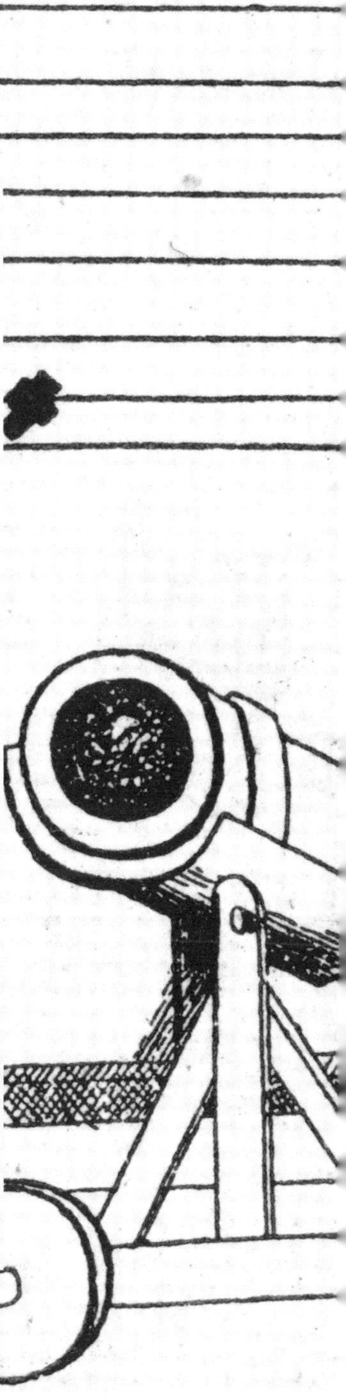

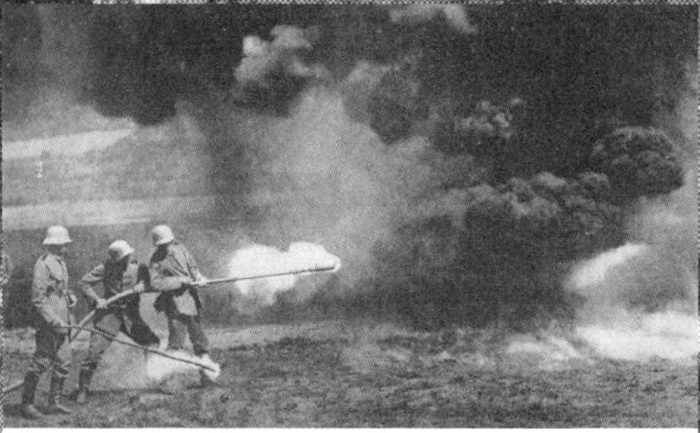
War technology, Flammenwerfer

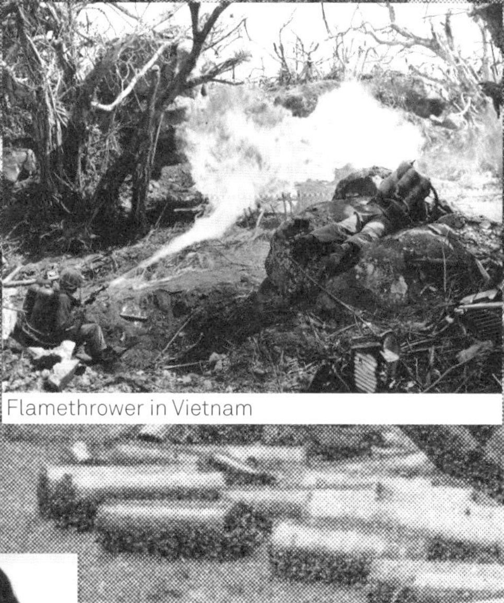
Flamethrower in Vietnam

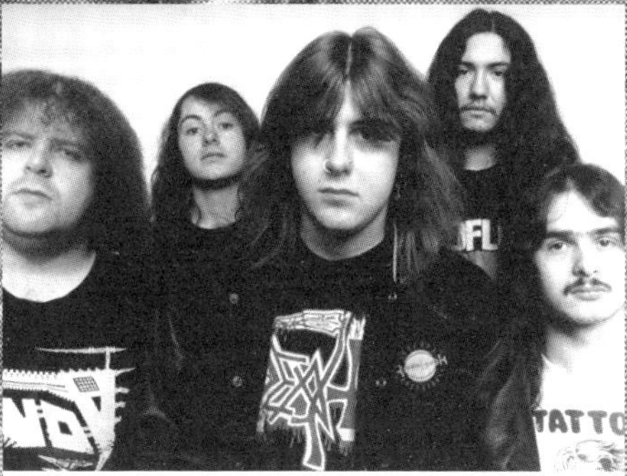
Napalm Death, early years

Empty shells

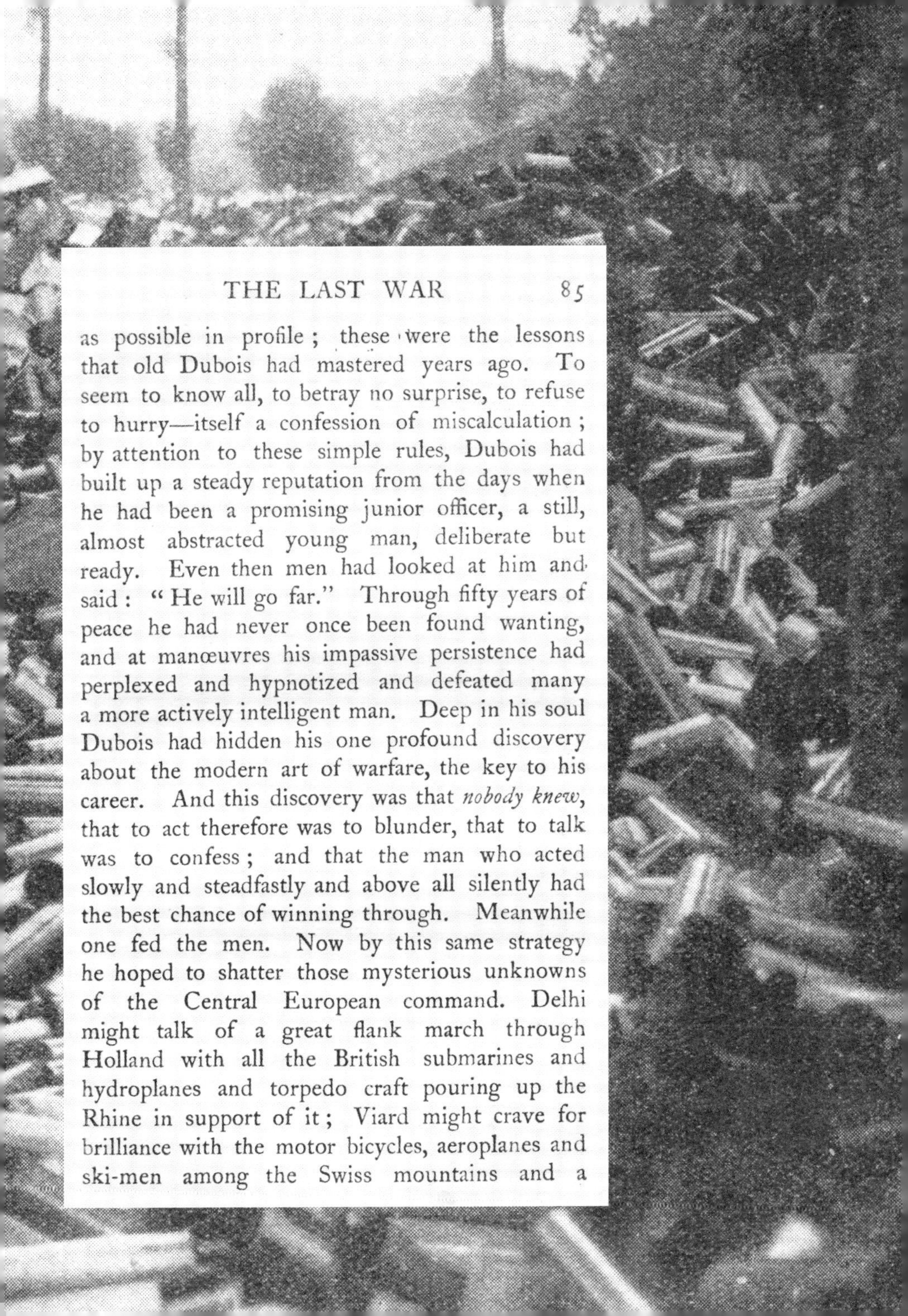

as possible in profile; these were the lessons that old Dubois had mastered years ago. To seem to know all, to betray no surprise, to refuse to hurry—itself a confession of miscalculation; by attention to these simple rules, Dubois had built up a steady reputation from the days when he had been a promising junior officer, a still, almost abstracted young man, deliberate but ready. Even then men had looked at him and said: "He will go far." Through fifty years of peace he had never once been found wanting, and at manœuvres his impassive persistence had perplexed and hypnotized and defeated many a more actively intelligent man. Deep in his soul Dubois had hidden his one profound discovery about the modern art of warfare, the key to his career. And this discovery was that *nobody knew*, that to act therefore was to blunder, that to talk was to confess; and that the man who acted slowly and steadfastly and above all silently had the best chance of winning through. Meanwhile one fed the men. Now by this same strategy he hoped to shatter those mysterious unknowns of the Central European command. Delhi might talk of a great flank march through Holland with all the British submarines and hydroplanes and torpedo craft pouring up the Rhine in support of it; Viard might crave for brilliance with the motor bicycles, aeroplanes and ski-men among the Swiss mountains and a

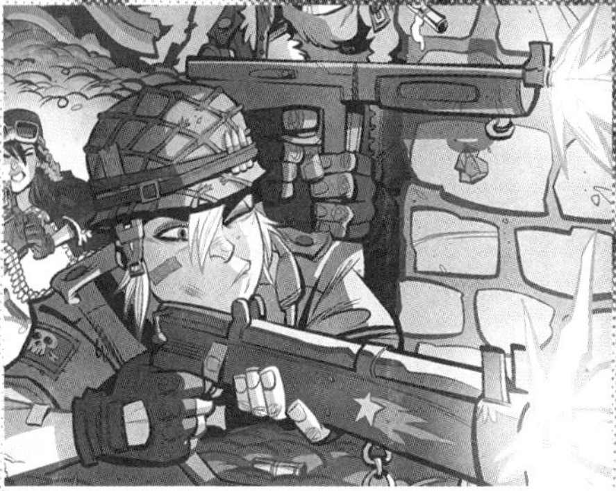

Tank Girl with gun

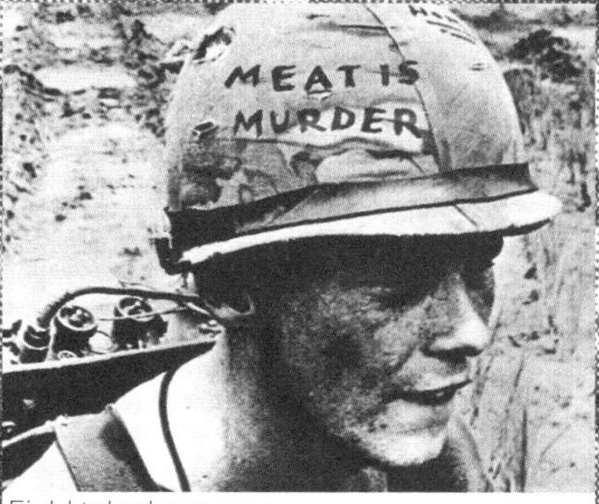

Field telephone guy

Granate girls

sudden swoop upon Vienna; the thing was to listen—and wait for the other side to begin experimenting. It was all experimenting. And meanwhile he remained in profile, with an air of assurance—like a man who sits in an automobile after the chauffeur has had his directions.

And every one about him was the stronger and surer for that quiet face, that air of knowledge and unruffled confidence. The clustering lights threw a score of shadows of him upon the maps, great bunches of him, versions of a commanding presence, lighter or darker, dominated the field, and pointed in every direction. Those shadows symbolized his control. When a messenger came from the wireless room to shift this or that piece in the game, to replace under amended reports one Central European regiment by a score, to draw back or thrust out or distribute this or that force of the allies, the Marshal would turn his head and seem not to see, or look and nod slightly, as a master nods who approves a pupil's self-correction. "Yes, that's better."

How wonderful he was, thought the woman at the window, how wonderful it all was. This was the brain of the western world, this was Olympus with the warring earth at its feet. And he was guiding France, France so long a resentful exile from imperialism, back to her old predominance.

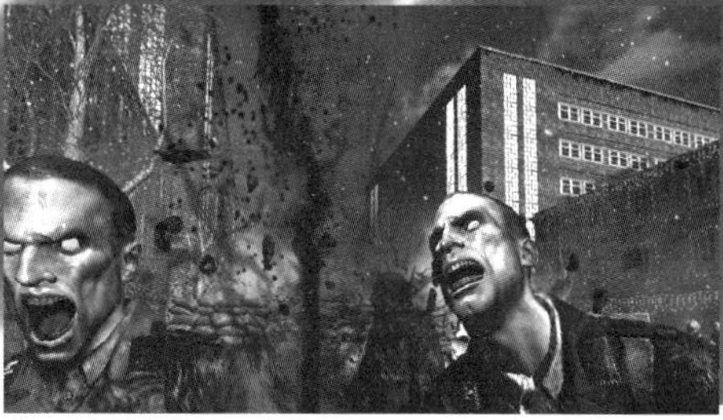

Zombie Wehrmacht

It seemed to her beyond the desert of a woman that she should be privileged to participate. . . .

It is hard to be a woman, full of the stormy impulse to personal devotion, and to have to be impersonal, abstract, exact, punctual. She must control herself. . . .

She gave herself up to fantastic dreams, dreams of the days when the war would be over and victory enthroned. Then perhaps this harshness, this armour would be put aside and the gods might unbend. Her eyelids drooped. . . .

She roused herself with a start. She became aware that the night outside was no longer still. That there was an excitement down below on the bridge and a running in the street and a flickering of searchlights among the clouds from some high place away beyond the Trocadero. And then the excitement came surging up past her and invaded the hall within.

One of the sentinels from the terrace stood at the upper end of the room gesticulating and shouting something.

And all the world had changed. A kind of throbbing. She couldn't understand. It was as if all the water-pipes and concealed machinery and cables of the ways beneath, were beating—as pulses beat. And about her blew something like a wind—a wind that was dismay.

Marching on ...

Her eyes went to the face of the Marshal as a frightened child might look towards its mother.

He was still serene. He was frowning slightly, she thought, but that was natural enough, for the Earl of Delhi with one hand gauntly gesticulating had taken him by the arm and was all too manifestly disposed to drag him towards the great door that opened on the terrace. And Viard was hurrying towards the huge windows and doing so in the strangest of attitudes, bent forward and with eyes upturned.

Something up there?

And then it was as if thunder broke overhead.

The sound struck her like a blow. She crouched together against the masonry and looked up. She saw three black shapes swooping down through the torn clouds, and from a point a little below two of them there had already started curling trails of red. . . .

Everything else in her being was paralyzed, she hung through moments that seemed infinities, watching those red missiles whirl down towards her.

She felt torn out of the world. There was nothing else in the world but a crimson-purple glare and sound, deafening, all-embracing, continuing sound. Every other light had gone out about her and against this glare hung slanting walls, pirouetting pillars, projecting fragments of

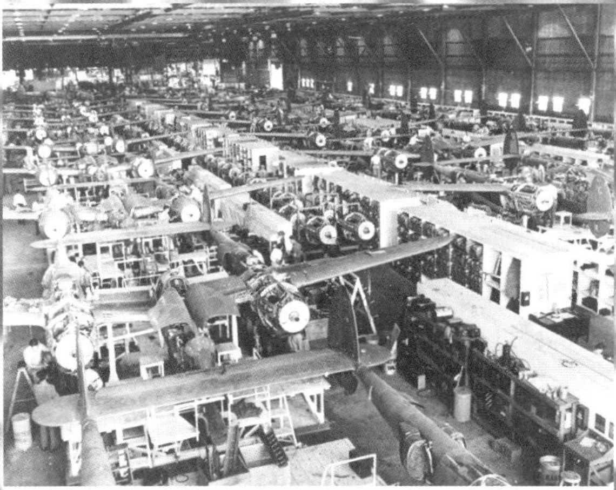
Warplane factory

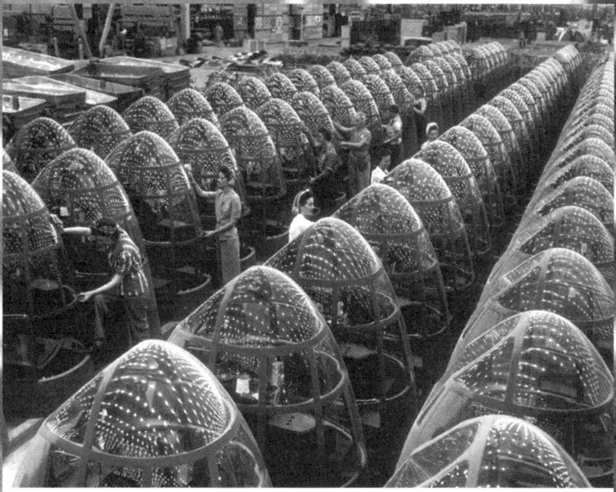
... new weapons

... in the factories on ...

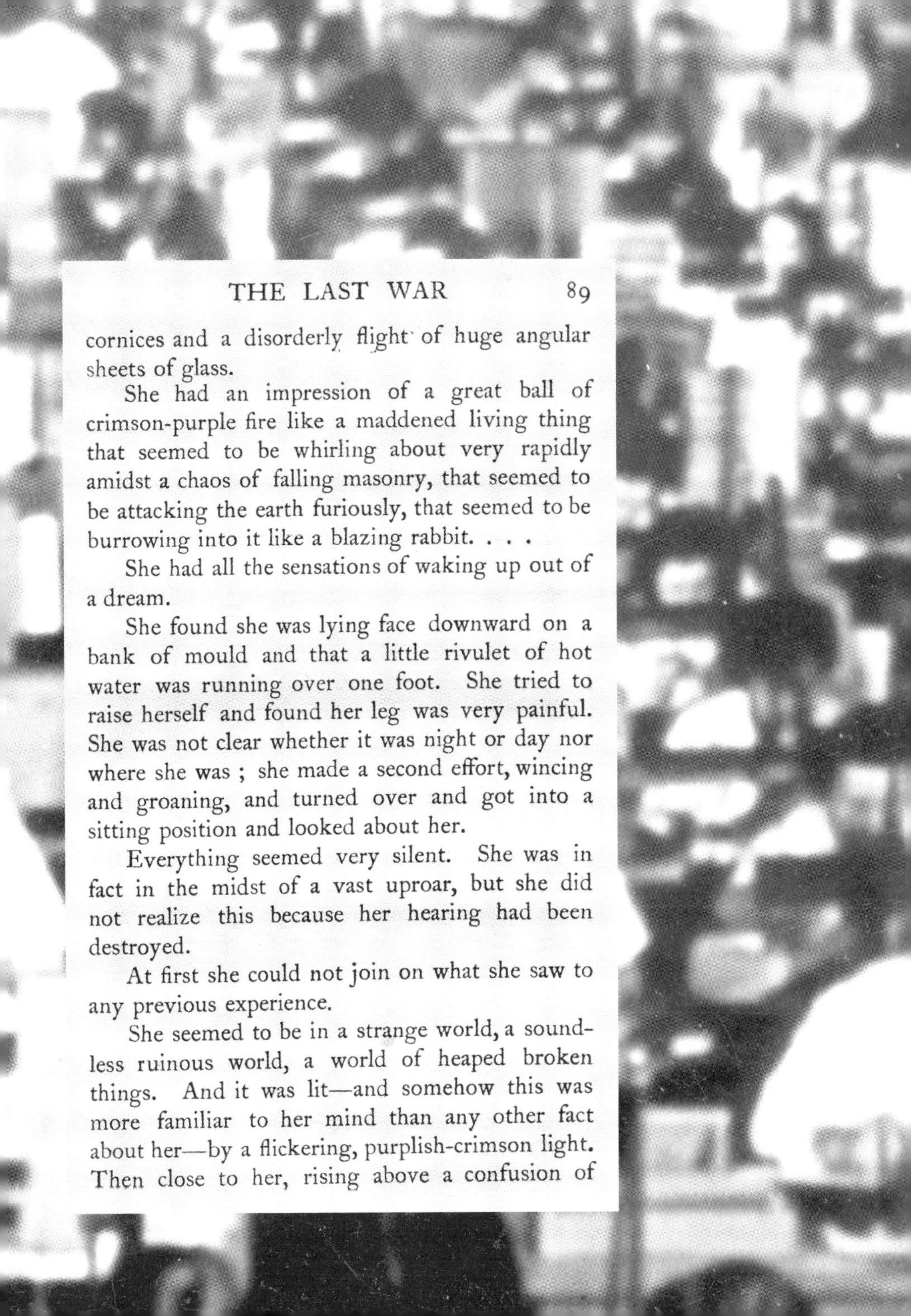

cornices and a disorderly flight of huge angular sheets of glass.

She had an impression of a great ball of crimson-purple fire like a maddened living thing that seemed to be whirling about very rapidly amidst a chaos of falling masonry, that seemed to be attacking the earth furiously, that seemed to be burrowing into it like a blazing rabbit. . . .

She had all the sensations of waking up out of a dream.

She found she was lying face downward on a bank of mould and that a little rivulet of hot water was running over one foot. She tried to raise herself and found her leg was very painful. She was not clear whether it was night or day nor where she was ; she made a second effort, wincing and groaning, and turned over and got into a sitting position and looked about her.

Everything seemed very silent. She was in fact in the midst of a vast uproar, but she did not realize this because her hearing had been destroyed.

At first she could not join on what she saw to any previous experience.

She seemed to be in a strange world, a soundless ruinous world, a world of heaped broken things. And it was lit—and somehow this was more familiar to her mind than any other fact about her—by a flickering, purplish-crimson light. Then close to her, rising above a confusion of

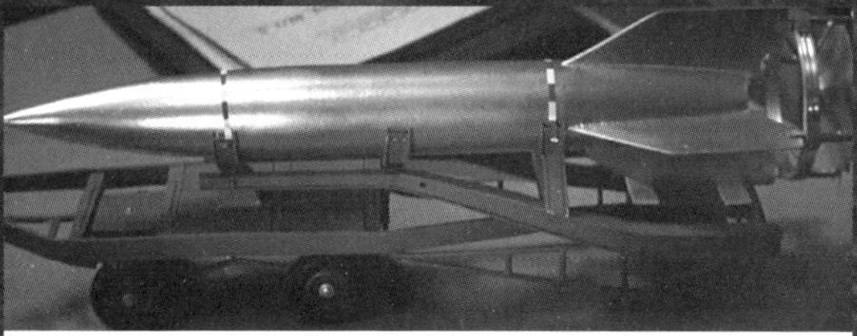

Long range bomb desktop model (DDDE 1967)

débris, she recognized the Trocadero; it was changed, something had gone from it, but its outline was unmistakable. It stood out against a streaming whirling uprush of red-lit steam. And with that she recalled Paris and the Seine and the warm overcast evening and the beautiful luminous organization of the War Control. . . .

She drew herself a little way up the slope of earth on which she lay and examined her surroundings with an increasing understanding. . . .

The earth on which she was lying projected like a cape into the river. Quite close to her was a brimming lake of dammed-up water from which these warm rivulets and torrents were trickling. Wisps of vapour came into circling existence a foot or so from its mirror-surface. Near at hand and reflected exactly in the water was the upper part of a familiar-looking stone pillar. On the side of her away from the water the heaped ruins rose steeply in a confused slope up to a glaring crest. Above and reflecting this glare towered pillowed masses of steam rolling swiftly upward to the zenith. It was from this crest that the livid glow that lit the world about her proceeded, and slowly her mind connected this mound with the vanished buildings of the War Control.

"*Mais!*" she whispered and remained with staring eyes quite motionless for a time, crouching close to the warm earth.

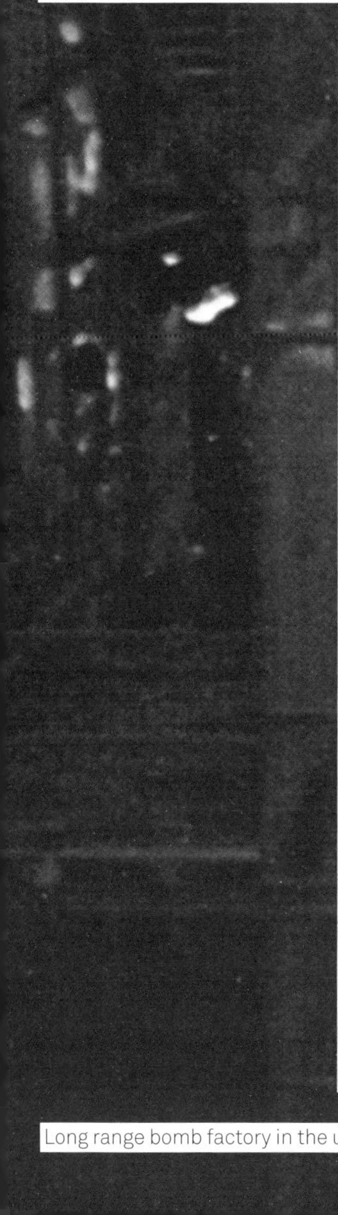

Long range bomb factory in the underground

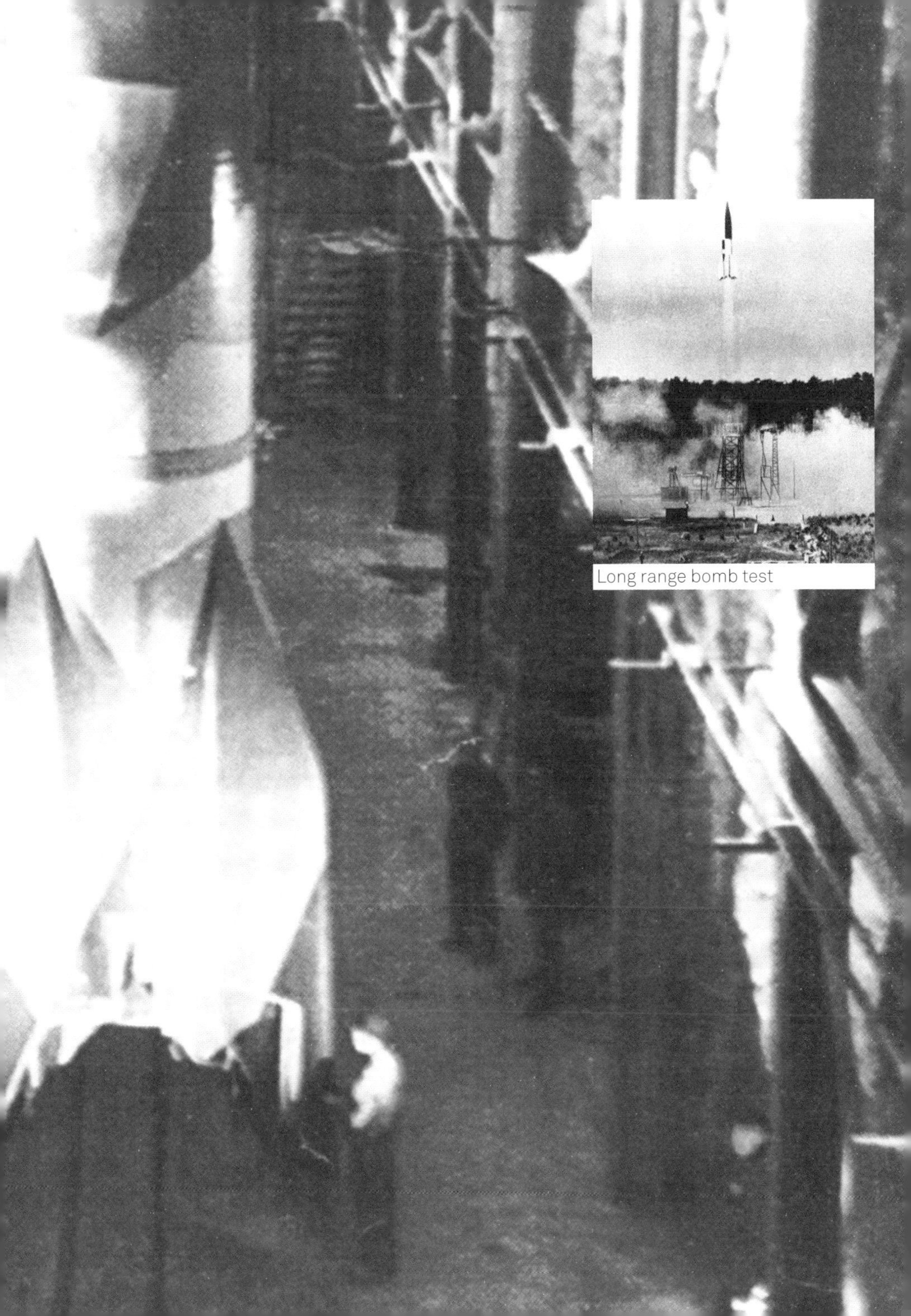

Long range bomb test

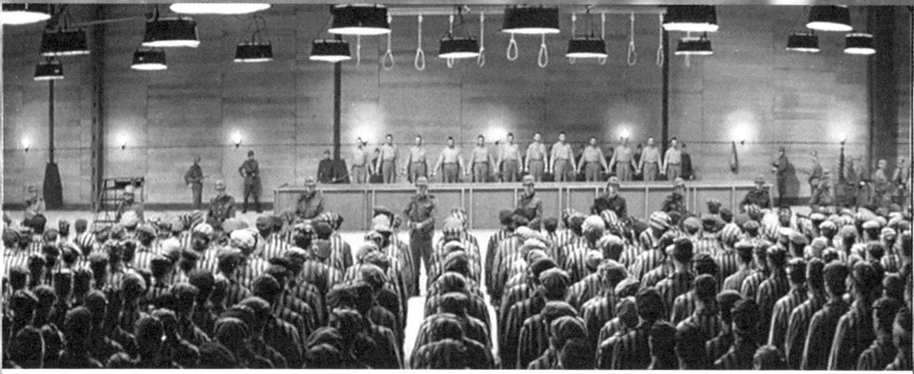
Forced labour, punishment on the resistance (DDDE 1967)

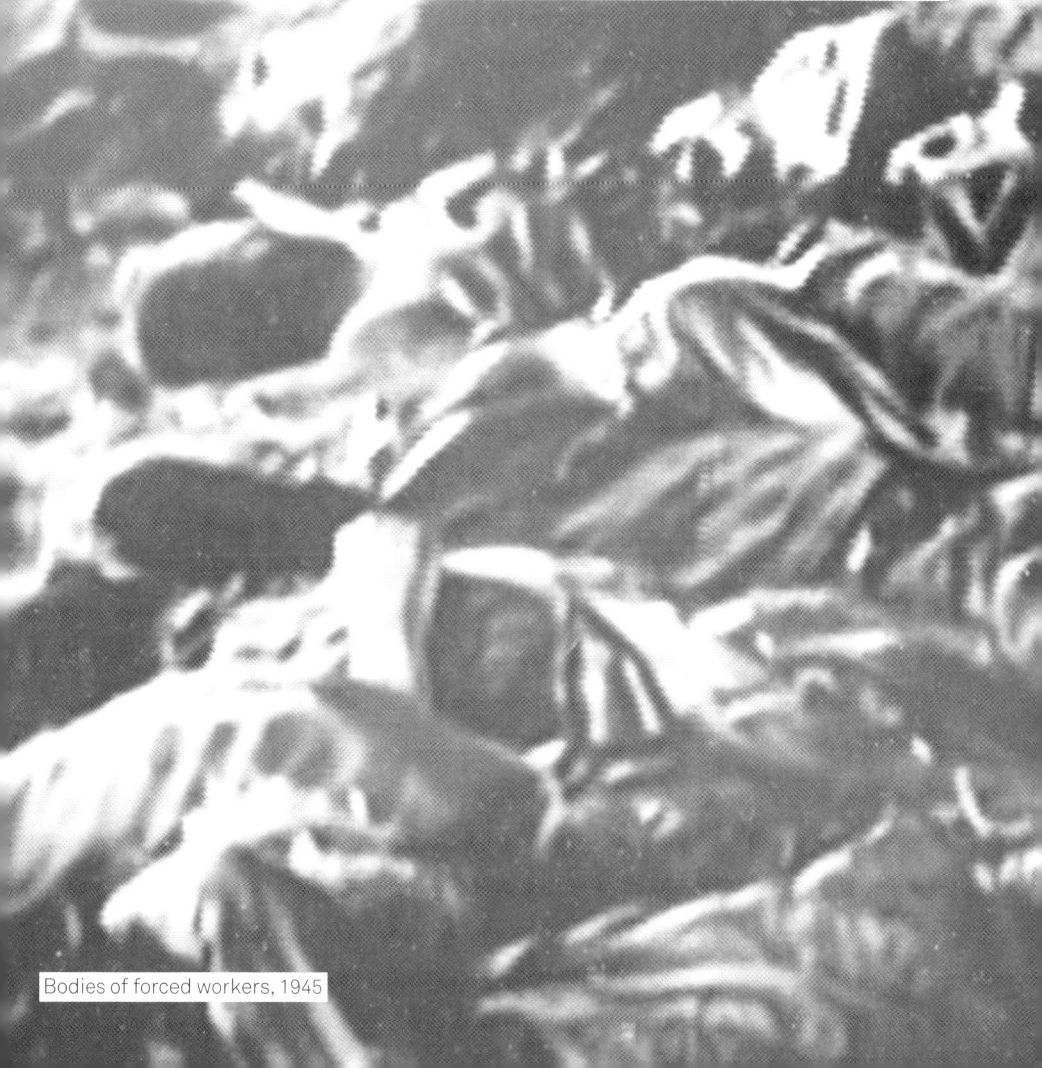
Bodies of forced workers, 1945

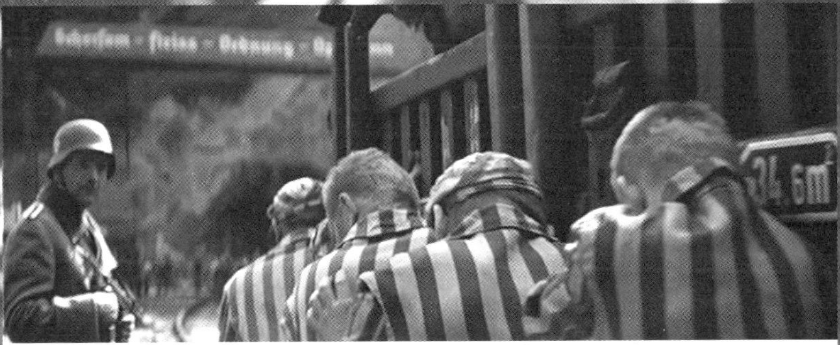

Forced labourers, walking into the rocket mountain (DDDE 1967)

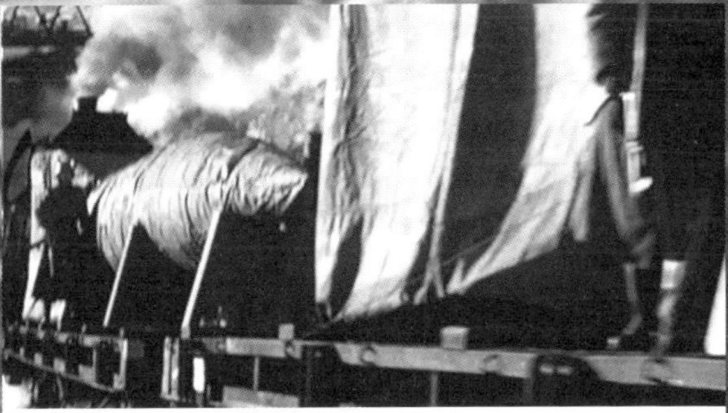

Rocket on a train (DDDE 1967)

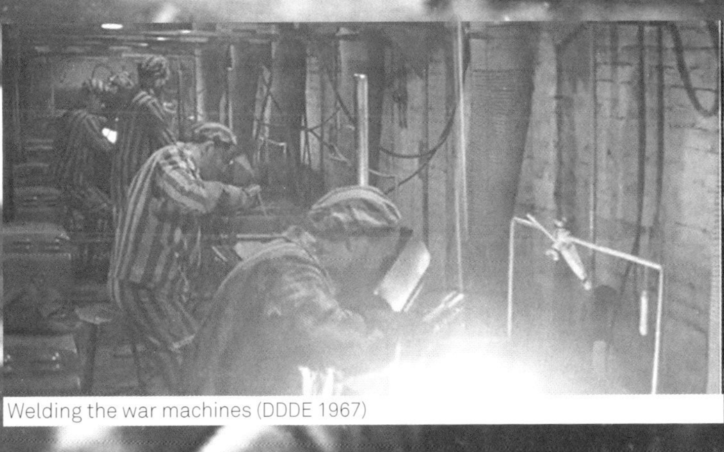

Welding the war machines (DDDE 1967)

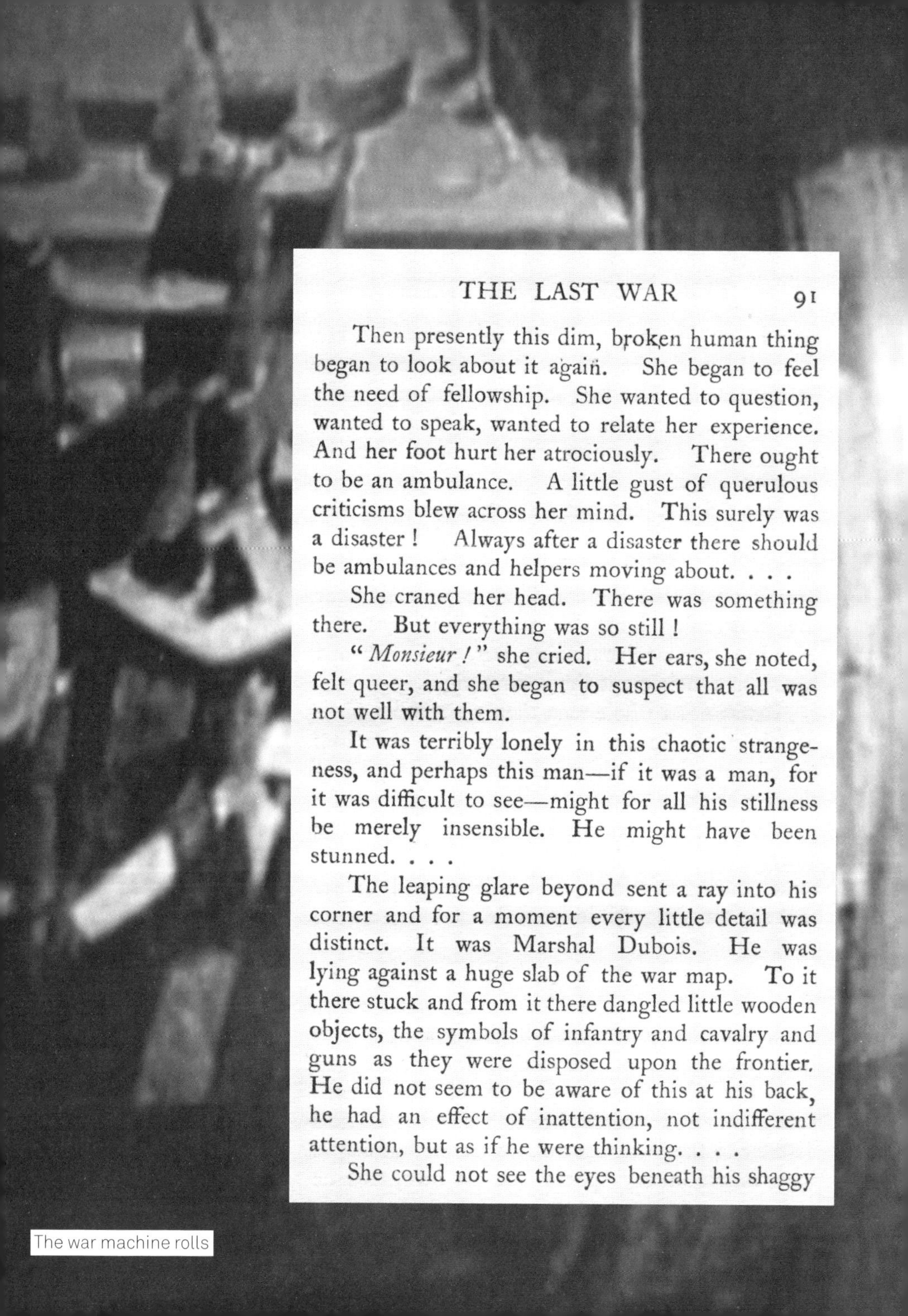

Then presently this dim, broken human thing began to look about it again. She began to feel the need of fellowship. She wanted to question, wanted to speak, wanted to relate her experience. And her foot hurt her atrociously. There ought to be an ambulance. A little gust of querulous criticisms blew across her mind. This surely was a disaster! Always after a disaster there should be ambulances and helpers moving about. . . .

She craned her head. There was something there. But everything was so still!

"*Monsieur!*" she cried. Her ears, she noted, felt queer, and she began to suspect that all was not well with them.

It was terribly lonely in this chaotic strangeness, and perhaps this man—if it was a man, for it was difficult to see—might for all his stillness be merely insensible. He might have been stunned. . . .

The leaping glare beyond sent a ray into his corner and for a moment every little detail was distinct. It was Marshal Dubois. He was lying against a huge slab of the war map. To it there stuck and from it there dangled little wooden objects, the symbols of infantry and cavalry and guns as they were disposed upon the frontier. He did not seem to be aware of this at his back, he had an effect of inattention, not indifferent attention, but as if he were thinking. . . .

She could not see the eyes beneath his shaggy

The war machine rolls

brows but it was evident he frowned. He frowned slightly, he had an air of not wanting to be disturbed. His face still bore that expression of assured confidence, that conviction that if things were left to him France might obey in security. . . .

She did not cry out to him again, but she crept a little nearer. A strange surmise made her eyes dilate. With a painful wrench she pulled herself up so that she could see completely over the intervening lumps of smashed-up masonry. Her hand touched something wet, and after one convulsive movement she became rigid.

It was not a whole man there; it was a piece of a man, the head and shoulders of a man that trailed down into a ragged darkness and a pool of shining black. . . .

And even as she stared the mound above her swayed and crumbled and a rush of hot water came pouring over her. Then it seemed to her that she was dragged downward. . . .

§ 3

When the rather brutish young aviator with the bullet head and the black hair close-cropped *en brosse* who was in charge of the French special scientific corps heard presently of this disaster to the War Control, he was so wanting in imagination in any sphere but his own, that he

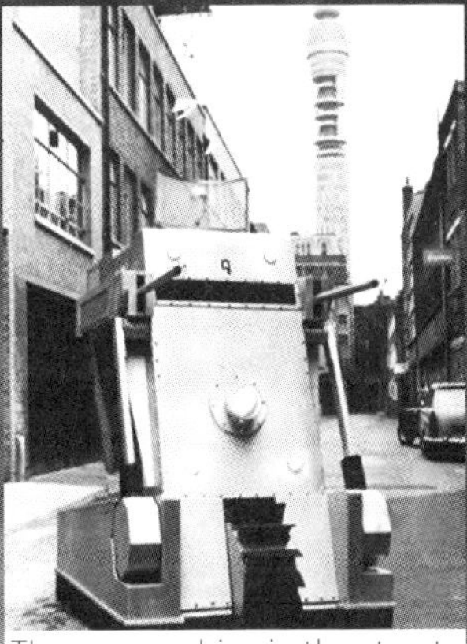
The war machine in the street

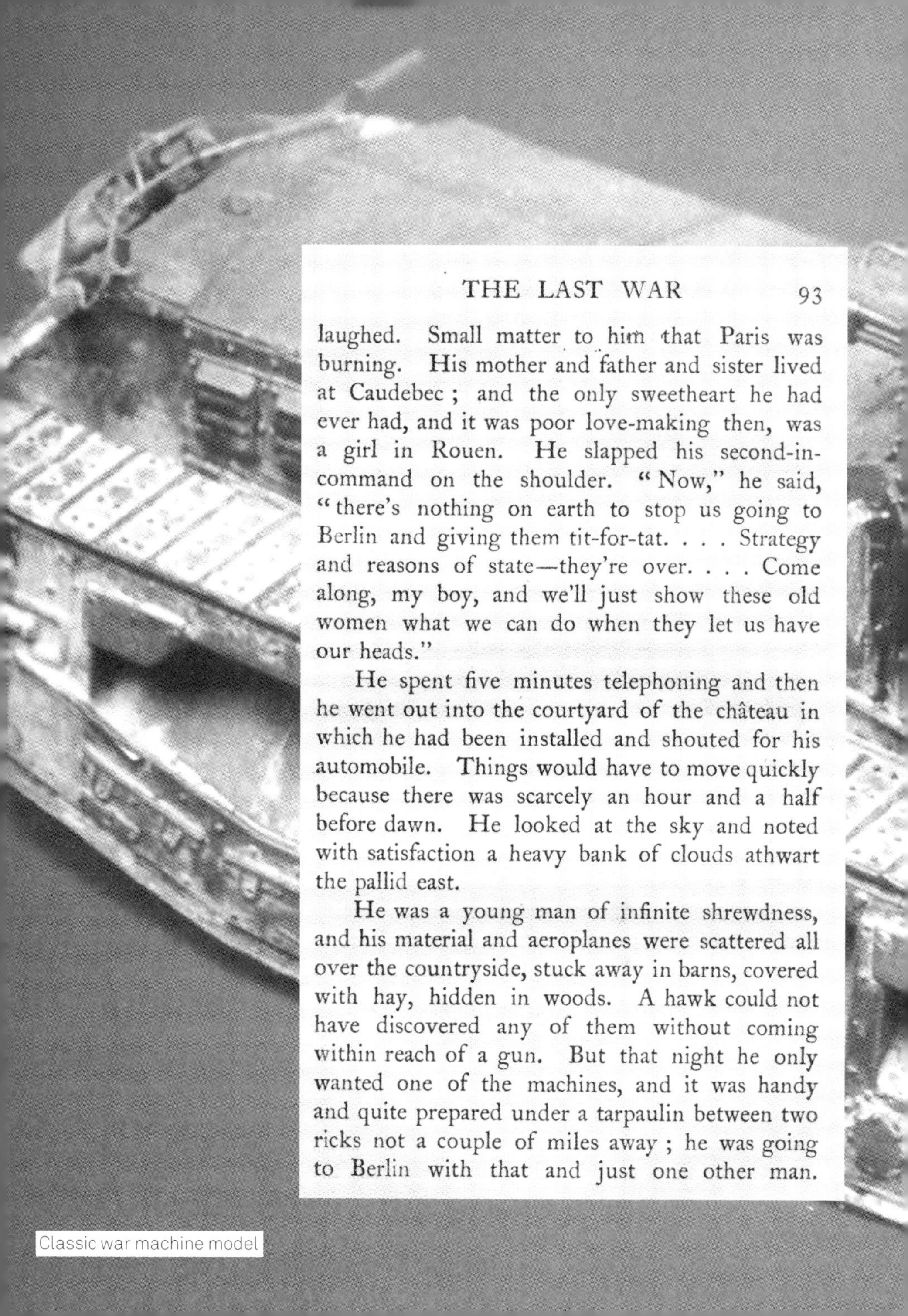

laughed. Small matter to him that Paris was burning. His mother and father and sister lived at Caudebec; and the only sweetheart he had ever had, and it was poor love-making then, was a girl in Rouen. He slapped his second-in-command on the shoulder. "Now," he said, "there's nothing on earth to stop us going to Berlin and giving them tit-for-tat. . . . Strategy and reasons of state—they're over. . . . Come along, my boy, and we'll just show these old women what we can do when they let us have our heads."

He spent five minutes telephoning and then he went out into the courtyard of the château in which he had been installed and shouted for his automobile. Things would have to move quickly because there was scarcely an hour and a half before dawn. He looked at the sky and noted with satisfaction a heavy bank of clouds athwart the pallid east.

He was a young man of infinite shrewdness, and his material and aeroplanes were scattered all over the countryside, stuck away in barns, covered with hay, hidden in woods. A hawk could not have discovered any of them without coming within reach of a gun. But that night he only wanted one of the machines, and it was handy and quite prepared under a tarpaulin between two ricks not a couple of miles away; he was going to Berlin with that and just one other man.

Classic war machine model

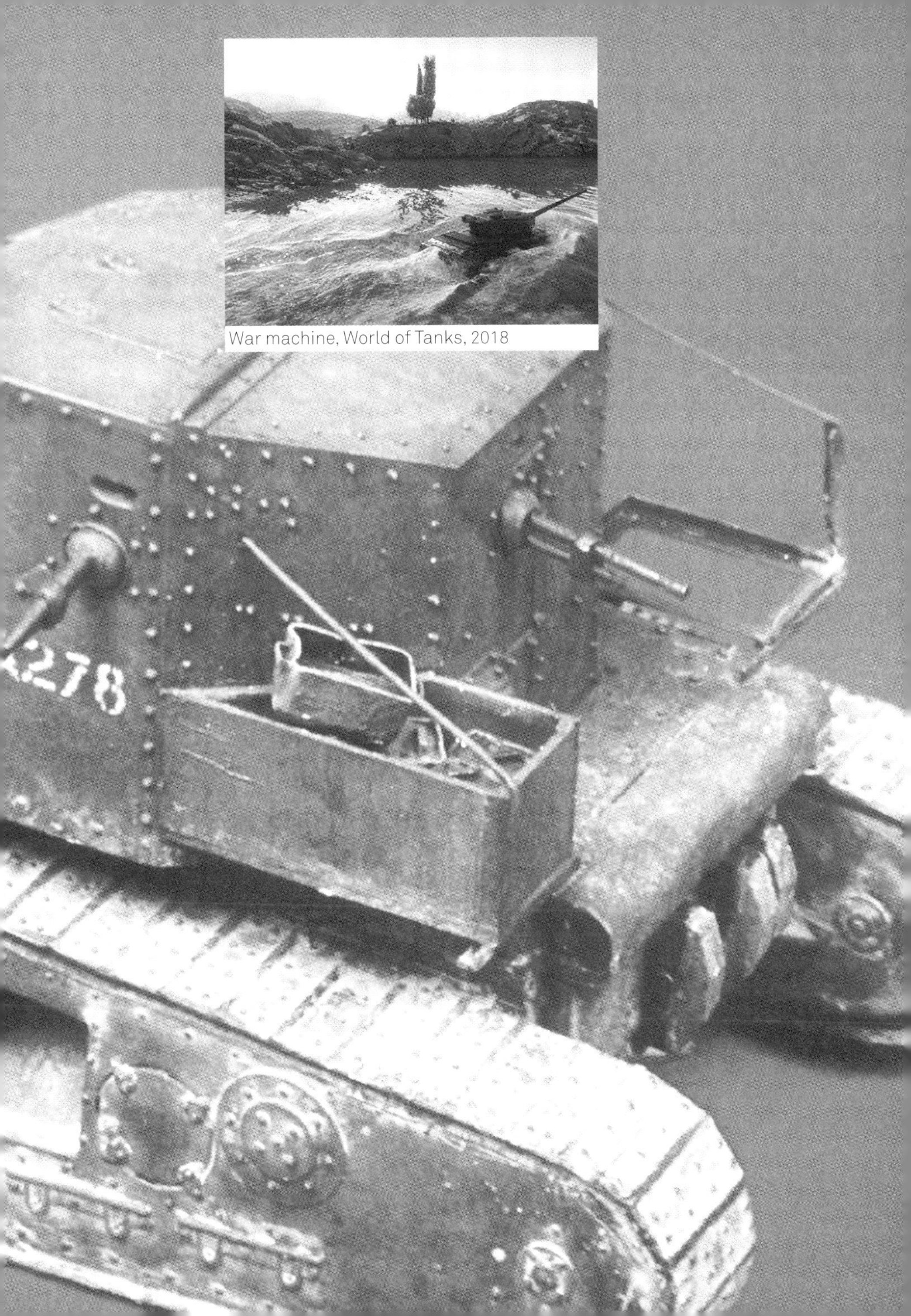

War machine, World of Tanks, 2018

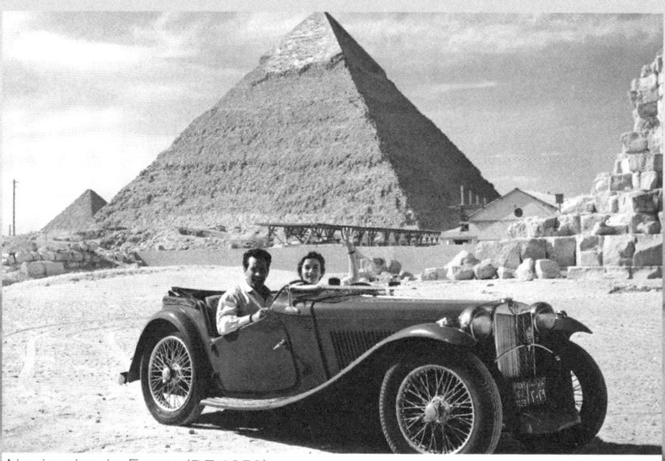

Nazi spies in Egypt (DE 1959)

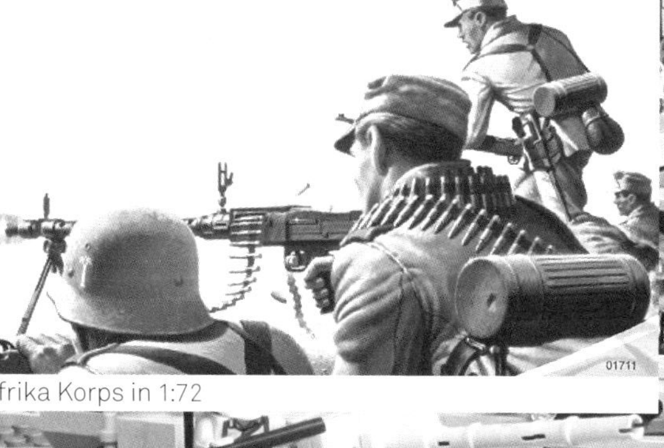

Afrika Korps in 1:72

Nazi toys

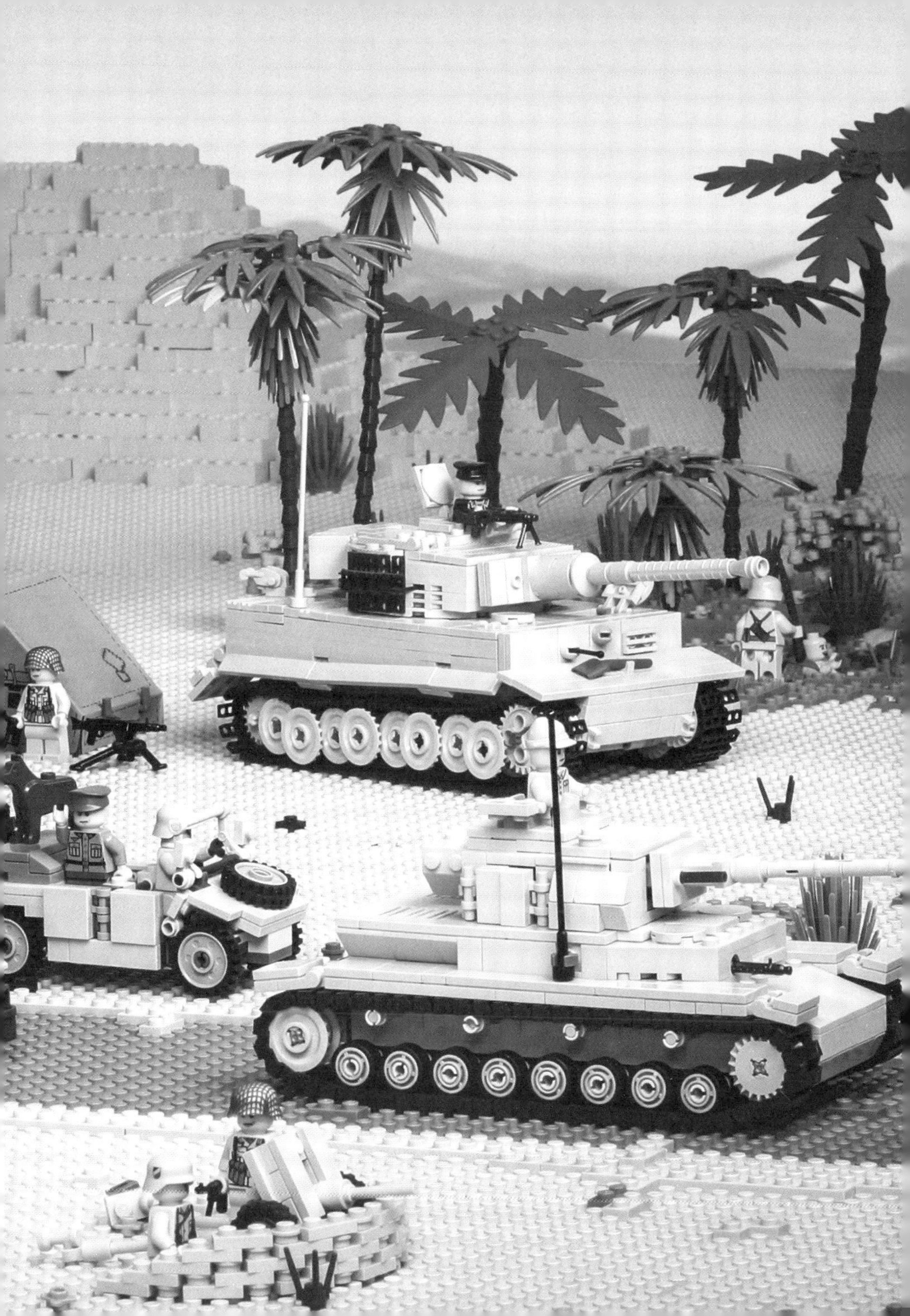

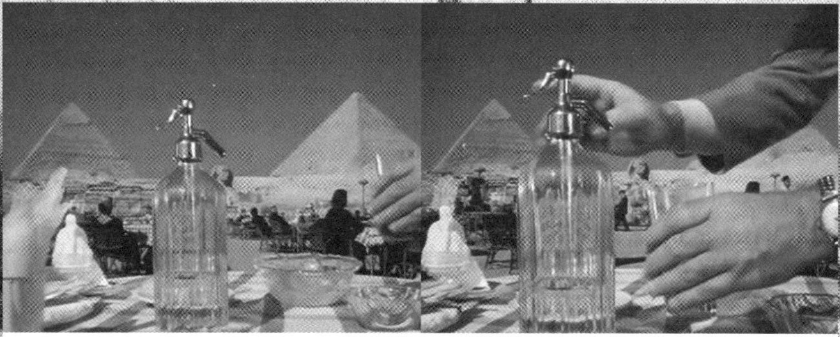
Refreshment during war time

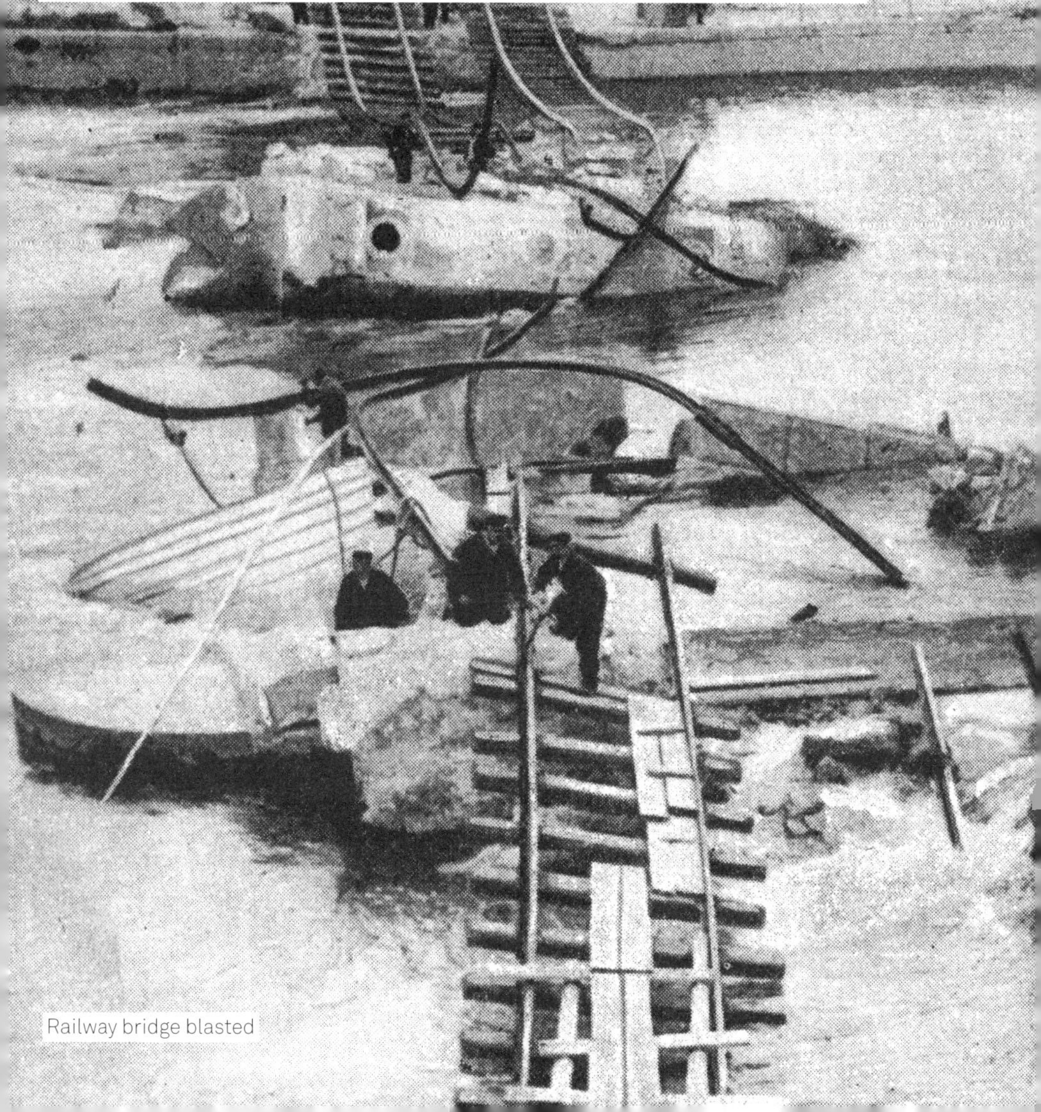
Railway bridge blasted

Two men would be enough for what he meant to do. . . .

He had in his hands the black complement to all those other gifts science was urging upon unregenerate mankind, the gift of destruction, and he was an adventurous rather than a sympathetic type. . . .

He was a dark young man with something negroid about his gleaming face. He smiled like one who is favoured and anticipates great pleasures. There was an exotic richness, a chuckling flavour, about the voice in which he gave his orders, and he pointed his remarks with the long finger of a hand that was hairy and exceptionally big.

"We'll give them tit-for-tat," he said. "We'll give them tit-for-tat. No time to lose, boys. . . ."

And presently over the cloud-banks that lay above Westphalia and Saxony the swift aeroplane, with its atomic engine as noiseless as a dancing sunbeam and its phosphorescent gyroscopic compass, flew like an arrow to the heart of the Central European hosts.

It did not soar very high ; it skimmed a few hundred feet above the banked darknesses of cumulus that hid the world, ready to plunge at once into their wet obscurities should some hostile flier range into vision. The tense young steersman divided his attention between the

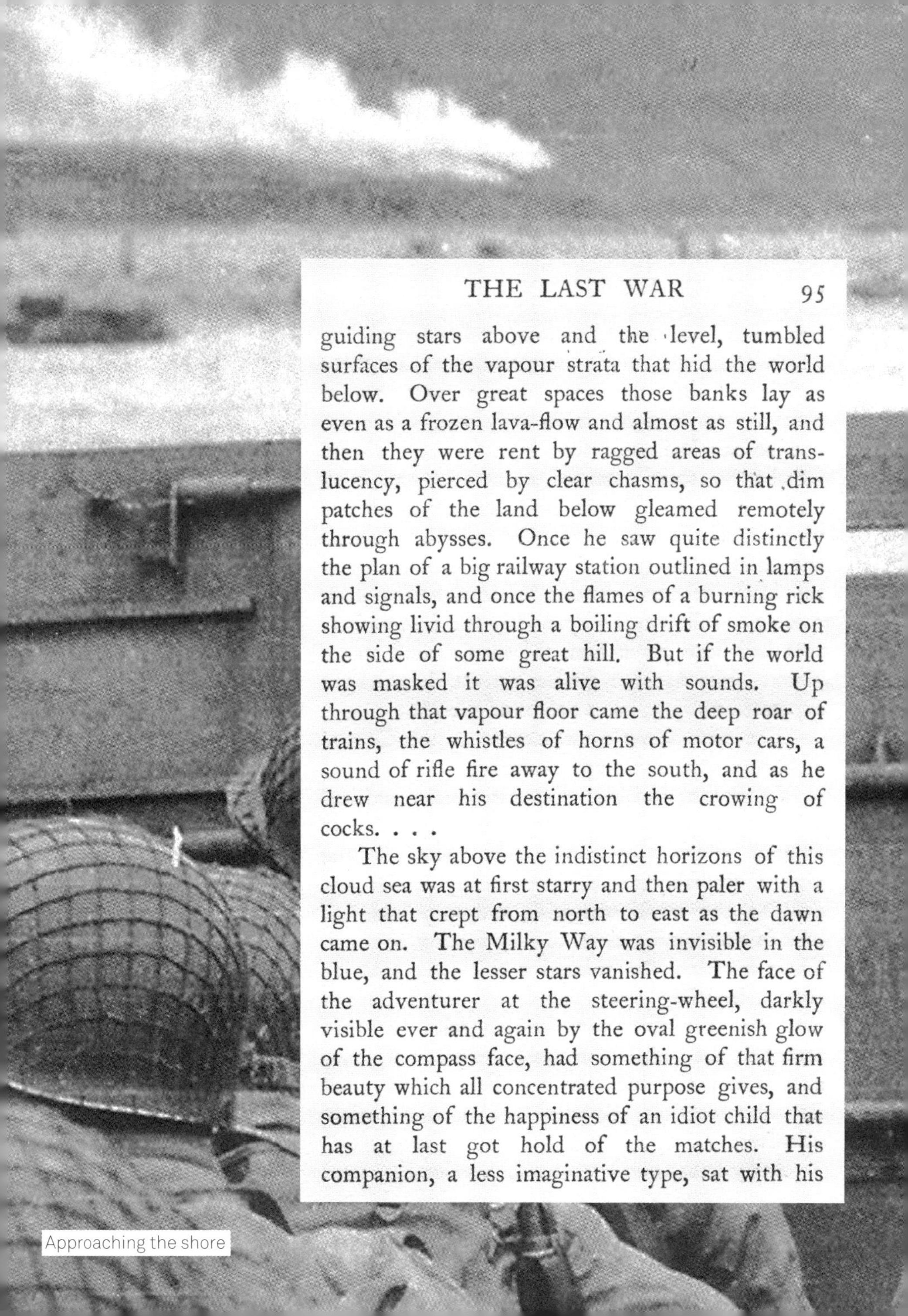

Approaching the shore

guiding stars above and the level, tumbled surfaces of the vapour strata that hid the world below. Over great spaces those banks lay as even as a frozen lava-flow and almost as still, and then they were rent by ragged areas of translucency, pierced by clear chasms, so that dim patches of the land below gleamed remotely through abysses. Once he saw quite distinctly the plan of a big railway station outlined in lamps and signals, and once the flames of a burning rick showing livid through a boiling drift of smoke on the side of some great hill. But if the world was masked it was alive with sounds. Up through that vapour floor came the deep roar of trains, the whistles of horns of motor cars, a sound of rifle fire away to the south, and as he drew near his destination the crowing of cocks. . . .

The sky above the indistinct horizons of this cloud sea was at first starry and then paler with a light that crept from north to east as the dawn came on. The Milky Way was invisible in the blue, and the lesser stars vanished. The face of the adventurer at the steering-wheel, darkly visible ever and again by the oval greenish glow of the compass face, had something of that firm beauty which all concentrated purpose gives, and something of the happiness of an idiot child that has at last got hold of the matches. His companion, a less imaginative type, sat with his

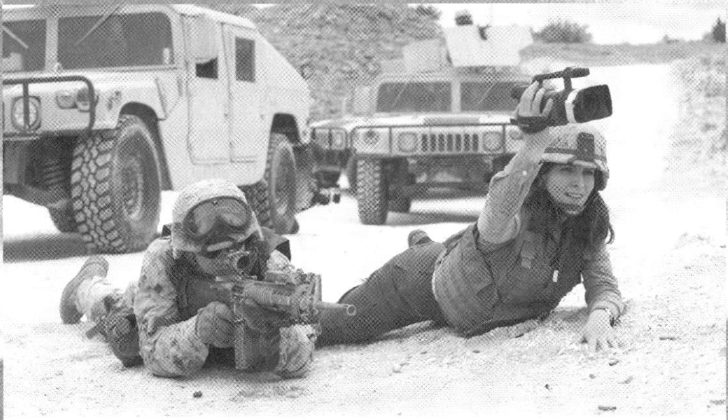

Embedded journalism (US 2016)

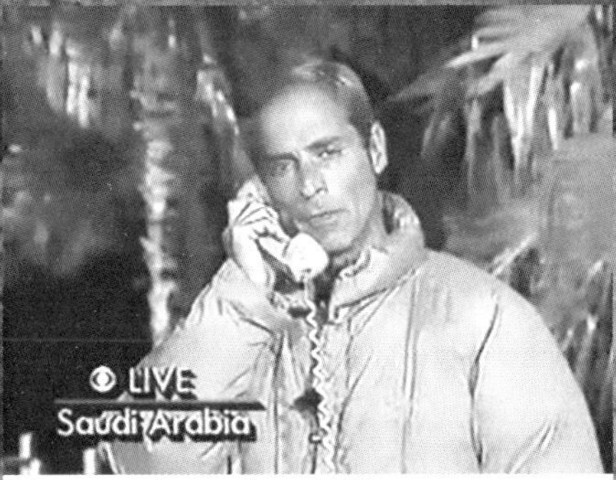

War scene journalism, 1993

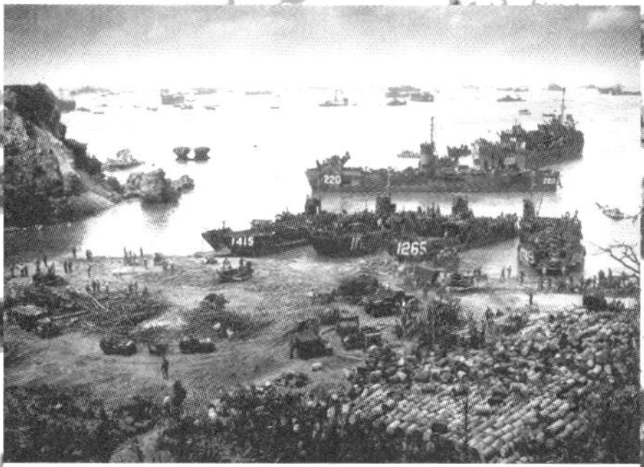
Troops landing

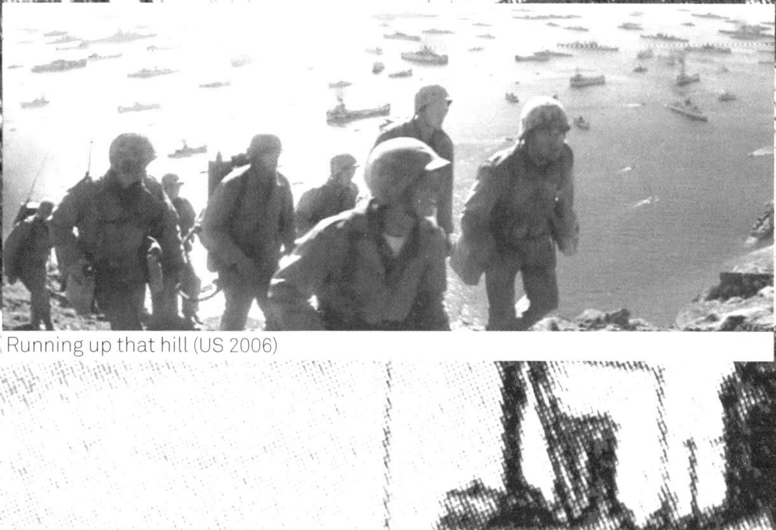
Running up that hill (US 2006)

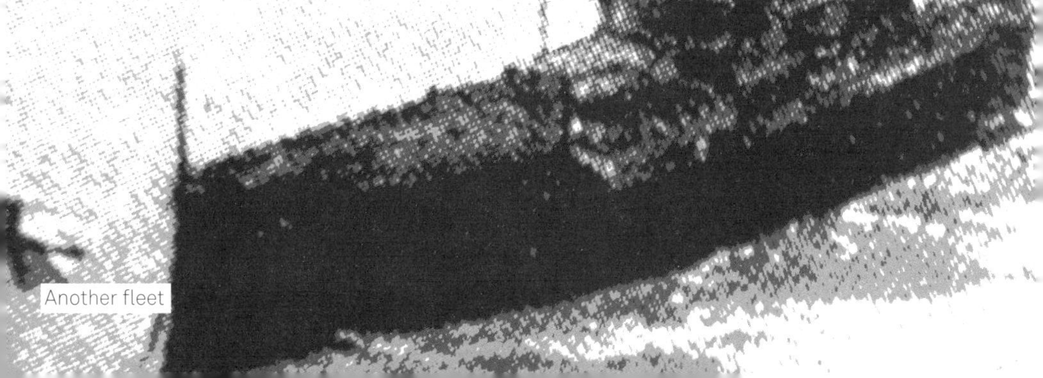
Another fleet

legs spread wide over the long coffin-shaped box which contained in its compartments the three atomic bombs, the new bombs that would continue to explode indefinitely and which no one so far had ever seen in action. Hitherto Carolinum, their essential substance, had been tested only in almost infinitesimal quantities within steel chambers embedded in lead. Beyond the thought of great destruction slumbering in the black spheres between his legs, and a keen resolve to follow out very exactly the instructions that had been given him, the man's mind was a blank. His aquiline profile against the starlight expressed nothing but a profound gloom.

The sky below grew clearer as the Central European capital was approached.

So far they had been singularly lucky and had been challenged by no aeroplanes at all. The frontier scouts they must have passed in the night; probably these were mostly under the clouds; the world was wide and they had had luck in not coming close to any soaring sentinel. Their machine was painted a pale grey that lay almost invisibly over the cloud levels below. But now the east was flushing with the near ascent of the sun, Berlin was but a score of miles ahead, and the luck of the Frenchmen held. By imperceptible degrees the clouds below dissolved. . . .

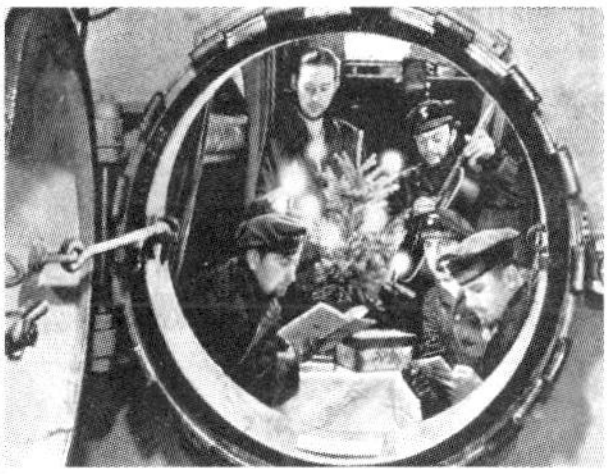

Christmas in a submarine

Away to the north-eastward, in a cloudless pool

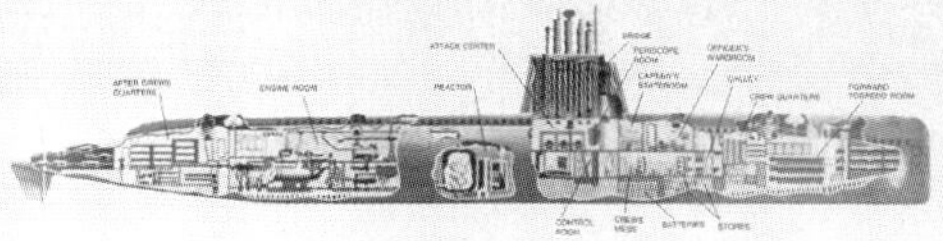

First nuclear submarine, 1957

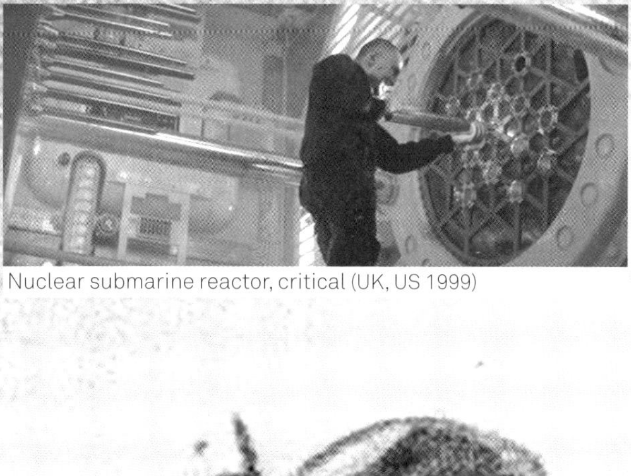
Nuclear submarine reactor, critical (UK, US 1999)

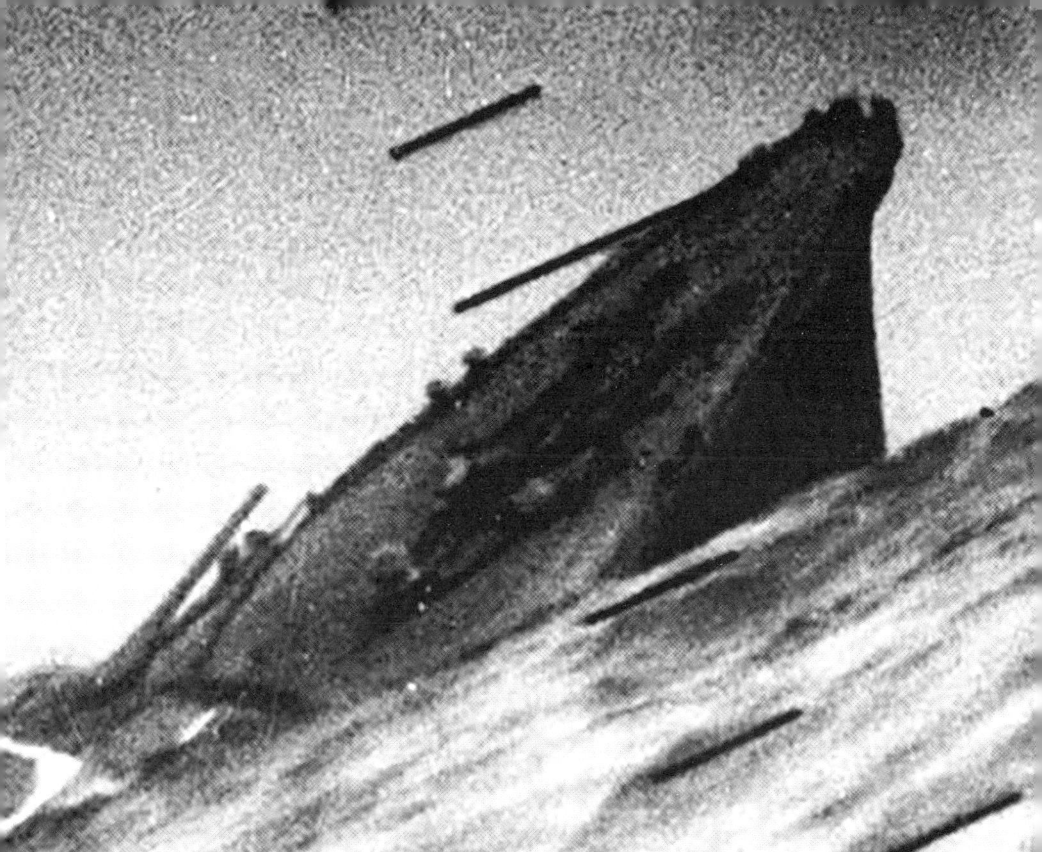

Dive the world by nuclear power, 1960

Submarine captain reporting a strike to his mother

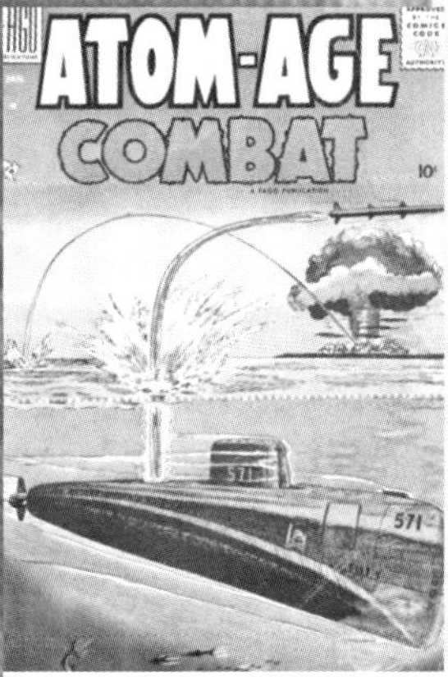

Golden Age comic, 1959

of gathering light and with all its nocturnal illuminations still blazing, was Berlin. The left finger of the steersman verified roads and open spaces below upon the mica-covered square of map that was fastened by his wheel. There in a series of lake-like expansions was the Havel away to the right; over by those forests must be Spandau; there the river split about the Potsdam island; and right ahead was Charlottenburg cleft by a great thoroughfare that fell like an indicating beam of light straight to the imperial head-quarters. There, plain enough, was the Thier-garten; beyond rose the imperial palace, and to the right those tall buildings, those clustering beflagged, bemasted roofs, must be the offices in which the Central European staff was housed. It was all coldly clear and colourless in the dawn.

He looked up suddenly as a humming sound grew out of nothing and became swiftly louder. Nearly overhead a German aeroplane was circling down from an immense height to challenge him. He made a gesture with his left arm to the gloomy man behind and then gripped his little wheel with both hands, crouched over it and twisted his neck to look upward. He was attentive, tightly strung, but quite contemptuous of their ability to hurt him. No German alive, he was assured, could outfly him, or indeed any one of the best Frenchmen. He imagined they might strike at him as a hawk strikes, but they

Pending: 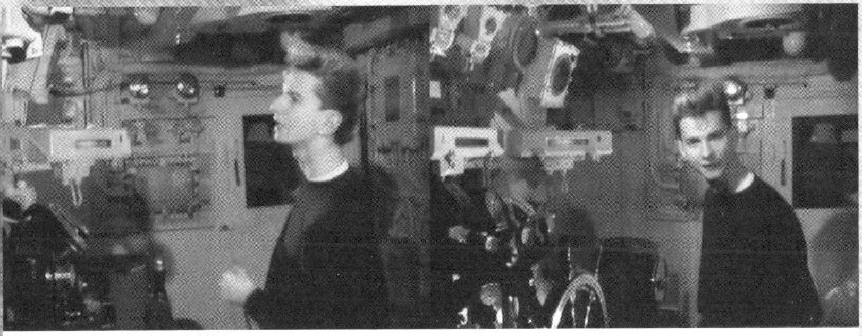
Dave at the helm, 1984

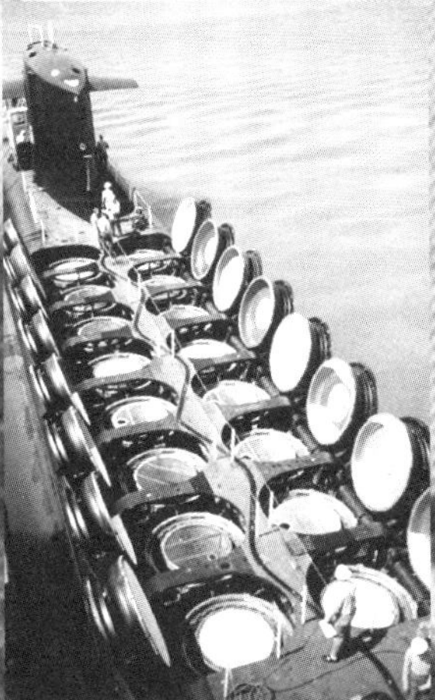
All rocket hatches open

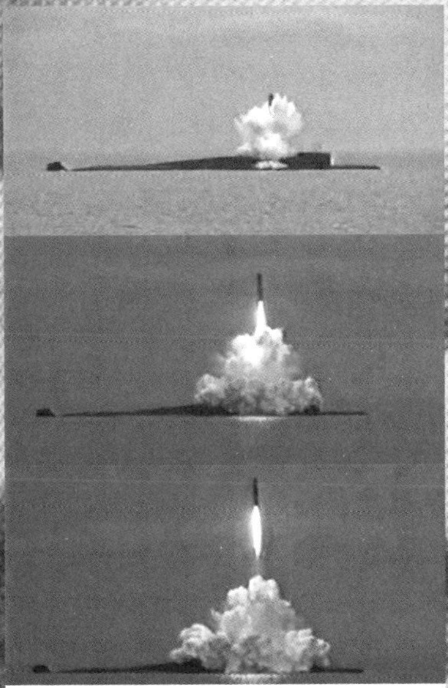
Submarine rocket launch

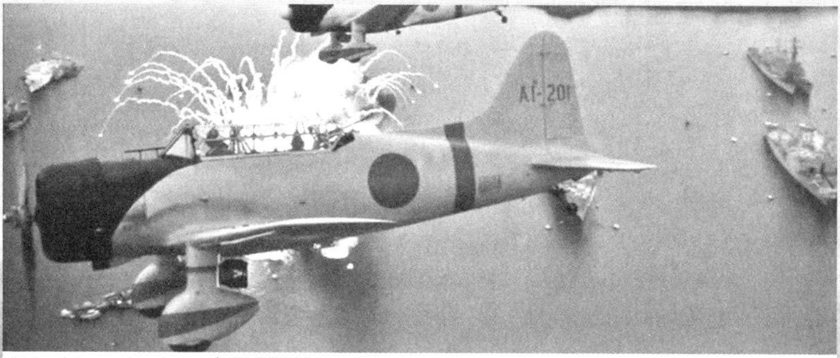

Attacking a harbour (US 2001)

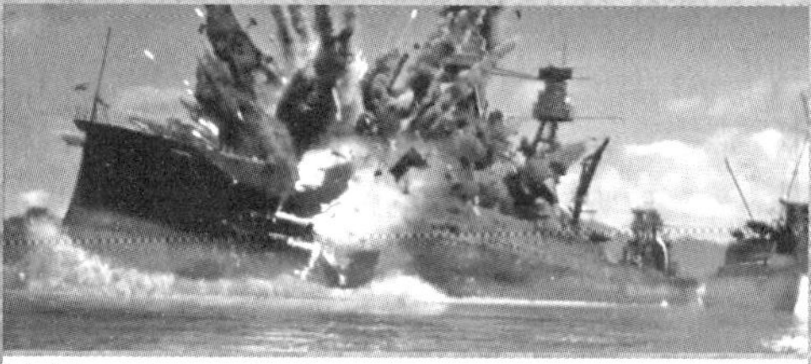
Battleship bombed

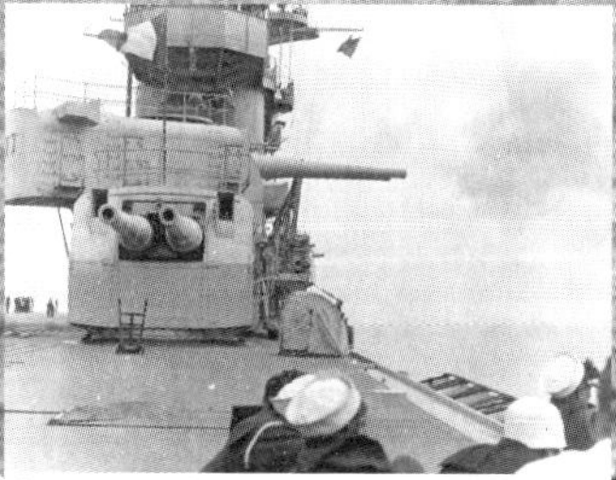
On deck of the Saratoga

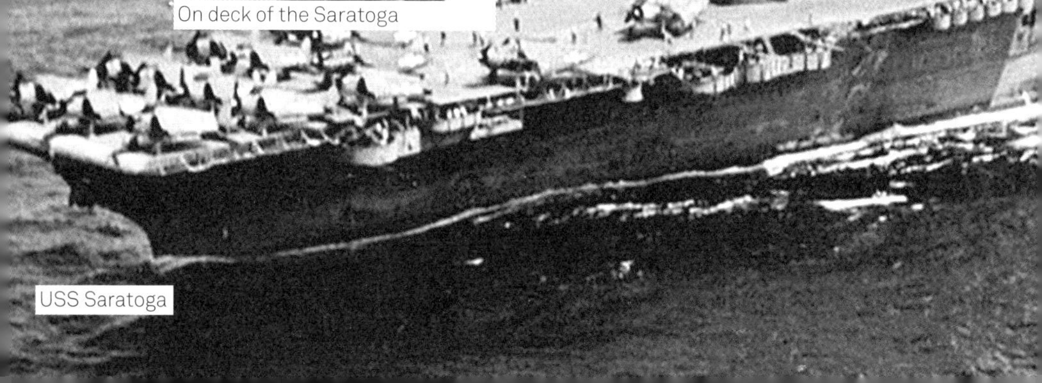
USS Saratoga

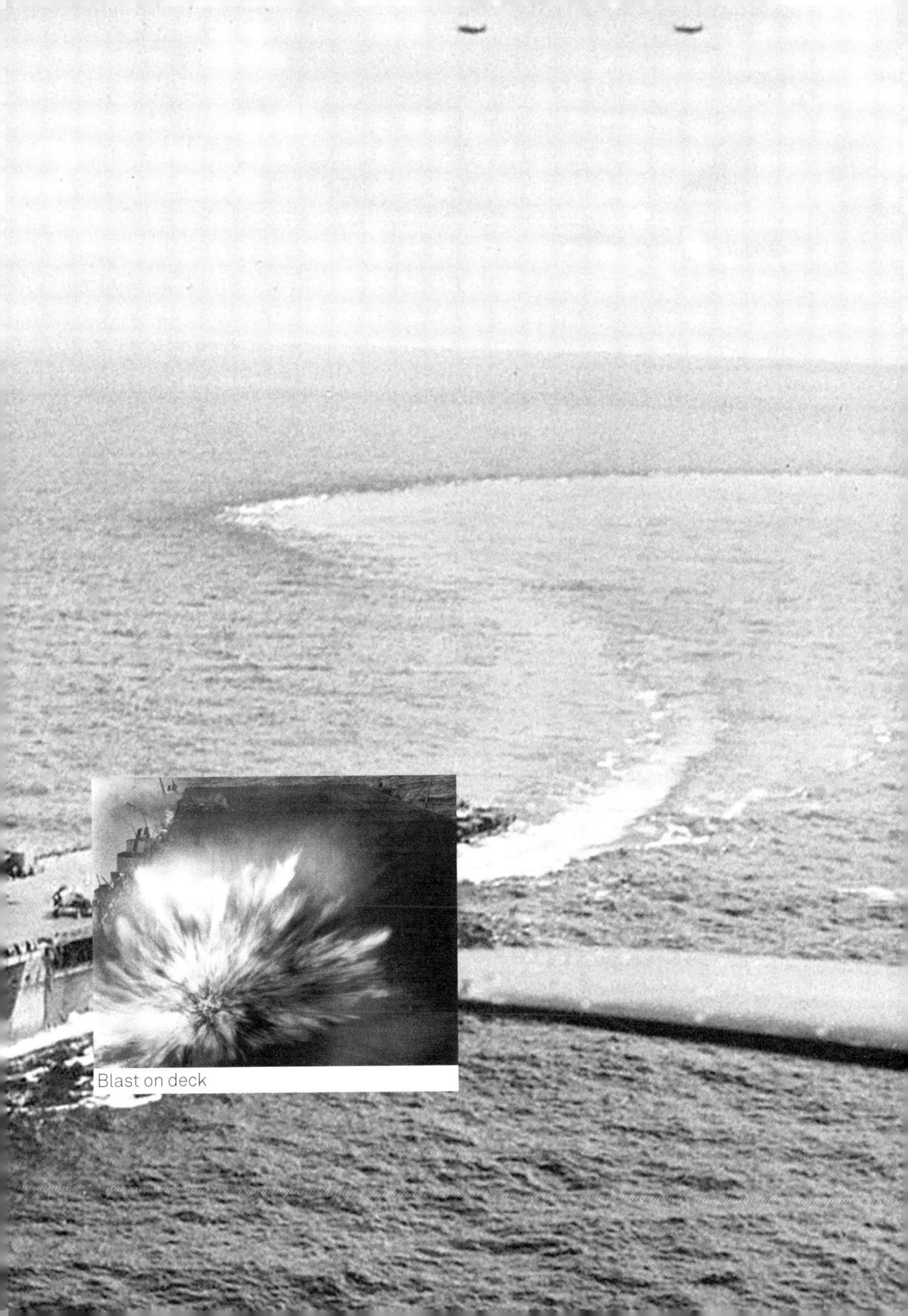

Blast on deck

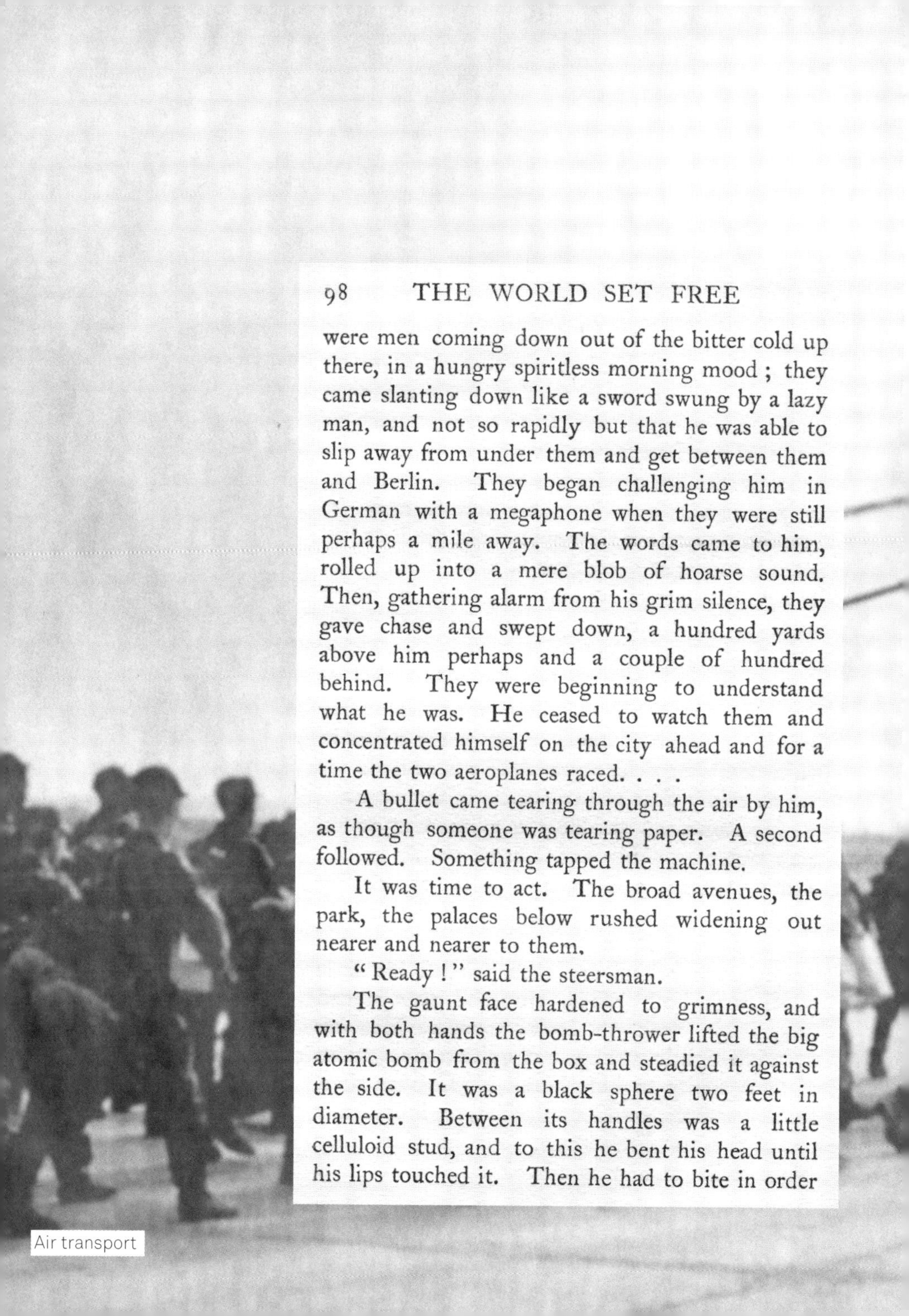

98 THE WORLD SET FREE

were men coming down out of the bitter cold up there, in a hungry spiritless morning mood ; they came slanting down like a sword swung by a lazy man, and not so rapidly but that he was able to slip away from under them and get between them and Berlin. They began challenging him in German with a megaphone when they were still perhaps a mile away. The words came to him, rolled up into a mere blob of hoarse sound. Then, gathering alarm from his grim silence, they gave chase and swept down, a hundred yards above him perhaps and a couple of hundred behind. They were beginning to understand what he was. He ceased to watch them and concentrated himself on the city ahead and for a time the two aeroplanes raced. . . .

A bullet came tearing through the air by him, as though someone was tearing paper. A second followed. Something tapped the machine.

It was time to act. The broad avenues, the park, the palaces below rushed widening out nearer and nearer to them.

"Ready !" said the steersman.

The gaunt face hardened to grimness, and with both hands the bomb-thrower lifted the big atomic bomb from the box and steadied it against the side. It was a black sphere two feet in diameter. Between its handles was a little celluloid stud, and to this he bent his head until his lips touched it. Then he had to bite in order

Air transport

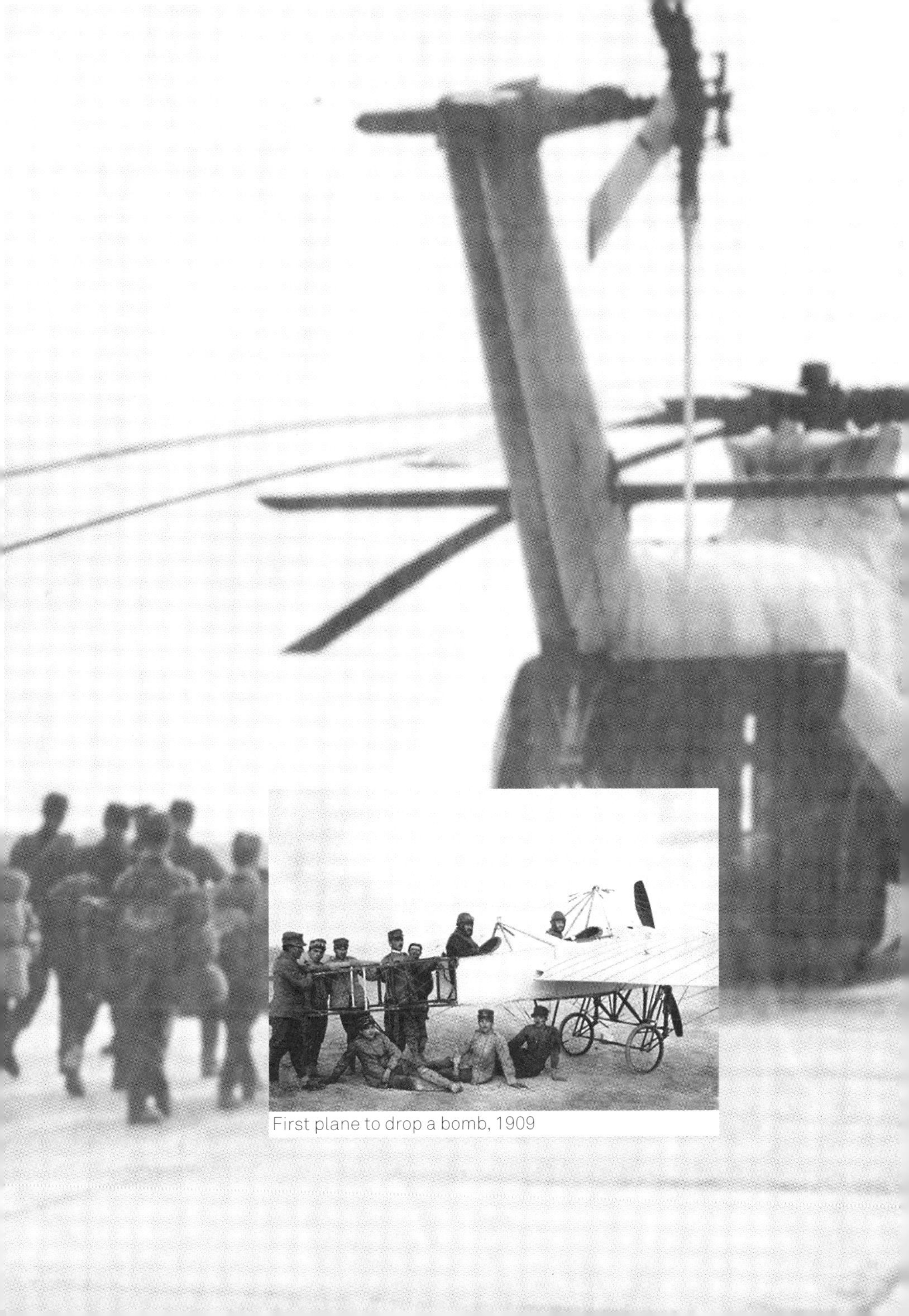

First plane to drop a bomb, 1909

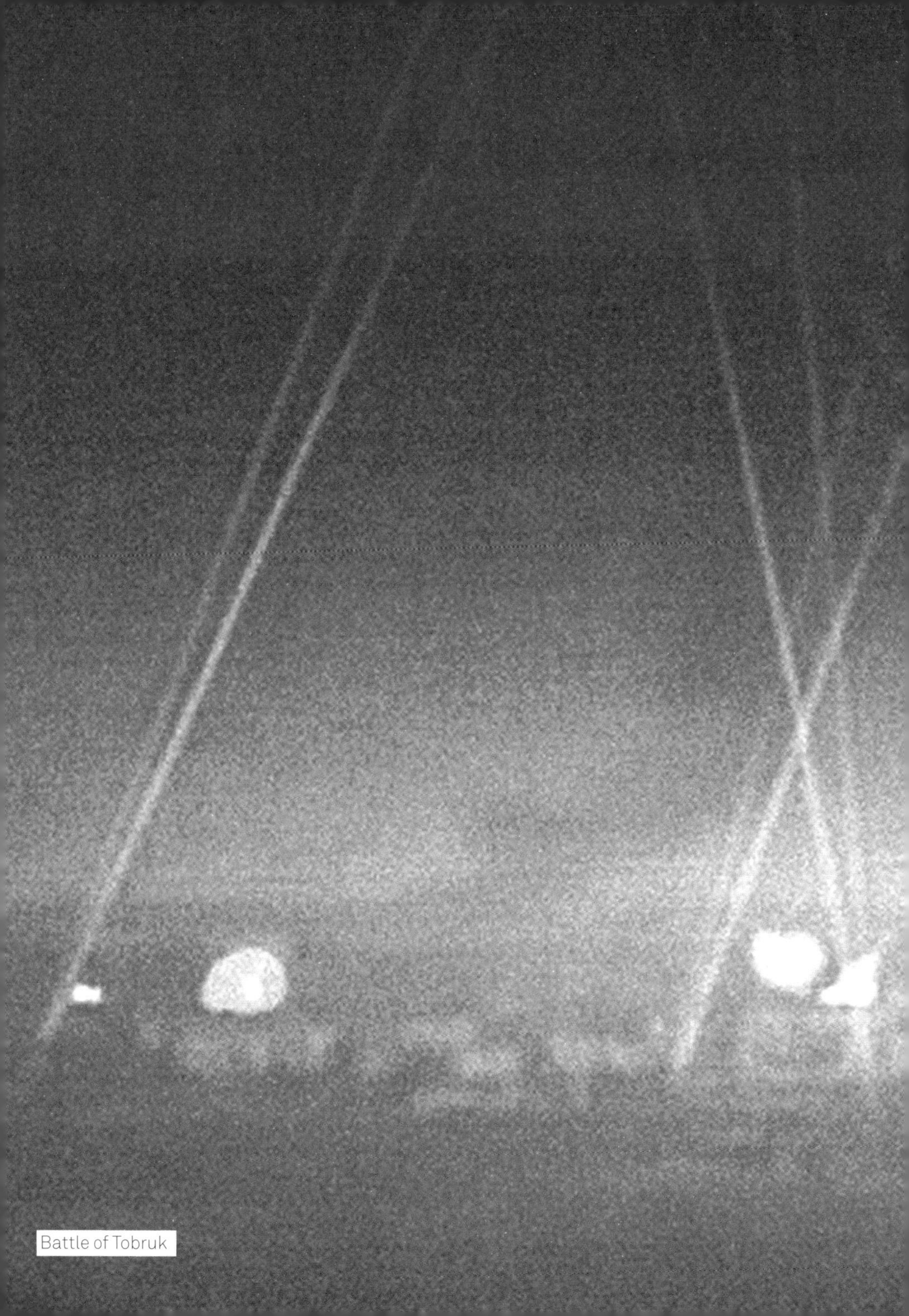

Battle of Tobruk

to let the air in upon the inducive. Sure of its accessibility, he craned his neck over the side of the aeroplane and judged his pace and distance. Then very quickly he bent forward, bit the stud and hoisted the bomb over the side.

"Round," he whispered inaudibly.

The bomb flashed blinding scarlet in mid-air and fell, a descending column of blaze eddying spirally in the midst of a whirlwind. Both the aeroplanes were tossed like shuttlecocks, hurled high and sideways; and the steersman with gleaming eyes and set teeth fought in great banking curves for a balance. The gaunt man clung tight with hand and knees; his nostrils dilated, his teeth biting his lips. He was firmly strapped. . . .

When he could look down again it was like looking down upon the crater of a small volcano. In the open garden before the Imperial castle a shuddering star of evil splendour spurted and poured up smoke and flame towards them like an accusation. They were too high to distinguish people clearly, or mark the bomb's effect upon the building until suddenly the façade tottered and crumbled before the flare as sugar dissolves in water. The man stared for a moment, showed all his long teeth, and then staggered into the cramped standing position his straps permitted, hoisted out and bit another bomb and sent it down after its fellow.

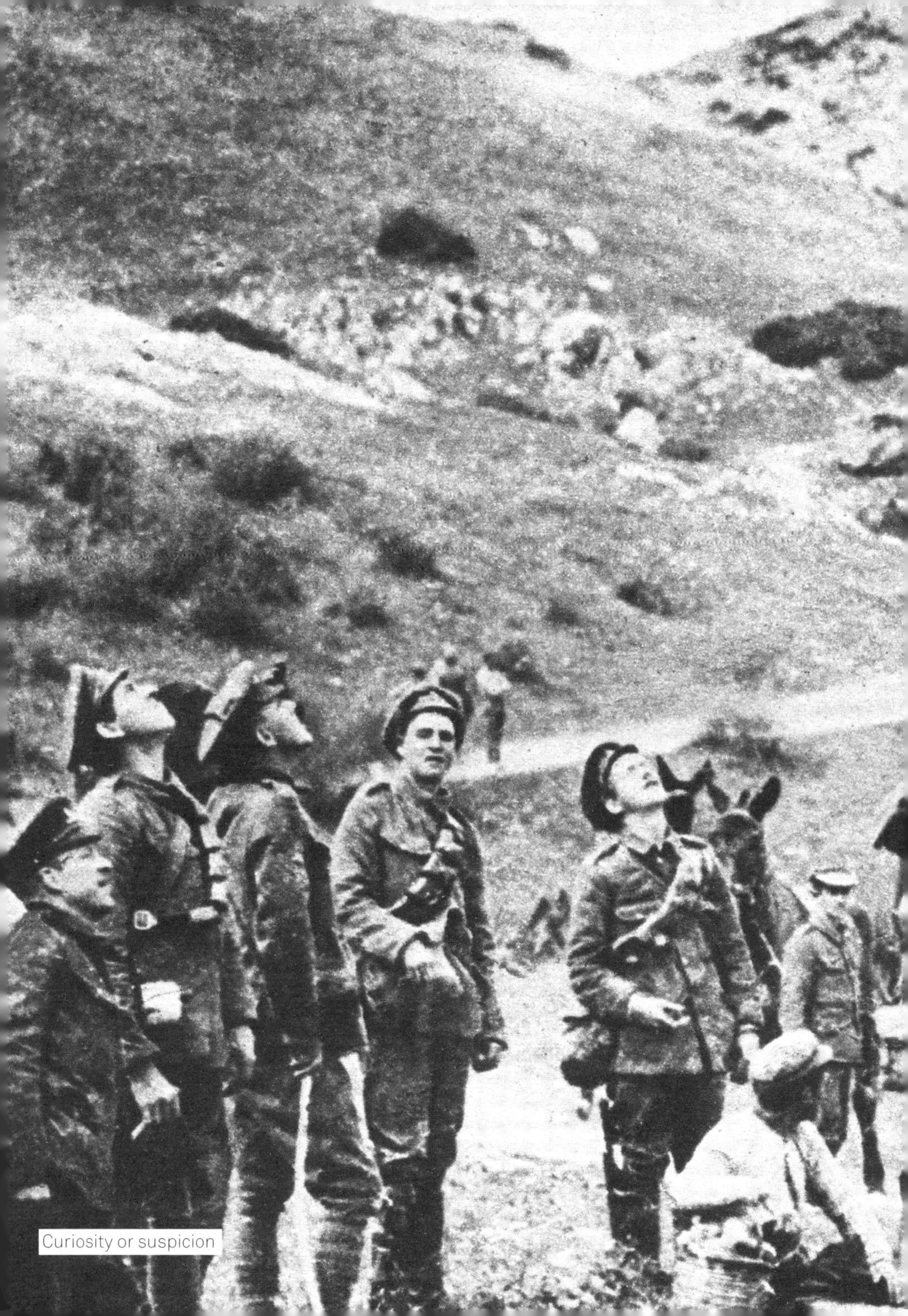

Curiosity or suspicion

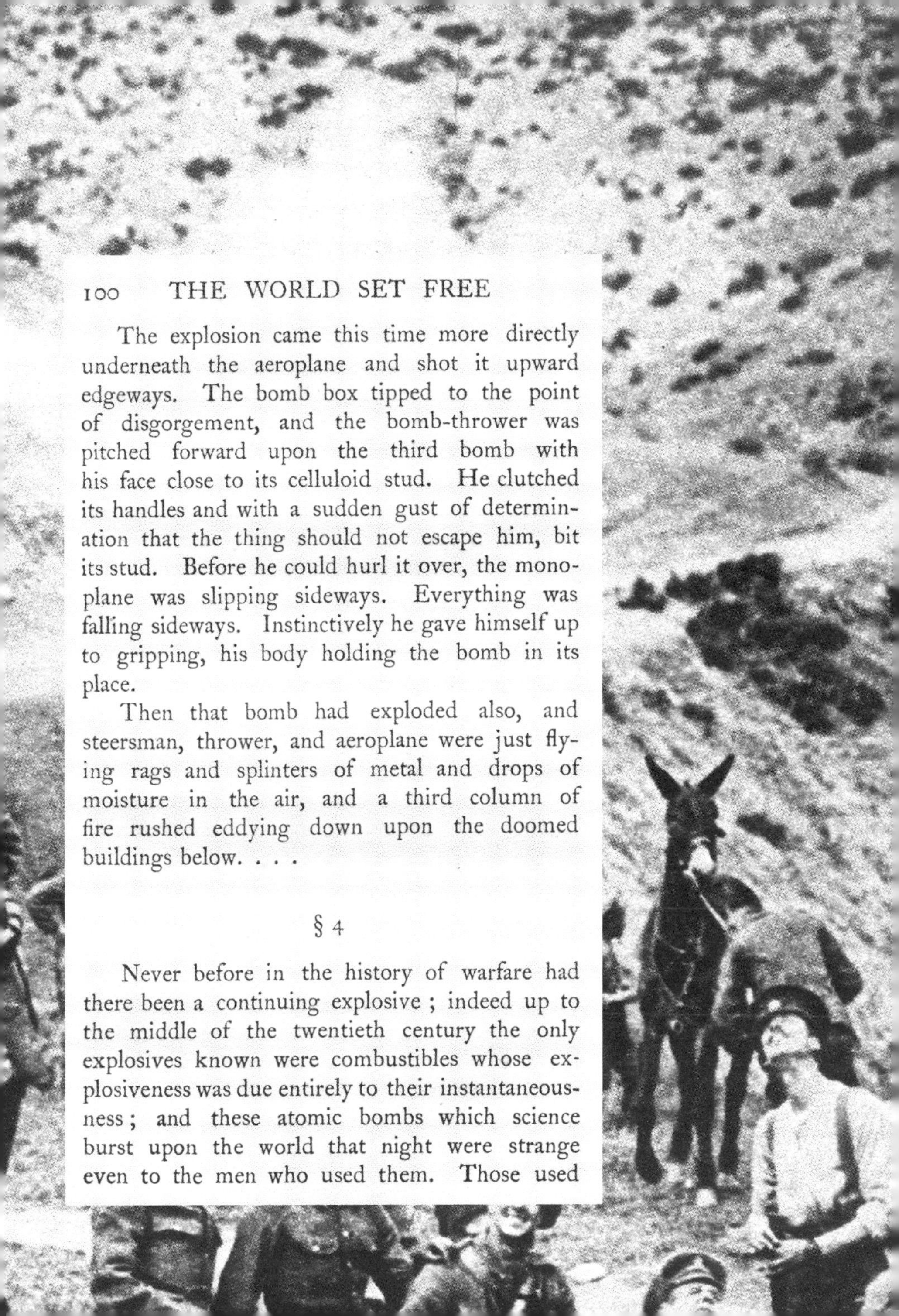

The explosion came this time more directly underneath the aeroplane and shot it upward edgeways. The bomb box tipped to the point of disgorgement, and the bomb-thrower was pitched forward upon the third bomb with his face close to its celluloid stud. He clutched its handles and with a sudden gust of determination that the thing should not escape him, bit its stud. Before he could hurl it over, the monoplane was slipping sideways. Everything was falling sideways. Instinctively he gave himself up to gripping, his body holding the bomb in its place.

Then that bomb had exploded also, and steersman, thrower, and aeroplane were just flying rags and splinters of metal and drops of moisture in the air, and a third column of fire rushed eddying down upon the doomed buildings below. . . .

§ 4

Never before in the history of warfare had there been a continuing explosive ; indeed up to the middle of the twentieth century the only explosives known were combustibles whose explosiveness was due entirely to their instantaneousness ; and these atomic bombs which science burst upon the world that night were strange even to the men who used them. Those used

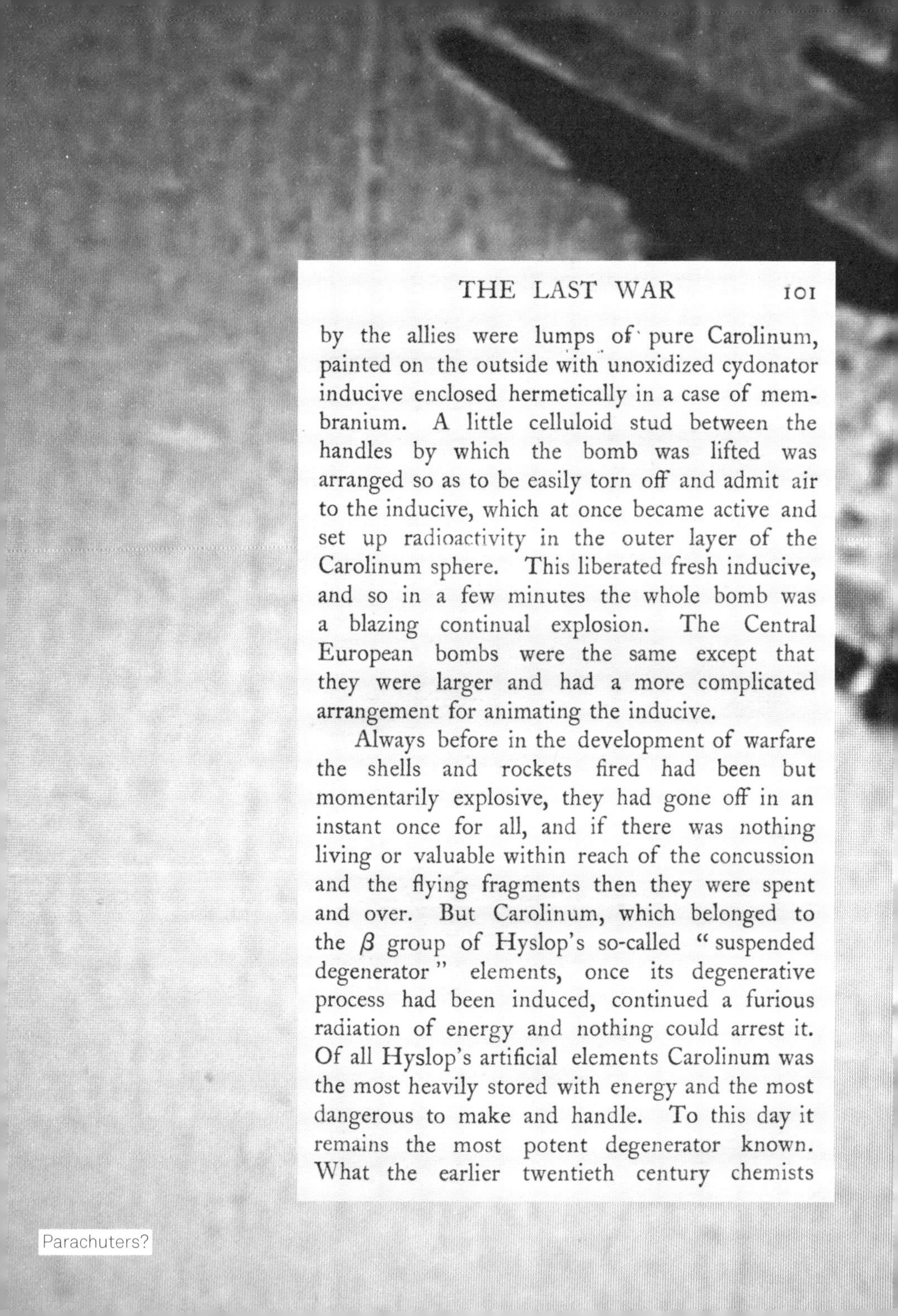

by the allies were lumps of pure Carolinum, painted on the outside with unoxidized cydonator inducive enclosed hermetically in a case of membranium. A little celluloid stud between the handles by which the bomb was lifted was arranged so as to be easily torn off and admit air to the inducive, which at once became active and set up radioactivity in the outer layer of the Carolinum sphere. This liberated fresh inducive, and so in a few minutes the whole bomb was a blazing continual explosion. The Central European bombs were the same except that they were larger and had a more complicated arrangement for animating the inducive.

Always before in the development of warfare the shells and rockets fired had been but momentarily explosive, they had gone off in an instant once for all, and if there was nothing living or valuable within reach of the concussion and the flying fragments then they were spent and over. But Carolinum, which belonged to the β group of Hyslop's so-called "suspended degenerator" elements, once its degenerative process had been induced, continued a furious radiation of energy and nothing could arrest it. Of all Hyslop's artificial elements Carolinum was the most heavily stored with energy and the most dangerous to make and handle. To this day it remains the most potent degenerator known. What the earlier twentieth century chemists

Parachuters?

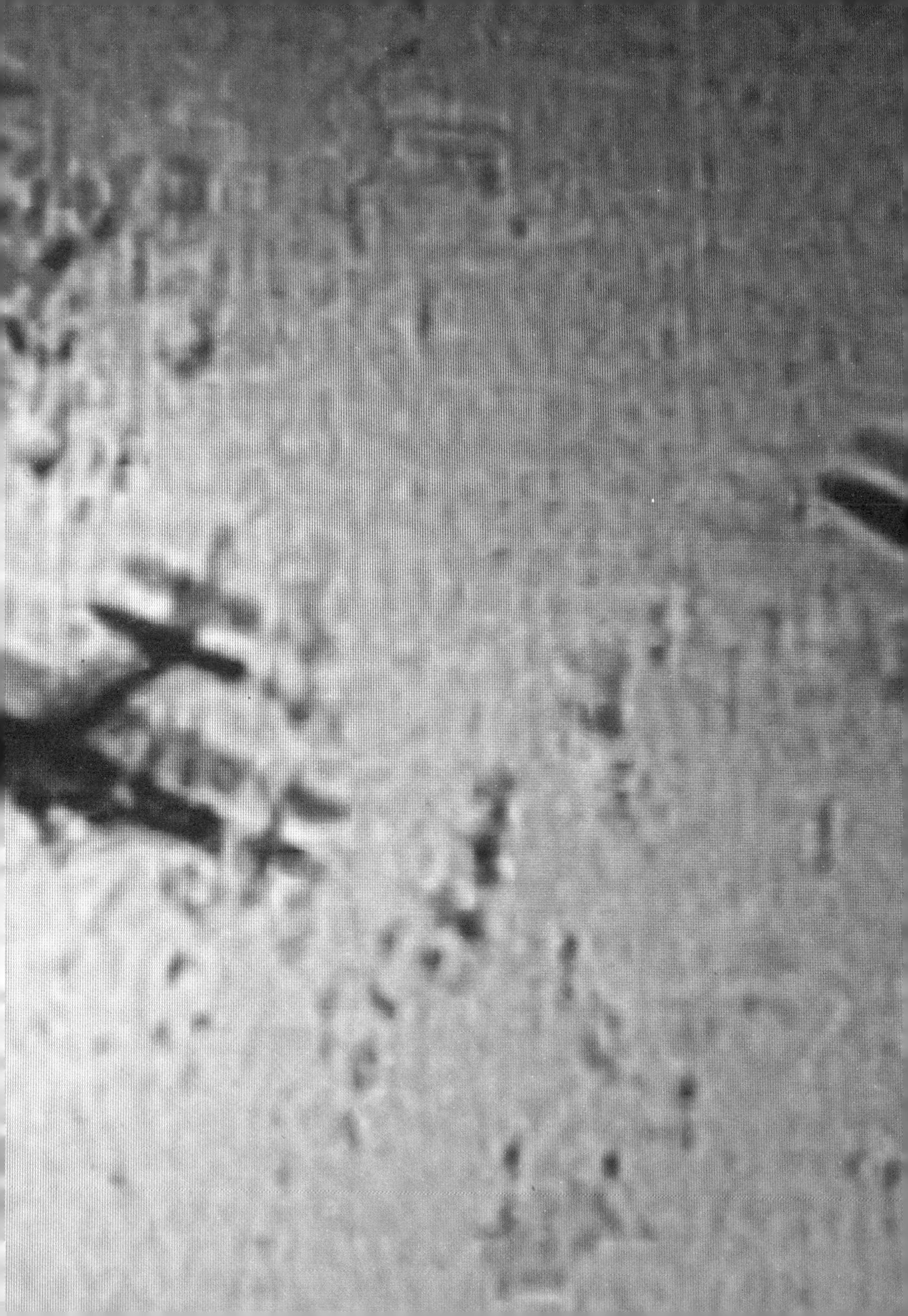

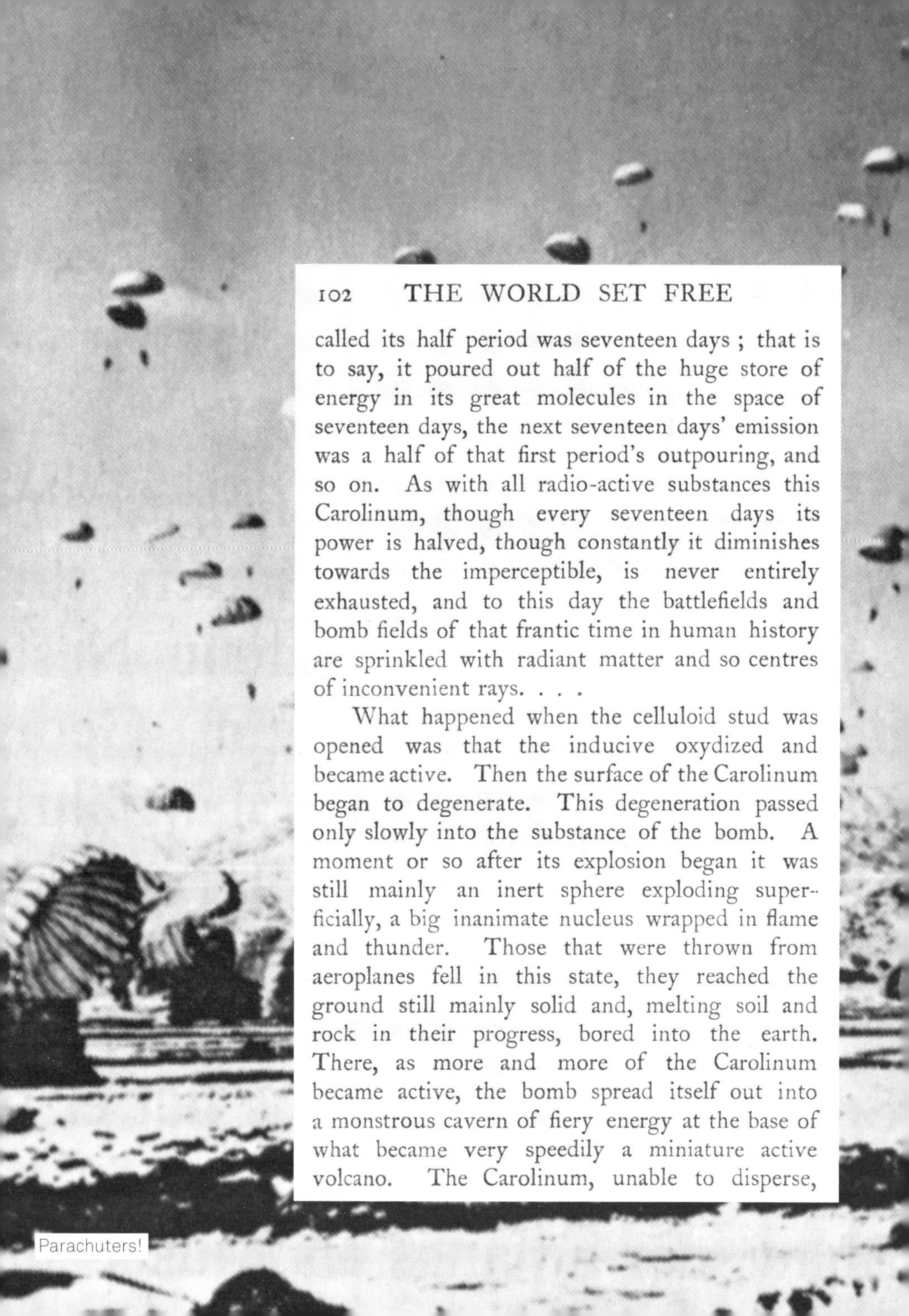

Parachuters!

called its half period was seventeen days ; that is to say, it poured out half of the huge store of energy in its great molecules in the space of seventeen days, the next seventeen days' emission was a half of that first period's outpouring, and so on. As with all radio-active substances this Carolinum, though every seventeen days its power is halved, though constantly it diminishes towards the imperceptible, is never entirely exhausted, and to this day the battlefields and bomb fields of that frantic time in human history are sprinkled with radiant matter and so centres of inconvenient rays. . . .

What happened when the celluloid stud was opened was that the inducive oxydized and became active. Then the surface of the Carolinum began to degenerate. This degeneration passed only slowly into the substance of the bomb. A moment or so after its explosion began it was still mainly an inert sphere exploding superficially, a big inanimate nucleus wrapped in flame and thunder. Those that were thrown from aeroplanes fell in this state, they reached the ground still mainly solid and, melting soil and rock in their progress, bored into the earth. There, as more and more of the Carolinum became active, the bomb spread itself out into a monstrous cavern of fiery energy at the base of what became very speedily a miniature active volcano. The Carolinum, unable to disperse,

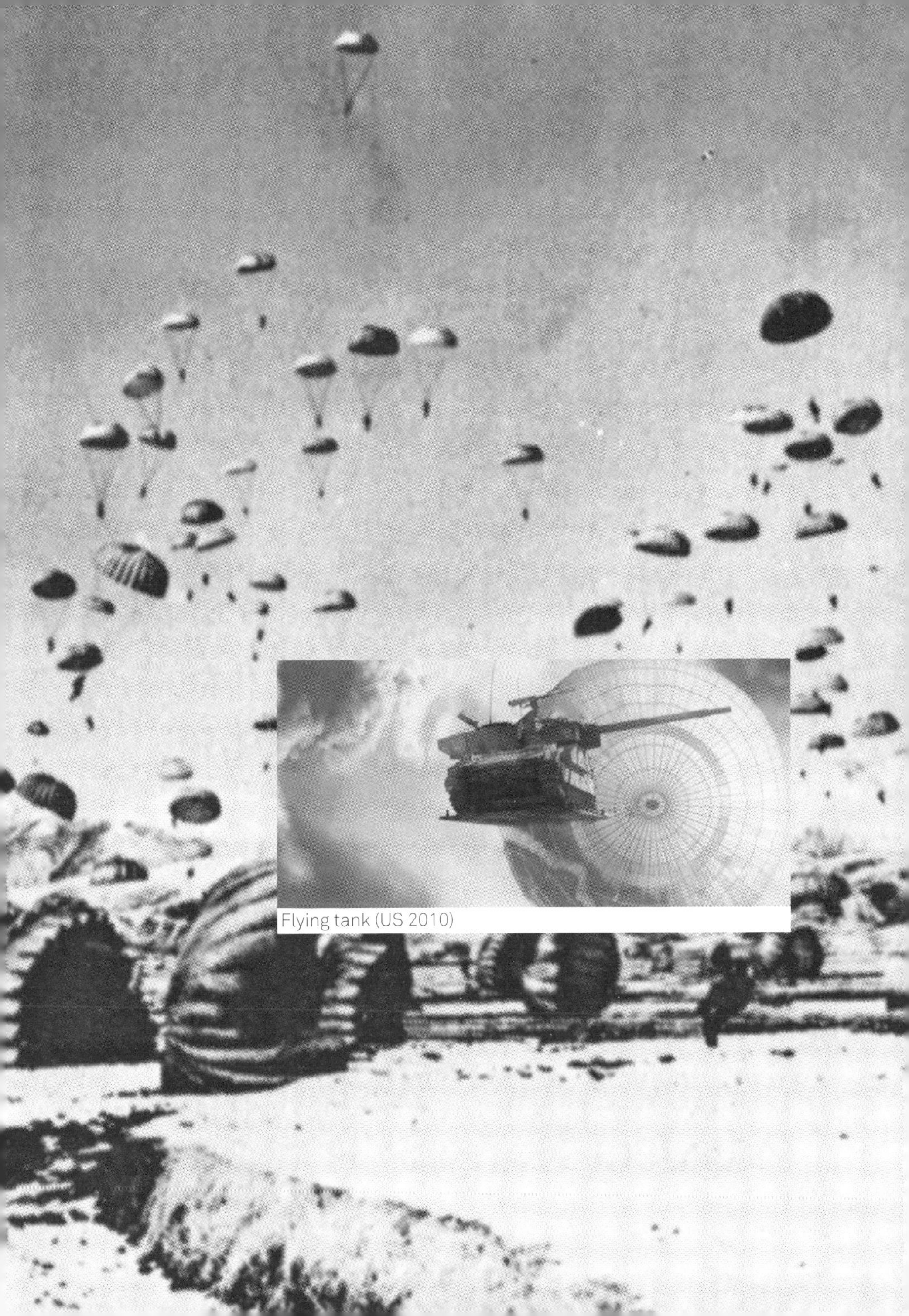

Flying tank (US 2010)

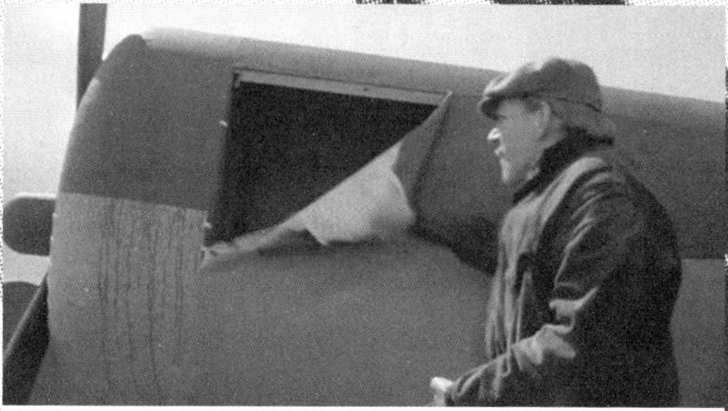

Spying on warplanes (UK 1981)

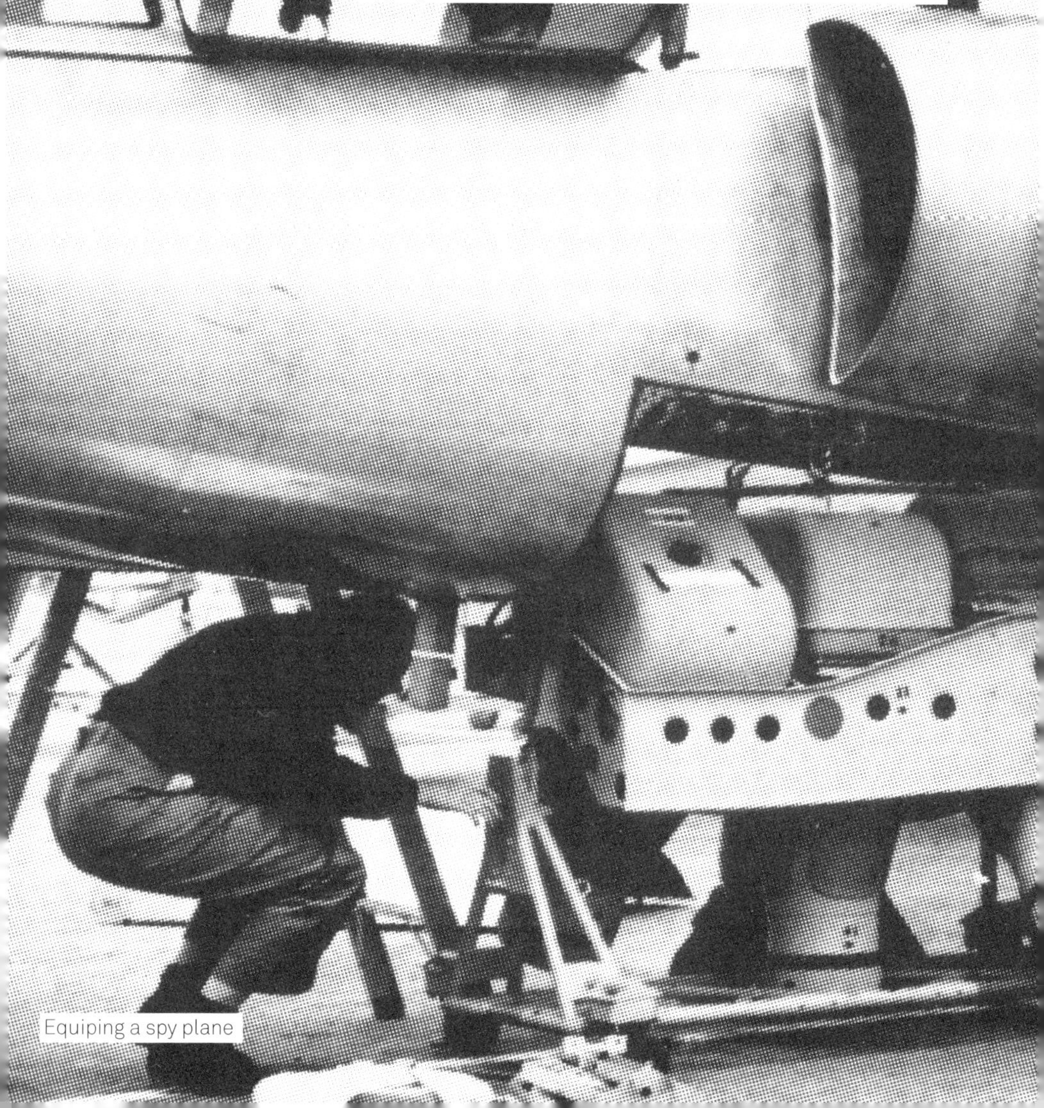

Equiping a spy plane

freely drove into and mixed up with a boiling confusion of molten soil and superheated steam and so remained spinning furiously and maintaining an eruption that lasted for years or months or weeks according to the size of the bomb employed and the chances of its dispersal. Once launched the bomb was absolutely unapproachable and uncontrollable until its forces were nearly exhausted, and from the crater that burst open above it, puffs of heavy incandescent vapour and fragments of viciously punitive rock and mud, saturated with Carolinum, and each a centre of scorching and blistering energy, were flung high and far.

Such was the crowning triumph of military science, the ultimate explosive that was to give the "decisive touch" to war. . . .

§ 5

A recent historical writer has described the world of that time as one that "believed in established words and was invincibly blind to the obvious in things." Certainly it seems now that nothing could have been more obvious to the people of the earlier twentieth century than the rapidity with which war was becoming impossible. And as certainly they did not see it. They did not see it until the atomic bombs burst in their fumbling hands. Yet the broad facts must have

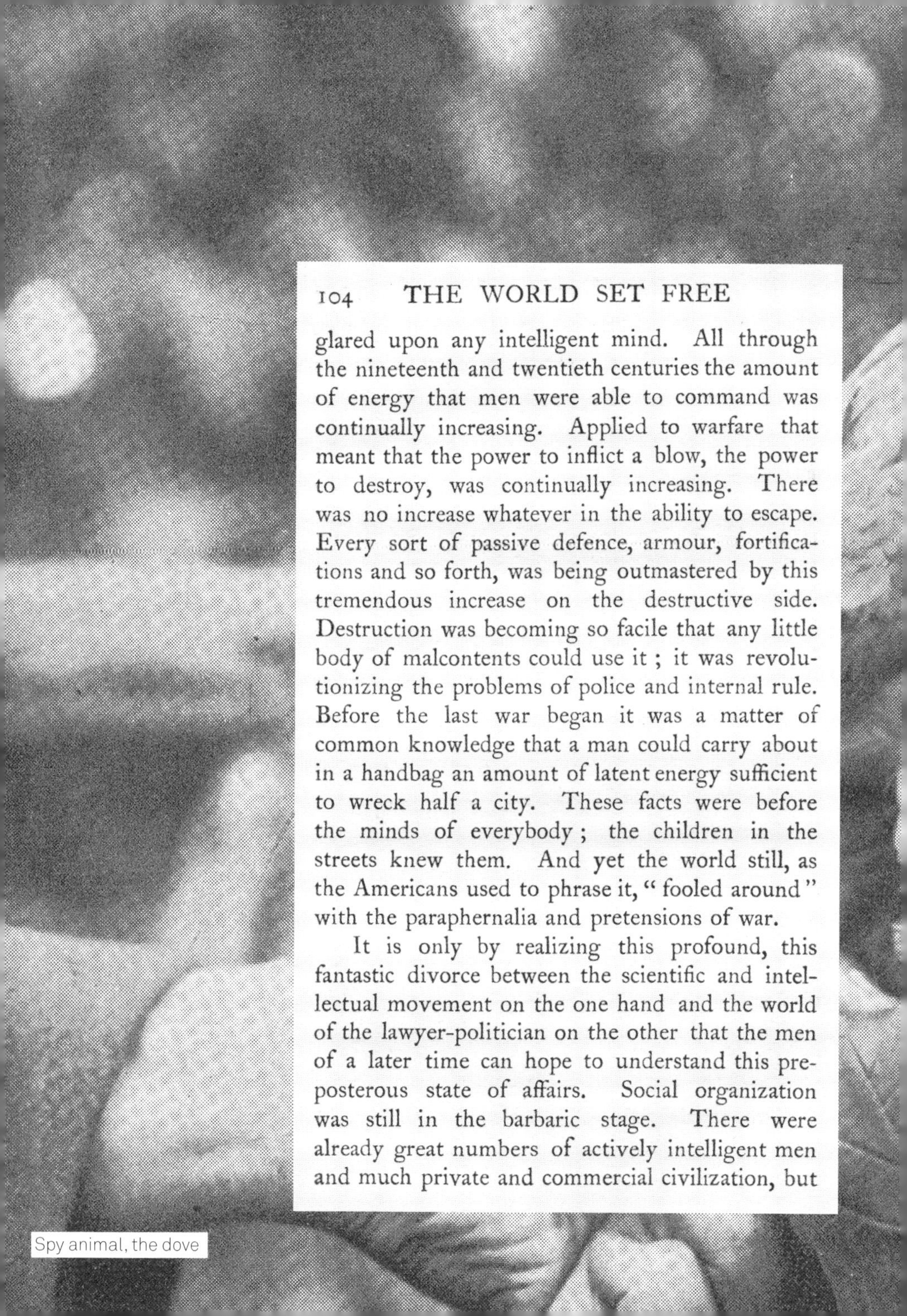

glared upon any intelligent mind. All through the nineteenth and twentieth centuries the amount of energy that men were able to command was continually increasing. Applied to warfare that meant that the power to inflict a blow, the power to destroy, was continually increasing. There was no increase whatever in the ability to escape. Every sort of passive defence, armour, fortifications and so forth, was being outmastered by this tremendous increase on the destructive side. Destruction was becoming so facile that any little body of malcontents could use it ; it was revolutionizing the problems of police and internal rule. Before the last war began it was a matter of common knowledge that a man could carry about in a handbag an amount of latent energy sufficient to wreck half a city. These facts were before the minds of everybody ; the children in the streets knew them. And yet the world still, as the Americans used to phrase it, " fooled around " with the paraphernalia and pretensions of war.

It is only by realizing this profound, this fantastic divorce between the scientific and intellectual movement on the one hand and the world of the lawyer-politician on the other that the men of a later time can hope to understand this preposterous state of affairs. Social organization was still in the barbaric stage. There were already great numbers of actively intelligent men and much private and commercial civilization, but

Spy animal, the dove

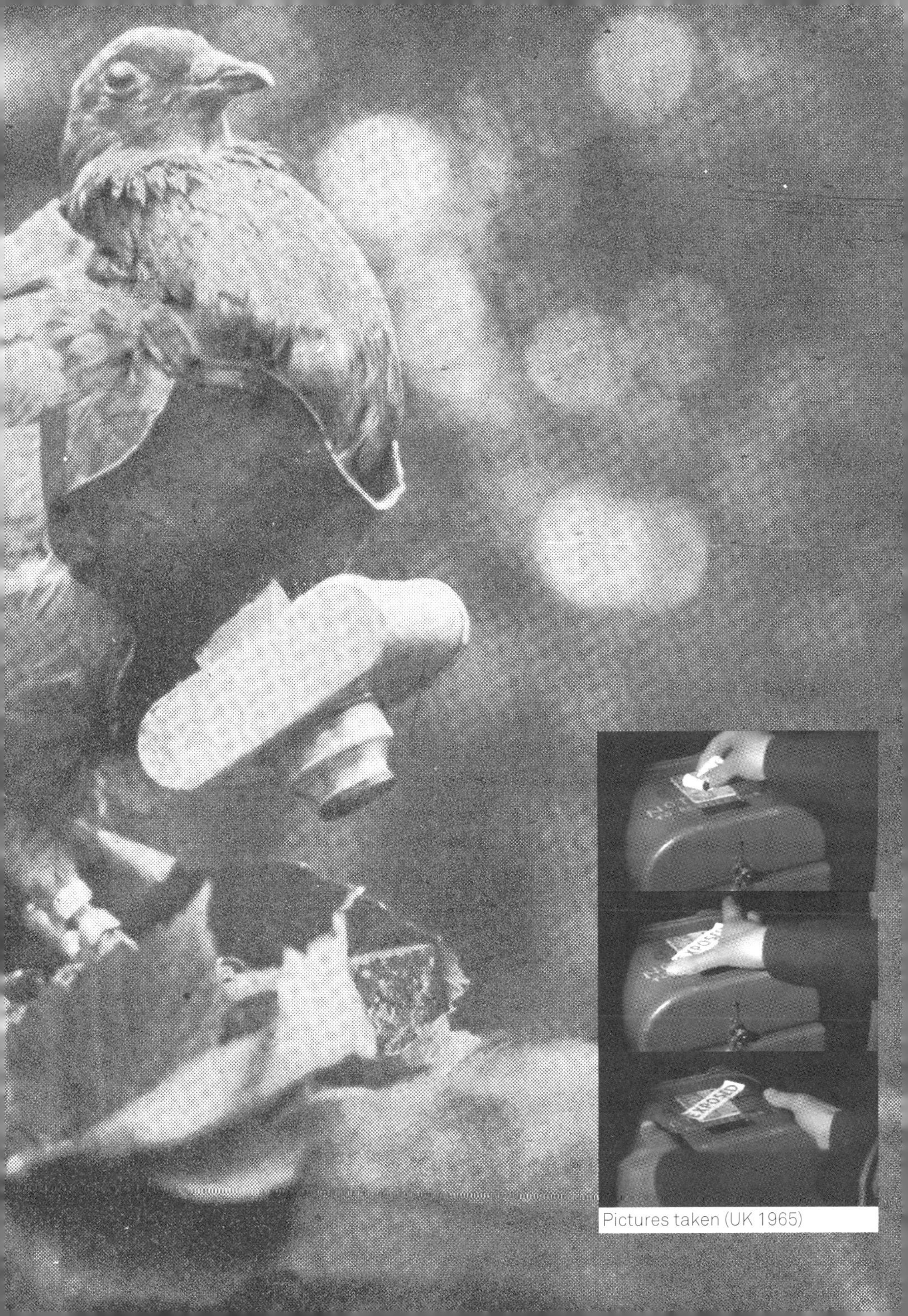

Pictures taken (UK 1965)

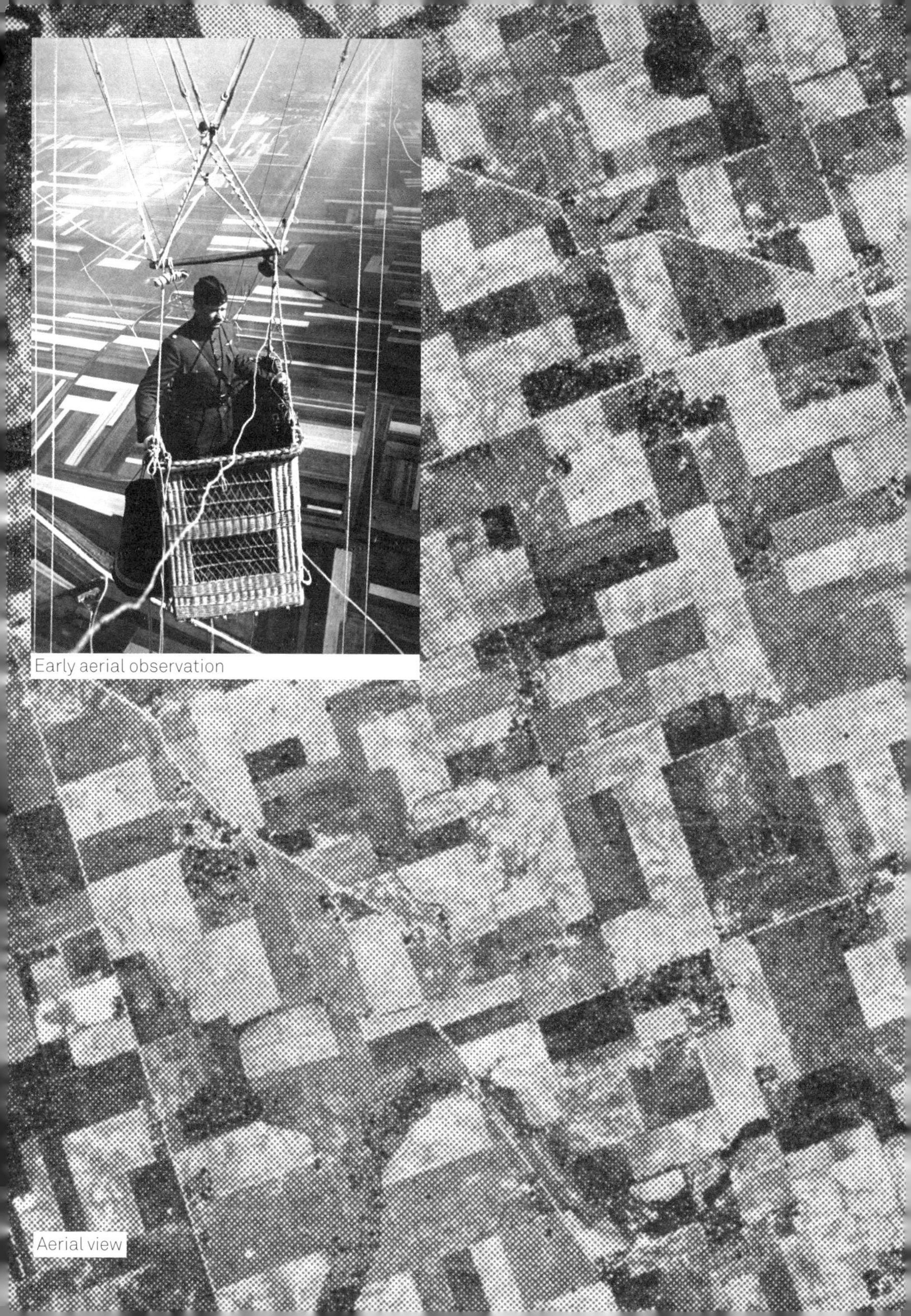
Early aerial observation

Aerial view

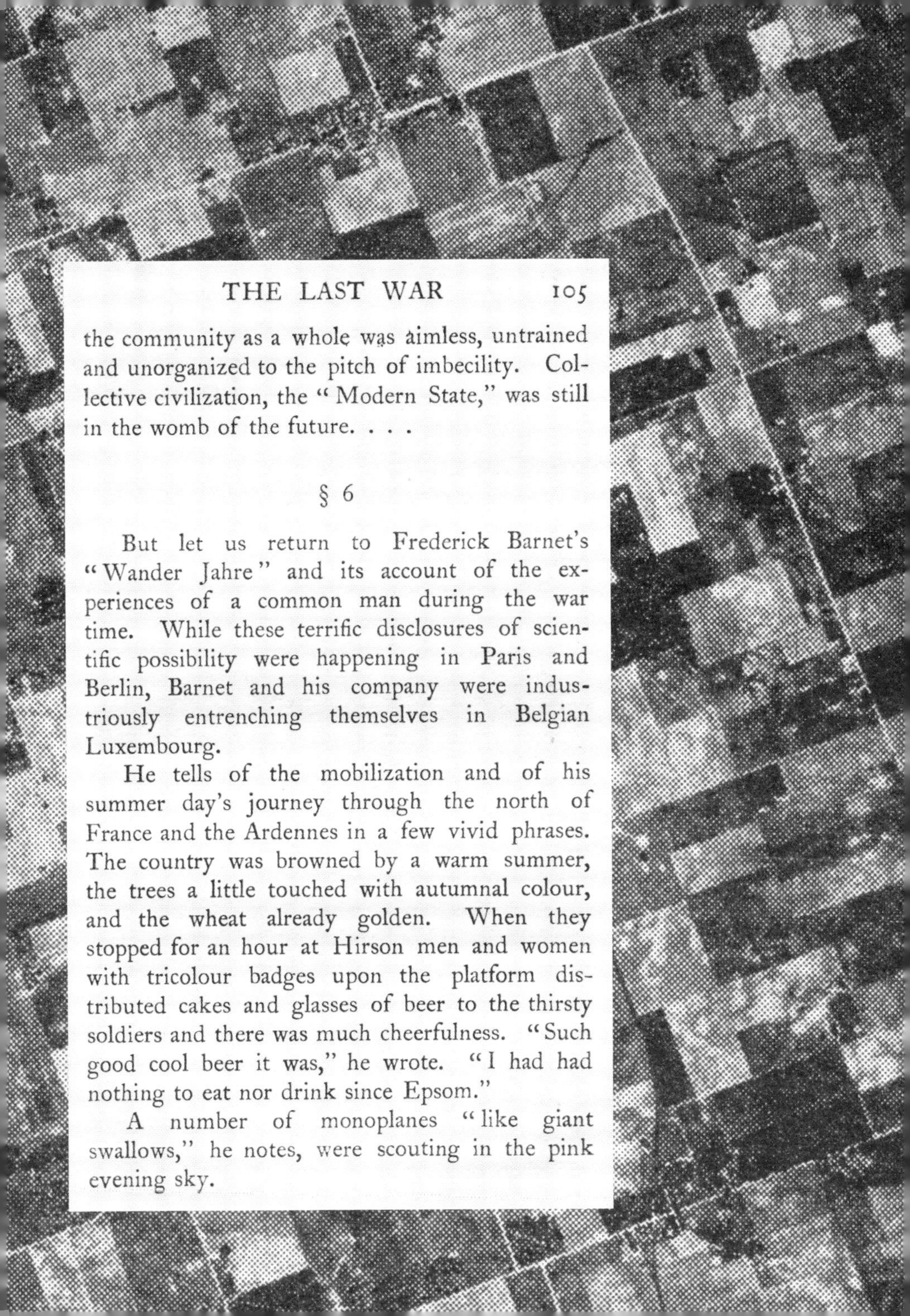

the community as a whole was aimless, untrained and unorganized to the pitch of imbecility. Collective civilization, the "Modern State," was still in the womb of the future. . . .

§ 6

But let us return to Frederick Barnet's "Wander Jahre" and its account of the experiences of a common man during the war time. While these terrific disclosures of scientific possibility were happening in Paris and Berlin, Barnet and his company were industriously entrenching themselves in Belgian Luxembourg.

He tells of the mobilization and of his summer day's journey through the north of France and the Ardennes in a few vivid phrases. The country was browned by a warm summer, the trees a little touched with autumnal colour, and the wheat already golden. When they stopped for an hour at Hirson men and women with tricolour badges upon the platform distributed cakes and glasses of beer to the thirsty soldiers and there was much cheerfulness. "Such good cool beer it was," he wrote. "I had had nothing to eat nor drink since Epsom."

A number of monoplanes "like giant swallows," he notes, were scouting in the pink evening sky.

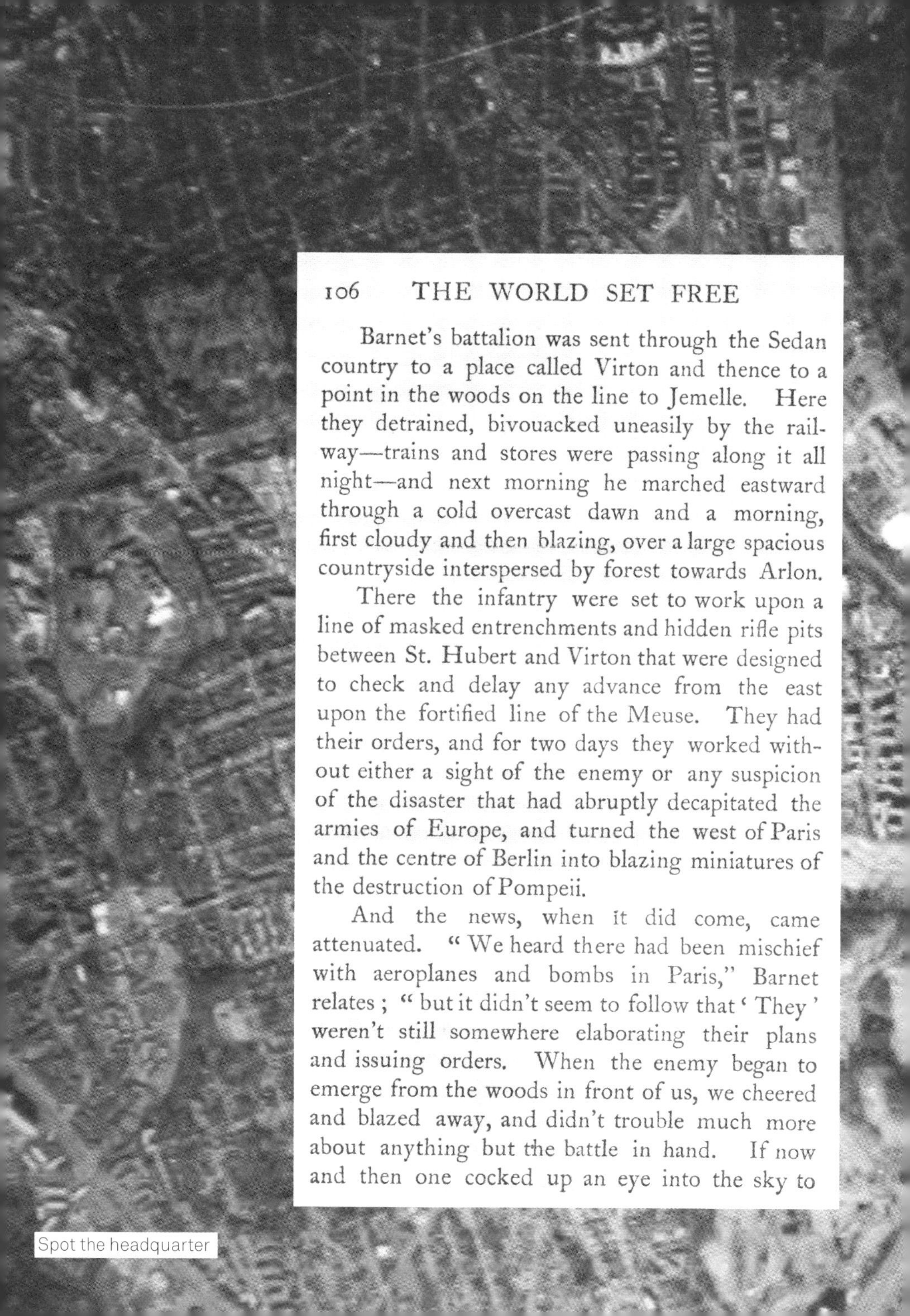

Barnet's battalion was sent through the Sedan country to a place called Virton and thence to a point in the woods on the line to Jemelle. Here they detrained, bivouacked uneasily by the railway—trains and stores were passing along it all night—and next morning he marched eastward through a cold overcast dawn and a morning, first cloudy and then blazing, over a large spacious countryside interspersed by forest towards Arlon.

There the infantry were set to work upon a line of masked entrenchments and hidden rifle pits between St. Hubert and Virton that were designed to check and delay any advance from the east upon the fortified line of the Meuse. They had their orders, and for two days they worked without either a sight of the enemy or any suspicion of the disaster that had abruptly decapitated the armies of Europe, and turned the west of Paris and the centre of Berlin into blazing miniatures of the destruction of Pompeii.

And the news, when it did come, came attenuated. "We heard there had been mischief with aeroplanes and bombs in Paris," Barnet relates; "but it didn't seem to follow that 'They' weren't still somewhere elaborating their plans and issuing orders. When the enemy began to emerge from the woods in front of us, we cheered and blazed away, and didn't trouble much more about anything but the battle in hand. If now and then one cocked up an eye into the sky to

Spot the headquarter

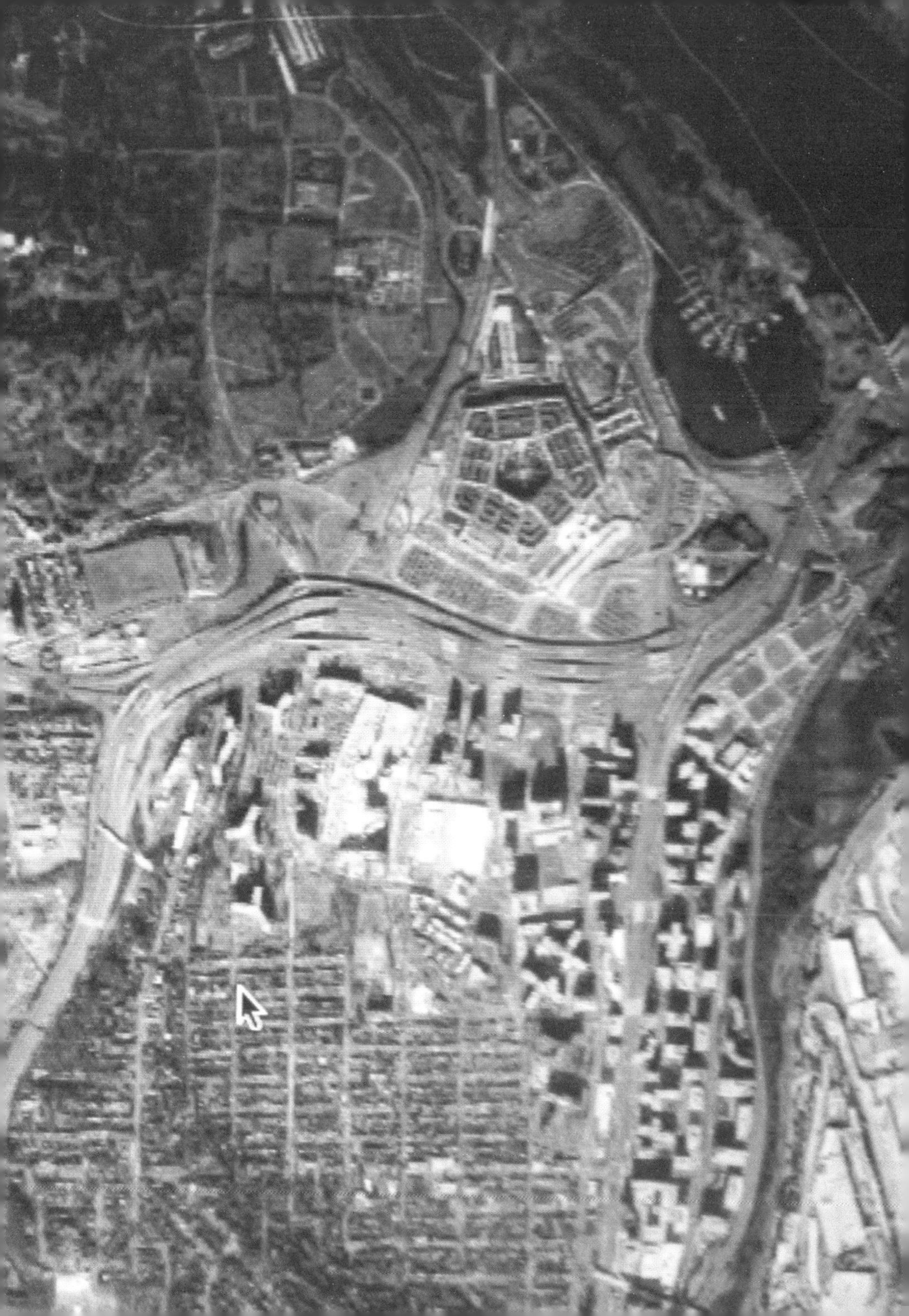

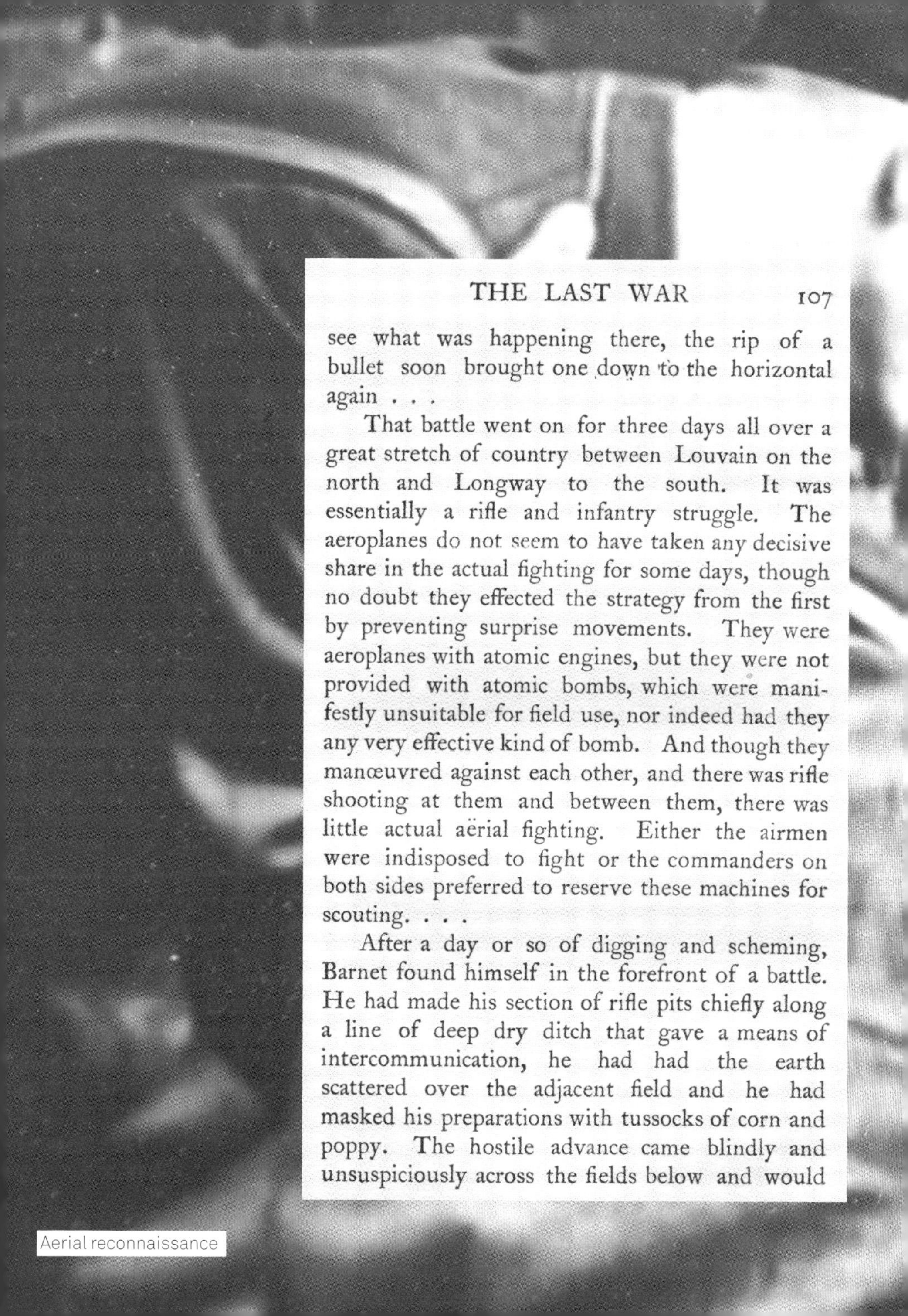

see what was happening there, the rip of a bullet soon brought one down to the horizontal again . . .

That battle went on for three days all over a great stretch of country between Louvain on the north and Longway to the south. It was essentially a rifle and infantry struggle. The aeroplanes do not seem to have taken any decisive share in the actual fighting for some days, though no doubt they effected the strategy from the first by preventing surprise movements. They were aeroplanes with atomic engines, but they were not provided with atomic bombs, which were manifestly unsuitable for field use, nor indeed had they any very effective kind of bomb. And though they manœuvred against each other, and there was rifle shooting at them and between them, there was little actual aërial fighting. Either the airmen were indisposed to fight or the commanders on both sides preferred to reserve these machines for scouting. . . .

After a day or so of digging and scheming, Barnet found himself in the forefront of a battle. He had made his section of rifle pits chiefly along a line of deep dry ditch that gave a means of intercommunication, he had had the earth scattered over the adjacent field and he had masked his preparations with tussocks of corn and poppy. The hostile advance came blindly and unsuspiciously across the fields below and would

Aerial reconnaissance

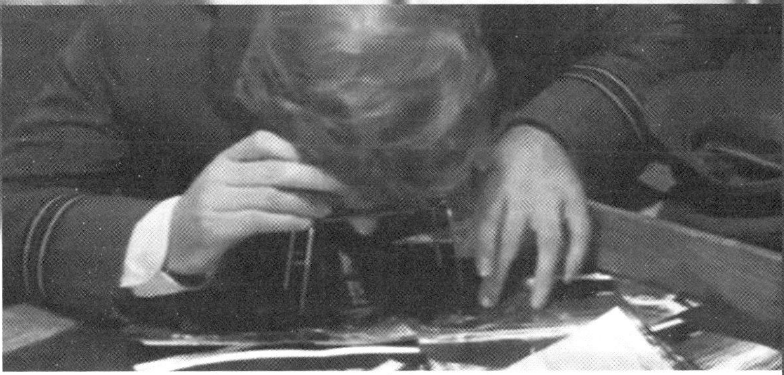

Image interpretation department at work (UK 1965)

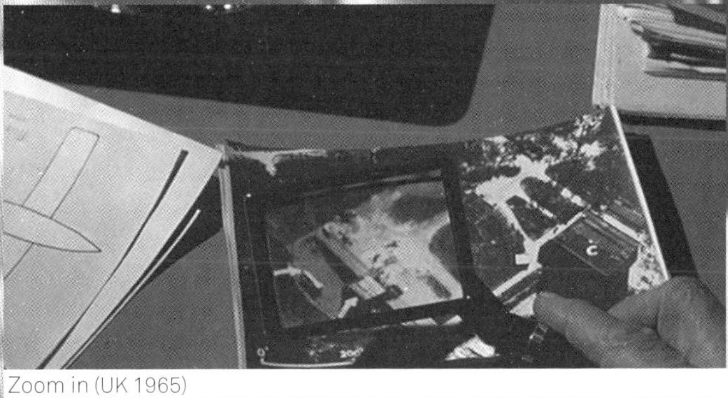

Zoom in (UK 1965)

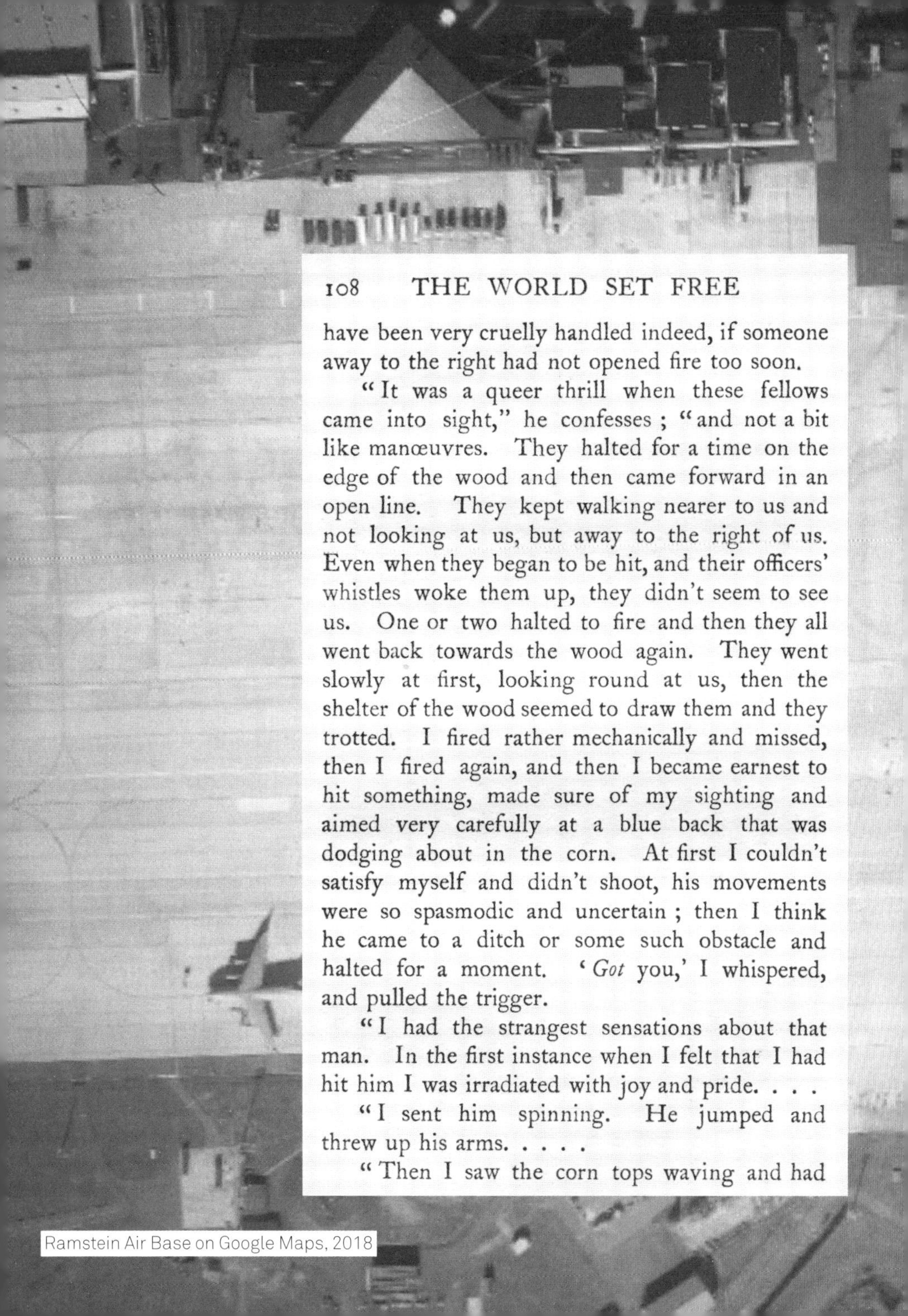

have been very cruelly handled indeed, if someone away to the right had not opened fire too soon.

"It was a queer thrill when these fellows came into sight," he confesses; "and not a bit like manœuvres. They halted for a time on the edge of the wood and then came forward in an open line. They kept walking nearer to us and not looking at us, but away to the right of us. Even when they began to be hit, and their officers' whistles woke them up, they didn't seem to see us. One or two halted to fire and then they all went back towards the wood again. They went slowly at first, looking round at us, then the shelter of the wood seemed to draw them and they trotted. I fired rather mechanically and missed, then I fired again, and then I became earnest to hit something, made sure of my sighting and aimed very carefully at a blue back that was dodging about in the corn. At first I couldn't satisfy myself and didn't shoot, his movements were so spasmodic and uncertain; then I think he came to a ditch or some such obstacle and halted for a moment. '*Got* you,' I whispered, and pulled the trigger.

"I had the strangest sensations about that man. In the first instance when I felt that I had hit him I was irradiated with joy and pride. . . .

"I sent him spinning. He jumped and threw up his arms. . . . .

"Then I saw the corn tops waving and had

Ramstein Air Base on Google Maps, 2018

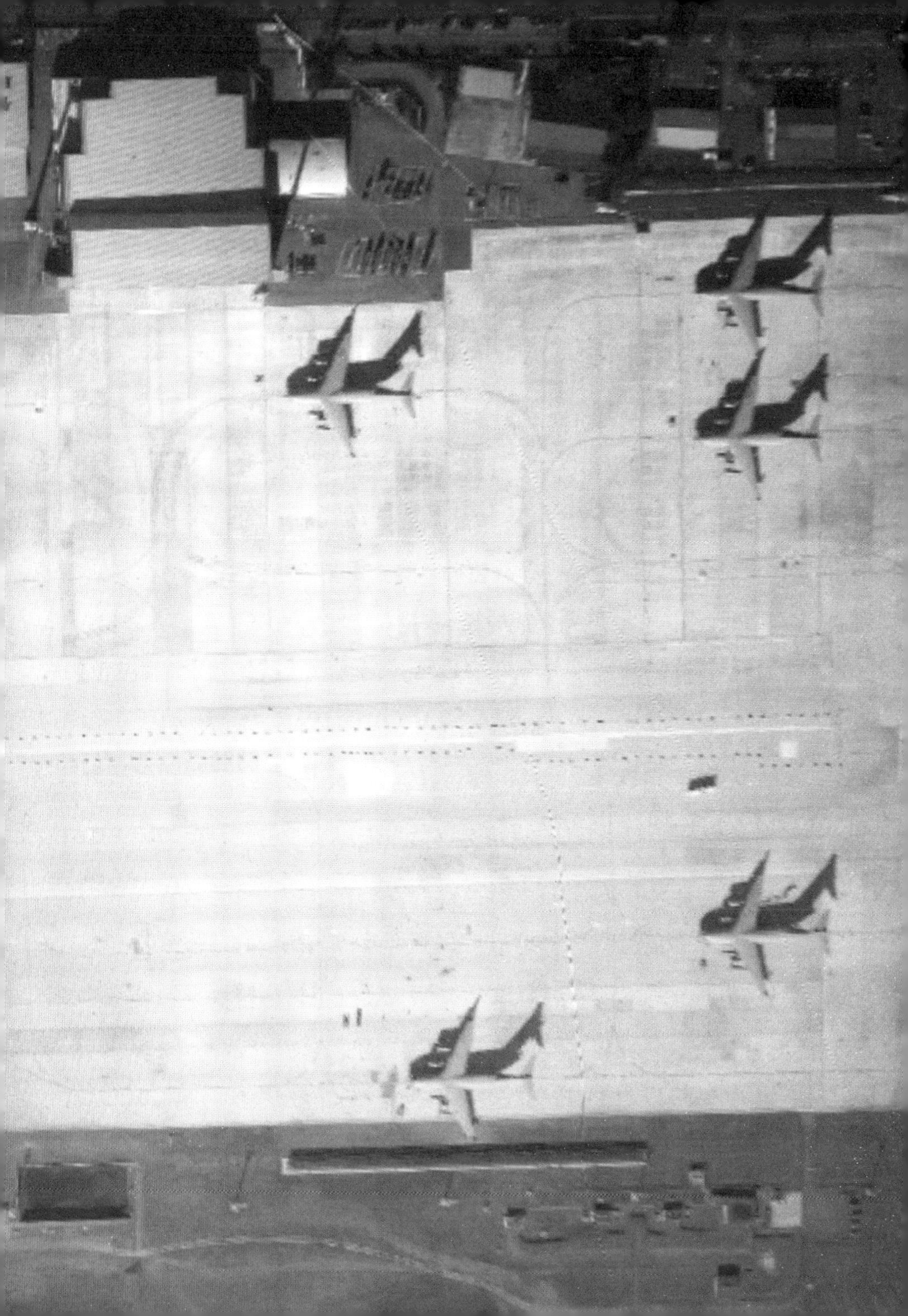

glimpses of him flapping about. Suddenly I felt sick. I hadn't killed him. . . .

"In some way he was disabled and smashed up and yet able to struggle about. I began to think. . . .

"For nearly two hours that Prussian was agonizing in the corn. Either he was calling out or someone was shouting to him. . . .

"Then he jumped up,—he seemed to try and get up upon his feet with one last effort; and then he fell like a sack and lay quite still and never moved again.

"He had been unendurable, and I believe someone had shot him dead. I had been wanting to do so for some time. . . ."

The enemy began sniping the rifle pits from shelters they made for themselves in the woods below. A man was hit in the pit next to Barnet and began cursing and crying out in a violent rage. Barnet crawled along the ditch to him and found him in great pain, covered with blood, frantic with indignation and with the half of his right hand smashed to a pulp. "Look at this," he kept repeating, hugging it and then extending it. "Damned foolery! Damned foolery! My right hand, sir! My right hand!"

For some time Barnet could do nothing with him. The man was consumed by his tortured realization of the evil silliness of war, the realization which had come upon him in a flash with the

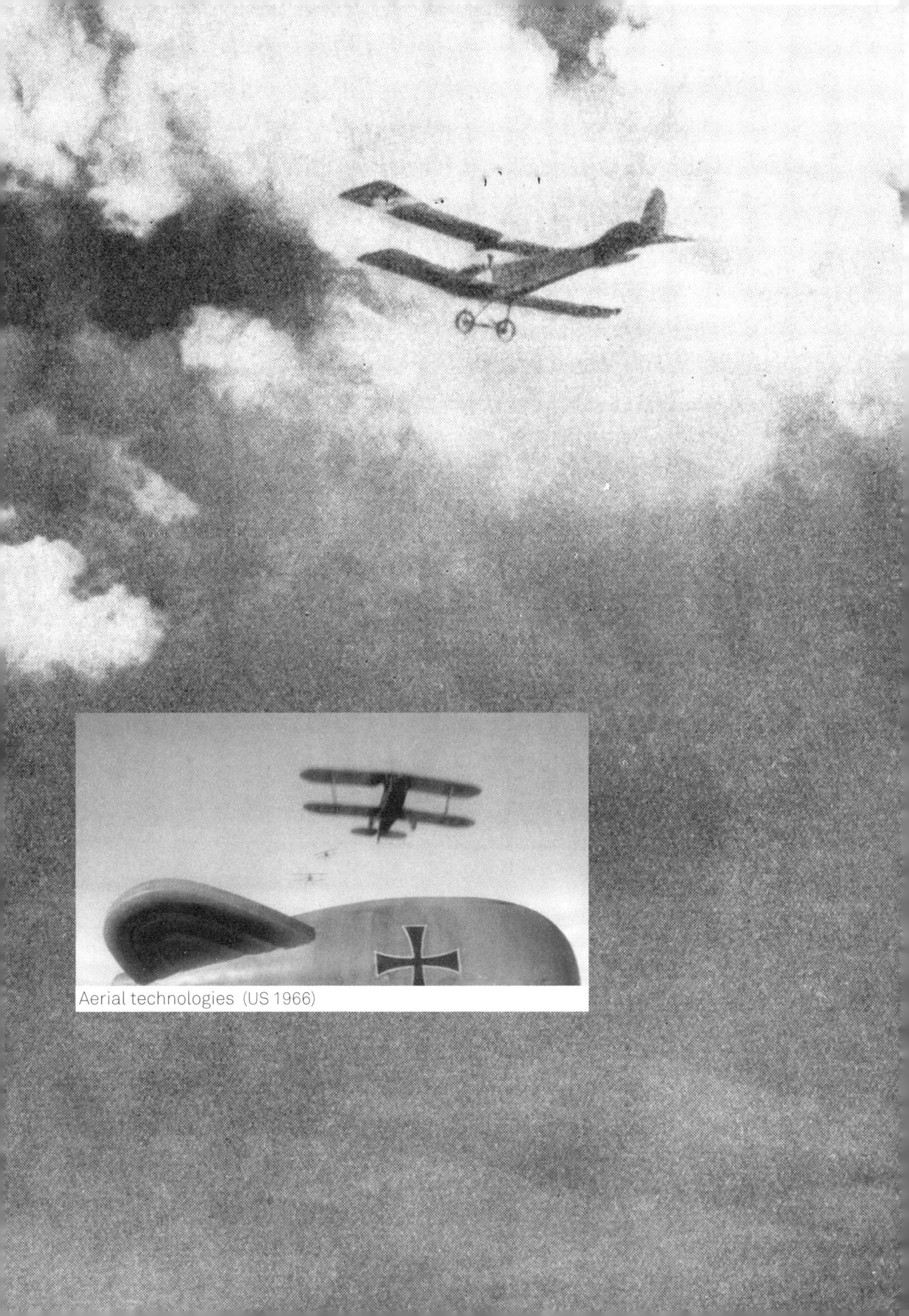

Aerial technologies (US 1966)

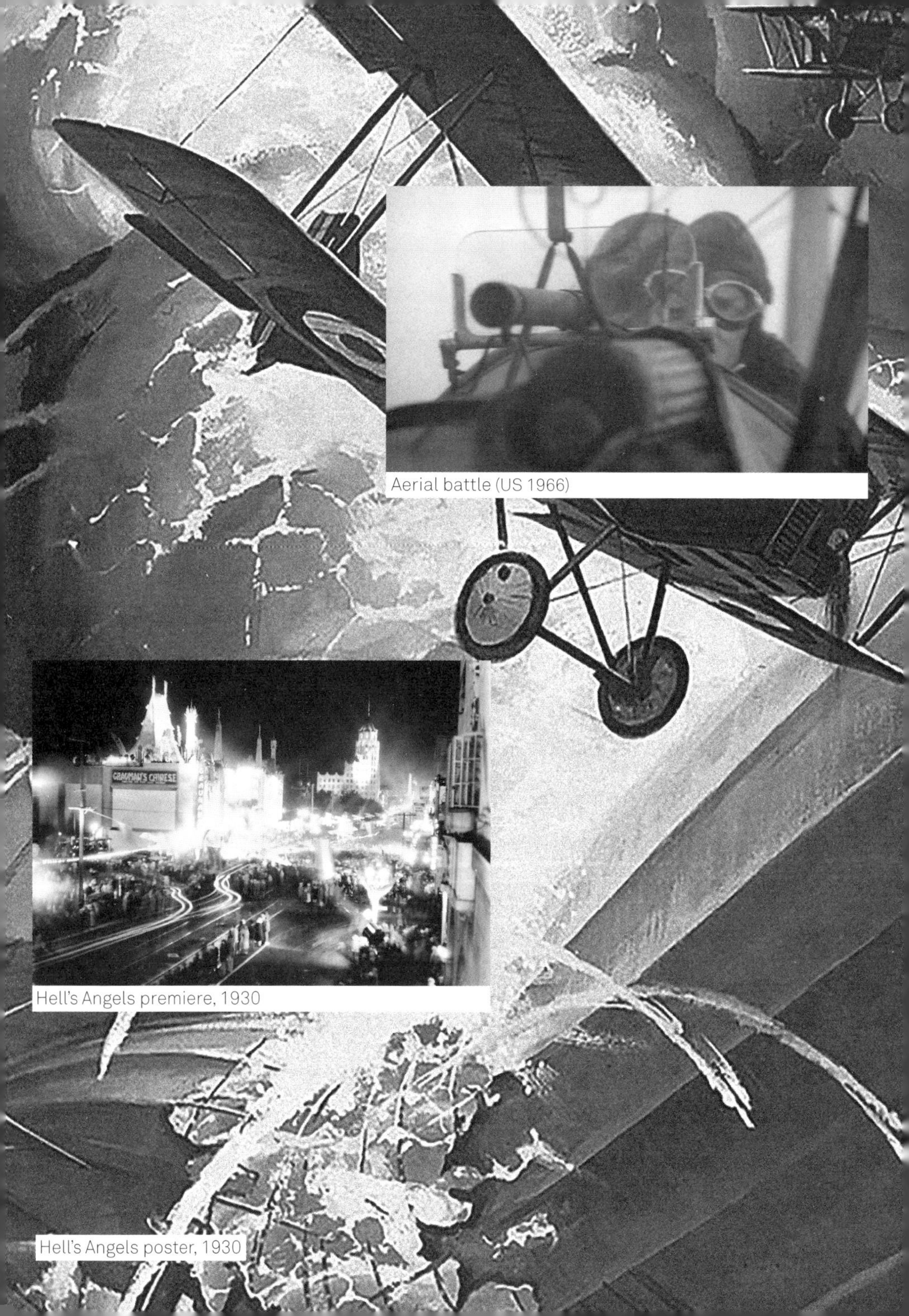

Aerial battle (US 1966)

Hell's Angels premiere, 1930

Hell's Angels poster, 1930

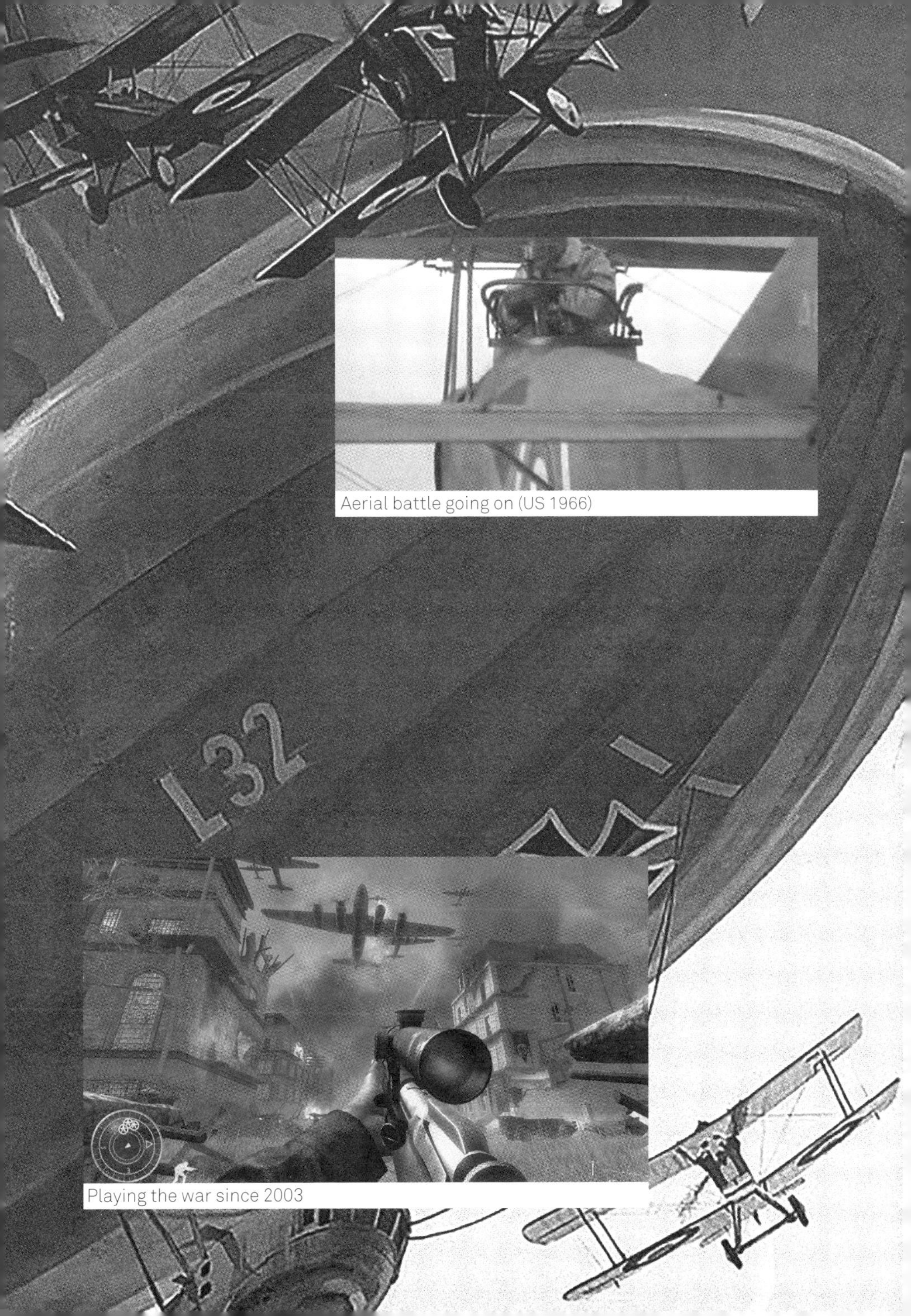

Aerial battle going on (US 1966)

Playing the war since 2003

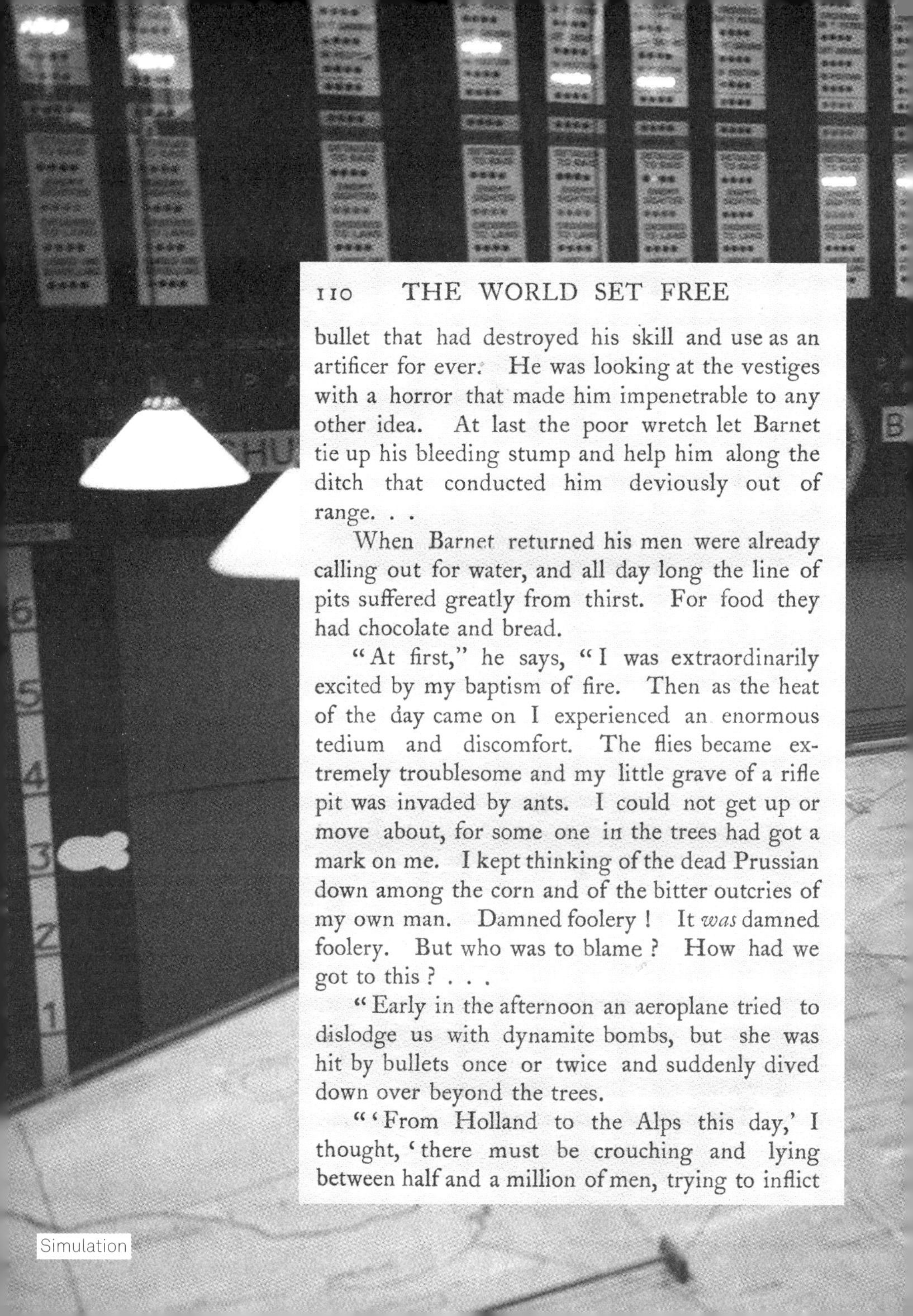

bullet that had destroyed his skill and use as an artificer for ever. He was looking at the vestiges with a horror that made him impenetrable to any other idea. At last the poor wretch let Barnet tie up his bleeding stump and help him along the ditch that conducted him deviously out of range. . .

When Barnet returned his men were already calling out for water, and all day long the line of pits suffered greatly from thirst. For food they had chocolate and bread.

"At first," he says, "I was extraordinarily excited by my baptism of fire. Then as the heat of the day came on I experienced an enormous tedium and discomfort. The flies became extremely troublesome and my little grave of a rifle pit was invaded by ants. I could not get up or move about, for some one in the trees had got a mark on me. I kept thinking of the dead Prussian down among the corn and of the bitter outcries of my own man. Damned foolery! It *was* damned foolery. But who was to blame? How had we got to this? . . .

"Early in the afternoon an aeroplane tried to dislodge us with dynamite bombs, but she was hit by bullets once or twice and suddenly dived down over beyond the trees.

"'From Holland to the Alps this day,' I thought, 'there must be crouching and lying between half and a million of men, trying to inflict

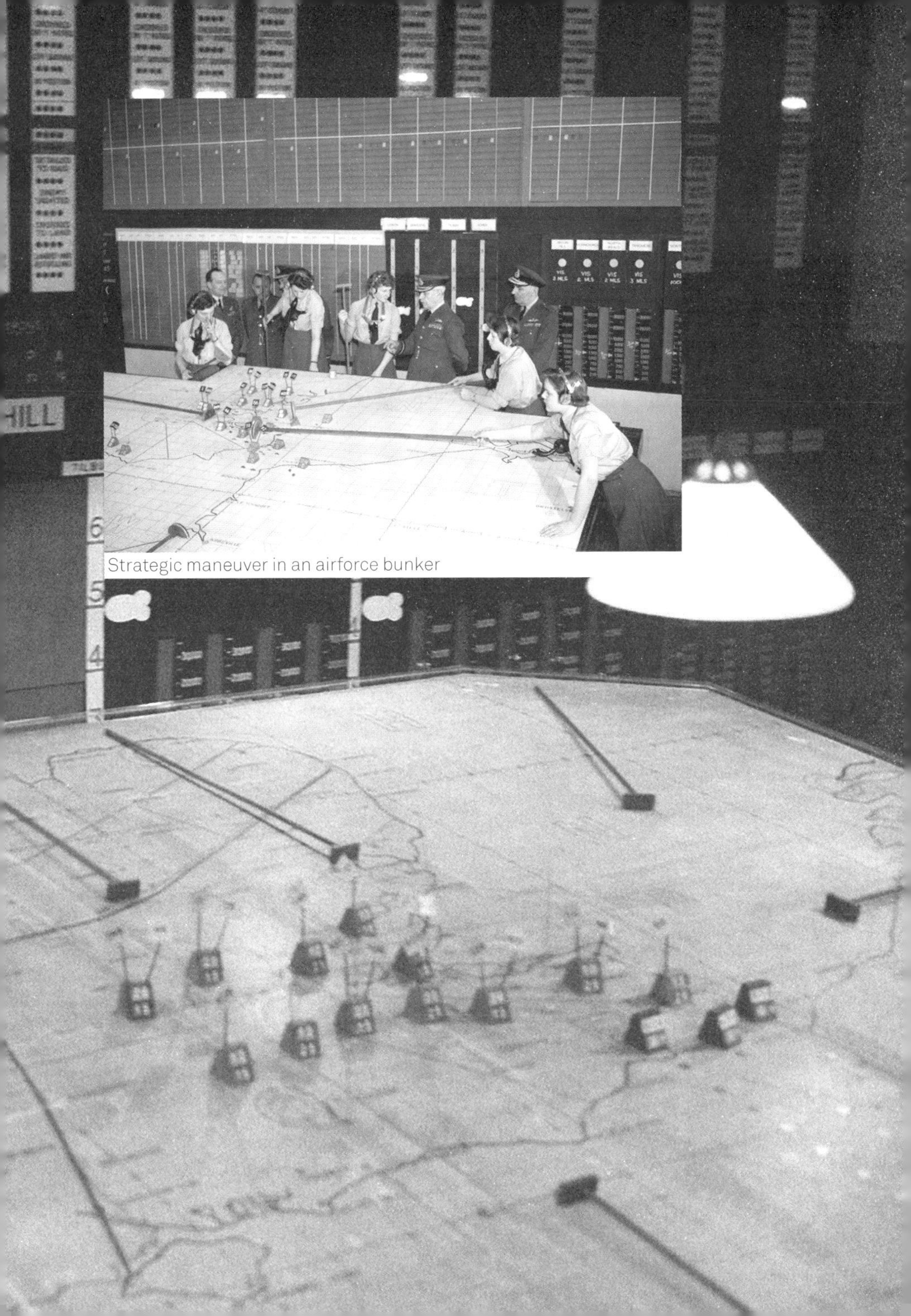

Strategic maneuver in an airforce bunker

irreparable damage upon one another. The thing is idiotic to the pitch of impossibility. It is a dream. Presently I shall wake up.' . . .

"Then the phrase changed itself in my mind. 'Presently mankind will wake up.'

"I lay speculating just how many thousands of men there were among these hundreds of thousands, whose spirits were in rebellion against all these ancient traditions of flag and empire. Weren't we perhaps already in the throes of the last crisis, in that darkest moment of a nightmare's horror before the sleeper will endure no more of it—and wakes?

"I don't know how my speculations ended. I think they were not so much ended as distracted by the distant thudding of the guns that were opening fire at long range upon Namur."

§ 7

But as yet Barnet had seen no more than the mildest beginnings of modern warfare. So far he had taken part only in a little shooting. The bayonet attack by which the advanced line was broken was made at a place called Croix Rouge more than twenty miles away, and that night under cover of the darkness the rifle pits were abandoned and he got his company away without further loss.

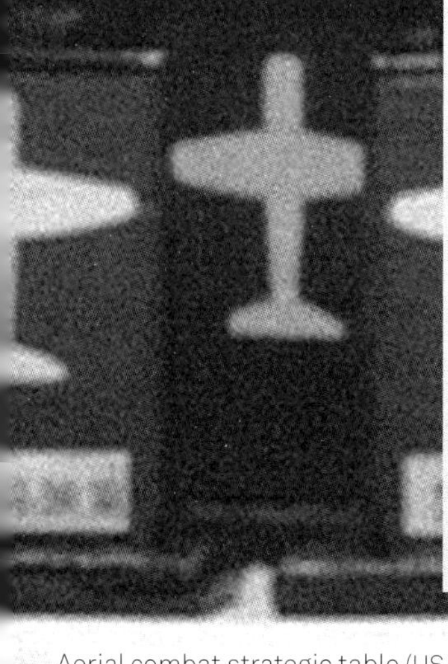

Aerial combat strategic table (US 2001)

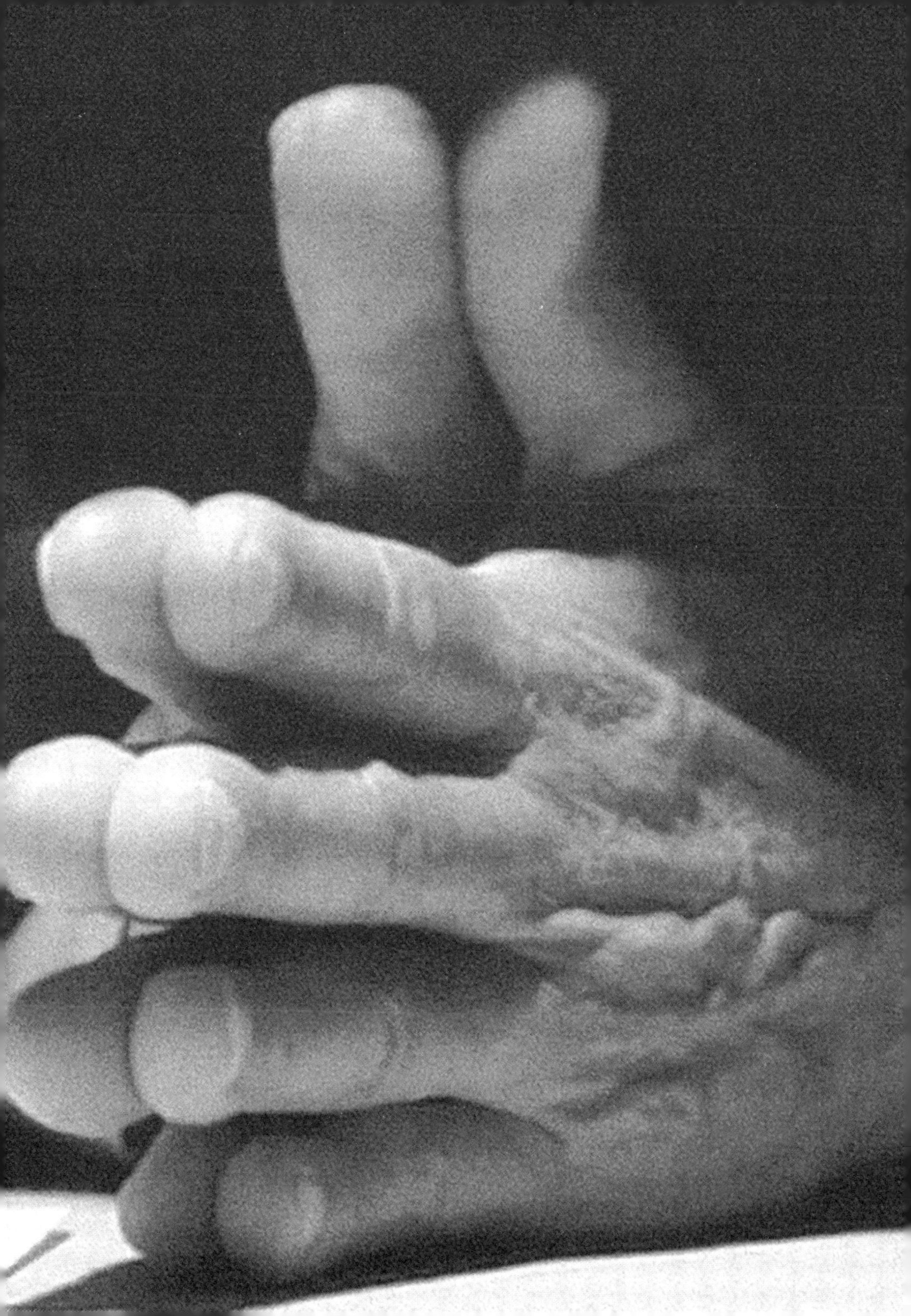

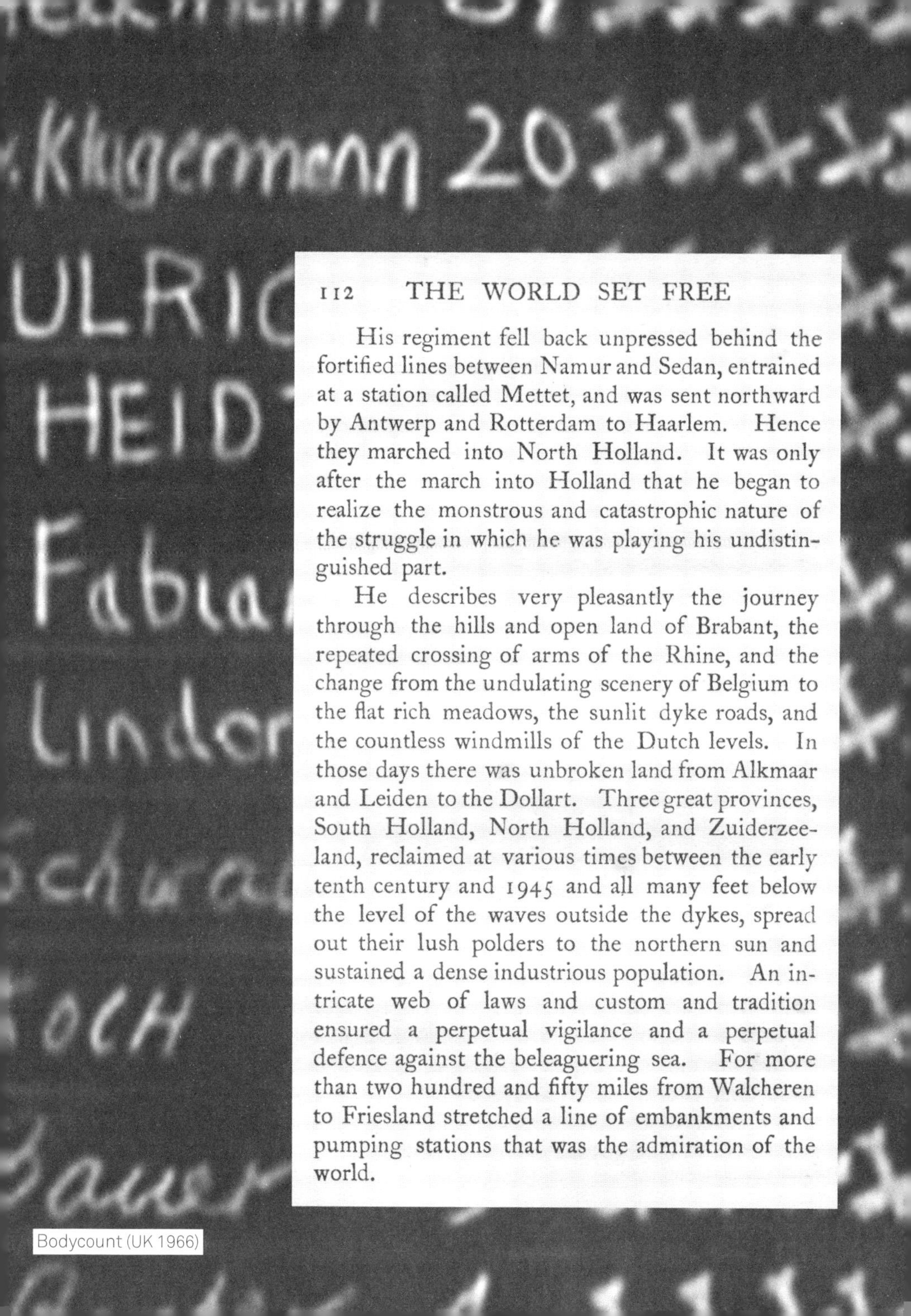

112 THE WORLD SET FREE

His regiment fell back unpressed behind the fortified lines between Namur and Sedan, entrained at a station called Mettet, and was sent northward by Antwerp and Rotterdam to Haarlem. Hence they marched into North Holland. It was only after the march into Holland that he began to realize the monstrous and catastrophic nature of the struggle in which he was playing his undistinguished part.

He describes very pleasantly the journey through the hills and open land of Brabant, the repeated crossing of arms of the Rhine, and the change from the undulating scenery of Belgium to the flat rich meadows, the sunlit dyke roads, and the countless windmills of the Dutch levels. In those days there was unbroken land from Alkmaar and Leiden to the Dollart. Three great provinces, South Holland, North Holland, and Zuiderzeeland, reclaimed at various times between the early tenth century and 1945 and all many feet below the level of the waves outside the dykes, spread out their lush polders to the northern sun and sustained a dense industrious population. An intricate web of laws and custom and tradition ensured a perpetual vigilance and a perpetual defence against the beleaguering sea. For more than two hundred and fifty miles from Walcheren to Friesland stretched a line of embankments and pumping stations that was the admiration of the world.

Bodycount (UK 1966)

If some curious god had chosen to watch the course of events in those northern provinces while that flanking march of the British was in progress, he would have found a convenient and appropriate seat for his observation upon one of the great cumulus clouds that were drifting slowly across the blue sky during all these eventful days before the great catastrophe. For that was the quality of the weather, hot and clear with something of a breeze, and underfoot dry and a little inclined to be dusty. This watching god would have looked down upon broad stretches of sunlit green, sunlit save for the creeping patches of shadow cast by the clouds, upon sky-reflecting meres, fringed and divided up by masses of willow and large areas of silvery weeds, upon white roads lying bare to the sun and upon a tracery of blue canals. The pastures were alive with cattle, the roads had a busy traffic of beasts and bicycles and gaily coloured peasants' automobiles, the hues of the innumerable motor barges in the canal vied with the eventfulness of the roadways; and everywhere in solitary steadings, amidst ricks and barns, in groups by the wayside, in straggling villages, each with its fine old church, or in compact towns laced with canals and abounding in bridges and clipped trees, were human habitations.

The people of this countryside were not belligerents. The interests and sympathies alike of Holland had been so divided that to the end

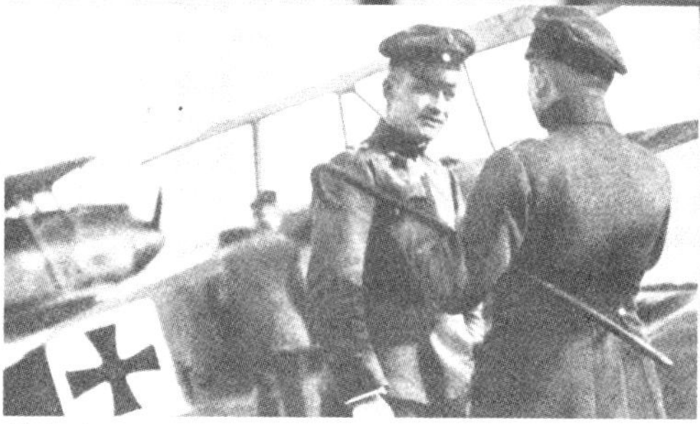
Flying ace

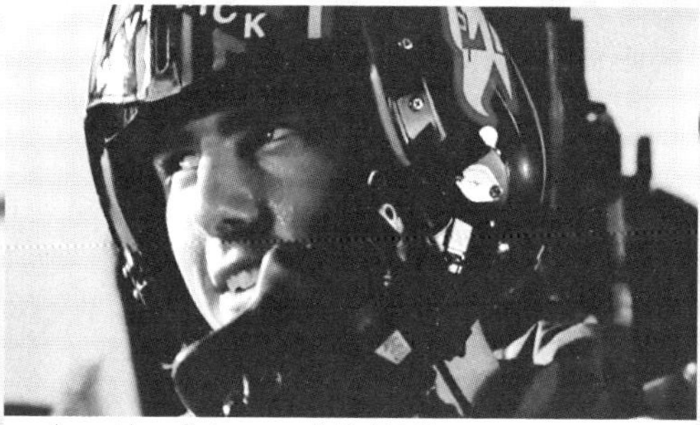
and another flying ace (US 1986)

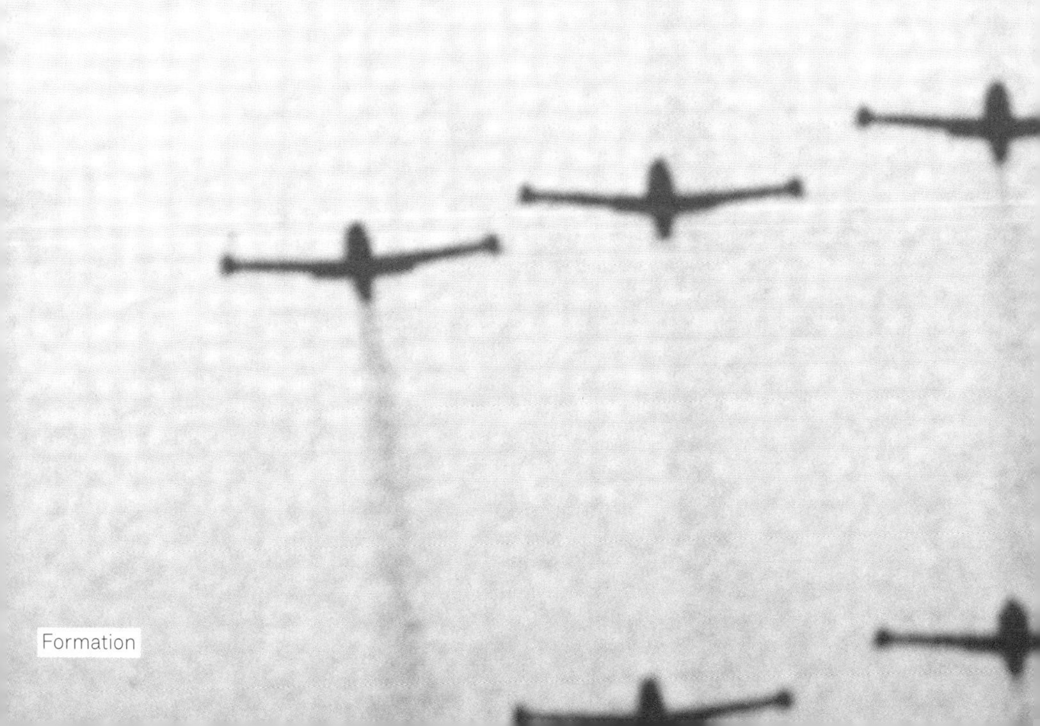
Formation

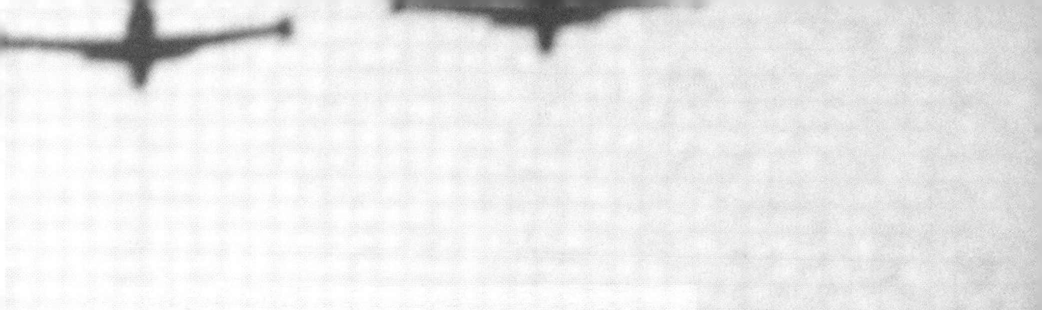

she remained undecided and passive in the struggle of the world powers. And everywhere along the roads taken by the marching armies clustered groups and crowds of impartially observant spectators, women and children in peculiar white caps and old-fashioned sabots, and elderly clean-shaven men quietly thoughtful over their long pipes. They had no fear of their invaders; the days when "soldiering" meant bands of licentious looters had long since passed away. . . .

That watcher among the clouds would have seen a great distribution of khaki-uniformed men and khaki-painted material over the whole of the sunken area of Holland. He would have marked the long trains, packed with men or piled with great guns and war material, creeping slowly, alert for train-wreckers, along the north-going lines; he would have seen the Scheldt and Rhine choked with shipping and pouring out still more men and still more material; he would have noticed halts and provisionings and detrainments, and the long bustling caterpillars of cavalry and infantry, the maggot-like waggons, the huge beetles of great guns, crawling under the poplars along the dykes and roads northward, along ways lined by the neutral, unmolested, ambiguously observant Dutch. All the barges and shipping upon the canals had been requisitioned for transport. In that clear bright warm weather it would all have looked from above like some extravagant festival of animated toys.

As the sun sank westward the spectacle must have become a little indistinct because of a golden haze; everything must have become warmer and more glowing, and because of the lengthening of the shadows more manifestly in relief. The shadows of the tall churches grew longer and longer until they touched the horizon and mingled in the universal shadow; and then, slow, and soft, and wrapping the world in fold after fold of deepening blue, came the night—the night at first obscurely simple, and then with faint points here and there, and then jewelled in darkling splendour with a hundred thousand lights. Out of that mingling of darkness and ambiguous glares the noise of an unceasing activity would have arisen, the louder and plainer now because there was no longer any distraction of sight.

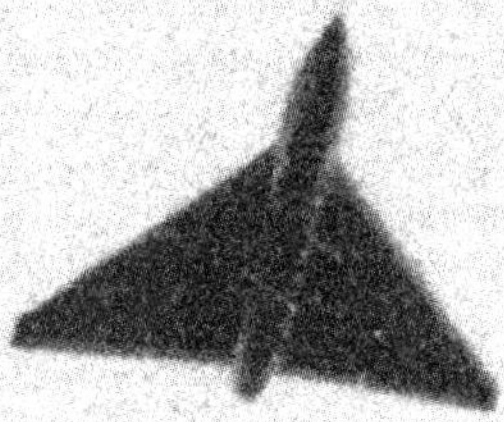

It may be that watcher drifting in the pellucid gulf beneath the stars watched all through the night; it may be that he dozed. But if he gave way to so natural a proclivity assuredly on the fourth night of the great flank march he was aroused, for that was the night of the battle in the air that decided the fate of Holland.

The aeroplanes were fighting at last, and suddenly about him, above and below, with cries and uproar rushing out of the four quarters of

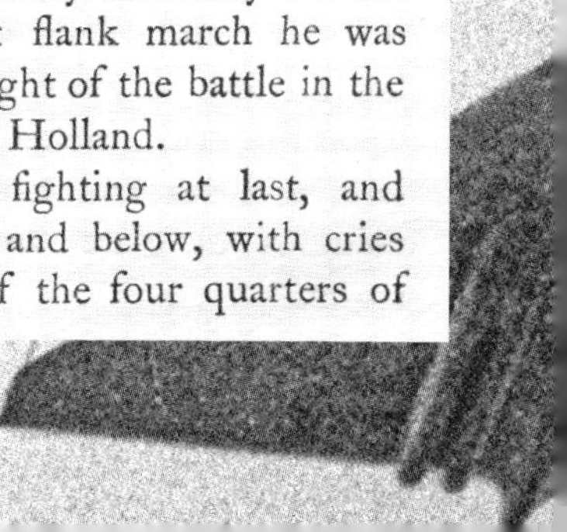

Next generation

heaven, striking, plunging, oversetting, soaring to the zenith and dropping to the ground, they came to assail or defend the myriads below.

Secretly the Central European power had gathered his flying machines together, and now he threw them as a giant might fling a handful of ten thousand knives over the low country. And amidst that swarming flight were five that drove headlong for the sea walls of Holland, carrying atomic bombs. From north and west and south the allied aeroplanes rose in response and swept down upon this sudden attack. So it was that war in the air began. Men rode upon the whirlwind that night and slew and fell like archangels. The sky rained heroes upon the astonished earth. Surely the last fights of mankind were the best. What was the heavy pounding of your Homeric swordsmen, what was the creaking charge of chariots, beside this swift rush, this crash, this giddy triumph, this headlong swoop to death?

And then athwart this whirling rush of aërial duels that swooped and locked and dropped in the void between the lamp-lights and the stars, came a great wind and a crash louder than thunder, and first one and then a score of lengthening fiery serpents plunged hungrily down upon the Dutchmen's dykes and struck between land and sea and flared up again in enormous columns of glare and crimsoned smoke and steam.

And out of the darkness leapt the little land, with its spires and trees, aghast with terror, still and distinct, and the sea, tumbled with anger, red-foaming like a sea of blood. . . .

Over the populous country below went a strange multitudinous crying and a flurry of alarm bells. . . .

The surviving aeroplanes turned about and fled out of the sky, like things that suddenly know themselves to be wicked. . . .

Through a dozen thunderously flaming gaps that no water might quench, the waves came roaring in upon the land. . . .

§ 8

"We had cursed our luck," says Barnet, "that we could not get to our quarters at Alkmaar that night. There, we were told, were provisions, tobacco, and everything for which we craved. But the main canal from Zaandam and Amsterdam was hopelessly jammed with craft, and we were glad of a chance opening that enabled us to get out of the main column and lie up in a kind of little harbour very much neglected and weedgrown before a deserted house. We broke into this and found some herrings in a barrel, a heap of cheeses, and stone bottles of gin in the cellar; and with this I cheered my starving men. We made fires and

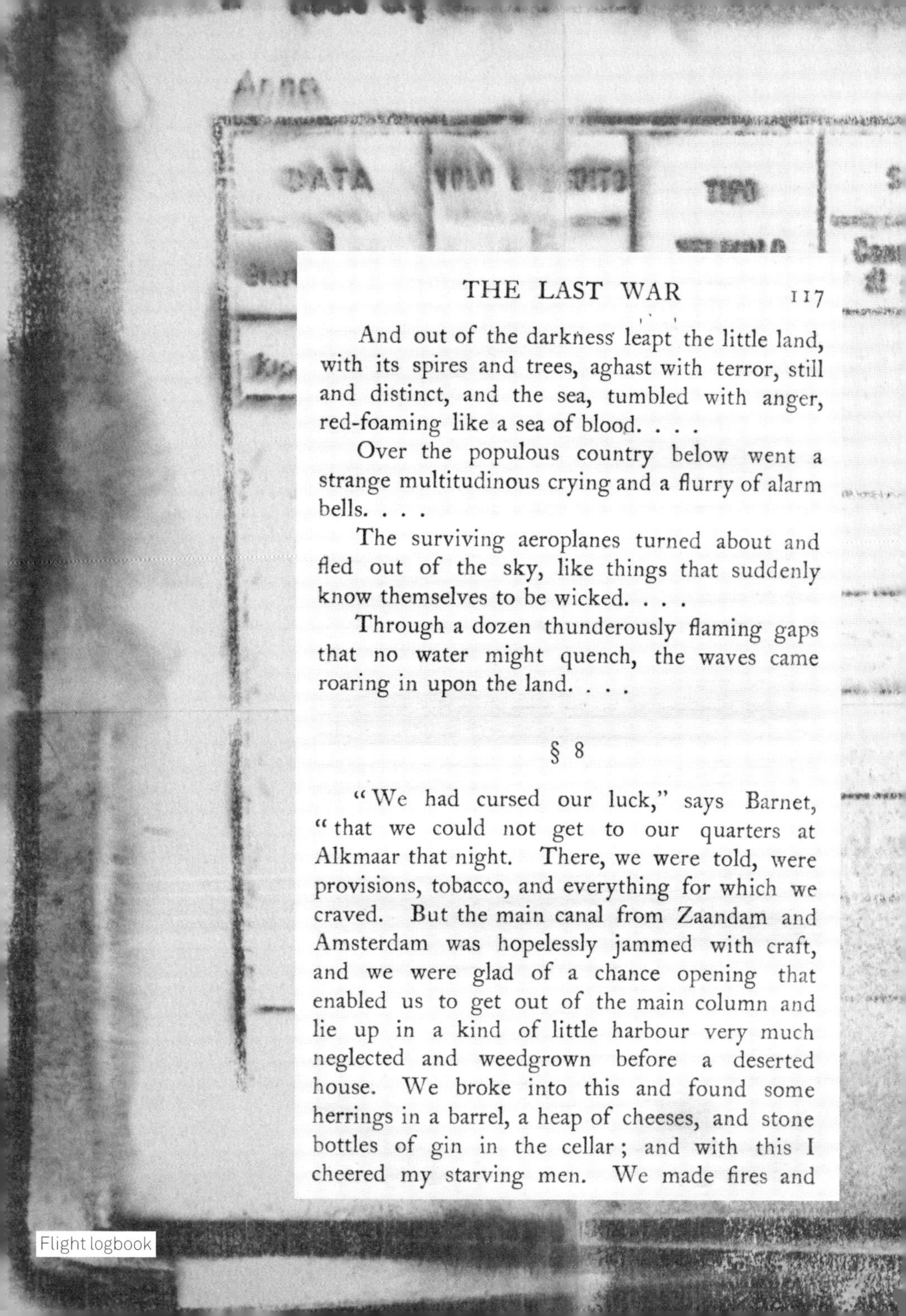

Flight logbook

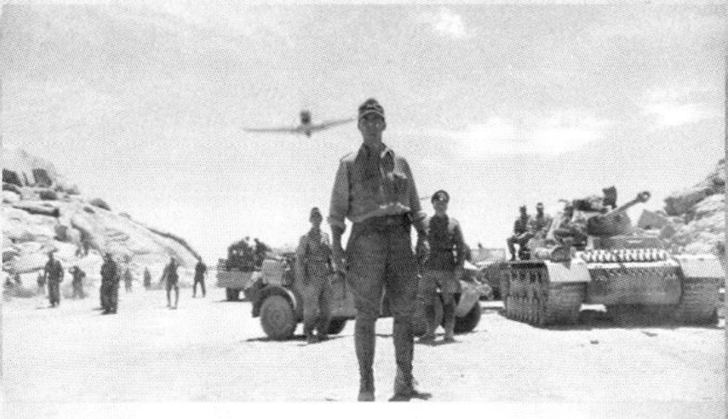

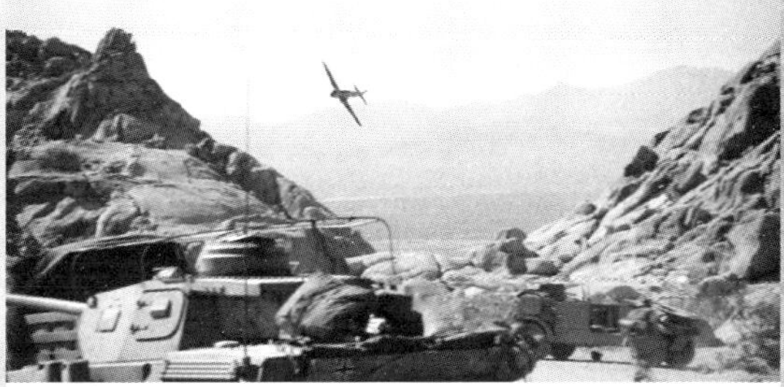

Out of the blue (US, DE 2008)

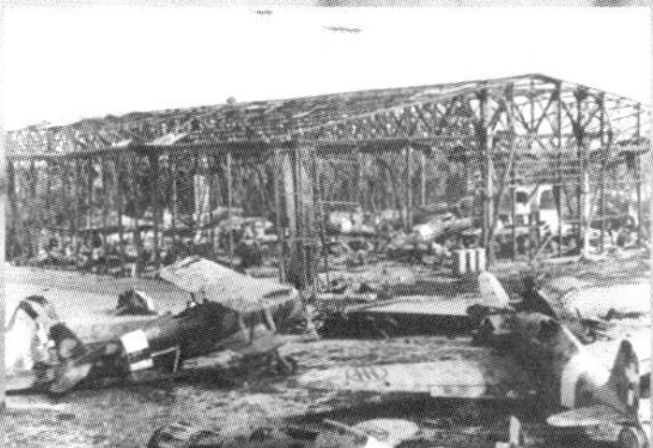

Bullseye

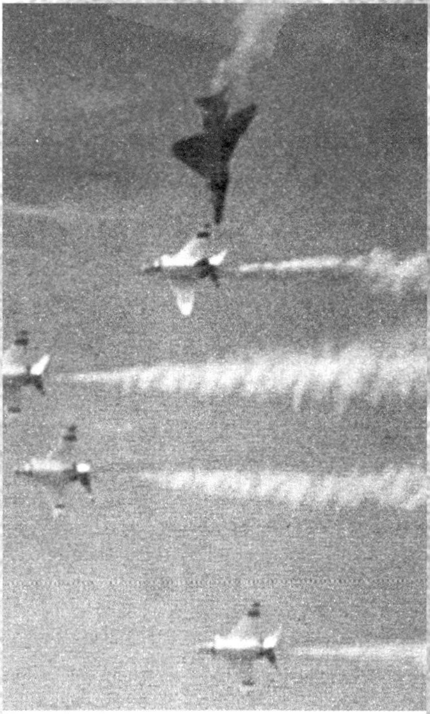

Direction down

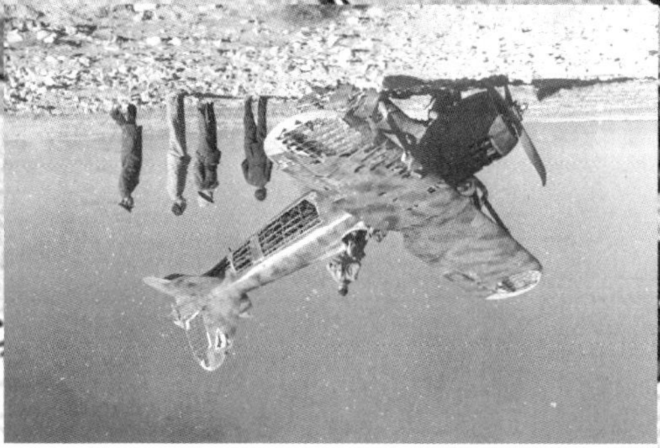

Crashed

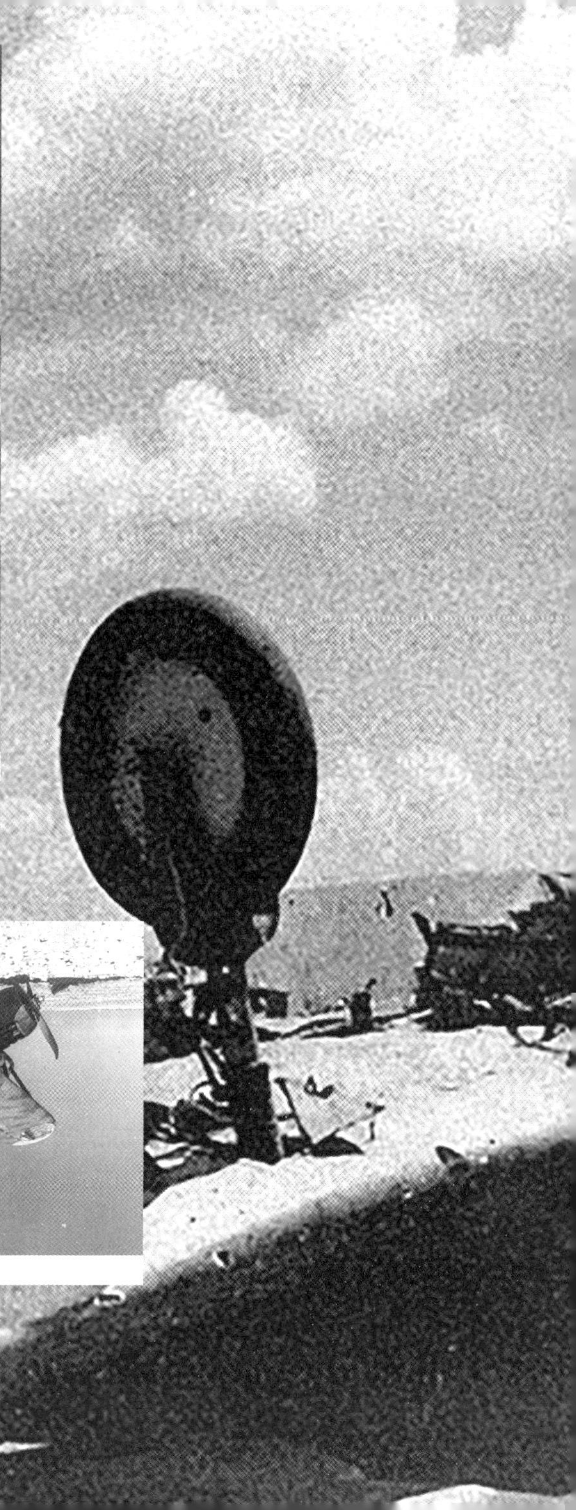

After the battle

toasted the cheese and grilled our herrings. None of us had slept for nearly forty hours and I determined to stay in this refuge until dawn and then if the traffic was still choked leave the barge and march the rest of the way into Alkmaar.

"This place we had got into was perhaps a hundred yards from the canal and underneath a little brick bridge we could see the flotilla still and hear the voices of the soldiers. Presently five or six other barges came through and lay up in the meer near by us and with two of these, full of men of the Antrim regiment, I shared my find of provisions. In return we got tobacco. A large expanse of water spread to the westward of us and beyond were a cluster of roofs and one or two church towers. The barge was rather cramped for so many men and I let several squads, thirty or forty perhaps altogether, bivouac on the bank. I did not let them go into the house on account of the furniture, and I left a note of indebtedness for the food we had taken. We were particularly glad of our tobacco and fires because of the numerous mosquitoes that rose about us.

"The gate of the house from which we had provisioned ourselves was adorned with the legend *Vreugde bij Vrede*, 'Joy with Peace,' and it bore every mark of the busy retirement of a comfort-loving proprietor. I went along his garden, which was gay and delightful with big bushes of

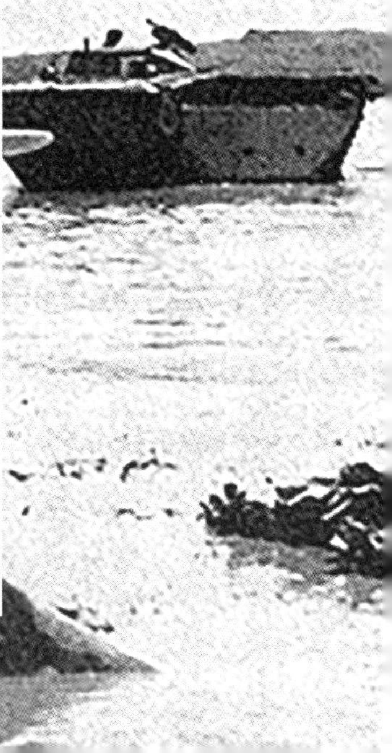

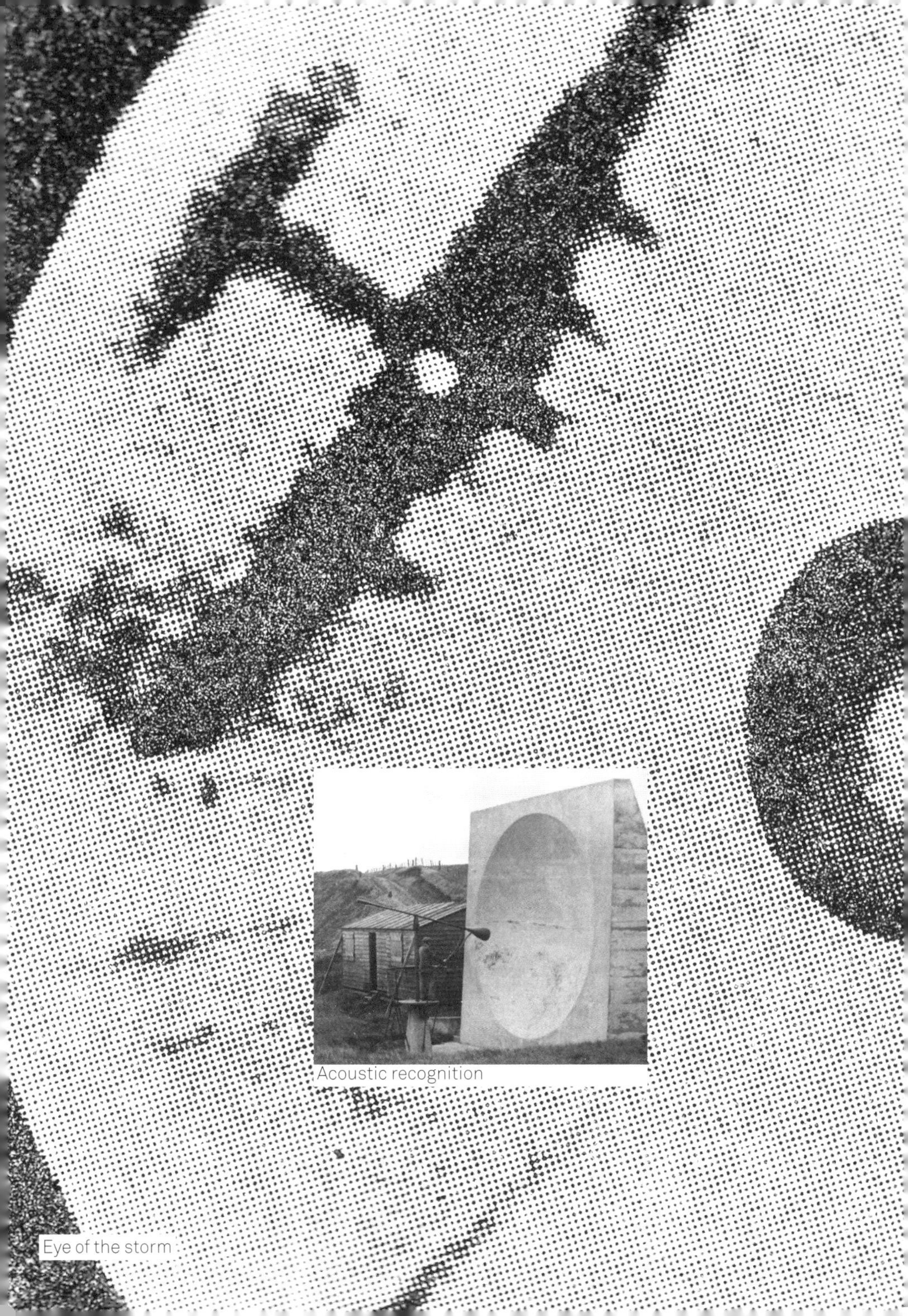

Acoustic recognition

Eye of the storm

rose and sweet briar, to a quaint little summer-house, and there I sat and watched the men in groups cooking and squatting along the bank. The sun was setting in a nearly cloudless sky.

"For the last two weeks I had been a wholly occupied man, intent only upon obeying the orders that came down to me. All through this time I had been working to the very limit of my mental and physical faculties and my only moments of rest had been devoted to snatches of sleep. Now came this rare unexpected interlude and I could look detachedly upon what I was doing and feel something of its infinite wonderfulness. I was irradiated with affection for the men of my company and with admiration at their cheerful acquiescence in the subordination and needs of our positions. I watched their proceedings and heard their pleasant voices. How willing those men were! How ready to accept leadership and forget themselves in collective ends! I thought how manfully they had gone through all the strains and toil of the last two weeks, how they had toughened and shaken down to comradeship together, and how much sweetness there is after all in our foolish human blood. For they were just one casual sample of the species—their patience and readiness lay, as the energy of the atom had lain, still waiting to be properly utilized. Again it came to me with overpowering force that the supreme need of our

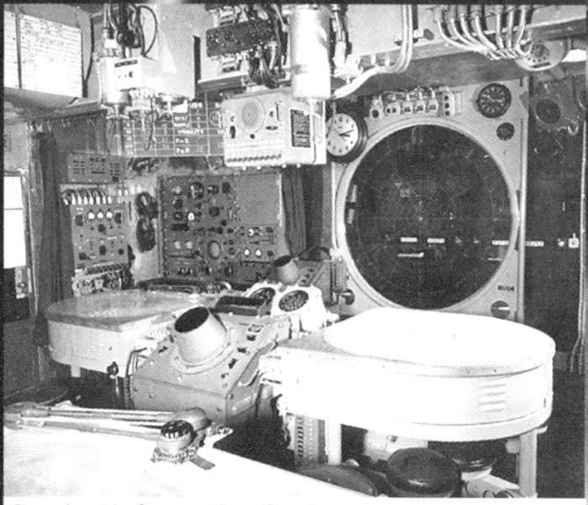

Combat Information Center

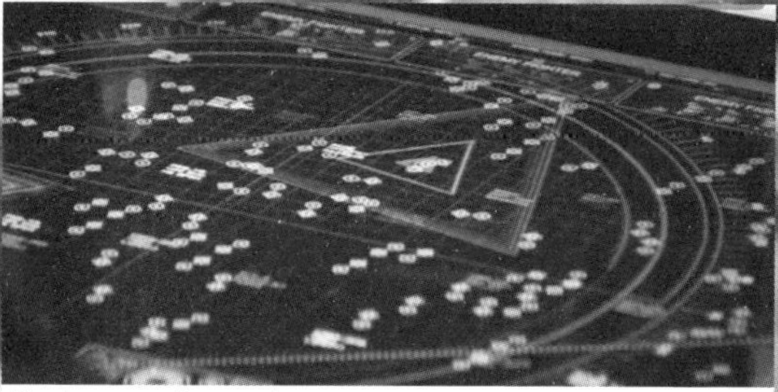

Next generation radar

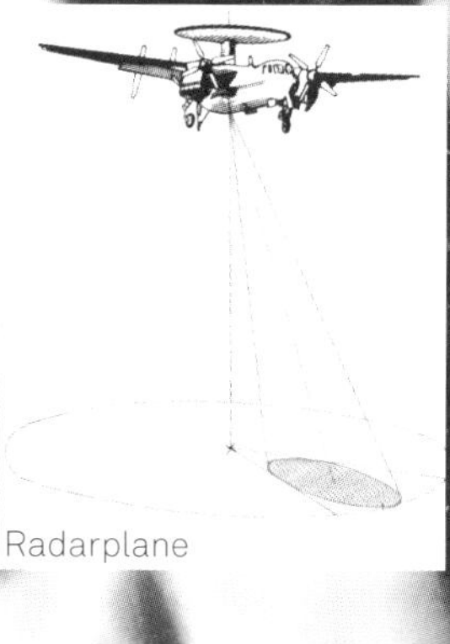

Radarplane

Plan and position

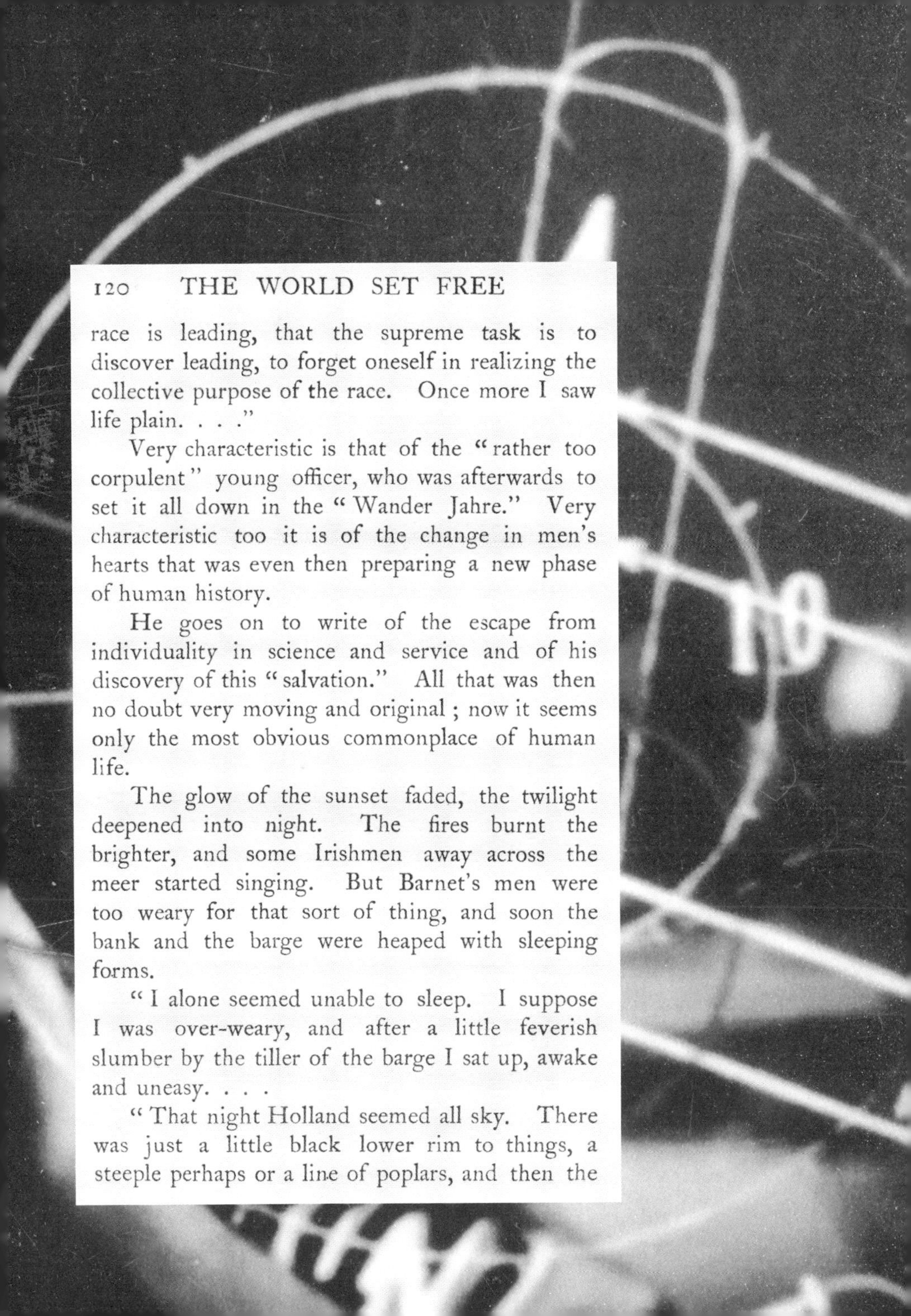

race is leading, that the supreme task is to discover leading, to forget oneself in realizing the collective purpose of the race. Once more I saw life plain. . . ."

Very characteristic is that of the "rather too corpulent" young officer, who was afterwards to set it all down in the "Wander Jahre." Very characteristic too it is of the change in men's hearts that was even then preparing a new phase of human history.

He goes on to write of the escape from individuality in science and service and of his discovery of this "salvation." All that was then no doubt very moving and original; now it seems only the most obvious commonplace of human life.

The glow of the sunset faded, the twilight deepened into night. The fires burnt the brighter, and some Irishmen away across the meer started singing. But Barnet's men were too weary for that sort of thing, and soon the bank and the barge were heaped with sleeping forms.

"I alone seemed unable to sleep. I suppose I was over-weary, and after a little feverish slumber by the tiller of the barge I sat up, awake and uneasy. . . .

"That night Holland seemed all sky. There was just a little black lower rim to things, a steeple perhaps or a line of poplars, and then the

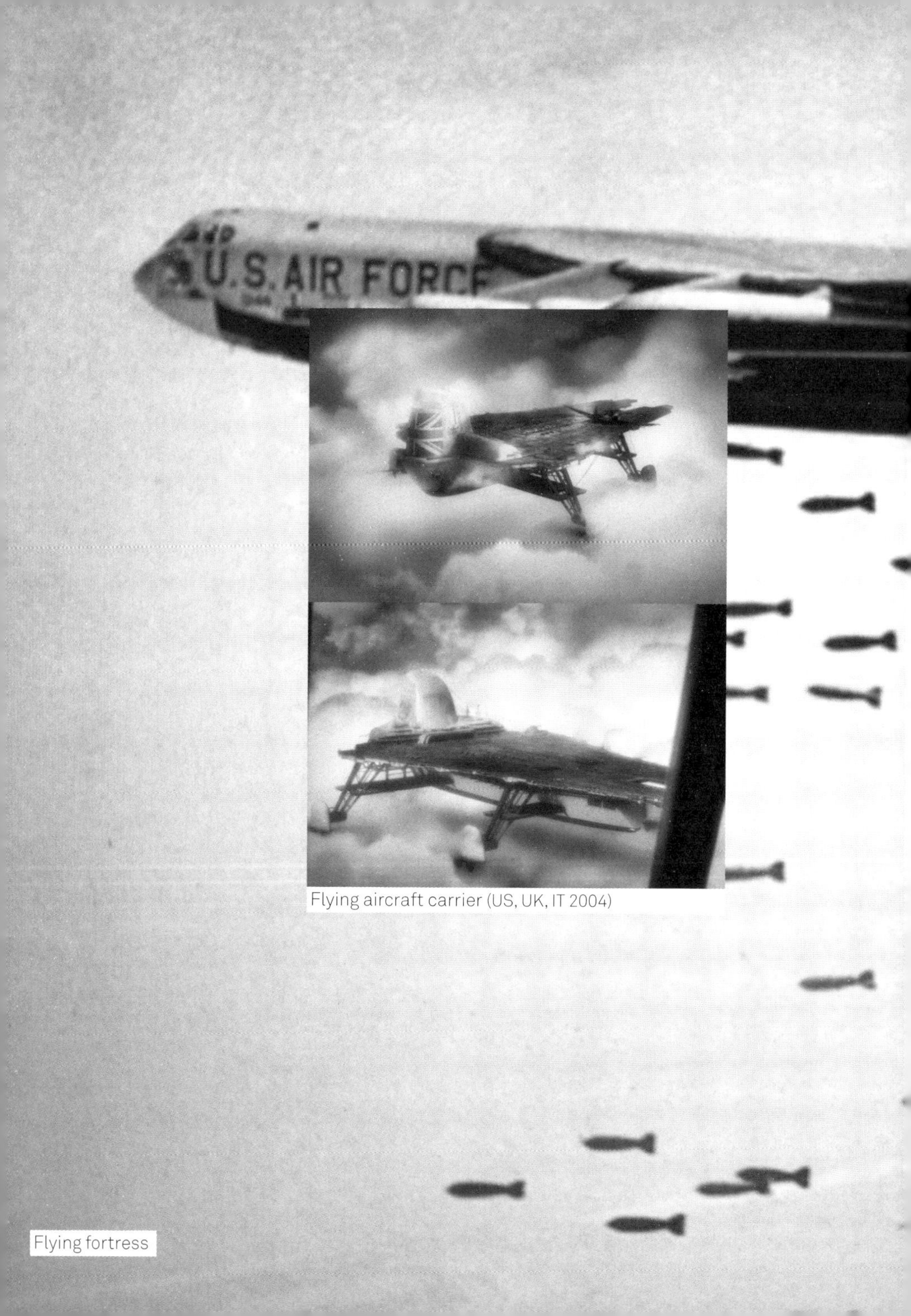

Flying aircraft carrier (US, UK, IT 2004)

Flying fortress

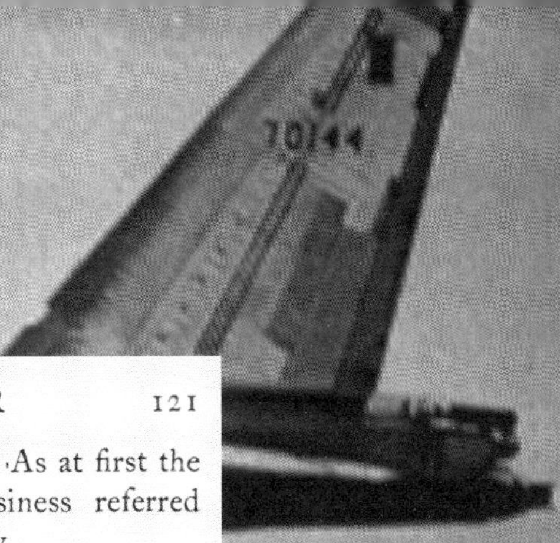

great hemisphere swept over us. As at first the sky was empty. Yet my uneasiness referred itself in some vague way to the sky.

"And now I was melancholy. I found something strangely sorrowful and submissive in the sleepers all about me, those men who had marched so far, who had left all the established texture of their lives behind them to come upon this mad campaign, this campaign that signified nothing and consumed everything, this mere fever of fighting. I saw how little and feeble is the life of man, a thing of chances, preposterously unable to find the will to realize even the most timid of its dreams. And I wondered if always it would be so, if man was a doomed animal who would never to the last days of his time take hold of fate and change it to his will. Always, it may be, he will remain kindly but jealous, desirous but discursive, able and unwisely impulsive, until Saturn who begot him shall devour him in his turn. . . .

"I was roused from these thoughts by the sudden realization of the presence of a squadron of aeroplanes far away to the north-east and very high. They looked like little black dashes against the midnight blue. I remember that I looked up at them at first rather idly—as one might notice a flight of birds. Then I perceived that they were only the extreme wing of a great fleet that was advancing in a long line very

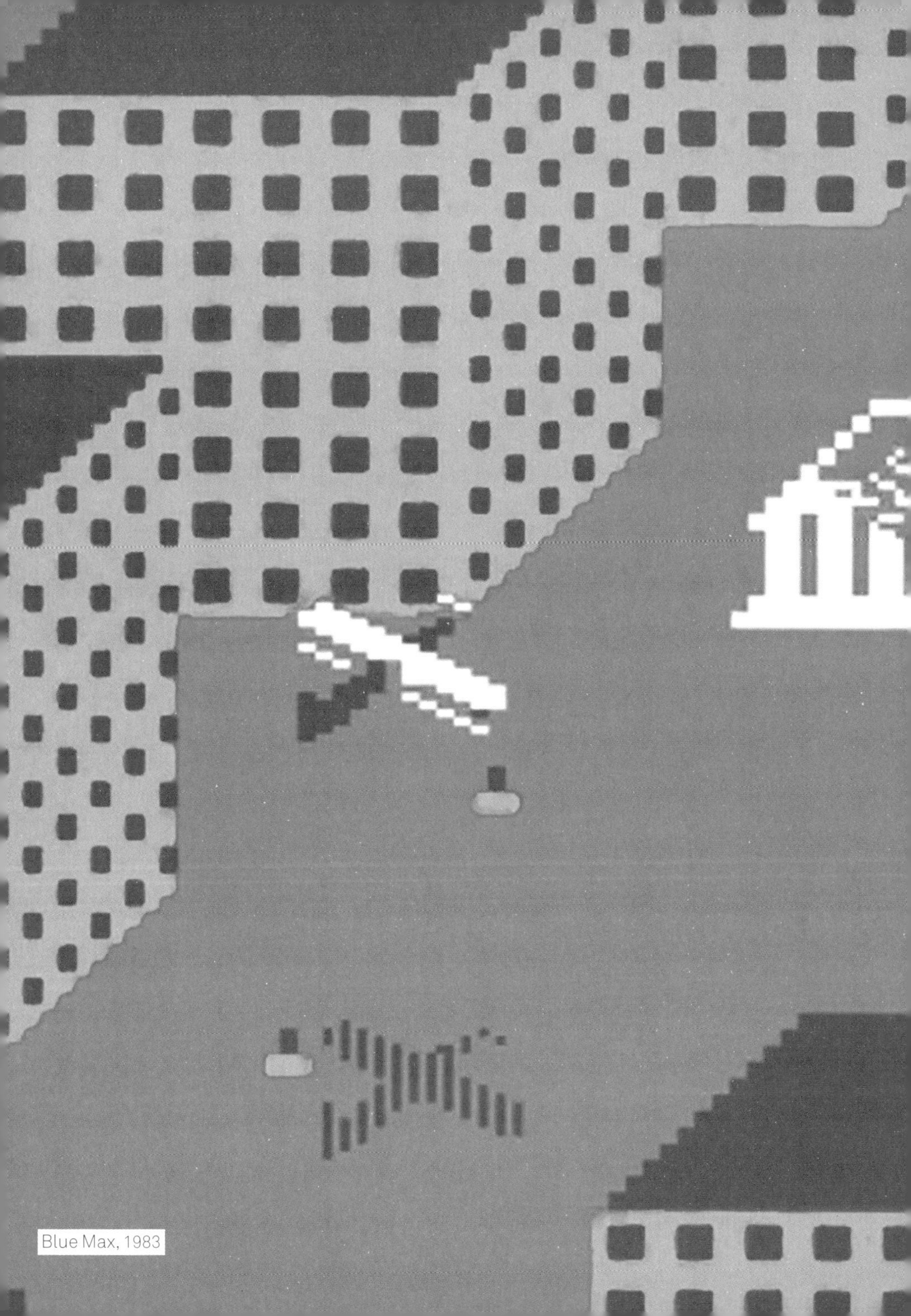

Blue Max, 1983

swiftly from the direction of the frontier and my attention tightened.

"Directly I saw that fleet I was astonished not to have seen it before.

"I stood up softly, undesirous of disturbing my companions, but with my heart beating now rather more rapidly with surprise and excitement. I strained my ears for any sound of guns along our front. Almost instinctively I· turned about for protection to the south and west, and peered; and then I saw coming as fast and much nearer to me, as if they had sprung out of the darkness, three banks of aeroplanes; a group of squadrons very high, a main body at a height perhaps of one or two thousand feet, and a doubtful number flying low and very indistinct. The middle ones were so thick they kept putting out groups of stars. And I realized that after all there was to be fighting in the air.

"There was something extraordinarily strange in this swift, noiseless convergence of nearly invisible combatants above the sleeping hosts. Everyone about me was still unconscious; there was no sign as yet of any agitation among the shipping on the main canal whose whole course, dotted with unsuspicious lights and fringed with fires, must have been clearly perceptible from above. Then a long way off towards Alkmaar I heard bugles, and after that shots, and then a wild clamour of bells. I determined to let

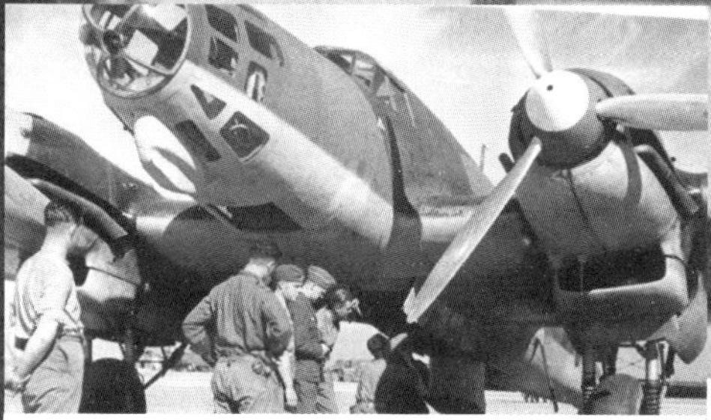

Secret bombing mission on a small town in Spain

my men sleep on for as long as they could. . . .

"The battle was joined with the swiftness of dreaming. I do not think it can have been five minutes from the moment when I first became aware of the Central European air fleet to the contact of the two forces. I saw it quite plainly in silhouette against the luminous blue of the northern sky. The allied aeroplanes—they were mostly French—came pouring down like a fierce shower upon the middle of the Central European fleet. They looked exactly like a coarser sort of rain. There was a crackling sound—the first sound I heard—it reminded one of the Aurora Borealis and I supposed it was an interchange of rifle shots. There were flashes like summer lightning; and then all the sky became a whirling confusion of battle that was still largely noiseless. Some of the Central European aeroplanes were certainly charged and overset; others seemed to collapse and fall and then flare out with so bright a light that it took the edge off one's vision and made the rest of the battle disappear as though it had been snatched back out of sight.

"And then while I still peered and tried to shade these flames from my eyes with my hand, and while the men about me were beginning to stir, the atomic bombs were thrown at the dykes. They made a mighty thunder in the air, and fell like Lucifer in the picture, leaving a flaring trail

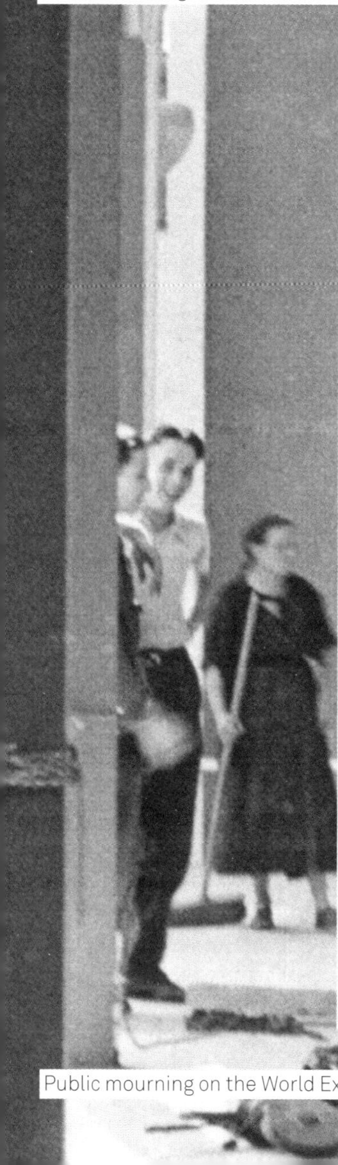

Public mourning on the World Exhibition, 1937

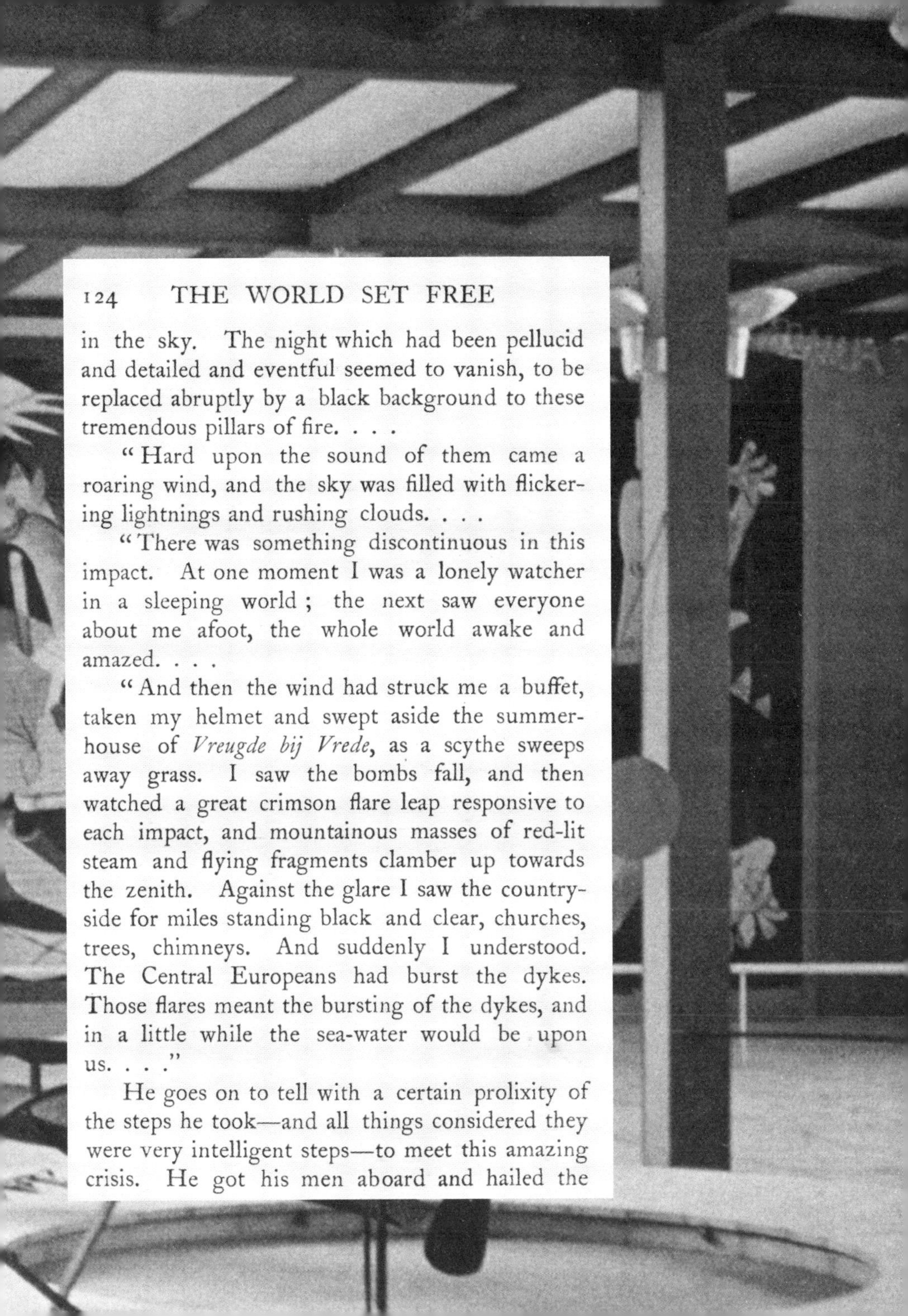

in the sky. The night which had been pellucid and detailed and eventful seemed to vanish, to be replaced abruptly by a black background to these tremendous pillars of fire. . . .

"Hard upon the sound of them came a roaring wind, and the sky was filled with flickering lightnings and rushing clouds. . . .

"There was something discontinuous in this impact. At one moment I was a lonely watcher in a sleeping world; the next saw everyone about me afoot, the whole world awake and amazed. . . .

"And then the wind had struck me a buffet, taken my helmet and swept aside the summerhouse of *Vreugde bij Vrede*, as a scythe sweeps away grass. I saw the bombs fall, and then watched a great crimson flare leap responsive to each impact, and mountainous masses of red-lit steam and flying fragments clamber up towards the zenith. Against the glare I saw the countryside for miles standing black and clear, churches, trees, chimneys. And suddenly I understood. The Central Europeans had burst the dykes. Those flares meant the bursting of the dykes, and in a little while the sea-water would be upon us. . . ."

He goes on to tell with a certain prolixity of the steps he took—and all things considered they were very intelligent steps—to meet this amazing crisis. He got his men aboard and hailed the

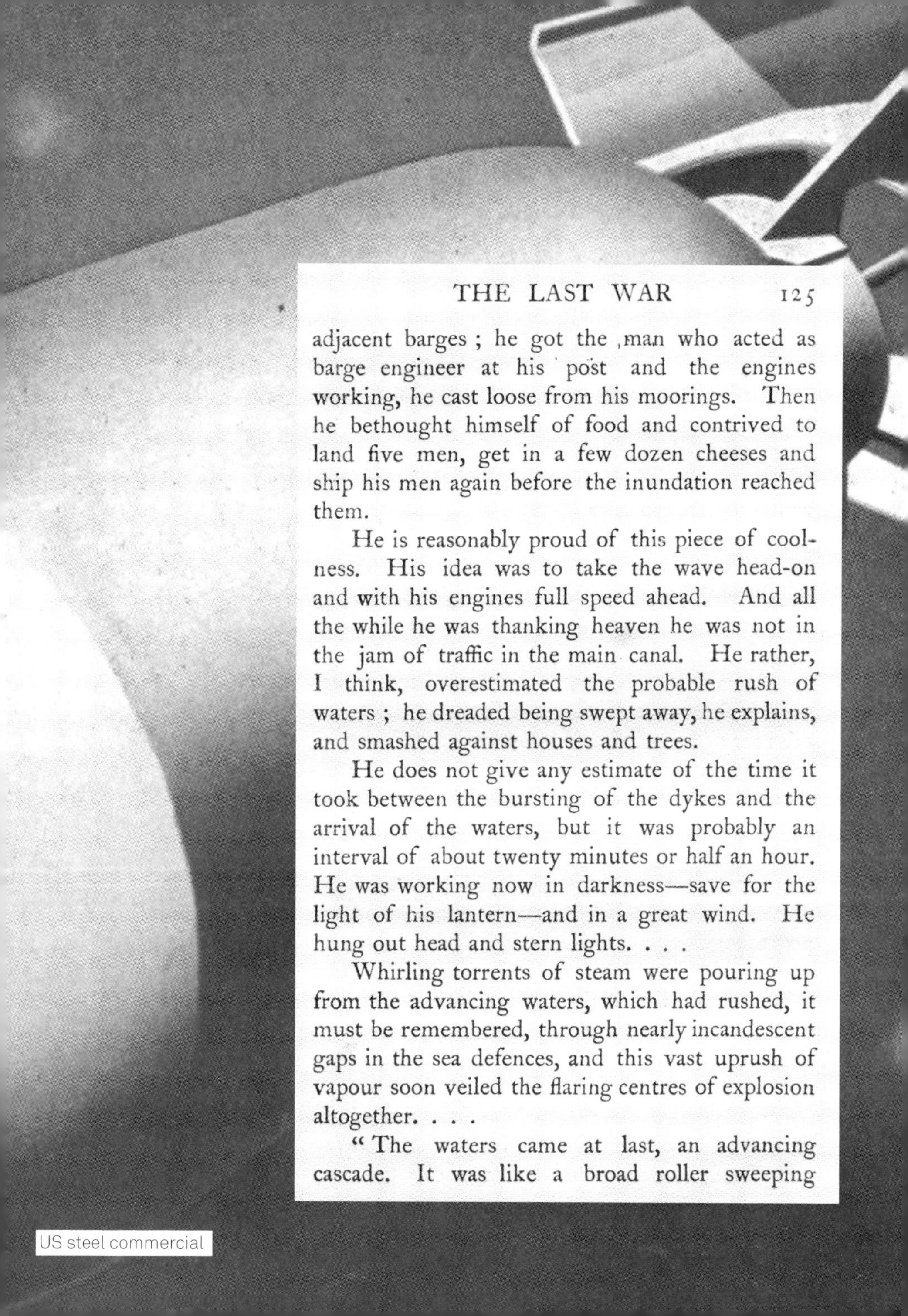

adjacent barges ; he got the man who acted as barge engineer at his post and the engines working, he cast loose from his moorings. Then he bethought himself of food and contrived to land five men, get in a few dozen cheeses and ship his men again before the inundation reached them.

He is reasonably proud of this piece of coolness. His idea was to take the wave head-on and with his engines full speed ahead. And all the while he was thanking heaven he was not in the jam of traffic in the main canal. He rather, I think, overestimated the probable rush of waters ; he dreaded being swept away, he explains, and smashed against houses and trees.

He does not give any estimate of the time it took between the bursting of the dykes and the arrival of the waters, but it was probably an interval of about twenty minutes or half an hour. He was working now in darkness—save for the light of his lantern—and in a great wind. He hung out head and stern lights. . . .

Whirling torrents of steam were pouring up from the advancing waters, which had rushed, it must be remembered, through nearly incandescent gaps in the sea defences, and this vast uprush of vapour soon veiled the flaring centres of explosion altogether. . . .

“ The waters came at last, an advancing cascade. It was like a broad roller sweeping

US steel commercial

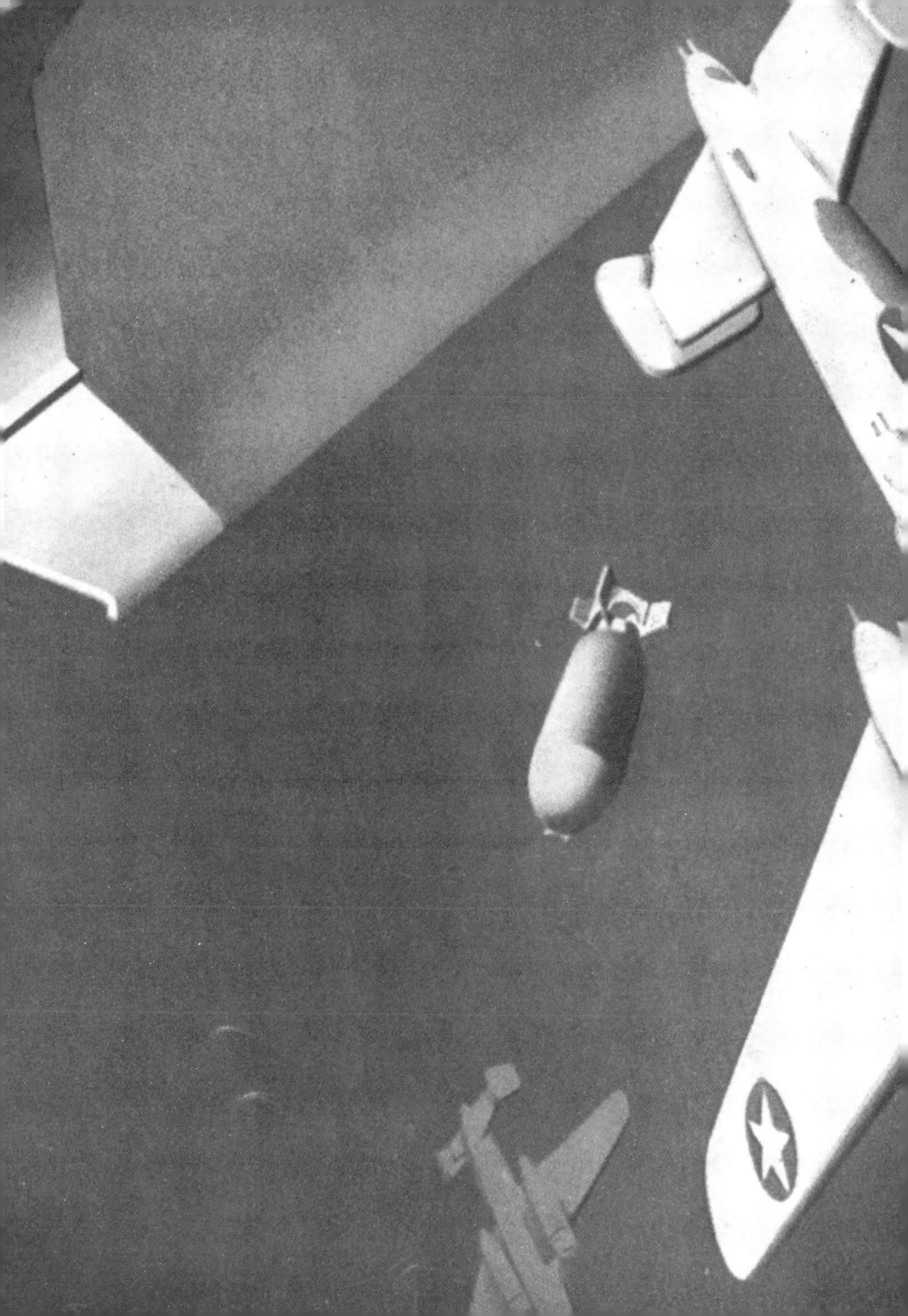

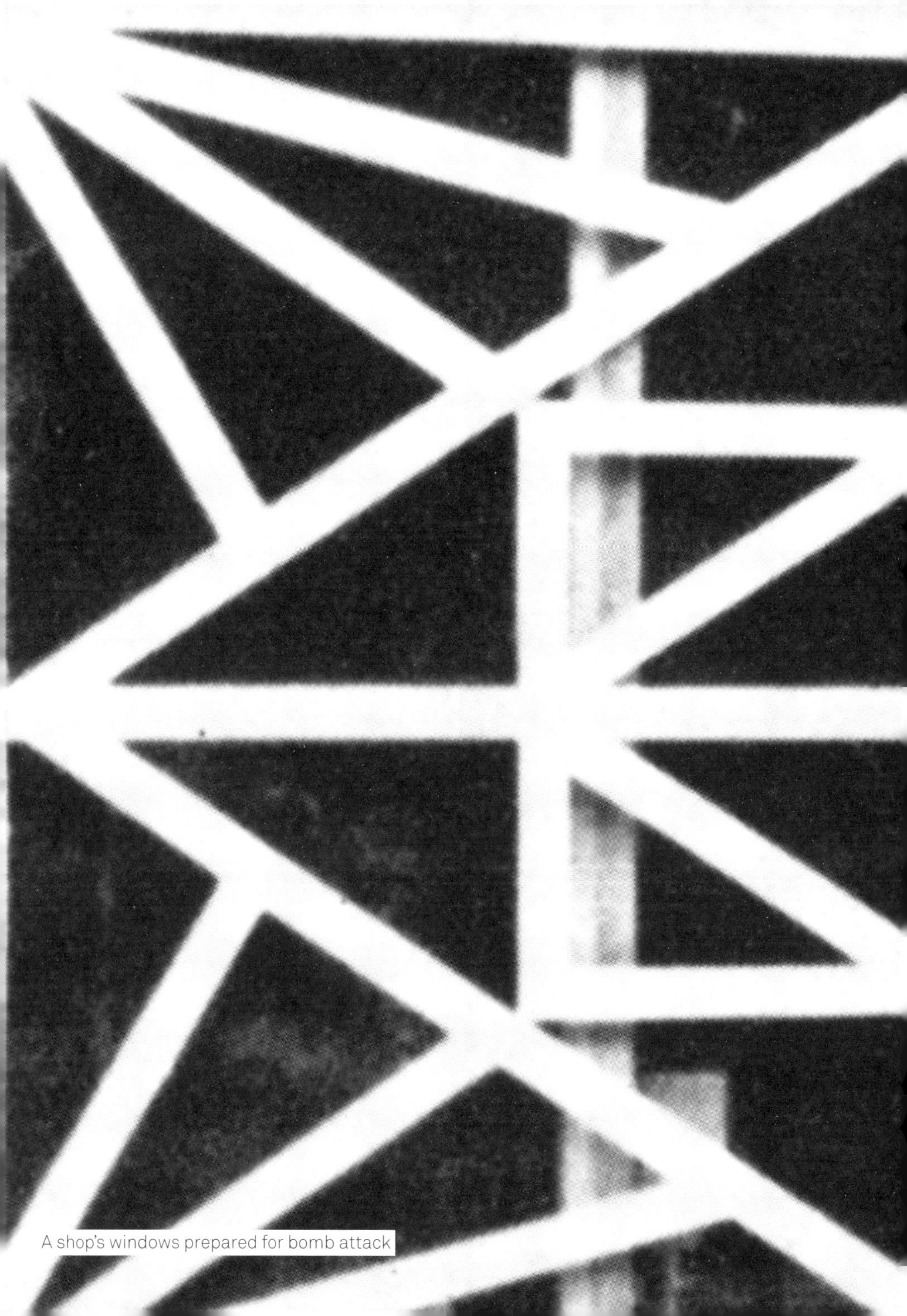

A shop's windows prepared for bomb attack

across the country. They came with a deep roaring sound. I had expected a Niagara but the total fall of the front could not have been much more than twelve feet. Our barge hesitated for a moment, took a dose over her bows and then lifted. I signalled for full speed ahead and brought her head up stream, and held on like grim death to keep her there.

"There was a wind about as strong as the flood and I found we were pounding against every conceivable buoyant object, that had been between us and the sea. The only light in the world now came from our lamps, the steam became impenetrable at a score of yards from the boat, and the roar of the wind and water cut us off from all remoter sounds. The black shining waters swirled by, coming into the light of our lamps out of an ebony blackness and vanishing again into impenetrable black. And on the waters came shapes, came things that flashed upon us for a moment, now a half-submerged boat, now a cow, now a huge fragment of a house's timberings, now a muddle of packing-cases and scaffolding. The things clapped into sight like something shown by the opening of a shutter, and then bumped shatteringly against us or rushed by us. Once I saw very clearly a man's white face. . . .

"All the while a group of labouring half-submerged trees remained ahead of us drawing very slowly nearer. I steered a course to avoid

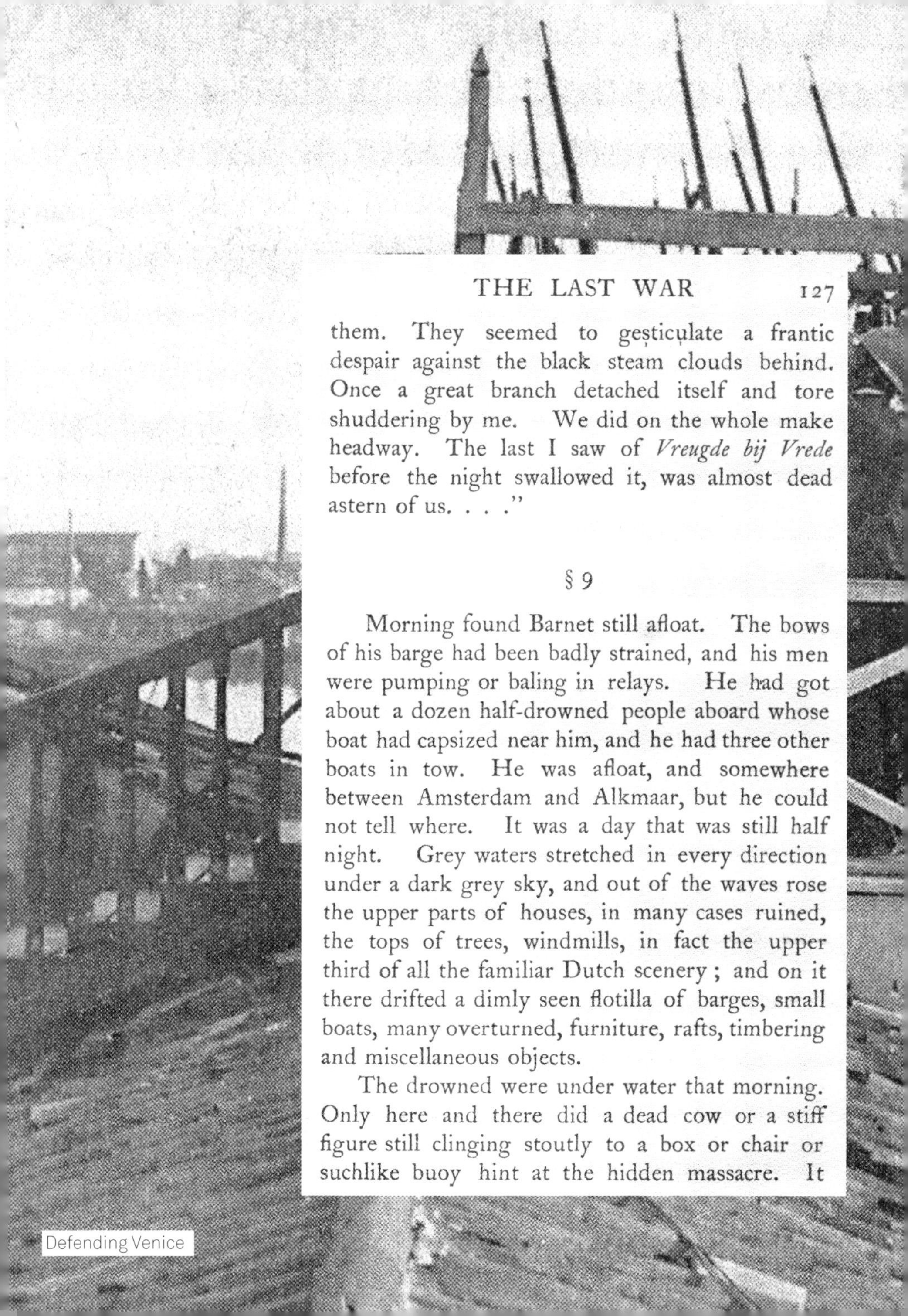

them. They seemed to gesticulate a frantic despair against the black steam clouds behind. Once a great branch detached itself and tore shuddering by me. We did on the whole make headway. The last I saw of *Vreugde bij Vrede* before the night swallowed it, was almost dead astern of us. . . ."

§ 9

Morning found Barnet still afloat. The bows of his barge had been badly strained, and his men were pumping or baling in relays. He had got about a dozen half-drowned people aboard whose boat had capsized near him, and he had three other boats in tow. He was afloat, and somewhere between Amsterdam and Alkmaar, but he could not tell where. It was a day that was still half night. Grey waters stretched in every direction under a dark grey sky, and out of the waves rose the upper parts of houses, in many cases ruined, the tops of trees, windmills, in fact the upper third of all the familiar Dutch scenery; and on it there drifted a dimly seen flotilla of barges, small boats, many overturned, furniture, rafts, timbering and miscellaneous objects.

The drowned were under water that morning. Only here and there did a dead cow or a stiff figure still clinging stoutly to a box or chair or suchlike buoy hint at the hidden massacre. It

Defending Venice

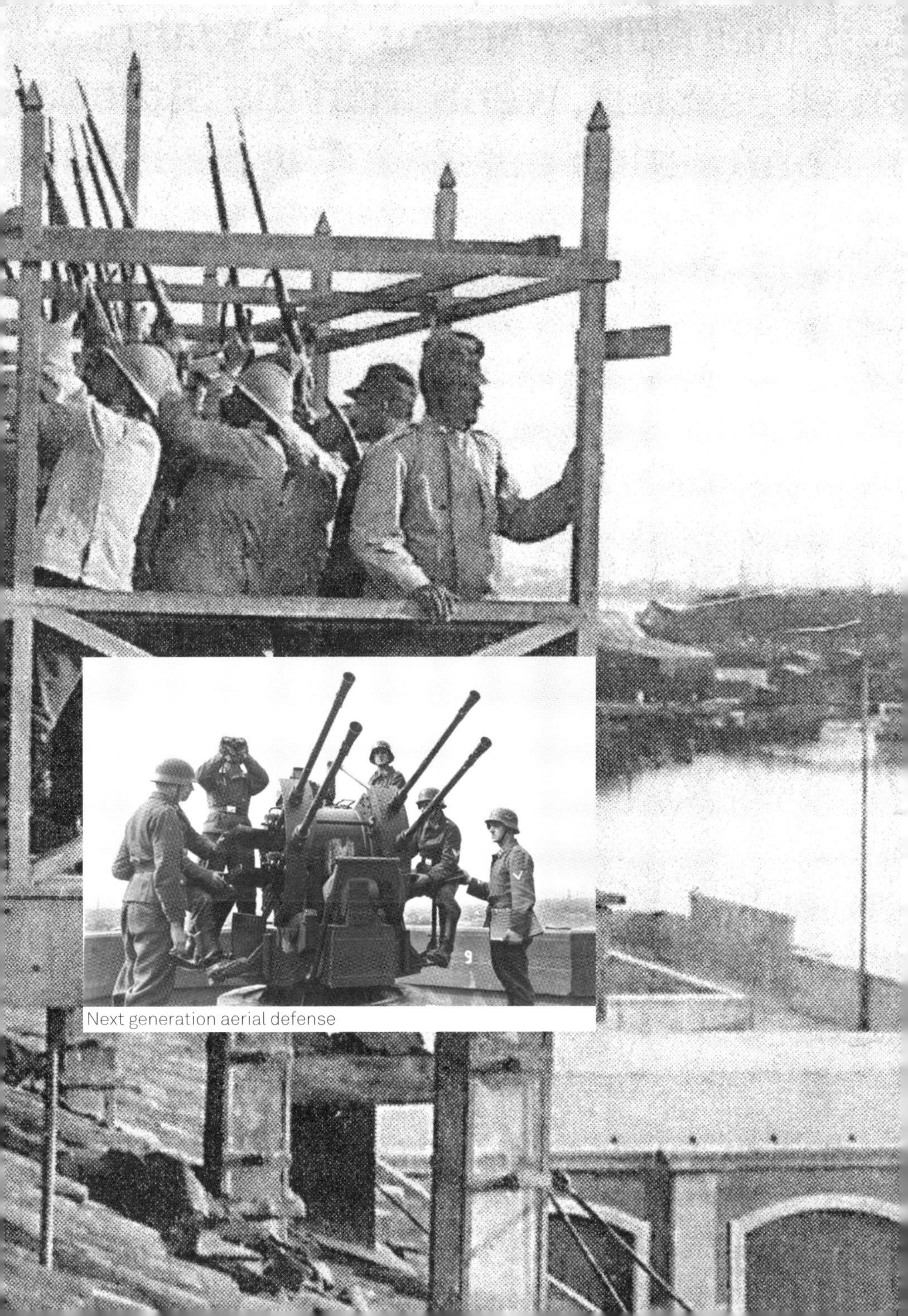

Next generation aerial defense

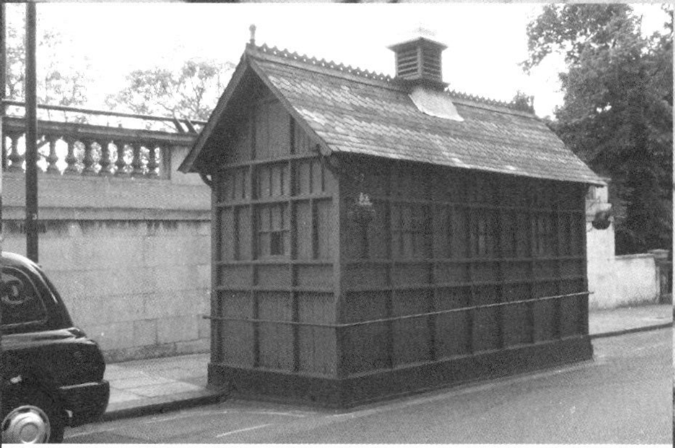

Entrance to a subterranean shelter

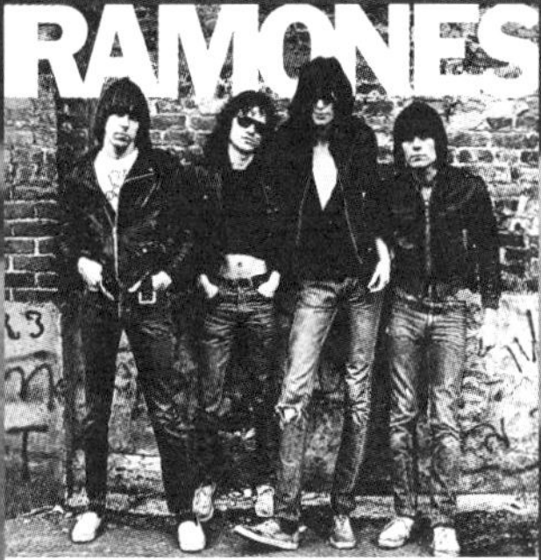

Blitzkrieg Bop

Underground shelter

was not till the Thursday that the dead came to the surface in any quantity. The view was bounded on every side by a grey mist that closed overhead in a grey canopy. The air cleared in the afternoon, and then, far away to the west under great banks of steam and dust, the flaming red eruption of the atomic bombs came visible across the waste of water.

They showed flat and sullen through the mist, like London sunsets. "They sat upon the sea," says Barnet, "like frayed-out waterlilies of flame."

Barnet seems to have spent the morning in rescue work along the track of the canal, in helping people who were adrift, in picking up derelict boats and in taking people out of imperilled houses. He found other military barges similarly employed, and it was only as the day wore on and the immediate appeals for aid were satisfied that he thought of food and drink for his men and what course he had better pursue. They had a little cheese but no water. "Orders," that mysterious direction, had at last altogether disappeared. He perceived he had now to act upon his own responsibility.

"One's sense was of a destruction so far-reaching and of a world so altered that it seemed foolish to go in any direction and expect to find things as they had been before the war began. I sat on the quarter-deck with Mylius my engineer

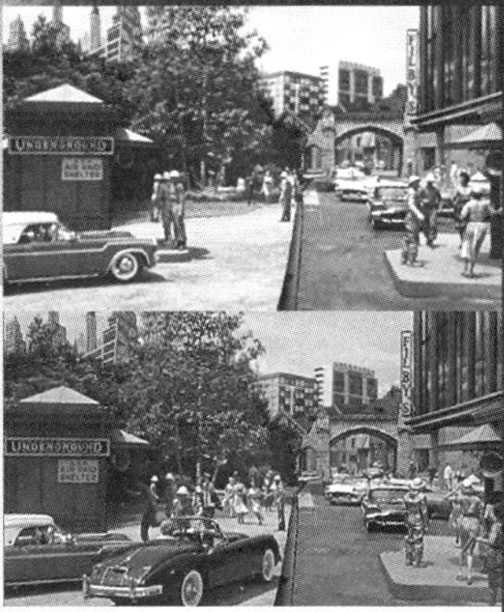

Air raid street scene (US 1960)

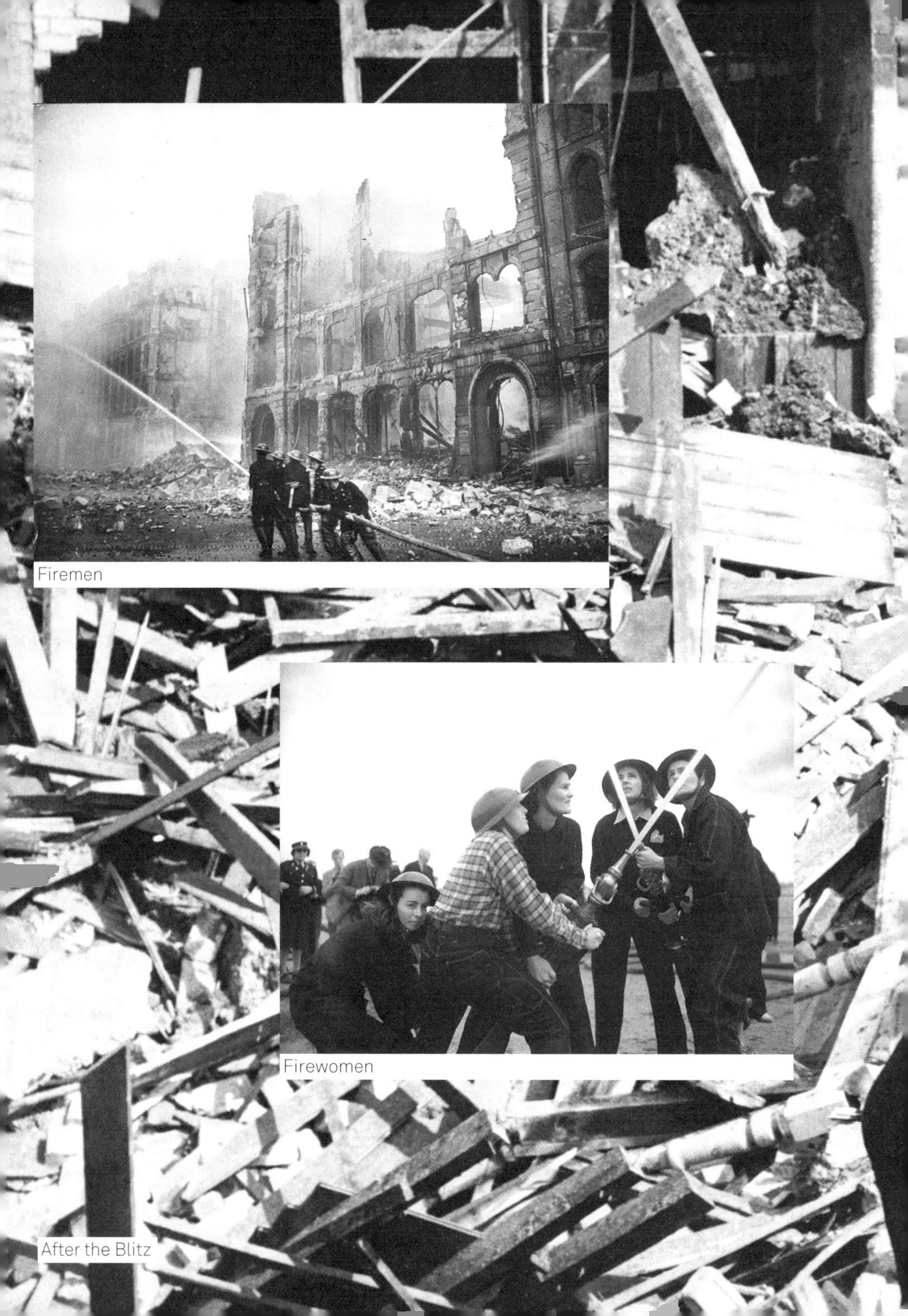
Firemen

Firewomen

After the Blitz

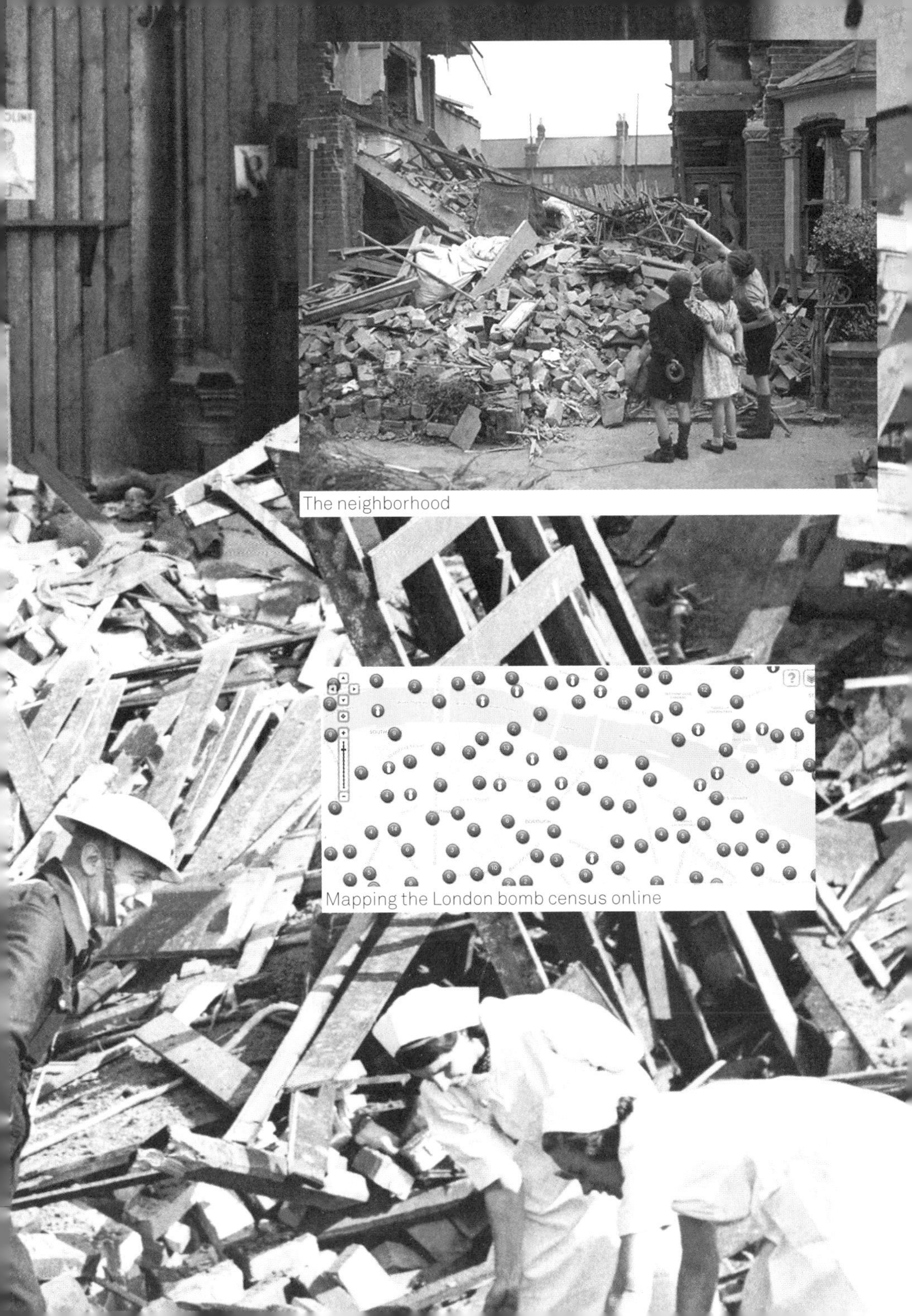

The neighborhood

Mapping the London bomb census online

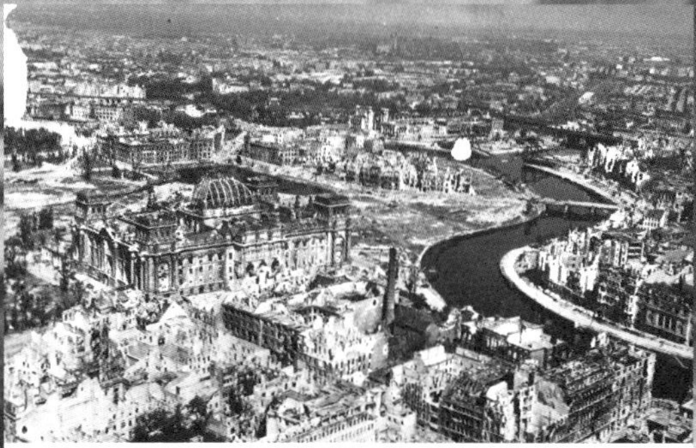

Berlin bombed

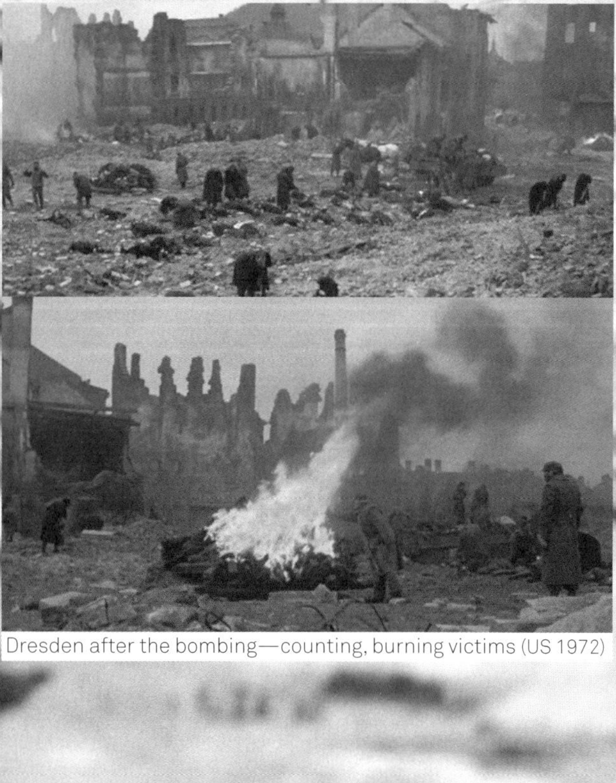

Dresden after the bombing—counting, burning victims (US 1972)

Devastated city of Rotterdam

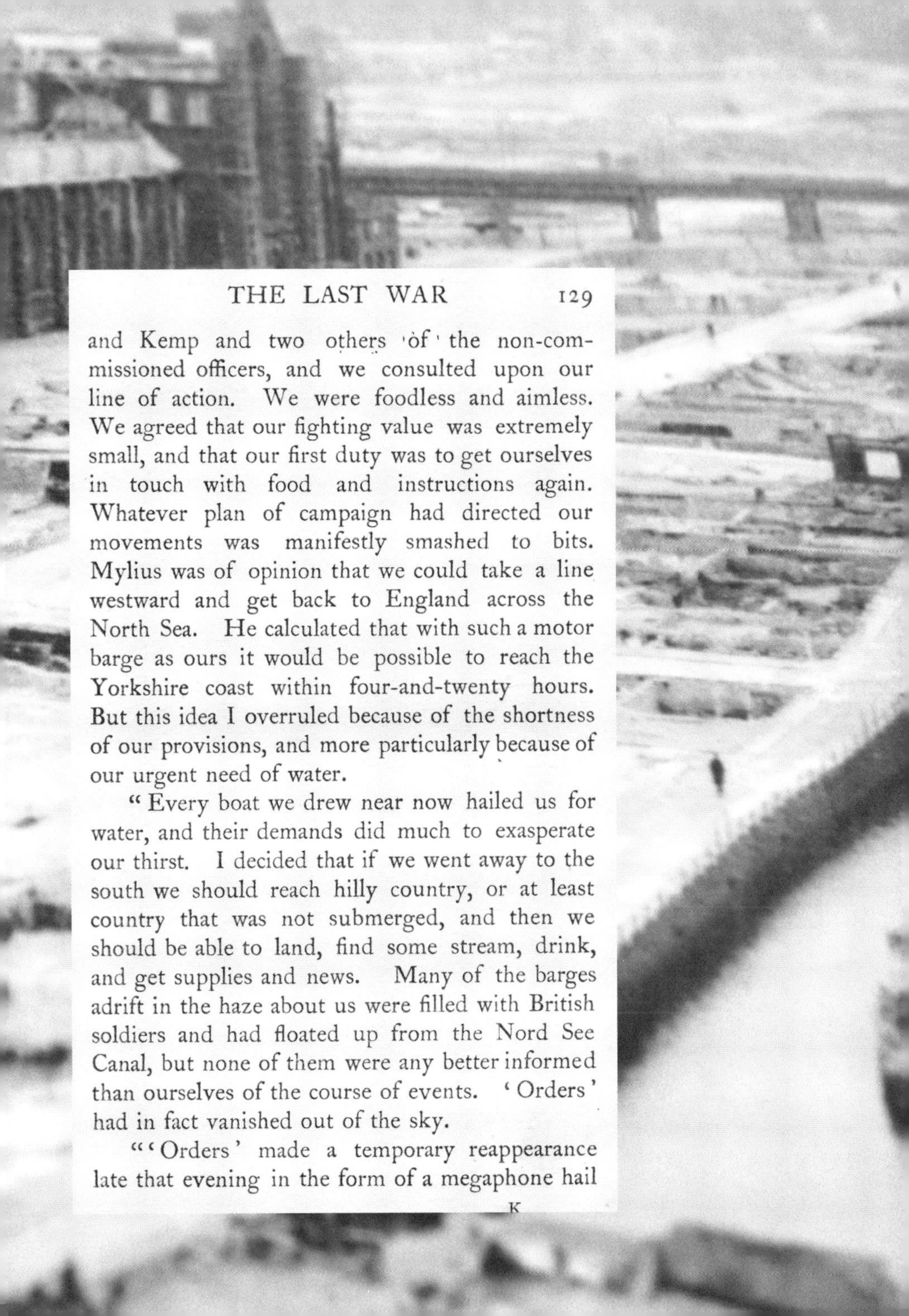

and Kemp and two others of the non-commissioned officers, and we consulted upon our line of action. We were foodless and aimless. We agreed that our fighting value was extremely small, and that our first duty was to get ourselves in touch with food and instructions again. Whatever plan of campaign had directed our movements was manifestly smashed to bits. Mylius was of opinion that we could take a line westward and get back to England across the North Sea. He calculated that with such a motor barge as ours it would be possible to reach the Yorkshire coast within four-and-twenty hours. But this idea I overruled because of the shortness of our provisions, and more particularly because of our urgent need of water.

"Every boat we drew near now hailed us for water, and their demands did much to exasperate our thirst. I decided that if we went away to the south we should reach hilly country, or at least country that was not submerged, and then we should be able to land, find some stream, drink, and get supplies and news. Many of the barges adrift in the haze about us were filled with British soldiers and had floated up from the Nord See Canal, but none of them were any better informed than ourselves of the course of events. 'Orders' had in fact vanished out of the sky.

"'Orders' made a temporary reappearance late that evening in the form of a megaphone hail

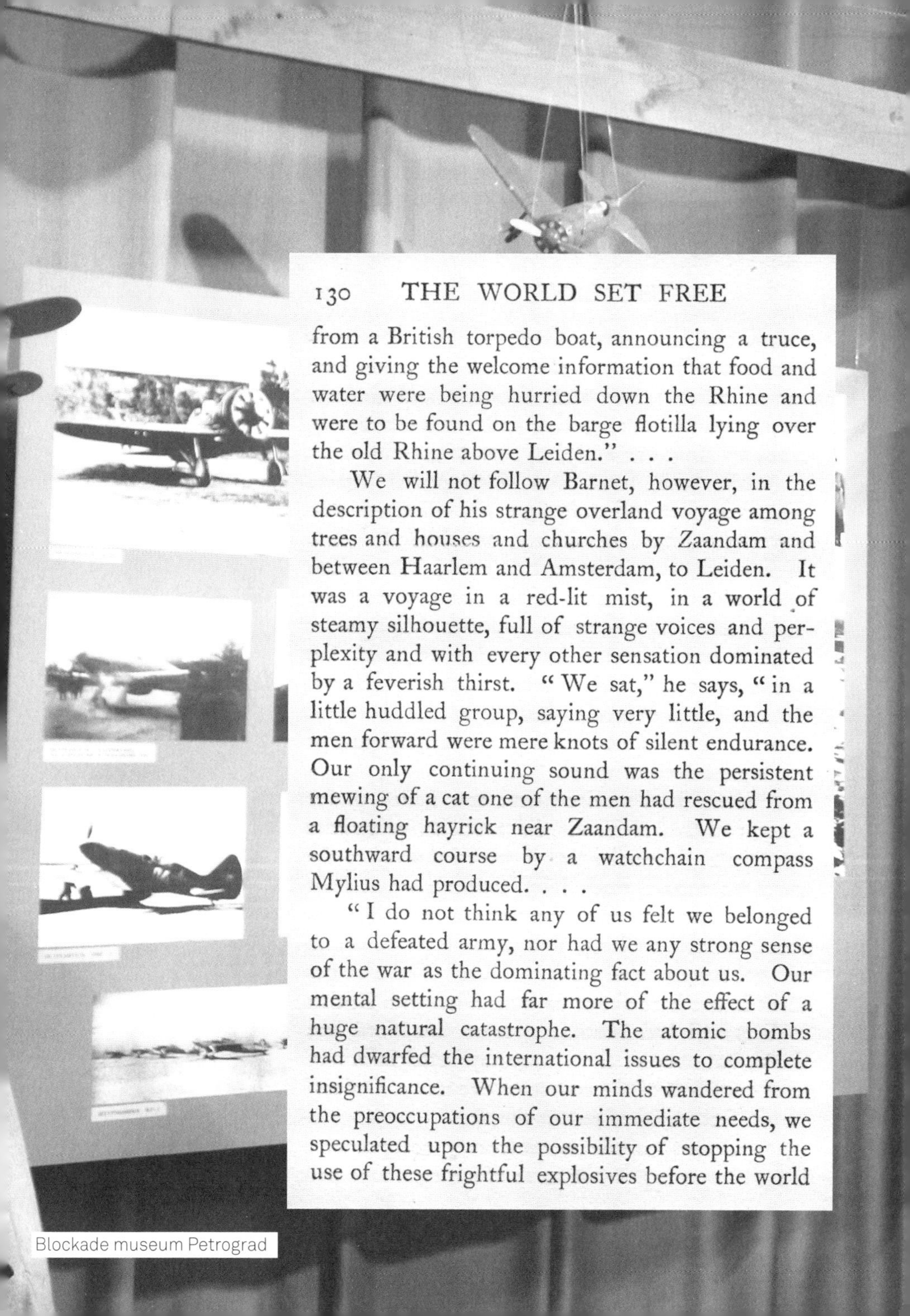

from a British torpedo boat, announcing a truce, and giving the welcome information that food and water were being hurried down the Rhine and were to be found on the barge flotilla lying over the old Rhine above Leiden." . . .

We will not follow Barnet, however, in the description of his strange overland voyage among trees and houses and churches by Zaandam and between Haarlem and Amsterdam, to Leiden. It was a voyage in a red-lit mist, in a world of steamy silhouette, full of strange voices and perplexity and with every other sensation dominated by a feverish thirst. "We sat," he says, "in a little huddled group, saying very little, and the men forward were mere knots of silent endurance. Our only continuing sound was the persistent mewing of a cat one of the men had rescued from a floating hayrick near Zaandam. We kept a southward course by a watchchain compass Mylius had produced. . . .

"I do not think any of us felt we belonged to a defeated army, nor had we any strong sense of the war as the dominating fact about us. Our mental setting had far more of the effect of a huge natural catastrophe. The atomic bombs had dwarfed the international issues to complete insignificance. When our minds wandered from the preoccupations of our immediate needs, we speculated upon the possibility of stopping the use of these frightful explosives before the world

Blockade museum Petrograd

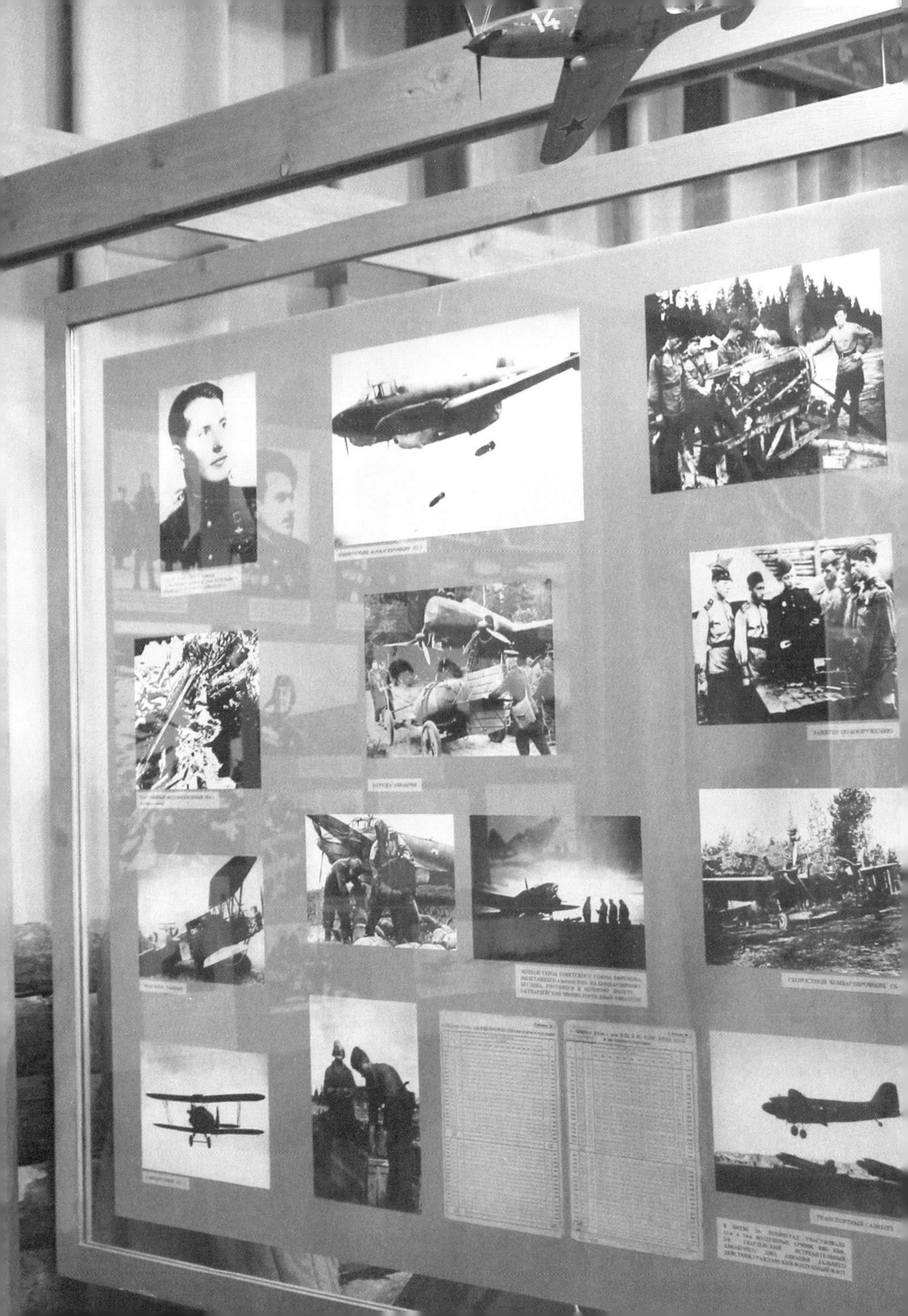

War proceeding

Supporting these troops

was utterly destroyed. For to us it seemed quite plain that these bombs and the still greater power of destruction of which they were the precursors might quite easily shatter every relationship and institution of mankind.

"'What will they be doing,' asked Mylius, 'what will they be doing? It's plain we've got to put an end to war. It's plain things have to be run some way. *This*—all this—is impossible.'

"I made no immediate answer. Something —I cannot think what—had brought back to me the figure of that man I had seen wounded on the very first day of actual fighting. I saw again his angry tearful eyes and that poor dripping bloody mess that had been a skilful human hand five minutes before, thrust out in indignant protest. 'Damned foolery,' he had stormed and sobbed, 'damned foolery. My right hand, sir! My *right* hand. . . .'

"My faith had for a time gone altogether out of me. 'I think we are too—too silly,' I said to Mylius, 'ever to stop war. If we'd had the sense to do it, we should have done it before this. I think this——' I pointed to the gaunt black outline of a smashed windmill that stuck up, ridiculous and ugly, above the blood-lit waters—'this is the end.'"

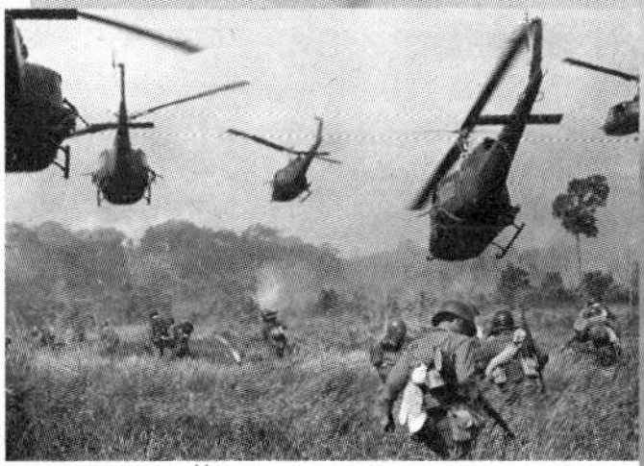

... proceeding ...

§ 10

But now our history must part company with Frederick Barnet and his barge-load of hungry and starving men.

For a time in western Europe at least it was indeed as if civilization had come to a final collapse. These crowning buds upon the tradition that Napoleon planted and Bismarck watered, opened and flared "like waterlilies of flame" over nations destroyed, over churches smashed or submerged, towns ruined, fields lost to mankind for ever and a million weltering bodies. Was this lesson enough for mankind, or would the flames of war still burn amidst the ruins?

Neither Barnet nor his companions, it is clear, had any assurance in their answers to that question. Already once in the history of mankind, in America, before its discovery by the whites, an organized civilization had given way to a mere cult of warfare, specialized and cruel, and it seemed for a time to many a thoughtful man as if the whole world was but to repeat on a larger scale this ascendancy of the warrior, this triumph of the destructive instincts of the race.

The subsequent chapters of Barnet's narrative do but supply body to this tragic possibility. He gives a series of vignettes of civilization,

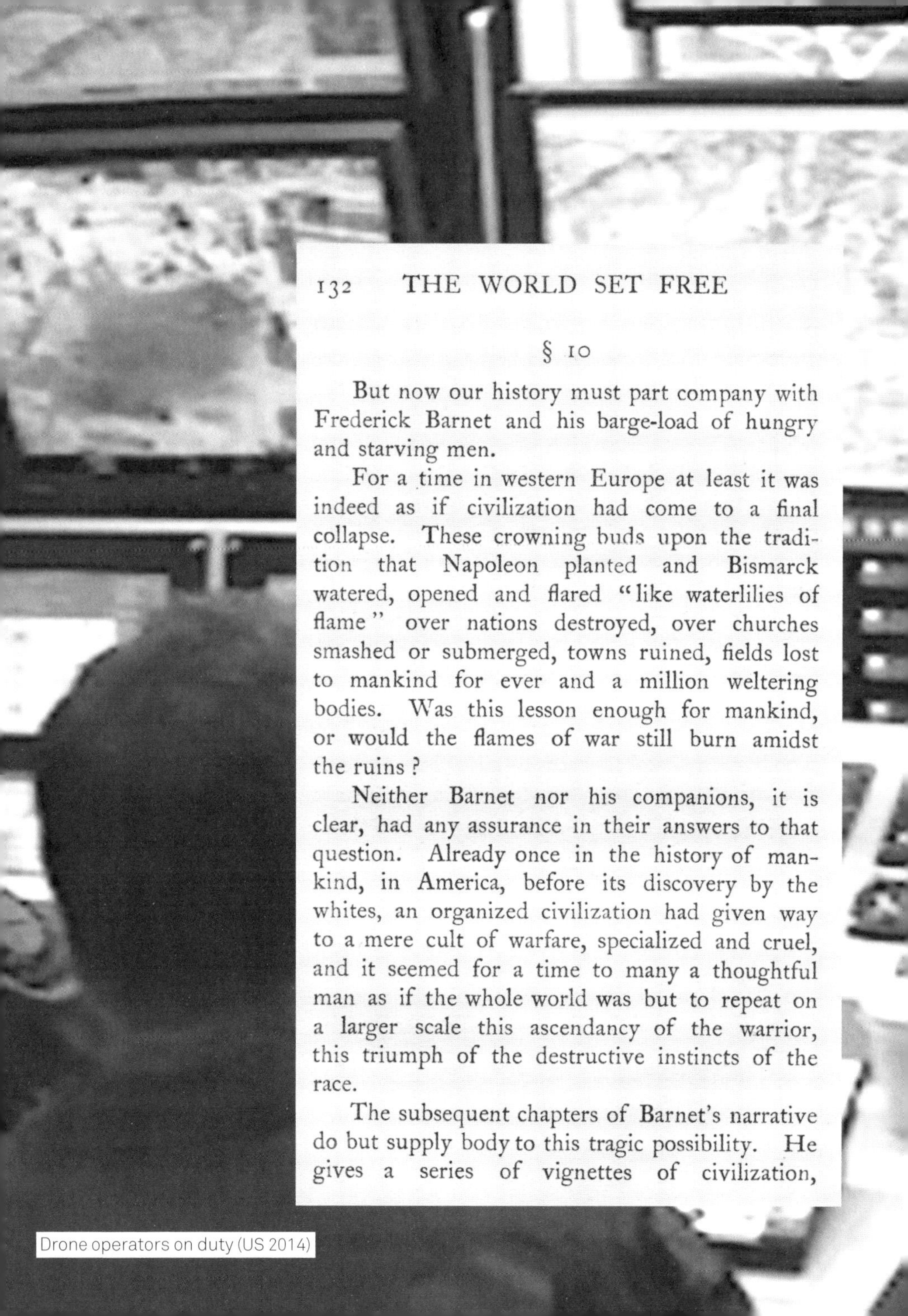

Drone operators on duty (US 2014)

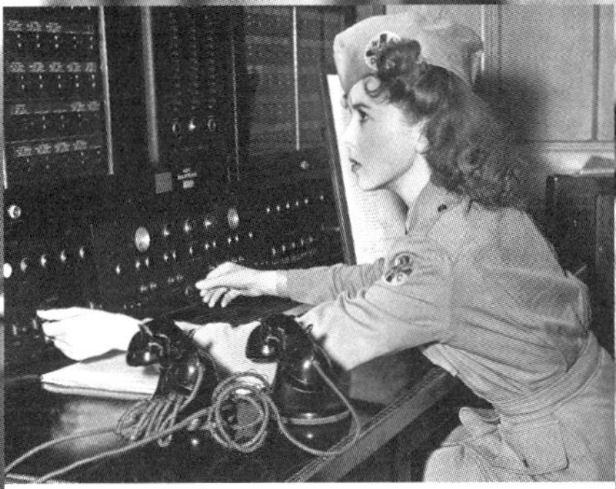

Wartime telephone operator

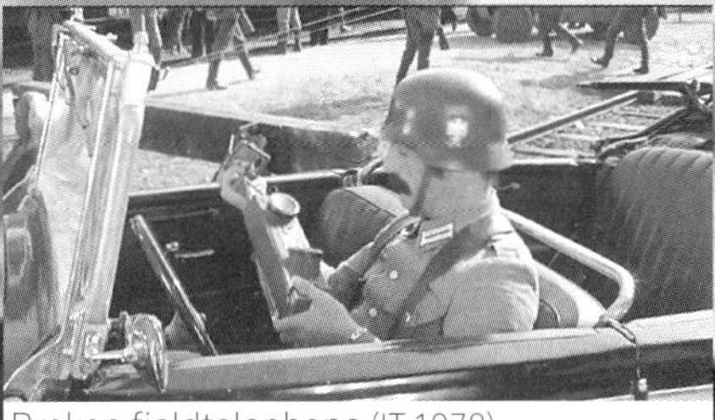

Broken fieldtelephone (IT 1978)

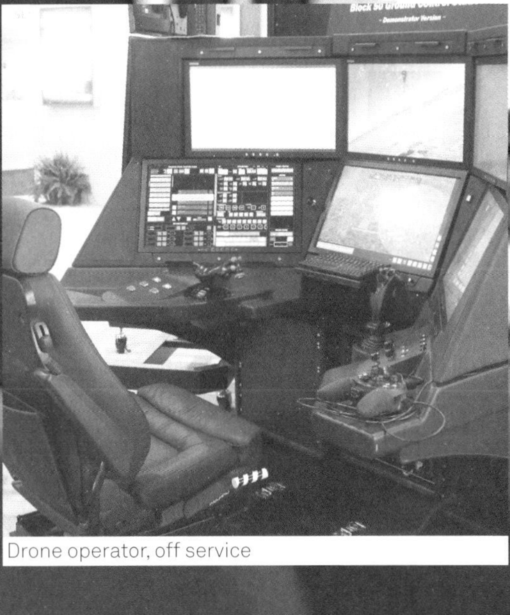

Drone operator, off service

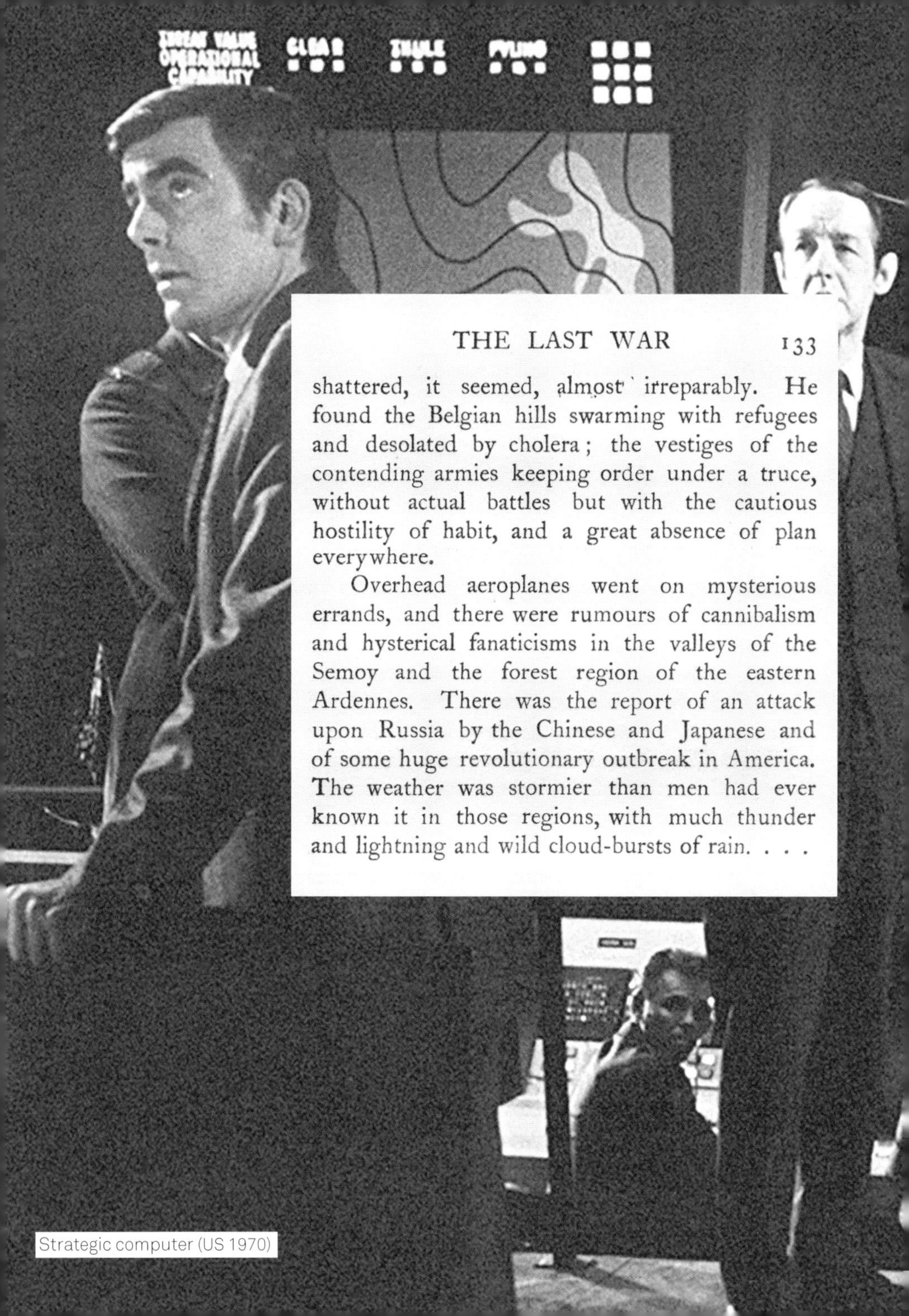

THE LAST WAR 133

shattered, it seemed, almost irreparably. He found the Belgian hills swarming with refugees and desolated by cholera; the vestiges of the contending armies keeping order under a truce, without actual battles but with the cautious hostility of habit, and a great absence of plan everywhere.

Overhead aeroplanes went on mysterious errands, and there were rumours of cannibalism and hysterical fanaticisms in the valleys of the Semoy and the forest region of the eastern Ardennes. There was the report of an attack upon Russia by the Chinese and Japanese and of some huge revolutionary outbreak in America. The weather was stormier than men had ever known it in those regions, with much thunder and lightning and wild cloud-bursts of rain. . . .

Strategic computer (US 1970)

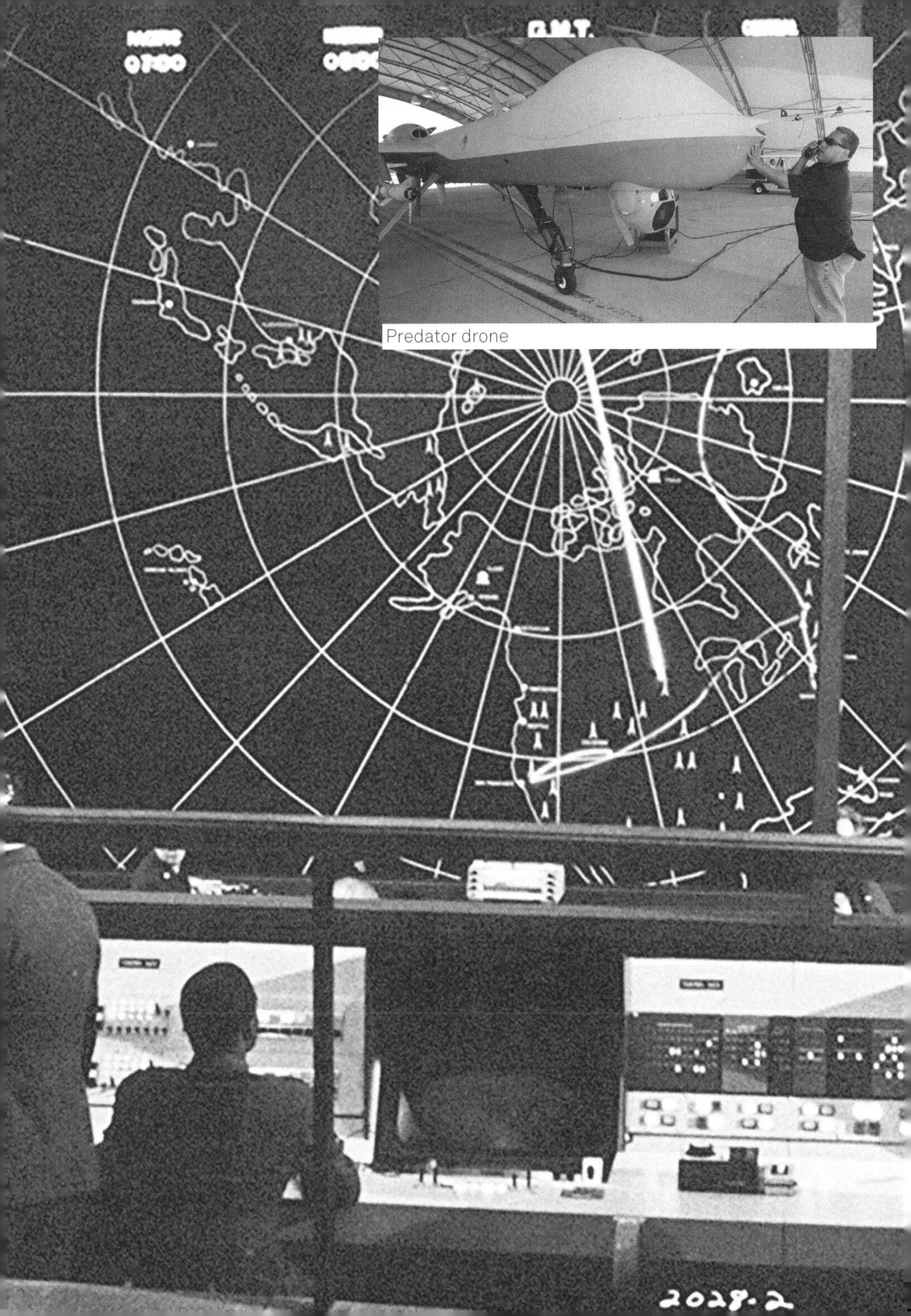

Predator drone

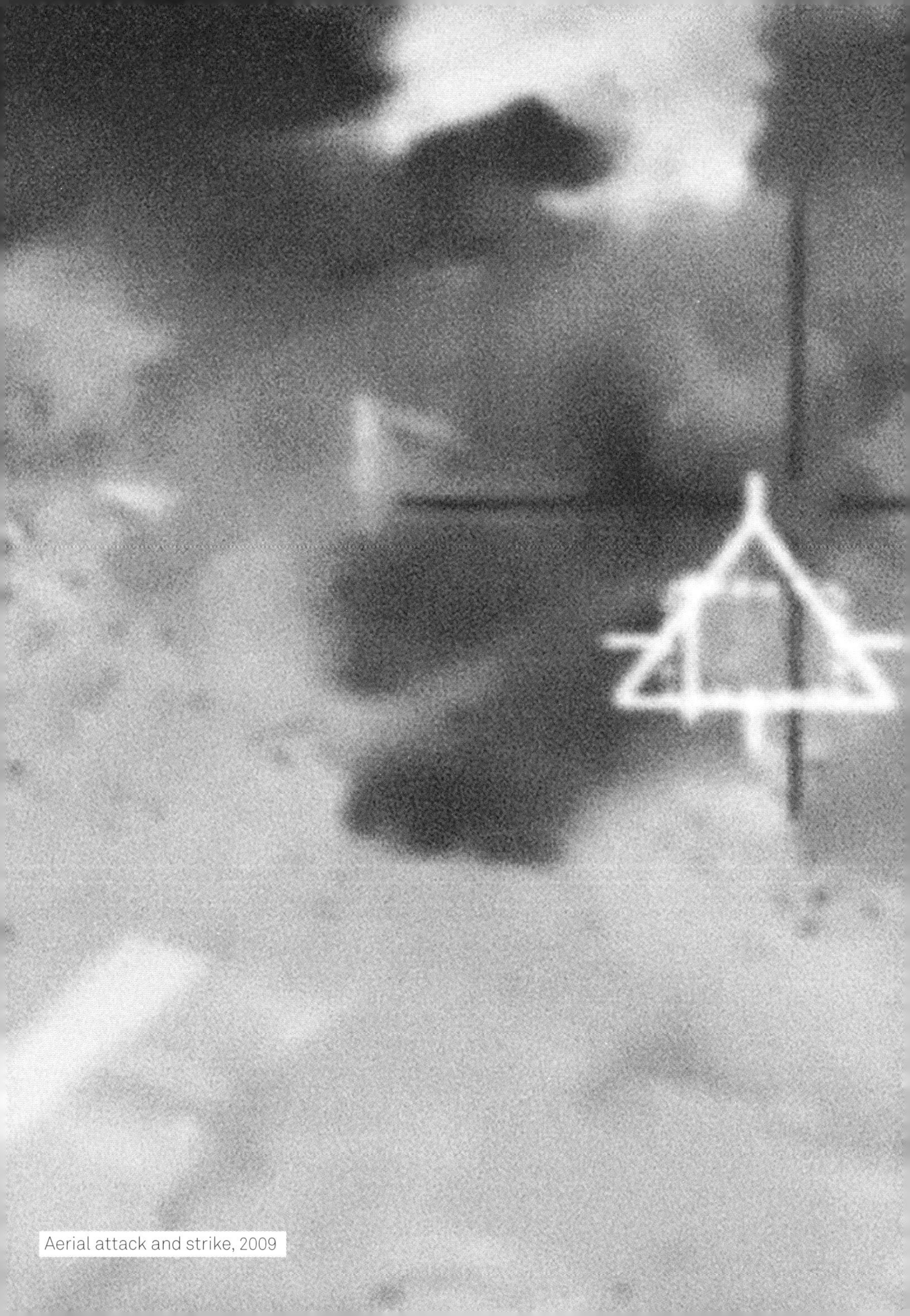

Aerial attack and strike, 2009

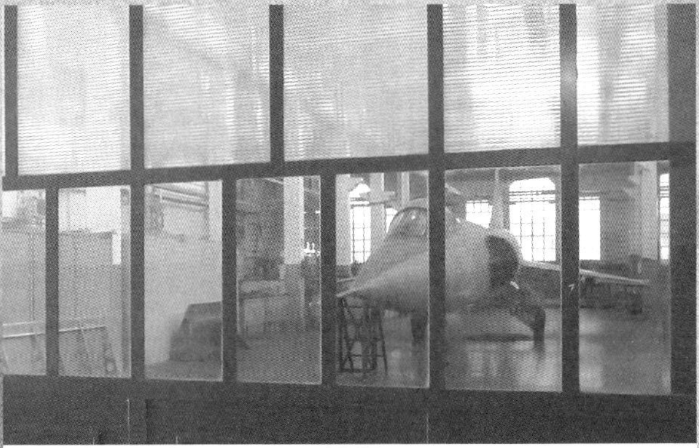

Starfighter jet in a museum, 2015

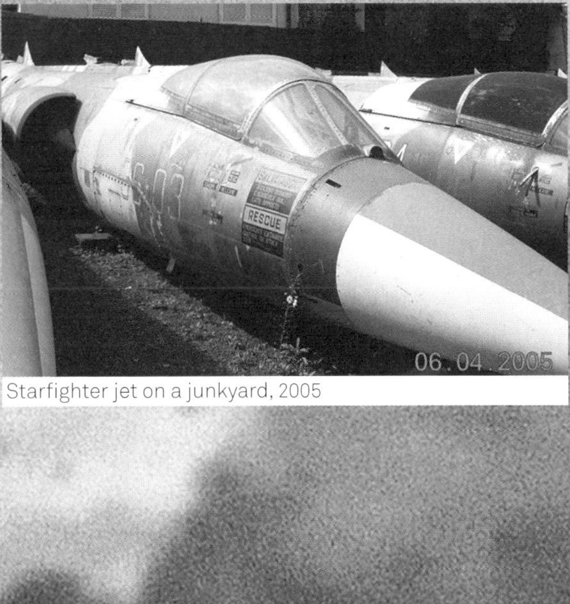

Starfighter jet on a junkyard, 2005

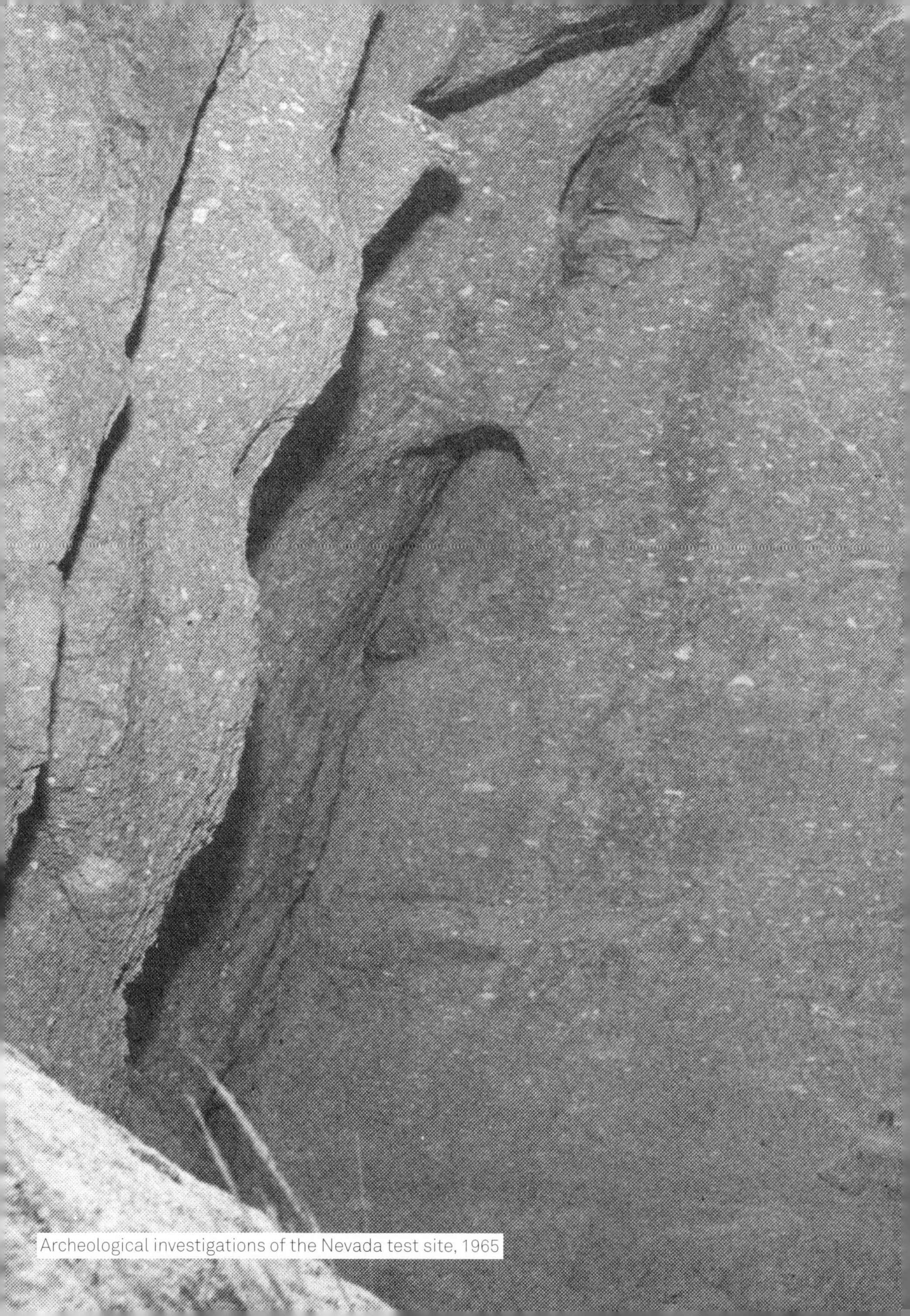

Archeological investigations of the Nevada test site, 1965

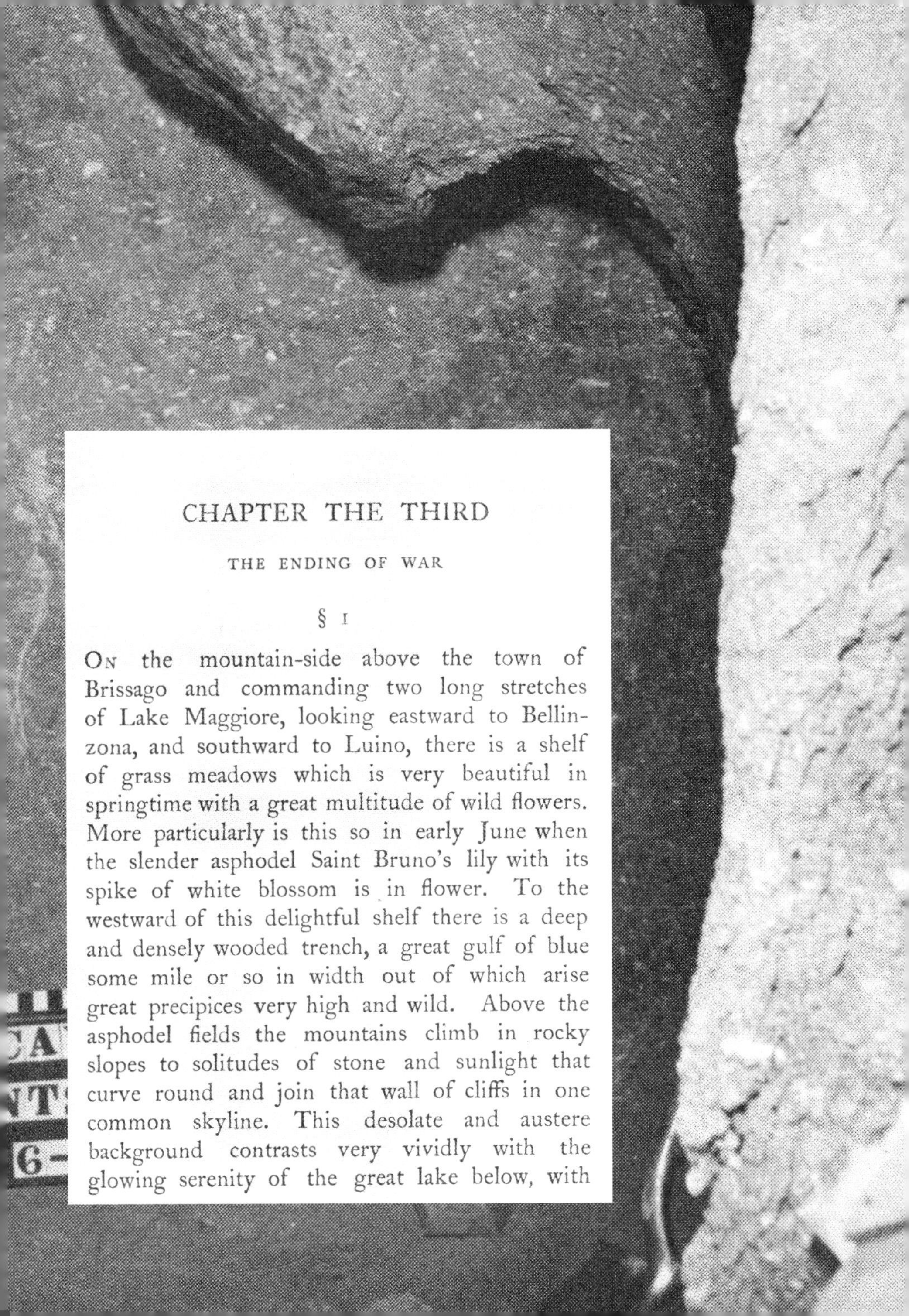

CHAPTER THE THIRD

THE ENDING OF WAR

§ I

On the mountain-side above the town of Brissago and commanding two long stretches of Lake Maggiore, looking eastward to Bellinzona, and southward to Luino, there is a shelf of grass meadows which is very beautiful in springtime with a great multitude of wild flowers. More particularly is this so in early June when the slender asphodel Saint Bruno's lily with its spike of white blossom is in flower. To the westward of this delightful shelf there is a deep and densely wooded trench, a great gulf of blue some mile or so in width out of which arise great precipices very high and wild. Above the asphodel fields the mountains climb in rocky slopes to solitudes of stone and sunlight that curve round and join that wall of cliffs in one common skyline. This desolate and austere background contrasts very vividly with the glowing serenity of the great lake below, with

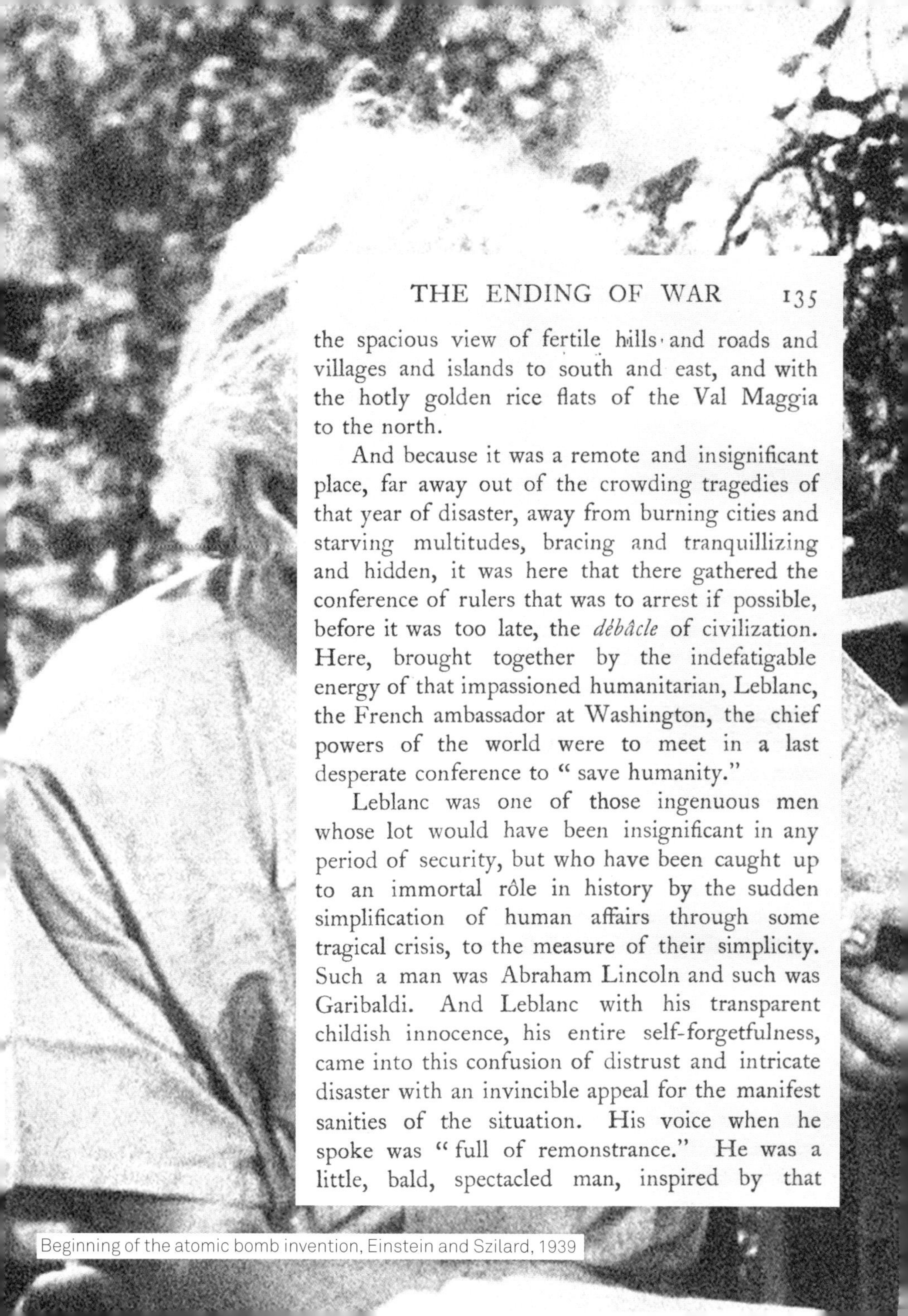

the spacious view of fertile hills and roads and villages and islands to south and east, and with the hotly golden rice flats of the Val Maggia to the north.

And because it was a remote and insignificant place, far away out of the crowding tragedies of that year of disaster, away from burning cities and starving multitudes, bracing and tranquillizing and hidden, it was here that there gathered the conference of rulers that was to arrest if possible, before it was too late, the *débâcle* of civilization. Here, brought together by the indefatigable energy of that impassioned humanitarian, Leblanc, the French ambassador at Washington, the chief powers of the world were to meet in a last desperate conference to "save humanity."

Leblanc was one of those ingenuous men whose lot would have been insignificant in any period of security, but who have been caught up to an immortal rôle in history by the sudden simplification of human affairs through some tragical crisis, to the measure of their simplicity. Such a man was Abraham Lincoln and such was Garibaldi. And Leblanc with his transparent childish innocence, his entire self-forgetfulness, came into this confusion of distrust and intricate disaster with an invincible appeal for the manifest sanities of the situation. His voice when he spoke was "full of remonstrance." He was a little, bald, spectacled man, inspired by that

Beginning of the atomic bomb invention, Einstein and Szilard, 1939

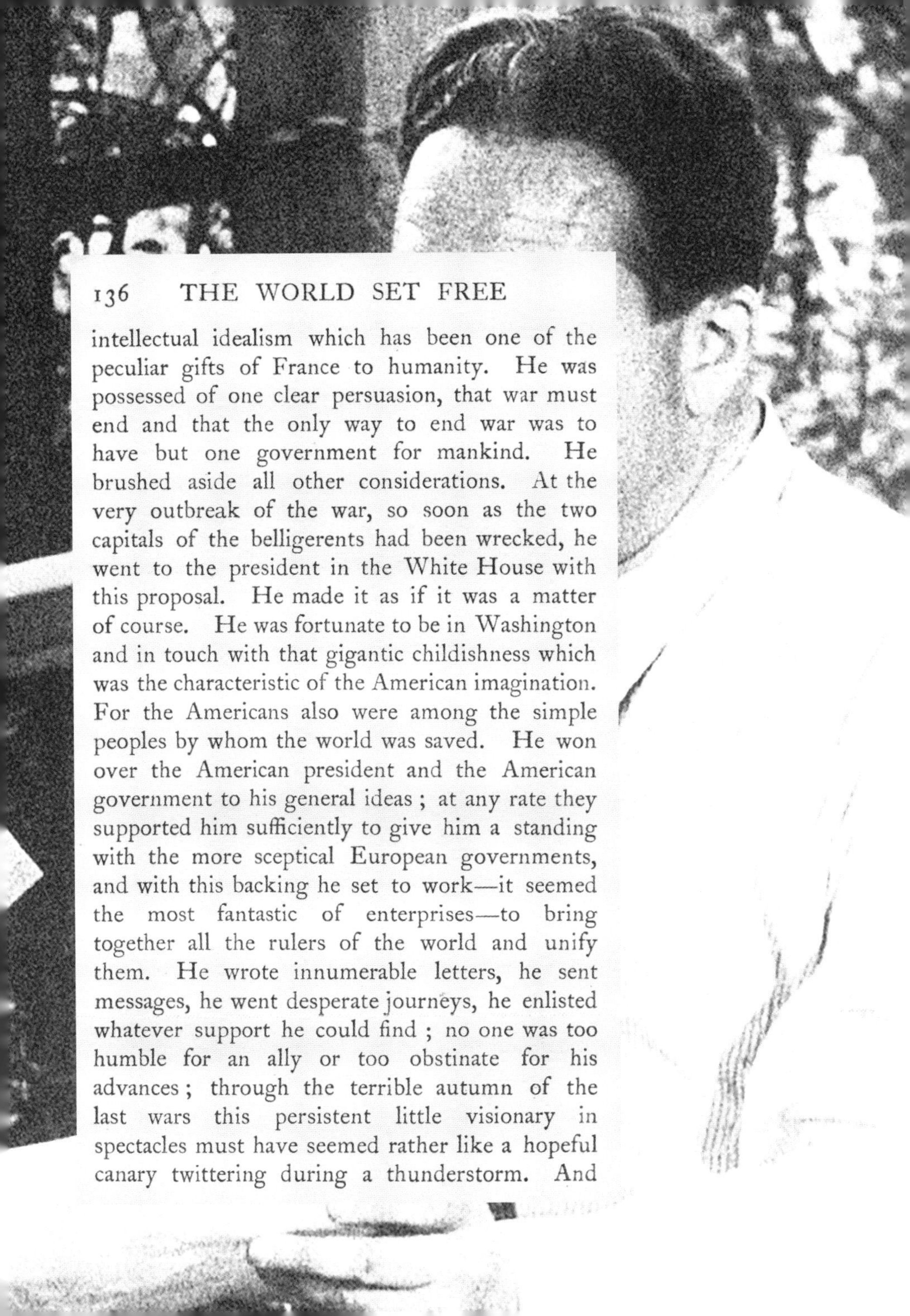

intellectual idealism which has been one of the peculiar gifts of France to humanity. He was possessed of one clear persuasion, that war must end and that the only way to end war was to have but one government for mankind. He brushed aside all other considerations. At the very outbreak of the war, so soon as the two capitals of the belligerents had been wrecked, he went to the president in the White House with this proposal. He made it as if it was a matter of course. He was fortunate to be in Washington and in touch with that gigantic childishness which was the characteristic of the American imagination. For the Americans also were among the simple peoples by whom the world was saved. He won over the American president and the American government to his general ideas ; at any rate they supported him sufficiently to give him a standing with the more sceptical European governments, and with this backing he set to work—it seemed the most fantastic of enterprises—to bring together all the rulers of the world and unify them. He wrote innumerable letters, he sent messages, he went desperate journeys, he enlisted whatever support he could find ; no one was too humble for an ally or too obstinate for his advances ; through the terrible autumn of the last wars this persistent little visionary in spectacles must have seemed rather like a hopeful canary twittering during a thunderstorm. And

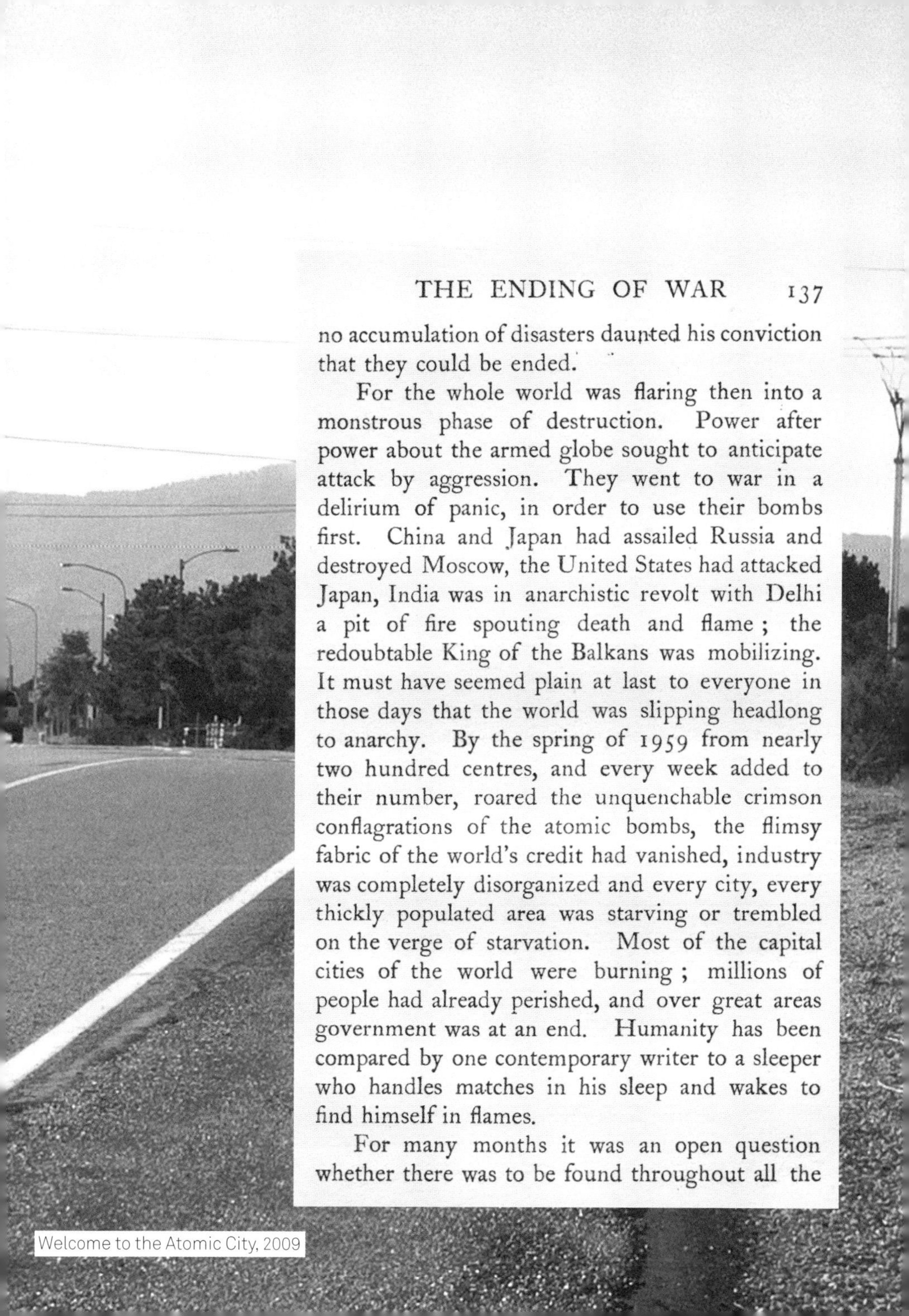

no accumulation of disasters daunted his conviction that they could be ended.

For the whole world was flaring then into a monstrous phase of destruction. Power after power about the armed globe sought to anticipate attack by aggression. They went to war in a delirium of panic, in order to use their bombs first. China and Japan had assailed Russia and destroyed Moscow, the United States had attacked Japan, India was in anarchistic revolt with Delhi a pit of fire spouting death and flame; the redoubtable King of the Balkans was mobilizing. It must have seemed plain at last to everyone in those days that the world was slipping headlong to anarchy. By the spring of 1959 from nearly two hundred centres, and every week added to their number, roared the unquenchable crimson conflagrations of the atomic bombs, the flimsy fabric of the world's credit had vanished, industry was completely disorganized and every city, every thickly populated area was starving or trembled on the verge of starvation. Most of the capital cities of the world were burning; millions of people had already perished, and over great areas government was at an end. Humanity has been compared by one contemporary writer to a sleeper who handles matches in his sleep and wakes to find himself in flames.

For many months it was an open question whether there was to be found throughout all the

Welcome to the Atomic City, 2009

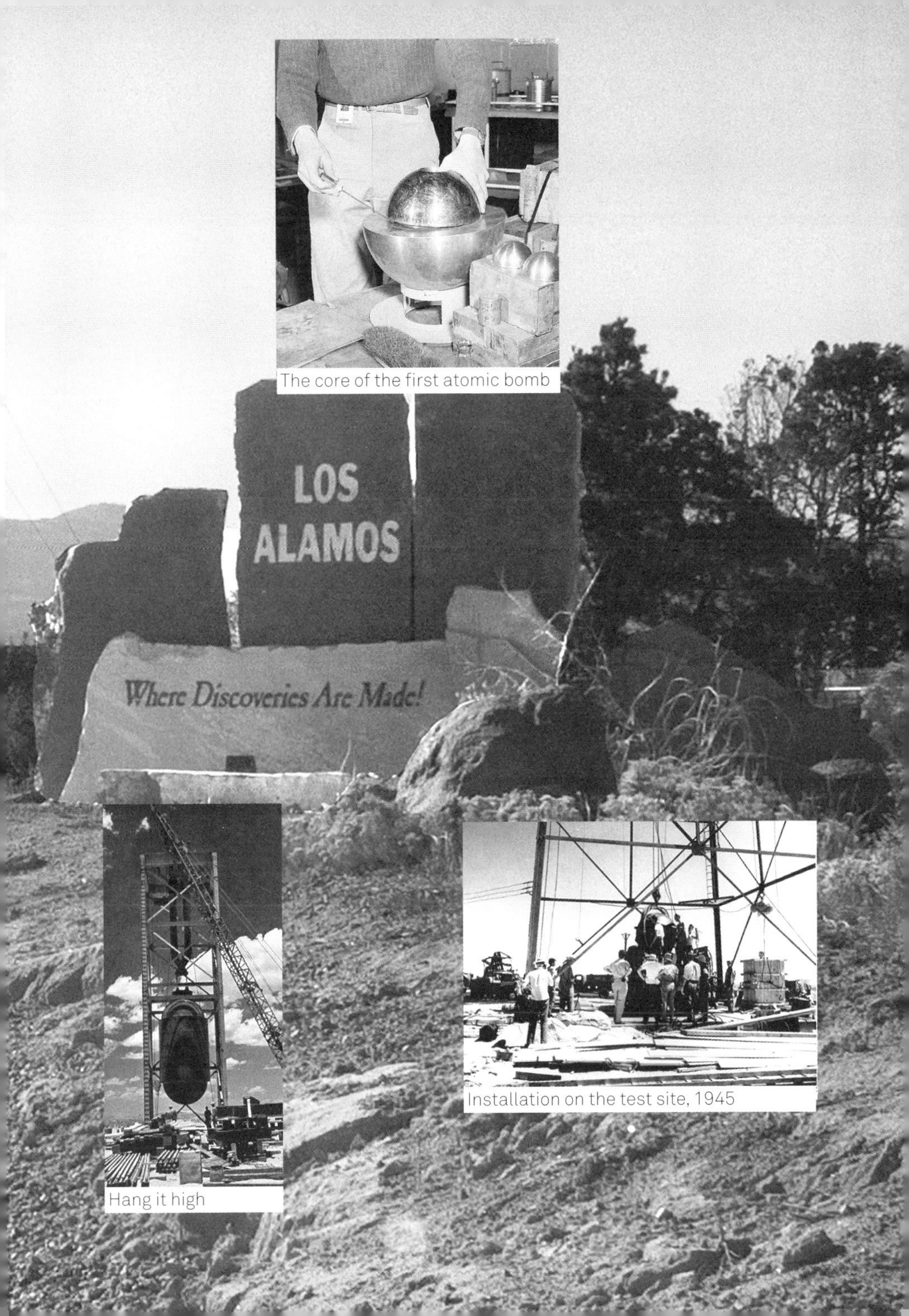

The core of the first atomic bomb

Hang it high

Installation on the test site, 1945

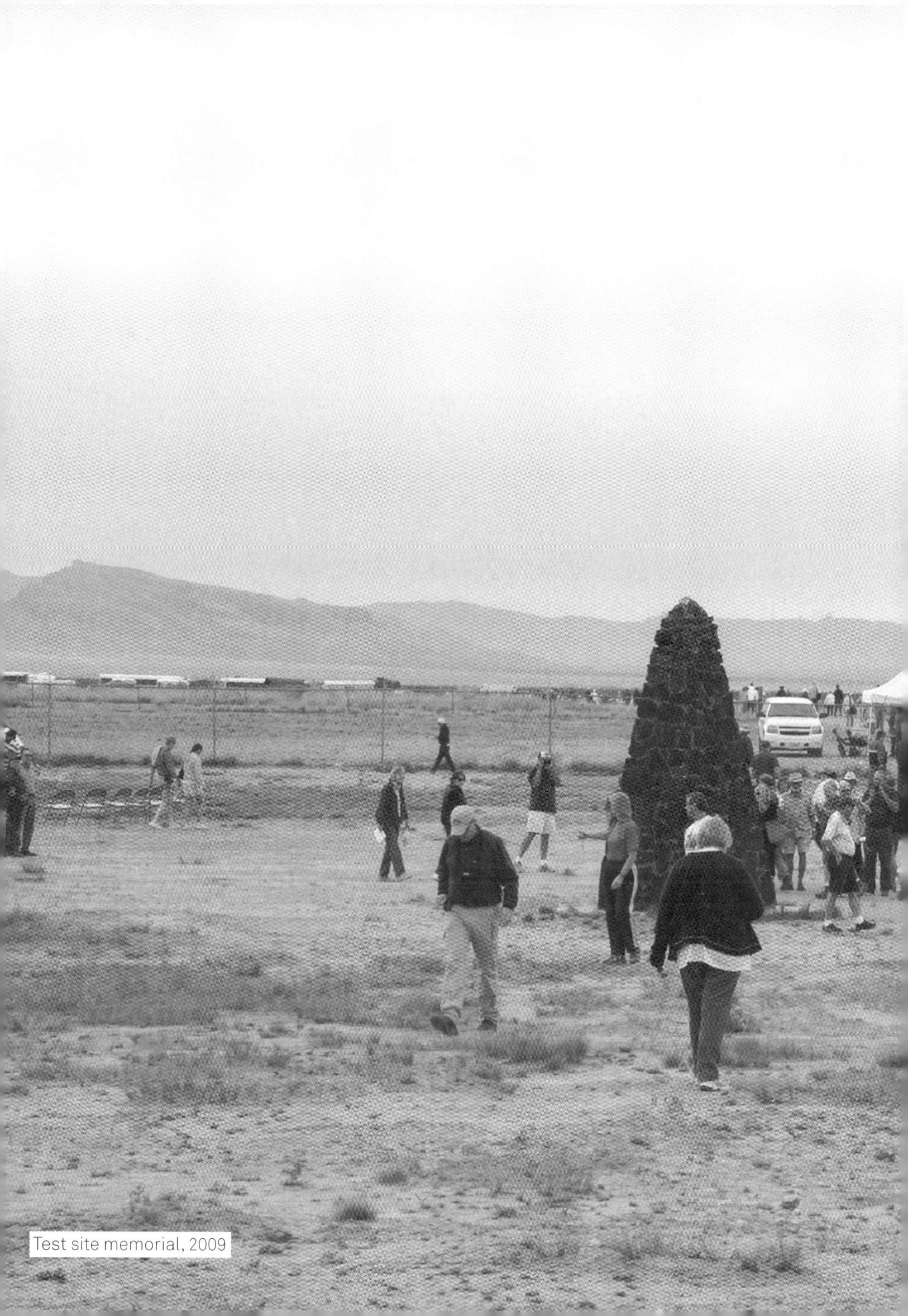

Test site memorial, 2009

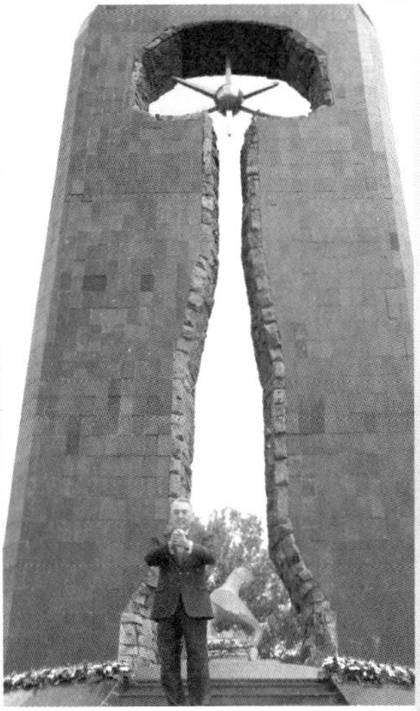
Semipalatinsk-21 monument

race the will and intelligence to face these new conditions and make even an attempt to arrest the downfall of the social order. For a time the war spirit defeated every effort to rally the forces of preservation and construction. Leblanc seemed to be protesting against earthquakes, and as likely to find a spirit of reason in the crater of Etna. Even though the shattered official governments now clamoured for peace, bands of irreconcilables and invincible patriots, usurpers, adventurers and political desperadoes, were everywhere in possession of the simple apparatus for the disengagement of atomic energy and the initiation of new centres of destruction. The stuff exercised an irresistible fascination upon a certain type of mind. Why should anyone give in while he can still destroy his enemies? Surrender? While there is still a chance of blowing them to dust? The power of destruction which had once been the ultimate privilege of government was now the only power left in the world—and it was everywhere. There were few thoughtful men during that phase of blazing waste who did not pass through such moods of despair as Barnet describes, and declare with him: "This is the end. . . ."

And all the while Leblanc was going to and fro with glittering glasses and an inexhaustible persuasiveness urging the manifest reasonableness of his view upon ears that ceased presently to be

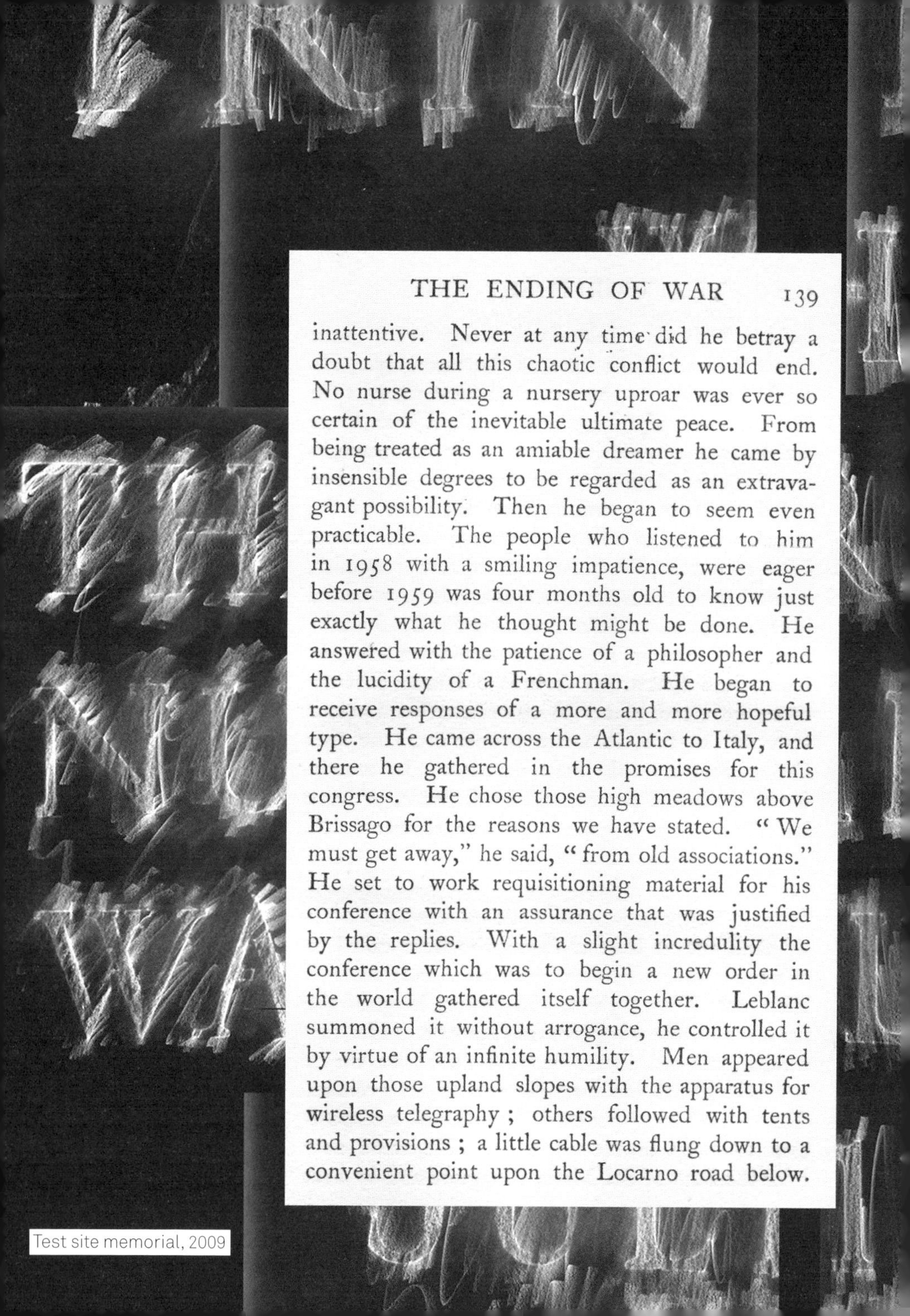

inattentive. Never at any time did he betray a doubt that all this chaotic conflict would end. No nurse during a nursery uproar was ever so certain of the inevitable ultimate peace. From being treated as an amiable dreamer he came by insensible degrees to be regarded as an extravagant possibility. Then he began to seem even practicable. The people who listened to him in 1958 with a smiling impatience, were eager before 1959 was four months old to know just exactly what he thought might be done. He answered with the patience of a philosopher and the lucidity of a Frenchman. He began to receive responses of a more and more hopeful type. He came across the Atlantic to Italy, and there he gathered in the promises for this congress. He chose those high meadows above Brissago for the reasons we have stated. " We must get away," he said, " from old associations." He set to work requisitioning material for his conference with an assurance that was justified by the replies. With a slight incredulity the conference which was to begin a new order in the world gathered itself together. Leblanc summoned it without arrogance, he controlled it by virtue of an infinite humility. Men appeared upon those upland slopes with the apparatus for wireless telegraphy ; others followed with tents and provisions ; a little cable was flung down to a convenient point upon the Locarno road below.

Test site memorial, 2009

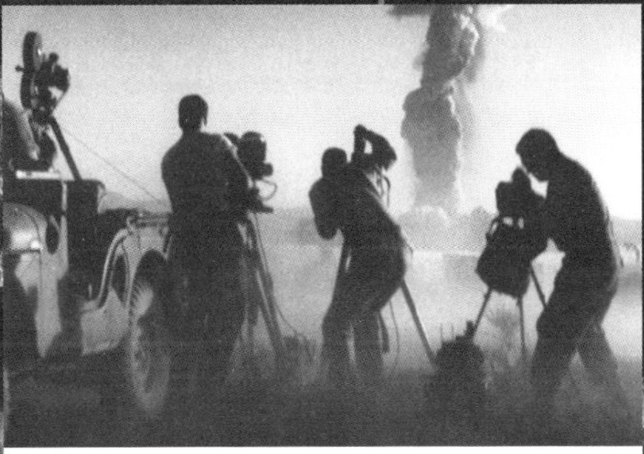
Professional spectators

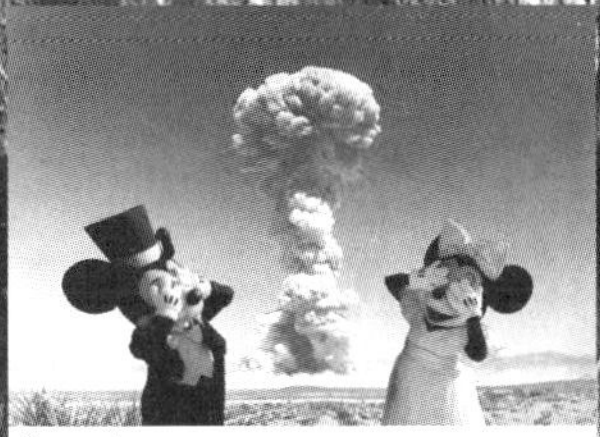
Oops!

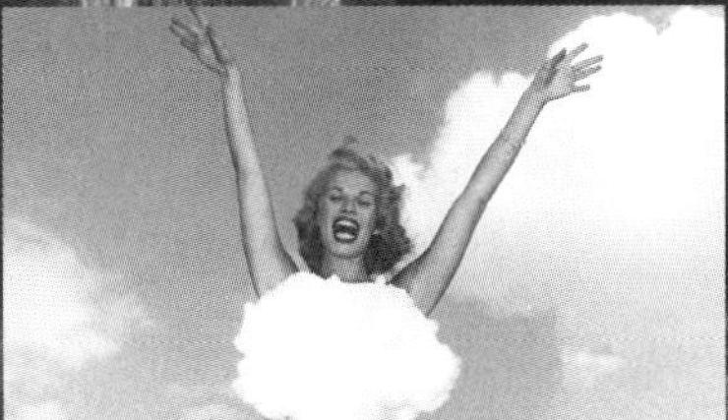
Miss Nevada test site, 1957

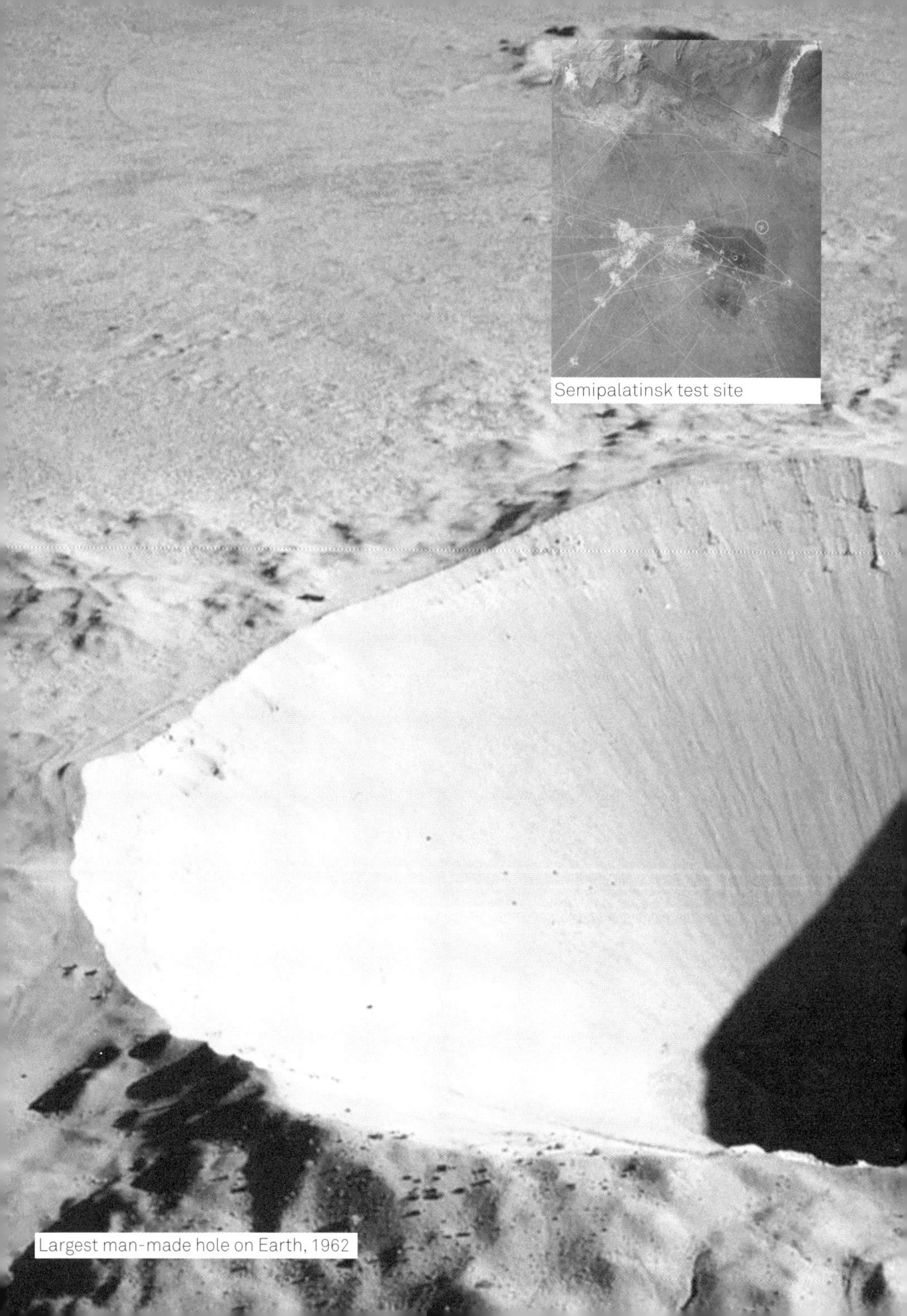

Semipalatinsk test site

Largest man-made hole on Earth, 1962

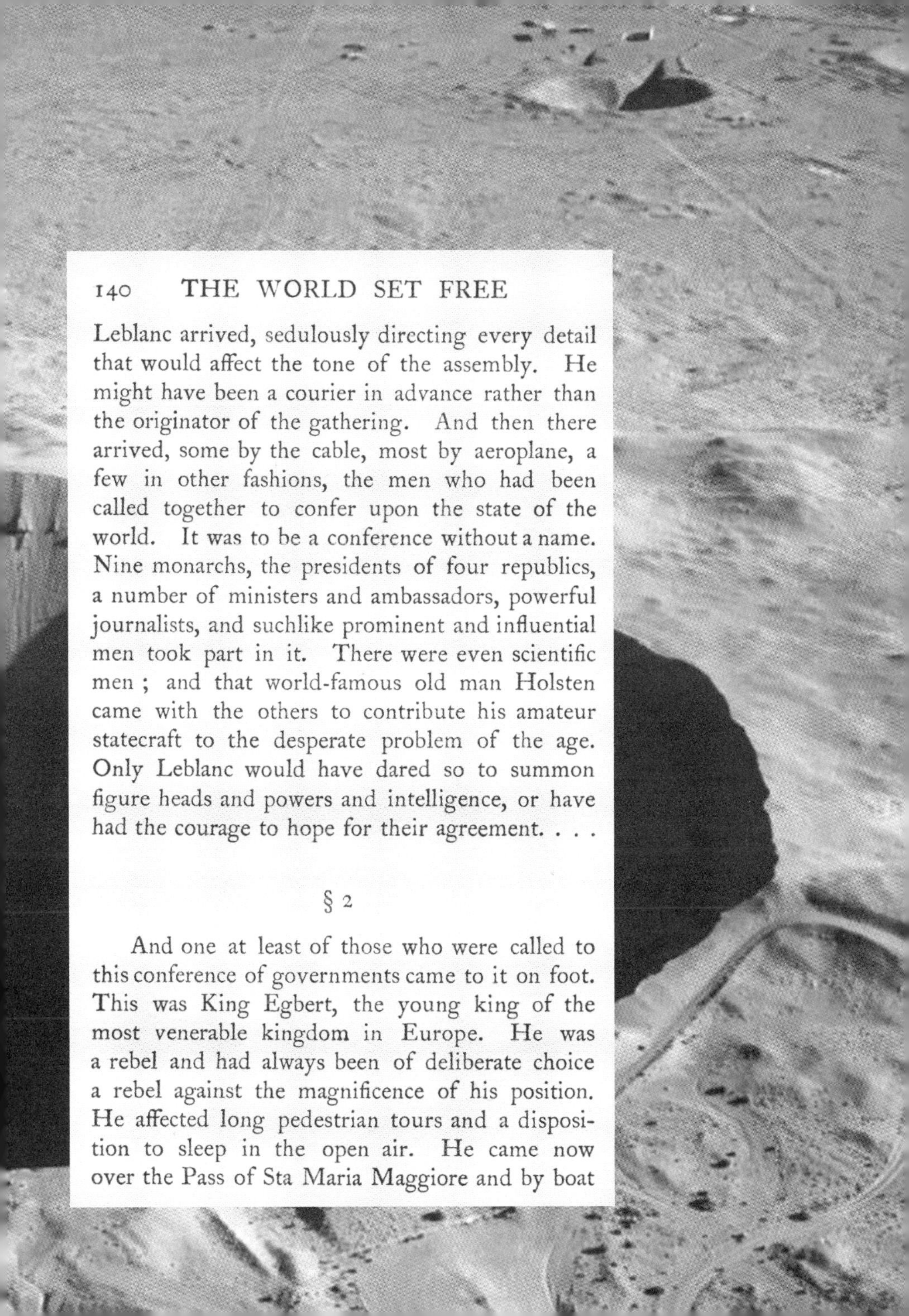

Leblanc arrived, sedulously directing every detail that would affect the tone of the assembly. He might have been a courier in advance rather than the originator of the gathering. And then there arrived, some by the cable, most by aeroplane, a few in other fashions, the men who had been called together to confer upon the state of the world. It was to be a conference without a name. Nine monarchs, the presidents of four republics, a number of ministers and ambassadors, powerful journalists, and suchlike prominent and influential men took part in it. There were even scientific men ; and that world-famous old man Holsten came with the others to contribute his amateur statecraft to the desperate problem of the age. Only Leblanc would have dared so to summon figure heads and powers and intelligence, or have had the courage to hope for their agreement. . . .

§ 2

And one at least of those who were called to this conference of governments came to it on foot. This was King Egbert, the young king of the most venerable kingdom in Europe. He was a rebel and had always been of deliberate choice a rebel against the magnificence of his position. He affected long pedestrian tours and a disposition to sleep in the open air. He came now over the Pass of Sta Maria Maggiore and by boat

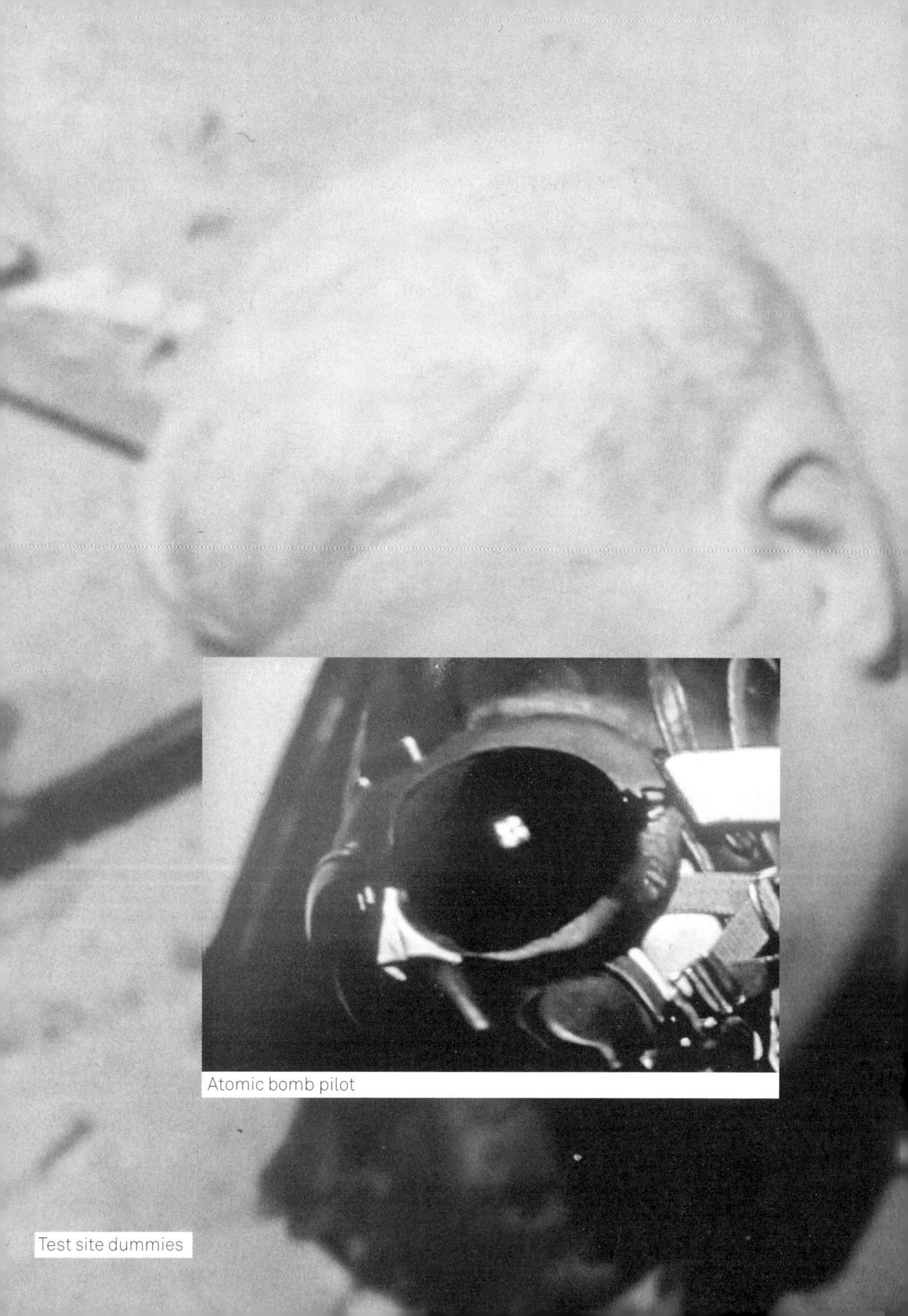

Atomic bomb pilot

Test site dummies

up the lake to Brissago ; thence he walked up the mountain, a pleasant path set with oaks and sweet chestnut. For provision on the walk, for he did not want to hurry, he carried with him a pocketful of bread and cheese. A certain small retinue that was necessary to his comfort and dignity upon occasions of state he sent on by the cable car, and with him walked his private secretary, Firmin, a man who had thrown up the Professorship of World Politics in the London School of Sociology, Economics and Political Science, to take up these duties. Firmin was a man of strong rather than rapid thought, he had anticipated great influence in this new position, and after some years he was still only beginning to apprehend how largely his function was to listen. Originally he had been something of a thinker upon international politics, an authority upon tariffs and strategy and a valued contributor to various of the higher organs of public opinion, but the atomic bombs had taken him by surprise and he had still to recover completely from his pre-atomic opinions and the silencing effect of those sustained explosives.

The king's freedom from the trammels of etiquette was very complete. In theory—and he abounded in theory—his manners were purely democratic. It was by sheer habit and inadvertency that he permitted Firmin, who had discovered a rucksack in a small shop in the town

142 THE WORLD SET FREE

below, to carry both bottles of beer. The king had never as a matter of fact carried anything for himself in his life and he had never noted that he did not do so.

"We will have nobody with us," he said, "at all. We will be perfectly simple."

So Firmin carried the beer.

As they walked up—it was the king made the pace rather than Firmin—they talked of the conference before them, and Firmin, with a certain want of assurance that would have surprised him in himself in the days of his Professorship, sought to define the policy of his companion. "In its broader form, sir," said Firmin; "I admit a certain plausibility in this project of Leblanc's, but I feel that although it may be advisable to set up some sort of general control for International affairs—a sort of Hague Court with extended powers—that is no reason whatever for losing sight of the principles of national and imperial autonomy."

"Firmin," said the king, "I am going to set my brother kings a good example."

Firmin intimated a curiosity that veiled a dread.

"By chucking all that nonsense," said the king.

He quickened his pace as Firmin, who was already a little out of breath, betrayed a disposition to reply.

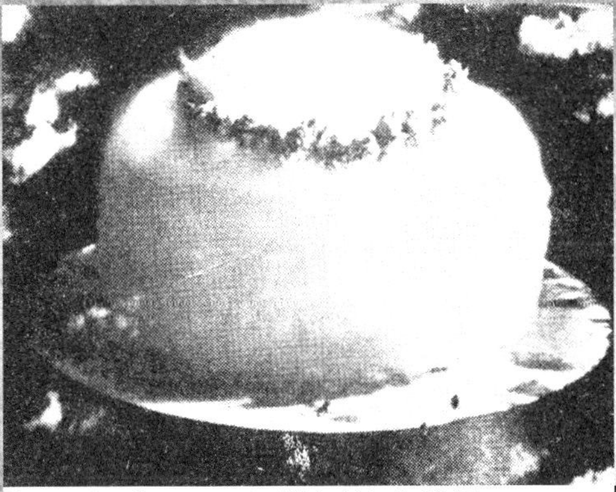

Operation Crossroads, Bikini Atoll, 1947

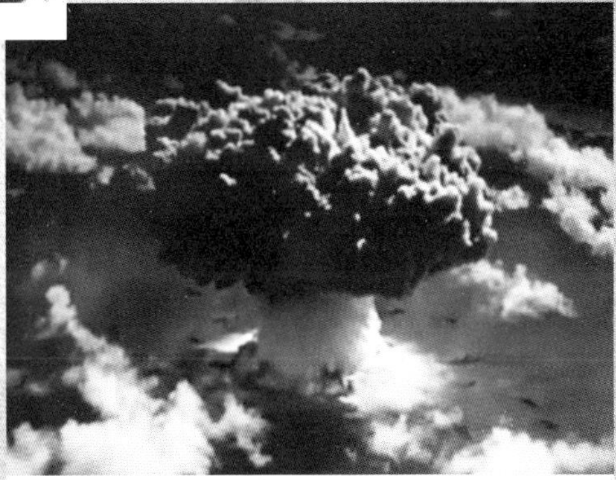

The mushroom cloud ...

"I am going to chuck all that nonsense," said the king as Firmin prepared to speak. "I am going to fling my royalty and empire on the table—and declare at once I don't mean to haggle. It's haggling—about rights—has been the devil in human affairs, for—always. I am going to stop this nonsense."

Firmin halted abruptly. "But, sir!" he cried.

The king stopped six yards ahead of him and looked back at his adviser's perspiring visage.

"Do you really think, Firmin, that I am here as—as an infernal politician to put my crown and my flag and my claims and so forth in the way of peace? That little Frenchman is right. You know he is right as well as I do. Those things are over. We—we kings and rulers and representatives have been at the very heart of the mischief. Of course we imply separation, and of course separation means the threat of war, and of course the threat of war means the accumulation of more and more atomic bombs. The old game's up. But, I say, we mustn't stand here, you know. The world waits. Don't you think the old game's up, Firmin?"

Firmin adjusted a strap, passed a hand over his wet forehead and followed earnestly. "I admit, sir," he said to a receding back, "that there has to be some sort of hegemony, some sort of Amphictyonic council——"

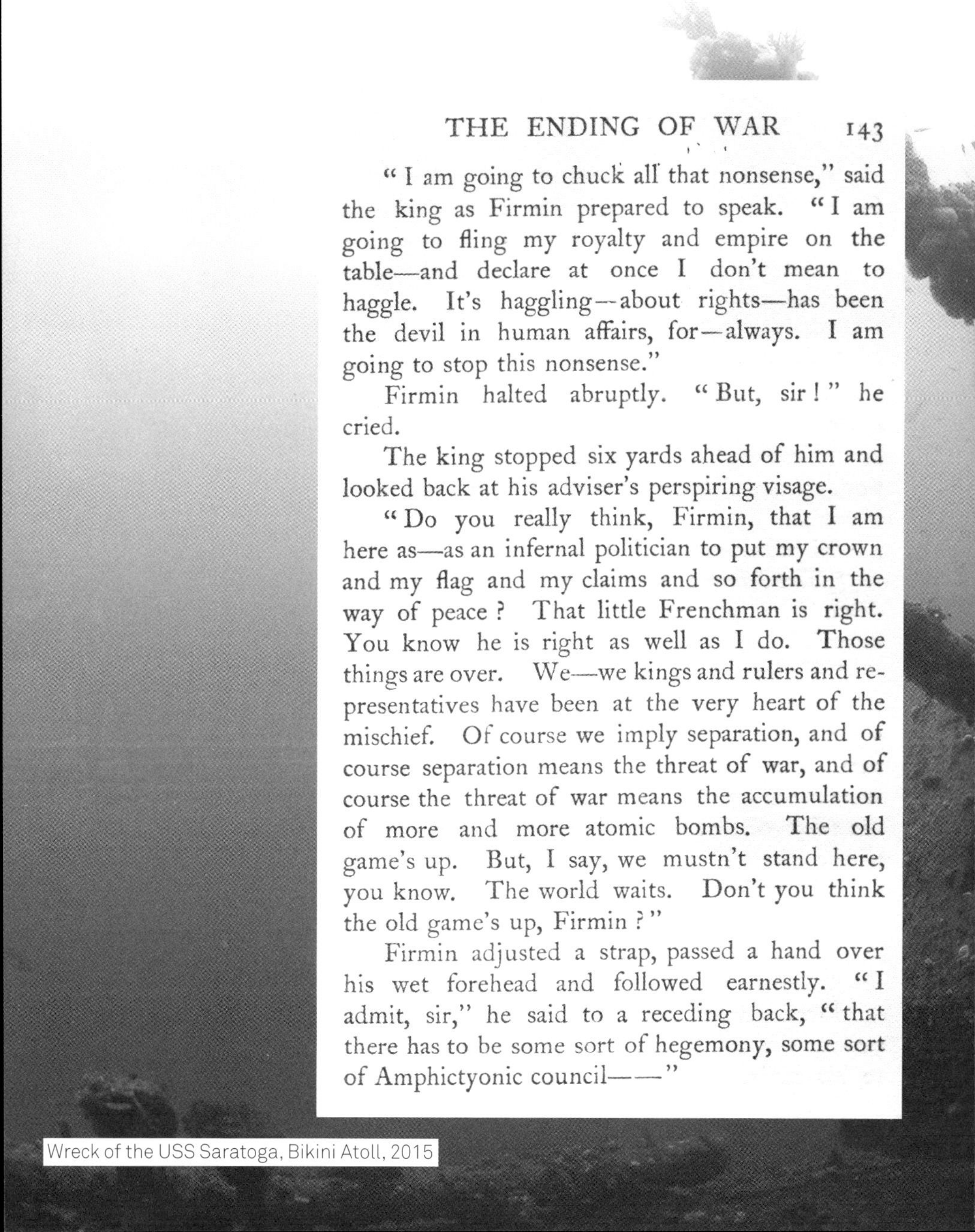

Wreck of the USS Saratoga, Bikini Atoll, 2015

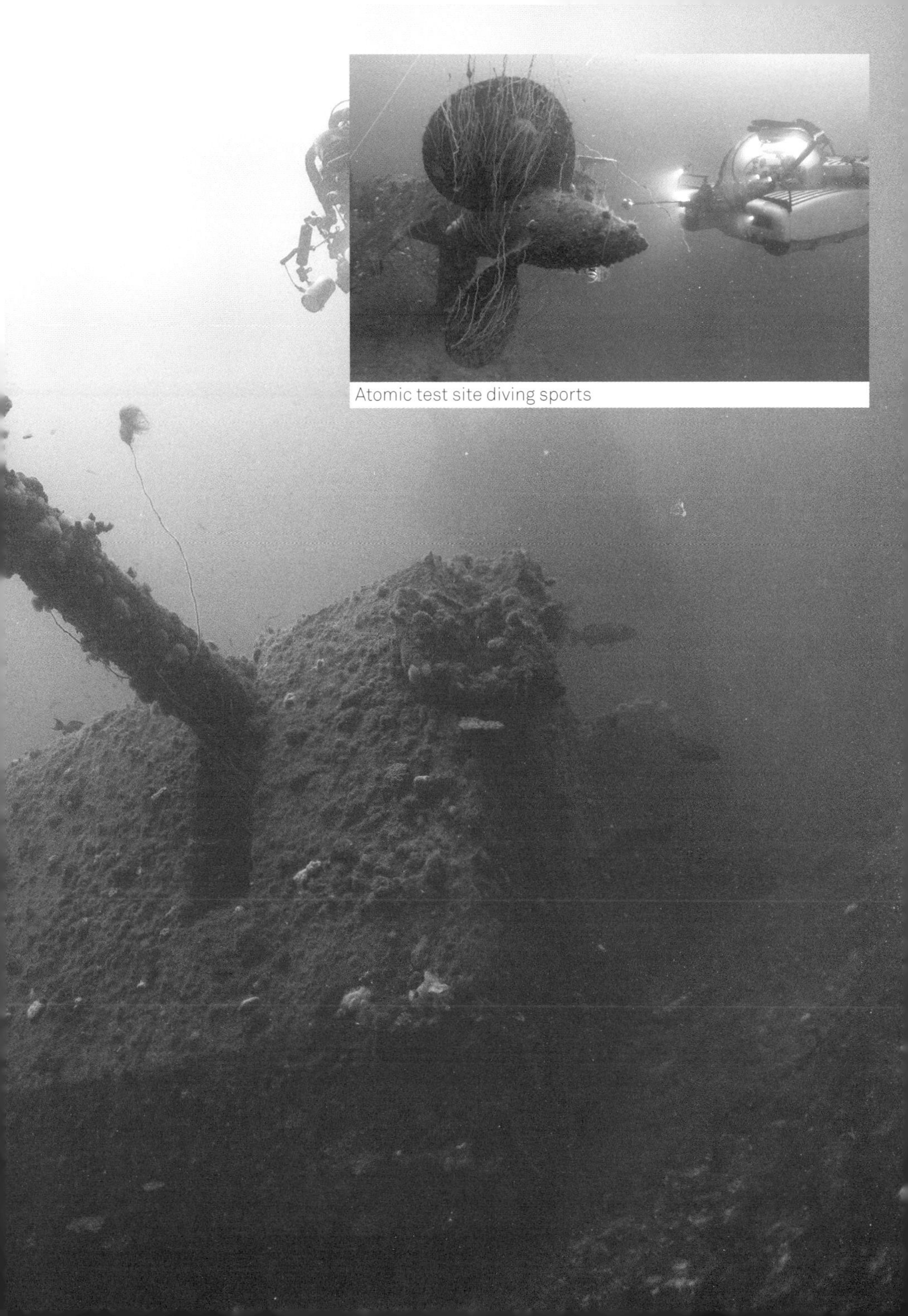

Atomic test site diving sports

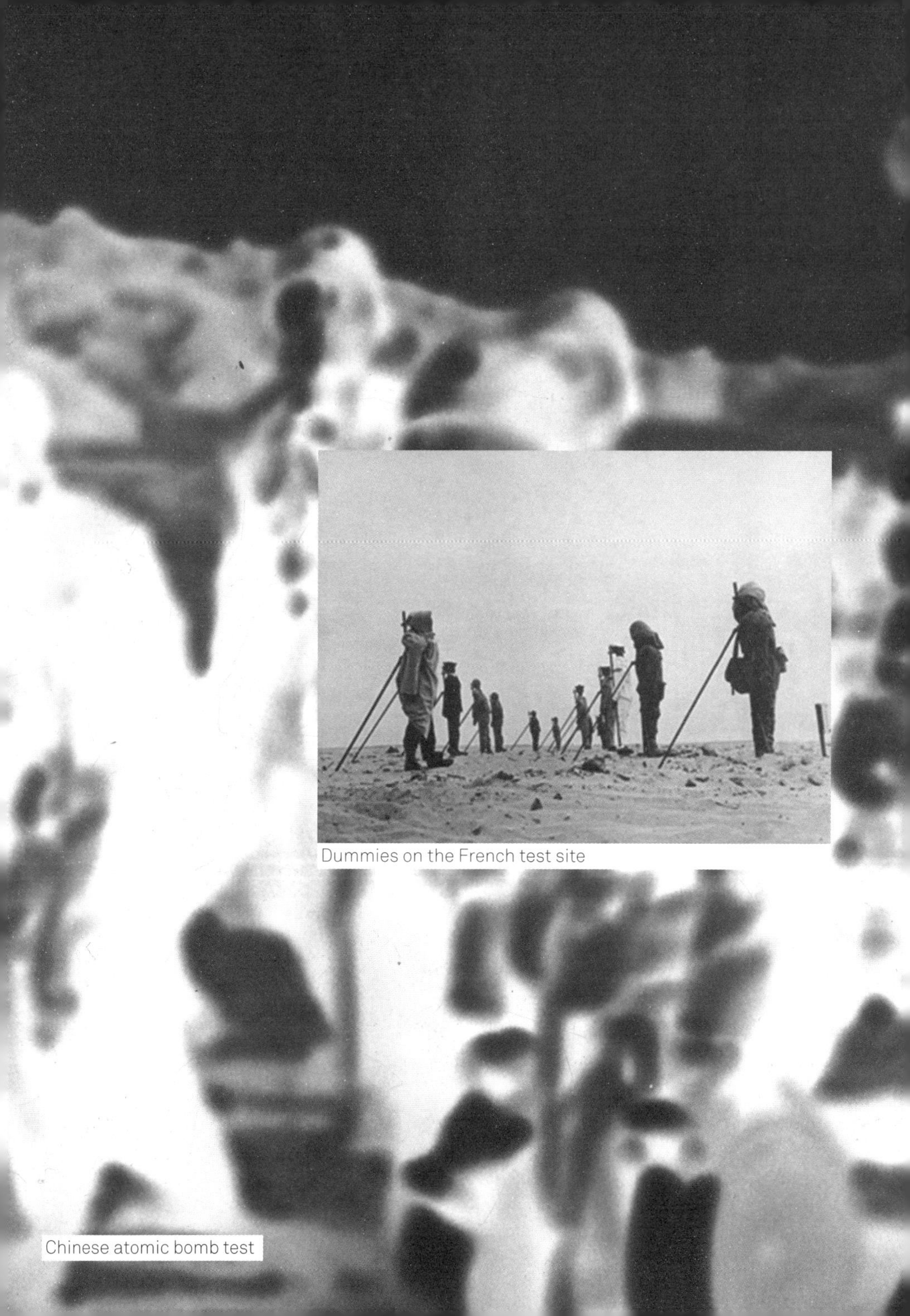

Dummies on the French test site

Chinese atomic bomb test

"There's got to be one simple government for all the world," said the king over his shoulder.

"But as for a reckless unqualified abandonment, sir——"

"*Bang!*" cried the king.

Firmin made no answer to this interruption. But a faint shadow of annoyance passed across his heated features.

"Yesterday," said the king by way of explanation, "the Japanese very nearly got San Francisco."

"I hadn't heard, sir."

"The Americans ran the Japanese aeroplane down into the sea and there the bomb got busted."

"Under the sea, sir?"

"Yes. Submarine volcano. The steam is in sight of the Californian coast. It was as near as that. And with things like this happening, you want me to go up this hill and haggle. Consider the effect of that upon my imperial cousin—and all the others!"

"*He* will haggle, sir."

"Not a bit of it," said the king.

"But, sir."

"Leblanc won't let him."

Firmin halted abruptly and gave a vicious pull at the offending strap. "Sir, he will listen to his advisers," he said, in a tone that in some

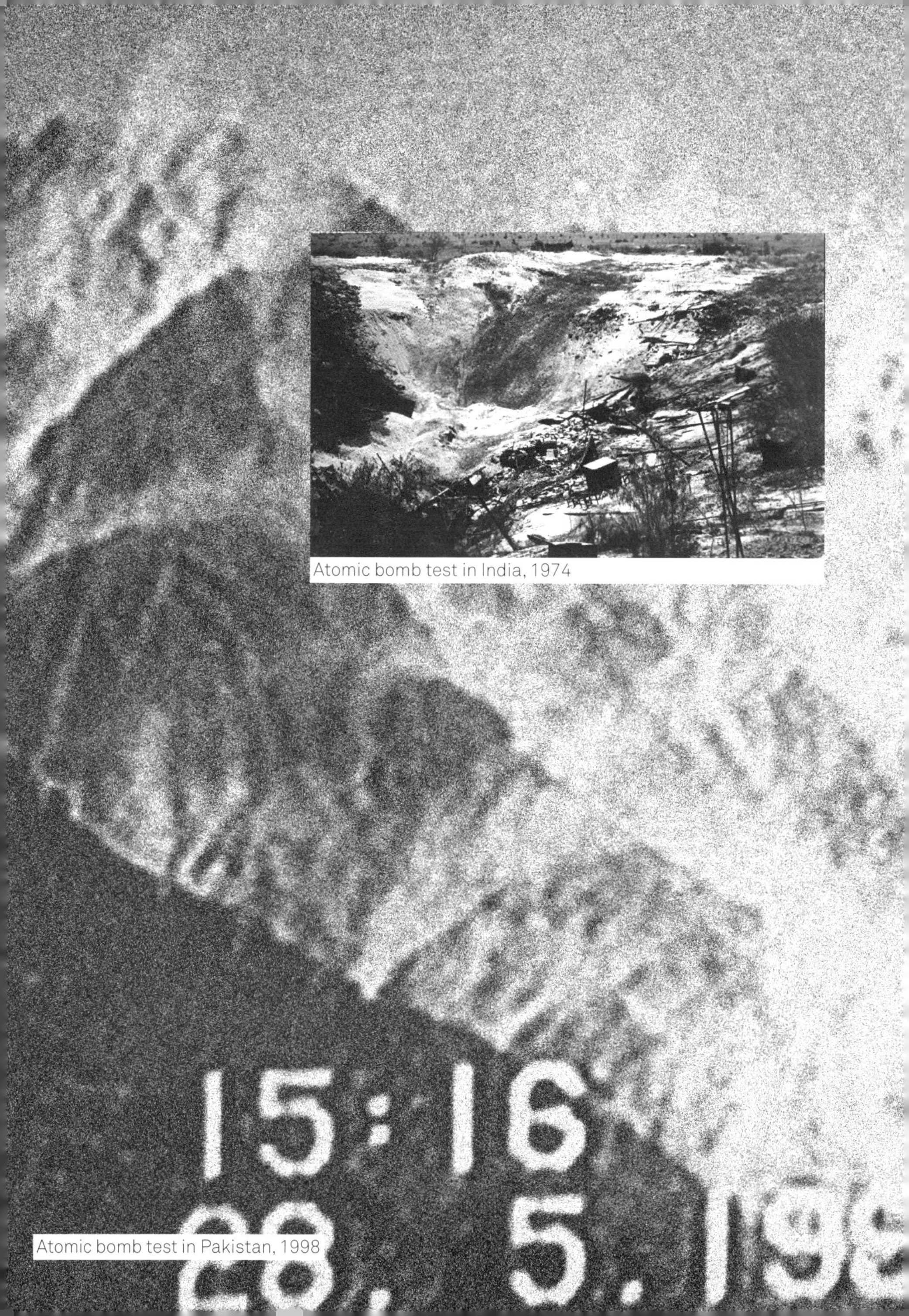

Atomic bomb test in India, 1974

Atomic bomb test in Pakistan, 1998

subtle way seemed to implicate his master with the trouble of the knapsack.

The king considered him.

"We will go just a little higher," he said. "I want to find this unoccupied village they spoke of, and then we will drink that beer. It can't be far. We will drink the beer and throw away the bottles. And then, Firmin, I shall ask you to look at things in a more generous light. . . . Because, you know, you must. . . ."

He turned about and for some time the only sound they made was the noise of their boots upon the loose stones of the way and the irregular breathing of Firmin.

At length, as it seemed to Firmin, or quite soon, as it seemed to the king, the gradient of the path diminished, the way widened out, and they found themselves in a very beautiful place indeed. It was one of those upland clusters of sheds and houses that are still to be found in the mountains of North Italy, buildings that were used only in the high summer, and which it was the custom to leave locked up and deserted through all the winter and spring and up to the middle of June. The buildings were of a soft-toned grey stone, buried in rich green grass, shadowed by chestnut trees and lit by an extraordinary blaze of yellow broom. Never had the king seen broom so glorious; he shouted at the light of it, for it seemed to give out more

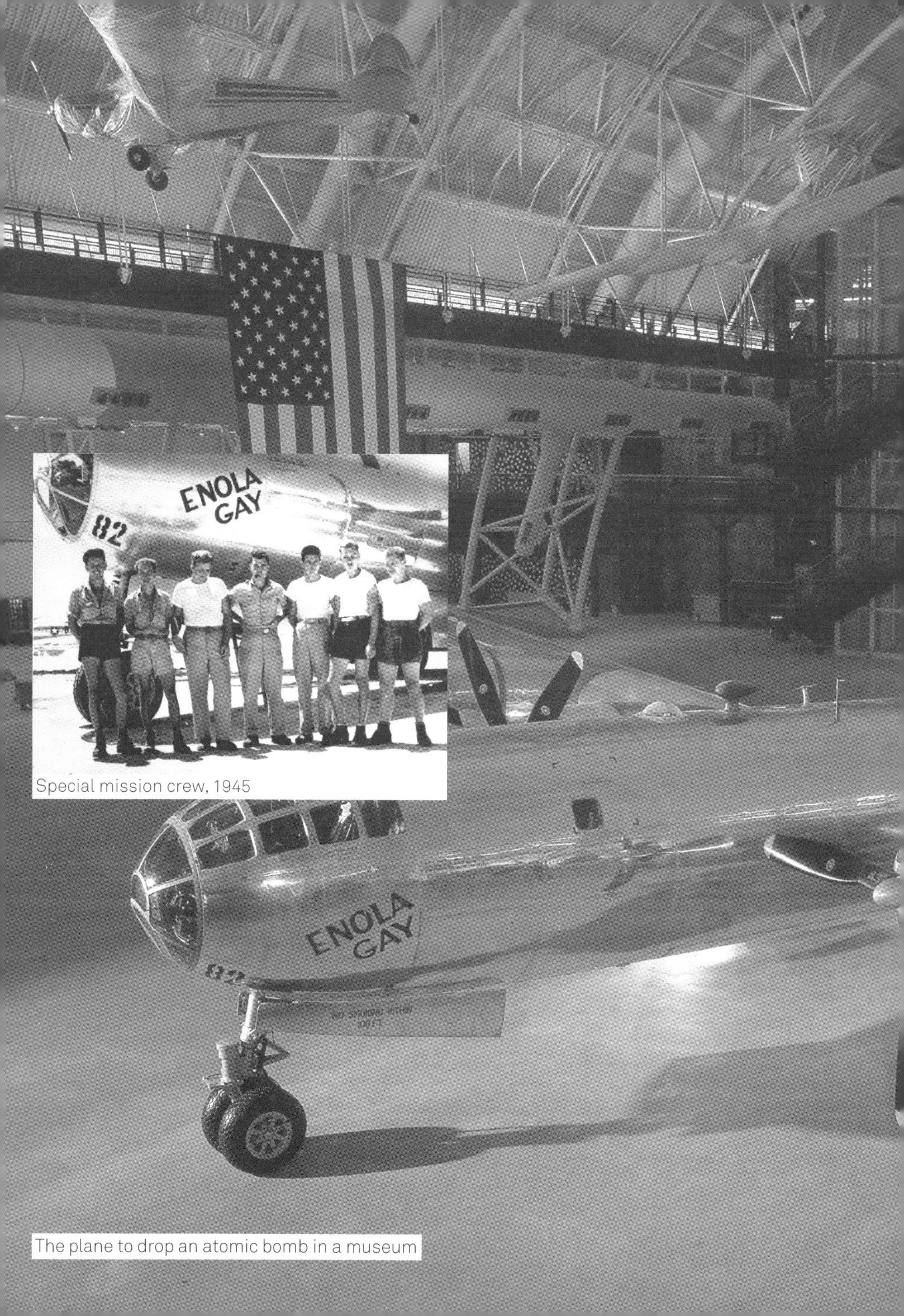

Special mission crew, 1945

The plane to drop an atomic bomb in a museum

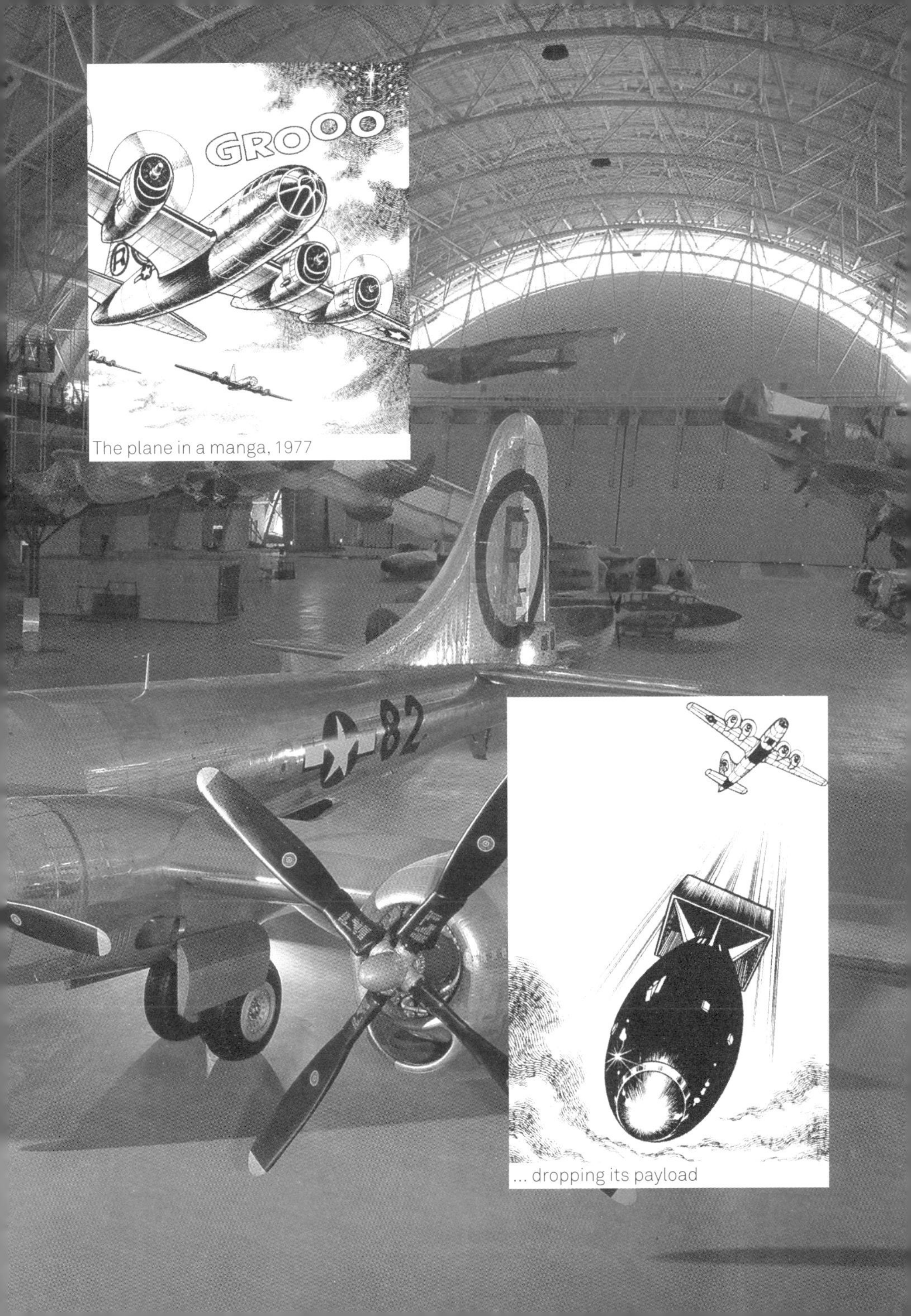

The plane in a manga, 1977

... dropping its payload

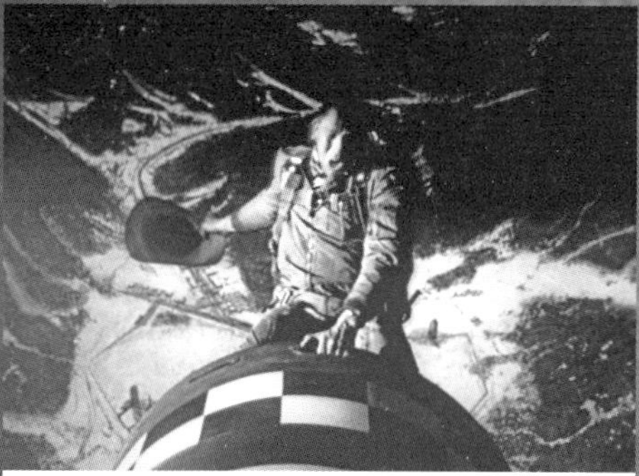
Atomic rodeo (US, UK 1963)

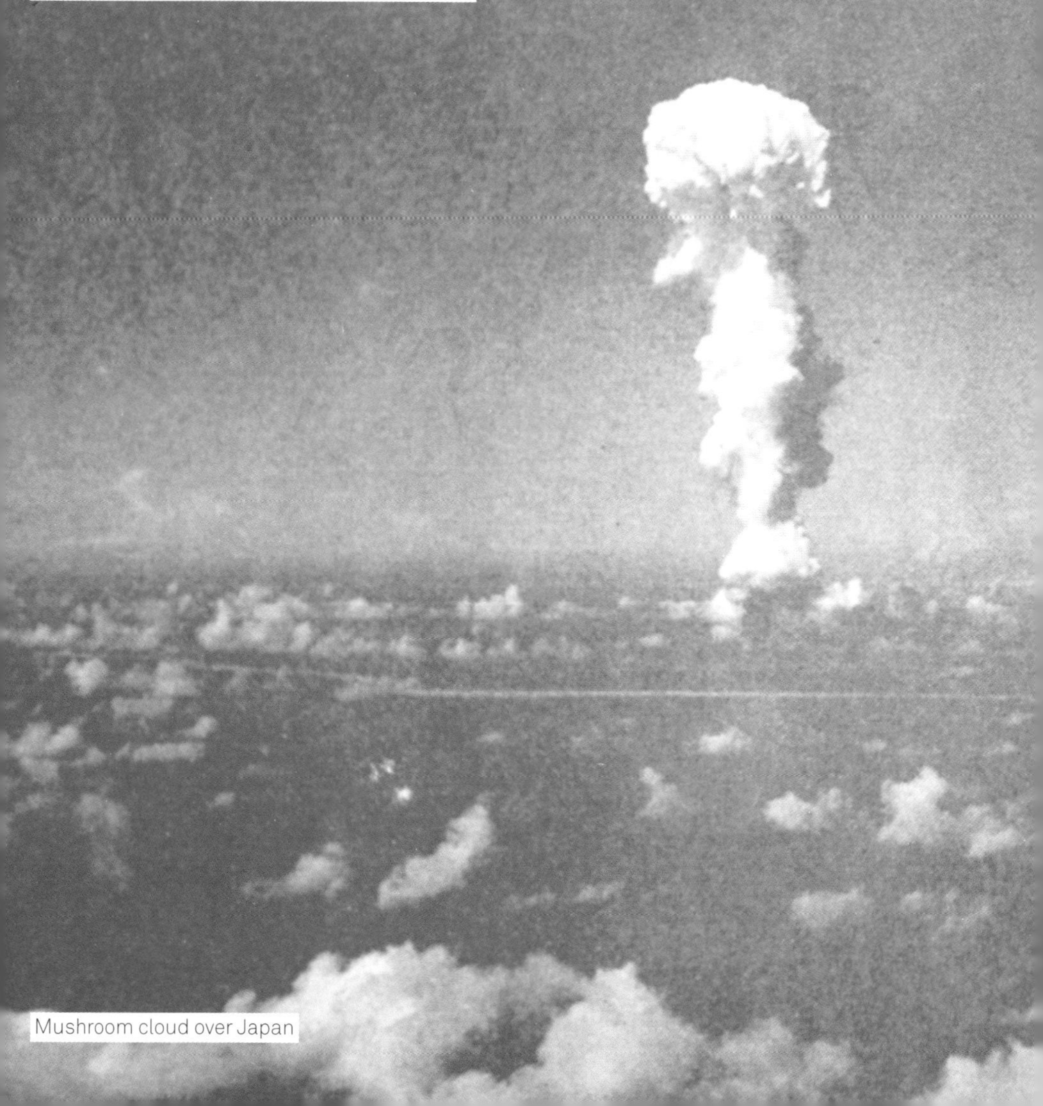
Mushroom cloud over Japan

sunlight even than it received; he sat down impulsively on a lichenous stone, tugged out his bread and cheese, and bade Firmin thrust the beer into the shaded weeds to cool.

"The things people miss, Firmin," he said, "who go up into the air in ships!"

Firmin looked around him with an ungenial eye. "You see it at its best, sir," he said, "before the peasants come here again and make it filthy."

"It would be beautiful anyhow," said the king.

"Superficially, sir," said Firmin. "But it stands for a social order that is fast vanishing away. Indeed, judging by the grass between the stones and in the huts, I am inclined to doubt if it is in use even now."

"I suppose," said the king, "they would come up immediately the hay on this flower meadow is cut. It would be those slow creamy-coloured beasts, I expect, one sees on the roads below, and swarthy girls with red handkerchiefs over their black hair. . . . It is wonderful to think how long that beautiful old life lasted. In the Roman times and long ages before ever the rumour of the Romans had come into these parts, men drove their cattle up into these places as the summer came on. . . . How haunted is this place! There have been quarrels here, hopes, children have played here and lived to

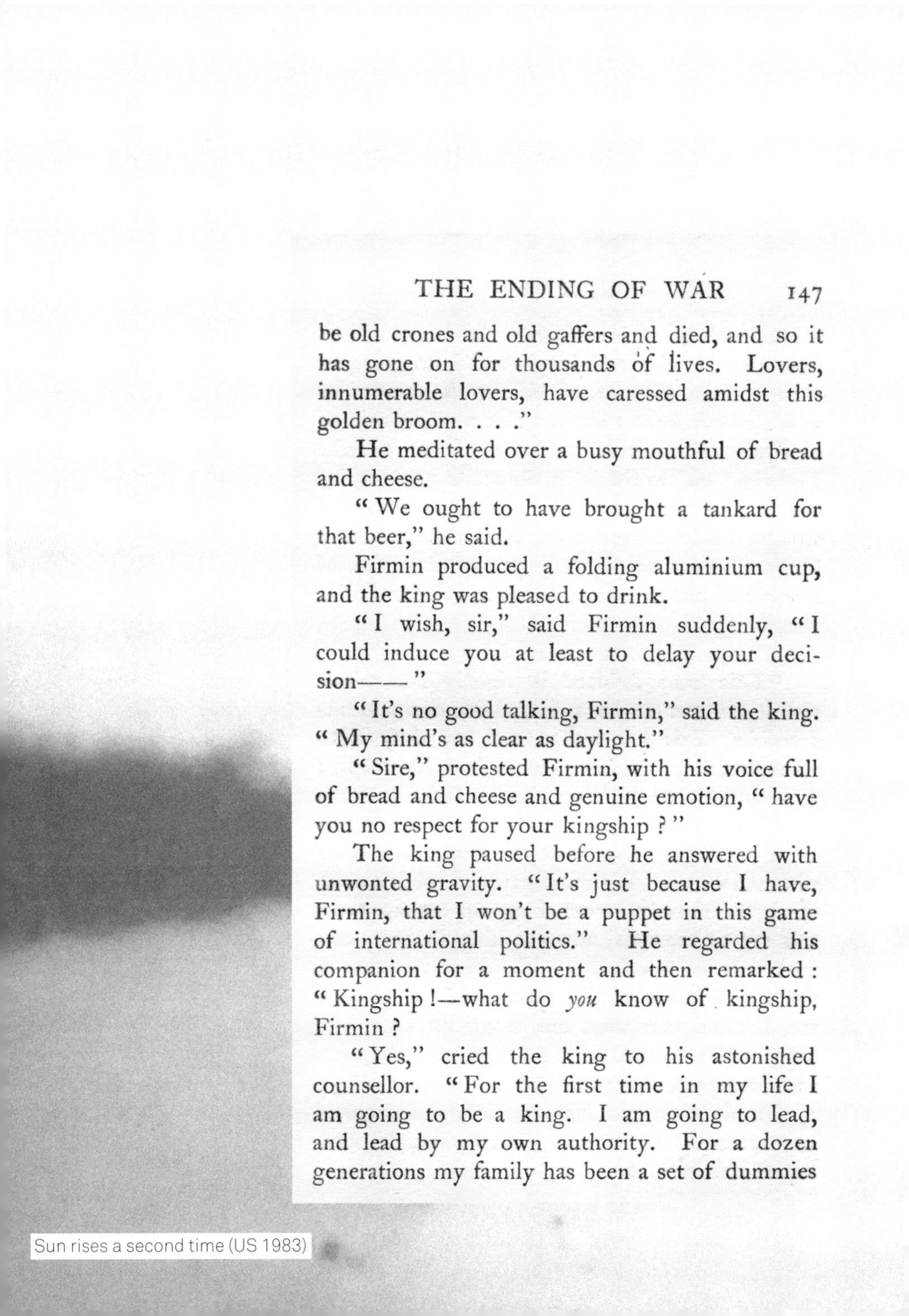

be old crones and old gaffers and died, and so it has gone on for thousands of lives. Lovers, innumerable lovers, have caressed amidst this golden broom. . . ."

He meditated over a busy mouthful of bread and cheese.

"We ought to have brought a tankard for that beer," he said.

Firmin produced a folding aluminium cup, and the king was pleased to drink.

"I wish, sir," said Firmin suddenly, "I could induce you at least to delay your decision——"

"It's no good talking, Firmin," said the king. "My mind's as clear as daylight."

"Sire," protested Firmin, with his voice full of bread and cheese and genuine emotion, "have you no respect for your kingship?"

The king paused before he answered with unwonted gravity. "It's just because I have, Firmin, that I won't be a puppet in this game of international politics." He regarded his companion for a moment and then remarked: "Kingship!—what do *you* know of kingship, Firmin?

"Yes," cried the king to his astonished counsellor. "For the first time in my life I am going to be a king. I am going to lead, and lead by my own authority. For a dozen generations my family has been a set of dummies

Sun rises a second time (US 1983)

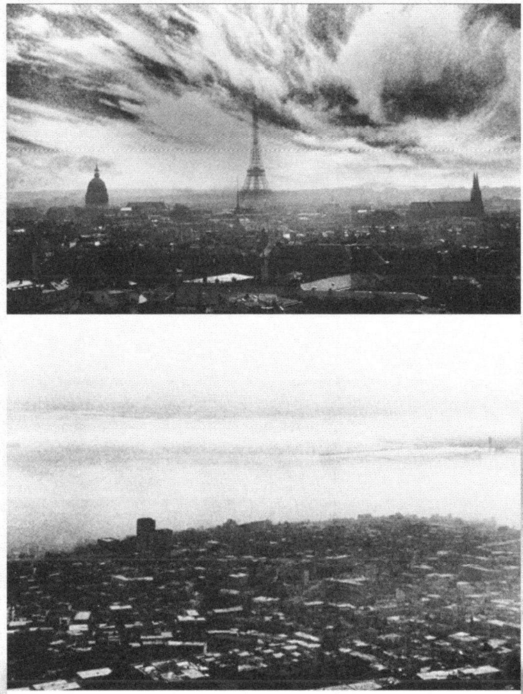
Paris disappears in a nuclear attack (FR 1962)

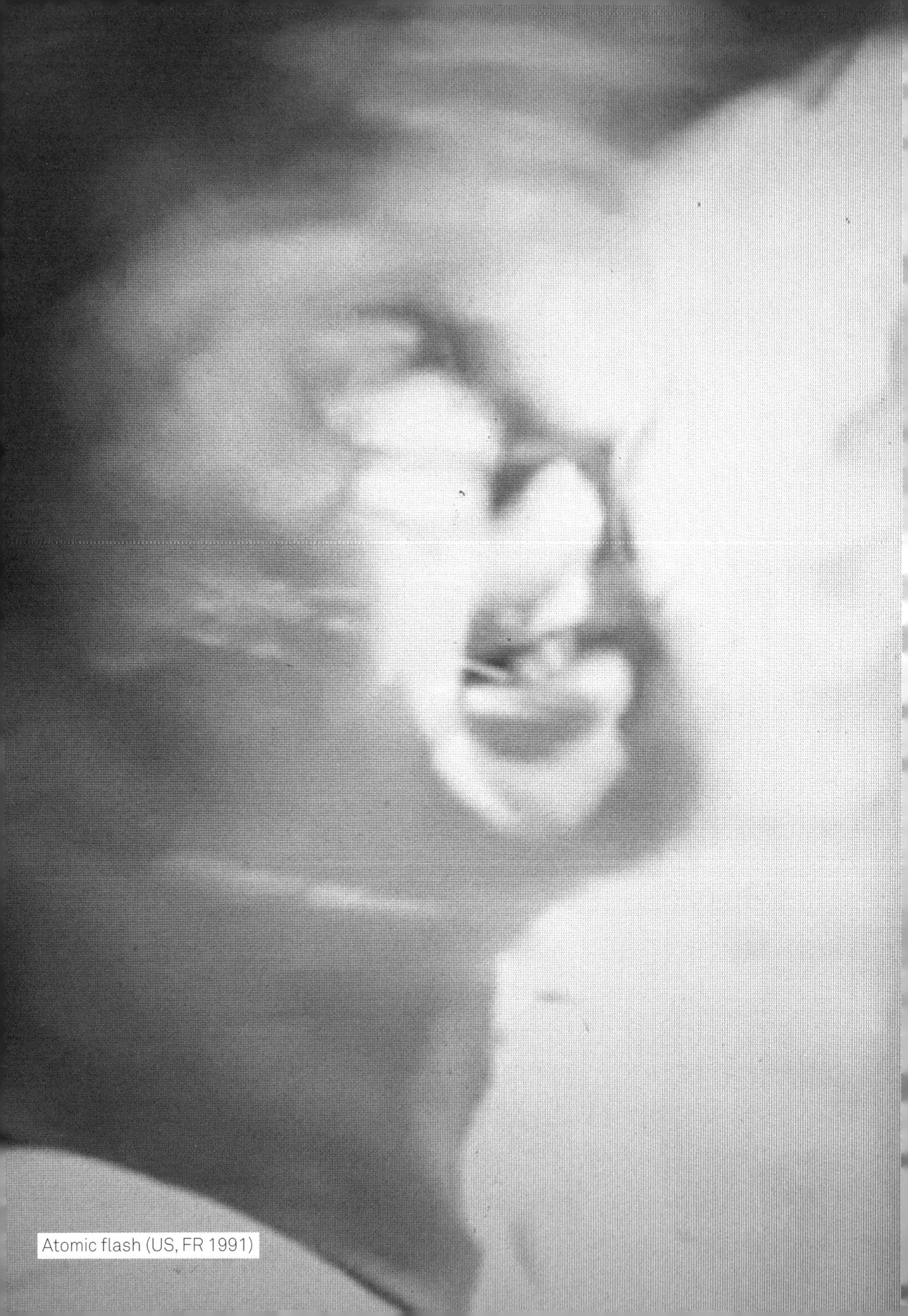

Atomic flash (US, FR 1991)

in the hands of their advisers. Advisers! Now I am going to be a real king—and I am going to—to abolish, dispose of, finish, the crown to which I have been a slave. But what a world of paralyzing shams this roaring stuff has ended! The rigid old world is in the melting-pot again, and I, who seemed to be no more than the stuffing inside a regal robe, I am a king among kings. I have to play my part at the head of things and put an end to blood and fire and idiot disorder."

"But, sir," protested Firmin.

"This man Leblanc is right. The whole world has got to be a Republic, one and indivisible. You know that, and my duty is to make that easy. A king should lead his people; you want me to stick on their backs like some Old Man of the Sea. To-day must be a sacrament of kings. Our trust for mankind is done with and ended. We must part our robes among them, we must part our kingship among them and say to them all, now the king in every one must rule the world. . . . Have you no sense of the magnificence of this occasion? You want me, Firmin, you want me to go up there and haggle like a damned little solicitor for some price, some compensation, some qualification. . . ."

Firmin shrugged his shoulders and assumed an expression of despair. Meanwhile, he conveyed, one must eat.

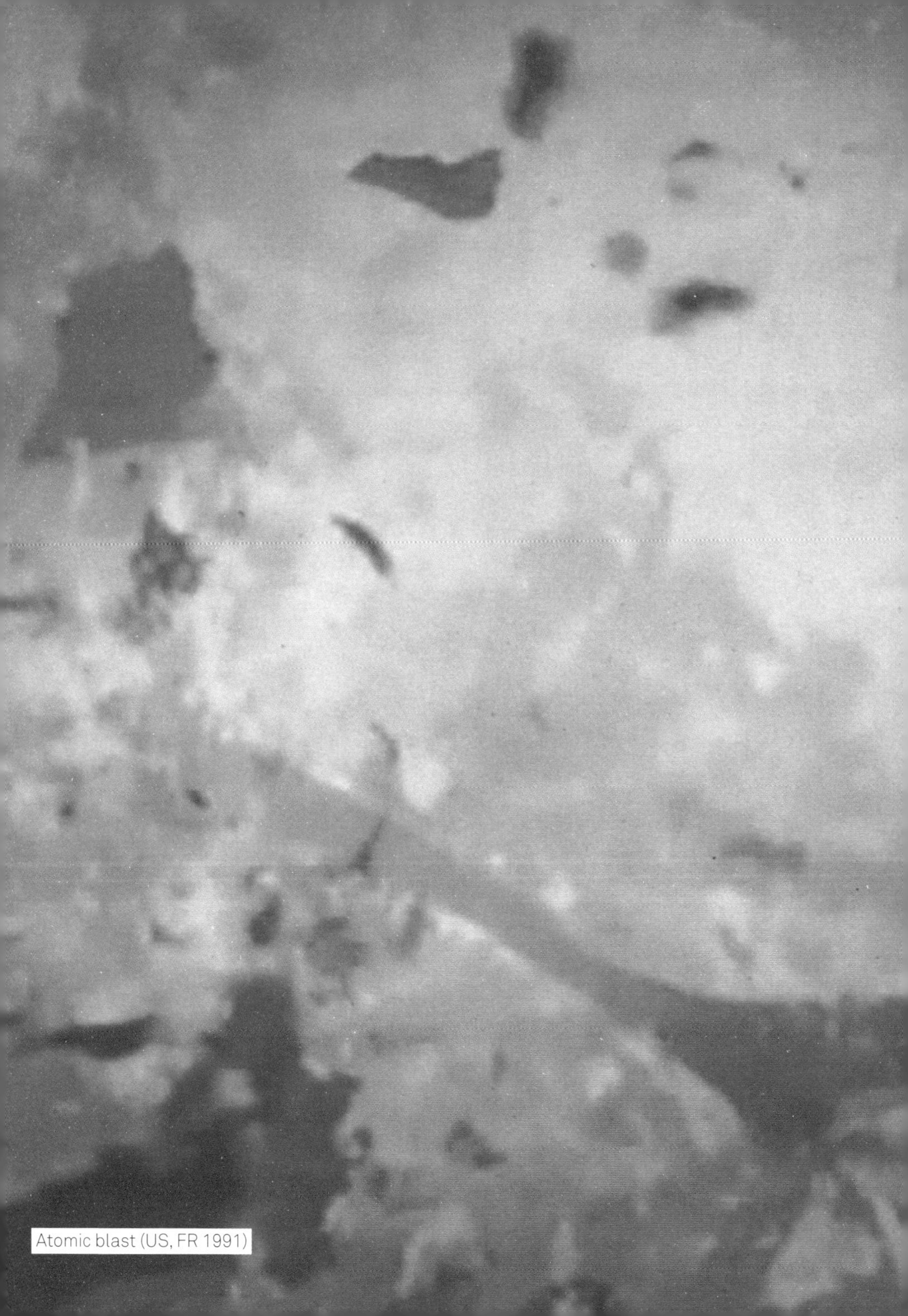

Atomic blast (US, FR 1991)

For a time neither spoke, and the king ate and turned over in his mind the phrases of the speech he intended to make to the conference. By virtue of the antiquity of his crown he was to preside, and he intended to make his presidency memorable. Reassured of his eloquence, he considered the despondent and sulky Firmin for a space.

"Firmin," he said, "you have idealized kingship."

"It has been my dream, sir," said Firmin, sorrowfully, "to serve."

"At the levers, Firmin," said the king.

"You are pleased to be unjust," said Firmin deeply hurt.

"I am pleased to be getting out of it," said the king.

"Oh, Firmin," he went on, "have you no thought for me? Will you never realize that I am not only flesh and blood but an imagination —with its rights. I am a king in revolt against that fetter they put upon my head. I am a king awake. My reverend grandparents never in all their august lives had a waking moment. They loved the job that you, you advisers, gave them; they never had a doubt of it. It was like giving a doll to a woman who ought to have a child. They delighted in processions and opening things and being read addresses to, and visiting triplets and nonagenarians and all that sort of thing.

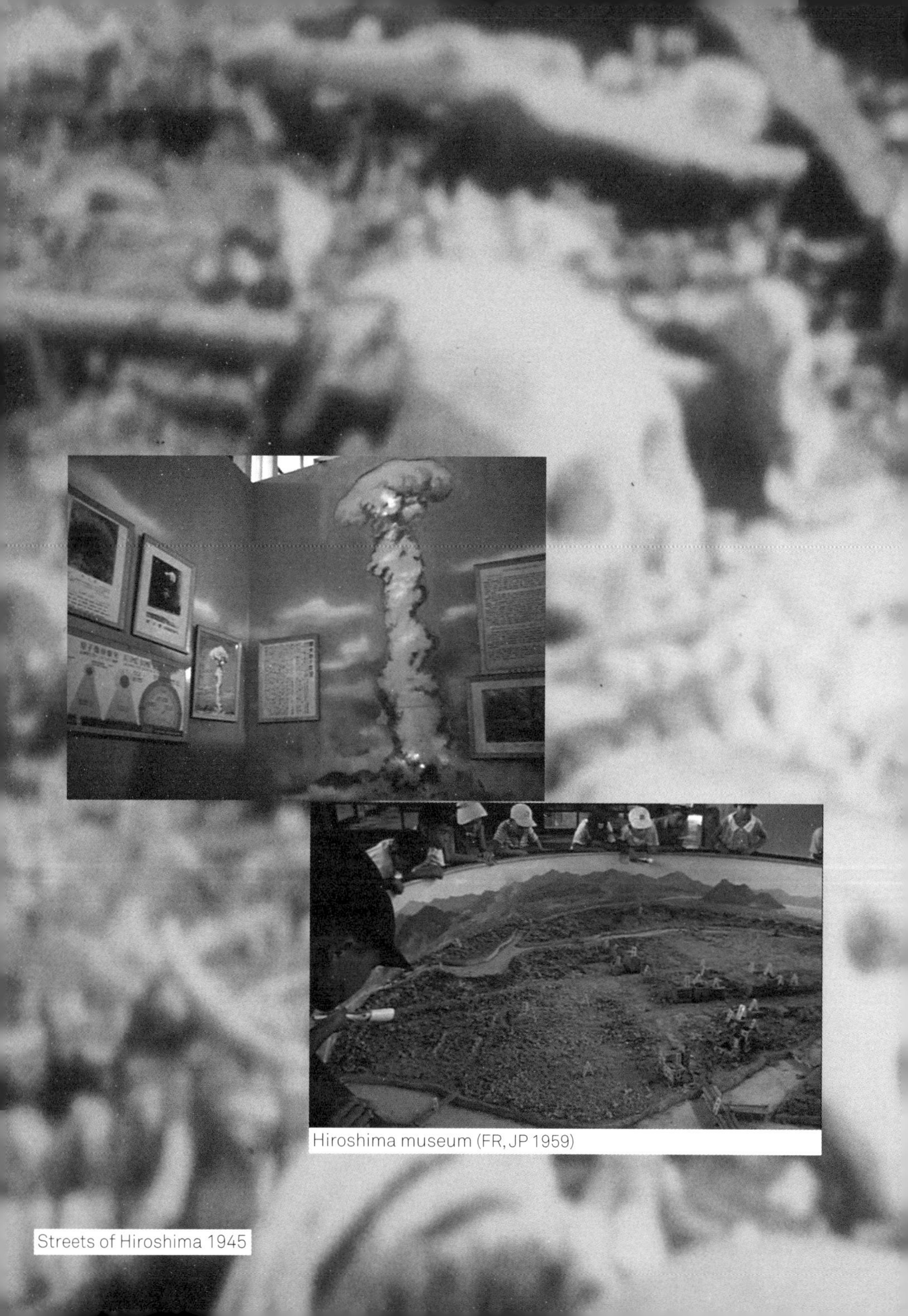

Hiroshima museum (FR, JP 1959)

Streets of Hiroshima 1945

Incredibly. They used to keep albums of cuttings from all the illustrated papers showing them at it, and if the press-cutting parcels grew thin they were worried. It was all that ever worried them. But there is something atavistic in me ; I hark back to unconstitutional monarchs. They christened me too retrogressively, I think. I wanted to get things done. I was bored. I might have fallen into vice, most intelligent and energetic princes do, but the palace precautions were unusually thorough. I was brought up in the purest court the world has ever seen. . . . Alertly pure. . . . So I read books, Firmin, and went about asking questions. The thing was bound to happen to one of us sooner or later. Perhaps, too, very likely I'm not vicious. I don't think I am."

He reflected. "No," he said.

Firmin cleared his throat. "I don't think you are, sir," he said. "You prefer———"

He stopped short. He had been going to say "talking". He substituted "ideas".

"That world of royalty!" the king went on. "In a little while no one will understand it any more. It will become a riddle. . . .

"Among other things it was a world of perpetual best clothes. Everything was in its best clothes for us and usually wearing bunting. With a cinema watching to see we took it properly. If you are a king, Firmin, and you go

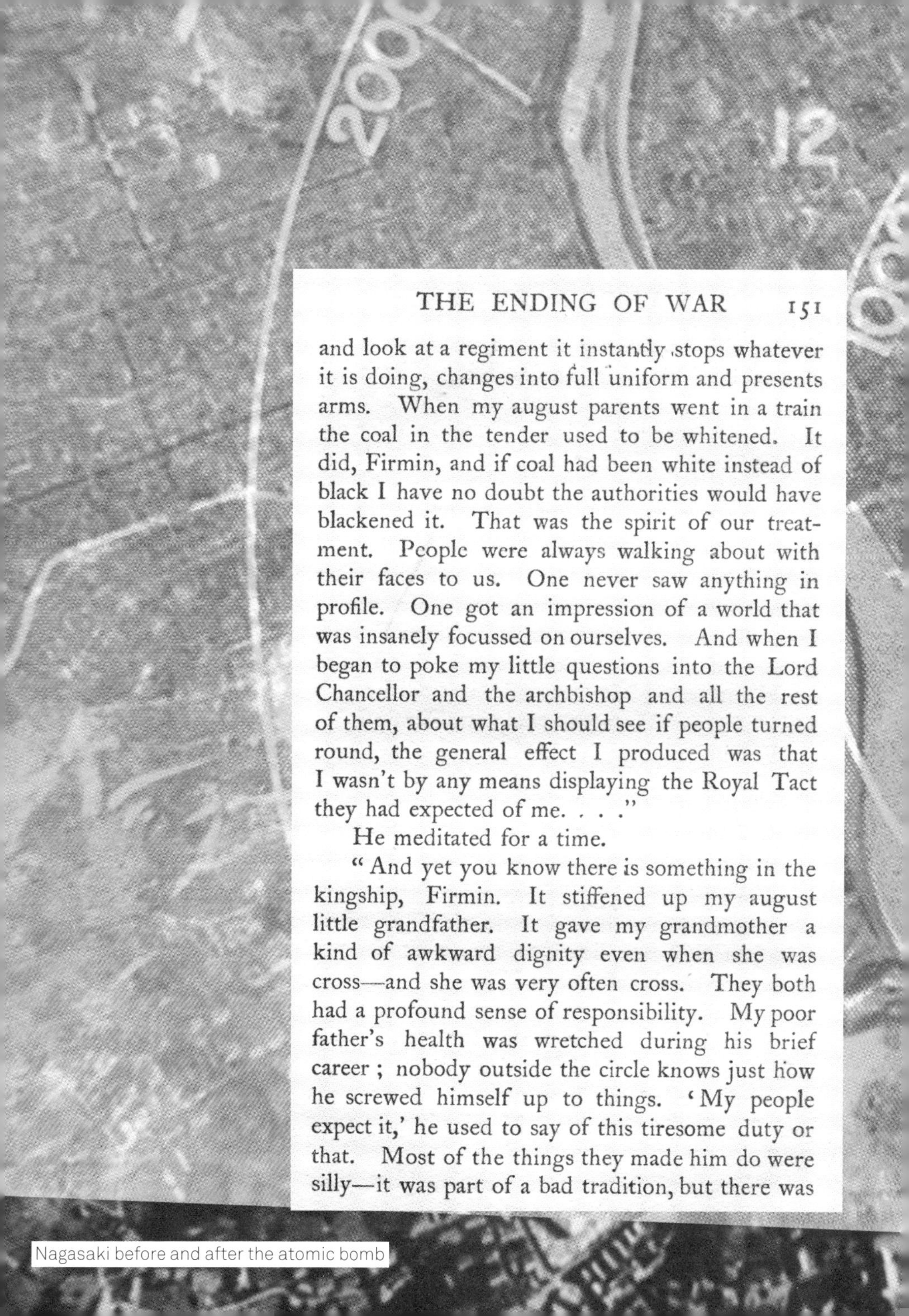

and look at a regiment it instantly stops whatever it is doing, changes into full uniform and presents arms. When my august parents went in a train the coal in the tender used to be whitened. It did, Firmin, and if coal had been white instead of black I have no doubt the authorities would have blackened it. That was the spirit of our treatment. People were always walking about with their faces to us. One never saw anything in profile. One got an impression of a world that was insanely focussed on ourselves. And when I began to poke my little questions into the Lord Chancellor and the archbishop and all the rest of them, about what I should see if people turned round, the general effect I produced was that I wasn't by any means displaying the Royal Tact they had expected of me. . . ."

He meditated for a time.

"And yet you know there is something in the kingship, Firmin. It stiffened up my august little grandfather. It gave my grandmother a kind of awkward dignity even when she was cross—and she was very often cross. They both had a profound sense of responsibility. My poor father's health was wretched during his brief career; nobody outside the circle knows just how he screwed himself up to things. 'My people expect it,' he used to say of this tiresome duty or that. Most of the things they made him do were silly—it was part of a bad tradition, but there was

Nagasaki before and after the atomic bomb

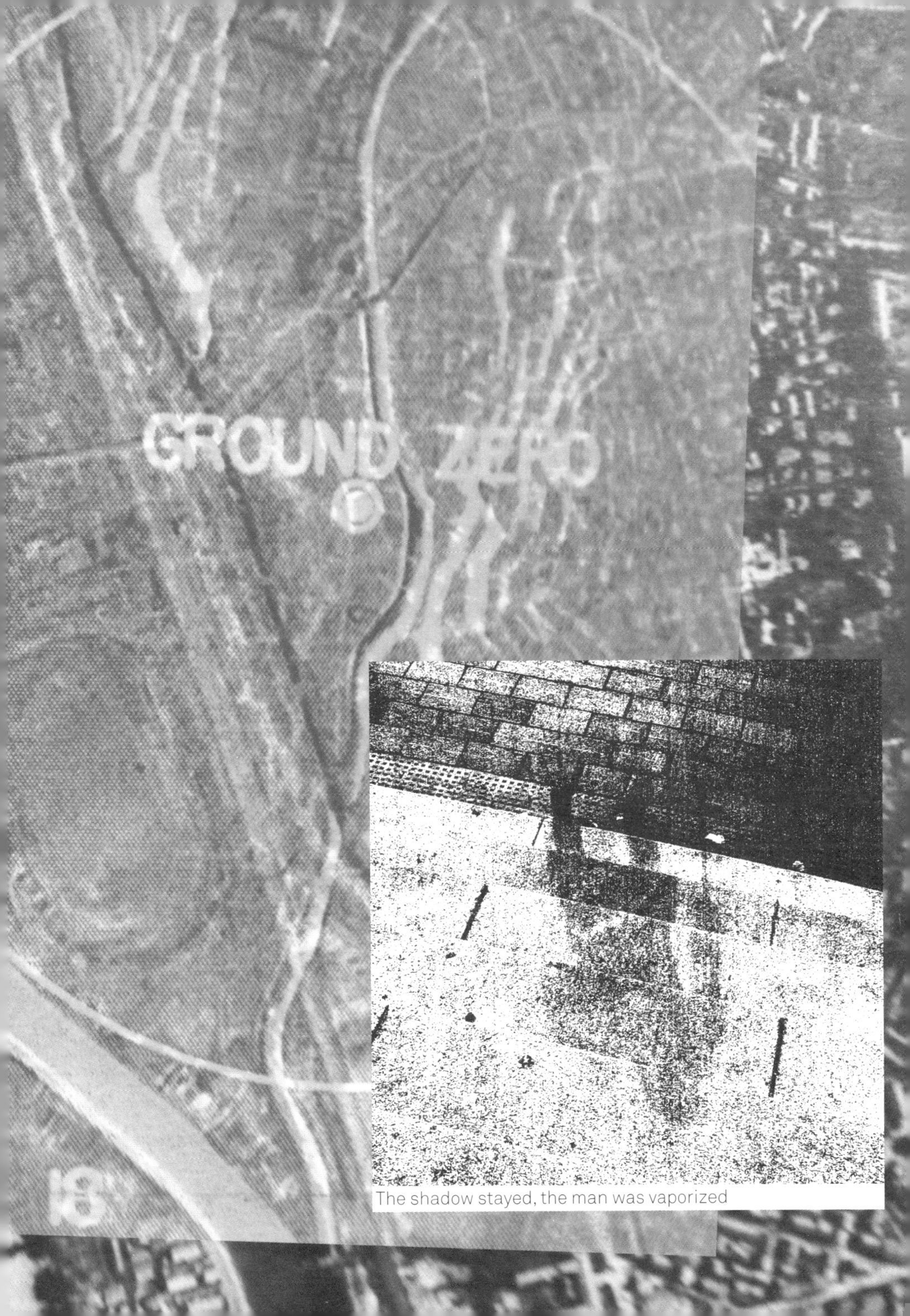

The shadow stayed, the man was vaporized

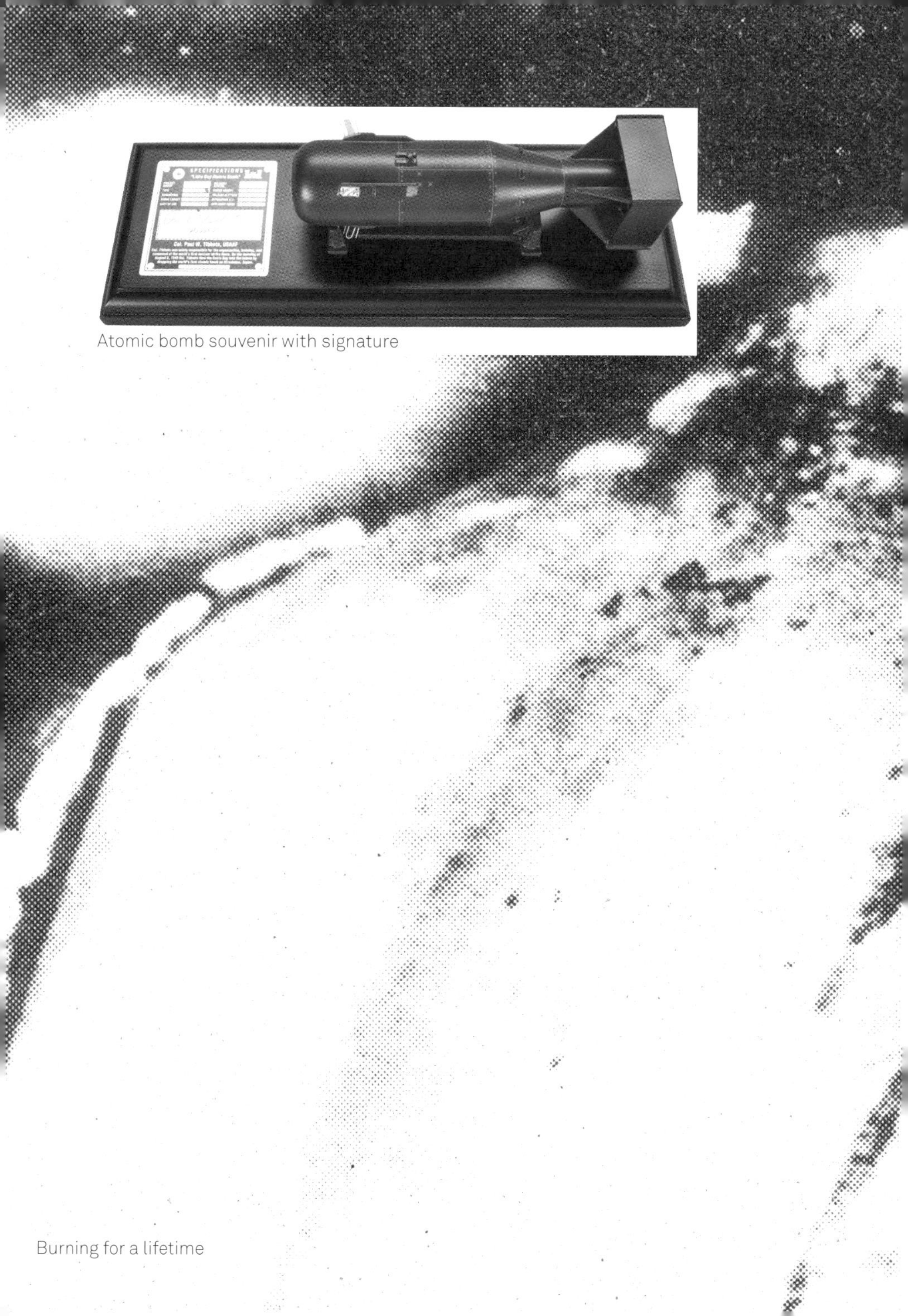

Atomic bomb souvenir with signature

Burning for a lifetime

nothing silly in the way he set about them. . . . The spirit of kingship is a fine thing, Firmin ; I feel it in my bones ; I do not know what I might not be if I were not a king. I could die for my people, Firmin, and you couldn't. No, don't say you could die for me, because I know better. Don't think I forget my kingship, Firmin, don't imagine that. I am a king, a kingly king, by right divine. The fact that I am also a chattering young man makes not the slightest difference to that. But the proper text-book for kings, Firmin, is none of the Court memoirs and Welt-Politik books you would have me read ; it is old Fraser's *Golden Bough*. Have you read that, Firmin ? "

Firmin had.

"Those were the authentic kings. In the end they were cut up and a bit given to everybody. They sprinkled the nations—with Kingship."

Firmin turned himself round and faced his royal master.

" What do you intend to do, sir ? " he asked. "If you will not listen to me, what do you propose to do this afternoon ? "

The king flicked crumbs from his coat.

" Manifestly war has to stop for ever, Firmin. Manifestly this can only be done by putting all the world under one government. Our crowns and flags are in the way. Manifestly they must go."

" Yes, sir," interrupted Firmin, " but *what*

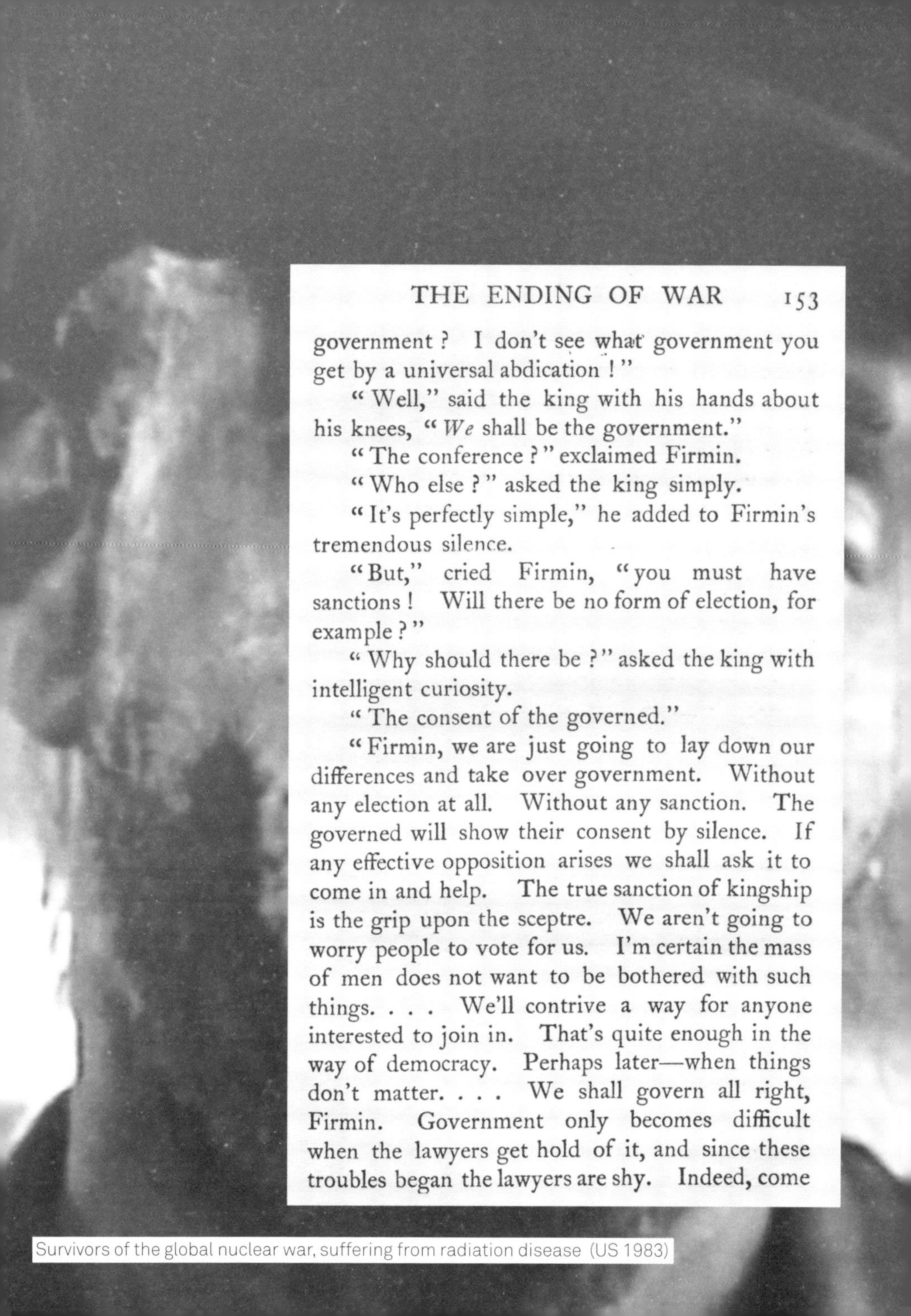

government? I don't see what government you get by a universal abdication!"

"Well," said the king with his hands about his knees, "*We* shall be the government."

"The conference?" exclaimed Firmin.

"Who else?" asked the king simply.

"It's perfectly simple," he added to Firmin's tremendous silence.

"But," cried Firmin, "you must have sanctions! Will there be no form of election, for example?"

"Why should there be?" asked the king with intelligent curiosity.

"The consent of the governed."

"Firmin, we are just going to lay down our differences and take over government. Without any election at all. Without any sanction. The governed will show their consent by silence. If any effective opposition arises we shall ask it to come in and help. The true sanction of kingship is the grip upon the sceptre. We aren't going to worry people to vote for us. I'm certain the mass of men does not want to be bothered with such things. . . . We'll contrive a way for anyone interested to join in. That's quite enough in the way of democracy. Perhaps later—when things don't matter. . . . We shall govern all right, Firmin. Government only becomes difficult when the lawyers get hold of it, and since these troubles began the lawyers are shy. Indeed, come

Survivors of the global nuclear war, suffering from radiation disease (US 1983)

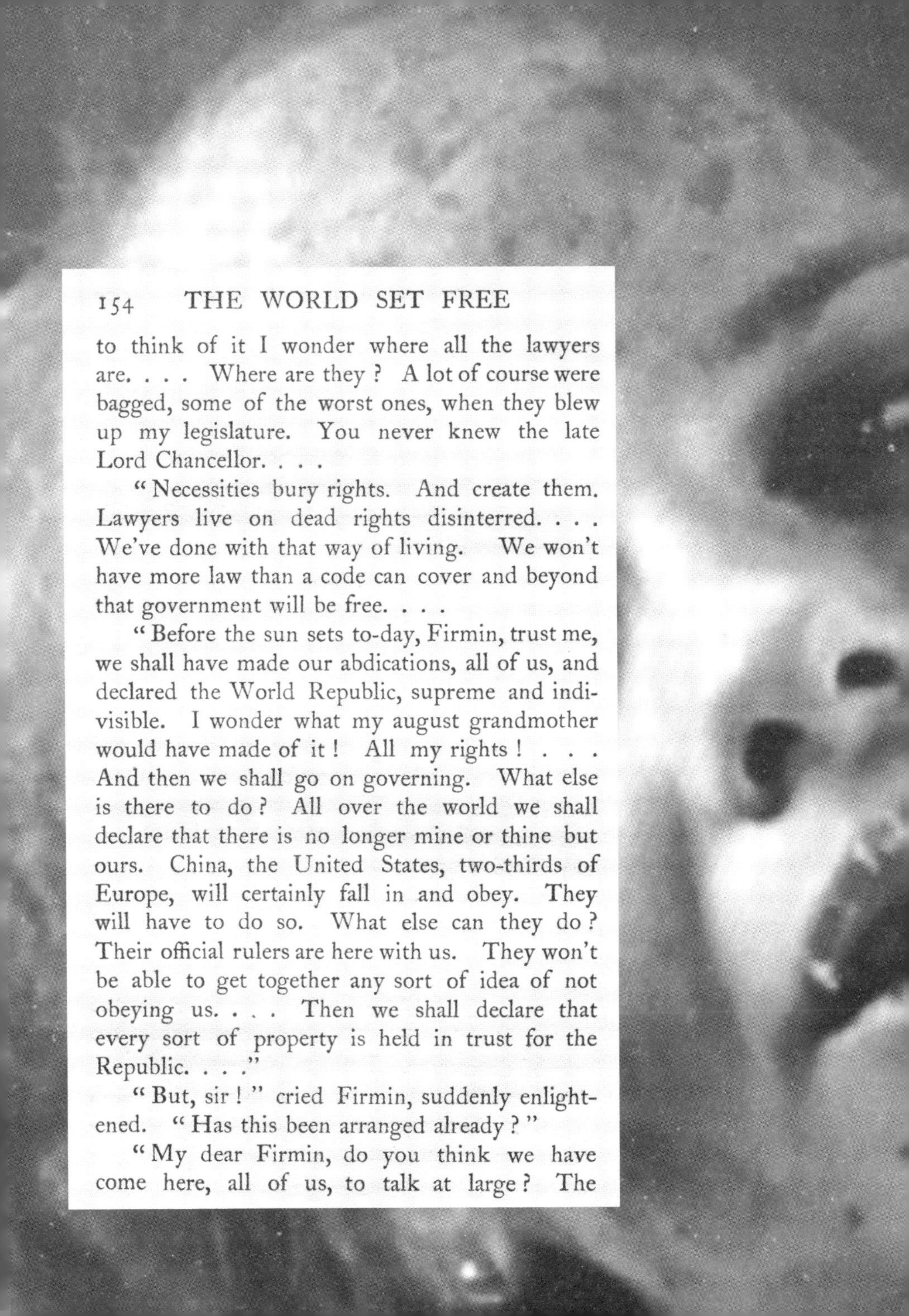

to think of it I wonder where all the lawyers are. . . . Where are they? A lot of course were bagged, some of the worst ones, when they blew up my legislature. You never knew the late Lord Chancellor. . . .

"Necessities bury rights. And create them. Lawyers live on dead rights disinterred. . . . We've done with that way of living. We won't have more law than a code can cover and beyond that government will be free. . . .

"Before the sun sets to-day, Firmin, trust me, we shall have made our abdications, all of us, and declared the World Republic, supreme and indivisible. I wonder what my august grandmother would have made of it! All my rights! . . . And then we shall go on governing. What else is there to do? All over the world we shall declare that there is no longer mine or thine but ours. China, the United States, two-thirds of Europe, will certainly fall in and obey. They will have to do so. What else can they do? Their official rulers are here with us. They won't be able to get together any sort of idea of not obeying us. . . . Then we shall declare that every sort of property is held in trust for the Republic. . . ."

"But, sir!" cried Firmin, suddenly enlightened. "Has this been arranged already?"

"My dear Firmin, do you think we have come here, all of us, to talk at large? The talking has been done for half a century. Talking and writing. We are here to set the new thing, the simple obvious necessary thing, going."

He stood up.

Firmin, forgetting the habits of a score of years, remained seated.

"*Well*," he said at last. "And I have known nothing!"

The king smiled very cheerfully. He liked these talks with Firmin.

§ 3

That conference upon the Brissago meadows was one of the most heterogeneous collections of prominent people that has ever met together. Principalities and powers, stripped and shattered until all their pride and mystery were gone, met in a marvellous new humility. Here were kings and emperors whose capitals were lakes of flaming destruction, statesmen whose countries had become chaos, scared politicians and financial potentates. Here were leaders of thought and learned investigators dragged reluctantly to the control of affairs. Altogether there were ninety-three of them, Leblanc's conception of the head men of the world. They had all come to the realization of the simple truths that the indefatigable Leblanc had hammered into them;

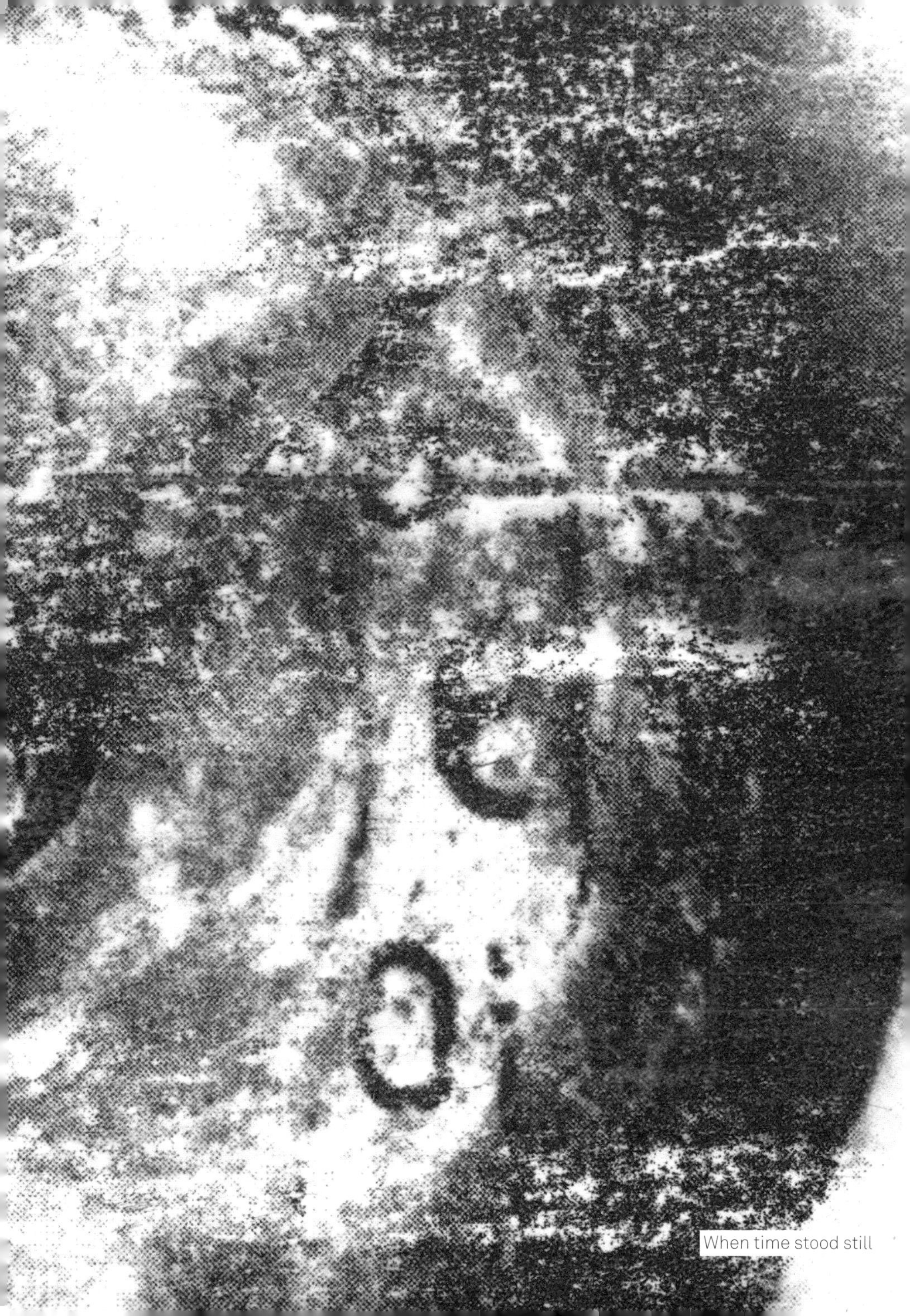

When time stood still

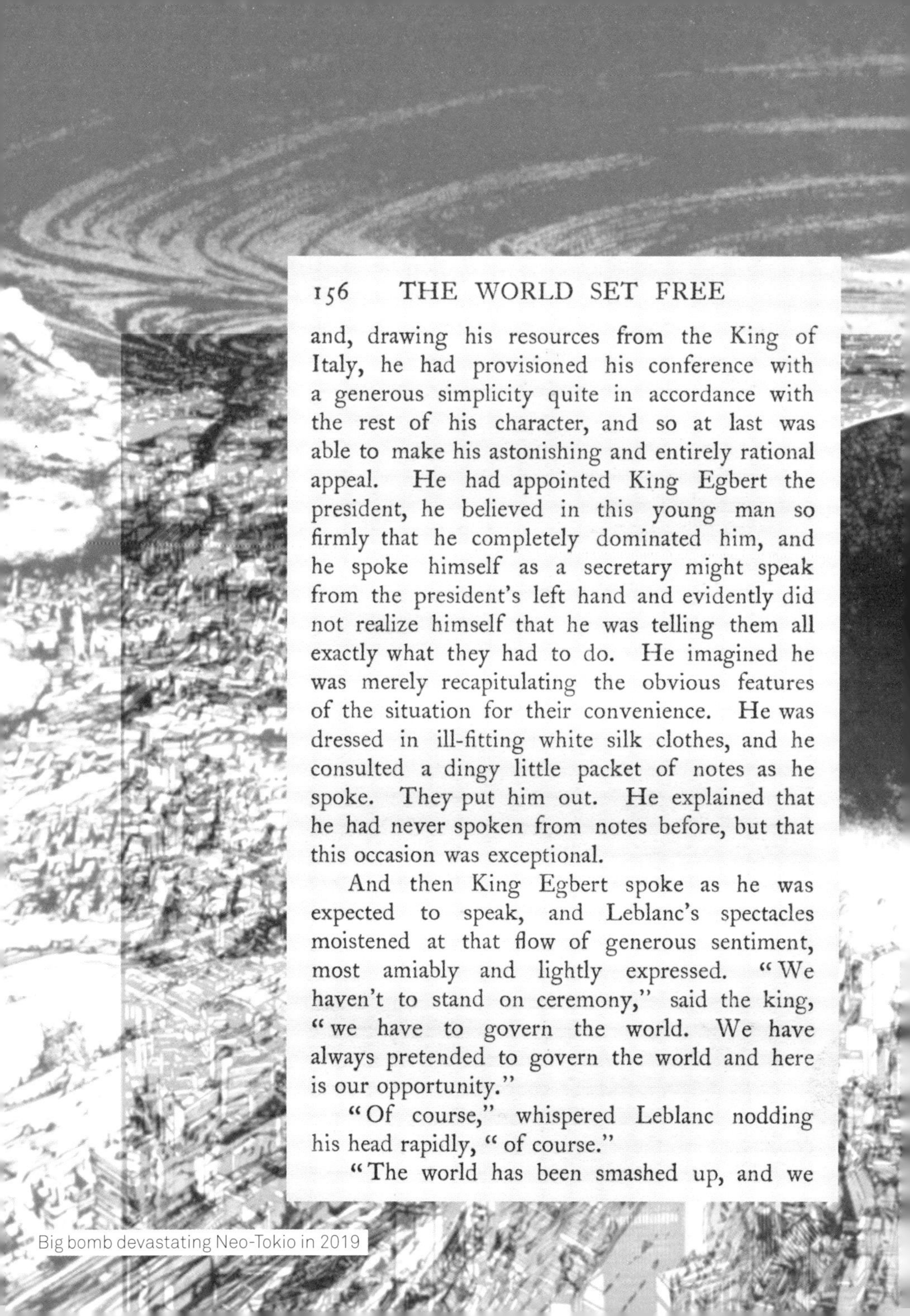

and, drawing his resources from the King of Italy, he had provisioned his conference with a generous simplicity quite in accordance with the rest of his character, and so at last was able to make his astonishing and entirely rational appeal. He had appointed King Egbert the president, he believed in this young man so firmly that he completely dominated him, and he spoke himself as a secretary might speak from the president's left hand and evidently did not realize himself that he was telling them all exactly what they had to do. He imagined he was merely recapitulating the obvious features of the situation for their convenience. He was dressed in ill-fitting white silk clothes, and he consulted a dingy little packet of notes as he spoke. They put him out. He explained that he had never spoken from notes before, but that this occasion was exceptional.

And then King Egbert spoke as he was expected to speak, and Leblanc's spectacles moistened at that flow of generous sentiment, most amiably and lightly expressed. "We haven't to stand on ceremony," said the king, "we have to govern the world. We have always pretended to govern the world and here is our opportunity."

"Of course," whispered Leblanc nodding his head rapidly, "of course."

"The world has been smashed up, and we

Big bomb devastating Neo-Tokio in 2019

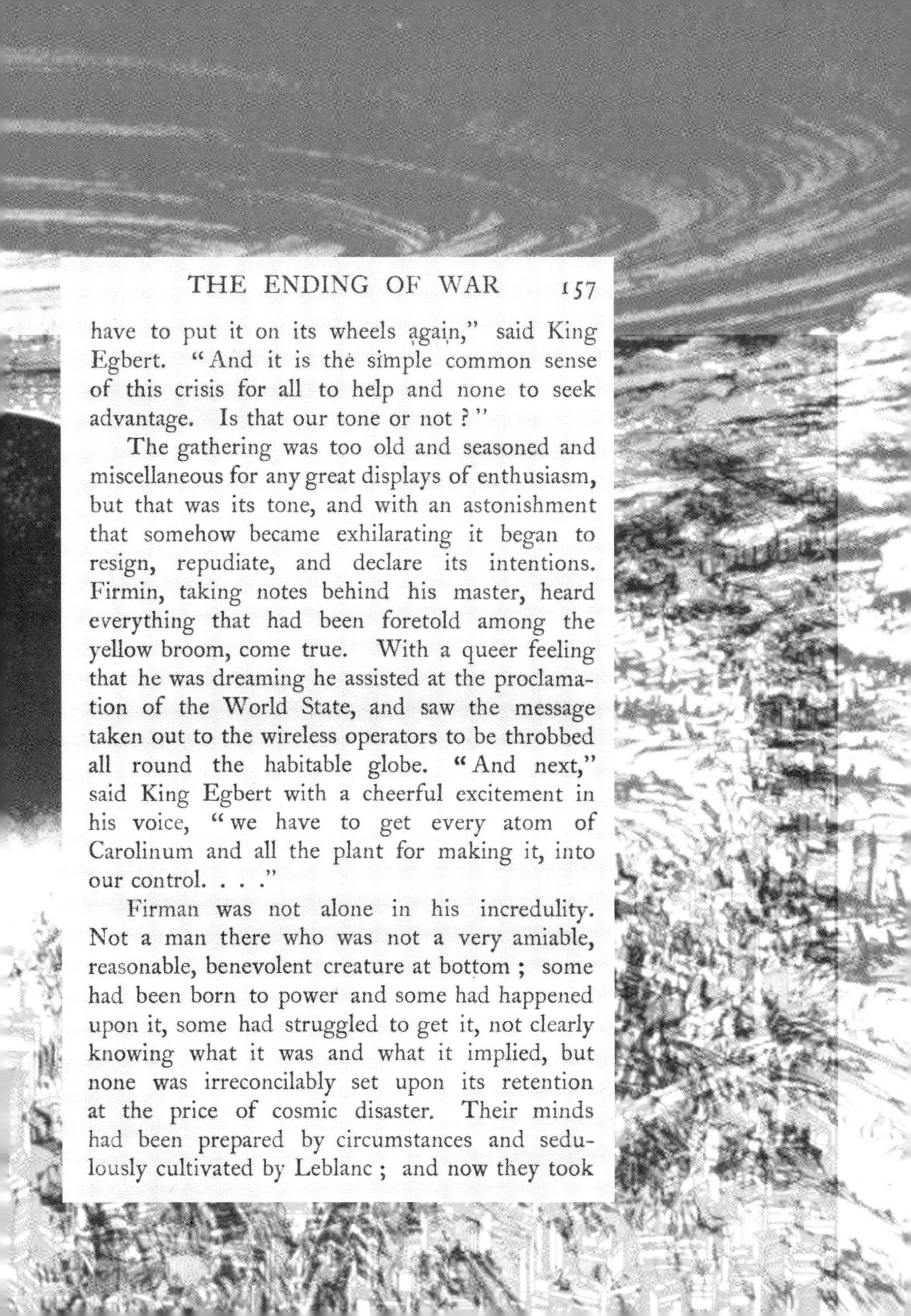

have to put it on its wheels again," said King Egbert. "And it is the simple common sense of this crisis for all to help and none to seek advantage. Is that our tone or not ?"

The gathering was too old and seasoned and miscellaneous for any great displays of enthusiasm, but that was its tone, and with an astonishment that somehow became exhilarating it began to resign, repudiate, and declare its intentions. Firmin, taking notes behind his master, heard everything that had been foretold among the yellow broom, come true. With a queer feeling that he was dreaming he assisted at the proclamation of the World State, and saw the message taken out to the wireless operators to be throbbed all round the habitable globe. "And next," said King Egbert with a cheerful excitement in his voice, "we have to get every atom of Carolinum and all the plant for making it, into our control. . . ."

Firman was not alone in his incredulity. Not a man there who was not a very amiable, reasonable, benevolent creature at bottom ; some had been born to power and some had happened upon it, some had struggled to get it, not clearly knowing what it was and what it implied, but none was irreconcilably set upon its retention at the price of cosmic disaster. Their minds had been prepared by circumstances and sedulously cultivated by Leblanc ; and now they took

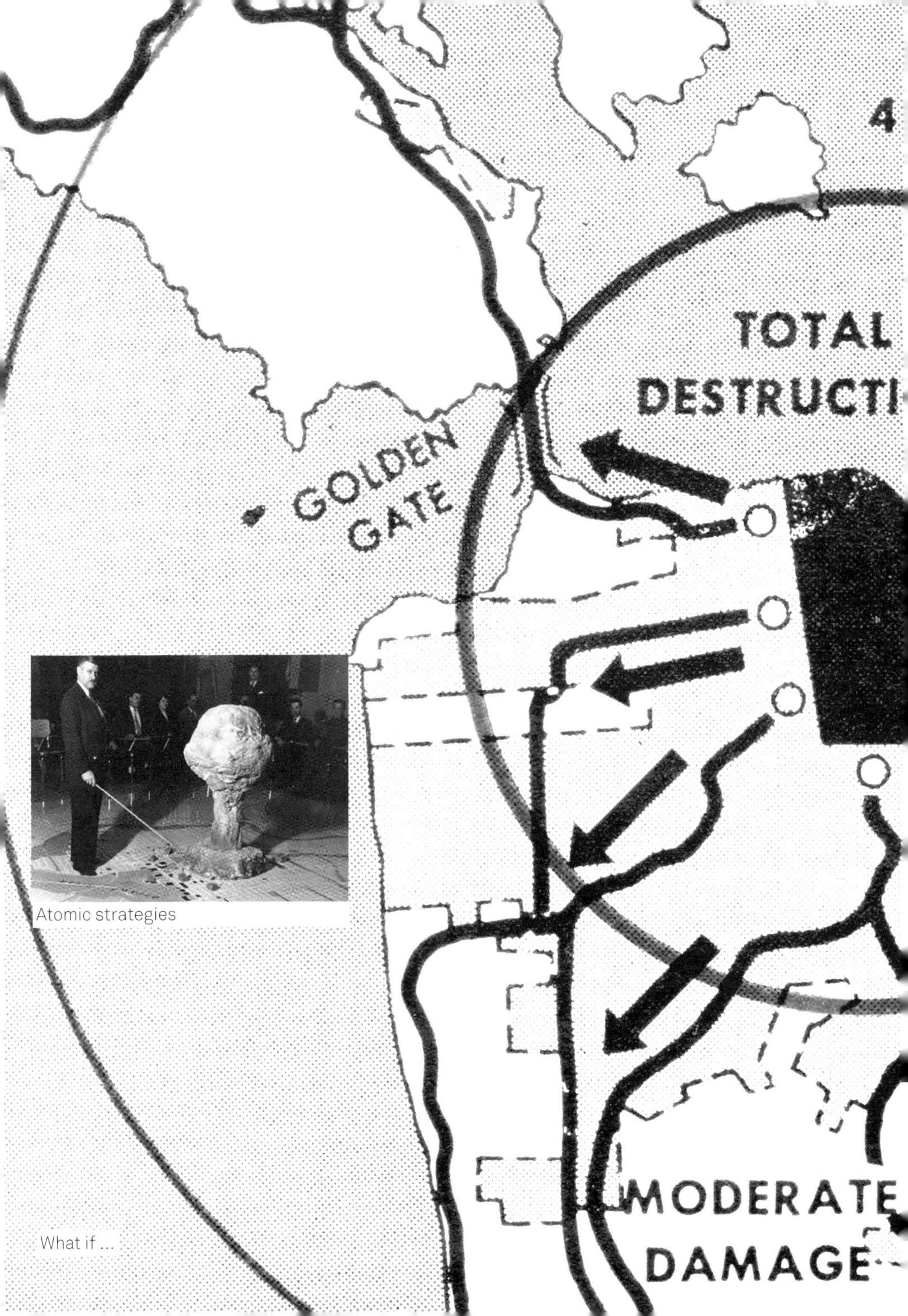

Atomic strategies

What if ...

the broad obvious road along which King Egbert was leading them, with a mingled conviction of strangeness and necessity. Things went very smoothly; the King of Italy explained the arrangements that had been made for the protection of the camp from any fantastic attack; a couple of thousand of aeroplanes, each carrying a sharpshooter, guarded them, and there was an excellent system of relays and at night all the sky would be searched by scores of lights, and the admirable Leblanc gave luminous reasons for their camping just where they were and going on with their administrative duties forthwith. He knew of this place because he had happened upon it when holiday-making with Madame Leblanc twenty years and more ago. "There is very simple fare at present," he explained, "on account of the disturbed state of the countries about us. But we have excellent fresh milk, good red wine, beef, bread, salad and lemons. . . . . In a few days I hope to place things in the hands of a more efficient caterer. . . ."

The members of the new world government dined at three long tables on trestles, and down the middle of these tables Leblanc in spite of the barrenness of his menu had contrived to have a great multitude of beautiful roses. There was similar accommodation for the secretaries and attendants at a lower level down the mountain. The assembly dined as it had debated, in the open air, and over the dark crags to the west the glowing June sunset shone upon the banquet. There was no precedency now among the ninety-three, and King Egbert found himself between a pleasant little Japanese stranger in spectacles and his cousin of Central Europe, and opposite a great Bengali leader and the President of the United States of America. Beyond the Japanese was Holsten the old chemist, and Leblanc was a little way down the other side.

The king was still cheerfully talkative and abounded in ideas. He fell presently into an amiable controversy with the American, who seemed to feel a lack of impressiveness in the occasion.

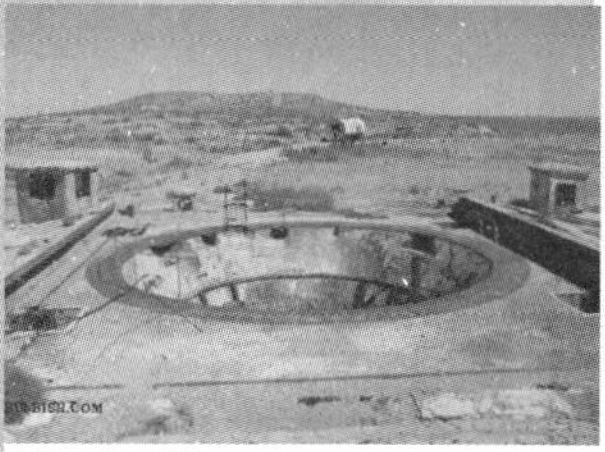
Missile silo

It was ever the Transatlantic tendency, due no doubt to the necessity of handling public questions in a bulky and striking manner, to over-emphasise and over-accentuate, and the president was touched by his national failing. He suggested now that there should be a new era, starting from that day as the first day of the first year.

The king demurred.

"From this day forth, sir, man enters upon his heritage," said the American.

"Man," said the king, "is always entering upon his heritage. You Americans have a

Effects of radiation on the human body

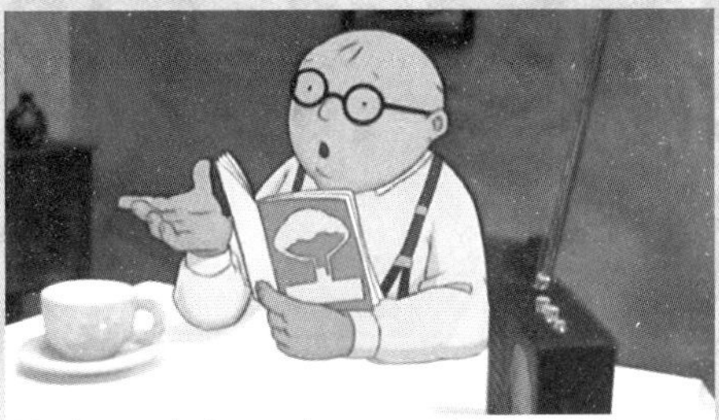

The hazard of a nuclear attack (UK 1986)

peculiar weakness for anniversaries—if you will forgive me saying so. Yes—I accuse you of a lust for dramatic effect. Everything is happening always, but you want to say this or this is the real instant in time and subordinate all the others to it."

The American said something about an epoch-making day.

"But surely," said the king, "you don't want us to condemn all humanity to a world-wide annual Fourth of June for ever and ever more. On account of this harmless necessary day of declarations. No conceivable day could ever deserve that. Ah! you do not know, as I do, the devastations of the memorable. My poor grandparents were—*rubricated.* The worst of these huge celebrations is that they break up the dignified succession of one's contemporary emotions. They interrupt. They set back. Suddenly out come the flags and fireworks and the old enthusiasms are furbished up—and it's sheer destruction of the proper thing that ought to be going on. Sufficient unto the day is the celebration thereof. Let the dead past bury its dead. You see in regard to the calendar I am for democracy and you are for aristocracy. All things I hold are august and have a right to be lived through on their merits. No day should be sacrificed on the grave of departed events. What do you think of it, Wilhelm?"

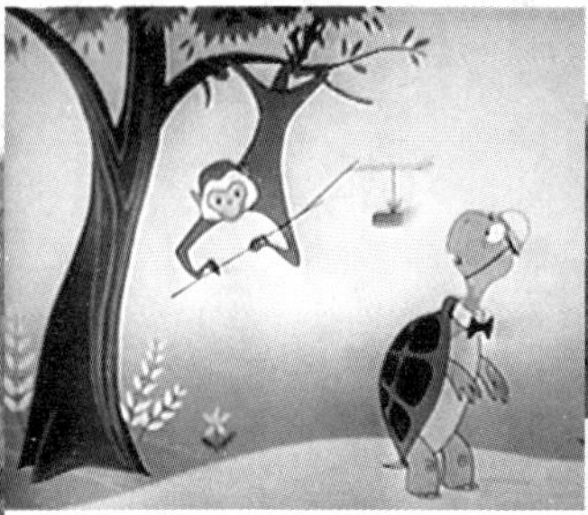

The know-how-turtle (US 1951)

"For the noble, yes, all days should be noble."

"Exactly my position," said the king, and felt pleased at what he had been saying.

And then since the American pressed his idea the king contrived to shift the talk from the question of celebrating the epoch they were making to the question of the probabilities that lay ahead. Here everyone became diffident. They could see the world unified and at peace, but what detail was to follow from that unification they seemed indisposed to discuss. This diffidence struck the king as remarkable. He plunged upon the possibilities of science. All the huge expenditure that had hitherto gone into unproductive naval and military preparations, must now, he declared, place research upon a new footing. "Where one man worked we will have a thousand." He appealed to Holsten. "We have only begun to peep into these possibilities," he said. "You at any rate have sounded the vaults of the treasure house."

"They are unfathomable," smiled Holsten.

"Man," said the American with a manifest resolve to justify and reinstate himself after the flickering contradictions of the king, "Man, I say, is only beginning to enter upon his heritage."

"Tell us some of the things you believe we shall presently learn, give us an idea of the things we may presently do," said the king to Holsten.

Advising the householder on protection against nuclear attack, 1963

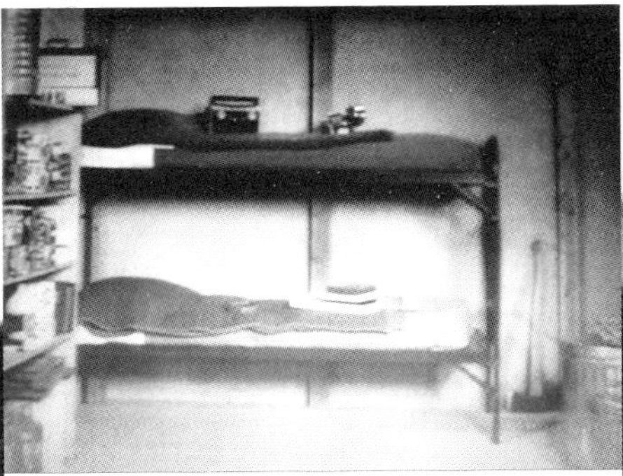

Good shelter, 1950s

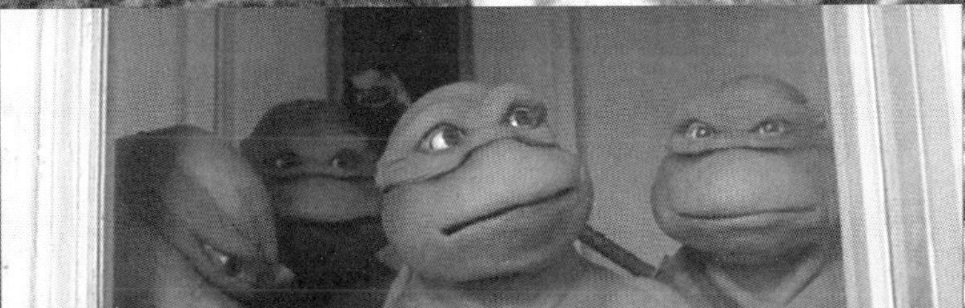

Friendly atomic mutants (US, HK 1990)

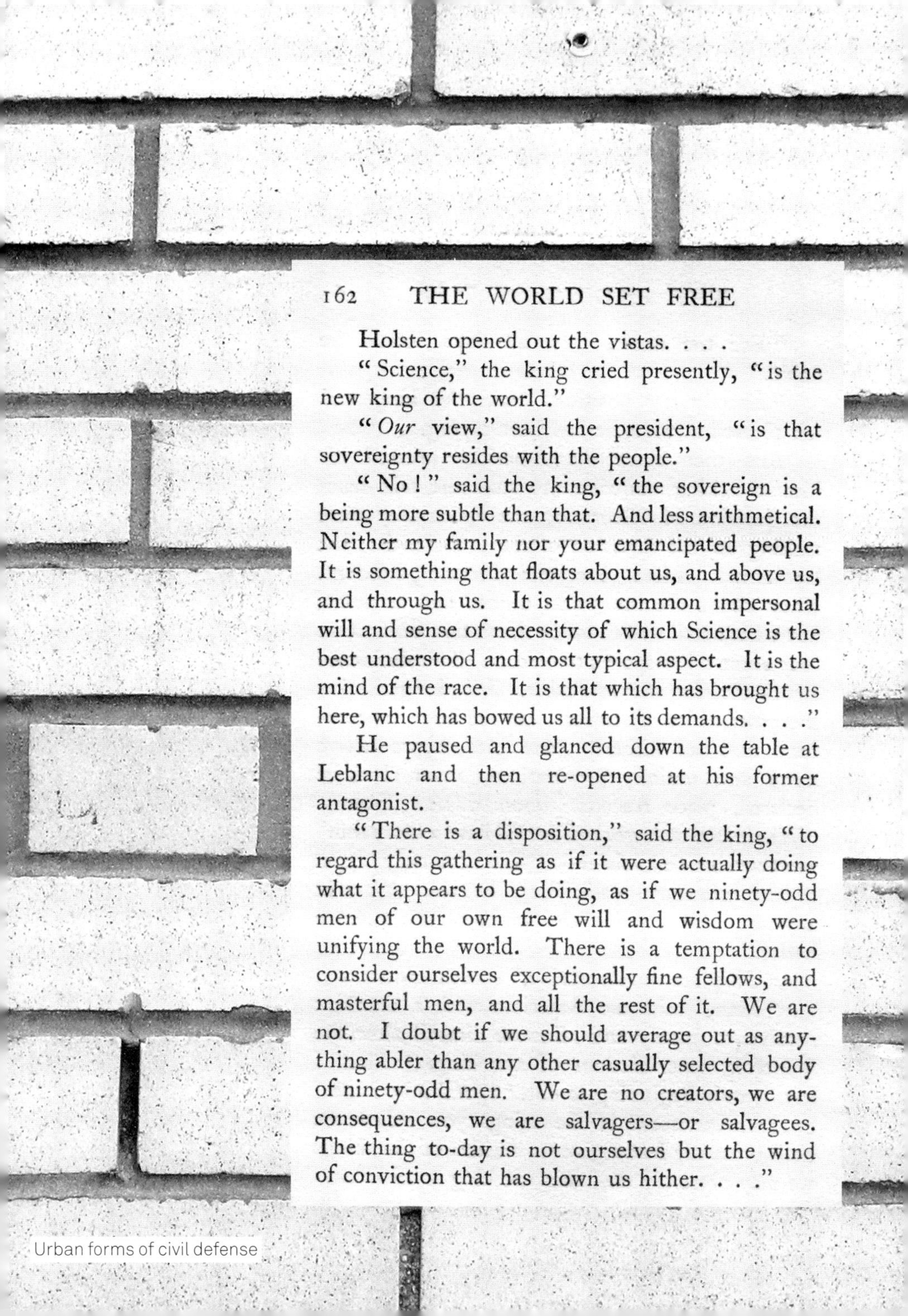

Holsten opened out the vistas. . . .

"Science," the king cried presently, "is the new king of the world."

"*Our* view," said the president, "is that sovereignty resides with the people."

"No!" said the king, "the sovereign is a being more subtle than that. And less arithmetical. Neither my family nor your emancipated people. It is something that floats about us, and above us, and through us. It is that common impersonal will and sense of necessity of which Science is the best understood and most typical aspect. It is the mind of the race. It is that which has brought us here, which has bowed us all to its demands. . . ."

He paused and glanced down the table at Leblanc and then re-opened at his former antagonist.

"There is a disposition," said the king, "to regard this gathering as if it were actually doing what it appears to be doing, as if we ninety-odd men of our own free will and wisdom were unifying the world. There is a temptation to consider ourselves exceptionally fine fellows, and masterful men, and all the rest of it. We are not. I doubt if we should average out as anything abler than any other casually selected body of ninety-odd men. We are no creators, we are consequences, we are salvagers—or salvagees. The thing to-day is not ourselves but the wind of conviction that has blown us hither. . . ."

Urban forms of civil defense

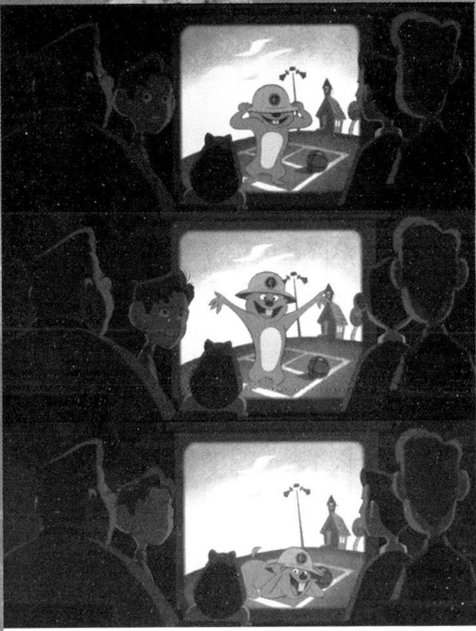

The Civil Defense educational program (US 1999)

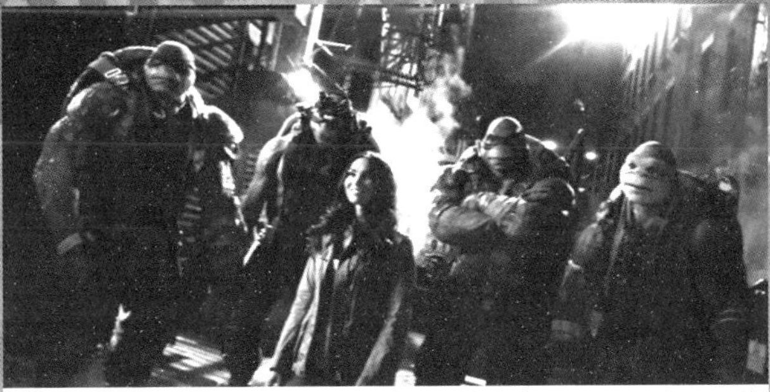

Atomic mutants on the streets of New York (US, HK, CN, CA 2016)

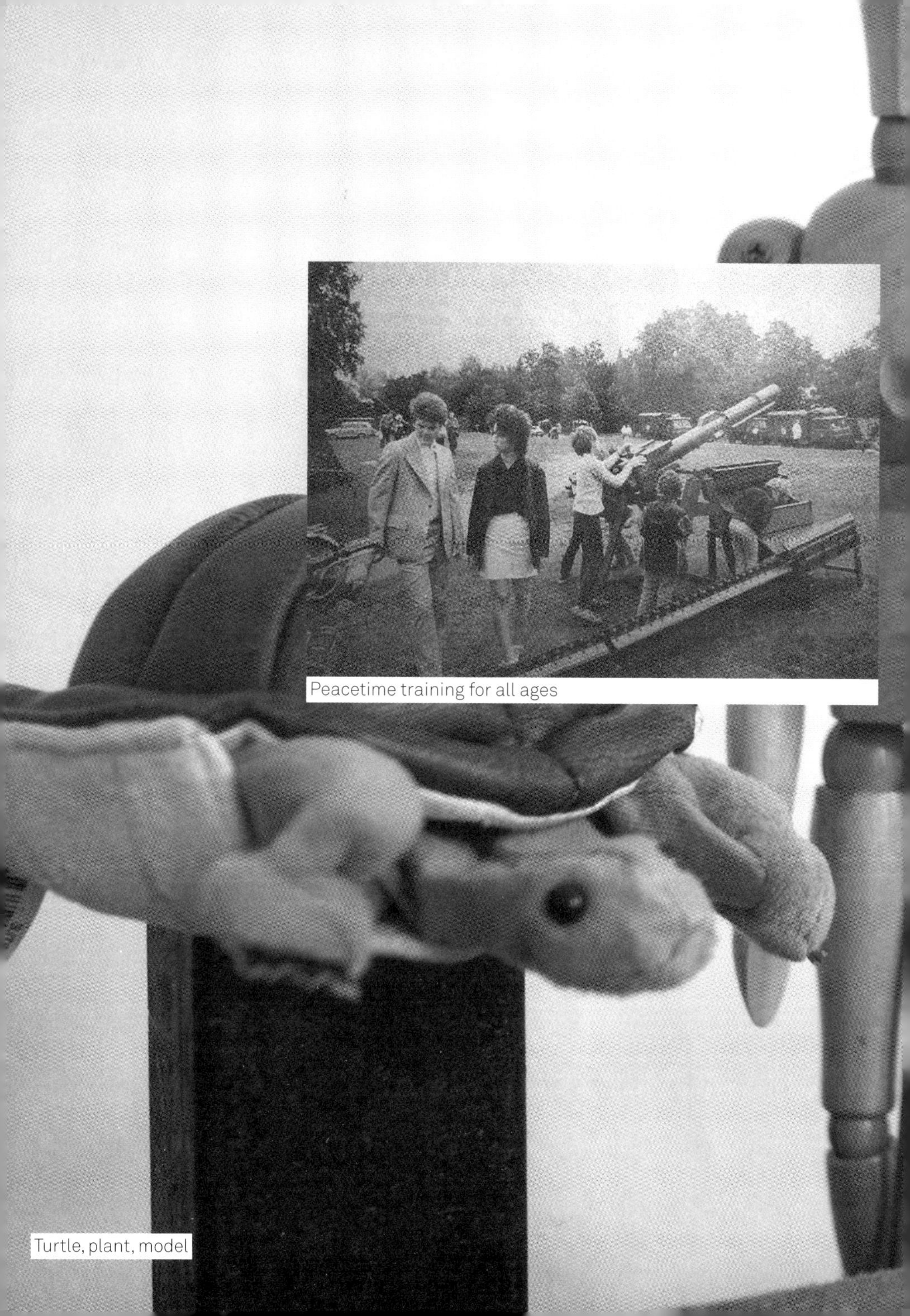

Peacetime training for all ages

Turtle, plant, model

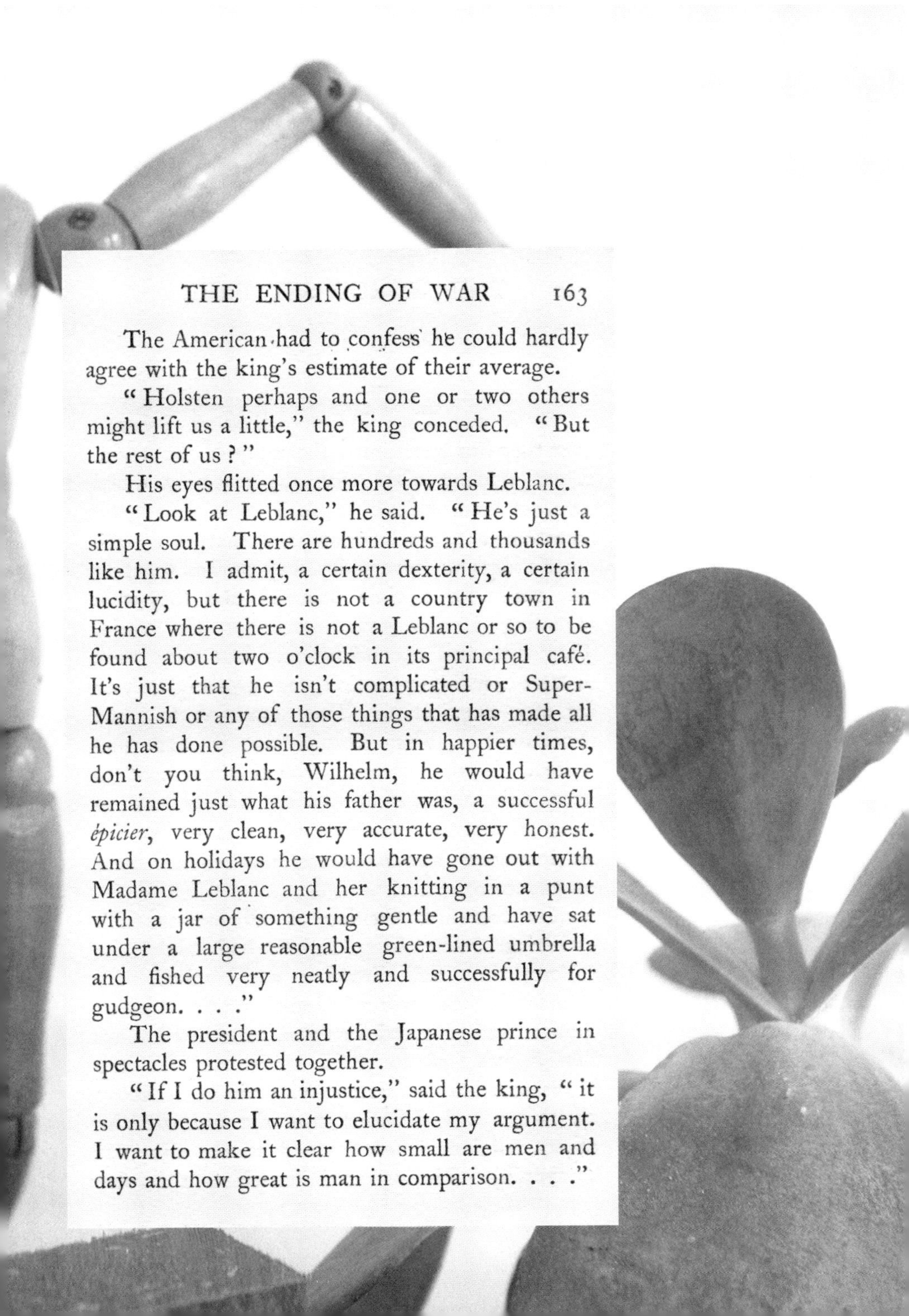

The American had to confess he could hardly agree with the king's estimate of their average.

"Holsten perhaps and one or two others might lift us a little," the king conceded. "But the rest of us?"

His eyes flitted once more towards Leblanc.

"Look at Leblanc," he said. "He's just a simple soul. There are hundreds and thousands like him. I admit, a certain dexterity, a certain lucidity, but there is not a country town in France where there is not a Leblanc or so to be found about two o'clock in its principal café. It's just that he isn't complicated or Super-Mannish or any of those things that has made all he has done possible. But in happier times, don't you think, Wilhelm, he would have remained just what his father was, a successful *épicier*, very clean, very accurate, very honest. And on holidays he would have gone out with Madame Leblanc and her knitting in a punt with a jar of something gentle and have sat under a large reasonable green-lined umbrella and fished very neatly and successfully for gudgeon. . . ."

The president and the Japanese prince in spectacles protested together.

"If I do him an injustice," said the king, "it is only because I want to elucidate my argument. I want to make it clear how small are men and days and how great is man in comparison. . . ."

§ 4

So it was King Egbert talked at Brissago after they had proclaimed the unity of the world. Every evening after that the assembly dined together and talked at their ease and grew accustomed to each other and sharpened each other's ideas, and every day they worked together and really for a time believed that they were inventing a new government for the world. They discussed a constitution. But there were matters needing attention too urgently to wait for any constitution. They attended to these incidentally. The constitution it was that waited. It was presently found convenient to keep the constitution waiting indefinitely as King Egbert had foreseen, and meanwhile with an increasing self-confidence, that council went on governing. . . .

On this first evening of all the council's gatherings, after King Egbert had talked for a long time and drunken and praised very abundantly the simple red wine of the country that Leblanc had procured for them, he fathered about him a group of congenial spirits and fell into a discourse upon simplicity, praising it above all things and declaring that the ultimate aim of art, religion, philosophy and science alike was to simplify. He instanced himself as a devotee

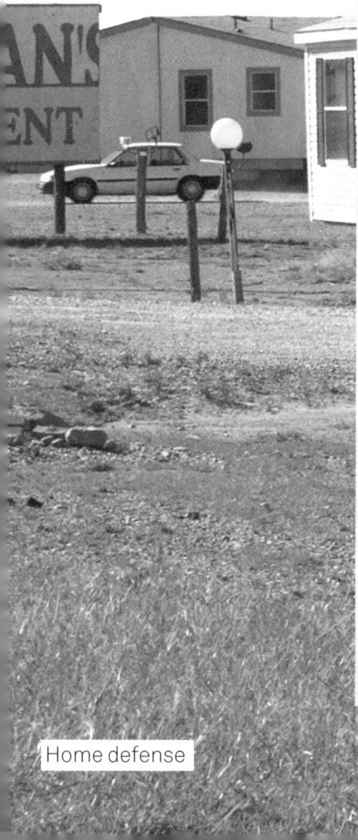

Home defense

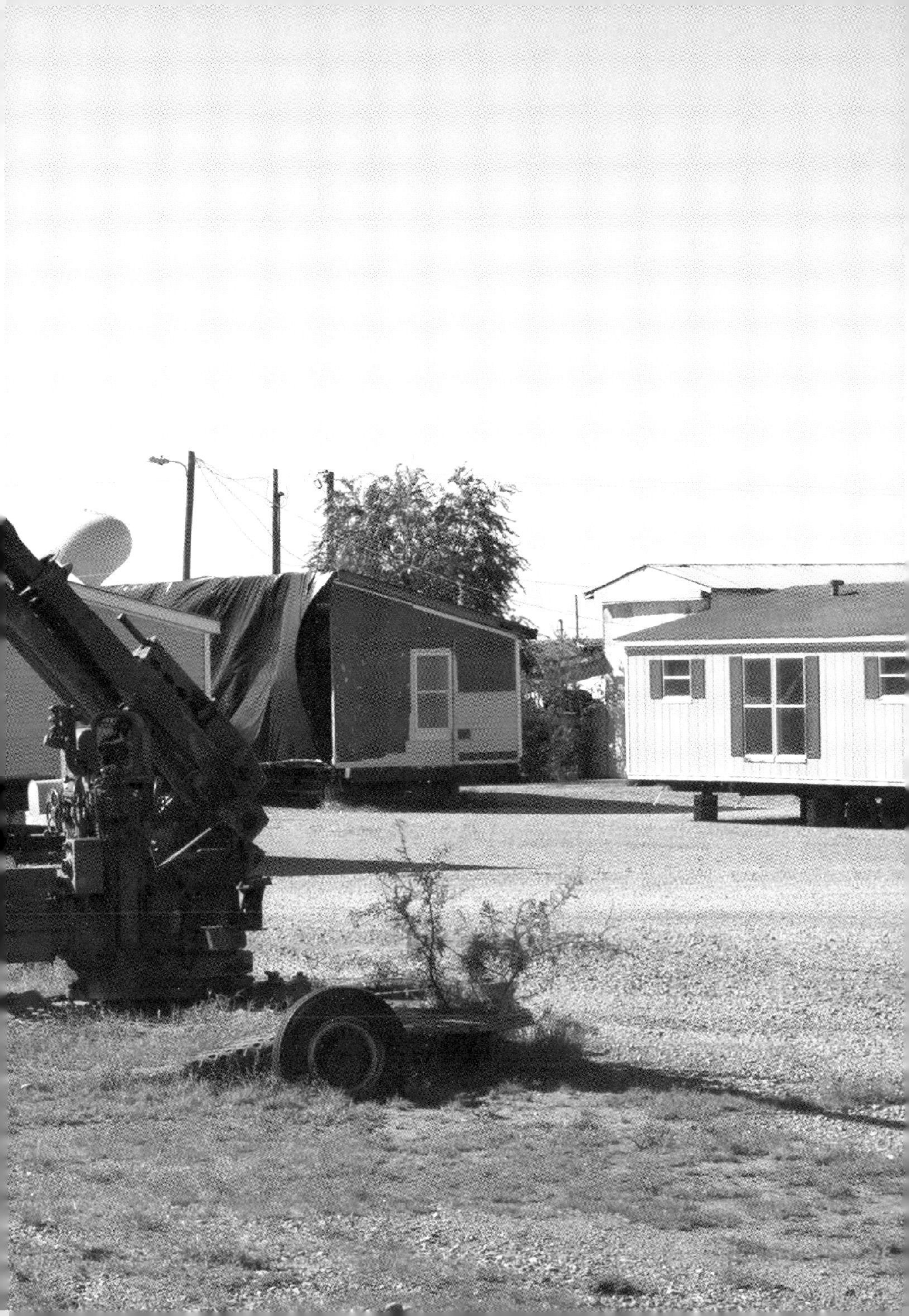

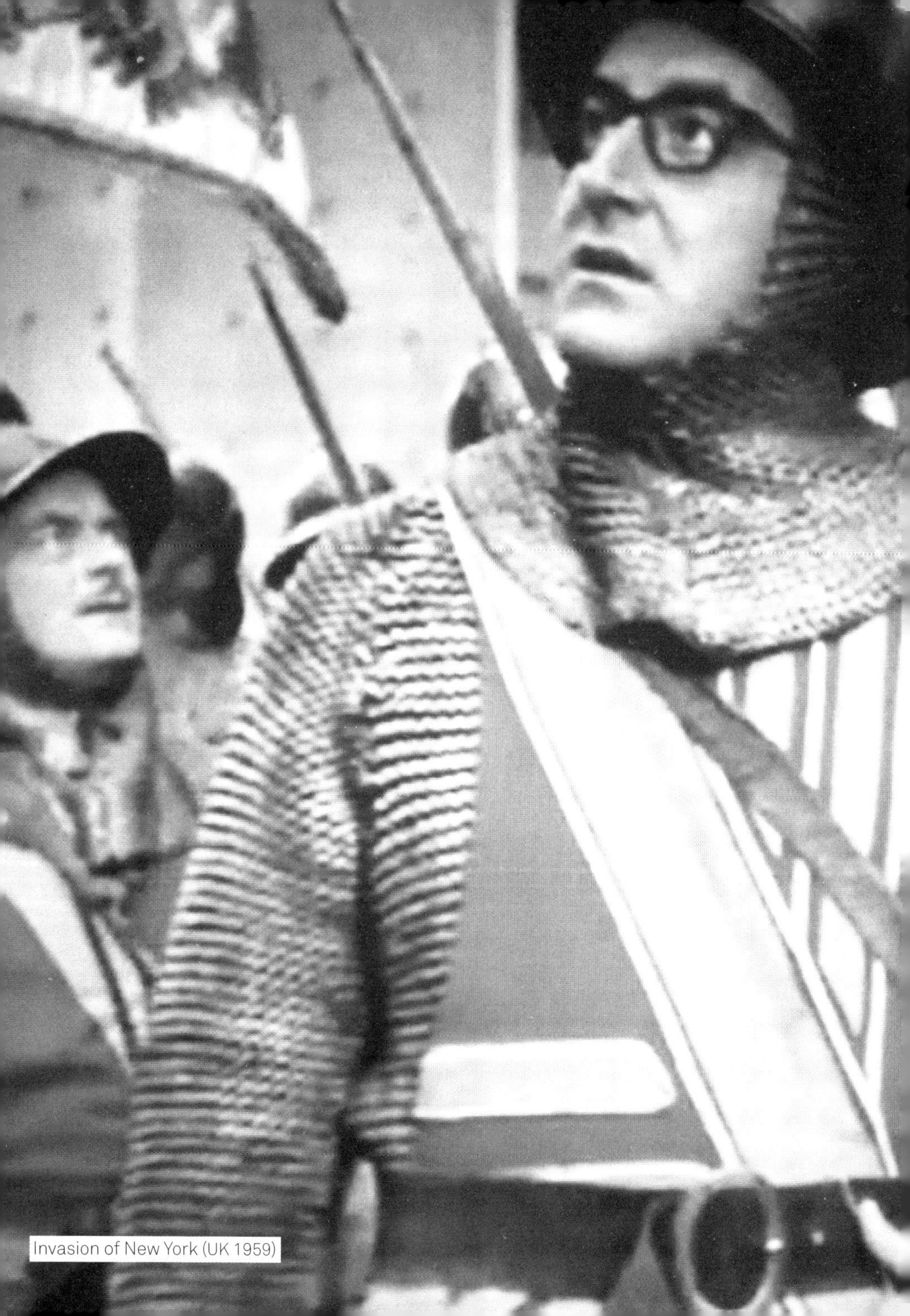

Invasion of New York (UK 1959)

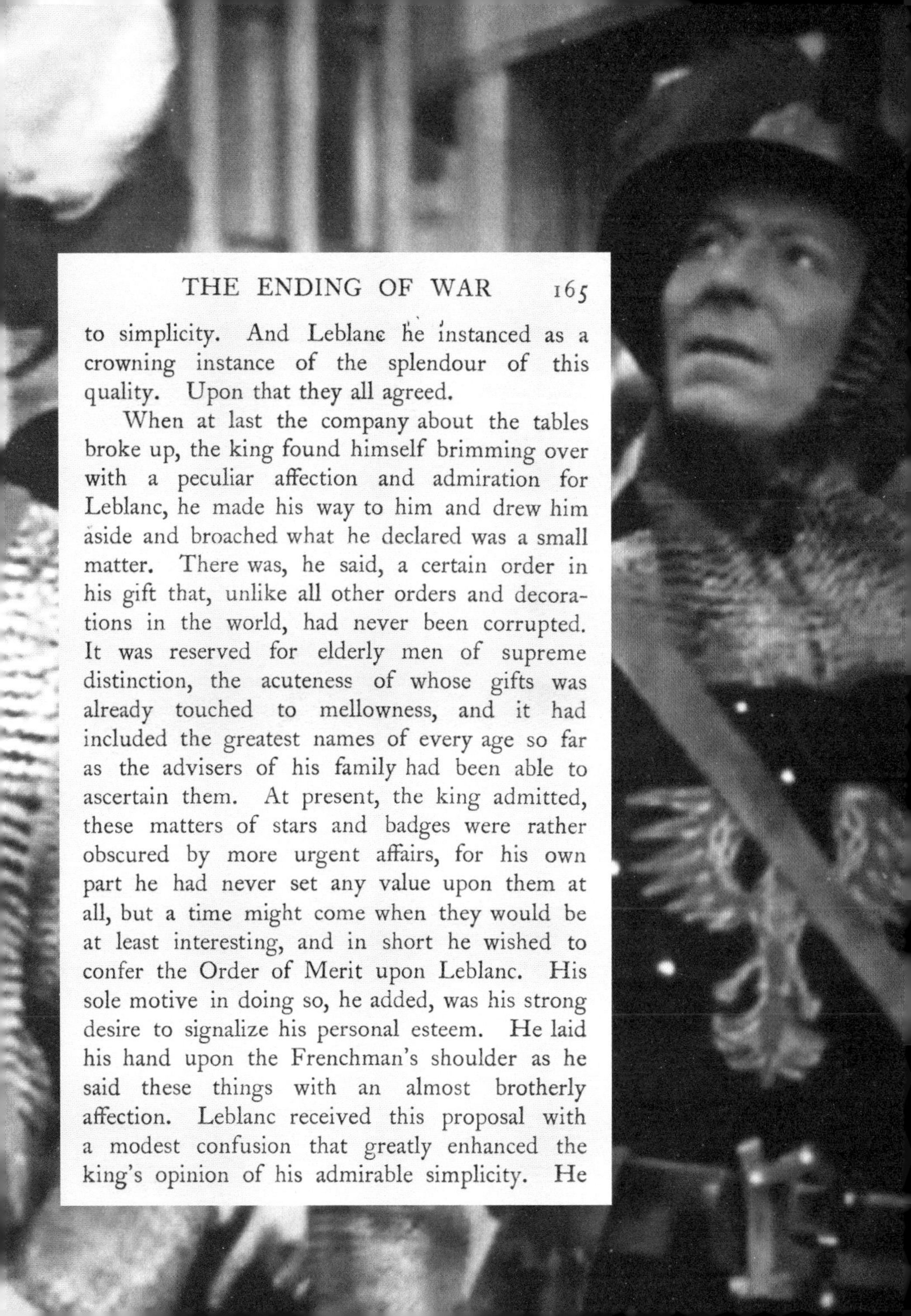

to simplicity. And Leblanc he instanced as a crowning instance of the splendour of this quality. Upon that they all agreed.

When at last the company about the tables broke up, the king found himself brimming over with a peculiar affection and admiration for Leblanc, he made his way to him and drew him aside and broached what he declared was a small matter. There was, he said, a certain order in his gift that, unlike all other orders and decorations in the world, had never been corrupted. It was reserved for elderly men of supreme distinction, the acuteness of whose gifts was already touched to mellowness, and it had included the greatest names of every age so far as the advisers of his family had been able to ascertain them. At present, the king admitted, these matters of stars and badges were rather obscured by more urgent affairs, for his own part he had never set any value upon them at all, but a time might come when they would be at least interesting, and in short he wished to confer the Order of Merit upon Leblanc. His sole motive in doing so, he added, was his strong desire to signalize his personal esteem. He laid his hand upon the Frenchman's shoulder as he said these things with an almost brotherly affection. Leblanc received this proposal with a modest confusion that greatly enhanced the king's opinion of his admirable simplicity. He

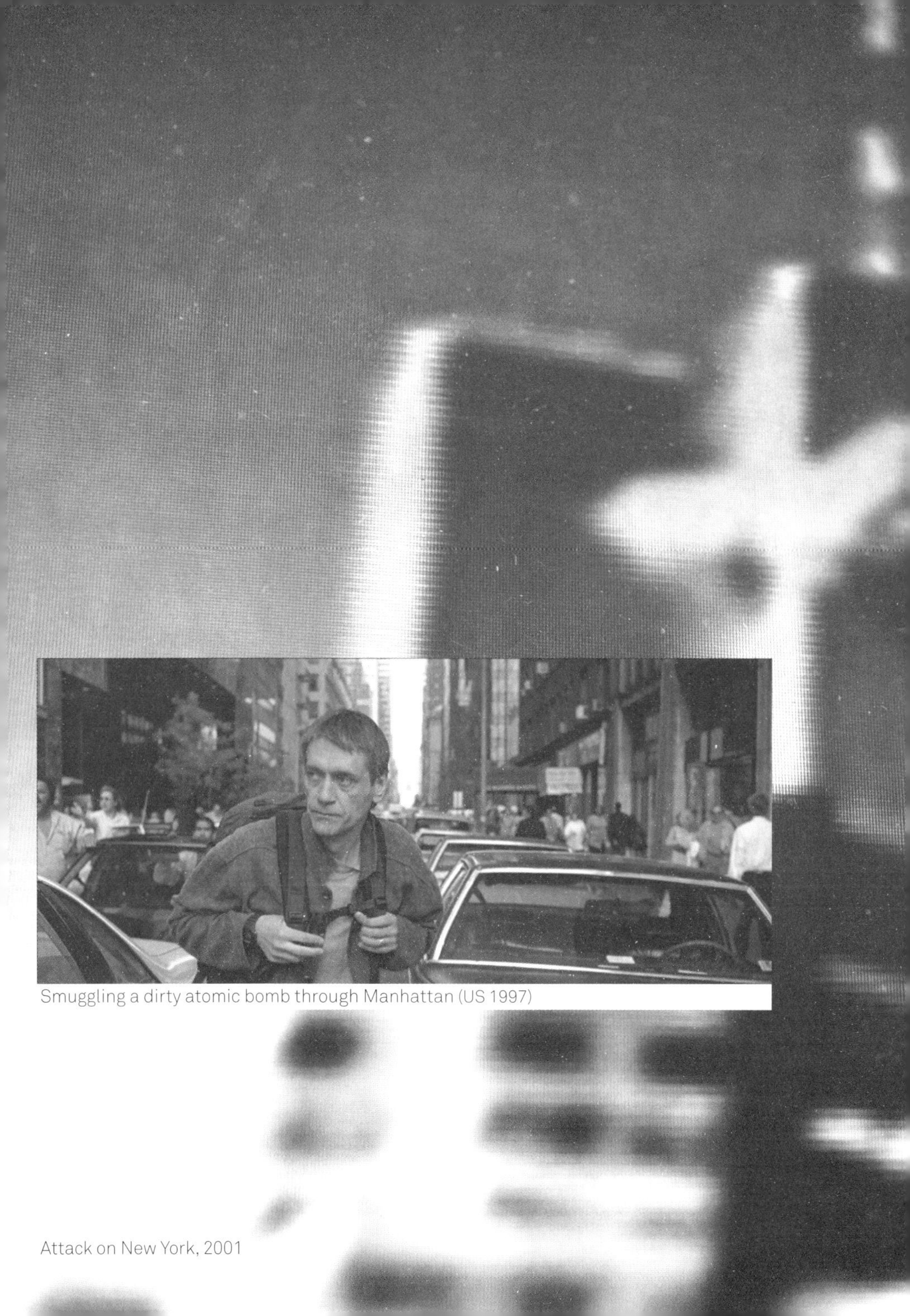

Smuggling a dirty atomic bomb through Manhattan (US 1997)

Attack on New York, 2001

pointed out that eager as he was to snatch at the proffered distinction, it might at the present stage appear invidious, and he therefore suggested that the conferring of it should be postponed until it could be made the crown and conclusion of his services. The king was unable to shake this resolution, and the two men parted with expressions of mutual esteem.

The king then summoned Firmin in order to make a short note of a number of things that he had said during the day. But after about twenty minutes' work the sweet sleepiness of the mountain air overcame him, and he dismissed Firmin and went to bed and fell asleep at once, and slept with extreme satisfaction. He had had an active agreeable day.

§ 5

The establishment of the new order that was thus so humanly begun, was, if one measures it by the standard of any preceding age, a rapid progress. The fighting spirit of the world was exhausted. Only here or there did fierceness linger. For long decades the combative side in human affairs had been monstrously exaggerated by the accidents of political separation. This now became luminously plain. An enormous proportion of the force that sustained armaments had been nothing more aggressive

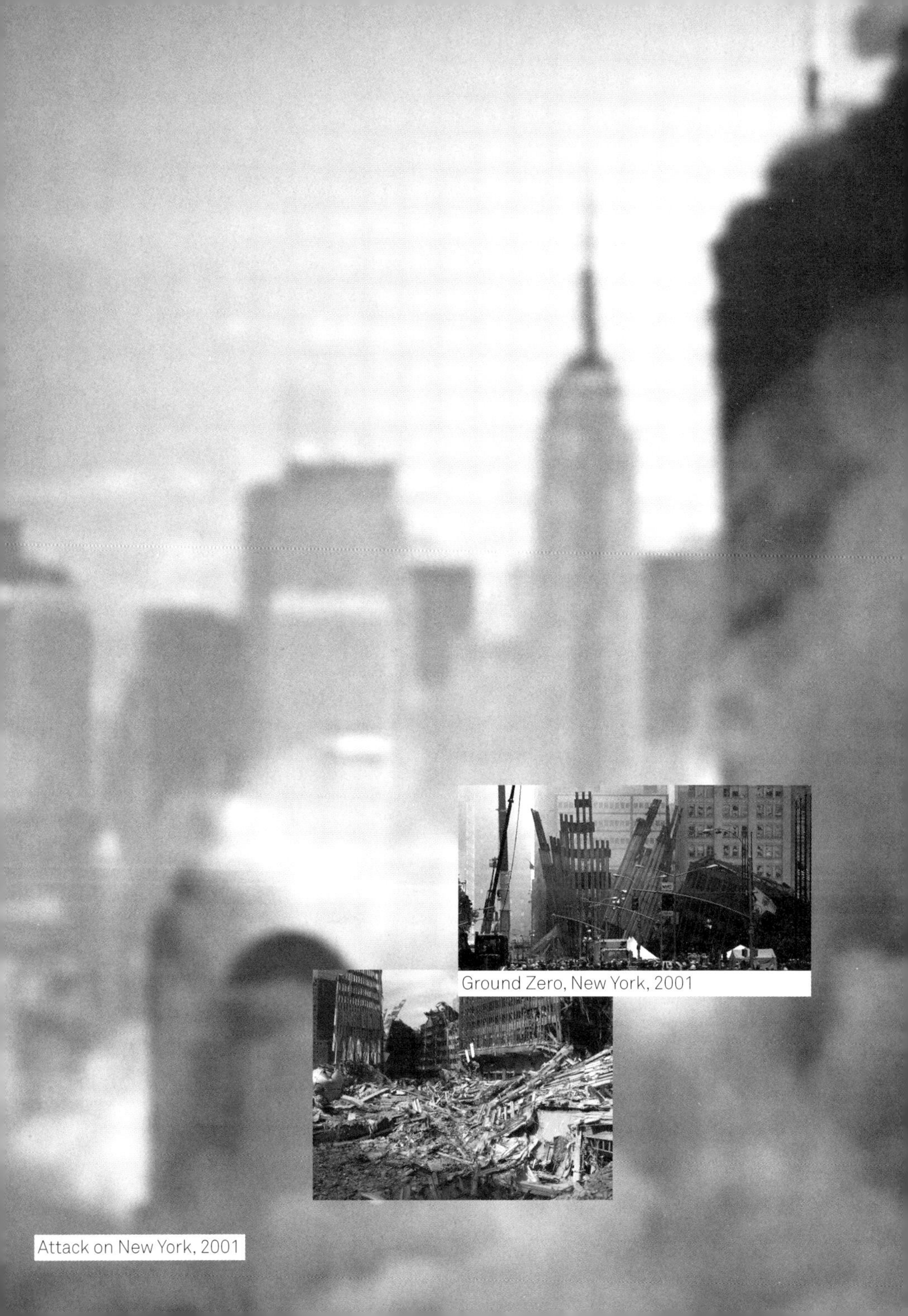

Ground Zero, New York, 2001

Attack on New York, 2001

than the fear of war and warlike neighbours. It is doubtful if any large section of the men actually enlisted for fighting ever at any time really hungered and thirsted for bloodshed and danger. That kind of appetite was probably never very strong in the species after the savage stage was past. The army was a profession, in which killing had become a disagreeable possibility rather than an eventful certainty. If one reads the old newspapers and periodicals of that time, which did so much to keep militarism alive, one finds very little about glory and adventure and a constant harping on the disagreeableness of invasion and subjugation. In one word militarism was funk. The belligerent resolution of the armed Europe of the twentieth century was the resolution of a fiercely frightened sheep to plunge. And now that its weapons were exploding in its hands Europe was only too eager to drop them, and abandon this fancied refuge of violence.

For a time the whole world had been shocked into frankness ; nearly all the clever people who had hitherto sustained the ancient belligerent separations had now been brought to realize the need for simplicity of attitude and openness of mind ; and in this atmosphere of moral renascence, there was little attempt to get negotiable advantages out of resistance to the new order. Human beings are foolish enough

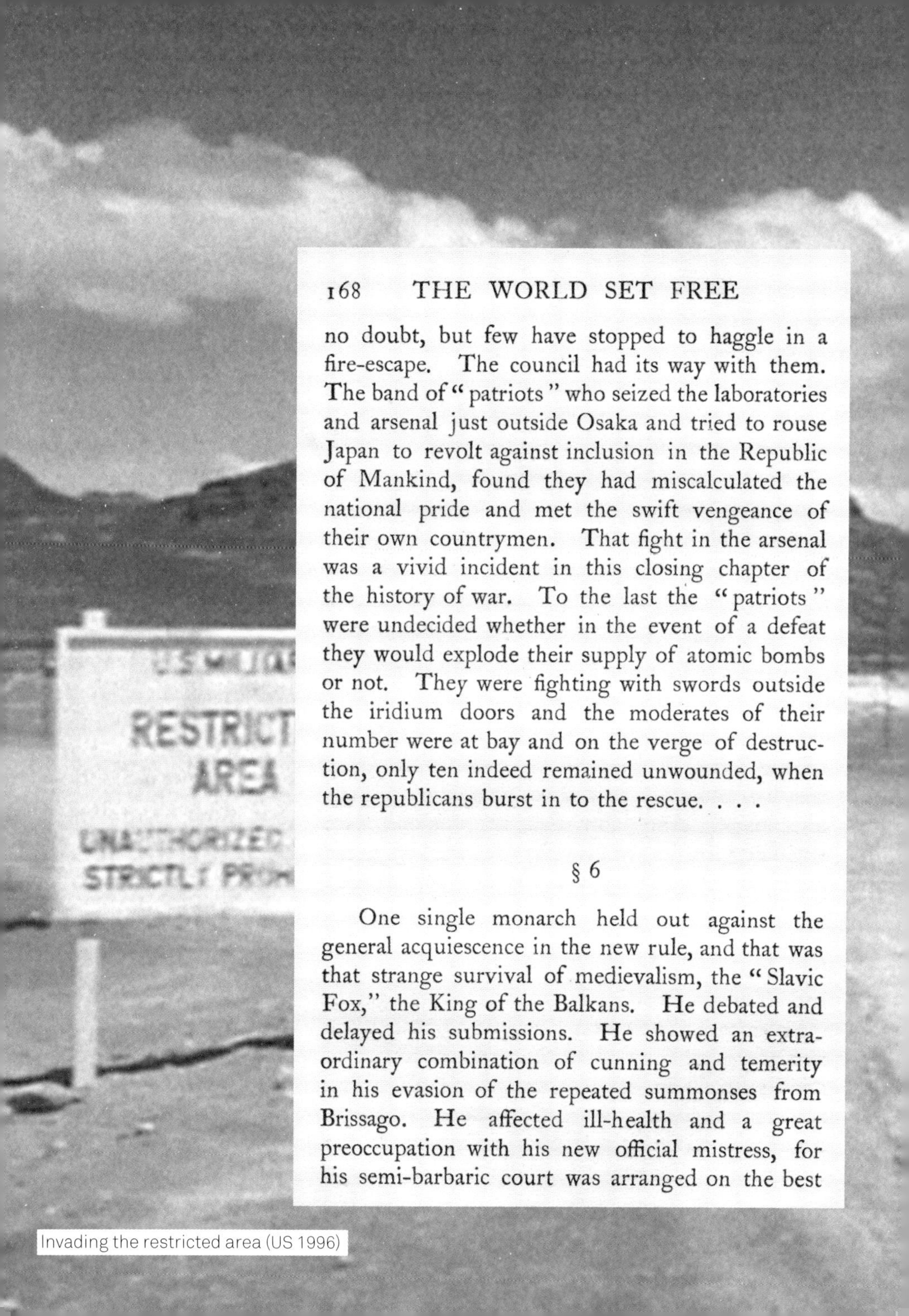

Invading the restricted area (US 1996)

no doubt, but few have stopped to haggle in a fire-escape. The council had its way with them. The band of "patriots" who seized the laboratories and arsenal just outside Osaka and tried to rouse Japan to revolt against inclusion in the Republic of Mankind, found they had miscalculated the national pride and met the swift vengeance of their own countrymen. That fight in the arsenal was a vivid incident in this closing chapter of the history of war. To the last the "patriots" were undecided whether in the event of a defeat they would explode their supply of atomic bombs or not. They were fighting with swords outside the iridium doors and the moderates of their number were at bay and on the verge of destruction, only ten indeed remained unwounded, when the republicans burst in to the rescue. . . .

§ 6

One single monarch held out against the general acquiescence in the new rule, and that was that strange survival of medievalism, the "Slavic Fox," the King of the Balkans. He debated and delayed his submissions. He showed an extraordinary combination of cunning and temerity in his evasion of the repeated summonses from Brissago. He affected ill-health and a great preoccupation with his new official mistress, for his semi-barbaric court was arranged on the best

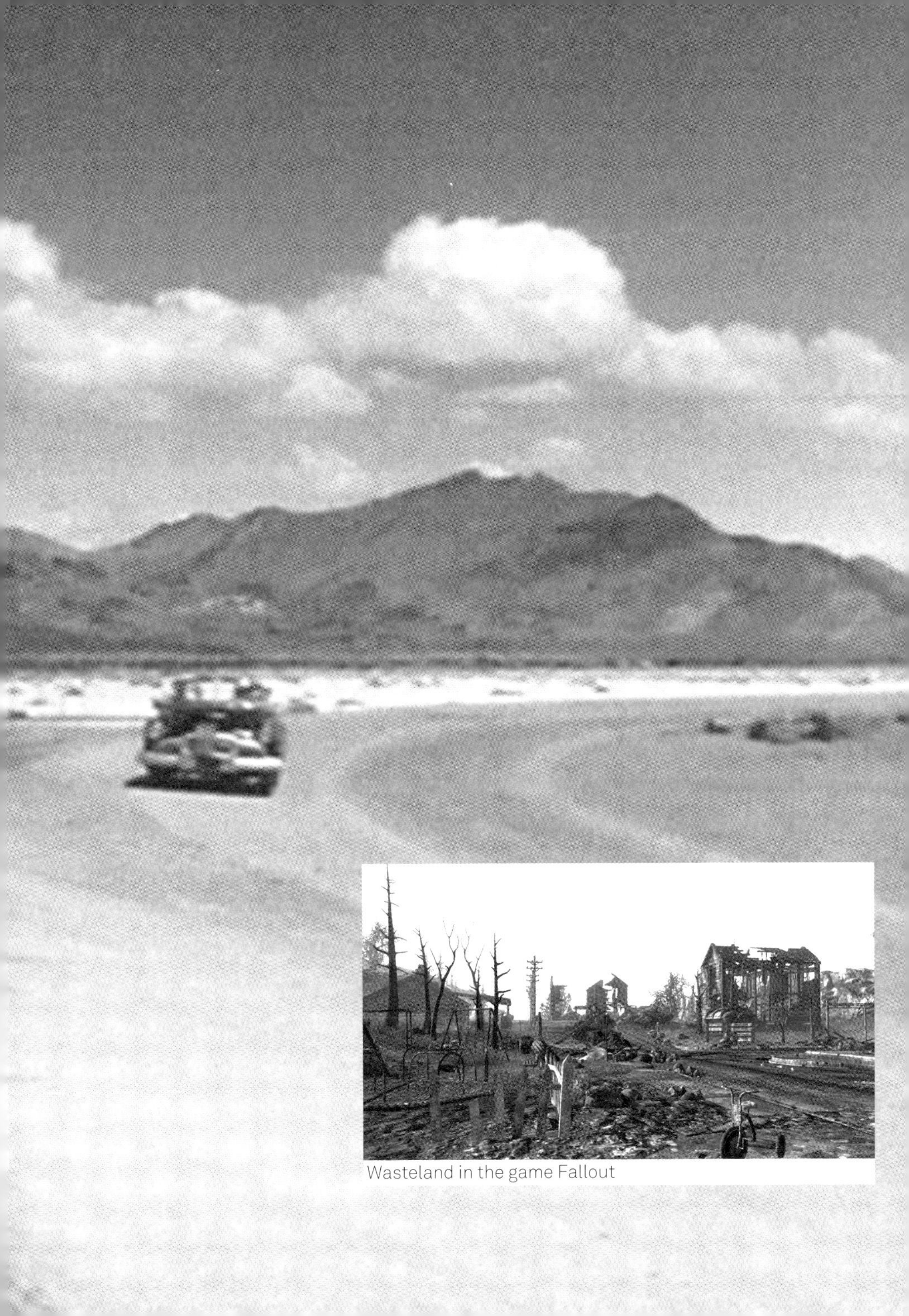

Wasteland in the game Fallout

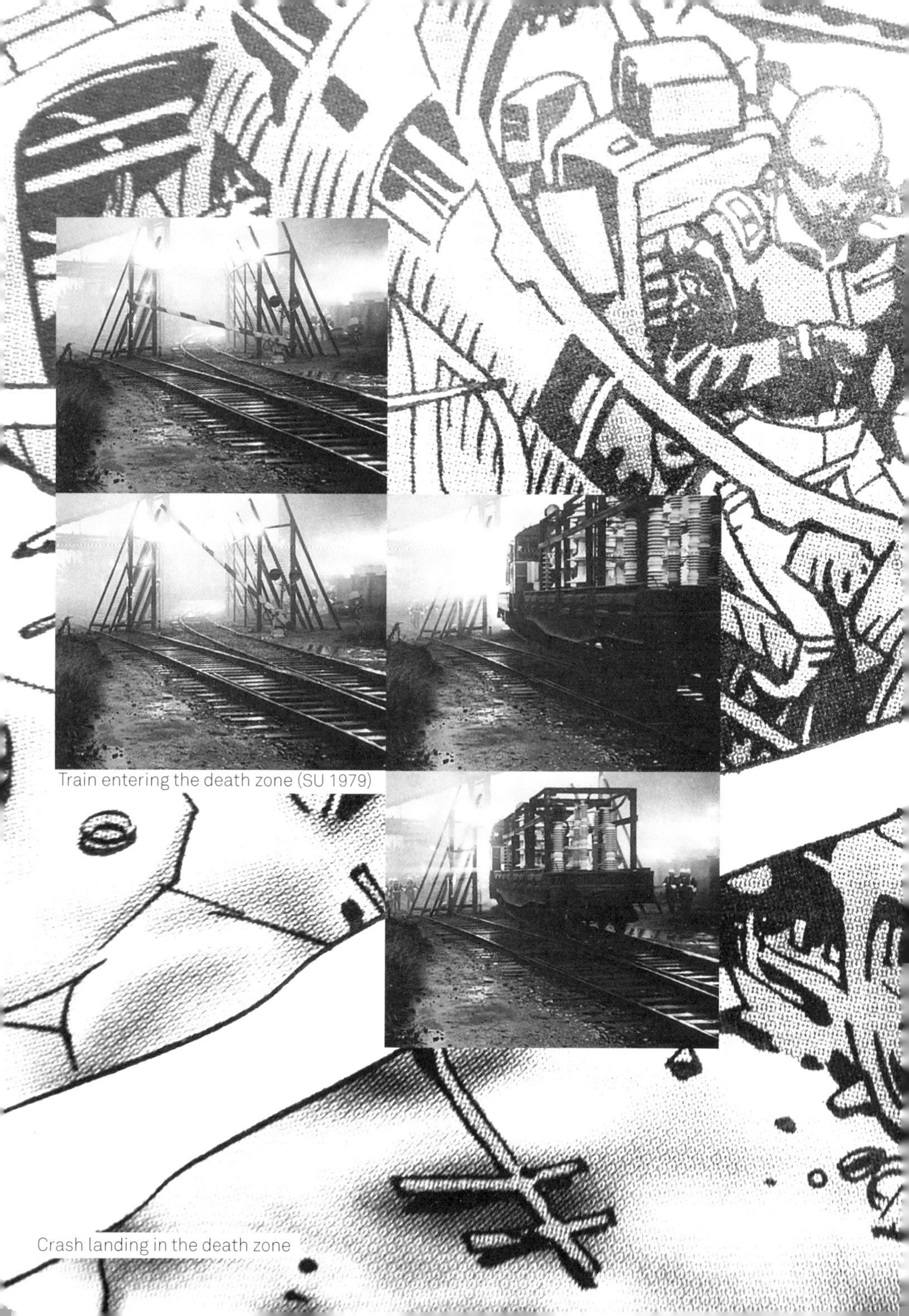

Train entering the death zone (SU 1979)

Crash landing in the death zone

romantic models. His tactics were ably seconded by Doctor Pestovitch, his chief minister. Failing to establish his claims to complete independence King Ferdinand Charles annoyed the conference by a proposal to be treated as a protected state. Finally he professed an unconvincing submission, and put a mass of obstacles in the way of the transfer of his national officials to the new government. In these things he was enthusiastically supported by his subjects, still for the most part an illiterate peasantry, passionately if confusedly patriotic and so far with no practical knowledge of the effect of atomic bombs. More particularly he retained control of all the Balkan aeroplanes.

For once the extreme naïveté of Leblanc seems to have been mitigated by duplicity. He went on with the general pacification of the world as if the Balkan submission was made in absolute good faith, and he announced the disbandment of the force of aeroplanes that hitherto guarded the council at Brissago upon the approaching fifteenth of July. But instead he doubled the number upon duty on that eventful day, and made various arrangements for their disposition. He consulted certain experts, and when he took King Egbert into his confidence there was something in his neat and explicit foresight that brought back to that ex-monarch's mind his half-forgotten fantasy of Leblanc as a fisherman under a green umbrella.

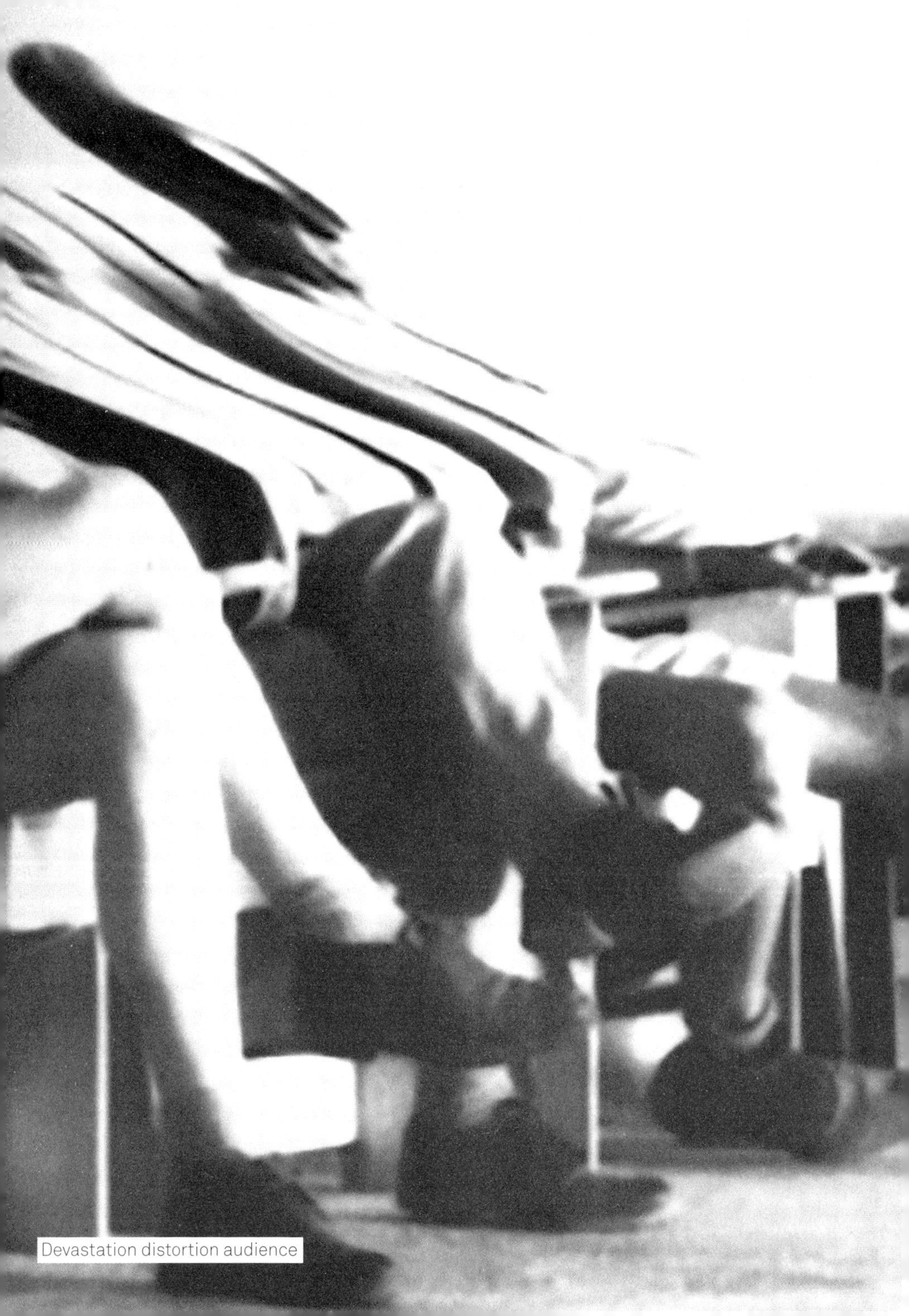

Devastation distortion audience

About five o'clock in the morning of the seventeenth of July one of the outer sentinels of the Brissago fleet, which was soaring unobtrusively over the lower end of the lake of Garda, sighted and hailed a strange aeroplane that was flying westward and, failing to get a satisfactory reply, set its wireless apparatus talking and gave chase. A swarm of consorts appeared very promptly over the westward mountains, and before the unknown aeroplane had sighted Como, it had a dozen eager attendants closing in upon it. Its driver seems to have hesitated, dropped down among the mountains and then turned southward in flight, only to find an intercepting biplane sweeping across his bows. He then went round into the eye of the rising sun, and passed within a hundred yards of his original pursuer.

The sharpshooter therein opened fire at once, and showed an intelligent grasp of the situation by disabling the passenger first. The man at the wheel must have heard his companion cry out behind him, but he was too intent on getting away to waste even a glance behind. Twice after that he must have heard shots. He let his engine go, he crouched down, and for twenty minutes he must have steered in the continual expectation of a bullet. It never came, and when at last he glanced round three great planes were close upon him, and his companion, thrice hit, lay dead across his bombs. His followers manifestly did not mean either to upset or shoot him, but inexorably they drove him down, down. At last he was curving and flying a hundred yards or less over the level fields of rice and maize. Ahead of him and dark against the morning sunrise was a village with a very tall and slender campanile and a line of cable bearing metal standards that he could not clear. He stopped his engine abruptly and dropped flat. He may have hoped to get at the bombs when he came down, but his pitiless pursuers drove right over him and shot him as he fell.

Three other aeroplanes curved down and came to rest amidst grass close by the smashed machine. Their passengers descended, and ran holding their light rifles in their hands towards the débris and the two dead men. The coffin-shaped box that had occupied the centre of the machine had broken, and three black objects, each with two handles like the ears of a pitcher, lay peacefully amidst the litter.

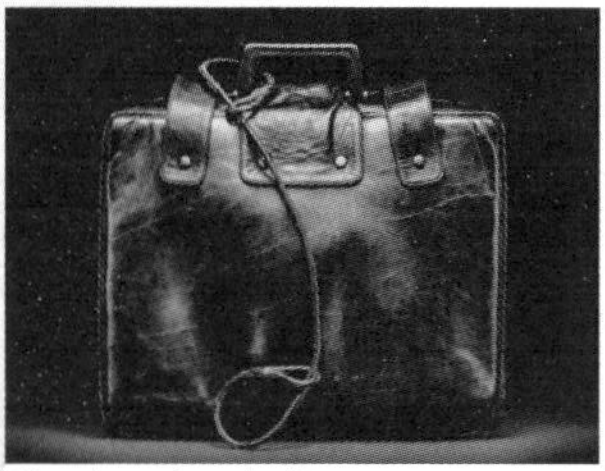
Nuclear football

These objects were so tremendously important in the eyes of their captors that they disregarded the two dead men who lay bloody and broken amidst the wreckage as they might have disregarded dead frogs by a country pathway.

"By God," cried the first. "Here they are!"

"And unbroken!" said the second.

"I've never seen the things before," said the first.

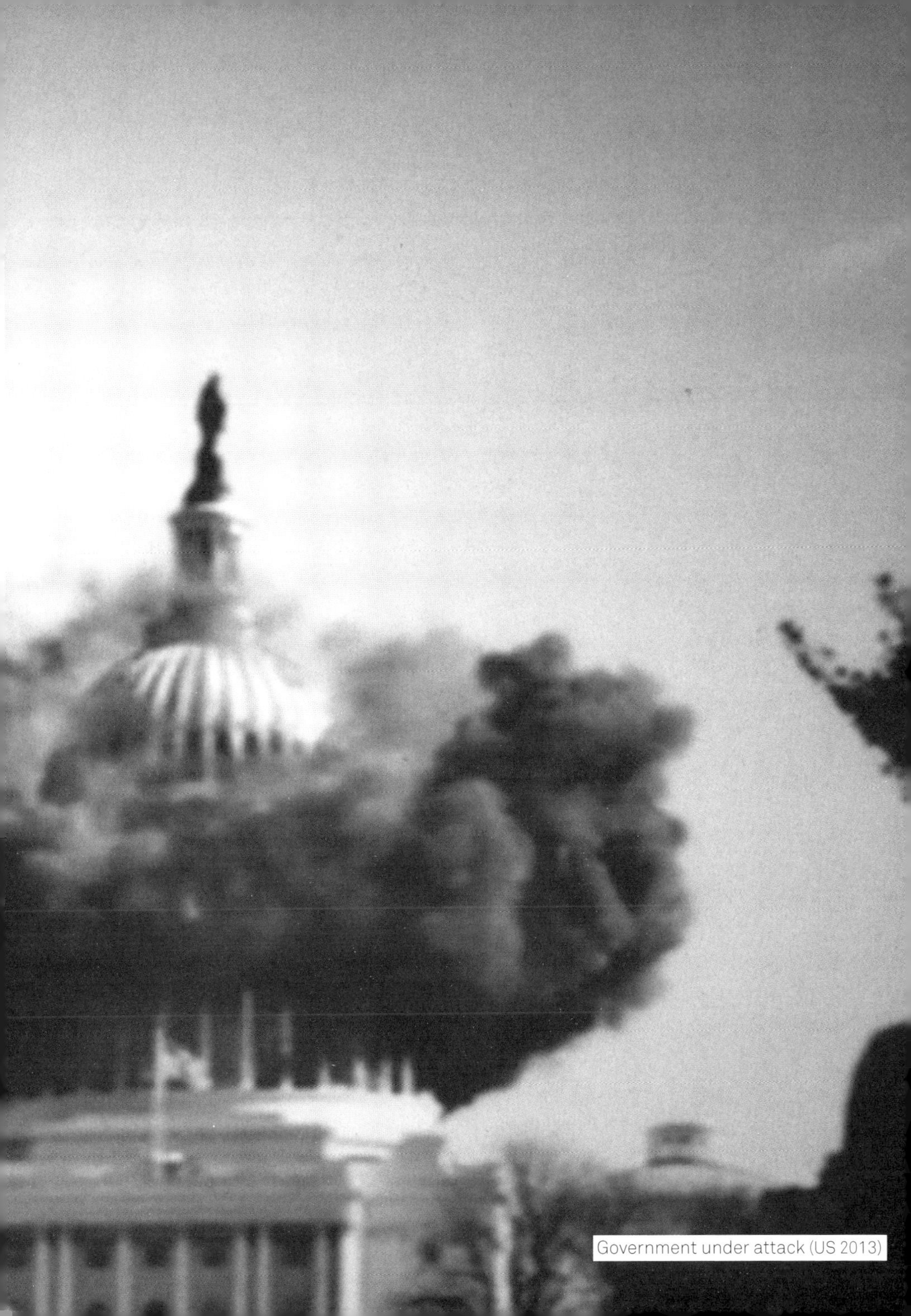

Government under attack (US 2013)

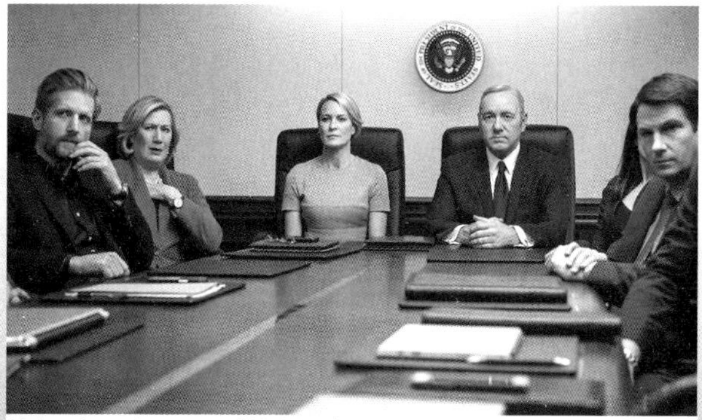

Fake situation room (US 2016)

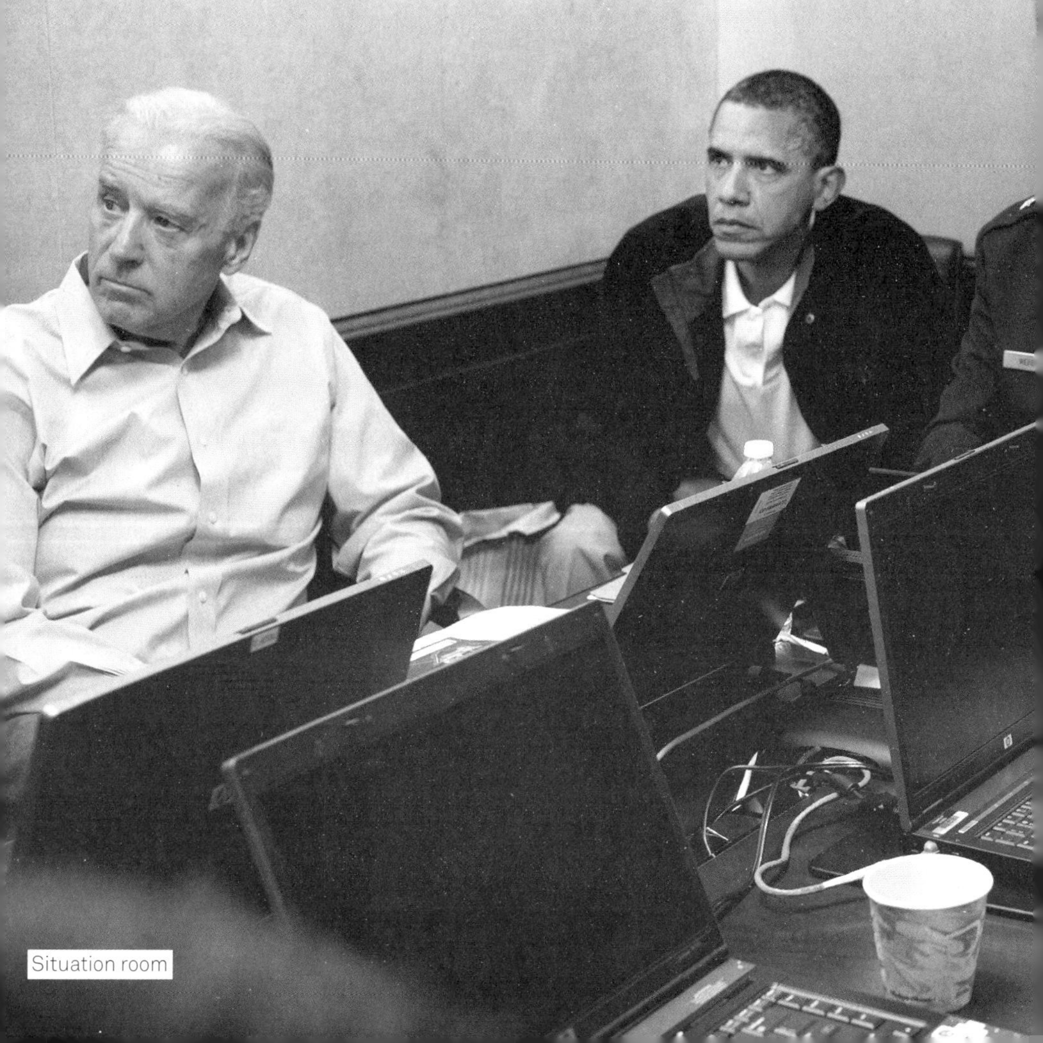

Situation room

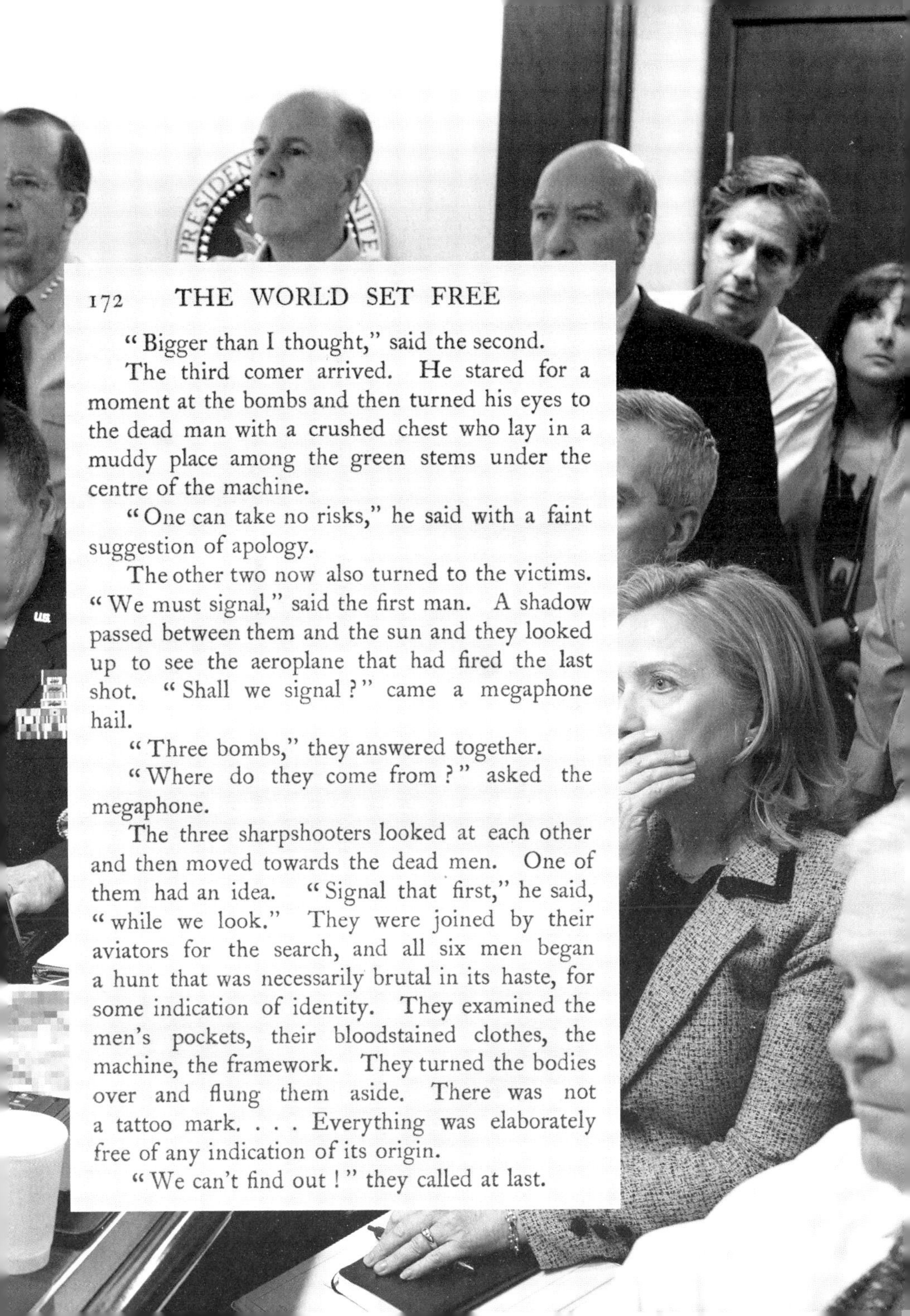

"Bigger than I thought," said the second.

The third comer arrived. He stared for a moment at the bombs and then turned his eyes to the dead man with a crushed chest who lay in a muddy place among the green stems under the centre of the machine.

"One can take no risks," he said with a faint suggestion of apology.

The other two now also turned to the victims. "We must signal," said the first man. A shadow passed between them and the sun and they looked up to see the aeroplane that had fired the last shot. "Shall we signal?" came a megaphone hail.

"Three bombs," they answered together.

"Where do they come from?" asked the megaphone.

The three sharpshooters looked at each other and then moved towards the dead men. One of them had an idea. "Signal that first," he said, "while we look." They were joined by their aviators for the search, and all six men began a hunt that was necessarily brutal in its haste, for some indication of identity. They examined the men's pockets, their bloodstained clothes, the machine, the framework. They turned the bodies over and flung them aside. There was not a tattoo mark. . . . Everything was elaborately free of any indication of its origin.

"We can't find out!" they called at last.

"Not a sign?"

"Not a sign."

"I'm coming down," said the man overhead. . . .

§ 7

The Slavic fox stood upon a metal balcony in his picturesque Art Nouveau palace that gave upon the precipice that overhung his bright little capital, and beside him stood Pestovitch, grizzled and cunning and now full of an ill-suppressed excitement. Behind them the window opened into a large room, richly decorated in aluminium and crimson enamel, across which the king, as he glanced ever and again over his shoulder with a gesture of enquiry, could see through the two open doors of a little azure walled antechamber the wireless operator in the turret working at his incessant transcription. Two pompously uniformed messengers waited listlessly in this apartment. The room was furnished with a stately dignity, and had in the middle of it a big green baize-covered table with the massive white metal inkpots and antiquated sandboxes natural to a new but romantic monarchy. It was the king's council chamber and about it now, in attitudes of suspended intrigue, stood the half dozen ministers who constituted his cabinet. They had been summoned for twelve o'clock, but

Defense condition (US 1983)

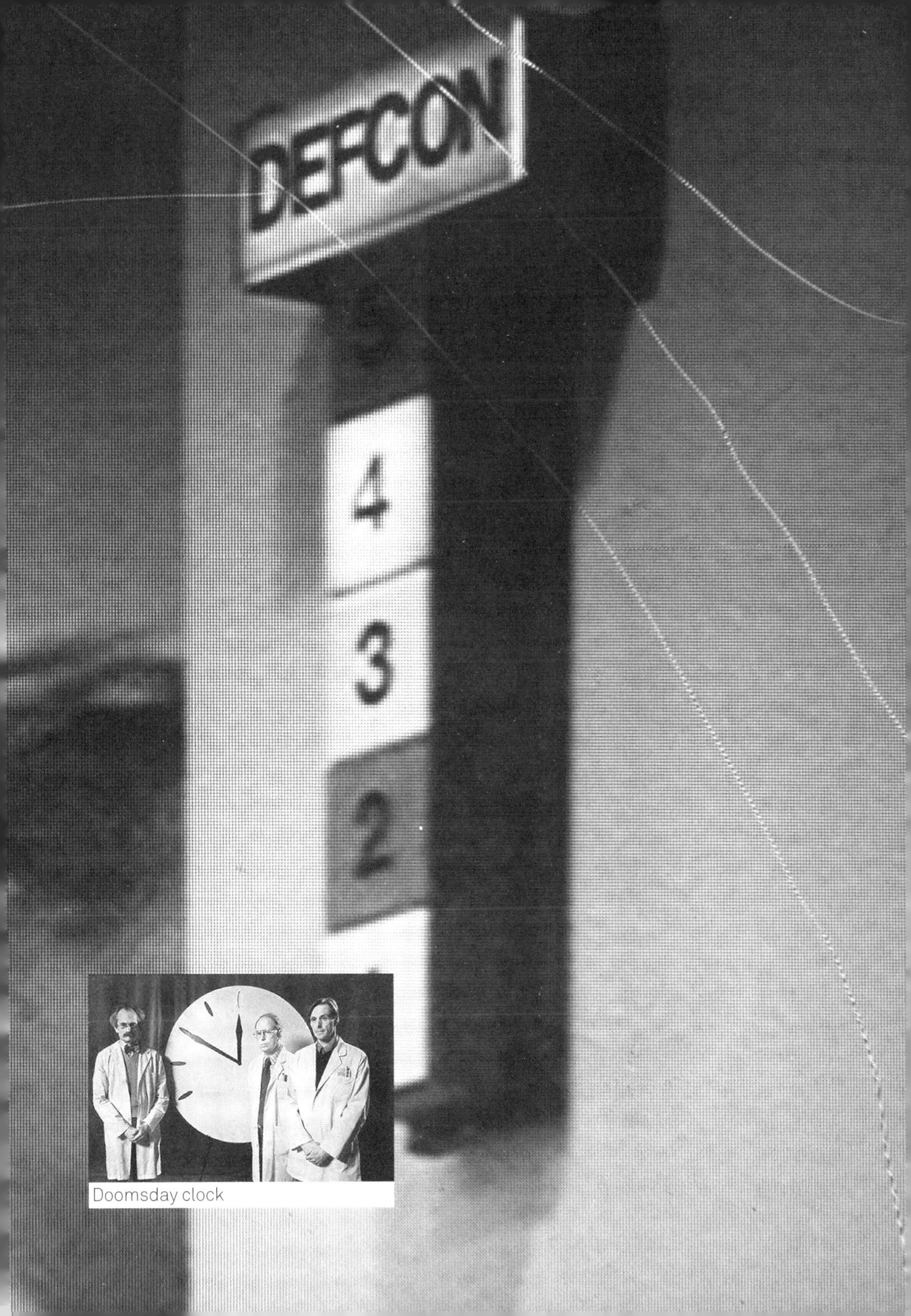

Doomsday clock

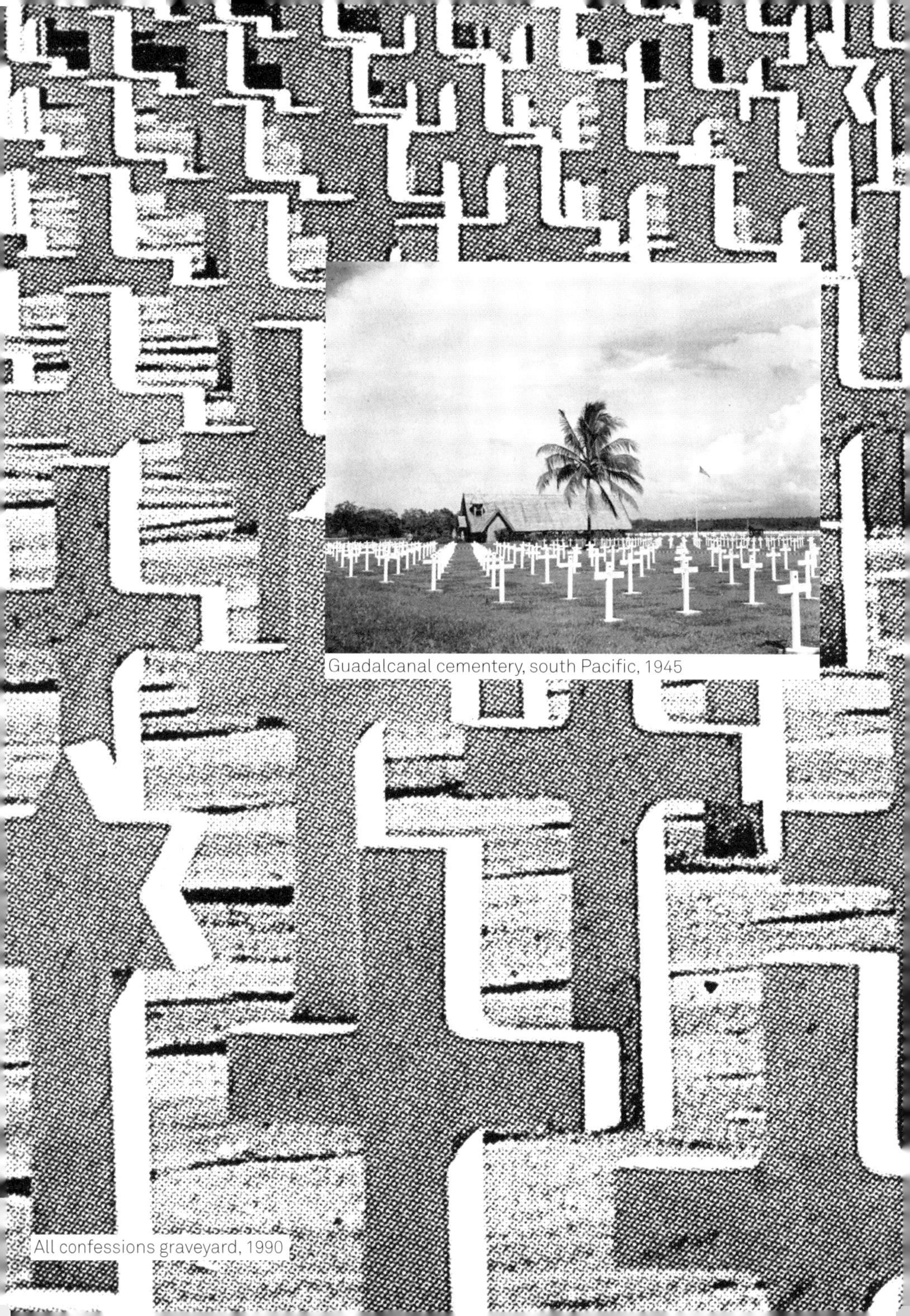

Guadalcanal cementery, south Pacific, 1945

All confessions graveyard, 1990

still at half-past twelve the king loitered in the balcony and seemed to be waiting for some news that did not come.

The king and his minister had talked at first in whispers ; they had fallen silent, for they found little now to express except a vague anxiety. Away there on the mountain side were the white metal roofs of the long farm buildings beneath which the bomb factory and the bombs were hidden. (The chemist who had made all these for the king had died suddenly after the declaration of Brissago.) Nobody knew of that store of mischief now but the king and his adviser and three heavily faithful attendants ; the aviators who waited now in the midday blaze with their bomb-carrying machines and their passenger bomb throwers in the exercising grounds of the motor-cyclist barracks below were still in ignorance of the position of the ammunition they were presently to take up. It was time they started if the scheme was to work as Pestovitch had planned it. It was a magnificent plan. It aimed at no less than the Empire of the World. The government of idealists and professors away there at Brissago was to be blown to fragments, and then east, west, north and south those aeroplanes would go swarming over a world that had disarmed itself, to proclaim Ferdinand Charles, the new Cæsar, the Master, Lord of the Earth.

It was a magnificent plan. But the tension

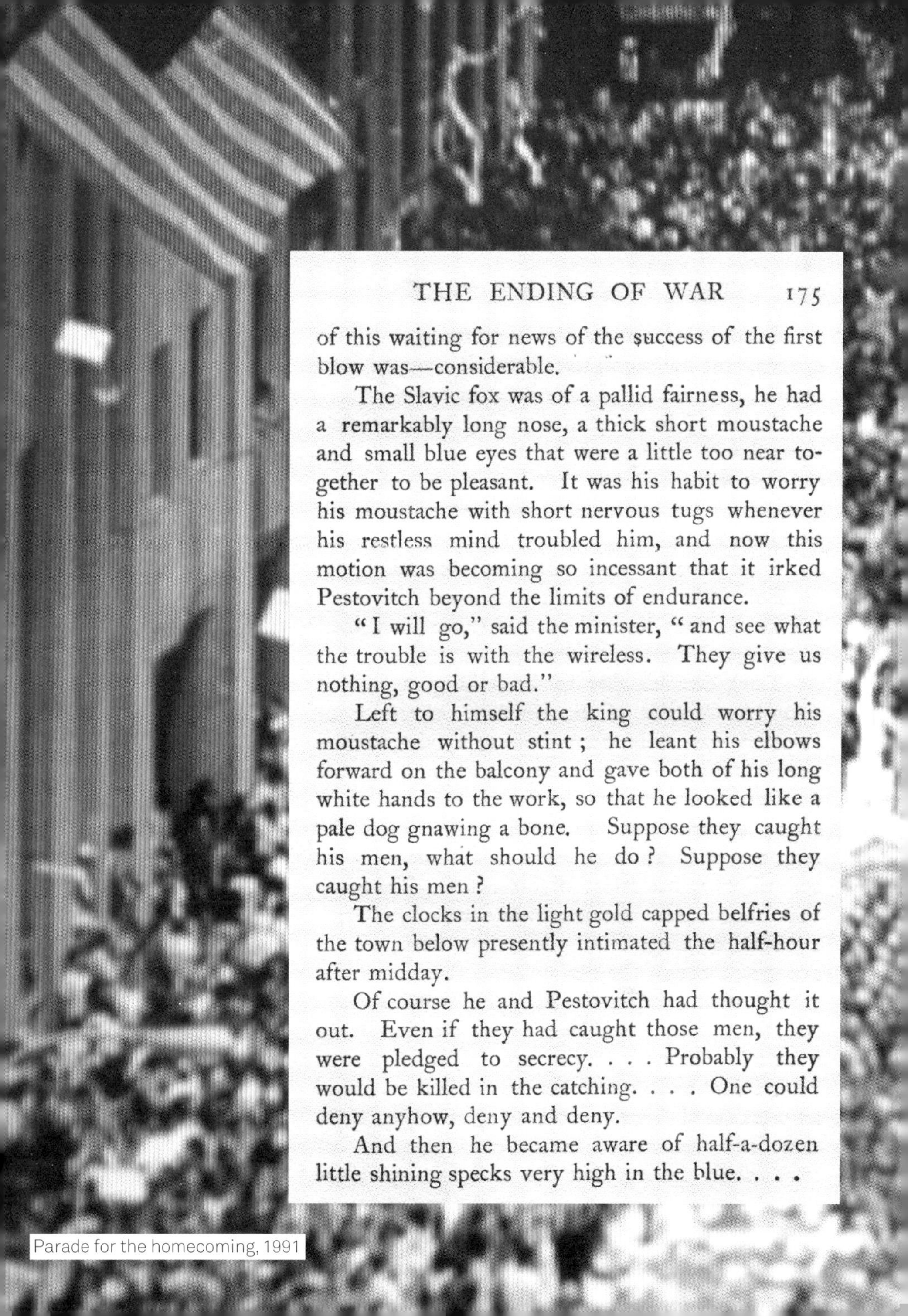

of this waiting for news of the success of the first blow was—considerable.

The Slavic fox was of a pallid fairness, he had a remarkably long nose, a thick short moustache and small blue eyes that were a little too near together to be pleasant. It was his habit to worry his moustache with short nervous tugs whenever his restless mind troubled him, and now this motion was becoming so incessant that it irked Pestovitch beyond the limits of endurance.

"I will go," said the minister, "and see what the trouble is with the wireless. They give us nothing, good or bad."

Left to himself the king could worry his moustache without stint; he leant his elbows forward on the balcony and gave both of his long white hands to the work, so that he looked like a pale dog gnawing a bone. Suppose they caught his men, what should he do? Suppose they caught his men?

The clocks in the light gold capped belfries of the town below presently intimated the half-hour after midday.

Of course he and Pestovitch had thought it out. Even if they had caught those men, they were pledged to secrecy. . . . Probably they would be killed in the catching. . . . One could deny anyhow, deny and deny.

And then he became aware of half-a-dozen little shining specks very high in the blue. . . .

Parade for the homecoming, 1991

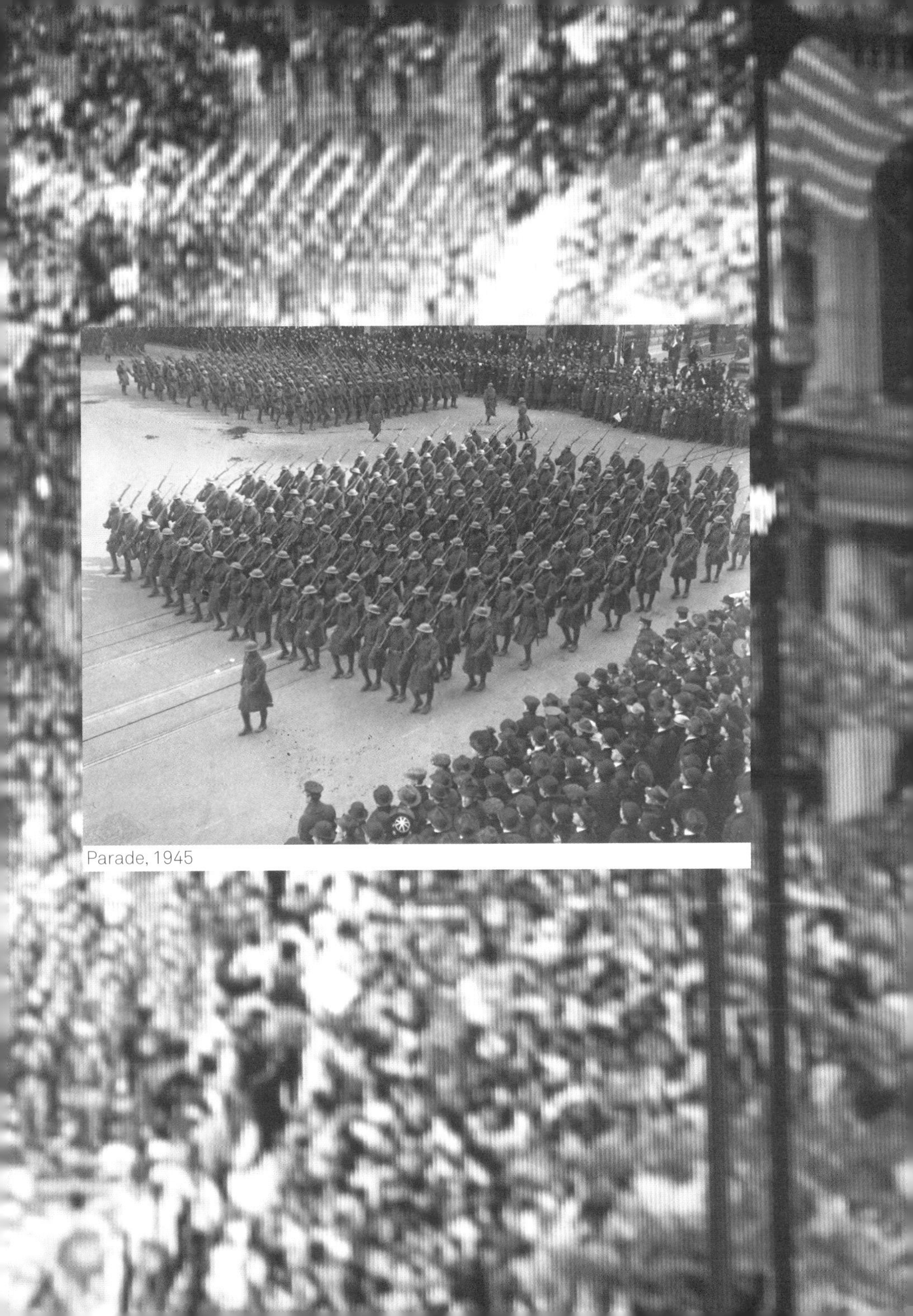

Parade, 1945

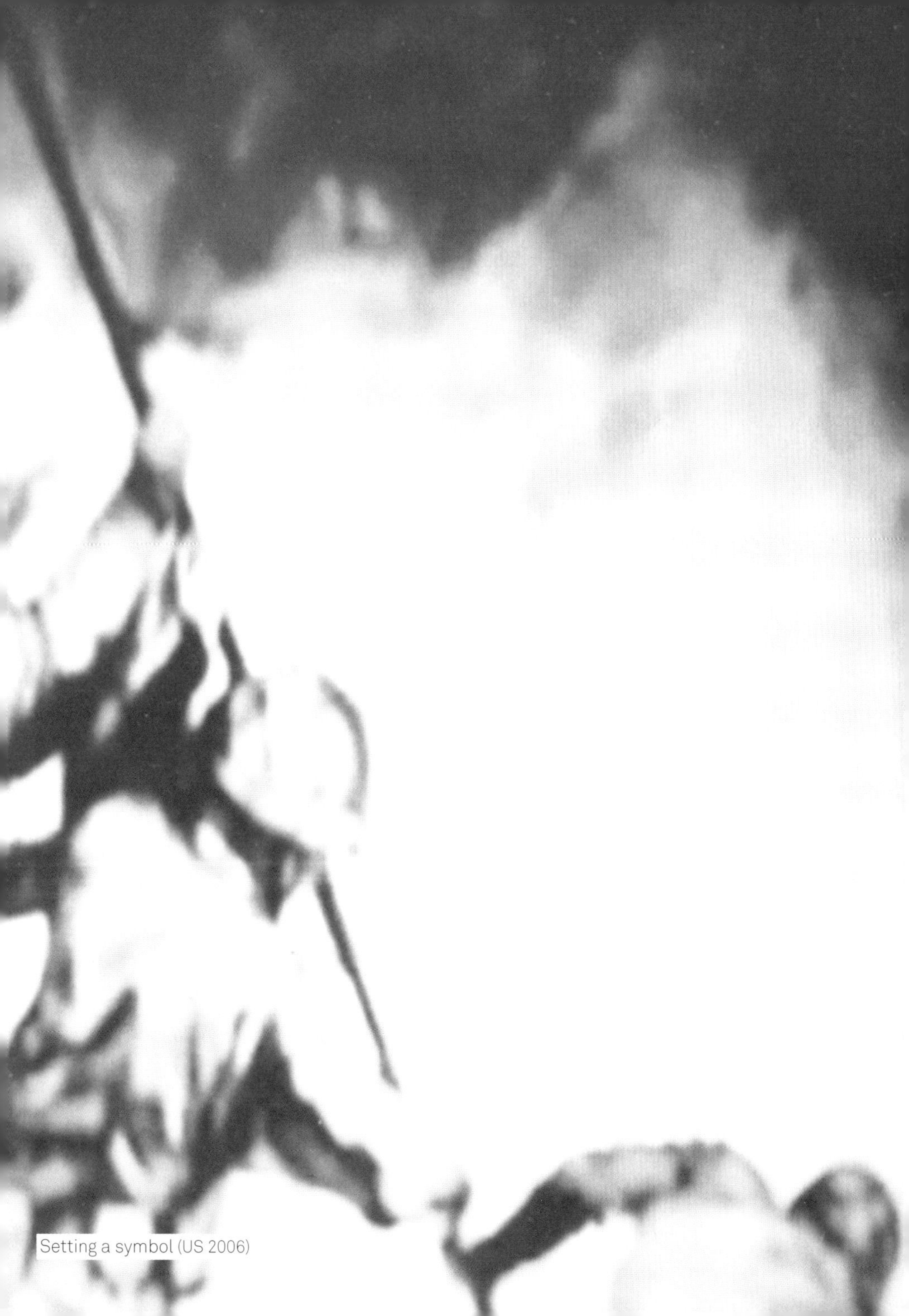

Setting a symbol (US 2006)

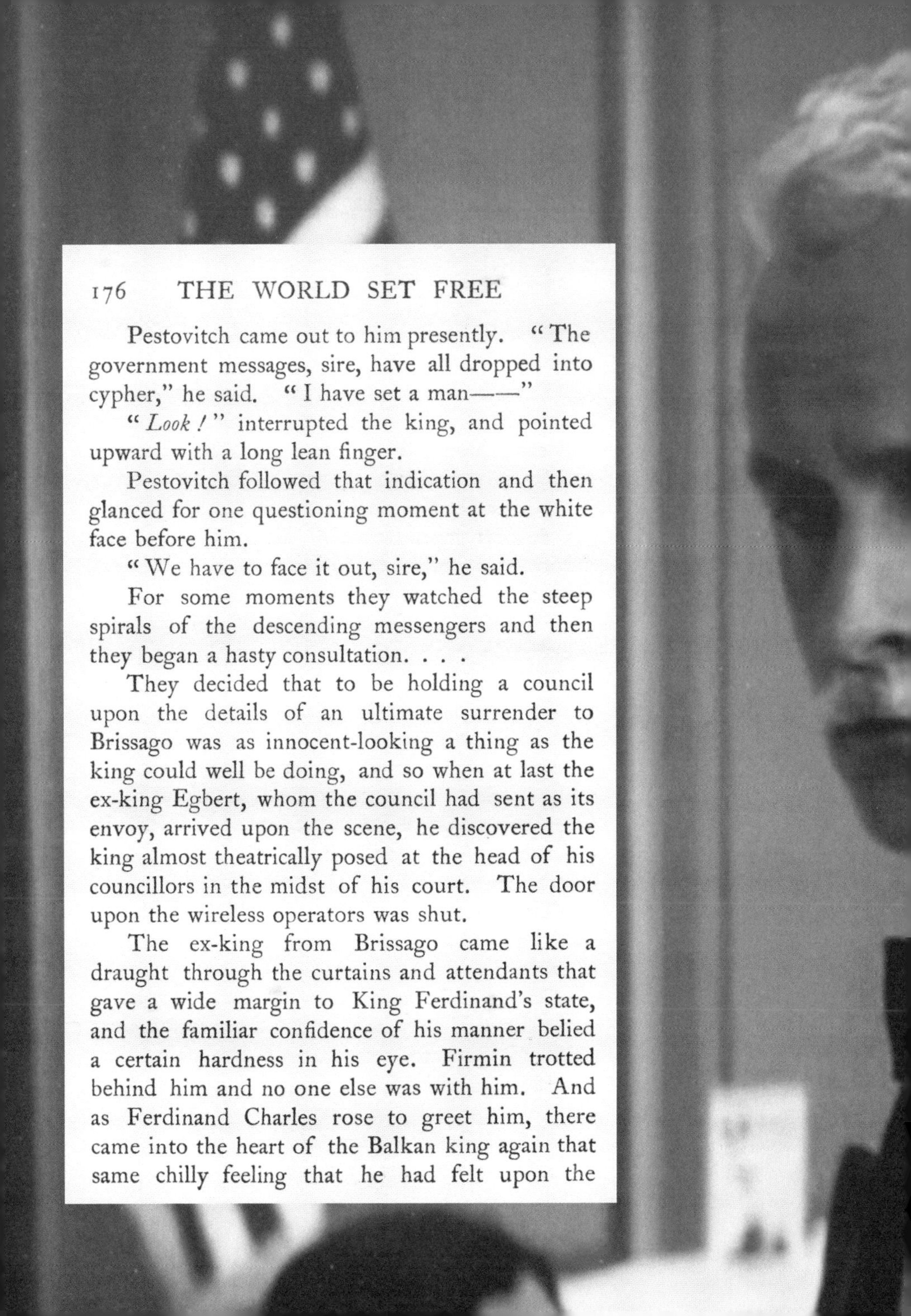

Pestovitch came out to him presently. "The government messages, sire, have all dropped into cypher," he said. "I have set a man——"

"*Look!*" interrupted the king, and pointed upward with a long lean finger.

Pestovitch followed that indication and then glanced for one questioning moment at the white face before him.

"We have to face it out, sire," he said.

For some moments they watched the steep spirals of the descending messengers and then they began a hasty consultation. . . .

They decided that to be holding a council upon the details of an ultimate surrender to Brissago was as innocent-looking a thing as the king could well be doing, and so when at last the ex-king Egbert, whom the council had sent as its envoy, arrived upon the scene, he discovered the king almost theatrically posed at the head of his councillors in the midst of his court. The door upon the wireless operators was shut.

The ex-king from Brissago came like a draught through the curtains and attendants that gave a wide margin to King Ferdinand's state, and the familiar confidence of his manner belied a certain hardness in his eye. Firmin trotted behind him and no one else was with him. And as Ferdinand Charles rose to greet him, there came into the heart of the Balkan king again that same chilly feeling that he had felt upon the

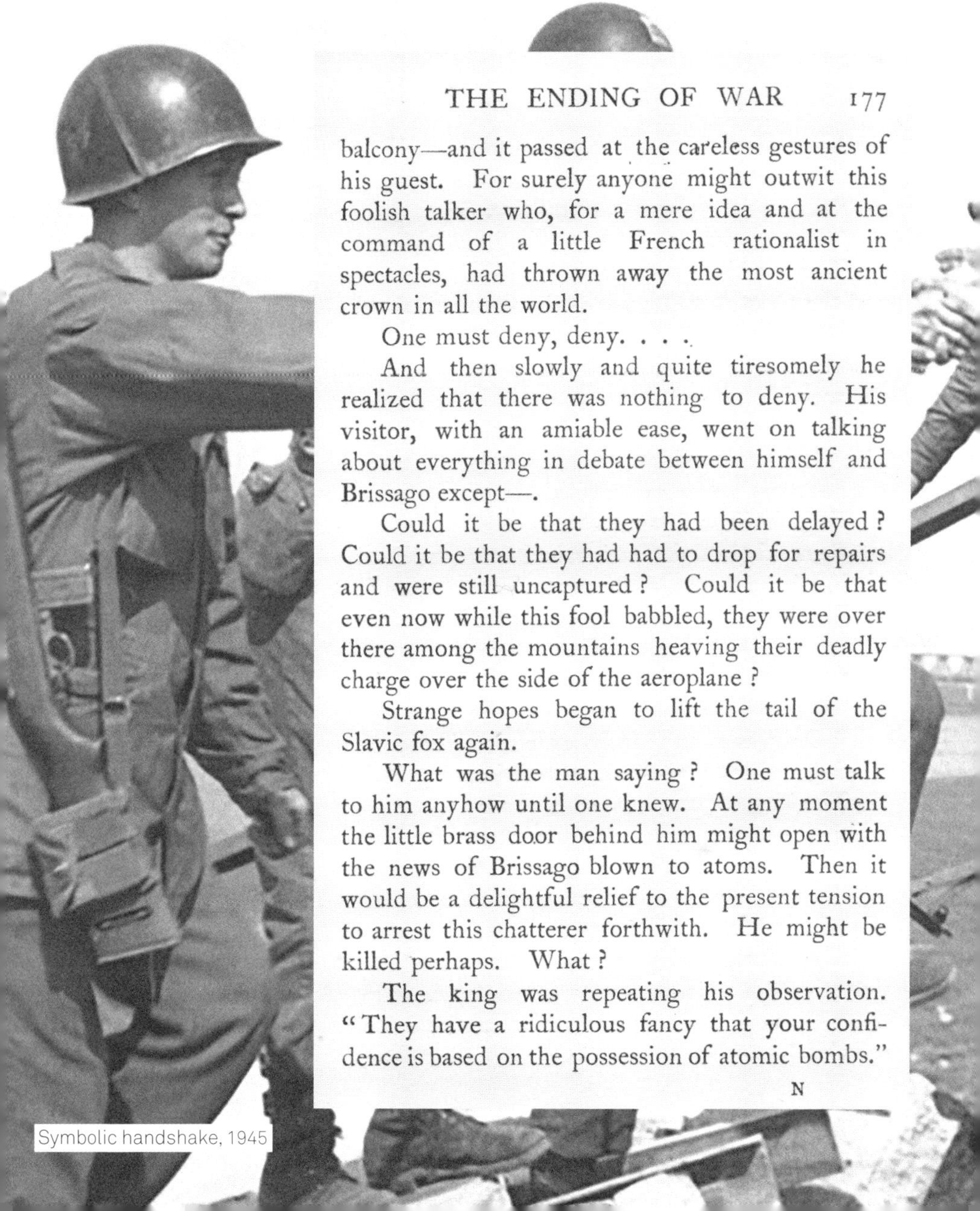

Symbolic handshake, 1945

balcony—and it passed at the careless gestures of his guest. For surely anyone might outwit this foolish talker who, for a mere idea and at the command of a little French rationalist in spectacles, had thrown away the most ancient crown in all the world.

One must deny, deny. . . .

And then slowly and quite tiresomely he realized that there was nothing to deny. His visitor, with an amiable ease, went on talking about everything in debate between himself and Brissago except—.

Could it be that they had been delayed? Could it be that they had had to drop for repairs and were still uncaptured? Could it be that even now while this fool babbled, they were over there among the mountains heaving their deadly charge over the side of the aeroplane?

Strange hopes began to lift the tail of the Slavic fox again.

What was the man saying? One must talk to him anyhow until one knew. At any moment the little brass door behind him might open with the news of Brissago blown to atoms. Then it would be a delightful relief to the present tension to arrest this chatterer forthwith. He might be killed perhaps. What?

The king was repeating his observation. "They have a ridiculous fancy that your confidence is based on the possession of atomic bombs."

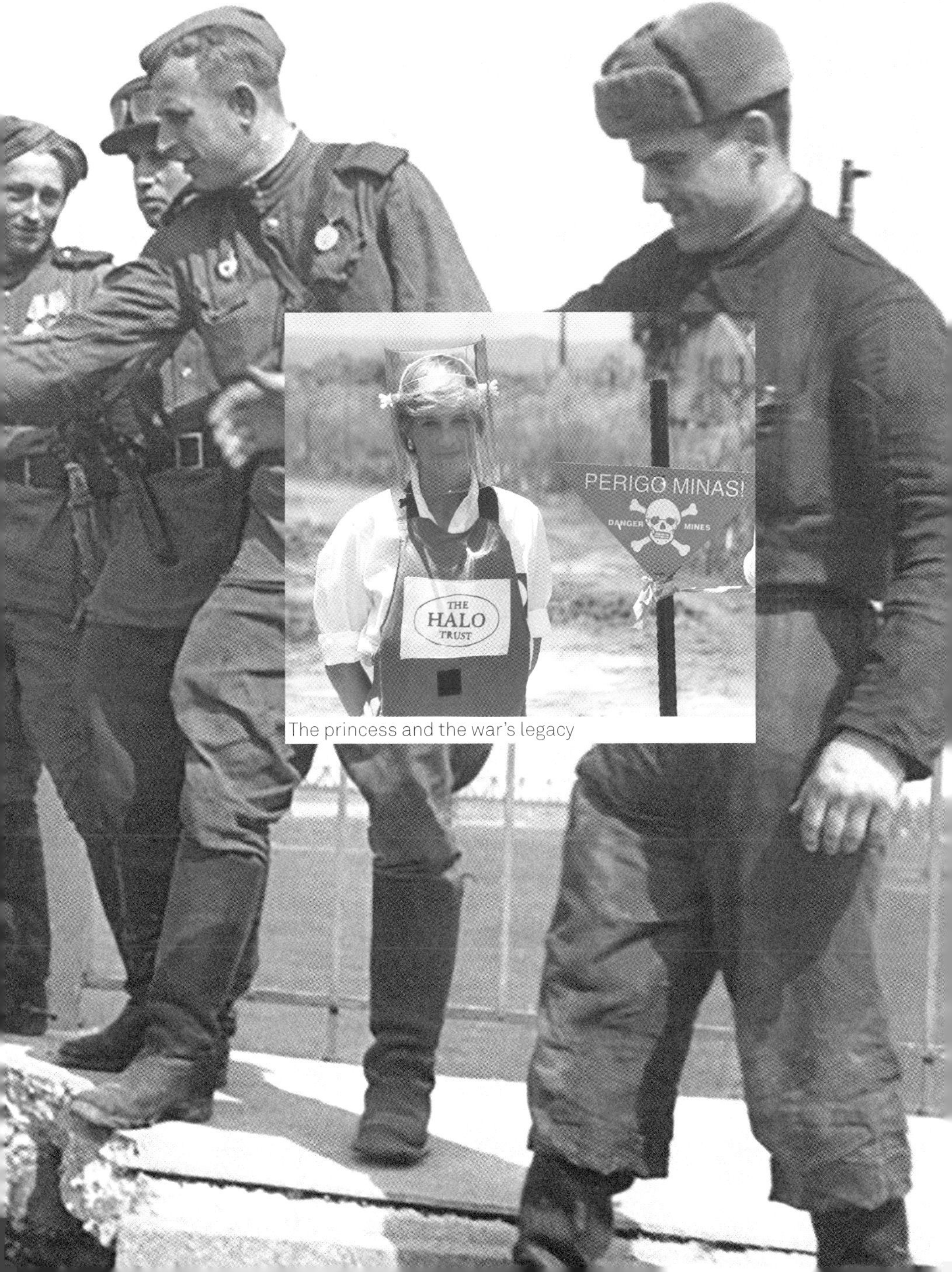

The princess and the war's legacy

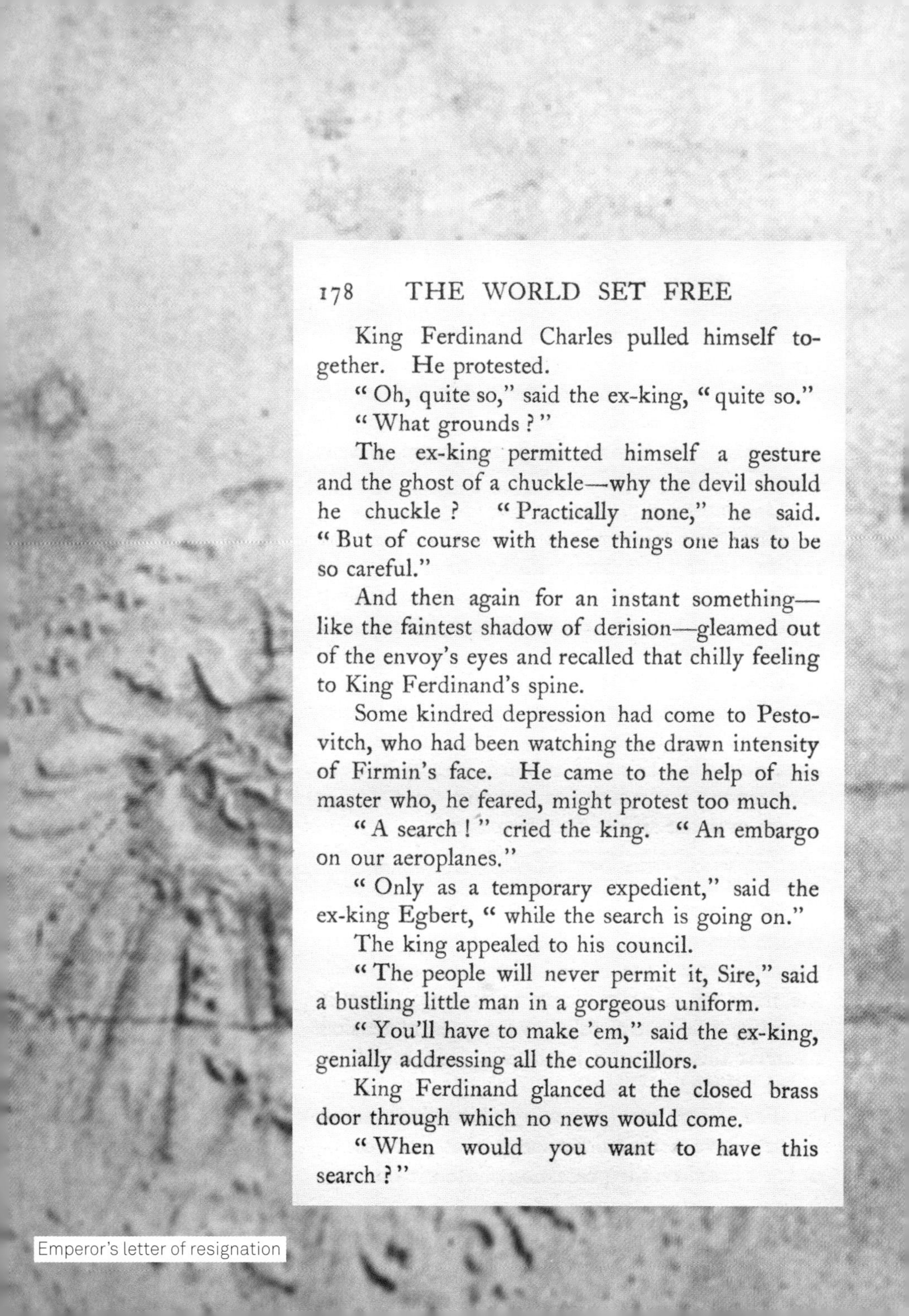

King Ferdinand Charles pulled himself together. He protested.

"Oh, quite so," said the ex-king, "quite so."

"What grounds?"

The ex-king permitted himself a gesture and the ghost of a chuckle—why the devil should he chuckle? "Practically none," he said. "But of course with these things one has to be so careful."

And then again for an instant something—like the faintest shadow of derision—gleamed out of the envoy's eyes and recalled that chilly feeling to King Ferdinand's spine.

Some kindred depression had come to Pestovitch, who had been watching the drawn intensity of Firmin's face. He came to the help of his master who, he feared, might protest too much.

"A search!" cried the king. "An embargo on our aeroplanes."

"Only as a temporary expedient," said the ex-king Egbert, "while the search is going on."

The king appealed to his council.

"The people will never permit it, Sire," said a bustling little man in a gorgeous uniform.

"You'll have to make 'em," said the ex-king, genially addressing all the councillors.

King Ferdinand glanced at the closed brass door through which no news would come.

"When would you want to have this search?"

Emperor's letter of resignation

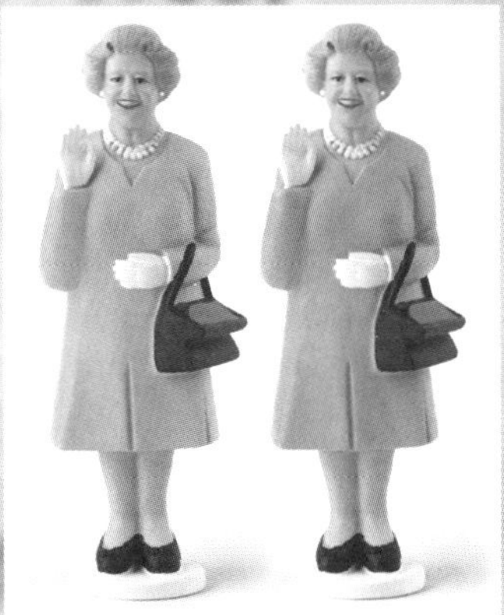
The Queen waves

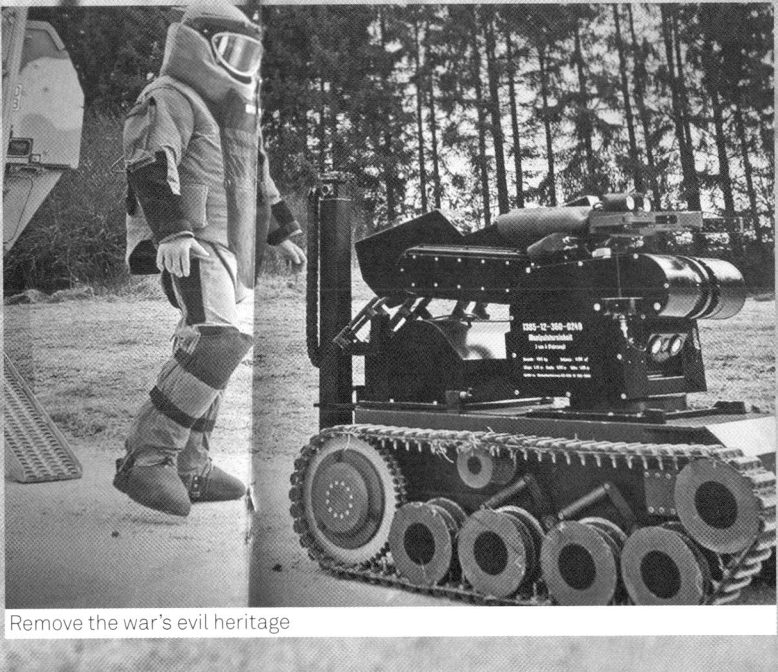
Remove the war's evil heritage

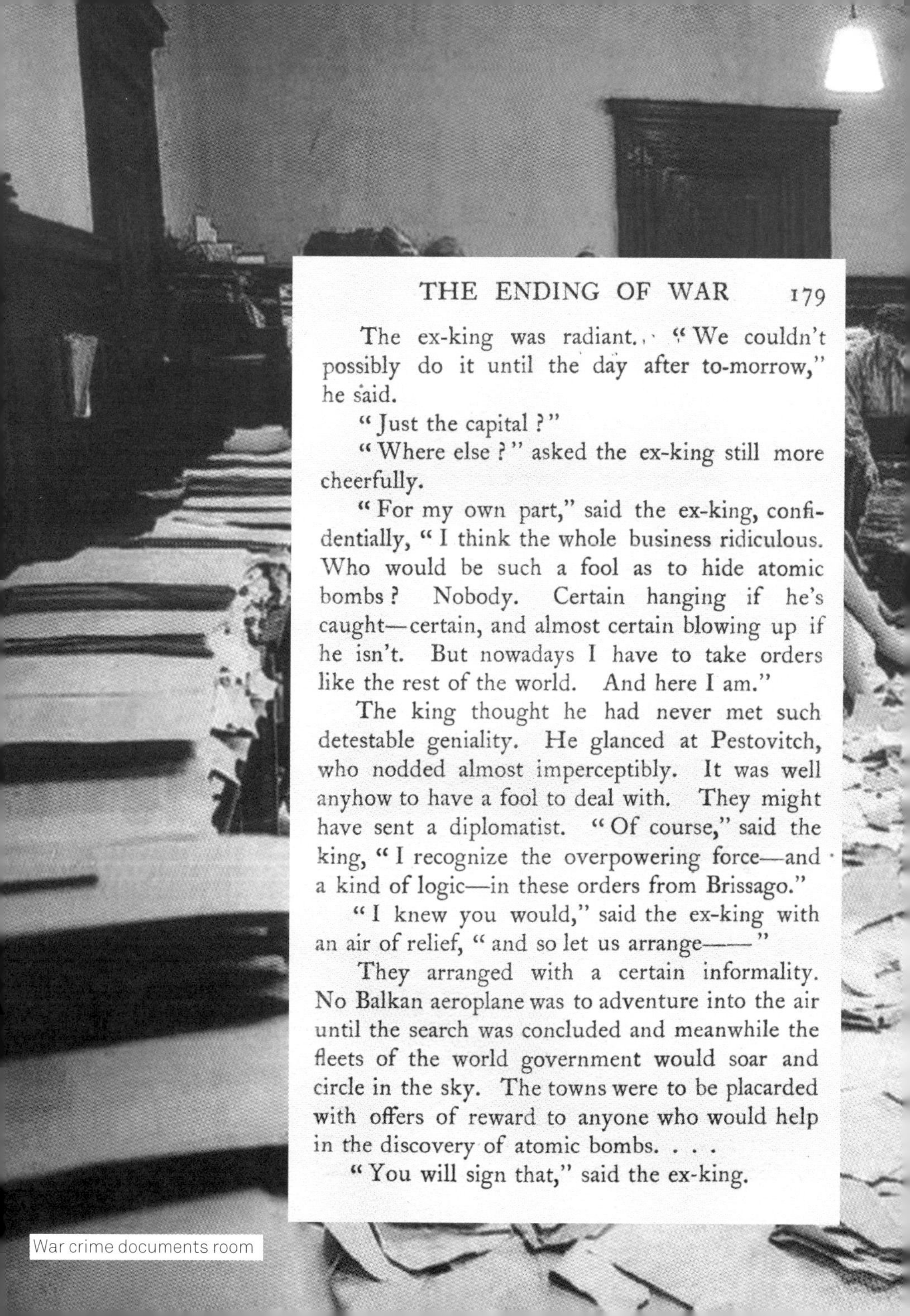

The ex-king was radiant. "We couldn't possibly do it until the day after to-morrow," he said.

"Just the capital?"

"Where else?" asked the ex-king still more cheerfully.

"For my own part," said the ex-king, confidentially, "I think the whole business ridiculous. Who would be such a fool as to hide atomic bombs? Nobody. Certain hanging if he's caught—certain, and almost certain blowing up if he isn't. But nowadays I have to take orders like the rest of the world. And here I am."

The king thought he had never met such detestable geniality. He glanced at Pestovitch, who nodded almost imperceptibly. It was well anyhow to have a fool to deal with. They might have sent a diplomatist. "Of course," said the king, "I recognize the overpowering force—and a kind of logic—in these orders from Brissago."

"I knew you would," said the ex-king with an air of relief, "and so let us arrange——"

They arranged with a certain informality. No Balkan aeroplane was to adventure into the air until the search was concluded and meanwhile the fleets of the world government would soar and circle in the sky. The towns were to be placarded with offers of reward to anyone who would help in the discovery of atomic bombs. . . .

"You will sign that," said the ex-king.

War crime documents room

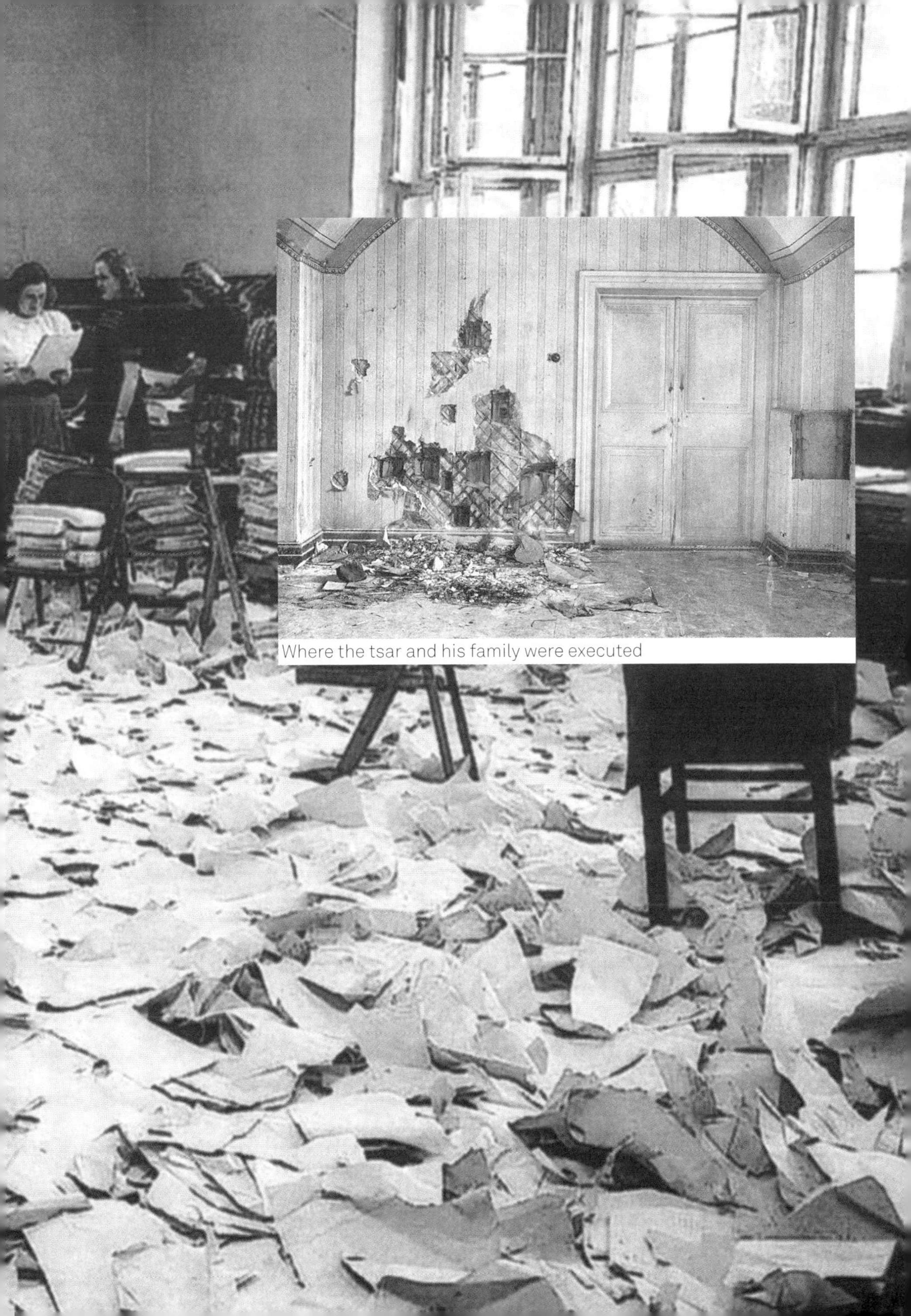

Where the tsar and his family were executed

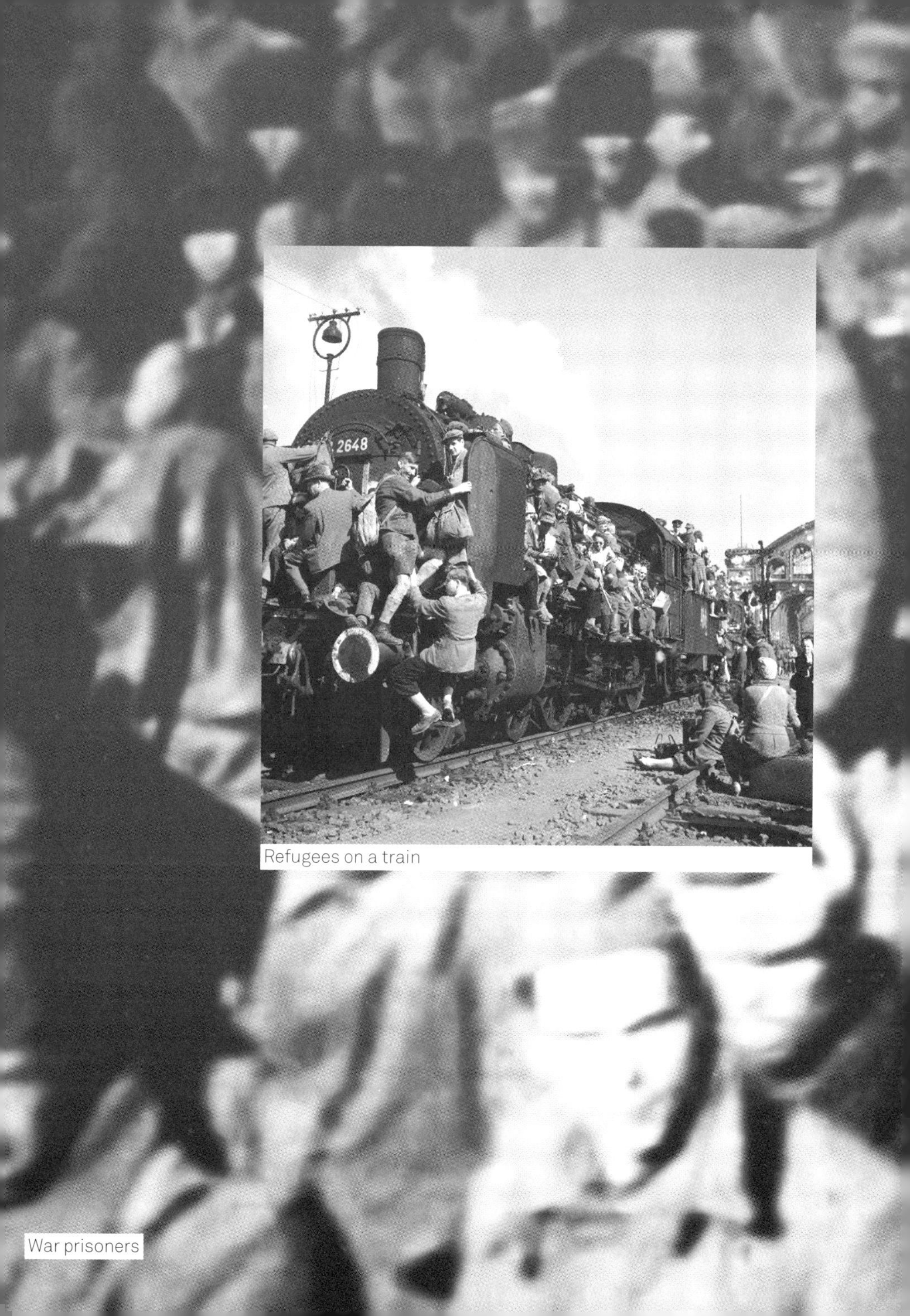

Refugees on a train

War prisoners

"Why?"

"To show that we aren't in any way hostile to you."

Pestovitch nodded "yes" to his master.

"And then you see," said the ex-king in that easy way of his, "we'll have a lot of men here, borrow help from your police and run through all your things. And then everything will be over. Meanwhile, if I may be your guest. . . ."

When presently Pestovitch was alone with the king again, he found him in a state of jangling emotions. His spirit was tossing like a wind-whipped sea. One moment he was exalted and full of contempt for "that ass" and his search; the next he was down in a pit of dread. "They will find them, Pestovitch, and then he'll hang us."

"Hang us?"

The king put his long nose into his councillor's face. "That grinning brute *wants* to hang us," he said. "And hang us he will, if we give him a shadow of a chance."

"But all their Modern State Civilization!"

"Do you think there's any pity in that crew of Godless, Vivisecting Prigs?" cried this last king of romance. "Do you think, Pestovitch, they understand anything of a high ambition or a splendid dream? Do you think that our gallant and sublime adventure has any appeal to them? Here am I, the last and greatest

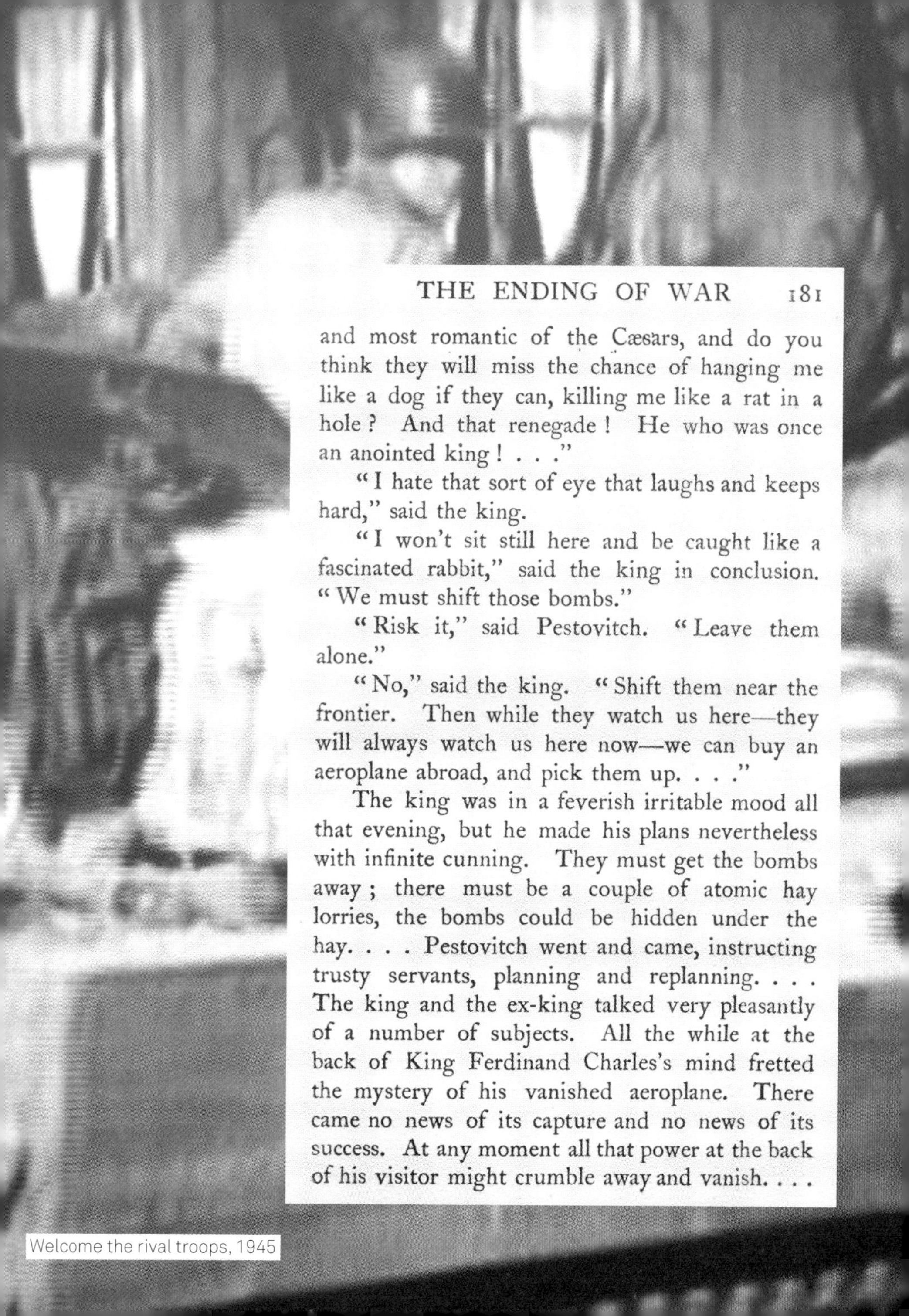

and most romantic of the Cæsars, and do you think they will miss the chance of hanging me like a dog if they can, killing me like a rat in a hole? And that renegade! He who was once an anointed king! . . ."

"I hate that sort of eye that laughs and keeps hard," said the king.

"I won't sit still here and be caught like a fascinated rabbit," said the king in conclusion. "We must shift those bombs."

"Risk it," said Pestovitch. "Leave them alone."

"No," said the king. "Shift them near the frontier. Then while they watch us here—they will always watch us here now—we can buy an aeroplane abroad, and pick them up. . . ."

The king was in a feverish irritable mood all that evening, but he made his plans nevertheless with infinite cunning. They must get the bombs away; there must be a couple of atomic hay lorries, the bombs could be hidden under the hay. . . . Pestovitch went and came, instructing trusty servants, planning and replanning. . . . The king and the ex-king talked very pleasantly of a number of subjects. All the while at the back of King Ferdinand Charles's mind fretted the mystery of his vanished aeroplane. There came no news of its capture and no news of its success. At any moment all that power at the back of his visitor might crumble away and vanish. . . .

Welcome the rival troops, 1945

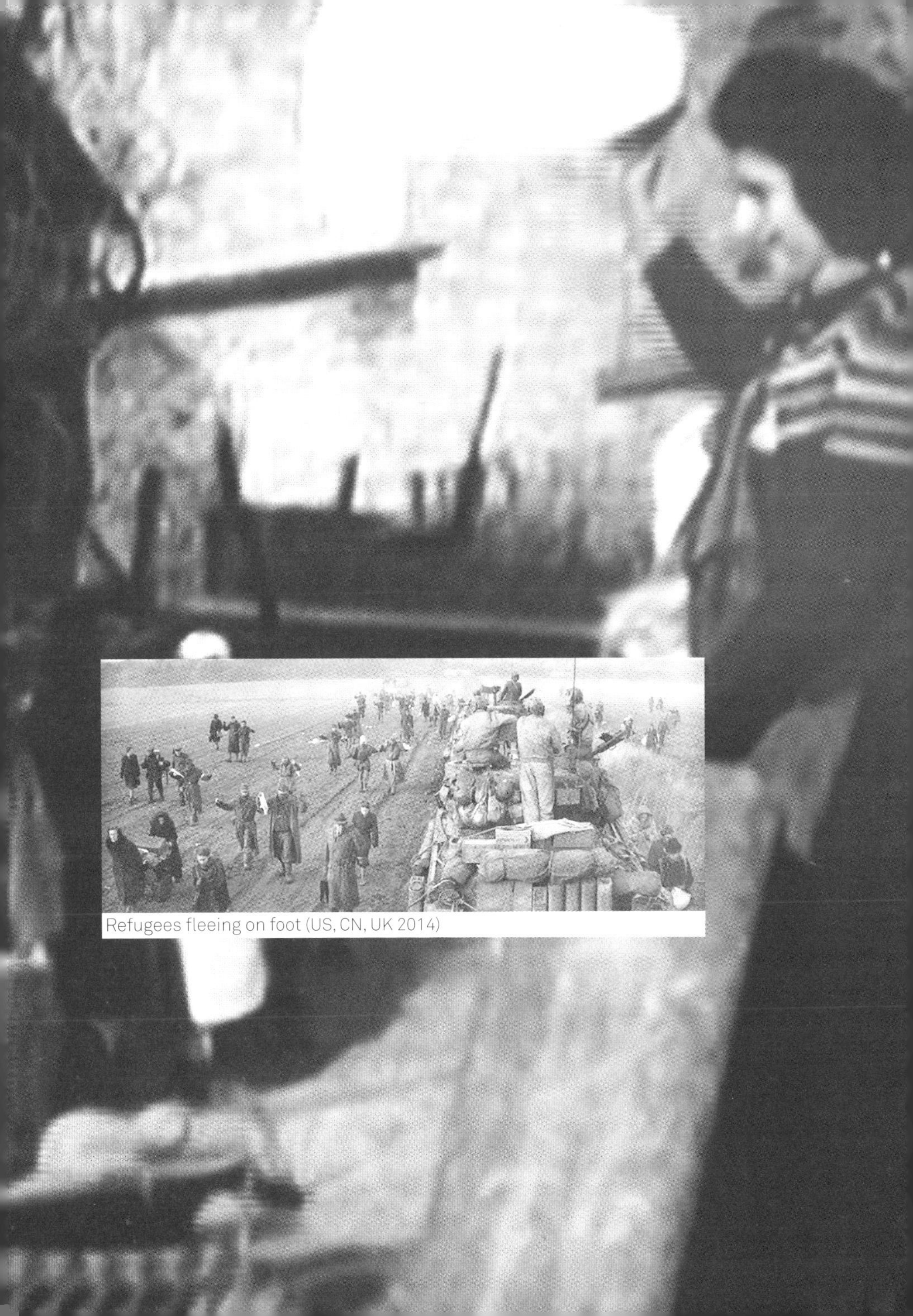

Refugees fleeing on foot (US, CN, UK 2014)

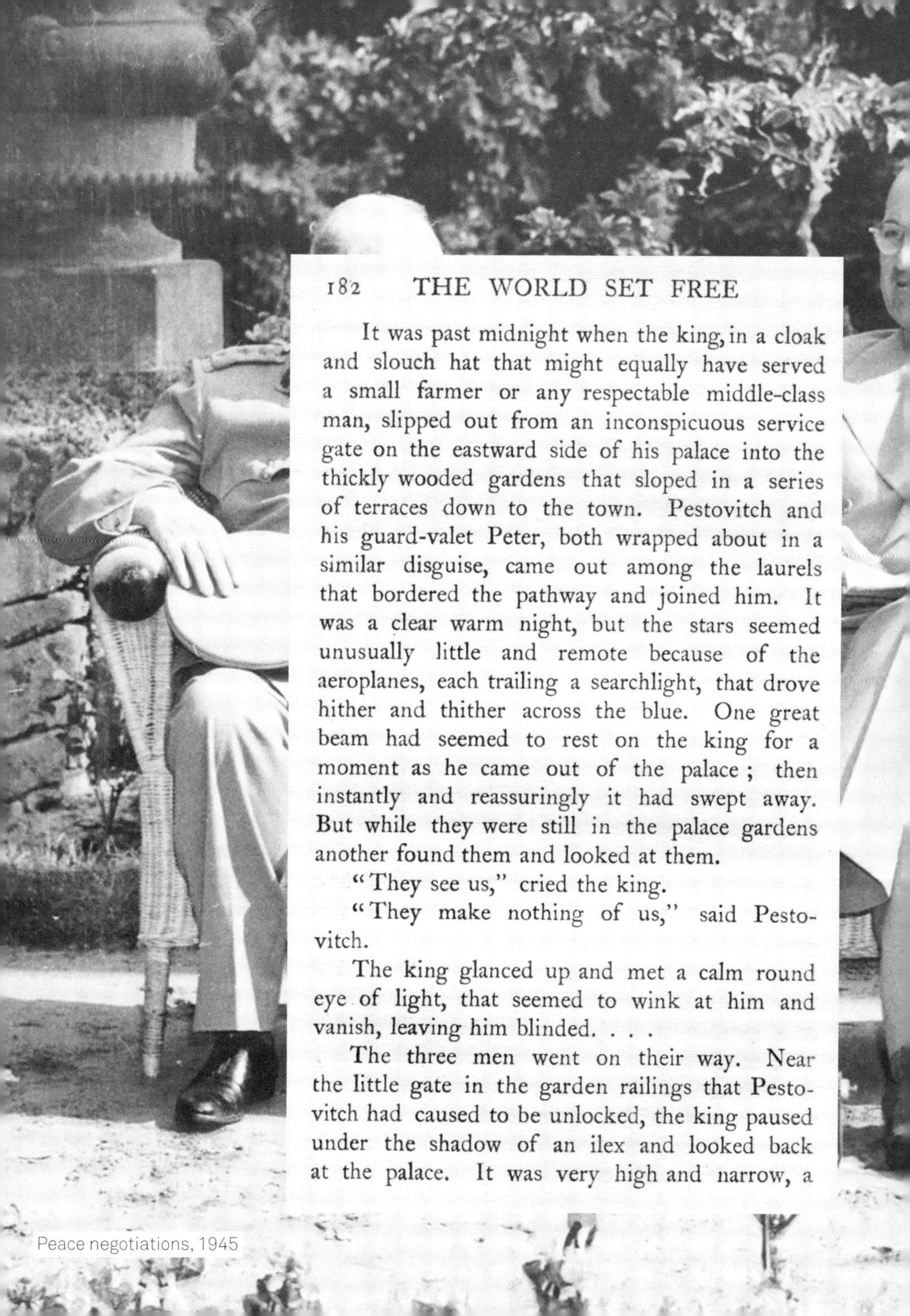

It was past midnight when the king, in a cloak and slouch hat that might equally have served a small farmer or any respectable middle-class man, slipped out from an inconspicuous service gate on the eastward side of his palace into the thickly wooded gardens that sloped in a series of terraces down to the town. Pestovitch and his guard-valet Peter, both wrapped about in a similar disguise, came out among the laurels that bordered the pathway and joined him. It was a clear warm night, but the stars seemed unusually little and remote because of the aeroplanes, each trailing a searchlight, that drove hither and thither across the blue. One great beam had seemed to rest on the king for a moment as he came out of the palace; then instantly and reassuringly it had swept away. But while they were still in the palace gardens another found them and looked at them.

"They see us," cried the king.

"They make nothing of us," said Pestovitch.

The king glanced up and met a calm round eye of light, that seemed to wink at him and vanish, leaving him blinded. . . .

The three men went on their way. Near the little gate in the garden railings that Pestovitch had caused to be unlocked, the king paused under the shadow of an ilex and looked back at the palace. It was very high and narrow, a

Peace negotiations, 1945

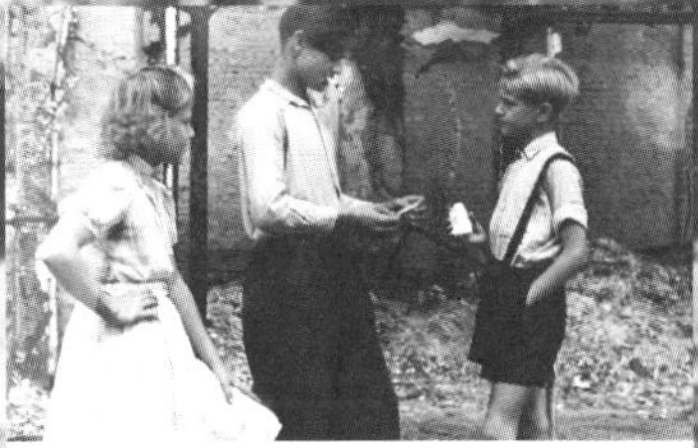
Daily postwar negotiations (IT 1948)

twentieth century rendering of medievalism, medievalism in steel and bronze and sham stone and opaque glass. Against the sky it splashed a confusion of pinnacles. High up in the eastward wing were the windows of the apartments of the ex-king Egbert. One of them was brightly lit now and against the light a little black figure stood very still and looked out upon the night.

The king snarled.

"He little knows how we slip through his fingers," said Pestovitch.

And as he spoke they saw the ex-king stretch out his arms slowly like one who yawns, knuckle his eyes and turn inward—no doubt to his bed.

Down through the ancient winding back streets of his capital hurried the king, and at an appointed corner a shabby atomic-automobile waited for the three. It was a hackney carriage of the lowest grade, with dinted metal panels and deflated cushions. The driver was one of the ordinary drivers of the capital, but beside him sat the young secretary of Pestovitch who knew the way to the farm where the bombs were hidden.

The automobile made its way through the narrow streets of the old town, which were still lit and uneasy—for the fleet of airships overhead had kept the cafés open and people abroad—over

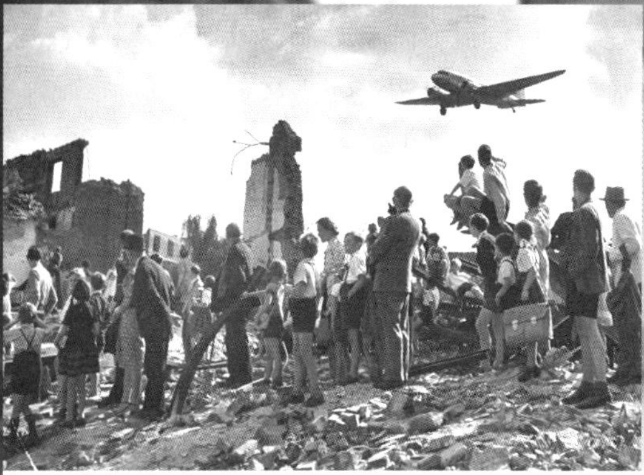
Luftbrücke Berlin

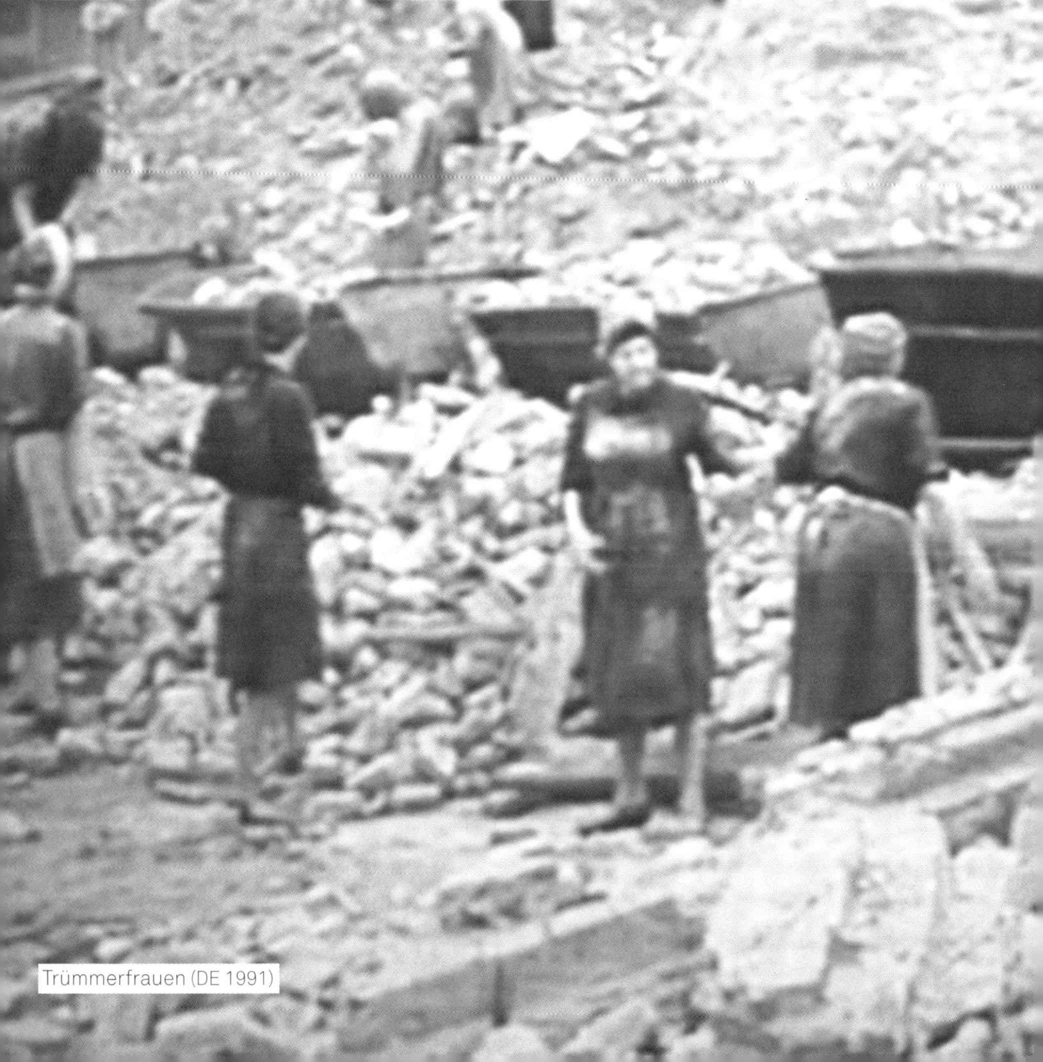
Trümmerfrauen (DE 1991)

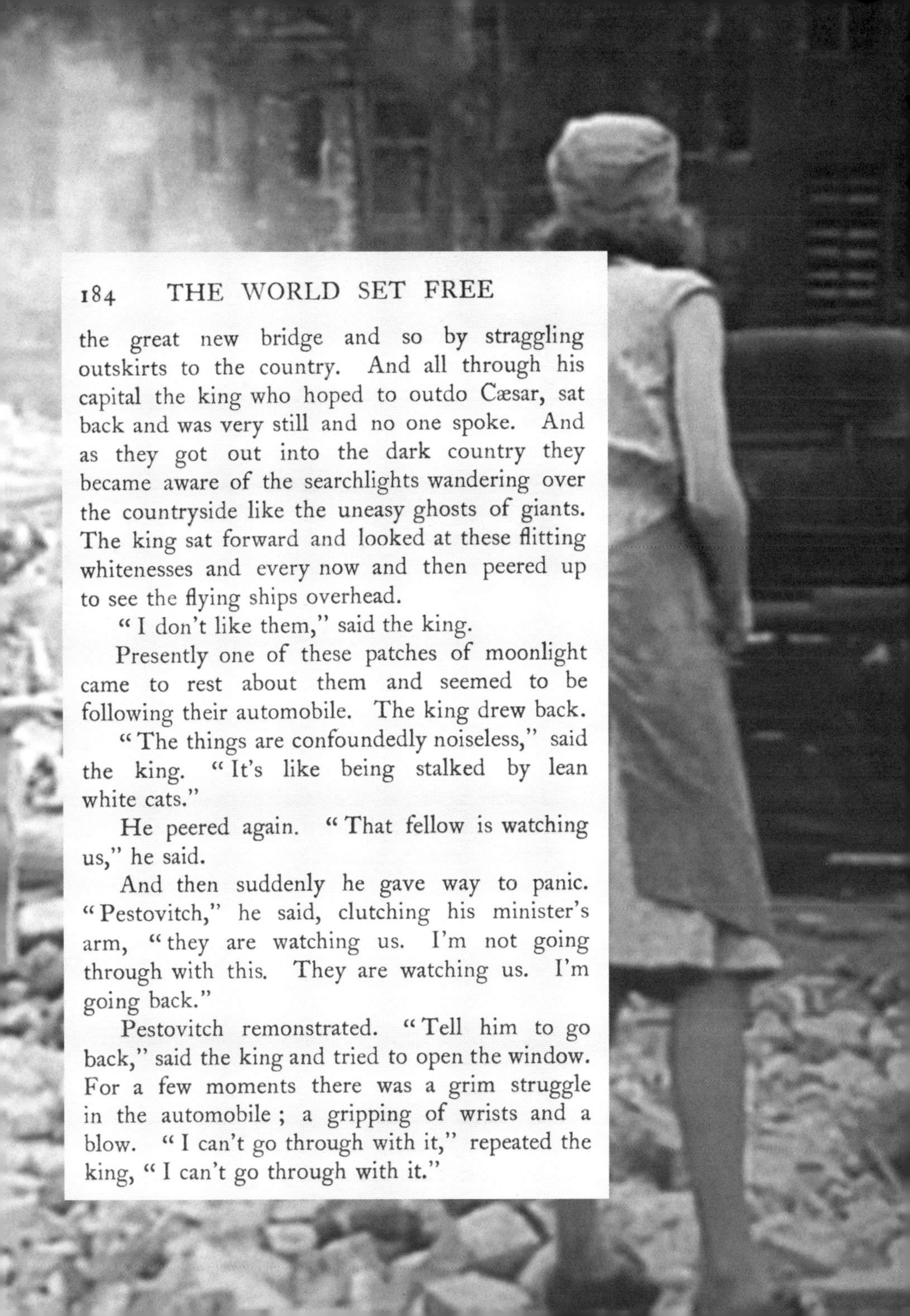

the great new bridge and so by straggling outskirts to the country. And all through his capital the king who hoped to outdo Cæsar, sat back and was very still and no one spoke. And as they got out into the dark country they became aware of the searchlights wandering over the countryside like the uneasy ghosts of giants. The king sat forward and looked at these flitting whitenesses and every now and then peered up to see the flying ships overhead.

"I don't like them," said the king.

Presently one of these patches of moonlight came to rest about them and seemed to be following their automobile. The king drew back.

"The things are confoundedly noiseless," said the king. "It's like being stalked by lean white cats."

He peered again. "That fellow is watching us," he said.

And then suddenly he gave way to panic. "Pestovitch," he said, clutching his minister's arm, "they are watching us. I'm not going through with this. They are watching us. I'm going back."

Pestovitch remonstrated. "Tell him to go back," said the king and tried to open the window. For a few moments there was a grim struggle in the automobile; a gripping of wrists and a blow. "I can't go through with it," repeated the king, "I can't go through with it."

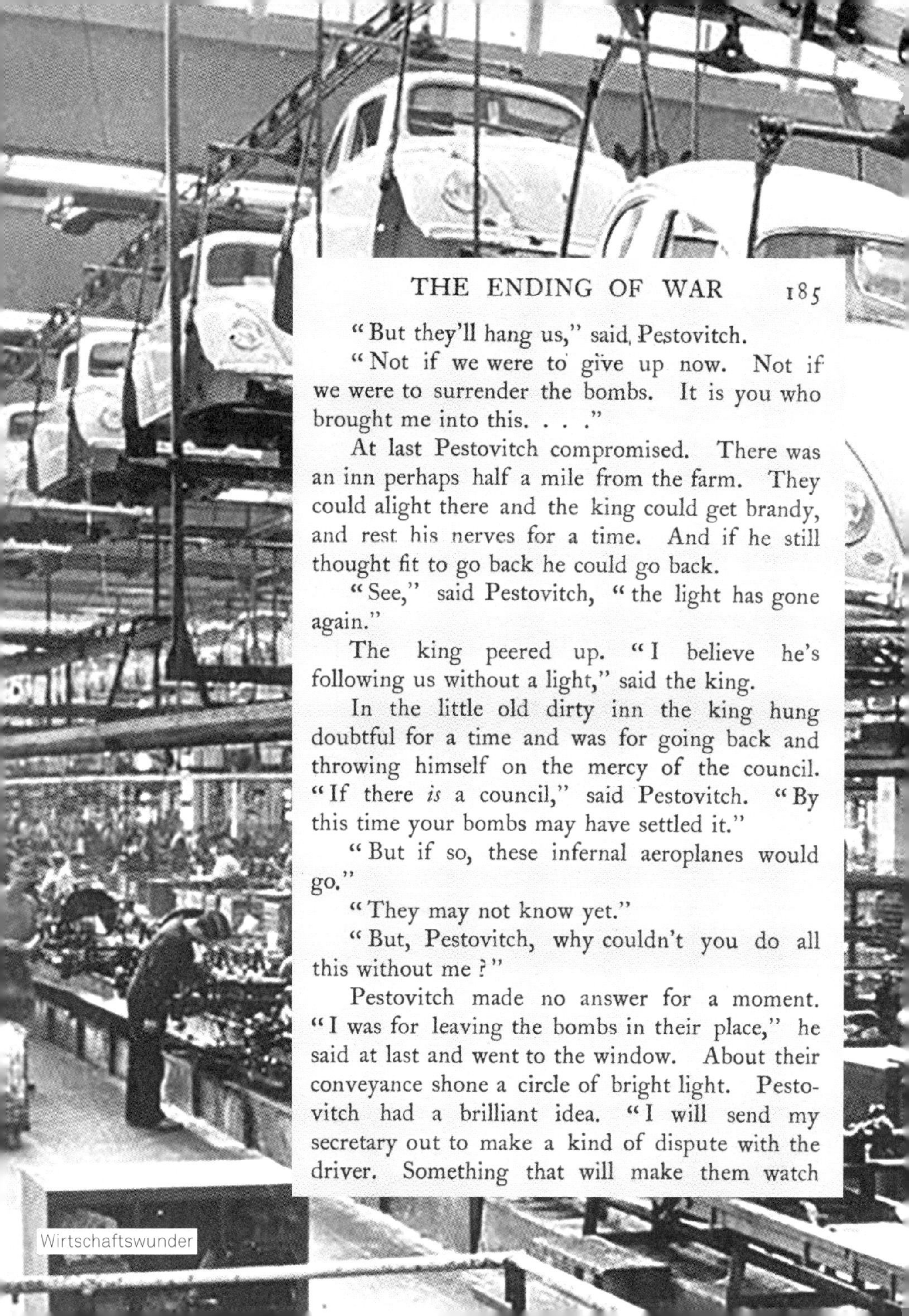

"But they'll hang us," said Pestovitch.

"Not if we were to give up now. Not if we were to surrender the bombs. It is you who brought me into this. . . ."

At last Pestovitch compromised. There was an inn perhaps half a mile from the farm. They could alight there and the king could get brandy, and rest his nerves for a time. And if he still thought fit to go back he could go back.

"See," said Pestovitch, "the light has gone again."

The king peered up. "I believe he's following us without a light," said the king.

In the little old dirty inn the king hung doubtful for a time and was for going back and throwing himself on the mercy of the council. "If there *is* a council," said Pestovitch. "By this time your bombs may have settled it."

"But if so, these infernal aeroplanes would go."

"They may not know yet."

"But, Pestovitch, why couldn't you do all this without me?"

Pestovitch made no answer for a moment. "I was for leaving the bombs in their place," he said at last and went to the window. About their conveyance shone a circle of bright light. Pestovitch had a brilliant idea. "I will send my secretary out to make a kind of dispute with the driver. Something that will make them watch

Wirtschaftswunder

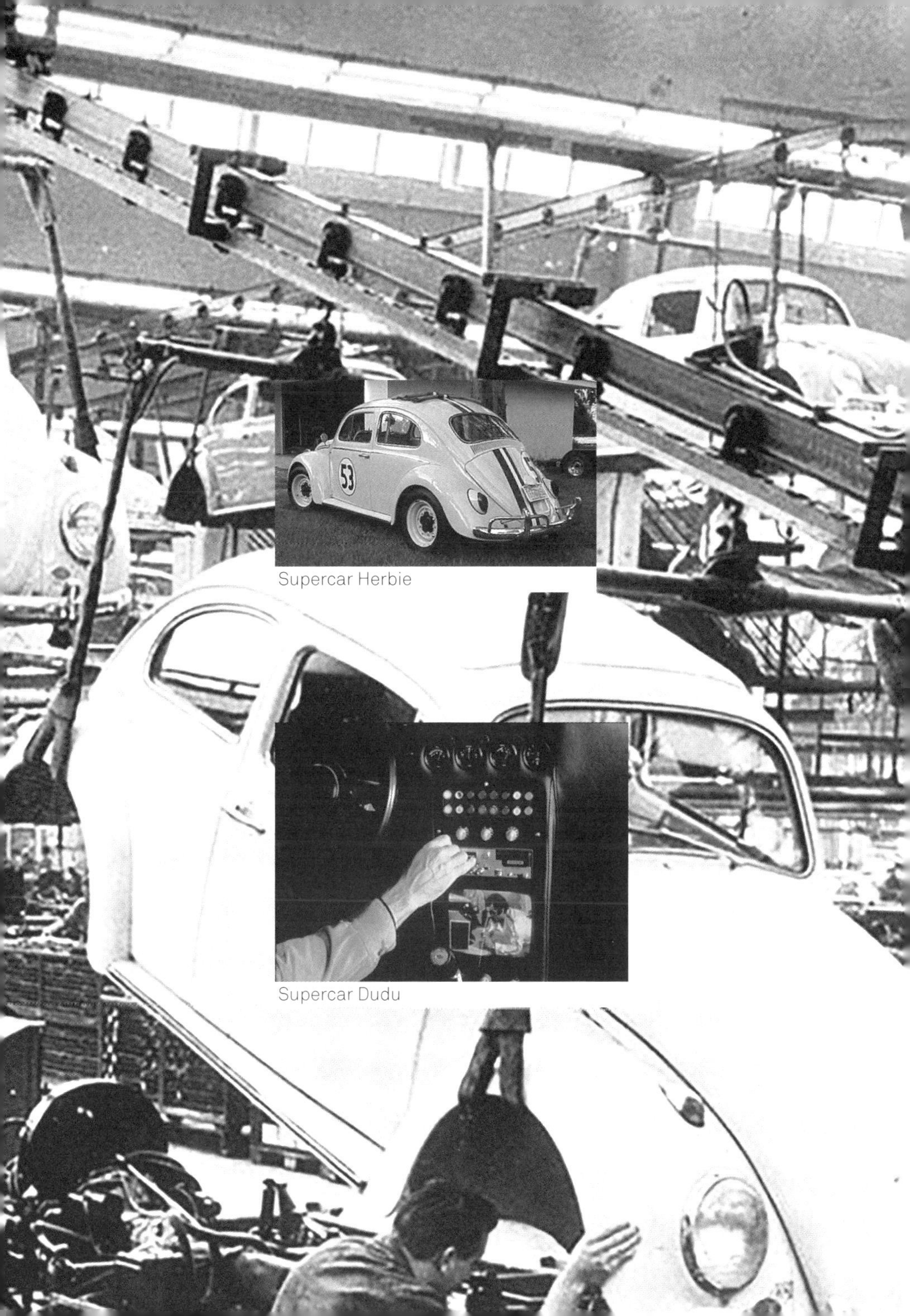

Supercar Herbie

Supercar Dudu

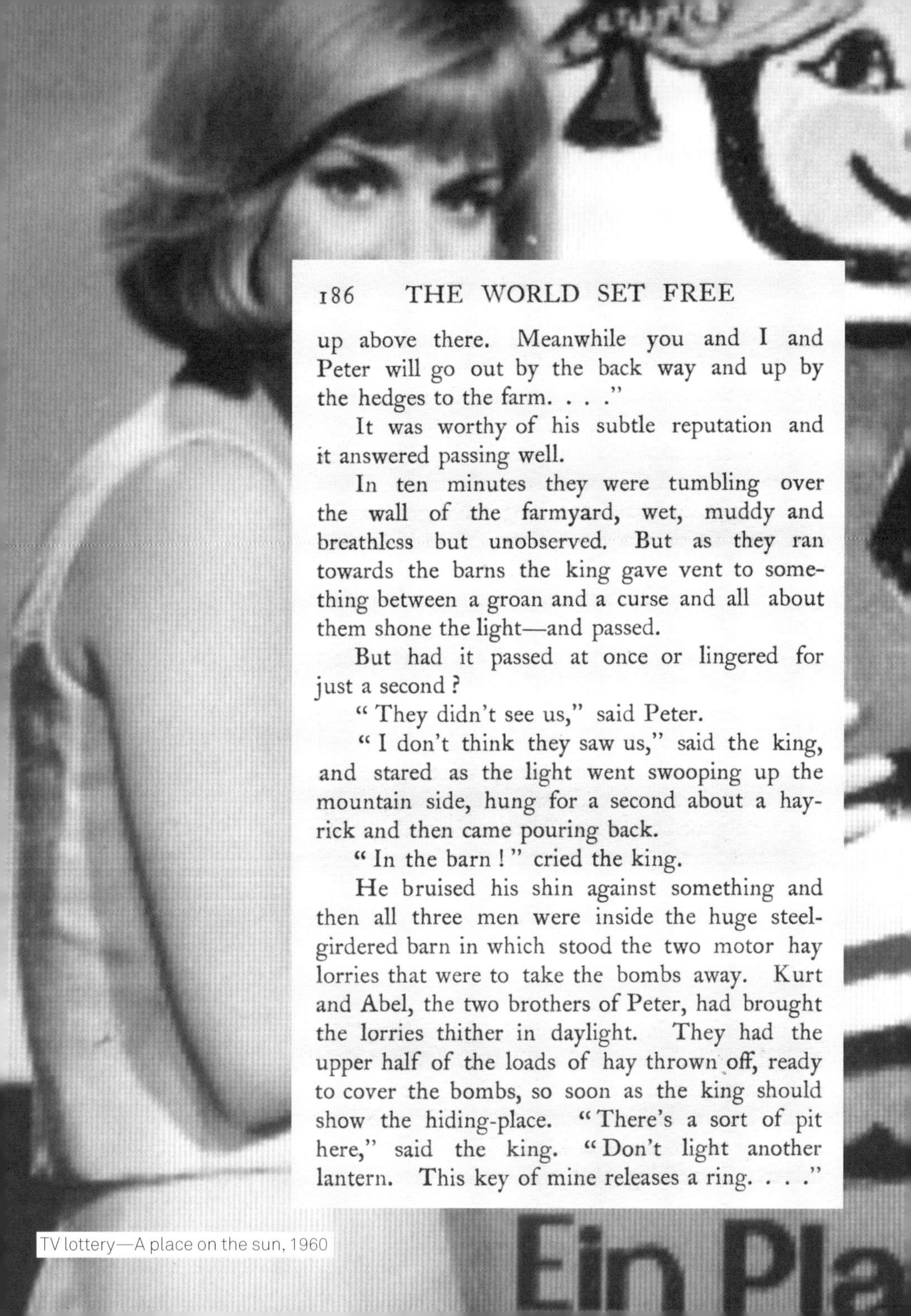

186 THE WORLD SET FREE

up above there. Meanwhile you and I and Peter will go out by the back way and up by the hedges to the farm. . . ."

It was worthy of his subtle reputation and it answered passing well.

In ten minutes they were tumbling over the wall of the farmyard, wet, muddy and breathless but unobserved. But as they ran towards the barns the king gave vent to something between a groan and a curse and all about them shone the light—and passed.

But had it passed at once or lingered for just a second?

"They didn't see us," said Peter.

"I don't think they saw us," said the king, and stared as the light went swooping up the mountain side, hung for a second about a hayrick and then came pouring back.

"In the barn!" cried the king.

He bruised his shin against something and then all three men were inside the huge steel-girdered barn in which stood the two motor hay lorries that were to take the bombs away. Kurt and Abel, the two brothers of Peter, had brought the lorries thither in daylight. They had the upper half of the loads of hay thrown off, ready to cover the bombs, so soon as the king should show the hiding-place. "There's a sort of pit here," said the king. "Don't light another lantern. This key of mine releases a ring. . . ."

TV lottery—A place on the sun, 1960

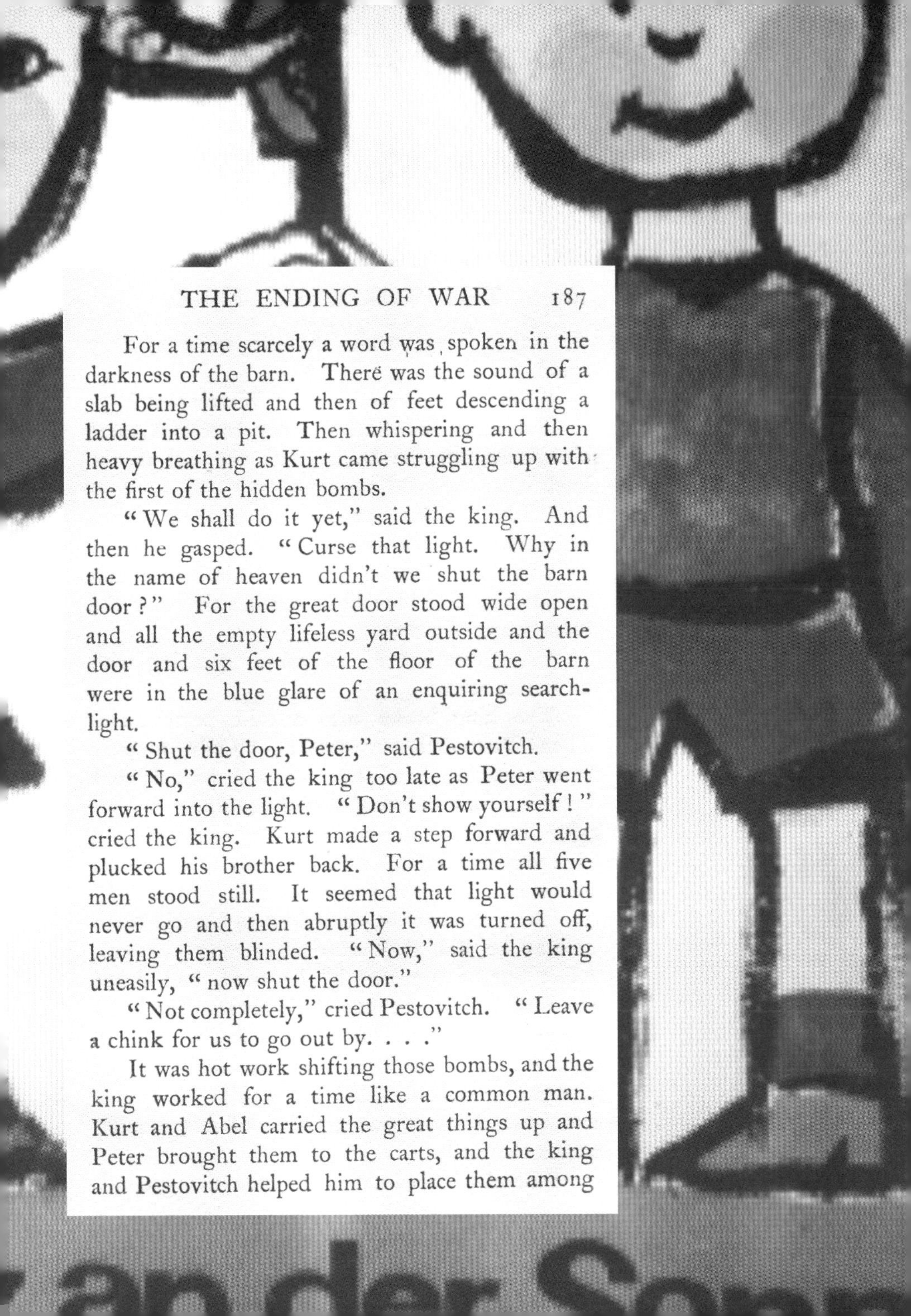

For a time scarcely a word was spoken in the darkness of the barn. There was the sound of a slab being lifted and then of feet descending a ladder into a pit. Then whispering and then heavy breathing as Kurt came struggling up with the first of the hidden bombs.

"We shall do it yet," said the king. And then he gasped. "Curse that light. Why in the name of heaven didn't we shut the barn door?" For the great door stood wide open and all the empty lifeless yard outside and the door and six feet of the floor of the barn were in the blue glare of an enquiring search-light.

"Shut the door, Peter," said Pestovitch.

"No," cried the king too late as Peter went forward into the light. "Don't show yourself!" cried the king. Kurt made a step forward and plucked his brother back. For a time all five men stood still. It seemed that light would never go and then abruptly it was turned off, leaving them blinded. "Now," said the king uneasily, "now shut the door."

"Not completely," cried Pestovitch. "Leave a chink for us to go out by. . . ."

It was hot work shifting those bombs, and the king worked for a time like a common man. Kurt and Abel carried the great things up and Peter brought them to the carts, and the king and Pestovitch helped him to place them among

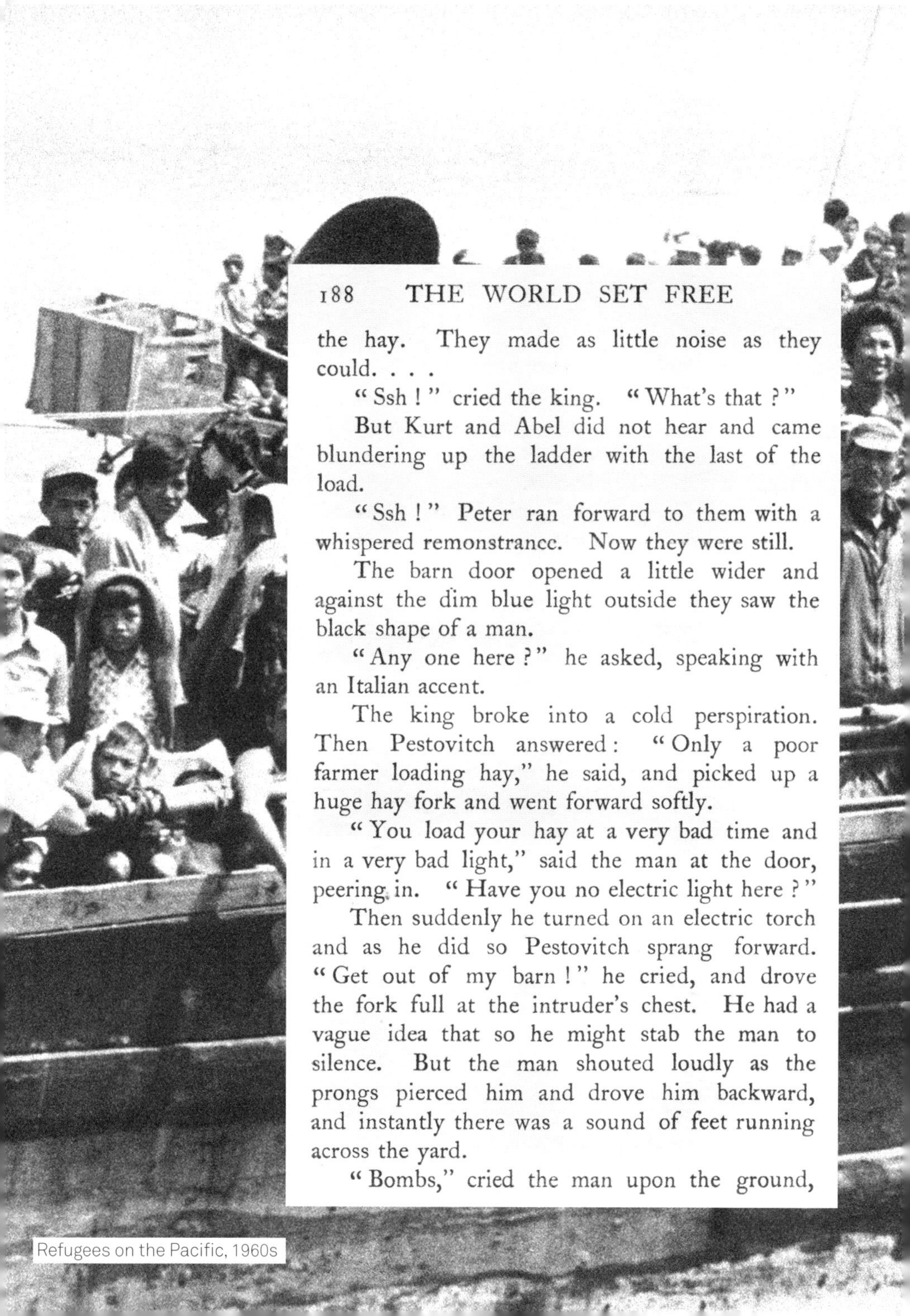

the hay. They made as little noise as they could. . . .

"Ssh!" cried the king. "What's that?"

But Kurt and Abel did not hear and came blundering up the ladder with the last of the load.

"Ssh!" Peter ran forward to them with a whispered remonstrance. Now they were still.

The barn door opened a little wider and against the dim blue light outside they saw the black shape of a man.

"Any one here?" he asked, speaking with an Italian accent.

The king broke into a cold perspiration. Then Pestovitch answered: "Only a poor farmer loading hay," he said, and picked up a huge hay fork and went forward softly.

"You load your hay at a very bad time and in a very bad light," said the man at the door, peering in. "Have you no electric light here?"

Then suddenly he turned on an electric torch and as he did so Pestovitch sprang forward. "Get out of my barn!" he cried, and drove the fork full at the intruder's chest. He had a vague idea that so he might stab the man to silence. But the man shouted loudly as the prongs pierced him and drove him backward, and instantly there was a sound of feet running across the yard.

"Bombs," cried the man upon the ground,

Refugees on the Pacific, 1960s

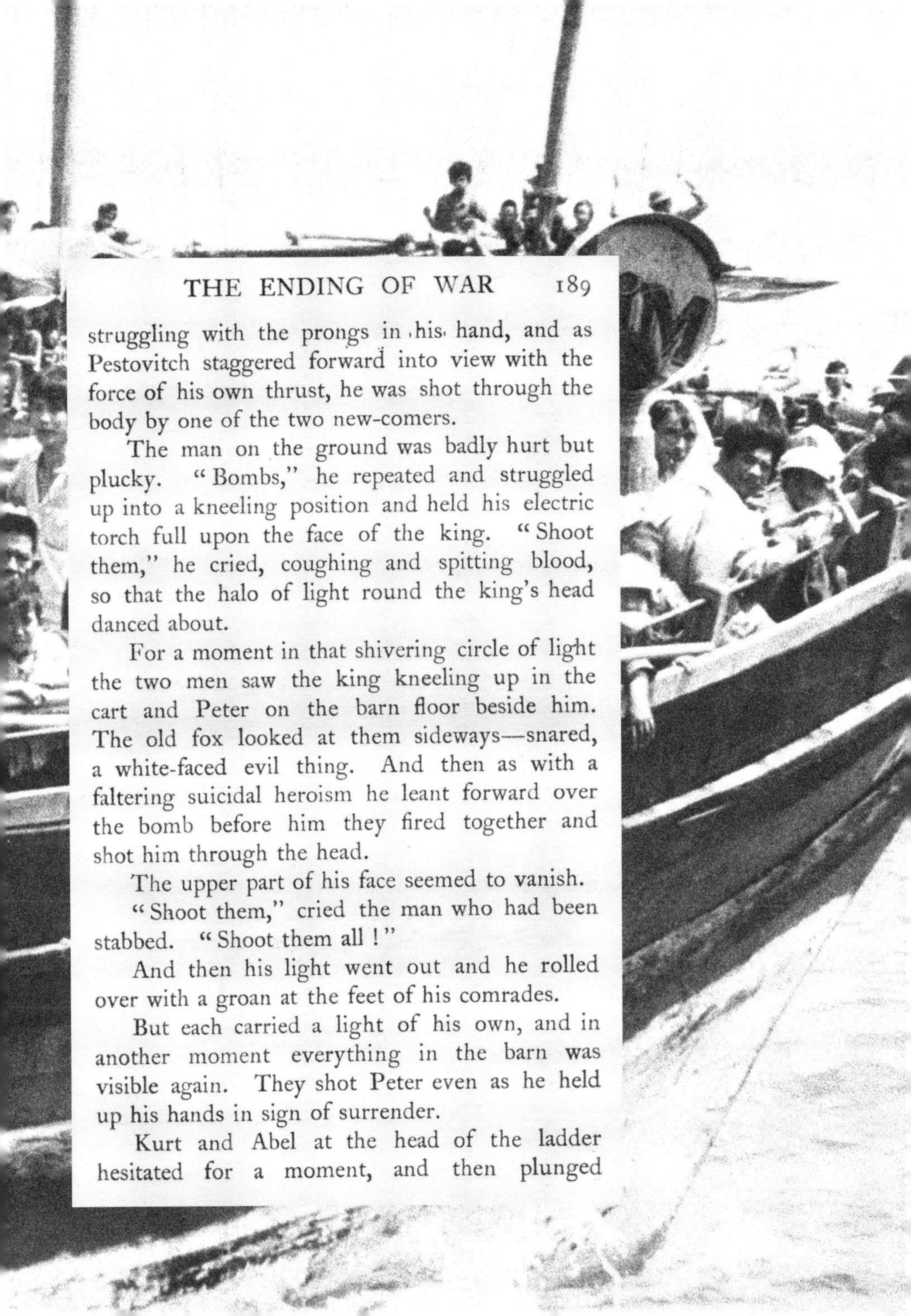

struggling with the prongs in his hand, and as Pestovitch staggered forward into view with the force of his own thrust, he was shot through the body by one of the two new-comers.

The man on the ground was badly hurt but plucky. "Bombs," he repeated and struggled up into a kneeling position and held his electric torch full upon the face of the king. "Shoot them," he cried, coughing and spitting blood, so that the halo of light round the king's head danced about.

For a moment in that shivering circle of light the two men saw the king kneeling up in the cart and Peter on the barn floor beside him. The old fox looked at them sideways—snared, a white-faced evil thing. And then as with a faltering suicidal heroism he leant forward over the bomb before him they fired together and shot him through the head.

The upper part of his face seemed to vanish.

"Shoot them," cried the man who had been stabbed. "Shoot them all!"

And then his light went out and he rolled over with a groan at the feet of his comrades.

But each carried a light of his own, and in another moment everything in the barn was visible again. They shot Peter even as he held up his hands in sign of surrender.

Kurt and Abel at the head of the ladder hesitated for a moment, and then plunged

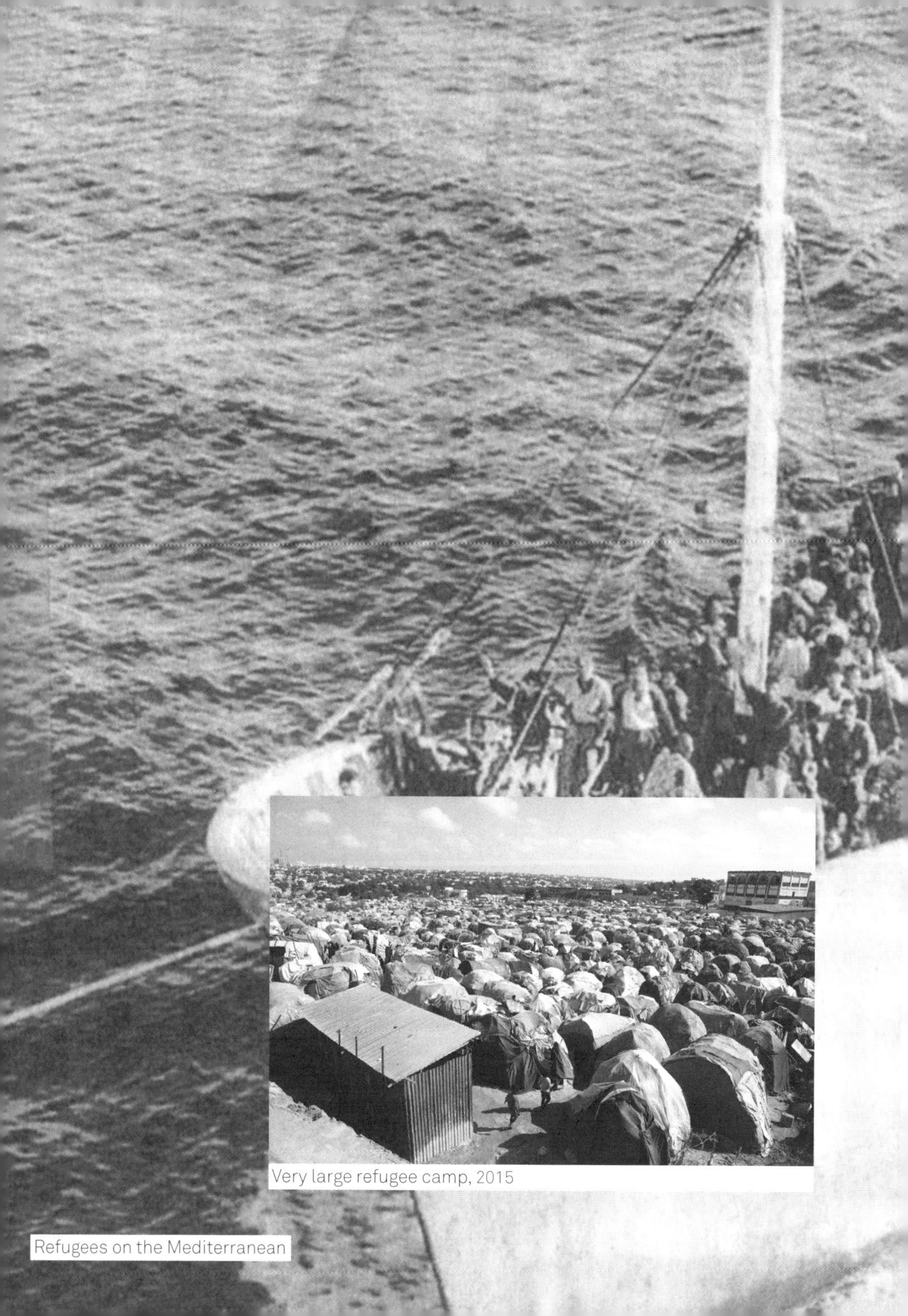

Very large refugee camp, 2015

Refugees on the Mediterranean

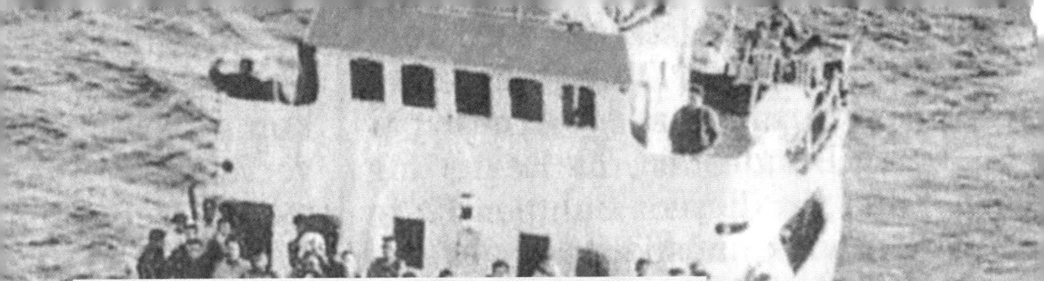

backward into the pit. "If we don't kill them," said one of the sharpshooters, "they'll blow us to rags. They've gone down that hatchway. Come! . . .

"Here they are. Hands up! I say. Hold your light while I shoot. . . ."

§ 8

It was still quite dark when his valet and Firmin came together and told the ex-king Egbert that the business was settled.

He started up into a sitting position on the side of his bed.

"Did he go out?" asked the ex-king.

"He is dead," said Firmin. "He was shot."

The ex-king reflected. "That's about the best thing that could have happened," he said. "Where are the bombs? In that farmhouse on the opposite hillside! Why! the place is in sight! Let us go. I'll dress. Is there any one in the place, Firmin, to get us a cup of coffee?"

Through the hungry twilight of the dawn the ex-king's automobile carried him to the farmhouse where the last rebel king was lying among his bombs. The rim of the sky flashed, the east grew bright, and the sun was just rising over the hills when King Egbert reached the farmyard. There he found the hay lorries drawn out from the barn with the dreadful bombs still

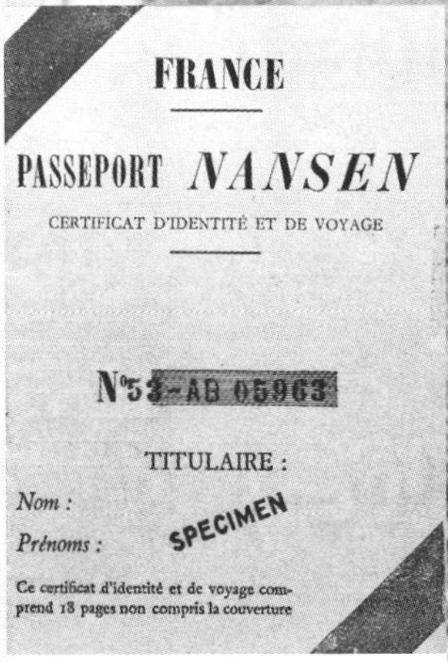

Refugee pass, since 1922

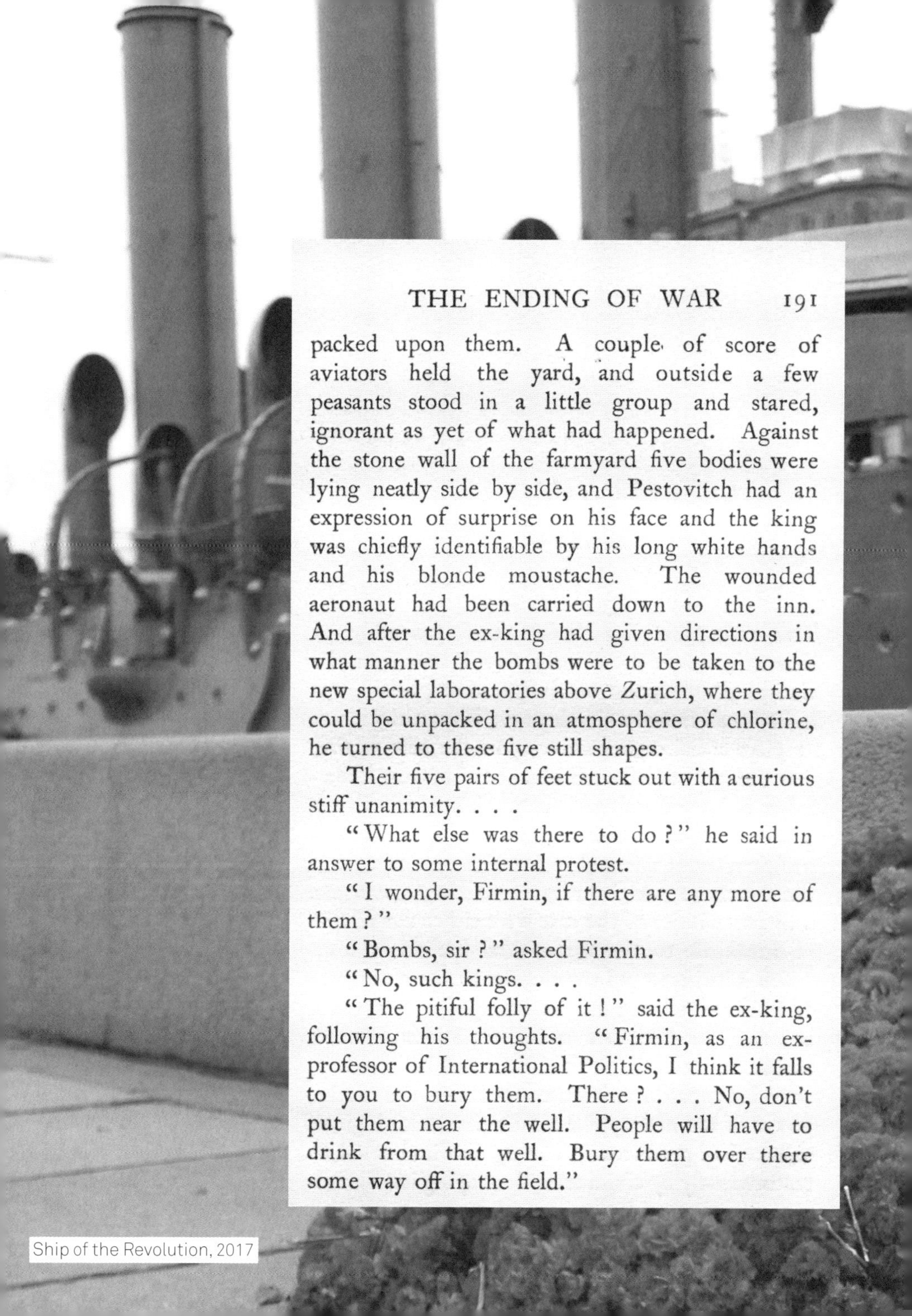

Ship of the Revolution, 2017

packed upon them. A couple of score of aviators held the yard, and outside a few peasants stood in a little group and stared, ignorant as yet of what had happened. Against the stone wall of the farmyard five bodies were lying neatly side by side, and Pestovitch had an expression of surprise on his face and the king was chiefly identifiable by his long white hands and his blonde moustache. The wounded aeronaut had been carried down to the inn. And after the ex-king had given directions in what manner the bombs were to be taken to the new special laboratories above Zurich, where they could be unpacked in an atmosphere of chlorine, he turned to these five still shapes.

Their five pairs of feet stuck out with a curious stiff unanimity. . . .

"What else was there to do?" he said in answer to some internal protest.

"I wonder, Firmin, if there are any more of them?"

"Bombs, sir?" asked Firmin.

"No, such kings. . . .

"The pitiful folly of it!" said the ex-king, following his thoughts. "Firmin, as an ex-professor of International Politics, I think it falls to you to bury them. There? . . . No, don't put them near the well. People will have to drink from that well. Bury them over there some way off in the field."

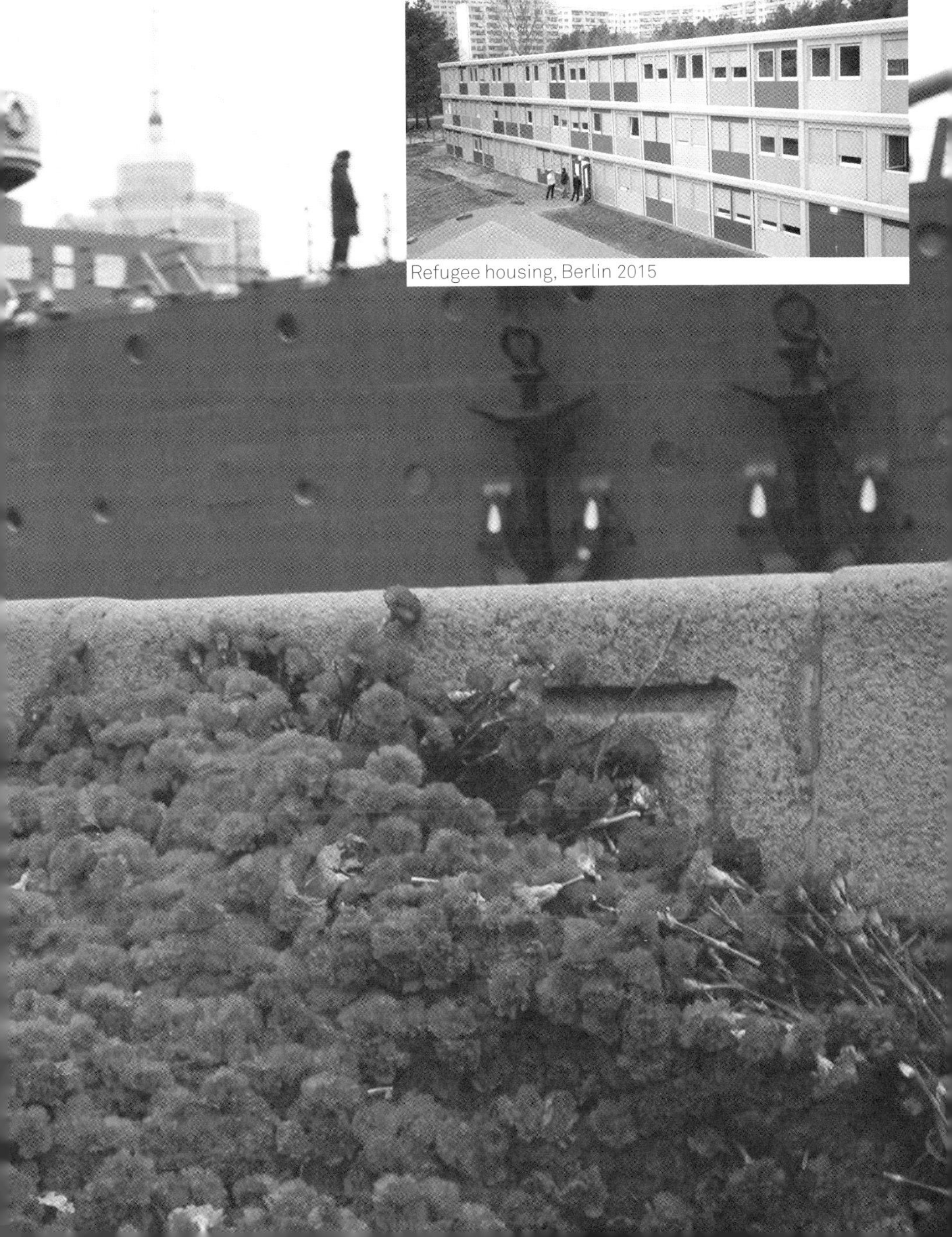

Refugee housing, Berlin 2015

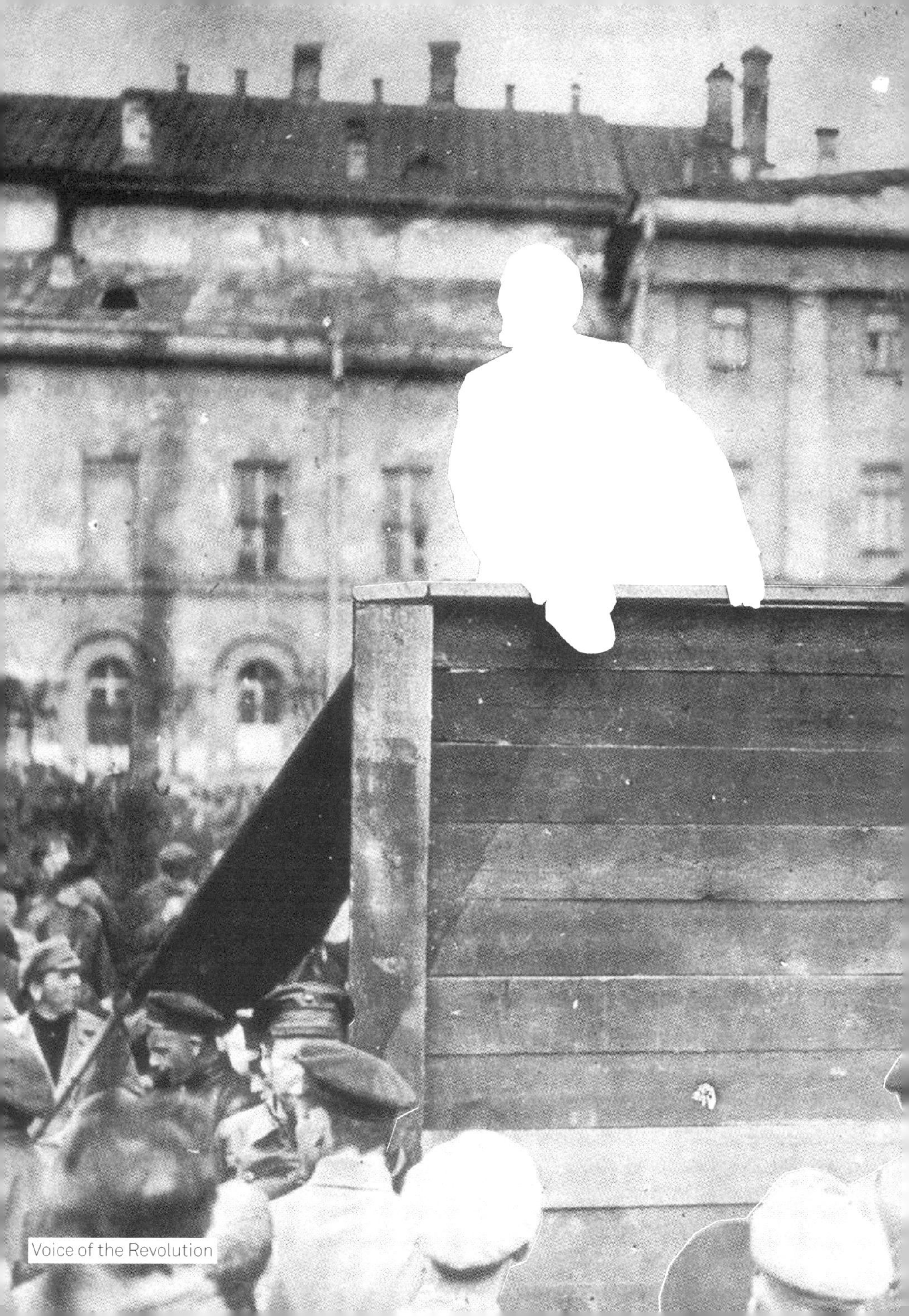

Voice of the Revolution

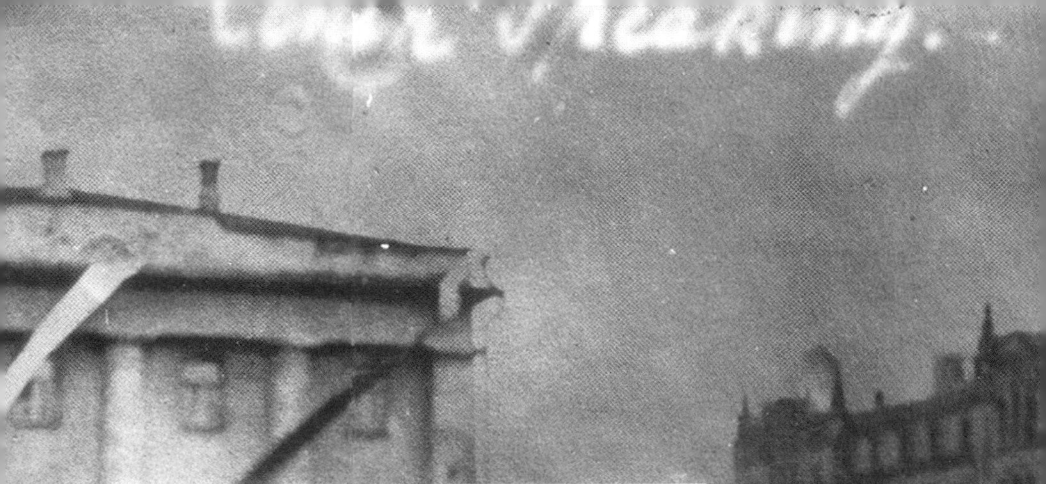

CHAPTER THE FOURTH

THE NEW PHASE

§ I

THE task that lay before the Assembly of Brissago, viewed as we may view it now from the clarifying standpoint of things accomplished, was in its broad issues a simple one. Essentially it was to place social organization upon the new footing that the swift accelerated advance of human knowledge had rendered necessary. The council was gathered together with the haste of a salvage expedition, and it was confronted with wreckage ; but the wreckage was irreparable wreckage, and the only possibilities of the case were either the relapse of mankind to the agricultural barbarism from which it had emerged so painfully or the acceptance of achieved science as the basis of a new social order. The old tendencies of human nature, suspicion, jealousy, particularism and belligerency, were incompatible with the monstrous destructive power of the new appliances the inhuman logic of science had produced. The equilibrium could be restored only by civilization destroying itself down

One World citizen number one, 1956

to a level at which modern apparatus could no longer be produced, or by human nature adapting itself in its institutions to the new conditions. It was for the latter alternative that the assembly existed.

Sooner or later this choice would have confronted mankind. The sudden development of atomic science did but precipitate and render rapid and dramatic a clash between the new and the customary that had been gathering since ever the first flint was chipped or the first fire built together. From the day when man contrived himself a tool and suffered another male to draw near him, he ceased to be altogether a thing of instinct and untroubled convictions. From that day forth a widening breach can be traced between his egotistical passions and the social need. Slowly he adapted himself to the life of the homestead, and his passionate impulses widened out to the demands of the clan and the tribe. But widen though his impulses might, the latent hunter and wanderer and wonderer in his imagination outstripped their development. He was never quite subdued to the soil nor quite tamed to the home. Everywhere it needed teaching and the priest to keep him within the bounds of the plough-life and the beast-tending. Slowly a vast system of traditional imperatives superposed itself upon his instincts, imperatives that were admirably fitted to make him that cultivator, that

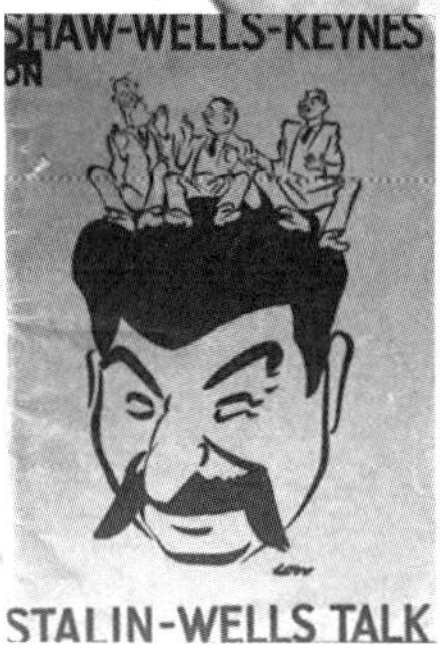

Conversation, 1934

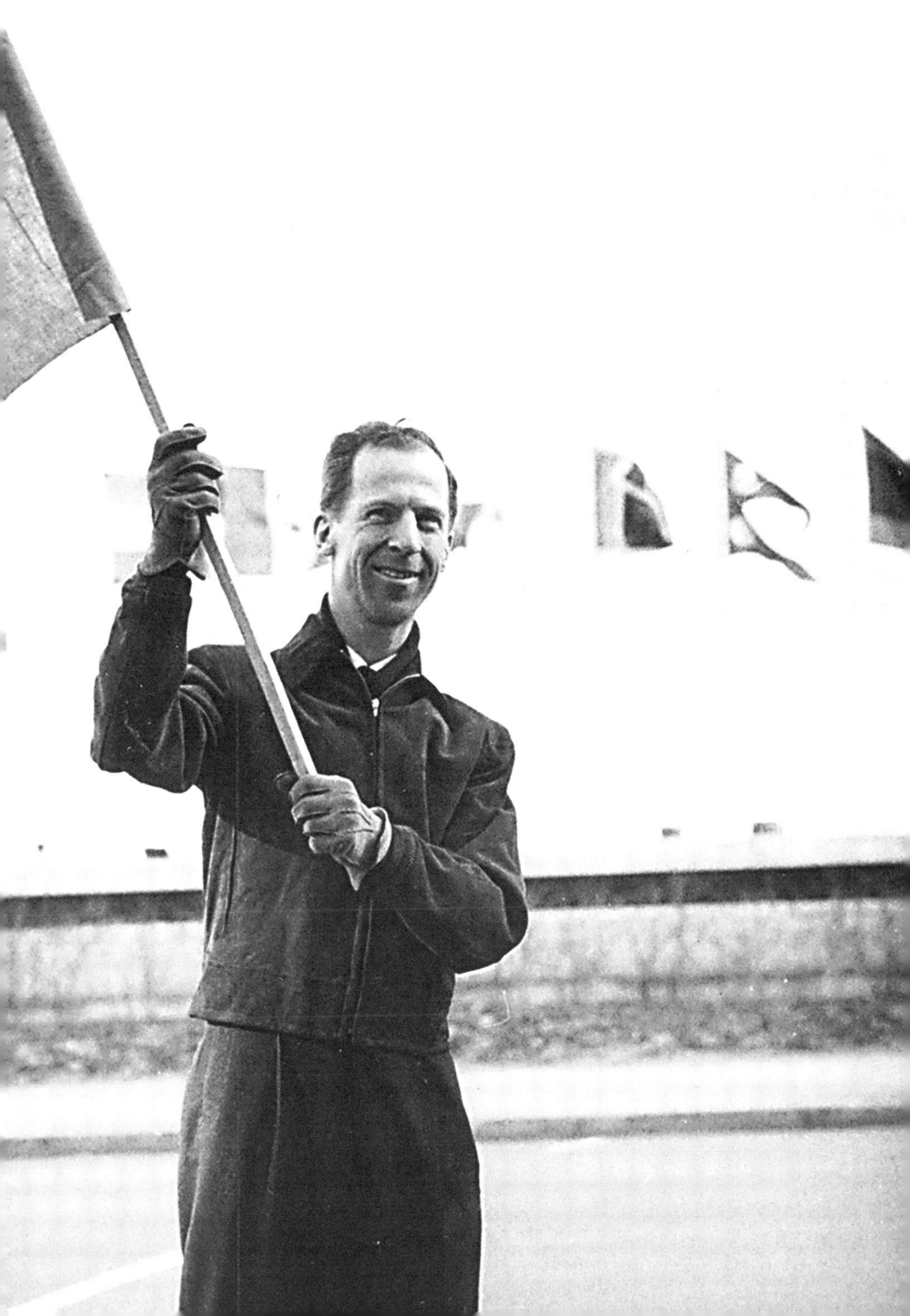

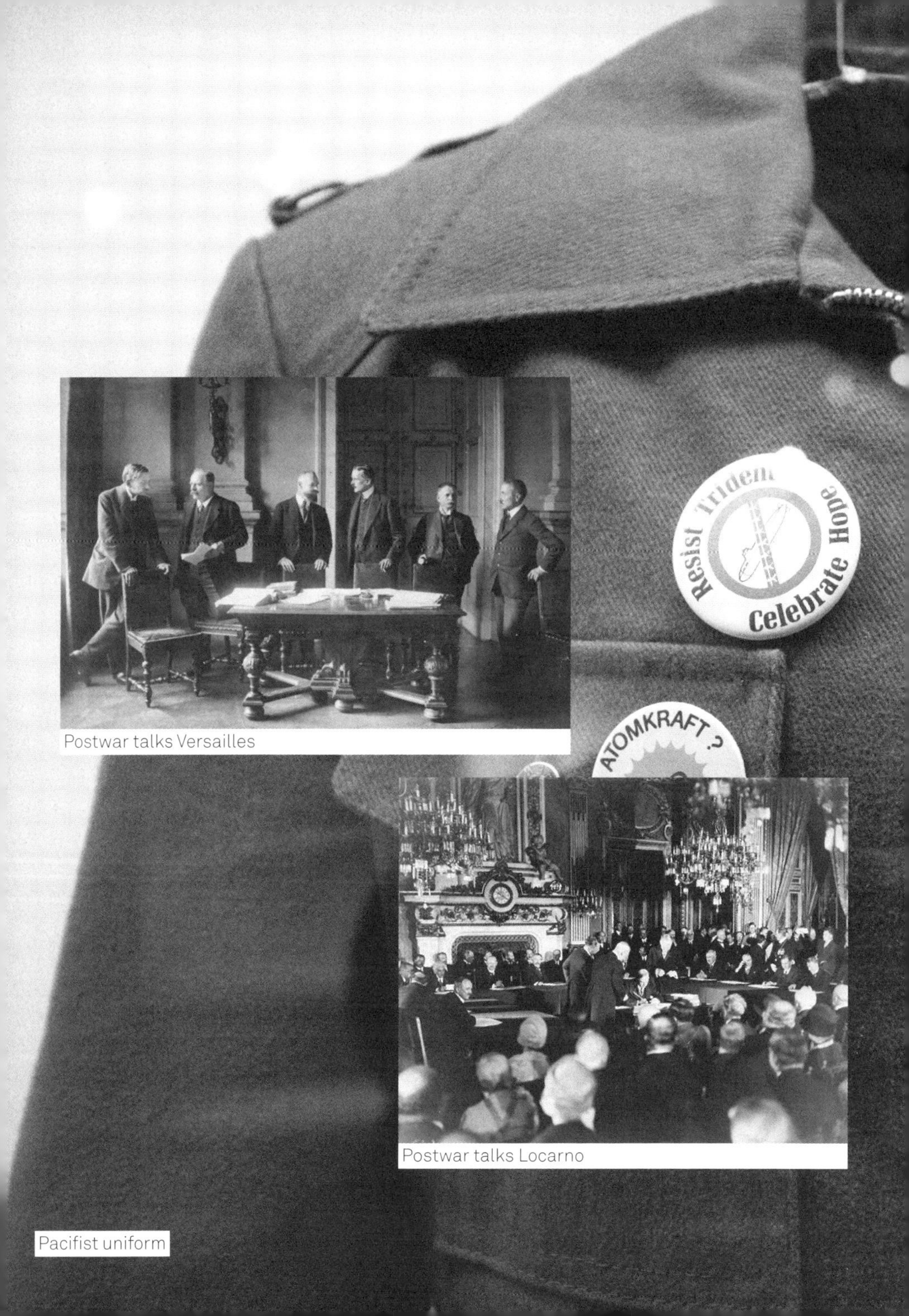

Postwar talks Versailles

Postwar talks Locarno

Pacifist uniform

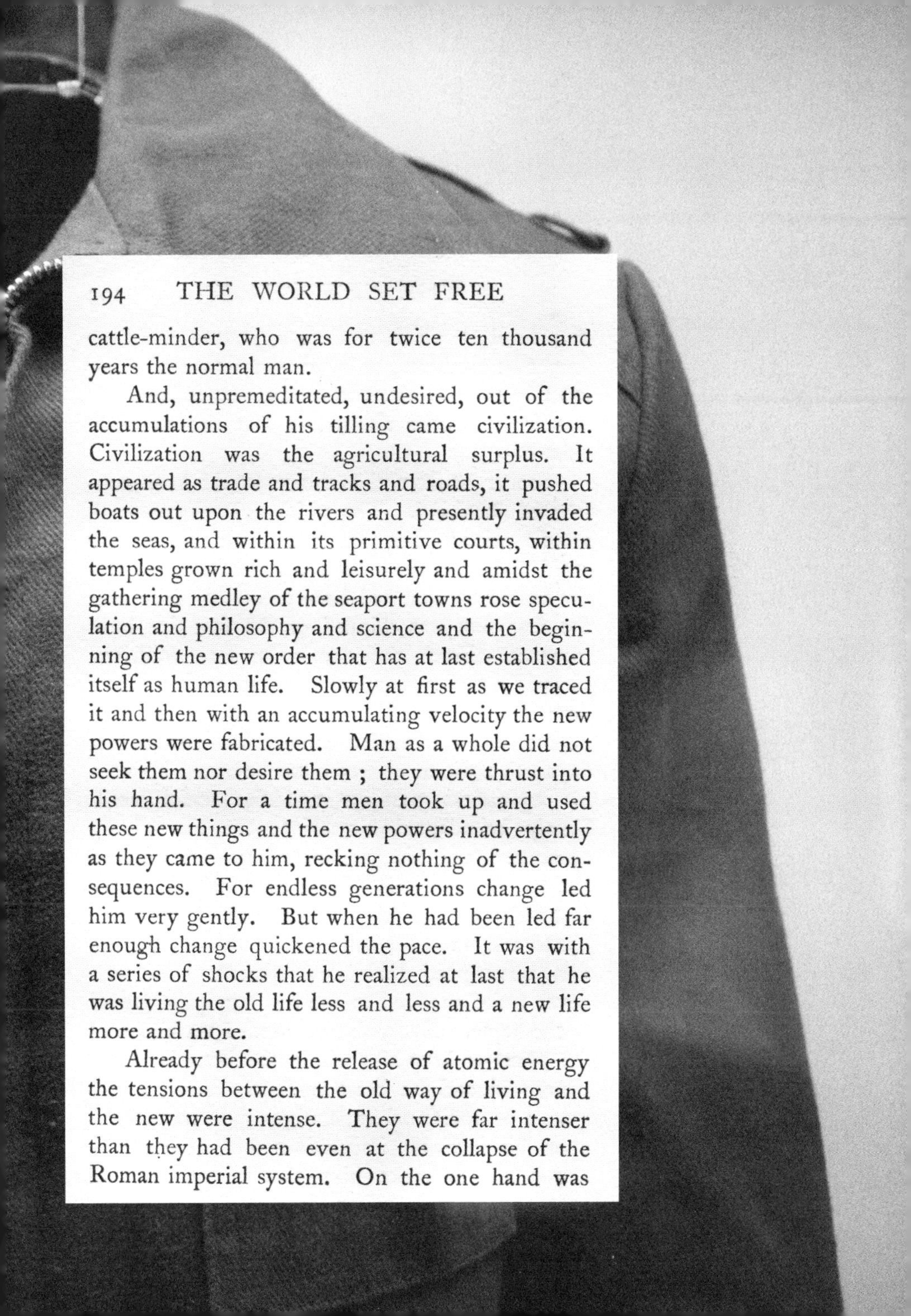

cattle-minder, who was for twice ten thousand years the normal man.

And, unpremeditated, undesired, out of the accumulations of his tilling came civilization. Civilization was the agricultural surplus. It appeared as trade and tracks and roads, it pushed boats out upon the rivers and presently invaded the seas, and within its primitive courts, within temples grown rich and leisurely and amidst the gathering medley of the seaport towns rose speculation and philosophy and science and the beginning of the new order that has at last established itself as human life. Slowly at first as we traced it and then with an accumulating velocity the new powers were fabricated. Man as a whole did not seek them nor desire them ; they were thrust into his hand. For a time men took up and used these new things and the new powers inadvertently as they came to him, recking nothing of the consequences. For endless generations change led him very gently. But when he had been led far enough change quickened the pace. It was with a series of shocks that he realized at last that he was living the old life less and less and a new life more and more.

Already before the release of atomic energy the tensions between the old way of living and the new were intense. They were far intenser than they had been even at the collapse of the Roman imperial system. On the one hand was

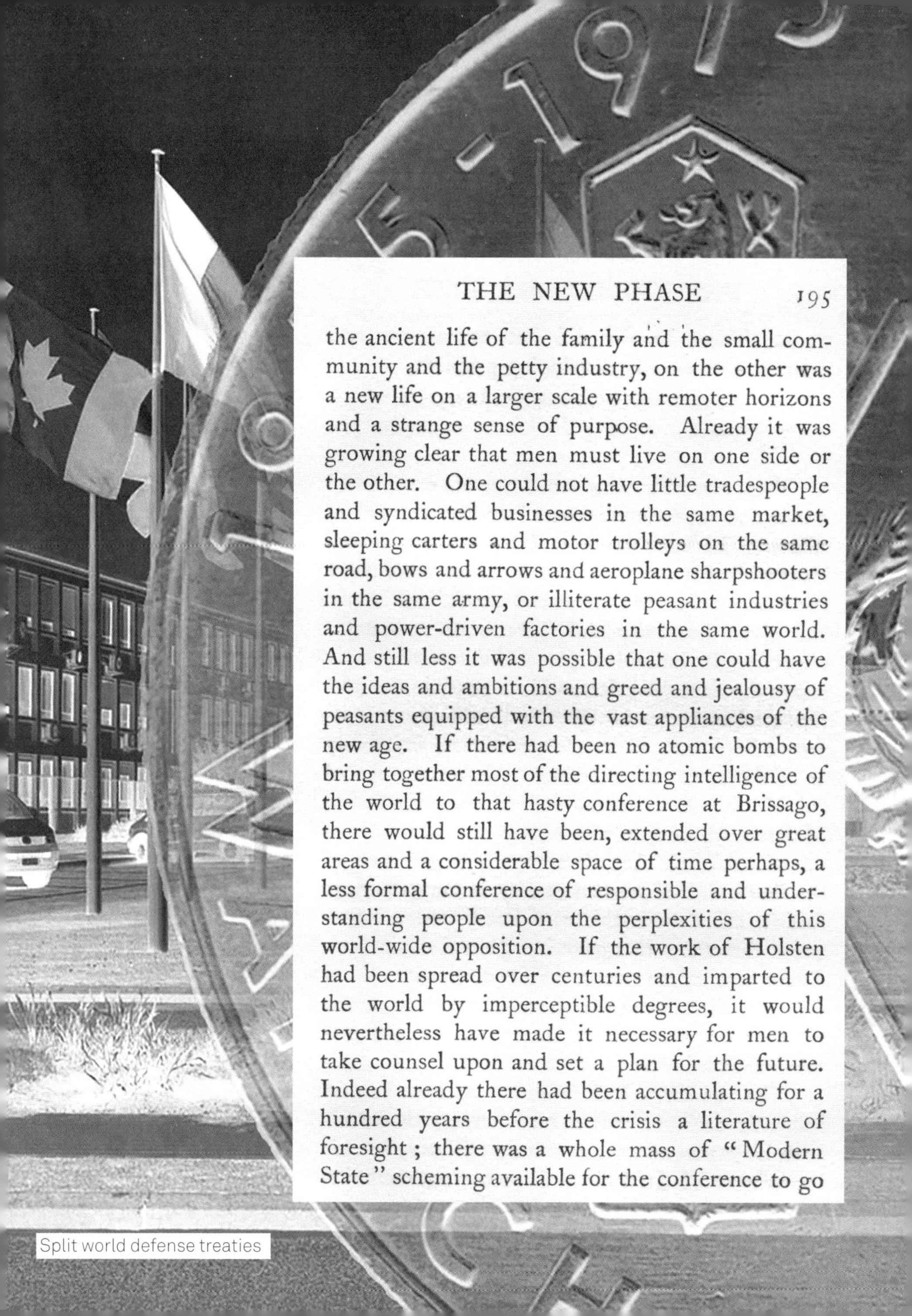

the ancient life of the family and the small community and the petty industry, on the other was a new life on a larger scale with remoter horizons and a strange sense of purpose. Already it was growing clear that men must live on one side or the other. One could not have little tradespeople and syndicated businesses in the same market, sleeping carters and motor trolleys on the same road, bows and arrows and aeroplane sharpshooters in the same army, or illiterate peasant industries and power-driven factories in the same world. And still less it was possible that one could have the ideas and ambitions and greed and jealousy of peasants equipped with the vast appliances of the new age. If there had been no atomic bombs to bring together most of the directing intelligence of the world to that hasty conference at Brissago, there would still have been, extended over great areas and a considerable space of time perhaps, a less formal conference of responsible and understanding people upon the perplexities of this world-wide opposition. If the work of Holsten had been spread over centuries and imparted to the world by imperceptible degrees, it would nevertheless have made it necessary for men to take counsel upon and set a plan for the future. Indeed already there had been accumulating for a hundred years before the crisis a literature of foresight; there was a whole mass of "Modern State" scheming available for the conference to go

Split world defense treaties

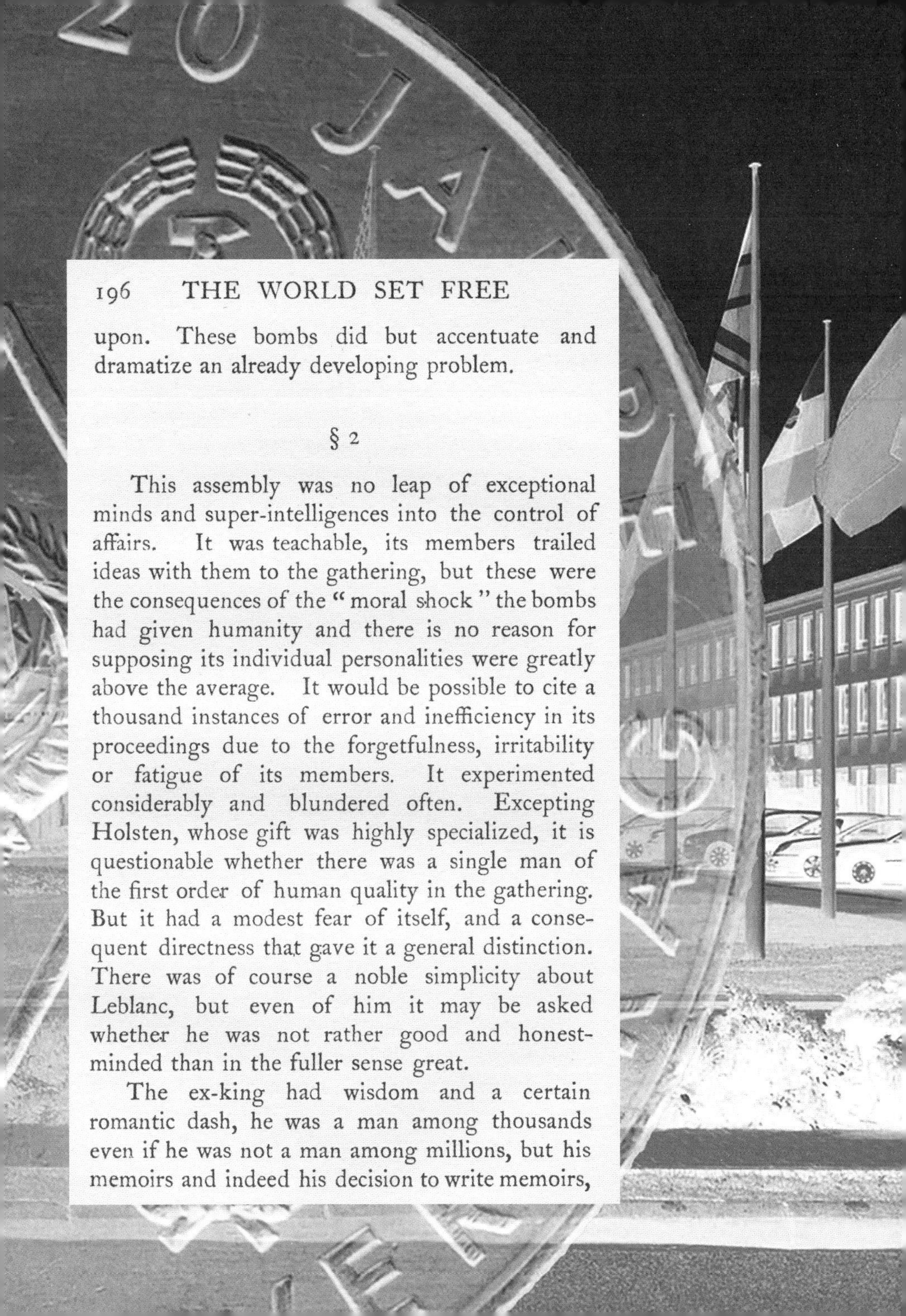

upon. These bombs did but accentuate and dramatize an already developing problem.

§ 2

This assembly was no leap of exceptional minds and super-intelligences into the control of affairs. It was teachable, its members trailed ideas with them to the gathering, but these were the consequences of the "moral shock" the bombs had given humanity and there is no reason for supposing its individual personalities were greatly above the average. It would be possible to cite a thousand instances of error and inefficiency in its proceedings due to the forgetfulness, irritability or fatigue of its members. It experimented considerably and blundered often. Excepting Holsten, whose gift was highly specialized, it is questionable whether there was a single man of the first order of human quality in the gathering. But it had a modest fear of itself, and a consequent directness that gave it a general distinction. There was of course a noble simplicity about Leblanc, but even of him it may be asked whether he was not rather good and honest-minded than in the fuller sense great.

The ex-king had wisdom and a certain romantic dash, he was a man among thousands even if he was not a man among millions, but his memoirs and indeed his decision to write memoirs,

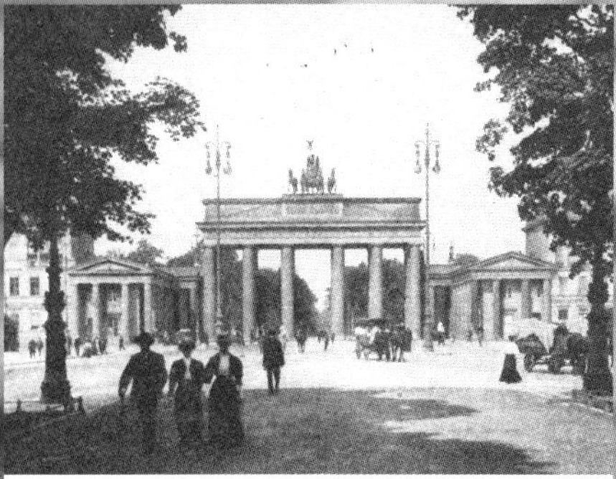

Peacetime

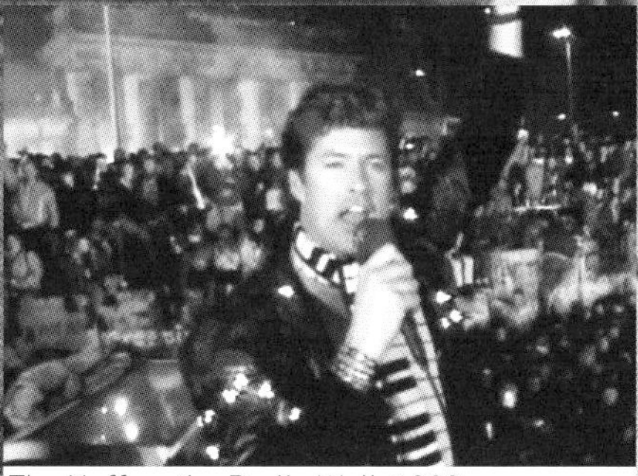

The Hoff on the Berlin Wall, 1989

Cold war time

give the quality of himself and his associates. The book makes admirable but astonishing reading. Therein he takes the great work the council was doing for granted as a little child takes God. It is as if he had no sense of it at all. He tells amusing trivialities about his cousin Wilhelm and his secretary Firmin, he pokes fun at the American president, who was indeed rather a little accident of the political machine than a representative American, and he gives a long description of how he was lost for three days in the mountains in the company of the only Japanese member, a loss that seems to have caused no serious interruption of the work of the council. . . .

The Brissago conference has been written about time after time as though it were a gathering of the very flower of humanity. Perched up there by the freak or wisdom of Leblanc, it had a certain Olympian quality, and the natural tendency of the human mind to elaborate such a resemblance would have us give its members the likenesses of gods. It would be equally reasonable to compare it to one of those enforced meetings upon the mountain-tops that must have occurred in the opening phases of the Deluge. The strength of the council lay not in itself but in the circumstances that had quickened its intelligence, dispelled its vanities, and emancipated it from traditional ambitions and antagonisms.

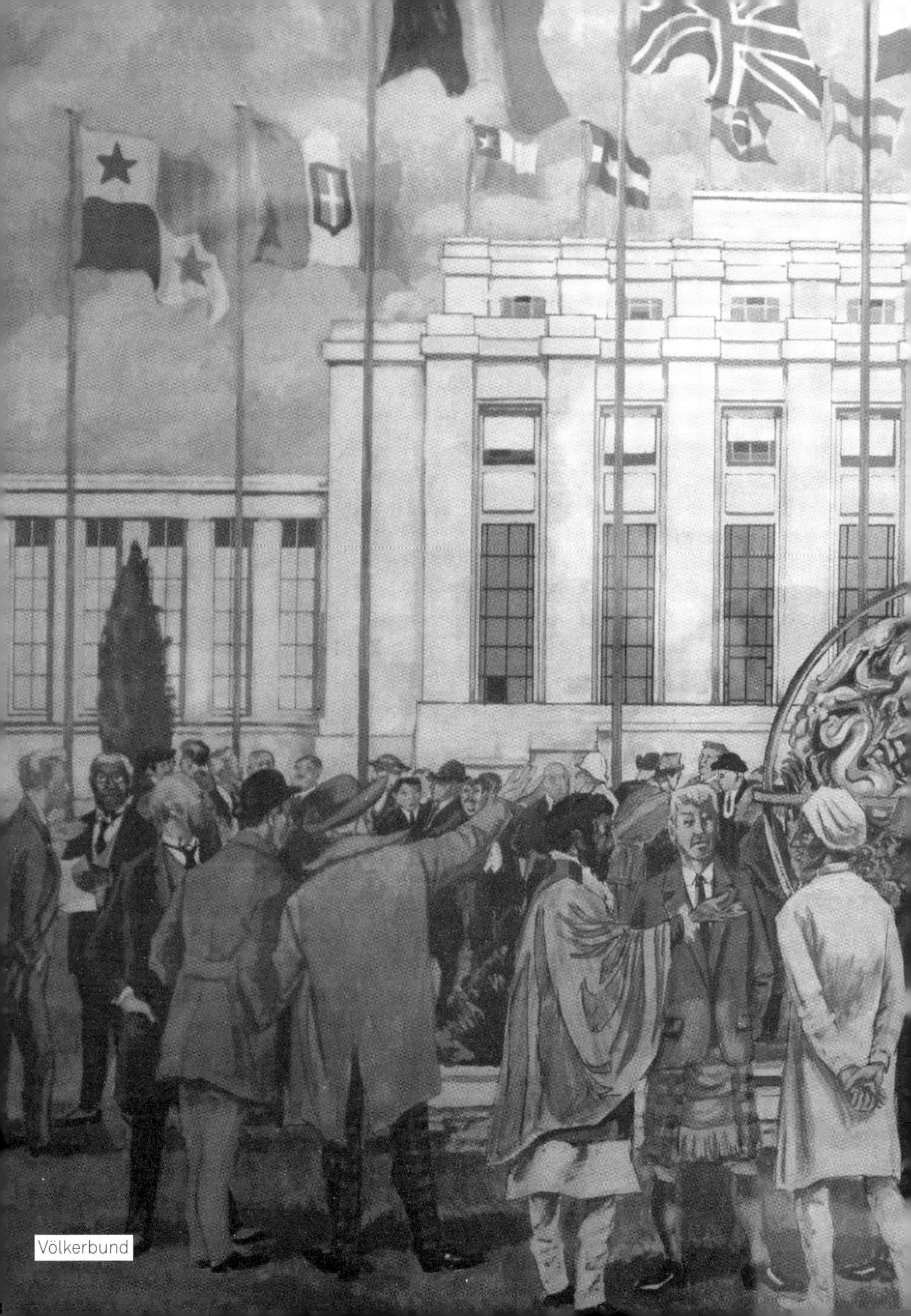

Völkerbund

It was stripped of the accumulations of centuries, a naked government with all that freedom of action that nakedness affords. And its problems were set before it with a plainness that was out of all comparison with the complicated and perplexing intimations of the former time.

§ 3

The world on which the council looked did indeed present a task quite sufficiently immense and altogether too urgent for any wanton indulgence in internal dissension. It may be interesting to sketch in a few phrases the condition of mankind at the close of the period of warring states, in the year of crisis that followed the release of atomic power. It was a world extraordinarily limited when one measures it by later standards, and it was now in a state of the direst confusion and distress.

It must be remembered that at this time men had still to spread into enormous areas of the land surface of the globe. There were vast mountain wildernesses, forest wildernesses, sandy deserts, and frozen lands. Men still clung closely to water and arable soil in temperate or sub-tropical climates, they lived abundantly only in river valleys, and all their great cities had grown upon large navigable rivers or close to ports upon the sea. Over great areas even of

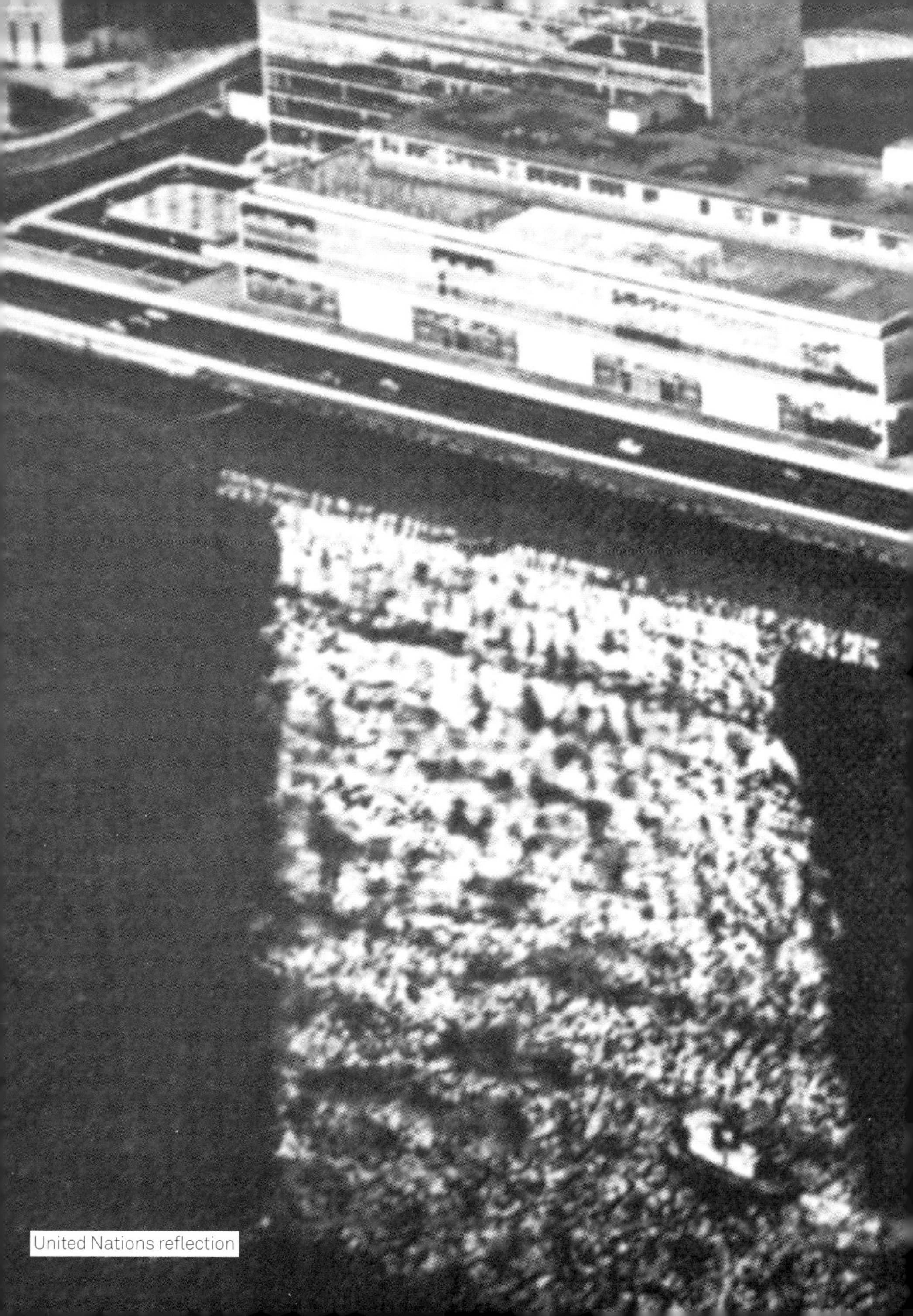

United Nations reflection

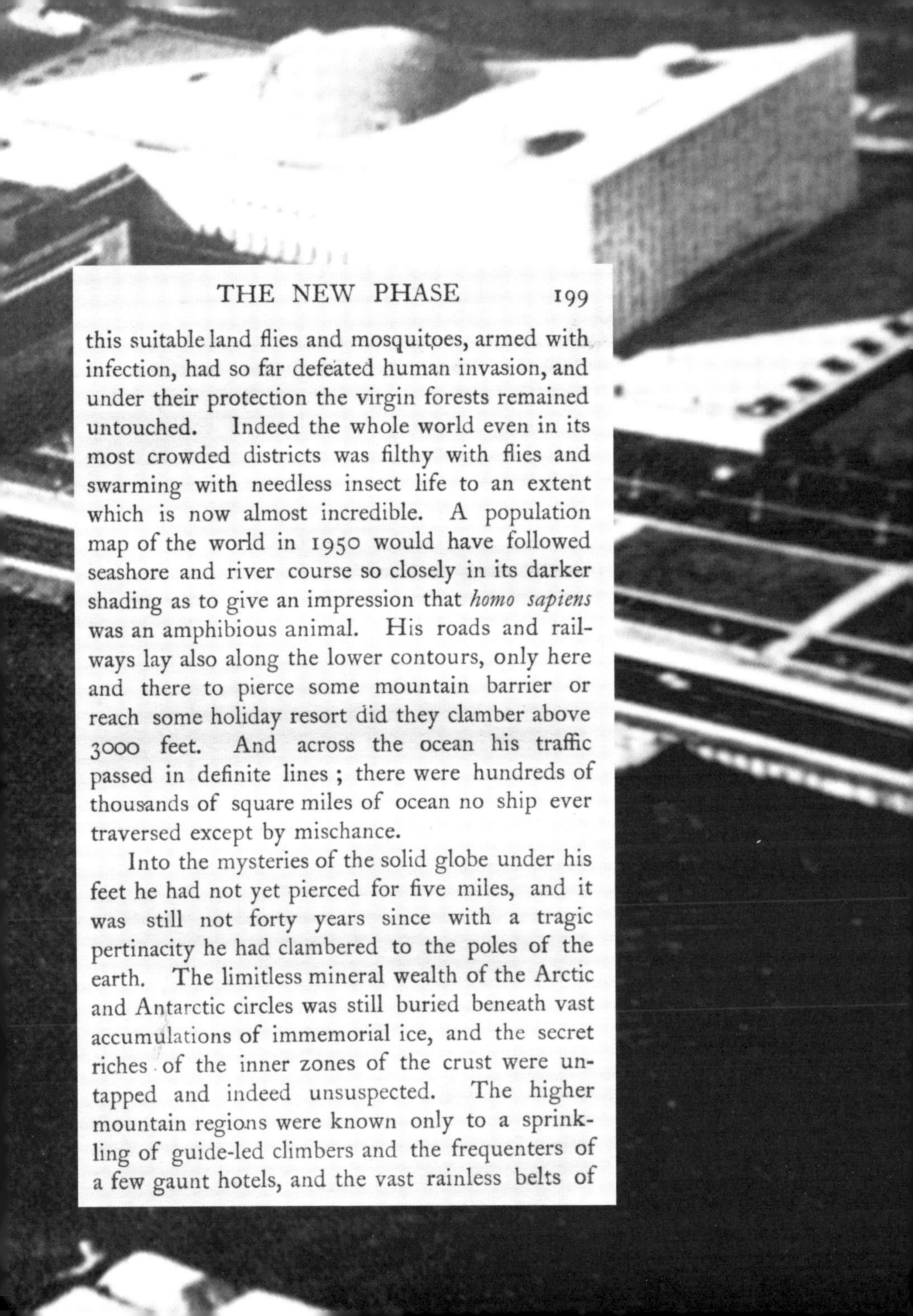

this suitable land flies and mosquitoes, armed with infection, had so far defeated human invasion, and under their protection the virgin forests remained untouched. Indeed the whole world even in its most crowded districts was filthy with flies and swarming with needless insect life to an extent which is now almost incredible. A population map of the world in 1950 would have followed seashore and river course so closely in its darker shading as to give an impression that *homo sapiens* was an amphibious animal. His roads and railways lay also along the lower contours, only here and there to pierce some mountain barrier or reach some holiday resort did they clamber above 3000 feet. And across the ocean his traffic passed in definite lines ; there were hundreds of thousands of square miles of ocean no ship ever traversed except by mischance.

Into the mysteries of the solid globe under his feet he had not yet pierced for five miles, and it was still not forty years since with a tragic pertinacity he had clambered to the poles of the earth. The limitless mineral wealth of the Arctic and Antarctic circles was still buried beneath vast accumulations of immemorial ice, and the secret riches of the inner zones of the crust were untapped and indeed unsuspected. The higher mountain regions were known only to a sprinkling of guide-led climbers and the frequenters of a few gaunt hotels, and the vast rainless belts of land that lay across the continental masses, from Gobi to Sahara and along the backbone of America, with their perfect air, their daily baths of blazing sunshine, their nights of cool serenity and glowing stars, and their reservoirs of deep-lying water, were as yet only desolations of fear and death to the common imagination.

And now under the shock of the atomic bombs, the great masses of population which had gathered into the enormous dingy town centres of that period were dispossessed and scattered disastrously over the surrounding rural areas. It was as if some brutal force, grown impatient at last at man's blindness, had with the deliberate intention of a rearrangement of population upon more wholesome lines, shaken the world. The great industrial regions and the large cities that had escaped the bombs were, because of their complete economic collapse, in almost as tragic plight as those that blazed, and the countryside was disordered by a multitude of wandering and lawless strangers. In some parts of the world famine raged, and in many regions there was plague. . . . The plains of north India, which had become more and more dependent for the general welfare on the railways and that great system of irrigation canals which the malignant section of the patriots had destroyed, were in a state of peculiar distress, whole villages lay dead together, no man heeding, and the very tigers

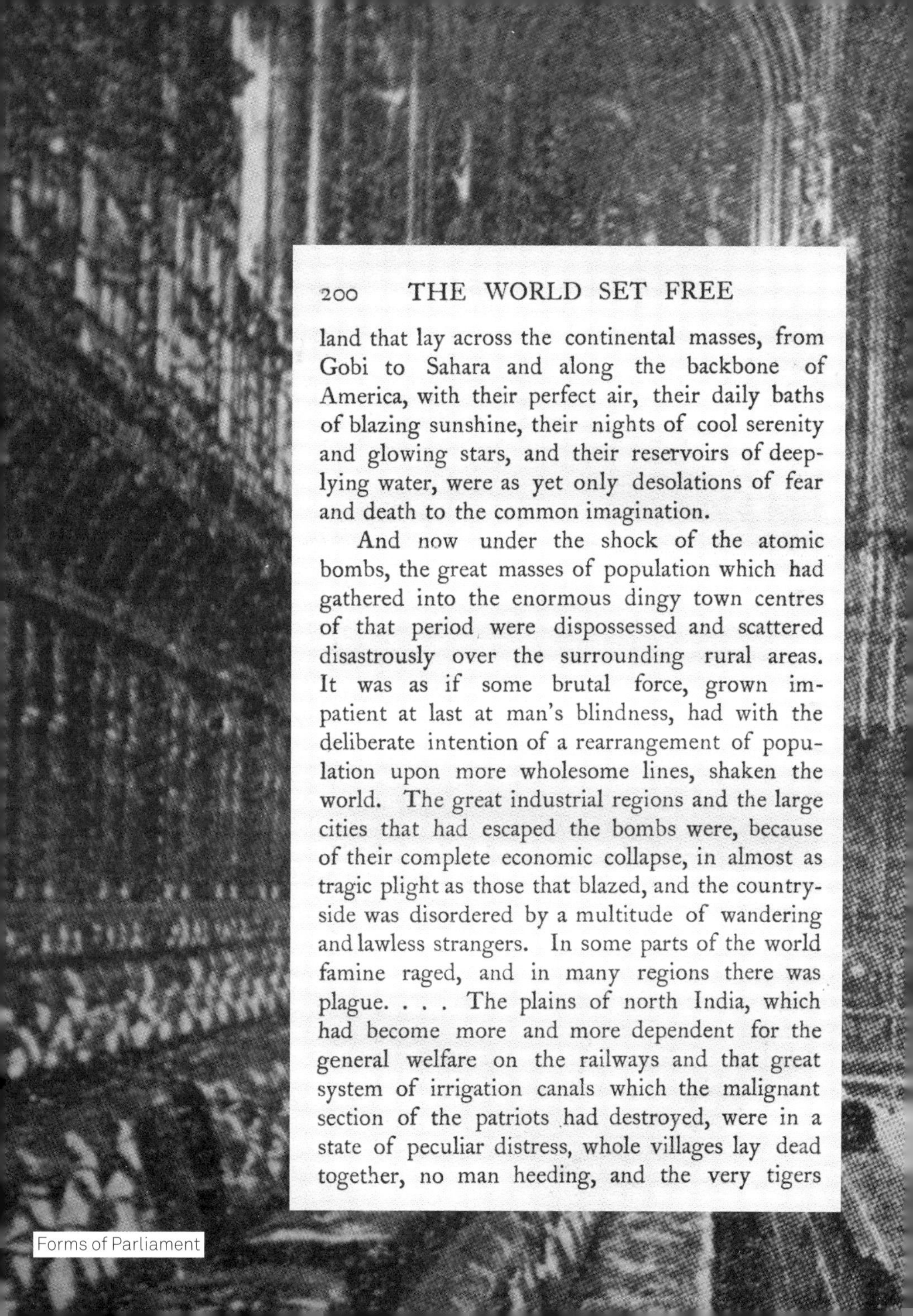

Forms of Parliament

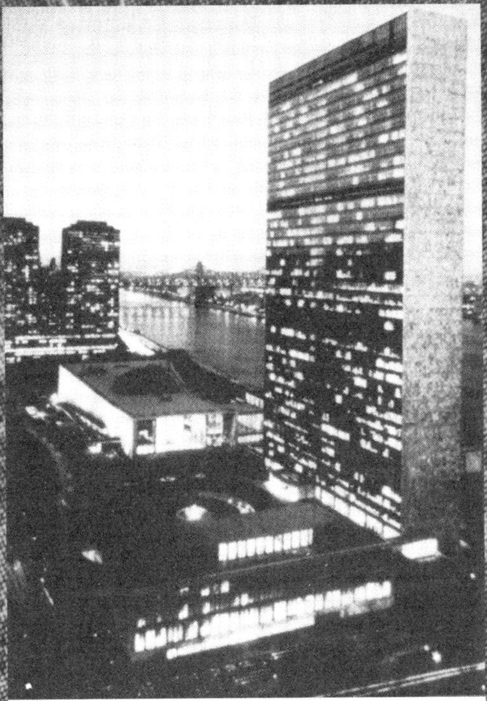
United Nations, New York

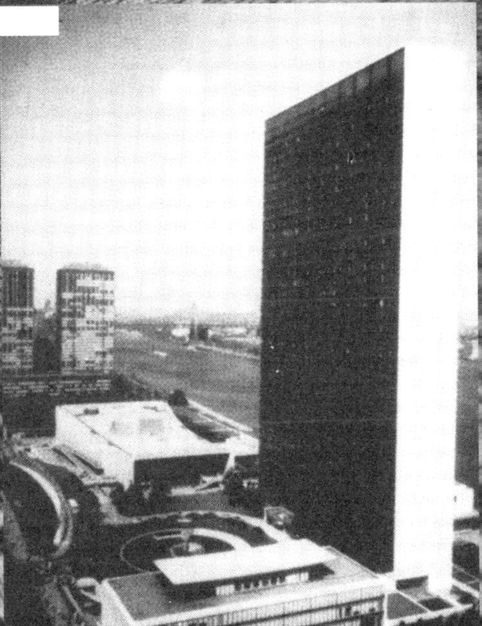
Night and day

and panthers that preyed upon the emaciated survivors crawled back infected into the jungle to perish. Large areas of China were a prey to brigand bands. . . .

It is a remarkable thing that no complete contemporary account of the explosion of the atomic bombs survives. There are of course innumerable allusions and partial records, and it is from these that subsequent ages must piece together the image of these devastations.

The phenomena, it must be remembered, changed greatly from day to day and even from hour to hour as the exploding bomb shifted its position, threw off fragments or came into contact with water or a fresh texture of soil. Barnet, who came within forty miles of Paris early in October, is concerned chiefly with his account of the social confusion of the country-side and the problems of his command, but he speaks of heaped cloud masses of steam "All along the sky to the south-west" and of a red glare beneath these at night. Parts of Paris were still burning, and numbers of people were camped in the fields even at this distance watching over treasured heaps of salvaged loot. He speaks too of the distant rumbling of the explosion—"like trains going over iron bridges."

Other descriptions agree with this; they all speak of the "continuous reverberations," or of the "thudding and hammering," or some such

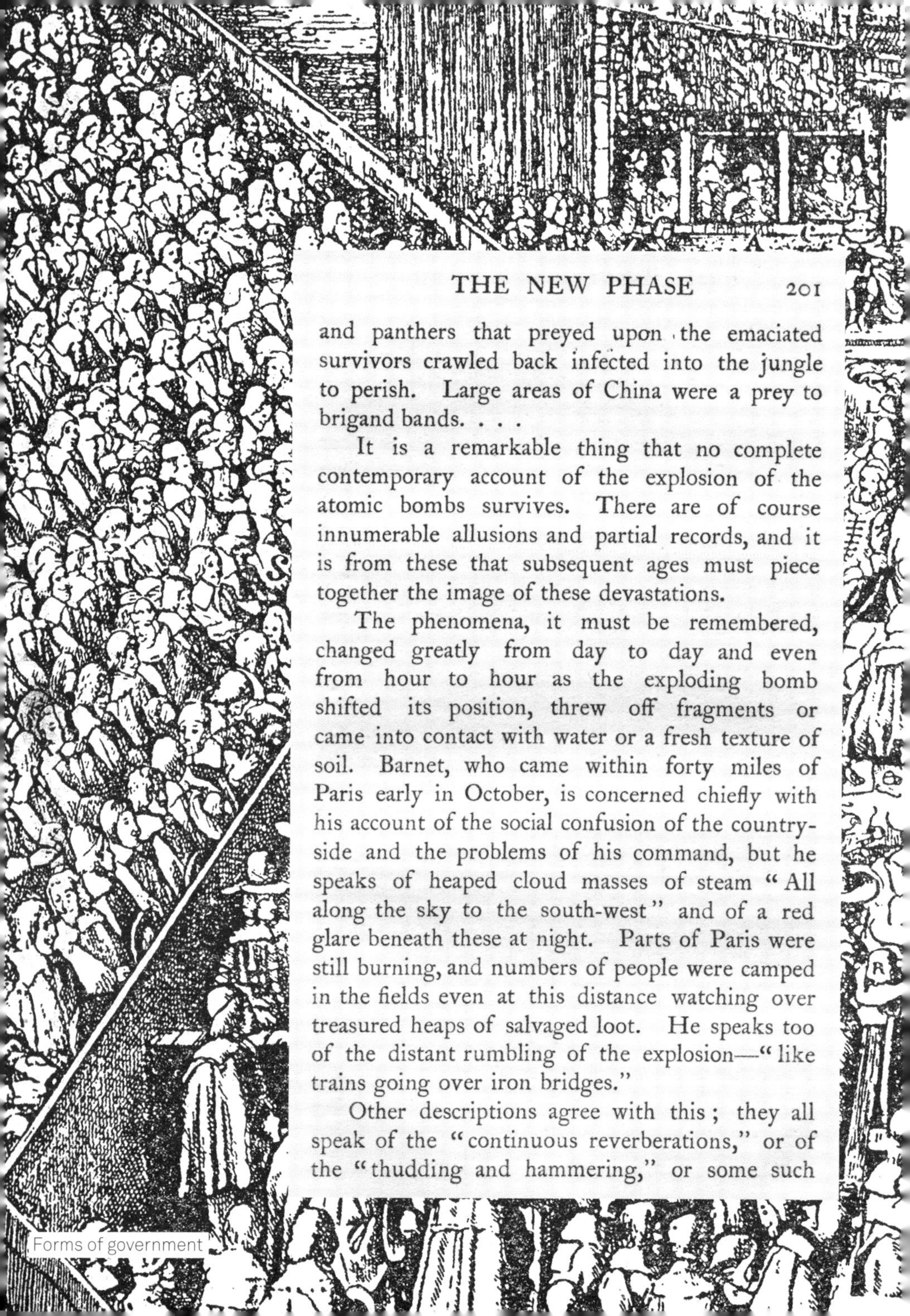

Forms of government

phrase; and they all testify to a huge pall of steam, from which rain would fall suddenly in torrents and amidst which lightning played. Drawing nearer to Paris an observer would have found the salvage camps increasing in number and blocking up the villages, and large numbers of people, often starving and ailing, camping under improvised tents because there was no place for them to go. The sky became more and more densely overcast until at last it blotted out the light of day and left nothing but a dull red glare "extraordinarily depressing to the spirit." In this dull glare, great numbers of people were still living, clinging to their houses and in many cases subsisting in a state of partial famine upon the produce in their gardens and the stores in the shops of the provision dealers.

Coming in still closer the investigator would have reached the police cordon, which was trying to check the desperate enterprise of those who would return to their homes or rescue their more valuable possessions within the "zone of imminent danger."

That zone was rather arbitrarily defined. If our spectator could have got permission to enter it, he would have entered also a zone of uproar, a zone of perpetual thunderings, lit by a strange purplish-red light, and quivering and swaying with the incessant explosion of the radio-active substance. Whole blocks of buildings were alight

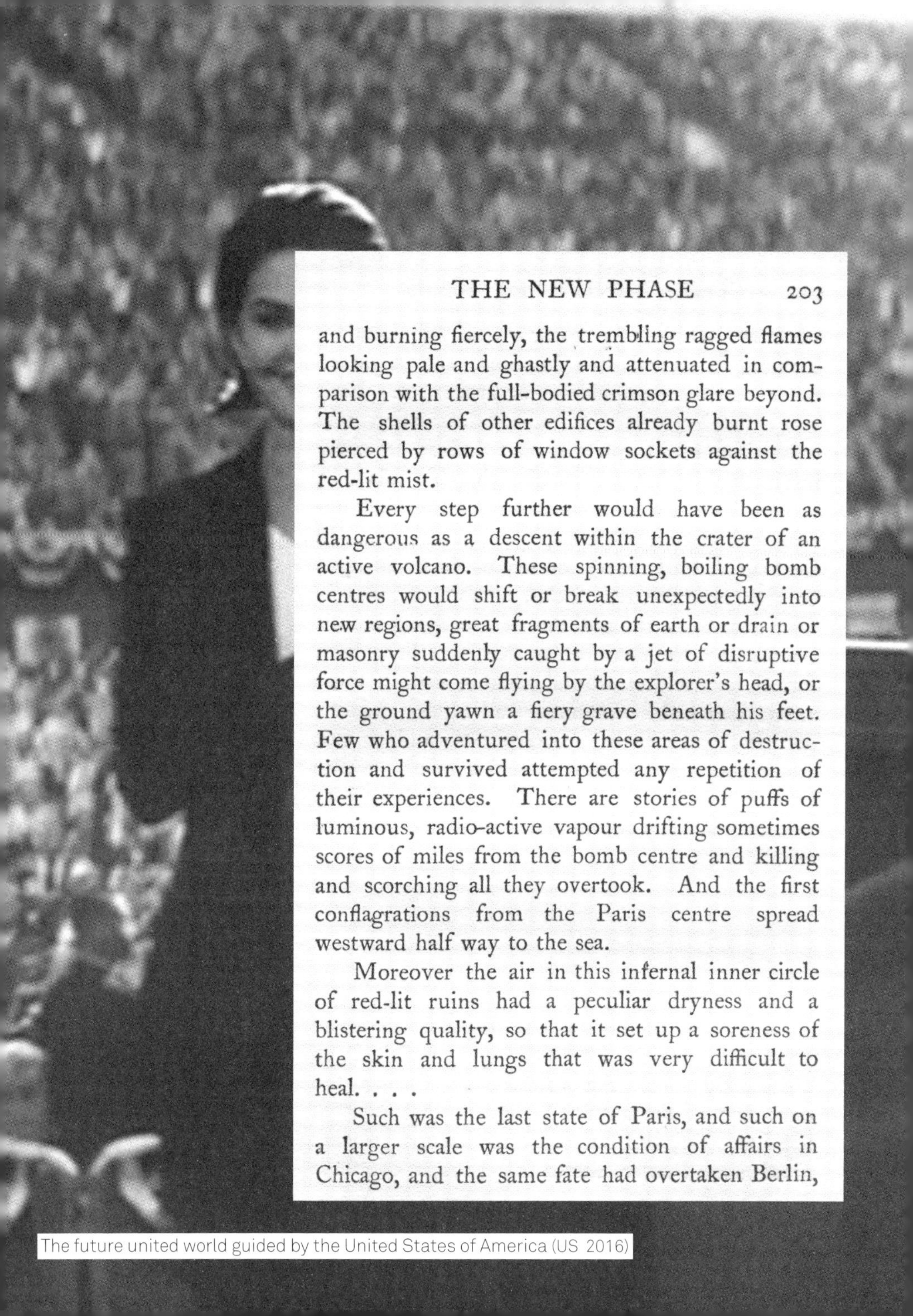

and burning fiercely, the trembling ragged flames looking pale and ghastly and attenuated in comparison with the full-bodied crimson glare beyond. The shells of other edifices already burnt rose pierced by rows of window sockets against the red-lit mist.

Every step further would have been as dangerous as a descent within the crater of an active volcano. These spinning, boiling bomb centres would shift or break unexpectedly into new regions, great fragments of earth or drain or masonry suddenly caught by a jet of disruptive force might come flying by the explorer's head, or the ground yawn a fiery grave beneath his feet. Few who adventured into these areas of destruction and survived attempted any repetition of their experiences. There are stories of puffs of luminous, radio-active vapour drifting sometimes scores of miles from the bomb centre and killing and scorching all they overtook. And the first conflagrations from the Paris centre spread westward half way to the sea.

Moreover the air in this infernal inner circle of red-lit ruins had a peculiar dryness and a blistering quality, so that it set up a soreness of the skin and lungs that was very difficult to heal. . . .

Such was the last state of Paris, and such on a larger scale was the condition of affairs in Chicago, and the same fate had overtaken Berlin,

The future united world guided by the United States of America (US 2016)

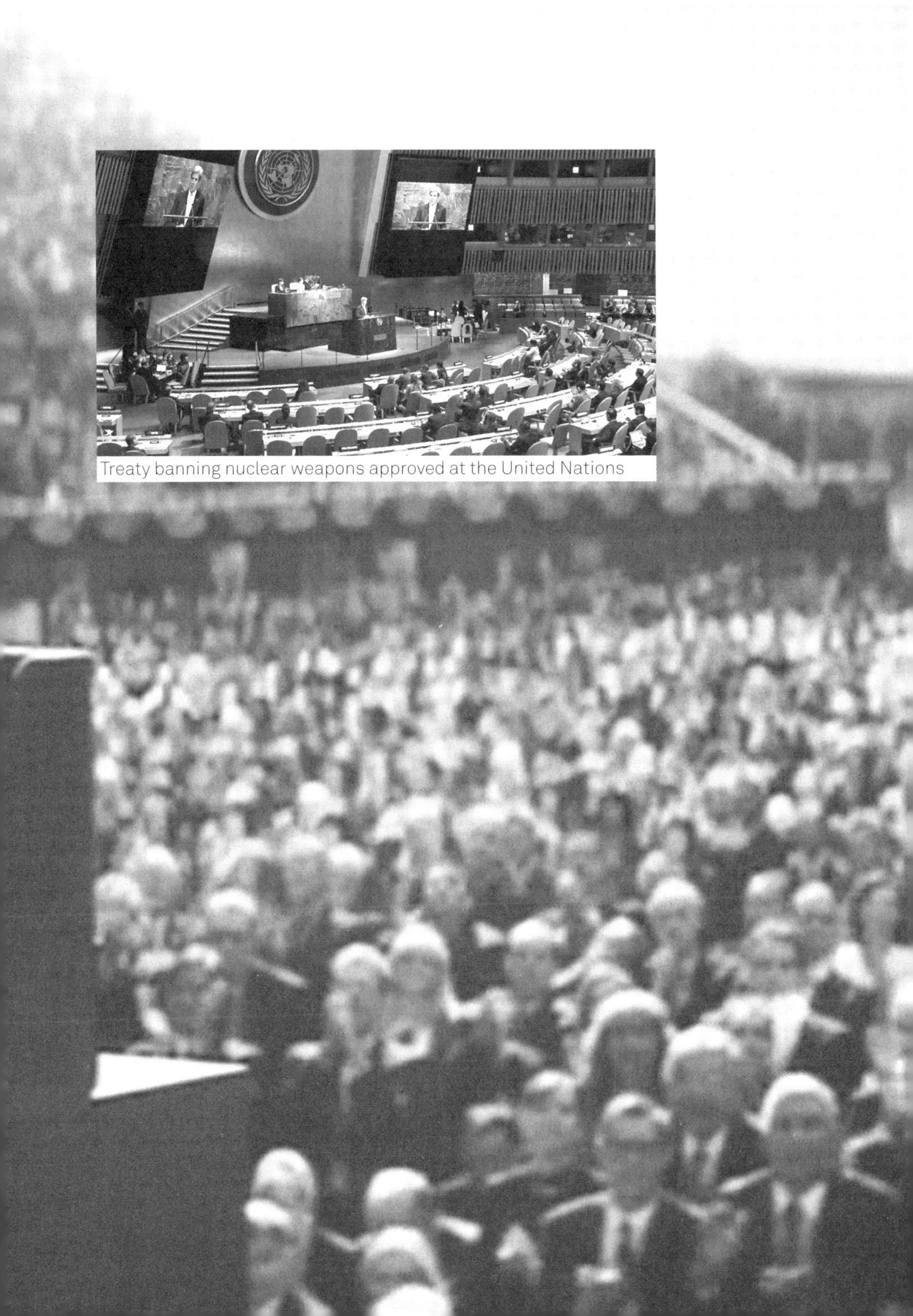

Treaty banning nuclear weapons approved at the United Nations

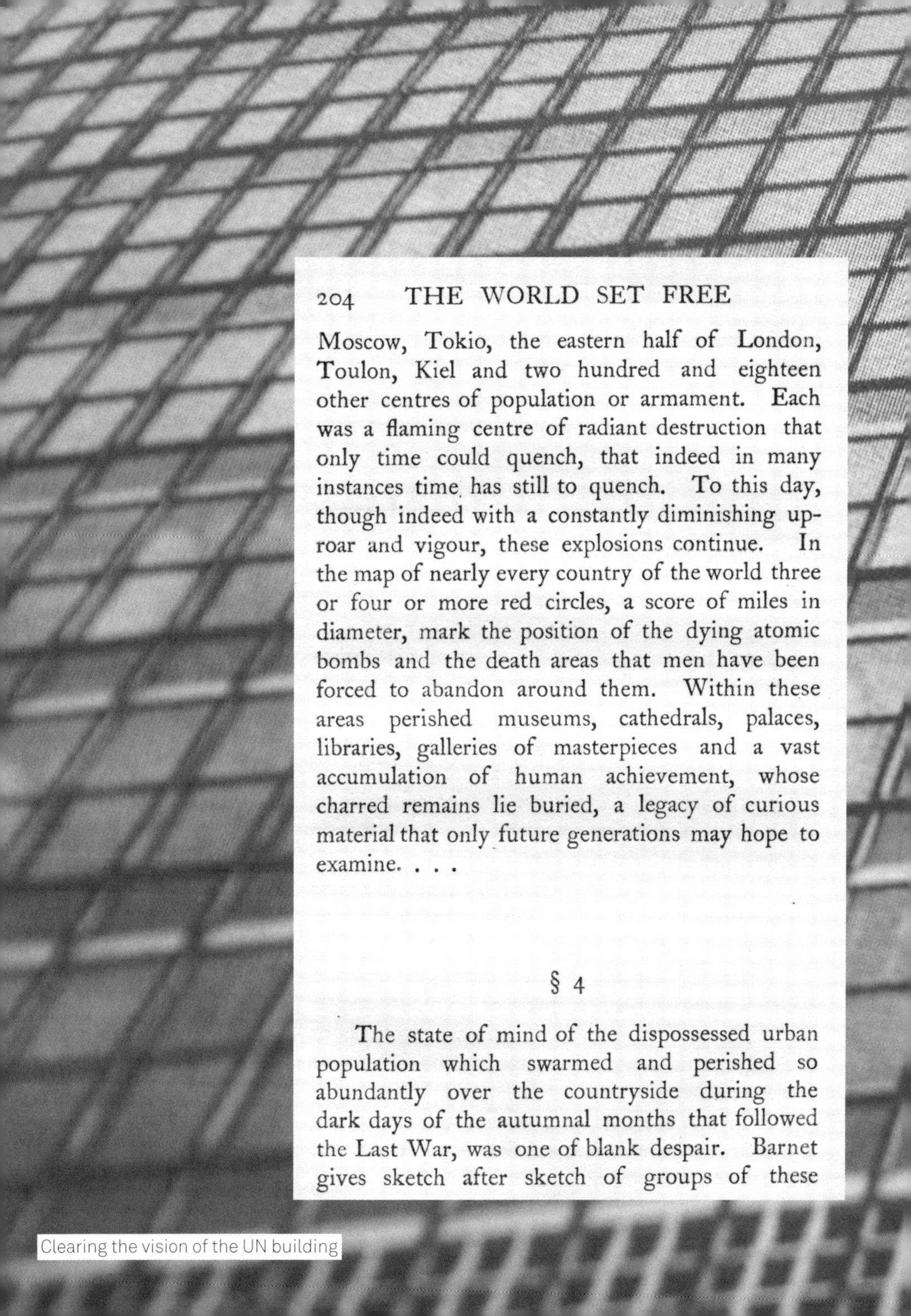

Moscow, Tokio, the eastern half of London, Toulon, Kiel and two hundred and eighteen other centres of population or armament. Each was a flaming centre of radiant destruction that only time could quench, that indeed in many instances time has still to quench. To this day, though indeed with a constantly diminishing uproar and vigour, these explosions continue. In the map of nearly every country of the world three or four or more red circles, a score of miles in diameter, mark the position of the dying atomic bombs and the death areas that men have been forced to abandon around them. Within these areas perished museums, cathedrals, palaces, libraries, galleries of masterpieces and a vast accumulation of human achievement, whose charred remains lie buried, a legacy of curious material that only future generations may hope to examine. . . .

§ 4

The state of mind of the dispossessed urban population which swarmed and perished so abundantly over the countryside during the dark days of the autumnal months that followed the Last War, was one of blank despair. Barnet gives sketch after sketch of groups of these

Clearing the vision of the UN building

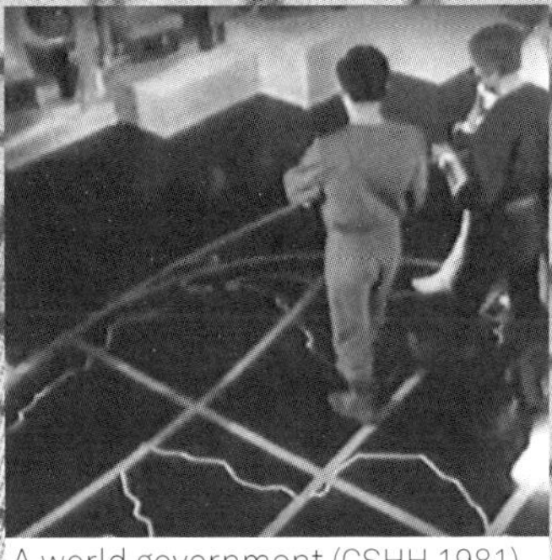

A world government (CSHH 1981)

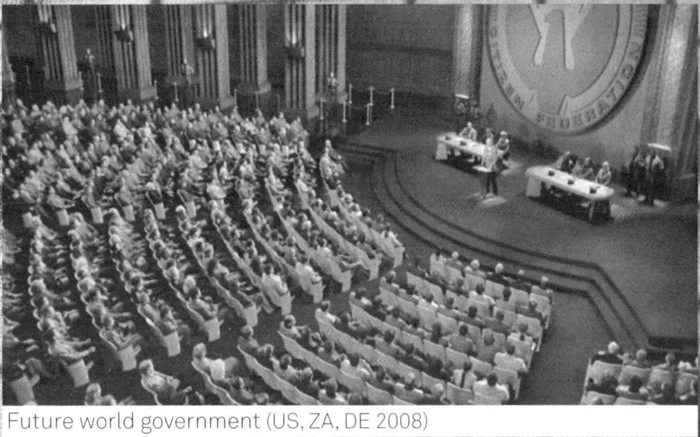

Future world government (US, ZA, DE 2008)

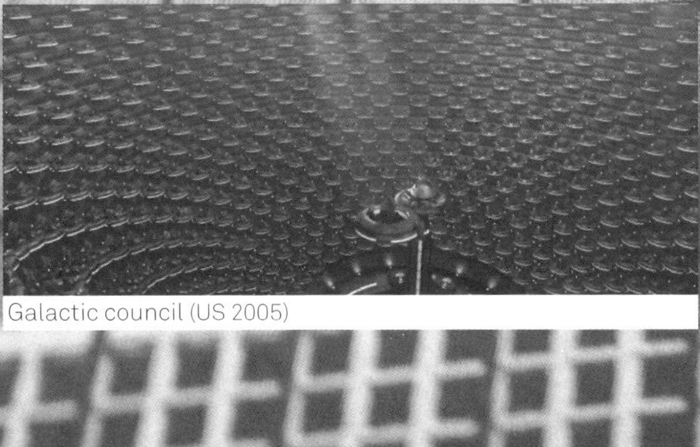

Galactic council (US 2005)

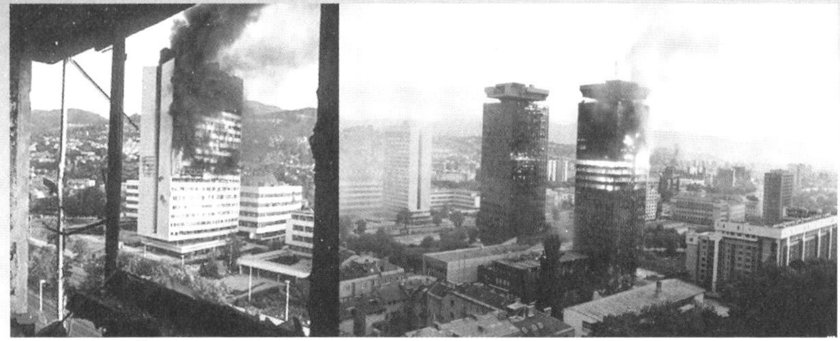

Sarajevo on fire

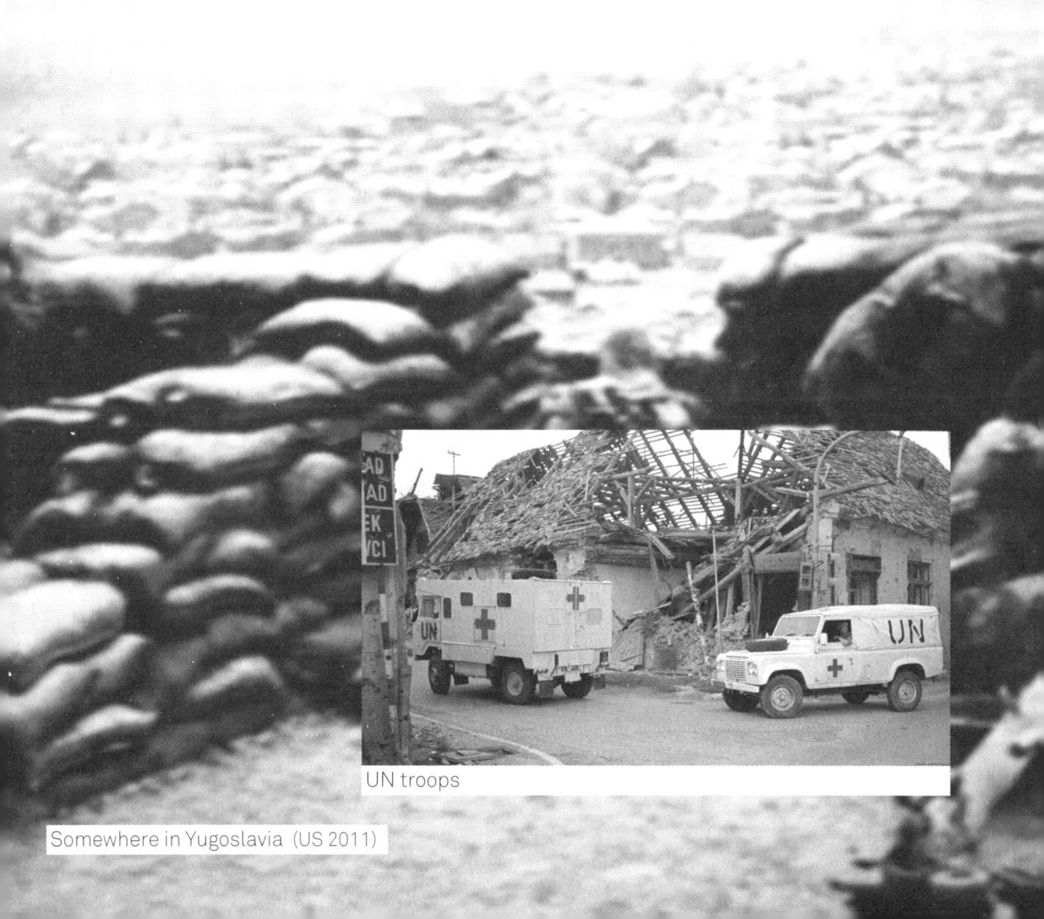

UN troops

Somewhere in Yugoslavia (US 2011)

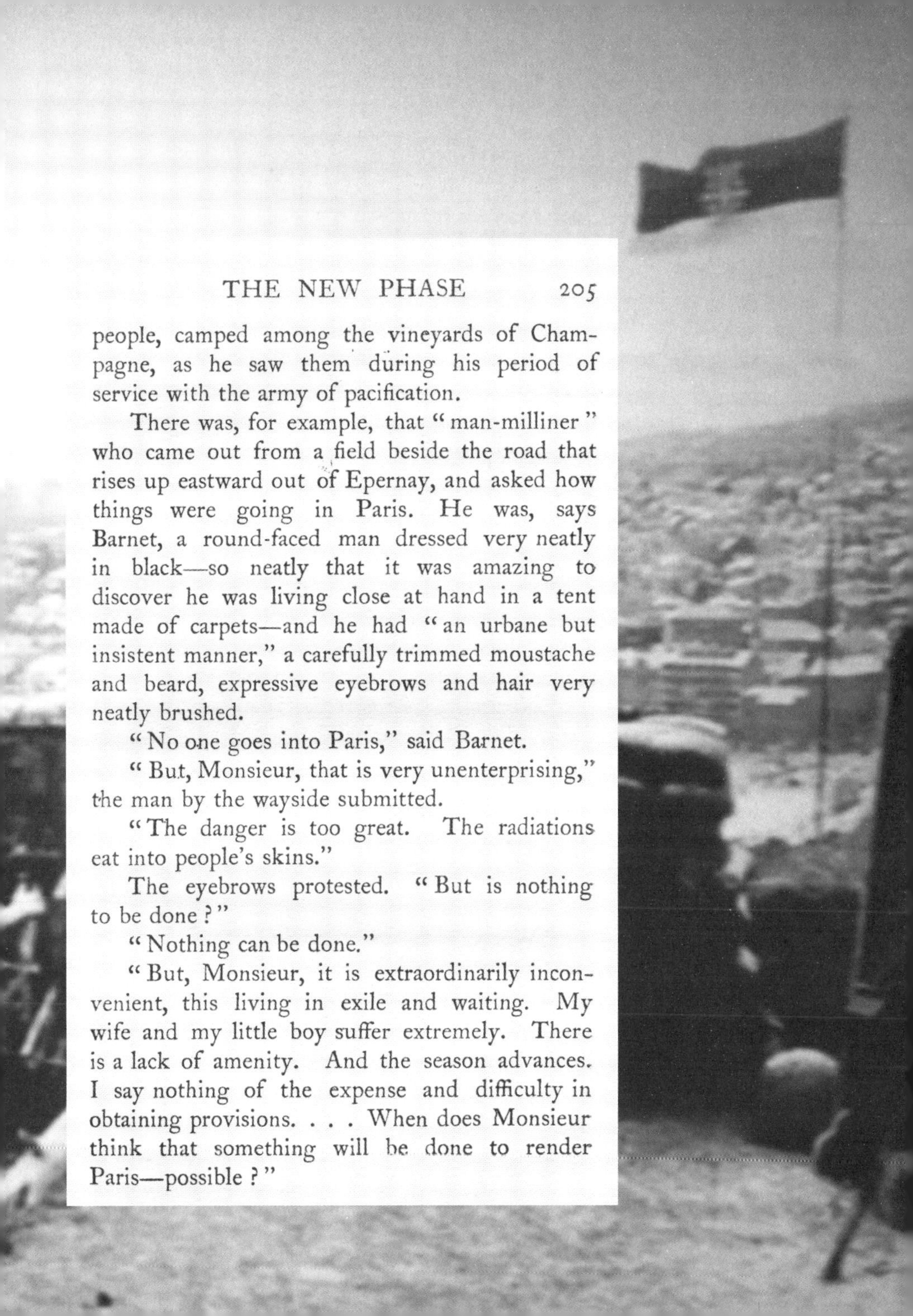

people, camped among the vineyards of Champagne, as he saw them during his period of service with the army of pacification.

There was, for example, that "man-milliner" who came out from a field beside the road that rises up eastward out of Epernay, and asked how things were going in Paris. He was, says Barnet, a round-faced man dressed very neatly in black—so neatly that it was amazing to discover he was living close at hand in a tent made of carpets—and he had "an urbane but insistent manner," a carefully trimmed moustache and beard, expressive eyebrows and hair very neatly brushed.

"No one goes into Paris," said Barnet.

"But, Monsieur, that is very unenterprising," the man by the wayside submitted.

"The danger is too great. The radiations eat into people's skins."

The eyebrows protested. "But is nothing to be done?"

"Nothing can be done."

"But, Monsieur, it is extraordinarily inconvenient, this living in exile and waiting. My wife and my little boy suffer extremely. There is a lack of amenity. And the season advances. I say nothing of the expense and difficulty in obtaining provisions. . . . When does Monsieur think that something will be done to render Paris—possible?"

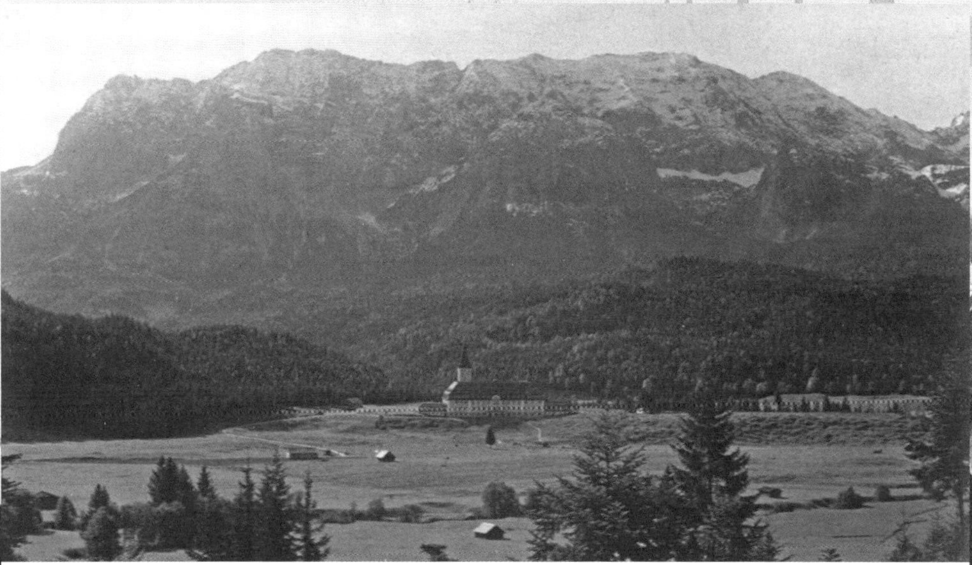

G8, 2015

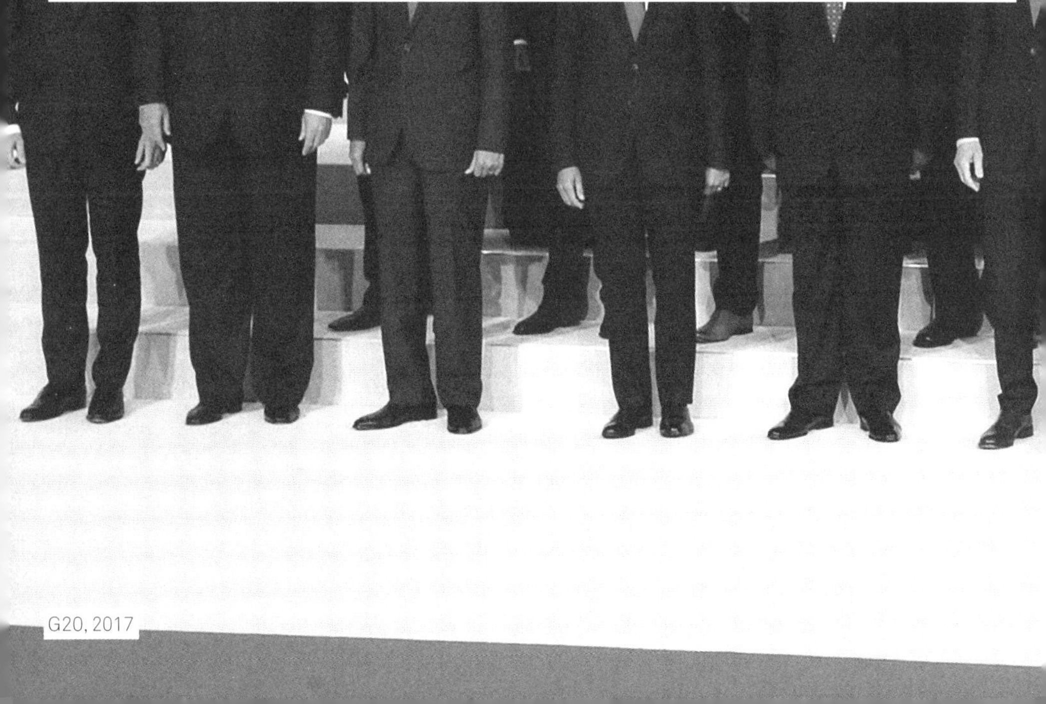

G20, 2017

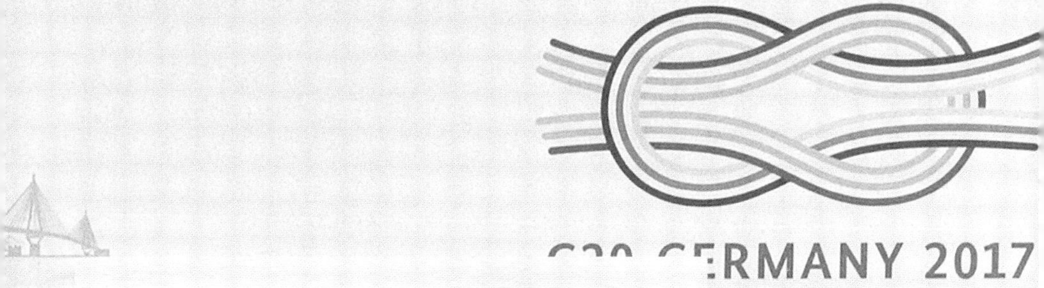

Barnet considered his interlocutor.

"I'm told," said Barnet, "that Paris is not likely to be possible again for several generations."

"Oh! but this is preposterous! Consider, Monsieur! What are people like ourselves to do in the meanwhile? I am a costumier. All my connections and interests, above all my style, demand Paris. . . ."

Barnet considered the sky, from which a light rain was beginning to fall, the wide fields about them from which the harvest had been taken, the trimmed poplars by the wayside.

"Naturally," he agreed, "you want to go to Paris. But Paris is over."

"Over!"

"Finished."

"But then, Monsieur—what is to become—of *me?*"

Barnet turned his face westward whither the white road led.

"Where else, for example, may I hope to find—opportunity?"

Barnet made no reply.

"Perhaps on the Riviera. Or at some such place as Homburg. Or some plage perhaps."

"All that," said Barnet, accepting for the first time facts that had lain evident in his mind for weeks; "all that must be over too."

There was a pause. Then the voice beside

him broke out. "But, Monsieur, it is impossible! It leaves—nothing."

"No. Not very much."

"One cannot suddenly begin to grow potatoes!"

"It would be good if Monsieur could bring himself——"

"To the life of a peasant! And my wife——. You do not know the distinguished delicacy of my wife, a refined helplessness, a peculiar dependent charm. Like some slender tropical creeper—with great white flowers. . . . But all this is foolish talk. It is impossible that Paris, which has survived so many misfortunes, should not presently revive."

"I do not think it will ever revive. Paris is finished. London too, I am told—Berlin. All the great capitals were stricken. . . ."

"But——! Monsieur must permit me to differ."

"It is so."

"It is impossible. Civilizations do not end in this manner. Mankind will insist."

"On Paris?"

"On Paris."

"Monsieur, you might as well hope to go down the Maelstrom and resume business there."

"I am content, Monsieur, with my own faith."

International Atoms Energy Agency—Atoms for Peace since 1958

"The winter comes on. Would not Monsieur be wiser to seek a house?"

"Further from Paris? No, Monsieur. But it is not possible, Monsieur, what you say, and you are under a tremendous mistake. . . . Indeed you are in error. . . . I asked merely for information. . . ."

"When last I saw him," said Barnet, "he was standing under the signpost at the crest of the hill, gazing wistfully yet it seemed to me a little doubtfully now towards Paris, and altogether heedless of a drizzling rain that was wetting him through and through. . . ."

§ 5

This effect of chill dismay, of a doom as yet imperfectly apprehended deepens as Barnet's record passes on to tell of the approach of winter. It was too much for the great mass of those unwilling and incompetent nomads to realize that an age had ended, that the old help and guidance existed no longer, that times would not mend again however patiently they held out. They were still in many cases looking to Paris when the first snowflakes of that pitiless January came swirling about them. The story grows grimmer. . . .

If it is less monstrously tragic after Barnet's return to England it is, if anything, harder.

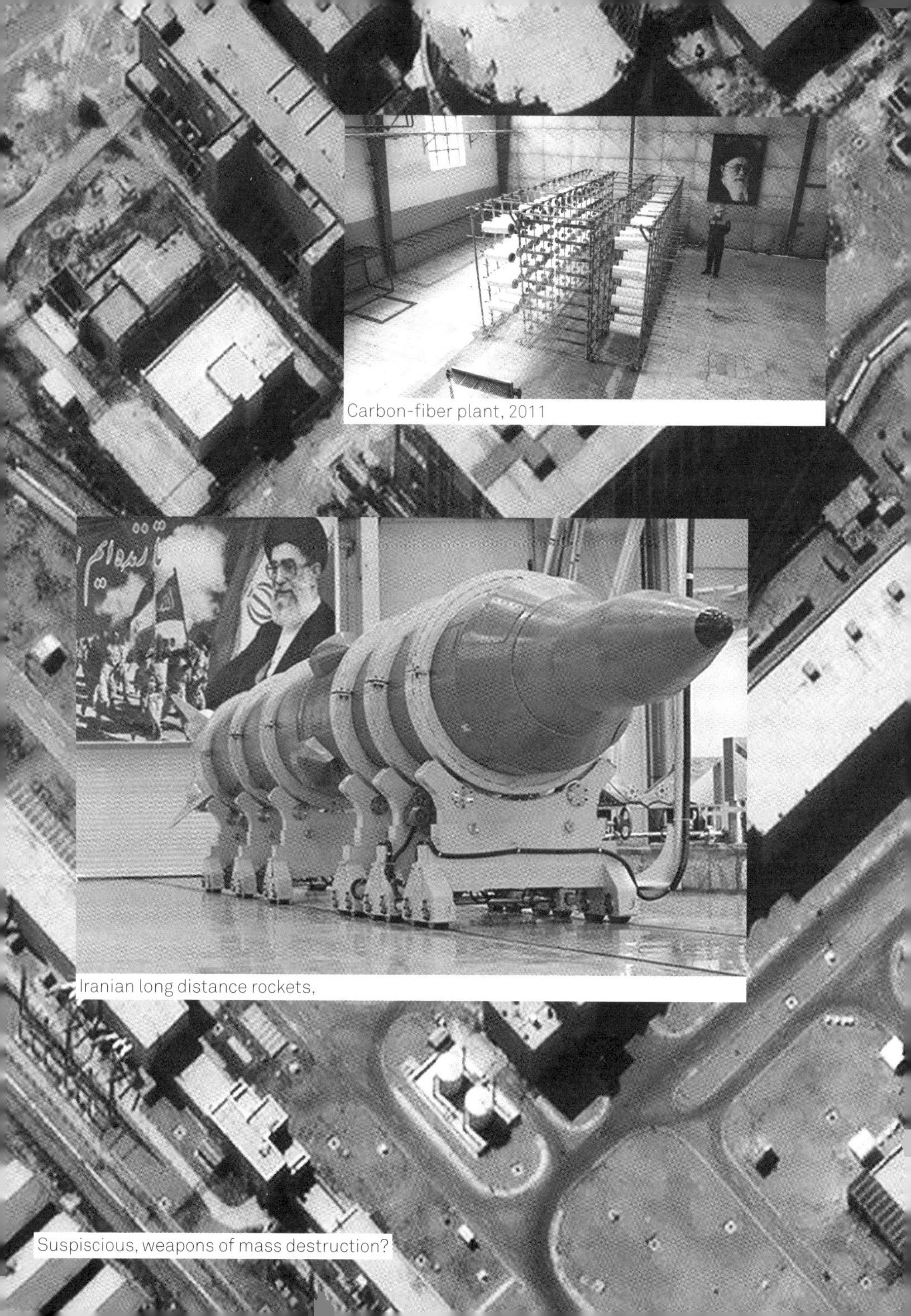

Carbon-fiber plant, 2011

Iranian long distance rockets,

Suspiscious, weapons of mass destruction?

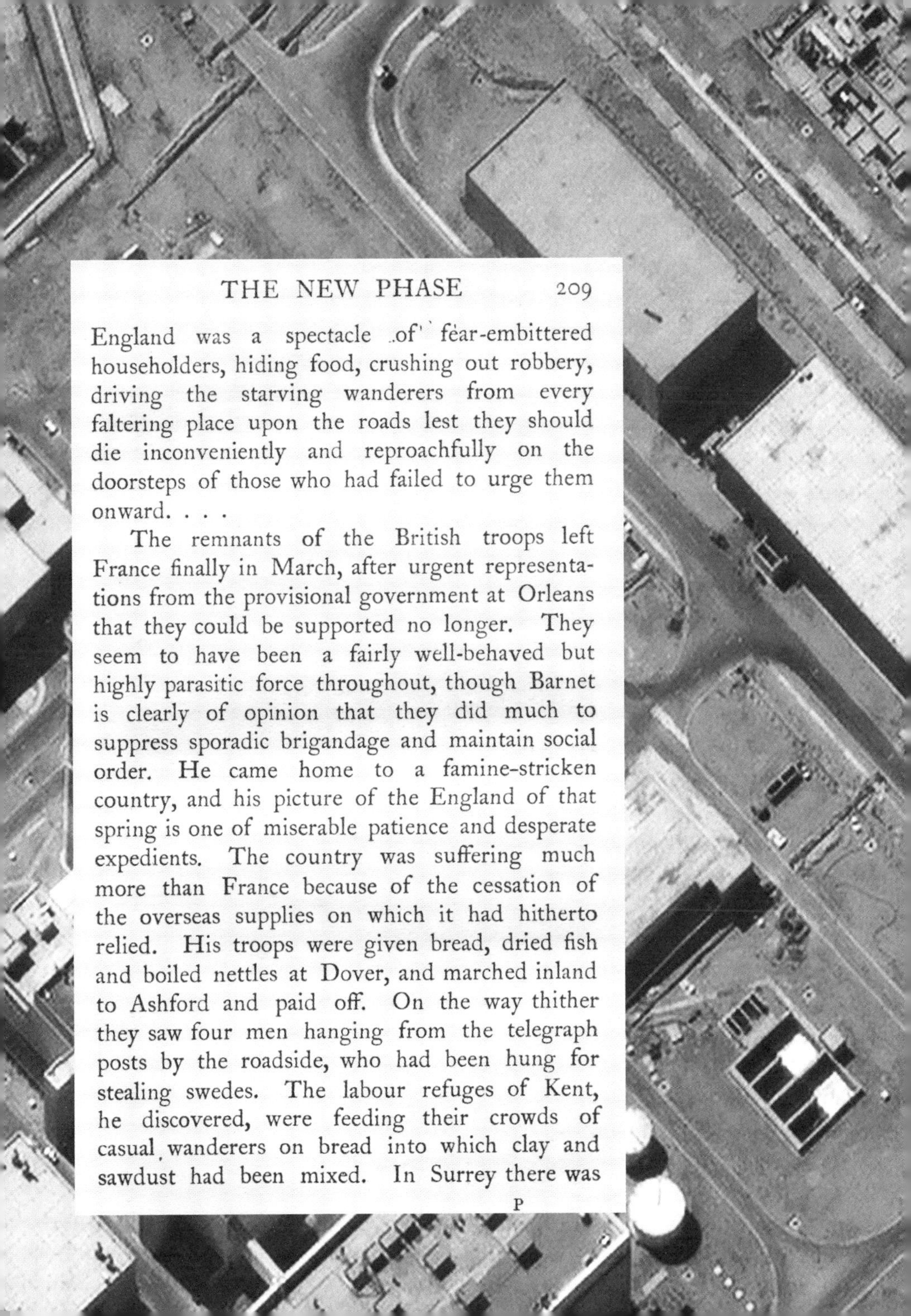

England was a spectacle of fear-embittered householders, hiding food, crushing out robbery, driving the starving wanderers from every faltering place upon the roads lest they should die inconveniently and reproachfully on the doorsteps of those who had failed to urge them onward. . . .

The remnants of the British troops left France finally in March, after urgent representations from the provisional government at Orleans that they could be supported no longer. They seem to have been a fairly well-behaved but highly parasitic force throughout, though Barnet is clearly of opinion that they did much to suppress sporadic brigandage and maintain social order. He came home to a famine-stricken country, and his picture of the England of that spring is one of miserable patience and desperate expedients. The country was suffering much more than France because of the cessation of the overseas supplies on which it had hitherto relied. His troops were given bread, dried fish and boiled nettles at Dover, and marched inland to Ashford and paid off. On the way thither they saw four men hanging from the telegraph posts by the roadside, who had been hung for stealing swedes. The labour refuges of Kent, he discovered, were feeding their crowds of casual wanderers on bread into which clay and sawdust had been mixed. In Surrey there was

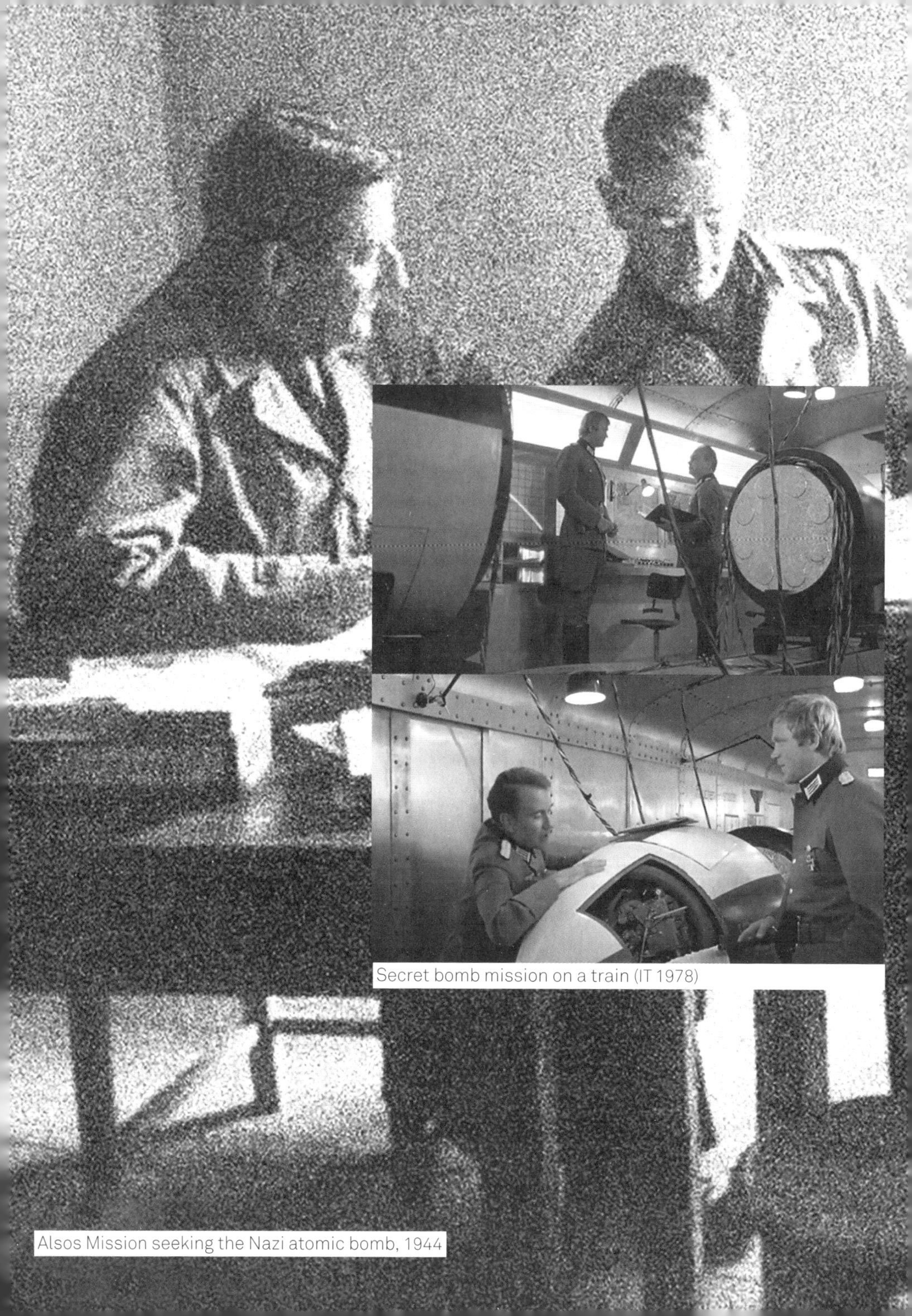

Secret bomb mission on a train (IT 1978)

Alsos Mission seeking the Nazi atomic bomb, 1944

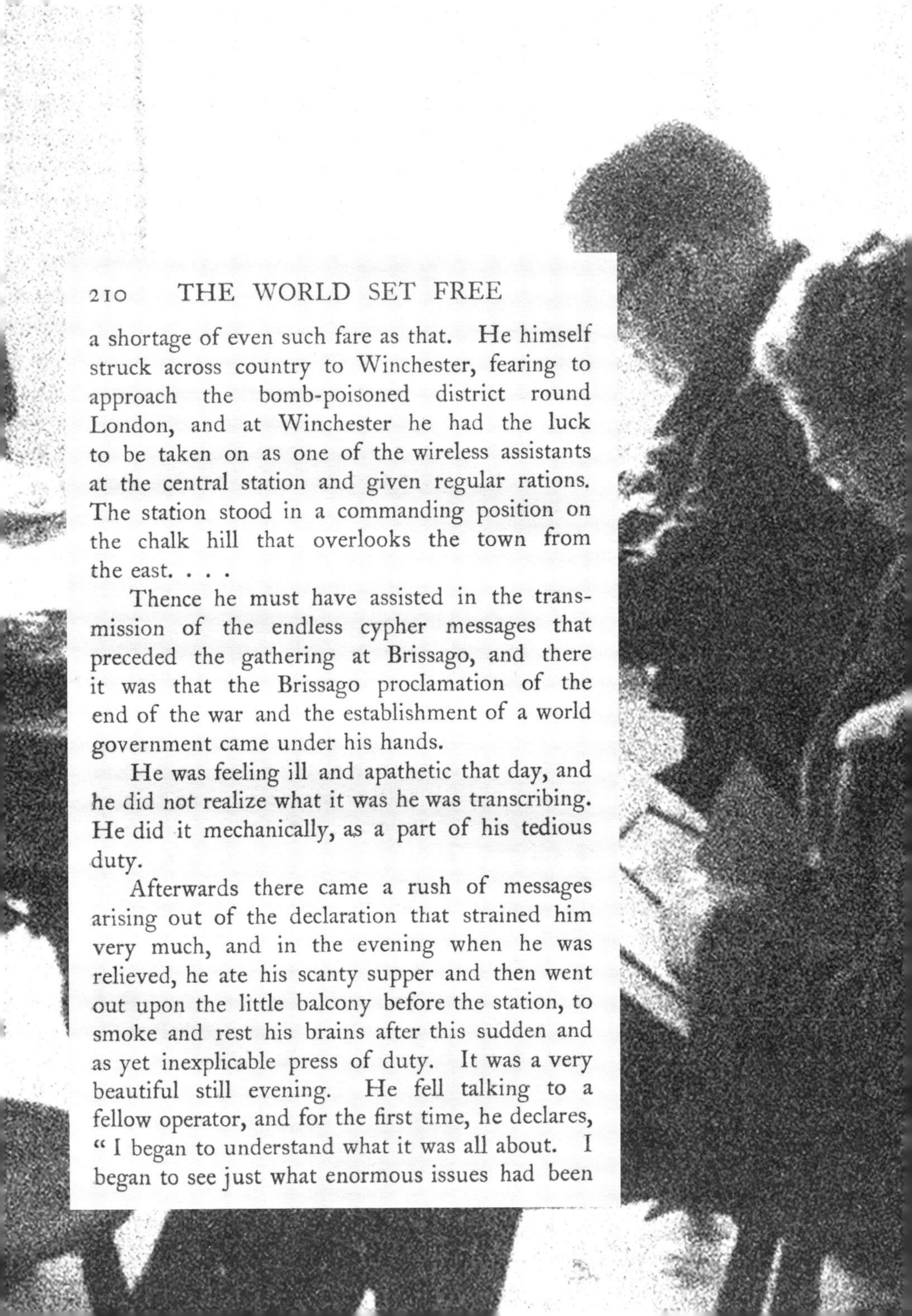

a shortage of even such fare as that. He himself struck across country to Winchester, fearing to approach the bomb-poisoned district round London, and at Winchester he had the luck to be taken on as one of the wireless assistants at the central station and given regular rations. The station stood in a commanding position on the chalk hill that overlooks the town from the east. . . .

Thence he must have assisted in the transmission of the endless cypher messages that preceded the gathering at Brissago, and there it was that the Brissago proclamation of the end of the war and the establishment of a world government came under his hands.

He was feeling ill and apathetic that day, and he did not realize what it was he was transcribing. He did it mechanically, as a part of his tedious duty.

Afterwards there came a rush of messages arising out of the declaration that strained him very much, and in the evening when he was relieved, he ate his scanty supper and then went out upon the little balcony before the station, to smoke and rest his brains after this sudden and as yet inexplicable press of duty. It was a very beautiful still evening. He fell talking to a fellow operator, and for the first time, he declares, "I began to understand what it was all about. I began to see just what enormous issues had been under my hands for the past four hours. But I became incredulous after my first stimulation. 'This is some sort of Bunkum,' I said very sagely.

"My colleague was more hopeful. 'It means an end to bomb-throwing and destruction,' he said. 'It means that presently corn will come from America.'

"'Who is going to send corn when there is no more value in money?' I asked.

"Suddenly we were startled by a clashing from the town below. The cathedral bells, which had been silent ever since I had come into the district, were beginning, with a sort of rheumatic difficulty, to ring. Presently they warmed a little to the work, and we realized what was going on. They were ringing a peal. We listened with an unbelieving astonishment and looking into each other's yellow faces.

"'They mean it,' said my colleague.

"'But what can they do now?' I asked. 'Everything is broken down. . . .'"

And on that sentence, with an unexpected artistry, Barnet abruptly ends his story.

§ 6

From the first the new government handled affairs with a certain greatness of spirit. Indeed it was inevitable that they should act greatly.

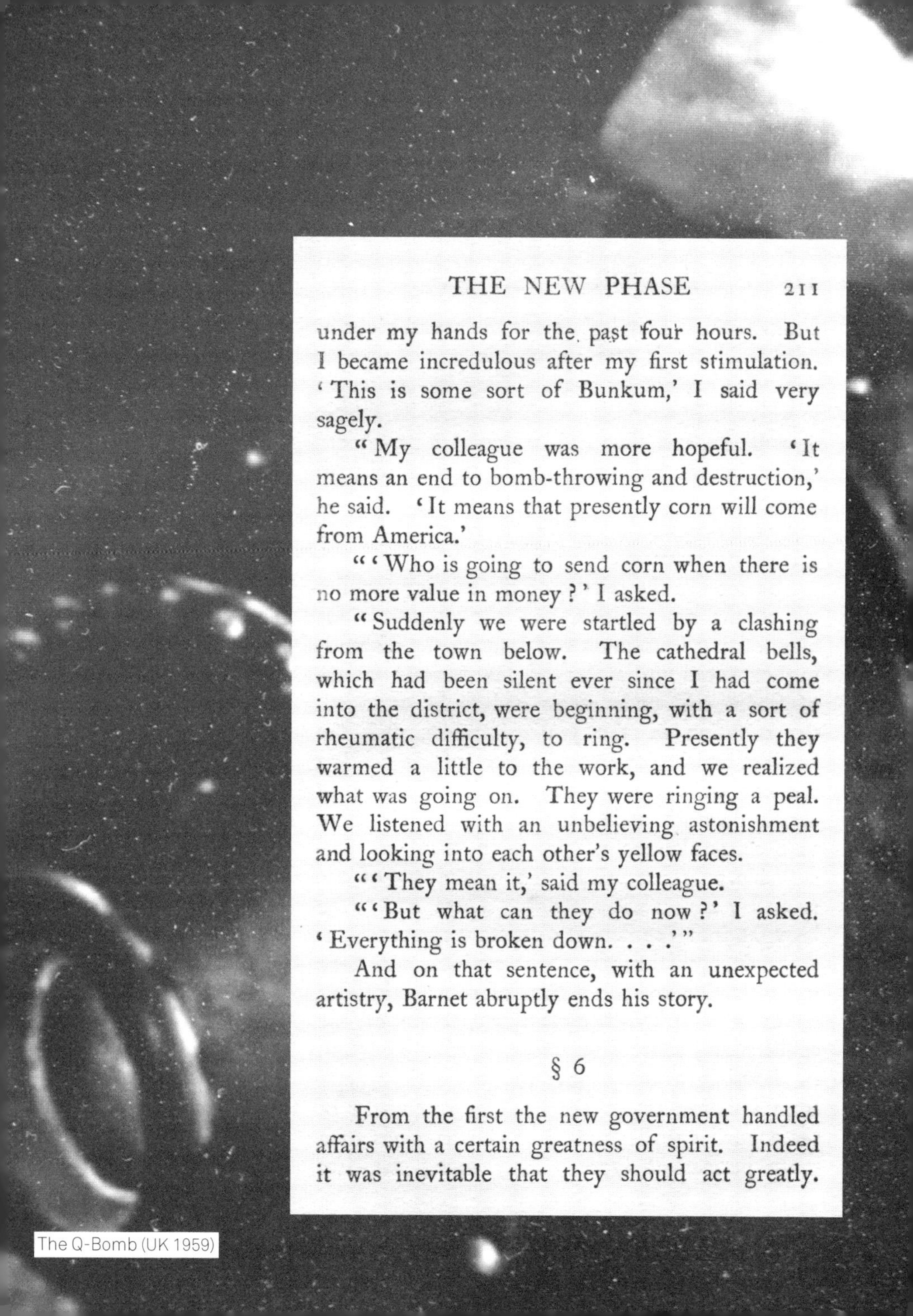

The Q-Bomb (UK 1959)

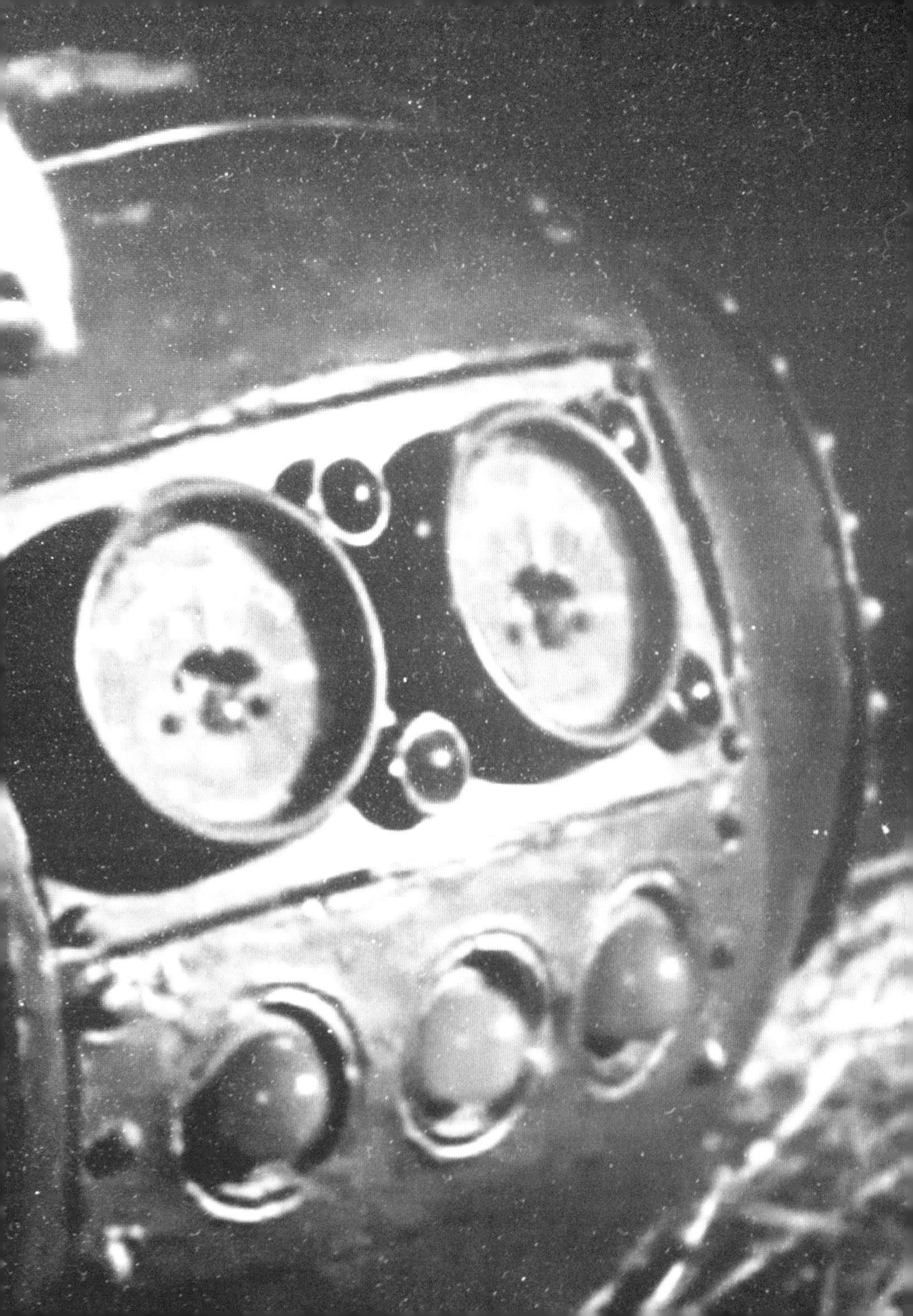

From the first they had to see the round globe as one problem; it was impossible any longer to deal with it piece by piece. They had to secure it universally from any fresh outbreak of atomic destruction, and they had to ensure a permanent and universal pacification. On this capacity to grasp and wield the whole round globe their existence depended. There was no scope for any further performance.

So soon as the seizure of the existing supplies of atomic ammunition and the apparatus for synthesizing Carolinum was assured, the disbanding or social utilization of the various masses of troops still under arms had to be arranged, the salvation of the year's harvests, and the feeding, housing and employment of the drifting millions of homeless people. In Canada, in South America and Asiatic Russia there were vast accumulations of provision that was immovable only because of the breakdown of the monetary and credit systems. These had to be brought into the famine districts very speedily if entire depopulation was to be avoided, and their transportation and the revival of communications generally absorbed a certain proportion of the soldiery and more able unemployed. The task of housing assumed gigantic dimensions, and from building camps the housing committee of the council speedily passed to constructions of a more permanent type. They found far less

New work (DE 1927)

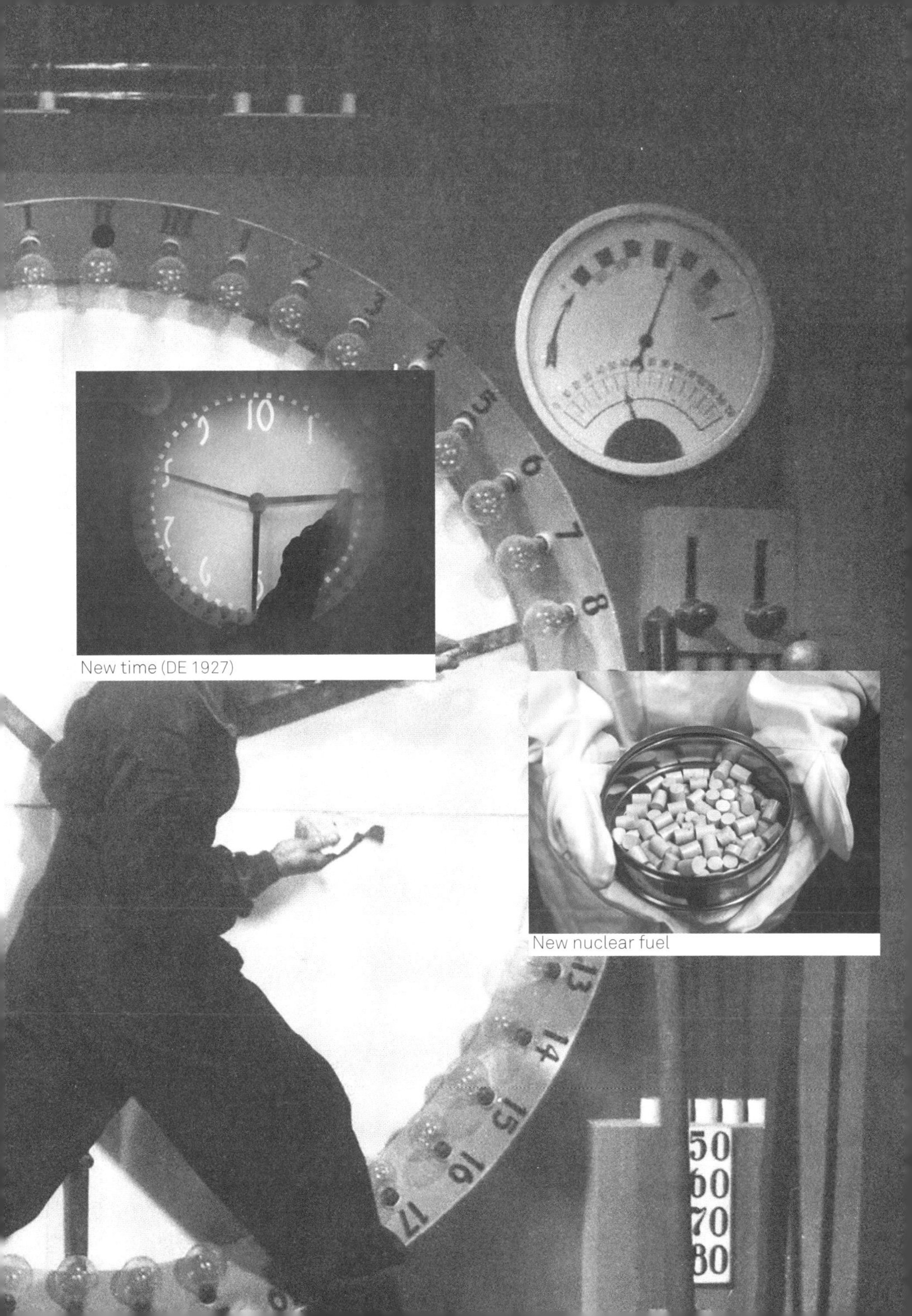

New time (DE 1927)

New nuclear fuel

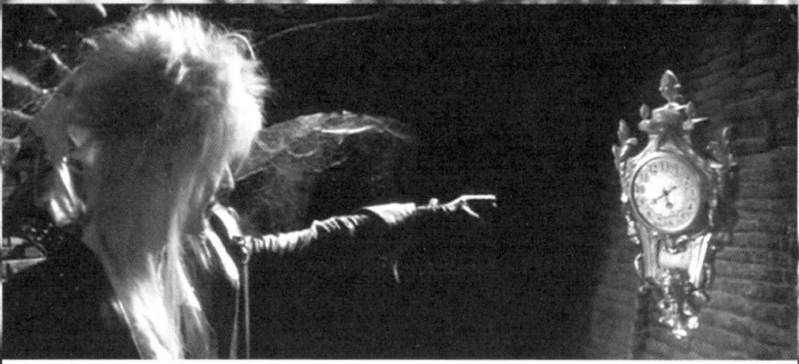

New time (UK, US 1986)

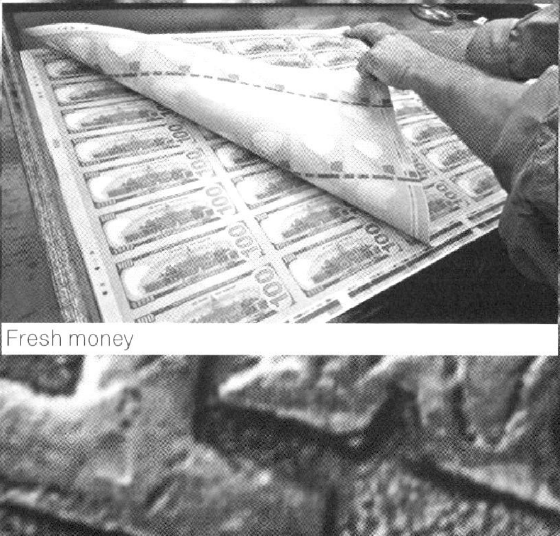

Fresh money

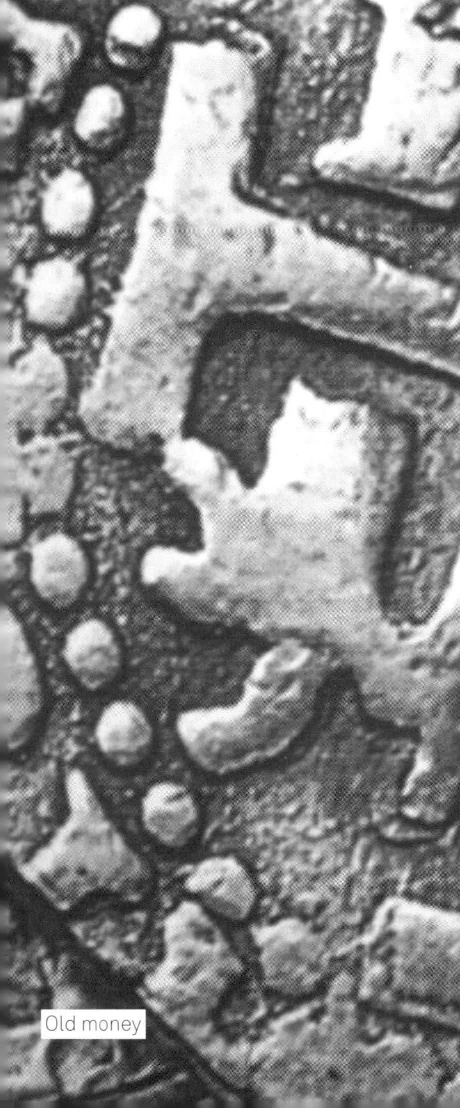

Old money

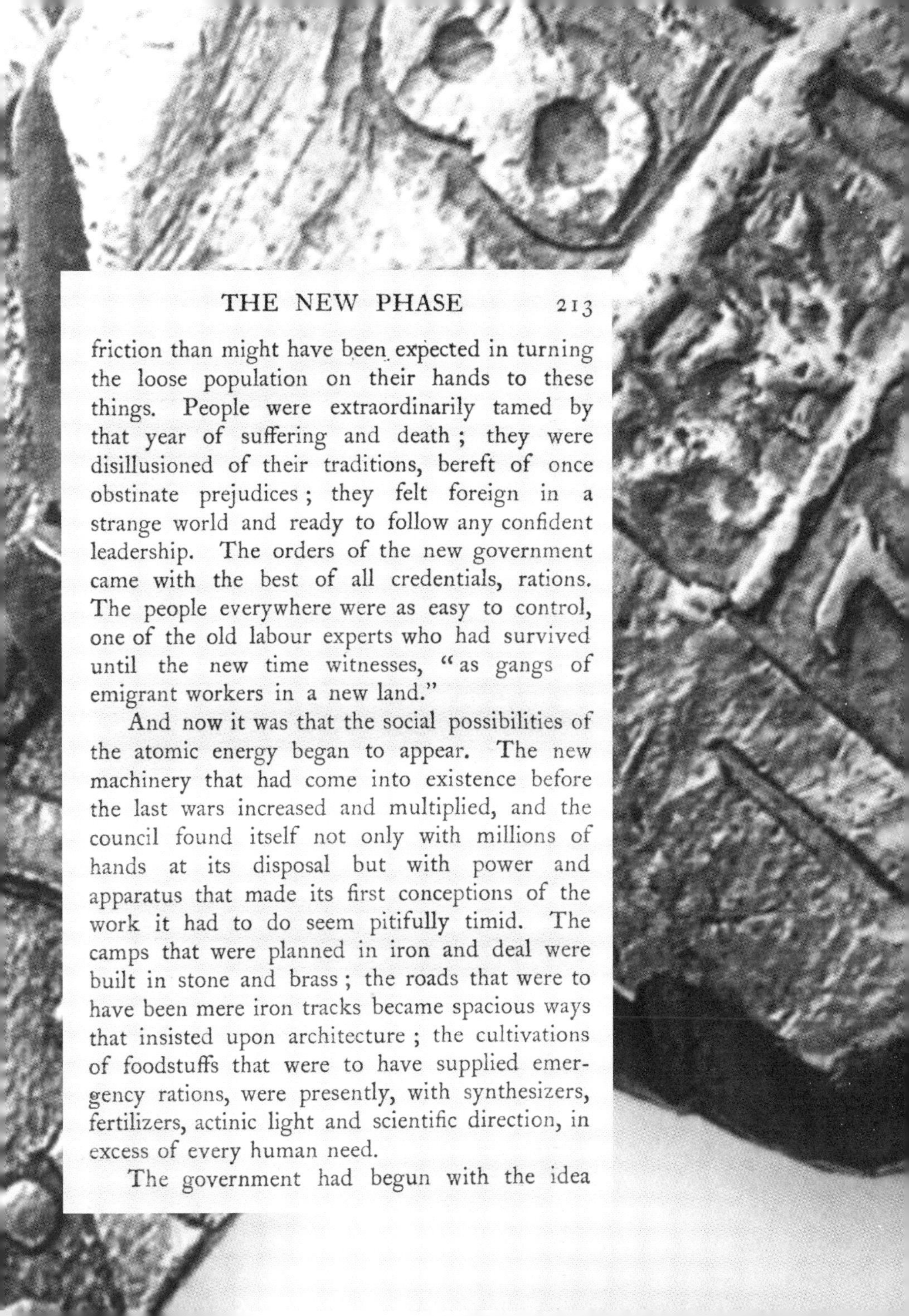

friction than might have been expected in turning the loose population on their hands to these things. People were extraordinarily tamed by that year of suffering and death ; they were disillusioned of their traditions, bereft of once obstinate prejudices ; they felt foreign in a strange world and ready to follow any confident leadership. The orders of the new government came with the best of all credentials, rations. The people everywhere were as easy to control, one of the old labour experts who had survived until the new time witnesses, "as gangs of emigrant workers in a new land."

And now it was that the social possibilities of the atomic energy began to appear. The new machinery that had come into existence before the last wars increased and multiplied, and the council found itself not only with millions of hands at its disposal but with power and apparatus that made its first conceptions of the work it had to do seem pitifully timid. The camps that were planned in iron and deal were built in stone and brass ; the roads that were to have been mere iron tracks became spacious ways that insisted upon architecture ; the cultivations of foodstuffs that were to have supplied emergency rations, were presently, with synthesizers, fertilizers, actinic light and scientific direction, in excess of every human need.

The government had begun with the idea

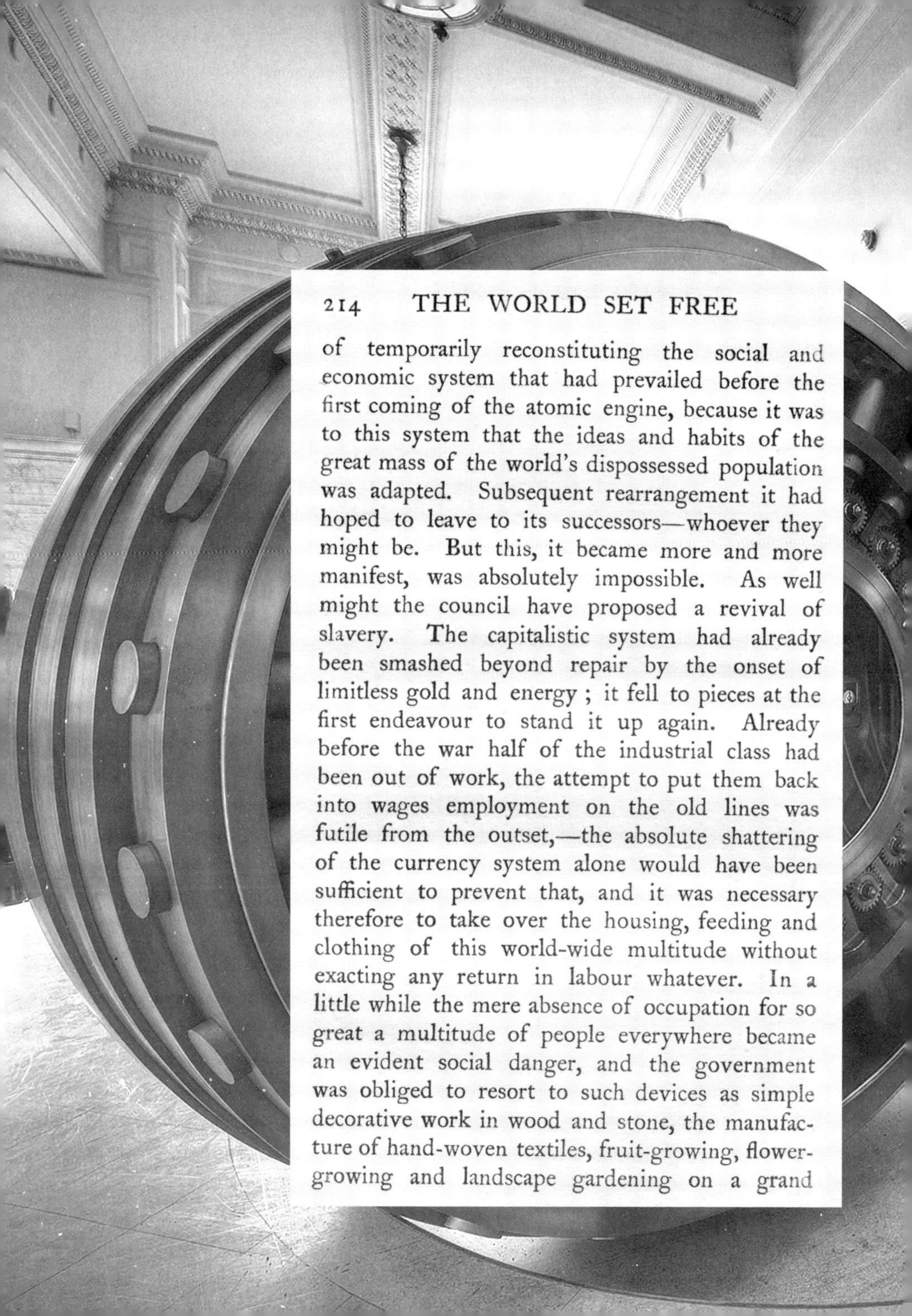

of temporarily reconstituting the social and economic system that had prevailed before the first coming of the atomic engine, because it was to this system that the ideas and habits of the great mass of the world's dispossessed population was adapted. Subsequent rearrangement it had hoped to leave to its successors—whoever they might be. But this, it became more and more manifest, was absolutely impossible. As well might the council have proposed a revival of slavery. The capitalistic system had already been smashed beyond repair by the onset of limitless gold and energy ; it fell to pieces at the first endeavour to stand it up again. Already before the war half of the industrial class had been out of work, the attempt to put them back into wages employment on the old lines was futile from the outset,—the absolute shattering of the currency system alone would have been sufficient to prevent that, and it was necessary therefore to take over the housing, feeding and clothing of this world-wide multitude without exacting any return in labour whatever. In a little while the mere absence of occupation for so great a multitude of people everywhere became an evident social danger, and the government was obliged to resort to such devices as simple decorative work in wood and stone, the manufacture of hand-woven textiles, fruit-growing, flower-growing and landscape gardening on a grand

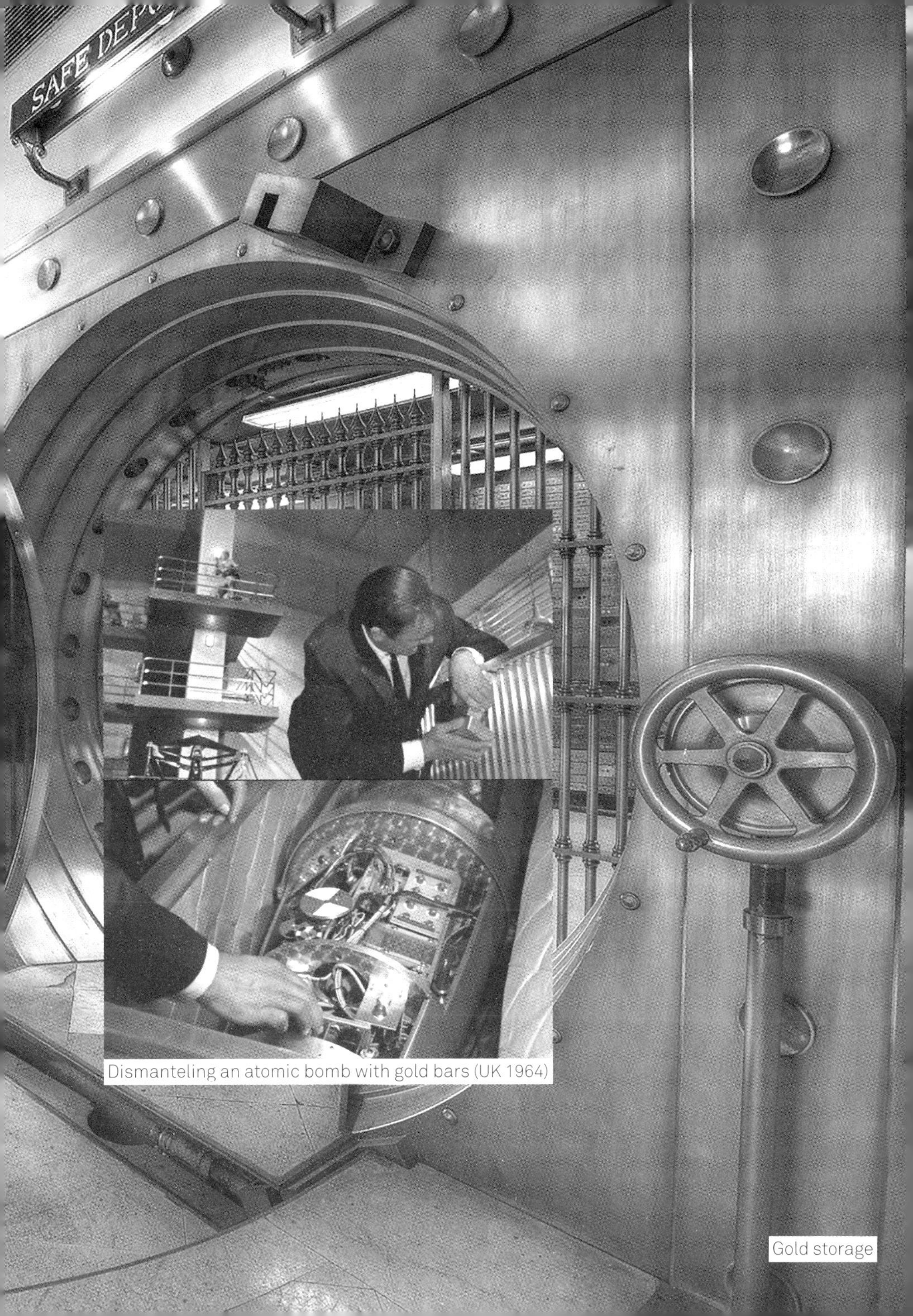

Dismanteling an atomic bomb with gold bars (UK 1964)

Gold storage

KNOTEN NACHMACHT ODER VERFÄLSCHT ODER NACHGEMACHTE ODE

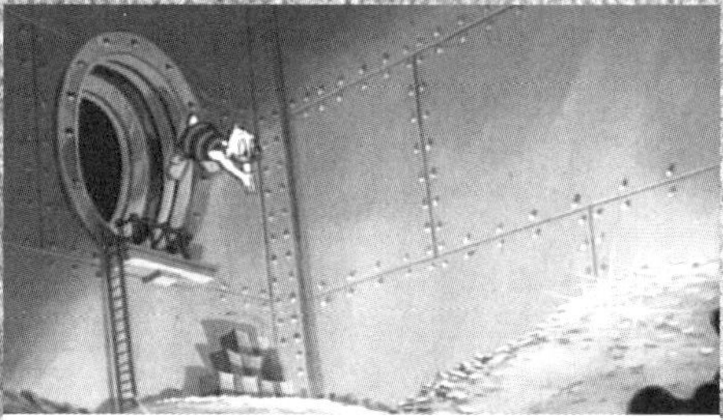

A gold bath

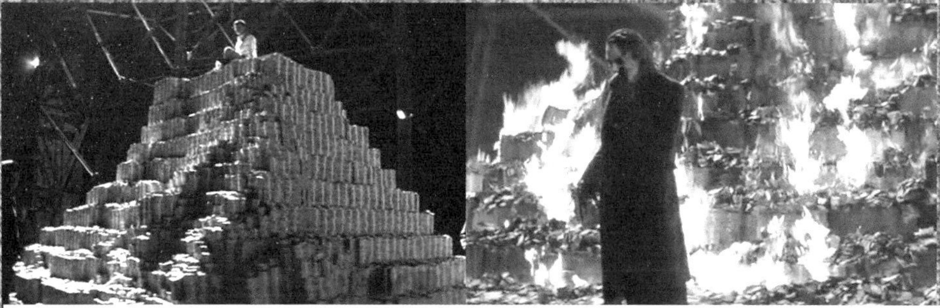

A mountain of money ... on fire (US, UK 2008)

100 HUN
DER DEUTSC

All the hundred deutsche Mark bills since 1945

UNDESBANK 1962

scale to keep the less adaptable out of mischief, and of paying wages to the younger adults for attendance at schools that would equip them to use the new atomic machinery. . . . So quite insensibly the council drifted into a complete re-organization of urban and industrial life, and indeed of the entire social system.

Ideas that are unhampered by political intrigue or financial considerations have a sweeping way with them, and before a year was out the records of the council show clearly that it was rising to its enormous opportunity, and partly through its own direct control and partly through a series of specific committees, it was planning a new common social order for the entire population of the earth. "There can be no real social stability or any general human happiness while large areas of the world and large classes of people are in a phase of civilization different from the prevailing mass. It is impossible now to have great blocks of population misunderstanding the generally accepted social purpose or at an economic disadvantage to the rest." So the council expressed its conception of the problem it had to solve. The peasant, the field-worker and all barbaric cultivators were at an "economic disadvantage" to the more mobile and educated classes, and the logic of the situation compelled the council to take up systematically the supersession of this stratum by a more efficient organization of production. It developed a scheme

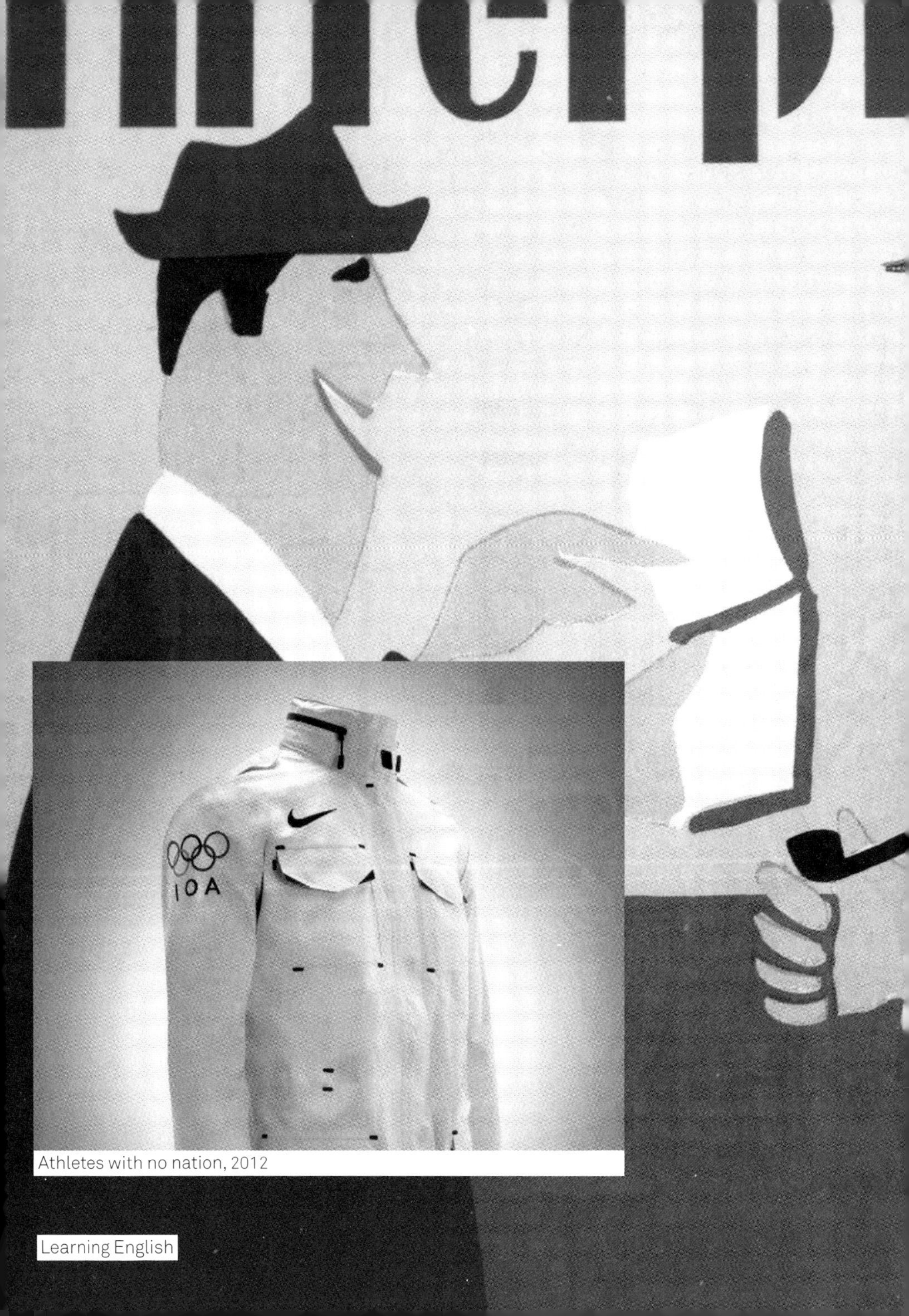

Athletes with no nation, 2012

Learning English

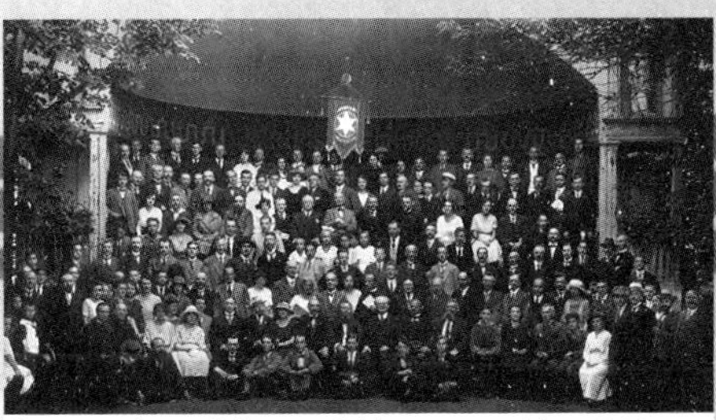

Convention of the world language Ido, 1922

for the progressive establishment throughout the world of the 'modern system' in agriculture, a system that should give the full advantages of a civilized life to every agricultural worker, and this replacement has been going on right up to the present day. The central idea of the modern system is the substitution of cultivating guilds for the individual cultivator and for cottage and village life altogether. These guilds are associations of men and women who take over areas of arable or pasture land, and make themselves responsible for a certain average produce. They are bodies small enough as a rule to be run on a strictly democratic basis and large enough to supply all the labour, except for a certain assistance from townspeople during the harvest, needed upon the land farmed. They have watchers' bungalows or châlets on the ground cultivated, but the ease and the costlessness of modern locomotion enables them to maintain a group of residences in the nearest town with a common dining-room and club house, and usually also a guild house in the national or provincial capital. Already this system has abolished a distinctively "rustic" population throughout vast areas of the old world where it has prevailed immemorially. That shy, unstimulated life of the lonely hovel, the narrow scandals and petty spites and persecutions of the small village, that hoarding, half inanimate existence away from books, thought or social participation and in constant contact with

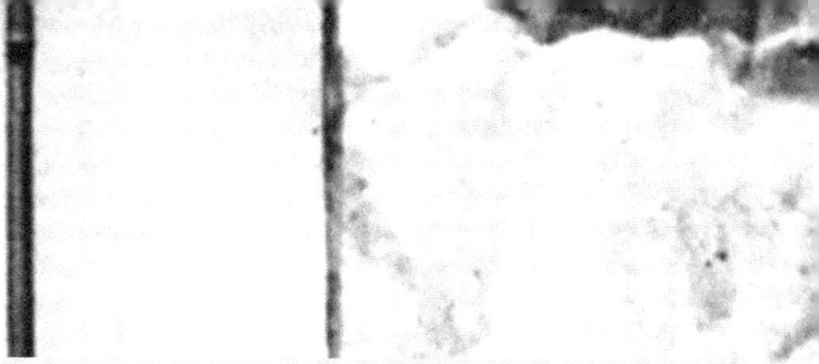

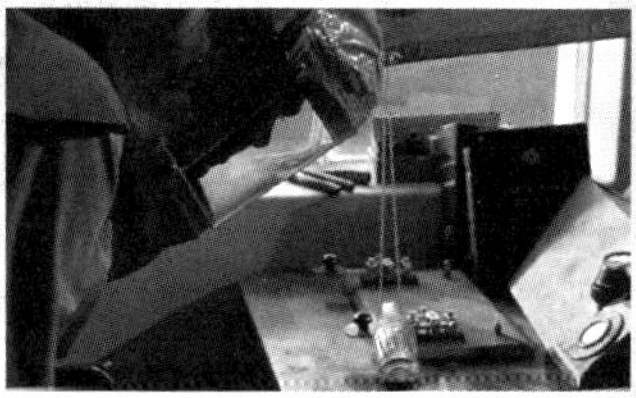

Radio signals from San Francisco

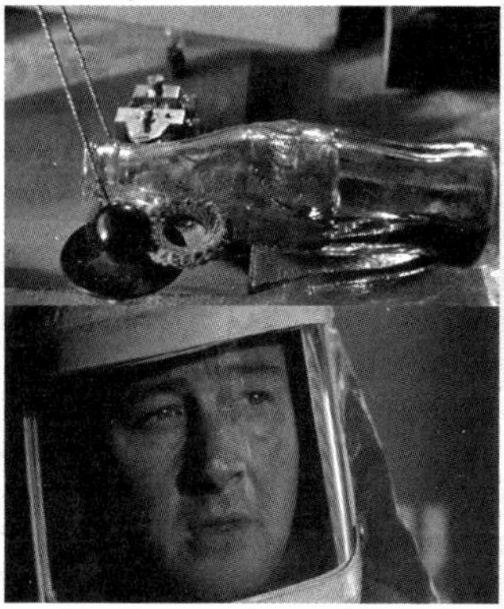

... after the atomic war (US 1959)

cattle, pigs, poultry and their excrement is passing away out of human experience. In a little while it will be gone altogether. In the nineteenth century it had already ceased to be a necessary human state, and only the absence of any collective intelligence and an imagined need for tough and unintelligent soldiers and for a prolific class at a low level, prevented its systematic replacement at that time. . . .

And while this settlement of the country was in progress, the urban camps of the first phase of the council's activities were rapidly developing, partly through the inherent forces of the situation and partly through the council's direction, into a modern type of town. . . .

§ 7

It is characteristic of the manner in which large enterprises forced themselves upon the Brissago council, that it was not until the end of the first year of their administration and then only with extreme reluctance that they would take up the manifest need for a lingua franca for the world. They seem to have given little attention to the various theoretical universal languages which were proposed to them. They wished to give as little trouble to hasty and simple people as possible, and the world-wide distribution of English gave them

Early transmitter

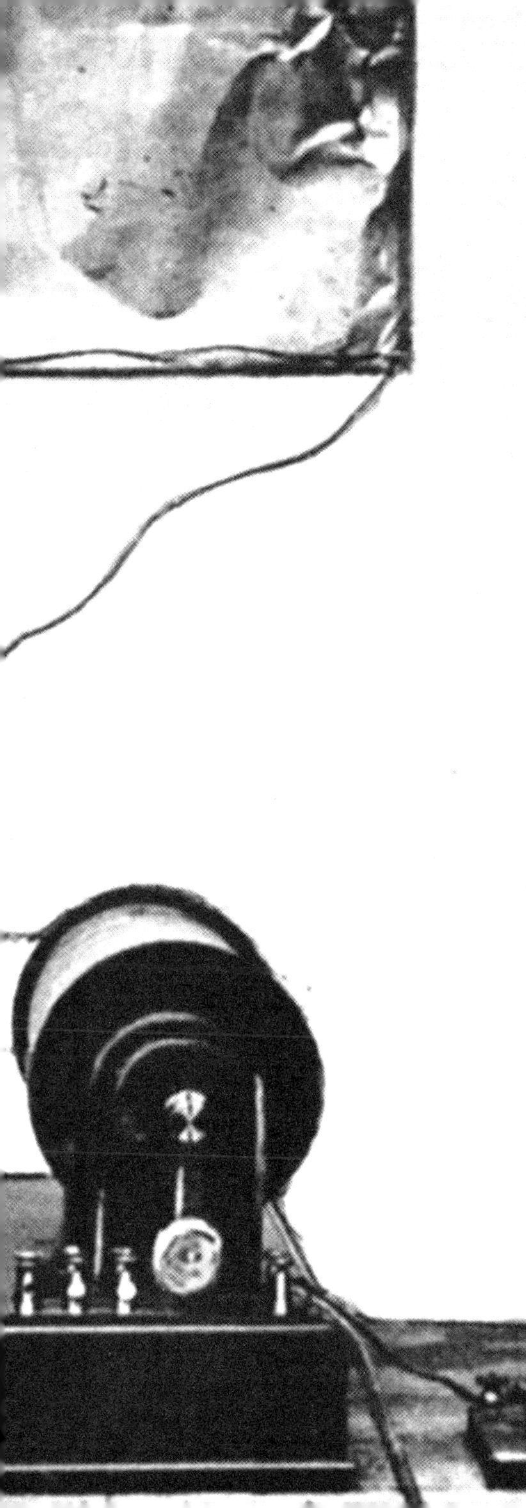

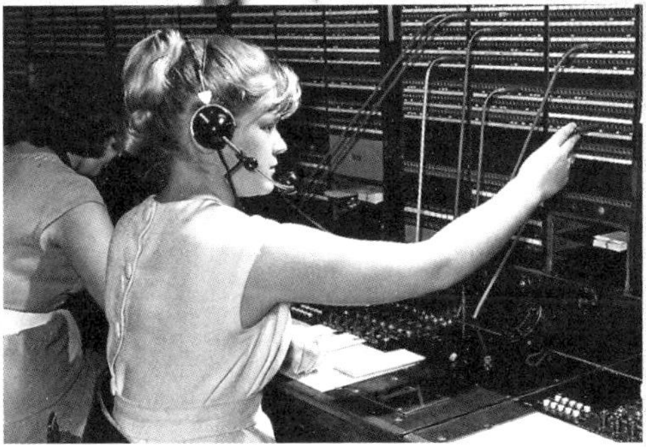

Operator

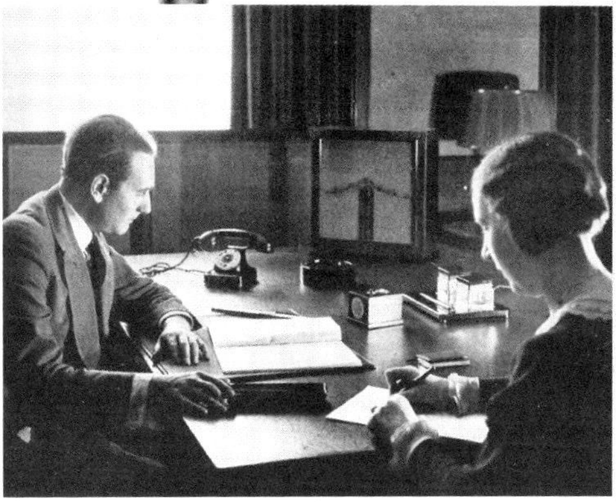

Phone conversation touchless

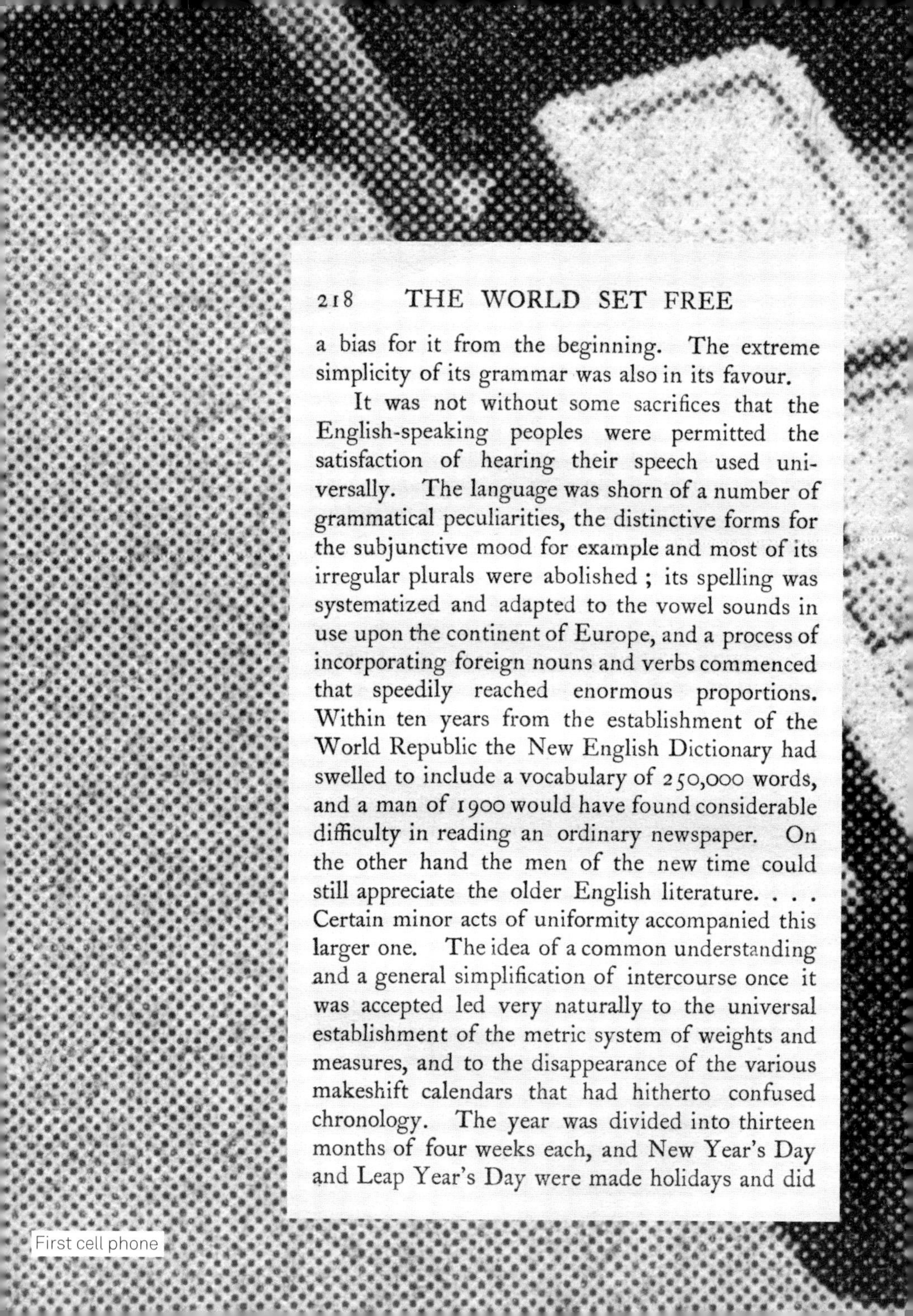

First cell phone

a bias for it from the beginning. The extreme simplicity of its grammar was also in its favour.

It was not without some sacrifices that the English-speaking peoples were permitted the satisfaction of hearing their speech used universally. The language was shorn of a number of grammatical peculiarities, the distinctive forms for the subjunctive mood for example and most of its irregular plurals were abolished ; its spelling was systematized and adapted to the vowel sounds in use upon the continent of Europe, and a process of incorporating foreign nouns and verbs commenced that speedily reached enormous proportions. Within ten years from the establishment of the World Republic the New English Dictionary had swelled to include a vocabulary of 250,000 words, and a man of 1900 would have found considerable difficulty in reading an ordinary newspaper. On the other hand the men of the new time could still appreciate the older English literature. . . . Certain minor acts of uniformity accompanied this larger one. The idea of a common understanding and a general simplification of intercourse once it was accepted led very naturally to the universal establishment of the metric system of weights and measures, and to the disappearance of the various makeshift calendars that had hitherto confused chronology. The year was divided into thirteen months of four weeks each, and New Year's Day and Leap Year's Day were made holidays and did

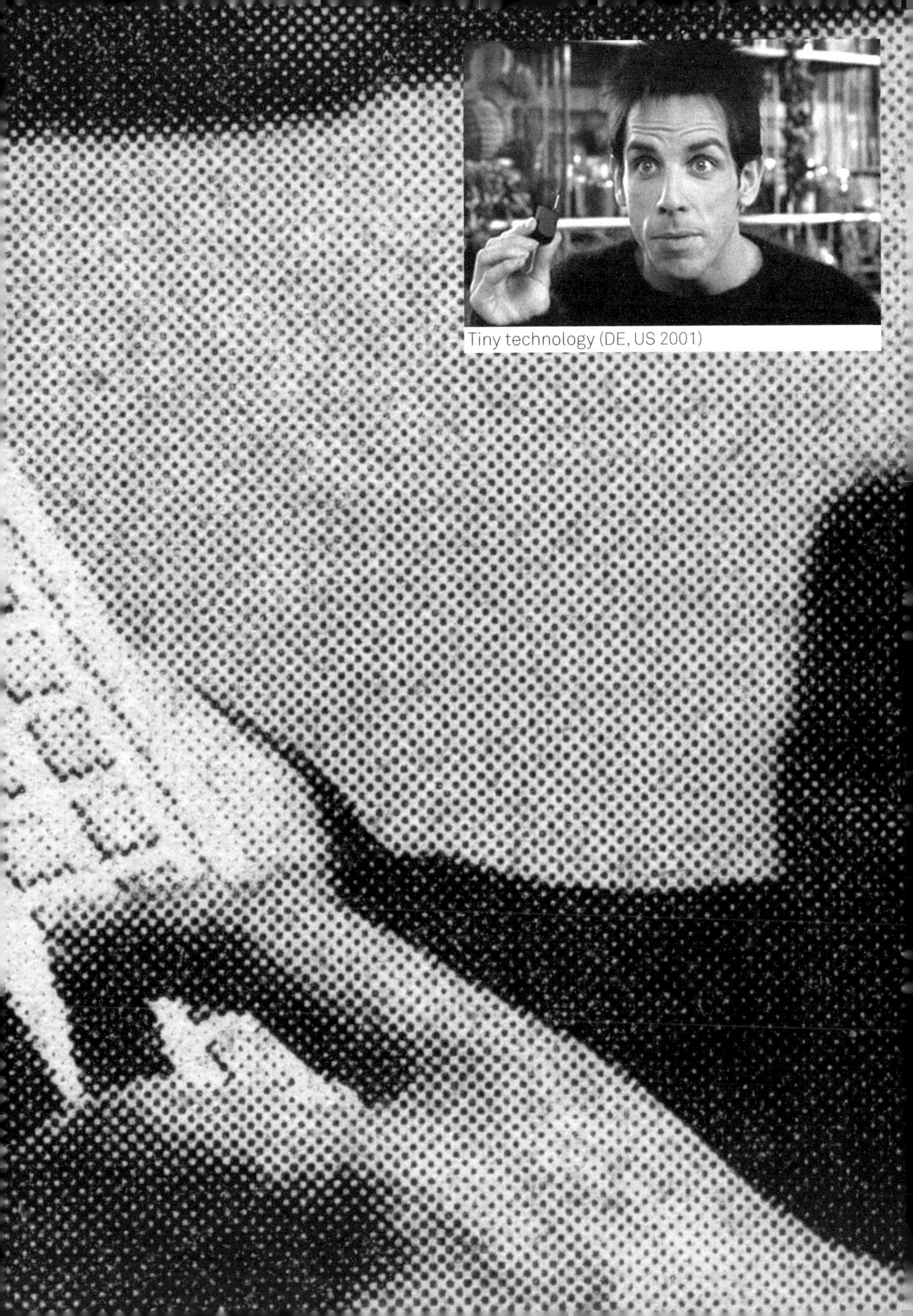

Tiny technology (DE, US 2001)

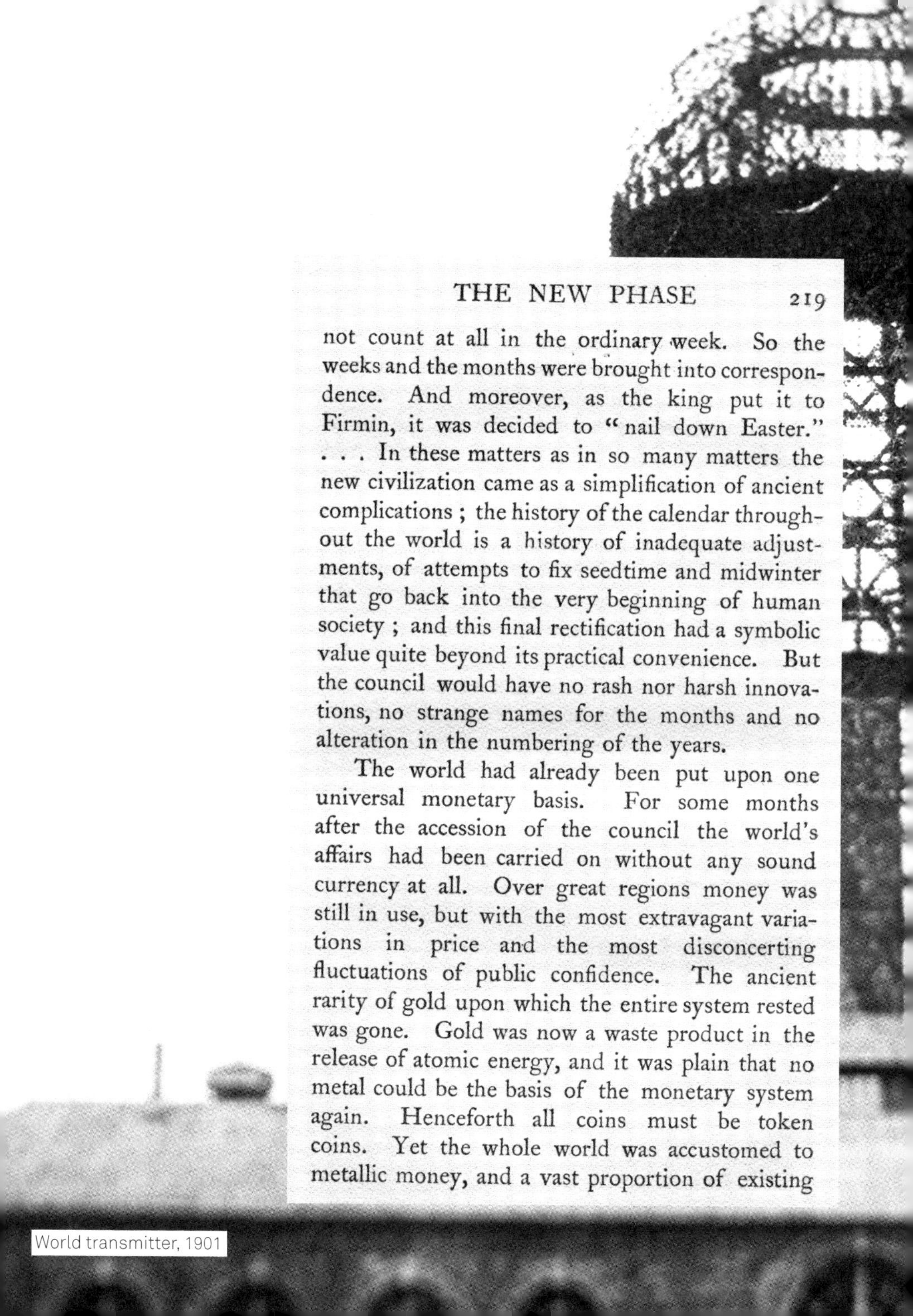

not count at all in the ordinary week. So the weeks and the months were brought into correspondence. And moreover, as the king put it to Firmin, it was decided to "nail down Easter." . . . In these matters as in so many matters the new civilization came as a simplification of ancient complications; the history of the calendar throughout the world is a history of inadequate adjustments, of attempts to fix seedtime and midwinter that go back into the very beginning of human society; and this final rectification had a symbolic value quite beyond its practical convenience. But the council would have no rash nor harsh innovations, no strange names for the months and no alteration in the numbering of the years.

The world had already been put upon one universal monetary basis. For some months after the accession of the council the world's affairs had been carried on without any sound currency at all. Over great regions money was still in use, but with the most extravagant variations in price and the most disconcerting fluctuations of public confidence. The ancient rarity of gold upon which the entire system rested was gone. Gold was now a waste product in the release of atomic energy, and it was plain that no metal could be the basis of the monetary system again. Henceforth all coins must be token coins. Yet the whole world was accustomed to metallic money, and a vast proportion of existing

World transmitter, 1901

human relationships had grown up upon a cash basis and were almost inconceivable without that convenient liquidating factor. It seemed absolutely necessary to the life of the social organization to have some sort of currency, and the council had therefore to discover some real value upon which to rest it. Various such apparently stable values as land and hours of work were considered. Ultimately the government, which was now in possession of most of the supplies of energy-releasing material, fixed a certain number of units of energy as the value of a gold sovereign, declared a sovereign to be worth exactly twenty marks, twenty-five francs, five dollars and so forth with the other current units of the world, and undertook, under various qualifications and conditions, to deliver energy upon demand as payment for every sovereign presented. On the whole this worked satisfactorily. They saved the face of the pound sterling. Coin was rehabilitated, and after a phase of price fluctuations began to settle down to definite equivalents and uses again, with names and everyday values familiar to the common run of people. . . .

§ 8

As the Brissago council came to realize that what it had supposed to be temporary camps of refugees were rapidly developing into great towns of a new type and that it was remoulding the world in spite of itself, it decided to place this work of redistributing then on-agricultural population in the hands of a compactor and better qualified special committee. That committee is now, far more than the council or any other of its delegated committees, the active government of the world. Developed from an almost invisible germ of "town-planning" that came obscurely into existence in Europe or America (the question is still in dispute) somewhere in the closing decades of the nineteenth century, its work, the continual active planning and replanning of the world as a place of human habitation, is now so to speak the collective material activity of the race. The spontaneous, disorderly spreadings and recessions of populations, as aimless and mechanical as the trickling of spilt water, which was the substance of history for endless years, giving rise here to congestions, here to chronic devastating wars, and everywhere to a discomfort and disorderliness that was at its best only picturesque, is at an end. Men spread now, with the whole power of the race to aid them, into every available region of the earth. Their cities are no longer tethered to running water and the proximity of cultivation, their plans are no longer affected by strategic considerations or thoughts of social insecurity. The aeroplane and the nearly costless mobile car

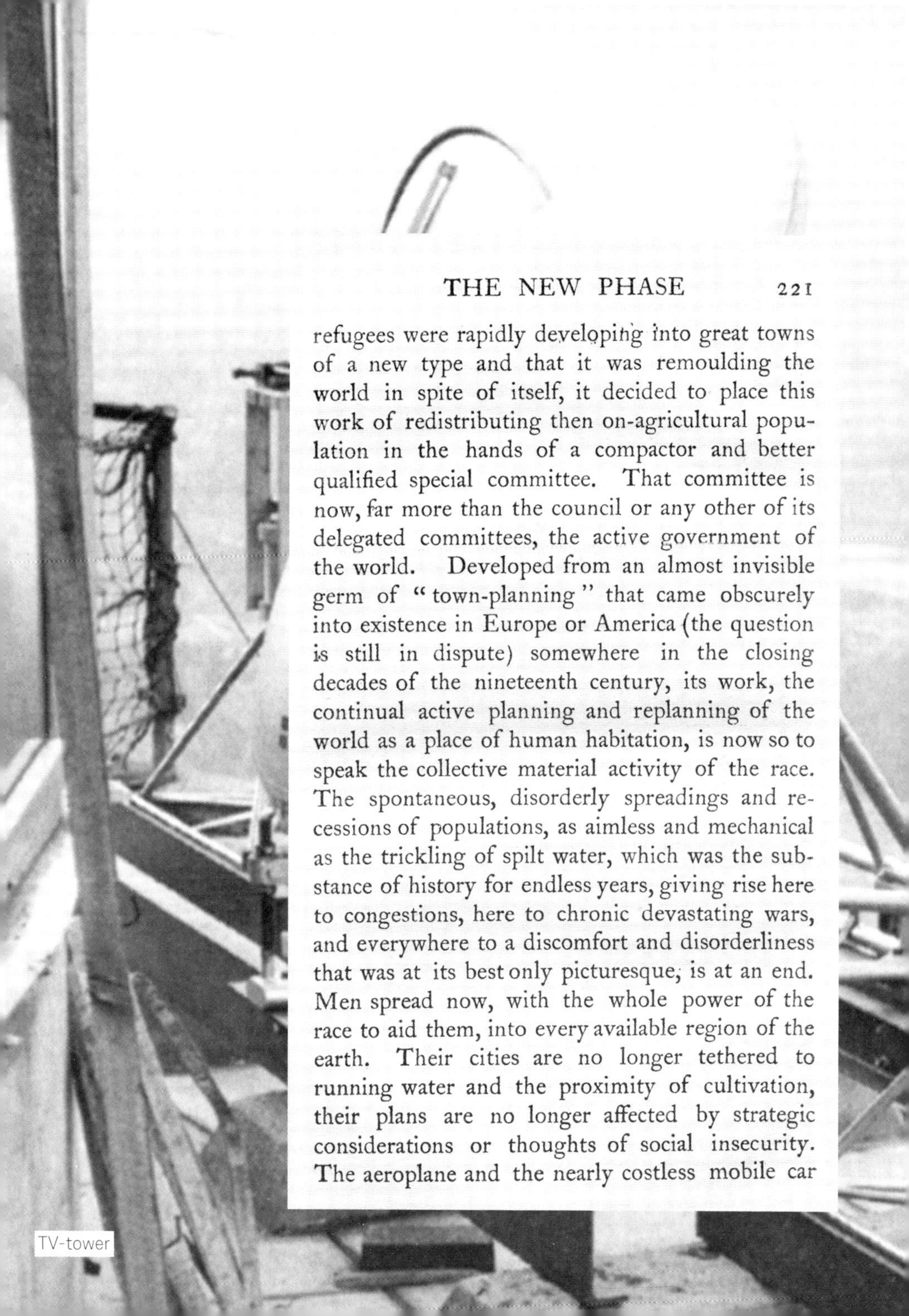

TV-tower

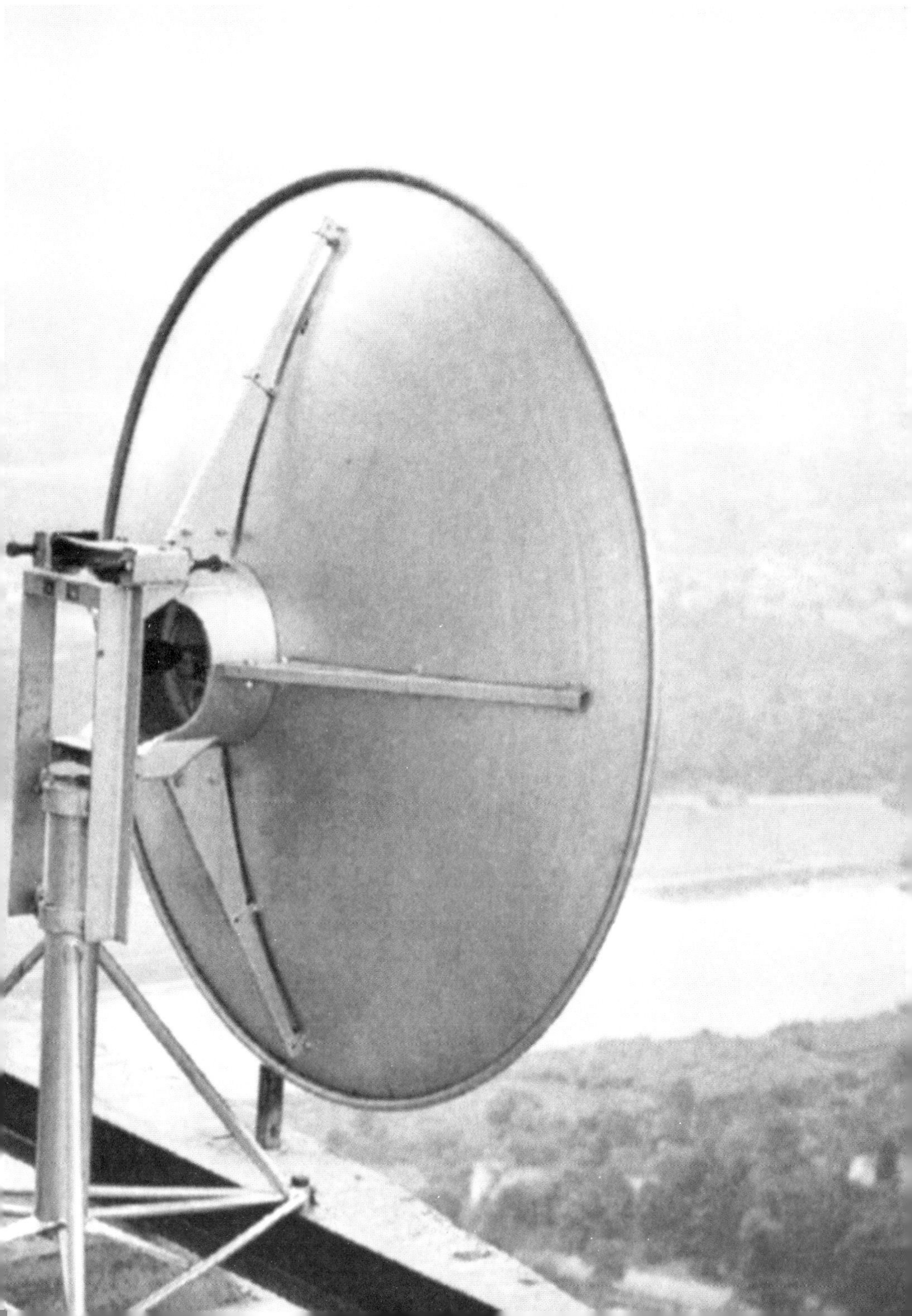

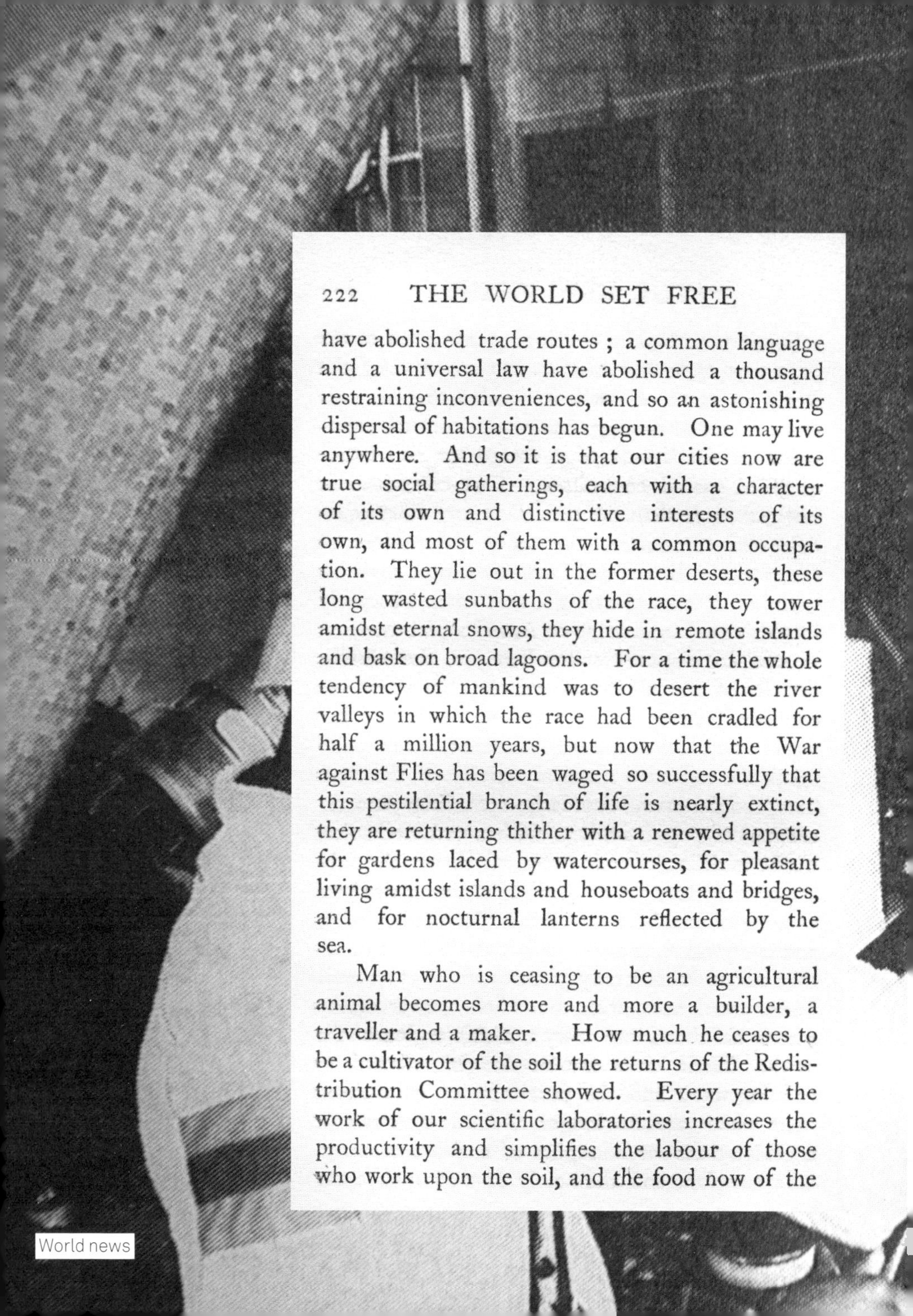

have abolished trade routes ; a common language and a universal law have abolished a thousand restraining inconveniences, and so an astonishing dispersal of habitations has begun. One may live anywhere. And so it is that our cities now are true social gatherings, each with a character of its own and distinctive interests of its own, and most of them with a common occupation. They lie out in the former deserts, these long wasted sunbaths of the race, they tower amidst eternal snows, they hide in remote islands and bask on broad lagoons. For a time the whole tendency of mankind was to desert the river valleys in which the race had been cradled for half a million years, but now that the War against Flies has been waged so successfully that this pestilential branch of life is nearly extinct, they are returning thither with a renewed appetite for gardens laced by watercourses, for pleasant living amidst islands and houseboats and bridges, and for nocturnal lanterns reflected by the sea.

Man who is ceasing to be an agricultural animal becomes more and more a builder, a traveller and a maker. How much he ceases to be a cultivator of the soil the returns of the Redistribution Committee showed. Every year the work of our scientific laboratories increases the productivity and simplifies the labour of those who work upon the soil, and the food now of the

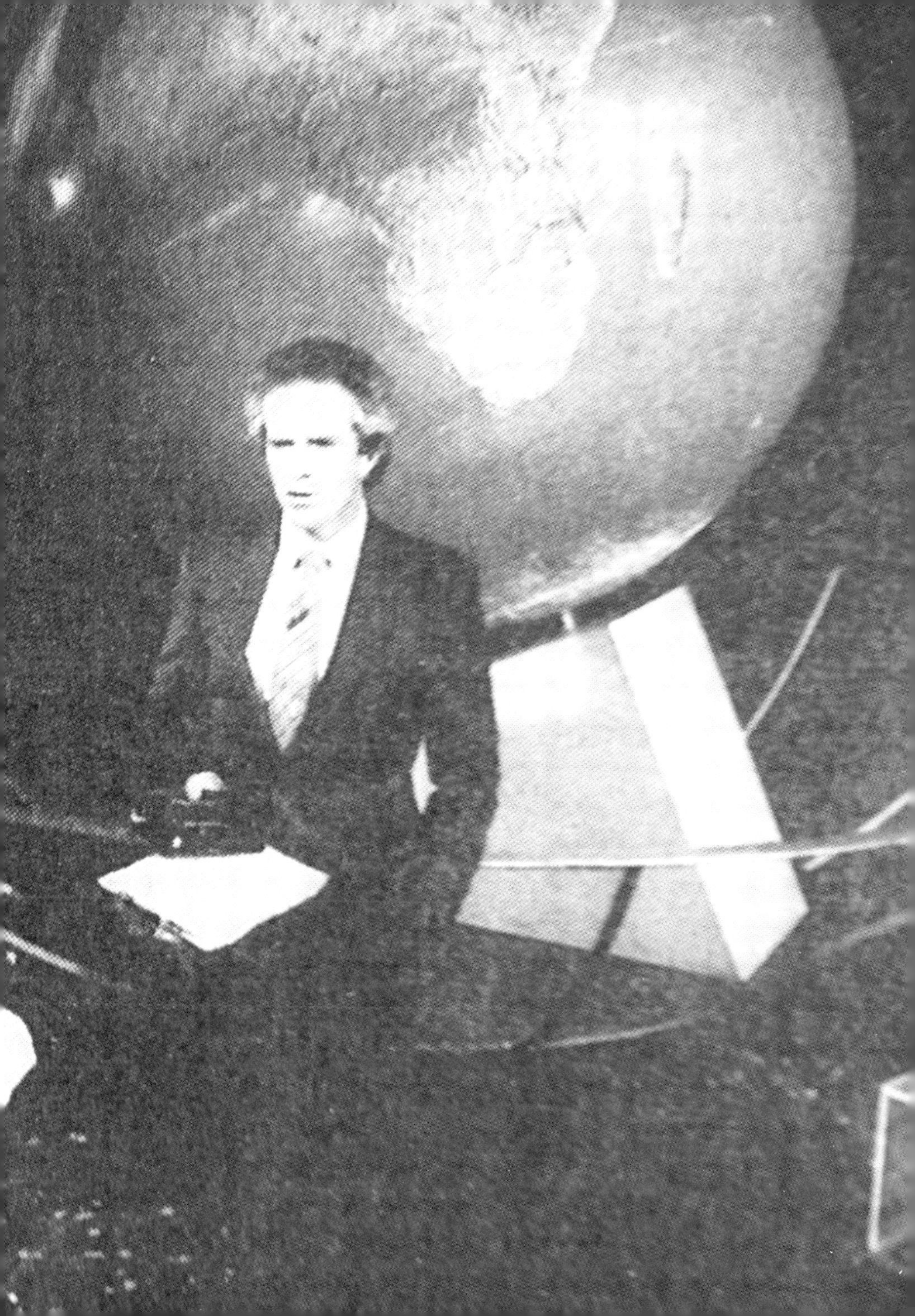

whole world is produced by less than one per cent. of its population, a percentage which still tends to decrease. Far fewer people are needed upon the land than training and proclivity dispose towards it, and as a consequence of this excess of human attention, the garden side of life, the creation of groves and lawns and vast regions of beautiful flowers has expanded enormously and continues to expand. For as agricultural method intensifies and the quota is raised one farm association after another, availing itself of the 1975 regulations, elects to produce a public garden and pleasaunce in the place of its former fields, and the area of freedom and beauty is increased. And the chemists' triumphs of synthesis which could now give us an entirely artificial food remain largely in abeyance because it is so much more pleasant and interesting to eat natural produce and to grow such things upon the soil. Each year adds to the variety of our fruits and the delightfulness of our flowers.

§ 9

The early years of the World Republic witnessed a certain recrudescence of political adventure. There was, it is rather curious to note, no revival of separatism after the face of King Ferdinand Charles had vanished from the sight of men, but in a number of countries, as the first

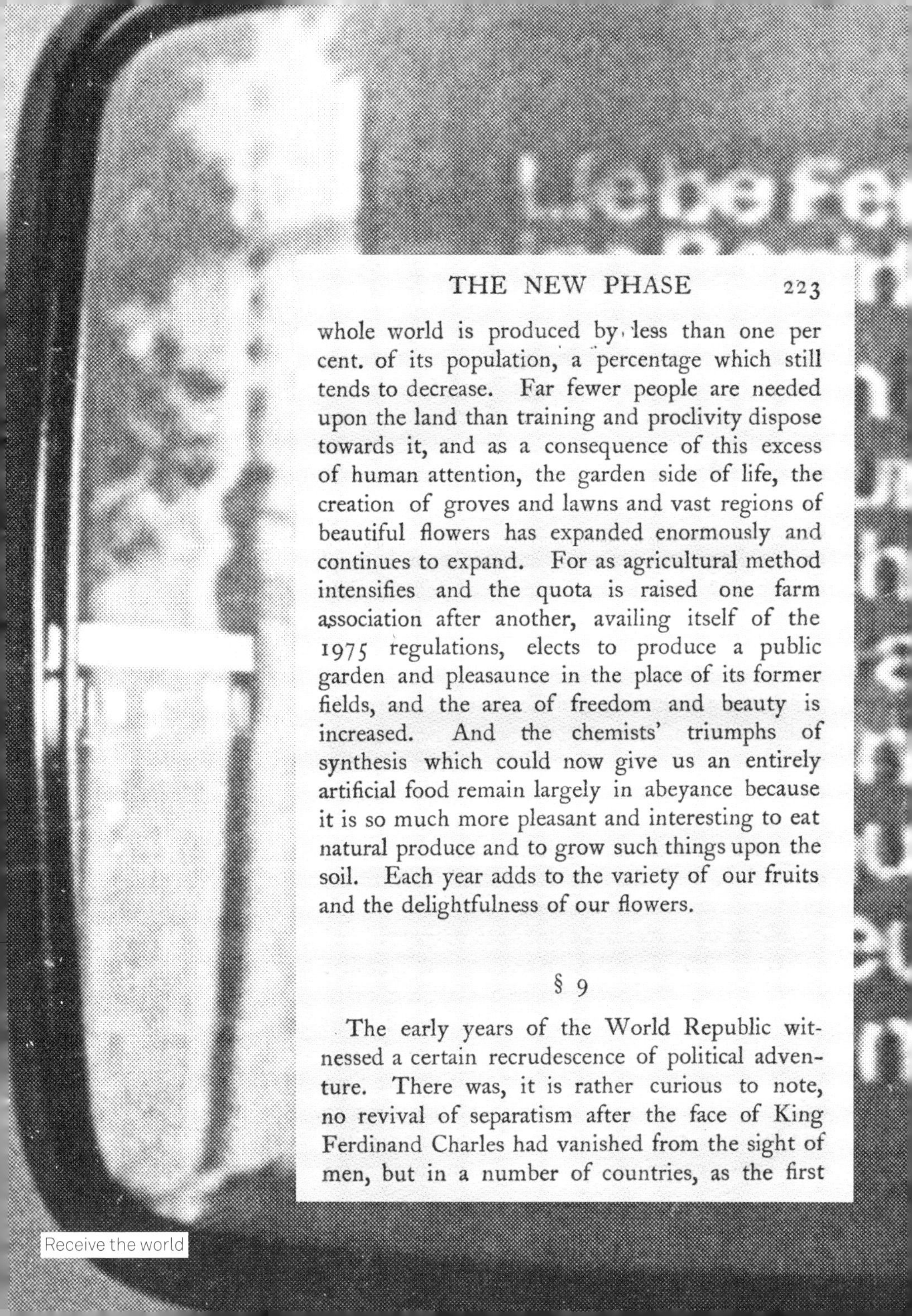

urgent physical needs were met, there appeared a variety of personalities having this in common, that they sought to revive political trouble and clamber by its aid to positions of importance and satisfaction. In no case did they speak in the name of kings, and it is clear that monarchy must have been far gone in obsolescence before the twentieth century began, but they made appeals to the large survivals of nationalist and racial feeling that were everywhere to be found, they alleged with considerable justice that the council was overriding racial and national customs and disregarding religious rules. The great plain of India was particularly prolific in such agitators. The revival of newspapers, which had largely ceased during the terrible year because of the dislocation of the coinage, gave a vehicle and a method of organization to these complaints. At first the council disregarded this developing opposition, and then it recognized it with an entirely devastating frankness.

Never of course had there been so provisional a government. It was of an extravagant illegality. It was indeed hardly more than a club, a club of about a hundred persons. At the outset there were ninety-three, and these were increased afterwards by the issue of invitations which more than balanced its deaths, to as many at one time as one hundred and nineteen. Always its constitution has been miscellaneous. At no time were

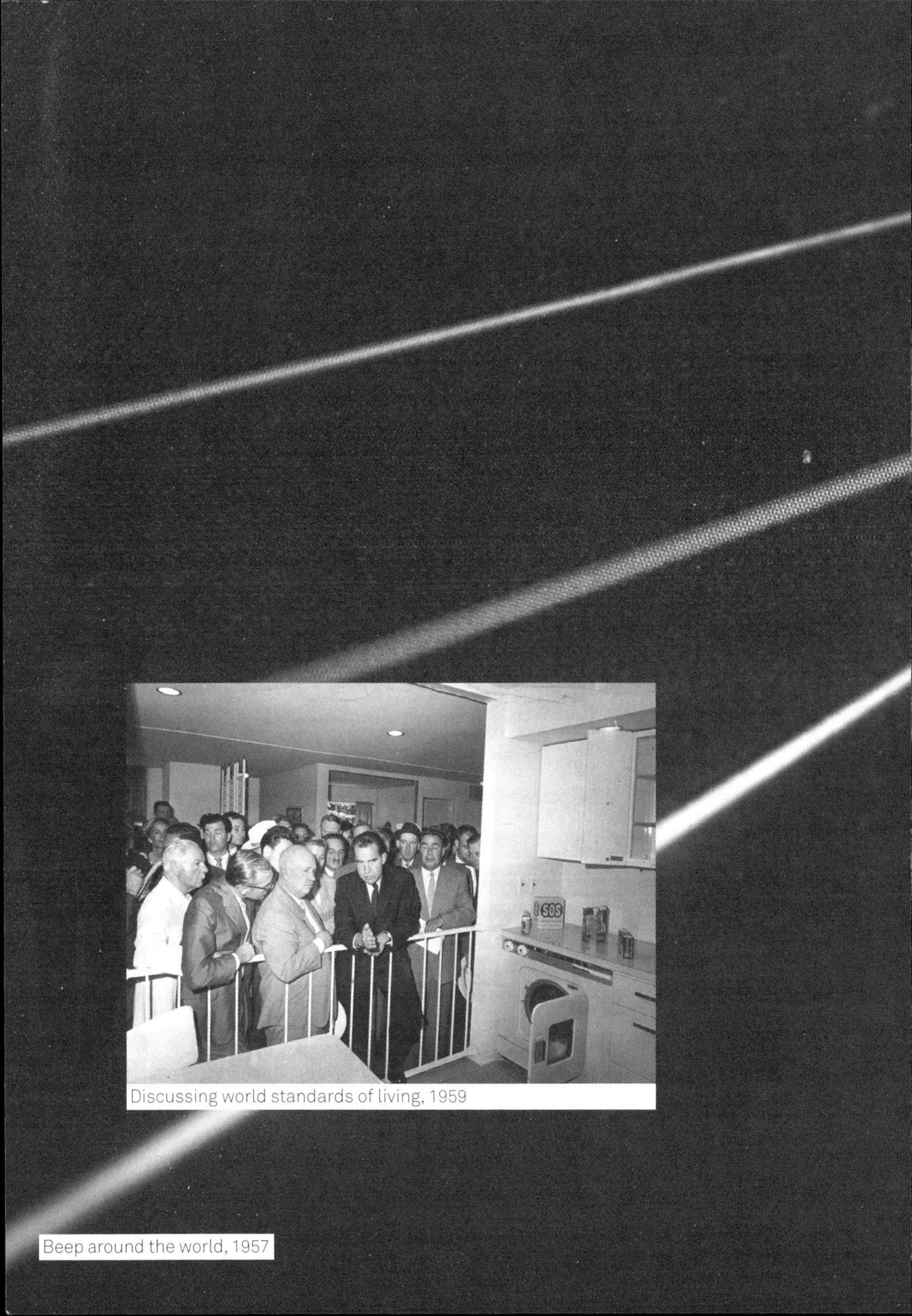

Discussing world standards of living, 1959

Beep around the world, 1957

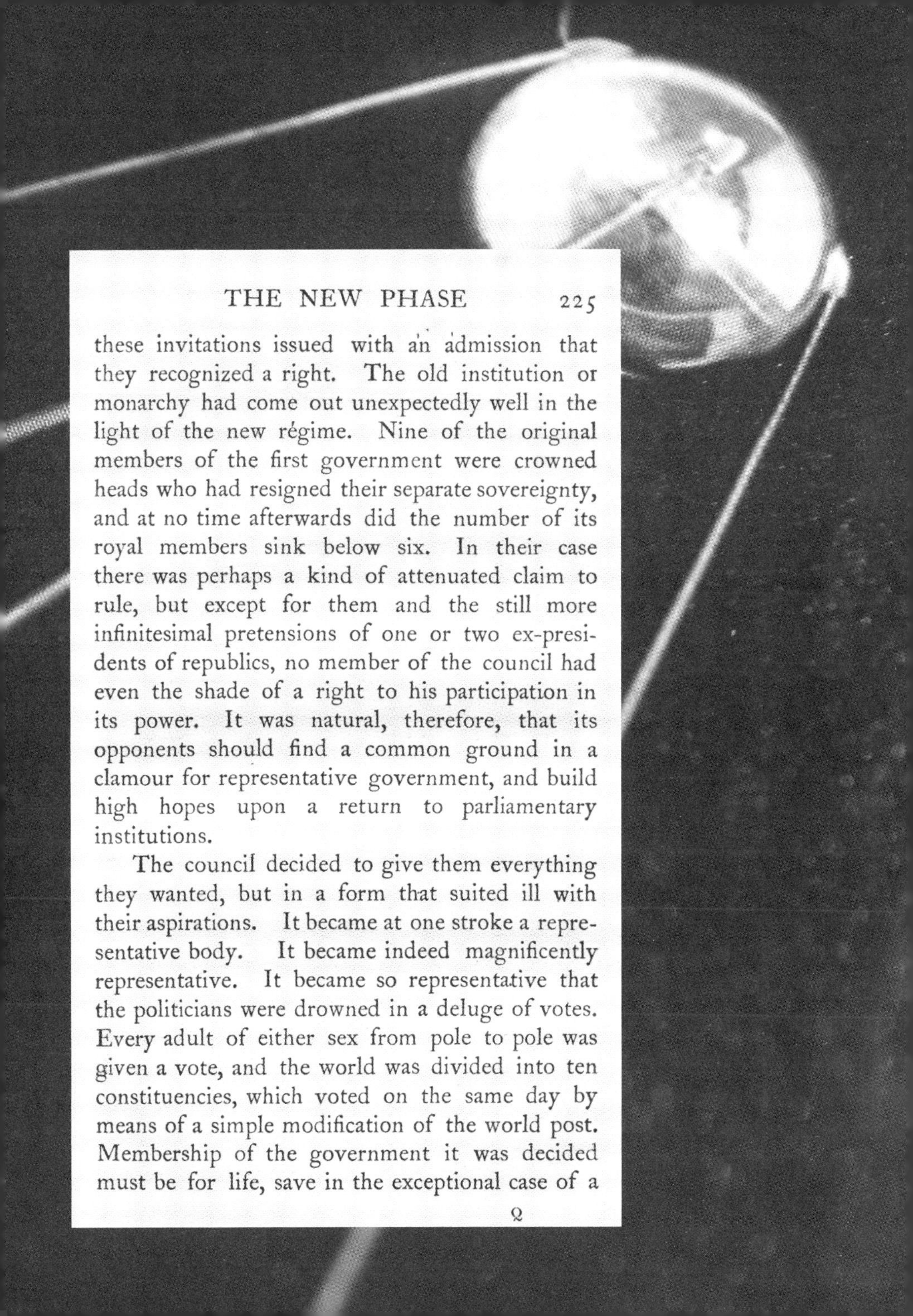

these invitations issued with an admission that they recognized a right. The old institution or monarchy had come out unexpectedly well in the light of the new régime. Nine of the original members of the first government were crowned heads who had resigned their separate sovereignty, and at no time afterwards did the number of its royal members sink below six. In their case there was perhaps a kind of attenuated claim to rule, but except for them and the still more infinitesimal pretensions of one or two ex-presidents of republics, no member of the council had even the shade of a right to his participation in its power. It was natural, therefore, that its opponents should find a common ground in a clamour for representative government, and build high hopes upon a return to parliamentary institutions.

The council decided to give them everything they wanted, but in a form that suited ill with their aspirations. It became at one stroke a representative body. It became indeed magnificently representative. It became so representative that the politicians were drowned in a deluge of votes. Every adult of either sex from pole to pole was given a vote, and the world was divided into ten constituencies, which voted on the same day by means of a simple modification of the world post. Membership of the government it was decided must be for life, save in the exceptional case of a

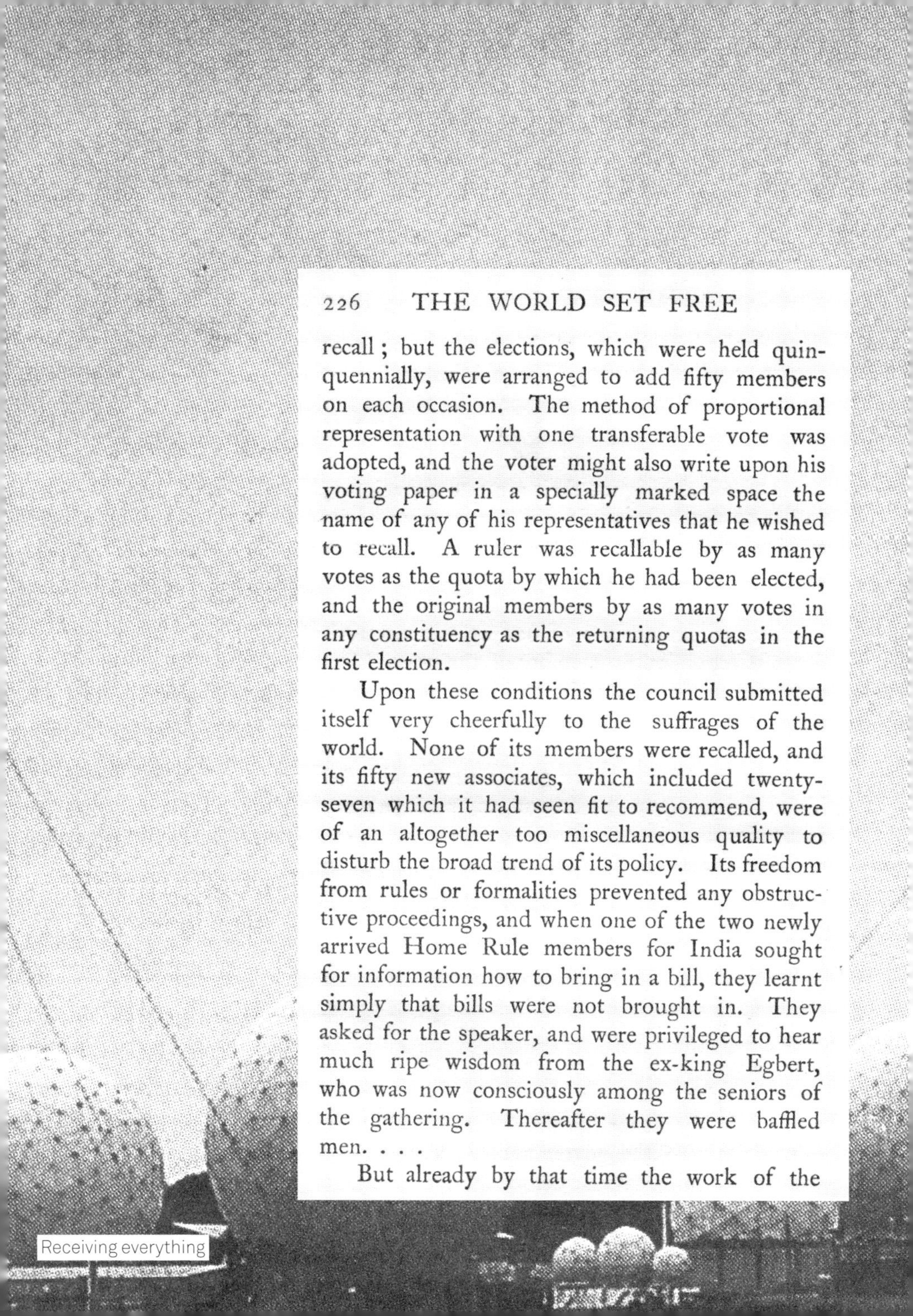

Receiving everything

recall; but the elections, which were held quinquennially, were arranged to add fifty members on each occasion. The method of proportional representation with one transferable vote was adopted, and the voter might also write upon his voting paper in a specially marked space the name of any of his representatives that he wished to recall. A ruler was recallable by as many votes as the quota by which he had been elected, and the original members by as many votes in any constituency as the returning quotas in the first election.

Upon these conditions the council submitted itself very cheerfully to the suffrages of the world. None of its members were recalled, and its fifty new associates, which included twenty-seven which it had seen fit to recommend, were of an altogether too miscellaneous quality to disturb the broad trend of its policy. Its freedom from rules or formalities prevented any obstructive proceedings, and when one of the two newly arrived Home Rule members for India sought for information how to bring in a bill, they learnt simply that bills were not brought in. They asked for the speaker, and were privileged to hear much ripe wisdom from the ex-king Egbert, who was now consciously among the seniors of the gathering. Thereafter they were baffled men. . . .

But already by that time the work of the

council was drawing to an end. It was concerned not so much for the continuation of its construction as for the preservation of its accomplished work from the dramatic instincts of the politician.

The life of the race becomes indeed more and more independent of the formal government. The council in its opening phase was heroic in spirit; a dragon-slaying body, it slashed out of existence a vast knotted tangle of obsolete ideas and clumsy and jealous proprietorships; it secured by a noble system of institutional precautions, freedom of enquiry, freedom of criticism, free communications, a common basis of education and understanding and freedom from economic oppression. With that its creative task was accomplished. It became more and more an established security and less and less an active intervention. There is nothing in our time to correspond with the continual petty making and entangling of laws in an atmosphere of contention that is perhaps the most perplexing aspect of constitutional history in the nineteenth century. In that age they seem to have been perpetually making laws when we should alter regulations. The work of change which we delegate to these scientific committees of specific general direction which have the special knowledge needed, and which are themselves dominated by the broad intellectual process of the community, was in

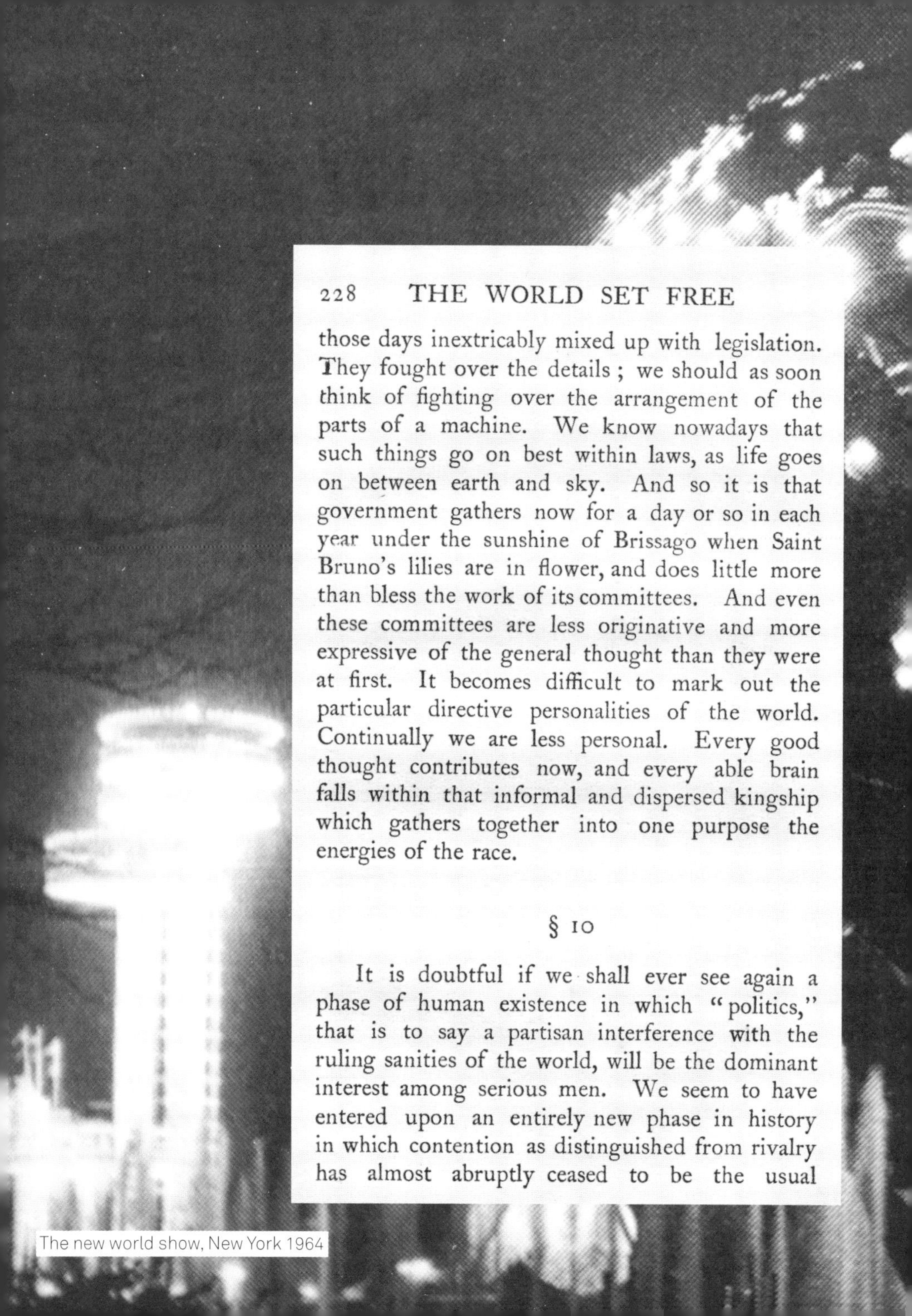

those days inextricably mixed up with legislation. They fought over the details; we should as soon think of fighting over the arrangement of the parts of a machine. We know nowadays that such things go on best within laws, as life goes on between earth and sky. And so it is that government gathers now for a day or so in each year under the sunshine of Brissago when Saint Bruno's lilies are in flower, and does little more than bless the work of its committees. And even these committees are less originative and more expressive of the general thought than they were at first. It becomes difficult to mark out the particular directive personalities of the world. Continually we are less personal. Every good thought contributes now, and every able brain falls within that informal and dispersed kingship which gathers together into one purpose the energies of the race.

§ 10

It is doubtful if we shall ever see again a phase of human existence in which "politics," that is to say a partisan interference with the ruling sanities of the world, will be the dominant interest among serious men. We seem to have entered upon an entirely new phase in history in which contention as distinguished from rivalry has almost abruptly ceased to be the usual

The new world show, New York 1964

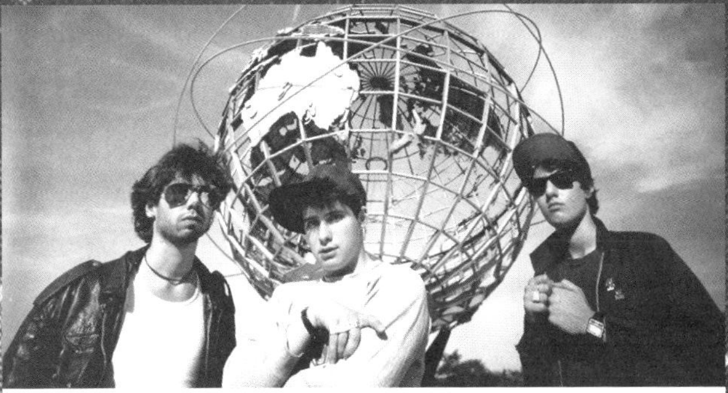

Youth of New York, 1986

The old new world show, New York 1939

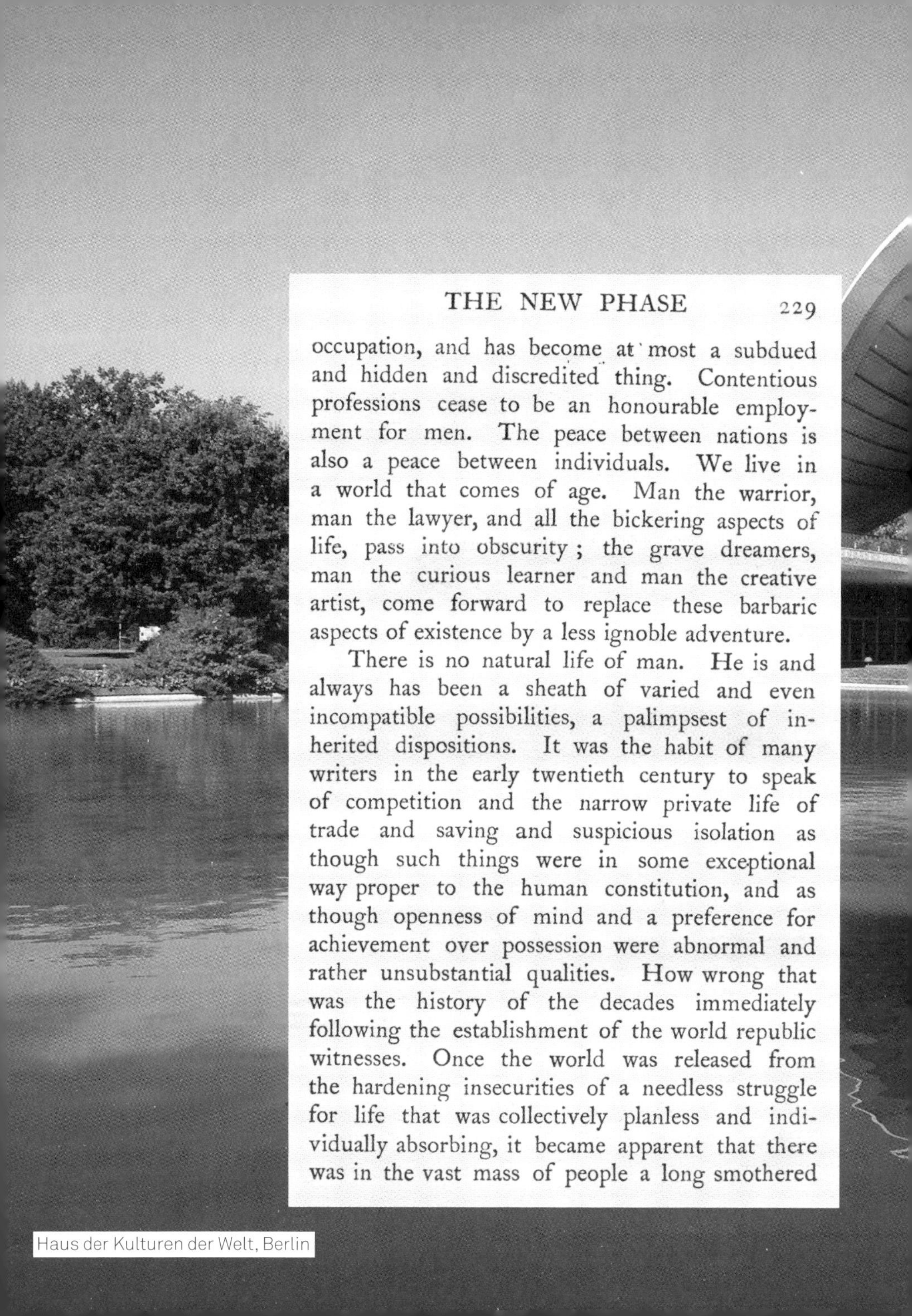

occupation, and has become at most a subdued and hidden and discredited thing. Contentious professions cease to be an honourable employment for men. The peace between nations is also a peace between individuals. We live in a world that comes of age. Man the warrior, man the lawyer, and all the bickering aspects of life, pass into obscurity; the grave dreamers, man the curious learner and man the creative artist, come forward to replace these barbaric aspects of existence by a less ignoble adventure.

There is no natural life of man. He is and always has been a sheath of varied and even incompatible possibilities, a palimpsest of inherited dispositions. It was the habit of many writers in the early twentieth century to speak of competition and the narrow private life of trade and saving and suspicious isolation as though such things were in some exceptional way proper to the human constitution, and as though openness of mind and a preference for achievement over possession were abnormal and rather unsubstantial qualities. How wrong that was the history of the decades immediately following the establishment of the world republic witnesses. Once the world was released from the hardening insecurities of a needless struggle for life that was collectively planless and individually absorbing, it became apparent that there was in the vast mass of people a long smothered

Haus der Kulturen der Welt, Berlin

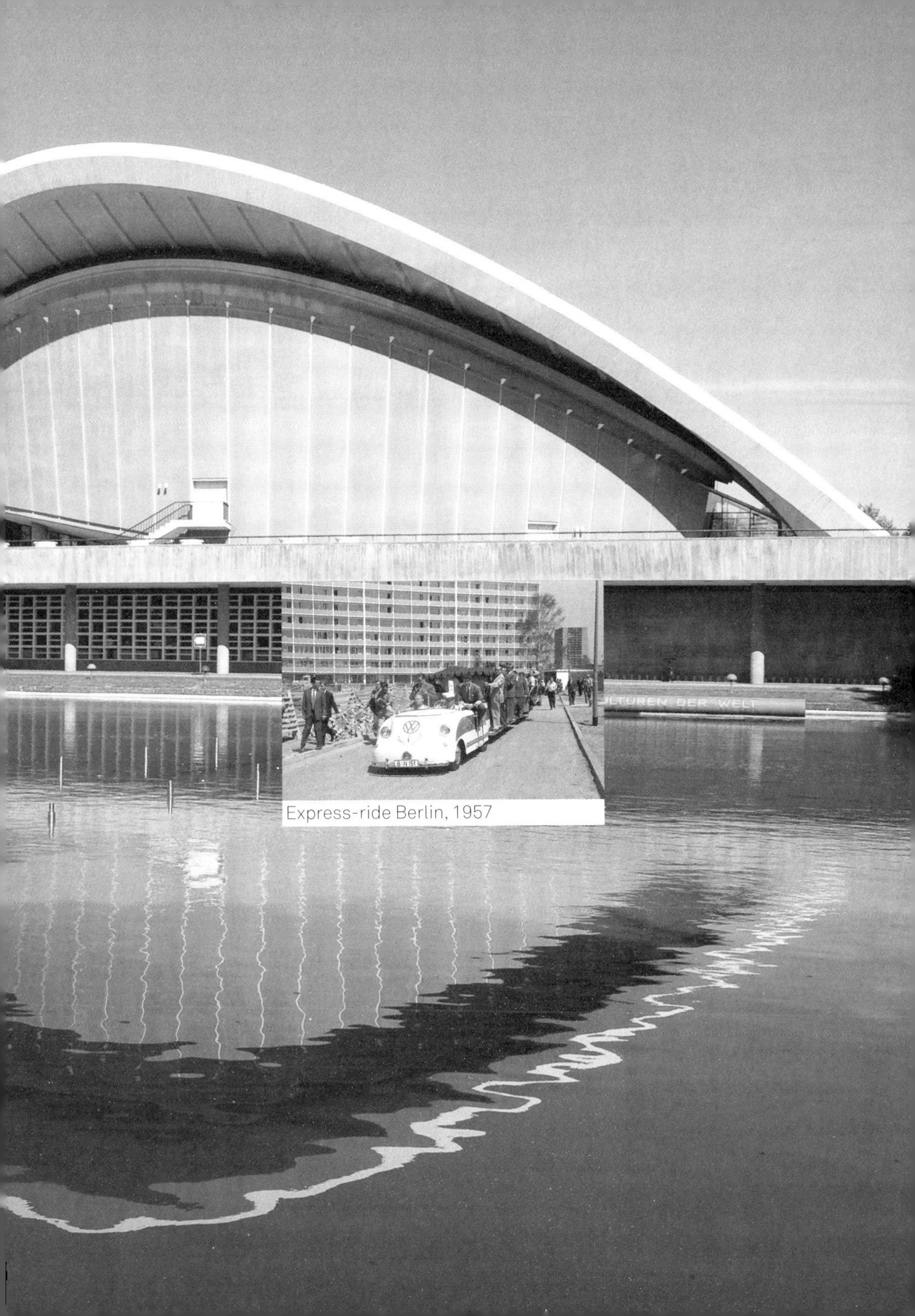

Express-ride Berlin, 1957

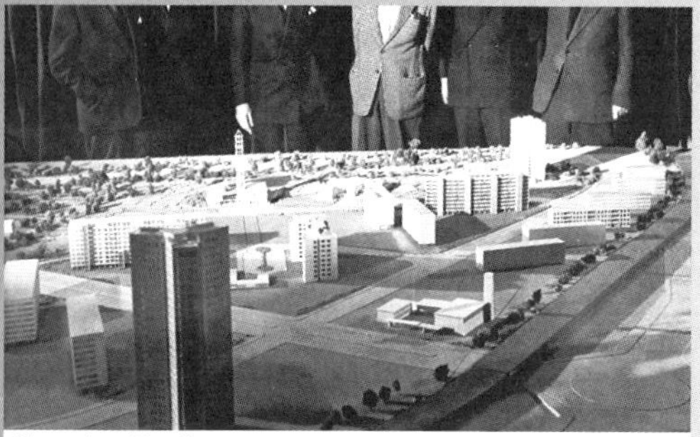
Planning Berlin

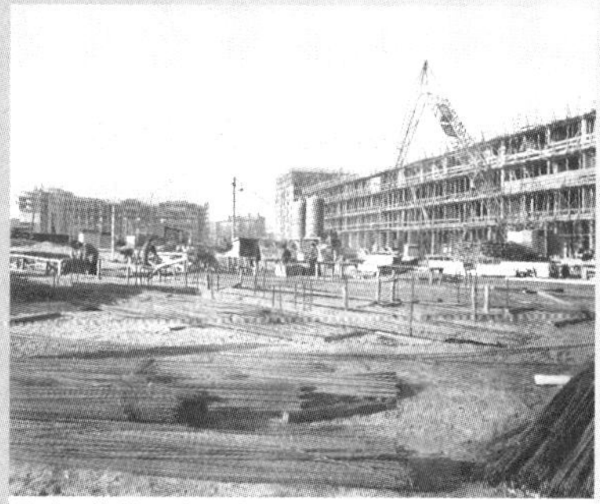
Rebuilding in 1957

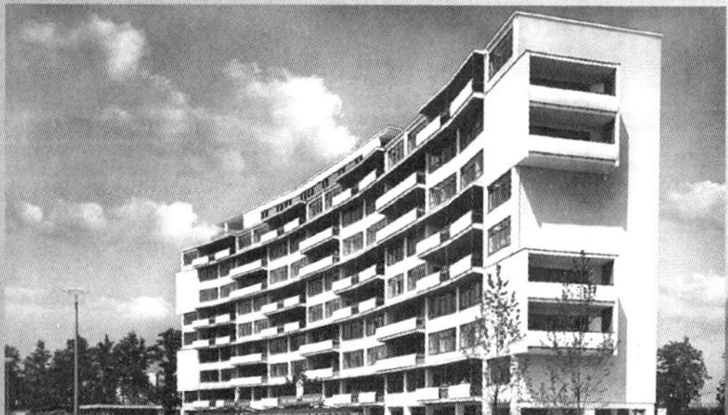
Interbau with express-tour, 1957

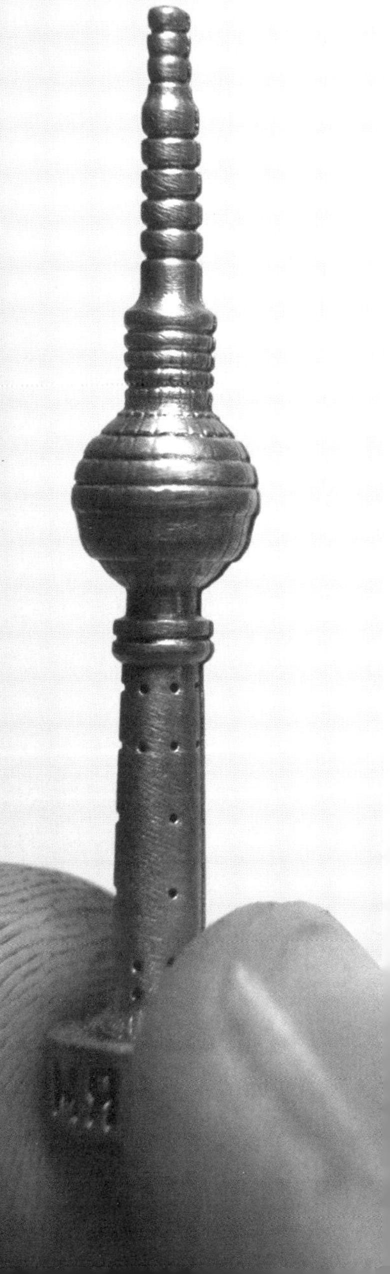
Transmission tower souvenir

passion to make things. The world broke out into making, and at first mainly into aesthetic making. This phase of history, which has been not inaptly termed the "Efflorescence," is still to a large extent with us. The majority of our population consists of artists, and the bulk of activity in the world lies no longer with necessities but with their elaboration, decoration and refinement. There has been an evident change in the quality of this making during recent years. It becomes more purposeful than it was, losing something of its first elegance and prettiness and gaining in intensity; but that is a change rather of hue than of nature. That comes with a deepening philosophy and a sounder education. For the first joyous exercises of fancy we perceive now the deliberation of a more constructive imagination. There is a natural order in these things, and art comes before science as the satisfaction of more elemental needs must come before art, and as play and pleasure come in a human life before the development of a settled purpose. . . .

For thousands of years this gathering impulse to creative work must have struggled in man against the limitations imposed upon him by his social ineptitude. It was a long smouldering fire that flamed out at last in all these things. The evidence of a pathetic, perpetually thwarted urgency to make something, is one of the most

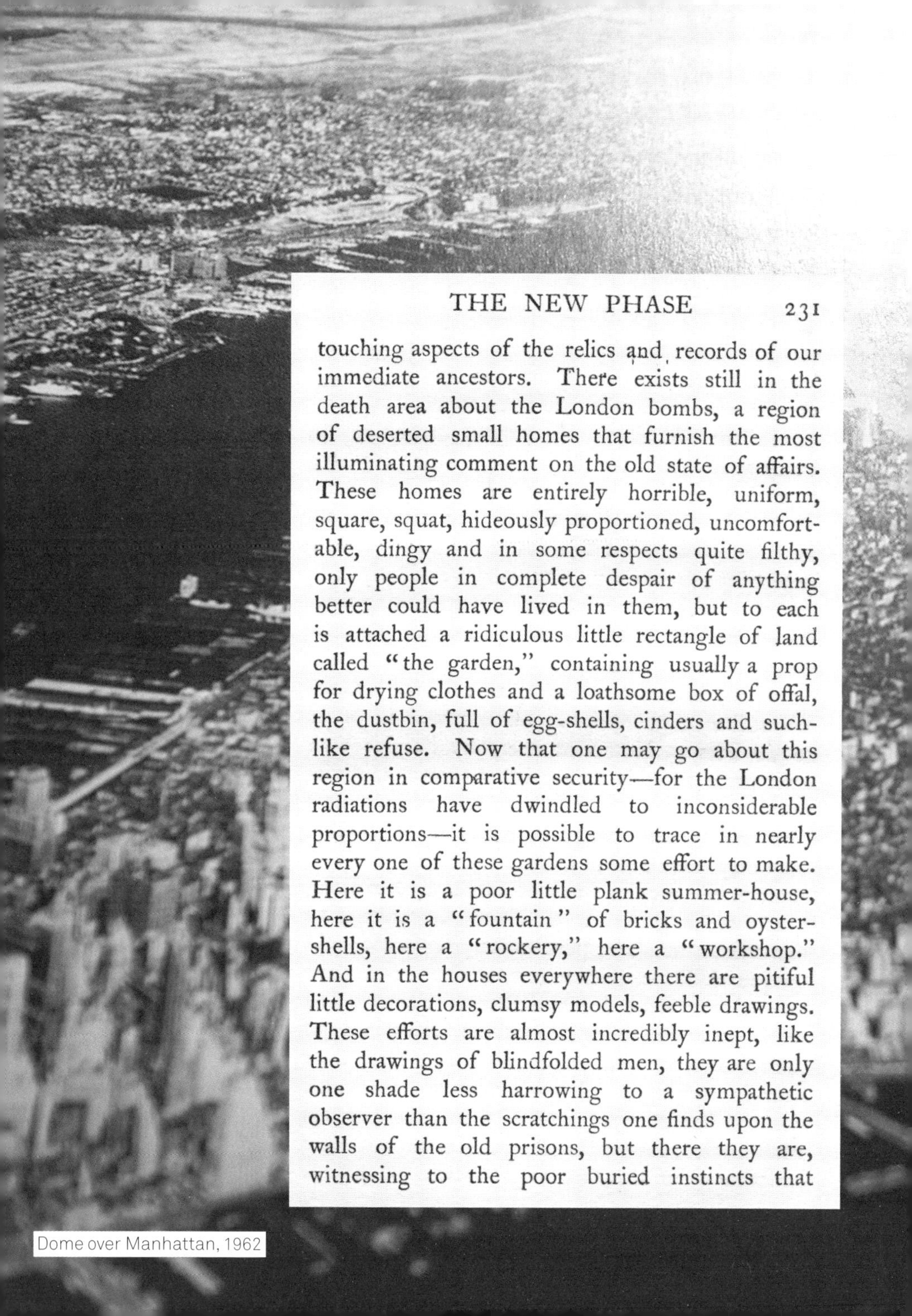

touching aspects of the relics and records of our immediate ancestors. There exists still in the death area about the London bombs, a region of deserted small homes that furnish the most illuminating comment on the old state of affairs. These homes are entirely horrible, uniform, square, squat, hideously proportioned, uncomfortable, dingy and in some respects quite filthy, only people in complete despair of anything better could have lived in them, but to each is attached a ridiculous little rectangle of land called "the garden," containing usually a prop for drying clothes and a loathsome box of offal, the dustbin, full of egg-shells, cinders and suchlike refuse. Now that one may go about this region in comparative security—for the London radiations have dwindled to inconsiderable proportions—it is possible to trace in nearly every one of these gardens some effort to make. Here it is a poor little plank summer-house, here it is a "fountain" of bricks and oyster-shells, here a "rockery," here a "workshop." And in the houses everywhere there are pitiful little decorations, clumsy models, feeble drawings. These efforts are almost incredibly inept, like the drawings of blindfolded men, they are only one shade less harrowing to a sympathetic observer than the scratchings one finds upon the walls of the old prisons, but there they are, witnessing to the poor buried instincts that

Dome over Manhattan, 1962

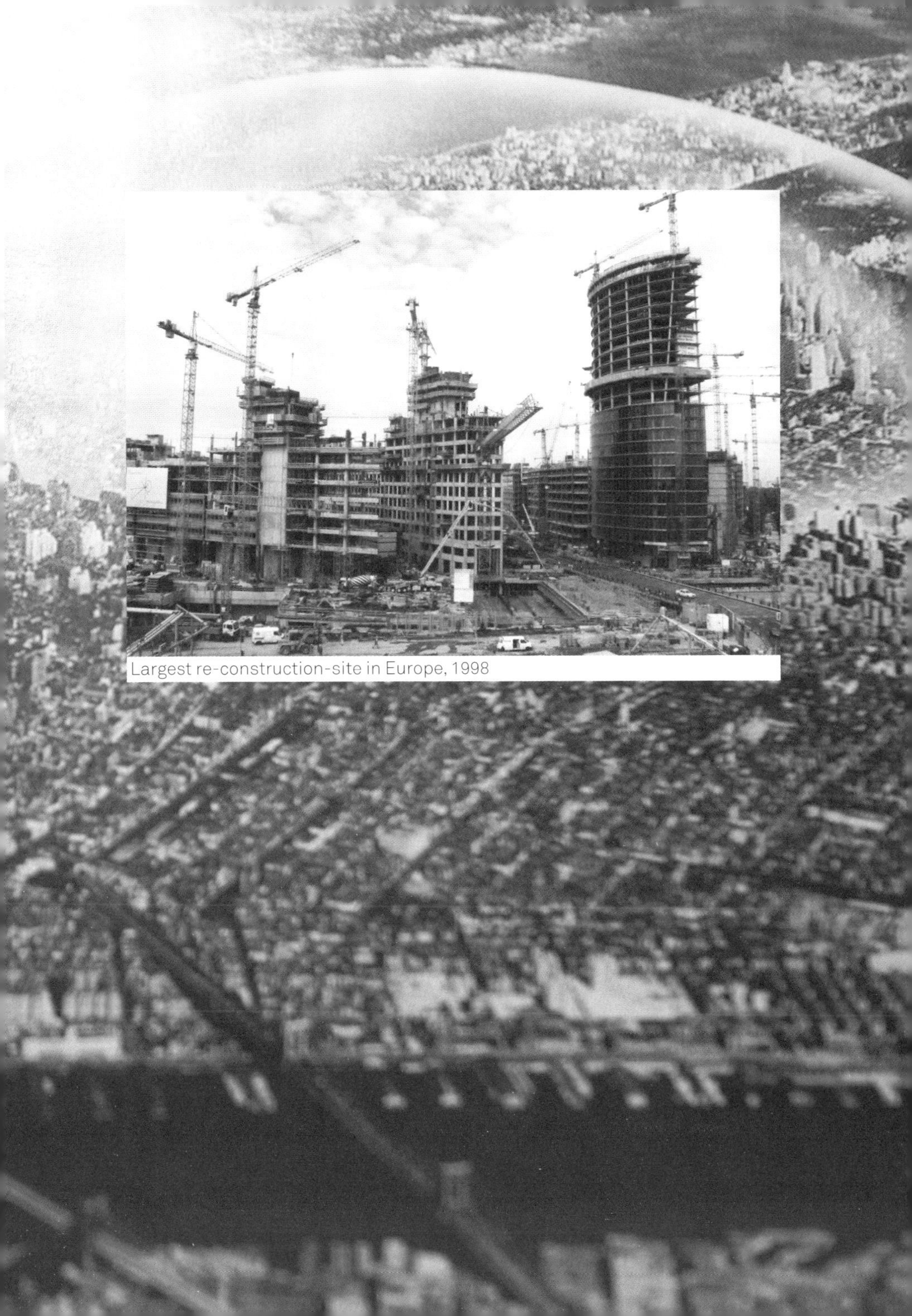

Largest re-construction-site in Europe, 1998

struggled up towards the light. That god of joyous expression our poor fathers ignorantly sought, our freedom has declared to us. . . .

In the old days the common ambition of every simple soul was to possess a little property, a patch of land, a house uncontrolled by others, an "independence" as the English used to put it. And what made this desire for freedom and prosperity so strong, was very evidently the dream of self-expression, of doing something with it, of playing with it, of making a personal delightfulness, a distinctiveness. Property was never more than a means to an end, nor avarice more than a perversion. Men owned in order to do freely. Now that everyone has his own apartments and his own privacy secure, this disposition to own has found its release in a new direction. Men study and save and strive that they may leave behind them a series of panels in some public arcade, a row of carven figures along a terrace, a grove, a pavilion. Or they give themselves to the penetration of some still opaque riddle in phenomena as once men gave themselves to the accumulation of riches. The work that was once the whole substance of social existence—for most men spent all their lives in earning a living—is now no more than was the burden upon one of those old climbers who carried knapsacks of provisions on their backs in order that they might ascend mountains.

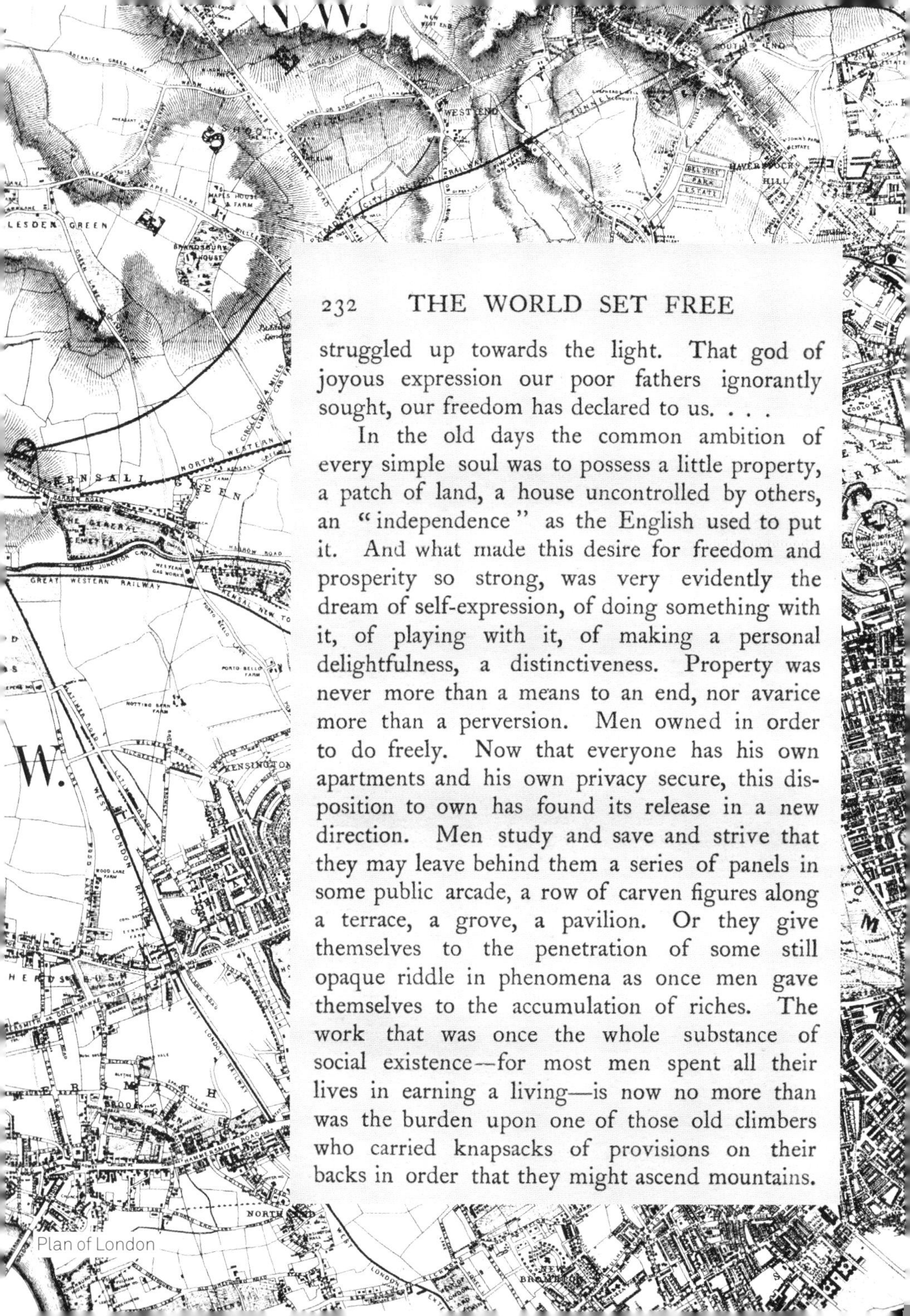

Plan of London

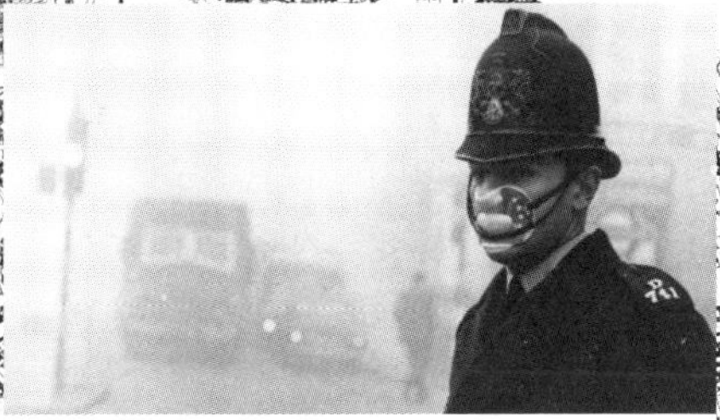

Air of the modern city

It matters little to the easy charities of our emancipated time that most people who have made their labour contribution produce neither new beauty nor new wisdom, but are simply busy about those pleasant activities and enjoyments that reassure them that they are alive. They help, it may be, by reception and reverberation, and they hinder nothing. . . .

§ 11

Now all this phase of gigantic change in the contours and appearances of human life which is going on about us, a change as rapid and as wonderful as the swift ripening of adolescence to manhood after the barbaric boyish years, is correlated with moral and mental changes at least as unprecedented. It is not as if old things were going out of life and new things coming in, it is rather that the altered circumstances of men are making an appeal to elements in his nature that have hitherto been suppressed, and checking tendencies that have hitherto been over-stimulated and over-developed. He has not so much grown and altered his essential being as turned new aspects to the light. Such turnings round into a new attitude the world has seen on a less extensive scale before. The Highlanders of the seventeenth century, for example, were cruel and bloodthirsty robbers, in the nineteenth their descendants were

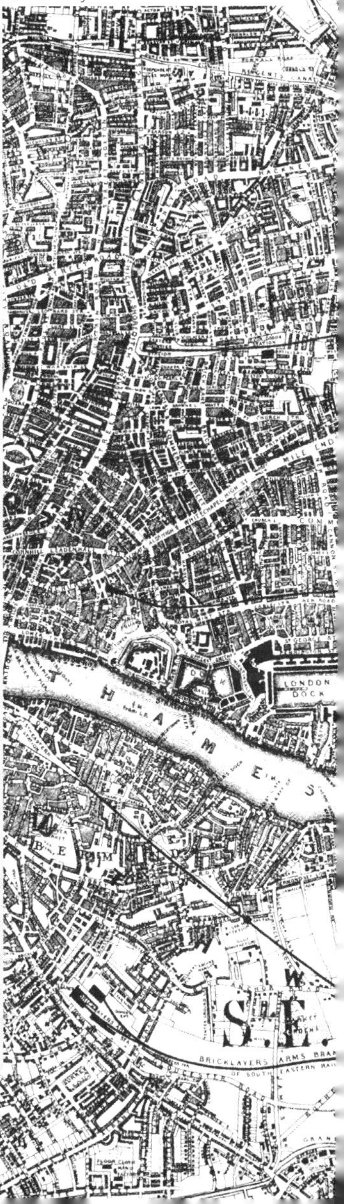

conspicuously trusty and honourable men. There was not a people in Western Europe in the early twentieth century that seemed capable of hideous massacres, and none that had not been guilty of them within the previous two centuries. The free frank kindly gentle life of the prosperous classes in any European country before the years of the last wars was in a different world of thought and feeling from that of the dingy, suspicious, secretive and uncharitable existence of the respectable poor, or the constant personal violence, the squalor and naïve passions of the lowest stratum. Yet there were no real differences of blood and inherent quality between these worlds; their differences were all in circumstances, suggestion, and habits of mind. And turning to more individual instances the constantly observed difference between one portion of a life and another consequent upon a religious conversion were a standing example of the versatile possibilities of human nature.

The catastrophe of the atomic bombs which shook men out of cities and businesses and economic relations shook them also out of their old established habits of thought, and out of the lightly held beliefs and prejudices that came down to them from the past. To borrow a word from the old-fashioned chemists, men were made nascent; they were released from old ties; for good or evil they were ready for new associations.

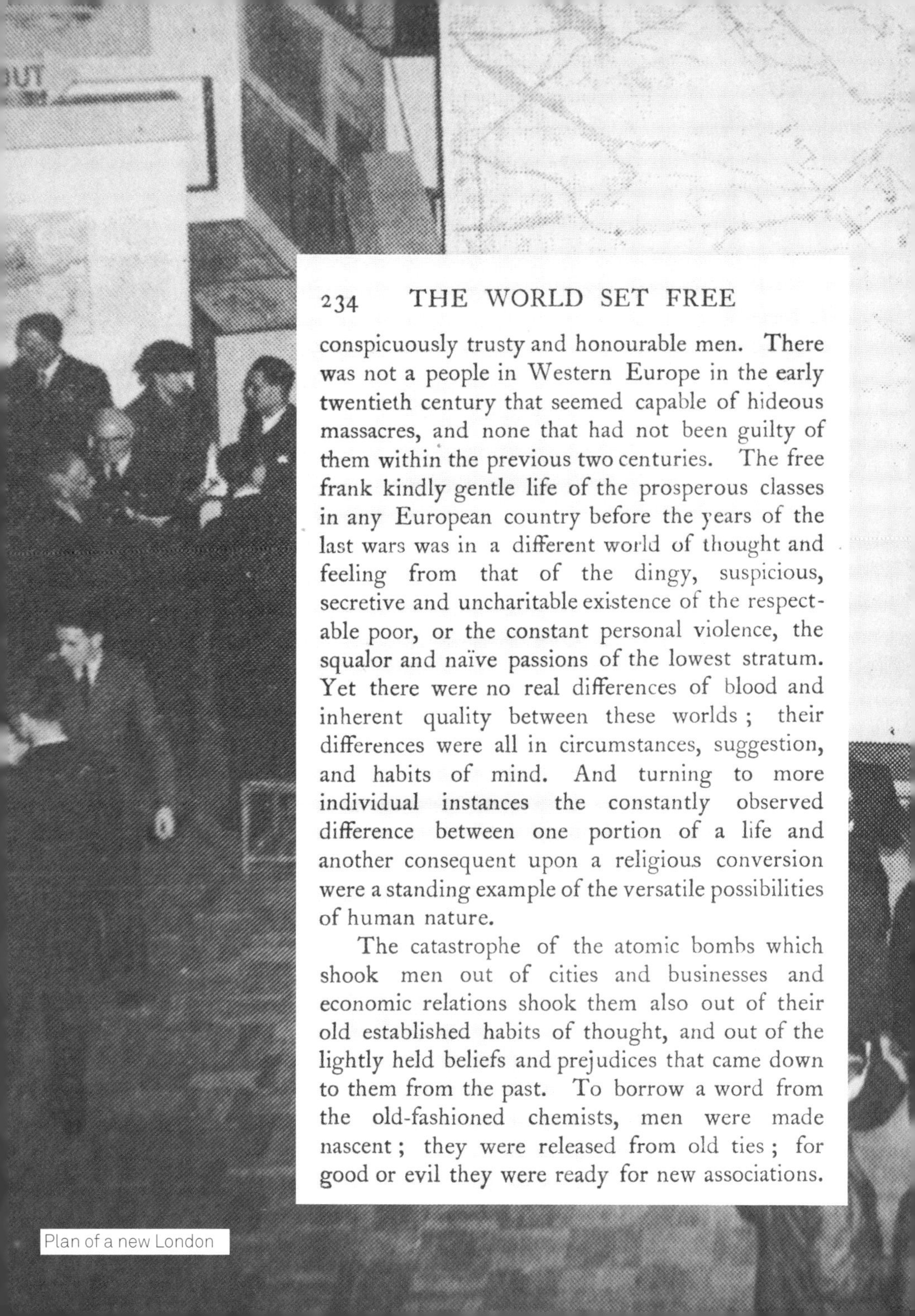

Plan of a new London

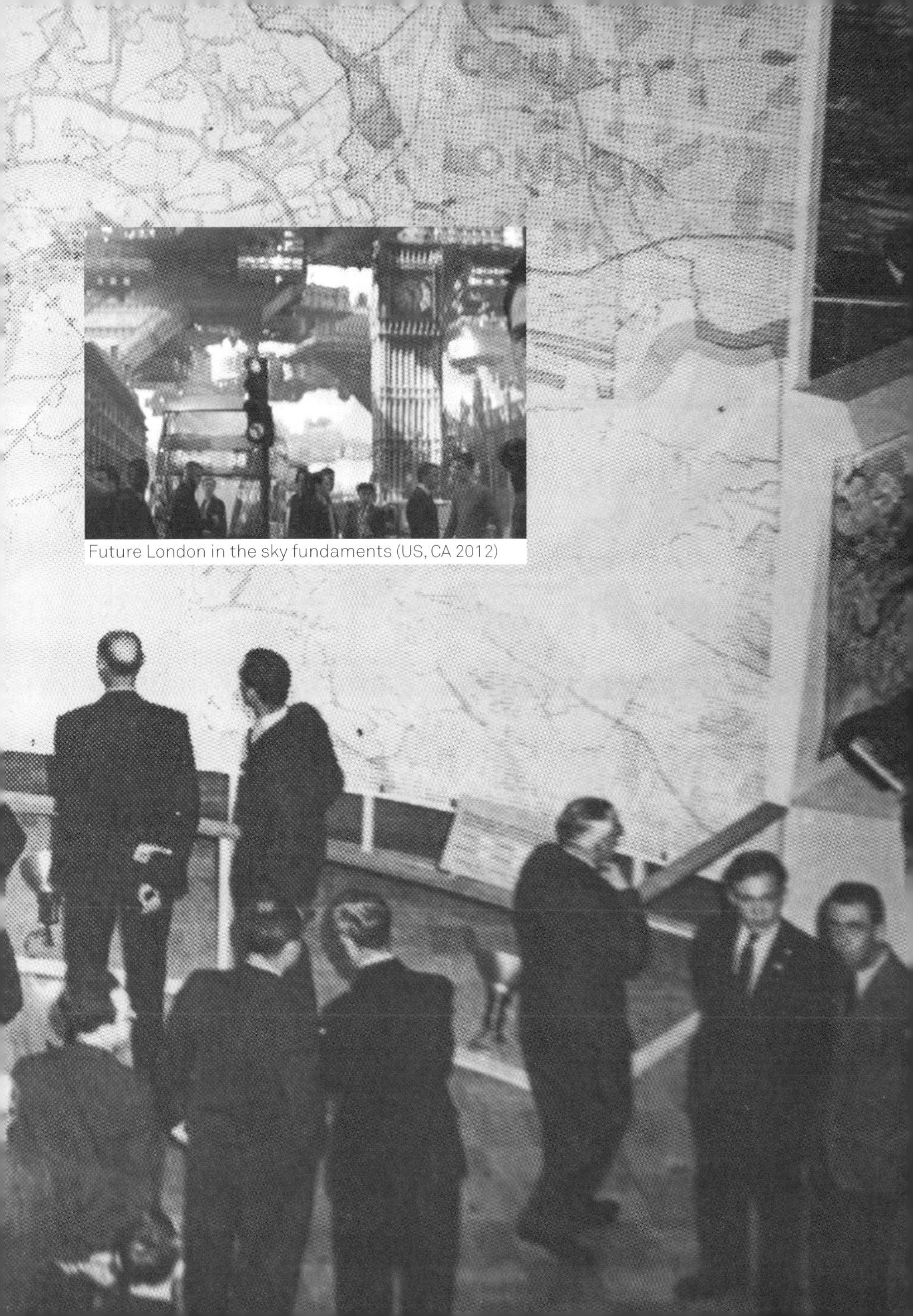

Future London in the sky fundaments (US, CA 2012)

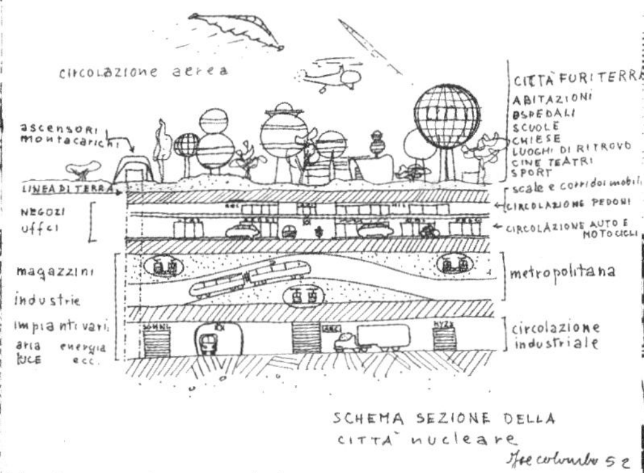

Nuclear underground city, 1952

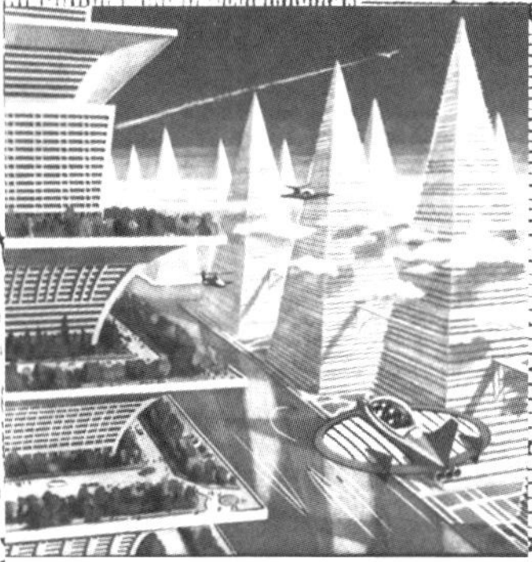

City in the clouds

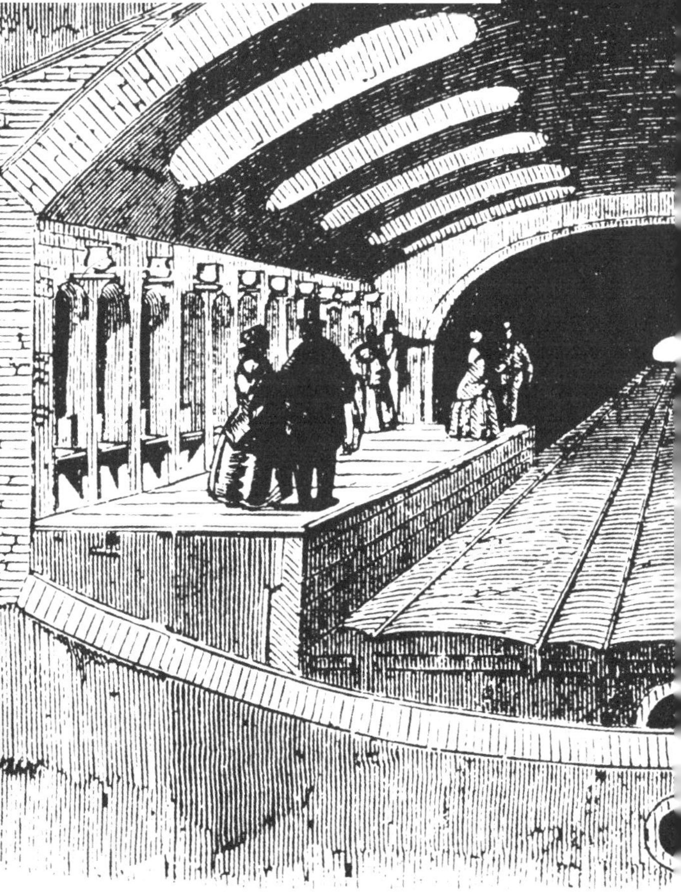

Underground, 1867

The council carried them forward for good; perhaps if his bombs had reached their destination King Ferdinand Charles might have carried them back to an endless chain of evils. But his task would have been a harder one than the council's. The moral shock of the atomic bombs had been a profound one, and for a while the cunning side of the human animal was overpowered by its sincere realization of the vital necessity for reconstruction. The litigious and trading spirits cowered together, scared at their own consequences; men thought twice before they sought mean advantages in the face of the unusual eagerness to realize new aspirations, and when at last the weeds revived again and "claims" began to sprout, they sprouted upon the stony soil of law-courts reformed, of laws that pointed to the future instead of the past, and under the blazing sunshine of a transforming world. A new literature, a new interpretation of history were springing into existence, a new teaching was already in the schools, a new faith in the young. The worthy man who forestalled the building of a research city for the English upon the Sussex downs by buying up a series of estates, was dispossessed and laughed out of court when he made his demand for some preposterous compensation; the owner of the discredited Dass patents makes his last appearance upon the scroll of history as the insolvent proprietor of a paper called *The Cry for Justice*, in which he duns the world for a

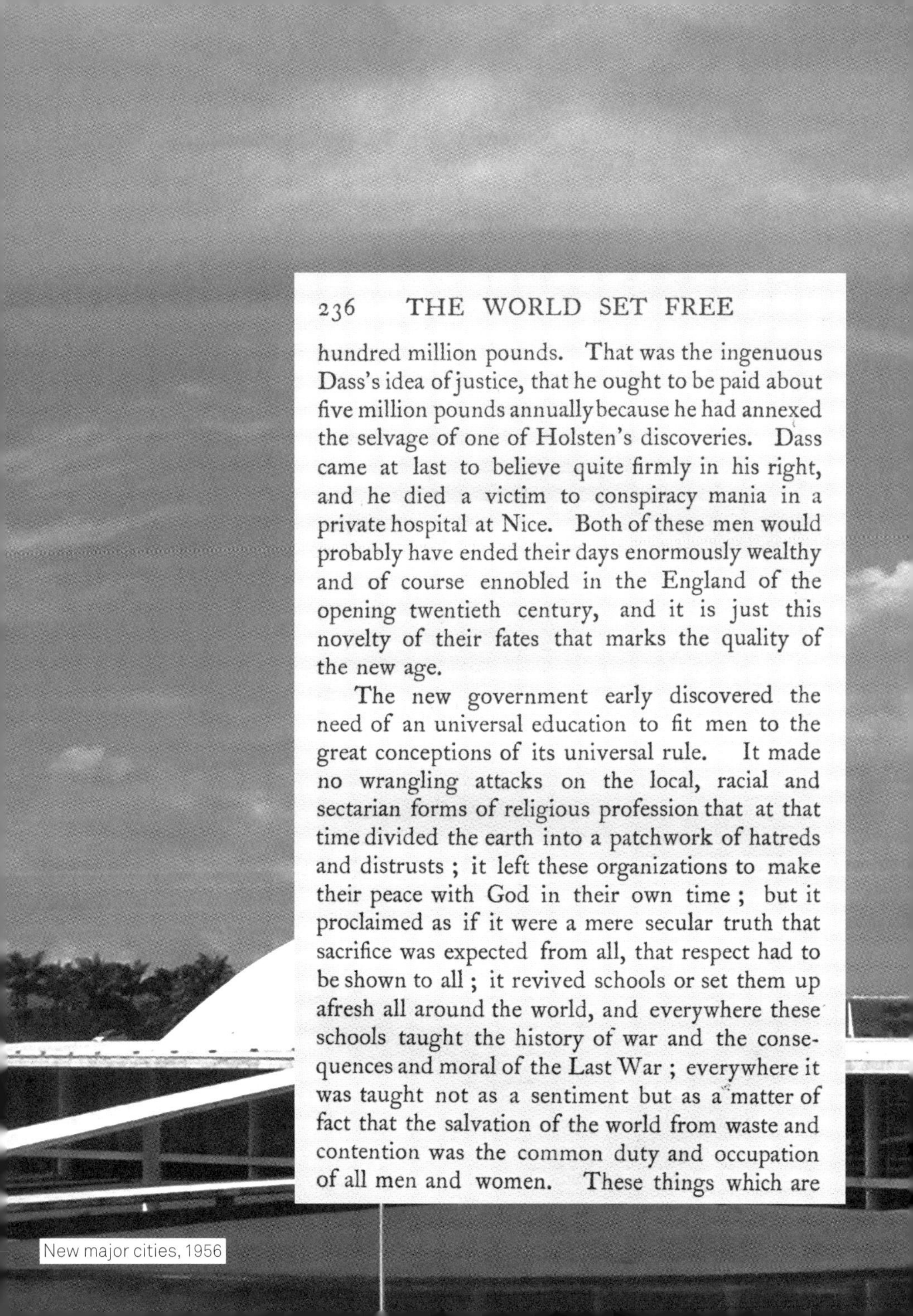

New major cities, 1956

hundred million pounds. That was the ingenuous Dass's idea of justice, that he ought to be paid about five million pounds annually because he had annexed the selvage of one of Holsten's discoveries. Dass came at last to believe quite firmly in his right, and he died a victim to conspiracy mania in a private hospital at Nice. Both of these men would probably have ended their days enormously wealthy and of course ennobled in the England of the opening twentieth century, and it is just this novelty of their fates that marks the quality of the new age.

The new government early discovered the need of an universal education to fit men to the great conceptions of its universal rule. It made no wrangling attacks on the local, racial and sectarian forms of religious profession that at that time divided the earth into a patchwork of hatreds and distrusts ; it left these organizations to make their peace with God in their own time ; but it proclaimed as if it were a mere secular truth that sacrifice was expected from all, that respect had to be shown to all ; it revived schools or set them up afresh all around the world, and everywhere these schools taught the history of war and the consequences and moral of the Last War ; everywhere it was taught not as a sentiment but as a matter of fact that the salvation of the world from waste and contention was the common duty and occupation of all men and women. These things which are

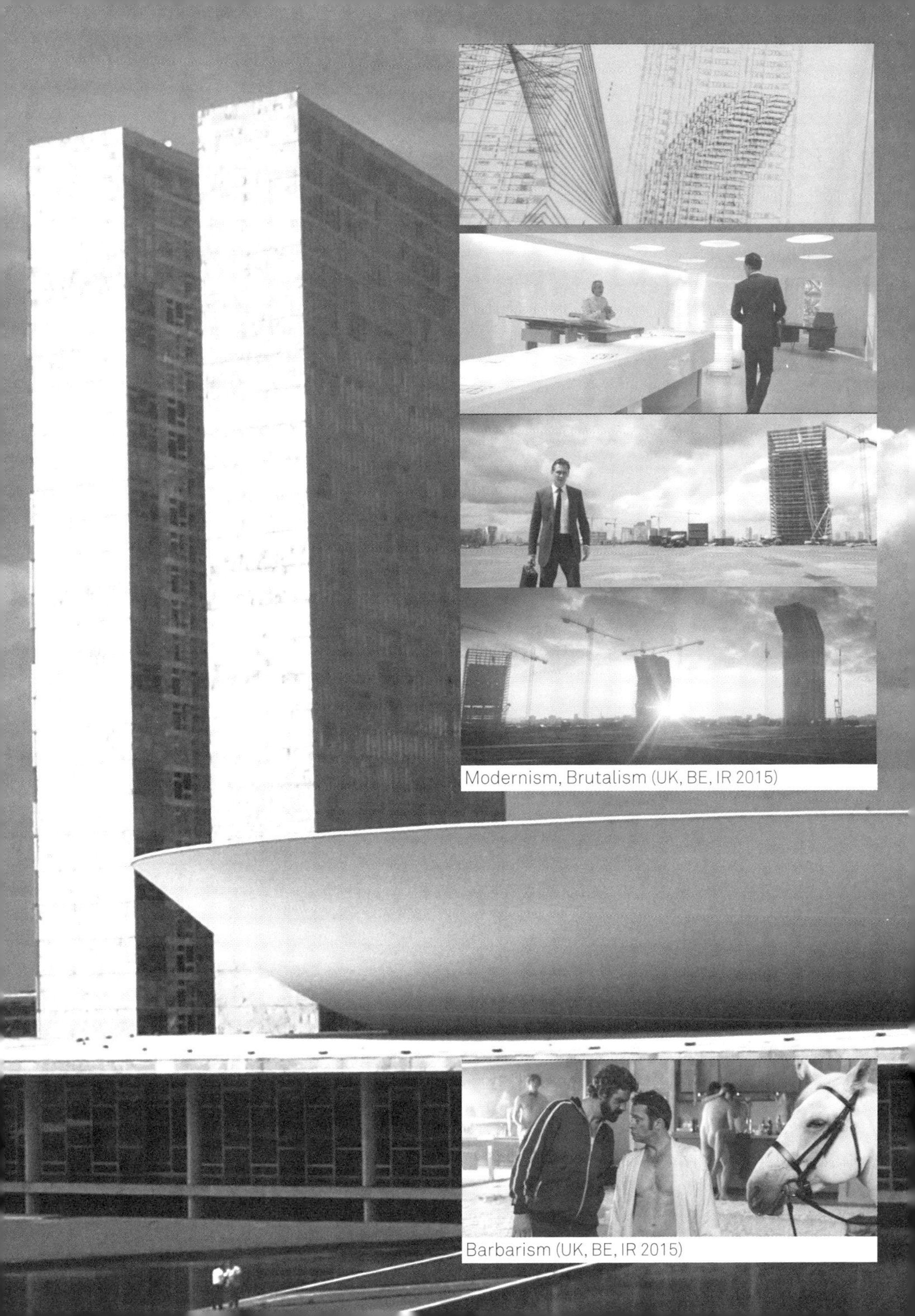

Modernism, Brutalism (UK, BE, IR 2015)

Barbarism (UK, BE, IR 2015)

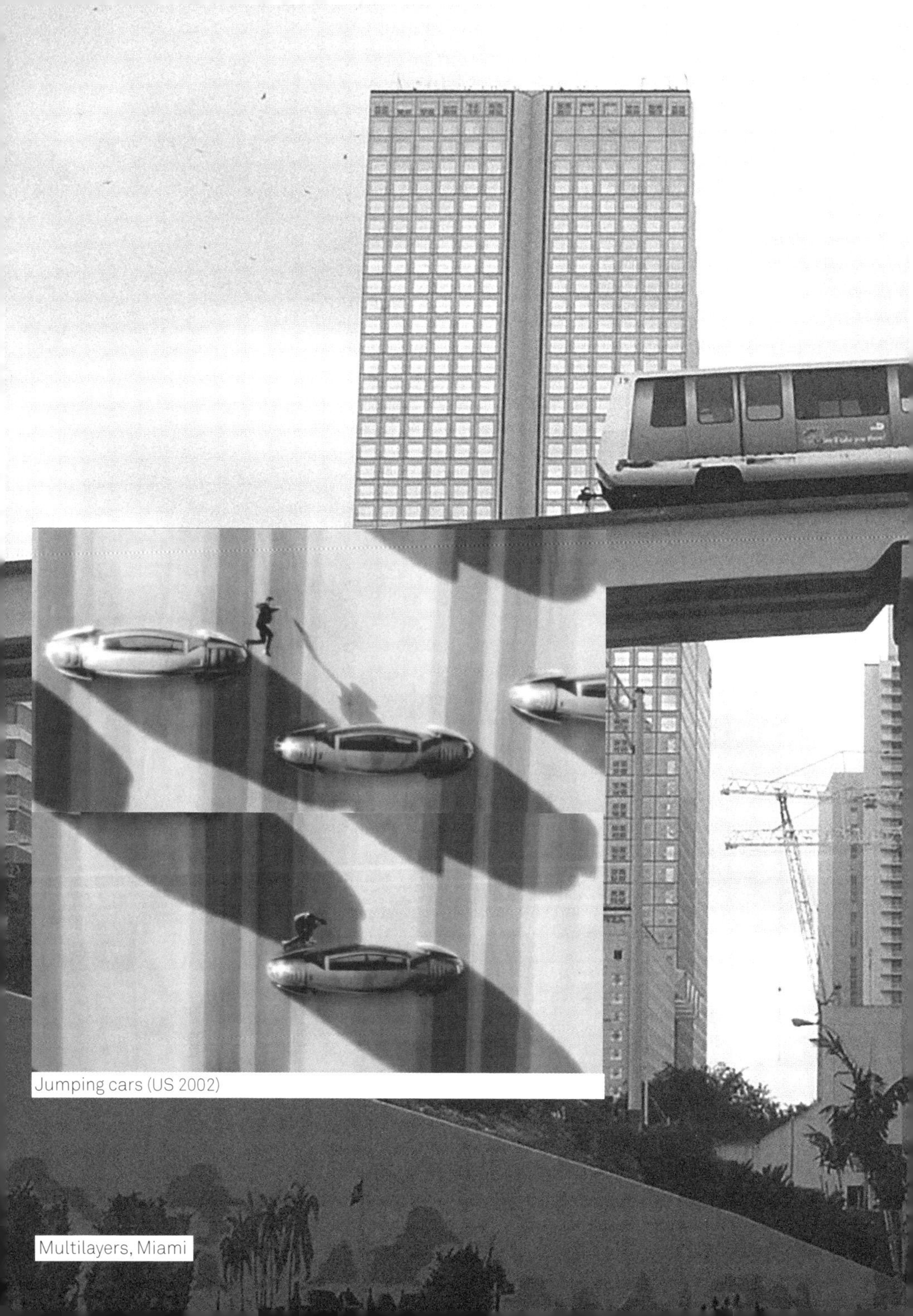

Jumping cars (US 2002)

Multilayers, Miami

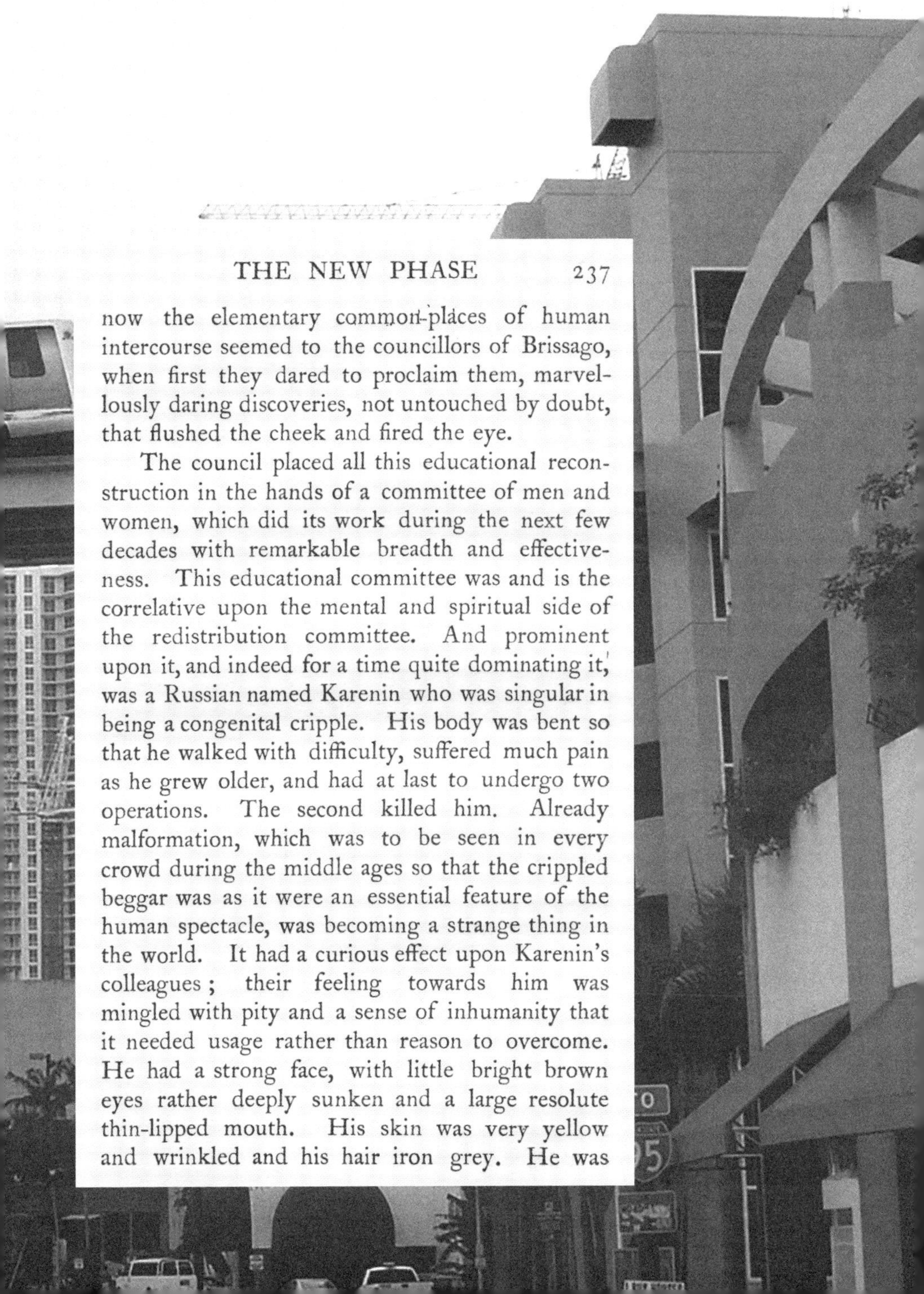

now the elementary common-places of human intercourse seemed to the councillors of Brissago, when first they dared to proclaim them, marvellously daring discoveries, not untouched by doubt, that flushed the cheek and fired the eye.

The council placed all this educational reconstruction in the hands of a committee of men and women, which did its work during the next few decades with remarkable breadth and effectiveness. This educational committee was and is the correlative upon the mental and spiritual side of the redistribution committee. And prominent upon it, and indeed for a time quite dominating it, was a Russian named Karenin who was singular in being a congenital cripple. His body was bent so that he walked with difficulty, suffered much pain as he grew older, and had at last to undergo two operations. The second killed him. Already malformation, which was to be seen in every crowd during the middle ages so that the crippled beggar was as it were an essential feature of the human spectacle, was becoming a strange thing in the world. It had a curious effect upon Karenin's colleagues; their feeling towards him was mingled with pity and a sense of inhumanity that it needed usage rather than reason to overcome. He had a strong face, with little bright brown eyes rather deeply sunken and a large resolute thin-lipped mouth. His skin was very yellow and wrinkled and his hair iron grey. He was at all times an impatient and sometimes an angry man, but this was forgiven him because of the hot wire of suffering that was manifestly thrust through his being. At the end of his life his personal prestige was very great. To him far more than to any contemporary is it due that self-abnegation, self-identification with the world spirit, was made the basis of universal education. That general memorandum to the teachers which is the key-note of the modern educational system was probably entirely his work.

"Whosoever would save his soul shall lose it," he wrote. "That is the device upon the seal of this document and the starting point of all we have to do. It is a mistake to regard it as anything but a plain statement of fact. It is the basis for your work. You have to teach self-forgetfulness, and everything else that you have to teach is contributory and subordinate to that end. Education is the release of man from self. You have to widen the horizons of your children, encourage and intensify their curiosity and their creative impulses, and cultivate and enlarge their sympathies. That is what you are for. Under your guidance and the suggestions you will bring to bear on them, they have to shed the old Adam of instinctive suspicions, hostilities and passions, and to find themselves again in the great being of the universe. The little circles of their egotisms have to be opened out until they become arcs in

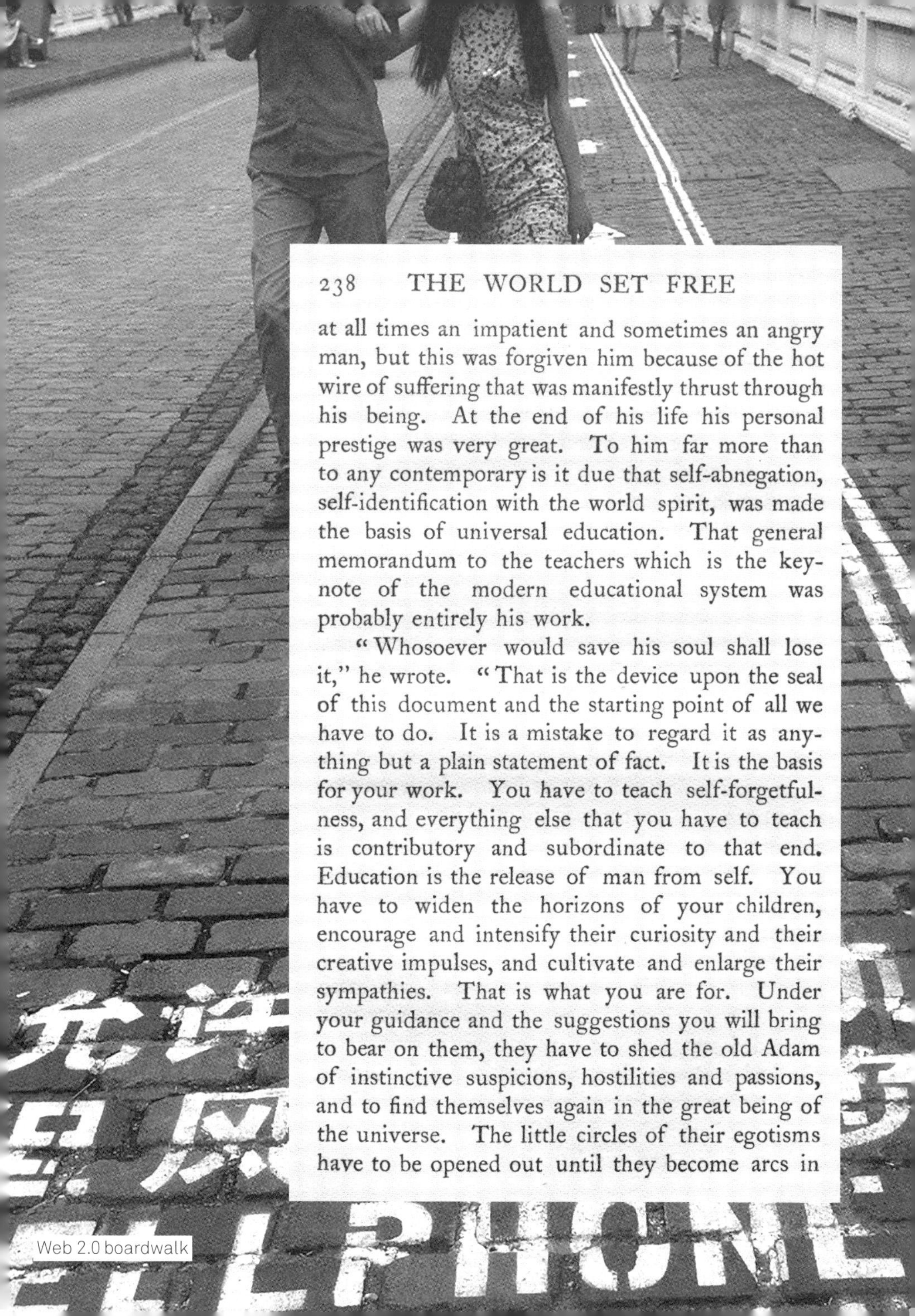

Web 2.0 boardwalk

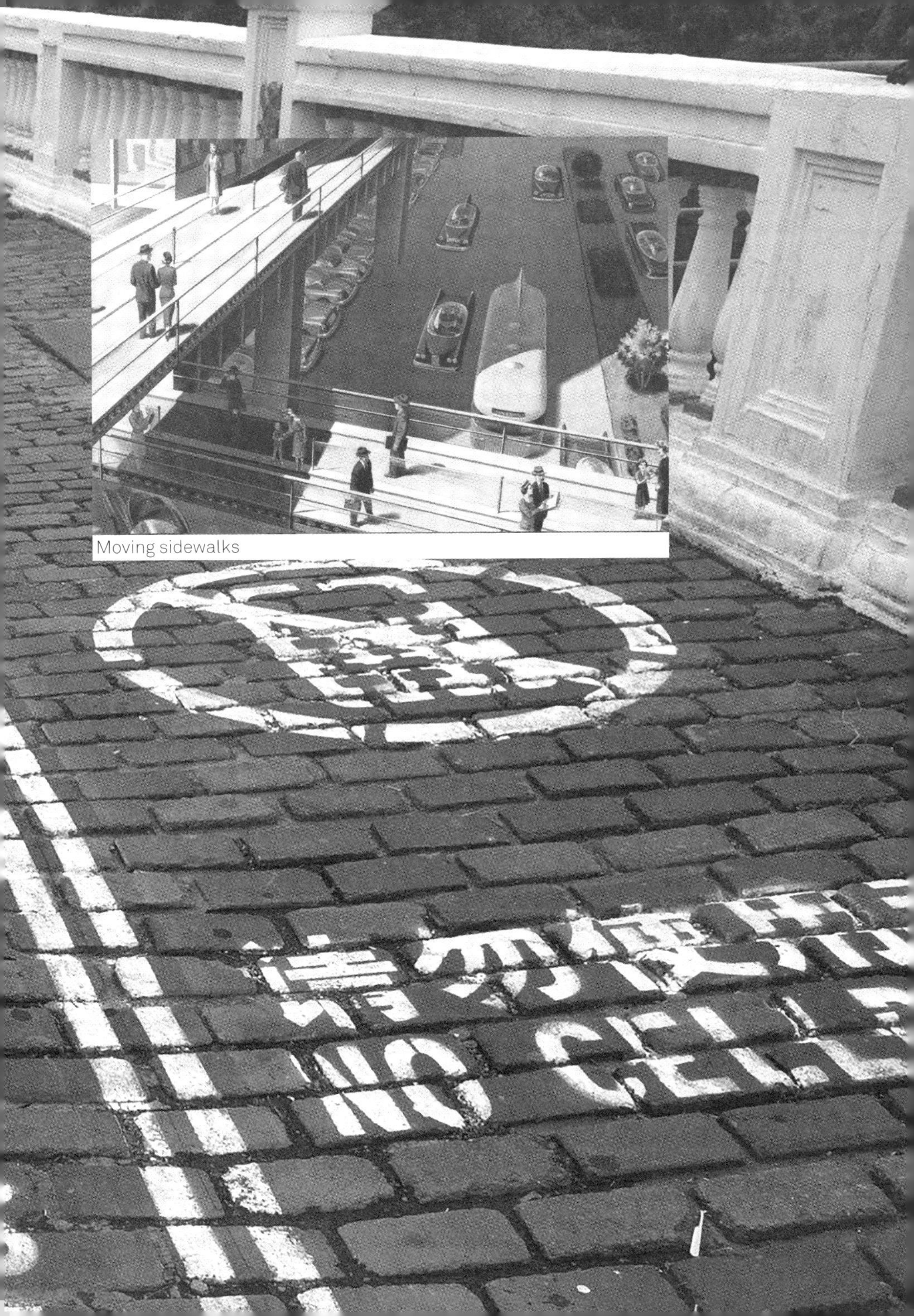

Moving sidewalks

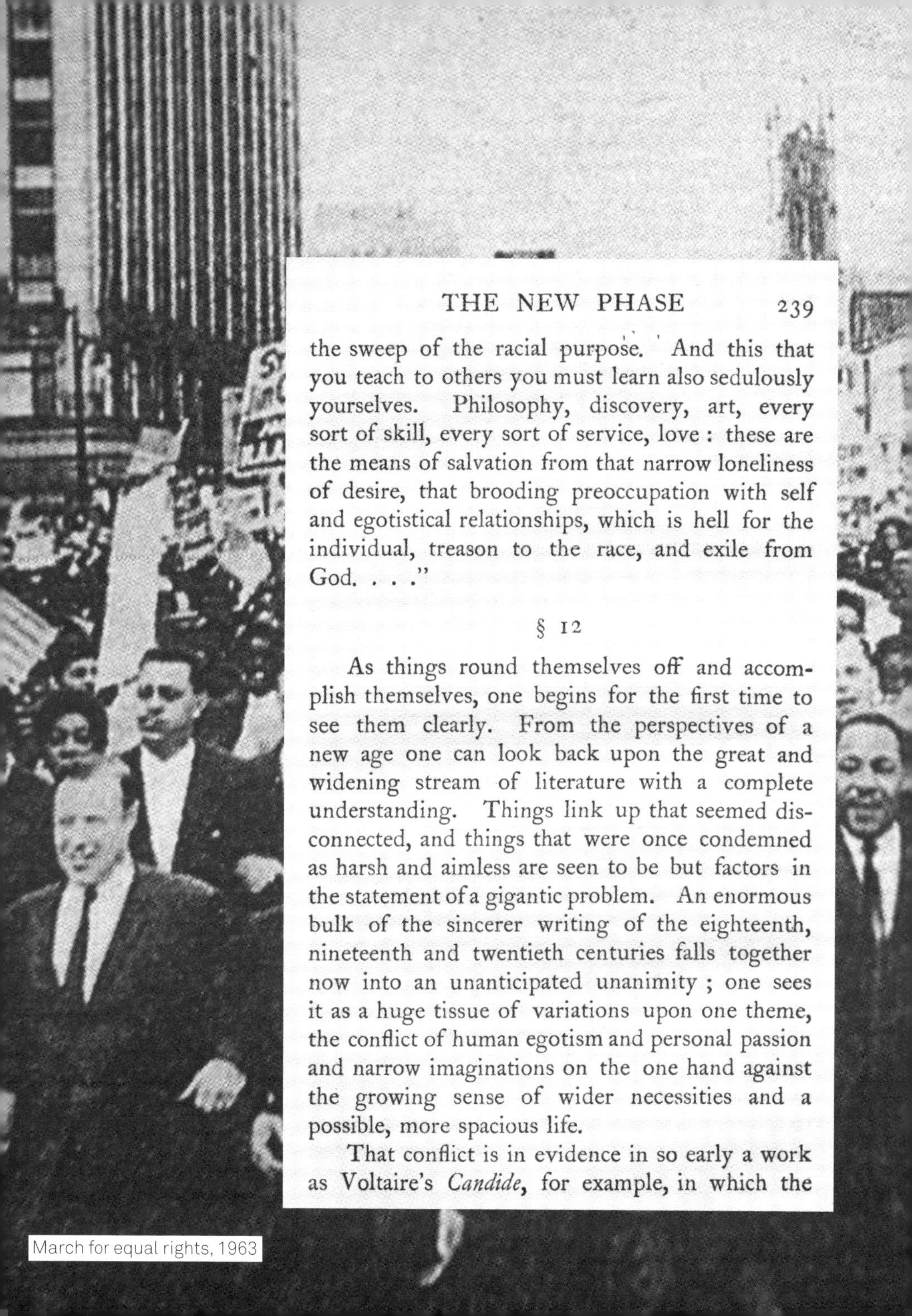

March for equal rights, 1963

the sweep of the racial purpose. And this that you teach to others you must learn also sedulously yourselves. Philosophy, discovery, art, every sort of skill, every sort of service, love : these are the means of salvation from that narrow loneliness of desire, that brooding preoccupation with self and egotistical relationships, which is hell for the individual, treason to the race, and exile from God. . . ."

§ 12

As things round themselves off and accomplish themselves, one begins for the first time to see them clearly. From the perspectives of a new age one can look back upon the great and widening stream of literature with a complete understanding. Things link up that seemed disconnected, and things that were once condemned as harsh and aimless are seen to be but factors in the statement of a gigantic problem. An enormous bulk of the sincerer writing of the eighteenth, nineteenth and twentieth centuries falls together now into an unanticipated unanimity ; one sees it as a huge tissue of variations upon one theme, the conflict of human egotism and personal passion and narrow imaginations on the one hand against the growing sense of wider necessities and a possible, more spacious life.

That conflict is in evidence in so early a work as Voltaire's *Candide*, for example, in which the

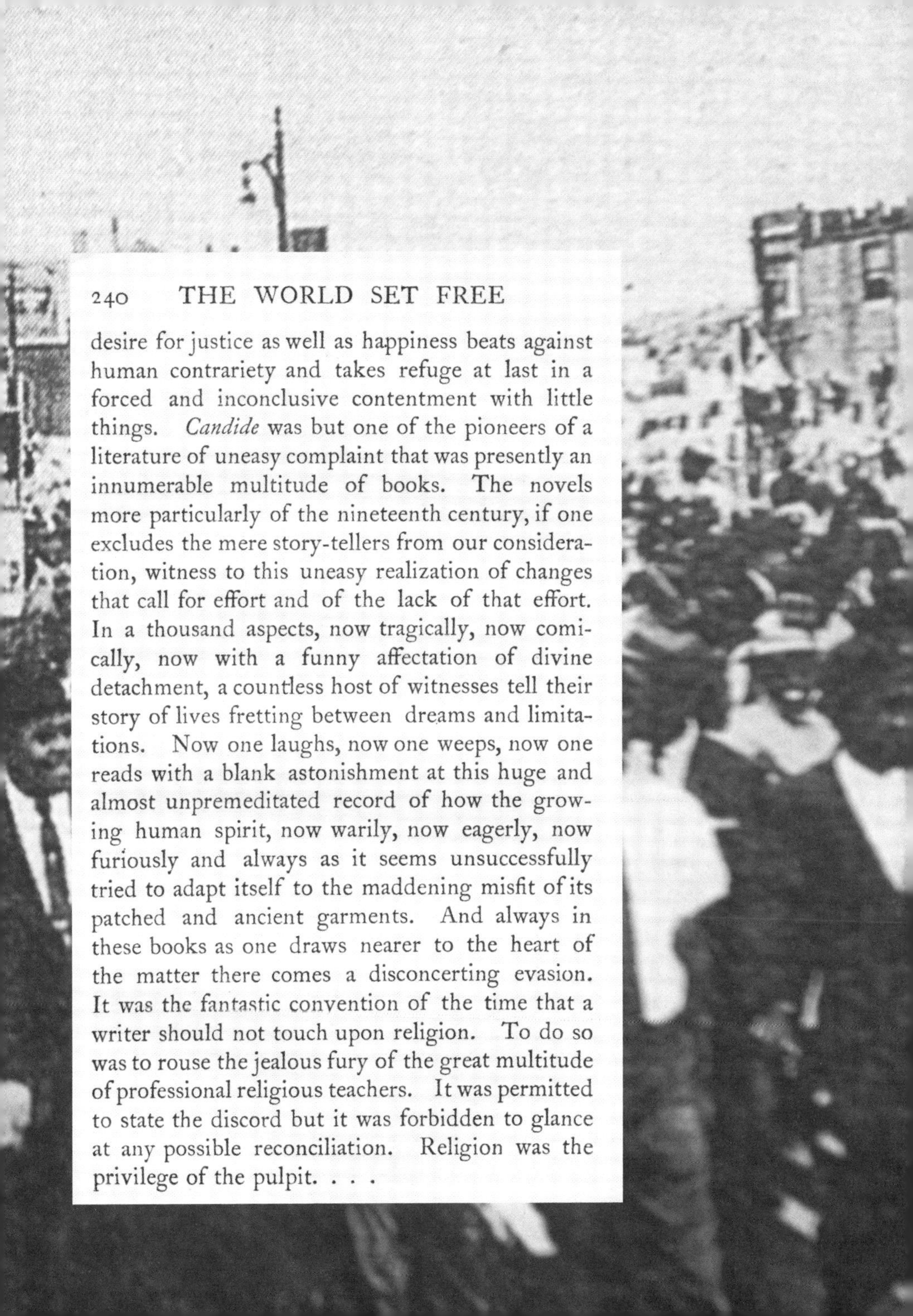

desire for justice as well as happiness beats against human contrariety and takes refuge at last in a forced and inconclusive contentment with little things. *Candide* was but one of the pioneers of a literature of uneasy complaint that was presently an innumerable multitude of books. The novels more particularly of the nineteenth century, if one excludes the mere story-tellers from our consideration, witness to this uneasy realization of changes that call for effort and of the lack of that effort. In a thousand aspects, now tragically, now comically, now with a funny affectation of divine detachment, a countless host of witnesses tell their story of lives fretting between dreams and limitations. Now one laughs, now one weeps, now one reads with a blank astonishment at this huge and almost unpremeditated record of how the growing human spirit, now warily, now eagerly, now furiously and always as it seems unsuccessfully tried to adapt itself to the maddening misfit of its patched and ancient garments. And always in these books as one draws nearer to the heart of the matter there comes a disconcerting evasion. It was the fantastic convention of the time that a writer should not touch upon religion. To do so was to rouse the jealous fury of the great multitude of professional religious teachers. It was permitted to state the discord but it was forbidden to glance at any possible reconciliation. Religion was the privilege of the pulpit. . . .

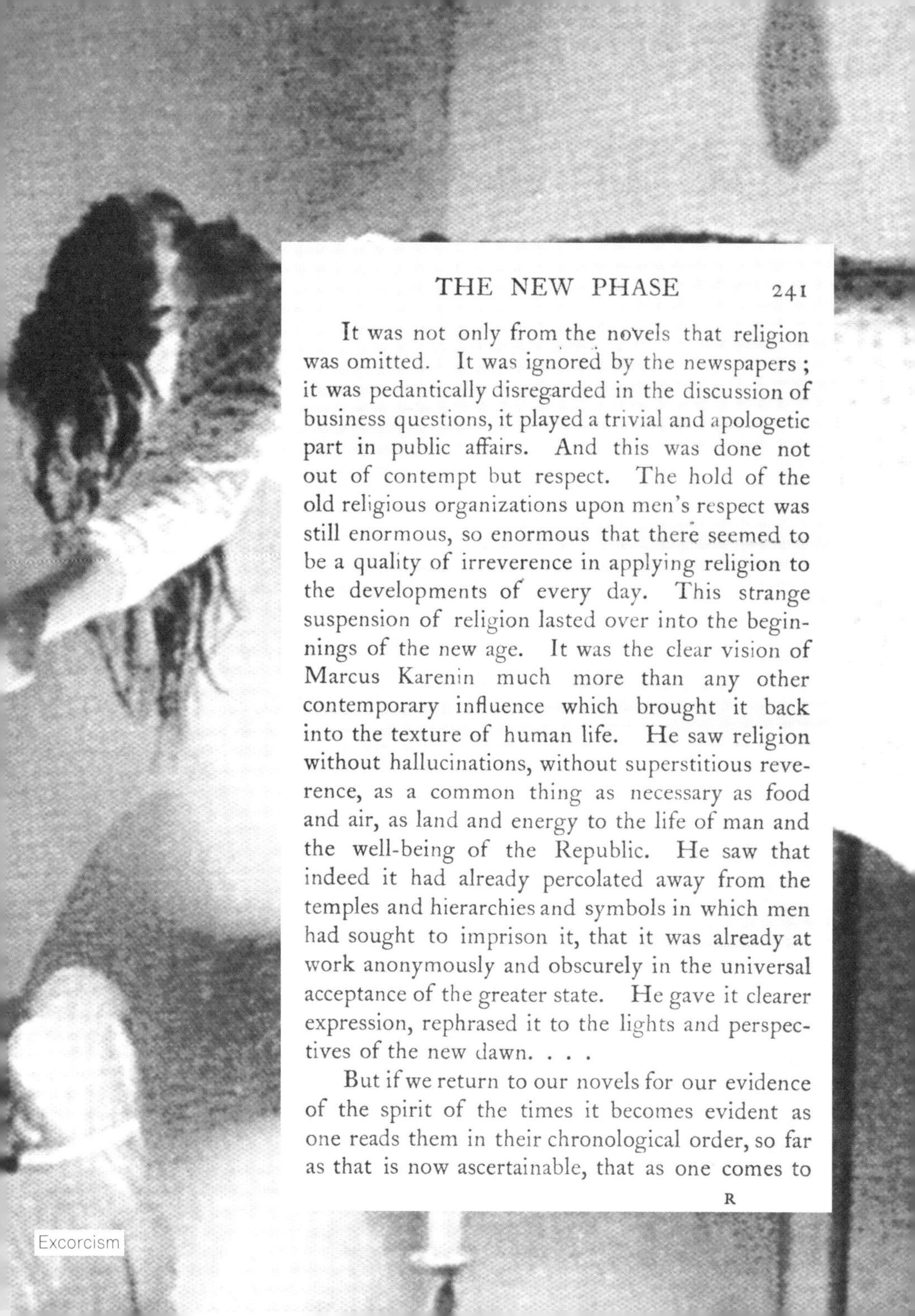

It was not only from the novels that religion was omitted. It was ignored by the newspapers; it was pedantically disregarded in the discussion of business questions, it played a trivial and apologetic part in public affairs. And this was done not out of contempt but respect. The hold of the old religious organizations upon men's respect was still enormous, so enormous that there seemed to be a quality of irreverence in applying religion to the developments of every day. This strange suspension of religion lasted over into the beginnings of the new age. It was the clear vision of Marcus Karenin much more than any other contemporary influence which brought it back into the texture of human life. He saw religion without hallucinations, without superstitious reverence, as a common thing as necessary as food and air, as land and energy to the life of man and the well-being of the Republic. He saw that indeed it had already percolated away from the temples and hierarchies and symbols in which men had sought to imprison it, that it was already at work anonymously and obscurely in the universal acceptance of the greater state. He gave it clearer expression, rephrased it to the lights and perspectives of the new dawn. . . .

But if we return to our novels for our evidence of the spirit of the times it becomes evident as one reads them in their chronological order, so far as that is now ascertainable, that as one comes to

Excorcism

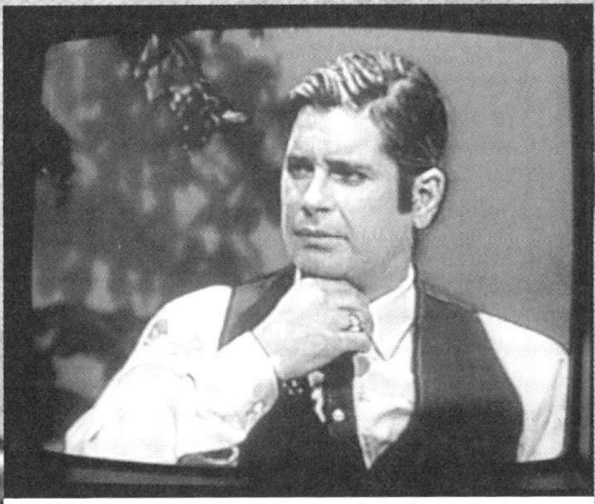

Ozzy Osbourne TV-priest (US 1986)

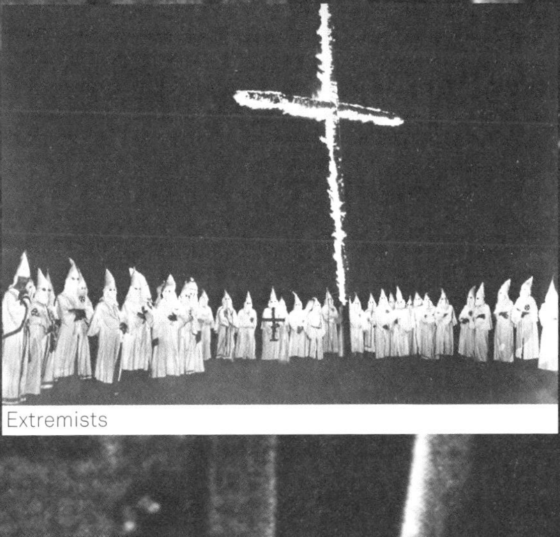

Extremists

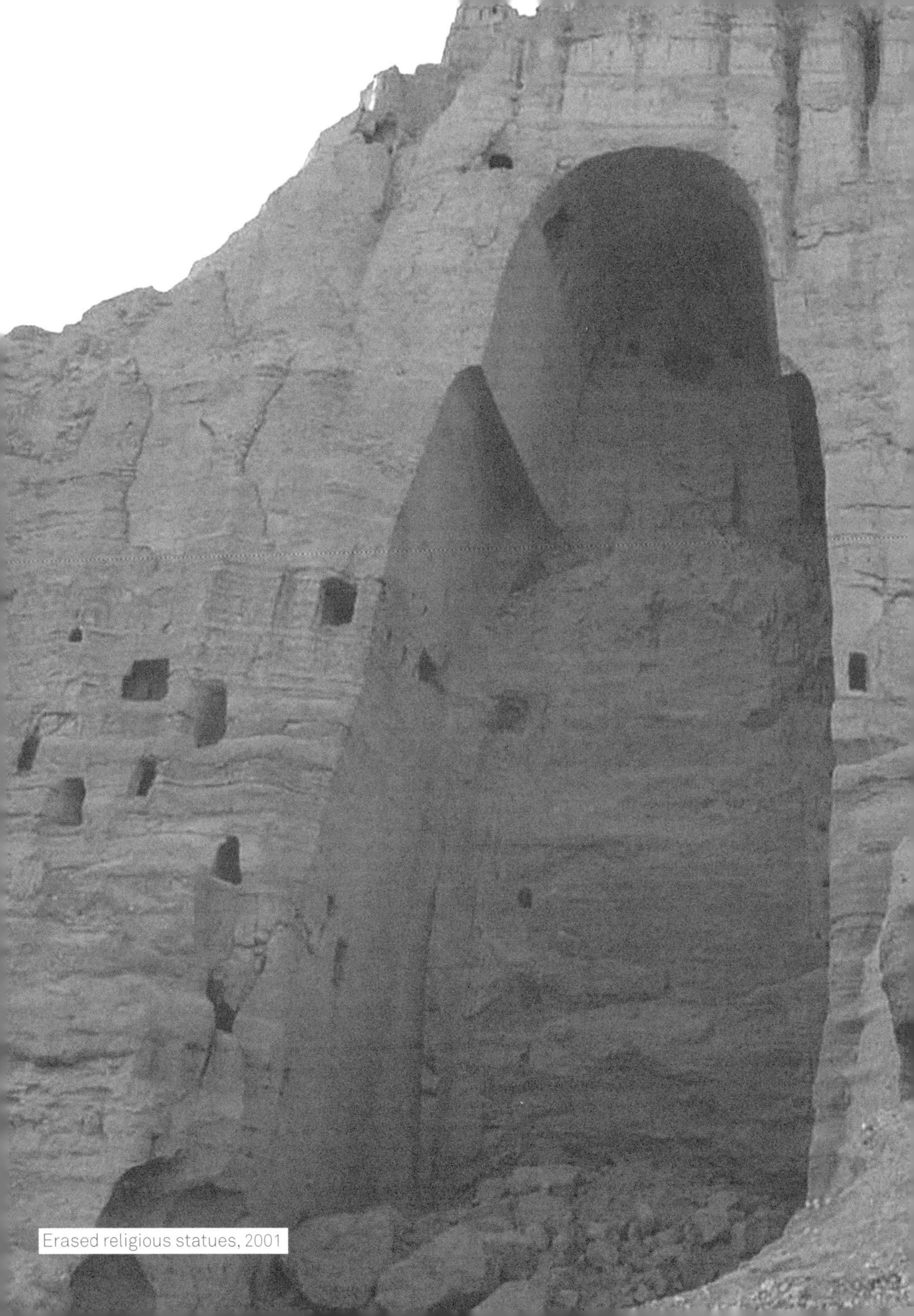
Erased religious statues, 2001

the latter nineteenth and the earlier twentieth century the writers are much more acutely aware of secular change than their predecessors were. The earlier novelists tried to show "life as it is," the latter showed life as it changes. More and more of their characters are engaged in adaptation to change or suffering from the effects of world changes. And as we come up to the time of the Last Wars, this newer conception of the everyday life as a reaction to an accelerated development is continually more manifest. Barnet's book, which has served us so well, is frankly a picture of the world coming about like a ship that sails into the wind. Our later novelists give a vast gallery of individual conflicts in which old habits and customs, limited ideas, ungenerous temperaments and innate obsessions are pitted against this great opening out of life that has happened to us. They tell us of the feelings of old people who have been wrenched away from familiar surroundings, and how they have had to make peace with uncomfortable comforts and conveniences that are still strange to them. They give us the discord between the opening egotisms of youths and the ill-defined limitations of a changing social life. They tell of the universal struggle of jealousy to capture and cripple our souls, of romantic failures and tragical misconceptions of the trend of the world, of the spirit of adventure and the urgency of curiosity and how these serve the universal

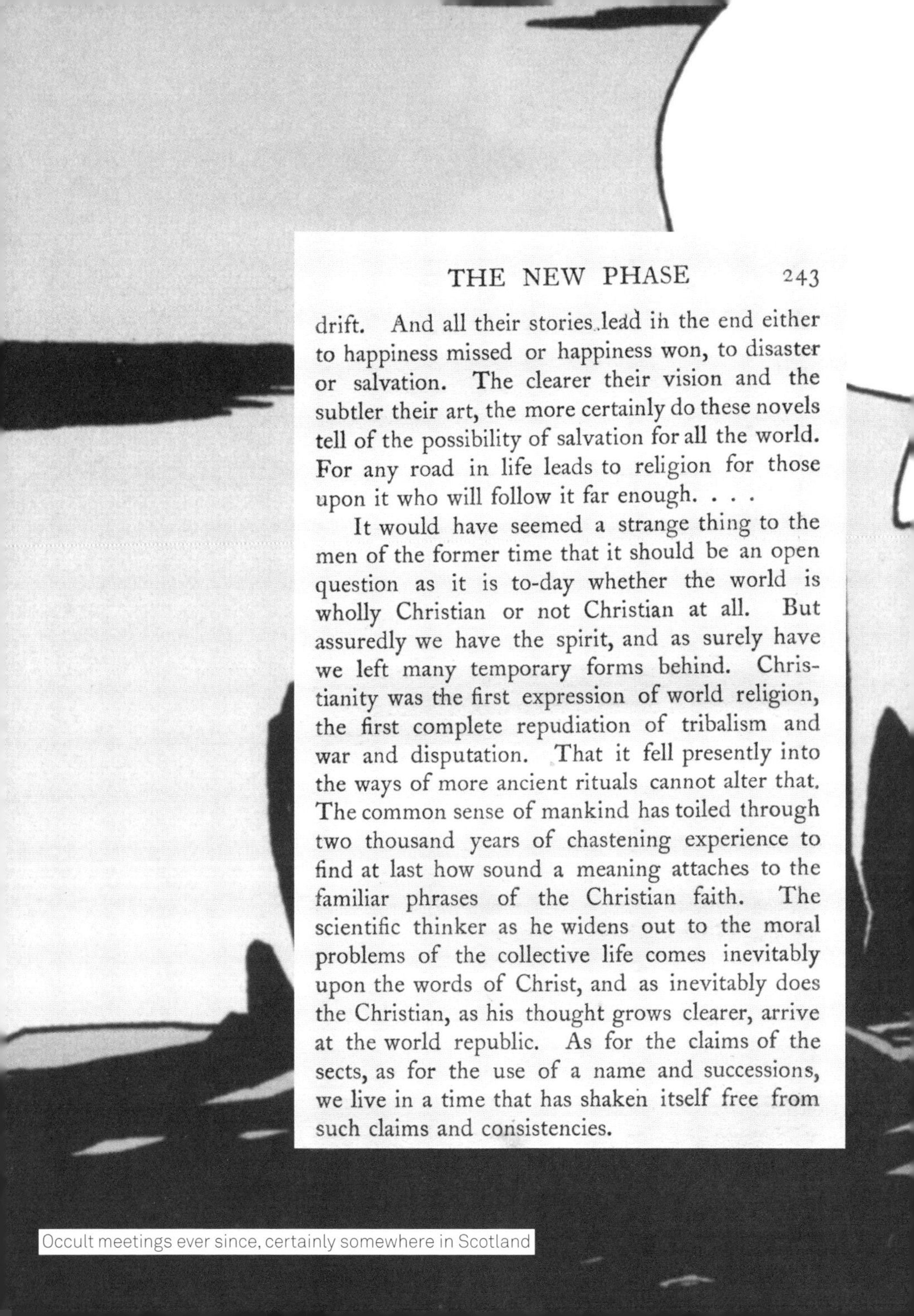

drift. And all their stories lead in the end either to happiness missed or happiness won, to disaster or salvation. The clearer their vision and the subtler their art, the more certainly do these novels tell of the possibility of salvation for all the world. For any road in life leads to religion for those upon it who will follow it far enough. . . .

It would have seemed a strange thing to the men of the former time that it should be an open question as it is to-day whether the world is wholly Christian or not Christian at all. But assuredly we have the spirit, and as surely have we left many temporary forms behind. Christianity was the first expression of world religion, the first complete repudiation of tribalism and war and disputation. That it fell presently into the ways of more ancient rituals cannot alter that. The common sense of mankind has toiled through two thousand years of chastening experience to find at last how sound a meaning attaches to the familiar phrases of the Christian faith. The scientific thinker as he widens out to the moral problems of the collective life comes inevitably upon the words of Christ, and as inevitably does the Christian, as his thought grows clearer, arrive at the world republic. As for the claims of the sects, as for the use of a name and successions, we live in a time that has shaken itself free from such claims and consistencies.

Occult meetings ever since, certainly somewhere in Scotland

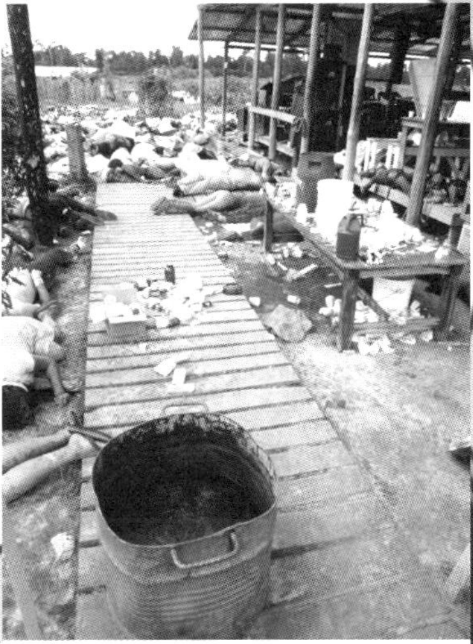

Cult of Death, 1978

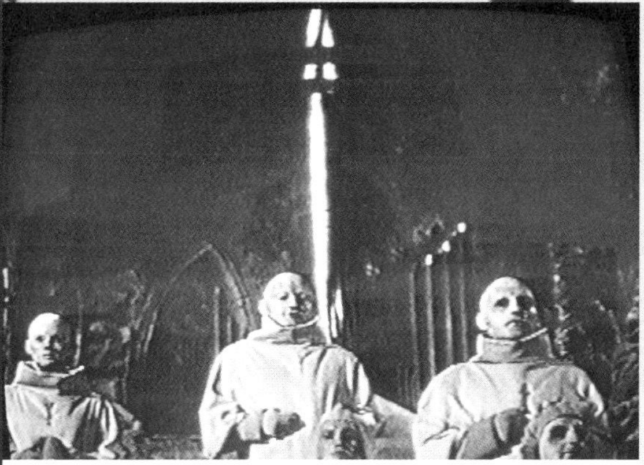

Mutant cult of the divine bomb (US 1970)

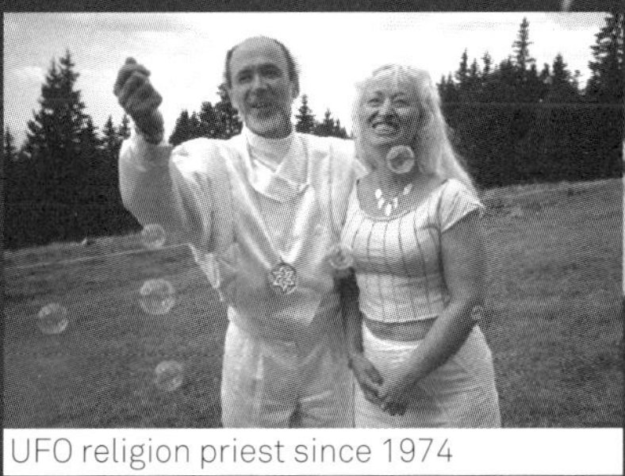

UFO religion priest since 1974

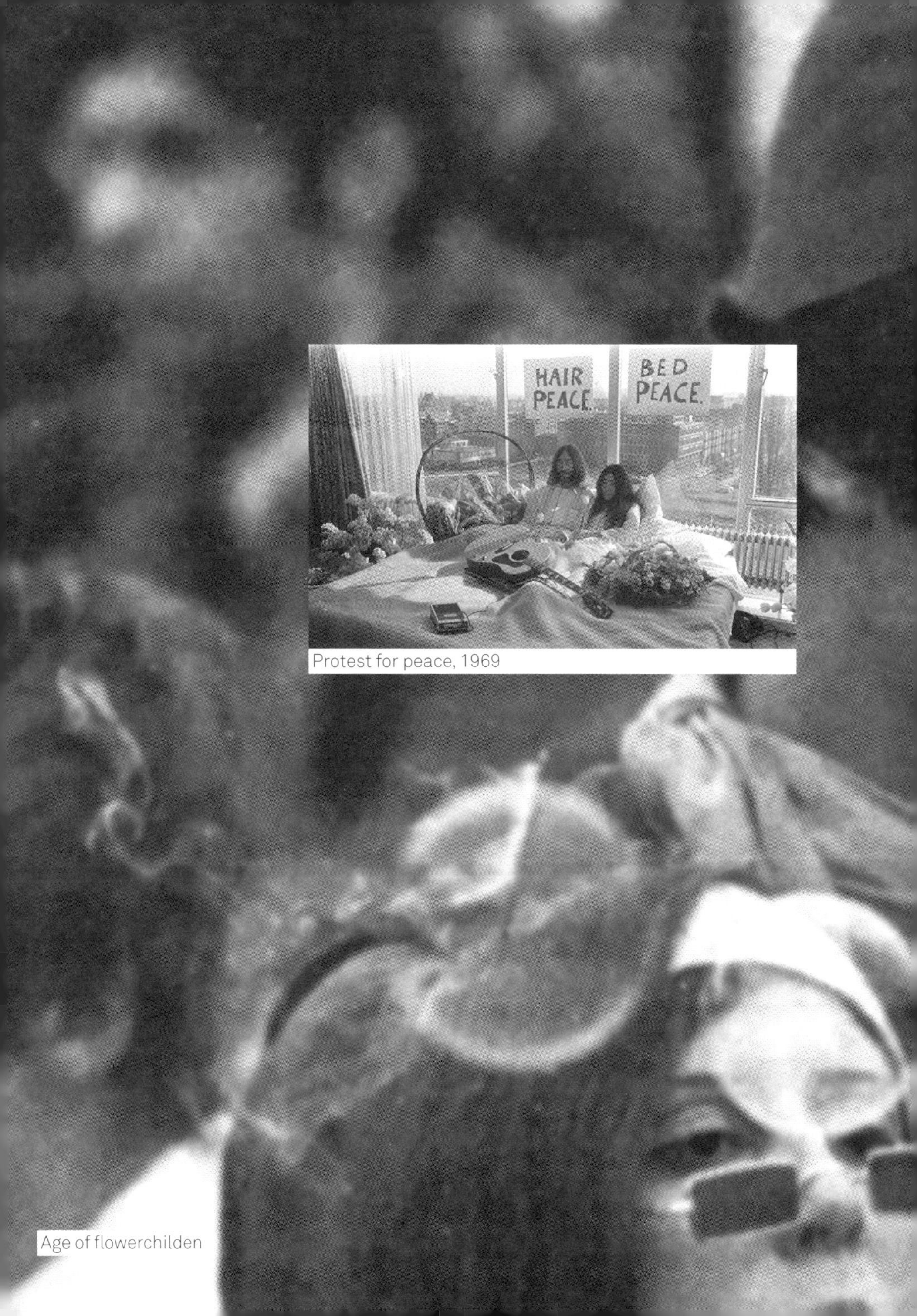

Protest for peace, 1969

Age of flowerchilden

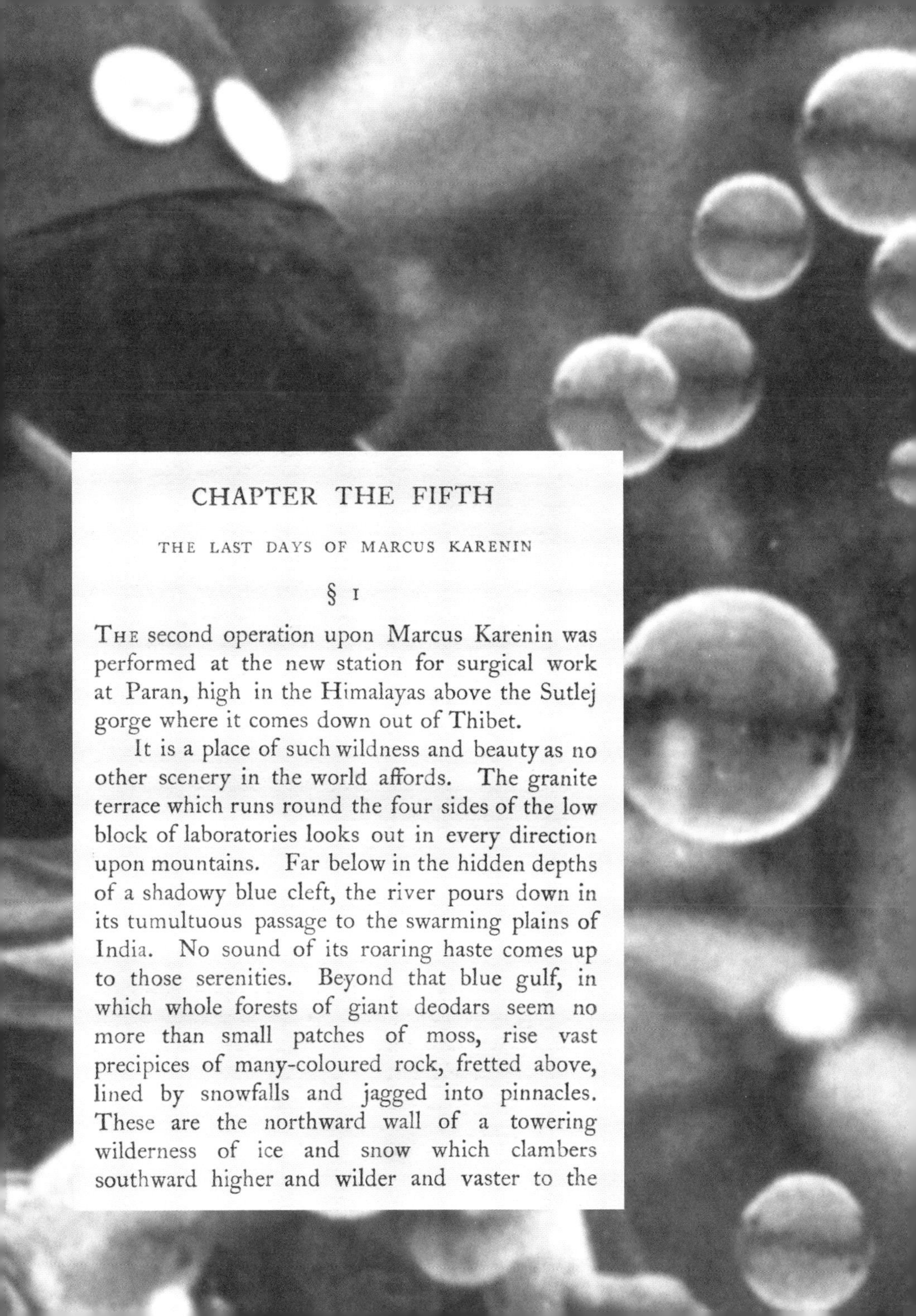

CHAPTER THE FIFTH

THE LAST DAYS OF MARCUS KARENIN

§ 1

THE second operation upon Marcus Karenin was performed at the new station for surgical work at Paran, high in the Himalayas above the Sutlej gorge where it comes down out of Thibet.

It is a place of such wildness and beauty as no other scenery in the world affords. The granite terrace which runs round the four sides of the low block of laboratories looks out in every direction upon mountains. Far below in the hidden depths of a shadowy blue cleft, the river pours down in its tumultuous passage to the swarming plains of India. No sound of its roaring haste comes up to those serenities. Beyond that blue gulf, in which whole forests of giant deodars seem no more than small patches of moss, rise vast precipices of many-coloured rock, fretted above, lined by snowfalls and jagged into pinnacles. These are the northward wall of a towering wilderness of ice and snow which clambers southward higher and wilder and vaster to the culminating summits of our globe, to Dhaulagiri and Everest. Here are cliffs of which no other land can show the like and deep chasms in which Mt. Blanc might be plunged and hidden. Here are icefields as big as inland seas on which the tumbled boulders lie so thickly that strange little flowers can bloom among them under the untempered sunshine. To the northward, and blocking out any vision of the uplands of Thibet, rises that citadel of porcelain, that gothic pile, the Lio Porgyul, walls, towers and peaks, a clear twelve thousand feet of veined and splintered rock above the river. And beyond it and eastward and westward rise peaks behind peaks, against the dark blue Himalayan sky. Far away below to the south the clouds of the Indian rains pile up abruptly and are stayed by an invisible hand.

Hither it was that with a dreamlike swiftness Karenin flew high over the irrigations of Rajputana and the towers and cupolas of the ultimate Delhi ; and the little group of buildings, albeit the southward wall dropped nearly five hundred feet, seemed to him as he soared down to it like a toy lost among these mountain wildernesses. No road came up to this place ; it was reached only by flight.

His pilot descended to the great courtyard, and Karenin assisted by his secretary clambered down through the wing fabric and made his

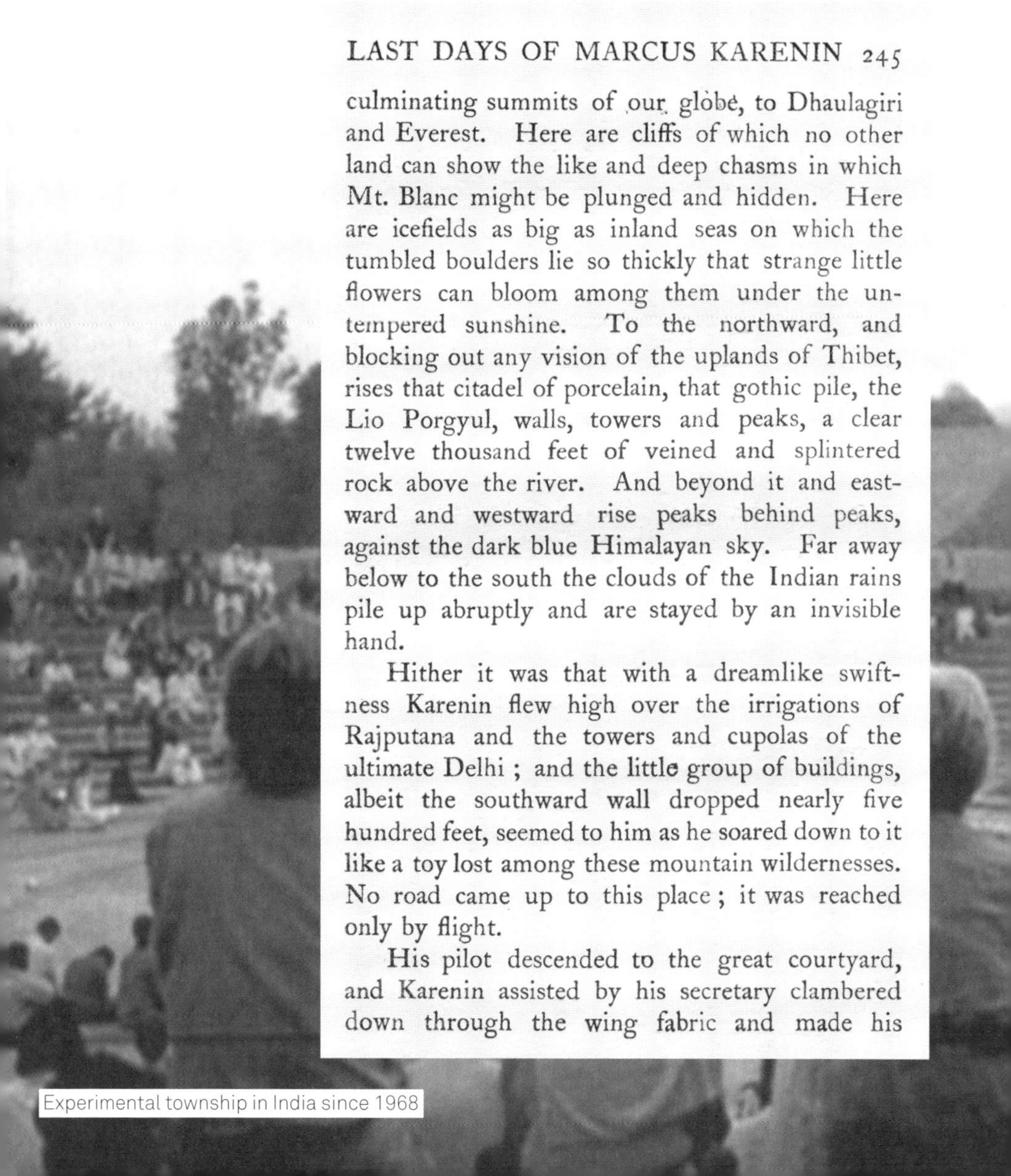

Experimental township in India since 1968

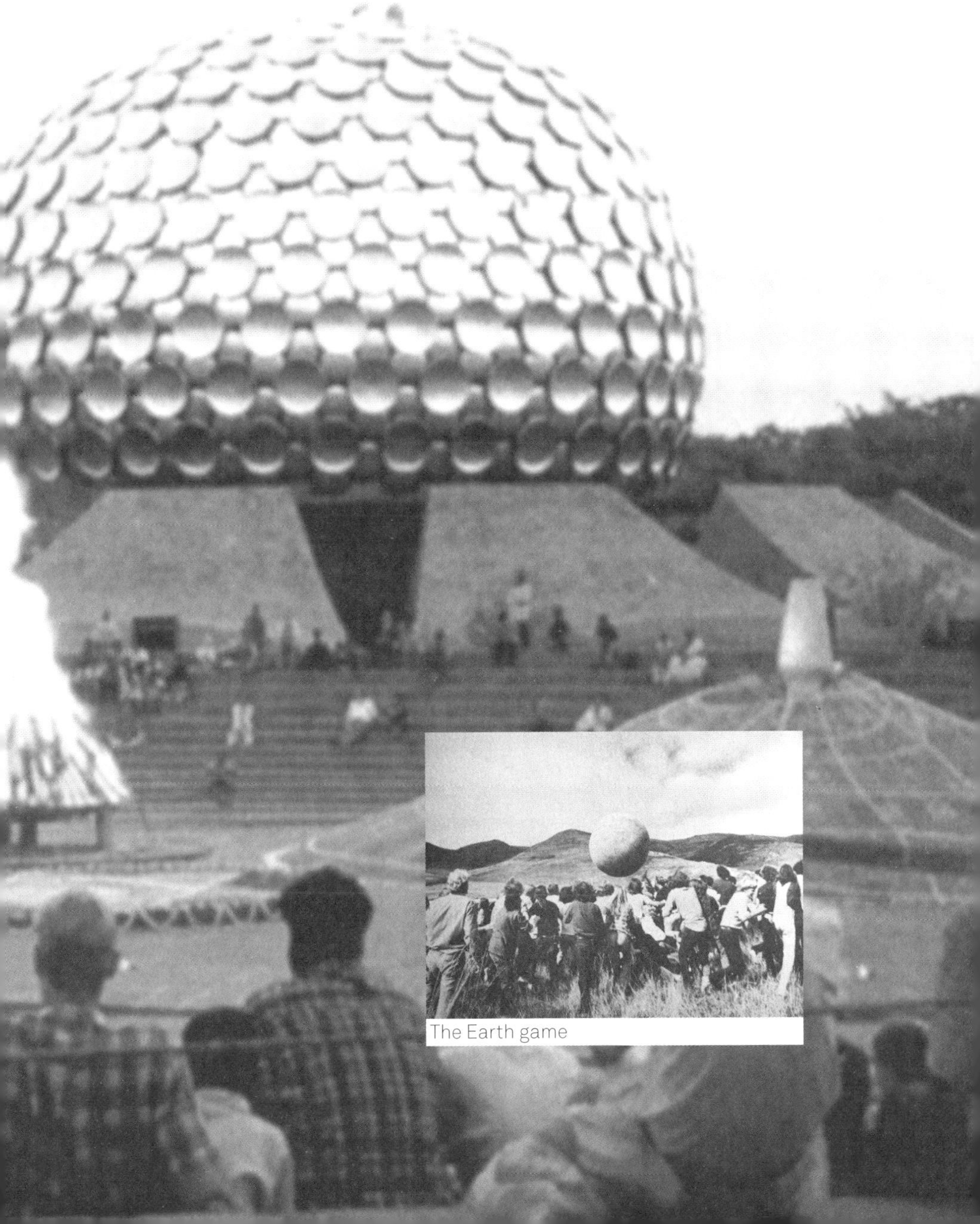

The Earth game

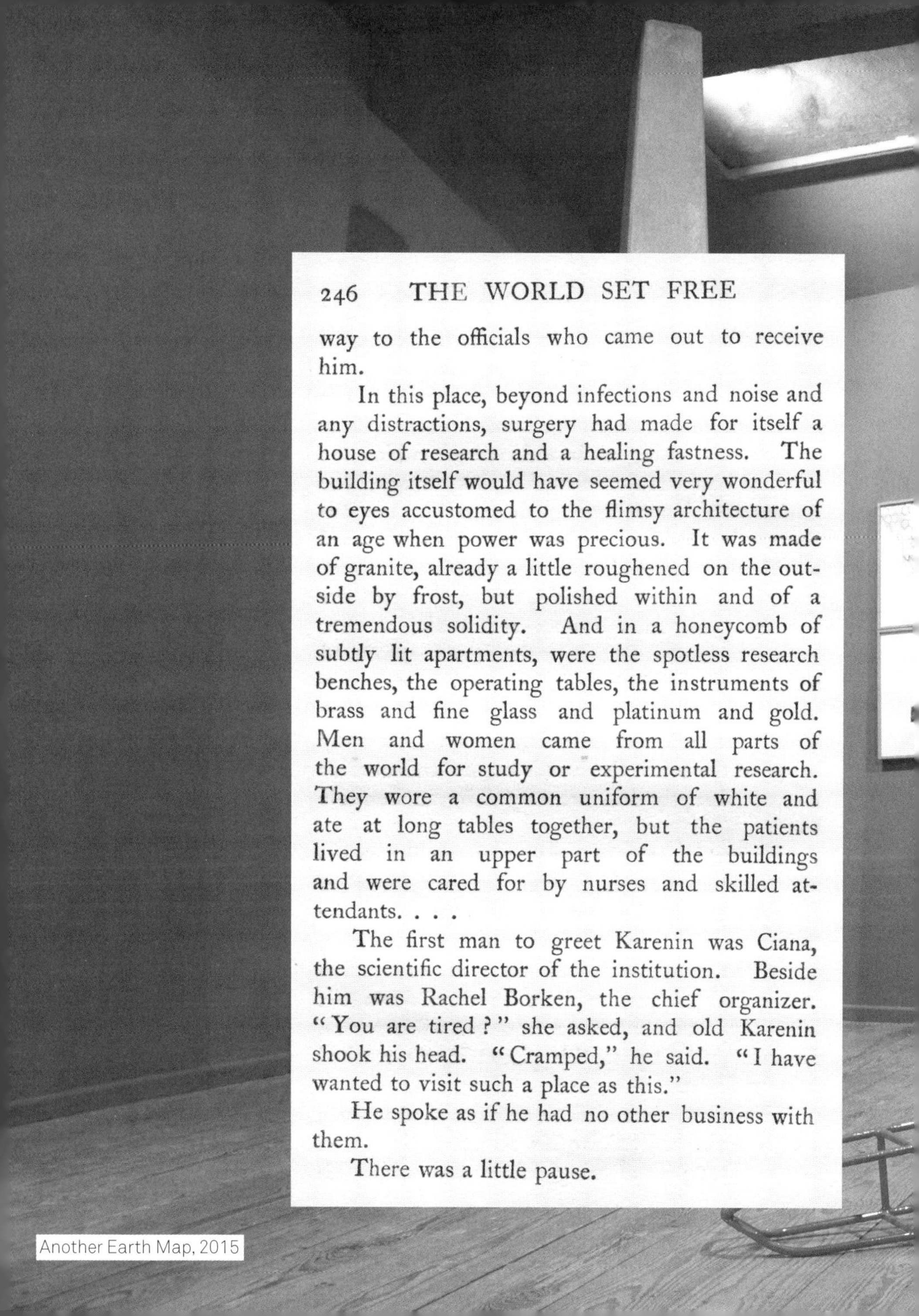

way to the officials who came out to receive him.

In this place, beyond infections and noise and any distractions, surgery had made for itself a house of research and a healing fastness. The building itself would have seemed very wonderful to eyes accustomed to the flimsy architecture of an age when power was precious. It was made of granite, already a little roughened on the outside by frost, but polished within and of a tremendous solidity. And in a honeycomb of subtly lit apartments, were the spotless research benches, the operating tables, the instruments of brass and fine glass and platinum and gold. Men and women came from all parts of the world for study or experimental research. They wore a common uniform of white and ate at long tables together, but the patients lived in an upper part of the buildings and were cared for by nurses and skilled attendants. . . .

The first man to greet Karenin was Ciana, the scientific director of the institution. Beside him was Rachel Borken, the chief organizer. "You are tired?" she asked, and old Karenin shook his head. "Cramped," he said. "I have wanted to visit such a place as this."

He spoke as if he had no other business with them.

There was a little pause.

Another Earth Map, 2015

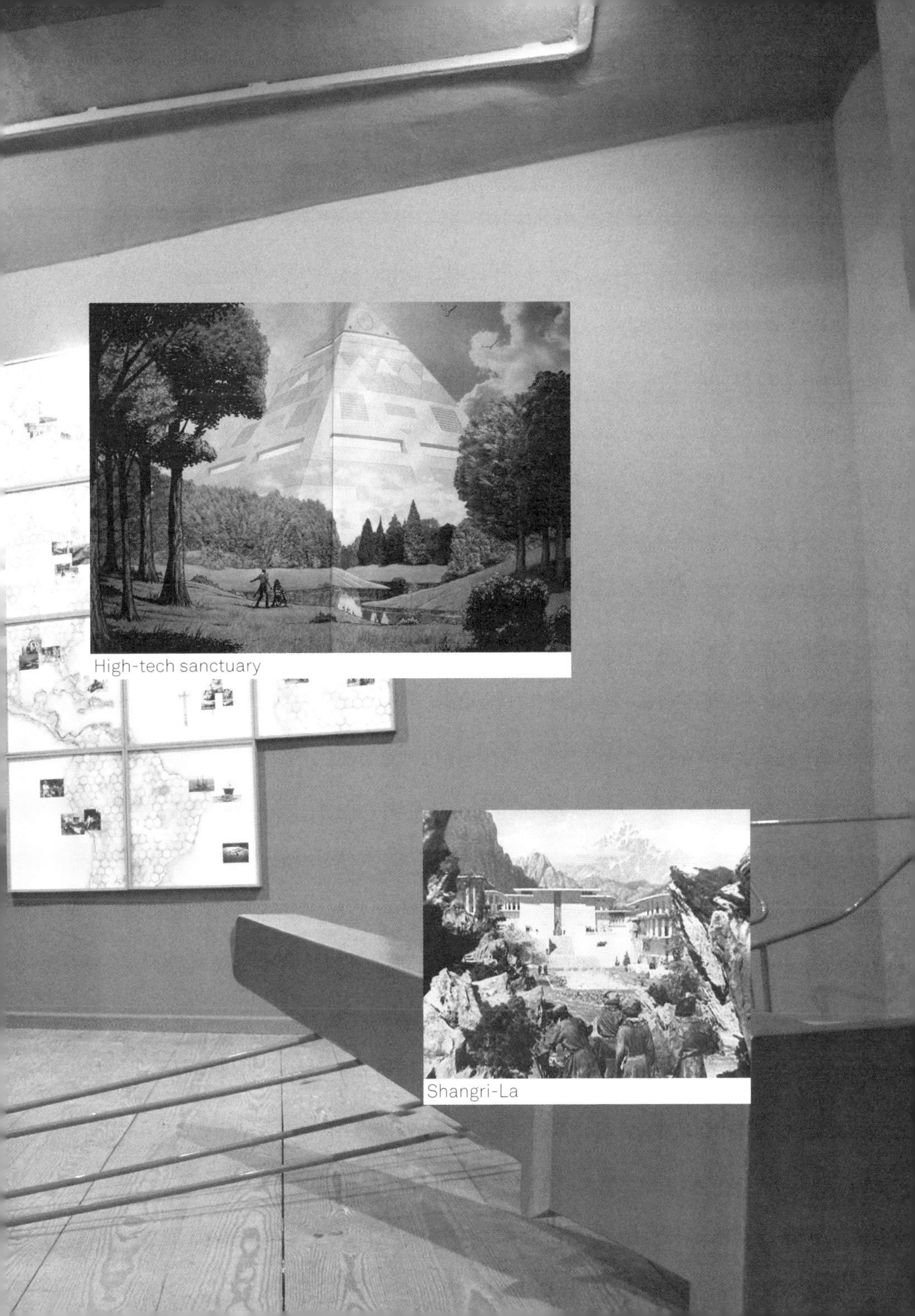
High-tech sanctuary
Shangri-La

"How many scientific people have you got here now?" he asked.

"Just three hundred and ninety-two," said Rachel Borken.

"And the patients and attendants and so on?"

"Two thousand and thirty."

"I shall be a patient," said Karenin. "I shall have to be a patient. But I should like to see things first. Presently I will be a patient."

"You will come to my rooms?" suggested Ciana.

"And then I must talk to this doctor of yours," said Karenin. "But I would like to see a bit of this place and talk to some of your people before it comes to that."

He winced and moved forward.

"I have left most of my work in order," he said.

"You have been working hard up to now?" asked Rachel Borken.

"Yes. And now I have nothing more to do —and it seems strange. . . . And it's a bother, this illness and having to come down to oneself. This doorway and that row of windows is well done; the grey granite and just the line of gold and then those mountains beyond through that arch. It's very well done. . . ."

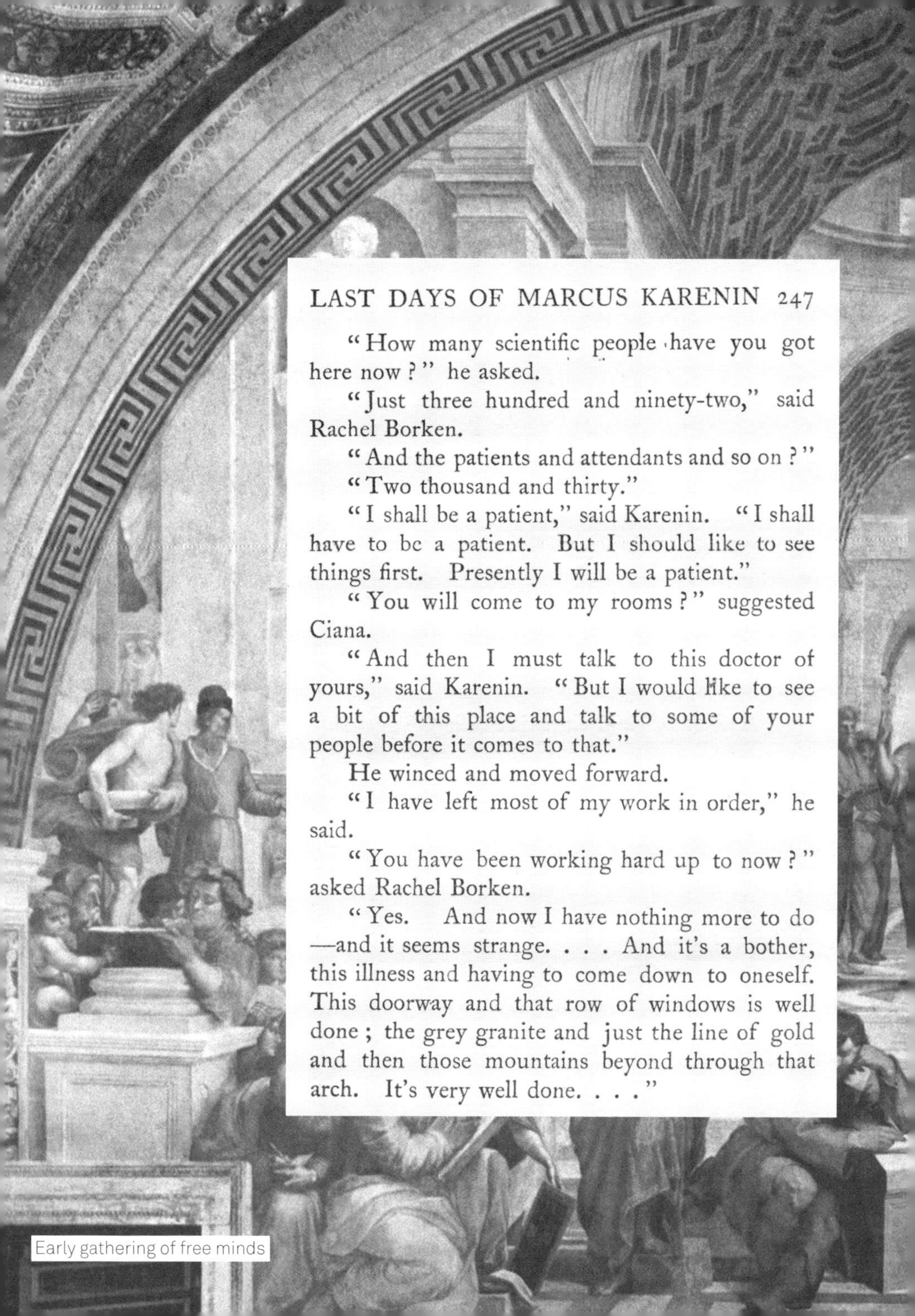

Early gathering of free minds

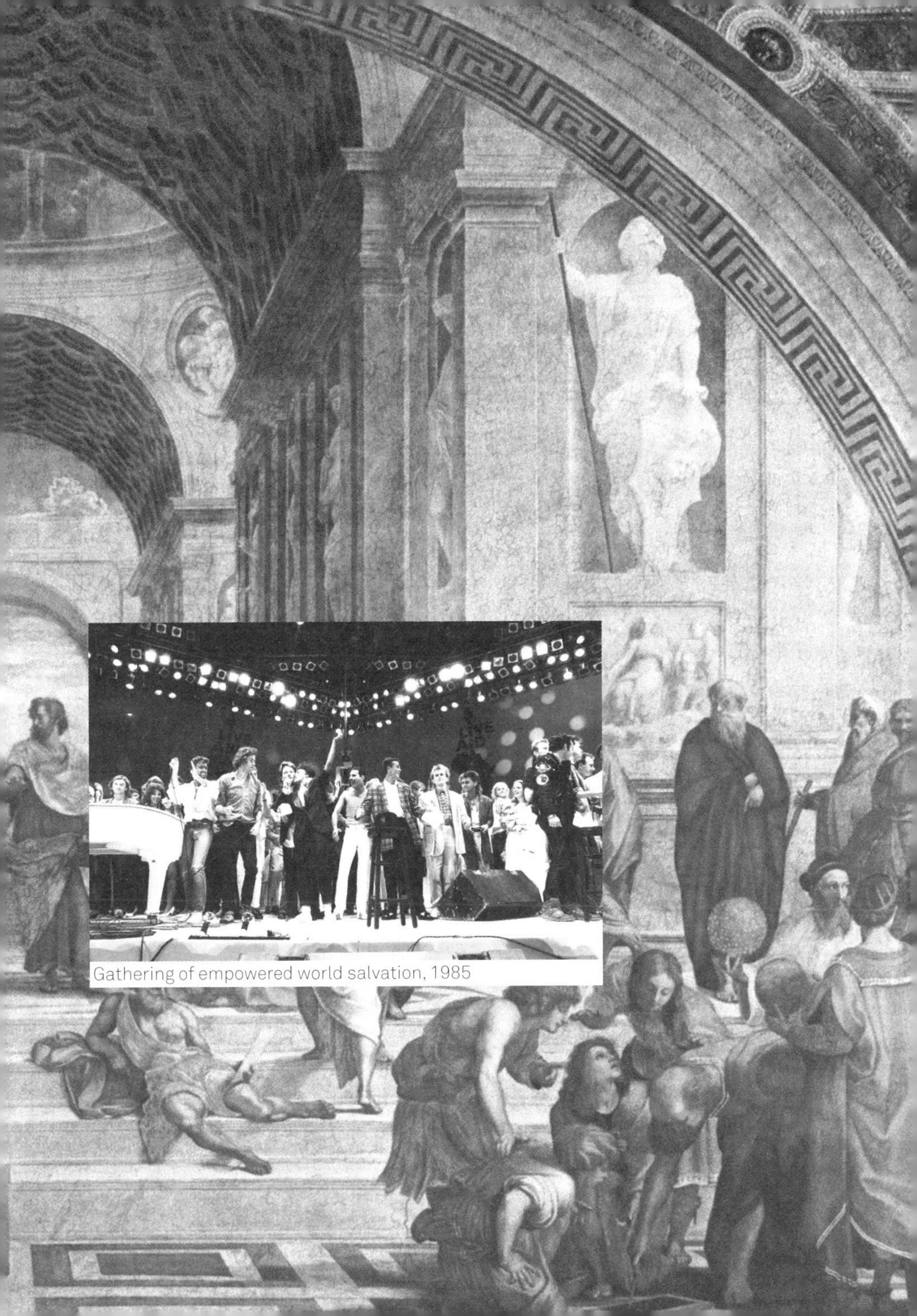

Gathering of empowered world salvation, 1985

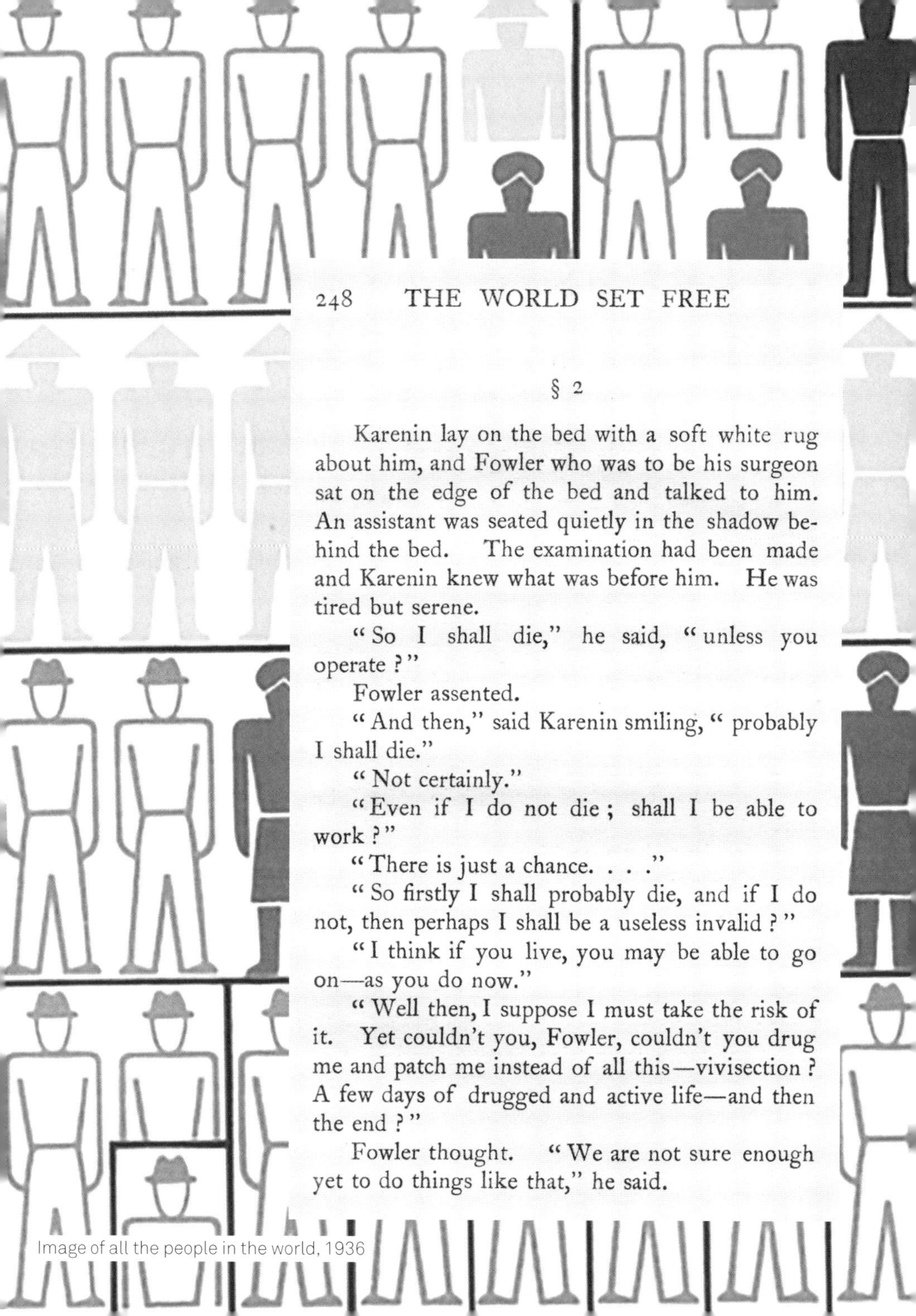

§ 2

Karenin lay on the bed with a soft white rug about him, and Fowler who was to be his surgeon sat on the edge of the bed and talked to him. An assistant was seated quietly in the shadow behind the bed. The examination had been made and Karenin knew what was before him. He was tired but serene.

"So I shall die," he said, "unless you operate?"

Fowler assented.

"And then," said Karenin smiling, "probably I shall die."

"Not certainly."

"Even if I do not die; shall I be able to work?"

"There is just a chance. . . ."

"So firstly I shall probably die, and if I do not, then perhaps I shall be a useless invalid?"

"I think if you live, you may be able to go on—as you do now."

"Well then, I suppose I must take the risk of it. Yet couldn't you, Fowler, couldn't you drug me and patch me instead of all this—vivisection? A few days of drugged and active life—and then the end?"

Fowler thought. "We are not sure enough yet to do things like that," he said.

Image of all the people in the world, 1936

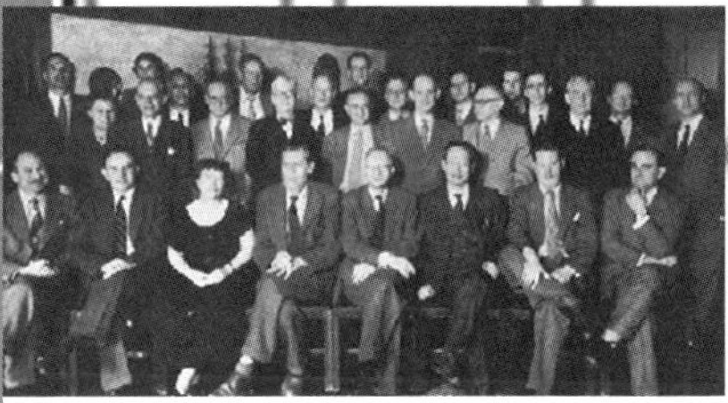
Cybernetic society meting

"But a day is coming when you will be certain."

Fowler nodded.

"You make me feel as though I was the last of deformity. Deformity is uncertainty—inaccuracy. My body works doubtfully, it is not even sure that it will die or live. I suppose the time is not far off when such bodies as mine will no longer be born into the world."

"You see," said Fowler after a little pause, "it is necessary that spirits such as yours should be born into the world."

"I suppose," said Karenin, "that my spirit has had its use. But if you think that is because my body is as it is I think you are mistaken. There is no peculiar virtue in defect. I have always chafed against—all this. If I could have moved more freely and lived a larger life in health I could have done more. But some day perhaps you will be able to put a body that is wrong altogether right again. Your science is only beginning. It's a subtler thing than physics and chemistry and it takes longer to produce its miracles. And meanwhile a few more of us must die in patience."

"Fine work is being done and much of it," said Fowler. "I can say as much because I have nothing to do with it. I can understand a lesson, appreciate the discoveries of abler men and use my hands, but those others, Pigou,

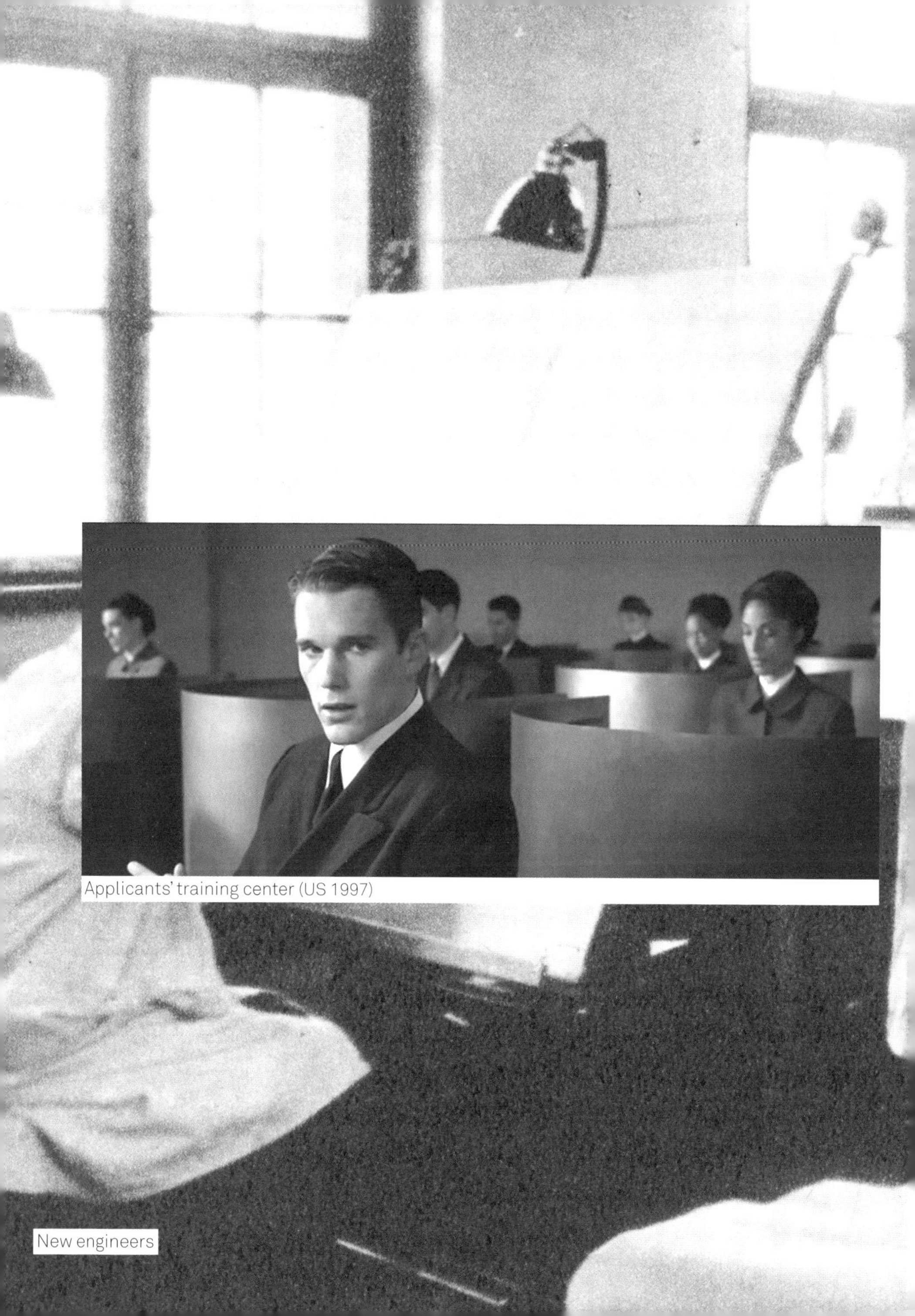

Applicants' training center (US 1997)

New engineers

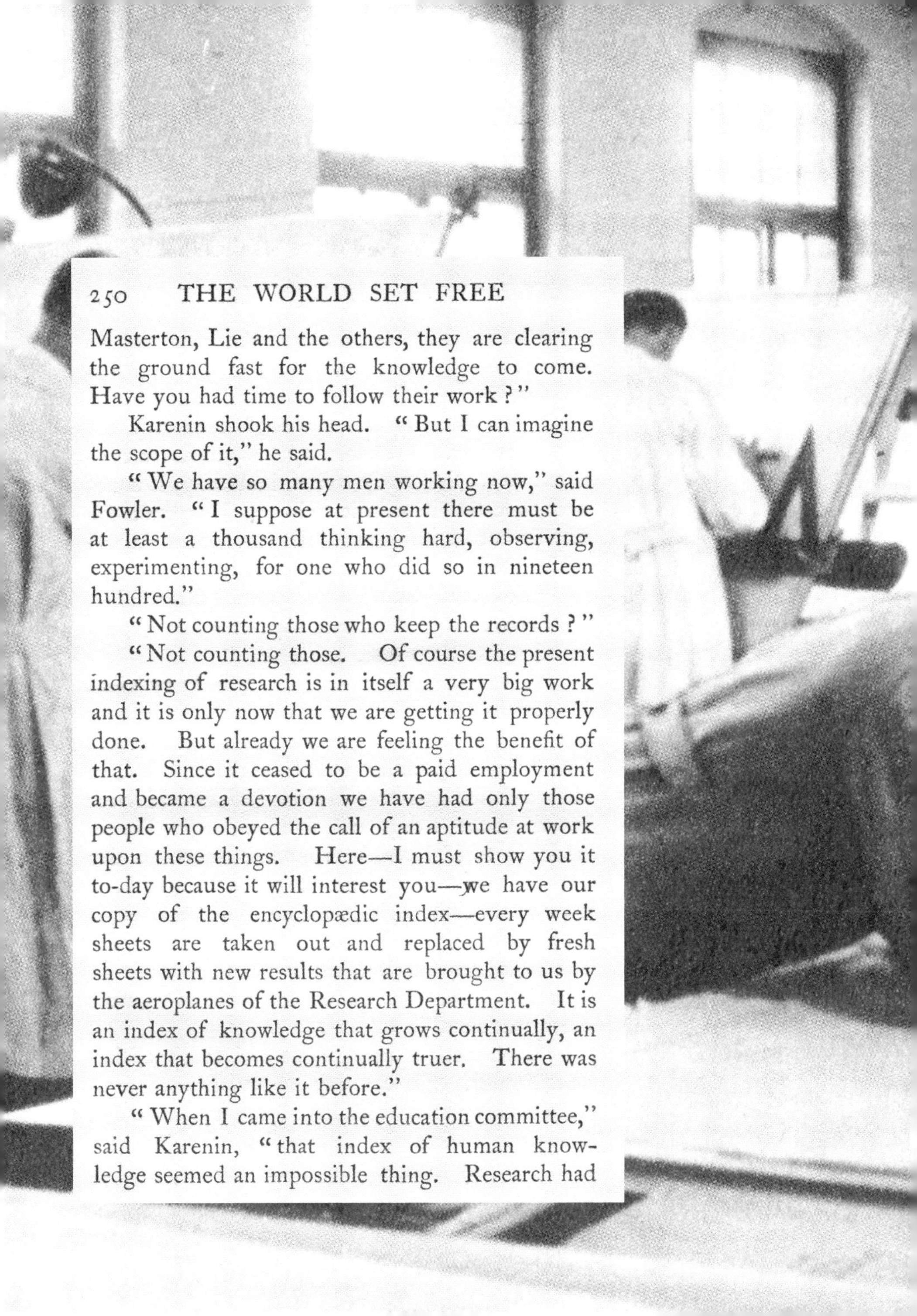

Masterton, Lie and the others, they are clearing the ground fast for the knowledge to come. Have you had time to follow their work?"

Karenin shook his head. "But I can imagine the scope of it," he said.

"We have so many men working now," said Fowler. "I suppose at present there must be at least a thousand thinking hard, observing, experimenting, for one who did so in nineteen hundred."

"Not counting those who keep the records?"

"Not counting those. Of course the present indexing of research is in itself a very big work and it is only now that we are getting it properly done. But already we are feeling the benefit of that. Since it ceased to be a paid employment and became a devotion we have had only those people who obeyed the call of an aptitude at work upon these things. Here—I must show you it to-day because it will interest you—we have our copy of the encyclopædic index—every week sheets are taken out and replaced by fresh sheets with new results that are brought to us by the aeroplanes of the Research Department. It is an index of knowledge that grows continually, an index that becomes continually truer. There was never anything like it before."

"When I came into the education committee," said Karenin, "that index of human knowledge seemed an impossible thing. Research had

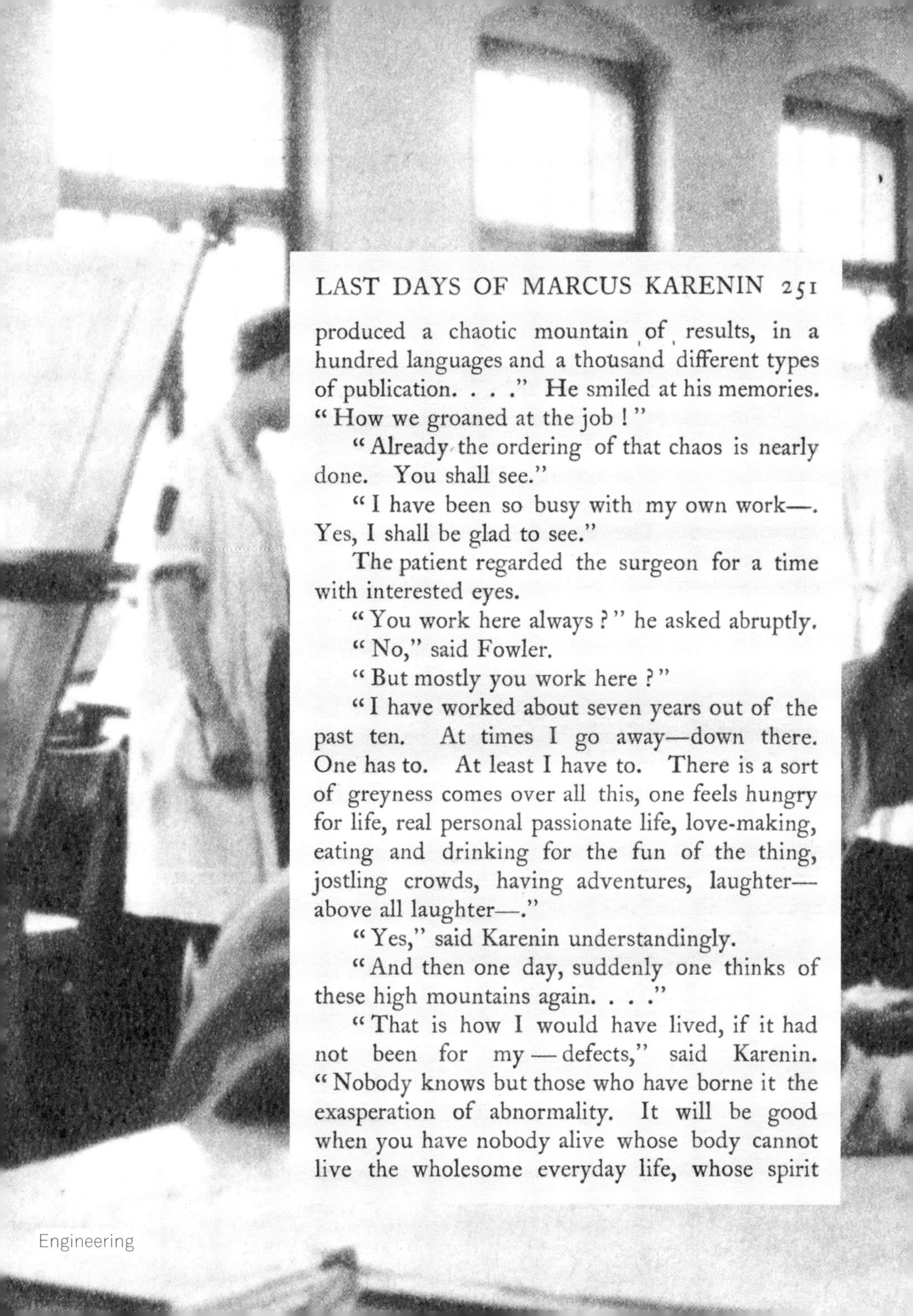

produced a chaotic mountain of results, in a hundred languages and a thousand different types of publication. . . ." He smiled at his memories. "How we groaned at the job!"

"Already the ordering of that chaos is nearly done. You shall see."

"I have been so busy with my own work—. Yes, I shall be glad to see."

The patient regarded the surgeon for a time with interested eyes.

"You work here always?" he asked abruptly.

"No," said Fowler.

"But mostly you work here?"

"I have worked about seven years out of the past ten. At times I go away—down there. One has to. At least I have to. There is a sort of greyness comes over all this, one feels hungry for life, real personal passionate life, love-making, eating and drinking for the fun of the thing, jostling crowds, having adventures, laughter—above all laughter—."

"Yes," said Karenin understandingly.

"And then one day, suddenly one thinks of these high mountains again. . . ."

"That is how I would have lived, if it had not been for my — defects," said Karenin. "Nobody knows but those who have borne it the exasperation of abnormality. It will be good when you have nobody alive whose body cannot live the wholesome everyday life, whose spirit

Engineering

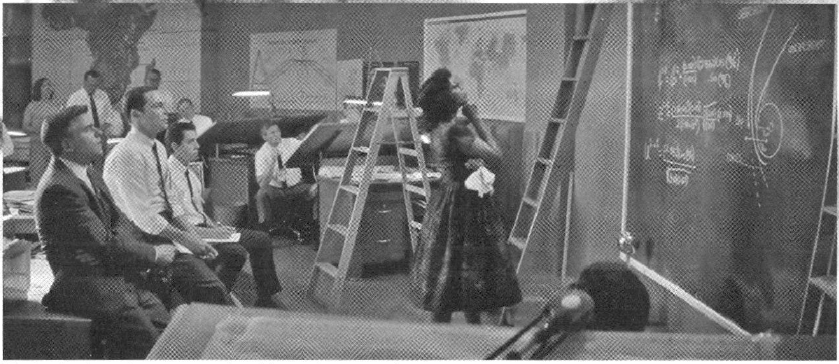

Calculating the way to the Moon (US 2016)

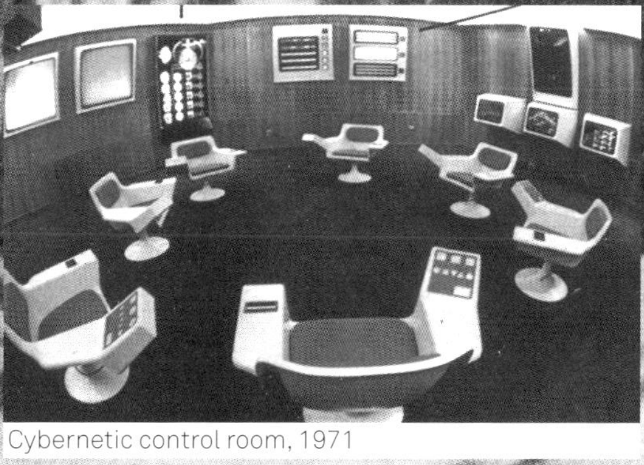

Cybernetic control room, 1971

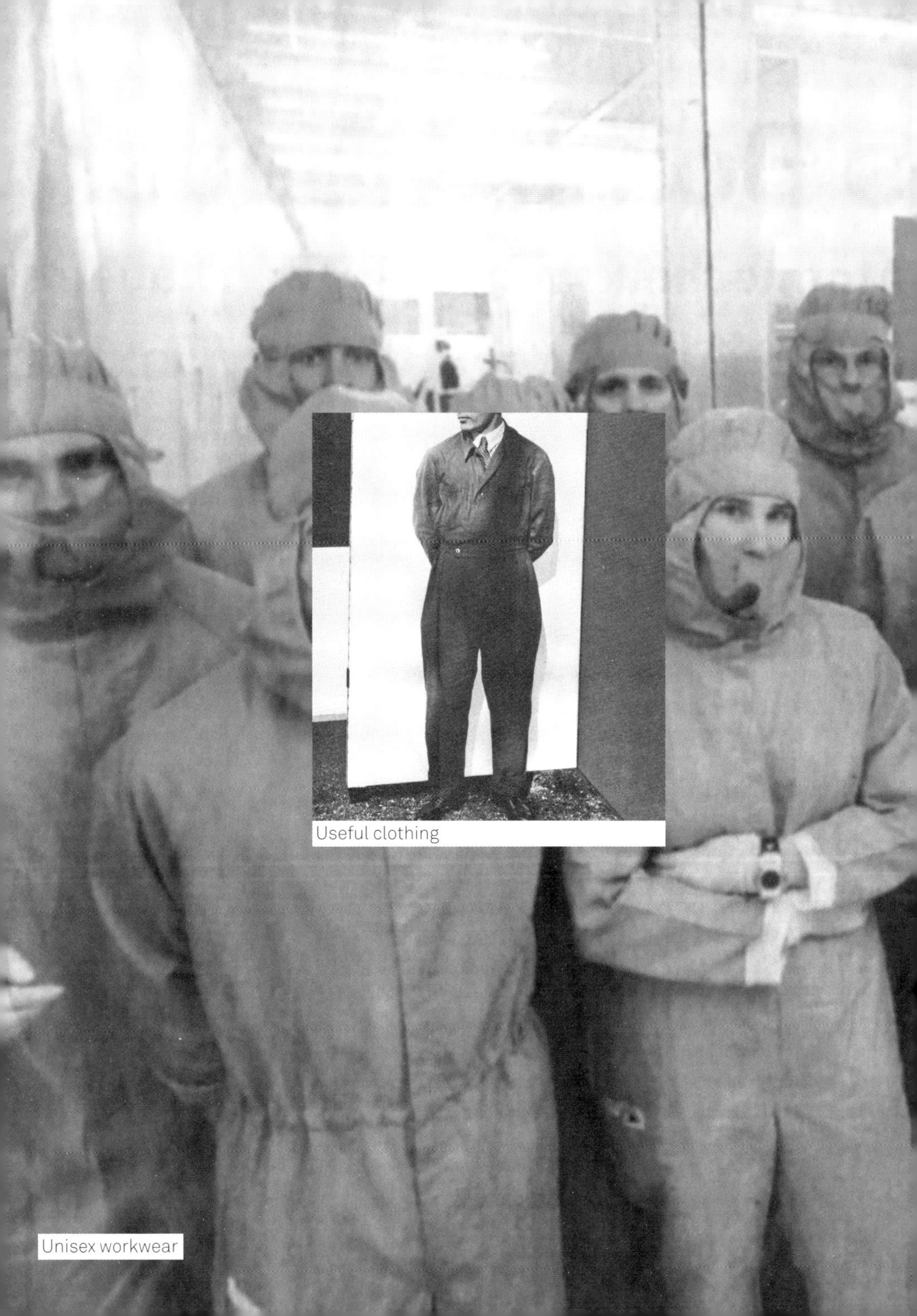

Useful clothing

Unisex workwear

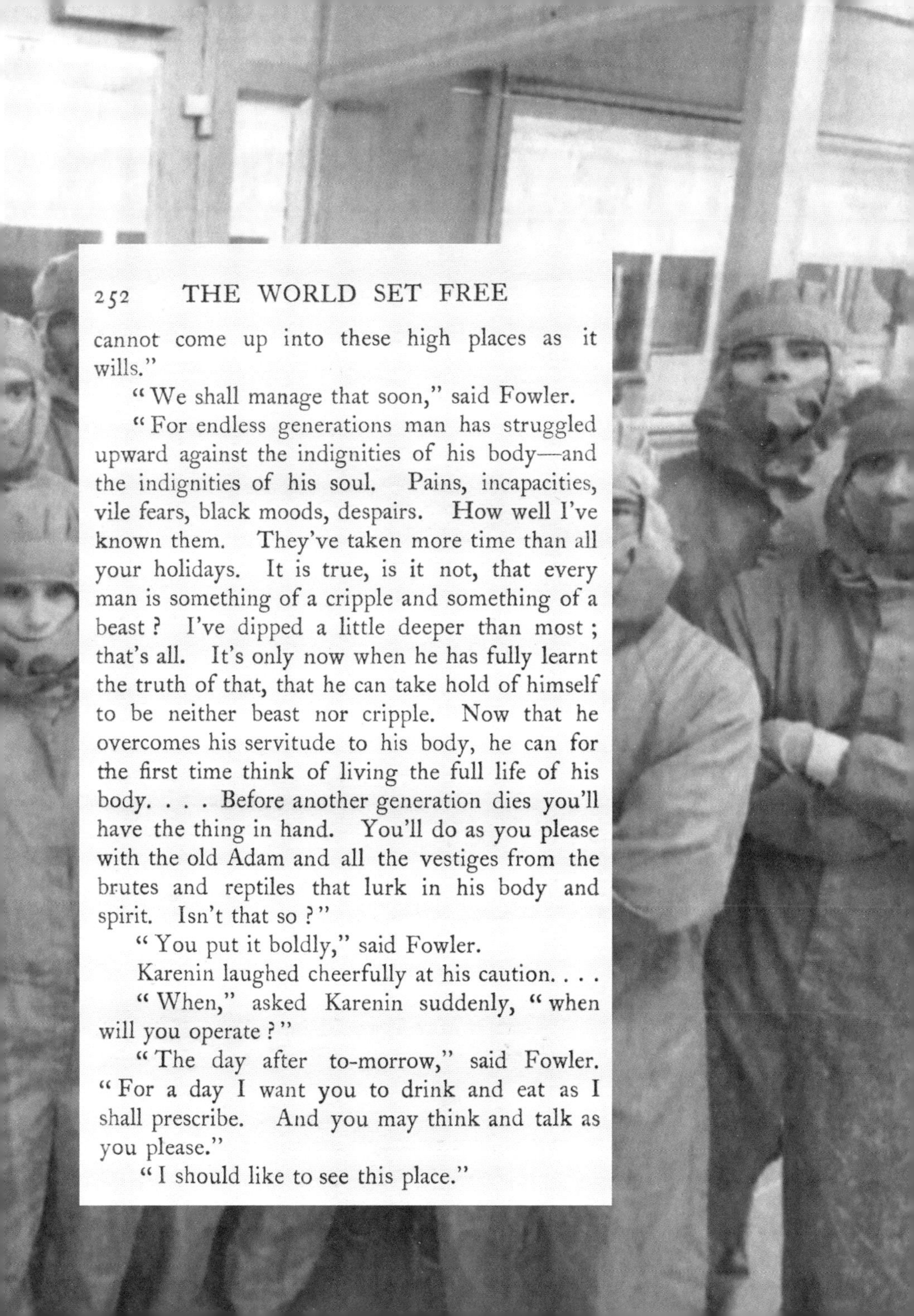

cannot come up into these high places as it wills."

"We shall manage that soon," said Fowler.

"For endless generations man has struggled upward against the indignities of his body—and the indignities of his soul. Pains, incapacities, vile fears, black moods, despairs. How well I've known them. They've taken more time than all your holidays. It is true, is it not, that every man is something of a cripple and something of a beast? I've dipped a little deeper than most; that's all. It's only now when he has fully learnt the truth of that, that he can take hold of himself to be neither beast nor cripple. Now that he overcomes his servitude to his body, he can for the first time think of living the full life of his body. . . . Before another generation dies you'll have the thing in hand. You'll do as you please with the old Adam and all the vestiges from the brutes and reptiles that lurk in his body and spirit. Isn't that so?"

"You put it boldly," said Fowler.

Karenin laughed cheerfully at his caution. . . .

"When," asked Karenin suddenly, "when will you operate?"

"The day after to-morrow," said Fowler. "For a day I want you to drink and eat as I shall prescribe. And you may think and talk as you please."

"I should like to see this place."

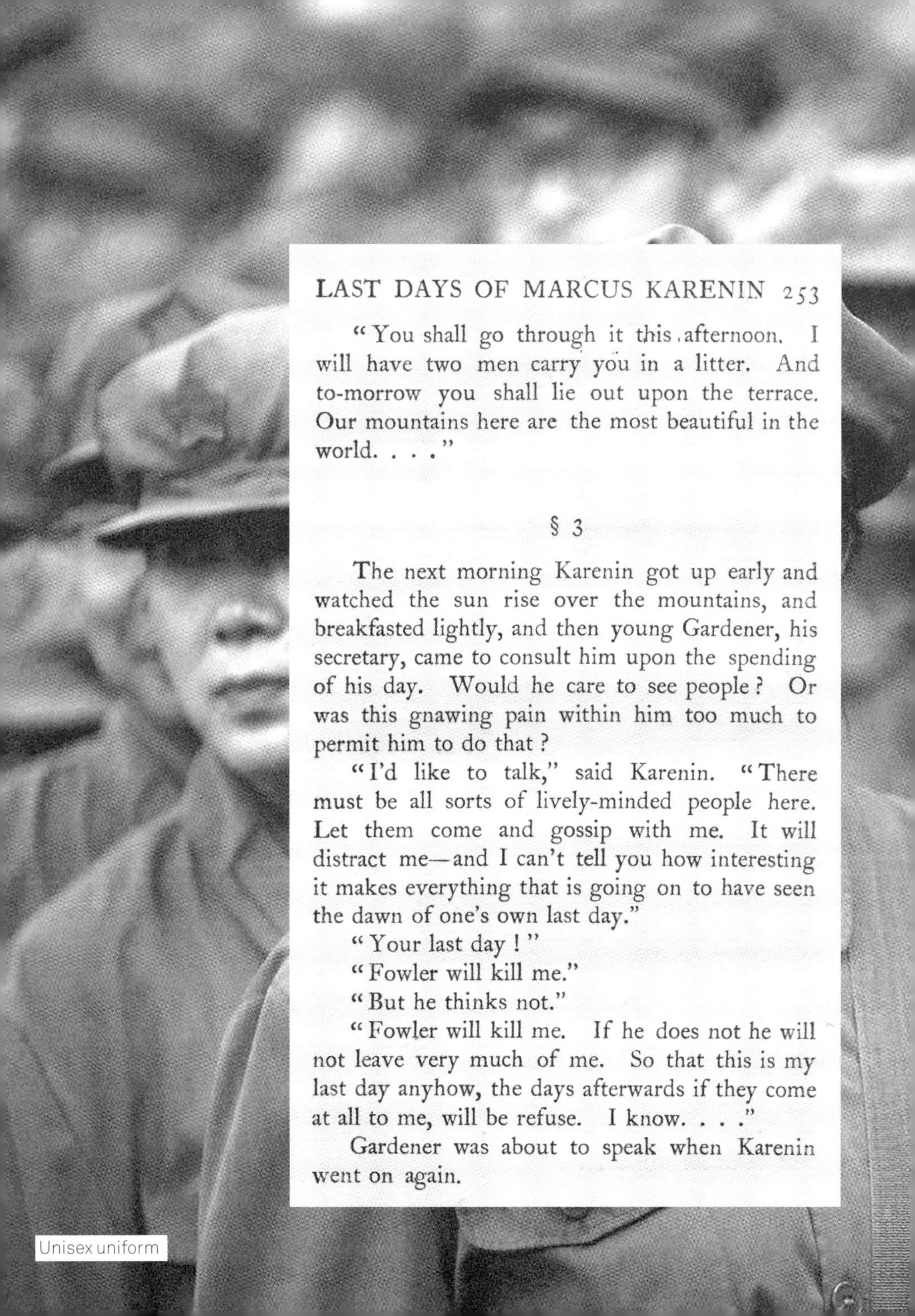

Unisex uniform

"You shall go through it this afternoon. I will have two men carry you in a litter. And to-morrow you shall lie out upon the terrace. Our mountains here are the most beautiful in the world. . . ."

§ 3

The next morning Karenin got up early and watched the sun rise over the mountains, and breakfasted lightly, and then young Gardener, his secretary, came to consult him upon the spending of his day. Would he care to see people? Or was this gnawing pain within him too much to permit him to do that?

"I'd like to talk," said Karenin. "There must be all sorts of lively-minded people here. Let them come and gossip with me. It will distract me—and I can't tell you how interesting it makes everything that is going on to have seen the dawn of one's own last day."

"Your last day!"

"Fowler will kill me."

"But he thinks not."

"Fowler will kill me. If he does not he will not leave very much of me. So that this is my last day anyhow, the days afterwards if they come at all to me, will be refuse. I know. . . ."

Gardener was about to speak when Karenin went on again.

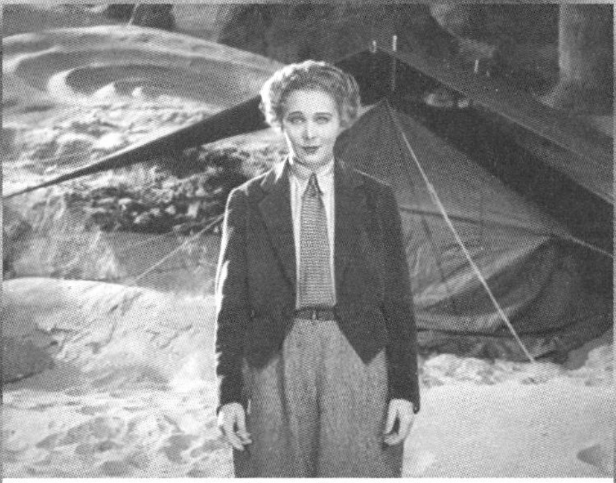

First woman on the Moon (DE 1929)

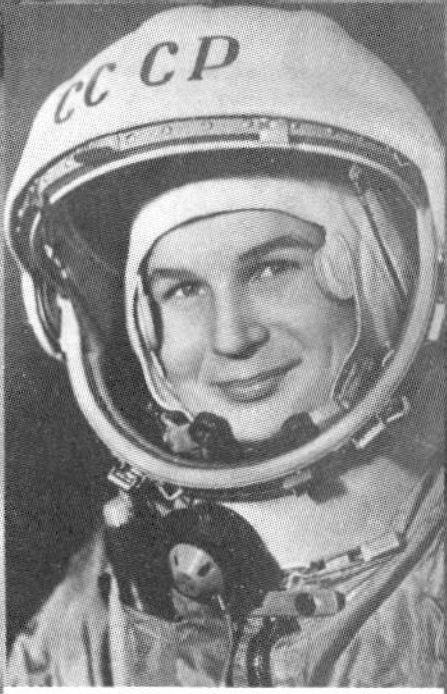

First woman in space

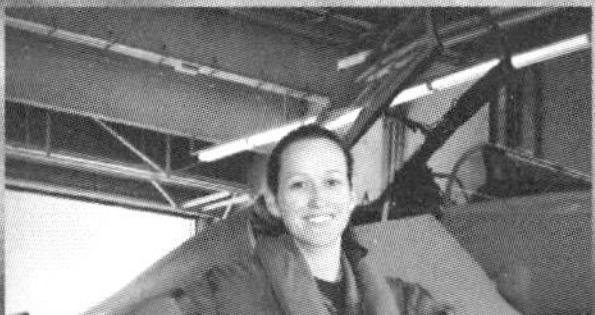

Astronaut in training

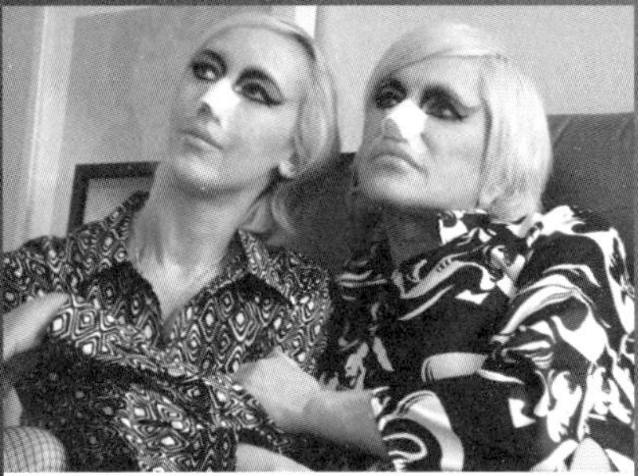

The ballad of becoming alike

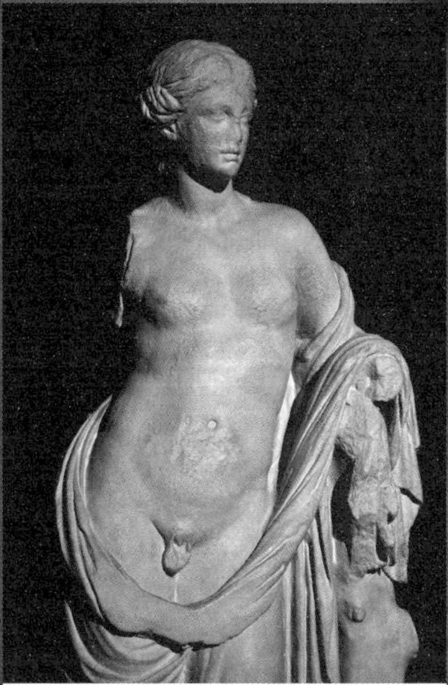

The third sex, ancient

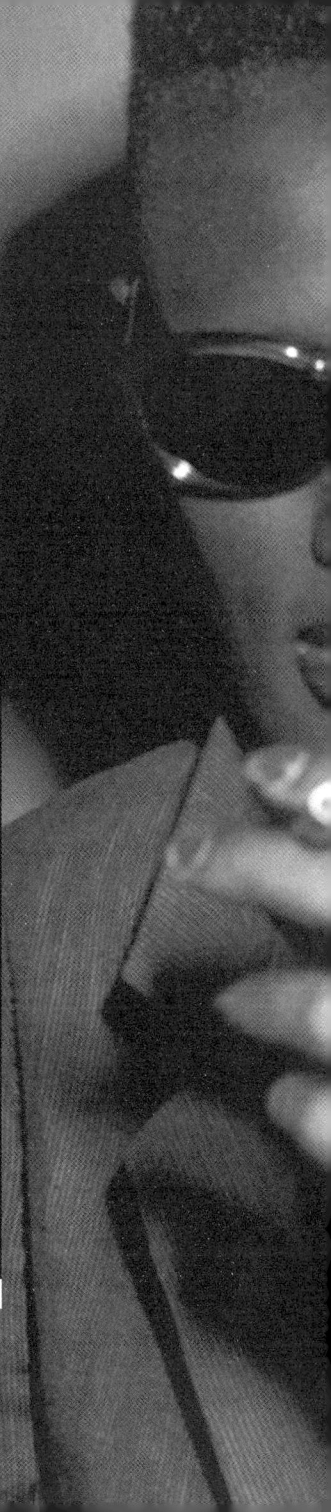

Twisting the gender

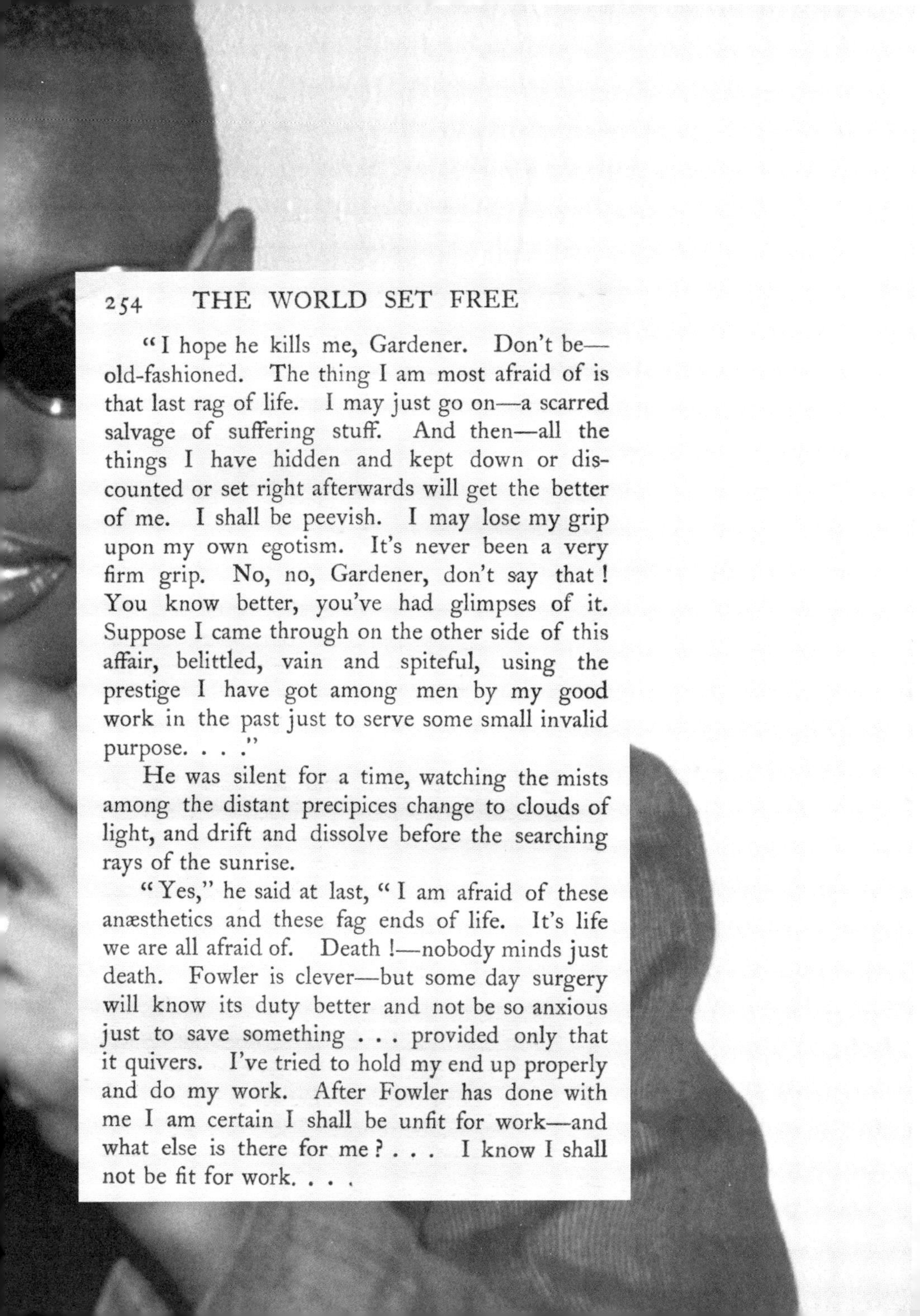

"I hope he kills me, Gardener. Don't be—old-fashioned. The thing I am most afraid of is that last rag of life. I may just go on—a scarred salvage of suffering stuff. And then—all the things I have hidden and kept down or discounted or set right afterwards will get the better of me. I shall be peevish. I may lose my grip upon my own egotism. It's never been a very firm grip. No, no, Gardener, don't say that! You know better, you've had glimpses of it. Suppose I came through on the other side of this affair, belittled, vain and spiteful, using the prestige I have got among men by my good work in the past just to serve some small invalid purpose. . . ."

He was silent for a time, watching the mists among the distant precipices change to clouds of light, and drift and dissolve before the searching rays of the sunrise.

"Yes," he said at last, "I am afraid of these anæsthetics and these fag ends of life. It's life we are all afraid of. Death!—nobody minds just death. Fowler is clever—but some day surgery will know its duty better and not be so anxious just to save something . . . provided only that it quivers. I've tried to hold my end up properly and do my work. After Fowler has done with me I am certain I shall be unfit for work—and what else is there for me? . . . I know I shall not be fit for work. . . .

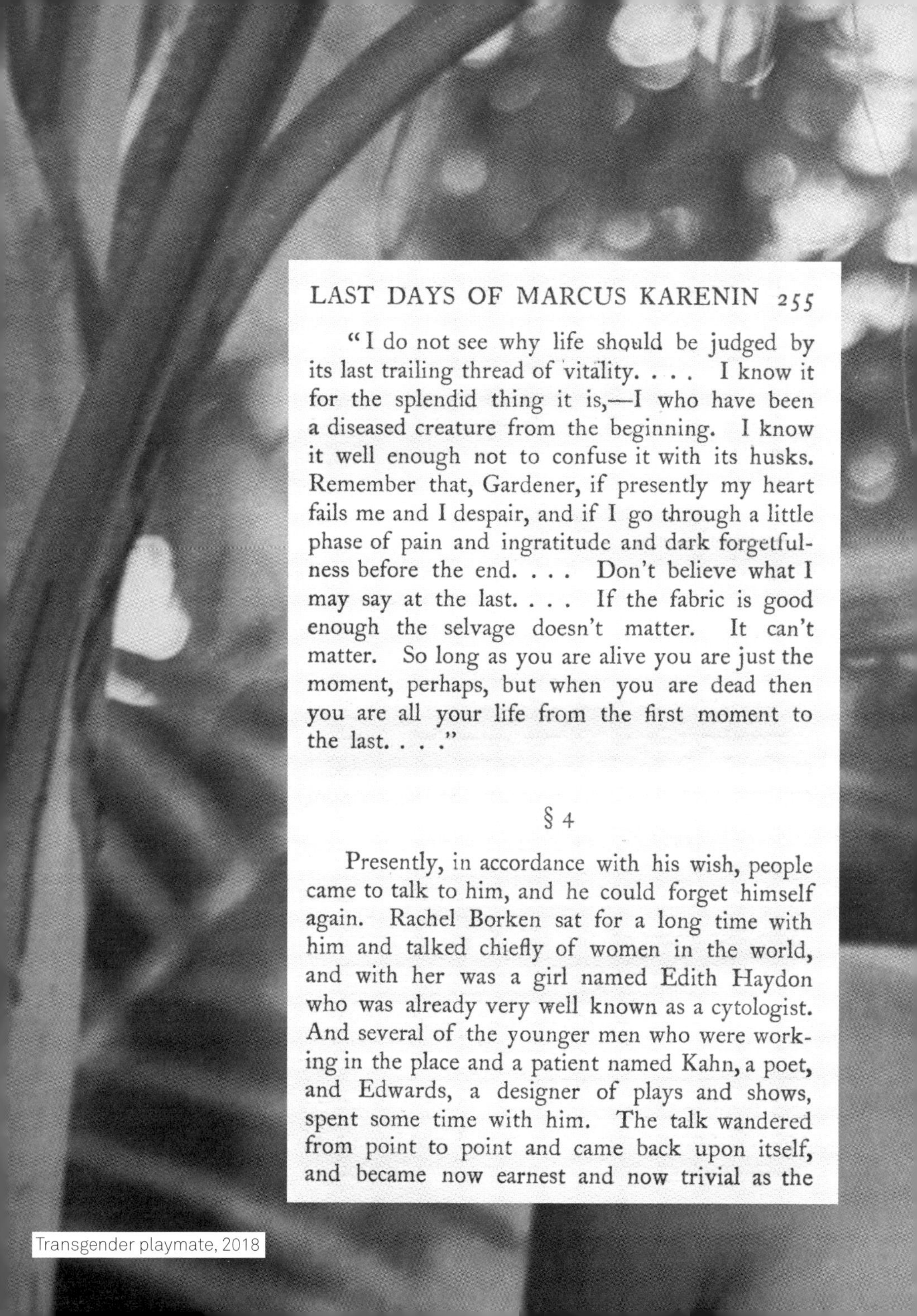

Transgender playmate, 2018

"I do not see why life should be judged by its last trailing thread of vitality. . . . I know it for the splendid thing it is,—I who have been a diseased creature from the beginning. I know it well enough not to confuse it with its husks. Remember that, Gardener, if presently my heart fails me and I despair, and if I go through a little phase of pain and ingratitude and dark forgetfulness before the end. . . . Don't believe what I may say at the last. . . . If the fabric is good enough the selvage doesn't matter. It can't matter. So long as you are alive you are just the moment, perhaps, but when you are dead then you are all your life from the first moment to the last. . . ."

§ 4

Presently, in accordance with his wish, people came to talk to him, and he could forget himself again. Rachel Borken sat for a long time with him and talked chiefly of women in the world, and with her was a girl named Edith Haydon who was already very well known as a cytologist. And several of the younger men who were working in the place and a patient named Kahn, a poet, and Edwards, a designer of plays and shows, spent some time with him. The talk wandered from point to point and came back upon itself, and became now earnest and now trivial as the

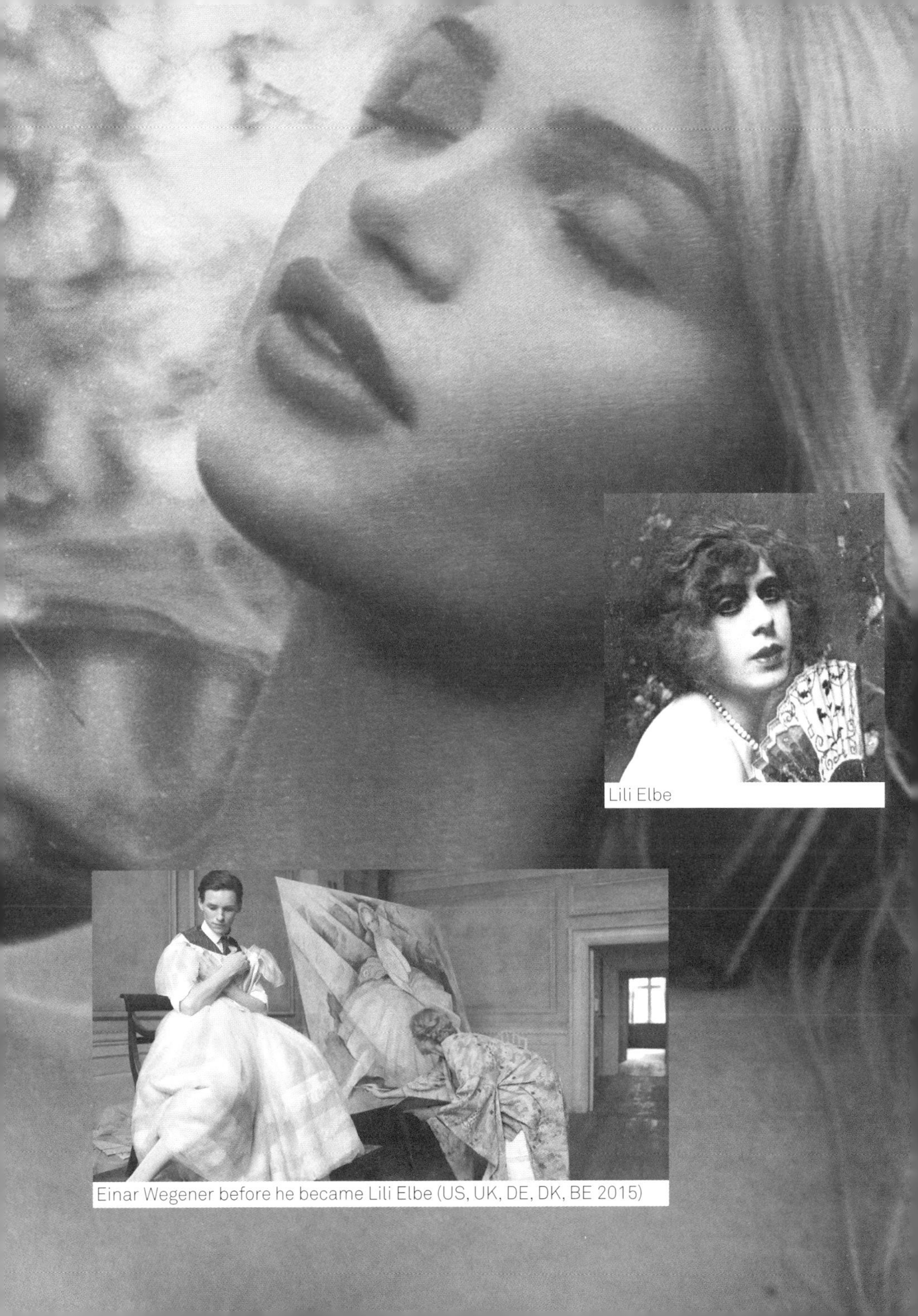

Lili Elbe

Einar Wegener before he became Lili Elbe (US, UK, DE, DK, BE 2015)

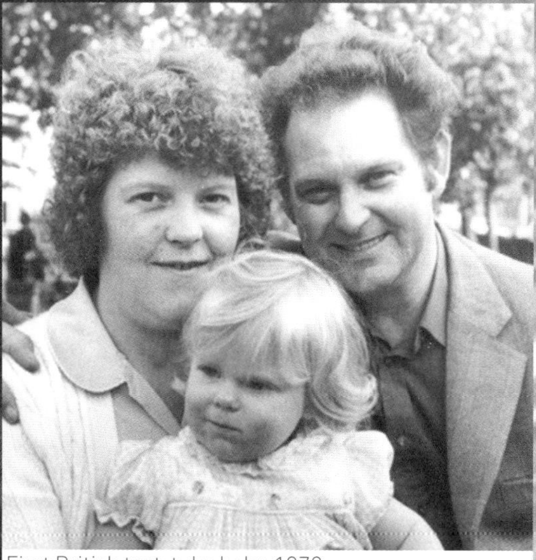

First British test-tube baby, 1978

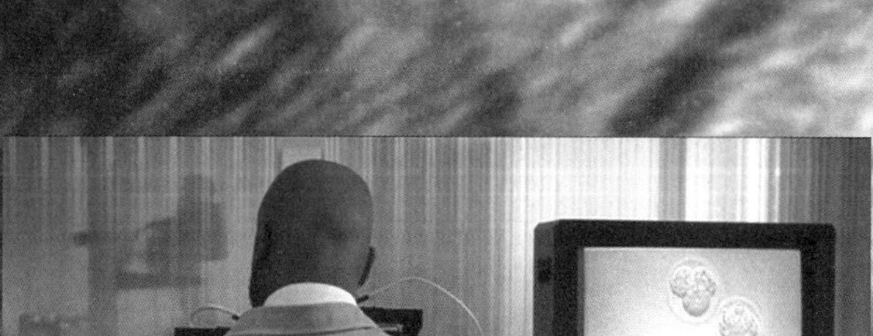

Designing a baby (US 1997)

Ultrasonic image

chance suggestions determined. But soon afterwards Gardener wrote down notes of things he remembered, and it is possible to put together again the outlook of Karenin upon the world and how he thought and felt about many of the principal things in life.

"Our age," he said, "has been so far an age of scene-shifting. We have been preparing a stage, clearing away the setting of a drama that was played out and growing tiresome. . . . If I could but sit out the first few scenes of the new spectacle. . . .

"How encumbered the world had become! It was ailing as I am ailing with a growth of unmeaning things. It was entangled, feverish, confused. It was in sore need of release, and I suppose that nothing less than the violence of those bombs could have released it and made it a healthy world again. I suppose they were necessary. Just as everything turns to evil in a fevered body so everything seemed turning to evil in those last years of the old time. Everywhere there were obsolete organizations seizing upon all the new fine things that science was giving to the world, nationalities, all sorts of political bodies, the churches and sects, proprietorship, seizing upon those great powers and limitless possibilities and turning them to evil uses. And they would not suffer open speech, they would not permit of education, they would let no one be educated to

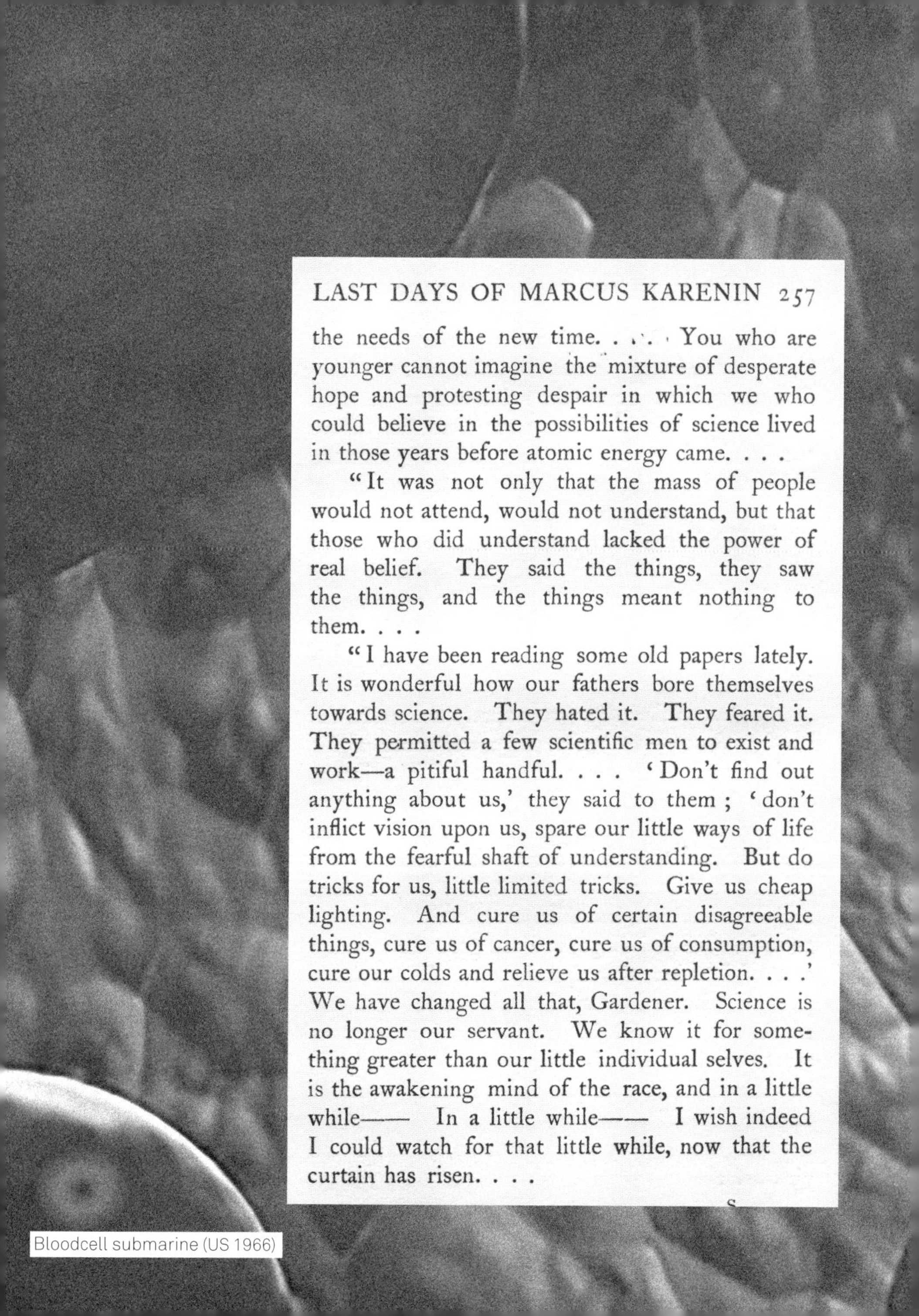

LAST DAYS OF MARCUS KARENIN 257

the needs of the new time. . . . . You who are younger cannot imagine the mixture of desperate hope and protesting despair in which we who could believe in the possibilities of science lived in those years before atomic energy came. . . .

"It was not only that the mass of people would not attend, would not understand, but that those who did understand lacked the power of real belief. They said the things, they saw the things, and the things meant nothing to them. . . .

"I have been reading some old papers lately. It is wonderful how our fathers bore themselves towards science. They hated it. They feared it. They permitted a few scientific men to exist and work—a pitiful handful. . . . 'Don't find out anything about us,' they said to them ; 'don't inflict vision upon us, spare our little ways of life from the fearful shaft of understanding. But do tricks for us, little limited tricks. Give us cheap lighting. And cure us of certain disagreeable things, cure us of cancer, cure us of consumption, cure our colds and relieve us after repletion. . . .' We have changed all that, Gardener. Science is no longer our servant. We know it for something greater than our little individual selves. It is the awakening mind of the race, and in a little while—— In a little while—— I wish indeed I could watch for that little while, now that the curtain has risen. . . .

Bloodcell submarine (US 1966)

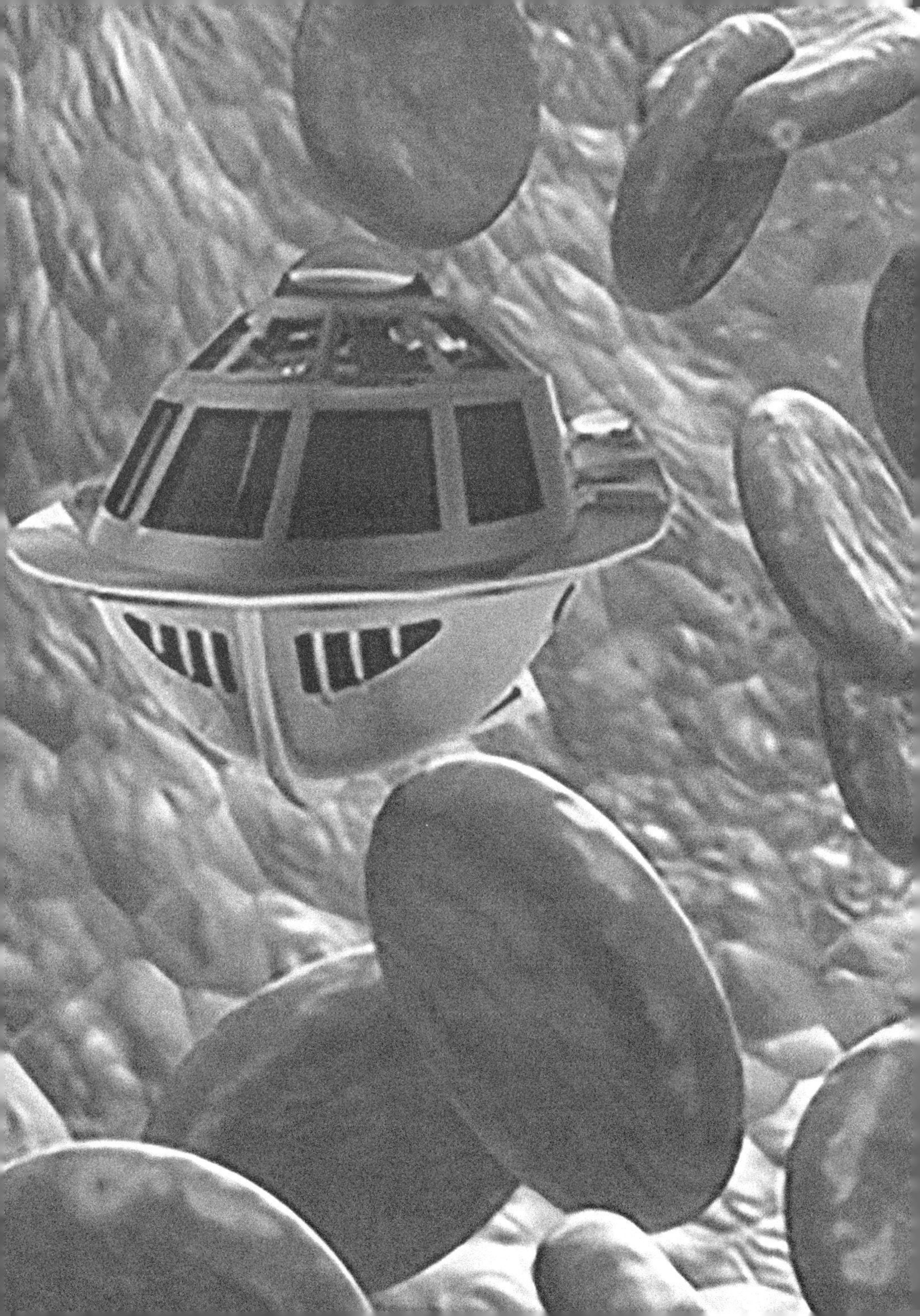

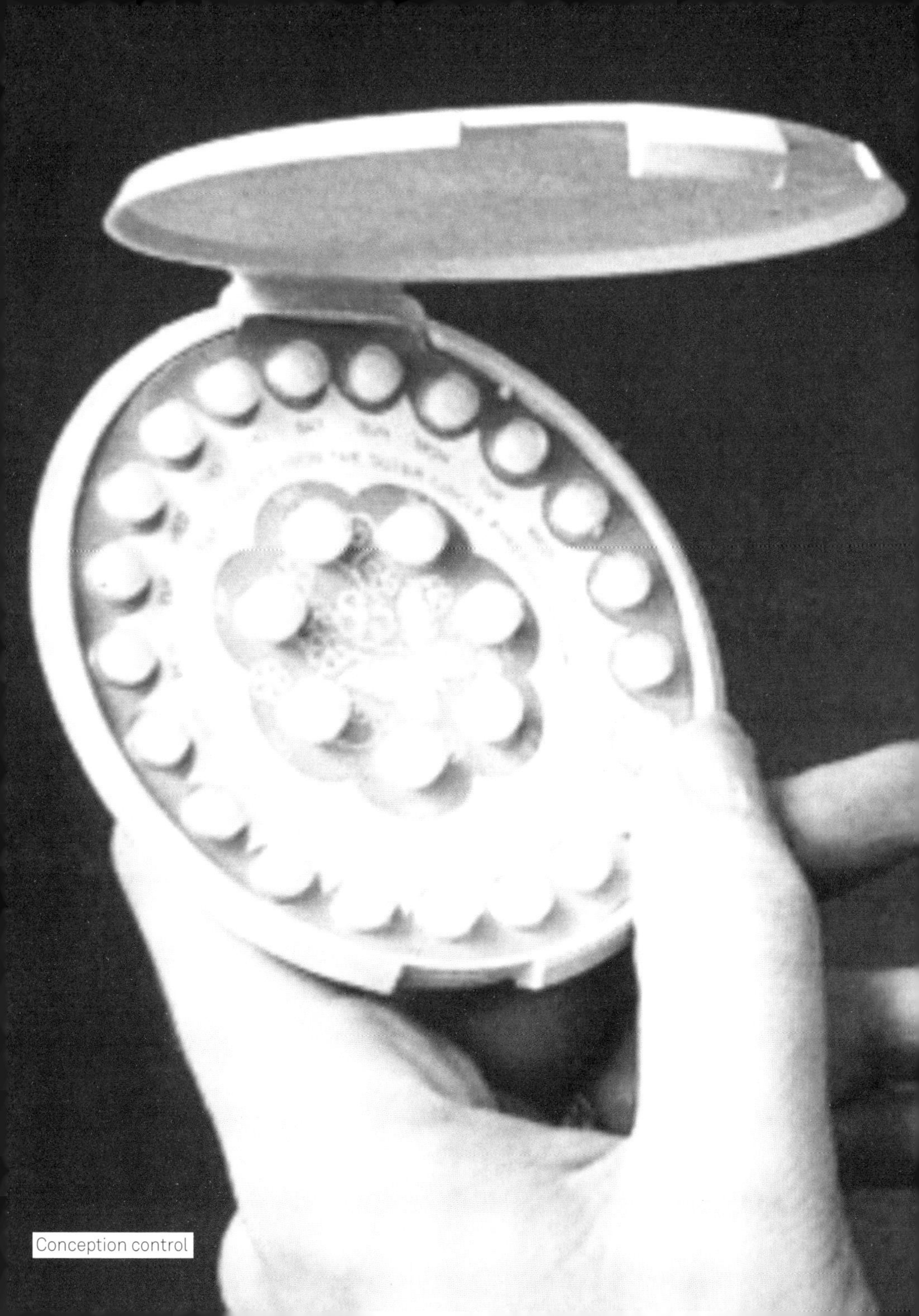

Conception control

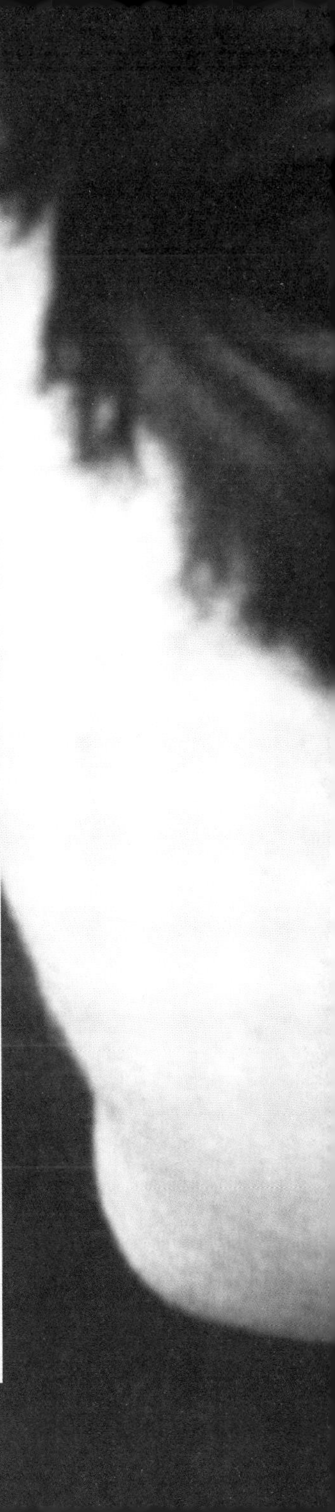

"While I lie here they are clearing up what is left of the bombs in London," he said. "Then they are going to repair the ruins and make it all as like as possible to its former condition before the bombs fell. Perhaps they will dig out the old house in St. John's Wood to which my father went after his expulsion from Russia. . . . That London of my memories seems to me like a place in another world. For you younger people it must seem like a place that could never have existed."

"Is there much left standing?" asked Edith Haydon.

"Square miles that are scarcely shaken in the south and north-west, they say; and most of the bridges and large areas of dock. Westminster, which held most of the government offices, suffered badly from the small bomb that destroyed the Parliament, there are very few traces of the old thoroughfare of Whitehall or the Government region thereabout, but there are plentiful drawings to scale of its buildings, and the great hole in the east of London scarcely matters. That was a poor district and very like the north and the south. . . . It will be possible to reconstruct most of it. . . . It is wanted. Already it becomes difficult to recall the old time—even for us who saw it."

"It seems very distant to me," said the girl. . . .

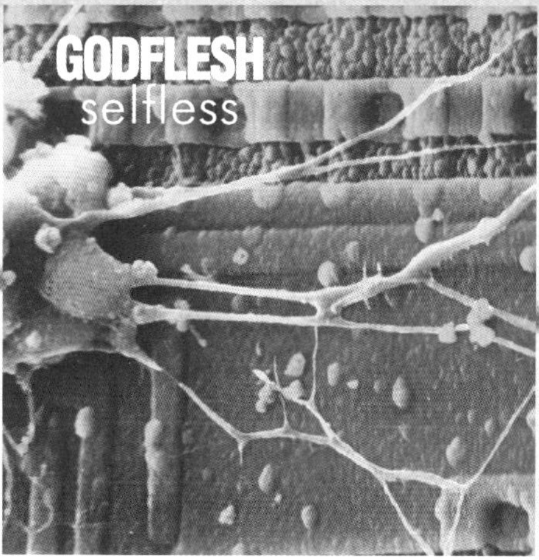

Human nerve cell growing on microchip, 1994

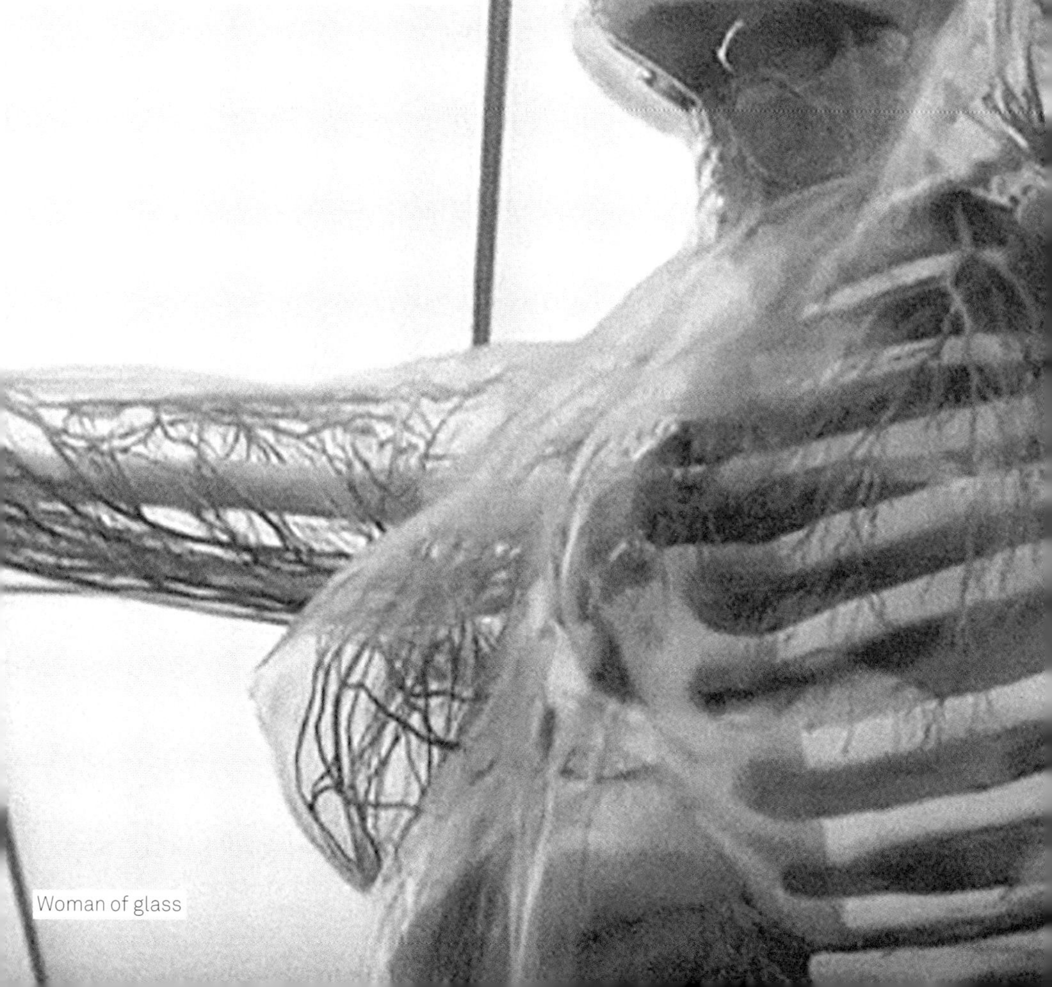

Woman of glass

"It was an unwholesome world," reflected Karenin. "I seem to remember everybody about my childhood as if they were ill. They were ill. They were sick with confusion. Everybody was anxious about money and everybody was doing uncongenial things. They ate a queer mixture of foods, either too much or too little, and at odd hours. One sees how ill they were by their advertisements. All this new region of London they are opening up now is plastered with advertisements of pills. Everybody must have been taking pills. In one of the hotel rooms in the Strand they have found the luggage of a lady covered up by falling rubble and unburnt, and she was equipped with nine different sorts of pill and tabloid. The pill-carrying age followed the weapon-carrying age. They are equally strange to us. People's skins must have been in a vile state. Very few people were properly washed; they carried the filth of months on their clothes. All the clothes they wore were old clothes; our way of pulping our clothes again after a week or so of wear would have seemed fantastic to them. Their clothing hardly bears thinking about. And the congestion of them! Everybody was jostling against everybody in those awful towns. In an uproar. People were run over and crushed by the hundred; every year in London the cars and omnibuses alone killed or disabled twenty thousand people, in Paris it was worse; people

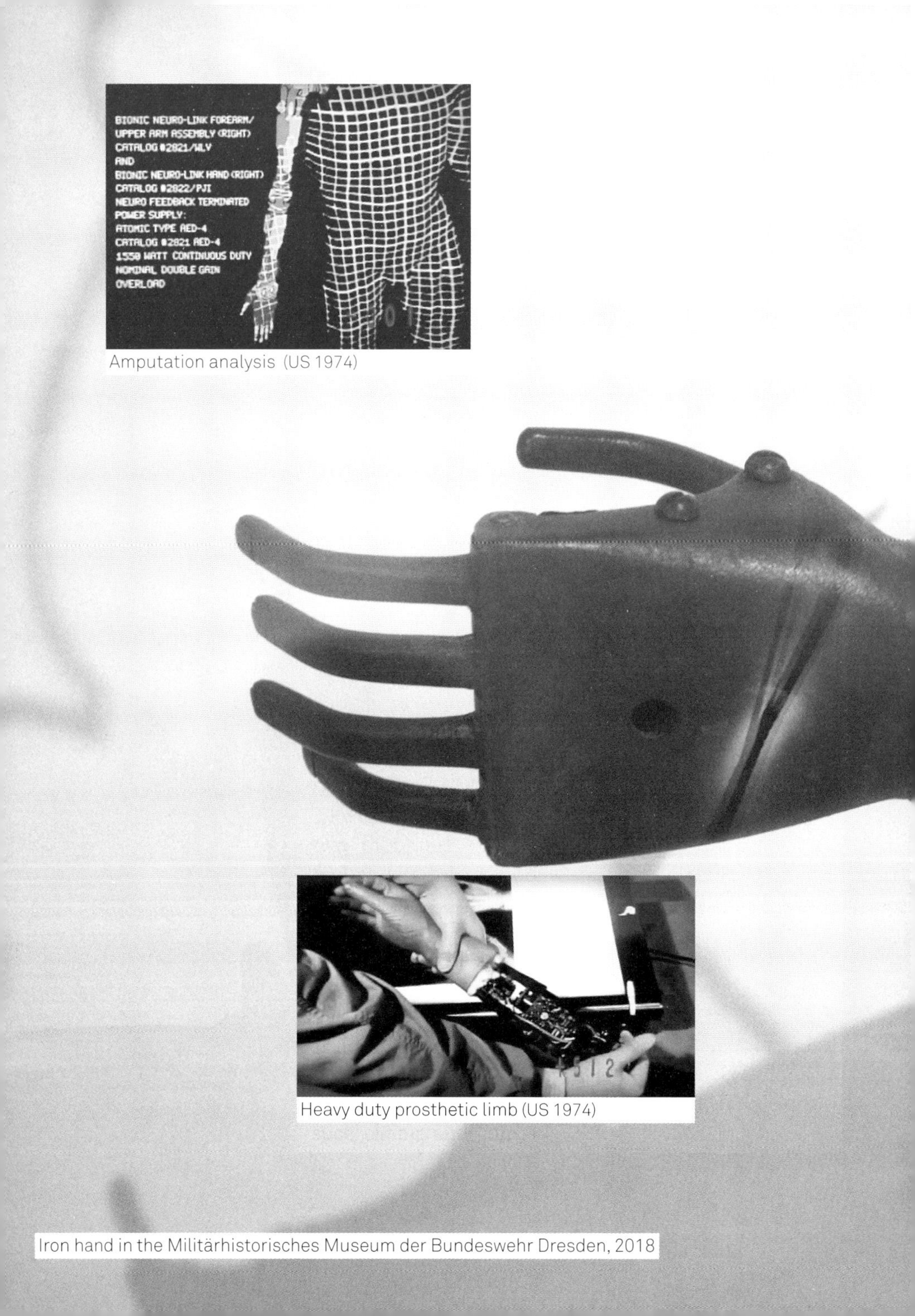

Amputation analysis (US 1974)

Heavy duty prosthetic limb (US 1974)

Iron hand in the Militärhistorisches Museum der Bundeswehr Dresden, 2018 used to fall dead for want of air in the crowded ways. The irritation of London, internal and external, must have been maddening. It was a maddened world. It is like thinking of a sick child. One has the same effect of feverish urgencies and acute irrational disappointments.

"All history," he said, "is a record of a childhood. . . .

"And yet not exactly a childhood. There is something clean and keen about even a sick child —and something touching. But so much of the old time makes one angry. So much they did seems grossly stupid, obstinately, outrageously stupid, which is the very opposite to being fresh and young.

"I was reading only the other day about Bismarck, that hero of nineteenth century politics, that sequel to Napoleon, that god of blood and iron. And he was just a beery, obstinate, dull man. Indeed that is what he was, the commonest, coarsest man who ever became great. I looked at his portraits, a heavy, almost froggish face, with projecting eyes and a thick moustache to hide a poor mouth. He aimed at nothing but Germany, Germany emphasized, indurated, enlarged; Germany and his class in Germany; beyond that he had no ideas, he was inaccessible to ideas; his mind never rose for a recorded instant above a bumpkin's elaborate cunning. And he was the most influential man in the

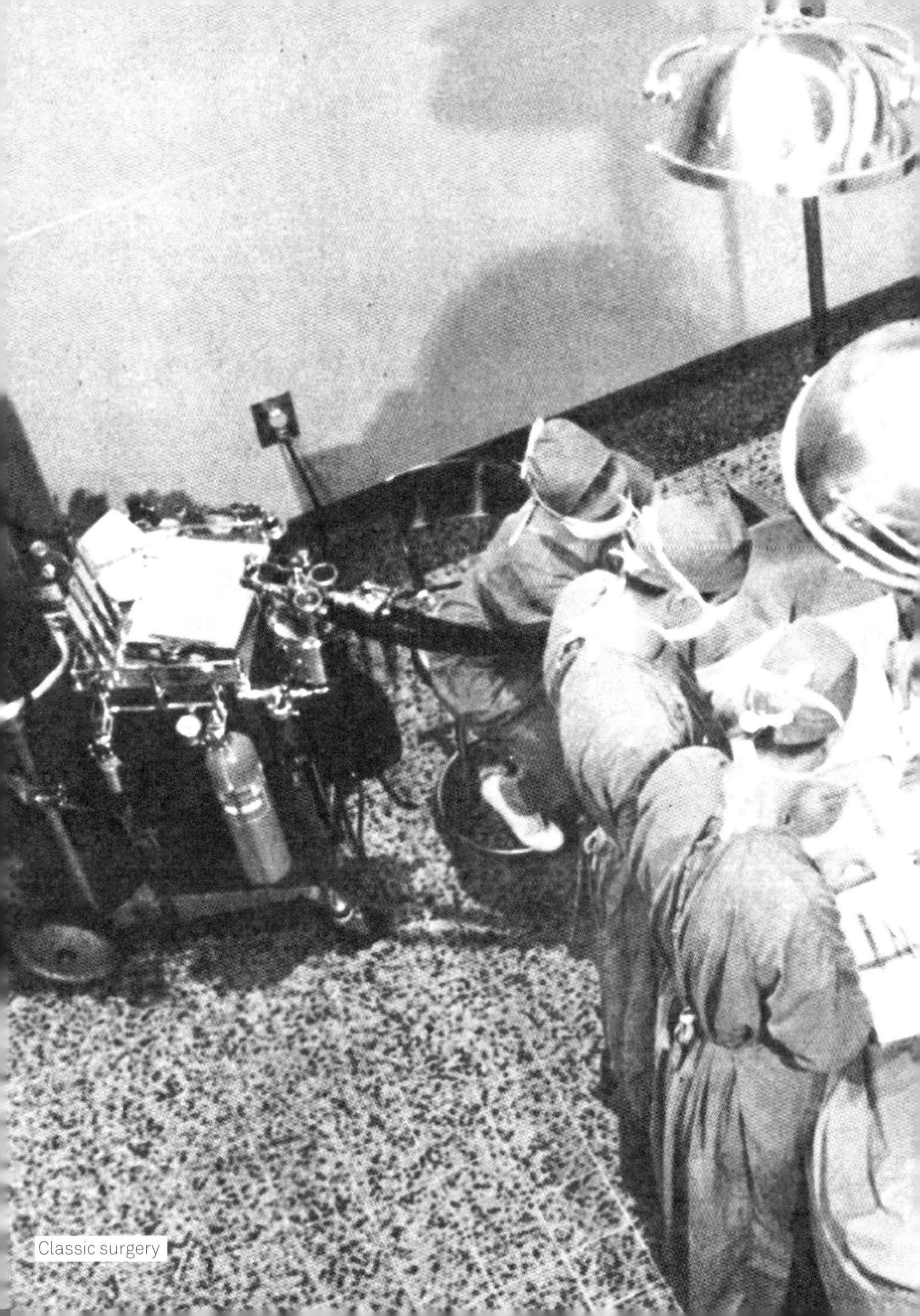
Classic surgery

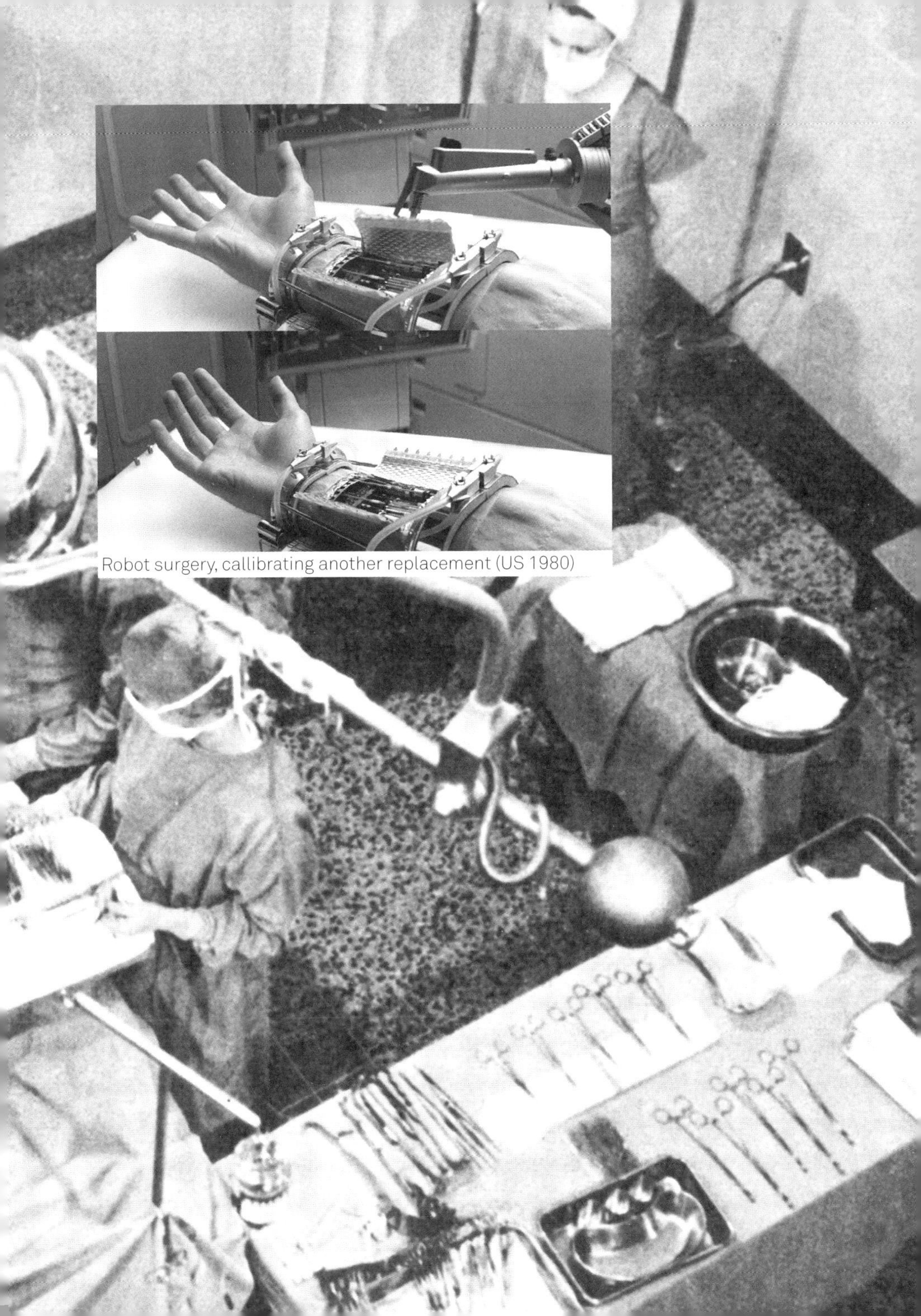

Robot surgery, callibrating another replacement (US 1980)

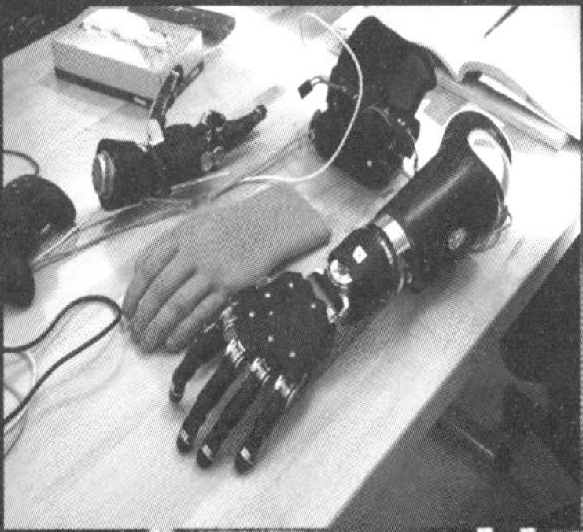

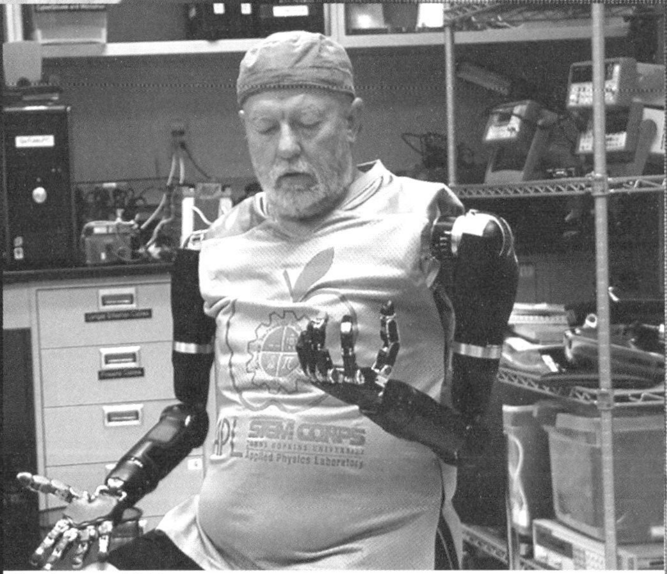

Bionic man, 2014

Computer added surgery (US 2017)

Veteran with robotic arm

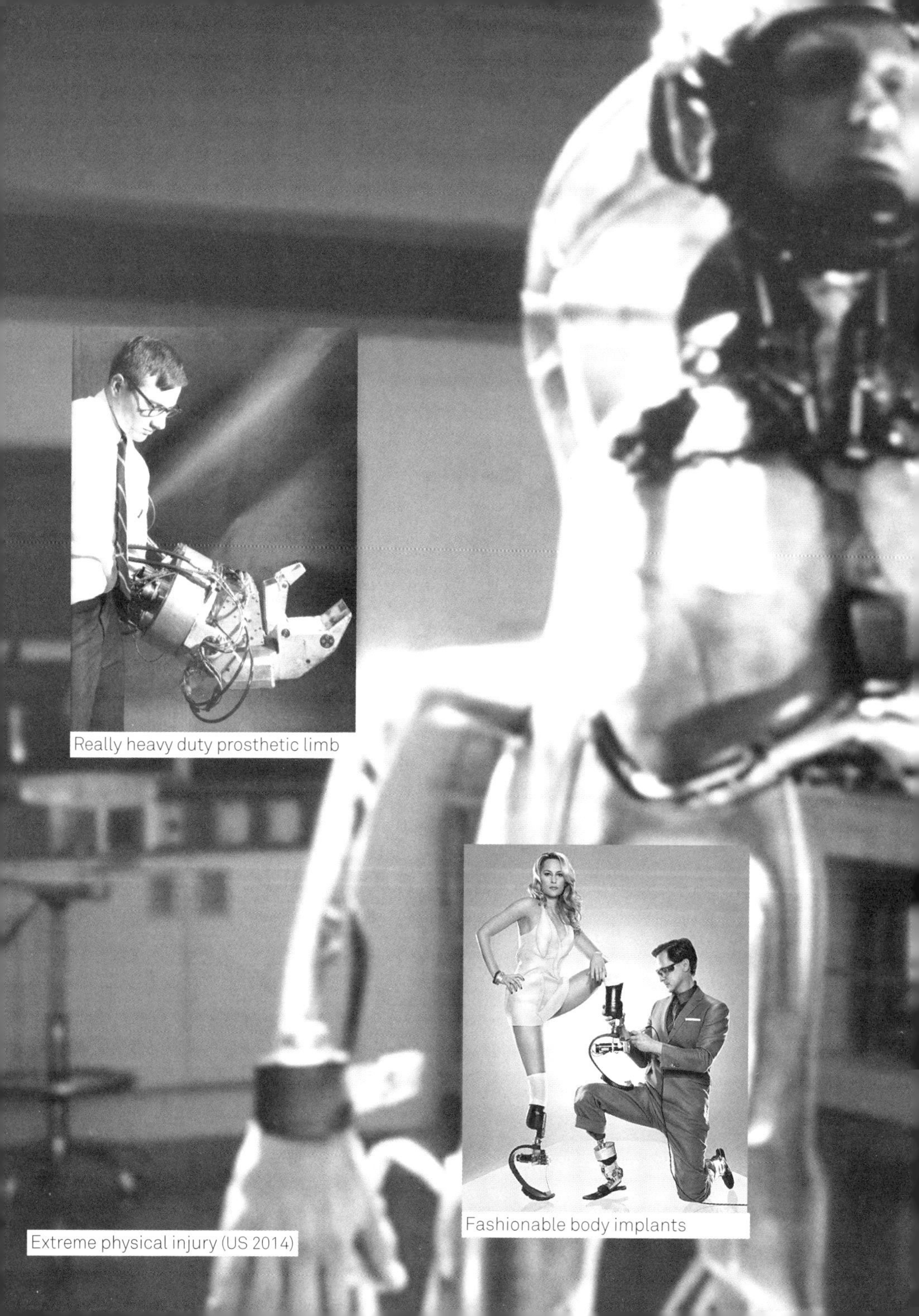

Really heavy duty prosthetic limb

Fashionable body implants

Extreme physical injury (US 2014)

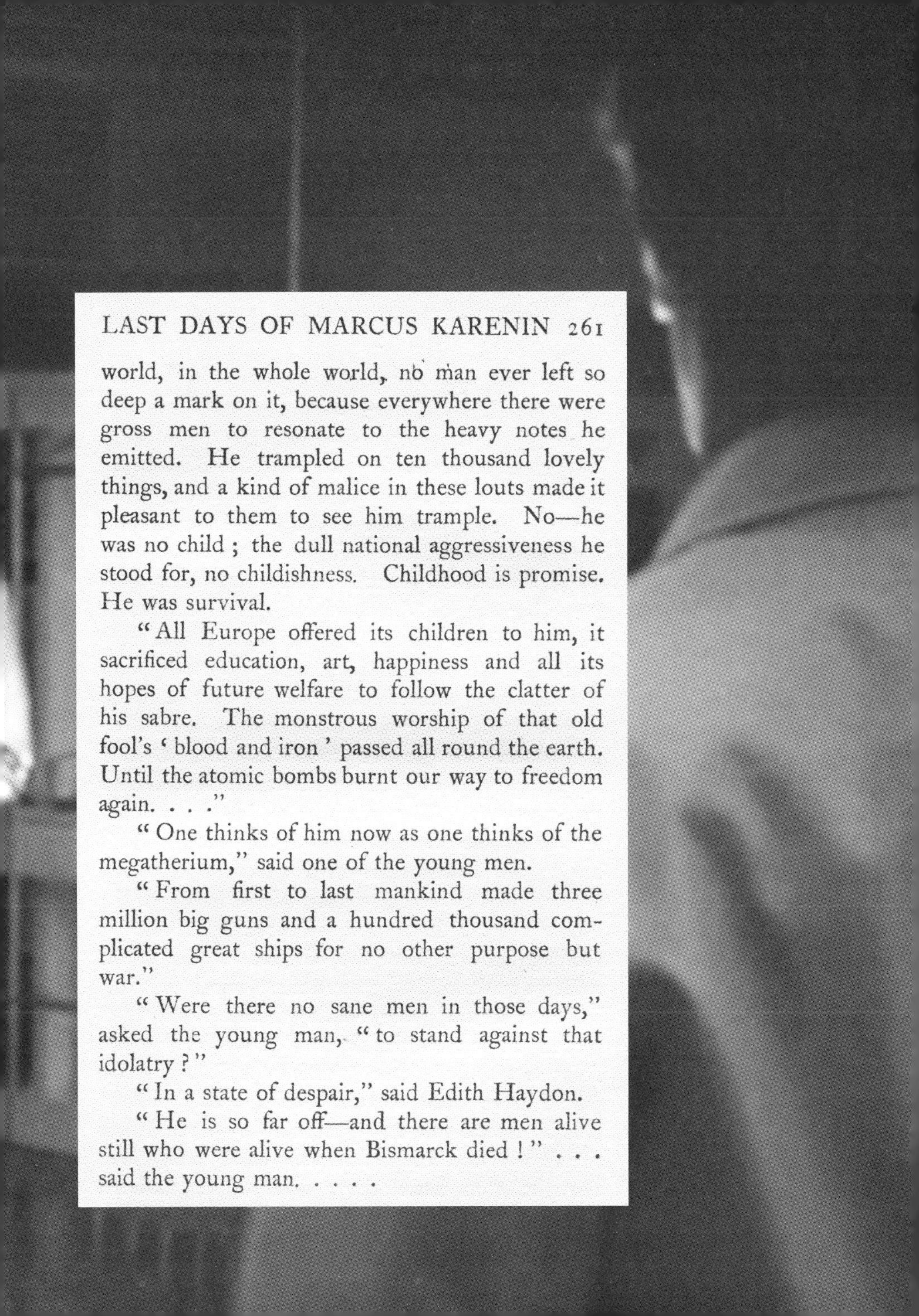

world, in the whole world, no man ever left so deep a mark on it, because everywhere there were gross men to resonate to the heavy notes he emitted. He trampled on ten thousand lovely things, and a kind of malice in these louts made it pleasant to them to see him trample. No—he was no child ; the dull national aggressiveness he stood for, no childishness. Childhood is promise. He was survival.

"All Europe offered its children to him, it sacrificed education, art, happiness and all its hopes of future welfare to follow the clatter of his sabre. The monstrous worship of that old fool's 'blood and iron' passed all round the earth. Until the atomic bombs burnt our way to freedom again. . . ."

"One thinks of him now as one thinks of the megatherium," said one of the young men.

"From first to last mankind made three million big guns and a hundred thousand complicated great ships for no other purpose but war."

"Were there no sane men in those days," asked the young man, "to stand against that idolatry ?"

"In a state of despair," said Edith Haydon.

"He is so far off—and there are men alive still who were alive when Bismarck died ! " . . . said the young man. . . . .

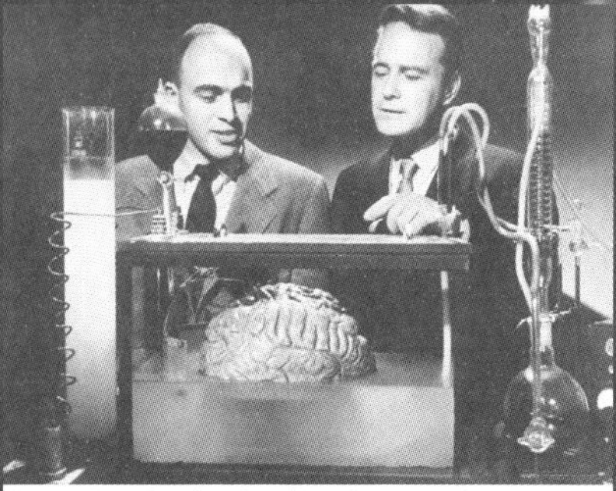
Keeping the brain alive (US 1953)

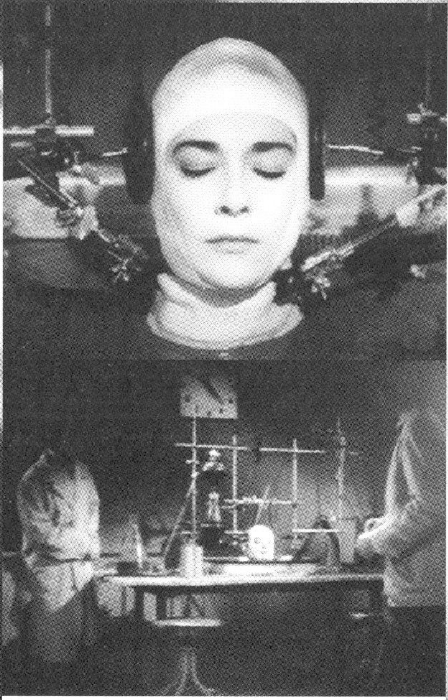
Keeping the mind alive (US 1962)

Confused (US 1931)

§ 5

"And yet it may be I am unjust to Bismarck," said Karenin, following his own thoughts. "You see men belong to their own age; we stand upon a common stock of thought and we fancy we stand upon the ground. I met a pleasant man the other day, a Maori, whose great-grandfather was a cannibal. It chanced he had a Daguerreotype of the old sinner, and the two were marvellously alike. One felt that a little juggling with time and either might have been the other. People are cruel and stupid in a stupid age who might be gentle and splendid in a gracious one. The world also has its moods. Think of the mental food of Bismarck's childhood; the humiliations of Napoleon's victories, the crowded crowning victory of the Battle of the Nations. . . . Everybody in those days, wise or foolish, believed that the division of the world under a multitude of governments was inevitable, and that it was going on for thousands of years more. It *was* inevitable until it was impossible. Anyone who had denied that inevitability publicly would have been counted—oh! a *silly* fellow. Old Bismarck was only just a little—forcible, on the lines of the accepted ideas. That is all. He thought that since there had to be national governments he would make one that was strong

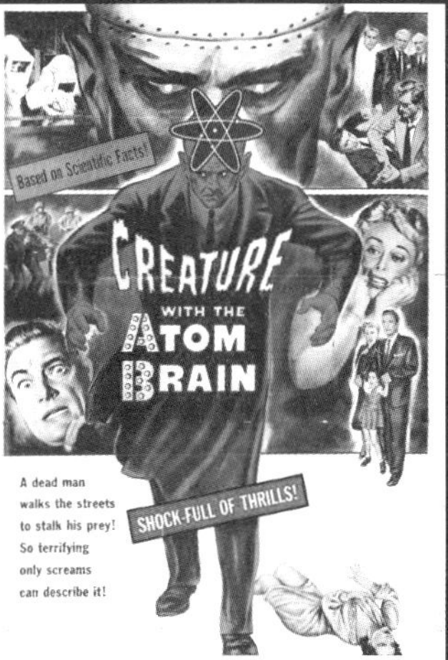

Golden age of B-movies, 1955

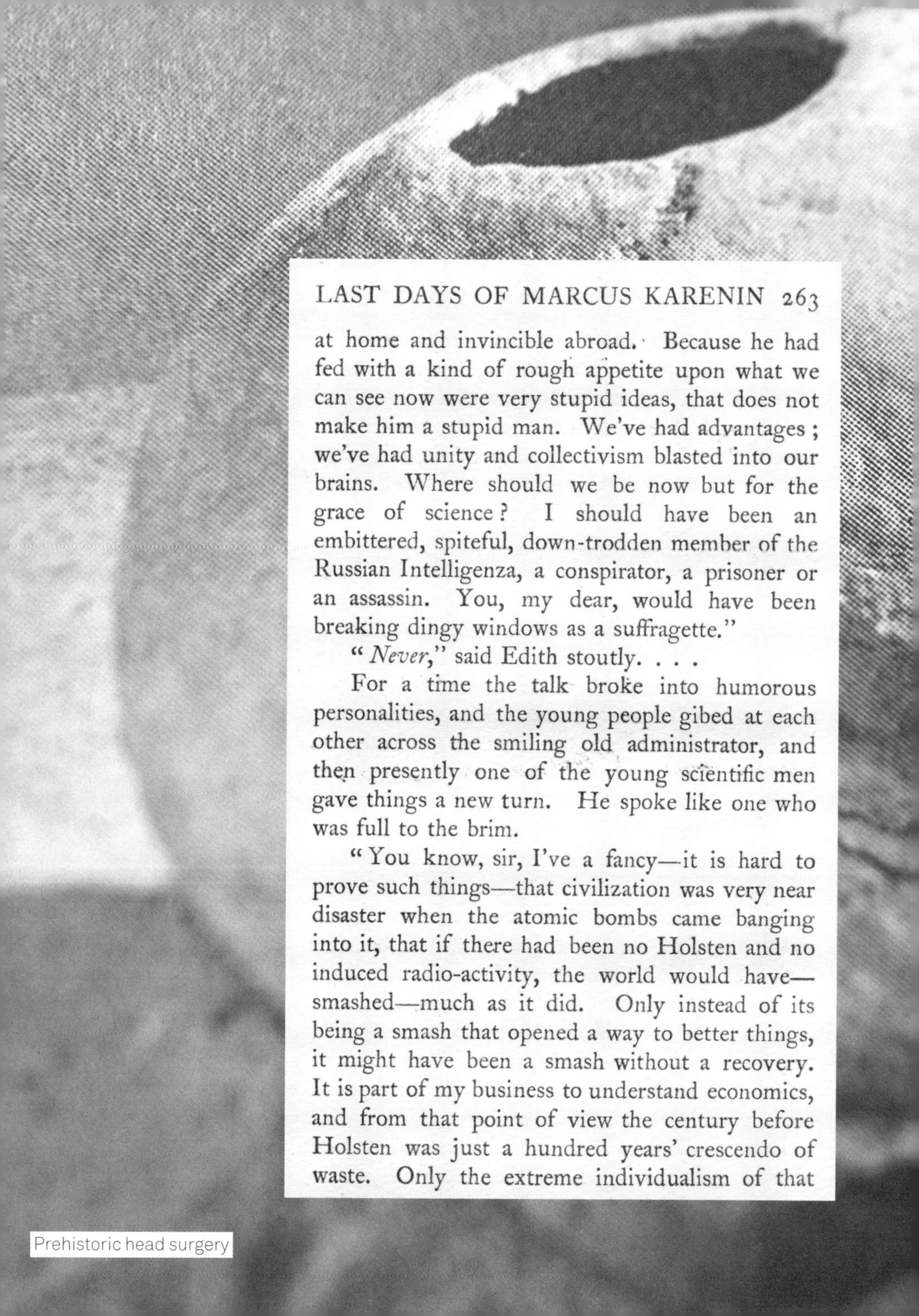

at home and invincible abroad. Because he had fed with a kind of rough appetite upon what we can see now were very stupid ideas, that does not make him a stupid man. We've had advantages; we've had unity and collectivism blasted into our brains. Where should we be now but for the grace of science? I should have been an embittered, spiteful, down-trodden member of the Russian Intelligenza, a conspirator, a prisoner or an assassin. You, my dear, would have been breaking dingy windows as a suffragette."

"*Never*," said Edith stoutly. . . .

For a time the talk broke into humorous personalities, and the young people gibed at each other across the smiling old administrator, and then presently one of the young scientific men gave things a new turn. He spoke like one who was full to the brim.

"You know, sir, I've a fancy—it is hard to prove such things—that civilization was very near disaster when the atomic bombs came banging into it, that if there had been no Holsten and no induced radio-activity, the world would have—smashed—much as it did. Only instead of its being a smash that opened a way to better things, it might have been a smash without a recovery. It is part of my business to understand economics, and from that point of view the century before Holsten was just a hundred years' crescendo of waste. Only the extreme individualism of that

Prehistoric head surgery

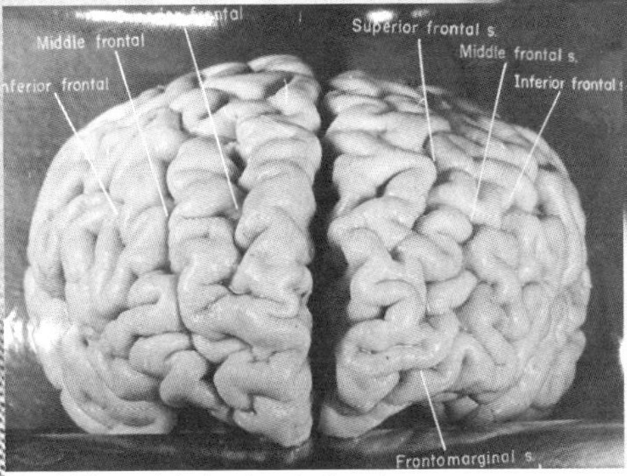

Prof. Einstein's brain, obviously

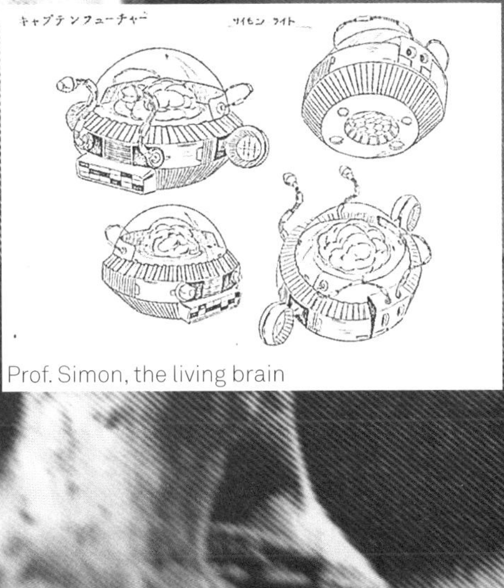

Prof. Simon, the living brain

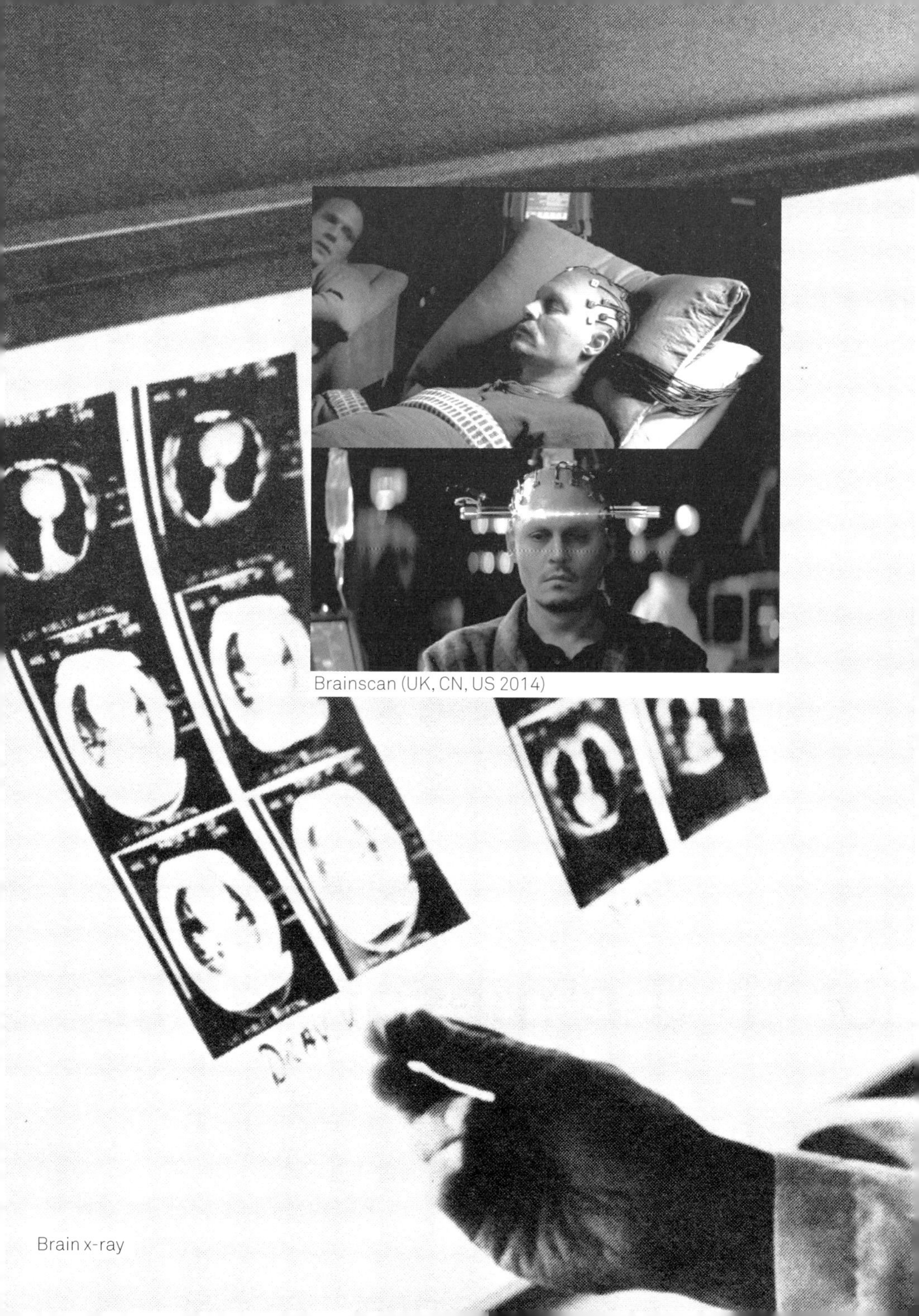

Brainscan (UK, CN, US 2014)

Brain x-ray

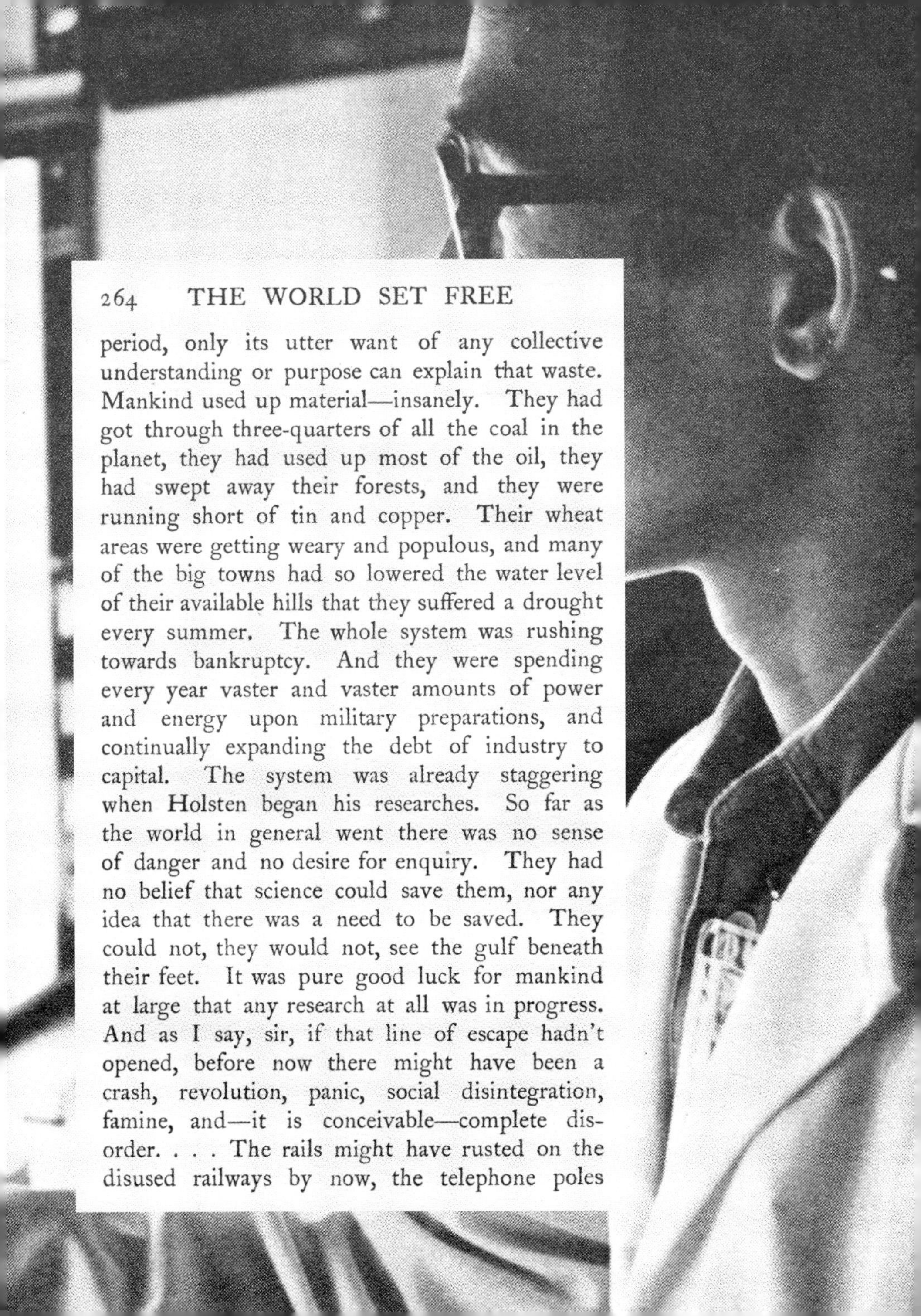

period, only its utter want of any collective understanding or purpose can explain that waste. Mankind used up material—insanely. They had got through three-quarters of all the coal in the planet, they had used up most of the oil, they had swept away their forests, and they were running short of tin and copper. Their wheat areas were getting weary and populous, and many of the big towns had so lowered the water level of their available hills that they suffered a drought every summer. The whole system was rushing towards bankruptcy. And they were spending every year vaster and vaster amounts of power and energy upon military preparations, and continually expanding the debt of industry to capital. The system was already staggering when Holsten began his researches. So far as the world in general went there was no sense of danger and no desire for enquiry. They had no belief that science could save them, nor any idea that there was a need to be saved. They could not, they would not, see the gulf beneath their feet. It was pure good luck for mankind at large that any research at all was in progress. And as I say, sir, if that line of escape hadn't opened, before now there might have been a crash, revolution, panic, social disintegration, famine, and—it is conceivable—complete disorder. . . . The rails might have rusted on the disused railways by now, the telephone poles

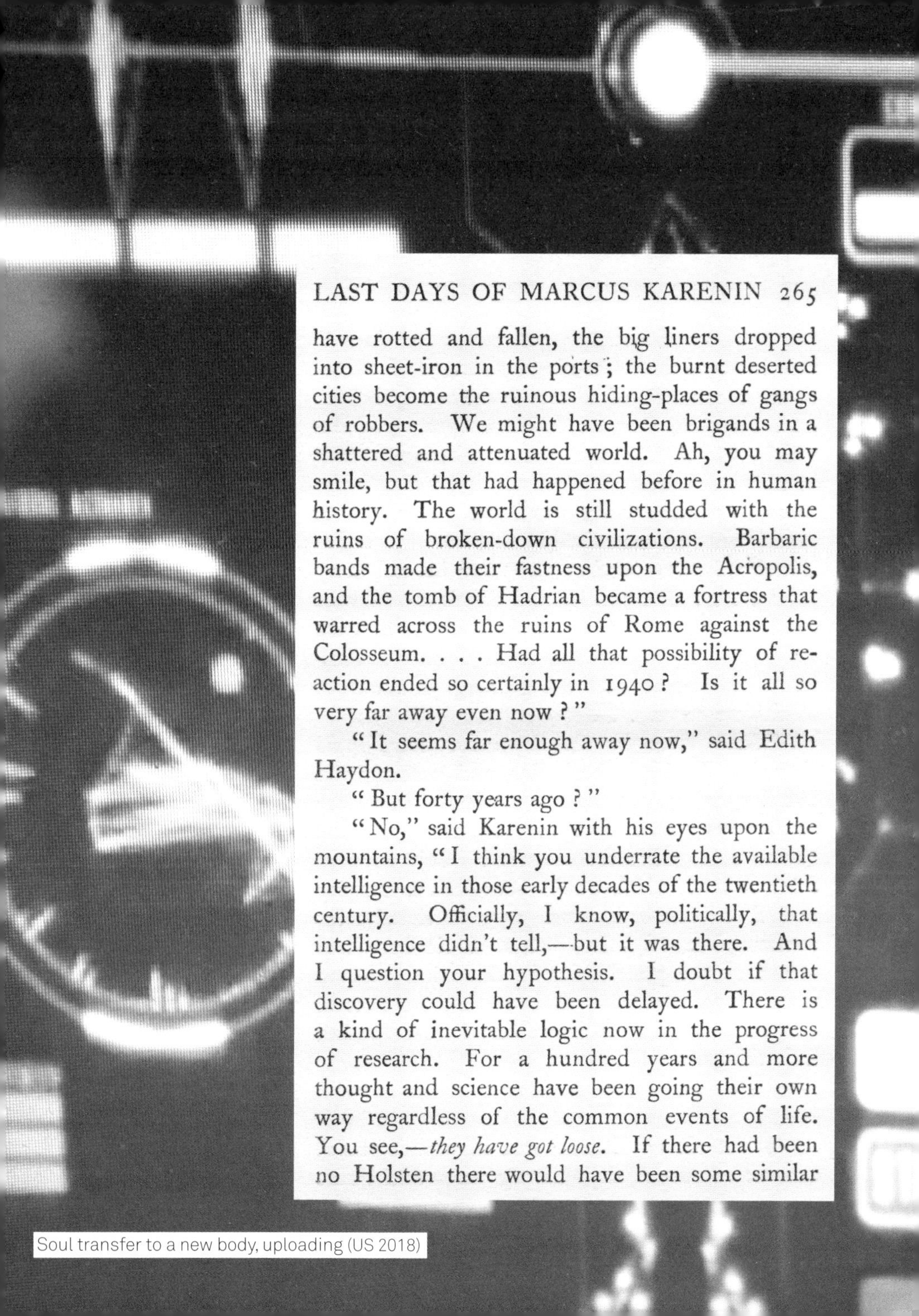

have rotted and fallen, the big liners dropped into sheet-iron in the ports; the burnt deserted cities become the ruinous hiding-places of gangs of robbers. We might have been brigands in a shattered and attenuated world. Ah, you may smile, but that had happened before in human history. The world is still studded with the ruins of broken-down civilizations. Barbaric bands made their fastness upon the Acropolis, and the tomb of Hadrian became a fortress that warred across the ruins of Rome against the Colosseum. . . . Had all that possibility of reaction ended so certainly in 1940? Is it all so very far away even now?"

"It seems far enough away now," said Edith Haydon.

"But forty years ago?"

"No," said Karenin with his eyes upon the mountains, "I think you underrate the available intelligence in those early decades of the twentieth century. Officially, I know, politically, that intelligence didn't tell,—but it was there. And I question your hypothesis. I doubt if that discovery could have been delayed. There is a kind of inevitable logic now in the progress of research. For a hundred years and more thought and science have been going their own way regardless of the common events of life. You see,—*they have got loose*. If there had been no Holsten there would have been some similar

Soul transfer to a new body, uploading (US 2018)

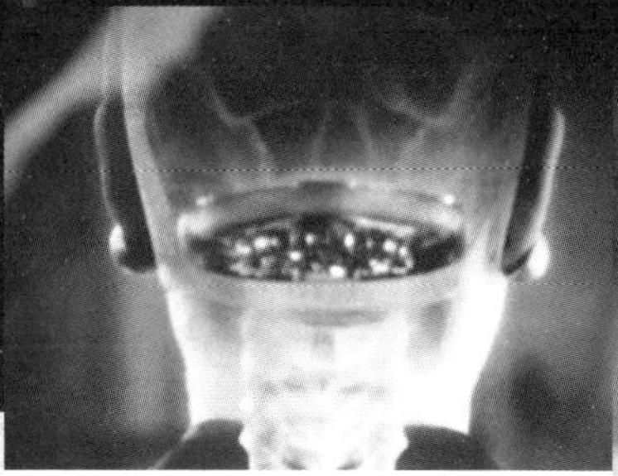
Mind-memory-implant (US 2018)

man. If atomic energy had not come in one year it would have come in another. In decadent Rome the march of science had scarcely begun. . . . Nineveh, Babylon, Athens, Syracuse, Alexandria, these were the first rough experiments in association that made a security, a breathing-space, in which enquiry was born. Man had to experiment before he found out the way to begin. But already two hundred years ago he had fairly begun. . . . The politics and dignities and wars of the nineteenth and twentieth centuries were only the last phœnix blaze of the former civilization flaring up about the beginnings of the new. Which we serve. . . .

"Man lives in the dawn for ever," said Karenin. "Life is beginning and nothing else but beginning. It begins everlastingly. Each step seems vaster than the last, and does but gather us together for the next. This Modern State of ours, which would have been a Utopian marvel a hundred years ago, is already the commonplace of life. But as I sit here and dream of the possibilities in the mind of man that now gather to a head beneath the shelter of its peace, these great mountains here seem but little things. . . ."

§ 6

About eleven Karenin had his midday meal, and afterwards he slept among his artificial furs

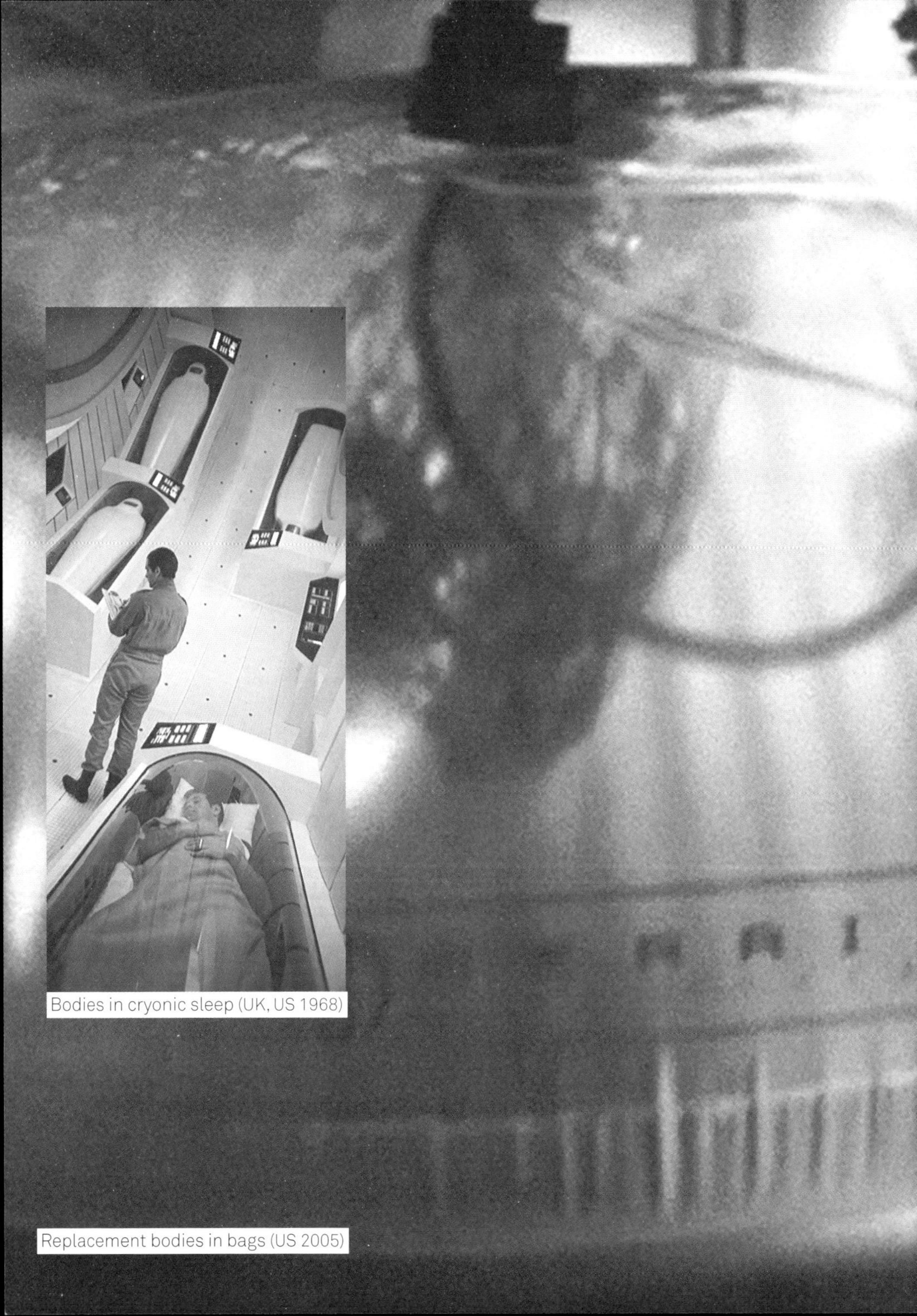
Bodies in cryonic sleep (UK, US 1968)

Replacement bodies in bags (US 2005)

and pillows for two hours. Then he awoke and some tea was brought to him, and he attended to a small difficulty in connection with the Moravian schools in the Labrador country and in Greenland that Gardener knew would interest him. He remained alone for a little while after that, and then the two women came to him again. Afterwards Edwards and Kahn joined the group, and the talk fell upon love and the place of women in the renascent world. The cloudbanks of India lay under a quivering haze, and the blaze of the sun fell full upon the eastward precipices. Ever and again as they talked some vast splinter of rock would crack and come away from these, or a wild rush of snow and ice and stone, pour down in thunder, hang like a wet thread into the gulfs below, and cease. . . .

§ 7

For a time Karenin said very little, and Kahn, the popular poet, talked of passionate love. He said that passionate personal love had been the abiding desire of humanity since ever humanity had begun, and now only was it becoming a possible experience. It had been a dream that generation after generation had pursued, that always men had lost on the verge of attainment. To most of those who had sought it obstinately it had brought tragedy. Now, lifted above sordid

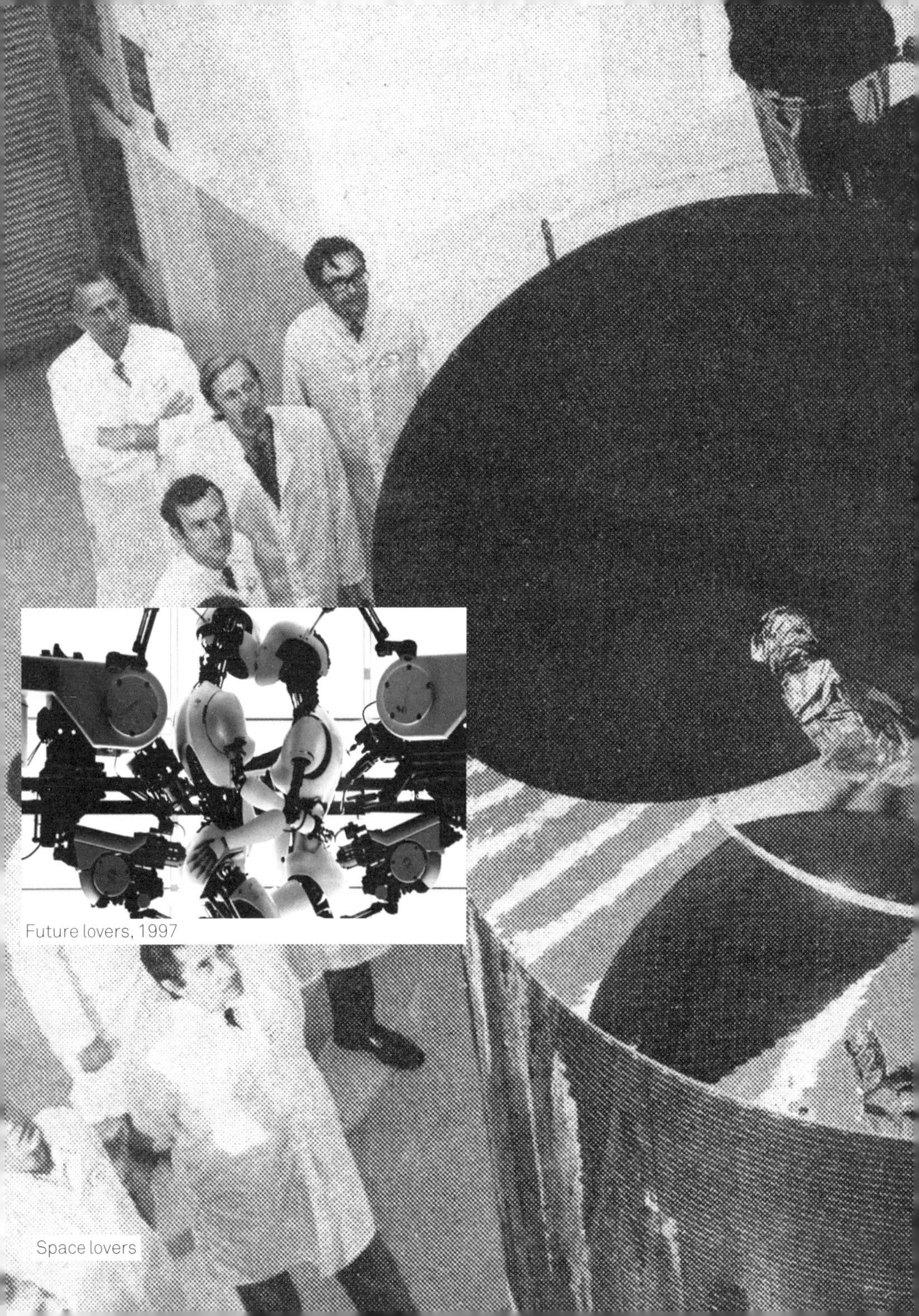

Future lovers, 1997

Space lovers

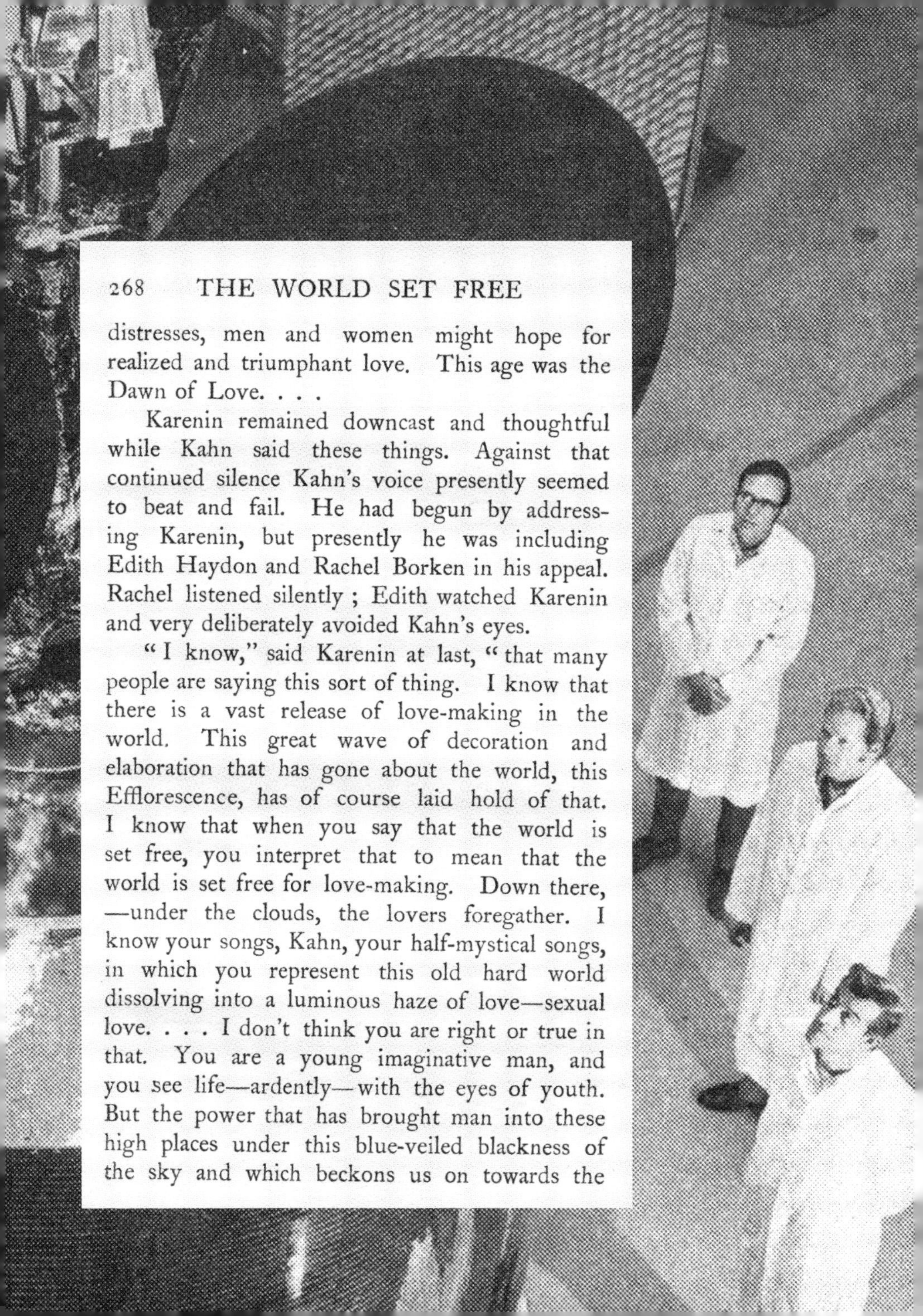

distresses, men and women might hope for realized and triumphant love. This age was the Dawn of Love. . . .

Karenin remained downcast and thoughtful while Kahn said these things. Against that continued silence Kahn's voice presently seemed to beat and fail. He had begun by addressing Karenin, but presently he was including Edith Haydon and Rachel Borken in his appeal. Rachel listened silently ; Edith watched Karenin and very deliberately avoided Kahn's eyes.

"I know," said Karenin at last, "that many people are saying this sort of thing. I know that there is a vast release of love-making in the world. This great wave of decoration and elaboration that has gone about the world, this Efflorescence, has of course laid hold of that. I know that when you say that the world is set free, you interpret that to mean that the world is set free for love-making. Down there, —under the clouds, the lovers foregather. I know your songs, Kahn, your half-mystical songs, in which you represent this old hard world dissolving into a luminous haze of love—sexual love. . . . I don't think you are right or true in that. You are a young imaginative man, and you see life—ardently—with the eyes of youth. But the power that has brought man into these high places under this blue-veiled blackness of the sky and which beckons us on towards the

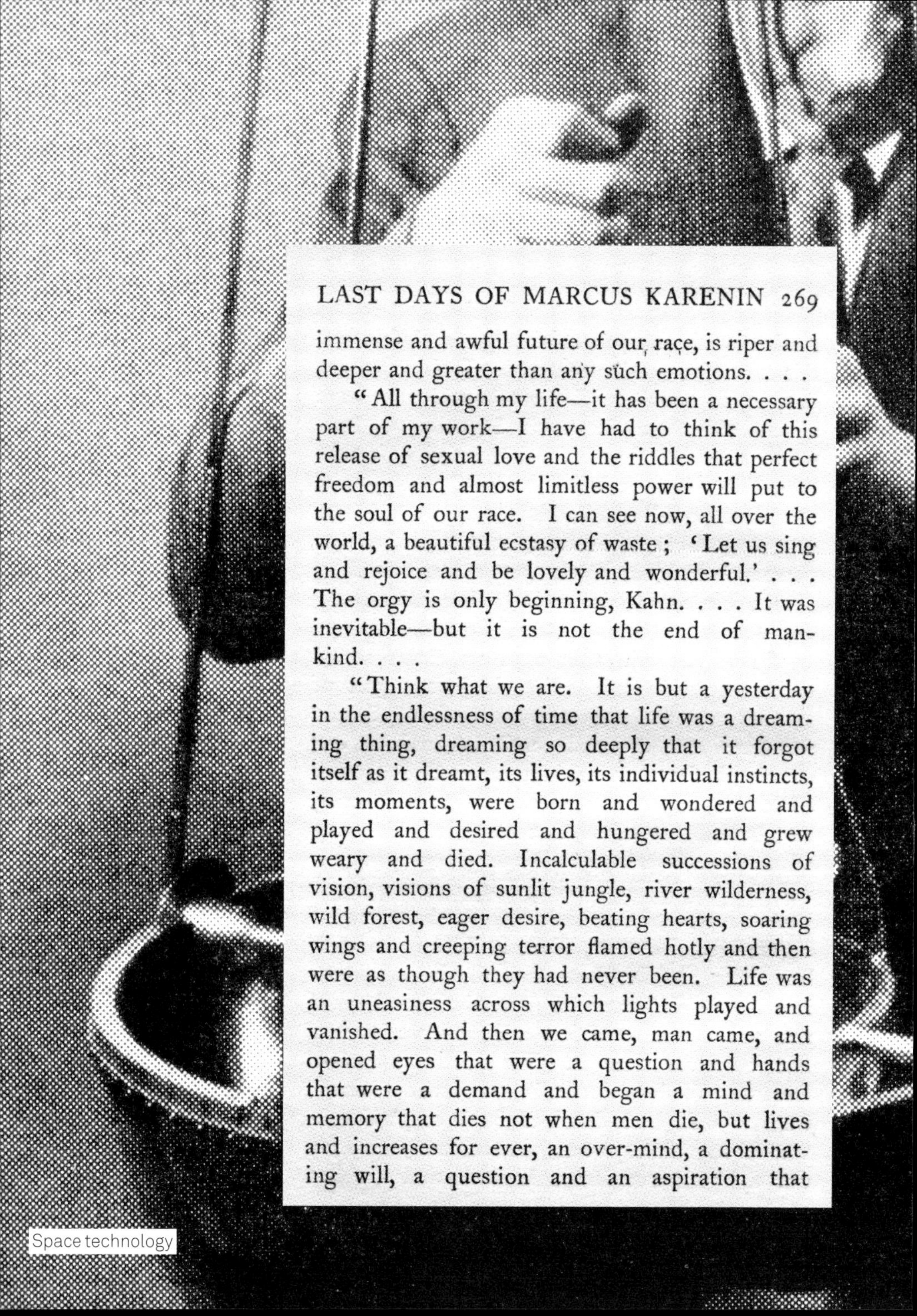

immense and awful future of our race, is riper and deeper and greater than any such emotions. . . .

"All through my life—it has been a necessary part of my work—I have had to think of this release of sexual love and the riddles that perfect freedom and almost limitless power will put to the soul of our race. I can see now, all over the world, a beautiful ecstasy of waste; 'Let us sing and rejoice and be lovely and wonderful.' . . . The orgy is only beginning, Kahn. . . . It was inevitable—but it is not the end of mankind. . . .

"Think what we are. It is but a yesterday in the endlessness of time that life was a dreaming thing, dreaming so deeply that it forgot itself as it dreamt, its lives, its individual instincts, its moments, were born and wondered and played and desired and hungered and grew weary and died. Incalculable successions of vision, visions of sunlit jungle, river wilderness, wild forest, eager desire, beating hearts, soaring wings and creeping terror flamed hotly and then were as though they had never been. Life was an uneasiness across which lights played and vanished. And then we came, man came, and opened eyes that were a question and hands that were a demand and began a mind and memory that dies not when men die, but lives and increases for ever, an over-mind, a dominating will, a question and an aspiration that

Space technology

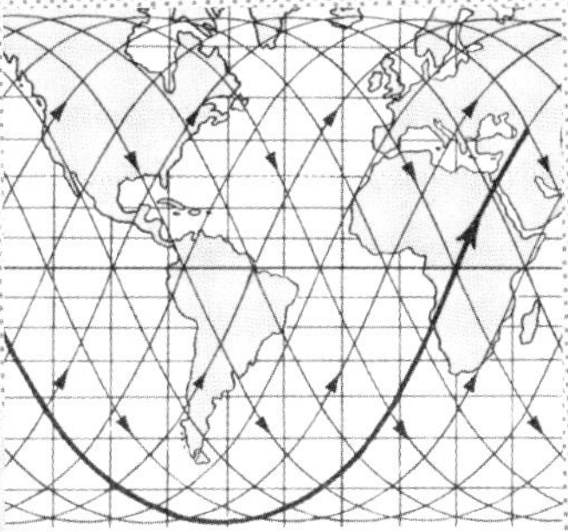
Orbits

reaches to the stars. . . . Hunger and fear and this that you make so much of, this sex, are but the elementals of life out of which we have arisen. All these elementals, I grant you, have to be provided for, dealt with, satisfied, but all these things have to be left behind."

"But Love," said Kahn.

"I speak of sexual love and the love of intimate persons. And that is what you mean, Kahn."

Karenin shook his head. "You cannot stay at the roots and climb the tree," he said. . . .

"No," he said after a pause, "this sexual excitement, this love story, is just a part of growing up and we grow out of it. So far literature and art and sentiment and all our emotional forms have been almost altogether adolescent, plays and stories, delights and hopes, they have all turned on that marvellous discovery of the love interest, but life lengthens out now and the mind of adult humanity detaches itself. Poets who used to die at thirty live now to eighty-five. You too, Kahn! There are endless years yet for you—and all full of learning. . . . We carry an excessive burthen of sex and sexual tradition still and we have to free ourselves from it. We do free ourselves from it. We have learnt in a thousand different ways to hold back death, and this sex, which in the old barbaric days was just sufficient to balance our dying, is now like a hammer that has lost

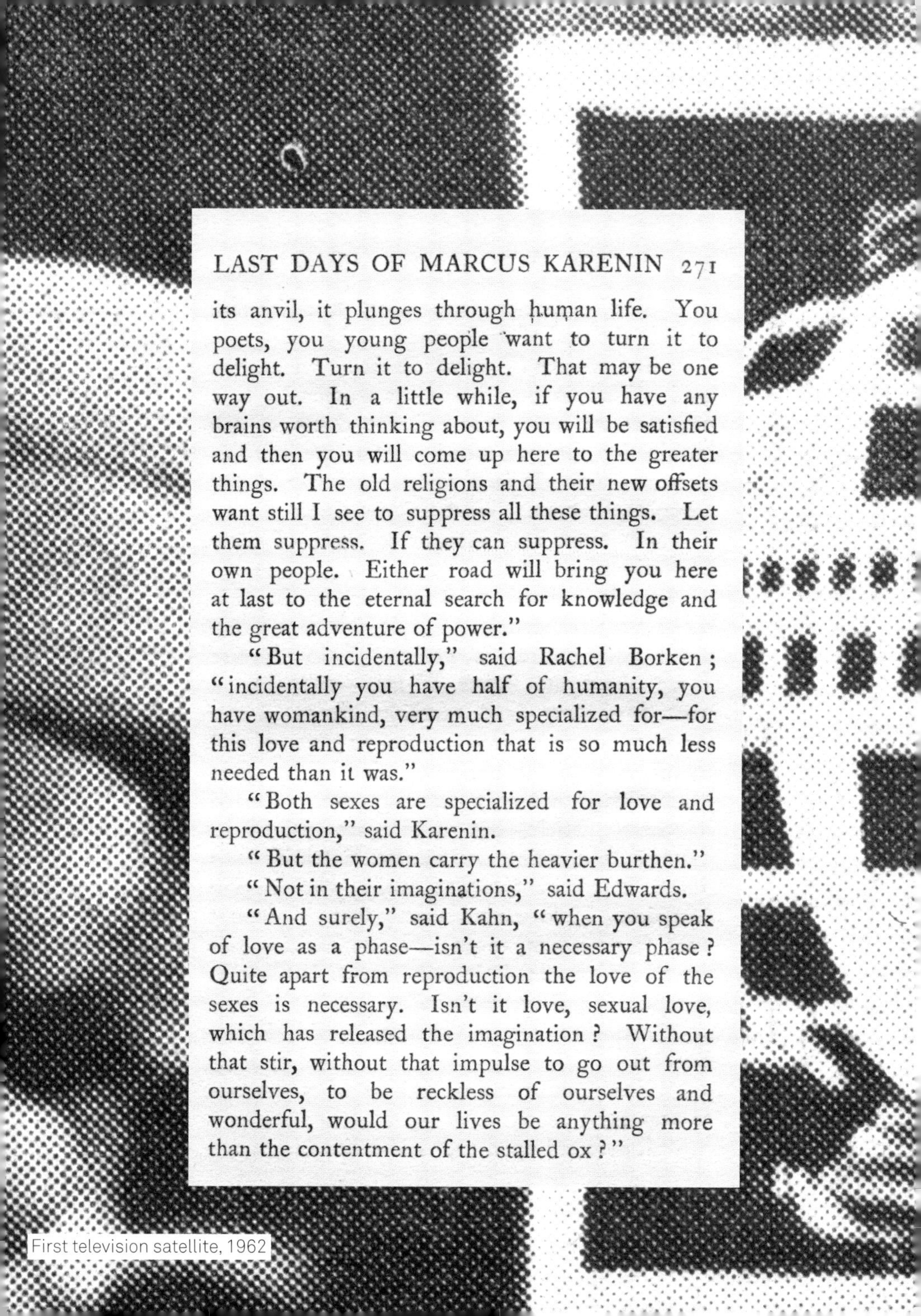

its anvil, it plunges through human life. You poets, you young people want to turn it to delight. Turn it to delight. That may be one way out. In a little while, if you have any brains worth thinking about, you will be satisfied and then you will come up here to the greater things. The old religions and their new offsets want still I see to suppress all these things. Let them suppress. If they can suppress. In their own people. Either road will bring you here at last to the eternal search for knowledge and the great adventure of power."

"But incidentally," said Rachel Borken; "incidentally you have half of humanity, you have womankind, very much specialized for—for this love and reproduction that is so much less needed than it was."

"Both sexes are specialized for love and reproduction," said Karenin.

"But the women carry the heavier burthen."

"Not in their imaginations," said Edwards.

"And surely," said Kahn, "when you speak of love as a phase—isn't it a necessary phase? Quite apart from reproduction the love of the sexes is necessary. Isn't it love, sexual love, which has released the imagination? Without that stir, without that impulse to go out from ourselves, to be reckless of ourselves and wonderful, would our lives be anything more than the contentment of the stalled ox?"

First television satellite, 1962

" The key that opens the door," said Karenin, " is not the goal of the journey."

" But women ! " cried Rachel. " Here we are ! What is our future—as women ? Is it only that we have unlocked the doors of the imagination for you men ? Let us speak of this question now. It is a thing constantly in my thoughts, Karenin. What do you think of us ? You who must have thought so much of these perplexities."

Karenin seemed to weigh his words. He spoke very deliberately. " I do not care a rap about your future—as women. I do not care a rap about the future of men—as males. I want to destroy these peculiar futures. I care for your future as intelligences, as parts of and contribution to the universal mind of the race. Humanity is not only naturally overspecialized in these matters, but all its institutions, its customs, everything, exaggerate, intensify this difference. I want to unspecialize women. No new idea. Plato wanted exactly that. I do not want to go on as we go now, emphasizing this natural difference ; I do not deny it, but I want to reduce it and overcome it."

" And—we remain women," said Rachel Borken.

" Need you remain thinking of yourselves as women ? "

" It is forced upon us," said Edith Haydon.

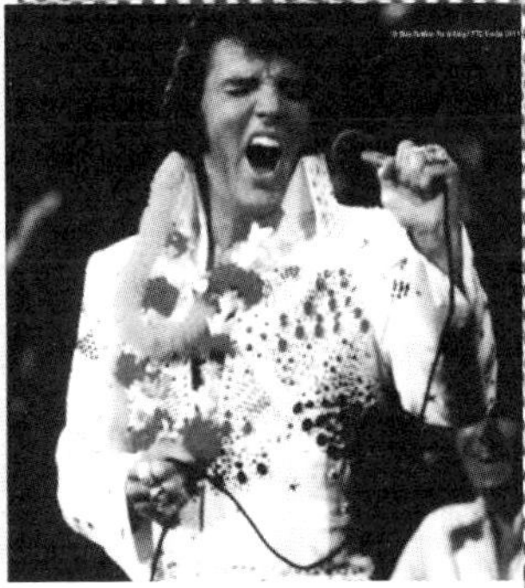

Worldwide transmission, 1973

"I do not think a woman becomes less of a woman because she dresses and works like a man," said Edwards. "You women here, I mean you scientific women, wear white clothing like the men, twist up your hair in the simplest fashion, go about your work as though there was only one sex in the world. You are just as much women, even if you are not so feminine, as the fine ladies down below there in the plains who dress for excitement and display, whose only thoughts are of lovers, who exaggerate every difference. . . . Indeed we love you more. . . ."

"But we go about our work," said Edith Haydon.

"So does it matter?" asked Rachel.

"If you go about your work and if the men go about their work then for Heaven's sake be as much woman as you wish," said Karenin. "When I ask you to unspecialize, I am thinking not of the abolition of sex, but the abolition of the irksome, restricting, obstructive obsession with sex. It may be true that sex made society, that the first society was the sex-cemented family, the first state a confederacy of blood relations, the first laws sexual taboos. Until a few years ago morality meant proper sexual behaviour. Up to within a few years of us the chief interest and motive of an ordinary man was to keep and rule a woman and her children and the chief concern of a woman was to get a man to do that. That

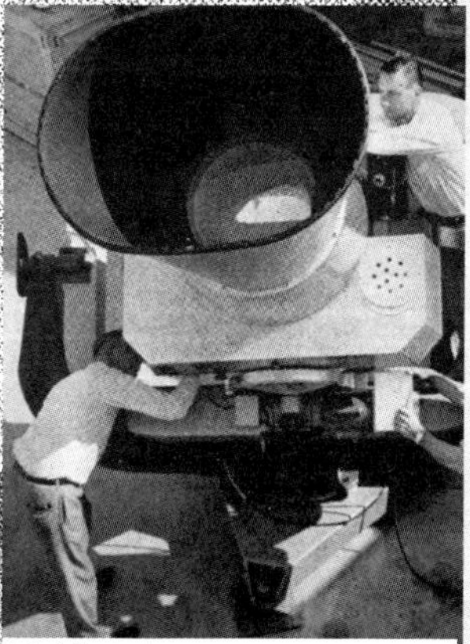

Mobile telescope

Big telescope in Hamburg

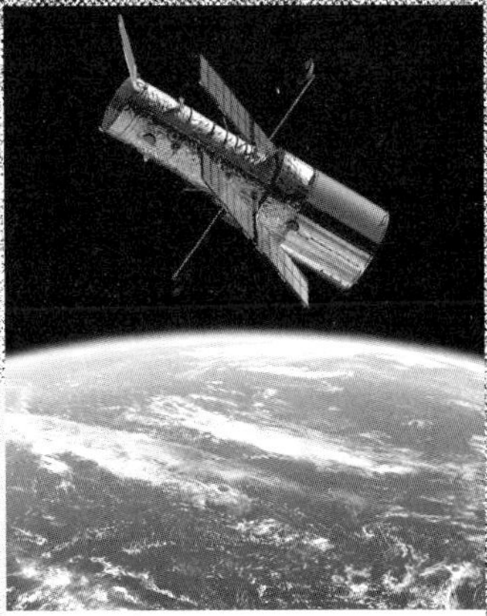

Space telescope

was the drama, that was life. And the jealousy of these demands was the master motive in the world. You said, Kahn, a little while ago that sexual love was the key that let one out from the solitude of self, but I tell you that so far it has only done so in order to lock us all up again in a solitude of two. . . . All that may have been necessary but it is necessary no longer. All that has changed and changes still very swiftly. Your future, Rachel, *as women*, is a diminishing future."

"Karenin?" asked Rachel, "do you mean that women are to become men?"

"Men and women have to become human beings."

"You would abolish women? But, Karenin, listen! There is more than sex in this. Apart from sex we are different from you. We take up life differently. Forget we are—females, Karenin, and still we are a different sort of human being with a different use. In some things we are amazingly secondary. Here am I in this place because of my trick of management, and Edith is here because of her patient, subtle hands. That does not alter the fact that nearly the whole body of science is man made; that does not alter the fact that men do so predominatingly make history, that you could nearly write a complete history of the world without mentioning a woman's name. And on

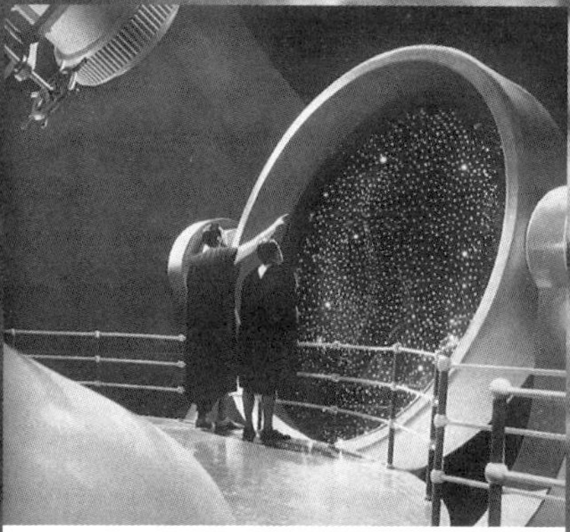

Tomorrow the stars

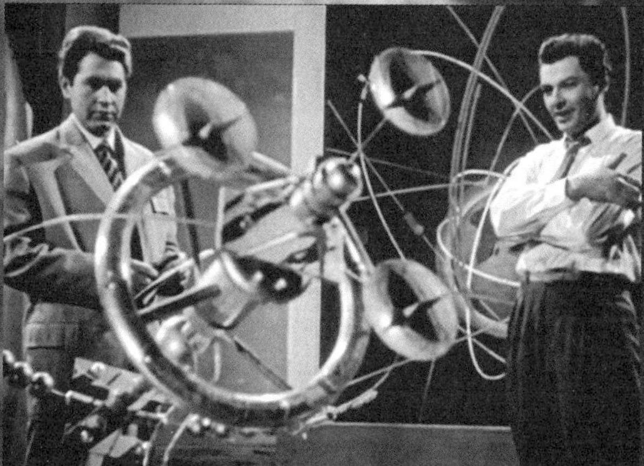

... and how this would have looked like (SU 1959)

Dream of days of future past (US 1977)

the other hand we have a gift of devotion, of inspiration, a distinctive power for truly loving beautiful things, a care for life and a peculiar keen close eye for behaviour. You know men are blind beside us in these last matters. You know they are restless—and fitful. We have a steadfastness. We may never draw the broad outlines nor discover the new paths, but in the future isn't there a confirming and sustaining and supplying rôle for us? As important perhaps as yours? Equally important. We hold the world up, Karenin, though you may have raised it."

"You know very well, Rachel, that I believe as you believe. I am not thinking of the abolition of woman. But I do want to abolish—the heroine, the sexual heroine. I want to abolish the woman whose support is jealousy and whose gift possession. I want to abolish the woman who can be won as a prize or locked up as a delicious treasure. And away down there the heroine flares like a divinity."

"In America," said Edwards, "men are fighting duels over the praises of women and holding tournaments before Queens of Beauty."

"I saw a beautiful girl in Lahore," said Kahn, "she sat under a golden canopy like a goddess and three fine men armed and dressed like the ancient paintings sat on steps below her to show

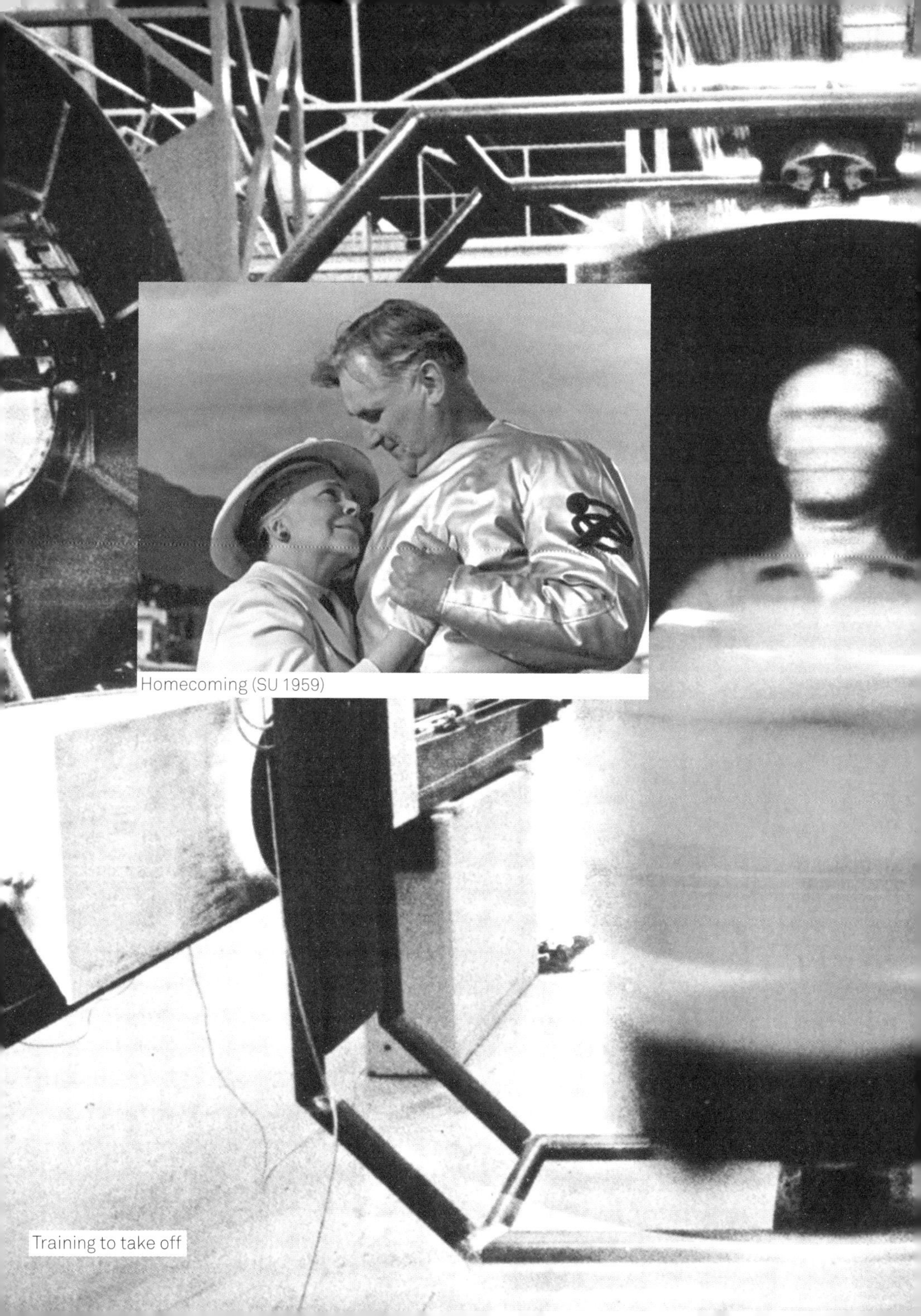

Homecoming (SU 1959)

Training to take off

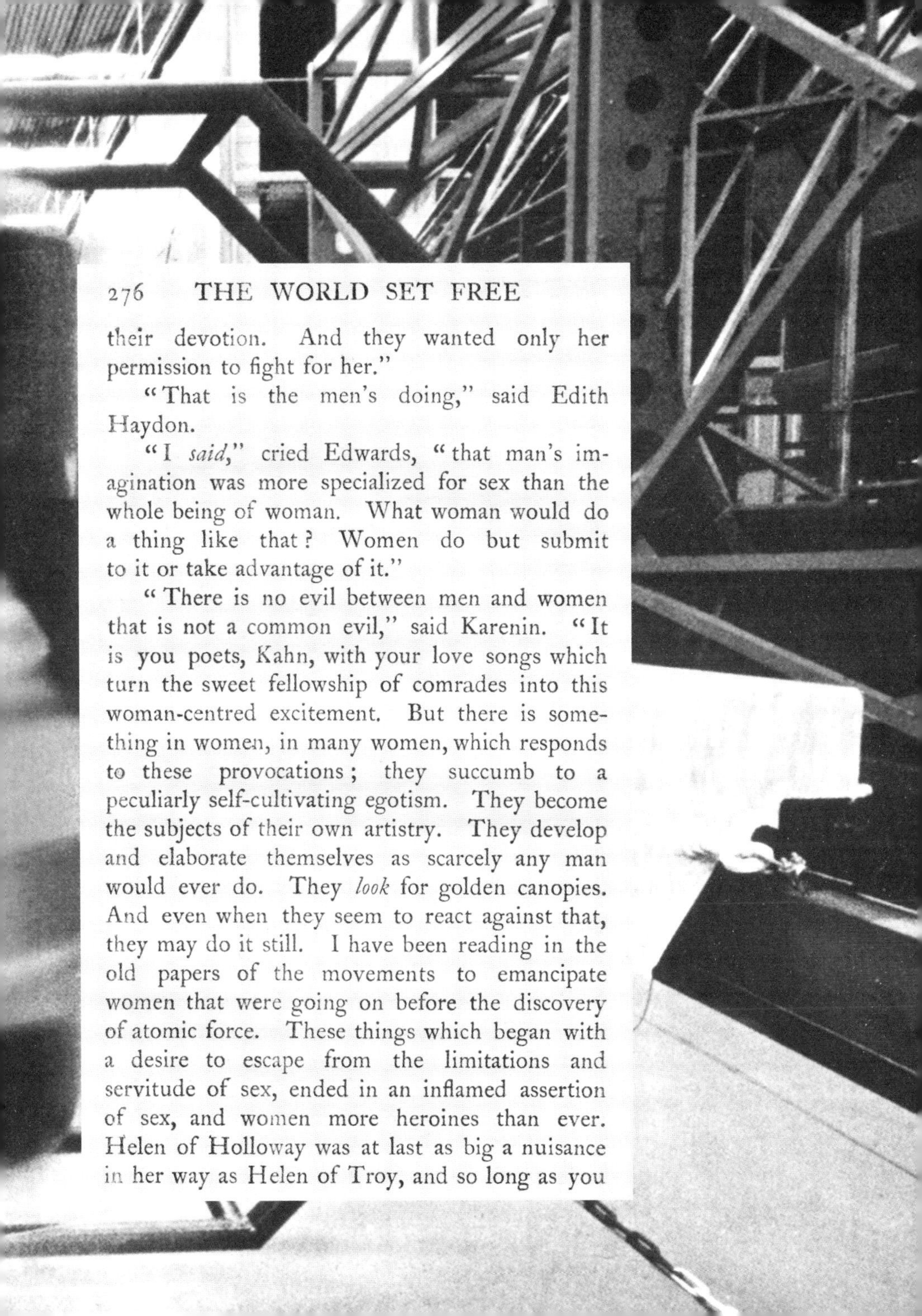

their devotion. And they wanted only her permission to fight for her."

"That is the men's doing," said Edith Haydon.

"I *said*," cried Edwards, "that man's imagination was more specialized for sex than the whole being of woman. What woman would do a thing like that? Women do but submit to it or take advantage of it."

"There is no evil between men and women that is not a common evil," said Karenin. "It is you poets, Kahn, with your love songs which turn the sweet fellowship of comrades into this woman-centred excitement. But there is something in women, in many women, which responds to these provocations; they succumb to a peculiarly self-cultivating egotism. They become the subjects of their own artistry. They develop and elaborate themselves as scarcely any man would ever do. They *look* for golden canopies. And even when they seem to react against that, they may do it still. I have been reading in the old papers of the movements to emancipate women that were going on before the discovery of atomic force. These things which began with a desire to escape from the limitations and servitude of sex, ended in an inflamed assertion of sex, and women more heroines than ever. Helen of Holloway was at last as big a nuisance in her way as Helen of Troy, and so long as you

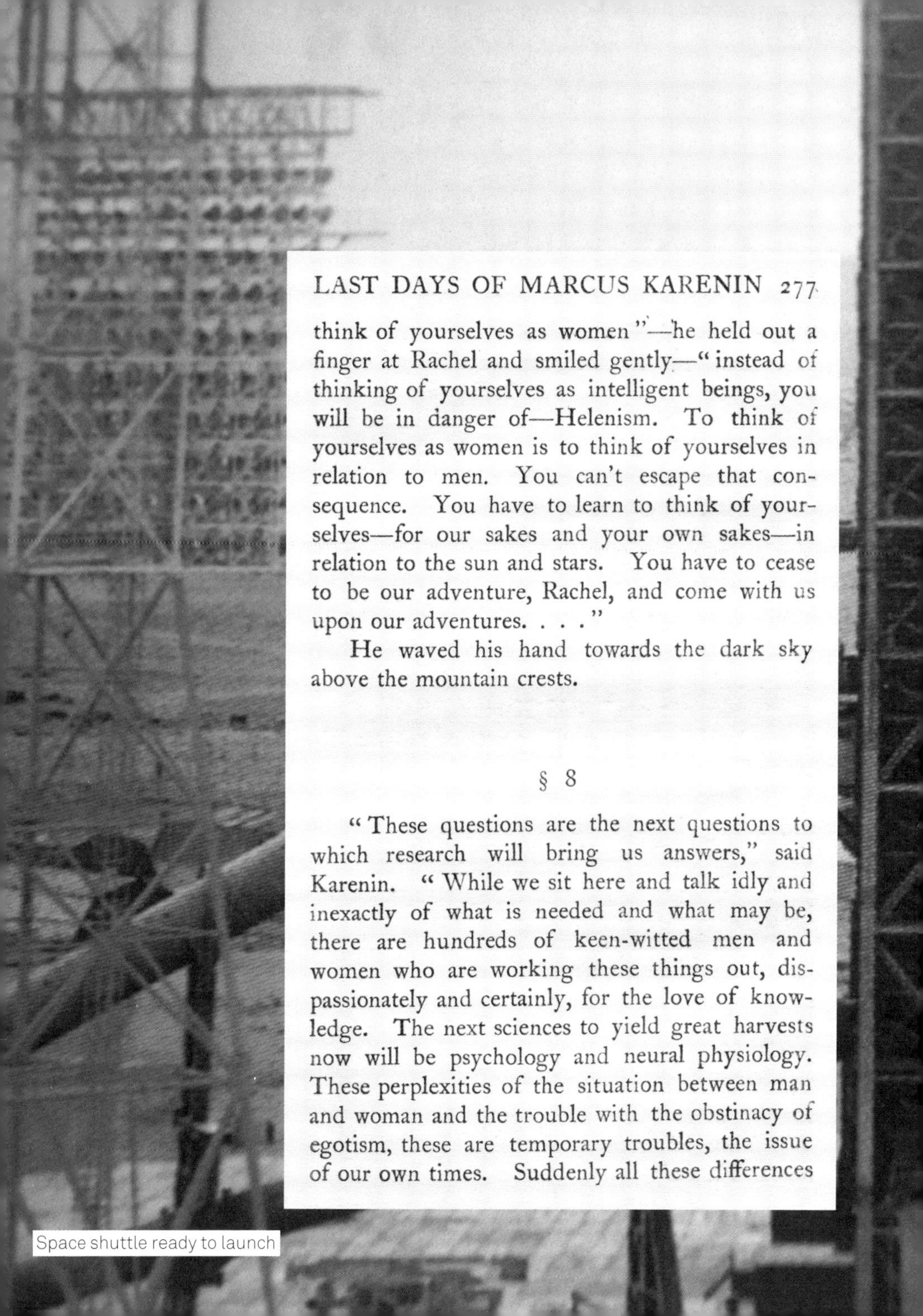

think of yourselves as women"—he held out a finger at Rachel and smiled gently—"instead of thinking of yourselves as intelligent beings, you will be in danger of—Helenism. To think of yourselves as women is to think of yourselves in relation to men. You can't escape that consequence. You have to learn to think of yourselves—for our sakes and your own sakes—in relation to the sun and stars. You have to cease to be our adventure, Rachel, and come with us upon our adventures. . . ."

He waved his hand towards the dark sky above the mountain crests.

§ 8

"These questions are the next questions to which research will bring us answers," said Karenin. "While we sit here and talk idly and inexactly of what is needed and what may be, there are hundreds of keen-witted men and women who are working these things out, dispassionately and certainly, for the love of knowledge. The next sciences to yield great harvests now will be psychology and neural physiology. These perplexities of the situation between man and woman and the trouble with the obstinacy of egotism, these are temporary troubles, the issue of our own times. Suddenly all these differences

Space shuttle ready to launch

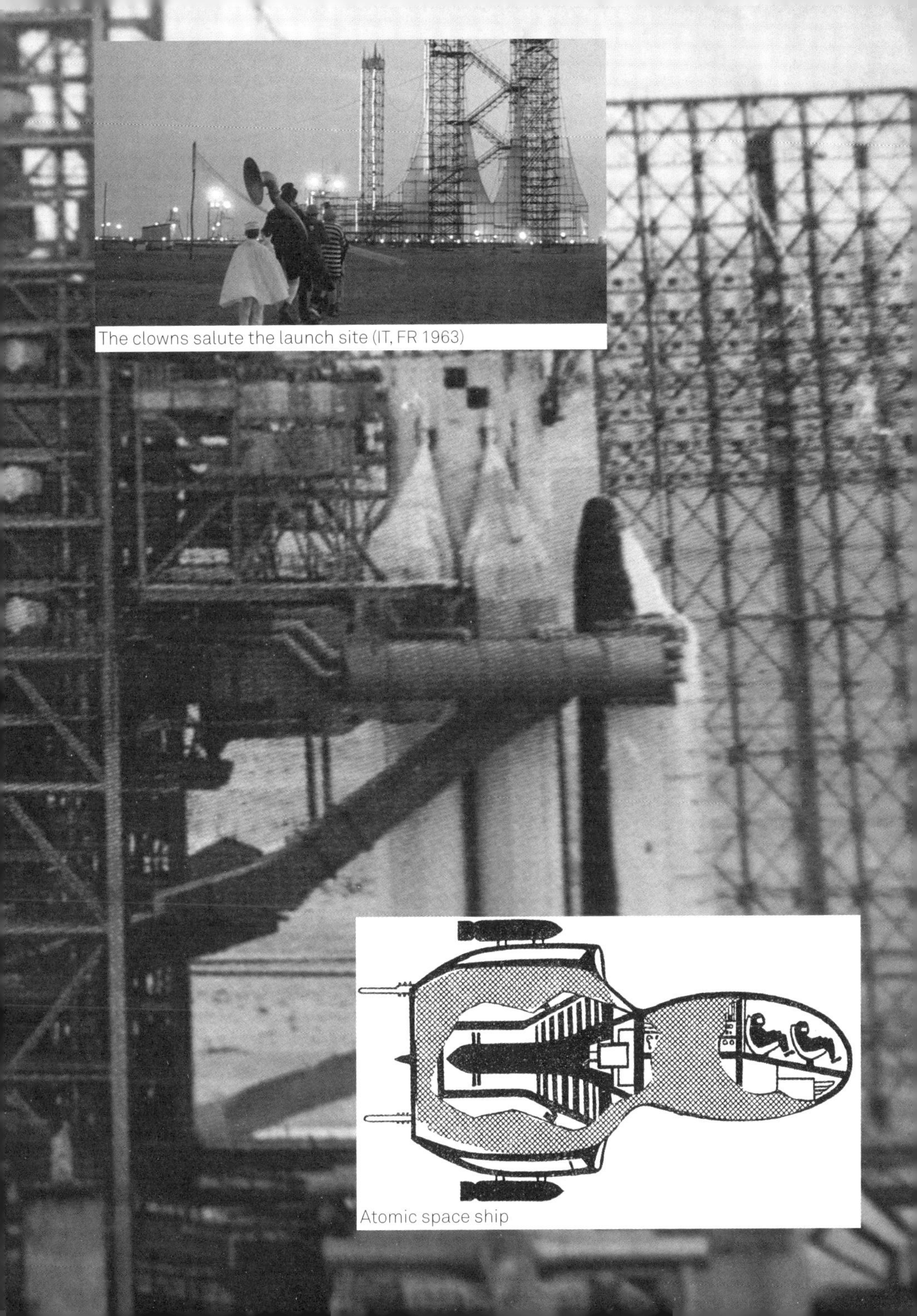
The clowns salute the launch site (IT, FR 1963)

Atomic space ship

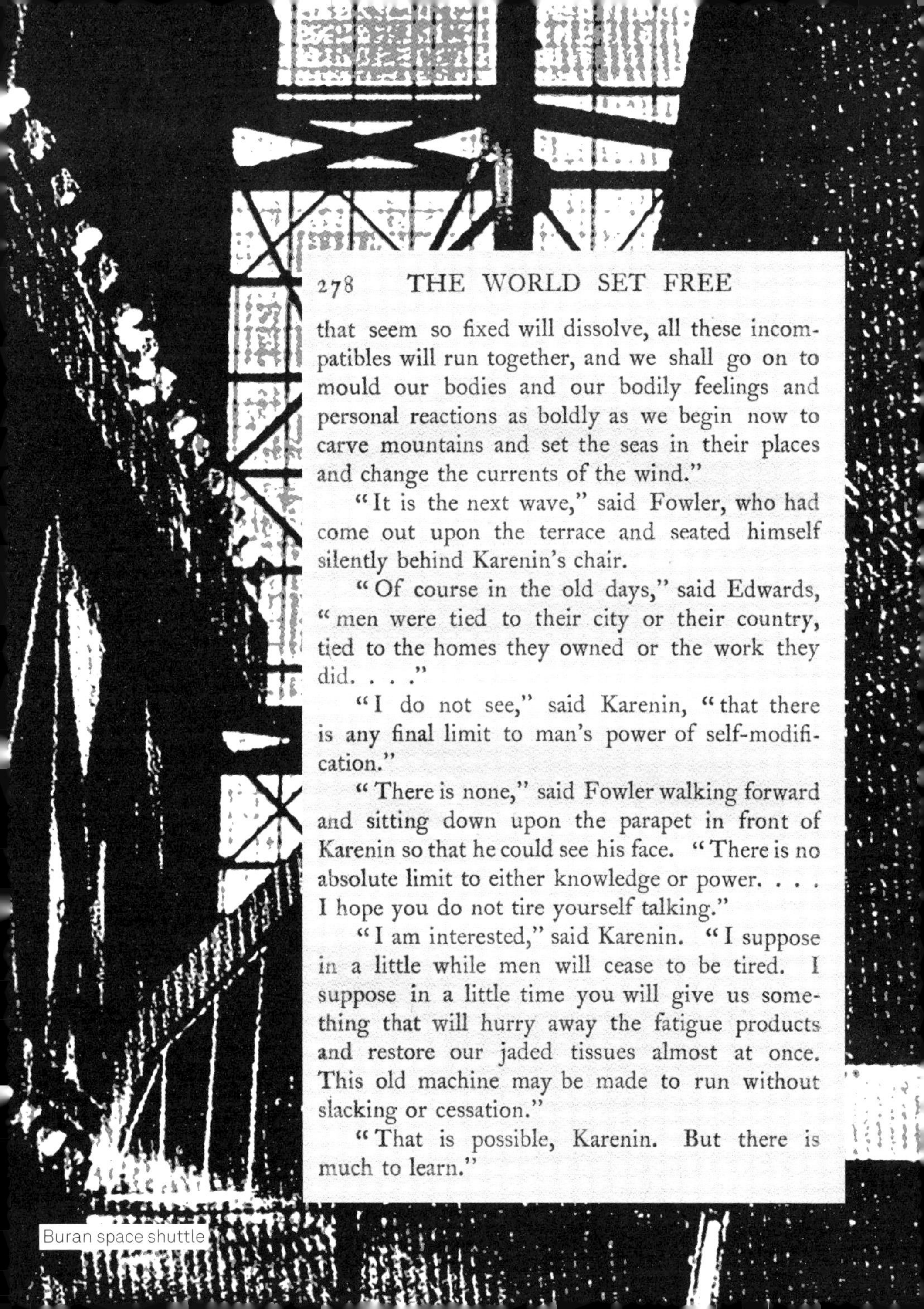

that seem so fixed will dissolve, all these incompatibles will run together, and we shall go on to mould our bodies and our bodily feelings and personal reactions as boldly as we begin now to carve mountains and set the seas in their places and change the currents of the wind."

"It is the next wave," said Fowler, who had come out upon the terrace and seated himself silently behind Karenin's chair.

"Of course in the old days," said Edwards, "men were tied to their city or their country, tied to the homes they owned or the work they did. . . ."

"I do not see," said Karenin, "that there is any final limit to man's power of self-modification."

"There is none," said Fowler walking forward and sitting down upon the parapet in front of Karenin so that he could see his face. "There is no absolute limit to either knowledge or power. . . . I hope you do not tire yourself talking."

"I am interested," said Karenin. "I suppose in a little while men will cease to be tired. I suppose in a little time you will give us something that will hurry away the fatigue products and restore our jaded tissues almost at once. This old machine may be made to run without slacking or cessation."

"That is possible, Karenin. But there is much to learn."

Buran space shuttle

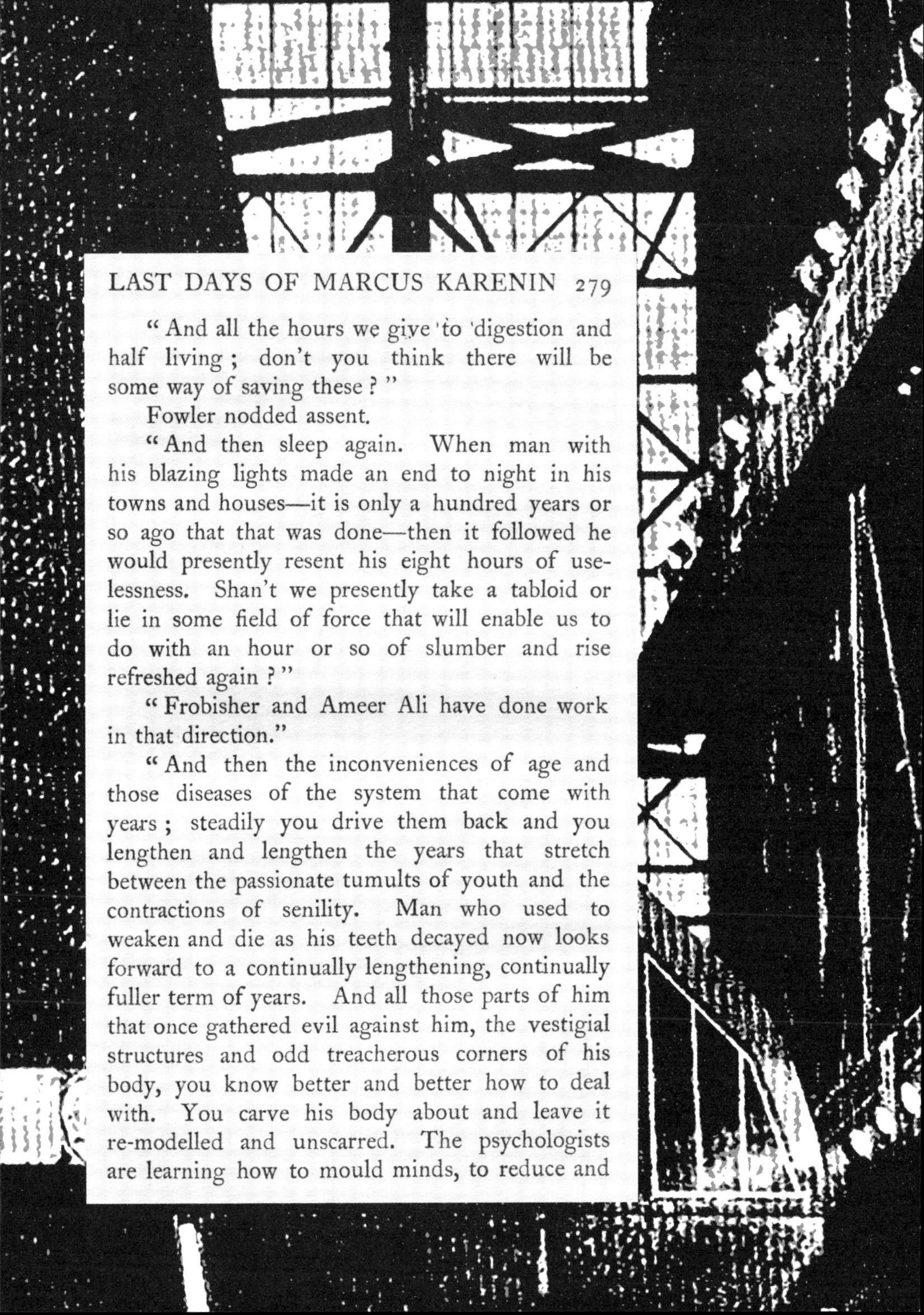

"And all the hours we give to digestion and half living; don't you think there will be some way of saving these?"

Fowler nodded assent.

"And then sleep again. When man with his blazing lights made an end to night in his towns and houses—it is only a hundred years or so ago that that was done—then it followed he would presently resent his eight hours of uselessness. Shan't we presently take a tabloid or lie in some field of force that will enable us to do with an hour or so of slumber and rise refreshed again?"

"Frobisher and Ameer Ali have done work in that direction."

"And then the inconveniences of age and those diseases of the system that come with years; steadily you drive them back and you lengthen and lengthen the years that stretch between the passionate tumults of youth and the contractions of senility. Man who used to weaken and die as his teeth decayed now looks forward to a continually lengthening, continually fuller term of years. And all those parts of him that once gathered evil against him, the vestigial structures and odd treacherous corners of his body, you know better and better how to deal with. You carve his body about and leave it re-modelled and unscarred. The psychologists are learning how to mould minds, to reduce and

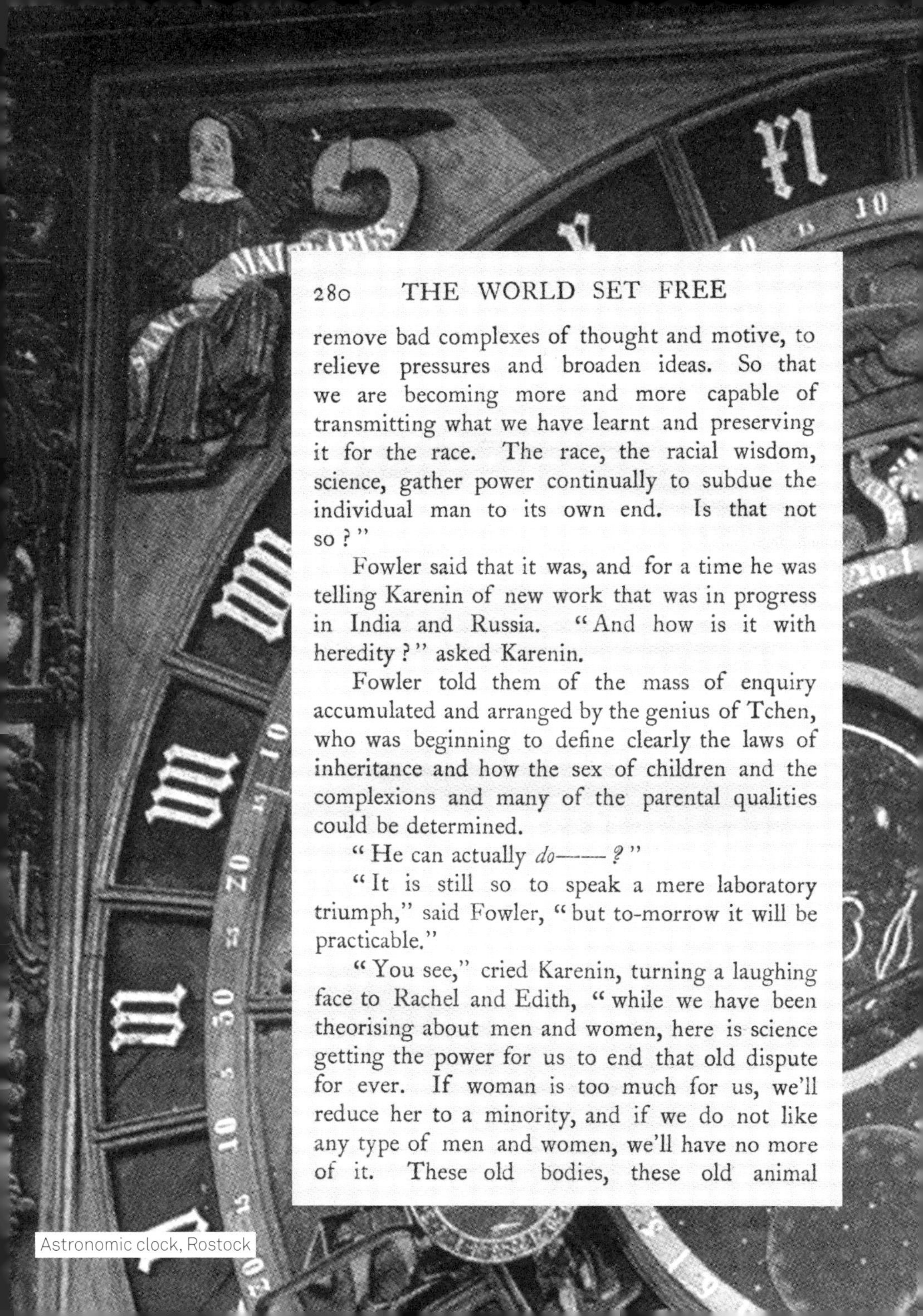

remove bad complexes of thought and motive, to relieve pressures and broaden ideas. So that we are becoming more and more capable of transmitting what we have learnt and preserving it for the race. The race, the racial wisdom, science, gather power continually to subdue the individual man to its own end. Is that not so ? "

Fowler said that it was, and for a time he was telling Karenin of new work that was in progress in India and Russia. "And how is it with heredity ?" asked Karenin.

Fowler told them of the mass of enquiry accumulated and arranged by the genius of Tchen, who was beginning to define clearly the laws of inheritance and how the sex of children and the complexions and many of the parental qualities could be determined.

" He can actually *do*—— ? "

" It is still so to speak a mere laboratory triumph," said Fowler, " but to-morrow it will be practicable."

" You see," cried Karenin, turning a laughing face to Rachel and Edith, " while we have been theorising about men and women, here is science getting the power for us to end that old dispute for ever. If woman is too much for us, we'll reduce her to a minority, and if we do not like any type of men and women, we'll have no more of it. These old bodies, these old animal

Astronomic clock, Rostock

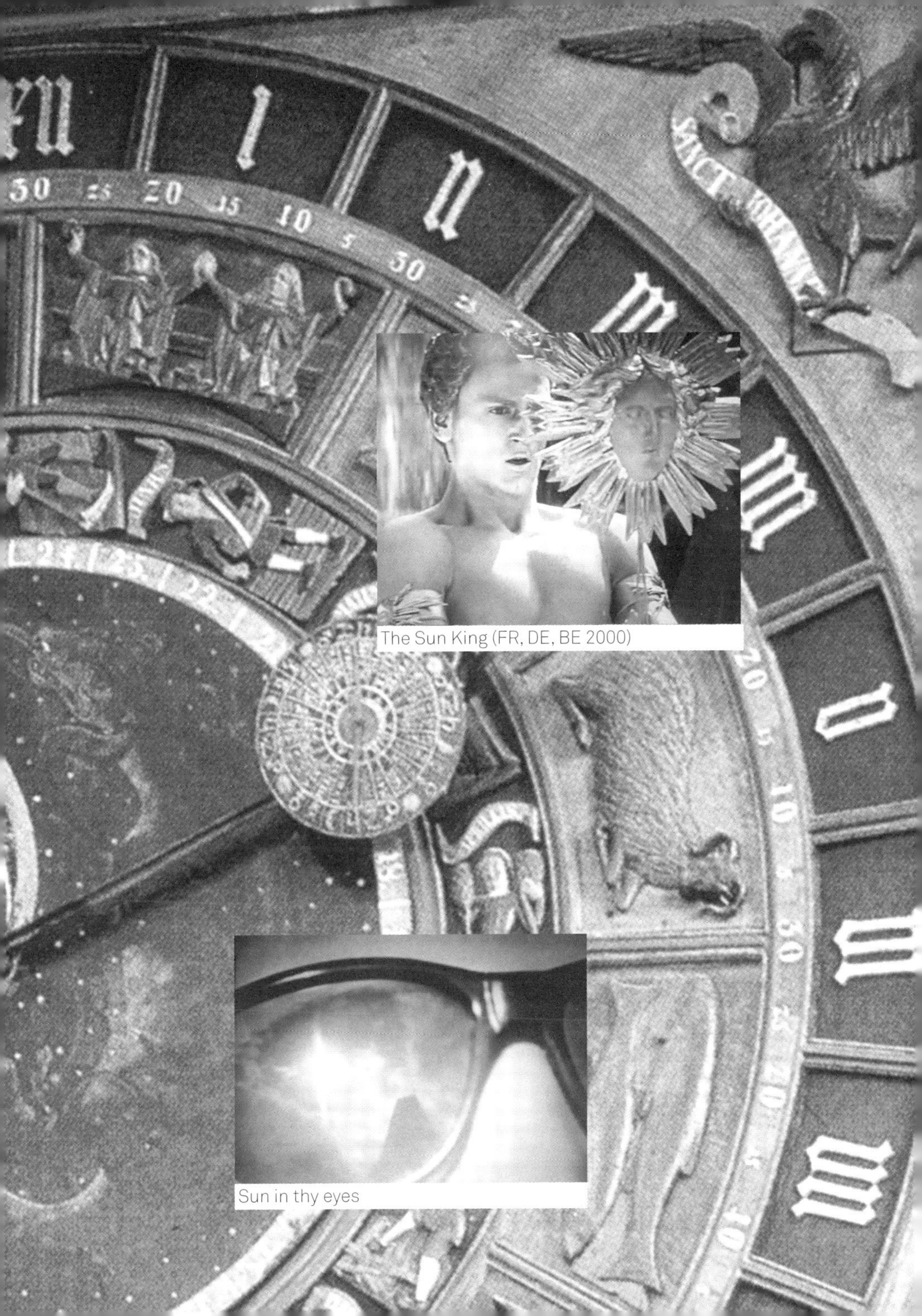

The Sun King (FR, DE, BE 2000)

Sun in thy eyes

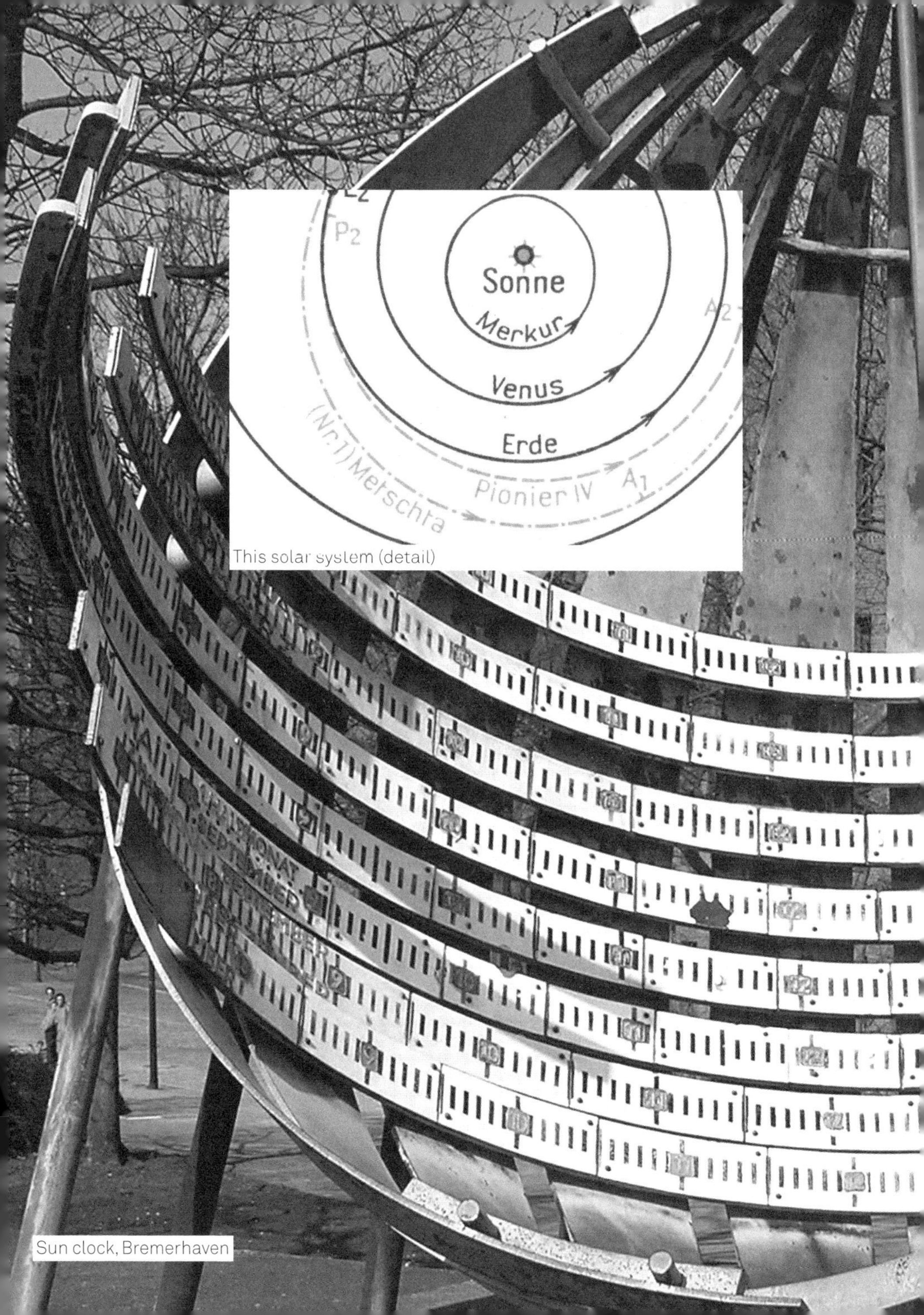

This solar system (detail)

Sun clock, Bremerhaven

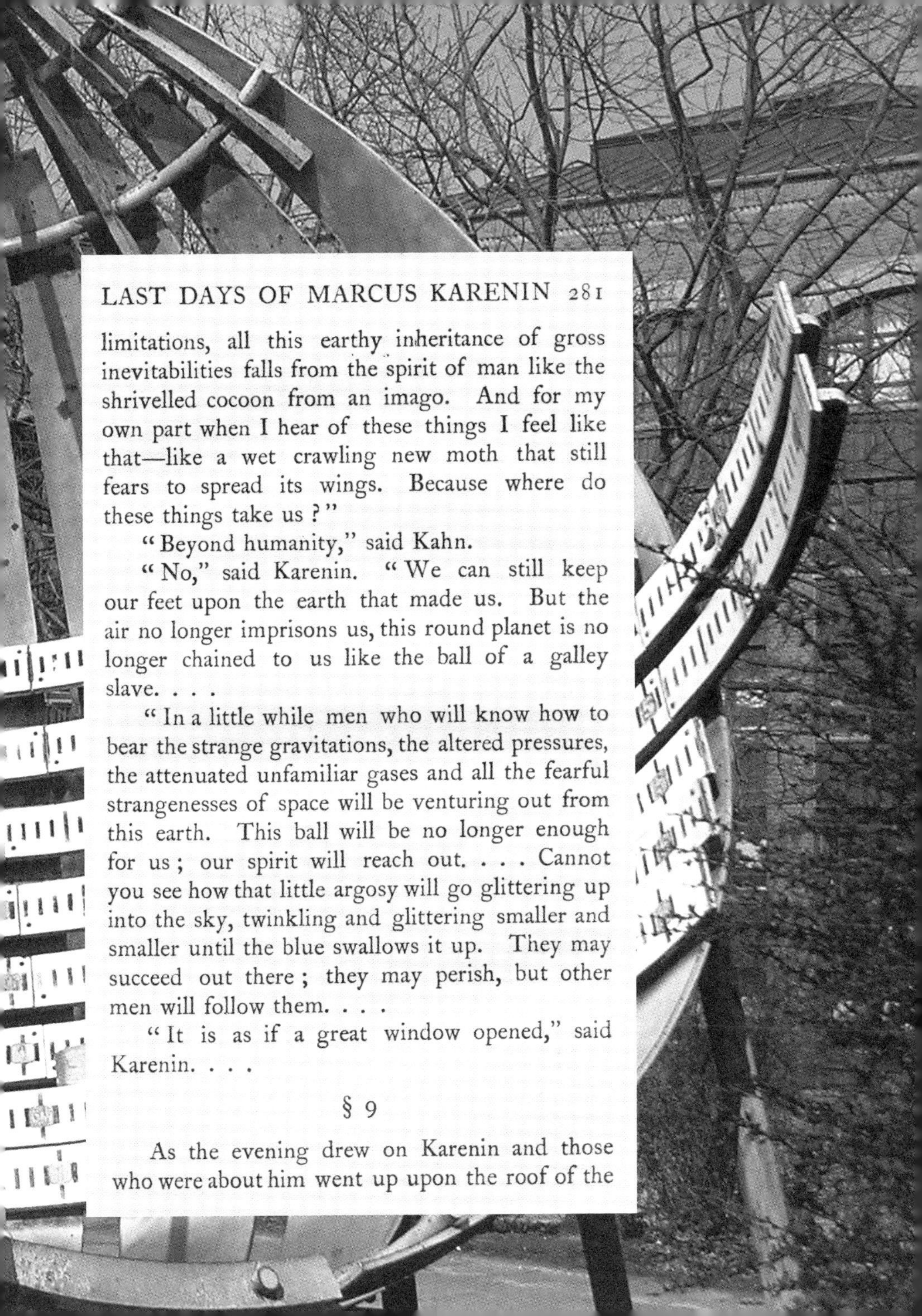

limitations, all this earthy inheritance of gross inevitabilities falls from the spirit of man like the shrivelled cocoon from an imago. And for my own part when I hear of these things I feel like that—like a wet crawling new moth that still fears to spread its wings. Because where do these things take us ?"

"Beyond humanity," said Kahn.

"No," said Karenin. "We can still keep our feet upon the earth that made us. But the air no longer imprisons us, this round planet is no longer chained to us like the ball of a galley slave. . . .

"In a little while men who will know how to bear the strange gravitations, the altered pressures, the attenuated unfamiliar gases and all the fearful strangenesses of space will be venturing out from this earth. This ball will be no longer enough for us ; our spirit will reach out. . . . Cannot you see how that little argosy will go glittering up into the sky, twinkling and glittering smaller and smaller until the blue swallows it up. They may succeed out there ; they may perish, but other men will follow them. . . .

"It is as if a great window opened," said Karenin. . . .

§ 9

As the evening drew on Karenin and those who were about him went up upon the roof of the

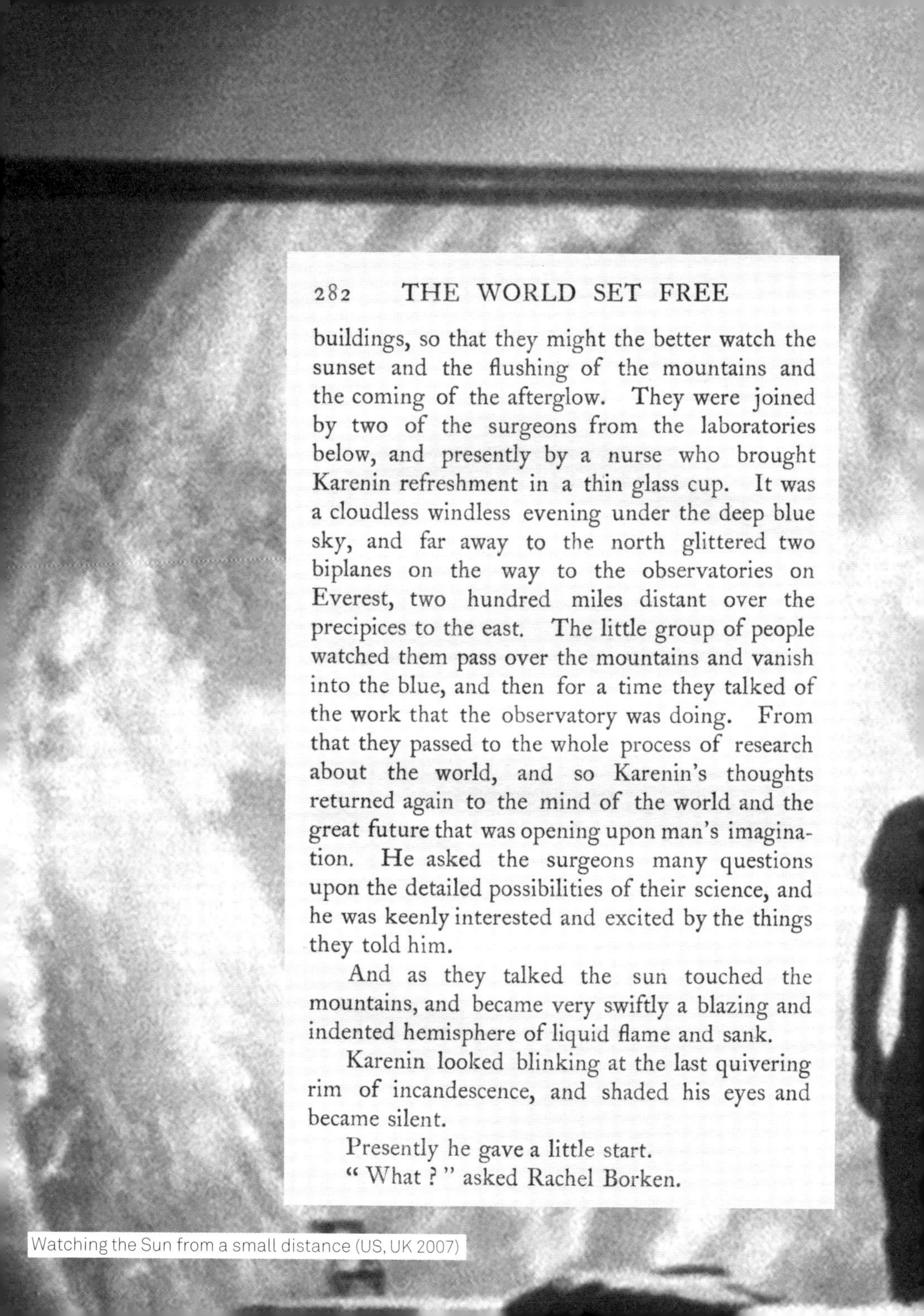

282 THE WORLD SET FREE

buildings, so that they might the better watch the sunset and the flushing of the mountains and the coming of the afterglow. They were joined by two of the surgeons from the laboratories below, and presently by a nurse who brought Karenin refreshment in a thin glass cup. It was a cloudless windless evening under the deep blue sky, and far away to the north glittered two biplanes on the way to the observatories on Everest, two hundred miles distant over the precipices to the east. The little group of people watched them pass over the mountains and vanish into the blue, and then for a time they talked of the work that the observatory was doing. From that they passed to the whole process of research about the world, and so Karenin's thoughts returned again to the mind of the world and the great future that was opening upon man's imagination. He asked the surgeons many questions upon the detailed possibilities of their science, and he was keenly interested and excited by the things they told him.

And as they talked the sun touched the mountains, and became very swiftly a blazing and indented hemisphere of liquid flame and sank.

Karenin looked blinking at the last quivering rim of incandescence, and shaded his eyes and became silent.

Presently he gave a little start.

" What ? " asked Rachel Borken.

Watching the Sun from a small distance (US, UK 2007)

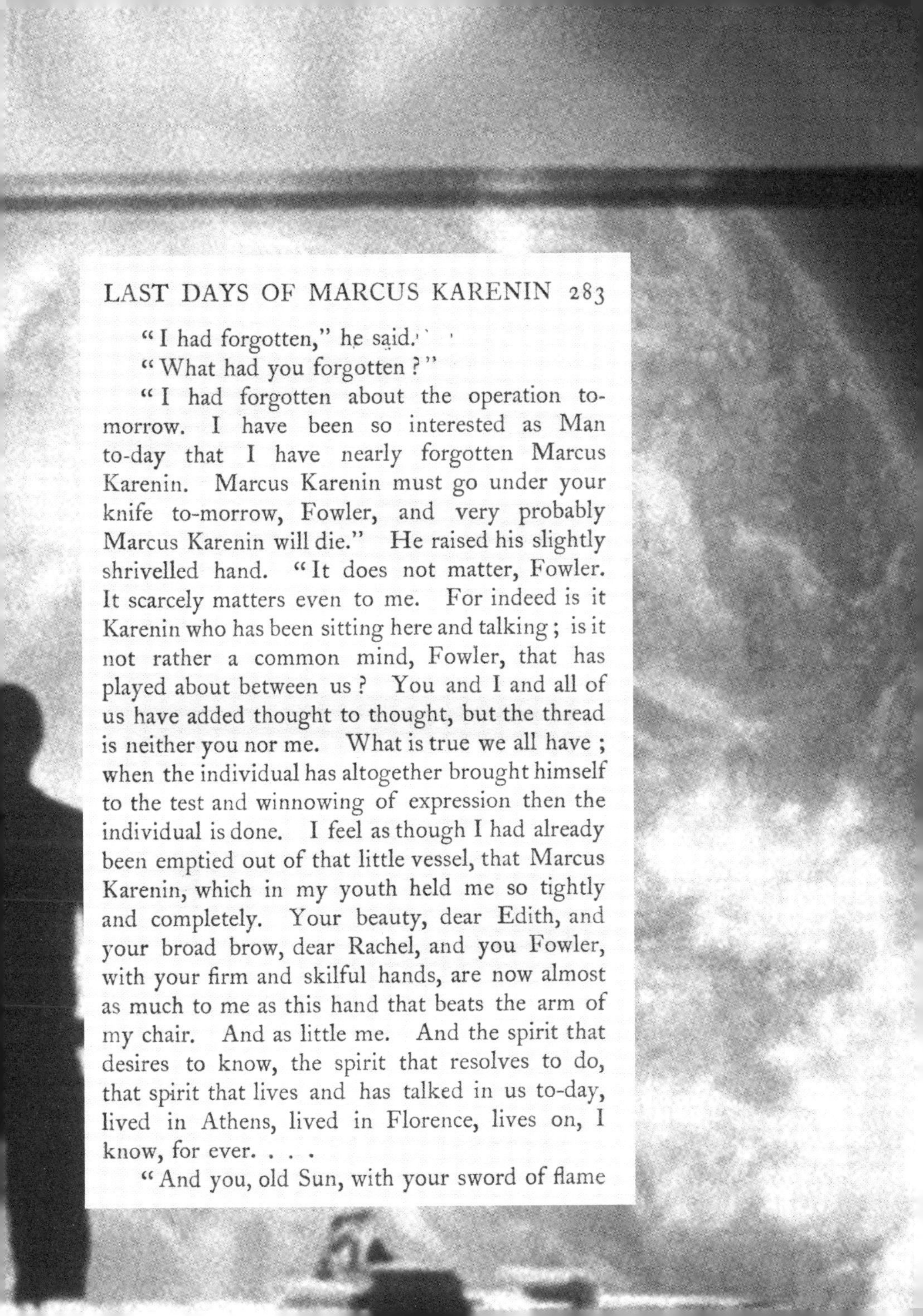

"I had forgotten," he said.

"What had you forgotten?"

"I had forgotten about the operation to-morrow. I have been so interested as Man to-day that I have nearly forgotten Marcus Karenin. Marcus Karenin must go under your knife to-morrow, Fowler, and very probably Marcus Karenin will die." He raised his slightly shrivelled hand. "It does not matter, Fowler. It scarcely matters even to me. For indeed is it Karenin who has been sitting here and talking; is it not rather a common mind, Fowler, that has played about between us? You and I and all of us have added thought to thought, but the thread is neither you nor me. What is true we all have; when the individual has altogether brought himself to the test and winnowing of expression then the individual is done. I feel as though I had already been emptied out of that little vessel, that Marcus Karenin, which in my youth held me so tightly and completely. Your beauty, dear Edith, and your broad brow, dear Rachel, and you Fowler, with your firm and skilful hands, are now almost as much to me as this hand that beats the arm of my chair. And as little me. And the spirit that desires to know, the spirit that resolves to do, that spirit that lives and has talked in us to-day, lived in Athens, lived in Florence, lives on, I know, for ever. . . .

"And you, old Sun, with your sword of flame

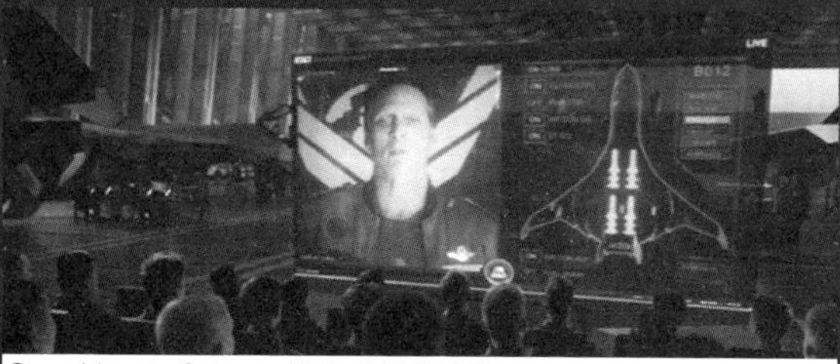

Speaking to future pilots (US 2016)

searing these poor eyes of Marcus for the last time of all, beware of me! You think I die—and indeed I am only taking off one more coat to get at you. I have threatened you for ten thousand years, and soon I warn you I shall be coming. When I am altogether stripped and my disguises thrown away. Very soon now, old Sun, I shall launch myself at you, and I shall reach you and I shall put my foot on your spotted face and tug you about by your fiery locks. One step I shall take to the moon, and then I shall leap at you. I've talked to you before, old Sun, I've talked to you a million times, and now I am beginning to remember. Yes,—long ago, long ago, before I had stripped off a few thousand generations, dust now and forgotten, I was a hairy savage and I pointed my hand at you and—clearly I remember it!—I saw you in a net. Have you forgotten that, old Sun? . . .

"Old Sun, I gather myself together out of the pools of the individual that have held me dispersed so long. I gather my billion thoughts into science and my million wills into a common purpose. Well may you slink down behind the mountains from me, well may you cower. . . ."

§ 10

Karenin desired that he might dream alone for a little while before he returned to the cell in

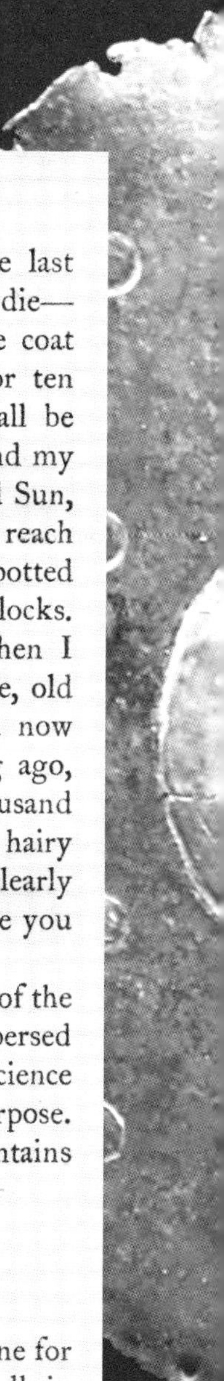

Nebra sky disc, about 4000 years B.C., found 1999

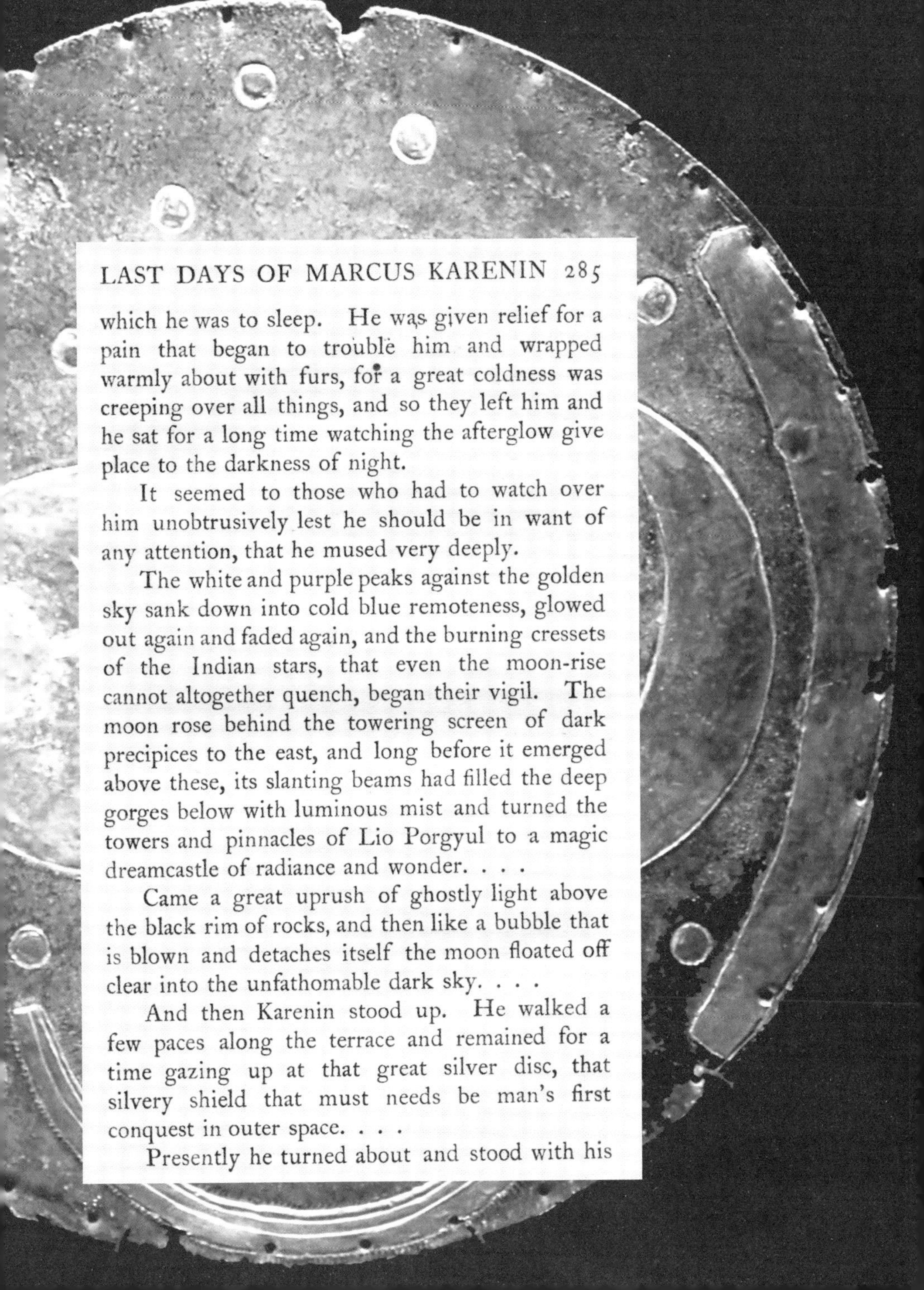

which he was to sleep. He was given relief for a pain that began to trouble him and wrapped warmly about with furs, for a great coldness was creeping over all things, and so they left him and he sat for a long time watching the afterglow give place to the darkness of night.

It seemed to those who had to watch over him unobtrusively lest he should be in want of any attention, that he mused very deeply.

The white and purple peaks against the golden sky sank down into cold blue remoteness, glowed out again and faded again, and the burning cressets of the Indian stars, that even the moon-rise cannot altogether quench, began their vigil. The moon rose behind the towering screen of dark precipices to the east, and long before it emerged above these, its slanting beams had filled the deep gorges below with luminous mist and turned the towers and pinnacles of Lio Porgyul to a magic dreamcastle of radiance and wonder. . . .

Came a great uprush of ghostly light above the black rim of rocks, and then like a bubble that is blown and detaches itself the moon floated off clear into the unfathomable dark sky. . . .

And then Karenin stood up. He walked a few paces along the terrace and remained for a time gazing up at that great silver disc, that silvery shield that must needs be man's first conquest in outer space. . . .

Presently he turned about and stood with his

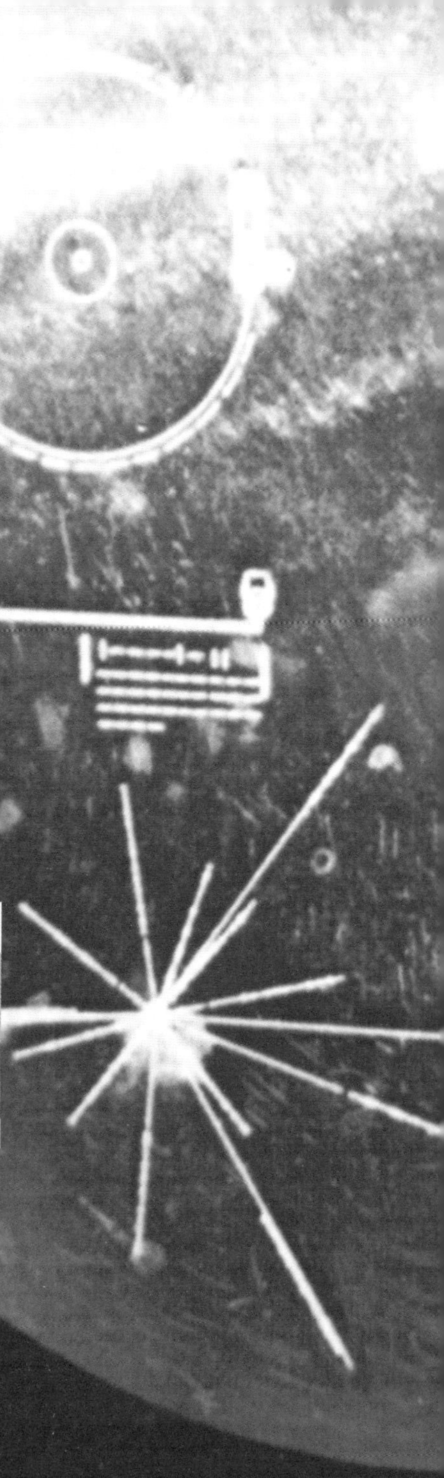

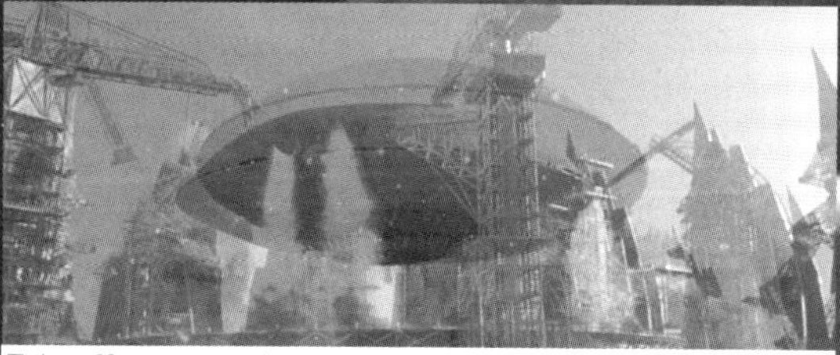

Takeoff to new galaxies (US 1998)

Voyager golden disc, 1977